MONTANA & WYOMING

CARTER G. WALKER

Contents

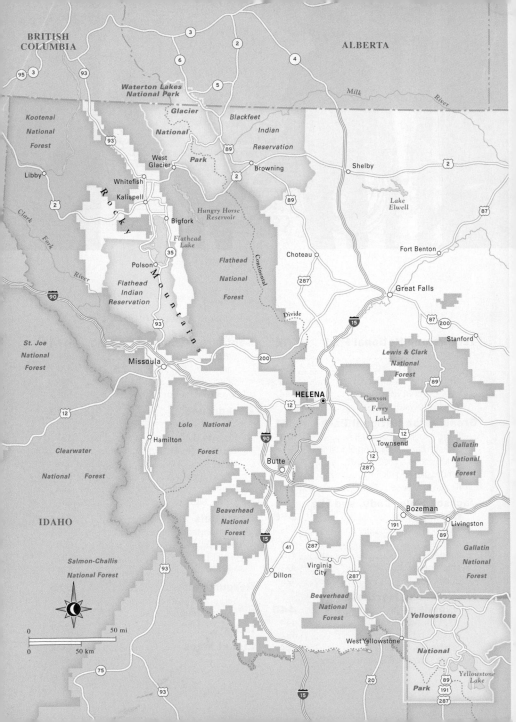

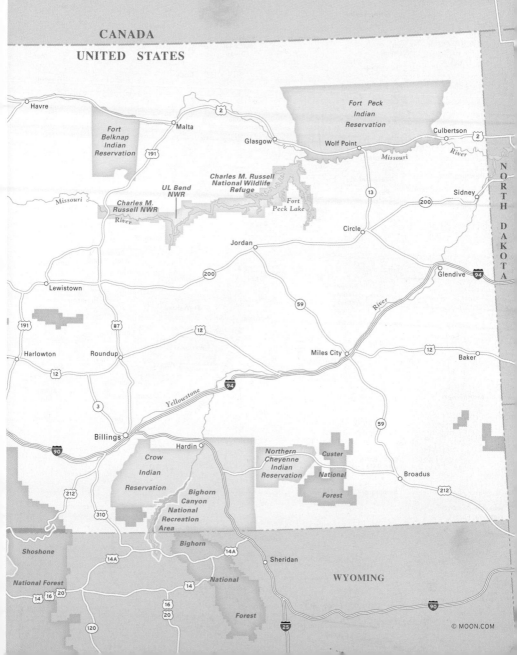

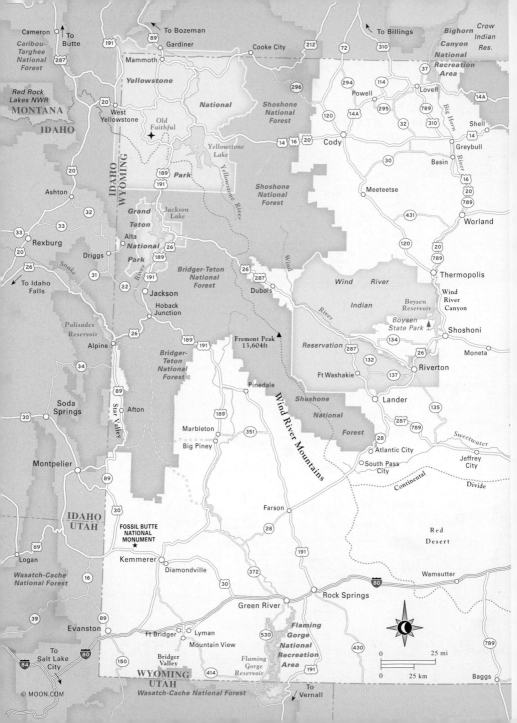

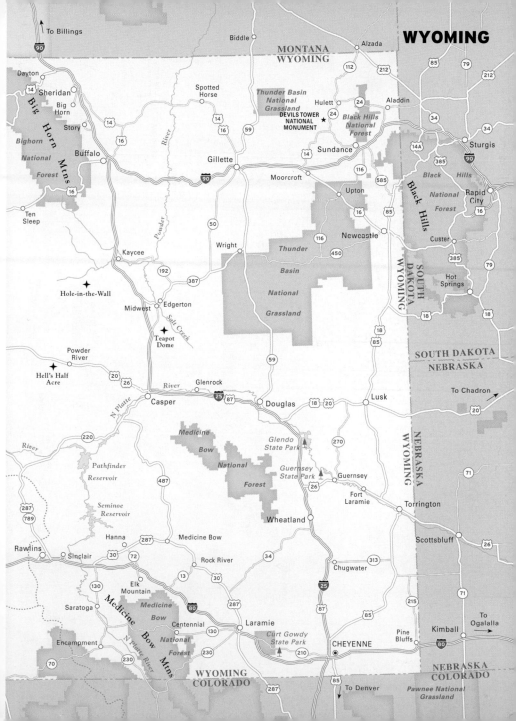

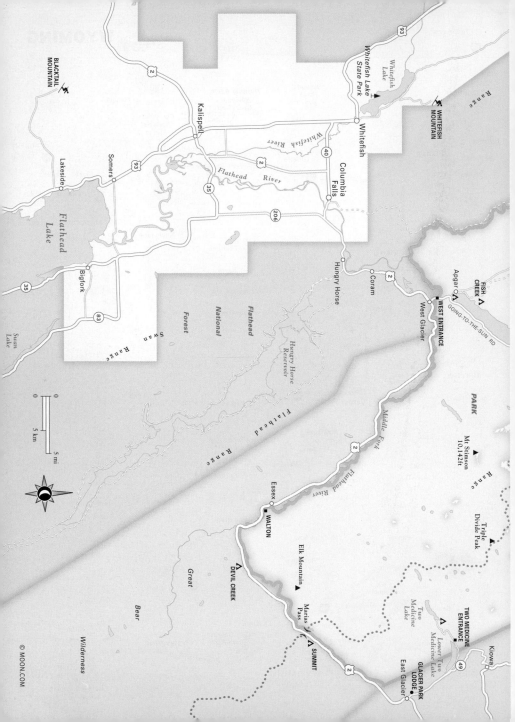

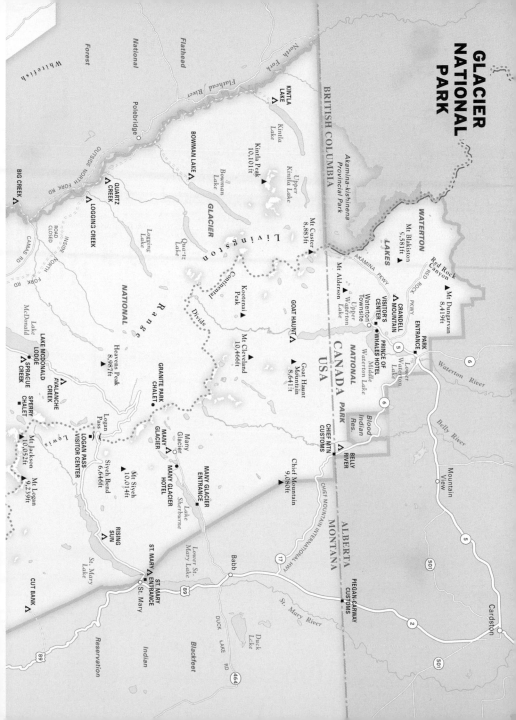

GLACIER NATIONAL PARK

Whitefish

Flathead

National

Forest

North Fork Flathead River

BRITISH COLUMBIA

Polebridge

Akamina-kishinena Provincial Park

KINTLA LAKE ▲

Kintla Lake

Upper Kintla Lake

Kintla Peak 10,101ft ▼

WATERTON LAKES

Mt Blakiston 9,581ft ▼

Red Rock Canyon

Mt Dungarvan 8,419ft ▶

BOWMAN LAKE ▲

Bowman Lake

Mt Custer 8,883ft ▼

AKAMINA PKWY

RED ROCK PKWY

Waterton Townsite

CRANDELL MOUNTAIN ▲

VISITOR'S CENTER ■

PARK ENTRANCE ▲

QUARTZ CREEK ▲

BIG CREEK ▲

LOGGING CREEK ▲

Quartz Lake

Logging Lake

GLACIER

Livingston

Continental

Kootenai Peak ▼

Mt Alderson ▼

Upper Waterton Lake

PRINCE OF WALES HOTEL ●

Middle Waterton Lake

Lower Waterton Lake

Waterton River

6

5

ROAD CLOSED

INSIDE NORTH FORK RD

OUTSIDE NORTH FORK RD

CAMAS RD

Lake McDonald

NATIONAL

Range

Divide

Heavens Peak 8,987ft ▼

GOAT HAUNT ▲

Mt Cleveland 10,466ft ▼

Goat Haunt Mountain 8,641ft ▼

CANADA

USA

NATIONAL PARK

Belly River

LAKE McDONALD LODGE ▲

SPRAGUE CREEK ▲

AVALANCHE CREEK ▲

SPERRY CHALET ■

Lewis

GRANITE PARK CHALET ▲

Logan Pass

LOGAN PASS VISITOR CENTER ■

Many Glacier

MANY GLACIER ○

Blood Indian Res.

CHIEF MTN CUSTOMS ▲

BELLY RIVER ▲

Mountain View

Mt Jackson 10,052ft ▼

Mt Logan 9,239ft ▼

Siyeh Bend 6,646ft

Mt Siyeh 10,014ft ▼

MANY GLACIER HOTEL ■

Lake Sherburne

MANY GLACIER ENTRANCE ▲

Chief Mountain 9,080ft ▼

CHIEF MOUNTAIN INTERNATIONAL HWY

ALBERTA

MONTANA

5

501

RISING SUN ▲

St. Mary Lake

Lower St. Mary Lake

Babb

17

89

Cardston

CUT BANK ▲

St. Mary Lake

ST. MARY ENTRANCE ▲

ST. MARY ○ St. Mary

Duck Lake

PIEGAN-CARWAY CUSTOMS ■

2

501

DUCK LAKE RD

St. Mary River

Reservation

Indian

Blackfeet

89

464

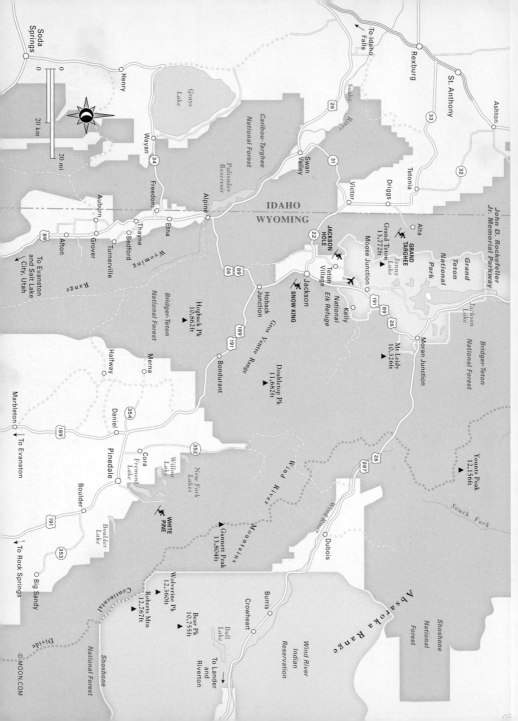

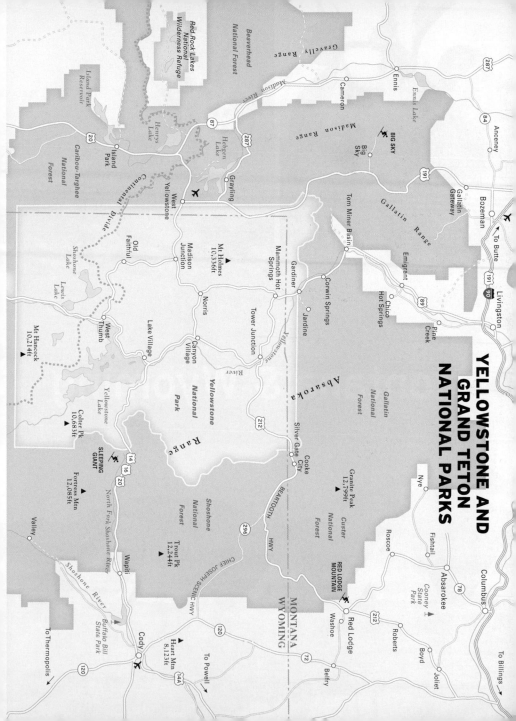

YELLOWSTONE AND GRAND TETON NATIONAL PARKS

Montana & Wyoming

The dramatic landscapes of Montana and Wyoming—from soaring mountains and narrow valleys to sweeping plains—were carved over eons by water, wind, fire, and ice. The culture was also shaped by conflict: between those who were from here and those who were not; those who valued the land itself and those who sought its riches. Although their distinct histories—both natural and cultural—are evident everywhere, not just tucked away in dusty museums, these states continue to redefine themselves. Wyoming's Tetons thrust skyward at the rate of an inch or so each year. Montana's blue-ribbon trout streams, tumbling and falling, etch themselves ever deeper into green valleys. The populations are perpetually shifting too, bringing new ideas, new conflicts, and an evolving culture.

Montana is as vast as the big sky that blankets it, rich with natural resources—fertile soil, rivers, gold, forests, wind—and overflowing with beauty. From Glacier National Park to the Little Bighorn, its sites are enchanting, and sometimes haunting. Its communities are diverse too, with pioneer traditions embraced by new generations of transplants in cities like Bozeman, where ski bums and artists mingle with fifth-generation farmers. Then there are tiny towns

Clockwise from top left: brown-eyed Susans; mountain goat; skiing at Montana Snowbowl; camping under a starry Wyoming sky; Lower Falls in Yellowstone National Park; row of tipis in Montana.

like Loma, at the confluence of the Milk and Marias Rivers, where the headline is still that Lewis and Clark camped just south of town in 1805. Montana's cities make us aware of the constant growth in the American West, while little dots on the map like Loma remind us of its almost magical timelessness.

Embodied by the bucking bronco on its license plates, Wyoming is a child's cowboy fantasy come to life, with rodeos aplenty and dude ranches where even city slickers can try their hand at riding and roping. But what strikes people most about Wyoming is its authenticity. The harsh climate and isolation that make Wyoming the least populated state in the union result in an uncommon grace in its residents. It's expressed not just in the weathered creases on their faces but in the way they do business and welcome visitors. There is glitz here too, in places like Jackson Hole and Cody, but it doesn't distract from the essence of Wyoming. Those towns are but a flash of silver, the shiny buckle on a well-worn belt.

Separated by history, culture, and sometimes even politics, Montana and Wyoming are still ideal neighbors, bound together by the forces of nature that make them so captivating.

Clockwise from top left: Mormon Row in Grand Teton National Park; National Bison Range in Moiese, Montana; grizzly bear in Glacier National Park; Yellowstone's Grand Prismatic Spring.

10 TOP EXPERIENCES

1 **Spot Wildlife in Yellowstone National Park:** Yellowstone is a wonderland of wildlife. Visit **Lamar Valley** (page 340) for the chance to see bears, bison, and bighorn sheep. This is also the best place to look for **wolves** (page 338).

2 **Hike in Glacier National Park:** Glacier is a hiker's paradise. Head to the west side of the park to explore its beloved trails (page 142).

>>>

3 **Go on an Adventure in Grand Teton National Park:** With the towering Tetons a near constant backdrop, the land here lends itself to superb hikes, bike rides, rock climbing, horseback adventures, fishing, and boating expeditions (page 361).

>>>

4 **Visit a Dude Ranch:** From rustic to luxe, there are dude ranches across the West where guests can saddle up and ride for their supper—or just ride to their heart's content (page 238).

5 **Go Skiing:** Skiing in Montana and Wyoming is a win-win: phenomenal terrain without the lines of big-name places. Hit up a ski resort like **Whitefish Mountain Resort** (page 209) or **Maverick Mountain** (page 249), or stay in a true ski town, like **Jackson Hole** (page 400).

>>>

6 **Take to the River:** Montana and Wyoming have an abundance of enviable rivers for fishing, boating, and both flat and whitewater river rafting. Kayak or canoe on **Oxbow Bend** (page 373) in Grand Teton, go rafting on the **Snake River** (page 399), or try fishing at the **Big Hole River** (page 249).

7 **Learn about Indigenous Cultures:** With seven reservations scattered across Montana, and one in Wyoming, there are many ways to experience Native American cultures (page 37).

>>>

8 **Scenic Drives:** The journey is the main event on **Going-to-the-Sun Road** (page 141), **Chief Joseph Scenic Highway** (page 432), and **Cloud Peak Skyway** (page 459).

<<<

9 **Soak in the Hot Springs:** From resort-style pools and thermally heated rivers to entire towns built on hot springs, this region offers infinite ways to get wet (page 35).

>>>

10 **See the Glaciers—While You Still Can:** Head to Glacier National Park's sublime **Many Glacier region** (page 155) and **Grinnell Glacier** (pictured; page 157) before 2030, when Montana's 62 glaciers are expected to disappear.

Planning Your Trip

Where to Go

Billings and the Big Open

Beyond **Billings,** the state's largest and most industrial city, much of eastern Montana is made up of small but tightly knit communities separated by vast swaths of **wide-open country.** It's also where four of the state's seven **Indian reservations** can be found. The landscapes are varied and dramatic—from the rimrocks in Billings and the rolling hills around the **Little Bighorn Battlefield** to the badlands of **Makoshika State Park** outside Glendive.

Great Falls and the Rocky Mountain Front

The **vast plains** erupt into **soaring peaks** along the **Rocky Mountain Front.** The **Bob Marshall Wilderness Complex** is one of the most spectacular and isolated mountainous areas in the Lower 48. Tiny towns like **Choteau** and **Fort Benton** offer a charming sense of community, along with fascinating sites like dinosaur mecca **Egg Mountain** and lovely **historic hotels.** Straddling the division between mountains and plains, **Great Falls** boasts two of the state's best museums: the **C. M. Russell Museum** and **Lewis and Clark National Historic Trail Interpretive Center.**

Glacier National Park

Known as the "Crown of the Continent," **Glacier National Park** embodies the Montana you've always imagined: **rugged mountains** piercing the sky, **crystalline lakes** and **plunging waterfalls, abundant wildlife,** gravity-defying roads, and miles upon miles of trails. For now, the park still lays claim to **25 glaciers.**

Glacier National Park boasts crystalline lakes.

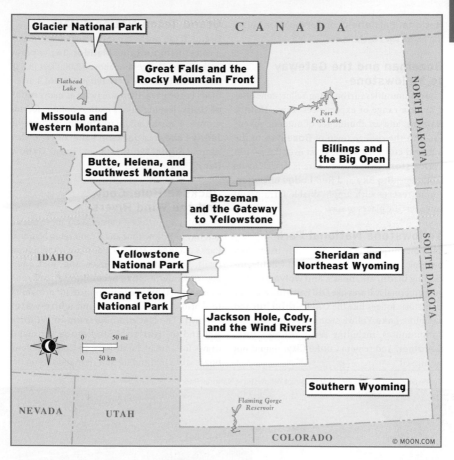

Missoula and Western Montana

Western Montana shows off with **lush green mountain ranges** and **towering forests.** In the far north, **Whitefish** is the ultimate mountain town, a **skier's paradise.** Just south, glittering **Flathead Lake** is Montana's Riviera, with sprawling mansions and luxe lodges at water's edge. The tiny hamlet of **Bigfork** serves up a surprisingly fine selection of both culture and cuisine, not to mention recreation. The scenic **National Bison Range** in Moiese can be visited en route to **Missoula,** a cultural hub and home of the **University of Montana,** with great restaurants and better bars. In the southwest corner of the state, the **Bitterroot Valley** combines a rich history with **world-class fly-fishing.**

Butte, Helena, and Southwest Montana

This corner of the state wears its history like a badge of honor in mining towns like **Bannack, Virginia City,** and **Nevada City.** Some of the other towns that survived the unforgiving boom-and-bust cycles include charming Victorian **Philipsburg** and **Butte,** and **Helena,** the venerable state capital. Then there is the sweeping **Big Hole Valley,** with **picturesque ranches** and **hot springs resorts,** and the **Big Hole**

National Battlefield, one of the most haunting battle sites in the state.

Bozeman and the Gateway to Yellowstone

The communities surrounding Yellowstone offer a diverse range of experiences. From **skiing, fishing,** and an abundance of outdoor adventures in the college town of **Bozeman** to the **art and culinary scenes** just over the pass in **Livingston,** the area's culture is as rich as its landscape. **Big Sky** and **Red Lodge** offer year-round resorts with ample skiable terrain and some terrific places to stay.

Yellowstone National Park

This magnificent park is constantly in motion; nothing here is static. See abundant wildlife, including **bison, elk, bears, and wolves;** marvel at geothermal features like **Old Faithful;** and stay in historic lodges like the **Old Faithful Inn** and rambling **Lake Yellowstone Hotel.** Perimeter communities, including **West Yellowstone, Gardiner,** and remote **Cooke City,** should not be missed.

Grand Teton National Park

Grand Teton packs a punch, particularly when it comes to **mountain splendor.** Twelve peaks in the Teton Range soar above 12,000 feet (3,658 m). While there are only 100 miles (161 km) of roads in the park, there are twice as many **miles of trails,** leaving hikers endless options for adventure. Favorite landmarks include picturesque **Jenny Lake,** vast **Jackson Lake,** drive-to-the-summit **Signal Mountain,** and serene **Oxbow Bend.**

Jackson Hole, Cody, and the Wind Rivers

Wyoming's northwest corner is far more than a gateway to Yellowstone and Grand Teton National Parks. **Jackson Hole** is a destination in and of itself, with **glitzy galleries** and boutiques, gourmet eateries, **luxe accommodations,** and a sensational art scene in immediate proximity to world-class **ski resorts** and **white-water rafting.** The **National Museum of Wildlife Art** and the **National Elk Refuge** are major draws for animal enthusiasts. In **Cody** the cowboy is still king, and the sun rises and sets on the

Castle Geyser in the Upper Geyser Basin of Yellowstone National Park

Buffalo Bill Center of the West and its five museums. Farther south, outdoors enthusiasts will find hot springs and mountain meccas.

Sheridan and Northeast Wyoming

Where the prairies meet the mountains, cowboy culture comes alive. This is where you'll find dude ranches and Sheridan, one of the most charming and authentic Western towns in the state. The spectacular Cloud Peak Skyway Scenic Byway climbs into the mountains toward the pictograph-rich Medicine Lodge State Archeological Site and more mysterious Medicine Wheel National Historic Landmark. The isolated and enigmatic Devils Tower National Monument draws climbers, geologists, and Native Americans who consider it a sacred site.

Southern Wyoming

Southern Wyoming contains everything from sweeping deserts, sand dunes, and wild mustang herds to lush river valleys and green mountains. The southwest corner is noted for fabulous recreational opportunities along the Green River and in the Flaming Gorge National Recreation Area. It's also home to three of the state's largest cities: capital Cheyenne, synonymous with its legendary Frontier Days rodeo, college town Laramie, and onetime frontier town Casper.

High and Low Seasons

Summer is the easiest and busiest time to travel the roads, both front- and backcountry, in Montana and Wyoming. Thoughtful planning and advance reservations, particularly for hotels and campgrounds, are essential. Hotel rooms are particularly hard to find during local events such as Frontier Days in Cheyenne or the Fourth of July celebration in Livingston.

Rates for accommodations are generally lower and rooms more available when snow is on the ground, except around ski areas, but winter road travel can be challenging because of the inevitable storms and possible closures.

The shoulder seasons can be a delightful time to travel in both states. The national parks are heavenly and much less crowded in autumn, but keep in mind that winter comes very early at high elevations. There are also little-known ways to enjoy the parks by bicycle in the spring, before they open to cars. Opening and closing times for the parks can vary by year (weather and federal budget too), so make sure to check with the parks before travel.

Don't try to see too much in too short a time; this cannot be overstated. Consider that the drive from Montana's eastern border to its western border is 550 miles (890 km), about the same distance as from New York City to Charlotte, North Carolina. Don't spend so much time on the road that you miss the small details—idyllic hikes, roadside burger joints, the locals who give small towns their true character—that make Montana and Wyoming what they are.

The 14-Day Greater Yellowstone Loop

With Yellowstone National Park at its heart, this generous two-week itinerary starts and ends in Bozeman, Montana, never exceeding 200 miles (320 km) of travel in a single day. See and experience this breathtaking region without getting stuck behind the wheel.

Day 1
Bozeman

Start your trip in Bozeman, equal parts college town and mountain town. Fit in a trip to the **Museum of the Rockies** to see where dinosaur guru Jack Horner did much of his work. Throw in a hike up the **M** or on the **Drinking Horse Mountain Trail,** just northeast of town, and end with a shopping stroll on historic **Main Street.** Enjoy a game of pool, a local brew, and an excellent meal at the popular **Montana Ale Works.** After a pre-bed ice-cream cone from the **Genuine Ice Cream** truck, bed down for the night at **The Lark,** a hip, artistically driven hotel.

Day 2
Bozeman to Red Lodge
174 MILES (280 KM), 2.5 HOURS

Start your morning with a quick jaunt up **Peet's Hill,** then walk a few blocks for breakfast at the old-school **Western Café** or the new-school **Little Star Diner.** Head east toward Red Lodge, a much smaller but equally historic ski town. Along the way, stop in **Livingston** to peruse **art galleries,** look for celebrities, or even fish or raft the Yellowstone. Continue on to **Big Timber** for a late lunch at **The Grand Hotel.** Arrive in Red Lodge in time for a quick outdoor meal at the **Red Box Car** and a downy bed at the historic **Pollard Hotel.**

Bozeman

Beartooth Scenic Highway

Day 3
Red Lodge

After a leisurely breakfast, stroll by the shops up and down Broadway, and check out the critters at the **Yellowstone Wildlife Sanctuary.** Later, grab some picnic supplies at **Café Regis** and head out on a scenic hike in the Beartooths, perhaps the **Basin Lakes Trail #61.** Back in town, refuel on simple but delicious Mexican fare at **Más Taco** or settle in for a more sumptuous meal in the dining room at **The Pollard Hotel.**

Day 4
Red Lodge to Cody
114 MILES (184 KM), 2 HOURS

Experience two of the most breathtaking drives in the region. Pack a picnic lunch and head up and over the **Beartooth Scenic Highway** (U.S. 212). Be sure to make plenty of stops along the way. Look for **mountain goats** at the summit. Consider an alpine hike: The **Clay Butte Fire Lookout Tower,** only 1 mile (1.6 km) from the highway, puts you above 11,000 feet (3,353 m); the 8-mile (12.9-km) scenic loop around **Beartooth Lake** offers level terrain with spectacular scenery.

Stop in **Cooke City** if you need a shot of civilization (or espresso), or continue to the **Chief Joseph Scenic Highway** (Hwy. 296) south to Cody. Arrive in time for a fantastic dinner at **The Local** and a cozy room at the **Chamberlin Inn.**

Day 5
Cody

After breakfast, head out on the hour-long **Cody Trolley Tour,** which can include tickets to the **Buffalo Bill Center of the West.** Spend most of the day exploring its five museums. Before dinner at the celebrated **Irma Hotel,** grab a cocktail and step outside to watch the **Cody Gunfighters.** After dinner, head over to the **Cody Nite Rodeo** for a two-hour action-packed show with local cowboys and cowgirls.

Day 6
Cody to Tower Junction
111 MILES (179 KM), 3 HOURS

On your way out of town, stop by **Old Trail Town.** Then head farther west on the **Buffalo Bill Scenic Byway** toward the east entrance of **Yellowstone National Park.** Stop for a bite at

Where the Wild Things Are

Appreciating wildlife is as much a part of the culture as mountains are part of the landscape. The most obvious choice for prime wildlife-viewing is Yellowstone National Park, where animals have the right-of-way; just try telling a herd of rutting bison that you have to be somewhere. Grand Teton and Glacier National Parks are also great bets, although the restricted roads and dense forests can limit visibility. Both states are packed with public lands and refuges (Wyoming has 7 national wildlife refuges, and Montana has 19) that offer prime habitat to any number of species.

MONTANA

- **Medicine Lake National Wildlife Refuge** is in fact two wildlife refuges and a wetland management district that host more birds than you could ever imagine.

- About 30 miles (48 km) south of Missoula in **Stevensville,** the **Lee Metcalf National Wildlife Refuge** provides habitat for migratory birds including ospreys, eagles, and hawks as well as larger animals including wolves, coyotes, black bears, and badgers.

- Located in **Moiese** between the Flathead and Missoula, the **National Bison Range** is home to around 400 bison, along with whitetailed and mule deer, bighorn sheep, pronghorn antelope, and elk.

- Near **Lima,** the **Red Rock Lakes National Wildlife Refuge** hosts more than 230 species of birds—including the once-endangered trumpeter swan—and other wildlife including bears, wolves, and moose.

WYOMING

- Just outside **Jackson,** the **National Elk Refuge** is home to 6,000-7,000 elk or more throughout the winter months.

- In **Dubois,** the **National Bighorn Sheep Interpretive Center** offers winter tours of

National Bison Range is home to bighorn sheep.

the nearby **Whiskey Mountain Habitat Area.** Self-guided tours take visitors into prime sheep country, where waterfowl, raptors, and moose can often be seen as well.

- Just north of **Rock Springs,** the **White Mountain Herd Management Area** is home to 1,100-1,600 wild mustangs which can sometimes be seen on a 24-mile (39-km) self-guided driving tour. Pronghorn, sage grouse, coyotes, and eagles also frequent the region.

- North of **Green River,** the wetland habitat of the **Seedskadee National Wildlife Refuge** hosts some 200 bird species, including Canada geese, great blue herons, and swans.

a bison in Lamar Valley

Yellowstone's Mammoth Hot Springs Terraces

Buffalo Bill Cody's historic **Pahaska Tepee** resort. Once inside the park, check out the phenomenal **Grand Canyon of the Yellowstone** and the wildlife-rich **Hayden Valley** on your way to **Tower Junction** and the classic **Roosevelt Lodge Cabins.** Arrive in time to ride horseback (or travel by covered wagon) to the **Old West Dinner Cookout.** Then retire to your rustic cabin under the stars.

Day 7
Tower Junction to Paradise Valley
59 MILES (95 KM), 1.5 HOURS

Early birds will delight in a sunrise drive through the famed **Lamar Valley** for amazing opportunities to spot wildlife, including wolves and bears. Consider a hike up to **Trout Lake** or maybe meander along the trout waters of **Slough Creek.** Turn around and head back north to **Mammoth and the Mammoth Hot Springs Terraces,** where you can amble around the colorful geothermal features. For lunch, try the bison burger or elk sliders at the **Mammoth Hotel Dining**

Room, just below the geothermal terraces. On your way out of the park, perhaps you'll want to soak in the **Boiling River** between Mammoth and Gardiner, or just wait until you arrive at **Chico Hot Springs Resort** to enjoy the naturally heated waters. After a gourmet dinner in the Chico dining room, settle in for the night and listen for Percy, the resident ghost.

Day 8
Paradise Valley to Lake, Wyoming
91 MILES (147 KM), 3 HOURS

Backtrack through the park's northern entrance. River rats should take a morning **raft trip** on the Yellowstone River through Yankee Jim Canyon. Inside the park, head to **Norris Geyser Basin** for another education in geology and supervolcanology. Then head to **Canyon**—check out the canyon or the falls from another angle, or even on a trail like **Uncle Tom's Trail,** which will take you to the spectacular **Lower Falls.** Wind up your day with a cocktail on the porch and a relaxing dinner at the idyllic **Lake Yellowstone Hotel.**

Rent a canoe at Jenny Lake.

Old Faithful

Day 9
Lake to Jackson
95 MILES (153 KM), 2.5 HOURS

After a morning stroll at water's edge, head down to **West Thumb Geyser Basin,** an incredible selection of geothermal features. From there, continue south to **Grand Teton National Park.** You'll pass this way again in two days, so don't feel pressured to stop at every scenic turnout. Grab lunch along the way and try a hike along the gentle **Lakeshore Trail** at Colter Bay. Continue down to Jackson and settle in at the **Anvil Motel.** Walk just a few blocks for small plates and communal seating at **Bin 22,** or sit down to a long and sumptuous meal at the **Snake River Grill.** Before tucking in for the night, stop for a nightcap at the famous **Million Dollar Cowboy Bar.**

Day 10
Jackson Hole

Hit the local favorite—**The Bunnery**—for a hearty breakfast. White-water enthusiasts will have no shortage of options on the **Snake River.** Mountain bikers and hikers can hit the alpine slopes at either **Snow King** in town or off the fabulous **gondola** at **Jackson Hole Mountain Resort,** or consider **horseback riding.** If you have the energy in the afternoon, visit the **National Museum of Wildlife Art** before grabbing a margarita and some Mexican fare at **Pica's Mexican Taqueria.** Wednesday and Saturday nights you can catch the **Jackson Rodeo.**

Day 11
Jackson to Old Faithful
98 MILES (158 KM), 2.5 HOURS

After breakfast, head north toward Grand Teton and Yellowstone. Stop at **Jenny Lake** for a hike to **Hidden Falls and Inspiration Point,** a boat ride, or just a picnic. Continue north through **Grand Teton,** checking out the sights you missed on the way down. Once in **Yellowstone,** drive north and west to Old Faithful and stay at the **Old Faithful Inn** for the night. There are great trails along the way, including an easy jaunt to **Lone Star Geyser.** Explore the area before settling in for dinner and a bed at the inn. If you can keep your eyes open, Old Faithful erupts in the moonlight are pretty unforgettable.

Day 12
Old Faithful to West Yellowstone
32 MILES (52 KM), 0.75 HOUR

After a leisurely morning, head north and then west to the town of West Yellowstone. Enjoy this small but dense section of the park on your way out. Don't miss the opportunity to swim in the thermally heated waters of the **Firehole River.** In West Yellowstone, check out the **Grizzly and Wolf Discovery Center** and the adjacent **Yellowstone Giant Screen Theatre.** Grab a bison burger at **Buckaroo Bill's Ice Cream** or a gourmet meal at **Bar N Ranch** before calling it a night in a cozy safari tent at **Yellowstone Under Canvas.**

Day 13
West Yellowstone to Big Sky
51 MILES (82 KM), 1 HOUR

Head over to the **Freeheel & Wheel** to rent a bike and then hit the famous **Rendezvous Ski Trails,** where Olympic Nordic skiers have trained. After lunch, continue north through the scenic **Gallatin Canyon** toward Big Sky Resort. There are countless hiking trails and fishing spots along the way. Plan on spending the night at **Big Sky Resort;** head to dinner at **Olive B's Big Sky Bistro.**

Day 14
Big Sky to Bozeman
44 MILES (71 KM), 1 HOUR

Start your day with a short hike to scenic **Ousel Falls** and then jump in a **Geyser Whitewater** raft to white-knuckle it down the Gallatin River canyon. Then head back to Bozeman to enjoy the mountain vistas and toast your trip over a bison steak or burger at **Ted's Montana Grill** or rustic Italian fare at **Blackbird Kitchen.**

Missoula

Seven-Day Glacier Road Trip

Start your tour of Montana's magnificent northwest corner in Missoula, the hometown of *A River Runs Through It* author Norman Maclean and dozens of the state's literary heroes. Although the city is surrounded by wilderness, the University of Montana community gives the town something of an urban vibe. Those who want to spend less time on the road could start and finish the journey in Kalispell. Because of the mountain terrain, the driving time is often much longer than the mileage suggests.

Day 1
Missoula to Bigfork
100 MILES (161 KM), 2 HOURS

Arrive in Missoula; check out the shops on **Higgins Avenue** and the hip **Missoula Art Museum,** grab a pastry or sandwich from **Bernice's Bakery,** and walk along the lovely **riverfront trails.** Next, head north toward Glacier country. At Ravalli, choose your direction—northwest toward the **National Bison Range** at Moiese or northeast to the historic mission at **St. Ignatius.** The forks come together again just south of Ronan, where you'll continue north along the east shore of **Flathead Lake** to the waterfront village of Bigfork. Stop along the way to gorge yourself on seasonal **Flathead cherries** or just to stretch your legs and dip your toes in the lake. Just south of Bigfork, settle in at the **Mountain Lake Lodge** for two restful nights.

Day 2
Bigfork

Try **white-water rafting** on the Flathead River or **kayaking** on the lake with the **Flathead Raft Company,** or rent your own craft at **Bigfork Outdoor Rentals.** Take an incredible hike—maybe to **Black Lake** or **Twin Lakes**—in the nearby **Jewel Basin.** Leave some time for browsing the cute shops around town, and reward yourself with a gourmet northern Italian meal at **Moroldo's Ristorante Italiano.**

Twin Lakes

Get Yourself in Hot Water

In the middle of winter, when the cold works its way into your bones, there's nothing quite like soaking in a natural hot spring to restore your energy and wellbeing. Thanks to the geothermal and hydrothermal activity that put Yellowstone National Park on the map, both Montana and Wyoming offer an abundance of hot springs, most of which can be enjoyed year-round. Options range from middle-of-nowhere holes in the ground to well-known natural features and developed pools in resort-like settings. In general, the closer you get to Yellowstone, the more options there are.

A good site for a diverse range of hot springs in Montana is Montana Hot Springs (http://montanahotsprings.net). Montana's official tourism site (www.visitmt.com) regularly updates their page on hot springs around the state (navigate to Things to Do, then Hot Springs). To find spots in Wyoming, visit the state tourism site (www.travelwyoming.com), which also has a page on hot springs (navigate to Things to Do, then Hot Springs).

Here are five favorite hot springs in Montana and Wyoming.

- Set in the middle of nowhere about halfway between Helena and Butte, **Boulder Hot Springs** (page 265) has both indoor and outdoor pools of varying temperatures and mineral content. There are also separate men's and women's plunge pools and steam baths. The on-site hotel offers simple rooms and great food).

- Just up the road from Yellowstone in Montana's Paradise Valley, **Chico Hot Springs Resort** (page 300) is a classic. Founded in the late 1800s and known then for offering miners a bath, a clean bed and fresh strawberries at every meal, Chico today is known for its wonderful outdoor pools, cozy accommodations, fabulous dining room, and lively tavern.

- The **Boiling River** (page 326)—which is not, in fact, boiling—is a magical place and an experience you will not soon forget. Located just inside Yellowstone's north entrance at Gardiner, Montana, the Boiling River is actually a small stretch of the Gardner River where thermally heated water from nearby Mammoth Hot Springs flows into the icy waters of the Gardner, mixing to make perfect a swimming temperature any time of year. The snowcapped peaks and great plumes of steam coming off the water make winter an especially unforgettable time to swim here.

- Located between Jackson Hole and Pinedale, Wyoming, **Granite Hot Springs** (page 410) was built in 1933 by the CCC and boasts a lovely mountainous setting and a family-friendly ambience. Access in winter is limited to skiers, snowmobilers and dogsledders, and there's a campground nearby.

- The entire town of Thermopolis, Wyoming, is built around natural hot springs and **Hot Springs State Park** (page 423) is a wonderful place to enjoy them. Originally part of the Wind River Indian Reservation, the area was sold to the U.S. Government in 1896 with the stipulation from Shoshone chief Washakie that the waters would always be freely available so that anyone could benefit from their healing properties. Today, the park houses a variety of developed pools, including **State Bath House**, which offers the only free thermal pools in the park.

Day 3
Bigfork to Whitefish
34 MILES (55 KM), 0.75 HOUR

Start your day at the **Echo Lake Café** before heading north toward **Kalispell**, where you can check out the contemporary art scene at the **Hockaday Museum of Art.** Consider a hike or bike ride at **Whitefish Mountain Resort,** perhaps hiking the **Danny On Trail,** just 3.8 miles (6.1 km) to the summit, and then a **gondola** ride down. For dinner, try **Latitude 48,** then wander the **art galleries and boutiques.** Settle in for the night, lakeside, at the **Lodge at Whitefish Lake.**

Many Glacier

Day 4
Whitefish to Many Glacier
112 MILES (180 KM), 3 HOURS

Get a hearty breakfast and a great piece of pie at **Loula's Café** before heading into **Glacier National Park.** Stop at **Lake McDonald** to soak in the majestic beauty and prepare yourself for the vistas still ahead on the **Going-to-the-Sun Road.** Stop for a hike; the **Hidden Lake Overlook** from Logan Pass is a stunner. Continue east out of the park through **St. Mary** and **Babb,** where you can treat yourself to dinner at **Two Sisters Café** before heading back into the phenomenal Many Glacier Valley to camp or stay at the historic **Many Glacier Hotel.**

Day 5
Many Glacier

Plan to spend the day adventuring around Many Glacier. Possible activities include an endless number of **hiking trails** and **canoeing, kayaking,** or **cruising** on **Swiftcurrent Lake.** One option is to combine a scenic cruise with a hike to **Grinnell Glacier.** Other options include **ranger-led hikes** and **Red Bus Tours.**

For dinner, try the bison tenderloin or the wild mushroom stroganoff in the **Ptarmigan Dining Room** at the Many Glacier Hotel.

Day 6
Many Glacier to East Glacier
63 MILES (101 KM), 1.75 HOURS

After a morning hike, head south toward East Glacier. Stop for recreation in **St. Mary** or continue farther south into the isolated **Two Medicine Valley.** Consider combining a 45-minute **cruise** on Two Medicine Lake, cutting 6 miles (9.7 km) off the hike to **Twin Falls.** Another option is to cruise and then hike to **No Name Lake.** Finish the day in East Glacier with a hearty meal at the **Two Medicine Grill** and a room at the historic **Glacier Park Lodge.**

Day 7
East Glacier to Missoula
222 MILES (355 KM), 4 HOURS

This is the longest day by far in the car, but there is some magnificent scenery and plenty of places to stop along the way. From East Glacier, drive southwest on U.S. 2 over **Marias Pass,** then

The culture and history of indigenous people have powerfully defined the identities of both Montana and Wyoming. Both states offer tremendous opportunities for those interested in learning about and experiencing Native American history, traditions, and contemporary culture.

LITTLE BIGHORN BATTLEFIELD NATIONAL MONUMENT

This is where thousands of Cheyenne, Sioux, and Arapaho warriors fought under such legendary figures as Sitting Bull and Crazy Horse. Lieutenant Colonel George Armstrong Custer and more than 200 men from his 7th Cavalry died in the brief battle. A wonderful way to explore the monument is by hiring a Native American guide through **Apsalooke Tours.**

CROW FAIR

Held the third week in August since 1904, Crow Fair is considered the largest outdoor powwow in the world. More than 45,000 people come to watch, and many camp out in more than 1,000 tipis erected on the banks of the Little Bighorn River.

BLACKFEET CULTURAL HISTORY TOURS

Step-on guided trips of the Blackfeet Reservation take guests to buffalo jumps, tipi rings, and medicine lodges. Tours often include visits to the **Museum of the Plains Indian.**

BIG HOLE NATIONAL BATTLEFIELD

This moving historic site bears witness to the battle between Chief Joseph's band of Nez Perce and the U.S. Army.

WIND RIVER RESERVATION

Wyoming's only reservation is home to about 8,600 Northern Arapaho and some 3,900 Eastern Shoshone. Sights of interest include the **Shoshone Tribal Cultural Center** and the gravesites of the two most prominent Shoshone, **Chief Washakie** and Lewis and Clark's guide **Sacagawea.**

The best time to visit is during the annual three-day powwows. The largest Shoshone powwow is the **Eastern Shoshone Indian Days**

performer at Eastern Shoshone Indian Days Powwow

Powwow and Rodeo, held the fourth weekend in June. The largest Arapaho powwow is the **Ethete Celebration,** usually held in late July.

MEDICINE WHEEL NATIONAL HISTORIC LANDMARK

This mysterious carved stone wheel has spiritual but unexplained significance to many Native American tribes. Interpretive tours are offered by local Native American guides.

DEVILS TOWER NATIONAL MONUMENT

This iconic rocky sentinel, the first national monument in the country, is considered sacred by numerous tribes, all of whom have unique origin stories for it. A voluntary climbing closure is in effect each June out of respect for various Native American ceremonies.

With more than 100 annual events on the calendar between May and November, it's hard to drive through Montana and Wyoming without running into rodeo action somewhere. Stop. Buy a ticket. The bleachers are fine. These small-town rodeos offer a unique window into life here: Locals wear their Sunday best, and no one seems to mind the dust. Sitting on a sunbaked wooden bench, cold beer in one hand and a bag of popcorn in the other, is the best first date in small towns like Livingston, Montana, or Ten Sleep, Wyoming, where they show off their best without hiding what's real.

MONTANA

Miles City Bucking Horse Sale (third full weekend in May)

Since 1914, the country's best bucking stock—and the most ambitious cowboys—have been showcased at this world-famous event in Miles City. The party atmosphere follows the crowds from the rodeo into town and every bar throughout the long weekend for concerts, street dances, and a good old small-town parade. Don't be surprised if you see cowboys, carrying their saddles, hitching a ride to this event: For horses, bulls, and riders, this is *the* place to get noticed.

Annual NRA Gardiner Rodeo (mid-June)

Just outside Yellowstone's north entrance, in the shadow of Electric Peak, the annual rodeo in tiny Gardiner includes all the standards—bull riding, saddle bronc riding, bareback bronc riding, steer wrestling, barrel racing, and breakaway roping—with a timeless small-town charm.

Augusta American Legion Rodeo and Parade (last Sunday in June)

Held in the hamlet of Augusta, at the edge of the spectacular Rocky Mountain Front, this is the largest and oldest one-day rodeo in the state. The town throws its biggest party of the year with rodeo action, a barbecue, a street dance, and even an art show.

Livingston Roundup Rodeo (July 2-4)

Offering small-town charm and a big-city purse over the Fourth of July holiday, this festive event puts Livingston on the map with big-name rodeo action, a popular parade, nightly fireworks, and more than 10,000 spectators that flood this riverfront community.

Wolf Point Wild Horse Stampede (second weekend in July)

Montana's oldest rodeo, the Wild Horse Stampede in Wolf Point, on the Fort Peck Indian Reservation, is a three-day event that includes professional rodeo, daily parades and a carnival, the famous wild horse race, street dances, and a kids' stick-horse rodeo.

WYOMING

Thermopolis Cowboy Rendezvous (weekend after Father's Day)

From tailgate parties and a Western dance to a pancake breakfast and parade, the small-town rodeo in Thermopolis ushers in the pro rodeo circuit for the Big Horn Basin with plenty of action and family fun.

Cody Stampede Rodeo (July 1-4)

With all the showmanship one would expect from a town named after Buffalo Bill Cody, this professional rodeo lets the town shine with all the classic events including bareback riding, roping, steer wrestling, barrel racing, and saddle bronc and bull riding. The rest of the summer, visitors can get a true sense of small-town rodeo at the Cody Nite Rodeo.

Ten Sleep Fourth of July Rodeo (two days over Fourth of July)

With a rodeo history that dates back to 1908 and includes some of the biggest names in the sport, Ten Sleep boasts rodeo action throughout the summer. Special events at the annual Fourth of July shindig include a Pony Express Ride from nearby Hyattville, a Main Street parade, an old-fashioned rodeo, fireworks, and a sometimes-bloody wild horse race.

Sheridan WYO Rodeo (usually the second week in July)

This is the biggest week of the year for Sheridan. There is a golf tournament, art show, rodeo royalty pageant, carnival, Indian relay races, parade, and street dance on top of four nights of pro-rodeo action.

Medicine Wheel National Historic Landmark

north along the west side of Glacier National Park. As you enter Columbia Falls, turn south onto Highway 206 and continue on Highway 35 toward Creston. Take Highway 83, the Swan Highway, south through the scenic **Seeley-Swan Valley.** You'll pass **Swan and Seeley Lakes,** among others. Time it right and you can stop for an incredible lunch and hike at **Holland Lake Lodge.** At Highway 200, continue west back to Missoula, where you can recall the highlights of your trip over an indulgent supper at the **Pearl Café & Bakery.**

Cowboys, Hot Springs, and Wide-Open Spaces

Though it is not as vast as Montana, Wyoming feels remarkably spacious. This 10-day road trip includes two tried-and-true cowboy towns, a geological wonder, an outdoors mecca, four days at a working ranch, and all the beautiful and historical sights in between. As is true of the other itineraries, the goal is to minimize driving time while maximizing wonderful stops along the way.

Day 1
Sheridan

Ease into your cowboy experience with a visit to the **Trail End State Historic Site.** Check out the Western duds at the legendary **King's Saddlery,** and don't leave without a **King Ropes baseball cap,** which is de rigueur in the West. Wander around town, nosing into some of the shops and galleries along **Main Street.** Then enjoy a hearty meal at **Rib & Chop House.** Wind things down at the classic **Mint Bar** and find a comfy bed at the historic **Sheridan Inn.**

10 Best Hikes

The best way to see this place and to know it is to get out and hike. Explore the wilderness. Climb the mountains. Run your fingertips along the bark of trees. Feel the whisper of high grasses on your legs. Earn the best view you've ever seen. Here are 10 of the top hikes in Montana and Wyoming.

BILLINGS AND THE BIG OPEN

- High in the Beartooth Mountains, not far from Roscoe, **East Rosebud Trail #15 to Elk Lake** is a 6.7-mile (10.8-km) trail with diverse terrain—forest, canyon, alpine cirque—and a rushing creek nearly the whole way. Wildlife is abundant, views are sublime, and a dip in Elk Lake makes every step worthwhile.

GLACIER NATIONAL PARK

- **Highline Trail** is popular for good reason. Best in midsummer when the wildflowers explode with color, the shorter version of this strenuous hike climbs a total of 1,950 feet (594 m) over 11.8 miles (19 km) and offers outstanding scenery, including a stretch along the Garden Wall, a ledge that will delight thrill seekers.

- A short and easy hike through alpine meadows known as the Hanging Gardens, the **Hidden Lake Overlook Trail,** also known as the Hidden Lake Nature Trail, offers extraordinary views of Clements Mountain, the Garden Wall, and Mount Oberlin. The 2.7-mile (4.3-km) round-trip hike crosses the Continental Divide and is often snow-covered, even in midsummer.

BUTTE, HELENA, AND SOUTHWEST MONTANA

- A lesser-known but stunning spot for hiking is the **Humbug Spires Wilderness Trail,** south of Butte. There are quartz monzonite towers, a primeval Douglas fir forest, and a gurgling stream. The 3.5-mile (5.6-km) hike travels through dense, lush greenery, even late in summer.

BOZEMAN AND THE GATEWAY TO YELLOWSTONE

- **Sacajawea Peak** towers above Fairy Lake and affords hikers spectacular views and a good shot at seeing mountain goats. The trail is just 4 miles

(6.4 km) round-trip—but steep, gaining 2,000 feet (610 m) in elevation. For more, continue on the winding **Bridger Mountains National Recreation Trail.** Those who want less can amble around **Fairy Lake,** a flat 1.2-mile (1.9-km) loop.

YELLOWSTONE NATIONAL PARK

- Starting with a steep descent to a suspension bridge over the rushing Yellowstone River, the backcountry **Hellroaring Trail** is beautiful but strenuous. Enjoy a 6.2-mile (10-km) stretch through scenic sagebrush plateau to the confluence of Hellroaring Creek and the Yellowstone River.

GRAND TETON NATIONAL PARK

- The **Taggart Lake-Bradley Lake Loop** takes hikers to two glacially formed lakes at the base of the Tetons. With only 585 feet (178 m) of elevation gained over 5.5 miles (8.9 km), this moderate trail along water and through forest offers up views of Nez Perce peak, Middle and Grand Tetons, and Teewinot Mountain.

- **Hidden Falls Trail** offers the best of the park—access to Jenny Lake, pristine conifer forests, rushing creeks, soaring alpine views, and a chance to encounter wildlife. The moderately challenging trail is 4.9 miles (7.9 km), but can be shortened to 1 mile (1.6 km) by taking the shuttle across Jenny Lake.

SHERIDAN AND NORTHEAST WYOMING

- Hiking is a great way to appreciate the stark beauty of Devils Tower. The 1.5-mile (2.4-km) **Joyner Ridge Trail** takes in beautiful views of the tower, particularly at sunset, and can be linked to the 2.8-mile (4.5-km) Red Beds Trail, which is steep, but lovely.

SOUTHERN WYOMING

- In the Vedauwoo climbing area near Laramie, **Turtle Rock Loop Trail** is an easy 2.8-mile (4.5-km) loop with plenty of options for more mileage. The trail winds through aspen forests, open country, and around dramatic rock formations.

Day 2
Sheridan to Thermopolis
160-205 MILES (260-330 KM), 3 HOURS

To get from Sheridan to Thermopolis, there are a couple of starkly beautiful drives, both offering access to interesting sights and countless trails in the **Bighorn National Forest.**

The **Bighorn Scenic Byway** (about 205 miles/330 km) climbs up and over the mountains past such sights as the **Medicine Wheel National Historic Landmark** and **Bighorn Canyon National Recreation Area,** where **mustangs** can be spotted. This route follows Highway 14 to Lovell and then south toward Thermopolis.

The shorter route (about 160 miles/260 km) is higher but no less scenic. It heads south to **Buffalo** past the impressive **Fort Phil Kearny State Historic Site,** then over the **Cloud Peak Skyway Scenic Byway** through Ten Sleep to Worland and eventually south to Thermopolis.

As you pull into Thermopolis, head to the colorful and otherworldly **Hot Springs State Park.** Stroll along the **Spirit Trail** or stop into the historic **State Bath House** for a swim before checking in to the **Best Western Plaza Hotel.** For dinner, grab a burger at the **One Eyed Buffalo Brewing Company.**

Day 3
Thermopolis to Casper
134 MILES (216 KM), 2 HOURS

Spend the day in Thermopolis, exploring the park and soaking in the medicinal waters. Arrange for a tour of the **Wyoming Dinosaur Center and Dig Sites.** You can even participate in their **archaeological digs.** Fill your belly at the **Black Bear Café** before heading south through some of the oldest rock formations on the planet. Consider planning a **white-water excursion** with Wind River Canyon Whitewater and Fly Fishing, the only outfitter licensed to operate on the Wind River Reservation. Keep your eyes peeled for **bighorn sheep.** At Shoshoni, head east toward Casper. After a thick steak at the **FireRock Steakhouse,** or surprisingly good pan-Asian food at **Dsasumo,** settle in for two nights at the **Sunburst Lodge** on **Casper Mountain.**

Bighorn National Forest

Day 4
Casper

Wake up to wilderness on **Casper Mountain.** There are endless options for ways to enjoy it: Hike or bike the trails, or fish on the well-recovered **North Platte River.** For a more cultural experience, head to the **Nicolaysen Art Museum and Discovery Center** and wonderful **National Historic Trails Interpretive Center.** Lunch at **The Cottage Café** or **Sherrie's Place,** and plan for dinner at **Guadalajara.** Back on the mountain, if the **Crimson Dawn Museum** is open, stop in to drink in the lore of the mountain.

Day 5
Casper to Buffalo
115 MILES (185 KM), 1.5 HOURS

Head north on I-87, which runs parallel to the old **Bozeman Trail.** This is stark open country, with the Thunder Basin National Grassland sweeping out east of the highway. In Buffalo, belly up to the bar in the historic **Occidental Hotel** for a meal and a cozy room for the night. For a little exercise, hit the 13-mile (20.9-km) **Clear Creek Trail System.** If you're lucky, you'll be able to catch the weekly **Cowgirl Rodeo,** on Tuesdays, June through August, at the Johnson County Fairgrounds.

Day 6
Buffalo to TA Guest Ranch
14 MILES (22.5 KM), 0.5 HOUR

Rise early and hightail it to the historic **TA Guest Ranch,** south of Buffalo off Highway 196, where you'll spend the next four days. This is where cowboy culture comes to life.

Days 7-9
TA Guest Ranch

Spend the next three nights enjoying an **authentic ranch experience.** Activities range from riding to fly-fishing, hiking, biking, and golf. You'll visit tipi rings and Bozeman Trail sites on the property, plus important battlefields nearby. Expect to work and play hard.

Day 10
TA Guest Ranch to Sheridan
61 MILES (98 KM), 1 HOUR

Trade your saddle for a bucket seat and head north to Sheridan. Consider a stop at **Fort Phil Kearny State Historic Site** and the tiny town of **Big Horn** to see the **Bradford Brinton Memorial and Museum.** Enjoy a last meal—Wyoming gourmet—at **Frackelton's** on Main Street in Sheridan.

Billings and the Big Open

Eastern Montana is a vibrant amalgam of history, landscapes, and cultures. It's home to the Little Bighorn Battlefield and four of the state's seven Indian reservations, as well as the city of Billings and starkly beautiful Missouri River Breaks terrain.

Sometimes referred to as Montana east of the mountains, rather than eastern Montana (in truth, the region occupies more than a third of the state's land mass), this region may not have the mountainous grandeur most people expect when they visit Montana, but it has a sense of authenticity, a grittiness that sets it apart from the rest of the state. Plenty of towns in eastern Montana were founded by accident, when someone's wagon broke down and options were limited. A day's drive in this region gives visitors a true sense of the hardscrabble life

Highlights

Look for ★ to find recommended sights, activities, dining, and lodging.

★ **Yellowstone Art Museum:** Housed in an old jail, this art museum is renowned for its permanent collection of Montana artists, both historical and cutting-edge (page 50).

★ **Pictograph Cave State Park:** The caves in this state park contain evidence of human habitation dating back more than 4,500 years, including pictographs of people, animals, and even weapons (page 51).

★ **Little Bighorn Battlefield National Monument:** This historic site is a moving tribute to one of the last armed battles in which Native Americans fought to preserve their land and way of life. An annual reenactment brings to life the terror and tragic meaning of the event (page 61).

★ **Crow Fair:** This five-day celebration on the Crow Indian Reservation features an all-Indian rodeo, daily parades, and horse racing (page 66).

★ **WaterWorks Art Museum:** This gem is housed in a century-old waterworks building (page 70).

★ **Miles City Bucking Horse Sale:** Held the third full weekend in May, this rodeo is packed with cowboy swagger (page 72).

★ **Makoshika State Park:** The colorful rock layers at Montana's largest state park are a fascinating lesson in geological time travel (page 77).

★ **Medicine Lake National Wildlife Refuge:** Walk or drive through this stunning blend of glacial-drift prairie and shallow wetland to see hundreds of migrating birds (page 78).

★ **Pioneer Town in Scobey:** More than 35 buildings from Scobey's past have been restored to their early 20th-century glory (page 82).

★ **Fort Peck Dam:** The dam's interpretive center and museum chronicle not only the remarkable structure itself but the staggering number of fossils unearthed during its construction, local dinosaur finds, and Sioux and Assiniboine culture (page 85).

in these parts, the unavoidable isolation and the enormous value placed on community. And there is beauty here that should not be overlooked. The often crumbling architecture of agriculture—leaning barns, lonely grain elevators, and rusted equipment—is as much a part of the landscape here as mountains are farther west. The tones of golden light are subtle but too plentiful to count. The clouds change their moods often and play tricks with shadows.

Though few and far between, the northern communities in this region—Malta, Scobey, Plentywood, and Wolf Point, to name a few—are strong and tightly knit. They have to be in the face of the Bakken Oil Field—and its ageless boom-and-bust cycle—just over the border in North Dakota. In the northeast corner of the state, the Fort Peck Indian Reservation is home to various bands of both Sioux and Assiniboine people. In this part of Montana, the hunting ethos is as deeply rooted as the agricultural way of life. Farther south, bigger towns like Glendive and Miles City boast strong cowboy culture and some surprisingly important art, and the Crow Indian Reservation is a carefully preserved, but living piece of Western history. Billings, Montana's largest city and frankly not known for its beauty, is not unpleasant in its size, modernity, and ease of access. Though decidedly industrial, the city is populated by fiercely loyal and proud residents, many of whom have been in the area for generations. Strong art, theater, and sports scenes are part of the city's pulse; with a number of excellent eateries and performing arts venues, Billings is a wonderful place for an evening out. Plus, outdoor pursuits—on the river and rimrocks or in the mountains—are always a good option.

Whether you see this region as the Big Sky, the Big Open, or just an obvious and easy access point, this is a part of the state that will enchant you with historical and geographic context for everything else Montana has to offer.

PLANNING YOUR TIME

For travelers who are willing to take their time and let the state unfold slowly as opposed to the drama of the one-two mountain-sky knockout punch, eastern Montana is an ideal place to start a Montana road trip. There is subtlety here in the landscape and the light as well as a feeling of timelessness. When you drive on the prairie, it is not such a stretch to imagine the first travelers to this region. In fact, some Lewis and Clark buffs suggest that the only landscape the explorers would recognize today is rural Montana, simply because it hasn't changed much. Even a stroll down almost any small-town Main Street can feel like a step back in time, with still-bustling local hardware stores and, instead of fast-food or chain restaurants, real bakeries, doughnut shops, and cafés. Take your time in eastern Montana: Stop for pie and to chat. Just slow down and enjoy.

Most visitors traveling by car from the east will arrive in Montana via either I-94 at Wibaux or I-90 near Wyola, just south of the **Little Bighorn Battlefield.**

Although "the Magic City" is the largest in Montana, and one of the easiest and least expensive to get to by air, **Billings** is not an altogether magical place. Still, the city has an authenticity and vitality that make a visit worthwhile. Its restaurants and art scene alone make Billings worth the trip. It is also an excellent place to launch explorations of eastern and central Montana. Many people opt to access Cody, Wyoming, or Yellowstone National Park by driving over the Beartooth Highway from Red Lodge, just over an hour's drive south of Billings.

Driving in this region, and throughout Montana and Wyoming, can eat up entire days, but the journey itself can be incredibly worthwhile. In 2010, the state introduced a tongue-in-cheek, in-state marketing campaign with the slogan "Get Lost," the signs of which are still evident on bumper stickers

---

Previous: Little Bighorn Battlefield National Monument; performers at Crow Fair on the Crow Indian Reservation; Pictograph Cave State Park.

Billings and the Big Open

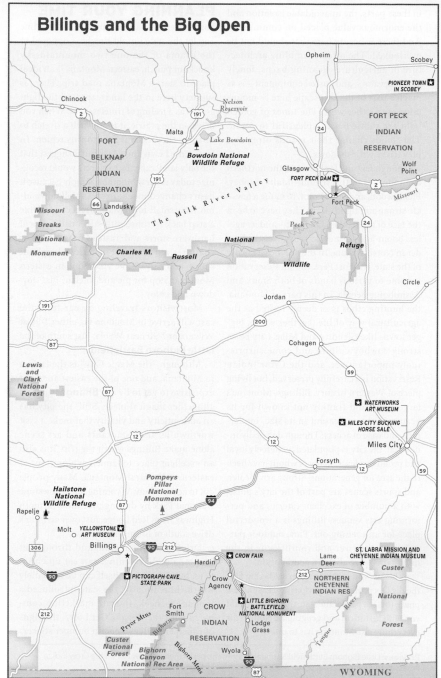

Opheim

Scobey

PIONEER TOWN IN SCOBEY ⭐

Chinook

Nelson Reservoir

(2)

(191)

Malta

Lake Bowdoin

(24)

FORT PECK

FORT

BELKNAP

Bowdoin National Wildlife Refuge

INDIAN

RESERVATION

INDIAN

(191)

Glasgow

Wolf Point

RESERVATION

FORT PECK DAM ⭐

Missouri

(66) Landusky

Fort Peck

(2)

Missouri

Breaks

The Milk River Valley

Lake Peck

National

(24)

National

Monument

Charles M.

Russell

Refuge

Wildlife

Circle

(191)

Jordan

(200)

(87)

Cohagen

Lewis and Clark National Forest

(87)

(59)

(12)

WATERWORKS ART MUSEUM ⭐

(12)

(12)

⭐ **MILES CITY BUCKING HORSE SALE**

Miles City

Forsyth

(12)

(59)

Pompeys Pillar National Monument

Hailstone National Wildlife Refuge

(87)

(94)

Rapelje

Molt ⭐ **YELLOWSTONE ART MUSEUM**

⭐ **CROW FAIR**

Lame Deer

ST. LABRA MISSION AND CHEYENNE INDIAN MUSEUM

(306)

Billings

(90) (212)

Hardin

Custer

(90)

⭐ **PICTOGRAPH CAVE STATE PARK**

Crow Agency

(212)

NORTHERN CHEYENNE INDIAN RES

National

Fort Smith

CROW

⭐ **LITTLE BIGHORN BATTLEFIELD NATIONAL MONUMENT**

(212)

Bighorn River

INDIAN

Lodge Grass

Forest

Tongue River

Custer National Forest

Bighorn Canyon National Rec Area

Bighorn Mtns

RESERVATION

Wyola

(90)

Pryor Mtns

(212)

(87)

WYOMING

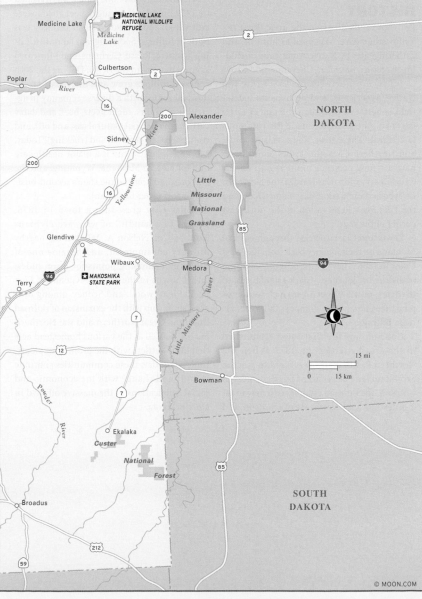

© MOON.COM

and the occasional painted barn. In eastern Montana, getting lost—in wide-open spaces, vast wilderness refuges, and friendly little towns—is the best way to get from one place to the next.

HISTORY

For thousands of years, the area along the Yellowstone River was used as hunting and gathering sites by Native Americans, including the Sioux, Blackfeet, Cheyenne, and Crow. Conflicts arose between the U.S. Army and Native Americans, and perhaps no battlefield is better known than the one at Little Bighorn where Custer made his infamous last stand. The Crow, Sioux, Assiniboine, and Northern Cheyenne tribes continue to have a strong presence in the region on the Crow Reservation near Hardin, the Northern Cheyenne Reservation near Lame Deer, and the Fort Peck Reservation in the northeast corner of the state.

Lewis and Clark traveled through eastern Montana on their journey back from the West Coast in 1806. They left the only physical sign of their entire journey—Clark's signature and the date—on a 200-foot (61-m) rocky outcropping that Clark named Pompeys Pillar, not far from Billings.

Coulson was the first town established in the area by settlers, in 1877. When the Northern Pacific Railway refused to pay the exorbitant land prices asked by the owners in Coulson, the railroad established a new town 2 miles (3.2 km) southeast of Coulson and named it after the Northern Pacific Railway's president, Frederick Billings. Within six months the city bustled with a population of 2,000, giving rise to the city's moniker, "the Magic City," which it still holds today.

When the Yellowstone Valley was irrigated in 1879, hundreds of sugar beet fields were cultivated, and by 1906 a sugar refinery was built in Billings. Soon migrant labor (including Japanese, Russo-Germans, and Mexicans) arrived to work in the fields. During the 20th century, Billings grew and thrived as an industrial center with a diverse economy in agriculture (grains, sugar beets, beef, and dairy cattle), energy (coal, natural gas, and oil), and transportation (air, rail, and trucking). Today, Montana's largest city is a major health care hub for eastern Montana, Wyoming, and the Dakotas and home to the state's second-busiest airport (after Bozeman).

Miles City grew into a town in 1876, thanks to a handful of wayward civilians fired by Col. Nelson A. Miles at his nearby military encampment, and became one of the largest shipping points for bison hides. Other towns in the region—Glendive, Fort Peck, Plentywood, and Scobey, among others—sprang up with the expansion of railroad lines, the Great Northern and the Northern Pacific, as well as the various homestead acts that lured settlers with the promise of plentiful land. Today, these communities continue to shift and change with the economic and social implications of the massive oil field in North Dakota.

Billings and Vicinity

Though not a tourist attraction per se, Billings (population 110,323; elevation 3,124 ft/952 m) is the largest city in the state and the hub for much of eastern Montana. The city is a center for industry, including oil refineries and stockyards, and serves much of eastern and central Montana with two major hospitals, three colleges, and significant shopping options. Billings used to be *the* place to buy a car, see a specialist doctor, or stock up at Costco. That has changed with growth across the state, but Billings still attracts visitors from around the state for both practical and decidedly more entertaining purposes.

The MetraPark is popular as a venue for concerts, trade shows, and rodeos and serves as the fairgrounds each summer. The Alberta Bair Theater for the Performing Arts is the largest of its kind between Minneapolis and Spokane. The Yellowstone Art Museum boasts an impressive collection of contemporary Montana art, in addition to past masters, and is worth a visit. The rimrocks around the city offer wonderful perspectives—you can see five mountain ranges—and there is a great network of hiking and biking trails. At the end of a full day, Billings's lively food and drink culture will sate any appetite.

SIGHTS
Guided Tours

Billings is not as easily navigated on foot as Montana's significantly smaller cities, but a number of tour companies offer opportunities to see its high points. The **Fun Express Bus** (406/254-7180, www.mtfunadventures. com, 11:30am, 2pm, and 7pm Mon.-Fri., 2pm Sat.-Sun. May 1-Labor Day, 2pm Sat.-Sun. Labor Day-April, $40/adults, $30/youth 6-14; custom tours available) offers 90-minute historical tours that feature underground tunnels, creepy cemeteries, haunted hotels, and the venerable Moss Mansion. Other tour options—including Lewis & Clark, Wild Mustangs, and Sunset Jeep Tours—can be arranged. The **Billings Trolley and Bus Company** (406/252-1778 or 800/698-1778, www.mttotaltransportation.com) offers customized and lighthearted tours of the Billings

Billings

Billings

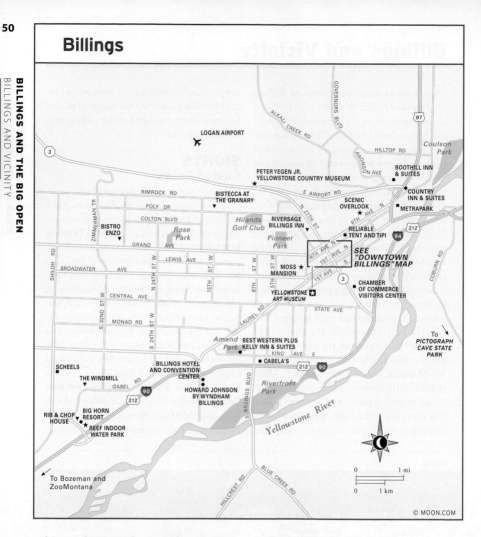

© MOON.COM

historic district and surrounding areas; the Christmas Light Tour is a winner.

★ Yellowstone Art Museum

The **Yellowstone Art Museum** (401 N. 27th St., 406/256-6804, www.artmuseum.org, 10am-5pm Tues.-Wed. and Sat., 10am-8pm Thurs.-Fri., 11am-4pm Sun., $6 adults, $3 children 6-18 and students, free for children under 6) is the region's largest contemporary art museum and offers changing exhibitions, education programs, a café, and an art sales gallery. The impressive permanent collection includes work by Russell Chatham, Freeman Butts, John Buck, Deborah Butterfield, and Theodore Waddell. The museum also houses a significant number of works by Will James and early Montana modernist Isabelle Johnson. The Visible Vault gives visitors a glimpse of how and where the museum stores its 7,400-object permanent collection.

Downtown Billings

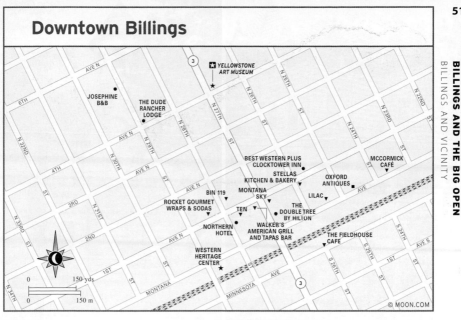

YELLOWSTONE
ART MUSEUM

JOSEPHINE
B&B

THE DUDE
RANCHER
LODGE

BEST WESTERN PLUS
CLOCKTOWER INN

STELLAS
KITCHEN & BAKERY

OXFORD
ANTIQUES

MCCORMICK
CAFÉ

BIN 119

MONTANA
SKY

LILAC

ROCKET GOURMET
WRAPS & SODAS

TEN

THE
DOUBLETREE
BY HILTON

NORTHERN
HOTEL

WALKER'S
AMERICAN GRILL
AND TAPAS BAR

THE FIELDHOUSE
CAFE

WESTERN
HERITAGE
CENTER

0   150 yds

0   150 m

© MOON.COM

Moss Mansion

For 87 years, the family of fabulously successful entrepreneur Preston Boyd Moss lived happily in Billings's **Moss Mansion** (914 Division St., 406/256-5100, www.mossmansion.com, guided tours 10am and 1pm Tues.-Sat. June-Aug., $15 adults, free for children under 5, self-guided tours noon-3pm Tues.-Sun. year-round, $12 adults, $10 seniors and military, $8 student, free for children under 5, extended summer hours 10am-4pm Tues.-Sat., noon-3pm Sun.). The 1903 home, designed by New York architect Henry Janeway Hardenbergh, who also designed New York City's original Waldorf Astoria and Plaza Hotels, was lovingly maintained by the family and turned into a museum. One-hour guided tours offer a fascinating glimpse into the Moss family's elegant lifestyle. Much of the original furnishings and art decorate the mansion today. Winter holiday tours (guided $20, children under 5 are free; self-guided, $15 adults, $12 seniors, military and students, free for children 5 and under) are a special treat starting in mid-November, when the mansion is decorated for Christmas.

Western Heritage Center

Beautifully housed downtown in the former Parmly Billings Memorial Library, the **Western Heritage Center** (2282 Montana Ave., 406/256-6809, www.ywhc.org, 10am-5pm Tues.-Sat., $5 adults, $3 students and seniors, $1 children under 12) is an affiliate of the Smithsonian Institution and has an extensive collection that documents the history of the Yellowstone River Valley, with more than 17,000 objects including historic photos and artifacts, Native American beadwork, architectural drawings, textiles, and Western art. The museum is one of the few dedicated to recording and collecting oral histories of various regional Native American groups.

★ Pictograph Cave State Park

Southeast of Billings among the sandstone cliffs that form the rimrocks, **Pictograph Cave State Park** (3401 Coburn Rd., 406/254-7342, www.stateparks.mt.gov, 9am-7pm daily Memorial Day-Labor Day, 10am-6pm daily Apr.-May and Sept., 10am-5pm daily Oct.-Mar., visitors center closes one hour before

park, $6/vehicle nonresidents, $4 walk-in, bicycle or bus passenger nonresident, free for Montana residents) contains three caves—Pictograph, Middle, and Ghost—with evidence of human habitation that dates back 5,000 years. Pictographs more than 2,000 years old can also be seen in one of the caves. Binoculars are helpful since visitors are kept some distance back in order to protect the ancient artwork. After the caves' discovery in 1936, a significant archaeological survey uncovered more than 30,000 artifacts from the site, including barbed harpoon points made from caribou horn. The park was vandalized in the 1950s and 1960s, when much of the artwork was covered with graffiti. Today it has been carefully restored, and in places, tracings from the initial archaeological study have been overlaid on the originals in order to make the vivid images more visible. A nice trail system winds through the park, and picnic facilities are available for day use only.

Pompeys Pillar National Monument

Twenty-five miles (40 km) east of Billings is **Pompeys Pillar** (3001 Hwy. 212 in Worden, 406/875-2400, www.pompeyspillar.org, vehicle access and interpretive center 9am-6pm daily early May-Sept., pedestrians permitted dawn-dusk Oct.-Apr. but no services available, $7/vehicle), an age-old landmark that bears the signature of Captain William Clark of the Lewis and Clark expedition. Named by Clark for Sacagawea's son, Jean Baptiste Charbonneau, nicknamed "Pomp," the sandstone pillar had a storied history both before and after Clark signed it on July 25, 1806: There were Indian pictographs on the 200-foot-tall (61-m) rock when he first laid eyes on it. In 1873, Custer's troops were camped opposite the pillar along the banks of the Yellowstone River when they were fired on by Sioux warriors. When the gate is locked, October-April, pedestrians can park along

the road and walk the mile from the gate to the pillar.

Every year on the last weekend in July, the Friends of Pompeys Pillar host **Clark Days** (406/969-5380), a celebration of the pillar's past with lively history lectures and presentations, nature walks, hot meals, and plenty of activities geared toward the whole family. It is the only night of the year that camping is allowed on the grounds of the pillar, and no admission fee is charged during the two-day festivities.

SPORTS AND RECREATION
Spectator Sports

Under the shadow of the rimrocks, **Dehler Park** (2611 9th Ave. N., 406/657-8371, www.billingsparks.org), built in 2008 to accommodate 6,000 baseball fans in stadium seats, bleachers, and grassy picnic areas, is home to the **Billings Mustangs** (406/252-1241, www.billingsmustangs.com). The stadium's predecessor, Cobb Field, built in 1948, was home to the Pioneer League rookie affiliates for the Brooklyn Dodgers, the Pittsburgh Pirates, and the St. Louis Cardinals. Since 1974 the Mustangs have been affiliated with the Cincinnati Reds. George Brett is among the most well-known alumni of Cobb Field.

Golf

There are a number of golf courses in Billings, perhaps because the winters here are milder than in much of western Montana and the summers are longer. Twice ranked first in the state by *Golf Digest,* **Briarwood Country Club**'s 18-hole course (3429 Briarwood Blvd., 406/248-2702, www.thebriarwoodgc.com) is open to members and, reciprocally, to members of other private golf facilities in the United States. **Eagle Rock Golf Course** (5624 Larimer Ln., 406/655-4445, www.eaglerockgolfcourse.com) is an 18-hole public course, as are the challenging par-3 **Exchange City Golf Course** (19 S. 19th St. W., 406/652-2553) and the **Lake Hills Golf Club** (1930 Clubhouse Way, 406/252-9244,

---

www.lakehillsgolf.com). Built in 1992, **Yegen Golf Club** (1390 Zimmerman Tr., 406/656-8099, www.yegengolfclub.com) is a beautiful course. Thirteen miles (20.9 km) northeast of Billings is the semiprivate **Pryor Creek Golf Club** (1292 Pryor Creek Rd., Huntley, 406/348-3900, www.pryorcreekgolf.com), one of only two 36-hole facilities in the state. The Elmer Link course is open to members and their guests, while the Johnny Walker course is open to the public.

Disc Golf

Also known as Diamond X Disc Golf Course, **Phipps Park** (Molt Rd., 4 mi/6.4 km west of Billings, www.billingsparks.org) is ranked among the top five disc golf courses in Montana. The 350-acre (141.6-hectare) city park offers 27 holes for disc golfers, panoramic views, and a network of rugged, challenging trails for both runners and mountain bikers. Right in town, **Riverfront Park** (S. Billings Blvd.) has a nice pond with hungry ducks and geese, some nice walking trails, and undeveloped areas.

Hiking

Hikers can find plenty of trails winding around the rimrocks, including the 2.8-mile (4.5-km) trail at the **Four Dances Natural Area** (2 mi/3.2 km east of downtown Billings, 406/896-5013, www.blm.gov/visit/four-dances), which offers up a wonderful view of the Yellowstone River and valley beyond from the top of the cliffs. It was named for what a Crow who did a vision quest here in the 1830s saw. Between April and August there are often peregrine falcons nesting so hikers are asked to stay away from cliff's edge. The trail drops down to the river as well. From Billings, head east on Highway 90 to exit #452, turn right on Highway 87, then take the first right on Coburn Road for 1.4 miles (2.3 km) to reach the entrance to Four Dances.

For more extreme terrain, there are some phenomenal mountain trails less than an hour from town. The **Island Lake Trail** (trailhead at Mystic Dam Power Station, end of W. Rosebud Rd.), 40 miles (64 km) southwest of Billings in the **Custer National Forest's Beartooth Ranger District** (406/446-2103, www.fs.fed.us/r1/custer), is a 12-mile (19.3-km) out-and-back round-trip in the West Rosebud Valley. There are numerous trout-laden mountain lakes in the region, but the climb is significant, so allow ample time.

Farther afield, 85 miles (137 km) from Billings, but well worth the drive, the **East Rosebud Trail #15 to Elk Lake** (406/446-2103, www.fs.fed.us/r1/custer) winds along a stream, through meadows and beneath jagged peaks to an alpine lake. There are waterfalls and sparse conifer forests along the route, which is frequented by hikers and wildlife alike. It's about 3.4 miles (5.5 km) to Elk Lake. There are established campsites at the lake, or ambitious hikers can go on another 2.5 miles (4 km) to the turquoise waters of Rimrock Lake. The out-and-back hike to Elk Lake is 6.7 miles (10.8 km) round-trip; it's 12 miles (19.3 km) to Rimrock Lake and back. To get there from Billings, head east on I-90 to exit #408 for Columbus. Head south on North 9th Street until it ends in a T at Old Highway 10/East Pike Avenue. Take a right and then the first left onto MT 78. Continue for about 27 miles (43 km) until the town of Roscoe. Turn right onto East Rosebud Road. Watch signs to stay on East Rosebud Road, as there are a few forks and deceptive turns. After 3.8 miles (6.1 km), just after crossing a bridge, turn right to stay on East Rosebud. Continue 10.6 miles (17 km) to the trailhead at the end of the road.

ENTERTAINMENT AND EVENTS
The Arts

Billings offers a host of urban culture options. Numerous theatrical performances and concerts are held at the **Alberta Bair Theater** (2801 3rd Ave. N., 406/256-6052, www.albertabairtheater.org), including the **Billings Symphony Orchestra and Chorale** (406/252-3610, www.billingssymphony.org, Sept.-June). The **NOVA Center for the Performing Arts** (2317 Montana Ave.,

406/591-9535, www.novabillings.org) hosts drama, musical theater, improv comedy, opera, and a youth conservatory all under one roof. The **Billings Studio Theatre** (1500 Rimrock Rd., 406/248-1141, www. billingsstudiotheatre.com) offers excellent theater with tremendous community support.

Festivals and Events

A great resource for finding specific events during your visit to Billings is www. Billings365.com, which highlights every sort of daily happening from concerts and food-related events to readings, sport, and recreation.

Few artificial objects enhance a skyline as spectacularly as a flock of hot-air balloons. Billings's annual **Big Sky International Balloon Rendezvous** (Pierce RV Supercenter Field off Zoo Drive and Shiloh, www.bigskyballoonrally.com), held on a weekend in late July or early August, lights up the sky with early-morning flights, dusk Balloon Glows, and plenty of camaraderie. Check the website as location can change from year to year.

Sponsored by the Yellowstone Art Museum, **Summerfair** (Veteran's Park, corner of Poly Dr. and 13th St. W., 406/256-6804, ext. 222, www.artmuseum.org, 4pm-9pm Fri., 9am-5pm Sat., 10am-4pm Sun., $5 adults, free for children under 6) is the largest arts and crafts festival in the region. Typically held on a weekend in mid-July, the fair includes more than 100 artist booths, loads of activities for kids, live entertainment, and a food court. The weekend pass ($25) admits two adults and three children for all three days.

The state's largest annual event, **MontanaFair** (MetraPark, 308 6th Ave. N., 406/256-2400 or 800/366-8538, www. montanafair.com, $9 adults, $5 seniors 65 and over and children 6-12, free for children 5 and under), running for nine days starting the second week of August, is an agricultural fair in the classic tradition. In addition to arts and crafts competitions and displays on everything from pigs and tomato-growing to pickles and crochet, MontanaFair events include major concerts, motorsports, bull riding, rodeo, and a good old-fashioned carnival. Check online or call ahead for special deals and concert tickets.

For beer lovers, **Ales for Trails** (downtown Billings, 406/281-1244, www.billingstrailnet. org) in late September offers 60 microbrews, local food vendors, and great local music. The event benefits the city's more than 43 miles (69 km) of multiuse trails and 24 miles (39 km) of bike lanes.

Growing like mad since its origins in 2001, the two-day **Magic City Blues** (main gate on the 2500 block of Montana Ave., 406/534-0400, www.magiccityblues.com, general admission from $59) music festival held in mid-August offers an impressive lineup of big-name artists in a unique outdoor setting.

SHOPPING

While Billings is more often thought of as a place for supplies rather than boutique shopping, there are a number of interesting shops worth visiting. The **Toucan Gallery** (2505 Montana Ave., 406/252-0122, www. toucanarts.com, 10am-5:30pm Tues.-Fri., 10am-4pm Sat.) is part gallery, part gift shop and showcases the work of more than 40 emerging and established contemporary artists, both local and regional. In addition to fine art, there are beautiful artisan crafts ranging from jewelry and cards to hats and home decor. They also offer various art classes and workshops.

AAA Oxford Hotel Antiques (2411 Montana Ave., 406/248-2094, www.oxford-hotel-antiques.business.site, 10:30am-4:30pm Wed.-Sat.) is Billings's oldest single-owner antiques store. The building is a 1908 Victorian Italianate and suits the inventory perfectly. In addition to two floors of furniture, the store has an endless assortment of Montana-related items and other collectibles, including record albums.

A unique piece of Montana can be ordered at **Reliable Tent & Tipi** (501 N. 23rd St., 406/252-4689 or 800/544-1039, www.reliabletent.com), which has been family-owned since 1945. Its tents are designed for the often rugged hunting conditions in Montana, and its specialty Crow and Sioux tipis are designed by Native Americans according to family and tribal traditions. The company also makes a wonderful Backyard Tipi for kids.

The 80,000-square-foot (7,430-sq-m) **Cabela's** (4550 King Ave. E., 406/373-7300, www.cabelas.com, 9am-9pm Mon.-Sat., 9am-7pm Sun.) offers a wealth of educational and entertaining displays—including a 7,000-gallon (26,495-liter) aquarium, indoor archery range, gun library, and museum-quality animal mounts—in addition to the company's top-notch outdoor gear. There's an express deli inside, as well as dog kennels and horse corrals, in case you plan to spend some time. Not to be outdone, **Scheels** (1121 Shiloh Crossing Blvd., 406/656-9220, www.scheels.com, 9am-9pm Mon.-Sat., 10am-6pm Sun.) is 220,000 square feet (20,440 sq m) of sporting goods paradise housing a collection of entertainment venues in addition to individual sport and game shops, brand-name concept shops, and a full-service shop for bikes, skis, skates, and so on. Amenities include a Ferris wheel, saltwater aquarium, shooting gallery, a deli and fudge shop, plus Starbucks.

FOOD

As Montana's largest city, Billings has a lively dining scene and is a good place to splurge. Right downtown, **Bin 119** (119 N. Broadway, 406/294-9119, www.bin119.net, 11am-10pm Mon.-Thurs., 11am-10:30pm Fri.-Sat., 10am-9pm Sun., $10-28) is an American bistro and wine bar with 180 labels and more than 30 wines sold by the glass. Started by local students, it's stylish but not at all pretentious. The food, primarily inspired by Spanish tapas, is geared toward appetizer-size dishes ($10-16). An expanded menu of entrées includes everything from roasted duck and braised short ribs to rib eye steaks and salmon fillets, a wide selection of pastas, plus soups, salads, and sandwiches.

★ **Walkers American Grill and Tapas**

Bar (2700 1st Ave. N., 406/245-9291, www.walkersgrill.com, dining room 4pm-10pm Mon.-Thurs., 4pm-10:30pm Fri., 5pm-10:30pm Sat., 5pm-10pm Sun., $9-37) is big-city chic with excellent food and award-winning wine. The menu is cosmopolitan (lamb meatball risotto) and entirely Montana (grilled Angus rib eye), and the ambience is elegant but vibrant; Sunday evenings are enhanced by live jazz starting at 7pm.

Bistro Enzo (1502 Rehberg Ln., 406/651-0999, 5pm-close Tues.-Sat., $10-30) serves up hearty fusion fare—American, Asian, French, Italian—in a comfortable farmhouse. The restaurant imports fresh fish from both coasts daily and cooks many of the entrées on a wood-fired grill; the eclectic menu is a local favorite.

Located in the Northern Hotel, **TEN** (19 N. Broadway, 406/867-6774, www.northernhotel.com/ten, 5pm-10pm daily, lounge opens at 3pm daily, $20-54) offers guests a sophisticated dining experience that emphasizes fresh local produce and meat in decidedly creative ways. From the elk nachos and hushpuppies on the lounge menu to Hutterite pork porterhouse and a phenomenal range of Angus and Kobe beef steaks, the red-hued restaurant offers an urban and very upscale take on the Montana culinary scene.

Another elegant choice for fine dining is **Bistecca at the Granary** (1500 Poly Dr., 406/259-3488, www.bisteccagranary.com, dining room 11:30am-2pm and 5pm-close Tues.-Fri., 5pm-close Sat.-Mon., lounge 3:30pm-close Mon.-Fri., 5pm-close Sat.-Sun., $17-30), which has several dining rooms, a fantastic outdoor patio in summer, and classic bistro fare.

Billings has plenty of casual and entirely family-friendly options as well that are open for both lunch and dinner. **The Windmill** (3429 TransTech Way, 406/252-8100, www.windmillbar51.com, 11am-9pm Sun.-Thurs., 11am-10pm Fri., 4pm-10pm Sat., lunch $8-35, dinner $11-40) offers an extensive seafood, steak, chicken, and ribs menu as well as a children's menu. The creekside patio can't be beat when the weather is good. Not far away, and right across from The Reef Indoor Water Park, is **Montana's Rib & Chop House** (1849 Majestic Ln., 406/839-9200, 11am-10pm daily, $9-30), an excellent chain with locations across Montana and Wyoming (and now Pennsylvania and Utah too). The menu is packed (and usually so is the restaurant) with plenty of steaks, seafood, and ribs.

For breakfast and lunch, **McCormick Café** (2419 Montana Ave., 406/255-9555, www.mccormickcafe.com, 7am-3pm Mon.-Fri., 8am-3pm Sat., 8am-2pm Sun., $8-11) is another local favorite, offering everything from French crepes and wonderful pastries to savory sandwiches, wraps, and healthy salads.

Rocket Gourmet Wraps & Sodas (2809 1st Ave. N., 406/248-5231, www.rocketwraps.com, 10am-3pm Mon.-Fri., $7-11) is an excellent place for a fast and filling meal. The hot and cold wraps and burritos are made from fresh ingredients like roasted chicken, andouille sausage, and albacore tuna. There is an ample selection of salads and kids' meals, and diners can wet their whistles with specialty coffees and Italian sodas.

★ **The Fieldhouse Cafe** (2601 Minnesota Ave., 406/534-2556, www.thefieldhousemt.com, 11am-2pm and 5pm-9pm Tues.-Fri., 9am-2pm and 5pm-9pm Sat., 9am-2pm Sun., $16-22) offers weekend brunch and a farm-to-table tapas-style dinner menu that changes weekly based on the freshest local and organic ingredients. From quinoa salad and fish tacos to truffle fries and cashew-parmesan brussels sprouts, you will want to lick your plate before you surrender it. The happy hour is 4pm-6pm Tuesday through Saturday. Another phenomenal spot for from-scratch local cuisine like rye gnocci and flat-iron steaks is **Lilac** (2515 Montana Ave., 406/969-4959, www.lilacmt.com, 5pm-close Tues.-Sat., $16-22).

Not exactly healthy—unless your body runs on cinnamon rolls, sour cream coffee cake, sugar cookies, or warm-from-the-oven bread—but completely homemade and utterly delicious, ★ **Stella's Kitchen & Bakery** (2525 1st Ave. N., 406/248-3060, 5:30am-5pm Mon.-Sat., 7am-1pm Sun., $10-12) is an excellent choice for warm, doughy comfort food and all-day breakfast. Stella's serves just breakfast items on Sunday.

ACCOMMODATIONS

When it comes to combining luxury and historical grandeur, the only choice is the magnificently restored 1902 ★ **Northern Hotel** (19 N. Broadway, 406/867-6767, www.northernhotel.com, from $129 low season, $189 high season). Reopened in 2013 as part of the Preferred Hotel Group and listed on the National Register of Historic Places, it is indeed a Western boutique hotel, with 160 guest rooms and two excellent restaurants, including the elegant **TEN**. It is Billings's only four-star hotel, and amenities include 24-hour room service, valet service, triple-sheeted beds, and piles of pillows.

The Double Tree by Hilton (27 N. 27th St., 406/252-7400, www.doubletree3.hilton.com/billings, from $115) in downtown Billings is difficult to miss: It is a towering brick building that dwarfs its neighbors. The hotel is geared to business travelers, and the guest rooms are plenty comfortable. It offers a large assortment of amenities, including complimentary high-speed Internet. The **Montana Sky** restaurant is situated on the 20th floor with terrific views of the city and rimrocks.

On the southwest side of town, the **Billings Hotel and Convention Center** (1223 Mullowney Ln., 406/248-7151, www.billingshotelmt.com, from $109 low season, $119 high season) is another large facility with all the standard amenities. Some rooms are pet-friendly (for a charge), and kids will love the curly-cue waterslides in the indoor pool.

There are two Best Western options in Billings, both of which offer clean, comfortable, and pet-friendly accommodations. In the heart of downtown, **Best Western Plus Clocktower Inn** (2511 1st Ave. N., 406/259-5511 or 800/238-4218, www.bwclocktowerinn.com, from $104 low season, $135 high season) offers guests a "Key to the City," which gives them 10 percent off at many area restaurants and bars within walking distance of the hotel. West of town, near the big-box shopping stores, the pet-friendly **Best Western Plus Kelly Inn & Suites** (4915 Southgate Dr., 406/256-9400 or 800/528-1234, www.bwbillings.com, from $124 low season, $165 high season) offers immaculately clean and spacious rooms, cozy fireplace suites, and an ideal water playland for younger kids.

When it comes to water parks, however, **Big Horn Resort** (1801 Majestic Ln., 406/839-9300 or 877/995-8999, www.thebighornresort.com, from $94 low season, $124 high season) is the real deal and a kid's dream come true. Parents will appreciate the clean, comfortable, quiet rooms and grown-up amenities like free wireless Internet and jetted bathtubs, and kids will delight in the enormous and loud **Reef Indoor Water Park** (406/839-9283, www.thereefindoors.com, 11am-7pm Mon.-Thurs., 11am-9pm Fri., 10am-9pm Sat., 10am-7pm Sun. June-Aug., 4pm-9pm Thurs.-Fri., 10am-9pm Sat., 10am-7pm Sun. Sept.-May, $14.95 all-day admission for anyone over 4 ft., $12.95 all-day admission under 4 ft., $12.95/swimmer after 4pm, $5 spectators, free for children under 2). The state's largest, this indoor facility includes three-story waterslides, a wave pool, interactive playhouse, basketball pool, 25-person hot tub, arcade, and café. There is outstanding dining just across the parking lot at the **Rib & Chop House,** so guests can leave the car parked during a stay here.

Additional hotel offerings worth looking at include the **Country Inn & Suites** (231 Main St., 406/245-9995, www.countryinns.com, from $101 low season, $118 high season) and **The Boothill Inn & Suites** (242 E. Airport Rd., 406/245-2000, from $128), which has great family suites with a king and queen as well as twin bunks.

Housed in a 1912 historic residence at the edge of downtown, **The Josephine Bed and Breakfast** (514 N. 29th St., 406/248-5898 or 800/552-5898, www.thejosephine.com, $95-170 d) offers a quiet stay in an intimate yet convenient setting. The inn provides airport pickup, free wireless Internet, passes to a 24-hour fitness center, and a gourmet breakfast. At times, the inn only accepts guests for one week or longer, so be sure to call ahead.

A 15-minute drive from downtown Billings in Huntley is **Somewhere in Time Bed & Breakfast** (266 Hogan Rd., Huntley, 406/348-2205, www.ourbedandbreakfast.com, $100-130), a lovely 1900 Victorian set in a ranch on Pryor Creek. Although the property is not handicapped-accessible, the rooms are comfortable and, unlike some Victorian establishments, not at all over-cluttered.

The Dude Rancher Lodge (415 N. 29th St., 406/545-0121, www.duderancherlodge.com, from $96) is a unique, independently owned frontier hotel built in 1949. It is within walking distance of downtown's shops, restaurants, and nightlife and prides itself on offering Western hospitality. Each guest room is individually furnished, and some come with refrigerators and microwaves.

Other budget-friendly hotels you may want to consider are the pet-friendly **Riversage Billings Inn** (880 N. 29th St., 406/252-6800 or 800/231-7782, from $84, with significant discounts for advance payment) and the **Howard Johnson by Wyndham Billings** (1345 Mullowney Ln., 406/252-2584, from $62-94, with discounts for advance payment).

CAMPING

Native Ways Primitive Campground (4055 High Trail Rd., 406/670-1209, nwpcmt@gmail.com, May 15-Nov. 1, weather dependent, $50-70), 4 (6.4 km) miles southeast of Billings, offers a unique take on camping: four tipis, both Crow and Sioux style, on 25 wooded acres (10.1 hectares). Each site has its own tipi and can be fully supplied with sleeping bags ($5) and other necessities if you need them, plus a washbasin, water, a picnic table, a lantern, and a garbage can.

The **Billings KOA** (547 Garden Ave., 406/252-3104 or 800/562-8546, www.billingskoa.com, Apr.-Oct. 15, limited service the rest of the year, from $31-51 tents, $45-85 RVs, from $95 cabins) is considered the world's first KOA and offers 40 tent sites, many of them on the banks of the Yellowstone River, along with 135 RV sites, 11 cabins, and two lodges that accommodate up to six people with bathroom, kitchen, and linens provided. There is a swimming pool and a spa for campers to use, a barbecue, miniature golf, a playground, and broadband Wi-Fi. The campground is conveniently close to town and offers pancake breakfasts and barbecue dinners mid-June-mid-August.

INFORMATION AND SERVICES

The **visitors center** is one floor below the **Billings Chamber of Commerce** (815 S. 27th St., 406/252-4016 or 800/735-2635, www.visitbillings.com, 8:30am-5pm Mon.-Sat., noon-4pm Sun. Memorial Day-Labor Day, 8:30am-5pm Mon.-Fri. Labor Day-Memorial Day).

The **main post office** (841 S. 26th St., 8:30am-5:30pm Mon.-Fri.) is just behind the chamber of commerce. There is also a **downtown post office** (2602 1st Ave. N., 406/657-5748, 8am-5:30pm Mon.-Fri.), and one **branch post office** (724 15th St. W., 406/657-5788) is open on Saturday (10am-2pm).

The **Parmly Billings Library** (510 N. Broadway, 406/657-8258, www.billings.lib. mt.us, 10am-9pm Mon.-Thurs., 10am-6pm Fri., 10am-5pm Sat., 1pm-5pm Sun., closed Sun. Memorial Day-Labor Day) offers free use of computers with Internet access.

You'll find Wi-Fi at **Starbucks** (27 N. 27th St., 6am-7pm Mon.-Fri, 7am-7pm Sat., 7am-3pm Sun.) in the Double Tree by Hilton Hotel and at **Rock Creek Roasters** (124 N. Broadway, 406/896-1600, 6am-6pm Mon.-Fri, 7am-3pm Sat.).

Two conveniently located coin-op laundries are **Speedy Wash** (2505 6th Ave. N., 406/248-4177, 7am-7:30pm daily) and **Spin Fresh Coin Laundry** (3189 King Ave. W., Ste. 4, 406/652-2993, www.spinfreshlaundry. com, 7am-9pm daily), which has a second self-serve-only location at 410 Lake Elmo Drive (6am-midnight daily).

For emergency medical assistance, **St. Vincent Healthcare** (1233 N. 30th St., 406/237-7000, www.svh-mt.org) and **Billings Clinic Hospital** (2800 10th Ave. N., 406/238-2501 or 800/332-7156, www.billingsclinic. com) both have 24-hour ER service. For minor medical care, the **Billings Clinic** also has walk-in service at three branch locations: Downtown (corner of 8th Ave. N. and N. 28th St., 406/238-2677, 7am-7:30pm Mon.-Fri., 9am-5pm Sat.-Sun.), West (2675 Central Ave., in Lamplighter Square next to Target, 406/238-2900, 7:30am-6pm Mon.-Fri., 9am-1pm Sat.), and Heights (760 Wicks Ln., across from Walmart, 406/238-2475, 7:30am-6pm Mon.-Fri.).

TRANSPORTATION
Getting There

Billings Logan International Airport (BIL, 1901 Terminal Cir., 406/247-8609 or 406/657-8495, www.flybillings.com) is situated atop the rimrocks off I-90 at the 27th Street exit. Delta, United, Allegiant, Alaska Airlines, American, and Cape Air offer regular flights.

If you arrive early at the airport or have some time to spare before you are picked up, visit the **Peter Yegen Jr. Yellowstone County Museum** (1950 Terminal Cir., 406/256-6811, www.pyjrycm.org, 10:30am-5pm Mon.-Fri., 10:30am-3pm Sat., free). Once outside the terminal, follow the road around the west parking lot; the museum is on the right before the airport exit. The museum has artifacts and exhibits highlighting the history of the northern plains from early Native American influence through westward expansion and mining up to the 1950s. There's even a two-headed calf! The museum's deck provides a splendid view of the city below.

The **Greyhound** (1830 4th Ave. N., 406/245-5117, www.greyhound.com) bus terminal and ticket offices are open 24 hours a day year-round.

As the largest city in Montana, Billings is an easy driving destination. It's intersected by I-90 and I-94 begins just outside the town. Billings is 142 miles (229 km) east of Bozeman, 81 miles (130 km) east of Big Timber, 60 miles (97 km) northeast of Red Lodge, and 46 miles (74 km) west of Hardin. In Wyoming, Cody is 106 miles (171) away, and it is 130 miles (209 km) to Sheridan.

Getting Around

At the Billings airport, **Enterprise, Thrifty, Dollar, Hertz, Alamo, Avis, Budget,** and **National** have on-site car-rental counters.

Two taxi services are available: **City Cab** (406/252-8700, www.willsonllc.com) and **Yellow Cab** (406/245-3033). There is no taxi stand at the airport, so call ahead if you want to be picked up.

MET transit (406/657-8218, www.mettransit.com, 5:50am-6:50pm Mon.-Fri., 8:10am-5:45pm Sat., $1.75 one-way fare adults 19 and up, $1.50 youth 6-18, $.85 seniors and disabled citizens, free for children 6 and under, $17.50 10-ride ticket, $4 day pass) offers bus service throughout Billings, and although there are marked bus stops around the city, you can also flag them down at any corner. Booklets with routes and schedules are available at most banks, convenience stores, grocery stores, the library, and government offices.

Crow and Northern Cheyenne Reservations

Southeastern Montana is a ruggedly beautiful part of the state, with vast prairies, dramatic canyons, and stark badlands. The land is dry and brittle in places, but the people are tenacious, having been ordered to occupy this region in the aftermath of the Fort Laramie Treaty of 1851. The two tribes in this part of the state—the Crow and the Northern Cheyenne—have managed to preserve their cultures with little more than steadfast determination. There is no better place to experience Native American culture—to see and hear their stories, their art, their traditions—than on the reservations.

The Crow Reservation occupies roughly 2.3 million acres (930,777 hectares) of land and is home to just over 7,000 Crow, which accounts for 75 percent of the tribe's enrolled members. Nearly 85 percent of those on the reservation speak Crow as their first language. The largest settlement by far and the county seat, **Hardin** (population 3,829; elevation 2,902 ft/885 m) is not on the reservation; communities on the reservation include **Crow Agency, Fort Smith, Garryowen, Lodgegrass, Pryor,** and **Wyola.**

Just east of the Crow Reservation is the much smaller **Northern Cheyenne Indian Reservation.** Today, the reservation is home to roughly 5,012 of the 11,266 enrolled tribal members. **Lame Deer** is the tribal and government agency headquarters; **Busby** is the other primary settlement on the reservation.

HISTORY

The story of the Crow Indian Reservation is all too familiar and tragic. The 1851 Fort Laramie Treaty recognized almost all of the Yellowstone Valley as Crow territory. Mining claims and a dramatic increase in the number of settlers traveling through the region led to conflict and a second treaty in 1868, which, even though unsigned by the vast majority of Crow, significantly reduced the size of their territory. The discovery of gold on Crow land shortly after the second treaty led to a third treaty in 1873, which moved the Crow again to a much smaller reservation in central Montana's Judith Basin. Neither the Crow nor the cattlemen settling in the region were pleased with the arrangement, and the Crow Reservation was moved farther east and reduced yet again in size.

The Northern Cheyenne are a division of the Cheyenne tribe who once ranged across the Great Plains from South Dakota to Colorado. The first Cheyenne territory dictated by the U.S. government was in the region around what is now Denver. The Cheyenne were repeatedly attacked by the U.S. government and sustained enormous casualties, all while living according to law in the territory the government had given them. Following the Battle of the Little Bighorn, in which the Cheyenne participated, the Army's attempts to capture the Cheyenne increased in intensity. Several Cheyenne chiefs surrendered, expecting to be returned to Colorado, but were instead sent to the reservation for the Southern Cheyenne in Oklahoma.

After disease decimated the tribe and starvation threatened the survivors, fewer than 300 Northern Cheyenne slipped out of the reservation with the intent of going back north. Nearly 10,000 soldiers and 3,000 settlers chased the band for six weeks across Kansas and Nebraska. In the fall of 1878, the remaining Northern Cheyenne split into two groups: those who were willing to surrender with Dull Knife and live at Red Cloud Agency and those under Little Wolf who wanted to continue fleeing. Dull Knife and his people were captured, brutalized, and ordered back to Oklahoma. Dull Knife refused and again made a daring attempt at escape. In the end, only nine of the people with Dull Knife survived. They were eventually allowed to go to Fort Keogh, near modern-day Miles City, Montana, where Little Wolf and his followers had ended up.

After assisting the Army in their pursuit of Chief Joseph and the Nez Perce, the Northern Cheyenne were given a reservation by the U.S. government in 1884. In an atypical move, the government actually expanded the reservation in 1890.

SIGHTS
★ Little Bighorn Battlefield National Monument

The **Little Bighorn Battlefield National Monument** (65 mi/105 km southeast of Billings, 15 mi/24 km southeast of Hardin, 1 mi/1.6 km east of I-90 on U.S. 212, 406/638-2621, www.nps.gov, entrance gate 8am-6pm daily Apr.-Memorial Day and Labor Day-end of Sept., 8am-8pm daily Memorial Day-Labor Day, 8am-4:30pm daily Oct.-Mar., $20/vehicle, $15/motorcycle, $10/pedestrian or bicyclist) is a desolate, somber, and terribly meaningful place, commemorating a tragic battle with no true victors, only bloodshed marking the end of an era. The monument memorializes the battlefield made famous by Lieutenant Colonel George Armstrong Custer, more than 200 men from his 7th Cavalry, and the thousands of Native American warriors who fought under Sitting Bull and Crazy Horse for their way of life against a foreign government that they perceived as dishonest, unreliable, and tyrannical.

In early 1876, thousands of Native Americans from numerous tribes slipped away from their reservations, restless and disgruntled at having been repeatedly lied to and mistreated by the U.S. government. Countless skirmishes throughout the winter and spring reinvigorated the Army's pursuit of the Native Americans, and four centuries of conflict between Native Americans and European Americans came to a head in June 1876 at the battle, when Custer and his men attacked an enormous force of Cheyenne, Sioux, and Arapaho and were quickly surrounded. Custer's infamous Last Stand actually lasted less than an hour, and every man under his command on that hill was killed.

The **Little Bighorn Battlefield Visitor Center and Museum** (8am-6pm daily Apr.-Memorial Day, 8am-7:30pm daily Memorial Day-Labor Day, 8am-6pm daily Labor Day-Sept. 30, 8am-4:30pm daily Oct. 1-Mar. 31) is a must for those visiting the site. The compact facility powerfully interprets the events leading up to and following the battle. Exhibited artifacts include weapons, photos of the key players, archaeological findings, and, during the off-season, a 25-minute video documentary. Rangers give frequent interpretive lectures, and bus tours of the site are available in summer.

Adjacent to the visitors center is the **Custer National Cemetery** for the military, which resembles Arlington National Cemetery on a much smaller scale. The actual monument on Last Stand Hill is on a paved trail within walking distance of the center, and a 4.5-mile (7.2-km) road open to car traffic connects the Custer Battlefield with the Benteen Battlefield.

The granite memorial on **Last Stand Hill** was built in July 1881, and in 1890 marble markers replaced stakes that stood where each soldier had fallen. Starting in 1999, red granite markers were placed to honor the Native Americans who died in the battle, including Cheyenne warriors Lame White Man and Noisy Walking and Lakota warriors Long Road and Dog's Back Bone. Another monument, titled "Peace Through Unity," was dedicated in 2003 to honor the Indian participants who fought and died in the Battle of the Little Bighorn. For those wanting to do a bit of homework before arriving at the site, the

Friends of the Little Bighorn Battlefield (www.friendslittlebighorn.com) maintain an excellent website.

A wonderful way to explore the monument, and the starkly beautiful windswept plains that surround it, is by hiring a Native American guide through **Apsalooke Tours** (406/638-3897 or 406/679-0041, daily Memorial Day-Labor Day, $10 adults, $8 seniors 65 and over, $5 children 4-12, free for children under 4), organized through the **Little Big Horn College.** The hour-long tours are generally held on the hour 10am-3pm, and guides can also be hired for group and private tours and as step-on guides.

Big Horn County Historical Museum and Visitor Center

Located in Hardin, 15 miles (24 km) north of the Battle of the Little Bighorn National Monument, the **Big Horn County Historical Museum** (1163 3rd St. E., 406/665-1671, www.bighorncountymuseum.org, 8am-6pm daily Memorial Day-Labor Day, 9am-5pm Mon.-Fri. Labor Day-Memorial Day, historic buildings closed Oct.-Apr., $6 adults, $5 seniors, $3 children 7-18, free for children under 6) contains 24 historic buildings outfitted from the periods in which they originated—a 1922

On Last Stand Hill, stone markers tell the story of where Custer's men fell.

Plenty Coups, Visionary Chief of the Crow

Born into the Crow tribe in 1848, Chief Plenty Coups had a life that spanned two eras. As a young warrior, he rode across the plains hunting, fighting, and conquering. As a middle-aged leader, he embraced life on the reservation as a farmer, trader, and negotiator. He is considered the last of the great Crow war chiefs and had a tremendous influence on the tribe's relations with settlers.

Plenty Coups was considered special even as a young child. His grandfather foresaw his role as a chief and named him Alaxchiiaahush, meaning "many accomplishments" or "plenty coups." When he was 11, Plenty Coups went into the mountains on a vision quest. He was gone for three days, and when he returned he shared his dream with the group's elders. He claimed he had seen large herds of buffalo disappearing across the plains and a new strange animal arriving to take their place. He described seeing all the trees in the forest blow over with a great gust of wind until only one remained standing straight and tall. Inside the tree was a single chickadee. The elders declared that his dream was a vision of the future and that it meant the buffalo would disappear and be replaced by settlers' cattle. They believed the forest represented all the Plains Indian tribes, and the settlers, like the wind, would tear through their land and way of life. The fallen trees were interpreted as the tribes that resisted and fought the settlers. The lone standing tree represented the Crow; they would survive because they would work with, rather than against, the settlers. The Crow used this dream as a guide for the next several years, and when it came time to fight, they joined the side of the settlers and fought against other tribes.

Plenty Coups earned several "coups" as a valiant and skilled warrior. He had a reputation for being intelligent and fearless and was believed to have had at least 80 feathers on his coup stick, each representing an act of bravery. In addition, he proved to be an eloquent and moving orator. When the Crow people were transferred to their reservation, Plenty Coups advocated that they ought to do their best to adapt to this new way of life. He led by example, cultivating his individual allotment of land, opening a general store, and building a log cabin in which to live. Plenty Coups was also a great promoter of education, reminding his people that "with education you will be the white man's equal; without it you will be the white man's victim." A persuasive advocate for his people, Plenty Coups negotiated a railroad line through the reservation and made several journeys to Washington DC to represent Native American interests. In turn, Washington recognized him as an important American leader. In 1921 he was invited to speak at the dedication of the Tomb of the Unknown Soldier, which was attended by other important international figures.

In 1928, four years before his death, Plenty Coups decided to dedicate a portion of his land as a memorial to the Crow Nation, stating, "It is given as a token of my friendship for all people, both red and white." Today it is a 195-acre (78.9-hectare) state park located on the Crow Reservation called **Chief Plenty Coups State Park** (1 Edgar Rd., 1 mi/1.6 km west of Pryor, 406/252-1289, www.stateparks.mt.gov, 8am-8pm daily mid-May-mid-Sept., 8am-5pm Wed.-Sun. mid-Sept.-mid-May, day use $6/vehicle nonresidents) and houses a **visitors center and museum** of Crow culture (10am-5pm daily mid-May-mid-Sept., 10am-5pm Wed.-Sun. mid-Sept.-mid-May, free), as well as a gift shop along with Chief Plenty Coups's log cabin home, general store, and grave.

schoolhouse, a 1917 Evangelical church built by German settlers, a 1906 depot, and buildings from a 1911 working farm. The museum offers excellent hands-on educational programs and a Montana state visitors center.

Chief Plenty Coups State Park

For his bravery and leadership, Plenty Coups was made chief of the Crow Nation when he was only 28 years old. In 1884, he became one of the first Crow to own and work a farm. Along with his wife, Strikes the Iron, Plenty Coups built a home, worked the land, and operated a general store on his 320-acre (129.5-hectare) plot of land just east of Pryor. Upon his death in 1932, and according to the wishes of the chief and his wife, 195 acres (78.9 hectares) of their land was turned into a public park known as **Chief Plenty Coups State Park** (1 Edgar Rd., 1 mi/1.6 km west

of Pryor, 406/252-1289, www.stateparks.
mt.gov, 8am-8pm daily mid-May-mid-Sept.,
8am-5pm Wed.-Sun. mid-Sept.-mid-May, $6/
vehicle nonresidents, free for Montana residents). The park is home to a **museum and
visitors center** (10am-5pm daily mid-May-
mid-Sept., 10am-5pm Wed.-Sun. mid-Sept.-
mid-May, free) celebrating Crow culture and a
gift shop, along with Chief Plenty Coups's log
cabin home, his general store, and his grave.

St. Labre Mission and Cheyenne Indian Museum

St. Labre Mission (1000 Tongue River Rd.,
Ashland, 406/784-4500, www.stlabre.org,
8am-5pm Mon.-Fri. Memorial Day-Labor
Day, 8am-4:30pm Mon.-Fri. Labor Day-
Memorial Day, free) began as the St. Labre
Indian School in 1884 under the guidance of
the Ursuline Sisters. The school and mission
were founded before the Northern Cheyenne
Indian Reservation was officially set up by
the U.S. government. George Yoakum, a for-
mer soldier and Roman Catholic from Miles
City, requested that Montana's bishop John
Brondel go to help the wandering Cheyenne
who were congregating in the Tongue River
Valley. Brondel purchased the land, and the
St. Labre School was founded in March 1884.

The original three-room cabin, of which
there is a replica today, served as the church,
the school, and the dormitory for both students and nuns. The school has always blended
Cheyenne culture with Roman Catholicism; in
1970 the Cheyenne language was added to the
elementary curriculum because many of the
children had never learned it. The course was
so well received that a night course was added
for adults. Today, the St. Labre Indian School
educates nearly 700 Northern Cheyenne and
Crow students from kindergarten through
high school on three campuses.

A 1971 church on the site was constructed
in tipi form, with a cross as the center pole.
The **Cheyenne Indian Museum** (8am-
5pm Mon.-Fri. Memorial Day-Labor Day,
8am-4:30pm Mon.-Fri. Labor Day-Memorial
Day, free) offers an opportunity to see various

Plains Indian artifacts as well as a short documentary film on the St. Labre School. The
museum is also open on Saturday on the
Memorial Day and Independence Day weekends (9am-3pm), and all weekend over Labor
Day (9am-3pm).

SPORTS AND RECREATION

Fishing

The fishing on the **Bighorn River** is legendary, and there is no shortage of fly shops and
outfitters available to help visitors find big,
beautiful trout. The Bighorn is known for
trout that are plentiful in both size and number: browns in this river average 15 inches (38
cm) and rainbows average 16 inches (41 cm).
Dry-fly fishing is almost always an option,
but nymphing and streamer fishing are useful
under certain water conditions as well. Trout
fishing on the Bighorn is generally best the
13 river miles (20.9 km) below the Yellowtail
Dam, and estimates put the fish population between 3,000 and 5,000 fish per mile.
Although fishing is certainly more popular
during the temperate season, the Bighorn is
a tailwater fishery—thanks to the Yellowtail
Dam—meaning that the river never freezes in
winter and stays fishable year-round.

The area's original fly shop and outfitter, **Bighorn Angler** (577 Parkdale Ct., Fort
Smith, 406/666-2233, www.bighornangler.
com) offers complete outfitting services,
with experienced guides, boat rentals, quality tackle, and packages including lodging—
ranging from simple but nice motel rooms
($85-125) or deluxe lodge rooms ($145) to river
cabins ($200-250 for up to 4 people) to deluxe
lodges ($435 for up to 6 people, $575 for up to
8 people). Stop in for the best advice on where
the fish are biting and what they're eating.

Established by Congress in 1966 after
the completion of the Yellowtail Dam, the
**Bighorn Canyon National Recreation
Area** (north entrance via Hwy. 313, Fort

1: Bighorn Canyon National Recreation Area
2: angler in the Bighorn River

Smith, headquarters 406/666-2414, visitor information 307/548-5406, www.nps.gov, $5/vehicle, $30 annual vehicle pass) includes 71 miles (114 km) of Bighorn Lake in a spectacular 55-mile (89 km) canyon. Fishing can be done from shore or in a boat either in the river or on Bighorn Lake—home to brown, rainbow, and lake trout as well as walleye, smallmouth bass, channel catfish, and even ling and shovelnose sturgeon.

Hiking and Boating

Bighorn Canyon National Recreation Area itself straddles the Montana-Wyoming border and also offers excellent boating, bird- and wildlife-watching, swimming, and picnicking. There are 28 miles (45 km) of hiking on 14 separate trails. Hiking guides and other information are available at the **Yellowtail Dam Visitor Center** (off Hwy. 313 near the top of the dam, 406/666-9961, www.nps.gov, 8:30am-5pm daily Memorial Day-Labor Day). Pontoon boats can be rented from the **Ok-A-Beh Marina** (near Fort Smith, 406/666-2349 or 406/629-9041, 10am-7pm Mon.-Fri., 9am-7pm Sat.-Sun., Memorial Day-Labor Day). Numerous free campgrounds are within the boundaries of the recreation area, many of which are open all year.

Horseback Riding

On the Northern Cheyenne Indian Reservation, **Cheyenne Trailriders** (N. Tongue River Rd. and Robinson Ln., Ashland, 406/784-6150) affords visitors an opportunity to explore the reservation on horseback. In order to increase awareness and appreciation of Cheyenne history and culture, it offers workshops on history, culture, and ethnobotany. Guides are also happy to teach you about gourd dancing, intertribal hand games, round dancing, and Indian sign language around an evening campfire. There are storytellers and flute players to entertain riders, and wagon trips are available for non-riders. Custom overnight trips (from $250 pp), with lodging in a tipi, can be arranged for riders as young as eight years old.

ENTERTAINMENT AND EVENTS

★ Crow Fair

Crow Fair (powwow grounds in Crow Agency, 406/638-3708 or 406/679-2108, www.crow-nsn.gov) is an annual powwow held on the Crow Indian Reservation the third week in August to celebrate the past, present, and future of the Crow people. The event is awash in vibrant color, sound, and taste and is certainly one of the best times to visit the reservation; it's called the "tipi capital of the world" for the more than 1,000 tipis that are erected at the site. Crow Fair is a major event not only for the Crow but also for Native Americans across North America, who come to participate in the competitive dancing and drumming and what is considered to be the largest all-Indian rodeo in the country. There are daily parades and evening grand entries, the ceremonial opening to the evening events, which include flag bearers and dancers in all their finery. There is also horse racing of many varieties and rodeo, in addition to nonstop food and music. Festivities take place mainly at the fairgrounds in Crow Agency, 60 miles (97 km) southeast of Billings off I-90.

Crow Native Days Powwow

A smaller and much newer event than Crow Fair, **Crow Native Days** (powwow grounds in Crow Agency, 406/638-3708, www.crow-nsn.gov) happens over a weekend in late June. The event includes evening grand entries and features the royalty from the upcoming Crow Fair. Like Crow Fair, the event hosts daily parades and dancing competitions for various age groups—from fancy dancing and chicken dancing categories for men to traditional and jingle dancing for women. Unique to Crow Native Days is an Ultimate Warrior competition for both men and women. Each male contestant runs, canoes, and rides three different horses for 6 (9.7 km) miles, wearing a breechcloth and moccasins. Women compete in teams of three, with each member completing one leg of the race.

The Tipi Capital of the World

Held annually since 1904 during the third week of August, **Crow Fair** is considered the largest outdoor powwow in the world. The five-day celebration was introduced to the Crow people—their traditional name is Apsáalooke, which means "children of the large-beaked bird" but was misinterpreted to mean "crow"—by S. C. Reynolds, an Indian Affairs agent assigned to the reservation around the turn of the 20th century. His goal was to encourage the nomadic Crow to become more settled and agrarian on the reservation, which was neither their traditional homeland nor particularly well suited for farming. He modeled the concept for the fair after the county fairs that were popular around the country at the time. The tribe's initial reaction was purportedly less than enthusiastic. In an effort to increase their willingness to participate, Reynolds relaxed the strict ban on "Indian doings" for the days of the Crow Fair, giving the Crow their only legal opportunity to dance, sing, and speak in their traditional ways. Recognizing it as an opportunity to openly pass on Crow culture to younger generations, the tribe eagerly accepted the opportunity, and Crow Fair has been held annually ever since, except during the world wars and the Great Depression. Today, close to 85 percent of the tribe speak Crow as their first language, a much higher percentage than among other Native American groups in the state.

The celebration itself is lively and colorful, with some 12,000 people camping out in more than 1,000 tipis erected on the banks of the Little Bighorn River. Native Americans from various tribes in the United States and Canada and visitors from around the world come to participate or just witness the competitive dancing and drumming, the all-Indian Championship Rodeo, the pari-mutuel horse racing, and the family reunion-like camaraderie that pervades this time-honored event. The hot, dusty late-summer air is thick with smells—from Indian fry bread to parade ponies—and sounds, including the bullhorn whine of the camp-crier and the jingling of the tobacco lids that decorate the elaborate costumes of some of the dancers. Crow Fair is a feast for the senses and a wonderful way to appreciate the traditions and culture of some of the people who were here long before the Europeans.

Little Big Horn Days and Battle of the Little Bighorn Reenactment

Little Big Horn Days (Hardin, 406/665-1672 or 888/450-3577, www.thehardinchamber.com) entails four days of celebrations close to the June 25 anniversary of the famous battle—some festive, others sober—commemorating the region's history and, in particular, its proximity to the Battle of the Little Bighorn. The festivities include a quilt show, a book fair, and a historical dance—the 1876 Grand Ball—as well as arts and crafts sales, a symposium, and a parade, all culminating in the dramatic and well-attended **Battle of the Little Bighorn Reenactment** (E. Frontage Rd. between Crow Agency and Garryowen, www.littlebighornreenactment.com). The reenactment requires more than 200 actors and is performed from the Indian perspective in a script written by historian Joe Medicine Crow.

The event takes place on a ranch 6 miles (9.7 km) west of Hardin, not far from the actual battlefield, and tickets ($20 adults, $10 children 6-16, free for children under 6) can be purchased at the gate only. Exact change is appreciated.

Powwows on the Northern Cheyenne Indian Reservation

Two powwows are held annually on the Northern Cheyenne Indian Reservation. The largest celebration for the tribe is the **Fourth of July Chief's Powwow and Rodeo** (Kenneth Beartusk Memorial Powwow Grounds, 3 mi/4.8 km south of Lame Deer, 406/477-8222 or 406/477-4847, www.cheyennenation.com, camping permitted), which happens over the course of four days around July 4. There are contests for princesses from all tribes, open dance and drum competitions, parades, grand entries, and daily gourd dancing. Traditional Native American food is available. Guests are welcome, and photography is allowed.

The **Ashland Labor Day Powwow** (at the arbor between St. Labre and Ashland, 0.5 mi/0.8 km off U.S. 212, 406/477-6824 or 406/477-8844, www.cheyennenation.com) happens every year for four days over Labor Day weekend. Drummers and dancers from tribes across the United States and Canada participate in the festivities. Flag-raising occurs each morning at 9am, and dancing concludes each night at midnight. The powwow welcomes visitors and provides an excellent opportunity to learn about and celebrate Northern Cheyenne culture.

FOOD

In much of Montana, especially in eastern Montana and on the Indian reservations, dining options are few and far between. You have to be willing to look hard and expand your culinary horizons now and again. There are some good places to be found.

Immediately off the highway near the Little Bighorn Battlefield National Monument is the **Custer Battlefield Trading Post and Café** (347 Hwy. 12, at exit 510 off I-90, 406/638-2270, www.laststand.com, 8am-9pm daily summer, 8am-8pm daily winter, $9-27), a tourist shop and restaurant that obviously appeals to locals. There is quite a selection of Crow handicrafts in the shop, and the restaurant offers Indian tacos, buffalo burgers, and plenty of variations on Montana beef.

In Hardin, you'll find a fantastic little pizza place called **3 Brothers Bistro** (316 N. Center Ave., 406/545-5133, www.3brothersbistro.com, 11am-9pm Mon.-Sat. summer, 11am-8pm Tues.-Fri, 4pm-8pm Sat. winter, $9-22), which offers a menu of pizza, sandwiches, and giant burgers. It also serves fresh salads, homemade pasta, and delicious desserts including Greek-style cheesecake with a glaze made from local sugar beets. Right next to the movie theater (meals can be taken to go), this place is small but cool.

In Ashland, you can try the **Hitching**

Post Café (206 Main St., 406/784-6840, 7:30am-10pm daily, $8-18) for everything from pancakes and chicken-fried steak to burgers and Mexican specialties. It's best to call ahead, as hours are subject to change seasonally. In Lame Deer, check out the **Dull Knife Café** (1 College Dr., 406/477-3179, 8am-3pm Mon.-Fri., $7-10) inside the college. Hours here can change daily according to the number of customers.

ACCOMMODATIONS

Lodging in this part of the state can be sparse, so day trips from Billings are not a bad idea unless you are an angler and need to be on the river from dusk until dawn. The closest town to the Little Bighorn Battlefield National Monument and easiest place to find accommodations in the area is Hardin. Safe bets include the **Super 8 by Wyndham Hardin** (201 W. 14th St., 406/665-1700 or 800/800-8000, www.hardinsuper8.com, from $68) and **Rodeway Inn** (1324 N. Crawford St., 406/665-1870, www.choicehotels.com, from $69). Both have clean and comfortable guest rooms; the kids will flip for the two-story waterslide that dominates the outdoor pool at the Rodeway Inn. The **Lariat Motel** (709 N. Center Ave., 406/665-2683, from $69) is convenient and pet-friendly.

A historical and worthwhile place to stay in Hardin is the **Kendrick House Inn** (206 N. Custer Ave., 406/665-3035, from $99), a 1915 Edwardian boardinghouse with five guest rooms and a couple of suites with private baths, all meticulously decorated with period furniture.

Just 3 miles (4.8 km) south of Hardin, the Orvis-endorsed **Eagle Nest Lodge** (879 Sawyer Loop, Hardin, 406/665-3711 or 866/258-3474, www.eaglenestlodge.com, packages from $1,900 for 3 nights) is a beautiful and traditional log lodge ideally suited for fishing and bird hunting. The lodge has seven well-appointed guest rooms, all with private baths, and the meals—breakfast, field lunch, and dinner—are superb. Guides are on-site, and owners John and Rebecca are exceedingly gracious and always available to point guests in the right direction. The lodge offers packages catering to fishing, hunting, and cast-and-blast. Shorter stays can be arranged.

Among the many (but still never enough) accommodations for anglers in the Fort Smith area is the Orvis-endorsed **Forrester's Bighorn River Resort** (40754 Hwy. 313, 406/333-1449 or 800/655-3799, www.forrestersbighorn.com, 3-night fishing packages from $1,800). When the fishing is good, you'll need to have booked well in advance.

CAMPING

Immediately adjacent to the Little Bighorn Battlefield National Monument and not far from the Crow Agency fairgrounds, **7th Ranch RV Camp** (Reno Creek Rd., Garryowen, 406/638-2438, www.historicwest.com, from $30 tent sites, from $41 RV sites, from $57 cabins without bedding) offers a great location and plenty of amenities including free Internet, free showers, cowboy cabins, horse stalls, and a tipi. Historical tours can be arranged.

INFORMATION

In some ways, visiting Native American reservations can be a bit like exploring another country. The tribes have worked fiercely to protect their culture and preserve their history. They also live according to their own values rather than any imposed on them. One result is that time can take on a different meaning: Few things happen precisely when it is stated they will. Travelers should adjust accordingly and learn to be more spontaneous. In addition, the technology that many of us rely on is not nearly as critical to some Native Americans; you may not get an answer the first few times you call someone. And there is no voicemail. Persistence pays off, and patience will serve you well.

The **Crow Tribal Council Headquarters** (406-638-3708, www.crow-nsn.gov) in Crow Agency is a good source of local information. The **Hardin Chamber of Commerce** (10. E. Railway St., 406/665-1672) is another source for visitor information.

The **Northern Cheyenne Tribal Office** (www.cheyennenation.com) can be reached at 406/477-6284. The **Northern Cheyenne Chamber of Commerce** (U.S. 212, Lame Deer, 406/477-8844) is another source of information on the reservation.

TRANSPORTATION

The **Crow Indian Reservation** is easily accessed from I-90, which runs the length of the reservation. The **Northern Cheyenne Indian Reservation** is accessed by U.S. 212, which runs east-west, or by Highways 39 or 314, both of which run north-south.

Miles City

Miles City (population 8,647; elevation 2,369 ft/722 m) has always been a cowboy town. After the 1876 campaign against the Indians, including the Battle of the Little Bighorn, the 5th Infantry established camp at the confluence of the Tongue and Yellowstone Rivers under the leadership of Col. Nelson A. Miles. In 1881 the arrival of the Northern Pacific Railway ensured the longevity of the settlement, and in 1884 the Montana Stockgrowers Association was formed, creating an important and long-lasting link to the cattle market. The brick buildings that line Main Street today are much as they were when this town boomed in the late 1800s and early 1900s.

The biggest event in Miles City, and its claim to fame today, is the annual Miles City Bucking Horse Sale, which at least doubles the population of the town each May and reflects its heritage and openness in all its glory. A Montana Mardi Gras with cowboys and chaps, the weekend celebration is probably one of the five best events in the state.

While Miles City has never shed its rough and weathered exterior or its boom-and-bust sensibility, there is much that makes it relevant. On top of its cowboy culture—stop in any diner before 8am to see the town's old guard—there is a youthful exuberance to the city evident in its cutting-edge art museum, the vitality of the Range Riders Museum, and its excellent recreation facilities. Indeed, surrounded by badlands and prairie, Miles City unites the best of Montana past and present.

SIGHTS
Range Riders Museum
The fabulous **Range Riders Museum** (435 L. P. Anderson Rd., 406/232-6146, 8am-5pm daily Apr.-Oct., or by appointment, $7.50 adults, $5 seniors, $1-3 students) is a gem. Plan to spend some time, and don't be bashful about striking up a conversation with caretaker-curator Bunny Miller or her husband,

Gary. Bunny's parents, Bob and Betty Ann Barthelmess, were the heart and soul of the Range Riders from 1976 until they were well in their 80s. Sadly, Bob passed away, but Bunny and Gary have kept his passion and spirit very much alive at the Range Riders.

The museum was founded in 1939 by a group of locals dedicated to preserving their heritage. Today it has 13 buildings and thousands of artifacts that include old saddles and clothing, machinery, dinosaur bones, phenomenal photographs by L. A. Huffman and Christian Barthelmess (Bunny's great-grandfather, an Army photographer born in Germany), and 400 antique firearms in the Bert Clark Gun Collection. Bob commandeered a team of volunteers to build four spectacular dioramas of the 1877 Battle of Lame Deer, Fort Keogh, the Milwaukee Railroad Roundhouse, and the famed L.O. Ranch, once southeast Montana's largest ranch. An almost life-size replica of Main Street in Miles City circa 1877 is another can't-miss exhibit. This museum has been a labor of love for so many, and it captures the spirit of this frontier town.

★ WaterWorks Art Museum
Quite a contrast to the Range Riders Museum but just as compelling is the **WaterWorks Art Museum** (85 Waterplant Rd., 406/234-0635, www.wtrworks.org, 9am-5pm Tues.-Sun. May.-Sept., 1pm-5pm Tues.-Sun. Oct.-Apr., free). Creatively housed in the 10,000-square-foot (929-sq-m) concrete basins of the 1910 waterworks that provided the city's drinking water for more than 60 years, the award-winning museum specializes in contemporary Montana artists but has regional and national changing shows. Part museum, part gallery, WaterWorks also owns the state's largest public collection of works by photographer L. A. Huffman in addition to photos by Lady Evelyn Cameron, E. S. Curtis, and Christian Barthelmess. Interesting local art,

Miles City

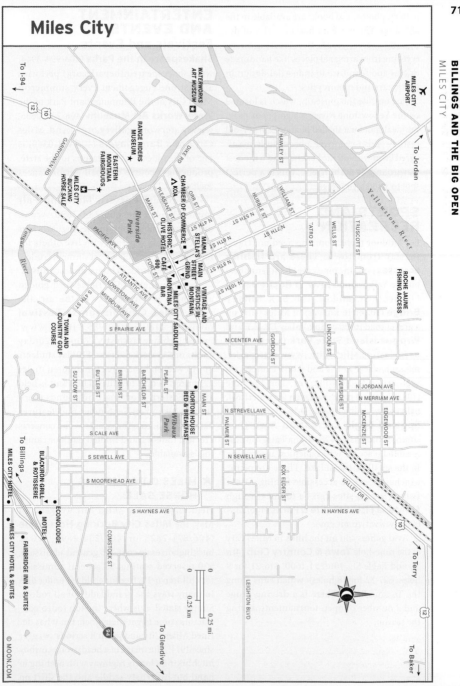

To I-94

WATERWORKS ART MUSEUM

MILES CITY AIRPORT

To Jordan

RANGE RIDERS MUSEUM

EASTERN MONTANA FAIRGROUDS

MILES CITY BUCKING HORSE SALE

GARRYOWEN RD

DIXIE RD

HAWLEY ST

WILLIAM ST

Yellowstone River

KOA

CHAMBER OF COMMERCE

ORR ST

HUBBLE ST

N 4TH ST

N 5TH ST

N 7TH ST

ATRIO ST

WELLS ST

TRUSCOTT ST

ROCHE JAUNE FISHING ACCESS

PLEASANT ST

N 4TH N

HISTORIC OLIVE HOTEL

MAIN ST

600

FORT ST

N 7TH ST

N 8TH N

N 10TH N

MAMA STELLA'S CAFE

MONTANA BAR

MAIN STREET GRIND

VINTAGE AND RUSTICS IN MONTANA

MILES CITY SADDLERY

PACIFIC AVE

Riverside Park

ATLANTIC AVE

YELLOWSTONE AVE

MISSOURI AVE

S 4TH ST

Tongue River

TOWN AND COUNTRY GOLF COURSE

S PRAIRIE AVE

N CENTER AVE

GORDON ST

LINCOLN ST

RIVERSIDE ST

SU JOLN ST

BUTLER ST

BRISBIN ST

BATCHELOR ST

PEARL ST

MAIN ST

N JORDAN AVE

N MERRIAM AVE

MCKENZIE ST

EDGEWOOD ST

HORTON HOUSE BED & BREAKFAST

Wibaux Park

N STREVELL AVE

S CALE AVE

PALMER ST

N SEWELL AVE

BOX ELDER ST

VALLEY DR E

To Billings

MILES CITY HOTEL

BLACKIRON GRILL & ROTISSERIE

S SEWELL AVE

S MOOREHEAD AVE

ECONOLODGE

MOTEL 6

S HAYNES AVE

N HAYNES AVE

To Terry

FAIRBRIDGE INN & SUITES

MILES CITY HOTEL & SUITES

COMSTOCK ST

LEIGHTON BLVD

To Glendive

To Baker

0   0.25 mi
0   0.25 km

© MOON.COM

pottery, photos, and books are available in the gift shop. The museum hosts a series of design shows every year or two, focusing on everything from artisanal pieces like handmade fiddles and furniture to industrial design in iconic cars and motorcycles.

Just outside the museum, which is located on the Yellowstone River, is a gorgeous park, the ideal spot for a shaded picnic. Century-old cottonwoods tower over a beautifully manicured lawn with picnic benches and a modest playground. If nothing else, this is a perfect spot to stretch your legs.

SPORTS AND RECREATION

For outdoor recreation, one need not travel too far from town. There are **fishing accesses** (and in some cases boat launches) on the Yellowstone River at **Roche Jaune** (Truscott St. and N. 6th St.), **Kinsey Bridge** (10 mi/16 km east of Miles City, on a gravel road intersecting Valley Dr. E.), and **Pirogue Island State Park** (3 mi/4.8 km northeast of Miles City, www.stateparks. mt.gov), where Lewis and Clark camped on their cross-country journey. The 269-acre (108.9-hectare) park is a haven for waterfowl, bald eagles, and white-tailed and mule deer. **Spotted Eagle Recreation Area** (just south of the Eastern Montana Fairgrounds) is a quiet place for walks, picnics, and fishing in the small artificial lake. There are picnic benches as well as accessible fishing. Other fishing access sites can be found through **Montana Fish, Wildlife & Parks** (406/234-0900, www.fwp.mt.gov).

Avid golfers can hit the links in Miles City at the nine-hole **Town & Country Club** (4th St. and Eagle St., 406/234-1600, $16-21 for 9 holes; $27-32 for 18 holes), which runs along the Tongue River. There is a driving range and a number of open tournaments during the season.

ENTERTAINMENT AND EVENTS

Festivals and Events

Shakespeare in the Parks (406/994-3944, www.shakespeareintheparks.org) performs at least one engagement every summer in Miles City at the Pumping Plant Park of the **WaterWorks Art Museum** (406/234-0635, www.waterworksgallery.org). And Miles City's own **Barn Players** (406/951-0560) is one of the oldest theater groups in the state, producing a couple of small performances each year.

The annual **Eastern Montana Fair** (406/421-5419 or 406/234-2890, www. milescitychamber.com) in late August brings Custer County together with five others for four days of nonstop entertainment, rodeo, concerts, fireworks, exhibits, and a carnival.

In September, as the fields turn golden and there is a crispness to the air, the small **Miles City Bluegrass Festival** (406/234-2480 or 406/853-1678, www. milescitybluegrassfestival.com, $20/day adults or $35 weekend pass, $10/day students or $15 weekend pass, free for children under 12) brings people together. The event is held at the Eastern Montana Fairgrounds every third weekend in September and features bands from across the country. The concerts are held indoors, and limited outdoor camping is available.

★ MILES CITY BUCKING HORSE SALE

Held annually the third full weekend in May, the **Miles City Bucking Horse Sale** (406/874-2825 or 406/234-2890, www. buckinghorsesale.com, $15 general admission, $20 reserved seating, $5 general admission for children 6-12, free for children under 6) is in many ways the granddaddy of all rodeos. Simply stated, it is where the top rodeo contractors come to get their stock, but it has defined Miles City and given it serious swagger since 1914. The image of a headstrong cowboy hitchhiking a lonely highway with nothing in hand but his trusty saddle and the shirt on his back is realized here year after year—they come to ride the best broncs in the business.

In addition to the central bronc sale, the event is rounded out by concerts, bull riding, pari-mutuel horse racing, street dances each night, and a good old-fashioned parade on Saturday morning. The whole affair can be slightly bawdy, and it's true that the town's many bars take out all their furniture to make room for thirsty cowboys. If you arrive Monday morning after the Bucking Horse Sale, you'll see what a hungover town looks like.

SHOPPING

In business since 1909, **Miles City Saddlery** (808 Main St., 406/232-2512, www. milescitysaddlery.com, 9am-6pm Mon.-Sat.) is famous for having originated the Coggshall Saddle. The shop is a step back in time with exceptional custom saddles, clothing, boots and belts, hats, tack, and gifts. Across the street, **Vintage and Rustics in Montana** (813 Main St., 406/234-7878, 6:30am-4:30pm Tues.-Thurs., 6:30am-5pm Fri.-Sat.) is a sprawling and eclectic antiques mall with more than 80 vendors, a soda fountain, bakery, and espresso.

FOOD

True to its cow-town status, Miles City is a meat-and-potatoes mecca. The **Black Iron Grill & Rotisserie** (2901 Boutelle St., 406/234-4766, www.milescityrestaurant. com, 11am-close daily, $12-35) does not disappoint. From the mouthwatering burgers and chicken-fried steak to applewood-smoked brisket, Black Iron uses local beef and serves it alongside Montana microbrews.

For diners looking for something besides steak, **Mama Stella's** (607 Main St., 406/234-2922, www.trailsinn.com, 10am-10pm daily, $8-23) serves up pizza, wings, hoagies, grinders, and, of course, burgers. It serves breakfast all day (try the ultimate biscuits and gravy), including a breakfast pizza. And for those who haven't had enough of burgers, there's a bacon cheeseburger pizza.

A great place for breakfast, lunch, or a cup of joe is **Main Street Grind** (713 Main St., 406/234-9200, 6:30am-5:30pm Mon.-Fri., 6:30am-3:30pm Sat., $7-11). From the homemade pastries, pies, and granola to the thick, juicy burgers, Main Street Grind is a great find in eastern Montana. They offer free Wi-Fi.

The gold standard in Miles City for a community café is **Café 600** (600 Main St., 406/234-3860, 5am-2pm Sun.-Thurs., 5am-2pm and 5pm-9pm Fri.-Sat., $9-28) which opened in 1946 and still serves up excellent cinnamon rolls, omelets, sandwiches, steak, and more.

A trip to Miles City would not be complete without a drink at the **Montana Bar** (612 Main St., 406/234-5809, 10am-2am daily). The bar has been serving thirsty patrons since 1902 and has managed to keep its incredible original back bar in beautiful shape all these years. The expansive leather booths, beveled leaded glass, and marble tile floors are all original. The bar stools and the jukebox are just about the only additions in the last century. It is a remarkable place to sip a cold drink and reflect on just how much things haven't changed in little pockets like this across the West. Inside the bar, Tubb's Pub serves standard bar fare. Breakfast is served Saturday and Sunday only from 2am to 4am.

ACCOMMODATIONS

The **Historic Olive Hotel** (501 Main St., 406/234-2450, from $79) is both a classic and a bargain. The rooms are neither fancy nor grand, but they are clean and accommodating, and the location is unbeatable. There's also a ghost to be reckoned with—but don't worry, she's friendly.

Far more elegant than the Olive, but an equally historic gem in the heart of Miles City, ★ **Horton House Bed & Breakfast** (1918 Main St., 406/234-4422, www. hortonhousebandb.com, $119-139) is a stunning property with rooms dedicated to local historical figures including artist Charlie Russell and photographer Evelyn Cameron.

Among the chain hotel offerings, the

pet-friendly **Fairbridge Inn & Suites** (3111 Steel St., 406/232-3661 www.fairbridgeinns. com, from $99) has 61 rooms, free Wi-Fi, and a complimentary hot breakfast. More upscale and locally owned, the **Miles City Hotel & Suites** (1720 S. Haynes Ave., 406/234-1000, www.milescityhotelandsuites.com, from $109) has a presidential suite with a copper ceiling and strict no-pets policy.

You'll find a number of larger chain hotels on the way into Miles City—**Best Western War Bonnet Inn** (1615 S. Haynes Ave., 406/234-4560, from $84), **Miles City Hotel** (1615 S. Haynes Ave., 406/234-1000, from $89), **EconoLodge** (1209 S. Haynes Ave., 406/234-8880, from $68), **Motel 6** (1314 S. Haynes Ave., 406/232-7040, from $55), and **Sleep Inn & Suites** (1006 S. Haynes Ave., 406/232-3000, from $152).

CAMPING

The **Miles City KOA** (1 Palmer St., 406/232-3991 or 800/562-3909, www.koa.com, from $28 tents, $41-65 RVs, from $65 cabins, Apr. 15-Oct. 15) is tucked in the cottonwood trees on the banks of the Tongue River just six blocks from downtown. Free wireless Internet is provided, along with an outdoor swimming pool and bicycle rentals.

Big Sky Camp and RV Park (1294 U.S. 12, 406/234-1511, www.bigskycampandrvpark. com, mid-Apr.-Oct., from $18 tents, from $25 water and electric, from $30 full hookup) offers standard amenities, including Wi-Fi, in a beautiful grassy setting alongside impressive rock formations.

INFORMATION AND SERVICES

The **Miles City Area Chamber of Commerce** (511 Pleasant St., 406/234-2890, www.milescitychamber.com, 9am-5pm Mon.-Fri.) is a block from Main Street and has maps, brochures for local businesses, restaurant and hotel listings, museum information, and very friendly staff.

The **main post office** is at 106 North 7th Street (406/232-1224, 8am-5:30pm Mon.-Fri., 9am-noon Sat.).

The historic 1902 **Miles City Library** (1 S. 10th St., 406/234-1496, www. milescitypubliclibrary.org, 10am-6pm Tues.-Fri., 9am-5pm Sat.) is at Main and 10th Streets; computers with Internet access are available.

The **Express Laundry Center** (1115 S. Haynes Ave., 406/234-9999, www. expresslaundrymc.com, 6am-11pm daily for self-serve, laundry service available 8am-5pm Mon.-Fri., 8am-4pm Sat., 10am-4pm Sun.) offers coin-operated machines and same-day or next-day drop-off service. Plus there's a dog wash and free Wi-Fi.

Holy Rosary Health Care (2600 Wilson St., 406/233-2600, www.holyrosaryhealthcare. org) has a 24-hour emergency room as well as a walk-in clinic (406/233-2500, 7:30am-5:30pm Mon.-Fri., 8am-5pm Sat.-Sun.).

TRANSPORTATION

After a few years of scrambling to keep commercial flights to Denver, and then Billings, Miles City lost all commercial service in May 2013, which means the nearest commercial airport is 140 miles (225 km) away in Billings.

I-94 runs through Miles City, making it an easy destination by car. It is 140 miles (225 km) east of Billings and 78 miles (126 km) southwest of Glendive.

Bus service to Miles City is provided by **Greyhound** (336 S. Haynes Ave., 800/451-5333, www.greyhound.com) and **Jefferson Lines** (336 S. Haynes Ave., 800/451-5333, www.jeffersonlines.com), which leave from the Arby's Restaurant.

1: digging for fossils in Eastern Montana
2: Montana Bar in Miles City 3: Makoshika State Park

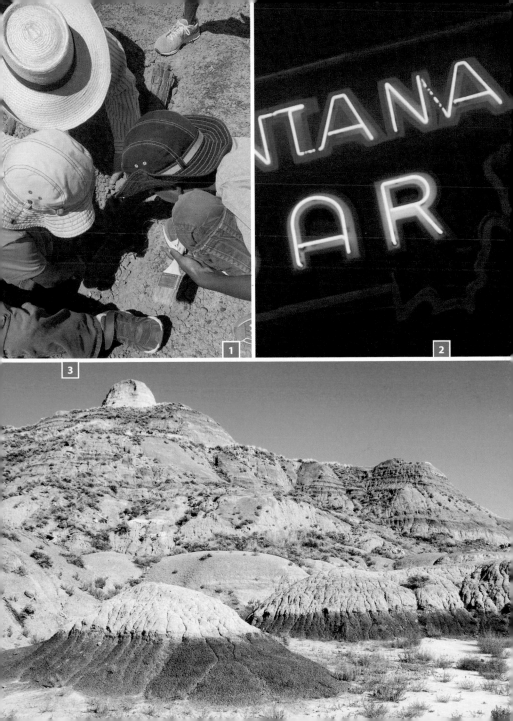

Miles City to Medicine Lake

The stretch of road from Miles City to Medicine Lake is sparsely populated and subtly beautiful. This is cattle country and the beginning of the badlands. The Yellowstone River cuts through the rugged country as it flows northeast to the North Dakota border. I-94 parallels the river, echoing the Yellowstone's onetime importance as a means of transportation and shipping. This area was once home to the country's last great bison herd, but the slaughter of these animals in the early 1880s nearly wiped out the species, ending a long and important chapter in North American history.

Though small towns dot the landscape here, there is more to the region than human settlements. With intact badlands, grasslands, and wetlands, this part of the state is a birder's paradise. The region is home to a number of national wildlife refuges, wildlife management areas, and tracts of public land, all of which provide marvelous habitat for an enormous number of avian species. Part wetland, part prairie, Medicine Lake National Wildlife Refuge is a spectacular place to see migrating birds at various times of year. Although it is not a common destination, driving through this part of the state is a magnificent way to enjoy the ride on the way from one place to the next.

HISTORY

The small, colorful towns in this part of the state have origins that date back to the Indian Wars and before. Terry, named for Gen. Alfred E. Terry, emerged from a dugout that offered food and lodging to soldiers fighting the Sioux. The town later became known for one of its esteemed residents, pioneering photographer Evelyn Cameron, a wealthy Englishwoman who ranched in the area with her husband and captured on film the often gritty life of local homesteaders. A museum in town honors her art and legacy. And the town's Kempton Hotel is the oldest continually operating hotel in the state.

The history of **Glendive** dates back even further. Lewis and Clark camped near the present-day town site in 1806 on their way back from Oregon, and they reportedly shot a huge white grizzly bear four times without killing it. An Irish nobleman hunting bison, bears, and ungulates in the region gave the name Glendive to a small tributary of the Yellowstone River. The town itself sprouted up with the arrival of the Northern Pacific Railway in 1880.

Just this side of the North Dakota border, **Wibaux** is named for French cattle king Pierre Wibaux, who left the family textile empire in Roubaix, France, for the wilds of Montana in 1883. Over time, he amassed a herd of 65,000 cattle. In 1884, with money from his father, Wibaux commissioned the construction of St. Peter's Catholic Church by Norman French immigrants, using stunning local fieldstone and lava rock. It is an exquisitely unexpected piece of noble architecture that still stands today. The tiny town is better known today for its Beaver Creek Brewery.

Farther north, towns such as **Sidney** and **Fairview** survive thanks to a robust sugar beet industry, and across the region, local people's lives are tied to the land through agriculture, ranching, and more recently, energy production. The influx of workers eager to make a fortune in North Dakota's Bakken Oil Field has brought money and more service jobs to the area, but is also responsible for sky-high rents, pressure on local infrastructure, and unfortunately, crime. While the population grew in Sidney by 20 percent between 2010 and 2013, the number of arrests in town during that same period rose by 167 percent and felony assaults increased by 825 percent. The downturn, thanks to plummeting oil prices starting in 2015, has yet to signal a reduction in the impact of Bakken on these small communities.

SIGHTS

Prairie County Museum and Evelyn Cameron Gallery

In Terry are the adjacent **Prairie County Museum** (101 Logan Ave., 406/635-4040, 9am-3pm Mon. and Wed.-Fri., 1pm-4pm Sat.-Sun. Memorial Day-Labor Day, free) and **Evelyn Cameron Gallery** (105 Logan Ave., 406/635-4040, www.evelyncameron. org, same hours as the museum, free, donations accepted). The latter pays homage to a fascinating woman who captured the spirit of the often hardscrabble life in eastern Montana with captivating photos and meticulous journals. Thousands of Cameron's negatives were discovered in the late 1970s by Time-Life Books editor Donna Lucey, who published them in her landmark work *Photographing Montana 1894-1928: The Life and Work of Evelyn Cameron.* The gallery is home to many of Cameron's images, both originals and reprints. Her work is a striking testament to the passage of time on the Western frontier and at the same time a reminder of how much remains the same in eastern Montana.

★ Makoshika State Park

Montana's largest state park at more than 11,000 acres (4,452 hectares), **Makoshika State Park** (1301 Snyder Ave., Glendive, 406/377-6256, www.makoshika.org, 10am-5pm daily Memorial Day-Labor Day, 10am-5pm Wed.-Sun. Labor Day-Memorial Day, $6/vehicle or $4/pedestrian for nonresidents, day use free for Montana residents, $8-20 for rustic and backcountry campsites) is literally at the perimeter of Glendive. The park is an intriguing if not altogether beautiful place, made up of colorful exposed rock layers that look like petrified anthills.

Makoshika (muh-KO-shi-kuh) was established in 1953 and named for the Lakota word for badlands, which literally translates as "pitiful earth." An impressive **interpretive center** gives an excellent overview of the park's geological significance and helps visitors easily navigate the rock layers according to color, distinguishing the Age of Reptiles

(dinosaurs!) from the Age of Mammals. Millions of years old, these badlands expose older rock layers than those in North Dakota and have produced some important dinosaur fossils, including a triceratops skull. Hikers have been known to find fossilized shark teeth and alligator teeth, but all rocks and fossils must stay in the park.

The park is well-suited for exploration in a number of different ways. There are 4 miles (6.4 km) of paved roads and 12 miles (19.3 km) of unpaved roads (which can be impassable at certain times of year). Three developed trails offer good hiking opportunities: the **Diane Gabriel Trail**, the **Cap Rock Nature Trail,** and the **Kinney Coulee Hiking Trail.** Trail guide pamphlets and free advice are available at the interpretive center. The park also has a number of picnic benches, shelters, and an 18-basket **disc golf course.** Although there are pines and junipers throughout the park, there is little shade in this compelling play of light and color, so bring water and a hat. The park ties the record for hottest place in Montana at 117°F (47.2°C).

Baisch's Dinosaur Digs

An outstanding place to schedule a dig for ages six and over is **Baisch's Dinosaur Digs** (323 Rd. 300, 406/365-4133, http:// dailydinosaurdigs.com, $120 pp, $80 half day, free for children under 12 with paying adult). The Baisch family—headed by matriarch Marge, whose father was on the last cattle drive from Wyoming to Montana—offers daily paleontological digs on their land in view of Makoshika State Park. They've uncovered remarkable specimens of *Tyrannosaurus rex,* edmontosaurus, and triceratops. A guide will take you out and show you the best places to dig (and the places to watch for rattlers!). When you've had your fill, head back to the ranch headquarters, a makeshift museum where Marge often goes through each of your finds and tells you exactly what she thinks it is. For visitors who want to take home their own fossil finds—including bone fragments, teeth, and petrified wood—this is the only legal way to do it. And the Baisch family makes the whole experience an absolute pleasure.

Frontier Gateway Museum

Tucked downtown in Glendive is the **Frontier Gateway Museum** (201 State St., 406/377-8168, www.frontiergatewaymuseum.org, 9am-5pm Mon.-Sat., 1pm-5pm Sun. Memorial Day-Labor Day, free). The classic small-town museum is home to a full-size stegosaurus replica, plus fossils from triceratops, hadrosaurs, and thescelosaurus.

Glendive Dinosaur & Fossil Museum

Visitors in search of dinosaur bones and fossil exhibits presented from a biblical perspective will find creationist exhibits at the **Glendive Dinosaur & Fossil Museum** (139 State St., 406/377-3228, www.creationtruth.org, 10am-5pm Tues.-Sat. mid-May-early Sept., 10am-5pm Fri.-Sat. Apr. 1-mid-May and Labor Day-late Oct., $8 adults, $7 seniors 60 and over and students 13 and over, $6 children 3-12). In addition to 20,000 square feet (1,858 sq m) of excellent dinosaur casts, nice fossil displays, and painstaking dioramas with much emphasis on the great flood as told in the Bible, the museum offers daylong and half-day dinosaur digs.

★ Medicine Lake National Wildlife Refuge

The Medicine Lake National Wildlife Refuge is a wetland oasis in a sea of prairie. It is a startlingly beautiful place on a breezy afternoon when the grasses sway in watery waves or on a stormy night when lightning flashes across the sky, illuminating clouds that are 15 shades of blue, pink, and purple—or any time, really; it's just that beautiful. And like so much of eastern Montana, it is not what you might expect to see in a state known for its mountains.

The **Medicine Lake National Wildlife Refuge** (223 North Shore Rd., 406/789-2305, www.fws.gov) comprises two wildlife refuges and a wetland management district. Established in 1935, the area provides a much-used breeding and stopover habitat for an enormous range of migratory birds, including ducks, geese, swans, cranes, white pelicans, and grebes. As such, the refuge is as much an oasis for landlocked ocean lovers and wildlife photographers as it is for migrating birds. The sounds and smells and even some of the sights can immediately conjure feelings of a favorite coastal haunt.

Opportunities for bird-watching abound, and what you see will depend on the time of year you visit. There are roads to cruise along and trails to explore. Hunting and fishing are permitted on the refuge as well; get up-to-date information about seasons and regulations, licensing, and necessary permits from the **U.S. Fish and Wildlife Service** (223 North Shore Rd., 406/789-2305, www.fws.gov). Camping is not permitted in the refuge, but sites are available in nearby Medicine Lake or Plentywood.

The refuge is on Highway 16, just south of the tiny town of Medicine Lake, which has very limited accommodations (www.medicinelakemt.com), most of which are modest rentals. The nearest towns with significant hotel and motel accommodations and services—Plentywood and Culbertson—are more than 20 miles (32 km) away to the north and south, respectively, so bring what you need for the time you plan to spend exploring the refuge.

SPORTS AND RECREATION
Fishing

Since I-94 parallels the Yellowstone River from Billings to Glendive, **fishing opportunities** are available at just about any exit. The Yellowstone is filled with trout and, oddly enough, paddlefish: These prehistoric monstrosities in the sturgeon family can live up to 60 years and weigh more than 100 pounds (45 kg). They are caught only by snagging and then fighting them, sometimes for hours. The paddlefishing season on the Yellowstone runs from early to mid-May to mid- to late June, assuming the target goal of fish (usually varying between 500-1,000) is not met in that time. When the

The Montana Dinosaur Trail

Before Montana had cowboys, Indians, ranchers, and homesteaders, even before the Missouri and Yellowstone Rivers were formed, this was dinosaur territory. The world's first *Tyrannosaurus rex* was discovered in Montana, as were the world's first baby dinosaur bones. Sites across the state are dedicated to celebrating this unique and rich history, and the **Montana Dinosaur Trail** (www.mtdinotrail.org), created in 2005, consists of 14 different facilities in 12 communities. The stops along the trail include museums, parks, educational centers, and field stations, all of which are committed to finding and preserving dinosaur specimens. These sites have numerous well-preserved fossils, complete dinosaur skeletons, perfectly honed replicas, and even some active dig sites that are open to the public.

Malta's **Great Plains Dinosaur Museum and Field Station** (405 N. 1st St. E., Malta, 406/654-5300, www.greatplainsdinosaur.org, 10am-5pm Tues.-Sat. May, 10am-5pm Mon.-Sat. and 12:30pm-5pm Sun. June-Aug., $5 adults 13 and over, $3 children 6-12, free for children under 6) displays rare fossils, including a "mummy" dinosaur considered the world's best-preserved dinosaur. Also in Malta, the **Phillips County Museum** (431 U.S. 2 E., Malta, 406/654-1037, www.phillipscountymuseum.org, 10am-5pm Mon.-Sat. Apr.-Dec., $5 adults, $3 children, free for children under 3) boasts a 700-pound (317.5-kg) apatosaurus femur, a complete *Tyrannosaurus rex* skull, and "Elvis," a 33-foot-long (10.1-m) brachylophosaurus.

In Jordan, the site of the first *T. rex* discovery in 1902, the **Garfield County Museum** (952 Jordan Ave., Montana Hwy. 200, Jordan, 406/557-2308, www.garfieldcounty.com/our-museum.html, 1pm-5pm daily June-Labor Day) showcases Cretaceous fossils from the Hell Creek Formation.

The **Fort Peck Dam Interpretive Center and Museum** (adjacent to the power-houses on Lower Yellowstone Rd., Fort Peck, 406/526-3493, 9am-5pm daily May-Sept., 10am-4pm Tues.-Sun. Oct., 10am-4pm Tues.-Fri. Nov.-Apr., free) owns one of the most complete *T. rex* skeletons ever found. You are greeted with a life-size model of the ferocious carnivore when you enter the museum.

Glendive is home to the **Frontier Gateway Museum** (201 State St., Glendive, 406/377-8168, www.frontiergatewaymuseum.org, 9am-5pm Mon.-Sat., 1pm-5pm Sun. Memorial Day-Labor Day, free) and **Makoshika State Park** (1301 Snyder Ave., Glendive, 406/377-6256, www.makoshika.org, 10am-5pm daily Memorial Day-Labor Day, 10am-5pm Wed.-Sun. Labor Day-Memorial Day, $6/vehicle or $4/pedestrian for nonresidents, day use free for Montana residents), where at least 10 different dinosaur species have been found; the museum displays an impressive collection of dinosaur fossils from around the world.

The farthest eastern stop on the Dinosaur Trail is in Ekalaka, the **Carter County Museum** (306 N. Main St., Ekalaka, 406/775-6886, www.cartercountymuseum.org, 9am-5pm Mon.-Fri. and 1pm-5pm Sat.-Sun. Apr.-Nov., 9am-5pm Tues.-Fri. and 1pm-5pm Sat.-Sun. Dec.-Mar., free). This is Montana's first county museum and displays complete dinosaur skeletons found in the nearby Hell Creek Formation.

harvest target is met, anglers will be allowed to catch and release only. As if to reinforce what remarkable adversaries these fish are, there is an archery season for paddlefish below Fort Peck Dam in early July. Paddlefish roe is considered a delicacy among caviar connoisseurs, but can only be purchased outside Montana.

The Missouri River also flows through the region and offers plenty of trout, salmon, pike, and the occasional paddlefish.

Golf

Despite the abundance of gentle terrain in the region, there are only a few golf courses in the area, most of them nine-holers. The **Cottonwood Country Club** (504 Country Club Dr., 406/377-8797, www.cottonwoodcc.com) in Glendive is a lovely course with long holes, wide fairways, and mature cottonwood trees.

FOOD

This is bar-food country and an excellent place for hamburger and chicken-fried steak lovers. Some of the fun is finding the best piece of pie, the juiciest burger, or the strongest coffee. Don't expect gourmet fare, but you can expect big portions and good, simple food.

In Glendive, the **Yellowstone River Inn** (1903 N. Merrill Ave., 406/377-4433, www. yellowstoneriverinn.net, 6am-close daily, $10-28) is inside a hotel and has a pretty complete menu including wraps, burgers, salads, and steak.

For delicious, authentic Mexican food, try **Los Amigos** (209 N. Merrill Ave., 406/377-5074, 11am-8:30pm Tues.-Sun., $7-28). The enormous menu (which includes a kids menu and American dishes like rib eye, T-bone steaks, and bacon cheeseburgers) has seafood, vegetarian options, combo plates, and a whole page of house specialties, including Carne Mexicana and Chile Colorado. You will not leave hungry.

A great family restaurant just across the street from the Holiday Inn Express is **CC's Family Café** (1902 N. Merrill Ave., Glendive, 406/377-8926, 6am-10pm daily summer, 6am-9pm daily winter, $10-28). The restaurant is decorated with photographs of Montana's beauty pageant winners, which is odd but kind of fun. It's the full menu, though, and the friendly service that make CC's a great stop. It features home cooking, daily specials, breakfast all day, and, yep, really good pie.

ACCOMMODATIONS AND CAMPING

Wherever you find communities in Montana, most often you'll find at least a couple of roadside motels; options in eastern Montana, however, can be somewhat limited. In Terry, the 1902 **Kempton Hotel** (204 Spring St., 406/635-5543, $50-100) has hosted such notable figures as Teddy Roosevelt and Calamity Jane. Stories of ghosts abound. The hotel is showing its age, and long-range plans are in place to restore it to its original glory; for now,

this is a choice you make for the experience rather than the comfort.

Glendive is a safe bet for a comfortable, clean room. There are a number of **chain motels** (including La Quinta Inn & Suites, Comfort Inn, Days Inn, Holiday Inn Express Hotel & Suites, and Super 8) thanks to traffic to and from the Bakken Oil Field, but the cream of the crop is the 89-room, pet-friendly **Astoria Hotel & Suites** (201 California St., 406/377-6000, www.glendive. stayastoria.com, $75-123), which offers a business center, indoor swimming pool and fitness center, free Wi-Fi, free breakfast, and on-site dining. All of the nicely appointed and oversize rooms have microwaves, refrigerators, and coffeemakers. This is indeed evidence of the New West.

Perhaps because of the Bakken traffic, campgrounds in Glendive have been changing hands and going out of business. The most reliable and interesting place to camp is **Makoshika State Park** (1301 Snyder Ave., Glendive, 406/377-6256, www.makoshika. org, $8-20 for rustic and backcountry campsites, day use free for Montana residents). Peak season at Montana's state parks is from the third Thursday in May to the third Monday in September.

INFORMATION AND SERVICES

The **Glendive Chamber of Commerce** (808 N. Merrill Ave., 406/377-5601, www. glendivechamber.com, 9am-5pm Mon.-Fri.) is an excellent resource for everything from guided excursions to daily fishing reports. One of the things that makes this chamber unique is that it offers to clean the paddlefish of any angler willing to donate the fish roe, which the chamber then processes into world-class caviar.

The 25-bed **Glendive Medical Center** (202 Prospect Dr., 406/345-3306 or 800/226-7623) offers 24-hour emergency care and a walk-in clinic (406/345-3311, 10am-6pm Mon.-Fri., 10am-2pm Sat.).

TRANSPORTATION

Glendive is off I-94 and at the southernmost point of Highway 16, west of the North Dakota border 35 miles (56 km) from Beach.

Bus service to Glendive is available through Greyhound (800/231-2222, www.greyhound.com) and **Jefferson Lines** (800/451-5333, www.jeffersonlines.com), which leave from **Robin's Service Station** (406/365-2600) at 1302 West Towne Street.

Fort Peck and the Hi-Line

In the extreme northeastern corner of the state, the Fort Peck Indian Reservation and the Hi-Line are tight-knit places that wear their histories like a badge of honor.

As the state's second-largest, the Fort Peck Indian Reservation encompasses more than 2 million acres (809,371 hectares) of land and is home to some 6,800 Assiniboine and Sioux tribe members. The land itself is made up of gently rolling hills and fertile agricultural land. Although the reservation was established in the late 1800s, the government negotiated a treaty with the tribes that each tribe member on the reservation would be given 320 acres (129.5 hectares) of land, not unlike the Homestead Act. The "surplus lands" were opened up to outside settlers, and by the 1920s the Indians retained ownership of only about half the original reservation. The integration of white settlers and Native Americans is more pronounced on Fort Peck than any other reservation in the state. The reservation is adjacent to the site of the Fort Peck Dam, the largest work-relief project to be undertaken during the Great Depression.

Just north of the reservation, the Hi-Line—a string of towns collectively named for their location along the northernmost railroad line in the region—sprouted up with the arrival of the Great Northern Railway in 1887. In fact, many of these small towns—Westby, Scobey, and Medicine Lake among them—up and moved to situate themselves alongside the tracks and make themselves places where the train could bring farmers in and move crops out. This is still a place where you make your own fate, where nothing comes easy.

U.S. 2 runs parallel to the railroad and is the access point for nearly all the communities of any size in this corner of Montana.

PLENTYWOOD

Like all the towns dotting the Hi-Line, Plentywood (population 1,904; elevation 2,024 ft/617 m) is primarily a farming community, known in recent years for pulse crops, including lentils, peas, and beans. Because of its size and proximity to nothing much larger, the town has become something of a trade center, a destination for Canadian bargain shoppers, and a stopping point for many of the oilfield workers. Plentywood also attracts a good number of bird hunters every autumn.

The town is proud of some unique chapters in its history—the famous Outlaw Trail ran right through here, bringing with it more than its fair share of unsavory characters; and in the 1920s and 1930s the Communist Party was one of the most active in local politics. An oil boom in the 1970s and 1980s caused a population spike, and for a time, poker chips from the many bars in the area were accepted as legal tender almost anywhere in the county.

Sights

The **Sheridan County Museum** (4642 Hwy. 16 S., 406/765-2145, 10am-5pm daily Memorial Day-Labor Day, free) is a small but pleasant county museum, conveniently located adjacent to a 24-hour rest area. The museum houses Montana's longest indoor mural at 74 feet (22.6 m), and nearby a historical monument commemorates Sitting Bull's surrender after five years living in Canada with his Sioux people.

Food

Just about everything in town is within walking distance of the Sherwood Inn, and **Randy's Restaurant** (323 W. 1st Ave., 406/765-1661, 6am-7pm daily, $8-16) offers three square meals a day. The 2-pound (0.9-kg) Randy Burger will leave you plenty full, but if you have room, the lemon meringue pie is exceptionally good. **Cousins Family Restaurant** (564 W. 1st Ave., 406/765-1690, www.cousinsplentywood.com, 6am-8pm Mon.-Sat., 6:30am-8pm Sun., $5-17) is another eatery known locally for good home cooking and breakfast all day. The pictures on the walls of the owners' family—early Plentywood settlers—are fun to see. The **Blue Moon Supper Club** (4316 Hwy. 16 S., 406/765-2491, 11am-2am daily, $7-46) is known for its prime rib and Montana-style fine dining. It's also one of the few places on the Hi-Line you can expect to find lobster tail on the menu.

Accommodations

Sherwood Inn (515 W. 1st Ave., 406/765-2810, www.sherwoodinnplentywood.com, $90-135), complete with a host of Robin Hood-themed businesses (the Robin Hood Lounge, Fryer Tuck's Restaurant, and Maid Marion's Hair Salon) is a rather large hotel with 120 guest rooms and extended-stay apartments in three separate buildings, the most recent of which opened in 2013. This pet-friendly hotel is a nice place for the night, perfectly situated within walking distance to eateries, and is ideal for hunters. Wireless Internet is available throughout the property.

SCOBEY

Just down the road from Plentywood is Scobey (population 1,032; elevation 2,450 ft/747 m), an agricultural town with Scandinavian roots, a wealth of wheat farms—in 1924, Scobey was the largest primary wheat-shipping point in North America—and a population of die-hard sports fans. The downtown area is compact and cute, with nice places to eat and a very welcoming attitude. The town has so many unique features because most of its residents are descendants of those who homesteaded the area around the turn of the 20th century. The 1913 Daniels County Courthouse, for example, was once known as One-Eyed Molly's House of Pleasure. There are a few legendary feuds, of course, but mostly people get along and are always willing to lend a hand. When Scobey residents get married, invitations are unheard of; rather, the event is published in the weekly paper, and the entire town shows up with hot dishes, salads, and everything else to make a party worth attending. It is as quaint as it is genuine. Scobey is a wonderful example of small-town Montana. The town achieved some minor fame thanks to an award-winning 2008 PBS documentary, *Class C,* which tells the story of vanishing small towns through the lens of five girls' basketball teams.

★ Pioneer Town

Just west of town is Scobey's beloved **Pioneer Town** (720 2nd Ave., 406/487-5965 or 406/487-2061, 12:30pm-4:30pm daily Memorial Day-Labor Day, by appointment only Labor Day-Memorial Day, $7 adults, $4 children under 12, free for preschool children, includes tour), an extension of the Daniels County Museum and a significant labor of love. It is a collection of more than 40 buildings from Scobey and the surrounding area that were saved from destruction and, to a lesser extent, the ravages of time. Some 35 of the buildings on-site—including a schoolhouse, a barbershop, two churches, and a saloon—have been restored and furnished with period pieces. Pioneer Town comes alive at the end of June each year with **Pioneer Days,** the town's biggest and arguably best event. The weekend includes the *Dirty Shame Show,* a musical variety show in the vaudeville tradition and still a rite of passage for many of Scobey's young women. There is a parade and plenty of food and celebration, and appropriately dressed pioneer guides will walk you through some of the town buildings.

Food

As you pull into town from the east, you'll encounter **Shu's Kitchen** (506 1st. Ave. E., no phone, 3pm-9pm daily, $8-16), a wonderful little place for surprisingly authentic Chinese cuisine. Owner Shu Mei Swenson has been known to select your meal for you; the wise will oblige and will not be sorry. Though hours are posted here, they aren't necessarily set, so you may have to take your chances and drive by. On the other side of town, **Burger Hut** (Hwy. 13 between 1st Ave. and Railroad Ave., 406/487-5030, 11am-8pm Mon.-Sat., 11am-4pm Sun., $5-12) is a summer-only establishment with classic curb service and a menu that puts full-size restaurants to shame. Don't miss the famous and enormous "Ugly Burgers" or the excellent ice cream.

The **Slipper Lounge** (608 Main St., 406/487-9973, 5pm-10pm Tues.-Sun., bar open until 2am, $7-24) offers sit-down meals (and a casino) in the classic supper-club tradition.

For a steak dinner and a nice drive, head 20 miles (32 km) west to the town of Peerless and **Dutch Henry's Club** (19 Main St., 406/893-4389, 11am-1:30pm Mon., 11am-1:30pm and 4:30pm-9pm Tues.-Sat., 1pm-9pm Sun., $8-30). This enormous place, named for one of the area's best-known outlaws, has a dance floor, full bar, and a menu offering everything from chicken and burgers to Montana steak.

Accommodations

Just south of town, the **Smoke Creek Inn** (Hwy. 13 S., 406/487-5332 or 800/562-2775, www.smokecreekinn.com, $80-90) offers 30 clean, basic rooms, free Wi-Fi, free continental breakfast, and free guest laundry. Pets are welcome with a $20 fee, and outside kennels are available too. Outside electric outlets are available to plug in your engine block during winter so that the car starts in the morning. No one said the winters were mild this far north.

WOLF POINT

Nestled on the banks of the Missouri River on the Fort Peck Reservation, Wolf Point (population 2,806; elevation 1,997 ft/609 m) has been many things over the course of Montana history: a fur trading post, a cow town, a refueling stop for wood-burning steamships, an Indian trading post, and, more recently, a community hub for the Fort Peck Reservation and an important storage site for much of the region's grain.

The community is made up of roughly equal numbers of tribe members and non-members, just as it was in the early 1900s when the U.S. government opened the reservation to homesteaders. The Native American population includes primarily Sioux and Assiniboine people.

Entertainment and Events

Among the most celebrated events in eastern Montana is the **Wild Horse Stampede** (Marvin Brookman Stadium, 0.25 mi/0.4 km east of Main St., 406/653-1770 or 406/653-2102, www.wolfpointchamber.com), Montana's oldest pro rodeo. Held annually the second weekend in July, this event has its origins in Native American celebration and is still an opportunity for participants to show off their equestrian skills. In addition to three nights of spine-tingling rodeo, there are daily parades, a carnival, the famous wild-horse race, and street dances.

The other major event for Wolf Point is the **Wadopana Celebration** (406/650-7104 or 406/650-8724, www.wolfpointchamber.com), the oldest traditional powwow in the state, held annually the first weekend in August. The event includes a special day of activities for young people and an annual community feed on Thursday evening.

Food

Old Town Grill (400 U.S. 2, 406/653-1031, 7am-8pm Mon.-Sat., 7am-2pm Sun., $8-15) is a clean, well-lit place with a curious but tasty assortment of Mexican, Asian, and American food. Don't miss the pastries, which are feasts for the eyes and the belly.

For more classic Montana fare and a slice of local life, try the restaurant at the **Sherman**

Inn (200 E. Main St., 800/653-1100, 6am-9pm daily, $10-25), where weekly specials include Wednesday prime rib and Saturday ribs, or the **Elk's Club Dining Room** (304 Main St., 406/653-1920, 5pm-9pm Thurs.-Sat., noon-10pm Sun. summer, 5pm-9pm Thurs.-Sat. fall-spring, $9-25), where the steak and the karaoke are the main draws.

For those inclined toward liquid nourishment, **Missouri Breaks Brewing, Doc'Z Pub** (326 Main St., 406/653-1467, www.missouribreaksbrewing.com, 5pm-8pm Mon., 4pm-8pm Tues.-Sat.) serves up six microbrew varieties, all made on-site, as well as homemade root beer for the under-21 crowd. Check their Facebook page for special events, including live music and trivia nights. Pizza can be ordered and brought in from the nearby **Wolf Point Café** (217 Main St., 406/653-1388, 11am-8pm Mon.-Fri., $6-27). Call ahead; listed hours can fluctuate based on customers and local happenings.

Accommodations

The Homestead Inn (101 U.S. 2 E., 406/653-1300 or 800/231-0986, www.homesteadinnmotel.com, from $69) is clean, comfortable, and affordable and offers free coffee and doughnuts every morning.

Right downtown, the **Sherman Inn** (200 E. Main St., 800/952-1100, www.shermaninn.com, from $88) offers 44 rooms, all with queen-size beds and cinder-block walls.

The Meadowlark (872 Nickwall Rd., 406/525-3289, www.meadowlarkcabin.com, $95-110) is a cozy spot 16 miles (26 km) south of town on the Lewis and Clark Trail. Options include a cabin rental and a daylight basement suite, set on a ranch with splendid views and abundant wildlife. Full breakfasts are available at an extra, per-person charge. Though pets cannot be accommodated in the cabin or suite, a heated, indoor facility can be made available on-property during inclement weather for kenneled pets.

1: Scobey's Pioneer Town 2: Fort Peck Lake

GLASGOW AND FORT PECK

Glasgow (population 3,364; elevation 2,090 ft/637 m) is another northeastern Montana town that has seen its share of heart-stopping boom and heartbreaking bust. Founded around 1887 with the arrival of the Northern Pacific Railway, the town was a supply center for the region's homesteaders before it exploded in 1933 with the construction of the Fort Peck Dam, the largest of President Roosevelt's Public Works Administration projects, which employed more than 10,000 workers at any given time. When the dam was complete, the population and the city dwindled until the mid-1960s, when the Glasgow Air Force Base was commissioned. The population doubled, and the city built an entirely new infrastructure to meet the needs of the new residents. When the Air Force pulled out suddenly in 1968, 16,000 people left Glasgow, and the city was left with the fallout. Today the mostly abandoned and deteriorated base operates intermittently as a testing facility for Boeing and is occupied by a couple hundred retirees.

Both the expansive **Fort Peck Lake**, with as many miles of shoreline as California has coastline, and the Charles M. Russell National Wildlife Refuge are nearby and offer residents and visitors alike a wealth of outdoor opportunities. And as the largest city in this part of the state, Glasgow has plenty of services for those looking for recreation at Fort Peck Lake.

The town of Fort Peck (population 247; elevation 2,100 ft/640 m) was an Indian trading post starting in 1867, and even though the settlement was bypassed by the railroad, it was a hub of activity during construction of the dam. Today the town has a few residents and a significant number of lake visitors. The historic Fort Peck Theatre is a magical place to watch a show during the summer season.

★ Fort Peck Dam

The **Fort Peck Dam Interpretive Center and Museum** (adjacent to the powerhouses on Lower Yellowstone Rd., 406/526-3493, www.fws.gov/refuge/Charles_M_Russell/,

9am-5pm daily May-Sept., 10am-4pm Tues.-Sun. Oct., 10am-4pm Tues.-Fri. Nov.-Apr., free) is a unique combination of exhibits created in a partnership among Fort Peck Paleontology Inc., the U.S. Fish and Wildlife Service, and the U.S. Army Corps of Engineers. The museum features the state's largest aquariums, with examples of the species native to Fort Peck Lake, a life-size model of the *T. rex* uncovered some 20 miles (32 km) southeast of Fort Peck, and the construction history of the Fort Peck Dam. The museum also offers excellent interpretive programs throughout the summer with weekend nature walks on a nice 3-mile (4.8-km) paved trail and experiential programs for kids. Visitors can also sign up for tours of the **Fort Peck Power Plants** (9am, 11am, 1pm, and 3pm Mon.-Fri. and on the hour weekends and holidays Memorial Day-Labor Day, 11am and 1pm daily Labor Day-Sept. 30, by appointment Oct.-Memorial Day), next to the interpretive center. A great day-use area is adjacent to the museum, complete with picnic shelters, playground equipment, and horseshoe pits. There is also a Class A campground.

The **Fort Peck Theatre** (201 Missouri Ave., 406/526-9943 or 406/228-9216, www.fortpecktheatre.org) was built as a temporary movie house in 1934 to entertain the huge number of workers building the dam. Over the years, the structure, designed and built by the Army Corps of Engineers in the style of a Swiss chalet, has become one of Montana's gems. The incredible craftsmanship, right down to the light fixtures, can be appreciated each summer during live performances produced by the Fort Peck Fine Arts Council.

In Glasgow, the **Valley County Pioneer Museum** (816 Hwy. 2, 406/228-8692, www.valleycountymuseum.com, 9am-5pm Mon.-Sat. summer, 1pm-5pm Tues.-Fri. fall-spring, closed Jan., $3 adults, $2 students, free for children 6 and under) houses everything from dinosaur fossils found nearby and Fort Peck Dam construction information to the country's largest Assiniboine collection and genealogical archives.

Sports and Recreation

With 50 different kinds of fish in **Fort Peck Lake Reservoir,** nearly 1,600 miles (2,575 km) of shoreline, and more than 1 million acres (404,686 hectares) of public land in the surrounding Charles M. Russell (CMR) National Wildlife Refuge, the area is a nature lover's paradise. **Hi-Line Charter Fishing** (6820 U.S. 2 E., Havre, 406/262-2195 or 406/390-6892, www.hilinecharterfishing.com, half day $400 for 3 people, full day $650-700 for 2-3 people) can provide fully equipped boats and guides for fishing expeditions. Depending on the season, fishers can angle for walleye, smallmouth bass, northern pike, sauger, lake trout, and king salmon, among others. To rent a boat, contact the **Hell Creek Marina** (1 Hell Creek Rd., 406/557-2345, www.hellcreekmarina.net), 26 miles (42 km) north of Jordan, or the **Rock Creek Marina** (625 S. Rock Creek Rd., 406/485-2560, www.rockcreekmarina.com), on the southeast end of the reservoir, which also offers stocked cabins (from $70), RV campsites (from $25), and an on-site restaurant and tavern.

Golfers can hit the links in nearby Glasgow at the fairly level nine-hole **Sunnyside Golf Club** (95 Skylark Rd., 406/228-9519, $15 for 9 holes, $22 for 18 holes, carts $12-18).

Food

An upscale burger and steak restaurant, **Durum Restaurant & Bar** (1015 U.S. 2, 406/228-2236, 11am-2pm and 5pm-9pm Tues.-Fri., 5pm-9pm Sat., bar 11am-2am Tues.-Sat., $15-35) is a nice surprise in this part of the state. The menu is diverse, and the preparations are creative—cowboy cut pork loin chop with rosemary molasses glaze—meaning the restaurant is often packed.

For a good, thin and crispy pizza with loads of create-your-own options, try **Eugene's Pizza** (193 Klein Ave., 406/228-8552, www.eugenespizza.com, 11am-2pm and 4pm-11pm daily, $10-21), which also serves up chicken dinners, burgers, steaks, and fried chicken by the bucket.

The best spot for a cup of coffee or tea in town is **The Loaded Toad** (527 2nd Ave. S., 406/228-4610, 7am-4pm Mon.-Fri., 7am-2pm Sat.), which also offers wonderful specialty salads ($5-10) and delicious pastries.

Accommodations

Right in Fort Peck is the rambling **Fort Peck Hotel** (175 S. Missouri St., 406/526-3266 or 800/560-4931, www.thefortpeckhotel. com, May-Nov., $71-160), built at the same time and in similar fashion to the Fort Peck Theatre. The wooden hotel certainly recalls a time gone by, and though the amenities are simple (double and single beds, bathrooms down the hall for the more basic rooms), they are perfectly suitable and quite charming. The hotel serves three wonderful meals daily in the quaint dining room, and guests tend to lounge in oversize Depression-era rockers on the expansive porch.

The **Cottonwood Inn & Suites** (45 1st Ave. NE, 406/228-8213 or 800/321-8213, www.cottonwoodinn.net, rooms from $105, RV sites from $40) in Glasgow is the town's newest and most modern addition. There are 168 guest rooms, an indoor heated pool with two hot tubs, free Wi-Fi, a dining room, lounge and casino, and an adjacent RV park which gives guests full access to hotel amenities.

INFORMATION AND SERVICES

The **Glasgow Area Chamber of Commerce** (313 Klein Ave., 406/228-2222, www.glasgowchamber.net, 9am-5pm Mon.-Fri. Memorial Day-Labor Day, 8:30am-4pm Mon.-Fri. Labor Day-Memorial Day) is happy to provide visitors with information for the surrounding area, including Fort Peck.

The **Daniels County Chamber of Commerce** (120 Main St., Scobey, 406/487-2061, www.scobeymt.com, 10am-2pm Mon.-Fri. May 15-Sept. 15) is located in downtown Scobey.

The **Sheridan County Chamber of Commerce** (108 N. Main St., 406/765-1733, www.sheridancountychamber.org, 9am-5pm Mon.-Sat.) is in Plentywood. There is also a **visitors information** rack filled with brochures and pamphlets at the **Sherwood Inn** (515 W. 1st Ave., Plentywood).

The **Wolf Point Chamber of Commerce and Agriculture** (218 3rd Ave. S., Ste. B, 406/653-2012, www.wolfpointchamber.com, 9am-4pm Mon., Wed., and Fri.) also has information about the Fort Peck Reservation.

TRANSPORTATION

Glasgow sits on U.S. 2, 270 miles (435 km) northeast of Great Falls and 50 miles (81 km) west of Wolf Point. Fort Peck is off Highway 24, 47 miles (76 km) southwest of Wolf Point and 18 miles (29 km) southeast of Glasgow.

The Milk River Valley

The Milk River flows from high in the Montana Rockies, north into Alberta, then east and south, through Havre and across prairie and riparian areas teeming with wildlife, through Fort Belknap, Malta, and Glasgow, eventually joining the Missouri River. The water is indeed milky colored, even late in summer, and it was named by Lewis and Clark, who thought the water looked like "a cup of tea with the admixture of a tablespoonful of milk."

Life along the river seems to follow an equally relaxed pace in nice little towns like Saco, Malta, and Fort Belknap. This is the country of Wallace Stegner, the beloved Western author who spent much of his childhood along Frenchman Creek, a tributary of the Milk River. He didn't always love the austere beauty of the place, but he always captured it in his spare, lovely prose.

This is also prime hunting territory for large game and birds, and there are a number of places to enjoy the water by boat or with a fishing rod. Many people simply come to drink it all in, visiting the scenic wildlife refuges, driving through the open country, stopping in friendly towns along the way, or relaxing at eastern Montana's only hot springs resort.

MALTA

A notable stop on the Montana Dinosaur Trail and something of a mecca for bird hunters, Malta (population 1,950; elevation 2,254 ft/687 m) is a hub for the myriad ranches in the area and a nice place to start day trips into the Bowdoin National Wildlife Refuge or organize an exciting fossil dig. Known among Native Americans in the region as "The Big Bend," for the curve of the Milk River here, the town eventually got its name when a blindfolded railroad employee in Minneapolis was told to point his finger at a spot on the globe—and landed on the Mediterranean island. Nearby Saco was named in the same way, when the man pointed to Saco, Maine.

Just west of town is the site of a great train robbery in 1901 by Kid Curry and his gang of outlaws, many of whom were known to frequent the area. The other most famous

The Montana skyline is often punctuated by weathered agricultural buildings.

residents of Malta were of the scaly variety: a 77-million-year-old mummified brachylophosaurus, a rare and precious find, was unearthed north of town in 2000 and has become something of a local hero, along with fellow duck-bills Elvis, Roberta, and Peanut, all of whom are on display in town.

The **Phillips County Museum** (431 U.S. 2 E., 406/654-1037, www.phillipscountymuseum.org, 10am-5pm Mon.-Sat. Apr.-Dec., $5 adults, $3 children, free for children under 6) is a stop on the Montana Dinosaur Trail and includes exhibits on mining, Native Americans, outlaws, and, most notably, dinosaurs. The collection includes Elvis, a brachylophosaurus found in 1994, in addition to a complete *Tyrannosaurus rex* skull and an upright full-size albertosaurus, a relative of the *T. rex* and the primary prey of the brachylophosaurus. A beautifully restored 1903 home, built by New York transplant H. G. Robinson, is adjacent to the museum and available for tours.

Another stop on the Montana Dinosaur Trail is the **Great Plains Dinosaur Museum and Field Station** (405 N. 1st St. E., 406/654-5300, www.greatplainsdinosaur.org, 10am-5pm Tues.-Sat. May, 10am-5pm Mon.-Sat. and 12:30pm-5pm Sun. June-Aug., $5 adults 13 and over, $3 children 6-12, free for children under 6). The museum includes rare dinosaur exhibits that show fossilized skin, tendon, and even stomach contents. It also offers excellent field programs as well as experiences in the paleo lab.

The nearby **Bowdoin National Wildlife Refuge** (194 Bowdoin Auto Tour Rd., 7 mi/11.3 km east of Malta off Old U.S. 2, 406/654-2863, www.bowdoin.fws.gov) is a landscape scoured by a runaway continental ice sheet more than 15,000 years ago. The area was established as a migratory bird refuge in 1936. Both saline and freshwater wetlands offer ideal habitat for the thousands of birds—from waterfowl and shorebirds to birds of prey and grassland songbirds—that soar along this flyway. More than 230 species have been identified in the refuge, including one of the largest colonies of inland American white pelicans, as well as double-crested cormorants, great blue herons, ring-necked pheasants, sandpipers, sharp-tailed grouse, and the occasional bald eagle. A 15-mile (24-km) self-guided auto tour route brings visitors face-to-face with much of the region's wildlife. Fishing and hunting in the refuge are strictly regulated and should be coordinated through the refuge office during business hours.

Two other impressive swaths of wildlife-rich land include the vast Charles M. Russell National Wildlife Refuge and the much newer American Prairie Reserve, which may eventually top 3 million acres (1.2 million hectares).

Twenty miles (32 km) northeast of Malta, near the tiny town of Saco, **Sleeping Buffalo Hot Springs** (699 Buffalo Trail, 406/527-3320, www.sbhotsprings.com, 10am-8pm Wed.-Thurs. and Sun., 10am-9pm Fri.-Sat. year-round, 10am-8pm Mon.-Tues. Memorial Day-Labor Day, $9.50 adults, $8.50 seniors and children 5-11, $5 children 4 and under) is a wonderfully restored slice of Montana history and a great place to soak in warm, medicinal waters. The only hot springs in eastern Montana, Sleeping Buffalo was discovered by a wildcat oil rigger in 1922 and became known as the local "Saturday night bathtub" for the region's cowboys before it was developed by a rancher whose son suffered from polio. The 108°F (42.2°C) mineral water, flowing from 3,200 feet (975 m) down, worked wonders on the boy, and it wasn't long before other swimmers started coming. The springs fell into grave disrepair and were closed before a massive 2015 renovation. Today there are three pools, all of which are drained nightly and refilled every day so that no chemicals are necessary. A snack bar is on-site, and towels and toys are available for rent. Deluxe cabins ($129-239) are available as are RV sites ($34-46) and tent sites ($24).

FORT BELKNAP INDIAN RESERVATION

Set between the Little Rockies and Milk River, the **Fort Belknap Ind**

Reservation, established in 1889, put together the Gros Ventre and the Assiniboine who refused to relocate to the Fort Peck Indian Reservation. The two tribes had long been enemies and only formed an alliance to fight the nearby Blackfeet. Today the reservation is a peaceful place encompassing 650,000 acres (263,046 hectares) of grasslands and gently rolling hills. There is an **1877 mission** in Hays as well as some significant recreation sites and a variety of festive celebrations. The nearby Charles M. Russell National Wildlife Refuge is a marvelous place for recreation and to appreciate the diverse and abundant wildlife.

CHARLES M. RUSSELL NATIONAL WILDLIFE REFUGE

The **Charles M. Russell (CMR) National Wildlife Refuge** (406/538-8706, ext. 221 or 406/526-3464, www.fws.gov) was established in 1936, and at 1.1 million acres (445,154 hectares), it is the second-largest U.S. wildlife refuge outside Alaska. In this place of uncommon beauty—from badlands to breaks, coulees to canyons—live thriving populations of mountain lions, coyotes, prairie dogs, pronghorn, and enormous numbers of birds. Twenty-five percent bigger than Rhode Island, the refuge has only two paved roads providing minimal access to the refuge. The 20-mile (32-km) paved auto tour begins and ends on U.S. 191 and offers two hours of scenery and, most often, abundant wildlife. All other travel is on dirt and gravel roads, on foot, on horseback, or by boat. The region was a frequent hiding place for a number of famous outlaws. The refuge encompasses Fort Peck Lake, a long stretch of the Missouri River, and the rugged Missouri Breaks, extending more than 100 miles (161 km) west to U.S. 191.

AMERICAN PRAIRIE RESERVE

The lofty mission for the **American Prairie Reserve** (406/585-4600 or 877/273-1123, www.americanprairie.org) is to create the largest wildlife reserve in the continental United States by piecing together more than 3.5 million acres (1.4 million hectares) of public and private land to be a functioning mixed-grass prairie ecosystem. Wild inhabitants of the area include bison, elk, deer, pronghorn, and even bighorn sheep. Smaller critters include badgers, prairie dogs, swift fox, and a multitude of birds. The reserve, very much

Pronghorn, also known as "speed goats," are the fastest land animal in North America.

a work in progress, is open to hiking, biking, horseback riding, wildlife-watching, and hunting. A multitude of guided trips and volunteer opportunities can be arranged and are well worth looking into for anyone seeking real solace in this ocean of grassland.

ENTERTAINMENT AND EVENTS

The **Milk River Indian Days** (406/353-2205 or 406/353-2281, www.ftbelknap.org) is a traditional powwow with colorfully clad dancers, Native American drummers, and music. The celebration is typically held in late July at the Fort Belknap Powwow Grounds. The **Hays Pow Wow** (406/353-2205) is another excellent celebration of Native American history and culture, staged annually 5 miles (8 km) south of Hays in Mission Canyon. The event features a weekend of Native dancing and singing, along with multiple contests for every age group. Both events are free and open to the public.

FOOD

As this is ranch country, diners often have the choice between steaks and burgers, and you can't really go wrong with either. The **Tin Cup Bar and Grill** (1652 U.S. 191 S., Malta, 406/654-5527, 10am-3pm and 5pm-10pm daily summer, limited hours fall-spring, $7-25) is an elegant full-service restaurant overlooking the Marian Hills Golf Course and the pastoral Milk River Valley. The **Great Northern Steak House** (2 S. 1st St. E., 406/654-2100, 6am-9:30pm Mon.-Sat, 6am-noon Sun., breakfast $4-13, lunch $4-23, dinner $13-42) serves the best surf and turf on the Hi-Line, including Saturday night prime rib. As the restaurant is in a hotel, it's open for breakfast and lunch as well, with an extensive menu for both, including Mexican specialties. A **coffee shop** in the hotel serves specialty coffees plus breakfast and lunch. And the **Great Northern Lounge** is a nice spot for a drink. **The Hitchin Post** (745 N. 1st Ave. E., Malta, 406/654-1882, 6am-3pm Mon.-Fri., 7am-2pm Sat., 8am-2pm Sun., $8-14) is a favorite for homemade soups, pies, rolls, muffins, and daily lunch specials. Breakfast is served all day.

ACCOMMODATIONS

A number of small motels are found in Malta, the nicest being the pet-friendly **Great Northern Hotel** (2 S. 1st St. E., 406/654-2100, from $78). It's not charming in a historical sense (the 1904 hotel was rebuilt after a catastrophic fire in 1971), but the rooms are quite comfortable and impeccably clean. There is also a nice steak house and nonsmoking coffee shop on the premises. The pet-friendly **Riverside Motel & RV Park** (8 Central Ave. N., 406/654-2310 or 800/854-2310, www.riversidemotel-rvpark.com, $62-95) is a good choice for more budget-conscious travelers. The modern rooms are clean and spacious and offer free Wi-Fi plus refrigerators and microwaves.

CAMPING

In Malta, basic motel rooms ($84-86), tent camping ($15-20), and RV sites ($36-45) are available at the **Edgewater Inn & RV Park** (47176 U.S. 2, 406/654 1302 or 800/821-7475). There is also an indoor pool, hot tub and health club on-site.

You'll find multiple primitive campgrounds in the vicinity of Malta: **Fourchette Bay Campground** is 60 miles (97 km) south of Malta, **Montana Gulch Campground** is 1 mile (1.6 km) south of Landusky, and **Nelson Reservoir** is 17 miles (27 km) east of Malta. But roads and access can be problematic in wet weather, and most sites advise campers to bring three days' worth of food in case they get stranded.

A newer and exciting option for camping in the region, with four tent sites and seven RV sites, is **Buffalo Camp at American Prairie Reserve** (44704 Regina Rd., 406/658-2252 or 877/273-1123, www.americanprairie.org, $10 without electricity, $15 with electri⸱⸱ 50 miles (81 km) south of Malta and in midst of excellent hiking and biking terr Tent sites include low-impact platforms w tie-down cleats. The campsite is primitive but does have non-potable water, vault toilets, and an amphitheater. There is no cell phone coverage on the reserve.

Inspired by tented African safaris, **Kestrel Camp at American Prairie Reserve** (44704 Regina Rd., 406/658-2252 or 877/273-1123, www.americanprairie.org, $2,400 adults for 2 nights, $1,200 children) offers several packaged tours each year and includes lodging in climate-controlled tented suites, guided activities, and gourmet meals. Past offerings have included close-up looks at the art of Charlie Russell, bison, wildlife-friendly ranching practices, and prairie conservation.

INFORMATION

The **Malta Chamber of Commerce** (2 S. 1st St. E., 406/654-1776, www.maltachamber. com, 10am-2pm Wed.) can provide brochures and information. The **Tourist Information Center** is open mid-May-mid-September in the **Phillips County Museum** (431 U.S. 2 E., 406/654-1037, 10am-5pm Mon.-Sat., 12:30pm-5pm Sun.).

TRANSPORTATION

The Milk River Valley can be accessed from U.S. 2, running east from Havre or west from Glasgow, or from U.S. 191 running north from Lewistown or south from Canada.

Great Falls and the Rocky Mountain Front

North-central Montana encompasses much of

the geographical diversity that defines the state, with vast plains along the Hi-Line, rolling agricultural fields in Montana's breadbasket, and the dramatic Rocky Mountain Front.

Although this stretch of Montana isn't often among the state's primary tourist destinations, there are many reasons why it should be (chief among them that the area is *not* a tourist destination). The region is rich with natural beauty, culturally significant landmarks, and history. Fort Benton, just east of Great Falls, is considered the birthplace of Montana due to its origins as an important inland port, the westernmost stopping point for steamers loaded with materials and pioneers traveling up the Missouri River. There are two major buffalo jumps

Highlights

Look for ★ to find recommended sights, activities, dining, and lodging.

★ **C. M. Russell Museum:** The most beloved and impressive art museum in the state is an extraordinary tribute to the life and work of the consummate Western artist (page 97).

★ **Lewis and Clark National Historic Trail Interpretive Center:** This compelling museum enables visitors to learn about the extraordinary challenges faced by Lewis and Clark and to appreciate how what they found parallels what exists today (page 99).

★ **Fishing on the Missouri River:** America's longest river attracts anglers from all over the world. The tailwater stretch between Holter Dam and Cascade serves up thousands of trout per mile (page 103).

★ **Bob Marshall Wilderness Complex:** More than 1 million acres (404,686 hectares) of pristine wilderness straddle the Continental Divide here. The topography is dramatic, the wildlife is plentiful, and the opportunities to explore are endless (page 112).

★ **Fort Benton:** Touted locally as the birthplace of Montana, this town was an important early trading post. A charming hotel, gourmet food, and a riverside setting make it an ideal destination (page 115).

★ **Havre Beneath the Streets:** Practically an entire city exists underneath the streets of downtown Havre. Guides show you around the 27-bed brothel, saloon, and opium den and the more genteel dentist's office, cigar shop, and bakery (page 118).

★ **Charlie Russell Chew Choo:** This three-hour narrated train ride travels from Lewistown through some of the most starkly beautiful terrain anywhere. The staged holdup might be

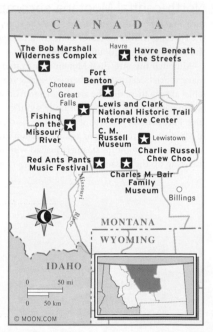

hokey, but the prime rib and splendid scenery are the real deal (page 123).

★ **Charles M. Bair Family Museum:** In the tiny agricultural town of Martinsdale, this remarkable home and museum tells the story of a Montana family and the way their history and art collection shaped the fabric of the West (page 126).

★ **Red Ants Pants Music Festival:** Voted Montana's best event of the year in 2018, this family-friendly weekend-long festival in late July offers pastoral beauty, fantastic music, and a real sense of community (page 127).

Great Falls and the Rocky Mountain Front

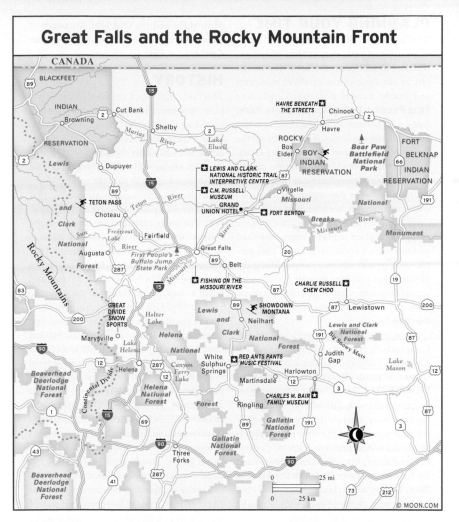

(butte-like geographical features that Native Americans used to hunt bison) worth seeing, Egg Mountain with its significant dinosaur discoveries, the vast Bob Marshall Wilderness, the placid Smith River, and outcroppings all along the Missouri River that hold the lore of the fur trapping era. Great Falls, the largest city in the region, is home to the C. M. Russell Museum and some intriguing contemporary art as well as the Lewis and Clark National Historic Trail Interpretive Center. Smaller towns, including Choteau, Lewistown, and White Sulphur Springs, have preserved their culture and history as they have fought to maintain their populations in boom-and-bust economies, and each offers a meaningful glimpse into Montana's agricultural life past and present. The Rocky Boy's and Fort Belknap Indian Reservations offer some wonderful ways to immerse yourself in Native American culture.

Previous: the Rocky Mountain Front; farmland near Fort Benton; the Missouri River.

PLANNING YOUR TIME

As with most of Montana, there is as much to do in Great Falls as your time will allow. Visitors should plan at least a day in the city to see some of the excellent museums and nearby natural attractions, including **First Peoples Buffalo Jump State Park.** Known for its consistent wind, this city is ideally located on the Missouri River between the Rocky Mountains and Montana's Big Open. Any number of outdoor adventures can be dreamed up and launched from Great Falls.

Other towns in this region, each with its own unique charm, are often best enjoyed en route from one destination to another. One notable exception is Fort Benton, less than an hour's drive from Great Falls. This picturesque hamlet sits in a canyon along the Missouri and is an ideal spot for visitors, with several museums, a quaint downtown, historic sites, and one of the handsomest old hotels in the state.

The country opens up significantly east of Great Falls. In places it looks as if the only occupants are cattle and oversize windmills. The **Upper Missouri River Breaks National Monument,** with some of the state's most interesting and isolated terrain, is best explored from the water. Havre is the largest city on the Hi-Line (a stretch of the state that parallels Montana's northernmost or "highest" railroad line) and offers plenty of accommodations and the fascinating **Havre Beneath the Streets Tour.** Farther south, Lewistown is small but colorful, with plenty of good fishing nearby and a couple of good restaurants.

West of Great Falls, the Rocky Mountains soar skyward, with towns such as Choteau and the reservation town of Browning in their shadows. Dude ranches are available for those who make this region their primary destination, but at the very least this is a magnificent corner to drive through en route to Glacier National Park or southwest toward Missoula. In the fall, this is a bird hunter's paradise. Dinosaur aficionados will want to allow enough time to visit some of the plentiful paleontological sites, including **Egg** Mountain and the **Old Trail Museum** in Choteau and the **Two Medicine Dinosaur Center** in Bynum.

HISTORY

This vast, largely open stretch of Montana was home to numerous Native American groups, including the Blackfeet, Sioux, Assiniboine, Gros Ventre, and Cree, who took up residence and battled for the land as early as the late 18th century. The Crow, Nez Perce, and Salish were known to hunt the region.

Settlers were brought by steamboats that navigated along the Missouri all the way to Fort Benton as early as 1859 and the rapid construction of the Great Northern Railway in 1887. Under the direction of James J. Hill, 643 miles (1,030 km) of track were laid in less than eight months by a crew of 9,000 men and 6,600 horses. In an attempt to populate the area, in 1908 Hill sent agents and exhibition cars to county fairs across the Midwest and on the East Coast to entice farmers. Settlers flocked to the region for their 320 acres (129.5 hectares) of "Poor Man's Paradise," a term made famous by Hill's promotional campaign, which piggybacked on the Homestead Act of 1891, giving every U.S. citizen the chance to claim 320 acres (129.5 hectares) of unoccupied land. Generous rainfall prompted enormous harvests of wheat and kept population growth steady until 1917, when a cyclical drought wreaked havoc on the land and broke the spirits of newcomers. Between 1909 and 1916, some 80,000 people had moved into the region; 60,000 of them were gone by 1922. North-central Montana is still subject to harsh weather and the unpredictable boom-and-bust cycle.

When Meriwether Lewis stood atop the rocks beneath the Great Falls of the Missouri River in June 1805, he pronounced the scene as "the grandest sight I ever beheld," a sentiment shared by Fort Benton businessman Paris Gibson some 75 years later. Gibson committed himself to building a city around the site of the falls. In 1883 he plotted the city, then urged his friend James J. Hill to bring his railroad through. Gibson envisioned a "new Minneapolis" on the banks of the Missouri River. By 1888, with plentiful industry in town and fertile farmland around it, the city of Great Falls, with Gibson as its mayor, boasted more than 2,000 residents. Two years later the population had doubled. But despite Gibson's best efforts and his intelligent and thoughtful city planning, Great Falls floundered when Hill opted not to bring the railroad to town. Though it never fulfilled Gibson's ultimate vision, the city did achieve industrial success with power-producing dams, copper smelting, and eventually an Air Force base.

Great Falls

At the edge of the mountains and the plains, Great Falls (population 58,638; elevation 3,674 ft/1,120 m) has more romantic origins than its modern-day grittiness may suggest. A few days ahead of William Clark, Meriwether Lewis stumbled on the region in June 1805, calling the falls themselves "the grandest sight I ever beheld." Seventy-five years later, Fort Benton merchant Paris Gibson sought the same views that had captivated Lewis and later recollected,

I had never seen a spot as attractive as this . . . I had looked upon this scene for a few moments only when I said to myself, here I would found a city.

Just three years later, in 1883, the city of Great Falls was named and platted.

With the falls long since dammed to create power—Great Falls is known as the "Electric City" for all its dams and power plants—the city has worked to capitalize on the beauty of the Missouri River with a scenic roadway (River Drive), trails, parks, and picnic areas along the waterway. The Lewis and Clark National Historic Trail Interpretive Center sits atop a bluff and affords visitors an unspoiled view of what the area might have looked like 200 years ago. Another kind of beauty celebrated by this city is art. There are a couple of excellent—and surprising—art museums to visit.

But Great Falls is still a rough-and-tumble Montana town. There is cowboy culture, military culture, and serious wind, all of which give the state's third-largest city a little bit of an edge. Its location between the mountains and plains and amid rivers is ideal for lovers of the outdoors, and Great Falls is an excellent launching point for adventures in any direction.

SIGHTS

Great Falls Historic Trolley

If you only have a few hours and want to see as much of the city as possible, the **Great Falls Historic Trolley** (406/868-2913, www. gftrolley.com, June-Sept., late Nov.-Dec. for holiday lights tours) takes you to the most important natural and human-built places. The company was sold in the spring of 2018. The new owner has updated the trolley and revamped the tour options, including ghost tours, brothel tours, and art tours.

★ C. M. Russell Museum

One of the best and most intimate Western art museums in the country, the **C. M. Russell Museum** (400 13th St. N., 406/727-8787, www.cmrussell.org, 10am-5pm Tues.-Sun. mid-May-Oct., 10am-5pm Wed.-Sat. Nov.-mid-May, $9 adults, $7 seniors and veterans, $4 students, free for children 5 and under) has amassed the world's largest collection of Charlie Russell art and personal objects, including his illustrated letters. His home (11am-4pm Tues.-Sun. mid-May-Oct.) has been meticulously maintained on the museum grounds and is open to visitors. In addition to a significant number of important works by Western masters, the museum takes an interesting approach to art through its permanent bison exhibit. The iconic western ungulate

Great Falls

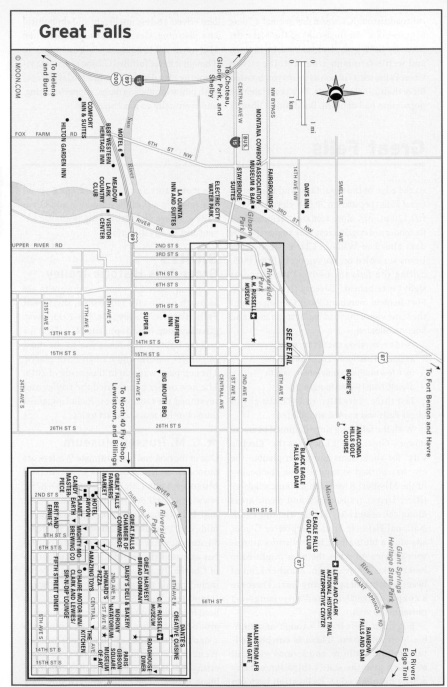

© MOON.COM

To Helena
and Butte

To Choteau,
Glacier Park, and
Shelby

CENTRAL AVE W

NW BYPASS

0
0   1 km
1 mi

FOX   FARM   RD

COMFORT
INN & SUITES

HILTON GARDEN INN

BEST WESTERN
HERITAGE INN

MOTEL 6

MEADOW
LARK
COUNTRY
CLUB

6TH   ST   NW

Sun   River

MONTANA COWBOY'S
ASSOCIATION
MUSEUM & BAR

STAYBRIDGE
SUITES

FAIRGROUNDS

14TH AVE NW

DAYS INN

SMELTER   AVE

3RD   ST   NW

Gibson
Park

ELECTRIC CITY
WATER PARK

LA QUINTA
INN AND SUITES

RIVER   DR

VISITOR
CENTER

UPPER   RIVER   RD

2ND ST S

3RD ST S

5TH ST S

6TH ST S

9TH ST S

13TH AVE S

17TH AVE S

21ST AVE S

13TH ST S

15TH ST S

24TH AVE S

SUPER 8

FAIRFIELD
INN

14TH ST S

15TH ST S

Park

Riverside

C. M. RUSSELL
MUSEUM

SEE DETAIL

BIG MOUTH BBQ

10TH AVE S

CENTRAL   AVE

1ST AVE N

2ND AVE N

8TH AVE N

BORRIE'S

87

To Fort Benton and Havre

To North 40 Fly Shop,
Lewistown, and Billings

26TH ST S

26TH ST S

38TH ST S

ANACONDA
HILLS GOLF
COURSE

BLACK EAGLE
FALLS AND DAM

Missouri

EAGLE FALLS
GOLF CLUB

87

56TH ST

LEWIS AND CLARK
NATIONAL HISTORIC TRAIL
INTERPRETIVE CENTER

MALMSTROM AFB
MAIN GATE

Giant Springs
Heritage State Park

River

GIANT SPRINGS RD

RAINBOW
FALLS AND DAM

To Rivers
Edge Trail

Detail

2ND ST S

CANDY
MASTER-
PIECE

BERT AND
ERNIE'S

5TH ST S

6TH ST S

FIFTH STREET DINER

14TH ST S

15TH ST S

HOTEL
ARVON

PLANET
EARTH

GREAT FALLS
FARMERS
MARKET

GREAT FALLS
CHAMBER OF
COMMERCE

MIGHTY MO
BREWING CO

AMAZING TOYS

O'HAIRE MOTOR INN/
CLARK AND LEWIS/
SIP-N-DIP LOUNGE

PARK   DR   N

Riverside
Park

GREAT HARVEST
BREAD COMPANY

DAISY'S DELI & BAKERY

HOWARD'S
PIZZA

2ND AVE N

MORONY
NATATORIUM

1ST AVE N

PARIS
GIBSON
SQUARE
MUSEUM
OF ART

RIVER   DR   N

C. M. RUSSELL
MUSEUM

8TH AVE N

CENTRAL   AVE

DANTE'S
CREATIVE CUISINE

ROADHOUSE
DINER

THE
KITCHEN
5TH AVE S

Nancy Russell:
The Force Behind the Artist

Charles M. Russell's name is synonymous with great Western art and Montana. He is not only the pride and joy of Great Falls but a hero to the entire state. Although today Charlie Russell's art is heralded around the world, there is little debate that the world may not have known him had it not been for his savvy and determined wife, Nancy.

Born Nancy Bates Cooper in 1878, she was 14 years younger than Charlie and worked as a housemaid for one of his friends when they met. Their pairing seemed an unlikely match, and when news of the engagement spread, it seemed clear that Charlie was marrying beneath himself. What soon became apparent was that not only could Nancy hold her own in any social circle, she would be the single greatest asset to her husband's career.

Nancy Russell had fended for herself from the age of 16, when her mother had died. She was a strong woman capable of achieving whatever she set her mind to; some would argue that's how she nabbed Charlie. In his book *More Rawhide*, Charlie wrote, "It's the women that make the men in this world," and in his case it was true. There is no doubt that he was a talented artist, but his wife's belief in his work and her drive to see him properly recognized are what made him a success. As his business-minded partner, Nancy ultimately organized the shows that gained him worldwide attention.

Nancy quickly earned the moniker "Nancy the robber" because of the high prices she would ask (and receive) for Charlie's work. Charlie once told a newspaper that the worst fight the couple ever had was when she had asked for $75 for a painting that he thought would sell for $5. Initially setting up a home in the town of Cascade, the couple moved to Great Falls to aid Charlie's burgeoning career. On their arrival, the mayor's wife commissioned a painting, and Nancy asked her husband if she could deliver it. He warned her that the painting was to be sold for $25, and she should not ask for a penny more or the painting would not sell. Nancy met the mayor's wife, delivered the painting, and with a lump in her throat asked for $35. The mayor's wife replied, "I'll get my checkbook."

Ultimately, it was evident that Charlie was proud of his wife and relieved to have her handle the financial part of his business. In 1919, when asked by a reporter if marriage hinders an artist's expression, Charlie replied, "I still love and long for the Old West, and everything that goes with it. But I would sacrifice it all for Mrs. Russell."

GREAT FALLS

had significance to Russell himself, and the importance of the animal and its near extinction is traced through more than 1,000 exquisite Native American artifacts. Don't leave Great Falls without spending a few hours at the C. M. Russell.

Paris Gibson Square Museum of Art

At the eastern end of downtown Great Falls, the **Paris Gibson Square Museum of Art** (1400 1st Ave. N., 406/727-8255, www.the-square.org, 10am-5pm Mon. and Wed.-Fri., 10am-9pm Tues., noon-5pm Sat., free) is known as "The Square" and occupies an entire city block. Built in 1896, the impressive structure served the community as Central High

School and later as Paris Gibson Junior High until it closed in 1975. Renovated, renamed after the city's founder, and reopened in 1977, this National Historic Landmark houses an impressive permanent collection of contemporary art as well as important traveling exhibitions. In addition to classes, lectures, tours, and performances, the museum has a café and gift shop. Don't miss a stroll through the sculpture garden out on the beautifully landscaped grounds.

★ Lewis and Clark National Historic Trail Interpretive Center

Beautifully built into a bluff overlooking the Missouri River, the **Lewis and Clark**

National Historic Trail Interpretive Center (4201 Giant Springs Rd., 406/727-8733, www.fs.usda.gov, 9am-6pm daily Memorial Day-Sept., 9am-5pm Tues.-Sat., noon-5pm Sun. Oct.-Memorial Day, $8 adults, free for children under 15 and Federal Pass holders) provides visitors with a hands-on interpretation of the intrepid explorers' cross-country journey. With a two-story diorama of the portage at the Missouri River's five great falls, impressive videos by Ken Burns and others, and ranger-led programs, the center does an excellent job of portraying the importance of Native Americans to the journey along with a comprehensive natural history exhibit. The center offers a wealth of worthwhile special events that include concerts, lectures, and reenactments (check the website for upcoming events). There is also a nice outdoor component to the center with a network of self-guided trails, one of which leads you to the nearby Giant Springs Heritage State Park.

Giant Springs Heritage State Park

Among the largest freshwater springs in the country, Giant Springs was discovered by Lewis and Clark in 1805. The spring, now in **Giant Springs Heritage State Park** (4600 Giant Springs Rd., 406/454-5840 or 406/727-1212, www.stateparks.mt.gov, 8am-sunset daily, $6/vehicle or $4/pedestrian or biker for nonresidents), produces 156 million gallons (590.5 million liters) of crystal clear water each day. The water stays at a constant 54°F (12.2°C) all year, making it an ideal spot for fishing. There is a fish hatchery on-site, a **visitors center** (8am-5pm daily), a picnic area, and several trails that wind through the lush area. For trivia buffs, the 201-foot-long **Roe River,** the second shortest in the world, flows from the springs.

1: Roe River at Giant Springs Heritage State Park
2: Great Falls

First Peoples Buffalo Jump State Park

Considered to be among the largest buffalo jumps in North America, and in use more than 1,000 years before Lewis and Clark explored the area, **First Peoples Buffalo Jump State Park** (342 Ulm-Vaughn Rd., Ulm, 406/866-2217 or 406/454-5840, www.stateparks.mt.gov, 8am-6pm daily Apr.-Sept., 10am-4pm Wed.-Sat., noon-4pm Sun. Oct.-Mar., $6/vehicle nonresidents) is exceptional in that it offers an extensive on-site education center that houses buffalo culture exhibits, a storytelling circle, a gallery, and an outdoor powwow area. The site itself is impressive, with a mile-long sandstone cliff from which the bison were chased to their deaths, but more than anything, this is the best place in the state to learn about buffalo jumps. Watch your step on or off the trails for both rattlesnakes and prickly pear cacti. An adjacent prairie dog town is home to protected black-tailed prairie dogs and worth the short detour. The park is 10 miles (16.1 km) south of Great Falls off I-15 at Ulm; follow signs for the state park 3.5 miles (5.6 km) northwest on a county road. Check the website for upcoming events like the guided **Rock Art Hike** ($4 pp), a strenuous hiking tour that takes visitors to prehistoric petroglyphs and pictographs by Native Americans as well as carvings in stone made by early European settlers.

SPORTS AND RECREATION
River's Edge Trail

The River's Edge Trail is the envy of nearly every town in Montana. With 60 miles (97 km) of trail, some 20 miles (32 km) of which are paved for wheelchair access, the River's Edge Trail accommodates single-track and double-track riders on 19 miles (31 km) of dirt, as well as walkers on graveled paths. Started in the 1990s, the trail winds along both sides of the Missouri River, past five waterfalls including Black Eagle Falls, Rainbow Falls, Crooked Falls, and the renowned Great Falls of the Missouri below Ryan Dam. The art-lined trail

The History of Buffalo Jumps

Used by Native Americans for more than 5,000 years, buffalo jumps are rocky cliff formations that entire herds of bison were driven over, causing mortal injury to the animals and providing the hunters with ample meat, fur, and bones to make into weapons, tools, and decorative objects. Throughout Montana, the jumps have become significant archaeological sites, with discoveries of bones and tools guiding scientists to a better understanding of the various cultures of the people who hunted in this way.

What is surmised about the process is that the hunters first would spot herds of bison within a reasonable distance of the jump. Using rock cairns, they would carefully construct an ever-narrowing pathway from the base of the jump, up the gradual slope to the cliff's edge. Several warriors would dress in animal hides and intersperse themselves undetected among the herd. At a specific moment, the warriors would throw off their hides and stand up to startle the bison into a stampede, hopefully in the direction of the jump. As the bison headed toward the jump, other hunters would line the way, waving a variety of things to frighten the animals and prevent them from leaving the trail. By the time the animals reached the precipice, they were moving so fast that they were unable to stop at the cliff's edge even when they saw it. Hundreds of bison could go over the jump in one event, providing a substantial harvest for the hunters.

All of the animals were processed on-site, a painstaking process since every piece of the animal was used for meat, clothing, shelter, tools, and even toys. Archaeologists have uncovered significant prehistoric camps at the base of many jumps. In some places, bison bones continue to be found more than 15 feet (4.6 m) beneath the surface.

Buffalo jumps were used by a great variety of Native American tribes until the 19th century, when the Spanish brought horses to North America and the Indians began hunting on horseback.

also provides access to numerous parks, reservoirs, and other attractions, including the **Lewis and Clark National Historic Trail Interpretive Center** (4201 Giant Springs Rd., 406/727-8733, www.fs.usda.gov). There are 11 parking areas for easy access, and a trail map can be downloaded online (www.thetrail. org) or picked up at the **visitor information center** (15 Overlook Dr.).

Swimming

Starting in 2000, the city of Great Falls went to great lengths to renovate all of its municipal pools. The **Electric City Water Park** (100 River Dr. S., 406/771-1265, www.greatfallsmt. net, noon-6pm daily, Wed. family nights until 8pm, early June-late Aug., $5-12 adults, $3-10 children 2-17, free for children under 2) is a favorite with kids and includes surfing features, giant slides, a lazy river, and a toddler-friendly water-play structure. The facility boasts the largest heated outdoor swimming pool in the state, **Mitchell Pool**, and

concessions are available on-site. Two other outdoor neighborhood pools in Great Falls with small splash parks are **Jaycee Pool** (4th St. and 26th Ave. NE, www.greatfallsmt. net, $3.50 adults, $2.50 children 3-17, free for children under 3) and **Water Tower Pool** (34th St. and 7th Ave. S., www.greatfallsmt. net, $3.50 adults, $2.50 children 3-17, free for children under 3). Both are open daily (1pm-5:45pm late June-mid-August) depending upon weather.

When the weather is not conducive to outdoor swimming, **Morony Natatorium** (111 12th St. N., 406/452-3733, www.greatfallsmt. net, $3.50 adults, $2.50 children 3-17, free for children under 3) is a good option for open swimming and classes. The pool is kept at 83-86°F (28.3-30°C). Life vests are provided free of charge at all municipal pools in Great Falls, but swimmers need to provide their own towels. Hours vary for lap swim, classes, and open swim, so call ahead or check online for the day's schedule.

Golf

Golfers not afraid of a stiff breeze can find a few places to play in Great Falls. There are three 18-hole public courses: **Eagle Falls Golf Club** (1025 25th St. N., 406/761-1078, www.greatfallsmt.net, $19 for 9 holes or $32 for 18 holes Mon.-Fri., $20 for 9 holes or $35 for 18 holes Sat.-Sun.), **Anaconda Hills Golf Course** (2315 E. Smelter Ave., Black Eagle, 406/761-8459, www.greatfallsmt.net, $16 for 9 holes or $26 for 18 holes Mon.-Fri., $18 for 9 holes or $30 for 18 holes Sat.-Sun.), and **Hickory Swing Golf Course** (1100 American Ave., 406/452-9400, www.hickoryswinggolf.com, $14 for 9 holes or $24 for 18 holes). **Meadow Lark Country Club** (300 Country Club Blvd., 406/454-3553, www.meadowlarkclub.com) is a lovely old private club at the confluence of the Missouri and Sun Rivers that allows reciprocal fees ($80) for members of other private clubs.

★ Fishing on the Missouri River

With no shortage of world-class waters in the region, including the Missouri and Sun Rivers, there are endless opportunities to wet a line in and around Great Falls. Among the fish that can be found in local waters are northern pike, walleye, perch, catfish, large- and smallmouth bass, plus, of course, the venerable trout. For trout fishing on the Missouri, the 30-mile (48-km) stretch of river running from **Holter Dam to Cascade** is the most productive (and the most heavily fished!) for both rainbows and browns. Average size for rainbows is 14-18 inches (36-46 cm), and browns are generally a bit bigger. Blue-winged olive hatches start in late April and often last through June, and then hit again in the fall. The river's biggest hatch, the pale morning dun, can happen anytime from June well into August and gives skilled anglers a thrilling chance to catch very big fish on very small flies. Fish in these parts see a lot of flies and thus are wary of clumsy anglers.

North 40 Outfitters (which used to be Big R) is one of the West's best all-around ranch supply stores, selling everything from baby chicks and barbed wire to snakeskin cowboy boots and also has a well-respected fly-fishing shop staffed by passionate local anglers. **North 40 Fly Shop** (4400 10th Ave. S., 406/761-7441, www.north40flyshop.com, 7am-7pm Mon.-Sat., 9am-5pm Sun.) is an excellent place to start for advice on local waters and current hatches.

For a guided trip on any number of local waters, try **Fin Fetchers Outfitters** (406/240-3715, www.finfetchers.com, from $425 half-day, $525 full-day for up to 2 people). Owner Brian Neilson was born in Bozeman and raised in Great Falls, and he knows as much as you could ever hope to learn about the sport. Another well-respected guide is Dirk Johnsrud of **Johnsrud Outfitters** (406/253-8408, www.johnsrudoutfitters.com, from $375 half-day, $495 full-day), who can take anglers to a variety of rivers and lakes in the region.

Skiing

Although Great Falls is not often considered a prime alpine skiing destination, with the Rocky Mountains in such close proximity, it is no surprise that there are in fact three developed ski areas within a couple of hours' drive.

High atop the Continental Divide, **Great Divide Ski Area** (7385 Belmont Dr., Marysville, 95 miles (153 km) southwest of Great Falls, 406/449-3746, www.skigd.com, $48 adults full-day, $40 students and military, $20 children and seniors, free for preschool children and beginner rope tow; partial-day tickets vary depending on arrival time) touts itself as "Montana's sunniest ski area" and offers an impressive 1,600 acres (647.5 hectares) and 140 trails accessed by six lifts. The hill averages 180 inches (457 cm) of snow annually and offers night skiing.

Showdown Montana Ski Area (2850 U.S. 89, south of Neihart, 1 hour southeast of Great Falls, 406/236-5522 or 800/433-0022, www.showdownmontana.com, $45 full-day or $40 half-day ages 18-69, $35 seniors, $35-40 students with ID, $25 children 6-10 beginner chair only, free for children 5 and under) is one of Montana's oldest ski hills, in operation since 1936. In the middle of the not-so-little Little Belts, Showdown sees an average of 245 inches (622 cm) of powder annually. There are four lifts and 34 trails on 620 skiable acres (151 hectares) at this family-friendly ski hill, with 40 percent of the runs geared to intermediates and 30 percent each aimed at beginners and experts. Mountain biking is also offered when the snow melts, with the primary season running mid-June-October.

Closest to Great Falls, **Teton Pass Ski Resort** (18 mi/29 km west of Choteau, 406/466-2209, www.tetonpassresort.com, $39 adults full-day or $36 half-day, $36 seniors, $33 youth 7-17, $15 beginner lift, free for kids 6 and under) is a small ski area—two lifts and 36 trails geared largely to experts—with an enormous amount of snow (the area averages 20 ft/6.1 m of snow annually) and some pretty fierce terrain.

ENTERTAINMENT AND EVENTS
Nightlife

An authentic and unforgettable tiki bar in the heart of cowboy country, the **Sip-N-Dip Lounge** (17 17th St. S., 406/454-2141 or 800/332-9819, www.ohairemotorinn.com, 11:30am-midnight Sun.-Mon., 11:30am-2am Tues.-Sat.) is housed in the O'Haire Motor Inn. You can sip exotic cocktails as you gaze at the glass window into the pool behind the bar, watch exhibitionist guests, or, most evenings depending on the season, see mermaid- and (occasionally) merman-costumed performers (6pm-9pm Mon., 6pm-10:30pm Tues., 6pm-midnight Wed.-Sat., 9:30am-2:30pm every second Sunday for mermaid brunch). Daryl Hannah, the quintessential mermaid, has even taken a dip here. You can catch Piano-Pat Spoonheim singing covers of Elvis, Neil Diamond, and other legendary crooners (starting around 9:30pm Wed.-Fri.)—she has been a mainstay at the lounge for close to 50 years. Once voted the best bar on the planet by *GQ* magazine and recognized as one of the world's best bars by *Condé Nast Traveler*, this kitschy, cool watering hole should not be missed.

Another one-in-a-million bar in Great Falls is the **Montana Cowboys Association Museum & Bar** (311 3rd St. NW, 406/453-0651, www.cowboysbarmca.com, 8am-2am daily). Whether this is a bar in a museum or a museum in a bar is open to debate, but either way there is no shortage of cool old stuff to look at while you sip something frosty. An authentic log cabin built in 1941, it boasts two fireplaces and hundreds of artifacts from the Old West, including a sizable gun collection, Charlie Russell's well-worn boots, a rare photo of Jeremiah "Liver-Eating" Johnson, and a handsome collection of saddles. An evening spent bellied up to the bar is bound to be unforgettable. Bring some friends; the bar closes earlier when the number of guests drops below five.

The Arts
GREAT FALLS SYMPHONY

The **Great Falls Symphony** (venues vary, 406/453-4102, www.gfsymphony.org) is a dynamic organization that has been in existence for more than half a century, offering marvelous year-round entertainment in the form of classical symphonic masterpieces and contemporary compositions, chamber music, a youth orchestra, a symphonic choir, and ballet. For an evening of refined culture in the heart of cowboy country, the symphony is a rare treat. Larger performances are held at the **Mansfield Theater** (2 Park Dr. S.) in the lovely 1930s Great Falls Civic Center.

Festivals and Events
WESTERN ART WEEK

With major art-related events held across Great Falls over a long weekend closest to Charlie Russell's birthday (Mar. 19), **Western Art Week** puts Great Falls on the map of top destinations for serious Western art collectors. In addition to three major auctions—which include **The Russell: The Sale to Benefit the C. M. Russell Museum** (400 13th St. N.,

406/727-8787, www.cmrussell.org), **Out West Art Show** (1700 Fox Farm Rd., 406/899-2958, www.outwestartshow.com), and **March in Montana** (1411 10th Ave. S., 307/635-0019, www.marchinmontana.com)—the weekend offers an impressive collection of fine art by living and deceased masters, as well as cowboy and Indian collectibles. Considered *the* social event of the year for lovers of Western art, the celebration takes over several hotels, where artists and art dealers set up mini galleries and provide a rare opportunity for collectors to mingle with the artists they collect. Lectures, tours, artist demonstrations, parties, and a quick draw event are scheduled throughout the week.

LEWIS AND CLARK FESTIVAL

For 25 years, Great Falls has been celebrating the Corps of Discovery's 1806 month-long stay in the city. The **Lewis and Clark Festival** (event venues vary, many held at Gibson Park on the River's Edge Trail, 406/791-7732, www.lewisandclarkfoundation.org) takes place each year, usually in mid-June. For a full weekend, history comes alive in various locations around the city. Highlighting events from Lewis and Clark's experience in Great Falls, the festival is as much about education as it is about fun. There are children's activities such as a discovery camp and storytelling, float trips, tours of Lewis and Clark sites, and presentations by Native American groups. Actors help re-create daily life from this period with dramatic readings and plays, and there is a traditional arts and crafts show, concerts, food, nature outings, and exhibits.

MONTANA STATE FAIR

The **Montana State Fair** (Montana ExpoPark, 400 3rd St. NW, 406/727-8900, www.goexpopark.com, general admission $8 adults, $5 youth 6-17) takes place in Great Falls around the end of July and into August. It is one of Montana's largest parties and a true celebration of the state's unique history and culture. It includes a five-day rodeo (the largest in the state), horse racing, carnival rides, and big-name entertainment at the Montana ExpoPark. There are more than 250 vendor booths selling arts, crafts, clothes, music, and plenty of food as well as local, national, and international exhibits.

GREAT FALLS ORIGINAL FARMER'S MARKET

During summer, wander over to the **Great Falls Original Farmer's Market** (Civic Center Park, 2 Park Dr. S., www.farmersmarketgf.com, 7:45am-noon Sat. June-Sept., 4:30pm-6:30pm Wed. mid-July-Sept.), which was started in 1982 by some of the local Hutterite colonists. Claiming to be the largest farmers market in the state, more than 150 vendors gather to sell their goods, and you'll find the best homegrown fruits and vegetables, delicious jams, tasty baked goods, and handmade gifts and crafts. Pony rides are available for the little ones, and musicians wander among the stalls to keep you entertained.

SHOPPING

Great Falls has a number of unique specialty stores that line either side of Central Avenue downtown. You can start at the beginning of Central Avenue at Park Drive and stroll down the avenue. If you have a sweet tooth, don't miss **Candy Masterpiece** (120 Central Ave., 406/727-5955, www.candymasterpiece.com, 9:30am-5:30pm Mon.-Fri., 9:30am-5pm Sat.). Friendly staff are extremely generous with samples, and you'll find a delicious array of sweets, from childhood favorites straight off the candy rack to mouthwatering handmade chocolates. There are 30 different types of fudge available: Try the Heavenly Goo (chocolate with marshmallow and caramel) or, for the more adventurous, jalapeño fudge. Leaving Montana without a bag of huckleberry saltwater taffy is a mistake.

Next door to the candy store is the fun and funky **Planet Earth** (116 Central Ave., 406/761-7000, 10am-5:30pm Mon.-Thurs. and Sat., 10am-7pm Fri.), a shop full of eclectic gifts. Browse the assortment of cards, accessories, and jewelry. It also has a fragrance bar where you can create your own scent from essential oils and add it to specific bath or skin-care products.

Every town should have a great toy store, and Great Falls certainly does. The aptly named **Amazing Toys** (515 Central Ave., 406/727-5557, www.amazingtoys.net, 9:30am-5:30pm Mon.-Thurs., 9:30am-6pm Fri., 9:30am-5pm Sat.) has an abundance of games, puzzles, and other toys and has been a local favorite since 1987.

FOOD

In a historic building downtown, **Bert & Ernie's Tavern and Grill** (300 1st Ave. S., 406/453-0601, www.bertandernies.com, 11am-8pm Mon.-Wed., 11am-9pm Thurs., 11am-10pm Fri.-Sat., $10-24) is something of a Great Falls institution. The food is simple and hearty with a variety of homemade soups, big salads, sandwiches, and burgers.

Another iconic restaurant in Great Falls is **Borrie's** (1800 Smelter Ave., 406/761-0300, www.borriesrestaurant.com, 5pm-9:30pm Mon.-Thurs., 4:30pm-10pm Fri., 4pm-10pm Sat., 4pm-9pm Sun., $10-40), an old-school supper club with excellent steaks, seafood specials (including Australian lobster), and legendary homemade pasta sauce and ravioli. The atmosphere leaves something to be desired, but this is a classic Montana dining experience with great specials several nights a week.

Though it has changed names and owners many times over the decades, the **Roadhouse Diner** (613 15th St. N., 406/788-8839, www.roadhousegf.com, 11am-8pm Wed.-Sat., last seating at 7:30pm, 9am-2pm Sun., $9-16) is the real deal when it comes to burgers and fries. It has inventive, and strangely delicious, options like the Bacon Mac-N-Cheeseburger and PB&J Burger—which pairs bacon, cheddar, peanut butter, and grape jelly—but the basics here are plenty good. Try the breakfast burrito and the hand-cut fries. A true mom-and-pop outfit, the Roadhouse gets as much of its ingredients as possible locally and makes most everything from scratch.

One of Great Falls's most well-known restaurants is a local pizza joint, **Howard's Pizza** (713 1st Ave. N., 406/453-1212, www. howardspizzamt.com, 4pm-midnight daily, $12-21), started in 1959. Much beloved for its signature thin crust, famous sauce, and homemade ranch dressing, four locations citywide are now available for dining in, take-out, or delivery.

Another Montana success story, **Great Harvest Bread Company** (515 1st Ave. N., 406/452-6941, www.greatharvestgreatfalls. com, 6am-5:30pm Mon.-Fri., 6am-4pm Sat.) is a national chain that started in Great Falls in 1976. Its motto starts, "Be loose and have fun," and the food follows suit with inventive offerings ranging from cranberry crunch bread with flaxseeds and oat bran to white chocolate cherry bread and the more savory buttery basil oregano bread. The menu revolves around fresh-baked bread and is filled with delicious hot and cold sandwiches. And the cinnamon rolls, muffins, and brownies will leave you begging for mercy.

For a step back in time, **Fifth Street Diner** (500 Central Ave., 406/727-1962, 8:30am-2:30pm Tues.-Sun., $4-11) is located in a refurbished Woolworth's and centered around the original F. W. Woolworth stainless steel lunch counter. The menu offers standard comfort food ranging from steak and eggs to burgers and meat loaf. The fries, called "smiles," are mashed potatoes shaped into smiley faces. The shakes and malts should not be missed—even for breakfast!

Newer on the scene, and an excellent addition to Great Falls, is **Mighty Mo Brewing Company** (412 Central Ave., 406/952-0342, www.mightymobrewing.com, 11am-8pm daily, $6-19). Housed in a beautifully refurbished historic building, this microbrewery serves fine beer with perfectly paired food—wings, pizza, nachos, bread sticks, pretzels, and the like.

Big Mouth BBQ (1720 10th Ave. S., 406/727-7095, www.greatfallsbbq.com, 11am-8pm Mon.-Thurs., 11am-9pm Fri.-Sat., $9-15) is not for the faint of heart. The

$20 Big John Challenge entices diners to eat three chicken-fried steaks with gravy sandwiched between two grilled cheese sandwiches served with 1 pound (0.5 kg) of fries topped with chili and cheese. Those who can finish in 30 minutes or less get the whole shebang (and some serious heartburn) for free. Less maniacal eaters can enjoy Texas-style pit-smoked meats, po'boys, fried pork tenderloin, ribs, and all the fixings. There's another location (215 3rd St. NW, 406/952-0872) west of the river.

A stark contrast to Big Mouth BBQ, **Dante's Creative Cuisine** (1325 8th Ave. N., 406/453-9599, 11am-9pm Mon.-Thurs., 11am-10pm Fri.-Sat., $16-25) is within a beautiful, old brick ironworks building. It's white linens all the way with Italian and Southwestern fare, seafood, and steak. The Thursday night lobster tail is a local favorite at this decidedly upscale establishment.

A weekday takeout restaurant with traditional family-style restaurant grub is **The Kitchen** (1225 Central Ave., 406/727-5820, 11am-6:30pm Mon.-Fri., $5-11), which offers two homemade soups daily, plus classic dinners like baked ham, meat loaf, cabbage rolls, and shepherd's pie. In the summer, picnic benches out front provide a place for on-site eating.

For healthy eating and gorgeous pastries for breakfast or lunch on weekdays, the best choice is **Daisy's Deli & Bakery** (508 1st Ave. N., 406/452-0361, 8am-3pm Mon.-Fri.). It offers organic and gluten-free menu items alongside specialties like a coconut chicken wrap with honey almonds.

ACCOMMODATIONS

If you are looking for a memorable motel stay in downtown Great Falls, look no further than the ★ **O'Haire Motor Inn** (17 7th St. S., 406/454-2141 or 800/332-9819, $90-150), with 68 guest rooms renovated in 2009, an indoor pool, indoor parking, and free Wi-Fi. Its full-service restaurant, **Clark and Lewie's** (6am-10pm Mon.-Thurs., 6am-midnight Fri.-Sat., 6am-9pm Sun., $13-25), offers up hearty

meals and even room service. The biggest draw at the inn is its authentic and unforgettable tiki bar, the Sip-N-Dip Lounge.

The upscale **Hotel Arvon** (118 1st Ave. S., 406/952-1101, www.hotelarvon.com, $129-189) is a 33-room boutique hotel with a coffee shop, wine bar, restaurant, and pub in the city's oldest commercial building.

Another option just south of downtown is the **La Quinta Inn & Suites** (600 River Dr. S., 406/761-2600 or 800/531-5900, www.laquintagreatfalls.com, $114-229), built in 2000 on the banks of the Missouri River. Ask for a room with a view of the river. The hotel is styled as a Western lodge, with a fireplace in the lobby, as well as an indoor pool and a fitness center. The guest rooms are large and comfortable with amenities such as high-speed Internet, microwaves, and fridges, and continental breakfast is included.

Along the River's Edge Trail, the spacious **Staybridge Suites** (201 3rd St. NW, 406/761-4903 or 877/238-8889, www.staybridgesuites.com/greatfallsmt, $145-300) is a pet-friendly, all-suite hotel offering fully equipped kitchens, free Wi-Fi, a 24-hour business center, and an indoor pool.

Among the chain hotel offerings in town, the **Best Western Heritage Inn** (1700 Fox Farm Rd., 406/761-1900, www.bestwestern.com, $109-149) offers 231 rooms plus an indoor swimming pool, fitness center, restaurant, casino, and sports bar. Other comfortable chain hotels in Great Falls include **Comfort Inn & Suites** (1801 Market Place Dr., 406/455-1000, www.choicehotels.com, from $120), the pet-friendly **Days Inn** (101 14th Ave. NW, 406/727-6565, www.daysinngreatfalls.com, $106-133), **Fairfield Inn** (1000 9th Ave. S., 406/454-3000, www.marriott.com/fairfieldinn, $114-145), and the **Hilton Garden Inn** (2520 14th St. SW, 406/452-1000, http://greatfalls.hgi.com, $134-404), which is located next to several restaurants, a shopping mall, and a 10-screen movie theater. More budget-friendly options include **Motel 6** (2 Treasure State Dr., 406/453-1602, www.motel6.com, from $67-78) and **Super 8** (1214 13th St. S., 406/727-7600, www.greatfallssuper8.com, $56-78).

INFORMATION AND SERVICES

Most services are conveniently located in a walkable downtown area. The **Great Falls Chamber of Commerce** (100 1st Ave. N., 406/761-4434, www.greatfallschamber. org, 8am-5pm Mon.-Fri.) and the **Visitor Information Center** (15 Overlook Dr., 406/771-0885, www.greatfallsmt.net, 10am-4pm Mon.-Fri., 10am-2pm Sat.-Sun. Oct.-Apr., 9am-6pm Mon.-Fri., 10am-4pm Sat.-Sun. May-Sept.), under the huge U.S. flag in Overlook Park, both have city brochures, books, Made in Montana goods for sale, and friendly, knowledgeable volunteers.

The **main post office** (215 1st Ave. N., 406/771-2160, 8:30am-5:30pm Mon.-Fri., 10am-1pm Sat.) is at 1st Avenue and 2nd Street.

The **public library** (301 2nd Ave. N., 406/453-0349, www.greatfallslibrary.org, 10am-8pm Tues.-Thurs., 10am-6pm Fri.-Sat.) is just two blocks from the post office and offers computers and free Internet access.

Falls Cleaners & Laundry Center (614 9th St. S., 406/453-9361, 8am-9pm daily) offers same-day laundry service, dry-cleaning service, and coin-op machines to do it yourself.

Benefis Health Systems (1101 26th St. S., 406/455-5000, www.benefis.org) is a first-class hospital with a 24-hour emergency room

as well as a **walk-in clinic** (1401 25th St. S., 406/731-8300, 7am-8pm Mon.-Fri., 9am-6:30pm Sat.-Sun.) for immediate medical care.

TRANSPORTATION
Getting There

The **Great Falls International Airport** (GTF, 2800 Terminal Dr., 406/727-3404, www.flygtf.com) is southwest of the city. It is served by Alaska Airlines, Allegiant, Delta, and United. The airport's on-site car-rental companies are **Alamo, Avis, Enterprise, Hertz,** and **National. Budget** also offers car-rental services off-site with shuttles to and from the airport.

Greyhound Bus Lines offers service to other major towns and cities in Montana.

Great Falls is situated directly off I-15, allowing easy access by car. It is 218 miles (355 km) northwest of Billings, 186 miles (300 km) north of Bozeman, 155 miles (250 km) northeast of Butte, and approximately 90 miles (145 km) from Helena (to the south) or Shelby (to the north).

Getting Around

Diamond Cab (406/453-3241) serves the Great Falls area and will pick you up from the airport (look for the direct phone in the terminal) or shuttle you around town. **Blacked Out 406 Taxi** (406/781-5218) is another option for airport transfers, regular taxi service, or crazy fancy limousine SUVs, buses, and the like.

Rocky Mountain Front

Spanning more than 100 miles (161 km) from Montana into Canada, the Rocky Mountain Front is the startling merger of prairie and mountain—in places the Rockies rise 4,000-5,000 feet (1,219-1,524 m). It is one of the few places in the Lower 48 where grizzly bears still wander onto the plains, much as they did when Lewis and Clark traveled the region. There is a strong cowboy culture in

Choteau and a rich Native American culture in Browning. The small agricultural towns have rugged mountain wilderness just a stone's throw away. It is rare to be able to appreciate natural diversity, undistracted by humankind's homogenous development.

The Rocky Mountain Front is also the gateway into the **Bob Marshall Wilderness Complex,** which comprises three wilderness areas totaling more than 1.5 million acres (607,028 hectares) of the remotest wilderness in the Lower 48. The complex runs 60 miles (97 km) north to south along the Continental Divide. The region, named for forester, wilderness preservationist, and Wilderness Society cofounder Bob Marshall, teems with wildlife and stunning topography. The Bob's Chinese Wall, for example, a rock escarpment that averages 1,000 feet (305 m) in height, follows the Continental Divide for 22 miles (35 km). For obvious reasons, including its 1,700 miles (2,736 km) of trails, this area is a mecca for outdoors enthusiasts.

BROWNING

Agency headquarters for the Blackfeet Indian Reservation, home to Montana's largest tribe, Browning (population 1,031; elevation 4,377 ft/1,334 m) has retained much of the culture of the Blackfeet people. The setting is spectacular, at the eastern edge of Glacier National Park, but the town doesn't offer anything in the way of striking architecture or high-end hotels. What it does offer, though, is an exceptional opportunity to learn about and experience Blackfeet culture. In addition to the significant Museum of the Plains Indian, there are a number of annual events open to visitors as well as tours given by well-versed local guides. There is even a place where guests can camp in tipis, feast on gourmet regional cuisine, and enjoy a thoughtfully cultivated Blackfeet experience.

Sights

Led by Blackfeet tribe member, historian, and well-known artist Darryl Norman, **Blackfeet Cultural History Tours** (www.blackfeetculturecamp.com, tipicamp@3rivers.net, half-day tours for 1-4 people from $100, full-day tours for 1-4 people $160) offers a remarkable opportunity to explore the reservation and its history. Norman operates as a step-on guide, joining guests in their own vehicles and taking them to various buffalo jumps, tipi rings, medicine lodges, and historic sites.

Just west of Browning at the junction of U.S. 2 and U.S. 89 is the **Museum of the Plains Indian** (19 Museum Loop, 406/338-2230, www.doi.gov/iacb/museum-plains-indian-location, 9am-4:45pm Tues.-Sat. June-Sept., 10am-4:30pm daily Oct.-May, $5 adults, $4 seniors 65 and over, $1 children 6-16 June-Sept., free Oct.-May). The museum exhibits the arts and crafts of the Northern Plains Indians. The permanent collection highlights the diversity of tribal arts and displays artifacts from everyday life, including clothing, weapons, toys, and household implements. Two galleries are dedicated to showcasing contemporary Native American artists. During summer, painted tipis are assembled on the grounds.

Entertainment and Events

Held annually the second week in July for four days, the **North American Indian Days** (406/338-7521 or 406/338-7103, www.blackfeetnation.com) is an excellent powwow giving insight into the Blackfeet culture and traditions. Events include contest dancing, games, sporting events, drum contests, and plenty of food.

Food

From Memorial Day to Labor Day, the Aspenwood Resort offers dining to the public in its **Outlaw Kitchen** (102 SW Boundary St., U.S. 89, 9.5 miles (15.3 km) west of Browning, 406/338-3370, 8am-11am and 1pm-close daily, $4-20). The Outlaw Kitchen offers standard fare ranging from fluffy pancakes to sandwiches, salads, burgers, pizza, and barbecue.

Right in town, across from the Museum of the Plains Indian, the **Junction Café** (Starr School Rd., 406/338-2386, 8am-2pm Mon.-Fri., $3-17) is locally owned and serves up hearty breakfasts of corned beef hash, breakfast burritos, and biscuits and gravy, as well as hamburgers and steaks. Try the fry bread! With usually only one server and a local clientele, the restaurant is very friendly. Don't be surprised if a neighboring diner offers to refill your coffee cup.

Another very friendly local restaurant serving everything from burgers to Indian tacos is **Nation's Burger Station** (205 Central Ave., 406/338-2422, www.nationsburgerstation. com, 10:30am-9:30pm Mon.-Fri., 10:30am-10:30pm Sat.-Sun. May-mid-Aug., 10:30am-8:30pm Mon.-Sat. mid-Aug.-Apr., $6-12). In addition to the aforementioned, Nation's Burger Station serves salads and wraps, plus an impressive menu of frozen treats including root beer floats, slushies, and snow cones. On a hot day, this is the place.

Accommodations

Browning itself doesn't offer a lot in the way of accommodations; the best bets are toward Glacier National Park. Just under 10 miles (16.1 km) west of Browning is the interesting **Aspenwood Resort** (U.S. 89, 406/338-3009, mid-May-early Oct., suites from $95-150), ideally located close to Glacier National Park between Browning and St. Mary. There are three suites in the rustic lodge in addition to RV sites ($40), a campground ($25), and a restaurant.

The ★ **Lodge Pole Gallery and Tipi Village** (U.S. 89, 2 mi/3.2 km west of Browning, www.blackfeetculturecamp.com, tipicamp@3rivers.net, tipis $70 for 1 person, $16 for each additional person; $10 children under 12, $12 to rent sleeping bag and mattress) is a rare and special place. Part art gallery and part tipi camp, the Lodge Pole offers an extraordinarily unique experience and a true taste of Blackfeet culture with Native American art, Spanish mustangs, and various cultural events. Two cabins ($135 d, $30 each additional person) that sleep up to four are available; tipis accommodate 6-8 people.

Information

The **Blackfeet Country Chamber of Commerce** (380 1st Ave. SW, 406/338-4015 or 406/338-7521, www.blackfeetnation.com, 8am-4:30pm Mon.-Fri.) is open year-round and has an active Facebook presence.

Transportation

Browning is 123 miles (198 km) northwest of Great Falls on U.S. 89.

CHOTEAU AND AUGUSTA

Established with a post office under the name Old Agency in 1875, Choteau (population 1,686; elevation 3,819 ft/1,164 m) is one of the region's oldest active towns. The name was changed in 1882 to honor Pierre Chouteau, president of the American Fur Company and responsible for bringing the first steamboat up the Missouri River. This ranching town at the edge of the Rockies is a dinosaur lover's dream, with paleontological museums and sites galore. It also provides unparalleled access to some of the state's most incredible wilderness areas. In addition to its obvious attractions, Choteau is simply a charming Montana town—small, friendly, and ideally situated for visitors.

Just under 30 miles (48 km) southwest of Choteau, is the wonderful little town of Augusta (population 315; elevation 4,068 ft/1,240 m), another gateway to the Bob Marshall and Scapegoat wilderness areas. The town—with classic Western storefronts and warm hospitality—hosts the state's oldest and biggest one-day rodeo, known as the "Wildest One Day Show on Earth," the last Sunday in June.

Sights

The remains of the most famous inhabitants of **Egg Mountain** (U.S. 287, between mileposts 57 and 58) were discovered in 1977 by Marion Brandvold and studied extensively by dinosaur guru Jack Horner. The discovery has yielded the largest collection of dinosaur eggs, embryos, and baby skeletons in the Western Hemisphere. The findings entirely changed our notion of how dinosaurs raised their young. The baby remains were found alongside an enormous number of adult remains, which scientists determined was a monumental herd of maiasaura (good mother reptile) along with a lesser number of troodons killed in a catastrophic event like a volcanic eruption or a hurricane. Egg Mountain is one of 16 sites in Montana deemed "geological wonders" by a team of historians, geologists, and paleontologists. An interpretive sign on U.S. 287 provides information about the site. There is also a small parking area, and visitors are welcome to wander the site, which is more a hill than a mountain. Naturalist guides occasionally offer narrated tours of the area; for more information contact the Museum of the Rockies in Bozeman (406/994-2251).

At the north end of Choteau, the **Old Trail Museum** (823 N. Main St., Choteau, 406/466-5332, www.oldtrailmuseum.com, 9am-5pm daily Memorial Day-Labor Day, $2, children under 3 are free) celebrates both the natural and cultural history of the Rocky Mountain Front. In the Dinosaurs of the Two Medicine paleontology gallery, there are dinosaur bones and fossils aplenty, along with a good maiasaura exhibit. The museum also has a number of other interesting local history exhibits, including Native American artifacts collected by A. B. Guthrie Jr. and details of Choteau's last hanging.

Between Choteau and Fairfield off U.S. 89 is **Freezeout Lake** (406/467-2646, www.fwp.mt.gov, mid-Mar.-autumn), a birder's paradise and for many Montanans the best place to gauge the imminent arrival of an ever-elusive spring. The scenic lake is a staging area for hundreds of thousands of snow geese and thousands of tundra swans on their way north. The snow geese typically arrive at Freezeout in early March. As with most wildlife, dawn and dusk offer the best viewing opportunities. A variety of other birds pass through the area, including raptors and upland game birds in winter, waterfowl in spring and fall, and shorebirds in summer. The interior roads have ample parking and pullouts, and are open to vehicles mid-March to the beginning of waterfowl season.

Entertainment and Events

Held annually the last Sunday in June, the **Augusta American Legion Rodeo and Parade** (American Legion Rodeo Grounds, Augusta, 406/562-3477, www.augustamontana.com) is the biggest and oldest one-day rodeo in the state. For more than 80 years, this small town has put on an amazing show with a parade, a Professional Rodeo Cowboys Association-sanctioned rodeo complete with bull riding, and a huge party atmosphere.

Shopping

Don't leave Choteau without a stop at **Choteau Trading Post** (106 N. Main Ave., Choteau, 406/466-5354 or 406/229-0279, 9am-5:30pm Mon.-Sat.) which offers Western wares, boots galore, work clothes, jewelry, and gifts. Another place to take a step back in time is **Days Gone By Antiques** (38 N. Main Ave., Augusta, 406/466-3435, 9am-5pm Tues.-Sat. winter, 9am-6pm daily spring and summer), which specializes in vintage furniture, but also has an abundance of glassware, dishes, linens, jewelry, old photos, and more. They also claim the largest collection of tobacco tins in the state.

One of the best gift shops in the state is **Latigo and Lace** (122 Main St., Augusta, 406/562-3665, 10am-5pm Wed.-Sun. Mar., 10am-6pm Tues.-Sun. Apr., 10am-6:30pm daily May-Dec.) which has books, clothing, an espresso bar, and fantastic local art including ceramics, photography, paintings, jewelry, rugs, baskets, and beadwork. Just up the street, **Allen's Manix Store** (10 Main St., Augusta, 406/562-3333, 7:30am-7:30pm daily Jan.-May and Sept.-Dec., 7am-8pm daily June-Aug.) is a classic country store with everything from groceries and meats to hunting and fishing licenses, sporting goods, and gifts. The staff are friendly and helpful, and just listening to the chatter as you wait in line to check out makes you feel like you know this place a little bit.

Food

Choteau has some good options for regional cuisine. The **Log Cabin Cafe** (102 Main Ave. N., Choteau, 406/466-2888, 11am-9pm Tues.-Fri., 8am-9pm Sat.-Sun., $5-11) is precisely what you would expect from its name: a cozy spot with hearty servings of good old-fashioned comfort food. The burgers are great, but so too are the salads, soups, and breakfast dishes. Don't miss the desserts!

For a quick, fresh lunch or snack, **9th and Main Gourmet** (825 Main Ave. N., Choteau, 406/466-3880, 11am-5pm Thurs.-Sun. summer, 7am-2pm Thurs.-Fri., 6am-3pm Sat.-Sun. winter) offers soups, sandwiches, lettuce wraps, smoothies, and a mouthwatering assortment of fresh-baked goodies. From the maple sticks and blueberry scones to the ham-and-cheese breakfast rolls and deli sandwiches, **Bylers Bakery** (425 Main Ave. S., Choteau, 406/466-9900, 6am-2pm Wed.-Sat., $2-8) is a great little coffee shop and café open for breakfast and lunch.

In Augusta, the **Buckhorn Bar** (120 Main St., Augusta, 406/562-3344, 7am-2am daily, $9-23) is a great place for burger and a microbrew and to soak in the scene, particularly during bird-hunting season.

Accommodations

Sadly, most of the small, mom-and-pop motels in Choteau have gone the way of the dinosaur. The best hotel in town today is the relatively new **Stage Stop Inn** (1005 Main Ave. N., Choteau, 406/446-5900, www.stagestopinn. com, $114-150), which is spacious, comfortable, and clean but without any of the charm of days gone by.

In Augusta, the **Bunkhouse Inn** (124 Main St., Augusta, 406/562-3387, www. bunkhouseinnmt.com, $60-79) is small and charming and old-fashioned in ambience, but relatively new and very clean. Some of the rooms have their own sink and vanity, but all share bathrooms at the end of the hall.

One charming old guest ranch 28 miles (45 km) west of Choteau is the **Deep Canyon Guest Ranch** (2055 Teton Canyon Rd., 406/466-2044, www.deepcanyonguestranch. com, from $2,190 weekly pp double occupancy, $1,380 children under 12), located in the heart of Teton Canyon with easy access to the Bob Marshall Wilderness Complex.

Some of the buildings date back to the 1920s, but others were constructed in the 1980s. Available daily activities include horseback riding, fishing, and hiking.

Another favorite family-friendly guest ranch west of Augusta is the **Triple J Wilderness Ranch** (80 Mortimer Rd., 406/562-3653, www.triplejranch.com, $2,300 weekly pp double occupancy all-inclusive, $2,100 kids 13-17, $2,000 children 6-12), tucked in the magnificent Sun River Canyon above Gibson Lake. In addition to all-inclusive vacations catering to riders, hikers, and fishers, the Triple J offers fantastic kids' programs and awesome pack trips in the Bob Marshall Wilderness Complex. Early June-late September, the ranch offers six-day stays with discounts for children and teens. Shorter stays may be available in June and September.

Information

The **Choteau Chamber of Commerce** (703 Main Ave. N., 406/466-5316 or 800/823-3866, www.choteaumontana.us, 10am-4pm Mon.-Fri.) has hours that can vary from season to season; call ahead to make sure it is open. The **Augusta Chamber of Commerce** (www.augustamontana.com) has a great website with information on the area, but no physical presence.

Transportation

Choteau is 52 miles (84 km) northwest of Great Falls along U.S. 89. Augusta is 26 miles (42 km) southwest of Choteau on U.S. 287.

★ BOB MARSHALL WILDERNESS COMPLEX

With more than 1.5 million acres (607,028 hectares), the Bob Marshall Wilderness Complex is one of the largest and remotest wilderness areas in the Lower 48. The mountains soar above 9,000 feet (2,743 m), and the Continental Divide splits the region into

1: the Chinese Wall and wildflowers in the Bob Marshall Wilderness Complex **2:** typical Montana highway

several headwater drainage areas. Numerous lakes and pristine trout-laden rivers are here along with copious animals, including elk, white-tailed and mule deer, gray wolves, Canada lynx, bobcats, bighorn sheep, mountain goats, wolverines, and cougars. The area was named for its first and perhaps most vociferous champion, Bob Marshall, a forester, author, explorer, and leader in the protection of wildlands. The area was first set aside in 1940, shortly after Marshall's death, and was designated as wilderness by the federal government in conjunction with the 1964 Wilderness Act.

Visiting the Bob

Encompassing three designated roadless wilderness areas, "the Bob," as it is known locally, is a magnificent place to explore. The most famous geological landmark is a dramatic 22-mile-long (35-km) escarpment known as the **Chinese Wall.** Technically referred to as the Lewis Overthrust, the incredible rock wall—it is 1,000 feet (305 m) high in places—is the result of a massive geologic upheaval in which the state split from Glacier National Park all the way down to Yellowstone. The Chinese Wall is where the eastern plate slid under the western plate.

Other popular areas for hikers and backpackers include the **South Fork of the Flathead River** valley, where most of the major trails leading into or out of the Bob can be picked up. **Big Salmon Lake** in the South Fork is among the more popular destinations. On the western edge of the wilderness complex, **Holland Lake** in the Swan Valley offers good access for backpackers and outfitters.

The **Sun River Game Preserve,** which lies at the eastern edge of the Bob, is the only portion of the complex where hunting is restricted. The area was established in the late 1920s as a refuge for elk, deer, and grizzlies, among other animals, and remains an important winter range for numerous species.

Access

Though the wilderness complex is roadless by definition, more than 1,000 miles (1,610 km) of trails crisscross the region and provide access for private visitors and commercial outfitters. Ten-day trips into the region to take advantage of hunting, fishing, or just unparalleled wild scenery are popular and can be arranged through a number of licensed outfitters. The **Bob Marshall Wilderness Outfitters** (41088 Roberts Rd., Charlo, 406/644-7889 or 406/240-2722, www.bobmarshallwildernessoutfitters.com) offers a range of guided pack trips into the Bob that cater to hunters, fishers, and nature lovers. Seven-day, six-night trips start at $2,625 per person. **Seven Lazy P Outfitters** (891 Teton Canyon Rd., Choteau, 406/466-2245, www.sevenlazyp.com, four-day trips from $1,750 pp, six-day trips from $2,600 pp) also offers guided trips into the wilderness area. Other outfitters can be found through the **Montana Outfitters & Guides Association** (406/449-3578, www.montanaoutfitters.org).

Information

Road access to the perimeter of the wilderness complex is on U.S. 2 to the north, U.S. 89 and U.S. 287 to the east, and Highways 200 and 83 to the south and west. The complex is managed by four national forests, including the **Flathead National Forest** (406/758-5208, www.fs.usda.gov) in Kalispell, and five ranger districts.

Transportation

The Bob Marshall Wilderness Complex is roughly 80 miles (129 km) west of Great Falls and can be accessed from numerous communities along the Rocky Mountain Front, including Choteau, Augusta, and Browning.

Fort Benton and the Hi-Line

The farther east you travel from Great Falls, the more the landscape opens up. From the edge of the towering Rockies the land is pulled tight into the Upper Missouri River valley and the rugged breaks that fracture the vast agricultural land and prairie. It is quiet in these parts but stunning, and there is a remarkable quality of light in which the weather can change the landscape in a moment.

Fort Benton, considered the oldest town in Montana, is a picturesque hamlet on the banks of the Missouri. Farther north, on the Milk River, is Havre, a rough-and-tumble railroad town with a colorful history. Tight-knit communities like Cut Bank, Shelby, and Chinook span the Hi-Line and reflect its boom-and-bust cycle.

★ FORT BENTON

Established in 1846 as an American Fur Company trading post, Fort Benton (population 1,456; elevation 2,644 ft/806 m) became one of the most important trading centers in the Northwest as a critical inland port. Starting in 1860, each year in spring and early summer some 50 steamboats would arrive, loaded with trappers, traders, gold seekers, and mountains of supplies destined for places across the West. When the Great Northern Railway arrived in Helena in 1887, the river traffic to Fort Benton all but dried up. The last steamboat to unload in Fort Benton left in 1922.

The infrastructure created in Fort Benton's heyday—including a glamorous hotel—still lures visitors today. In fact, the entire town is recognized as a National Historic Landmark, and the people of Fort Benton have done much to preserve and promote their storied past. The old steamboat levee, along what was once known as the "bloodiest block in the West," has been transformed into a tranquil walking path. The original fort has been partially rebuilt in the center of town, and there are two wonderful museums and one of the best historic hotels in the state.

Sights

Fort Benton has an inordinate number of museums for its population, all of which are worth seeing. A **two-day museum pass** ($15 adults, $12 seniors, $5 children 12-18, $1 children 6-11) can be purchased at any of the museums and enables you to visit both the Museum of the Upper Missouri and the Museum of the Northern Great Plain.

Dedicated to the region's 19th-century history, the **Museum of the Upper Missouri** (Old Fort Park, 406/622-5316, www.fortbenton.com, 10am-5pm Mon.-Sat., noon-4pm Sun. late May-late Sept.) has a number of exhibits that hark back to Fort Benton's glory days as the Northwest's most important inland port. Twice-daily guided tours take visitors on a walk around the fascinating Old Fort.

The **Museum of the Northern Great Plain** (1205 20th St., 406/622-5316, www.fortbenton.com, 10:30am-4:30pm Mon.-Sat., noon-4pm Sun. late May-late Sept.) pays tribute to the agricultural heritage and homestead era.

The **Upper Missouri River Breaks National Monument Interpretive Center** (701 7th St., 406/622-4000 or 877/256-3252, www.mt.blm.gov, 8am-4:30pm daily Memorial Day-late Sept., $5) is an impressive facility celebrating the natural and cultural history of the river and its surrounding environment. A must-see for boaters on the Missouri, the center offers technical information as well as historical and interactive exhibits. Among the other treasures here is Chief Joseph's surrender rifle. Winter hours can change according to budget so call ahead.

The **Upper Missouri River Breaks National Monument** (406/538-1900 or 877/256-3252, www.mt.blm.gov) comprises

The Legend of Shep

The story of a dog named Shep is a tear-jerking one, and Shep has become something of an icon for the town of Fort Benton. Some sort of border collie mix, Shep was born in Montana in the late 1920s. He was a sheepdog and, by all accounts, a very faithful companion. When his sheepherding master fell ill during the Great Depression and had to be taken by buckboard to the hospital in Fort Benton, Shep followed along and waited for days outside the hospital for his owner. A nurse at the hospital, Sister Genevieve, noticed the dog and began to leave scraps of food and drinking water for him. When his master was loaded onto an eastbound train at the Fort Benton depot in a casket, Shep began a nearly six-year vigil, meeting every train, waiting for his master to disembark. Each time a train pulled out of the station, Shep would vanish into the hills, only to return to greet the next arrival.

After several months, Shep stayed closer to the station, carving a little nook for himself under the platform. The son of one of the railroad workers made a point of bringing Shep regular meals, and the depot agent eventually coaxed the wary animal into the station with a warm bed. Another railroad worker recognized Shep as having belonged to a sheepherder whose lifeless body was shipped to his family back East. He explained to Shep's new caretakers that the dog had been waiting at the station since then. Over the span of a few years, the legend of Shep began to grow, along with the number of his admirers.

Shep was written up in newspapers around the world, and the Great Northern Railway had to hire a secretary just to handle the mail—which included everything from money to dog bones—addressed to Shep from people worldwide.

By 1942, Shep was quite old and deaf. Despite his celebrity, he still greeted every train in search of his master. On an icy January morning, Shep wandered out to the tracks and was tragically hit and killed by an inbound train. The whole town mourned his loss, and hundreds came to pay their respects at his funeral. His concrete gravestone still stands sentry high atop a hill next to where the depot once stood.

In 1994, the city fathers presented a beautiful bronze statue of Shep to the people of Fort Benton. His sweet story was immortalized in a wonderful children's book, *Shep: Our Most Loyal Dog,* by Sneed B. Collard III and Joanna Yardley.

378,000 acres (152,971 hectares) centered on a 149-mile (240-km) stretch of the Missouri, designated a National Wild and Scenic River. The remoteness of the region adds to its ecological and cultural significance. Boaters have the rare opportunity to travel in an area virtually untouched since Lewis and Clark's era, and the cliffs and sandy beaches have as much appeal today as they did 200 years ago. The water is wide and reasonably flat, so whitewater equipment and expertise are not necessary. However, because of its remoteness, great care should be taken, and careful planning is necessary. Day trips, shuttles, and full-service camping trips can be arranged through a number of outfitters, including **Upper Missouri River Guides** (406/582-9720 or 406/691-1135, www.uppermissouri. com), which offers three-day, two-night trips

from $825 per person and plenty of other options up to the full 149 miles (240 km) in eight days and seven nights for $2,200 per person. **Missouri River Outfitters** (406/622-3295 or 866/282-3295, www.mroutfitters.com, 3-day trip from $800, 4-day trip from $1,000, 6-day trip from $1,400) offers guided trips and shuttle service as well as canoe, kayak, and camping equipment rentals. Boaters interested in planning their own trips should contact the **Fort Benton River Management Station** (701 7th St., 877/256-3252, www.blm.gov).

For an altogether different experience, check out the tiny town of **Virgelle,** in the heart of the national monument and accessible by road or **river ferry** (406/378-3110 or 800/426-2926). This former ghost town has been restored without being overly modernized, and bed-and-breakfast-type accommodations in small cabins and even sheepherder wagons are available. The tiny town and its do-everything mercantile store truly offer a step back in time.

Food

Inside the Grand Union Hotel, ★ **The Union Grill** (1 Grand Union Sq., 406/622-1882 or 888/838-1882, www.grandunionhotel.com, 5pm-9pm daily summer, 5pm-9pm Wed.-Sun. winter, $13-37) is exquisite and offers some of the most innovative cuisine in this part of the state. In the summer you can sit on the riverside patio and indulge in everything from smoked trout hushpuppies and duck prosciutto to grilled bison coulette steak with fiddlehead ferns. The menu is ever-changing and incorporates as much fresh local fare as possible. The wine list and the desserts are equally exceptional, and even the bar menu is inspired.

For something decidedly more casual, **The Freeze** (722 Front St., 406/622-3739, 11am-8pm Tues.-Sat., 11am-7pm Sun. Apr.-Oct., open weekends in October "until the snow gets deep") has great burgers, pork chop sandwiches, onion rings, and phenomenal soft-serve ice-cream flavors like Blue Goo, which tastes like cotton-candy. There's even a cone for dogs.

Accommodations

If you could only stay in one place in Montana, the ★ **Grand Union Hotel** (1 Grand Union Sq., 406/622-1882 or 888/838-1882, www.grandunionhotel.com, $108-200) might be it. The hotel was built in 1882 at the height of Fort Benton's steamboat era and a full seven years before Montana became a state. After more than 100 years of operation, the hotel closed its doors in the mid-1980s and continued to decay. Montanans Jim and Cheryl Gagnon purchased the once-glorious hotel in 1997 and undertook a massive, award-winning renovation. Today the 26-room hotel lives up to its original splendor with gorgeous mahogany woodwork, lofty ceilings, and elegant furnishings throughout. It's interesting

to note that the 3rd floor was originally designed for cowboys, workers, and their occasional female companions. It's accessed by a back staircase, rather than the grand central staircase to the 2nd floor, which was occupied by VIPs. The entire hotel is lovely and worth the splurge.

Accommodations in Virgelle, in the heart of the Upper Missouri River Breaks National Monument, are available in rustic but comfy homestead-era cabins (from $70 pp) with a shared bathhouse or in charming B&B rooms ($140-250 including breakfast) above the **Virgelle Mercantile** (7485 Virgelle Ferry Rd. N., 406/378-3110 or 800/426-2926, www.virgellemontana.com).

Information

The **Fort Benton Chamber of Commerce** (1421 Front St., 406/622-3864, www.fortbentonchamber.org, 10am-4pm daily May-Sept.) is part of the Information Center inside the old fire station next to the walking bridge.

Transportation

Fort Benton is 40 miles (64 km) east of Great Falls on U.S. 87.

CUT BANK

At the edge of the Blackfeet Reservation between Browning and Shelby, Cut Bank (population 3,012; elevation 3,733 ft/1,138 m) is famous for being the site of Lewis and Clark's only armed encounter with Native Americans. On July 26, 1806, Meriwether Lewis, joined by George Drouillard, Joseph Fields, and Reuben Fields, met with eight Blackfeet. When Lewis revealed that the U.S. government intended to outfit all the Plains Indians with hunting rifles, the Blackfeet became angry because they had controlled the firearms trade among Native Americans through their relationship with the Hudson's Bay Company. The Blackfeet took off with the men's horses, a fight ensued, and two Blackfeet were killed.

In addition to the town's proximity to the reservation and its cultural influence, five

Hutterite colonies in the area also welcome visitors. The **Glacier County Historical Museum** (107 Old Kevin Hwy., 406/873-4904, 10am-5pm Tues.-Sat. Memorial Day-Labor Day, by appointment Labor Day-Memorial Day, donation) presents exhibits on Lewis and Clark, homesteading, artist John Clark, and the town's oil boom. On summer weekends, costumed guides reenact homestead life circa 1915.

The **Glacier Gateway Plaza** (1130 E. Main St., 406/873-2566 or 800/851-5541, www.glaciergateway.com, $65-89) has large, clean rooms. This place is nothing fancy, but they offer amenities like an indoor pool and high-speed Internet.

Cut Bank is 30 miles (48 km) south of the Canadian border on Highway 213, 106 miles (171 km) northwest of Great Falls via I-15 and U.S. 2, and 35 miles (56 km) east of Browning on U.S. 2.

SHELBY

The humble story of Shelby's origins involves a discarded boxcar around which a town eventually developed. The town saw enormous growth thanks to the railroad, the Homestead Act, and a 1921 oil discovery. Shelby even hosted the 1923 World Heavyweight Championship fight between Jack Dempsey and Tommy Gibbons. Today, Shelby (population 3,216; elevation 3,086 ft/941 m) is a small trade center that attracts plenty of Canadians through the state's busiest port of entry.

The **Marias Museum of History and Art** (1129 1st St. N., 406/424-2551, www.toolecountymt.gov, 1pm-7pm Mon.-Fri., 1pm-4pm Sat. June-Aug., 1pm-4pm Tues. Sept.-May, free) is a classic county history museum with plenty of interesting displays of Indian artifacts, dinosaur bones, homestead-era relics, and re-created historic interiors.

The **Shelby Chamber of Commerce** (100 Montana Ave., 406/434-7184, www.shelbymtchamber.org, 9am-noon Mon.-Fri.) and the **Shelby Visitors Information Center** (406/434-9151, 11am-6pm Mon.-Fri., 1pm-6pm Sat. mid-May-Sept.) are located in the historic Shelby Town Hall (100 Montana Ave.) at the eastern edge of town and can inform you about local events and guided tours. There is free Wi-Fi on the premises.

Shelby is 84 miles (135 km) north of Great Falls along I-15.

HAVRE

Named for the birthplace of the French homesteaders on whose land the town was sited, Havre (HAV-er, population 9,846, elevation 2,494 ft/760 m) is a railroad town anchoring the Hi-Line, with an economy that is increasingly diversifying. As with so many towns along the Hi-Line, the existence of the settlement can unquestionably be attributed to railroad titan James J. Hill, who sent his construction crew to the area in 1887.

The city itself is defined by various natural features: the Bears Paw Mountains to the south, the wide-open plains in every direction, and the Milk River, which borders Havre. With the exception of the Havre Beneath the Streets Tour, which is remarkably well done, Havre has not done well in preserving and promoting its historical attractions, many of which, in Havre's defense, were not actually discovered until the 1960s and 1970s. This is an agricultural and college town—Montana State University-Northern—as well as the trade center for many of the smaller towns in the region.

★ Havre Beneath the Streets

When the city of Havre nearly burned to the ground in 1904, business owners moved underground in an effort to stay afloat while the city was rebuilt. The **Havre Beneath the Streets Tour** (120 3rd Ave., 406/265-8888, 2-hour tours 9:30am-3:30pm daily late May-mid-Sept., 10:30am-2:30pm Mon.-Sat. mid Sept.-late May, call for specific tour times and reservations, $17 adults, $9 children 6-12, free for children under 6) takes visitors into this phenomenal maze of turn-of-the-20th-century establishments that include a faithfully re-created saloon, brothel, bakery, sausage factory, opium den, and more. The guides are passionate and have juicy stories of Havre's wild days and wilder characters. The underground passages were only discovered in 1976 when the city undertook a street-widening project, but the care with which the businesses have been restored is remarkable, making it one of the best historical tours in the state. Each year in early June, actors in period garb bring the underground city to life with a **Living History Weekend.**

Other Sights

If you don't get your fill of Havre history on the underground tour, visit the **H. Earl Clack Memorial Museum** (Holiday Village Mall, 1753 U.S. 2, 406/265-4000, www. hearlclackmuseum.org, 11am-5pm Mon.-Sat., noon-5pm Sun. May-mid-Sept., 1pm-5pm Tues.-Sat. mid-Sept.-Apr., free), oddly located in a shopping mall, for illustrative dioramas on the development of Havre, an assortment of dinosaur eggs and embryos, and most interestingly, artifacts from the adjacent **Wahkpa Chu'gn Archeological Site** (406/265-4000, www.buffalojump.org, 9am-4pm daily, weather permitting, June-Labor Day, $10 adults, $9 seniors, $7 students 13-18, $5 students 6-12, free for children under 6), a 2,000-year-old buffalo jump that was discovered in the early 1960s. Unfortunately the site is located immediately behind the mall and surrounded by a chain-link fence that detracts from the perceived significance of the place, but it is one of the best-preserved buffalo jump sites in the state. An hour-long guided tour—the only way visitors are permitted into the site—takes visitors through bison kill areas and campsite deposits, some of which are 20 feet (6.1 m) deep.

Sports and Recreation

Winter visitors to Havre, hardy souls indeed, should do whatever they can to ski at **Bear Paw Ski Bowl** (66 Saddle Butte Dr., Rocky Boy's Reservation, 29 miles (47 km) south of Havre, 406/395-4040, www.skibearpaw.com, 10:30am-4pm Sat.-Sun. Jan.-Mar., $25 adults, $20 children 9-17, free for children under 9

with paying adult). Known as the "Last Best Ski Hill," Bear Paw is an old-fashioned ski area with two lifts, excellent advanced terrain, and an entirely volunteer staff. No rentals are available, so pick skis up in Havre at **Master Sports** (301 1st St., 406/265-4712, 9am-6pm Mon.-Fri., 9am-5:30pm Sat.). The hill is open only on weekends, but it's a day of skiing with a side of nostalgia that you will never forget.

Entertainment and Events

The biggest event of the year by far in the Havre area is the **Rocky Boy Pow Wow and Rodeo** in Box Elder, usually held around the first weekend in August. The four-day event includes a rodeo, a dance, and costume and drumming competitions for more than $100,000 in prize money. There are cultural demonstrations, grand entries twice daily, and plenty of food vendors. The venues are decided each year and can be located through the **Rocky Boy Agency** (406/395-5705 or 406/395-5439), which also has a regular presence on Facebook.

Food

Murphy's Pub & Casino (1465 U.S. 2 NW, 406/265-4700, 11am-9pm Sun.-Thurs., 11am-10pm Fri.-Sat., $8-22) has a surprisingly international menu that ranges from the rather Irish fish-and-chips, beef pasties, and potato nachos, to Asian chicken salad, chicken quesadillas, Philly cheesesteak, and even a Maui Waui burger. The food is good, and the beer and liquor selection is excellent.

Equally inexplicable but just as delicious is **Nalivka's Original Pizza Kitchen** (1032 1st St., 406/265-4050, lunch and dinner Tues.-Sun., large pizza $19-27, sandwiches from $8), owned and operated by a Russian American family since 1957. Nalivka's serves outstanding pizza—the crust is rich and flaky like a quiche—along with sandwiches, soups, and salads. The service is takeout or delivery only.

For great sandwiches and homemade soup in the less-than-scenic ambience of the Atrium Mall, **Grateful Bread** (220 3rd Ave.

S., 406/265-2370, 7am-2pm Mon.-Sat., $4.25-12) is an excellent choice.

If you haven't had your fill of big, juicy burgers and hand-cut fries or old-fashioned milk shakes by this point, **Wolfer's Diner** (126 3rd Ave., 406/265-2111, 11am-8pm Mon.-Sat., $6.50-9.25) won't disappoint.

Accommodations

Havre has a plentiful assortment of hotels and motels, and surprisingly they are often fully booked with business travelers, so advance reservations are a good idea. On the west end of town, the **AmericInn** (2520 U.S. 2 W., 406/395-5000 or 877/634-3444, www.wyndhamhotels.com, $107-210) is relatively new and one of the largest, with an indoor pool, oversize rooms, Wi-Fi, and hearty breakfasts. Other options include **Best Western Plus** (1345 1st St., 406/265-4200 or 888/530-4100, www.bestwestern.com, $106-173), **Havre Super 8** (166 19th Ave. W., 406/265-1411 or 800/800-8000, $71-110), and **Quality Inn of Havre** (601 W. 1st St., 406/265-6711 or 800/442-4667, www.qualityinnhavre.com, $89-115).

In the center of downtown, **El Toro** (521 1st St., 800/422-5414, from $74) is a good bargain in an excellent location. The Spanish architecture is unexpected, but the rooms are basic and nice.

For campers, just 20 miles (32 km) south of town is **Beaver Creek Park** (17863 Beaver Creek Rd., 406/395-4565 or 406/265-5481, http://bcpark.org, permits $12/night), which has a special site on the north face of the Bears Paw Mountains. At 10,000 acres (4,047 hectares), it is the largest county park in the United States and offers nature trails, two lakes for fishing, and a private campground. The Bear Paw Nature Trail, leaving from the Lion's campground, has paneled signs over 2 miles (3.2 km) to interpret wildlife, archaeology, and history of the park.

A phenomenal option for luxury-loving bird hunters in the region is **Sage Safaris** (406/219-4025, www.sagesafaris.com, Sept.-Nov., from $6,950 pp for three-night trips), which offers a variety of all-inclusive guided wing-shooting safaris in luxurious wall tents with three gourmet meals daily.

Information

One block south of 1st Avenue at the corner of 5th Avenue is the **Havre Area Chamber of Commerce** (130 5th Ave., 406/265-4383, www.havrechamber.com, 9am-5pm Mon.-Fri.), which has a good selection of visitor and recreation information.

Transportation

The **Havre City-County Airport** (HVR, 5404 9th St. W., 406/265-4671) is 3 miles (4.8 km) west of the town. **Cape Air** (800/227-3247, www.capeair.com) offers two flights daily (only one on weekend days) to Billings from Havre.

Havre is 114 miles (184 km) northeast of Great Falls along U.S. 87.

BY TRAIN

The *Empire Builder* is the most popular **Amtrak** (800/872-7245, www.amtrak.com) long-distance train in the United States, traveling between Chicago and either Portland or Seattle. One train passes in each direction daily, and much of the route through Montana, known as the Hi-Line, runs in the north along U.S. 2. The first stop for westbound trains in Montana is Wolf Point, and the last is Libby. The route goes over the Continental Divide and along the southern border of Glacier National Park, a portion of the trip that is unforgettable, and trains are supposedly timed so that passengers are able to enjoy a view of the majestic Rockies regardless of which direction they are traveling. The busiest stops for the train are Whitefish, Shelby, and Havre. If you have plans to travel west and can spare the time, consider taking the train.

CHINOOK

With such an auspicious name—*chinook* is a Native American word meaning "warm wind"—it's no wonder that Chinook (population 1,233; elevation 2,428 ft/740 m) is a cattle town with more cows than people. Set on the rolling plains alongside the Milk River and just north of the Bears Paw Mountains, Chinook is a lovely and solemn place most closely associated with the heartbreaking battle and subsequent surrender of Chief Joseph.

Bear Paw Battlefield

Fifteen miles (24 km) south of Chinook and just 40 miles (64 km) south of the Canadian border on Highway 240 is the haunting **Bear Paw Battlefield** (sunrise-sunset daily year-round), one of three historic Nez Perce sites in the state and the site of a five-day battle between the U.S. Army and Chief Joseph's band of 700 Nez Perce, who had already traveled 1,300 miles (2,092 km) in an effort to escape the Army and were only 40 miles (64 km) from freedom in Canada. There is a self-guided 1.25-mile (2-km) trail, and ranger-guided tours can be arranged in summer by contacting the **National Park Service** (406/357-3130, www.nps.gov).

For a comprehensive introduction to the site, visit Chinook's **Blaine County Museum** (501 Indiana St., 406/357-2590, 8am-noon and 1pm-5pm Mon.-Sat., noon-5pm Sun. Memorial Day-Labor Day, 8am-noon and 1pm-5pm Mon.-Fri. Sept. and May, 1pm-5pm Mon.-Fri. Oct.-Apr., free) before you head to the battlefield. The museum offers a gripping multimedia presentation, *Forty Miles from Freedom,* as well as maps of the battlefield. The museum is also on the Montana Dinosaur Trail and houses a dozen exhibits from the area's once massive inland ocean.

Other Sights

Wildlife lovers will very much appreciate the artistic taxidermy of the **Wildlife Museum** (417 Indiana St., 406/357-3102, www.bcwildlifemuseum.com, 9am-5pm Mon.-Sat., 1pm-5pm Sun. June-Aug., $6 adults, $4 students, children 5 and under free, tours available by appointment), which includes an ever-growing number of exhibits covering everything from a buffalo jump and wetlands to peaks, plains, nocturnal woods, and a moose-grizzly encounter.

Entertainment and Events

Unlike the vast majority of Montana towns that pack the calendar with events during summer, Chinook offers worthwhile entertainment in the fall. The **Bear Paw Battle Commemoration** (406/357-3130, www.nps.gov) pays tribute to the 1877 battle with a traditional pipe ceremony. It is normally scheduled for 10am the first Saturday in October. Photos and filming of the pipe ceremony are not permitted.

Worth seeing during summer is the **Blaine County Fair & Bear Paw Roundup** (300 Cleveland Rd. W., 406/357-2988 or 406/357-3742), a small-town fair with a great rodeo, a carnival, country music, agricultural exhibits, and even lawn mower races.

Food

Rad's Pizza & Deli (315 Indiana St., 406/357-3606, 11am-9pm Mon.-Sat., $7-21) is a quaint little place with excellent soups and sandwiches as well as pizza, salads, wraps, nachos, and homemade cookies.

If you don't get too full at Rad's, just a couple of blocks away is **The Creamery** (415 U.S. 2 W., 406/357-4260, noon-9pm daily Apr.-Sept.), a perfect spot for any soft-serve ice-cream concoction imaginable when the weather is warm. In addition to its ice cream, The Creamery serves grilled hamburgers twice weekly.

Accommodations

The **Bear Paw Motel** (145 Cleveland Rd., 406/357-2221 or 888/357-2224, lawanna.harvey@hotmail.com, $60-75) has guest rooms with queen beds and free Wi-Fi. Pets are allowed for a fee. The nearby **Chinook Motor Inn** (100 Indiana St., 406/357-2248, www.chinookmotorinn.com, $74-100) is much bigger and slightly more modern, also with Wi-Fi.

The Battle of Bear Paw

Sixteen miles (26 km) south of Chinook is the historic Bear Paw Battlefield, an area that looks much as it did 130 years ago when the Nez Perce fought the last in a series of battles known as the Nez Perce War of 1877. Originally from the Wallowa Valley in northeastern Oregon, the Nez Perce, under the leadership of Chief Joseph, had refused to relocate to a reservation in Idaho. General Oliver O. Howard planned an attack to force Joseph's band onto the reservation. Before arriving at this site in Montana, the band of 700 Indians, 200 of whom were warriors, undertook a journey that has come to be known as one of the most spectacular military retreats in U.S. history. They spent three months covering more than 1,300 miles (2,092 km), crossed four states, and engaged in numerous skirmishes with the U.S. Army as they fled capture and sought refuge in Canada.

Bear Paw Battlefield in Nez Perce National Historical Park

On September 29, 1877, the Nez Perce chose to rest at Snake Creek, just north of the Bears Paw Mountains and 40 miles (64 km) from the Canadian border. General Howard had pursued them relentlessly, but believing that they had a good lead on his troops, the Nez Perce chose to set up camp. Unbeknownst to the Nez Perce, Col. Nelson A. Miles and his 7th Cavalry were quickly approaching from the southeast. With the help of Cheyenne and Lakota scouts, they spotted the Nez Perce camp. Although almost 300 troops attacked the Nez Perce, the skilled warriors were able to stand their ground and rapidly fortify the encampment.

The Nez Perce earned great praise not only for their fighting but also for their humane treatment of others. During this battle, as wounded Army soldiers lay on the battlefield, the Nez Perce moved among them looking for ammunition and weapons but did no further harm to the injured men. There is even a legend that an injured soldier kept crying out to his comrades for water. A warrior approached him, removed the soldier's ammunition belt, and left a container of water.

After five days of fighting, Joseph had seen enough. There may have been an opportunity to escape, but he refused to leave the wounded, sick, and elderly behind. On October 5, 1877, Joseph, Howard, and Miles spoke though translators. Joseph made a poignant speech, finishing with the famous words: "From where the sun now stands, I will fight no more forever." Although it was a conditional surrender and both Miles and Howard assured Joseph that he and his people would be returned to their home in the Northwest, that was not the case: The U.S. government moved the Nez Perce first to a reservation in Kansas and later to Indian Territory in present-day Oklahoma. Not until 1885 were they moved to Washington State, still not their original homeland. Joseph died there in 1904, the cause of death diagnosed by his doctor as "a broken heart."

The Bear Paw Battlefield is one of several sites located within the **Nez Perce National Historical Park** (406/357-3130 or 208/843-7009, www.nps.gov, year-round). A ranger is on-site beginning at noon each day late June-September.

Information

The **Chinook Chamber of Commerce** (85½ 2nd St., 406/357-2532, www.chinookmontana.com) has an informative website. Information is also available at the **Blaine County Museum** (501 Indiana St., 406/357-2590) and *Blaine County Journal* (217 Indiana St., 406/357-3573).

Transportation

Chinook is 135 miles (217 km) northeast of Great Falls via U.S. 87 and U.S. 2.

Lewistown and the Central Plains

In many ways, the heartland of Montana doesn't look all that different from the heartland of the United States. Small towns with strong identities and long, hard histories lie amid vast swaths of agricultural land, rolling fields, and—here is where things are different—humble mountains on the horizon. Though Lewistown is holding on to its population and the culture that accompanies it, other towns, like Judith Gap, Harlowton, and White Sulphur Springs, have struggled to hang on to their residents, most of whom earn a living on the land. There is great charm in the fact that some places don't change much, and visiting them can be like stepping back in time.

LEWISTOWN

Long the heart of this region both geographically and for trade, Lewistown (population 5,870; elevation 3,950 ft/1,204 m) was built by a diverse group of immigrants, something that is reflected in the town's beautiful architecture. The stonework, using local sandstone, was done largely by Croatians, and the interiors were crafted by Norwegians. The town itself was incorporated in 1899, and the area was settled by landless Métis, gold seekers, farmers, and ranchers. It is splendidly set amid open fields, rolling prairie, and three mountain ranges. Although there are three ghost towns in the area—access to which is limited because they are almost entirely on private land—Lewistown itself is thriving and has become something of a model for renaissance in Montana. The combination of beautiful scenery, old-fashioned hospitality, good fishing, and great food has served Lewistown well.

Lewistown Art Center

Across from the historic courthouse, the **Lewistown Art Center** (323 W. Main St., 406/535-8278, www.lewistownartcenter.org,

11:30am-5:30pm Tues.-Fri., 10am-4pm Sat., free) is the artistic hub of this artsy community. Monthly gallery shows feature primarily Montana artists, and the center is the site of numerous arts-related events throughout the year, including music and theater performances. The center's gift shop sells regional pottery, jewelry, fused glass, hitched horsehair, and fine art.

★ Charlie Russell Chew Choo

One of the best ways to see and appreciate the area is aboard the fabulous and kitschy **Charlie Russell Chew Choo** (406/535-5436 or 866/912-3980, www.montanadinnertrain.com, selection of Sat. evenings June-Sept., special events in the fall and Dec. holidays, $100 adults, $50 children 12 and under, VIP packages $135 adults and $70 children), a 56-mile (90-km), three-hour ride that takes visitors on a narrated tour through the mountains and prairies of the region aboard an elegant 1950s passenger train. A full-course dinner featuring prime rib and all the fixings is served. There is also entertainment in the form of musicians, cowboy poets, and the occasional good-natured train robber. The boarding station is a 40-minute drive from Lewistown. At Christmas time, the train runs as the **North Pole Adventure Train** (www.montananorthpoleadventure.com, 5pm and 7:30pm weekly late Nov.-Dec., $30 pp) on a 90-minute adventure that includes hot cocoa, cookies, a story, songs, games, and a visit from Santa and Mrs. Claus.

Ghost Towns

Three primary ghost towns are located outside Lewistown, all of which were gold-mining towns around the turn of the 19th century. **Maiden** (off U.S. 191, northeast of Lewistown, 406/535-5436) was home to some 6,000 people in 1881 and produced more than $18 million worth of gold in its heyday.

By 1896 the population had dwindled to 200, and after a fire destroyed every building in 1905, Maiden was never rebuilt. Today, the town's abandoned structures are entirely on private property, so you can only view them from the road.

The town of **Kendall** (on U.S. 87, north of Lewistown, at the base of the North Moccasin Mountains, 406/535-5436) took off in 1901 with the advent of the Kendall Gold Mining Company. It was among the first mines to use the cyanide process for separating gold and mined an average of $800 worth of gold daily in its prime. At its height, Kendall had a 23-room hotel complete with hot running water, hot-air heating, and electricity. There was also an opera house, several saloons, two churches, four stagecoach lines, and a number of other businesses. By 1920 the town had died, the mines were closed, and many of the buildings collapsed into the mine shafts. Today, only three stone buildings are left standing, and interpretive signs guide visitors at the ruins.

Built in 1893, **Gilt Edge** (off U.S. 191, 20 mi/32 km northeast of Lewistown, 406/535-5436) was considered to be among the premier towns in the country at its heyday in 1900. Calamity Jane was a frequent visitor, and not unlike Jane herself, who grew quite familiar with the town's jail, Gilt Edge's residents experienced a host of legal problems. The mine manager, Colonel Ammon, was eventually tried and convicted of stealing $25,000 worth of bullion intended as wages for the miners. He ultimately served time in New York's Sing Sing prison for stock swindling. Today, the jail and brothel are two of three buildings left standing. But beware: An open well behind one of the buildings poses a real danger for hikers.

Before you seek out any of the ghost towns, call the **Lewistown Chamber of Commerce** (406/535-5436) for precise directions and information about private land. For more history and detailed driving directions, visit www.montanahikes.com.

Sports and Recreation

The land, mountains, and rivers around Lewistown make this area an ideal destination for anglers, hunters, and nature lovers. It's one of the few cities in Montana that offers outstanding fishing within the city limits at **Big Spring Creek,** the area's premier water source, supplying water for the city and a significant trout hatchery. There are also numerous public and privately stocked ponds and springs. For a guided fishing trip on Big Spring Creek, contact **Brad Hanzel of S&W Outfitters** (406/640-1673, www.sandwoutfitters.com, $375 full-day walk/wade for up to 2 anglers, includes lunch) or stop by **Don's Sports and Western Store** (120 2nd Ave. S., 406/538-9408, 10am-6pm Mon.-Fri., 10am-4pm Sat.) for some flies and advice.

Entertainment and Events

Held in late July, the **Central Montana Horse Show, Fair and Rodeo** (1000 U.S. 191 N., 406/535-8841, www.centralmontanafair.com, $5 adults, free for children 12 and under) is a great small-town fair with an equestrian bent. In addition, there is live country music entertainment, PRCA rodeo, AMX auto racing, and a demolition derby.

The second-oldest such event after the National Cowboy Poetry Gathering in Elko, Nevada, the **Montana Cowboy Poetry Gathering & Western Music Rendezvous** (1001 Casino Creek Rd., 406/535-4575, www.montanacowboypoetrygathering.com) is held each year over four days in mid-August. The event—which features readings and musical performances—aims to preserve and celebrate the history, heritage, and values of the American cowboy in the upper Rocky Mountain West.

The **Annual Montana State Chokecherry Festival** (Main St., 406/535-5436, www.lewistownchokecherry.com) is held the first Saturday after Labor Day. Nearly 5,000 people attend the breakfast (pancakes with chokecherry syrup, of course) and other festivities, which include a fun run and walk, chokecherry culinary contests, kids' activities, chokecherry pit-spitting contests, and arts and crafts booths.

An awesome festival in central Montana is the **What the Hay Contest** held each year on the Sunday after Labor Day. Sponsored by the Friends of the Hobson Library, the event sees inventive and artistic farmers in the area—between Windham, Hobson, and Utica—build magnificent sculptures using hay bales along a 21-mile (34-km) loop south of U.S. 87 on Highways 239 and 541. The voting day takes place in conjunction with the **Utica Day Fair.** Oftentimes the sculptures stay up long after the voting, making this route the ideal choice for a Sunday drive.

Food

Lewistown is beginning to establish a reputation for fine dining, and among its gems is **The Mint Bar & Grill** (113 4th Ave. S., 406/535-9925, 5pm-8:30pm Wed.-Sat., $14-32), housed in a 1940s car dealership. The chefs specialize in savory sauces to accompany succulent steaks, ribs, seafood, and pasta. Like the best Montana restaurants, it uses fresh local ingredients and pairs hearty meals with an impressive wine list.

Another local favorite is the casual **Harry's Place** (631 NE Main St., 406/538-9510, 11am-9pm Mon.-Sat., $5.25-24), which serves sandwiches, salads, soups, wraps, burgers, chicken sandwiches, steak, and prime rib.

Open since 1952, the **Dash Inn** (207 NE Main St., 406/535-3892, 10am-10pm daily, $3-11) is a classic drive-through-only burger joint with everything you'd expect from a drive-in diner: ice-cream drinks, buckets of crispy chicken, and its famous wagon-wheel sandwich.

Accommodations

For in-town convenience, the pet-friendly **Yogo Inn of Montana** (211 E. Main St., 406/535-8721 or 800/860-9646, www.yogoinn. com, $82-150) has 123 well-appointed guest rooms and suites catering to technologically inclined business travelers. The indoor pool is a hit with kids.

Originally built as a girls' dormitory in 1912, **The Calvert Hotel** (216 7th Ave. S., 406/535-5411 or 877/371-5411, www. thecalverthotel.com, from $90) is a beautifully refurbished 28-room historic property.

The **Mountain View Motel** (1422 W. Main St., 406/535-3177 or 800/862-5786, www.mountainviewmontana.com, from $60) offers simple, quiet guest rooms in a building that was once a barracks for American and Russian pilots training during World War II. Pets are welcome for a $5 fee. There is also a **Super 8** (102 Wendell Ave., Hwy. 87 W., 406/538-2581, www.super8.com, $65-98) in town.

For more privacy on a ranch setting 10 miles (16.1 km) from town, **Cottonwood Cabins** (4197 Lower Cottonwood Creek Rd., 406/538-8411, rentals@cottonwoodlogcabins. com, $120) has four cute log cabins with kitchens, bathrooms, grills, and picnic benches. All the cabins are pet-friendly and two have hot tubs.

Information

The **Lewistown Area Chamber of Commerce** (408 NE Main St., 406/535-5436, www.lewistownchamber.com, 8am-5pm Mon.-Fri.) is housed in the Central Montana Museum building in Symmes Park, on the east side of town.

Transportation

Lewistown is 106 miles (171 km) southeast of Great Falls on Highway 3 and 125 miles (201 km) northwest of Billings via U.S. 87.

WHITE SULPHUR SPRINGS

Named for the white deposits found around the hot sulfur springs here, White Sulphur Springs (population 908; elevation 5,043 ft/1,537 m) was a gathering spot for various Native Americans tribes for years before James Brewer stumbled on the area in 1886 and developed the hot springs into a resort. The town boomed, first as the "Saratoga of the West," then with lead and silver mines, and then as a cattle town and commercial region for this vast agricultural area. There is nothing booming about White Sulphur Springs these days, but it does have its own charm. In the midst of the prairies, it is close to excellent floating on the Smith River and skiing at Showdown Ski Area, and there are wonderful relics from its glory days: A castle sits atop the hill in town, and the hot springs still gurgle with purportedly healing waters. And every summer the Red Ants Pants Music Festival brings great musicians (country, folk, bluegrass) to a dreamed-up stage in the middle of a cow pasture in the middle of nowhere.

Castle Museum

Built in 1892 by merchant Bryon Roger Sherman, **The Castle** is a remarkable Victorian mansion that now houses the **Meagher County Museum** (310 2nd Ave. NE, 406/547-2324, 10am-5pm daily Memorial Day-Labor Day, 10am-5pm Wed.-Sun. Labor Day-Oct., last guided tour of the day at 4pm, $5 adults, $3 seniors and children 4-12, free for children under 4). It was constructed with hand-cut granite blocks hauled by oxen from the Castle Mountains, 12 miles (19.3 km) away. It is appointed with period furniture and original fixtures—Italian marble sinks as well as crystal and brass light fixtures. Sherman supplied electricity to the entire town, making White Sulphur Springs one of the first towns in the state to have electricity.

★ Charles M. Bair Family Museum

Thirty-five miles (56 km) east of White Sulphur Springs off U.S. 12 in the little town of Martinsdale, the **Charles M. Bair Family Museum** (2751 Hwy. 294, 406/572-3314, 10am-5pm daily May 15-Sept. 15, $5 adults, $3 seniors, $2 children under 13) is a phenomenal little museum dedicated to preserving and perpetuating the historic

and artistic significance of the Bair family legacy. Charles Bair arrived in Montana in 1883 from Paris, Ohio, intent on making his fortune. He worked as a train conductor and sheep rancher (where he befriended the Crow chief Plenty Coups) before making it big with a ground-thawing device used in Alaska's gold rush. He used his earnings to buy land around Martinsdale, where he ran 300,000 sheep. Charles, his wife, Mary, and their daughters, Alberta and Marguerite, lived all over the country as he worked in mining, oil, and business, and traveled around the world, but they always came back to the ranch in Martinsdale. Avid art collectors and good friends with artists like Charlie Russell and Joseph Henry Sharp, the family filled their Montana home full to bursting with glorious artworks, antiques, and artifacts. After youngest daughter Alberta died in 1993 at the age of 97, the family home was opened to the public as a museum. In 2011, a 7,000-square-foot art museum containing the family's treasures opened. Visitors can tour both the home and the museum in summer and early fall to see family photos and memorabilia, original paintings, and Native American artifacts.

Sports and Recreation

One of Montana's most isolated, the **Smith River** is 59 miles (95 km) of dramatic canyons, open ranch land, and rugged forest between Camp Baker and Eden Bridge. The high season is when the water is high, typically late spring-early summer. On average, floaters take four days to travel through this spectacular roadless area.

Because of its popularity with Montanans, it is the only river in the state that can be used only with a permit. Permits are issued annually by Montana Fish, Wildlife & Parks (FWP) in a lottery that runs early January-mid-February. For more information, contact the **Great Falls FWP office** (406/454-5840). To inquire about remaining launch dates or cancelled permits, call the Smith River Reservation Line (406/454-5861) beginning in mid-March.

Floating the Smith River

In the center of Montana and the middle of nowhere runs the Smith River, a red-ribbon trout stream and one of the most sought-after rivers in the state for float trips. There are no services and no road access along the 59-mile (95-km) stretch of river between Camp Baker and Eden Bridge. The remoteness of the Smith, coupled with limestone canyons and giant swaths of ranch land, make this river an idyllic destination.

Aside from the splendid scenery, the fish add to the river's appeal. The rainbow and brown trout populations are thriving, as are the native whitefish, which are somewhat unfairly maligned. Perhaps because they are easier to catch (thanks in part to a bigger and more circular "sucker" mouth), or because they don't have the dramatic colors of a trout, or maybe just because they compete for food and space with trout, whitefish are often called "trash fish" by fly fishers. But anyone who's ever had the good fortune to eat smoked whitefish on crackers with horseradish would never stoop to name-calling.

Because of the river's popularity, it is closely managed by Montana Fish, Wildlife & Parks (FWP), which oversees a lottery system for the roughly 1,000 permits issued annually. There are 27 boat camps and 52 campsites scattered along the river, which can most often be floated in four days. The season varies dramatically depending on snowpack, rainfall, and the timing of irrigation use, but mid-April-early July is considered the prime season, and occasionally floaters can hit the Smith as late as September. To apply for a permit, which is due in mid-February, contact the **Montana FWP Smith River Reservation Line** (406/454-5861, www.fwp.mt.gov). Another option for those unlucky in the lottery is to book a Smith River trip with one of eight permitted outfitters. **Lewis and Clark Expeditions** (Twin Bridges, 406/684-5960, www.hwlodge.com, 4-day/5-night trips from $4,100) offers excellent trips with world-class guides and gourmet grub. In addition to his fantastic commercial trips and Healing Waters Lodge, owner Mike Geary has teamed with Project Healing Waters to sponsor river fishing trips for disabled veterans.

Entertainment and Events

★ **RED ANTS PANTS MUSIC FESTIVAL**

Voted the Best Event of the Year for the State of Montana in 2018, **Red Ants Pants Music Festival** (Jackson Ln., 3 mi/4.8 km northeast of White Sulphur Springs, 406/209-8135, www.redantspantsmusicfestival.com, $60 day pass, $160 3-day pass, $25 camping pass, free for kids 12 and under) is held in late July. It's a family-friendly, three-day weekend of music, food, and camping for those who don't mind the dust. Past headliners have included Dwight Yoakum, Shooter Jennings, Lucinda Williams, Lyle Lovett, and the Wailing Jennies. There's a kids' tent, a beer garden, hayrides, great food vendors, and room to dance. It can be hot and windy with very little shade (bring your own!), but this is a wholesome place to listen to great music. Tickets go on sale with early bird specials in early April. The festival was founded in 2011 by Sarah Calhoun, the genius behind the Red Ants Pants brand of workwear for women. Along with her staff and army of volunteers, she is transforming the region by bringing youth and vibrancy and music. In town, stop into **Red Ants Pants** (206 E. Main St., 406/547-3781, www.redantspants.com, 10am-5pm Mon.-Sat.) which sells T-shirts, gifts, and awesome work gear, including pants that don't wear out and are made for women's bodies.

Food

Dori's Café (112 E. Main St., 406/547-2280, 6am-2pm Mon.-Fri., 6am-1pm Sat., 6am-11am Sun., though hours can change without notice, $5-12) is just what you'd hope to find in a small, middle-of-nowhere Montana town: a friendly place with good hearty food and the ambience of a wildlife museum.

For dinner and a glimpse of the local nightlife, head to the **Stockman's Bar and Barnwood Steakhouse** (2nd Ave. NE,

406/547-9985, 5pm-10pm daily, bar opens 11am daily, $7-25) for a steak or juicy burger.

For a gourmet experience and a glimpse of the New West, try ★ **Bar 47** (24 E. Main St., 406/547-6330, 11am-2am daily, $10-29), which serves excellent and inspired comfort food including poutine, sea salt caramel fries, cheese curds, pulled pork sliders, phenomenal burgers, street tacos, and steaks. There's also a kids menu and awesome desserts. Try the grownup milk shakes too!

Accommodations

To enjoy White Sulphur Springs in the way the earliest settlers intended, make a point to visit the pet-friendly **Spa Hot Springs Motel** (202 W. Main St., 406/547-3366, www.spahotsprings.com, $99-139). The guest rooms are basic and clean, though some have been recently updated and have pillow-top mattresses, leather recliners, and flat-screen TVs. Some pet-friendly rooms are available for a $10 fee. It's the three hot springs pools that make this place special. Outside, two pools are kept at 98°F (26.7°C) and 103°F (39.4°C). Inside, the pool is 105°F (40.6°C), and all are drained and cleaned nightly so that no chemicals have to be added to the natural hot water. Nonguests can use the pools for a fee ($7 adults, $6 seniors, $6 children 13-17, $5 children 6-12, $3 children 3-5, $2 children under 3). The springs are open 6am-11pm daily year-round.

For nonswimmers, the nearby **All Seasons Inn & Suites** (U.S. 89 S., at the south end of town, 406/547-8888 or 877/314-0241, www.allseasonsinnandsuites.net, $89-160) is a smoke-free modern hotel with a hot tub, free Wi-Fi, and continental breakfast. Dogs are welcome for a $25 fee.

Information

For information about White Sulphur Springs, contact the **Meagher County Chamber of Commerce** (406/547-2250, www.meagherchamber.org). Hours here vary daily and seasonally, so please call before you visit.

Transportation

White Sulphur Springs is 97 miles (156 km) south of Great Falls and 79 miles (127 km) north of Bozeman on U.S. 89 and 75 miles (121 km) east of Helena via U.S. 12 and 89.

Glacier National Park

Known as the "Crown of the Continent," Glacier National Park is one of the largest intact ecosystems in the Lower 48, an amalgam of stunning landscapes that, for many visitors, defines the entire state.

The beauty of Glacier is rugged, raw, and dynamic. The mountains thrust skyward, and the gravity-defying roads are ribbons that snake toward the summits. The legendary Going-to-the-Sun Road is one of the West's most impressive engineering feats and one of the best scenic drives in the country. There are still 25 "active" glaciers (at least 25 acres/10.1 hectares in area) to be found within the park, along with countless waterfalls and hundreds of crystalline lakes. In summer the landscape is heavy with huckleberries and dotted with

Highlights

Look for ★ to find recommended sights, activities, dining, and lodging.

★ **Lake McDonald:** The largest lake in the park and arguably one of the most beautiful. Glacially carved Lake McDonald is easy to access. Pack a picnic for the rocky beach or cruise the waters on a boat tour (page 140).

★ **Going-to-the-Sun Road:** Stretching just over 50 miles (81 km), this phenomenal feat of engineering gives viewers an extraordinary overview of Glacier (page 141).

★ **Hiking:** Among the best-loved trails in the park is the Highline Trail, which climbs 690 feet (210.3 m) over 7.6 miles (12.2 km), then drops more than 2,200 feet (671 m) over the last 4 miles (6.4 km) back to Going-to-the-Sun Road. The views are staggering but not for the faint of heart (page 142).

★ **Many Glacier:** Prime hiking, canoeing, and horseback riding country, this stunning area in the northeast section of the park is popular but rarely crowded (page 155).

★ **Grinnell Glacier:** Since scientists anticipate that the glaciers in the park could disappear entirely by 2030, seeing Grinnell Glacier may be a once-in-a-lifetime opportunity. The ranger-led hike is especially worthwhile (page 157).

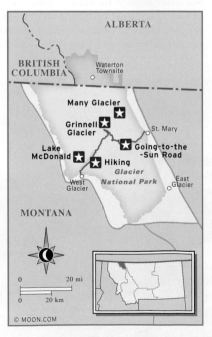

fuzzy, white bear grass. While wildlife-viewing from the road can be challenging in this mountainous terrain, the animals—grizzly and black bears, mountain goats, bighorn sheep, wolves, and more—are here in abundance. With 1,583 square miles (4,100 sq km) of alpine majesty, the scenery, if not the altitude, will leave you breathless.

Glacier National Park is a haven for nature lovers, and visitors can enjoy the natural beauty in a number of ways—hiking, bicycling, boating, and cross-country skiing, to name a few. There are 745.6 miles (1,210 km) of trails throughout the park and a smattering of historic lodges and chalets for cozy accommodations. Yet despite its extensive offerings, Glacier still provides visitors a rare and precious sense of solitude. The crowds are gone as soon as your feet hit the trail, and there are miles of shoreline where the only other picnickers are four-legged. More than just the Crown of the Continent, Glacier is like no place on earth.

PLANNING YOUR TIME

Depending on the amount of time you have to spend in Montana, Glacier National Park could easily absorb all of it, but often it is a spectacular route to get from one side of the Continental Divide to the other, in which case some sights take priority.

The 50-mile (81-km) **Going-to-the-Sun Road** is one of the most scenic drives you will ever take and the best way to get an overview of the park if your time is limited. The alpine vistas provide a marvelous sense of the geography, and the park's history comes alive for those who stop to notice the architecture of the road itself. The drive will likely take at least two hours, not accounting for construction, traffic, or weather-related delays, but if time permits even just an extra hour, there are plenty of turnouts and hiking opportunities along the way. **Hidden Lake Overlook** is a wonderful 2.7-mile (4.3-km) round-trip hike

from the **Logan Pass Visitor Center** that provides opportunities to view seasonal wildflowers and wildlife. Any time in Glacier's backcountry will be time well spent, but visitors should be prepared for changes in the weather (dress in layers and bring water) and wildlife encounters.

With more than a day, visitors can see some of the park's idyllic corners. **Many Glacier** is a launching spot for day hikes to numerous alpine lakes and glaciers. **Lake McDonald,** the park's largest, is a favorite place to spend the day. The southern section of the park, accessed from U.S. 2, is especially popular in winter with cross-country skiers who make tracks from the **Izaak Walton Inn** in Essex.

Planning is critical in Glacier, as accommodations within and immediately surrounding the park fill up months in advance. The 1,004 campsites throughout the park, on the other hand, are filled primarily on a first-come, first-served basis (with a few notable exceptions: Fish Creek and St. Mary can be reserved in advanced, as can half the group sites at Apgar and some of the campsites at Many Glacier). Still, last-minute travelers are not necessarily out of luck. For park brochures, which can be immensely helpful in planning your trip, visit www.nps.gov/glac. For those who are willing to stay outside of the park and launch day trips, the gateway towns of Whitefish and Kalispell have many more choices for accommodations.

INFORMATION AND SERVICES

If you have questions before arriving in Glacier, visit the Plan Your Visit section on the **Glacier National Park website** (www.nps.gov/glac) or call the **Park Headquarters** (406/888-7800, 8am-4:30pm daily year-round).

Park Fees and Passes

Entrance to **Glacier National Park**

GLACIER NATIONAL PARK

Previous: Hidden Lake; one of Glacier's historic red buses; hiker above Grinnell Lake.

Glacier National Park

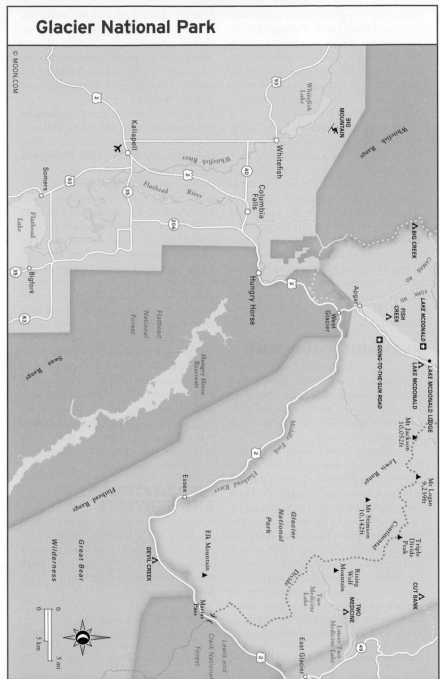

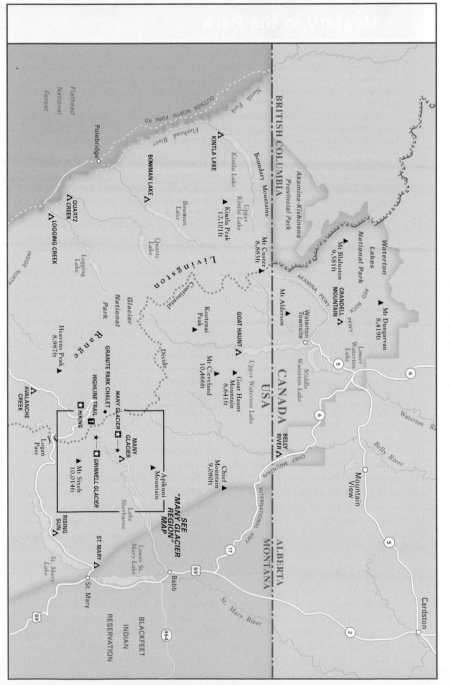

Flathead
National
Forest

BRITISH COLUMBIA

North Fork

OUTSIDE NORTH FORK RD

Flathead River

Polebridge

KINTLA LAKE

Kintla Lake

Upper
Kintla Lake
▲ Kintla Peak
11,101ft

BOWMAN LAKE ⋀

Bowman
Lake

QUARTZ
⋀ CREEK

Quartz
Lake

⋀ LOGGING CREEK

Logging
Lake

INSIDE NORTH

Boundary Mountains

Akamina-Kishinena

Provincial Park

Mt Custer
8,883ft ▲

Livingston

Continental

Kootenai
Peak ▲

Glacier
National
Park

Range

Divide

Heavens Peak
8,987ft ▲

GRANITE PARK CHALET ●

HIGHLINE TRAIL 🚺

⋀ AVALANCHE
CREEK

✚ HIKING

Logan
Pass

MANY GLACIER
✚
★ —
✚ GRINNELL GLACIER

▲ Mt Siyeh
10,014ft

RISING
SUN ⋀

ST MARY ⋀

St. Mary

St. Mary
Lake

89

Mt Alderson

GOAT HAUNT ⋀

Upper Waterton Lake

Goat Haunt
Mountain
8,641ft ▲

Mt Cleveland
10,466ft ▲

MANY
GLACIER ⋀

★

Apikuni
Mountain ▲

Lake
Sherburne

SEE
"MANY
GLACIER
REGION"
MAP

Lower St.
Mary Lake

Babb

89

464

Mt Blakiston
9,581ft ▲

AKAMINA PKWY

Waterton
Townsite

Waterton
Lakes
National Park

RED ROCK PKWY

CRANDELL
MOUNTAIN ⋀

Mt Dungarvan
8,419ft ▲

Lower
Waterton
Lake

Middle
Waterton Lake

CANADA

USA

5

6

6

BELLY
RIVER ⋀

Chief
Mountain
9,080ft ▲

CHIEF MOUNTAIN

INTERNATIONAL HWY

17

ALBERTA

MONTANA

BLACKFEET
INDIAN
RESERVATION

St. Mary River

Waterton Ri

Belly River

Mountain
View

5

Cardston

2

A Mystery in the Park

Although there are a handful of woeful stories about bear attacks, restless ghosts, drownings, and freak accidents in Glacier, few are as chilling as the tales of those souls who simply vanish. Though there have been well over 260 deaths in Glacier since 1900, only 13 people have disappeared. Among those were Joseph and William Whitehead, two brothers from Chicago who vanished without a trace in Glacier's backcountry in 1924.

Joseph Whitehead, 29, was an engineer, and his younger brother, William, 22, was a student at the Massachusetts Institute of Technology. They had come to Glacier as thoughtful adventurers for a well-planned two-week journey. The trip had gone exceedingly well, and in their last letter to their mother, the boys wrote, "Don't worry . . . we won't go into any danger."

Early in the morning on August 24, 1924, the boys set out from Granite Park Chalet on a reasonably ambitious 22-mile (35-km) hike to the Lewis Hotel at Lake McDonald. When they failed to return to Chicago on September 1, their mother, Dora, alerted park authorities that her sons were missing. An extensive manhunt followed, with countless park employees and volunteers covering nearly every corner of the park. No trace of them was found.

Dora refused to give up the search; even President Calvin Coolidge got involved, instructing the Park Service to continue the search with no expense spared. Dora offered a $500 reward, and Louis Hill, son of railroad magnate James Hill, promised an additional $1,000 to anyone with information. False leads flooded in, but nothing else.

In late September, nearly a month after the young men had been reported missing, a horse party reported having met the brothers on the afternoon of August 24 hiking along Logan Creek, just 10 miles (16.1 km) from their destination and only a few miles from the road to Lake McDonald. As winter set in, the FBI assumed control of the investigation.

The following summer, Dora and her daughter traveled to Glacier to follow the route the young men had taken. They didn't find a single clue, and the following year FBI director J. Edgar Hoover closed the case, which remains unsolved to this day.

There was some initial speculation that the Whiteheads had drowned, but the theory seemed less likely as no bodies were ever found. The prevailing conjecture is that the brothers followed the trail from Logan Creek, where they met the horse party, to the road, northeast of the Lewis Road. It is thought likely that the young men were then abducted in an automobile by unknown assailants for unknown reasons. It is a mystery, and a tragedy, that haunts Glacier to this day.

(406/888-7800, www.nps.gov/glac) costs $35 per vehicle for seven days May 1through October 31, $30 for motorcycles, and $20 for hikers and bikers. An annual park pass for Glacier costs $70, and an annual America the Beautiful Pass is $80 and will gain you entrance into any and all national parks for one year.

Visitors Centers

At the park entrance, visitors are given a copy of *Vacation Planner*, which provides important general information about the park. Once inside the park, visitors centers and ranger stations are the best sources of information. Hours of operation vary, but during the summer the centers and stations are open every day.

The **Visitor Information Headquarters Building** (64 Grinnell Dr., 8am-4:30pm Mon.-Fri., excluding holidays, year-round) is just inside the West Glacier park entrance before the actual entrance station; turn right after passing the "Glacier National Park" sign. They can issue a variety of passes and permits as well as answer most questions.

The park's visitors centers all have knowledgeable staff, guidebooks and maps, and basic amenities. In West Glacier, visit the **Apgar Visitor Center** (9am-4:30pm daily mid-May-mid-Oct., only open Sat.-Sun. winter) in the central part of Apgar Village. It is two doors down from the **Backcountry**

Permit Center (406/888-7800, open daily late May-mid-Sept., or by appointment when closed for the season), which also provides trip planning. The **St. Mary Visitor Center** (8am-5pm daily late May-mid-Sept.) inside the eastern park entrance, is the park's largest visitors center and offers backcountry permit services.

The **Two Medicine Ranger Station** and **Many Glacier Ranger Station** (both 7am-5pm daily late May-mid-Sept., backcountry permits available), close to the campgrounds, provide visitor information and permits.

Entrance Stations

The two main entrances to Glacier National Park are at either end of Going-to-the-Sun Road. **West Glacier,** on the west side of the park, can be accessed from U.S. 2, and **St. Mary,** on the park's east side, can be accessed from U.S. 89. Entrance stations on the west side are at **Camas Creek** and the **Polebridge Ranger Station** off Outside North Fork Road, and on the east side at **Two Medicine** off Highway 49, **Many Glacier** off U.S. 89, and at **Waterton Lakes National Park** accessible from Alberta Provincial Highways 5 and 6. Entrance fees must be paid even when entrance stations are closed.

Services

Lodging in Glacier is available through three separate providers. **Xanterra** (303/265-7010, www.xanterra.com) operates the Village Inn at Apgar, Lake McDonald Lodge, Rising Sun Motor Inn & Cabins, Swiftcurrent Motor Inn & Cabins, and Many Glacier Hotel. **Glacier Park Collection** (844/868-7474, www.glacierparkcollection.com) operates Grouse Mountain Lodge, Glacier Park Lodge, St. Mary Village, Prince of Wales Hotel, Apgar Village Lodge & Cabins, West Glacier Motel & Cabins, and Motel Lake McDonald. **Belton Chalet** (406/888-5000 or 888/235-8665, http://beltonchalet.com) operates the Belton Lodge and the Lewis and Clark Cottages. You can book accommodations as well as a variety of tours and park transportation online or by phone.

If you arrive and discover you are missing some important piece of recreational equipment—or more important, bear spray—almost anything you need can be rented from **Glacier Outfitters** (196 Apgar Loop, 406/219-7466, www.goglacieroutfitters.com). From camping gear and backpacks to a variety of bicycles, paddleboards, kayaks, canoes, fishing rods, GoPro cameras, and, yep, bear spray, this is the place to make sure you have what you need in the way of toys and gear.

hiking the Hidden Lake Trail

Ranger Programs

Some of the best resources on Glacier National Park are the Park Service rangers—encyclopedias in hiking boots. Their stations are conveniently located at major sites throughout the park, and the rangers host a number of outdoor educational events geared to the whole family. The ranger programs in Glacier begin in late spring and run throughout the summer, with most activities offered at St. Mary, Apgar, Logan Pass, Many Glacier, Goat Haunt, and Two Medicine. Rangers lead several guided hikes each day that allow visitors to learn about the park's geology, history, wildlife, flora, fauna, and more. The St. Mary Visitor Center, Fish Creek Amphitheater, Lake McDonald Lodge, and Many Glacier Hotel host slide lectures as part of the ranger program. Full-day hikes, boat tours, and Junior Ranger programs also are available.

One of the most noteworthy park programs is "Native America Speaks," where members from the Blackfeet, Salish, Kootenai, and Pend d'Oreille tribes provide campfire talks about their life, culture, and influence in Glacier. The speakers range from artists and musicians to historians who intersperse their talks with personal stories and Native American legends. These talks are given at the Apgar, Many Glacier, Two Medicine, and Rising Sun Campgrounds. During July-August, the St. Mary Visitor Center also hosts weekly Native American dance troupes. For times, locations, and descriptions of the ranger programs offered, pick up the free "Ranger-led Activity Schedule" available at any of the park's visitors centers.

For information on ranger stations or programs and to download park brochures, contact **Park Service Headquarters** (406/888-7800, www.nps.gov/glac).

Pets

Although pets are allowed in drive-in campgrounds, picnic areas, and on roads open to car traffic, they are required to be on a leash no longer than 6 feet (1.8 m) at all times. They are not permitted on any trails within the park, and park officials strongly discourage the presence of pets in Glacier. Because of this policy, it is nearly impossible to find pet-friendly accommodations in the area.

TRANSPORTATION
Getting There
BY AIR

The closest airport to Glacier is 30 miles (48 km) away in Kalispell. The **Glacier Park International Airport** (FCA, www.iflyglacier.com) is served by Delta, Alaska Airlines, United, and Allegiant. At the airport **Avis, Budget, Hertz,** and **National/Alamo** have car-rental counters, and **Dollar, Thrifty,** and **Enterprise** have car-rental lots off-site but near the airport. **Glacier Taxi** (406/250-3603) and **Wild Horse Limousine** (406/756-2290 or 800/841-2391, www.wildhorselimo.com) offer taxi and limo services, respectively.

Great Falls International Airport is 130-165 miles (209-265 km) to the southeast of entrances at St. Mary, Two Medicine, and Many Glacier.

Missoula International Airport is roughly 150 miles (242 km) south of the park entrance at West Glacier.

BY CAR

By car, the park is accessible from U.S.s 2 and Highway 89. It is about 150 miles (252 km) north of Missoula and 150 miles (252 km) northwest of Great Falls.

BY TRAIN

Amtrak runs the *Empire Builder* from Chicago to Seattle, with daily stops in both directions in East Glacier (summer only), Essex, and West Glacier.

Getting Around
PRIVATE VEHICLES

Vehicles and vehicle combinations longer than 21 feet (6.4 m), including bumpers, and wider than 8 feet (2.4 m), including mirrors, are not permitted on Going-to-the-Sun Road between

Hands-On Learning

Founded in 1983, the **Glacier Institute** (406/755-1211, www.glacierinstitute.org) is a private nonprofit organization that offers hands-on educational experiences using Glacier National Park and Flathead National Forest as its classrooms. Its mission is to provide "an objective and science-based understanding of the area's ecology and its interaction with people." The Glacier Institute fulfills its mission by providing field-based experiences in and around the park for all ages and levels of fitness.

The Glacier Institute offers 3- to 5-day youth camps, starting at $150, which have a variety of focuses. Whether it is the first overnight camp experience for children away from their parents, an introduction to the basic concepts of ecology, or a focus on art and nature, the institute offers experienced guides and experts to foster each child's learning. It also has a variety of outdoor education courses open to young and old. You can enroll for a daylong course (from $65) with expert instructors on topics such as, for instance, wolves of the North Fork Valley, for a unique learning experience.

To peruse the institute's extensive and fascinating offerings, visit its website; if you see a course that interests you but is not being offered when you plan to be in Glacier, the Glacier Institute creates custom programs and can plan a half-day to several-day course just for your group (1-6 people, $425) based on the courses or expert instructors that you select.

Avalanche Campground and the Rising Sun Parking Area. Vehicles and vehicle combinations taller than 10 feet (3 m) may have difficulty navigating Going-to-the-Sun Road westbound from Logan Pass to the Loop because of rock overhangs. Stock trucks and trailers can access Packers Roost on the west side and Siyeh Bend on the east side.

SHUTTLES

Glacier's **free shuttle system** (406/892-2525, 7:30am-7pm daily July-September 23) picks up and drops off at 16 different stops, including Apgar Visitor Center, Avalanche Creek, Logan Pass, St. Mary Visitor Center, and a number of trailheads. West-side shuttles depart every 15-30 minutes and east-side shuttles depart every 40 minutes. The shuttle is an excellent option for hiking from the Logan Pass Visitor Center, which often has a full parking lot otherwise, or for doing trails that start at one trailhead and end at another. To travel the entire Going-to-the-Sun Road from the Apgar Visitor Center to the St. Mary Visitor Center and back, or vice versa, takes approximately seven hours on the shuttle. The last service to Logan Pass with time to visit and return departs Apgar Visitor Center at

4:15pm and St. Mary Visitor Center at 6:31pm. Check daily schedules for early morning express service from Apgar Visitor Center to Logan Pass.

TOURS

Scenic, interpretive **Red Bus Tours** (855/733-4522 or 303/265-7010 from outside the U.S., www.glaciernationalparklodges.com, from $36 adults, $18 children) are another way to see the park. These snazzy vintage buses, known locally as "Jammers," were originally built by the White Motor Company 1936-1939. The vehicles, which have been overhauled for safety purposes, are 25 feet (7.6 m) long, seat 17 passengers, and have the added bonus of roll-back canvas tops, ideal for sunny summer days. Numerous tours of varying lengths are available, and informative guides entertain with facts and stories about Glacier. It's an excellent way to leave the driving to someone else.

Slightly less flashy but quite comfortable are the air-conditioned and large-windowed coaches of **Sun Tours** (406/226-9220 or 800/786-9220, www.glaciersuntours.com, June-Sept. 1, $55-100 adults, $35-52 children 5-12, free for children under 5). Tours last four, six, or eight hours, and what makes them unique is that they are guided from a Blackfeet perspective. Plants and roots used for Blackfeet medicine are pointed out, for example, as are the natural features that relate to the Blackfeet Nation. The coaches can accommodate 25 passengers and depart daily from East Glacier, Browning, St. Mary, and West Glacier. Sun Tours also offers a hiker shuttle service and private custom tours.

PLANTS AND ANIMALS
Plants
With more than 1 million acres (0.4 million hectares), Glacier National Park offers a staggering number of microclimates, including forests, alpine meadows, lakes, rocky peaks, and glacial valleys, that are home to an incredible diversity of plant and animal life.

With two climate zones (Pacific maritime and prairie/arctic), three major watersheds (Pacific, Atlantic, and Arctic), and a range of biomes at various elevations, Glacier is home to a broad selection of plantlife. There are 20 different tree species and at least 1,132 species of vascular plants, 858 nonvascular, including 127 nonnative species. There are nearly 900 species of moss and lichen, almost 1,000 species of wildflowers, and more than 100 species of plants that are listed by the state as "sensitive." Amazingly, some of the tiny, seemingly delicate alpine plants that are beaten and battered by the harsh climate year after year can live to be more than 100 years old.

Visitors from the northern part of North America will find familiar flora in Glacier. Divided into four floristic provinces, Glacier's plant species are 49 percent cordilleran (which includes the southern and central Rockies as well as the Cascade Mountains in Washington), 39 percent boreal (which includes much of Canada), 10 percent arctic-alpine, and 1 percent Great Plains. The continent's easternmost hemlock forest thrives in the moist environment around Lake McDonald on the park's west side, offering a stark contrast to the wind-sculpted open forests and grasslands of the east side. There are

also significant shifts in plantlife from the north to the south as a result of changes in annual precipitation.

Animals
Glacier's diversity of habitats is a critical factor in the spectrum of wildlife that calls the park home. From the minute pygmy shrew, which weighs about as much as a dime, to indicator species like the grizzly bear, gray wolf, and mountain lion, Glacier is home to 71 species of mammals and more than 260 species of birds. Missing are bison and woodland caribou, both of which were grossly overhunted in the region prior to the park's designation in 1910.

Today the park is a safe haven for the Canada lynx and the grizzly bear, both of which are threatened, and the once-endangered gray wolf. There are healthy populations of elk, primarily in the grasslands of the park's eastern side, as well as moose, mountain goats, and bighorn sheep. Though rarely seen and few in number, wolverines, cougars, and fishers also live here. Glacier's tailed frog is considered the most primitive frog in North America, and the only one that fertilizes the female's eggs internally. It is most closely related to frogs in New Zealand, which has led scientists to believe that its origins date back 250 million years.

The addition of nonnative species and removal of native species can have far-ranging and catastrophic results. The healthy red-backed vole population on the park's west side eats primarily fungus and consequently spread fungal spores as they travel. The rootlets of the spores are almost entirely responsible for the regeneration of conifer trees in the region. Without the voles, there would be no forest. Without the fungus, there would be no voles. The ecosystem is as delicately balanced as it is captivating.

HISTORY
Recently discovered evidence indicates that this area was inhabited as far back as 10,000 years ago, and the Salish, Kootenai, Flathead,

Bear Safety

Glacier has significant concentrations of both grizzly and black bears, both of which can be threatening in any encounter. The keys to safe travel in the backcountry are acting to prevent bear encounters and knowing what to do in the event you do meet a bear. The following are simple guidelines for responsible behavior in bear country:

- **Don't surprise bears.** Make noise, even on well-traveled trails, to allow bears the opportunity to get away from you. Bells can be effective, as can singing, hand-clapping, and loud talking. Never assume that a bear has better senses than you and will see, hear, or smell you coming.

- **Don't approach bears.** Be aware of their feeding opportunities and behavior so that you can avoid potential feeding locations and times of day. Avoid hiking through berry patches, cow parsnip thickets, or fields of glacier lilies. Never approach a carcass, which could be under the surveillance of a bear. Try not to hike before sunrise or at dusk, both active times for bears. Always keep children in close proximity.

- **Minimize the possibility that a bear would be attracted to your belongings or campsite.** Abide by all the park regulations about hanging your food and garbage away from your sleeping area. Don't carry odiferous food, and never bring anything potentially edible, including medicines and toothpaste, into your tent. Take special care with used feminine hygiene products by sealing them in several zip-top bags with baking soda to absorb the odor.

- **Be prepared for an encounter.** Carry pepper spray that is not out of date and know how to use it. Familiarize yourself with the behaviors most likely to ensure your safety in a bear encounter.

If you do surprise a bear, keep your wits about you. While there is no easy and universal answer about how to react—bears are as individual and unpredictable as humans—the following are accepted behaviors outlined on Glacier's website:

- **Talk quietly and calmly.** If you have surprised a bear, don't attempt to threaten it; if possible, try to detour around it.

- **Never run.** Don't turn your back; instead, back away slowly, unless it agitates the bear. Running could trigger its predator instincts.

- **Use peripheral vision.** Bears may perceive direct eye contact as aggressive behavior on your part.

- **Drop something (not food) to distract the bear and keep your pack on for protection in case of an attack.** If you have bear spray, grab it and be prepared to use it in the event of an attack.

- **Protect yourself if the bear attacks.** Protect your chest and abdomen by falling to the ground on your stomach or assuming the fetal position. Cover the back of your neck with your hands, and if the bear tries to roll you over, attempt to stay on your stomach. If the attack is defensive, the bear will leave once it has determined you are not a threat. If the attack is prolonged, fight back!

and Blackfeet have all called Glacier home. The Blackfeet came to the region later than the others, entering the region sometime in the early 1700s and extending their territory through the eastern part of the park and onto the plains. The Blackfeet fought quite a few battles for territory with other tribes; the French, British, and Spanish fur trappers who entered the region in the 1800s in search of beaver pelts were wary of the Blackfeet.

When the Blackfeet Indian Reservation was created in 1855, it included the eastern part of the park up to the Continental Divide. In 1895 the Blackfeet sold the land to the U.S.

government for $1.5 million with the agreement that they would still have unrestricted access for hunting, ceremonies, and other use. Today the Blackfeet Indian Reservation borders the eastern edge of the park, and the Flathead Indian Reservation—which is home to the Confederated Salish, Pend d'Oreille, and Kootenai tribes—lies to the southwest.

In 1891, the Great Northern Railway completed its route over Marias Pass in the southern part of the park. By the turn of the 20th century it had become a tourist destination; visitors arrived by train and ventured into the park on horseback, on foot, or by boat. In 1910 the railroad started building hotels, lodges, and chalets to further entice visitors. There were few roads at the time, and visitors spent days working their way through the mountains, spending nights in different hotels and chalets. As the Great Northern Railway worked to attract visitors, George Bird Grinnell, a journalist who had first come west to cover the plight of the Blackfeet and who also founded the first Audubon Society, worked arduously to see this magnificent area achieve national park status, and in 1910 President Taft made Glacier the nation's 10th national park.

With the railroad, tourist facilities, and national park status, Glacier did attract a fair number of visitors, and soon there was demand for road access into the park. Going-to-the-Sun Road, a 50-mile (81-km) highway across the Continental Divide that runs from West Glacier to St. Mary, was completed in 1932 after years of treacherous surveying and more than a decade of construction. The road is an impressive engineering feat, now designated a National Historic Landmark, and offers visitors breathtaking (or stomach-churning, depending upon your tolerance for heights) views of the park. With the addition of the road, the number of visitors to the park skyrocketed, and the experience shifted. Now people were able to spend less than a day driving through the park as one of many stops on a cross-country car trip.

In 1932, as a gesture of goodwill between the United States and Canada, the park was joined with Canada's Waterton Lakes National Park to become Waterton-Glacier International Peace Park.

West Glacier Area

A bustling entrance to Glacier, West Glacier (population 227; elevation 3,220 ft/982 m) has the feeling of "last chance to get bug spray" and "first non-PB and J in a while." It is clearly not a destination but a portal, and a good place to find lodging, dining, and supplies in immediate proximity to the park.

The town itself grew up around the Belton Chalet, a lodge built by the Great Northern Railway in 1910, the same year Glacier became a national park. The Belton, an arts and crafts-style gem, was the first permanent lodging on the west side of Glacier, and thanks to a painstaking restoration in 2000 and a wonderful restaurant, it remains one of the best accommodations in the area.

SIGHTS
★ Lake McDonald

The largest lake in the park at 9.4 miles (15.1 km) long and 464 feet (141 m) deep, Lake McDonald was gouged out by a glacier that was likely 2,200 feet (671 m) thick. Surrounded by jagged peaks on three sides, it is bordered by the Lewis Range to the east, which creates a rain block and makes the Lake McDonald Valley one of the mildest and lushest environments in the region. Not unlike the Pacific Northwest, the Lake McDonald Valley boasts dense forests of towering western red cedars and hemlocks.

Although the lake and surrounding forests are exquisitely serene, the area is a hub of activity in the summer months for human visitors and the bear population alike. Modeled after a Swiss chalet and opened in 1914, the grand and slightly worse-for-wear **Lake McDonald Lodge** sprawls along the northeast shore and provides relatively expensive lodging with unmatched views. The dining room, lounge, and pizzeria are open to nonguests. Stop in to warm yourself by the massive fireplace, check out the animal mounts that have decorated the place since its origins, or lounge lakeside on the veranda with a beverage.

There are many great hiking trails around the lake, including those to Fish Lake, Mount Brown Lookout, and the mellow Johns Lake Loop. Plenty of fish swim in the lake—17 varieties in all, mainly trout. Boat tours also depart from the lodge, as well as Red Bus Tours and ranger-led activities.

Bowman Lake

Some 32 miles (52 km) north of the west entrance to Glacier in the North Fork area, and only 30 miles (48 km) south of Canada, is Bowman Lake, another crystalline alpine gem ringed with mountains and forest. A long bumpy ride is required to get here, and as a result it is never crowded. The density of mosquitoes tends to discourage visitors, too. But the 7-mile-long (11.3-km) lake is beautiful, and there is such a thing as bug spray. Boats are permitted, with restrictions on engines. Kayaks and canoes are a wonderful way to explore this photogenic setting. The lake is filled with fish, primarily kokanee and cutthroat trout, and the fishing is legendary, particularly in late spring. There are plenty of worthwhile hikes from the area, including the arduous 13.1-mile (21.1-km) round-trip **Quartz Lakes Loop,** but be warned that this is the heart of grizzly country, and visitors should come prepared. Camping is available on a first-come, first-served basis at the primitive **Bowman Lake Campground** (48 sites, late May-mid-Sept., $15), where several of the trailheads can be accessed.

TOP EXPERIENCE

★ Going-to-the-Sun Road

Completed in 1932, the famed Going-to-the-Sun Road is a marvel of modern engineering. Spanning 50 miles (81 km) from West Glacier to St. Mary, the road snakes up and around mountains that include its namesake, Going-to-the-Sun Mountain, giving viewers some of the most dramatic vistas in the country. The road, which crosses the Continental Divide, required more than

Lake McDonald shoreline

two decades of planning and construction. It climbs more than 3,000 feet (914 m) with only a single switchback, known as **The Loop.** Going-to-the-Sun is an architectural accomplishment as well: All of the bridges, retaining walls, and guardrails are built of native materials, so the road itself blends seamlessly into its majestic alpine setting.

In addition to being an experience all on its own, Going-to-the-Sun is also the primary access road to the park and the only way to get to some of the park's best-known highlights: the visitors center at Logan Pass, the Highline Trail, Lake McDonald, and an array of hiking trails. For visitors who are not keen on driving the road themselves, there are a few excellent options, including free shuttles, vintage tours, and Blackfeet tours, to see the road as a sightseer.

SPORTS AND RECREATION

TOP EXPERIENCE

★ Hiking

Glacier is a hiker's paradise, and the west side of the park around the Lake McDonald Valley offers a unique opportunity to hike through primeval forests of western red cedars, hemlocks, and other species that thrive in this moist, moderate climate. For a number of reasons—including wildlife, weather conditions, and maintenance—hiking trails can be closed at any time. To check on the status of many of the park's most popular trails, visit www.nps.gov/glac.

Among the most popular and well-traveled trails near Lake McDonald is the **Johns Lake Loop,** a relatively flat 1.8-mile (2.9-km) round-trip through prime moose habitat. It can be found just northeast of Lake McDonald Lodge. Also popular is **Trail of the Cedars,** an easy 0.7-mile (1.1-km) loop on a wheelchair-accessible boardwalk through spectacular forest. Leaving from Avalanche Campground, less than 5 miles (8 km) east of Lake McDonald Lodge,

the trail crosses an impressive footbridge over Avalanche Gorge. Also leaving from Avalanche Campground, **Avalanche Creek Trail,** 4 miles (6.4 km) round-trip with a 500-foot (154-m) elevation gain, takes hikers to the picturesque, mountain-ringed Avalanche Lake. Because trailhead parking tends to fill early, the park's free shuttles to both of these trailheads are available from Lake McDonald Lodge or Apgar Village.

A longer and somewhat more strenuous hike is the trail to **Akokala Lake,** climbing roughly 600 feet (183 m) over 5.5 miles (8.9 km) one-way. The trailhead is at the north end of **Bowman Lake Campground** (32 bumpy mi/52 km north of West Glacier on Inside North Fork Rd. and Bowman Lake Rd.), and the trail runs over moderate terrain, through burned areas, and to the remote Akokala Lake, which is filled with native cutthroat trout. The fishing is great, especially halfway around the west side of the lake, where the water is deep next to the shore. Reuter and Numa Peaks tower over the lake and provide a sublime backdrop. As with many of the trails in Glacier, this one cuts through grizzly country, and hikers should be well prepared.

Certainly among the best-loved trails in the park is the **Highline Trail.** Leaving from Logan Pass at the summit of Going-to-the-Sun Road, the high-altitude trail to Granite Park Chalet is 15.2 miles (24.5 km) round-trip, out and back, over moderate terrain with a 500-foot (154-m) elevation gain. A **shorter option,** which requires a shuttle, is to hike one way from Logan Pass to the Loop Trail, for a total hiking distance of 11.8 miles (19 km). Those who start at The Loop will hike up 2,300 feet (701 m), whereas those who start at Logan Pass will have more downhill than up. The trail is well traveled and breathtakingly scenic. The first part of the trail cuts into the Garden Wall above Going-to-the-Sun Road and is not for those with a fear of heights; the ledge can be frightening but provides remarkable views. En route to Granite Park Chalet (7.6 mi/12.2 km), the trail passes in the shadow of Haystack Butte, Mount Gould, and

Mount Grinnell. Mountain goats and bighorn sheep often share the trail with a good number of hikers. If you're making it a day hike, plan on lunch at the chalet (888/345-2649, www. graniteparkchalet.com) before returning to the trailhead.

An alternate day-hike option is to make a loop using the park's shuttle service. At Granite Park Chalet, the **Granite Park Trail** drops more than 2,200 feet (671 m) over 4 miles (6.4 km) back to Going-to-the-Sun Road at The Loop, where you can catch a shuttle back to Logan Pass.

Another popular and scenic hike from Logan Pass is along **Hidden Lake Overlook Trail,** sometimes referred to as Hidden Lake Nature Trail. It's a 2.7-mile (4.3-km) roundtrip hike that starts as paved pathway from the west side of the Logan Pass Visitor Center. The paved trail becomes boardwalk, which allows passage even when there is snow, ice, and melt water on the trail. The trail offers views of the striking Clements Mountain, the Garden Wall, and Mount Oberlin. After a little more than half a mile, the boardwalk ends and the trail heads toward Bearhat Mountain. At just over 1.2 miles (1.9 km), hikers arrive at the Continental Divide; the Hidden Lake Overlook is at 1.35 miles (2.2 km). On clear days, Sperry Glacier can be seen in the distance. Mountain goats frequent the area and wildlife encounters can happen anytime. Be prepared for bighorn sheep, marmots, wolverine, and even grizzly bears.

Boating

Before Going-to-the-Sun Road was completed, most of Glacier's adventurous visitors saw the park by boat. Today this nostalgic mode of travel offers benefits all its own. Both Lake McDonald and Bowman Lake offer excellent boating and fishing opportunities in the form of kayaking, canoeing, and even semi-restricted motorboating. Boat rentals are available at Apgar and Lake McDonald Lodge. For hour-long boat tours—think sunset cocktail cruises in a historic wooden boat on Lake McDonald—and rentals, the **Glacier Park Boat Company** (406/257-2426, www. glacierparkboats.com, tours $18.25 adults, $9.25 children 4-12, free for children under 4) is the ultimate resource. Rowboats can be rented for $18 per hour and fishing motorboats for $23 per hour.

Rafting

Although there is no rafting inside the park, a number of white-water outfitting services in West Glacier offer trips on the 87-mile (140-km) Middle Fork of the Flathead River. The North Fork of the Flathead, which forms the western boundary of the park, can be rafted as well. **Glacier Raft Company** (106 Going-to-the-Sun Rd., West Glacier, 406/888-5454 or 800/235-6781, www.glacierraftco.com, half-day from $59 adults, $49 children 12 and under, full-day from $99 adults, $79 children 12 and under) offers everything from half-day and dinner floats to multiple-day expeditions. The company caters to all floaters, from novices to adrenaline junkies. In addition, the company offers horseback riding excursions, fly-fishing, and kayaking.

Montana Raft Company (11970 U.S. 2, West Glacier, 406/387-5555 or 800/521-7238, www.glacierguides.com, all-inclusive half-day from $61 adults, $51 children, full-day from $99 adults, $76 children) is the sister company of Glacier Guides and has some of the most well-rounded and knowledgeable guides in the area. Group numbers tend to be smaller (9 in a boat as opposed to 14), and the company offers an expansive range of options including rafting and horseback riding, overnight adventures, inflatable kayak trips, family-friendly day trips, and scenic floats. Because of water conditions, in June the minimum age for rafters is eight; from July through the rest of the season, rafting is available to those ages six and up.

Another noteworthy outfitter offering rafting trips in the region is **Wild River Adventures** (11900 U.S. 2 E., 406/387-9453 or 800/700-7056, www.riverwild.com, half-day from $58 adults, $48 children). All-day trips, including lunch, are $97 for adults and

$77 for children. Minimum age for rafters in May and June is 12, and 6-year-olds and up can raft from July onward.

Bicycling

Biking in Glacier is not for the nonchalant. The climbs are treacherous, the edges precipitous, and the automobile traffic even worse. But the thrill of reaching the summit of Going-to-the-Sun Road, seeing how far you've come, soaking in the scenery, and whooshing back down again is unrivaled.

Still, as with any activity in Glacier, cyclists should be well aware of the conditions, restrictions, and potential hazards. Common sense prevails: Use helmets and reflectors; wear brightly colored and highly visible clothing; and watch for falling rocks, wildlife, and ice on the road. Bicycles are prohibited 11am-4pm daily June 15-Labor Day between Apgar Campground and Sprague Creek Campground. From Logan Creek to Logan Pass, eastbound (uphill) bicycle traffic is prohibited 11am-4pm daily June 15-Labor Day. It takes roughly 45 minutes to ride from Sprague Creek to Logan Creek, and three hours from Logan Creek to the summit of Logan Pass. Bicycles cannot be ridden on any of the hiking trails, other than on a few marked trails in Waterton Lakes National Park. For more information on restrictions and current road closures, check online at www.nps.gov/glac.

Bicycles can be rented at Apgar Village from **Glacier Outfitters** (196 Apgar Loop, 406/219-7466, www.goglacieroutfitters.com). It rents cruiser bikes ($12 for 2 hours, $22 for 4 hours, $42 for 24 hours), mountain bikes ($18 for 2 hours, $32 for 4 hours, $47 for 25 hours), hybrid road-mountain bikes ($18 for 2 hours, $32 for 4 hours, $47 for 24 hours), tandem bikes ($22 for 2 hours, $32 for 4 hours, $45 for 24 hours), kids' bikes ($16 for 2 hours, $26 for 4 hours, $36 for 24 hours), and even child trailers ($10 for 2 hours, $20 for 4 hours, $30 for 24 hours).

1: rafting the Middle Fork of the Flathead River
2: Heaven's Peak from The Loop

Helicopter Tours

If seeing the park from atop Going-to-the-Sun Road is not quite dramatic enough, consider a **Kruger Helicopter Tour** (11892 U.S. 2 E., West Glacier, 406/387-4565, half-hour tours from $140/pp based on four people, $280/pp based on four people), which can give adventuresome visitors a bird's-eye view of Iceberg Lake and Gunsight Pass, the Chinese Wall, and more.

Golf

Golfers not afraid of a little distraction in the form of stunning mountain scenery can hit the links at the 18-hole **Glacier View Golf Club** (640 Riverbend Dr., 406/888-5471, www.glacierviewgolf.com, $32 for 18 holes, $20 for 9 holes, $28 for cart for 18 holes) in West Glacier.

Horseback Riding

Another historic form of transportation in Glacier can be enjoyed even today: Guided horseback rides, from one hour to a full day, are available in good weather late May-mid-September at the corrals at Apgar, Lake McDonald, and Many Glacier from **Swan Mountain Outfitters** (406/387-4405 or 877/888-5557, www.swanmountainoutfitters.com), the only outfitter that can offer trail rides inside the park. Options include hour-long rides ($45), half-day trips ($125, 4-person minimum), and full-day trips ($225). Rates do not include gratuities, which are encouraged. Reservations are required.

Cross-Country Skiing

When the white stuff blankets the park, cross-country skiers and snowshoers find themselves in a winter paradise. Many of the hiking trails double as ski and snowshoe trails, but nothing is groomed, so keen and constant orientation is critical. The **Lower McDonald Creek** trailhead is just south of McDonald Creek Bridge, and the trail is 2-3 miles (3.2-4.8 km) round-trip of gentle, forested terrain that parallels the creek in some spots. Another fairly level but longer option is the

Rocky Point trail, which is 6 miles (9.7 km) round-trip and rewards skiers with a phenomenal view of Lake McDonald. The trailhead can be found 0.2 mile (0.3 km) north of Fish Creek Campground. Farther north, toward Avalanche Campground, McDonald Falls (4 mi/6.4 km round-trip), Sacred Dancing Cascades (5.3 mi/8.5 km round-trip), and the Avalanche Picnic Area (11.6 mi/18.7 km round-trip) make excellent day trips.

Since many of the roads in the park are unplowed and impassable for cars in winter, they can make excellent ski trails. Going-to-the-Sun Road is one of the best, although because of avalanche danger, it can often be closed east of Avalanche Creek.

Although it's not in the park, one of the region's best-known and beloved areas for cross-country skiing is the Izaak Walton Inn (off U.S. 2, Essex, between East Glacier and West Glacier, 406/888-5700, www.izaakwaltoninn. com), which has repeatedly been named one of the best cross-country ski resorts in the Rockies. The resort boasts approximately 20 miles (32 km) of groomed trails, and its proximity to the park invites backcountry travel. Ski rentals are available, and a night or two at the inn will be something to remember.

FOOD

Even if you are not planning to stay at the Belton Chalet, the hotel offers two distinct and rich dining experiences that are definitely worth a visit in this land of burgers and grilled cheese. The Belton Grill Dining Room (12575 U.S. 2 E., 406/888-5000 or 888/235-8665, www.beltonchalet.com, 5pm-9pm daily summer, $22-41) provides an intimate, exquisite dining experience in the historic 1910 chalet. The menu changes seasonally, and Chef James offers innovative dishes incorporating the freshest ingredients from local Montana growers and the chalet's own Flathead Lake orchard. For dinner you could sample a Foie Gras Torchon appetizer, Wagyu sirloin strip, or pan-seared wild king salmon. For equally delicious lighter fare and a more moderately priced experience, you can visit the hotel's

Belton Tap Room (3pm-9pm daily summer, $8-12), where you may choose to accompany a locally brewed Montana beer with pork belly sliders or a lamb burger.

The Glacier Highland Restaurant (U.S. 2, 406/888-5427, www.glacierhighland.com, 7:30am-10pm daily July-Aug., off-season days and hours vary, $13-33) is an authentic West Glacier diner experience. Located just before the entrance to the park and across from the Amtrak depot, this is an easy stop if you are craving a 5-ounce (142-g) burger with all the toppings and fresh-cut fries. Hearty homemade soups and a variety of delicious sweet treats, baked each day in the bakery, are also on offer.

For breakfast and lunch with outdoor seating options in Apgar Village, Eddie's Café & Mercantile (1 Fish Creek Rd., 406/888-5361, www.eddiescafegifts.com, 7:00am-9pm daily summer, $16-25) serves up excellent grub including steak and eggs, breakfast burritos, buffalo burgers, and fried chicken.

The closest restaurant to the entrance at West Glacier is the West Glacier Restaurant (200 Going-to-the-Sun Rd., 406/888-5359, 7am-9pm daily mid-May-Sept., $8-18). Set in a classic Park Service-like building, the restaurant offers casual dining with homemade soups, burgers, sandwiches, and yummy baked goods. An attached bar has a selection of liquor, wine, and beer, not to mention sports on satellite TV for those who are so inclined.

A long ways down a dirt road in Glacier's North Fork Valley is a special off-the-grid spot that is worth every bump and then some. The remote and wonderful Polebridge Mercantile (265 Polebridge Loop, 406/888-5105, www.polebridgemercantile.com, 7am-9pm daily Memorial Day-Labor Day, 9am-6pm daily Labor Day-Thanksgiving and mid-Apr.-Memorial Day, 10am-5pm Fri.-Sun. Jan.-late Mar., $3.50-7.25) offers world-class baked goods—don't leave without at least a couple of huckleberry bear claws—sandwiches, soups, and other goodies in addition to groceries and gifts. Lodging is also available.

ACCOMMODATIONS

The West Glacier area has a good selection of places to stay, but once inside the park, or even within view of it, accommodations do not come cheap. If you are on a tight budget, camping is the best option. The hotels listed are only open during the summer season, when Glacier is busiest. However, for avid cross-country skiers who want to take advantage of the park during the winter, the **Izaak Walton Inn** (off U.S. 2, Essex, between East Glacier and West Glacier, 406/888-5700, www.izaakwaltoninn. com, $159-409), a charming old railroad hotel that is on the National Register of Historic Places, is open year-round. In addition to homey rooms in the lodge, guests can select from unique accommodations including family cabins and restored railcars.

Also in Essex, 20 miles (32 km) from West Glacier and 35 miles (56 km) from East Glacier, is **Glacier Haven Inn & Healthy Haven Café** (14305 U.S. 2 E., 406/888-5720, www.glacierhaveninn.com, $99 cabins without bathrooms, $169-349 lodge rooms and cabins with full bath and kitchen), which offers clean, comfy accommodations in addition to great home-style cooking.

A reasonably priced motel in the West Glacier area is the **Apgar Village Lodge & Cabins** (Lake View Dr., West Glacier, 406/888-5484 or 844/868-7474, www. glacierparkcollection.com, $82-323), 2 miles (3.2 km) east of West Glacier village at the south end of Lake McDonald. There are 28 cabins that sleep up to eight with Western decor, most with kitchens with stoves and refrigerators, and each with its own picnic table. Ask for a cabin on McDonald Creek; you can literally fish from your front door. There are also 20 modestly furnished, clean motel rooms, some overlooking the creek, with either a queen or two twin beds.

On the shores of Lake McDonald, the **Village Inn at Apgar** (1.3 mi/2.1 km from the entrance at West Glacier, 855/733-4522, www. glaciernationalparklodges.com, $171-279) is a quaint, 1950s motor inn that is listed on the National Register of Historic Places.

West Glacier Motel & Cabins (200 Going-to-the-Sun Rd., West Glacier, 844/868-7474, www.glacierparkcollection. com, motel rooms from $129, cabins from $159) is divided between two properties— half the motel units are about 1 mile (1.6 km) from the park entrance in West Glacier, and the cabins and other motel units are on a secluded bluff that overlooks the Flathead River. It's a great value for the price and location. Pets are not allowed. The cabins on the bluff require a minimum stay of two nights and offer kitchenettes but no air-conditioning or television.

Also in West Glacier, just across the street from the Amtrak depot, is the **Glacier Highland Resort** (12555 U.S. 2 E., 406/888-5427, www.glacierhighland. com, May-Oct., $128-176), which offers 33 clean, simple rooms.

If you are willing to spend a bit more, there are two historic lodges that are worth a night's stay. **Lake McDonald Lodge** (Going-to-the-Sun Rd., 12 miles (19.3 km) from West Glacier, 855/733-4522, www. glaciernationalparklodges.com, $113-364) was built in 1914 by the furrier John Lewis and adheres to the Swiss chalet-style of architecture. Though the lodge and cabins are showing their age, they still outshine the 1950s motor inn on-site. The 82-room lodge emanates rustic charm and still has personal touches, such as Lewis's hunting trophies displayed in the lobby. Built before there were roads running through Glacier, visitors arrived at the lodge by boat, and the hotel's original entrance faced the lake. Today most guests arrive by car, and the hotel is conveniently located off Going-to-the-Sun Road on the shore of Lake McDonald. Upon entering the lodge, visitors are struck by its warmth and charm. The spacious lobby is surrounded by balconies on three sides. Guests and visitors can enjoy sipping a cocktail on the sprawling veranda, a serene setting that affords a beautiful view of the lake. The guest rooms are rustic yet comfortable, and the location allows easy access to trailheads and boat tours. Fishing lessons and

Rooms in Glacier's historic lodges and chalets can already be full up to a year ahead, but spontaneous travelers are not necessarily out of luck. Last-minute cancellations and room openings are possible and well worth a couple of phone calls. **Glacier Park Inc.** (844/868-7474, www.glacierparkcollection.com) is the booking service for the Grouse Mountain Lodge, Glacier Park Lodge, St. Mary Village, Apgar Village Lodge & Cabins, Motel Lake McDonald, West Glacier Motel & Cabins, and Prince of Wales Hotel. Call and ask specifically for cancellations. You may have better luck if you are open to whatever they have to offer, but you just may get the property you were hoping for. Being flexible with your dates helps.

Glacier National Park Lodges (855/733-4522, www.glaciernationalparklodges.com) is the booking service for Cedar Creek Lodge, Many Glacier Hotel, Swiftcurrent Motor Inn & Cabins, Rising Sun Motor Inn & Cabins, Lake McDonald Lodge, and Village Inn at Apgar. In this case, too, a phone call to ask about cancellations can lead to a windfall.

view from Granite Park Chalet

For visitors willing to hike in to their accommodations, **Granite Park Chalet** (888/345-2649, www.graniteparkchalet.com, from $108 pp, $80 additional person in same room, optional linen and bedding service $20 pp) is a fantastic option and well worth a call to see if they have last-minute openings.

For true spontaneity, pitch a tent in one of Glacier's 1,000-plus campsites in 13 campgrounds, at least some of which are open May-mid-October. With the exception of St. Mary, Fish Creek, half the campsites at Many Glacier, and half the group sites at Apgar, all campgrounds are available on a first-come, first-served basis, with nightly fees of $10-23. An excellent page on the National Park Service website (www.nps.gov/glac) shows updated availability at campsites across the park, and even gives the time of day each campground was filled the day before. Apgar is the largest campground, with 194 sites, followed by Fish Creek (178 sites), St. Mary (146 sites), and Many Glacier (110 sites). For advance reservations no more than six months ahead of time at Fish Creek or St. Mary, contact the **National Park Reservation System** (877/444-6777, www.recreation.gov).

In the spirit of spontaneity, almost anything you need for your recreational purposes can be rented from **Glacier Outfitters** (196 Apgar Loop, 406/219-7466, www.goglacieroutfitters.com), from bear spray to camping gear.

day trips by horseback are available and can be arranged by the hotel.

The most memorable stay in West Glacier is at the family-owned ★ **Belton Chalet** (12575 U.S. 2 E., 406/888-5000 or 888/235-8665, www.beltonchalet.com, rooms $180-205, cottages $335) at the west entrance to the park. This was the first hotel built by the Great Northern Railway and dates to 1910. It was fully restored in 2000 and is a National Historic Landmark. Guests can experience a piece of history while enjoying modern amenities. All 25 guest rooms come with a queen bed and private bathroom and are beautifully furnished with antiques. The two cabins on the grounds each have three bedrooms to accommodate up to six people. Although the lodge is mostly closed during the winter season, the cabins are available to rent throughout the year. The hotel does not provide TVs, phones, or air-conditioning, as they can detract from the natural setting, but Wi-Fi is available at no charge. The lodge is immediately adjacent to both the highway and the train tracks, so silence is not possible. A fabulous restaurant on-site offers innovative and satisfying meals, and a fully stocked taproom specializes in Montana brews. You can enjoy a good book in the lobby's reading area, or curl up by the large stone fireplace. The incredibly friendly staff even offer wake-up calls for northern lights and bear sightings. Visitors looking for a bit of luxury, or relief for sore hiking muscles, will find a spa offering massages on-site. For an elegant vacation rental—complete with full kitchen, Wi-Fi, and flat-screen TV—the Belton's beautifully restored **Adobe House** is available off-site ($250-425 nightly with minimum stays required in high season and four-wheel drive necessary in low season).

CAMPING

Glacier has 13 front-country campgrounds with more than 1,000 sites, at least some of which are open May-mid-October. With the exception of St. Mary and Fish Creek, half the group sites at Apgar, and half the campsites at Many Glacier, all campgrounds are available on a first-come, first-served basis, with nightly fees ranging $10-23. You'll increase your chances of finding a site by showing up earlier in the day and scheduling your trip midweek rather than on the weekend. An excellent page on the National Park Service website (www.nps.gov/glac) shows updated availability at campsites across the park. **Apgar** ($20) is the largest campground, with 194 sites; followed by **Fish Creek** ($23), with 178 sites; **St. Mary** ($23), with 148 sites; and **Many Glacier** ($23) with 109 sites. For advance reservations at Fish Creek or St. Mary, contact the **National Park Reservation System** (877/444-6777, www.recreation.gov).

If your decision to camp is last-minute and you find yourself without such critical items as a tent or sleeping bag, **Glacier Outfitters** (196 Apgar Loop, 406/219-7466, www.goglacieroutfitters.com) can help with its stock of rentable items.

East Glacier Area

Located on the Blackfeet Indian Reservation at the southeast corner of the park, East Glacier (population 363; elevation 4,799 ft/1,463 m) has long been a primary entrance into Glacier National Park. Early visitors from the east often arrived by rail at East Glacier and spent the night in the grand Glacier Park Lodge before heading into the wilds of the park.

Today the town of East Glacier bustles year-round and is a hub of activity during the summer months as visitors stream in and out of the park. There are numerous accommodations, including the still-majestic Adirondack-style Glacier Park Lodge, several good restaurants, local outfitters, and a smattering of shops. There is also a tremendous amount of wilderness to be explored both inside the park and in immediate proximity to East Glacier. The stunning Two Medicine Valley is just a few miles away, and hiking, skiing, and even snowmobiling trails are within steps of the main drag.

SIGHTS
Two Medicine Valley

Geographically, Two Medicine Valley is not at the heart of Glacier, but this remote southeastern corner is staggeringly beautiful and seemingly less known among the mass of summer visitors. The rocky peaks and glacially carved valleys meet in clear alpine lakes, and the area offers plenty of activity. There are boat tours that intersect with hiking trails, numerous waterfalls to ogle, fishing, and a lovely campground.

Backcountry Camping

That Glacier National Park is a wild place cannot be overstated. Backcountry camping in this wild and potentially dangerous place requires thoughtful planning and meticulous attention to the rules and regulations. A strong dose of common sense can go a long way. Backcountry campers have to be smart about orientation, wildlife encounters, rapidly changing and adverse weather, and stream and snowfield crossings, all of which can be potentially deadly. Here is a list of simple but critical guidelines and etiquette for backcountry travel.

- **Make a plan and chart your route.** Carefully examine elevation gain and loss. Carrying a heavy pack more than 10 miles (16.1 km) in a day with a 2,500-foot (762-m) elevation change is an extremely ambitious and perhaps overly rigorous endeavor. Topographical maps and hiking guides are available at park visitors centers and ranger stations as well as online through the **Glacier National Park Conservancy** (www.glacier.org). Make sure you are aware of trail and campsite closures, fire restrictions, weather forecasts, local bear activity, and so on. Glacier offers an excellent online trip planner at www.nps.gov/glac.

- **Secure all your permits.** All backcountry campers must camp in established campsites and have a backcountry-use permit ($7 pp per night) for the duration of the trip. Campsites can be reserved in advance when you apply for the permit, or within 24 hours of the trip. Application forms can be downloaded (www.nps.gov/glac), but are accepted starting March 15 online only, and cost $40, not including the $7 per person per night camping fee, which must be paid in person when you pick up the permit. Permits must be picked up at one of five permit-issuing stations (St. Mary Visitor Center, Many Glacier Ranger Station, Two Medicine Ranger Station, Polebridge Ranger Station, and Waterton Lakes National Park Visitor Reception Centre) no sooner than one day before the trip and no later than 4:30pm on the day of departure.

- **Pack intelligently.** All campers should be prepared for a dramatic range of weather conditions by packing appropriate footwear and layered clothing, rain jacket and pants, and footwear for crossing streams. Other items to remember when packing include an appropriate amount of low-odor food, a tent and sleeping bag with pad, a compass and topographical maps, a first-aid kit, weatherproof food and garbage bags, 25 feet (7.6 m) of rope to hang bags, a water container and purifying system, a camp stove and fuel, an emergency signaling device, and a trowel. Bear spray is an absolute necessity.

- **Obey all rules and practice the seven principles of Leave No Trace.** Plan ahead and prepare, travel and camp on durable surfaces, leave what you find, properly dispose of waste, minimize campfire impacts, respect wildlife, and be considerate of other visitors. The goal anytime you are in the backcountry is to use your skills and be motivated by an ethic of responsibility for the natural resource, taking care of it conscientiously.

For visitors seeking the backcountry experience without all the preparatory work, guided trips can be arranged through **Glacier Guides** (406/387-5555 or 800/521-7238, www.glacierguides.com), and equipment can be rented from **Glacier Outfitters** (196 Apgar Loop, 406/219-7466, www.goglacieroutfitters.com).

SPORTS AND RECREATION
Hiking

More of a stroll than a hike, the trail to **Running Eagle Falls** is 0.6 mile (1 km) round-trip, kid-friendly, and wheelchair-accessible. The waterfall is interesting, as it changes from a double fall in spring and early summer to a single one by late summer; it appears to emerge from within the rock wall. The trailhead for this easy but scenic hike is on the park road roughly 1 mile (1.6 km) west of the Two Medicine entrance.

One particularly exquisite, and perhaps nostalgic, way to explore Glacier is by combining a boat ride with a hike. An excellent place to do so is in the Two Medicine Valley. The **Glacier Park Boat Company**

(406/257-2426, www.glacierparkboats.com,
$13.75 adults, $6.50 children 4-12, free for
children under 4) offers 45-minute cruises,
with optional guided hikes, from the Two
Medicine Lake boat dock to the far end of the
lake, cutting 6 miles (9.7 km) off the hike to
Twin Falls and **Upper Two Medicine Lake.**
It's backcountry hiking without the blisters.
From the upper (unloading) dock, the hike
to Twin Falls is just 0.9 mile (1.4 km), and an
additional 2.2 miles (3.5 km) to the gorgeous
upper lake. **No Name Lake,** at the base of
the sheer Pumpelly Pillar, is another spectacular hike made easier with a boat shuttle.
Instead of 5 miles (8 km) one-way, with the
boat it is 2.2 miles (3.5 km) with an 800-foot
(244 m) elevation gain. For those looking to
put more miles on their feet, there are trails
on either side of Two Medicine Lake, making a variety of loops possible. Farther north
of Two Medicine, the **Cut Bank Trailhead**
offers fantastic hiking with even fewer visitors—perfect for solitude seekers.

Bicycling

There aren't many places in the country where
you can hop on a bike, head to the nearest highway, and pedal through spectacular
scenery in every direction. Although the inclines can be steep and the declines precipitous around East Glacier, the air is fresh and
the mountain vistas unrivaled. The traffic—
human and animal—needs to be minded.

For avid cyclists, it's possible to do a 137-
mile (221-km) loop in and around the park:
Head southwest from East Glacier on U.S. 2
to West Glacier, then over Going-to-the-Sun
Road to St. Mary, then south on U.S. 89 and
Highway 49 back to East Glacier. Remember
that eastbound Going-to-the-Sun Road is
closed to cyclists from Logan Creek to Logan
Pass, 11am-4pm daily June 15-Labor Day,
so plan accordingly. In the vicinity of East
Glacier, biking to the Two Medicine Valley,
12 miles (19.3 km) northwest of town, is also
a popular route.

The closest place from which to rent
bicycles is the west side of the park, at

Apgar Village, from **Glacier Outfitters**
(196 Apgar Loop, 406/219-7466, www.
goglacieroutfitters.com).

Golf

Somewhat surprisingly, the **Glacier Park
Lodge** (U.S. 2 and Hwy. 49, 406/226-5642
or 406/892-2525, www.glacierparkcollection.
com, late-May-Sept. as weather permits, $40
for 9 holes with cart) has a unique nine-hole
golf course. Built in 1928 by Great Northern
Railway tycoon James J. Hill, the course is the
oldest grass course in Montana and permits
soft spikes only. The course was originally
named Oom-coo-ska-pes-che (Big Green
Blanket) by Chief Earl Old Person. It was designed by a New York architect, but because
the course was built within the boundaries
of the Blackfeet Indian Reservation, each of
the holes is named after a former chief of the
Blackfeet Nation. Clubs, carts, and pull carts
can be rented from the pro shop. A pitch-and-
putt course is on-site as well.

Horseback Riding

For horseback riding outside the park on
the Blackfeet Indian Reservation, **Glacier
Gateway Trailrides** (Hwy. 49, across from
the Glacier Park Lodge, 406/226-4408, off-
season 406/338-5560, $35-190 pp) offers ex-
cellent guided rides through magnificent
country June-September. Trips range from
one hour to full-day excursions; children
must be at least seven years old. The guides
are Native Americans, who offer a unique cultural perspective on places like Looking Glass
and Two Medicine River Gorge.

Boating

As on the west side of the park, the **Glacier
Park Boat Company** (406/257-2426, www.
glacierparkboats.com, tours $13.75 adults,
$6.75 children 4-12, free for children under
4) is the ultimate resource. Rowboats can
be rented for $18 per hour and fishing mo-
torboats for $23 per hour, and guided tours
are available on the company's fleet of classic
wooden launches. Excellent 45-minute cruises

on Two Medicine Lake take place at least four times daily mid-June-early September. The 2.5-hour guided hike to Twin Falls can be added at no extra cost.

FOOD

For a town with just over 300 year-round residents, East Glacier has a number of good restaurants that cater to Glacier-bound visitors. Often the best way to select a spot to eat is to walk around and see where the wait is shortest. **Serrano's Mexican Restaurant** (29 Dawson Ave., 406/226-9392, www.serranosmexican. com, 5pm-9pm daily May 1-Memorial Day and Labor Day-early Oct., 5pm-10pm daily Memorial Day-Labor Day, $11-20) is inside the oldest house in East Glacier. Nothing is old-fashioned, however, about the menu: There are classic and delicious Mexican favorites alongside local offerings that include Indian tacos and huckleberry carrot cake. A selection of American plates, including chicken, steaks, and burgers, is available too. The food here is good, and the atmosphere is quite festive. The fact that it's been in business for more than 25 years means something in this part of the world. As an aside, the on-site **Backpacker's Inn** offers nightly hostel-type lodging starting at $20 and private cabins starting at $50.

Two Medicine Grill (314 U.S. 2 E., 406/226-9227, www.seeglacier.com, 6:30am-9pm daily summer, 6:30am-8pm daily winter, breakfast $5-10, lunch $8-11, dinner $8-15) is a great spot for budget travelers. The menu has pretty standard fare for the region—bison burgers, homemade chili, chicken-fried steak—but the quality is excellent, and the staff are friendly and generous with advice and insights on the area. The huckleberry shakes are the stuff of legend, as is the double-crusted huckleberry pie.

Getting rave reviews from locals and tourists alike is **Summit Mountain Lodge Steakhouse** (16900 U.S. 2, 406/226-9319, www.summitmtnlodge.com, 5pm-9pm

---

1: Two Medicine Lake 2: hikers in Two Medicine Valley

Tues.-Sun., $19-38) housed in an old train station with a beautiful outside dining area. The food is marvelous and locally sourced whenever possible. There is a good wine list, and pairing suggestions are offered. Entrées include saltimbocca, grilled beef tenderloin, wild prawns piccata and a variety of salads and pasta. You could eat dirt on a summer night, with a view like this, and be happy. But luckily, you don't have to.

ACCOMMODATIONS

East Glacier has several small, kitschy motels that are ideal for a night or two before heading into the park, but they are not well suited for a week's stay. The standout alternative is the stately ★ **Glacier Park Lodge** (U.S. 2 and Hwy. 49, 844/868-7474, www. glacierparkcollection.com, late May-late Sept., $159-499), which opened to guests in 1913. An Adirondack-style hotel commissioned by the Great Northern Railway, it was constructed of massive fir and cedar timbers, each weighing at least 15 tons. The local Blackfeet who watched the structure go up called it *omah-koyis,* or "big-tree lodge." The grounds are beautifully manicured—there's even a historic and very playable golf course in addition to a pitch-and-putt. The 161-room hotel offers fine and casual dining, a cocktail lounge, a gift shop, an outdoor swimming pool, and a day spa. The rooms are modest but comfortable. Travelers with children will appreciate the family rooms with multiple beds. Although the setting at the edge of East Glacier village is not quite as captivating, the Glacier Park Lodge is certainly in the same class as the Lake McDonald Lodge and even the Old Faithful Lodge in Yellowstone National Park.

Slightly off the main drag is the tidy and comfortable **Mountain Pine Motel** (909 Hwy. 49, 1 mi/1.6 km north of U.S. 2, 406/226-4403, www.mtnpine.com, May-Sept., $102-180), with 25 units and relatively modern amenities.

The **Whistling Swan Motel** (314 U.S. 2, 406/226-4412, www.seeglacier.com, $89-149 motel rooms, $169-249 cabins) is a long, skinny building that feels a bit like train cars—somewhat appropriate given that the Amtrak station is just across the street. The guest rooms are spotlessly clean and quite comfortable. Hosts Mark and Colleen are exceptionally hospitable and go out of their way to make every guest feel welcome and accommodated. This motel is also within easy walking distance of the local eateries and shops.

Another clean, comfortable lodging option right in town is the **Sears Motel** (1023 Hwy. 49 N., 406/226-4432, June-mid-Sept., $118-138). In addition to its 16 rooms, the motel also offers campsites for both tent campers and RVs.

The **East Glacier Motel & Cabins** (1107 Hwy. 49, 406/226-5593, www. eastglaciermotel.com, June-July 1 $118-188, July 2-Aug. 15 $138-238) offers six motel units and 11 cabins at an excellent value.

On the east side of town, offering cute, park-style cabins complete with kitchenettes, gas fireplaces, and covered front porches, **Traveler's Rest Lodge** (20987 U.S. 2, 406/226-9143 summer or 406/378-2414 winter, www.travelersrestlodge.net, Apr. 15-Oct. 1, $129-160) is a great choice.

Two miles (3.2 km) west of town on what used to be a dude ranch is **Bison Creek Ranch** (20722 U.S. 2, 406/226-4482, www. bisoncreekranch.com, $89-140), a bed-and-breakfast offering simple sleeping cabins and larger A-frames. The same family has been pouring heart and soul into the ranch for more than 60 years, and it shows in every detail from the artwork to the meals to the housekeeping. The breakfasts—from cinnamon rolls and huckleberry pancakes to crepes—are excellent.

A few miles from town is **Summit Mountain Lodge** (16900 U.S. 2, 406/226-9319, www.summitmtnlodge.com, 5pm-9pm Tues.-Sun., from $159), which offers eight cabins with modern amenities. Single cabins have one queen bed and a full kitchenette. Double units have two queen beds and a living area. There are also family cabins ($285) that sleep six. The setting and the views are world-class. And the on-site steak house, housed in an old train station, is a special place for a memorable meal.

If you are willing to hike in to your accommodations, **Granite Park Chalet** (888/345-2649, www.graniteparkchalet.com, from $108 pp, $80 each additional person, optional linen and bedding service $20 pp) is a fantastic option. The last of the railroad chalets to be built, Granite Park Chalet is a hiker's hostel geared toward do-it-yourselfers. The rooms are private; hikers prepare their own meals and, although linens can be ordered ahead of time, generally sleep in their own sleeping bags. The most popular trail in to Granite Park is the 7.6-mile (12.2-km) Highline Trail, accessed from Logan Pass. A shorter 4-mile (6.4-km) trail through burned country and with a steep 2,300-foot (701-m) climb can be accessed from Going-to-the-Sun Road switchback known as The Loop.

CAMPING

Less than 20 miles (32 km) from East Glacier are a couple of scenic and shady campgrounds. Set on the lake, **Two Medicine Campground** (mid-May-late Sept., $20), with 100 sites and 10 RV sites, is 13 miles (20.9 km) outside town in some of Glacier's most breathtaking wilderness. It is well developed with potable water and flush toilets, an amphitheater for nightly ranger presentations, and one of the original Great Northern Chalets, which has been converted into a camp store and gift shop. Outside the regular season, primitive camping ($10) is possible late September-late October. Shuttle service, boat tours, and Red Bus Tours are all available from the campground. Sites are available on a first-come, first-served basis, and hiking in the area is as limitless as it is sublime.

Farther north is a smaller (14 sites) and more secluded spot, **Cut Bank Campground** (June-Aug. 23, $10), accessed 5 miles (8 km) down a dirt road from U.S. 89. The campground has no water, so campers have to bring their own. Sites are available on a first-come, first-served basis, and day hikes in the area are top-notch. RVs are not recommended due to the nature of the road and the campground layout. Shuttles are only available from the highway.

St. Mary to Many Glacier

This place feels like it's at the edge of two worlds: mountains to the west, vast plains to the east. St. Mary is a small village nestled between St. Mary Lake and Lower St. Mary Lake that marks another entrance to the park and the start of Going-to-the-Sun Road. With all the splendor of the jagged peaks and the wide-open vistas created by sparse stands of aspen and sweeping prairie, the recreational opportunities are abundant and the scenery spectacular.

Farther north, Many Glacier is the ideal base camp for avid and active outdoors lovers, with extensive opportunities for hiking, canoeing, and horseback riding. The popular boat tours and Red Bus Tours are also accessible from Many Glacier. Grinnell Glacier is a dwindling but still phenomenal work of nature, and daily ranger-led hikes take visitors up to its toe. The Many Glacier Hotel is a historic 1915 Great Northern Railway Swiss chalet-style lodge that welcomes guests with a rambling veranda and cozy guest rooms.

SIGHTS

St. Mary Lake

One of the most photographed lakes in the park for its absurdly beautiful mountain backdrop, St. Mary Lake is among the best places in Glacier to watch the sun rise. The lake and its many hiking trails are accessible from Going-to-the-Sun Road. The **Sun Point Nature Trail** is 1.4 miles (2.3 km) round-trip, and the trailhead is 9.5 miles (15.3 km) west of the St. Mary Visitor Center. It is worth the short walk for views of Baring Falls and the lake itself. An even quicker stop is **Sunrift Gorge,** 0.6 mile (1 km) west of Sun Point, an incredible cascade slicing between two rock walls; it is just 200 feet (61 m) from the parking area. Baring Falls is another 0.3-mile (0.5-km) walk down the trail.

TOP EXPERIENCE

★ Many Glacier

The Many Glacier region is a palpable reminder of why Glacier has long been known as the Switzerland of America. Marked by

early morning at Swiftcurrent Lake

Many Glacier Region

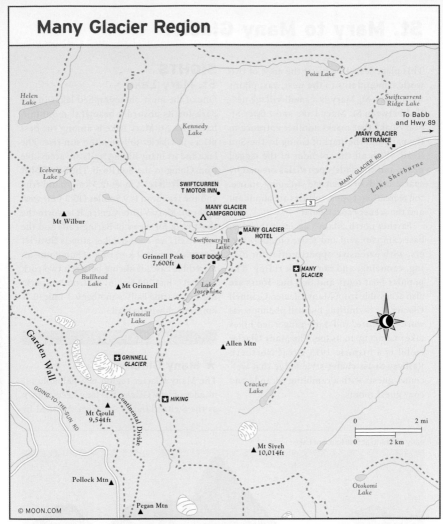

Poia Lake

Helen Lake

Swiftcurrent Ridge Lake

To Babb and Hwy 89 →

Kennedy Lake

MANY GLACIER ENTRANCE

MANY GLACIER RD

Lake Sherburne

Iceberg Lake

SWIFTCURRENT MOTOR INN

MANY GLACIER CAMPGROUND

3

Mt Wilbur

Swiftcurrent Lake

MANY GLACIER HOTEL

Grinnell Peak 7,600ft

BOAT DOCK

MANY GLACIER

Bullhead Lake

Mt Grinnell

Lake Josephine

Grinnell Lake

Allen Mtn

Garden Wall

GRINNELL GLACIER

GOING-TO-THE-SUN RD

Continental Divide

Cracker Lake

HIKING

Mt Gould 9,544ft

Mt Siyeh 10,014ft

0   2 mi

0   2 km

Pollock Mtn

Otokomi Lake

© MOON.COM

Pegan Mtn

grand accommodations and a landscape that was visibly scoured and carved by glaciers, from the U-shaped valleys and milky-blue glacial lakes to the rocky moraines and the last remaining glaciers themselves, this region is among the most dramatic and startlingly beautiful in the park.

This is not a place to be enjoyed from inside a car, although those on a tight schedule would still benefit from making the journey just to walk around the hotel to drink in the stunning surroundings. Many Glacier is best suited for active travelers: The hiking and boating are exceptional, and it is one of the rare places in the Lower 48 where a day hike can lead you to an actual glacier. Come to Many Glacier to see the splendid scenery, but if possible, stay a few days to truly enjoy it.

★ Grinnell Glacier

Named for conservationist and explorer George Bird Grinnell, Grinnell Glacier lies in the heart of Many Glacier and is a symbol both of the park's wilderness and of the dramatic climatic changes that are occurring. Because the glacier is accessible within a day's hike, its startling shrinkage—from 710 acres (287.3 hectares) in 1850 to 220 acres (89 hectares) in 1993 and 152 acres (61.5 hectares) in 2005—has been captured on film. Still, as long as it exists, this glacier is well worth visiting.

The options for seeing the glacier up close and personal are to hoof it from the **Many Glacier Hotel** (5.5 mi/8.9 km one-way with a 1,600-ft/488-m elevation gain) or to take a boat across Lake Josephine with **Glacier Park Boat Company** (406/257-2426, www.glacierparkboats.com, $27.50 adults, $13.75 children 4-12, free for children under 4) and hike the remainder of the trail from the head of Lake Josephine (3.8 mi/6.1 km one-way with a 1,600-ft/488-m elevation gain). There is also an excellent ranger-guided hike to the glacier that makes use of the boat, leaving the Many Glacier dock daily at 8:30am starting in mid-July (weather and conditions permitting). The 8.5-mile (13.7-km) round-trip outing lasts almost nine hours. The trail twists and climbs above impossibly blue alpine lakes and within sight of the aptly named Salamander Glacier. In the early season, hikers will get wet with runoff from the overhanging waterfalls along the trail. Come prepared! Though the trail is one of the oldest and most popular hikes in the park, and thus heavily trafficked, wildlife is plentiful in the area too, and grizzly bears are commonly spotted on or near the trail. The trail often does not open until late July and is seldom clear of snow until well into August.

Upper Waterton Lake and Goat Haunt

You won't necessarily need your passport to see one of the natural highlights of Canada's Waterton Lakes National Park, although the fjord-like valley is reminiscent of Norway, especially when it is shrouded in fog and mist. Upper Waterton Lake runs north-south, straddling the border. Boats run between the Canadian town of Waterton (headquarters for the park) and **Goat Haunt** at the lake's southern end, accessible only by hiking or by boat.

On the Canadian side, **Crypt Lake Trail** (10.8 mi/17.4 km round-trip) is an ambitious hike that includes a natural tunnel through a rock wall, stomach-dropping heights, waterfalls galore, and a dazzling hidden cirque. There are several hikes, ranging from mellow to death-defying, from the Goat Haunt ranger station, and several ranger-led hikes daily in summer. A few favorites are **Rainbow Falls** (2 mi/3.2 km round-trip, no elevation gain), **Kootenai Lakes** (5 mi/8 km round-trip, 200-ft/61-m elevation gain), **Lake Janet** (6.6 mi/10.6 km round-trip, 750-ft/229-m elevation gain), and **Lake Francis** (12.4 mi/20 km round-trip, 1,050-ft/320-m elevation gain). For those willing to huff and puff, but only briefly, **Goat Haunt Overlook** (2 mi/3.2 km round-trip, 800-ft/244-m elevation gain) offers a phenomenal view of the valley. The isolation and lack of roads tends to keep visitor numbers down around Upper Waterton Lake, but the mosquitoes are abundant; come prepared.

SPORTS AND RECREATION
Hiking

One could quite literally spend a lifetime hiking in the St. Mary, Many Glacier, and Upper Waterton Lake region. For a close-up look at a couple of stunning waterfalls in the St. Mary area, head to the **St. Mary Falls** trailhead, just west of Sunrift Gorge. The trail is just 0.8 mile (1.3 km) one-way, with a 260-foot (79.3-m) elevation drop, to St. Mary Falls, and another 0.7 mile (1.1 km) one-way, with a 285-foot (86.9-m) elevation gain, to the taller **Virginia Falls,** making a relatively easy and lovely 3-mile (4.8-km) round-trip hike.

For bear-savvy hikers with a penchant for floating ice, **Iceberg Lake** is an extraordinary day hike. The trail, 5 miles (8 km)

Waterton Lakes: Glacier's Canadian Sister

Just north of Glacier, across the Canadian border in the southwest corner of Alberta, lies Waterton Lakes National Park. Similar in terrain to Glacier, the park is much smaller (about 203 sq mi/525.8 sq km compared to Glacier's 1,600 sq mi/4,144 sq km) and houses a small town, Waterton Park, within its borders. Like its neighbor to the south, the stunning landscape of this park was formed by melting alpine glaciers more than 10,000 years ago and later shaped by floods, fires, wind, and its natural wildlife and flora.

Before European settlement, various nomadic groups of indigenous people passed through the area, gathering plants and hunting local wildlife. The most prominent in the area were the Kootenai, who eventually clashed with the Blackfeet that had followed the buffalo into Alberta and taken control of the plains. In 1858 the English explorer Thomas Blakiston was looking for a railroad pass through the Rockies. He encountered some members of the local Kootenai tribe, who directed him to a pass in the south. Traversing this path, he eventually came to an opening that looked on a chain of three lakes. He named the lakes after fellow British explorer and naturalist Charles Waterton, known to be quite eccentric. It became a national park in 1895, and the Great Northern Railway established the Prince of Wales Hotel in 1926, helping put the park on the map for tourists traveling from Glacier to Banff and Jasper in Alberta.

The star of Waterton's lakes is **Upper Waterton Lake,** situated on the U.S.-Canada border. It is the deepest lake in the Canadian Rockies and can be explored on a two-hour cruise that leaves from the Waterton marina and dips down into Montana before venturing back. If you have the time, you can disembark from the boat to follow the **Crypt Lake Trail,** considered one of the best hikes in Canada. Numerous trails around the lake lead past waterfalls, through valleys, and on to spectacular vistas.

Arguably one of the most photographed hotels in the world for its sublime setting, the **Prince of Wales Hotel** (Alberta 5, Waterton Park, 844/868-7474, www.glacierparkcollection.com) is a magnificent Swiss chalet-inspired lodge that overlooks the lake and the town below. Although pricey, it is a great place to stay to have the full Waterton experience. If a night's stay is not in your budget, try to stop in for high tea, which is served daily in the hotel lobby.

During the summer of 2017, two major wildfires roared through Glacier and Waterton Lakes National Parks. The Sprague Fire burned roughly 17,000 acres (6,880 hectares), primarily in Glacier's backcountry. The Kenow Fire burned more than 47,500 acres (19,223 hectares) in Waterton Lakes, blackening entire valleys and altering the landscape for decades to come. The slopes on both sides of the Akamina Highway were burned and are visible to tourists. It's worth remembering that fire is a critical part of the ecosystem here; many species of trees rely on fire to reseed. So even though the scars are prominent, healthy regrowth is happening already and provides visitors a unique lens into the forces of nature here.

As you enter the town on the Waterton highway, the **Visitors Reception Centre** (403/859-5133) is on the right. It is open early May-mid-October and can provide you with plenty of information on the region. Construction on a new visitors center is expected to begin in 2019. During the off-season, the park's operations building (403/859-2224), located next to the visitors center, provides visitor information and assistance.

one-way, with a 1,300-foot (396-m) elevation gain, is well traveled by hikers of the two-legged variety, but it also has one of the densest concentrations of grizzly bears in the park thanks to an abundance of huckleberries. Bear encounters are not uncommon, and no overnight camping is allowed. The well-marked trailhead is found at the very end of Many Glacier Road, the only road in this section of the park.

The lake itself is a sublime glacial blue with chunks of ice floating in it, often as late as September, but the chunks are bigger and more plentiful in July-August. The elevation is gained slowly, except for a short steep stretch at the beginning, which is enough to turn some hikers around, and passes through meadows bursting with wildflowers. Mountain goats and bighorn sheep are often visible on the last stretch of the hike. Ptarmigan Falls is halfway to the lake—a perfect resting spot. The bridge over Iceberg Creek is erected each summer and taken down each fall to prevent it washing out in spring. Most mornings in July-August, hikers can join a ranger-led hike to the lake, an especially good option for those with more than a healthy fear of bears.

It's always a good idea in Glacier, and this area in particular, to have a backup plan in place for trail closures, which are exceedingly common here due to bears, other wildlife, and trail conditions.

Boating

Boats are permitted on St. Mary Lake, but you'll have to bring your own as there are no rentals on-site. There are 90-minute tours available several times daily through the **Glacier Park Boat Company** (406/257-2426, www.glacierparkboats.com, $27.50 adults, $13.75 children 4-12, free for children under 4). The tours depart from the Rising Sun boat dock, 6 miles (9.7 km) inside the east entrance on Going-to-the-Sun Road,

and offer views of various waterfalls, Sexton Glacier, and Wild Goose Island. A 15-minute walk to Baring Falls is also an option on the St. Mary Lake cruise. Twice daily, the cruises can be combined with a guided hike to St. Mary Falls (less than 2 miles (3.2 km) round-trip, 200-ft/61-m elevation gain) for a 3.5-hour outing.

In the Many Glacier area, rowboats ($18/hour), kayaks ($15/hour), and canoes ($18/hour) are available to rent at **Swiftcurrent Lake,** adjacent to the Many Glacier Hotel. The **Glacier Park Boat Company** (406/257-2426, www.glacierparkboats.com, $27.50 adults, $13.75 children 4-12, free for children under 4) also provides a number of scenic cruises on Swiftcurrent Lake and Lake Josephine. There are up to seven trips daily during summer, and cruises can be combined with guided hikes or used as a shuttle for hiking trips. A highlight for many is seeing the Grinnell Glacier on a cruise across Lake Josephine.

Fishing

While fishing permits or licenses are not necessary in Glacier National Park, it is imperative that anyone fishing abides by the regulations. A brochure can be picked up at any of the visitors centers or downloaded from

touring Swiftcurrent Lake

the **National Park Service website** (www. nps.gov/glac).

Because of the altitude in Glacier, the water is colder, and some of the lakes in the park are sterile. St. Mary Lake is not especially productive water, but it sure is nice to stand in and soak up the scenery. There are some rainbow trout, brook trout, whitefish, and the rare bull trout populations in the lake for the patient angler. Shore fishing is possible, but the chances for catching increase significantly out in the deeper waters. St. Mary Lake can get rough quickly, with 2- to 3-foot (0.6-0.9 m) swells, so keep a constant eye on the conditions.

In Many Glacier, presumably because of its proximity to the hotel and the road, the trout in crystal clear **Swiftcurrent Lake** see the most action, but they seem to have wised up. Brook trout in the 10-inch (25-cm) range are the most common catches here. **Lake Josephine** and **Grinnell Lake** have brook trout populations that seem more willing to take the bait or go for flies.

There are some backcountry lakes worth hiking into if fishing is the goal. **Red Rock Lake,** located along Swiftcurrent Creek, for example, is accessible by a fairly level 2-mile (3.2-km) hike and holds plenty of brook trout in the 10- to 12-inch (31-cm) range. Dry-fly anglers will do best in the morning or evening, but will have to go deep in the afternoons.

FOOD

Without a doubt, the fanciest (and priciest!) place to go for a meal in St. Mary is the **Snowgoose Grille** (844/868-7474, www. glacierparkcollection.com, 7am-10pm daily late May-late Sept., $18-40) in the St. Mary Village. This slightly modern take on the Western steak house offers porterhouse pork chop, bison stroganoff and elk sausage gnocci. There are also plenty of vegetarian options for both lunch and dinner. The adjacent **Curly Bear Café** is primarily a sandwich and ice-cream joint. Outside seating is available and highly desirable when the weather cooperates. **Two Dog Flats Grill** (1380

Wisconsin Ave., 855/733-4522, www. glaciernationalparklodges.com, 6:30am-10am and 11am-10pm daily, $10-26) at the Rising Sun Motor Inn & Cabins is operated by Glacier National Park Lodges. It offers standard fare, from burgers and chicken to steak and pasta, and is open for three meals daily during the season. Basic boxed lunches are available with no substitutions.

The nearby ★ **Park Café** (U.S. 89 and Going-to-the-Sun Rd., 406/732-9979, www. parkcafe.us, 8am-7pm daily early June-mid-June, 7:30am-9pm June 20-Aug., 8am-7pm daily Sept. 1-mid-Sept., $14-22), in St. Mary, is staffed by people who know and really love Glacier National Park. The pies—nine flavors daily—are mouthwatering and worth every mile on the trail you'll need to work them off. The food is mostly American, from steaks and fish to outrageous baked potatoes, and for the most part as healthy as it is inventive and delicious. There's also a fantastic gift store and grocery on-site. This place should not be missed!

Up the road in Babb is the ★ **Two Sisters Café** (U.S. 89, 4 mi/6.4 km north of St. Mary, 406/732-5535, www. twosistersofmontana.com, 11am-9pm daily June-Sept., $8-29), a colorful place that is worth the scenic drive along Lower St. Mary Lake. Although the decor is rather outrageous, the food is sublime—a hiker's dream come true. Try a Red Burger and a slice of homemade huckleberry pie.

For those not cooking their own supper over a fire pan in Many Glacier, there are only a few options. The **Ptarmigan Dining Room** (Many Glacier Hotel, 855/733-4522, www.glaciernationalparklodges.com, 6:30am-10am, 11:30am-2:30pm, and 5pm-9:30pm daily mid-June-mid-Sept., $20-44) offers such flavorful entrées as Rocky Mountain trout, a variety of salads, bison tenderloin, Alaska salmon, and more. Lighter fare, including appetizers, burgers, salads, and cocktails, are available in its **Swiss Lounge** (11:30am-10pm daily, drinks until 11pm, $11-21).

In the nearby Swiftcurrent Motor Inn &

Cabins is a casual eatery, **'Nell's** (855/733-4522, www.glaciernationalparklodges.com, 6:30am-10am and 11am-10pm daily mid-June-mid-Sept., $10-21). It serves standard fare for three meals daily including pizza, pasta, and chicken, all of which can taste outstanding after a long day on the trail. Boxed lunches are available when ordered a day ahead.

ACCOMMODATIONS

Although options abound in both St. Mary and Many Glacier for hotels, motels, and cabins, there are not many budget-friendly choices. The prices seem to reflect the scenery, which is spectacular, rather than the amenities, which can be quite modest. Campgrounds and RV parks are more common, but small cabins can be found as well. The **Cottages at Glacier** (106 West Shore Dr., St. Mary, 855/684-3402, www.nationalparkreservations.com, late May-late Sept., from $250) offer views of St. Mary Lake and comfortable two-bedroom accommodations with a steep price tag. Still, for those who want a full kitchen, Wi-Fi, and satellite TV, these cottages are excellent. In nearby Babb, about 2 miles (3.2 km) north of St. Mary, the **Glacier Trailhead Cabins** (U.S. 89,

406/732-4143, www.glaciertrailheadcabins.com, mid-May-mid-Oct., $179-398) offers clean, modern cabins in a quiet setting without TVs or phones. If you can get a cabin here, you will not be disappointed with the amenities, the location, or the rate. In business for more than 70 years, the **St. Mary Village** (U.S. 89 and Going-to-the-Sun Rd., 844/868-7474, www.glacierparkcollection.com, mid-June-late Sept., from $99) is a full resort with all the modern amenities. From tipis to cabins to luxury lodge rooms, this resort has 127 guest rooms among six facilities.

Adjacent to St. Mary Lake is the 1940s-era **Rising Sun Motor Inn & Cabins** (Going-to-the-Sun Rd., 855/733-4522, www.glaciernationalparklodges.com, mid-June-early Sept., $165-177), offering simple, clean, motel-style rooms and on-site dining.

In Many Glacier, the standout is clearly the **Many Glacier Hotel** (855/753-4522, www.glaciernationalparklodges.com, mid-June-mid-Sept., $207-476), a historic Swiss chalet-style lodge built in 1915 by the Great Northern Railway. The hotel is right on the shore of Swiftcurrent Lake, and there is no limit to the natural beauty of the region or the number of ways in which to enjoy it. The hotel is being refurbished, wing by wing, but

camping at Many Glacier

the rooms are still simple and charming; the steep prices speak more to the hotel's setting in the Many Glacier Valley than its amenities. There are no televisions in the rooms and the Wi-Fi is extremely limited. There is nightly entertainment and a wealth of activities that include boat cruises, ranger-led hikes, evening programs, Red Bus Tours, and horseback riding from the lodge.

Nearby, the **Swiftcurrent Motor Inn & Cabins** (855/753-4522, www. glaciernationalparklodges.com, mid-June-mid-Sept., $102-177) is decidedly less grandiose and equally less expensive. But this place also has a history; it was established as a tipi camp in 1911 by the Great Northern Railway. Three main lodgings are available: motel rooms, duplex-type cottages, and one-bedroom cabins without private baths. It has its own charm as a longtime stopping point for adventurers and road-trippers, and the location cannot be beat. For the price, it is an excellent place to stay.

CAMPING

Two park campgrounds are available near the village of St. Mary. **St. Mary Campground** (www.recreation.gov, $23) has 148 sites, including 22 sites that can accommodate RVs and truck-trailer combinations up to 35 feet (10.7 m), as well as water and flush toilets. It is the park's largest campground, only 0.5 mile (0.8 km) from the St. Mary Visitor Center, and has limited shade but superb views. The regular season is late May-mid-September, but primitive camping ($10) is available early April-late May and mid-September-November. Winter camping is also possible December-March. Sites can be reserved up to six months in advance for June 1-the first Sunday in September online at www.recreation.gov.

The second is **Rising Sun** (www.recreation.gov, mid-June-early-Sept., $20), which has 84 sites with 10 sites for RVs, water, flush toilets, and showers. It is halfway along St. Mary Lake in the shadow of Red Eagle Mountain. Some sites are exposed, while others are tucked into the trees. All are available on a first-come, first-served basis.

Not far from the Many Glacier Hotel, the **Many Glacier Campground** ($23) has 109 sites, including 13 sites for RVs up to 35 feet (10.7 m), as well as water, flush toilets, and showers available at the nearby Swiftcurrent Motor Inn & Cabins. The regular season is late May-late September, but primitive camping ($10) is available late September-October. Half the sites can be reserved (www.recreation.gov) in advance mid-June-September 4, and the others fill up on a first-come, first-served basis. The views are phenomenal, and the access to hiking and boating is amazing. Arguably the most popular campground in the park, Many Glacier fills up early, so plan accordingly.

Missoula and Western Montana

From the towering pines and massive cedars to the mountain of huckleberry ice cream clinging to your cone, just about everything is larger than life in western Montana.

The region is home to three Native American tribes on one major reservation, an assortment of wildlife refuges, and enticing towns such as Missoula and Whitefish. The craggy Mission Mountains beside Flathead Lake and the Bitterroots, just south of Missoula, are but two of the ranges that make up the spine of the Rockies in this lush, green corner of Montana, the only place in the state that boasts some promising wineries. Western Montana is steeped in Western history, from Lewis and Clark to the Nez Perce and the state's earliest missions, and home to one of the state's fastest-growing areas, the Bitterroot

Highlights

Look for ★ to find recommended sights, activities, dining, and lodging.

★ **Carousel for Missoula and Caras Park:** Built from the dream of one man and the outpouring of the entire community, this extraordinary hand-built carousel is a magical place to spend a beautiful summer day (page 167).

★ **St. Ignatius Mission:** The jewel of a mission founded by Fathers Pierre-Jean De Smet S.J. and Adrian Hoecken S.J., this massive brick Catholic church from 1891 is still impressive, with 58 murals painted by Brother Joseph Carignano S.J. (page 192).

★ **Cherry Picking:** Timing your visit to Flathead Lake for the annual cherry harvest promises sweet, juicy memories to savor (page 196).

★ **Hiking at Jewel Basin:** With 27 lakes, 35 miles (56 km) of trails, and no motorized vehicles or horses permitted, this is a hiker's paradise (page 197).

★ **Skiing at Whitefish Mountain Resort:** This phenomenal ski area has a view over Whitefish Lake and perhaps the best après-ski scene in the state (page 209).

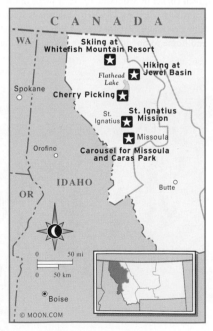

© MOON.COM

Valley, as well as the National Bison Range. The region feels like the Pacific Northwest in some ways—lush greenery, ancient trees, snowcapped peaks, and, rather unfortunately, the scars of hyper-ambitious logging, which often led to catastrophic wildfires that, as recently as 1910, devoured entire cities in a matter of minutes.

As is true of the state in general, western Montana is a slice of paradise for outdoors enthusiasts. From the sublime Flathead Lake in the north with its boating, fishing, and unbeatable swimming and the nearby Jewel Basin, famous for hiking, huckleberries, and grizzly bears, to the Rattlesnake National Recreation Area and Wilderness just outside Missoula and the rugged Bitterroot Mountains in the south, this corner of the state, some 12,000 square miles (31,080 sq km) of diverse and magnificent habitat, is for many the embodiment of the Wild West and the Montana dream brought to life.

PLANNING YOUR TIME

Missoula is a natural stopping point along both east-west I-90 and north-south U.S. 93, and it's easier to get here by air than much of the state, but the city is also a great destination in itself. From boutique shopping and hip eateries near the **University of Montana** to adventurous athletic pursuits in town and nearby, Missoula is Montana with an urban edge.

Using Missoula as a base, many visitors cruise down the **Bitterroot Valley** for an active day trip with fishing opportunities, historic missions and mansions, and cool little mountain towns like **Hamilton** and **Stevensville.** Another option is to stay at one of the numerous guest ranches in the Bitterroot Valley that have quick and easy access to Missoula.

Almost any part of western Montana can be accessed within a day's drive of Missoula, including the tiny but bustling villages lining

the sandy shores of **Flathead Lake**—don't miss charming **Bigfork** with its galleries, eateries, and theater—as well as **Glacier National Park** and its gold-letter gateway town of **Whitefish,** a marvelous destination with great restaurants and world-class recreation. Whitefish's proximity to Glacier Park and the **Flathead National Forest** makes it an obvious vacation spot for outdoors enthusiasts. Just south of Whitefish, the larger and slightly less picturesque **Kalispell** has plenty of lodging options, easy air access, and a couple of interesting, offbeat museums.

HISTORY

Because of harsh winters, unforgiving terrain, and territorial Native Americans, this land was not as quick to be settled by Europeans as other parts of Montana. The earliest inhabitants were the Salish, Kootenai, and Pend d'Oreille people, who fished in the crystal lakes and hunted in the forests and valleys. Fur trappers and traders—attracted by the abundance of beaver in the lakes—entered the area in the early 1800s. David Thompson, the famous Canadian explorer and fur trapper, set up trading posts in the area 1807-1812, including the first trading post established west of the Rockies.

When the Salish traveled through the Missoula valley in search of bison, the Blackfeet would ambush them as they entered the canyon. French trappers who passed through the canyon in the early 1800s encountered the gruesome remains of various massacres and dubbed the area "Hell Gate." Not far from Hellgate Canyon, Lewis and Clark met the Blackfeet, who introduced them to the main flower of the valley, a staple of the Indian diet, but Lewis found it bitter and inedible, thus giving the bitterroot lily, and eventually the valley, its name.

The Flathead (or Salish) were responsive to conversion by missionaries, and by 1840 St. Mary's Mission had been established; the

WESTERN MONTANA

Missoula and Western Montana

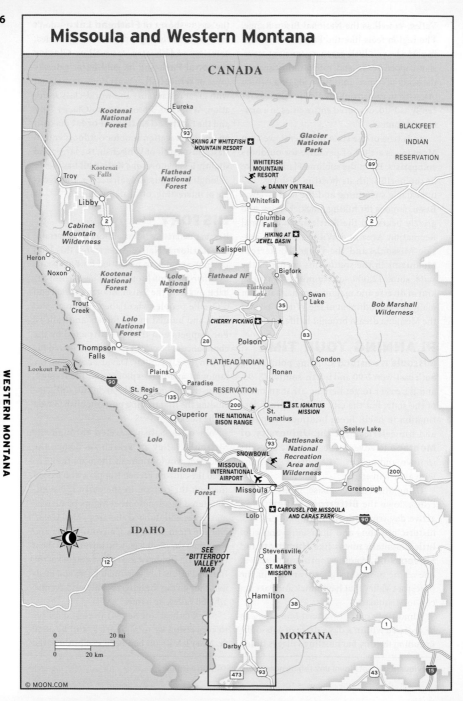

CANADA

Kootenai
National
Forest

Eureka

93

SKIING AT WHITEFISH
MOUNTAIN RESORT

Glacier
National
Park

89

BLACKFEET

INDIAN

RESERVATION

Troy

Kootenai
Falls

Flathead
National
Forest

WHITEFISH
MOUNTAIN
RESORT

★ DANNY ON TRAIL

Whitefish

Libby

Columbia
Falls

2

2

Cabinet
Mountain
Wilderness

HIKING AT
JEWEL BASIN

Kalispell

★

Heron

Noxon

Kootenai
National
Forest

Lolo
National
Forest

Flathead NF

Flathead
Lake

Bigfork

Swan
Lake

Bob Marshall
Wilderness

Trout
Creek

Lolo
National
Forest

35

CHERRY PICKING

★

28

Polson

83

Thompson
Falls

FLATHEAD INDIAN

Condon

Lookout Pass

90

Plains

Paradise

Ronan

St. Regis

135

RESERVATION

200

ST. IGNATIUS
MISSION

Superior

THE NATIONAL
BISON RANGE

★ St.
Ignatius

Seeley Lake

Lolo

93

SNOWBOWL

Rattlesnake
National
Recreation
Area and
Wilderness

200

National

MISSOULA
INTERNATIONAL
AIRPORT

Forest

Missoula

Greenough

Lolo

CAROUSEL FOR MISSOULA
AND CARAS PARK

90

IDAHO

SEE
"BITTERROOT
VALLEY"
MAP

Stevensville

ST. MARY'S
MISSION

1

12

Hamilton

38

1

0   20 mi

0   20 km

Darby

MONTANA

473   93

43

15

© MOON.COM

St. Ignatius Mission was moved from Lake Pend d'Oreille to Mission Creek in 1854. The Flathead Indian Reservation was created in 1855 on the condition that the Kootenai, Salish, and Pend d'Oreille share the territory. Although their leaders begrudgingly agreed, most of the members of these groups refused to move to the reservation until many years later. Two-thirds of the land originally assigned to the reservation was later taken back to create the many national forests in the area. The Native Americans contributed to the development of the area by selling a small portion of reservation land to the Northern Pacific Railway, at the time believing that their willingness to sell would lead the government to expand their reservation territory north, which did not happen.

In 1885 steamboats began to travel across Flathead Lake, and by the 1890s settlements had appeared on the lake's eastern side. The Northern Pacific Railway laid tracks through the town of Missoula at the same time, and by 1891 the railroad had arrived at Flathead. In response, Charles Conrad, a wealthy entrepreneur who stopped his westward travels when he fell in love with the Flathead Valley, established the town of Kalispell, where the main railroad junction would be. The railroad's entry into this region also marked the beginning of its timber industry: Not only were the trees used to lay railroad lines, but they could now be transported across the state to the rest of the nation. The wood played an integral part in the state's mining industry, used in building mine shafts and fueling numerous smelters. But like the rest of the state's natural resources, the timber industry would create boom-and-bust cycles that endure to present day.

Missoula

Given its site at the hub of five river valleys—the Jocko and Blackfoot Rivers to the north, the upper and lower Clark Fork east and west of the city, and the Bitterroot to the south—Missoula's longtime status as an important trade center makes perfect sense. About halfway between Yellowstone and Glacier National Parks, Missoula (population 72,364; elevation 3,200 ft/975 m) is on the way to just about everywhere in this part of the state and a natural stopping point for visitors to the region.

In addition to its history of logging and paper milling, the other defining element of the city—the University of Montana—keeps Missoula young, vibrant, and relatively liberal. Perhaps because the school is best known for its creative writing, art, drama, and dance programs, Missoula is decidedly arts-oriented.

In addition to its proximity to both the Flathead and Bitterroot Valleys, Missoula offers outdoors enthusiasts abundant options right in town—hike the "M" on Mount Sentinel or hang glide off it, kayak the Clark Fork or bike along its shores. There is world-class fishing on a number of rivers, hot-potting (the art of getting to and swimming in natural hot springs), mountain biking, and no end of places to hike.

SIGHTS

★ Carousel for Missoula and Caras Park

Aside from being a beautiful hand-carved carousel, one of the first built in the United States since the Great Depression, what makes the **Carousel for Missoula** (101 Carousel Dr., 406/549-8382, www.carrouselformissoula. com, 11am-7pm daily June-Aug., 11am-5:30pm daily Sept.-May, $2.25 adults, $0.75 children under 16, $1.50 adult with child on lap) so sweet is the way in which it came to be. Local cabinetmaker Chuck Kaparich vowed to the city of Missoula in 1991 that if they would "give it a home and promise no one will ever

Missoula and Vicinity

To Holiday Inn
and Jellystone Park

WINGATE
BY WYNDHAM

C'MON INN

LA QUINTA · BEST WESTERN
PLUS GRANT CREEK INN

ECONO LODGE

COURTYARD
BY MARRIOTT · HILTON GARDEN
INN MISSOULA

HOLIDAY INN
EXPRESS

MISSOULA KOA

W BROADWAY ST

90

200

10

CAROUSEL
FOR MISSOULA
AND CARAS PARK

KETTLE HOUSE
BREWING CO.

HIAWATHA
LN

MULLAN RD

COTE LN

93

Clark Fork River

SEE
"MISSOULA"
MAP

S RUSSELL

BLOSSOM'S
BED & BREAKFAST

S 3RD ST W   S 3RD ST W

Kelly
Island

S 7TH ST W

12   90

SPURGIN RD

ROCKIN RUDY'S

CLARK FORK
RIVERFRONT TRAIL

Spurgin
Park

TOWER ST

S RESERVE ST

14TH ST W

MISSOULA
FARMERS MARKET

SOUTH AVE W   SOUTH AVE W   12

CAFFE
DOLCE

Larchmont
Golf
Course

EATON ST

BROOKS ST

BANCROFT ST

University
of Montana
Golf Course

93   12

39TH ST

GIBSON MANSON

0   1 mi

0   1 km

© MOON.COM

take it apart," he would build a carousel by hand. As a child, Kaparich had spent summer days in Butte at the Columbia Gardens riding the carousel. For four years, he carved ponies, taught others to carve, and worked to restore and piece together the more than 16,000 pieces of an antique carousel frame he had purchased. The town raised funds and collectively contributed more than 100,000 volunteer hours. In May 1995 the carousel opened with 38 ponies, three replacement ponies, two chariots, 14 gargoyles, and the largest band organ in continuous use in the United States.

The jewel-box building opens to the surrounding green of **Caras Park** in summer and keeps the cold and wind out during the rest of the year. A fantastic adjacent play area, **Dragon Hollow,** was built with the same remarkable volunteerism over a substantially shorter time period. The entire playground was constructed by volunteers in just nine days in 2001.

Missoula Art Museum

With the tagline "Free Expression Free Admission," the **Missoula Art Museum** (MAM, 335 N. Pattee St., 406/728-0447, www.missoulaartmuseum.org, 10am-5pm Tues.-Sat., free) honors the past and celebrates the future. The building itself represents such a marriage, brilliantly combining a 110-year-old Carnegie library with a contemporary glass, steel, and wood addition. The museum has six exhibition spaces that host 20-25 solo and group exhibitions annually, most of them quite contemporary and

Missoula

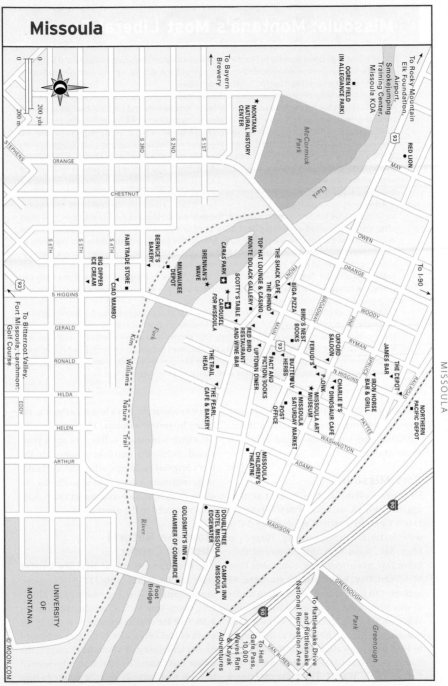

WESTERN MONTANA

MISSOULA

To Rocky Mountain
Elk Foundation,
Airport,
Smokejumping
Training Center,
Missoula KOA

To Bayern
Brewery

OGREN FIELD
(IN ALLEGIANCE PARK)

★ MONTANA
NATURAL HISTORY
CENTER

McCormick
Park

Clark

STEPHENS

ORANGE

CHESTNUT

S 3RD

S 2ND

S 1ST

93

RED LION

MAY

OWEN

ORANGE

To I-90

BERNICE'S
BAKERY ▼

FAIR TRADE STORE ▼

MILWAUKEE
DEPOT ■

BRENNAN'S
WAVE

CARAS PARK ★

★ CAROUSEL
FOR MISSOULA

SCOTTY'S TABLE ▼

MONTE DOLACK GALLERY ▼

TOP HAT LOUNGE & CASINO ▼

THE RHINO ▼

THE SHACK CAFÉ ▼

KIOWA

MAIN

BIGA PIZZA ▼

BIRD'S NEST
BOOKS

FACT AND
FICTION BOOKS

RED BIRD
RESTAURANT
AND WINE BAR

▼ UPTOWN DINER

BROADWAY

BUTTERFLY
HERBS

FERDINI'S ▼

OXFORD
SALOON ▼

N HIGGINS

PINE

RYMAN

WOODY

SPRUCE

CHARLIE B'S ▼
DINOSAUR CAFÉ ▼

IRON HORSE
BAR & GRILL

JAMES BAR ●

THE DEPOT ▼

P.ONK

★ MISSOULA
ART
MUSEUM

MISSOULA
SATURDAY MARKET

PATTEE

WASHINGTON

NORTHERN
PACIFIC DEPOT ■

RAILROAD

S 6TH

S 5TH

S 4TH

BIG
DIPPER
ICE CREAM ▼

CIAO MAMBO ▼

S HIGGINS

GERALD

RONALD

HILDA

HELEN

ARTHUR

93

To Bitterroot Valley,
Fort Missoula, Larchmont
Golf Course

Kim

Williams

Nature

Trail

Fork

THE TRAIL
HEAD ■

▼ THE PEARL
CAFÉ & BAKERY

POST
OFFICE ■

ADAMS

MADISON

MISSOULA
CHILDREN'S
THEATRE ■

GOLDSMITH'S INN ●
CHAMBER OF COMMERCE ■

DOUBLETREE
HOTEL MISSOULA
EDGEWATER ●

CAMPUS INN
MISSOULA ●

River

Foot
Bridge

UNIVERSITY
OF
MONTANA

90

90

VAN BUREN

GREENOUGH

To Hell
Gate Pass,
10,000
Waves Raft
& Kayak
Adventures

To Rattlesnake Drive
and Rattlesnake
National Recreation Area

Greenough
Park

0   200 yds
0   200 m

© MOON.COM

Missoula: Montana's Most Liberal Town?

In 1992, when I decided to move to Montana and was vacillating between Missoula and Bozeman, my older brother broke it down according to an age-old and surprisingly right-on generalization when he asked which I liked better: "cowboys or hippies?"

Missoula has long been associated with a hippie lifestyle (the herbs store is one of the busiest shops in town), but its origins as a center for labor movements and civil disobedience go back more than a century. In 1909 a pregnant 19-year-old by the name of Elizabeth Gurley Flynn came to Missoula on behalf of the Industrial Workers of the World to organize the region's lumber and migrant farm workers. She and her husband organized heated rallies around town. Eventually city leaders passed a law making public speaking on Missoula streets a crime. Flynn's plan to start a freedom-of-speech battle across the Northwest worked, and before long people willing to be arrested for the cause arrived by the trainload. City jails quickly filled and overflowed, forcing the city to back down and reinstate the right to speak publicly.

Among the Missoula locals who have contributed to its reputation was Jeannette Rankin who, in 1916, became the first woman to be elected to the U.S. House of Representatives, two years after Montana granted women the right to vote but four years *before* the 19th Amendment gave women across the country the right to vote. Among the early graduates from the University of Montana in 1902, Rankin was a tried-and-true pacifist, casting one of 50 votes against the resolution to enter World War I in 1917 and the lone vote against entering World War II, a move that sealed her political demise. Rankin famously stated, "You can no more win a war than you can win an earthquake." She was a founding vice president of the American Civil Liberties Union and an outspoken antiwar activist during the Vietnam War era.

The university has also contributed significantly to Missoula's reputation for liberal leanings. When the school was dedicated in 1895, speaker William Fisk Sanders implored, "Hold not up to these pupils hopes of money or office … their high service is to save the world from shame and thrall." In 1915, the removal of the University of Montana's popular president, Edwin Craighead, triggered the first of many organized protests on campus, including major incidents around freedom of speech, freedom of the press, civil rights, and the Vietnam War.

provocative. Don't miss the museum's own impressive Contemporary American Indian Art Collection, among the largest of its kind in the country.

Fort Missoula

Originally established to protect settlers against Indian attacks, **Fort Missoula** (3400 Captain Rawn Way, 406/728-3476, www.fortmissoulamuseum.org, 10am-5pm Mon.-Sat., noon-5pm Sun. Memorial Day-Labor Day, noon-5pm Tues.-Sun. Labor Day-Memorial Day, $4 adults, $2 students, $3 seniors, $10 family, free for children under 6) was never used for its intended purpose. When no attacks occurred, the fort was used to house the African American 25th Infantry in 1888 and as an alien detention center for Italian Americans and Japanese Americans during World War II. The museum houses

exhibits about the fort's history as well as rotating historical exhibits. The fort grounds, for which admission is free, are open year-round. While the museum is housed in the fort's original buildings, other historic buildings, including a one-room schoolhouse, an 1860s church, and a homesteader cabin, have been relocated to the grounds.

Montana Natural History Center

The **Montana Natural History Center** (120 Hickory St., 406/327-0405, www.montananaturalist.org, 9am-5pm Mon.-Fri., noon-4pm Sat., $3 adults, $1 children 4-18, free for children under 4) is one block south of McCormick Park. Originally housed on the University of Montana's campus, the center was created by educators who wanted to work with schools and the public to help nurture an understanding and appreciation of nature. It offers workshops, including children's activities, as well as field trips and evening lectures conducted by local scientists and naturalists. To see what is being offered on specific dates, look under "Community Activities" on the website.

University of Montana

The **University of Montana** (32 Campus Dr., 406/243-0211, www.umt.edu) was founded in 1895 at the base of Mount Sentinel. To secure Missoula as the site of the state's university, city leaders bribed state legislators with 5 gallons (18.9 liters) of whiskey, a case of beer, a case of wine, and 350 cigars. Regardless of its shady beginnings, the university has flourished into a well-respected liberal arts institution with a top-notch football team, a broad interest in the performing arts, a well-known creative writing program, and an ability to produce numerous Fulbright and Rhodes scholars each year.

The university has a fun campus to explore. **University Center,** on the east side of the campus almost directly under the M on the hillside, is the hub of campus life. Wander in to grab a bite at the food court, or peruse the well-stocked bookstore. To find out what lectures, plays, concerts, or other entertainment is happening on campus, visit the website (http://events.umt.edu).

Rocky Mountain Elk Foundation Visitor Center

Strengthening the view that hunters are often the most resolute conservationists, the **Rocky Mountain Elk Foundation Visitor Center** (5705 Grant Creek Rd., 406/523-4500 or 800/225-5355, www.rmef.org, 8am-5pm Mon.-Fri., 10am-5pm Sat. Jan.-Apr., 8am-6pm Mon.-Fri., 9am-6pm Sat.-Sun. May-Dec., free) has protected and enhanced millions of acres of wildlife habitat across North America since its humble origins in 1984. The center does an impressive job of putting the elk in the context of a wide range of wildlife and emphasizing the importance of habitat conservation. A favorite among hunters due to its wealth of trophy mounts, the visitors center is like a natural history museum, and in addition to a pleasant wooded walking trail on the property's 22 acres (8.9 hectares), there are some great kid-friendly interactive exhibits and wildlife conservation films. Tours can be arranged by emailing in advance, and free youth seminars are held monthly on such subjects as fire, archery, big game, and horns versus antlers.

Aerial Fire Depot and Smokejumper Center

Sharing space with the largest smokejumper training base in the country, the **Aerial Fire Depot and Smokejumper Center** (5765 W. Broadway, 0.5 mi/0.8 km west of the Missoula airport, 406/329-4934, www.smokejumpers. com, 8:30am-5pm daily Memorial Day-Labor Day, by appointment Labor Day-Memorial Day, free admission, free tours daily in summer) is a fascinating place for those interested in wildfires and the firefighters who parachute in to battle them. There is a memorial to those killed on duty and a replica of a 1930s fire lookout; visitors on the 45-minute tour have access to the smokejumper loft where the jumpers work when they are not fighting fires.

Brennan's Wave

Although there is no street address, everyone in Missoula knows exactly where Brennan's Wave is. Located on the Clark Fork River, right next to Caras Park, this engineered white-water masterpiece was built in honor of Brennan Guth, a Missoula native and world-class kayaker who perished in 2001 while paddling in Chile. Brennan's Wave hosts big competitions—the 2010 U.S. Freestyle Kayaking Championship brought 200 competitors to town and thousands of spectators—and plenty of everyday paddlers looking for a thrill. The banks are always lined with enthusiastic spectators, and the Wave is a popular gathering spot whenever the river is not covered by ice.

SPORTS AND RECREATION

Rattlesnake National Recreation Area and Wilderness

Less than 5 miles (8 km) north of town, the 60,000-acre (24,281-hectare) **Rattlesnake National Recreation Area and Wilderness** (406/329-3814, www.fs.usda.gov) is fed by some 50 creeks and has 30 lakes, waterfalls, and many miles of trails, some of which lead up to McLeod Peak, the highest spot in the area at 8,620 feet (2,627 m). The area is a dream for hikers, runners, mountain bikers, campers, cross-country skiers, and anglers; it is home to deer, elk, coyotes, mountain goats, bighorn sheep, black bears, and more than 40 species of birds in spring and fall. Camping is permitted anywhere beyond the 3-mile (4.8-km) radius from the Rattlesnake's main trailhead.

To get to the area from Missoula, take the I-90 Van Buren Street exit at the east end of town and travel 4.5 miles (7.2 km) north on Rattlesnake Drive.

Missoula Osprey Baseball

At Ogren Field in **Allegiance Park** (700 Cregg Ln.), the **Missoula Osprey** (406/543-3300, www.milb.com/missoula, $10 adults) take on other Pioneer League teams in some great small-town minor league baseball. Missoula is known for its softball, so it's no surprise that the community shows up in force to watch their hometown Ospreys, a farm team for the Arizona Diamondbacks.

Hiking and Biking

Hugely popular with walkers, runners, and bikers, the flat **Clark Fork Riverfront Trail** (www.ci.missoula.mt.us/2209/Riverfront-Trails) is 3.8 miles (6.1 km) long and provides access to **Caras Park, Bess Reed Park,** and **Kiwanis Park** on the river's north bank and **McCormick Park, Clark Fork Natural Park, John Toole Park,** the **University of Montana River Bowl,** and **Jacob's Island Park** on the south bank. The trail, graveled in places and paved in others, connects to a number of other intersecting trails and runs on both the north and south sides of the Clark Fork River. It is easily accessible throughout town, but the most abundant parking can be found at Caras Park near the Carousel for Missoula. The trail on the river's north side is about 0.5 mile (0.8 km) longer than on the south side.

The Clark Fork Riverfront Trail connects

Brennan's Wave draws boaters and spectators in downtown Missoula.

to the 2.5-mile (4-km) **Kim Williams Nature Trail,** a converted railroad bed near the base of Mount Sentinel (where you can hike the M) that winds through a 134-acre (54.2-hectare) natural area in Hellgate Canyon. The trail is wide and level, and it is open to pedestrians, equestrians, and cyclists. It's also frequented by wildlife, so keep your eyes open. The trail runs through Hellgate Canyon and connects to the Deer Creek-Pattee Canyon Loop. The trail can be accessed easily from Jacob's Island Park near the Van Buren Pedestrian Bridge. Leashed dogs are welcome on all of Missoula's trails.

M TRAIL ON MOUNT SENTINEL

For a bird's-eye view of the city, hike up the **M Trail on Mount Sentinel.** It is a popular trail, so there will likely be others huffing and puffing up the hill with you. There are 13 switchbacks on the west-facing slope, and the views over Missoula and the Bitterroot Valley at sunset are worth the sweat.

Skiing

Twenty minutes north of Missoula, **Snowbowl** (1700 Snowbowl Rd., 406/549-9777 or 800/728-2695, www.montanasnowbowl.com, $48 adults full-day or $43 half-day, $45 students and seniors full-day or $43 half-day, $22 children 6-12 full- or half-day, free for children under 6) is a nice little ski hill with an average of 300 inches (762 cm) of snow annually, 2,600 feet (793 m) of vertical drop, and a run that covers 3 miles (4.8 km). In summer, the mountain is open Friday-Sunday late June-mid-September for mountain biking, disc golf (folf), and diggler, which is a cross between mountain biking and snowboarding (rentals available).

There is no shortage of cross-country ski trails around Missoula. One unique destination is the **Garnet Resource Area** (406/329-3914, www.garnetghosttown.net), with 50 miles (81 km) of trails in a ghost town. In summer, hiking and mountain biking are popular. To get to Garnet, follow Highway 200 east of town and turn south at the Garnet Range Road, located between mile markers 22 and 23, about 30 miles (48 km) east of Missoula. Follow the range road approximately 12 miles (19.3 km) to the parking area. The road is closed January-April, when access is limited to snowshoers, cross-country skiers, and snowmobilers.

There are also more than 150 miles (242 km) of cross-country ski trails in the **Lolo National Forest** (406/329-3814, www.fs.usda.gov/lolo).

hiking the M Trail on Mount Sentinel

Hang Gliding in Missoula

While it makes some people crazy, for others the combination of wind and mountains in Missoula means only one thing: hang gliding. It's not uncommon to see these colorful oversize-kite contraptions launching off Mount Sentinel and soaring over the city. But what goes up must come down, and when Bill Johnson (widely considered to have been the first hang gliding pilot in the state) landed on top of the university fieldhouse, reports of a plane crash swiftly clogged the emergency services switchboard. When the fire department arrived, Johnson had broken down his glider, packed it neatly in a bag, and even asked the firefighters for help getting down. The firefighters were too busy scanning the scene for a crashed plane to realize that they were aiding Johnson in his getaway.

The sport took hold in the state in the 1970s when gear was cheap and mostly homemade. By October 2006 the number of launches off Mount Sentinel gave pause to Missoula's air traffic controllers, who feared a plane-versus-glider crash, and the area was closed to flight for nearly a year. The state's hang glider pilots joined with people in Missoula who appreciated the life and color that the sport brought to town, and in July 2007 Mount Sentinel opened again to hang gliding. **Missoula Paragliders and Hanggliders** (406/529-5135) is actively working to secure launch sites in the valley.

Local pilot Paul Roys from **Five Valley Hang Gliding** (406/203-2695) keeps the sport alive with his own gravity-defying flights as well as tandem flights ($175) for the curious and introductory lessons ($250). On a windy day in Missoula, there may not be a more unique way to see the city and the valleys around it.

Fishing

While access to the Clark Fork River right in town is easy, the river is still recovering from decades of pollution. Better bets are the Bitterroot River, the Blackfoot River, and Rock Creek. One guiding outfit that does them all is **Classic Journey Outfitters** (877/327-7878, www.montanaflyfishingguide.com, $550 full-day float, $395 half-day float, multiday trips with lodging available). Owner Joe Cummings grew up fishing on a ranch in nearby Stevensville and left to play professional football. But his heart has always been where the big, wild trout are. He and his guides fish year-round, have a passion for dry flies, and know the area backward and forward. Another guide who is a phenomenal naturalist in addition to being a world-class fishing instructor is Tom Jenni of **Tom Jenni's Reel Montana** (406/539-6610 or 866/885-6065, www.tomjenni.com). Jenni grew up in Missoula and has been fishing its rivers for more than 30 years.

Boating and Water Sports

With five rivers in the vicinity, Missoula is a boater's town. There is even an artificial practice wave, Brennan's Wave, right in town for kayakers to play safely in. **10,000 Waves Raft & Kayak Adventures** (131 E. Main St., 406/549-6670 or 800/537-8315, www.10000-waves.com) offers everything from scenic rafting to white-water adventures, sit-on-top kayaks, and kayak instruction on numerous sections of the Blackfoot and Clark Fork Rivers. There are also overnight trips ($595 adults, $565 children 5-12) and gourmet dinner trips ($115 adults, $90 children 5-12), plus half-day trips ($70 adults, $50 children 5-12) and full-day trips ($85 adults, $65 children 5-12) on the Blackfoot River. Another local outfitter that specializes in all things whitewater is **Zoo Town Surfers** (3067 Fleet St. in Missoula, or river headquarters 5077 Old U.S. 10 W., Alberton, 406/546-0370, www.zootownsurfers.com). It offers scenic and white-water rafting trips, kayak clinics, and stand-up paddleboarding experiences on local lakes and rivers.

Golf

Although there are a couple of nine-hole courses in town including **University of Montana Golf Course** (515 South Ave. E., 406/728-8629, $17 for 9 holes, $30 for 18) and **Linda Vista Public Golf Course** (4915 Lower Miller Creek Rd., 406/251-3655, $15 for 9 holes, $20 for 18), the only 18-hole public course in Missoula is the **Larchmont Golf Course** (3200 Old Fort Rd., 406/721-4416, $34 for 18 holes on foot, carts $18-36).

Horseback Riding

Less than 30 minutes south of Missoula in Lolo, amazing trail ride experiences can be had at **Dunrovin Ranch** (5001 Expedition Dr., 406/273-7745, www.dunrovinranchmontana.com), where the emphasis is on community, education, science, and the arts. Animals are at the center of the experience here and make every visit remarkable, from the family of smooth-gaited Tennessee Walking Horses to "diva donkeys," beloved dogs, and ospreys and other wild animals that call the ranch home. Though Dunrovin offers lodging and the full guest ranch experience, it also offers riding opportunities for nonguests. Corral sessions ($50) are great for children as young as three, and give new riders the opportunity to start slow. Trail rides off the ranch are available to anyone older than eight, ranging from one hour ($80 pp) or two hours ($115 pp) to half-day (4-6 hours, $160 pp) and full-day (6-9 hours, $260 pp). Rides might climb up to magnificent mountain views or travel along and across the river or through lush forests, and private rides can be arranged as well. Dunrovin Ranch also offers a historical ride perfect for history buffs and mountain men wannabes.

ENTERTAINMENT AND EVENTS

Nightlife

Home to college students and artists, there is no shortage of watering holes in Missoula, and a brief walk will take you to establishments that are pulsing with activity. Microbrew enthusiasts will enjoy the **Bayern Brewing's Edelweiss Bistro** (1507 Montana St., 406/721-1482, www.bayernbrewery.com, 11am-8pm Mon.-Sat.), which always has six of its beers available along with its own coffee blends and a small but delectable sampling of German food, including sausages, meats, cheeses, and pretzels. The beer garden is a great place to relax in summer, and brewery tours are available by appointment. The **Kettle House Brewing Co.** (313 N. 1st St. W. and 602 Myrtle St., 406/728-1660, www.kettlehouse.com, noon-8pm daily, growlers to-go sold until 9pm) is home of the famous Cold Smoke and has two locations for visitors to sample excellent local brews.

For more of a late-night scene, try tried-and-true favorites like **The Rhino** (158 Ryman St., 406/721-6061, 11am-2am Mon.-Sat., noon-2am Sun.), with more than 50 beers on tap; **Feruqi's** (318 N. Higgins Ave., 406/728-8799, 4pm-2am Mon.-Sat., 7pm-2am Sun.), an intimate spot known for its martinis and setting in a historic building; or the **Oxford Saloon** (337 N. Higgins Ave., 406/549-0117, www.the-oxford.com, 24 hours daily), which dates back to the 1880s and still offers live poker nightly at 8pm. Though it no longer serves brains and eggs, the Oxford still makes a pretty tasty Garbage Omelet. **Charlie B's** (428 N. Higgins Ave., 406/549-3589, 11am-2am daily) is a longtime favorite and has a reputation for hard drinking that starts early in the day. The adjacent **Dinosaur Café** offers inexpensive and excellent Cajun food to go with your booze. Complete with a Hunter S. Thompson quote etched on the outside of the building, **James Bar** (127 W. Alder St., 406/721-8158, 11am-2am daily) is a classy joint for cocktails and good, local cuisine—including elk, bison, lobster, and lamb sliders—instead of standard bar fare.

Music lovers will do well at the **Top Hat Lounge & Casino** (134 W. Front St., 406/830-4640, www.logjampresents.com, 11:30am-10pm Mon.-Wed., 11:30am-2am Thurs.-Sat.), which has been bringing live music of every

Montana Wineries

Since 1984, when Tom Campbell Jr. and his father first started experimenting with growing grapes along the shores of Flathead Lake, in prime Montana cherry territory, several other wineries have sprouted up across the state, primarily in the western region. Many have disappeared after hard winters and rough economies, but a handful are proving that Montana vintners have what it takes. Though many vintners buy grapes from out of state, there are several growers among them, including a few that opt for unconventional but delicious base fruits like cherries, huckleberries, chokecherries, apples, pears, currants, and rhubarb.

- **Glacier Sun Winery & Tasting Room** (3250 U.S. 2 E., Kalispell, 406/257-8886, www. glaciersunwinery.com, 8am-5pm Mon.-Fri.) grew out of the idea of a small, roadside fruit and veggie stand. Today the winery still sells fruits, veggies, and prepared foods, but also produces 18 varietals from locally grown fruits and regionally grown grapes.

- **Mission Mountain Winery** (82420 U.S. 93, Dayton, 406/849-5524, www. missionmountainwinery.com, tastings 10am-5pm daily May-Oct., 10am-6pm daily July-Aug., $5 tasting fee) is the state's first bonded winery and produces more than 6,500 cases annually of more than 10 different award-winning varietals. Its vineyards grow the grapes for its highly regarded pinot noir, pinot gris, and small amounts of riesling, chardonnay, and gewürztraminer. The tasting fee is waived with purchase of a bottle.

- **Ten Spoon Vineyard and Winery** (4175 Rattlesnake Dr., Missoula, 877/549-8703, www. tenspoon.com, tastings by appointment) is among the fastest-growing wineries in the state and has a marvelous origin story. Owner Connie Poten bought some pastureland in the Rattlesnake Valley outside Missoula to protect the rapidly disappearing open space. She met Andy Sponseller on a local preservation campaign, and their shared love of wine led to the backbreaking work that built the vineyard and set the stage for their subsequent success with varietals including Moonlight pinot noir, Ranger Rider Red, Blind Curve sauvignon blanc, Flathead cherry dry, Farm Dog Red, and Fat Cat.

- **Hidden Legend Winery** (1345 U.S. 93 N., Ste. 5, Victor, 406/363-6323, www. hiddenlegendwinery.com, tours and tastings 11am-6pm Tues.-Sat.) in the Bitterroot Valley specializes in honey-based mead with Montana twists like chokecherry and elderberry.

- **Trapper Peak Winery** (75 Cattail Ln., Darby, 406/821-1964, tours and tastings by appointment), also in the Bitterroot Valley, produces an affordable selection of cabernet sauvignon, petite sirah, merlot, cabernet franc, and muscat using California grapes.

- **Tongue River Winery** (99 Morning Star Ln., Miles City, 406/853-1028, www. tongueriverwinery.com, 8am-6pm Mon.-Sat., 2pm-7pm Sun.) is the only winery in southeastern Montana. It offers an expansive list of award-winning wines, and tours of both the vineyard and winery can be arranged.

genre to Missoula since 1952. The place can pack in 700 bodies, and the tapas-style menu does not disappoint. A bit mellower and far more upscale is **Plonk** (322 N. Higgins Ave., 406/926-1791, www.plonkwine.com, 11:30am-2am Tues.-Sat., 4pm-2am Sun.-Mon.), which pairs exquisite wine, inspired cocktails, and elegant food with eclectic music. Too pricey for the average college student, Plonk tends to appeal to an older crowd.

The Arts

MISSOULA CHILDREN'S THEATRE

Certainly one of the state's most beloved theater companies, the **Missoula Children's Theatre** (200 N. Adams St., 406/728-7529 or 406/728-1911, www.mctinc.org) mounts several productions annually of such family favorites as *Hansel and Gretel* and *Snow White and the Seven Dwarfs* with children as cast members. Most significantly, MCT has become known for its performances in 16 countries around the world that include local children. The company arrives in town the Monday before a Friday performance, casting and rehearsing local children to light up the stage (or the gym, as is often the case in small-town Montana). At the same time, the company performs pieces that include Broadway musicals and poignant comedies in its home performance space.

Festivals and Events

WEEKLY SUMMER EVENTS

With an active, outdoorsy, and independent population, Missoula hosts a number of weekly events during summer that encourage everything from outdoor dining to art appreciation. **First Friday Gallery Night** (406/532-3240) is held 5pm-8pm on the first Friday of every month. Some 15-20 galleries open their doors, often to display new exhibitions, and they provide complimentary hors d'oeuvres and refreshments to art strollers. **Out to Lunch** (406/543-4238, www.missouladowntown.com, 11am-2pm Wed. June-Aug.) in Caras Park is a riverside performing arts picnic for the whole city, with talented local musicians and more than 20 food vendors. Also in Caras Park and run by the Missoula Downtown Association, **Downtown ToNight** (406/543-4238, www.missouladowntown.com, 5:30pm-8:30pm Thurs. June-Aug.) features live music, food vendors, and a beverage garden.

Known as the Garden City, Missoula boasts three fabulous farmers markets, including the **Clark Fork Market** (under the Higgins St. Bridge in downtown, 406/396-0593, www.clarkforkmarket.com, 8am-1pm Sat. May-Sept., 9am-1pm Oct.), which offers an abundance of local produce, meat, and other products, including hot prepared food. There is live music 10am-12:30pm, and plenty of parking is available. The **Missoula Farmers Market** (Circle Square, north end of Higgins Ave., 406/274-3042, www.missoulafarmersmarket.com, 8am-12:30pm Sat. May-Oct., 5:30pm-7pm Tues. June 19-Sept.) features more than 100 vendors of fresh local produce, flowers, eggs, honey, and more. The **Missoula People's Market** (E. Pine St. between Higgins Ave. and Pattee St., 406/830-3216, www.missoulapeoplesmarket.org, 9am-1pm Sat. May-Sept.) has prepared food and features art and crafts by local artisans.

INTERNATIONAL WILDLIFE FILM FESTIVAL AND CINE

Since 1977, the **International Wildlife Film Festival** (718 S. Higgins Ave., 406/728-9380, www.wildlifefilms.org) has been celebrating conservation and film with an eight-day event based at Missoula's famed Roxy Theatre. The event runs annually in late April and features a phenomenal array of wildlife films from around the globe. In October, the Montana CINE International Film Festival features films on a broad range of topics relating to the environment and cultures of our planet.

INTERNATIONAL CHORAL FESTIVAL

Held every three years (the next one is scheduled for 2019), the **International Choral Festival** (406/721-7985, www.choralfestival.org) is a true Missoula community event. Nonprofit and noncompetitive, it began in 1987 with the goal of promoting cultural awareness and understanding through music. The four-day event takes place at different venues around the city, and the first day usually includes free preview concerts. Hundreds of international and national choral groups apply each year, but only a handful are selected to participate. In 2016, participants came from Hong Kong, Cuba, Costa Rica, Estonia, and Canada, among others.

SHOPPING

The Fair Trade Store (519 S. Higgins Ave., 406/543-3955, 10am-6pm Mon.-Sat., noon-4pm Sun.) is operated by the Jeannette Rankin Peace Center and promotes equitable and fair partnerships between producers and distributors of goods. There is a distinctive and colorful selection of merchandise from around the globe, including textiles, pottery, silver, and handmade cards.

In addition to being Missoula's oldest espresso bar, **Butterfly Herbs** (232 N. Higgins Ave., 406/728-8780, www.butterflyherbs.com, 7am-7pm daily) is a fun and eclectic gift shop. It sells whole herbs, teas, coffee, and spices in bulk as well as soaps, handmade jewelry, candles, and other decorative goods.

Rockin Rudy's (237 Blaine St., 406/542-0077, www.rockinrudys.com, 9am-9pm Mon.-Sat., 11am-6pm Sun.) uses as a tagline, "A place. Sort of." More than just a place, Rockin Rudy's is *the* place in Missoula for music, posters, cards, gag gifts, jewelry, and on and on. Big and random, this place is part of Missoula culture.

The Trail Head (221 E. Front St., 406/543-6966, www.trailheadmontana.net, 9:30am-8pm Mon.-Fri., 9am-6pm Sat., 11am-6pm Sun.) is a part of the Missoula community and thrives by knowing the area as well as its activities and specific conditions. Trail Head staff participate regularly in volunteer efforts to preserve and enhance recreational opportunities in the region. The store has fantastic gear for nearly every activity in the area, including skiing, boating, camping, and climbing. Since 1974, great adventures have started here.

One of the most recognizable artists in the region, Monte Dolack shows his work and that of his partner, Mary Beth Percival, at **Monte Dolack Gallery** (139 W. Front St., 406/549-3248, www.dolack.com, by appt. only). The artists travel frequently, which is reflected in their primarily nature-based, often whimsical and witty works, which include tranquil watercolors and vivid posters.

Bookstores

In a famously literary town, **Fact and Fiction Books** (220 N. Higgins Ave., 406/721-2881, www.factandfictionbooks.com, 10am-6pm Mon.-Fri., 10am-5pm Sat., noon-4pm Sun.) is a Missoula institution and a good place to learn about local culture and regional authors.

For used, rare, and out-of-print books, **The Bird's Nest** (219 N. Higgins Ave., 406/721-1125, 10am-4pm Tues.-Sat.) is a real find, next door to Fact and Fiction.

FOOD

Missoula's dining scene offers more cultural diversity than much of the rest of the state, with plenty of sushi and Thai offerings, but its strong suit is still fresh Rocky Mountain cuisine. Among the best is **Red Bird Restaurant and Wine Bar** (111 N. Higgins Ave., Ste. 100, 406/549-2906, www.redbirdrestaurant.com, 5pm-10pm Tues.-Sat., $13-41), an elegant little bistro in a historic hotel building. Everything is fresh, creative, and made on the premises, including steaks, seafood, house-made pasta, and soups. For a dress-up and hit-the-town evening, this is a wonderful spot.

Serving American bistro fare with a global twist, **Scotty's Table** (131 S. Higgins Ave., 406/549-2790, www.scottystable.net, 11:30am-2:30pm and 5pm-9pm Tues.-Fri., 9am-2pm and 5pm-9pm Sat-Sun., $26-32) is an upscale dining spot for the whole family. The gourmet kids' menu was inspired by the chef's own child. Entrées include mouthwatering cioppino and local pork confit, but the appetizers are enchanting—try the fried risotto known as arancini, walnut-encrusted blue cheese cakes, mussels and fries, or the charcuterie plate; you might not even make it to the main course.

For a creative take on Italian food, **Ciao Mambo** (541 S. Higgins Ave., 406/543-0377, www.ciaomambo.com, 5pm-10pm daily, $7-32), a Montana-started franchise, serves up everything from Italian nachos and fried mozzarella balls to wood-fired pizza, pasta, and steaks.

The **Pearl Café & Bakery** (231 E. Front St., 406/541-0231, www.pearlcafe.us, 5pm-9pm Mon.-Sat., $14-32) boasts "country fare with an urban flair." The cuisine is creative, fresh, and absolutely gorgeous. From rabbit with red wine mushroom sauce to classic filet mignon, the Pearl is indeed a standout.

For the best local pizza, you can't beat the

Montana's Literary Treasure

Few states can boast a nearly 1,200-page, 5-pound (2.3-kg) tome dedicated to the remarkable literature that has come from and defined the state. (The state's "Big Sky" moniker even came courtesy of A. B. Guthrie Jr.'s classic 1947 novel *The Big Sky*.) Montana's literary anthology, *The Last Best Place*, was published in 1988, and the state's literary status only continues to grow. This may partly be attributed to poet and professor Richard Hugo, who directed the University of Montana's renowned creative writing program from 1964 until his death in 1982. The less prosaic might ascribe the inordinate number of well-known authors and poets to things like the light, space, and quality of life here, or the long cold winters and limited distractions. Among the state's best-known writers are Wallace Stegner, Norman Maclean, Bill Kittredge, James Welch, Tom McGuane, James Crumley, Richard Brautigan, Ivan Doig, Mary Clearman Blew, Richard Ford, David Quammen, and Rick Bass.

Montana's literary heritage is very much alive in Missoula, where one of the area's softball teams goes by the name "The Montana Review of Books," which once had an outfield lineup with 12 published novels among them. The city boasts some fabulous independent bookstores that promote and often host local writers, including **Fact and Fiction** (220 N. Higgins Ave., 406/721-2881). But perhaps the literary spirit is most alive in any number of watering holes, some more savory than others. **Charlie B's** (428 N. Higgins Ave.), a favorite haunt of the late James Crumley, has no sign, tinted windows, and a big wooden door. Crumley was also a regular at **The Depot** (201 Railroad St. W.). During his tenure at the University of Montana, Bill Kittredge and plenty of creative writing students frequented **Diamond Jim's Eastgate Casino and Lounge** (900 E. Broadway) just over the Van Buren footbridge from campus. **The Rhino** (158 Ryman St.) was identifiable in Jeff Hull's short stories and his 2005 novel. Probably the best-known among Missoula's thirsty literary geniuses, Dick Hugo often wrote about bars—**The Dixon Bar** (Hwy. 200, Dixon), which is, for the moment anyway, a bar and grill; **Trixi's Antler Saloon** (Hwy. 200, Ovando); and more famously, the **Milltown Union Bar** (11 Main St., Milltown), which is now the Milltown Moose Lodge, home to the fraternal Moose club, and is virtually unrecognizable.

wood-fired offerings from **Biga Pizza** (241 W. Main St., 406/728-2579, www.bigapizza.com, 11am-3pm and 5pm-9:30pm Mon.-Thurs., 11am-3pm and 5pm-10pm Fri., 5pm-10pm Sat., pizzas $10-20). From the simple house pie with garlic oil, tomato sauce, fresh basil, and fresh mozzarella to the caramelized goat cheese and the house-made fennel marmalade with local bacon, its combinations are nothing short of mouthwatering. Gluten-free crusts are available too, as are calzones and antipasti.

A thriving brewpub in Missoula, the **Iron Horse Bar & Grill** (501 N. Higgins Ave., 406/728-8866, www.ironhorsebrewpub.com, 11am-2am daily, $12-22) is set in the old train depot. The place is always hopping, and terrific outdoor seating is available when the weather permits. The menu is extensive, serving up everything from ahi tuna and nachos

to spicy tandoori chicken, salads, burgers, and small plates.

A community favorite since 1949 and serving three meals a day in a classic Pontiac-Oldsmobile dealership setting, **The Shack Café** (222 W. Main St., 406/549-9903, www.theshackcafe.com, 7am-3pm Mon.-Wed., 7am-9pm Thurs.-Sun. $11-20) specializes in food grown and raised locally. Don't miss the huckleberry pancakes for breakfast; it may be the best breakfast in town. Lunch includes hefty sandwiches, and dinner entrées range from sandwiches and salads to Mexican fare and pasta.

For a quick and scrumptious bite with a killer cup of coffee, try **Bernice's Bakery** (190 S. 3rd St. W., 406/728-1358, www.bernicesbakerymt.com, 6am-8pm daily, sandwiches $6-10), a real-butter and from-scratch kind of place featuring high-quality organic ingredients, menus that change daily, and sheer artistry in everything it does. The staff support a strong coffeehouse vibe and a commendable commitment to community. If you leave without indulging your sweet tooth, you've made an enormous mistake. **Caffé Dolce** (500 Brooks St., 406/830-3055, www.caffedolce.com, 8am-3pm Mon., 8am-9pm Tues.-Sat., 9am-2pm Sun., $15-29) offers fresh, healthy, and utterly delicious fare for breakfast, lunch, and dinner. The pasta is homemade, the wine list is enormous and fabulous, and the traditional Italian coffee service goes from morning until evening. There's also a location at **Southgate Mall** (2901 Brooks St., 406/830-3055, 8am-9pm Mon.-Fri., 9am-9pm Sat., 10am-6pm Sun.).

If you're just starting your Montana adventure, you'll need to get in shape for all the ice-cream offerings. A great place to start is **Big Dipper Ice Cream** (631 S. Higgins Ave., 406/543-5722, www.bigdippericecream.com, $3-8), which has unexpected but out-of-this-world flavors like cardamom, El Salvador coffee, Mexican chocolate, and mango habanero sorbet in addition to the lip-smacking classics. Don't miss daily special flavors like cotton candy, Thai peanut curry (really), and Elvis (peanut butter, banana, chocolate chip, chocolate, and bacon). During summer, the walk-up window is open 11am-11pm daily. Hours vary the rest of the year, so call ahead.

ACCOMMODATIONS

As one of Montana's bigger cities, Missoula has plenty of lodging options. The old-school independent motels line much of East and West Broadway, while some of the newer chain hotels can be found on Reserve Street. Among the well-known and well-maintained chains in town are the **C'Mon Inn Hotel & Suites** (2775 Expo Parkway, 406/543-4600 or 888/989-5569, www.cmoninn.com, $140-230), **Courtyard by Marriott** (4559 N. Reserve St., 406/549-5260, www.marriott.com, $169-247), the pet-friendly **Econo Lodge** (4953 N. Reserve St., 406/542-7550, www.choicehotels.com, $81-112), **Hilton Garden Inn Missoula**

(3720 N. Reserve St., 406/532-5300 or 877/782-9444, www.hiltongardeninn3.hilton.com, $149-313), **Holiday Inn Express & Suites** (150 Expressway Blvd., 406/830-3100 or 800/315-2605, www.hiexpress.com, $142-198), and **La Quinta** (5059 N. Reserve St., 406/549-9000 or 800/753-3757, www.laquintamissoula.com, $134-189).

In the heart of Missoula on the banks of the Clark Fork River is the pet-friendly **Doubletree by Hilton Missoula Edgewater** (100 Madison St., 406/728-3100 or 800/222-8733, www.missoulaedgewater.doubletree.com, $154-413), an enormous hotel with all the amenities.

A couple of medium-size hotels offering good value near the university and downtown, respectively, are **Campus Inn Missoula** (744 E. Broadway, 406/549-5134 or 800/232-8013, www.campusinnmissoula.com, $77-227) and **Red Lion** (700 W. Broadway, 406/728-3300 or 800/733-5466, www.redlion.com/missoula, $92-173).

A few miles from downtown is the quiet, comfortable, and pet-friendly **Best Western Plus Grant Creek Inn** (5280 Grant Creek Rd., 406/543-0700 or 800/780-7234, www.bestwestern.com, $146-259). Kids will love the indoor-outdoor heated pool. But for avid swimmers, the only hotel to consider in Missoula is **Wingate by Wyndham** (5252 Airway Blvd., 406/541-8000 or 866/832-8000, www.wingatemissoula.com, $129-269), which boasts extremely clean and comfortable rooms with an indoor water park that will delight little ones with a kiddie pool, froggy slide, and mushroom waterfall. Bigger kids will like the three-story waterslides.

As a university town with some beautiful old homes, Missoula has an abundance of appealing B&Bs. One of the best, and right on the river, is a vast 1911 home built for the University of Montana's president. Since then, the home has been a fraternity, a lab, and an office. But now it is the wonderful **Goldsmith's Inn** (803 E. Front St., 406/728-1585, www.missoulabedandbreakfast.com, $139-202), a charming turn-of-the-20th-century bed-and-breakfast within easy walking distance of the university and downtown. Much smaller but equally inviting is the dog-friendly **Blossom's Bed & Breakfast** (1114 Poplar St., 406/721-4690, www.blossomsbnb.com, $150-195), a 1910 Craftsman gem not far from the trails of the Rattlesnake Recreation Area and Wilderness. Nestled on a mountainside outside of town is **Blue Mountain Bed & Breakfast** (6980 Deadman Gulch Rd., 406/251-4457 or 877/251-4457, www.bluemountainbb.com, $150-186), a tranquil spot where you can explore nature and even bring your own horse. By far the most dramatic B&B in town is the four-room **Gibson Mansion** (823 39th St., 406/251-1345 or 866/251-1345, www.gibsonmansion.com, $179-324), designed and built in 1903 by architect A. J. Gibson, who was responsible for many of the buildings on the university campus. The period details are spot-on, the gardens exquisite, and the breakfasts decadent.

Twenty minutes north of Missoula is the **Gelandesprung Lodge at Snowbowl** (1700 Snowbowl Rd., 406/549-9777, www.montanasnowbowl.com, from $44 shared bath, $56 private bath, $88 two-room suite), a European-style lodge right on the mountain and open throughout the ski season and on weekends in summer. Rates are announced seasonally, so call ahead or check online.

At the other end of the spectrum is an ultraluxe experience that will thin your wallet considerably. The **Resort at Paws Up** (40060 Paws Up Rd., 406/244-5200, luxury tents $980-1,670/night for 2 people) in Greenough, about 32 miles (52 km) east of Missoula, is among the most glamorous spots in the state. There are luxury homes and luxury tents that are unimaginably elegant, with heated floors, electricity, king-size feather beds, a dining pavilion with your own personal chef, a camping butler, and nightly bonfires with s'mores. This is camping fit for a high-maintenance king. The food is exquisite, as is the spa, and the activities and adventures are limitless.

CAMPING

There are only a handful of private campgrounds in Missoula, but the **Lolo National Forest** (406/329-3750, www.fs.usda.gov/lolo) has a wide range of campsites in beautiful settings, among them Lolo Creek, Ninemile, and Rock Creek. Camping is also permitted in certain sections of the **Rattlesnake National Recreation Area and Wilderness** (406/329-3814) beyond a 3-mile (4.8-km) radius from the main trailhead.

For in-town convenience with RV-specific sites, try the **Missoula KOA** (3450 Tina Ave., 406/549-0881 or 800/562-5366, www.missoulakoa.com, year-round, $35-44 tents, $44-79 RVs, $65-153 cabins). The tree-lined property offers 200 RV and tent sites in addition to amenities like a heated pool, two hot tubs, bike rentals, minigolf, free Wi-Fi, nightly ice cream, and a café that serves breakfast daily in summer. Another great option for Yogi and Booboo fans is the award-winning **Jellystone Park** (9900 Jellystone Ave., 800/318-9644, www.campjellystonemt.com, $36 tents, $47 RVs, $66 cabins), which offers an expansive menu of amenities including air-conditioned cabins, heated swimming pool, playground, minigolf, game room, and nightly visits with Yogi. Offering nice, shady sites just outside of town is the Good Sam-recognized **Jim and Mary's RV Park** (9800 Hwy. 93 N., 406/549-4416, www.jimandmarys.com, RV sites $49, including water, sewer, electric, cable TV, and Wi-Fi).

INFORMATION AND SERVICES

The **Missoula Chamber of Commerce** (825 E. Front St., 406/543-6623, www.missoulachamber.com, 8am-5pm Mon.-Fri.) and **Destination Missoula** (101 E. Main St., 800/526-3465 for travel consultation, www.destinationmissoula.org) are both great sources of information for visitors.

The **U.S. Forest Service** (26 Fort Missoula Rd., 406/329-3511) and the **Montana Department of Fish, Wildlife and Parks** (3201 Spurgin Rd., 406/542-5500,

8am-5pm Mon.-Fri.) offices offer good information about hiking, camping, and fishing in the national forests.

The **main post office** is at 1100 West Kent Avenue; the downtown location is 200 East Broadway. The **Missoula Public Library** (301 E. Main St., 406/721-2665, www.missoulapubliclibrary.org, 10am-9pm Mon.-Wed., 10am-6pm Thurs.-Sat., 1pm-5pm Sun.) is open daily.

The main hospitals are **St. Patrick's** (500 W. Broadway, 406/543-7271) and **Community Medical Center** (2827 Fort Missoula Rd., 406/728-4100), both of which have 24-hour emergency rooms. There are several walk-in urgent care facilities in town. The **CostCare Family Practice Walk-In Clinic** (2819 Great Northern Loop, 406/541-3046, www.costcare.com, 8:30am-5pm Mon.-Fri., 9am-2pm Sat.-Sun.) has several locations and expanded hours, including weekends.

The **Green Hanger** laundry (960 E. Broadway St. and 146 Woodford St., 406/728-1919 and 406/728-1948, www.greenhangermissoula.com, 7:30am-9:30pm daily) offers two locations with dry cleaning and laundry facilities (including Wi-Fi and free laundry soap), plus drop-off laundry services and a car wash.

TRANSPORTATION
Getting There
Just 4 miles (6.4 km) northwest of the university, **Missoula International Airport** (MSO, 5225 U.S. 10 W., 406/728-4381, www.flymissoula.com) is served by Alaska, Allegiant, American, Delta, Frontier, and United. On the first floor of the terminal are **Alamo, Avis, Budget, Enterprise, National, Thrifty**, and **Hertz** car-rental agencies. **Dollar** has shuttles to and from the airport. Most hotels offer free shuttle service to and from the airport; the **Airport Shuttler** (406/543-9416 or 406/880-7433, www.msoshuttle.com) also provides transportation into town.

The **Greyhound** bus station (1660 W. Broadway, 406/549-2339) has several buses in and out of town daily.

I-90 runs directly through Missoula, making it an easy destination by car. Missoula is 115 miles (185 km) west of Helena and the same south of Kalispell, 120 miles (193 km) northwest of Butte, and about 200 miles (320 km) northwest of Bozeman.

Getting Around
The **Mountain Line** (406/721-3333, www.mountainline.com, 6am-8:45pm Mon.-Fri., 9am-6pm Sat., free) is the free city bus service; the city has worked hard to make this a zero-fare public transportation system.

For taxi service, call **Yellow Cab** (406/543-6644, www.yellowcabmissoula.com) or **Green Taxi** (406/728-8294), which only uses hybrid cars.

Hamilton and the Bitterroot Valley

The peaceful and dramatically beautiful valley known as the Bitterroot, named by Meriwether Lewis, has a fascinating history; the region's past has been filled with promise and heartbreak since Lewis and Clark's visit in 1805.

In 1854, John Mullan, who masterminded the Mullan Road overland route to the Pacific, predicted that while much of the region was unpopulated rugged wilderness, the Bitterroot Valley would soon be "one villaged valley, teeming with life, and bustle and business." Nearly 160 years later, his prediction has panned out; the Bitterroot Valley is one of the fastest-growing regions in Montana but still retains a gorgeous swath of green-drenched mountains with sparkling rivers, quaint little towns, and no end of opportunities for outdoor adventures. The drive through towns like Florence, Stevensville,

Victor, Corvallis, Hamilton, and Darby is utterly scenic and a splendid way to spend a day or two. The largest of the towns in the Bitterroot Valley, Hamilton was founded by copper king Marcus Daly and named for James Hamilton, one of Daly's employees. Calamity Jane was among the town's most notorious residents.

The climate here is milder than in other parts of the state, sandwiched as it is between the Bitterroot and Sapphire mountain ranges. Anglers, cyclists, and hikers will not want to leave, and history buffs and antiques hunters will be content here as well.

LOLO HOT SPRINGS RESORT

Although not among the state's fanciest, the hot springs at **Lolo Hot Springs Resort** (38500 W. U.S. 12, 800/273-2290 or 877/541-5117, www.lolohotsprings.com, deluxe cabins $120-180, heated camping cabins $55) are among those that were known to indigenous people long before Lewis and Clark arrived in the region. The area was a natural mineral lick for wildlife and an ancient meeting spot for Native Americans. It was also a well-known rendezvous site for trappers and prospectors. As early as 1888, the springs were advertised in Missoula newspapers for board, room, and bath for $11 per week. Today the resort offers deluxe cabins, heated camping cabins, tipis, and RV and tent sites (from $16). There is a restaurant on-site too.

In summer this is a great camping spot, with immediate access to both the Lolo and Bitterroot National Forests as well as many miles of prime river access. In winter the area is popular for snowmobilers, and snowmobile rentals are available daily on-site. The naturally heated mineral pools (10am-10pm Mon.-Thurs., 10am-midnight Fri.-Sun. summer, 10am-9pm Mon.-Thurs., 10am-midnight Fri.-Sat., 10am-9pm Sun. winter, $7 adults, $6 seniors 55 and over, $5 children 5-12) are sublime at any time of year. Entrance to the pools is included with cabin rentals.

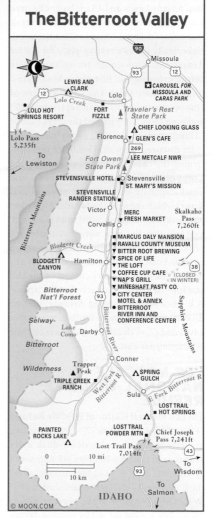

TRAVELERS' REST STATE PARK

Just 0.5 mile (0.8 km) west of the town of Lolo on U.S. 12, **Travelers' Rest State Park** (406/273-4253, www.travelersrest.org, 9am-5pm daily year-round, visitors center 9:30am-4:30pm daily spring-summer, 10am-4pm daily fall-winter, $6/vehicle, free with Montana license plates) is a critical stop for any Lewis and Clark buff. The park is a large grassy area with a tree-lined creek that occupies about 50 acres (20.2 hectares). Historically it was a resting place for Native Americans, who would set up camp here before crossing the Bitterroot Mountains; it is also where Lewis and Clark's Corps of Discovery camped twice, in September 1805 and June 1806. They named the creek nearby "Travellers Rest." In 2002 an archaeological team discovered physical evidence that confirmed the campsite had been used by the Corps of Discovery—it's the only Lewis and Clark campsite with verified physical evidence, which came in the form of high mercury levels. It was determined from the Corps' journals that the men were given mercury pills, which caused immediate evacuation of their bowels, to cure any number of ailments. The high mercury content of the soil was limited to a pit that served as the latrine. A kitchen was discovered Army regulation distance away. It was also at this campsite that Lewis and Clark decided to part ways on their return journey east.

LEE METCALF NATIONAL WILDLIFE REFUGE

The **Lee Metcalf National Wildlife Refuge** (4567 Wildfowl Ln., 406/777-5552, www.fws. gov/refuge/lee_metcalf/, dawn-dusk daily year-round) is about 30 miles (48 km) south of Missoula on U.S. 93 in Stevensville, along the Bitterroot River. It was established in 1963 by locals in response to the negative effects on wildlife habitat caused by ranches, farms, and the logging industry, and it was named in 1978 after a U.S. senator from Montana who was dedicated to the conservation movement. Its main purpose is as a refuge for migratory birds, including ospreys, eagles, and hawks. Larger animals such as white-tailed deer and coyotes can be spotted in the area as well. In the summer, after the nesting season has finished, a 2-mile (3.2-km) hiking trail is opened that loops through the wildlife-viewing area; two shorter trails are available year-round.

Wildfowl Lane, a county road, runs through the refuge and provides many viewing opportunities from the car.

STEVENSVILLE

Known primarily for the beautifully preserved mission built by Belgian-born Jesuit priest Pierre-Jean De Smet, **Stevensville** (population 1,963; elevation 3,323 ft/1,013 m) is surrounded by the Bitterroot and Sapphire Mountains and the Lee Metcalf National Wildlife Refuge. It provides superb access to hiking, biking, and fishing for outdoors enthusiasts. The town's history comes to life at Fort Owen, St. Mary's Mission, and the Stevensville Museum.

St. Mary's Mission

As the first permanent settlement in the state, many see **St. Mary's Mission** (315 Charlos St., 406/777-5734, www.saintmarysmission. org, Apr. 15-Oct. 15, tours 10am-4pm Tues.-Fri., 11am-3pm Sat., gift shop 10am-5pm Tues.-Fri., 11am-3pm Sat., grounds free, museum $3 adults, $2 students, free for children under 6, tours $8 adults, $7 seniors 60 and over, $6 students, free for children under 6) as the birthplace of modern Montana. Its origin dates to the winter of 1823-1824 when two dozen Iroquois were employed as trappers by the Hudson's Bay Company. Twelve of the Iroquois stayed in the Bitterroot Valley that winter, were adopted by the Salish people, and married Salish women. Having been introduced to Christianity 200 years earlier, the Iroquois shared stories of the men they called "blackrobes," who could speak to God. The Salish and neighboring Nez Perce were so riveted by the stories that they wanted to bring the blackrobes to their encampments. Four separate missions were dispatched to make contact with the blackrobes in St. Louis; all were futile until 1839, when the Indians met Father Pierre-Jean De Smet S. J. In 1841, De Smet arrived in the Bitterroot Valley with two

1: St. Mary's Mission **2:** the Marcus Daly Mansion in Hamilton

other priests and three laypeople. When they reached what would become Stevensville, De Smet and his men erected a cross and built the church, naming it St. Mary's Mission.

Four years later, the mission was commandeered by an Italian Jesuit priest named Anthony Ravalli. Ravalli was a physician, surgeon, pharmacist, architect, and artist who built the first flour mill and sawmill in the state. He respected the Salish, and although he was loved by his constituents, the mission was temporarily closed in 1850 when many of the Salish rebelled against practices meant to diminish their own traditions and way of life. During its closure the facility was sold to John Owen, and when the Jesuits could not return, as stipulated in the conditions of the sale, the church was burned; in its place Owen built a trading post known as Fort Owen. Ravalli stayed among the Native Americans in western Montana as their physician and spiritual guide.

In 1866, Ravalli built a new chapel and hospital just 1 mile (1.6 km) south of Fort Owen; it was doubled in size in 1879 to include Ravalli's house and pharmacy, a cabin for Salish chief Victor, and a cemetery where Jesuits and Salish were buried side by side. After Ravalli's death in 1884 and the subsequent forced exodus of the Salish from their homeland, the mission was permanently shuttered.

Today the buildings have been painstakingly restored to their original simple beauty. The chapel's colorful interior reflects the Italian Renaissance and re-creates the original colors Ravalli achieved using vermillion clay for the reds, blue from indigo traded among the Native Americans, and yellow from a sacred cave near the Judith River in central Montana. This place has been so lovingly restored that its sacred spirit is palpable; a visit here is time well spent. Mass is said in this historic chapel twice annually, on opening day and the third Sunday in September, in conjunction with the Salish pilgrimage.

Fort Owen State Park

Established in 1850 on the grounds of the original St. Mary's Mission, **Fort Owen State Park** (100 Stevensville Cutoff Rd. E., 406/273-4253, 8am-9pm daily May-Aug., 9am-5pm daily Sept.-Apr., free) is a great place for a picnic. Considered to be the site of the first permanent white settlement in the state, the site was a trading post established by Major John Owen, and visitors can wander around the restored rooms of the east barracks, which are appointed with period furnishings. Pets are welcome, and there is a picnic table and a vault toilet. Donations are appreciated.

Entertainment and Events

The third weekend of June is the time for **Western Heritage Days** (406/777-3773, www.mainstreetstevensville.com), a celebration of old-time traditions with historic home tours, wagon rides, a parade, cook-off, and more, in downtown Stevensville.

HAMILTON

The business and trading center of the Bitterroot Valley, Hamilton (population 4,674; elevation 3,572 ft/1,089 m) is a bustling and vibrant little community with a significant historic house, the Marcus Daly Mansion, as well as a museum set in a beautiful old courthouse, an important national research laboratory that arose from government concern over a spotted fever outbreak around the turn of the 20th century, and an abundance of great restaurants and art galleries. If you want to spend more than a day in the area, Hamilton makes an excellent base.

Marcus Daly Mansion

Among the original copper kings, Marcus Daly was an Irish immigrant who came to Butte and founded the Anaconda Copper Company, which dominated Montana's economy for more than 50 years. Daly became fabulously wealthy and built a dream life for himself in the Bitterroot Valley, with elaborate horse barns complete with hospitals and Turkish baths for his world-class racehorses, 15,000 acres (6,070 hectares) of farmland that included extensive livestock holdings, and a 24,000-square-foot (2,230-sq-m) mansion with more than 25 bedrooms. So many hundreds of people staffed the mansion, the racehorse operation, and the ranching and farming outfits that Daly had to build a town—Hamilton—to accommodate them all.

The home itself was purchased by the Daly family in 1886 and remodeled extensively several times until 1910, when it was transformed into its present Georgian revival style. The **Marcus Daly Mansion** (251 Eastside Hwy., 406/363-6004, www.dalymansion.org, tours on the hour 10am-3pm daily mid-May-early Oct., holiday tours Nov. 28-Dec. 20, $10 adults, $9 seniors, $7 children 6-17, free for children under 6, grounds open during tour season 9am-5pm) has been impeccably maintained and can be visited only on tours, which include the mansion itself, the laundry house, the greenhouse, the playhouse, the swimming pool, and the tennis courts. Weddings and parties are often held on the magnificently landscaped grounds, known as the **Margaret M. Daly Memorial Arboretum and Botanic Garden.** Check the website for scheduled events ranging from lawn parties to Shakespearean performances to murder mystery weekends. Daly Days, a two-day celebration of the Daly family and the town of Hamilton's heritage held in late July, is an ideal time to visit. But the mansion is a lovely, quiet place to spend any afternoon, imagining the kind of lives that were once lived here.

Ravalli County Museum

The **Ravalli County Museum** (205 Bedford St., 406/363-3338, www.ravallimuseum.org, 10am-4pm Tues.-Wed. and Fri., 10am-8pm Thurs., 9am-1pm Sat., $3 adults, $6 families, free for children, free for everyone on Thurs. and Sat.) is housed in the 1900 county courthouse. Operated by the Bitterroot Valley Historical Society, it is dedicated to preserving the cultural heritage of the valley. In addition to their rotating exhibits, the museum's permanent collection focuses on telling the stories of the Salish, Kootenia, and Pend d'Orielle people, as well as early settlers in the area.

Entertainment and Events

The **Hamilton Farmers Market** (205 Bedford St. between 2nd St. and 3rd St., 406/961-0004, www.hamiltonfarmersmarket. org, 9am-12:30pm Sat. early May-early Oct.) offers a bounty of local produce, much of it organic, along with local baked goods, arts and crafts, prepared food, and family entertainment. **First Friday Hamilton** (406/360-9124, www.hamiltondowntownassociation. org) happens the first Friday of each month in summer and is an arts-oriented street party with special sales and great food and drinks. Keep an eye open for Hamilton's **Music on Main** (406/360-9124, www. hamiltondowntownassociation.org), which closes down Main Street for a townwide party with live music and street vendors selling food, wine, and beer. It generally happens the second Friday of the month in summer, but visit the website for specific dates and band names.

DARBY

Once the terminus of the Northern Pacific Railway, Darby (pop. 763, elevation 3,888 ft/1,185 m) is perhaps best known for its place in some of the great logging debates of the 1960s-1980s, along with one of the largest pro-logging organized protests in the country in 1988. Referred to as "the Great Log Haul," some 300 fully loaded logging trucks delivered their loads to the Darby Lumber Company on May 13, 1988, to call attention to the plight of the loggers and mill workers who were affected by the big timber companies' flooding of the market, which led to plummeting prices and the subsequent closure of public land to prevent further logging. Much of western Montana, and the Bitterroot Valley in particular, had relied on logging for nearly a century; layoffs and mill closings had an enormous impact.

Entertainment and Events

A great regional event is **Darby Logger Days** (http://darbyloggerdays.com), held annually the third weekend in July. The two-day event celebrates the region's logging history with logger sports, kids' activities, a parade, and a concert. Admission is $15 Friday, $20 Saturday, and kids under 12 are free when accompanied by an adult.

SPORTS AND RECREATION

Fishing

Without a doubt, this valley offers some of the best fishing in the West. The Bitterroot River runs north from Connor, where the East Fork and West Fork (both of which offer great fishable waters) join to form the Bitterroot, up the valley to Missoula, where it flows into the Clark Fork River. In addition to its breathtaking beauty and relatively easy access via its close proximity to the road, the Bitterroot River offers diverse waters, with everything from riffles and pools to flats and gravel bars. Rainbow trout are the most plentiful fish, but browns and cutthroats can be found in the upper portion of the river, upstream from Hamilton. The best-known insect hatch is probably the spring Skwala hatch, which usually starts in March, one of the earliest in the state, and lasts well into April. All fishing during the Skwala hatch is strictly catch-and-release. In late June-early July, after the river has cleared of spring runoff, the big hatches are the Green Drake and Brown Drake hatches, which can last for several weeks. In the fall, September-October, the tiny Trico hatch offers some of the best (and toughest) fishing on the river. In general, the farther you get from Missoula, the fewer the anglers and the better the fishing. Still, there is wonderful wading and floating all along the river.

With so much productive water, it's no surprise that there are plenty of guides in the region. **Freestone Fly Shop** (701 S. 1st St., Hamilton, 406/363-9099, www. freestoneflyshop.com, $525/day for 1-2 anglers, $450/half-day for 1-2 anglers) is a good place to start, both for guided fishing and for equipment and flies. It provides lodging and fishing packages as well. Missoula native Tom Jenni of **Tom Jenni's Reel Montana** (406/539-6610 or 866/885-6065, www. tomjenni.com) guides in the area and is an exceptional all-around guide.

Hiking and Biking

With two mountain ranges on either side of the valley, the hiking and biking opportunities in the Bitterroot are endless. The **Stevensville Ranger Station** (88 Main St., Stevensville, 406/777-5461, www.fs.usda. gov) and the **Bitterroot National Forest Office** (1801 N. 1st St., Hamilton, 406/363-7100, www.fs.usda.gov) are great places to get maps and ideas.

It's possible in this valley to hike portions of both the **Lewis and Clark Trail** through the Bitterroot Mountains and the **Nee-Me-Poo Trail** (www.fs.usda.gov), the route of the Nez Perce on their fateful 1877 flight from the U.S. Army. The Nee-Me-Poo Trail is at the southern end of the valley near Sula, and the Lewis and Clark Trail is farther north near Lolo Pass.

Among the most popular areas to hike because of its supremely rugged beauty is **Blodgett Canyon,** 5 miles (8 km) northwest of Hamilton in the Bitterroot Mountains. The out-and-back hike is spectacular from the get-go with a nice stream and canyon walls. There are several waterfalls along the way, including a beautiful one at 3.6 miles (5.8 km), and the most dedicated can hike a full 12.5 miles (20.1 km) to Blodgett Lake, making it a 25-mile (40-km) trip. The trail is never too steep, and there is plenty of wildlife—including moose, deer, and elk—farther into the canyon. To find the trailhead, turn west off U.S. 93 2 miles (3.2 km) north of Hamilton onto Bowman Road, and follow it for 0.6 mile (1 km). Turn left onto Richetts Road, follow it for 2 miles (3.2 km), and then turn west onto Forest Road 736 for 2.4 miles (3.9 km) to the intersection of Blodgett Canyon Road. Turn right and drive 1.5 miles (2.4 km) to the trailhead.

Another wonderful quick hike that offers an excellent overlook of Blodgett Canyon and signs of the great fires of 2000 is the **Blodgett Canyon Overlook**. It is a short 3-mile (4.8-km) round-trip trail, but it is steep, with 1,100 feet (335 m) of elevation gain on a switchbacking trail to a heart-stopping overlook. There are benches along the way and an interpretive exhibit on forest fire ecology. To find the trailhead, follow the directions to the Blodgett Canyon Trailhead above, but at Blodgett Canyon Road, turn left (west) and drive 3 miles (4.8 km) to the trailhead.

The U.S. Forest Service maintains three mountain bike trails in the valley: the 10-mile (16.1-km) **Bass Creek Recreation Area Day Use Trail** (Bass Creek Rd., 5 miles northwest of Stevensville), the 17-mile (27-km) **Hart Bench Mountain Bike Loop** (off Forest Rd. 5711) near Darby, and the 19-mile (31-km) **Railroad Creek Mountain Bike Loop** (Skalkaho-Rye Rd., 16 mi/26 km southeast of Hamilton). Road cyclists will be grateful for the paved path between Lolo and Florence that eliminates the need to ride on the highway. Rentals, service, and repairs are available at **Valley Bicycles and Ski** (219 S. 1st St., Hamilton, 406/363-4428, 10am-6pm Mon.-Fri., 10am-3pm Sat.). The best resource in the area for race-worthy mountain bikes is **Red Barn Bicycles** (399 McCarthy Loop, Hamilton, 406/363-2662, www. redbarnbicycles.com, 10am-6pm Tues.-Fri., 10am-4pm Sat.).

Horseback Riding

In addition to numerous guest ranches in the area (listed at www.montanadra.com), guided trail rides are available in Lolo, about 30 minutes' drive north of Hamilton, from the **Dunrovin Ranch** (5001 Expedition Dr., Lolo, 406/273-7745, www.dunrovinranchmontana. com). Corral sessions ($50) are great for children as young as three, and give new riders the opportunity to start slow. Trail rides off the ranch are available to anyone older than eight, ranging from one hour ($80 pp) or two hours ($115 pp) to half-day (4-6 hours, $160

pp) and full-day (6-9 hours, $260 pp). Rides might climb up to magnificent mountain views or travel along and across the river or through lush forests, and private rides can be arranged as well. Dunrovin Ranch also offers a historical ride perfect for history buffs and mountain men wannabes.

Golf

The 18-hole **Hamilton Golf Club** (1004 Golf Course Rd., 406/363-4251, www. golfhamiltonmt.com, Mar. 1-Oct. 31, $29 for 18 holes, $17 for 9 holes), 3 miles (4.8 km) east of Hamilton, was established in 1924 and is still considered among the best public courses in the Northwest. The mild weather in the valley gives this course more playable days than almost any other in the state. A snack bar serves everything from breakfast sandwiches to burgers.

Winter Recreation

For downhill skiing, head down the valley to **Lost Trail Powder Mountain** (Conner, 406/821-3211, www.losttrail.com, 9:30am-4pm Thurs.-Sun. Dec.-Apr., extended hours around holidays and in spring, $46 adults full-day or $41 half-day morning or afternoon, $36 children 6-12 full-day or $32 half-day, free for children 5 and under), which sits high atop the Continental Divide and straddles the Idaho-Montana border. It is a great small-town Montana family-friendly mountain with fantastic terrain and more than 300 inches (762 cm) of snow annually. There are one-ride passes and discounts for afternoon-only and morning-only skiing as well as discounts for seniors and almost-seniors.

Cross-country skiers will be in heaven in the Bitterroot with places like **Chief Joseph Cross-Country Ski Trail** (Hwy. 43, 40 mi/64 km south of Hamilton), which offers 19 miles (31 km) of groomed trails for every level of ability. Groomed by the Bitterroot Cross-Country Ski Club, the trails and warming hut are open December-mid-April or as the snow permits.

At the end of a long winter's day, why not soak in the warm waters at **Lost Trail Hot Springs** (283 Lost Trail Hot Springs Rd., Sula, 406/821-3574, www.losttrailhotsprings. com, $8.25 ages 13-59, $6.25 seniors 60 and over, $6.25 children 3-12, $2.25 children 1-2) in Sula, not far from either ski area. The rustic resort offers a marvelous hot pool in any weather as well as lodging, food, and plenty of history.

FOOD

It is possible to get the impression that Bitterroot Valley residents live on a liquid diet of coffee and beer, as there is plenty of both to be had. But with its comparatively milder climate and abundance of local produce, the valley also boasts some excellent restaurants.

In Hamilton, **Bitter Root Brewing** (101 Marcus St., 406/363-7468, www. bitterrootbrewing.com, 11:30am-8pm daily, $7-11) offers great local beer, brewed on-site, along with some delicious tacos, burgers, and standard pub food. For eclectic ethnic food, Hamilton's **Spice of Life** (163 S. 2nd St., 406/363-4433, www.thespiceinhamilton. com, 11am-2pm Mon.-Fri., 5pm-9pm Tues.-Sat., $14-31) serves a compelling assortment of dishes, as suggested by the giant neon chili pepper outside. Don't miss the daily specials, and both kids and their parents will be happy with the children's menu. For fresh-baked goods in Hamilton, you can't go wrong at **Coffee Cup Cafe** (500 S. 1st St., 406/363-3822, 6am-10pm daily, $5-17), which serves breads, cakes, muffins, soups, and more made from scratch daily. For pie lovers, this is the place. **The Loft Café** (217 Main St., 406/375-5871, 7am-4pm daily, $7-11) serves breakfast all day in a big way. The menu offers fresh, hearty dishes—from crepes and wraps to scrambles and breakfast sandwiches. The salads are yummy too. For a unique Montana meal, **Mineshaft Pasty Co.** (111 N. 2nd St., 406/361-8170, 8:30am-6:30pm Mon.-Fri., 10am-4pm Sat., $6-8) serves traditional Cornish meat pies, called pasties (PASS-tees), long favored for their hearty taste and convenience by Montana miners. You can get yours filled with everything from eggs, cheese, onions, and potatoes to beef tenderloin and mushrooms. Mineshaft also has a full-service coffee bar. For Montana takeout, nothing beats **Nap's Grill** (220 N. 2nd St., 406/363-0136, www.napsgrill.com, 11am-9pm Mon.-Thurs., 11am-10pm Fri.-Sat., 11am-8pm Sun., $6-34) for its burgers, cheesesteaks, and steaks. Diehards might like to try the $35 Bitterroot Beast, which is three 12-ounce (340-g) patties topped with mushrooms, onions, and bacon, served with a pound of fries and a 16-ounce (473-ml) milk shake. Finish it all in 25 minutes and your meal is free, as is the bellyache.

In Florence, **Glen's Café** (157 Long Ave., 406/273-2534, www.glenscafe.com, 9am-3pm daily, $7-11) is a wonderful old log cabin that serves up hearty meals, homemade pies, and local art in equally delicious amounts.

In Corvallis, **The Merc Fresh Market** (1000 Main St., 406/961-4830, 6:30am-9pm daily) is a terrific market with fantastic prepared foods. Dine-in service and takeout are available.

ACCOMMODATIONS

The greatest number of hotels can be found in the valley's largest town, Hamilton, but the valley overall offers a handsome range of accommodations, from the ultraluxe, adults-only **Triple Creek Ranch** (5551 West Fork Rd., near Darby, 406/821-4600 or 800/654-2943, www.triplecreekranch. com, $1,121-2,759/night/couple all-inclusive) to the budget-friendly and pet-friendly **City Center Motel & Annex** (415 W. Main St., Hamilton, 406/363-1651, www. remlcsportsmanslodging.com, $50-91), which has standard rooms with microwaves and mini-refrigerators or full kitchenettes.

Among the larger properties in Hamilton is the pet-friendly, 65-room **Bitterroot River Inn and Conference Center** (139 Bitterroot Plaza Dr., 406/375-2525 or 877/274-8274, www.bitterrootriverinn.com, $139-179), which has all the standard amenities and comfortable, Western log decor.

A historic property that is long on charm is the **Stevensville Hotel** (107 E. 3rd St., Stevensville, 406/777-3087 or 888/816-2875, www.stevensvillehotel.com, $95-150), housed in the 1910 Thornton Hospital building. In bed-and-breakfast tradition, the rooms are individually decorated with period furnishings, and the continental breakfast is delicious. Dogs are welcome in two of the rooms for an additional fee.

A delightful, homey, one-bedroom rental within easy walking distance to downtown shops and restaurants, and the River Park Trail System is **Withy Gate** (701 S. 3rd St., Hamilton, 406/360-7019, www.vbro.com/275459, from $85).

For vacation rentals throughout the valley, ranging from cozy, remote cabins to condos and farmhouses, try **Cardinal Properties** (320 S. 2nd St., Hamilton, 406/363-4430, www.cardinalproperties.net) or **Sweet Sage MT** (406/369-0644, www.sweetsagemt.com).

CAMPING

Camping options in the valley are almost unlimited, with dozens of Forest Service campgrounds nearby. A good place to start is to contact the **U.S. Forest Service** (406/363-7100, www.fs.usda.gov) for camping in the Bitterroot National Forest.

A really beautiful campground is the **Lake Como Campgrounds** (County Rd. 82, 4 mi/6.4 km north of Darby, 406/363-7100, early June-early Sept., $16), which has 12 tent sites and 12 RV sites.

The **Bitterroot Valley RV Park and Campground** (1744 U.S. 93 S., 406/363-2430 or 406/531-1390, www.bitterrootvalleyrv.com, year-round, $18 tents, $18-28 RVs) is a pleasant and budget-friendly private campground 8 miles (12.9 km) south of Hamilton.

INFORMATION AND SERVICES

The **Bitterroot Valley Chamber of Commerce** (105 E. Main St., Hamilton, 406/363-2400, 8am-5pm Mon.-Fri.) is in Hamilton.

The nearest 24-hour emergency rooms are in Missoula, 47 miles (76 km) north of Hamilton and about an hour's drive, at **St. Patrick's** (500 W. Broadway, 406/543-7271) and **Community Medical Center** (2827 Fort Missoula Rd., 406/728-4100). **Bitterroot Valley Urgent Care** (1230 N. 1st St., 406/363-4120, 8:30am-6pm Mon.-Tues. and Fri., 10am-3pm Sat., 10am-2pm Sun.) is in Hamilton.

TRANSPORTATION
Getting There

The best way to visit the valley is by car. No major bus lines serve the area, and the closest international airport is **Missoula International Airport** (MSO, 5225 U.S. 10 W., 406/728-4381, www.flymissoula.com), served by Alaska, Allegiant, American, Delta, Frontier, and United.

U.S. 93 runs directly through the valley and can often be congested. To get a beautiful view of the Bitterroot Mountains and a sense of this historic part of Montana, take scenic Highway 269 between Stevensville and Hamilton. South from Missoula, Lolo is 9 miles (14.5 km), Hamilton is 50 miles (81 km), and Darby is 64 miles (103 km).

Getting Around

On the 1st floor of the Missoula International Airport terminal are the **Alamo, Avis, Budget, Enterprise, National, Thrifty,** and **Hertz** car-rental agencies. **Dollar** has shuttles to and from the airport.

The Flathead and Mission Valleys

Home to the largest freshwater lake in the western United States, a mountain range that will take your breath away, and the wide-open space of the National Bison Range, this part of Montana truly is God's country. The Flathead Valley, home to such towns as Kalispell, Whitefish, Polson, and Bigfork, is situated just west of the Continental Divide amid the Swan, Mission, Salish, and Whitefish mountain ranges. The Mission Valley is south of Flathead Lake and the Flathead Valley and includes the communities of St. Ignatius, Ronan, and Hot Springs, all three of which are located on the Flathead Indian Reservation. All tiny, with populations ranging from 557 in Hot Springs to 2,016 in Ronan, these are fascinating places with rich histories, but not too many services. St. Ignatius is home to a remarkable Catholic mission, built in 1854. Ronan was settled in 1883 and provides excellent access into the Mission Mountains Wilderness Area and the Ninepipe and Pablo National Wildlife Refuge complex. Hot Springs was founded in 1910 around the natural mineral springs in the area that still attract visitors today.

Between the wildlife refuges and the 1.3-million-acre (526,091-hectare) Flathead Indian Reservation, the area is of great significance, historically and today. Time spent in these valleys is often quiet and contemplative; there are many opportunities to learn. Flathead Lake has created a vacation culture all its own, with luxe lodges, sprawling lakeside manses, and high-end shops and eateries in and around Bigfork. Endless recreational opportunities are available as well, including hiking, boating, and soaking in hot springs. On the way to Glacier, these valleys and their small but vibrant communities should not be overlooked.

ST. IGNATIUS

The oldest town on the Flathead Reservation, and among the oldest settlements in the state, St. Ignatius (population 824; elevation 2,939 ft/896 m) is the site of the St. Ignatius Mission, built in 1854 by Jesuit priest Adrian Hoecken, who moved from Washington State to be closer to the indigenous people he wanted to reach. The town grew quickly as nearly 1,000 Native Americans resettled near the mission, and in 1864 a group of nuns added schools and a hospital to the community.

The building considered to be the oldest in the state, constructed in 1846, is at Fort Connah, just 6 miles (9.7 km) north of St. Ignatius on U.S. 93. It is all that remains of the last trading post built in the United States by the Hudson's Bay Company. The post was in operation until 1871.

★ St. Ignatius Mission

The beloved redbrick chapel standing today on the **St. Ignatius Mission** (300 Bear Track Ave., 406/745-2768, 9am-7pm daily summer, 9am-5pm daily winter, mass 9am Sun., free, donations accepted) was built in the 1890s, but the mission itself was settled as early as 1854 by Jesuit priest Adrian Hoecken and hundreds of Native Americans who set up camp near him. In 1864, a group of nuns from Montreal, the Sisters of Providence, came to the mission to open a boarding school for girls, a hospital, and eventually, with the help of Ursuline nuns, an orphanage, a kindergarten, and a school for boys. At its peak in the mid-1890s, some 320 children attended school at the mission. Sadly, the schools were burned down by one of the students, and when the federal government ceased aiding the mission, they could not be rebuilt and were shut down altogether.

The handsome brick chapel was completed in 1894 with 58 original murals painted by Joseph Carignano, who worked in the kitchen and as a handyman for the mission.

Carignano taught himself to paint and managed to complete the frescoes in only 14 months despite working on them only when he wasn't doing his primary job. The paintings tell the life story of St. Ignatius Loyola. In the summer of 2016, significant cracks in the frescoes were being monitored, and the church is hoping to raise the money to preserve them.

In addition to the chapel, a small museum and gift shop can be found in the log house that was the original residence of the Sisters of Providence.

National Bison Range

Established in 1908 when the population of bison across North America had dropped from upward of 30 million animals down to just a few hundred, the **National Bison Range** (58355 Bison Range Rd., 406/644-2211, www.fws.gov, gate hours 6:30am-10pm daily summer, exact hours vary depending on sunlight, year-round, $5/vehicle May-Oct.) is one of the oldest animal refuges in the country and well worth a visit. Located off Highway 212 in Moiese, the refuge comprises 18,500 acres (7,487 hectares) and is home to around 400 bison, not to mention white-tailed and mule deer, bighorn sheep, pronghorn, and elk.

There are two driving routes: The year-round West Loop and Prairie Drive is a short 5-mile (8-km) tour that takes about 30 minutes, and the other is a 17-mile (27-km) one-way loop, Red Sleep Mountain Drive, that climbs about 2,000 feet (610 m) and takes close to two hours. The longer route, open in summer, is incredibly scenic and definitely worth the time. The roads through the refuge are gravel; no bicycles or motorcycles are permitted on them, but parking is available at the **visitors center** (9am-5pm daily). Several short hiking trails leave from the day-use area as well as from Red Sleep Mountain Drive.

Before beginning your tour, stop in at the visitors center for informative displays, knowledgeable park rangers, and a large relief map of the refuge marked with small lights indicating where bison can likely be seen that day.

RONAN

Named for the first Indian agent, Major Peter Ronan, who wrote the history of the Flathead people and was respected by them, the town of Ronan (population 2,016; elevation 3,048 ft/929 m) was once part of the Flathead Reservation before it was opened to sale and settlement in 1910.

Ronan's history is marked by tragedy and travesty. In 1912, a fire erupted in an automobile garage on a particularly windy afternoon. Within hours, the entire town lay in ruins. In June 1929, a robbery at the Ronan State Bank made a group of seven 20-something robbers $3,000 richer. They went on a spree of robberies across the state with police always a few steps behind. Eventually all but the ringleader were caught and either killed during the pursuit or sent to prison. A woman who accompanied them, known dramatically as "the woman in white," was eventually found murdered in a Helena brothel.

Today Ronan is known for its proximity to two of the state's most beautiful wildlife refuges: the Ninepipe National Wildlife Refuge and, farther south, the National Bison Range.

Ninepipe National Wildlife Refuge

Five miles (8 km) south of Ronan and just north of the National Bison Range on land of the Confederated Salish and Kootenai Tribes, the **Ninepipe National Wildlife Refuge** (www.fws.gov/refuge/nine-pipe) is a waterfowl preserve. Established in 1921, these wetlands are at the base of the Mission Mountains and situated around a large reservoir. The marshlands are difficult to walk through, but good bird-watching is possible from the parking areas surrounding the reservoir. The refuge is situated on a popular migratory path for numerous birds, including mallards, gadwalls, great blue herons, and swans. It has become an important breeding and resting area for the Flathead Valley Canada goose population. The refuge is closed during waterfowl hunting season (fall) and the nesting season (spring). Signed access to the

Preserving the American Bison

The National Bison Range is a wonderful place to learn about these giant animals.

Before Lewis and Clark set foot in the West, more than 50 million bison roamed the Great Plains and most of North America, from southern Canada into northern Mexico. Early settlers recorded seeing herds so large it took a full day for the animals to pass by. Lewis and Clark came across herds covering entire plains and valleys. By 1900, however, it was believed that less than 100 wild bison existed in the United States.

Indispensable to the Native American way of life, the bison provided Indians with everything—food, clothing, shelter, weapons, and utensils. The eradication of the bison devastated their culture, making it easier to force them onto reservations. Land was also freed up for cattle grazing, railroads, and pioneers. During "the Great Slaughter" of 1820-1880, bison were hunted for their meat, hides, or just for sport. Their massive carcasses were often left to rot on the open plains.

William T. Hornaday, with the support of fellow conservationist President Theodore Roosevelt, founded the American Bison Society in 1905. In 1908, the government bought land from the Flathead Nation along with five individual allotments. That same year, the National Bison Range was established, marking the first time a refuge had been created to preserve a single species in Montana.

Once they had the land, the American Bison Society needed to acquire the bison for it. They solicited donations through letter-writing campaigns, newspaper ads, and neighborhood women's groups—many received came from individuals in the amount of $1-5. By year's end, they had the equivalent of almost $250,000 in today's dollars. The majority of the first 40 bison to enter the range came from the private herd of Charles Conrad in Kalispell, direct descendants of six orphaned bison calves brought to the Mission Valley by a Pend d'Oreille 20 years earlier. The first bison arrived on the range in 1909, and 11 calves were born by the spring of 1910. Between 1910 and 1922, white-tailed and mule deer, pronghorn, and elk were also donated to the range in small numbers. The last animals added to the refuge were mountain goats, in 1964.

Today there are 325-350 bison on the range with 50-95 bison removed each year. This protects the genetic integrity of the bison and ensures the land can support all of its inhabitants. The bison that are removed are either sold or donated to other refuges or private herds. The range also donates bison to the Flathead tribal government to support bison restoration on Native American land.

refuge is off U.S. 93. Other roads allowing access to the area from U.S. 93 are Olsen Road and Highway 212.

Ninepipes Museum of Early Montana

The **Ninepipes Museum of Early Montana** (69316 U.S. 93, Charlo, 406/644-3435, www.ninepipesmuseum.org, 9am-5pm Mon.-Sat. Mar.-Oct., $7 adults, $6 seniors and veterans, $5 students, $3 children 6-12, group rates available) is halfway between Missoula and Kalispell next to the Ninepipe waterfowl refuge. It documents daily life on the Flathead Reservation over the last 100-plus years and even includes a complete replica of a Native American camp. In addition to Native American life, the history of early trappers, miners, loggers, and ranchers is on display, including photos, artwork, costumes, and artifacts from people in these different walks of life.

HOT SPRINGS

At the western edge of the reservation, in the shadow of Baldy Mountain, Hot Springs (population 557; elevation 2,841 ft/866 m) is a town whose main attraction is evident from its name. Known as "the Little Bitterroot," the region is home to numerous natural hot springs and mud pots that for centuries have been thought to possess healing powers. Native Americans camped in the area to make use of the "big medicine." When the area opened to settlers in 1910, the springs became increasingly commercial and were advertised around the West. The local newspaper's slogan, printed beneath the masthead, read, "Limp In? . . . Hop Out!" The original bathhouse closed in 1985, but if hot mineral water is your thing, there are a number of modern versions worth soaking in.

The largest and most developed of the local hot springs, **Symes Hot Springs Hotel & Mineral Baths** (209 N. Wall St., 406/741-2361, www.symeshotsprings.com, 7am-10pm Sun.-Thurs., 7am-midnight Fri.-Sat., $10 nonguests, $5.50 children 12 and under, rooms $60-150) was built in 1929 as a grand Mission-style hotel. In addition to the outside mineral pools, two of which have been recently renovated, spa treatments are offered in private pools. The guest rooms are modest and quaint, and there is often live music at the hotel.

Camas Hot Springs (north end of Spring St. by the abandoned Camas Bathhouse, free) is run by the tribe and offers two outdoor

The Ninepipe National Wildlife Refuge was established in 1921.

pools and a very laid-back atmosphere. In the distance the original bathhouse has long been shuttered. The water in the pools stays at about 104°F (40°C). For information, contact the **Hot Springs Chamber of Commerce** (406/741-2662).

Developed in the 1930s, **Alameda's Hot Springs Retreat** (308 N. Spring St., 406/741-2283, www.alamedashotsprings.com, $75-155) is part motel and part spa with in-room soaking tubs filled with natural hot spring water. The retreat is popular for health-related gatherings and workshops, and the rooms are simple but clean. Although the retreat does not have an outdoor pool, it can direct guests to other places to soak within walking distance.

POLSON

Polson feels like the kind of town where there is almost always a fair going on or some other reason to celebrate. Historically the economy has been based on lumber, steamboat trade, and ranching. Founded around a trading post at the southern end of Flathead Lake in 1880, the town was named for David Polson, a local rancher who married a Nez Perce woman and who played the fiddle at dances and powwows across the region. Settlement from 1910 greatly increased the size of the town, and when much of the state was losing population during the Great Depression, Polson actually doubled in size with farmers who came to try their luck with the Flathead Irrigation Project and people seeking work at the Kerr Dam construction project.

Today Polson (population 4,777; elevation 2,931 ft/893 m) is a lakeside town, the heart of Montana's cherry-growing district, and the busiest town along Flathead Lake. Its proximity to the magnificent lake, the Flathead River, and the Mission Mountains makes Polson a natural playground.

Miracle of America Museum

An eclectic little museum, to say the least, the **Miracle of America Museum** (36094 Memory Ln., 406/883-6804, www.

miracleofamericamuseum.org, 9am-5pm daily, $6 adults, $3 children 2-12) likes to think of itself as the "Smithsonian of the West." Indeed, the founders were passionate collectors of Western artifacts, and the inspired museum is packed to the rafters with more than 100,000 objects including moonshine stills, antique motorcycles, entire buildings, and military paraphernalia. The museum is kid-friendly, with coin-operated music machines and other paraphernalia children love. Behind the main building is the museum's Pioneer Village, which has 35 buildings spread across 4 acres (1.6 hectares). There's a helicopter to play in, a replica of Laura Ingalls Wilder's sod-roofed home, and a couple of kiddie trains that still operate.

BIGFORK

Arguably the most beautiful of the lakeside hamlets, year-round resort town Bigfork (population 4,270; elevation 2,979 ft/908 m) was named for its location along the fork of the Swan River. At the northeast corner of Flathead Lake, Bigfork has unlimited outdoor recreation opportunities, a handsome offering of live theater, art, fine dining, boutique shopping, and elegant accommodations. The feeling here is of an East Coast beach village 50 years ago—small, quaint, and lovely.

SPORTS AND RECREATION

The thing about the beauty in this part of the state is that it's all very user-friendly. The mountains can be climbed, the rivers fished, the lake swum. And although public land is harder to find, especially along Flathead Lake, there are still plenty of great places to hike.

★ Cherry Picking

Picking fresh, sweet Flathead cherries, or just eating them, is an idyllic way to spend an afternoon. Several orchards dot the east side of the lake between Polson and Bigfork, so don't be shy about stopping at roadside stands to do a little taste-testing; in this valley, you can't go wrong. The primary harvest is late July-mid-August. The average season lasts just 7-10 days. Try **Bowman Orchards** (19944 East Shore Rd./Hwy. 35, 10 mi/16.1 km south of Bigfork at mile marker 21.5 on the east shore of Flathead, 406/982-3246, 9am-6pm daily), a family-owned business since 1921 that grows a variety of cherries and sells both the fresh fruit and a number of delicious cherry products. **Hockaday Orchards** (45 Hockaday Ln., Lakeside, 406/844-3547, www.hockadayorchards.com, 8am-6pm daily as long as crop lasts) lets cherry lovers climb up the ladders to harvest their own crop. Bring your own bucket or box, as the cherries will get crushed in a bag. At just $1.25 per pound, you can afford to eat cherries all day long.

★ Hiking at Jewel Basin

One of the best and most unique places in the state to hike is **Jewel Basin** (Forest Rd. 5392, 10 mi/16.1 km northeast of Bigfork, 406/387-3800, www.fs.usda.gov), a wilderness area with high peaks, lush forests, 27 lakes, and 35 miles (56 km) of dedicated hiking trails. Camping is permitted, and the trails can be crowded on weekends. Some of the best day hikes include those into **Black Lake** (8 mi/12.9 km round-trip), the **Jewel Lakes** (9 mi/14.5 km round-trip), or the **Twin Lakes** (5 mi/8 km round-trip). The best map for the area is published by the **Glacier National Park Conservancy** (406/892-3250, www.glacier.org). Note that grizzlies frequent the area, particularly in late summer when the huckleberries are ripe.

Boating

Polson offers rafting opportunities on the warm, clear lower **Flathead River.** The only outfitter on the river, **Flathead Raft Company** (50362 U.S. 93 N., 406/883-5838 or 800/654-4359, www.flatheadraftco.com, full-day raft trips $80 adults, $65 children 6-12, full-day kayak trips $99 adults, $89 children 8-12, paddleboard rentals $30 half-day) offers great scenic and white-water trips as well as white-water kayak instruction, riverboarding, or sea-kayaking trips on **Flathead Lake.**

A couple of outfits rent boats in Polson, including **Absolute Watersports Rentals** (303 Hwy. 93, Somers, 406/883-3900) and the **Flathead Boat Company** (50230 Hwy. 93 S., Polson, 406/883-0999, www.flatheadboatcompany.com, $250-350 for 4 hours).

In Bigfork, you can rent ski boats, WaveRunners, kayaks, paddleboards and pontoon boats from **Bigfork Outdoor Rentals** (110 Swan River Rd., 406/837-2498, www.bigforkoutdoorrentals.com) and have them delivered. At **Marina Cay Resort** (180 Vista Ln., Bigfork, 406/837-5861, www.marinacay.com), you can also rent a variety of watercraft, including fishing charters. For more information on Flathead Lake and the work being done to protect it, contact the non-profit **Flathead Lakers** (406/883-1346, www.flatheadlakers.org).

Golf

With so many resorts, there are a number of golf courses in the area. The **Polson Bay Golf Club** (111 Bayview Dr., Polson, 406/883-8230, www.polsonbaygolf.com, $39-54 for 18 holes, $24-29 for 9 holes, carts $34 for 18 holes, $22 for 9 holes) has two courses with a total of 27 holes. The twilight deal, available daily after 3pm, offers 18 holes with a cart and a drink in the clubhouse afterward for $39-54, depending on season and day of week. In Bigfork, golfers can hit the links at the renowned 27-hole **Eagle Bend Golf Course** (279 Eagle Bend Dr., 406/837-7310, www.eaglebendgolfclub.com, $49-111 for 18 holes, $29-59 for 9 holes).

ENTERTAINMENT AND EVENTS

One of the most important events on the Flathead Reservation is the annual **Fourth of July Powwow** (888/835-8766, www.arleepowwow.com) at Arlee. The celebration has played out each year since 1898 with camping, competition dancing, drumming and singing, traditional games, and a host of food and arts and crafts vendors. Though the

U.S government ban on "Indian doings" in the 19th and 20th centuries forbade such celebrations, Native Americans held the event on the Fourth of July so that the Army would see it as a patriotic display. The **People's Center Annual Powwow** (53253 U.S. 93, Pablo, 406/675-0160) is held the third Saturday in August in nearby Pablo.

In Polson, the **Polson Farmers Market** (3rd Ave. W., 406/675-0177, 9am-1pm Fri. May-mid-Oct.) features local produce, crafts, jewelry, photography, handmade soaps, and more. The **Mission Mountain NRA Rodeo** (320 Regatta Rd., 406/883-1100, www.polsonfairgroundsinc.com) is generally held in late June; the professional rodeo action and small-town fun always ensures a big crowd. The biggest event of the year in Polson is probably the **Polson Main Street Flathead Cherry Festival** (Main St., 406/883-3667, www.flatheadcherryfestival.com). It has a fair-like environment and celebrates everything cherry, including pie-eating contests, seed-spitting contests, exhibitions, and entertainment throughout the weekend. The event is typically held the third weekend in July, and it is among the best ways to enjoy the phenomenal cherry harvest.

The repertory theater at **Bigfork Summer Playhouse** (526 Electric Ave., 406/837-4886, www.bigforksummerplayhouse.com, performances 8pm Mon.-Sat. plus occasional matinees 2pm Sun., mid-May-Labor Day, $26-30 adults, $22-26 seniors 65 and older, $17 children 10 and under) is a standout in the Northwest. For more than 50 years the company has been staging award-winning productions of musical classics like *Fiddler on the Roof, Dirty Rotten Scoundrels,* and *Sugar Babies.* The contemporary theater is quite comfortable and roomy with 400 seats and air-conditioning. Also running all summer in Bigfork is the **Riverbend Concert Series** (Everit Slider Park, downtown Bigfork, 406/837-5888, www.bigfork.

1: Flathead Lake 2: Flathead cherries 3: Flathead Lake overlook 4: Jewel Basin viewpoint over the Flathead Valley

org, 7pm Sun. late-June-late-Aug., $3 adults, $1 children), held every Sunday. The bring-your-own-seating concerts range from jazz to big band and light opera. Held annually the first weekend in August, Bigfork's **Festival of the Arts** (406/881-4636, www.bigforkfestivalofthearts.com, 9am-4:30pm Sat.-Sun.) has been attracting visitors and artists alike since 1978 with more than 150 booths, food, and entertainment.

SHOPPING

In St. Ignatius, the **Four Winds Indian Trading Post** (U.S. 93, 3 mi/4.8 km north of St. Ignatius, 406/745-4336, www.fourwindsindiantradingpost.com, 10am-6pm daily summer, noon-5pm daily winter) is the oldest operating Indian trading post in the state. Opened in 1870, the Four Winds has long supplied local Native Americans with a variety of wares, including beads, face paint, animal hides, and dance bells. The store is authentic and sells traditional Native American crafts alongside history books and made-in-Montana products.

A good place to stop in Polson for some warm Montana bedding is **Three Dog Down** (48841 U.S. 93, 406/883-3696 or 800/364-3696, www.threedogdown.com, 9am-6pm daily), known in the region for custom-made comforters and pillows. Shopping here is a Montana experience—you can buy everything from soap to moccasins to saltwater taffy—and bargain hunters should know that singing the "Star-Spangled Banner" will earn you a discount. A number of art galleries, gift shops, and jewelry stores are also in town.

In tiny Bigfork, art is the thing, so stop in at a few galleries during your visit. You could cover the entire town, easily, in a day. Several artists have their own galleries in Bigfork to represent their work exclusively. Other galleries include **Collage Gallery** (573 Electric Ave., 406/837-0866, www.collagebigfork.com, 11am-5pm Mon.-Sat., noon-4pm Sun. May-Dec.), which offers rolling shows every month in addition to an eclectic and handsome collection of antiquities, books, Mexican textiles, and works by deceased masters. The colorful and playful **ArtFusion** (471 Electric Ave., 406/837-3526, www.bigforkartfusion.com, 10am-5:30pm Mon.-Sat., 11am-5pm Sun.) represents more than 60 Montana artists including ceramicists, painters, jewelers, and photographers.

Persimmon Gallery (537 Electric Ave., 406/837-2288, www.persimmongallery.com, 11am-5pm Mon.-Sat., noon-4pm Sun. June-Sept., 11am-5pm Tues.-Sat., noon-4pm Sun. Oct.-Dec., 11am-5pm Wed.-Sat., noon-4pm Sun. Feb.-May) has a wonderful collection of more than 70 Montana and Northwest artists working in such media as jewelry, painting, mixed media, ceramics, glass, and fabric. One favorite is Judy Colvin, from St. Ignatius, who uses wool from the sheep raised on their ranch to make felted items that include gorgeous purses, scarves, wraps, hats, and wall hangings.

FOOD

If you cannot survive on cherries alone, there are a number of good restaurants concentrated around Bigfork. Steeped in local history, **Bigfork Inn** (604 Electric Ave., 406/837-6680, 4:30pm-midnight daily, $17-36) is a lovely spot for a hearty meal. Choose from specialties like smoked mixed grill, Haus or Gypsy Schnitzel, Crispy Country Inn Duck, or prime rib.

★ **Moroldo's Ristorante Italiano** (7951 Hwy. 35, 406/837-2720, www.moroldos.info, 5:30pm-9pm Wed.-Sat., $22-32) offers an elegant and authentic approach to Italian cooking using fresh, local Montana ingredients in dishes including salads, pastas, steak, and fish. The restaurant is owned and operated by Fabrizio Moroldo and his family, and every dish is cooked to order, so meals can take some time. Reservations are strongly encouraged.

Flathead Lake Brewing Company (116 Holt Dr., 406/837-2004, wwwflatheadlakebrewing.com, 11am-10pm daily, $13-18) serves casual but delicious fare—from seared scallops with beet puree to braised pork shank,

rib eye, and house-made pizzas and pastas in a festive environment.

For breakfast and lunch, the hands-down favorite in the Flathead Valley is the ★ **Echo Lake Café** (1195 Hwy. 83, Bigfork, 406/837-1000, www.echolakecafe.com, 6:30am-2:30pm daily, $6-14), where everything is homemade and fabulous. Be prepared to wait in line with locals for a table.

In Polson, lovers of all things pink will delight in the pinkaliciousness at **Betty's Diner** (49779 Hwy. 93, 406/883-1717, www.bettysdiner.net, 7am-8pm Mon.-Sat., 7am-3pm Sun.). The goodness starts with breakfast ($6-11) including specialties for "kids and old farts." Lunch ($8-10) includes such classic diner favorites as burgers, cheesesteaks, patty melts, and other sandwiches. Dinner ($10.50-15) is everything from New York strip to shrimp baskets and chicken-fried steak.

For authentic Thai food in Polson, try **Hot Spot Thai** (50440 Hwy. 93, 406/883-4444, 11:30am-2:30pm and 5pm-8pm daily, $10.50-13). It has a wonderful Thai chef and is open for lunch, dinner, and takeout. The spot doesn't have a liquor license, but diners can bring their own wine.

Lake City Bakery & Eatery (49493 Hwy. 93, 406/883-5667, 7am-3pm daily, $7-12) is a wonderful spot for breakfast all day or lunch. The great old brick building was a grocery store in 1939. Everything is made from scratch. For a great beer, try **Glacier Brewing Company** (6 10th Ave. E., 406/883-2595, www.glacierbrewing.com, 3pm-8pm Tues.-Sat.), a German-style ale house serving its own impressive line of beer and homemade soda. Hours here change with the seasons and without advance notice, but are posted on its Facebook page.

ACCOMMODATIONS

There are a handful of places to stay in the vicinity of St. Ignatius, including the no-frills, roadside **Sunset Motel** (333 Mountain View Dr., St. Ignatius, 406/745-3900, $74-111). The **Bear Spirit Lodge B&B** (38712 St. Mary's Lake Rd., 406/745-3089, www.bearspiritlodge.

com, $119-122) is a cozy place in a phenomenal setting, and the hosts, Ann and Great Bear, are beyond compare. Take a sauna or a hot tub under the starry skies, and you will never want to leave this welcoming place.

About 12 miles (19.3 km) up the road in Charlo is **Ninepipes Lodge** (69286 Hwy. 93, 406/644-2588, www.ninepipeslodge.com, $94-183), set against the backdrop of the Mission Mountains and adjacent to the Ninepipes Reservoir. It's a full-service resort with a great restaurant, **Allentown Restaurant** (breakfast $7-13, lunch $9-15, dinner $15-27) serving steaks, pasta, seafood, and salads. On warm nights, eat outside on the deck overlooking the kettle pond with unrivaled mountain views.

Plenty of choices for lodging exist in Polson and Bigfork, but a room with a view in these parts can get pretty expensive. Among the best bargains in the area is the rustic **Mission Mountain Resort** (3 minutes from Polson on Hwy. 35, 406/883-1883, www.polsonmtresort.com, from $80-200 for 2 people, $10 each additional person), a collection of cabins and lodge rooms on 80 acres (32.4 hectares) set back from the lake.

The waterfront **Best Western KwaTaqNuk Resort and Casino** (49708 U.S. 93 E., Polson, 406/883-3636 or 800/882-6363, www.kwataqnuk.com, $180-319), which is owned and operated by the Flathead Nation, has 107 guest rooms and an extensive menu of activities that includes lake cruises, boat rentals, fishing tours, and plenty of gaming at the on-site casino. Pets are permitted for a $20-per-night fee. For standard pet-friendly accommodations right on the lake, try **America's Best Value Port Polson Inn** (49825 U.S. 93, Polson, 406/883-5385 or 800/654-0682, www.bestvalueinn.com, $112-124).

Luxuriousness and prices rise as you get closer to Bigfork. Depending on the size of your group, a vacation rental can be the most economical choice. In addition to listings on Airbnb, there are a few vacation rental companies in town, including **Bayside Property**

Management (406/883-4313, www.rentalsinpolson.com) and **Flathead Lake Vacation Rentals** (406/883-3253, www.flatheadvacationrentals.com), which offers a variety of properties around the lake.

Five miles (8 km) south of Bigfork, the **Mountain Lake Lodge** (14735 Sylvan Dr., Bigfork, 406/837-3800 or 877/823-4923, www.mountainlakelodge.com, $189-259) is elegant and cozy with great vistas of the lake and plenty of amenities, including an outdoor infinity pool, a hot tub, a putting green, and a fire pit along with two restaurants on-site. Pets are welcome for $15 per day per pet. Also south of town, just a short walk from the pebbled shores of Flathead Lake is **Flathead Lake Resort** (14871 Hwy. 35, Bigfork, 406/837-3333, www.flatheadlakeresort.com, $87-298), which offers modest accommodations from queen motel rooms to two-bedroom cabins, plus RV and tent sites, in an idyllic setting. Just down the road is the funky **Islander Inn** (14729 Shore Acres Drive, Bigfork, 406/837-5472, www.sleepeatdrink.com, $177-205), which boasts colorful and cozy boutique-style bungalows, each designed to reflect Anguila, Crete, Jamaica, Maui, Wild Horse, Zanzibar, or Bali. A gift shop, bakery, and restaurant is on the property, so you may not want to leave. Right in town, and on the water, is **Marina Cay Resort** (180 Vista Ln., 406/837-5861, www.marinacay.com, $109-545). The largest property in the vicinity, and the hub of water sports activities, Marina Cay boasts a number of accommodations, including condos and townhomes, as well as dining. The resort is within easy walking to the lake and the town's shops and restaurants. For a phenomenal guest ranch experience, **Averill's Flathead Lake Lodge** (150 Flathead Lodge Rd., 406/837-4391, www.flatheadlakelodge, weeklong all-inclusive trips from $3,998 adults, $2,984 children 6-17, $1,675 children 3-5, $200 infants) is a historic family ranch set right on the water. From sailing to horseback riding, fly-fishing to mountain biking, this ranch is exceptional.

CAMPING

If you can get a tent site, camping is one of the best ways to stay as close to Flathead Lake as possible and truly enjoy the region. Among the most popular are **Wayfarers State Park** (8600 Hwy. 35, 0.5 mi/0.8 km south of Bigfork, 406/837-4196, www.stateparks.mt.gov/wayfarers, mid-Mar.-mid-Nov., $10-72), **Finley Point State Park** (31543 S. Finley Point Rd., 11 mi/17.7 km north of Polson, then 4 mi/6.4 km west on County Rd., 406/887-2715, May 1-Sept. 30, $10-72), and **Yellow Bay State Park** (23861 Hwy. 35, 15 mi/24 km north of Polson at mile marker 17, 406/982-3034, mid-May-mid-Sept., $10-72). All the parks and camping amenities can be seen online at www.stateparks.mt.gov.

INFORMATION AND SERVICES

The **Polson Chamber of Commerce** (418 Main St., 406/883-5969, www.polsonchamber.com, 10am-3pm Mon.-Fri., 10am-2pm Sat. Memorial Day-Labor Day, 10am-2pm Mon.-Fri. Labor Day-Memorial Day) is an excellent resource for the south end of the Flathead Valley, and the **Bigfork Area Chamber of Commerce and Visitor's Center** (Old Town Center, 8155 Hwy. 35, 406/837-5888, www.bigfork.org, 9am-5pm Mon.-Fri., 10am-3pm Sat.-Sun. Memorial Day-Labor Day, 10am-2pm daily Labor Day-Memorial Day) is open to visitors on the east side of Flathead Lake.

Kalispell Regional Medical Center (310 Sunnyview Ln., 406/752-5111, www.krh.org) is 20 miles (32 km) north of Bigfork, just north of downtown Kalispell.

TRANSPORTATION

Nestled between lake and mountains south of Whitefish and north of Missoula, Polson and Bigfork can be accessed from U.S. 93. Polson is 70 miles (113 km) north of Missoula and 67 miles (108 km) south of Whitefish. Bigfork is 33 miles (53 km) north of Polson on Highway 35, known as the East Shore Route.

Seeley-Swan Valley

Much quieter than Flathead and nestled in between the magnificent Mission and Swan mountain ranges, the Seeley-Swan Valley is a remarkable destination. Visitors feel like they are stepping back in time 50 years or more. There are unlikely to be any towns you've ever heard of in this valley, and no chain hotels, fast-food restaurants, and interstate highways. Instead you'll find pristine lakes and seemingly endless forests, wonderful old lodges, and handsome guest ranches. The communities in this valley—Swan Lake (pop. 113), Condon (pop. 351), and Seeley Lake (pop. 1,659)—are old timber camps that now cater to lake-loving summer crowds and outdoors enthusiasts, cross-country skiers, and snowmobilers.

This is a place to spend lazy lakeside days and cozy fireside evenings, and if lazy isn't your style, there are mountains in every direction for hiking as well as rivers and lakes for boating and fishing. For those who want to venture into the **Bob Marshall Wilderness Complex,** this valley is an excellent launching point. If you don't have time to stop and stay awhile, at least plan to drive this route from the Flathead and places north to Missoula, Helena, or Bozeman. In fact, the 91-mile (147-km) stretch of Highway 83 through the Seeley-Swan Valley is the shortest route between Yellowstone and Glacier National Parks. The scenery and solitude make the trip worthwhile.

SEELEY LAKE

Seeley Lake (population 1,659; elevation 4,028 ft/1,228 m) is clearly a recreation town, and the lake itself is among the chain of lakes through which the Clearwater River flows. A resort town in the most classic sense— think rustic lodges and lakeside retreats with cabins dotting the forest—Seeley Lake is popular but relatively uncrowded. There are plenty of fish in the lake, including bass, kokanee salmon, bull trout, perch, and bluegills, in addition to year-round activities that include boating, hiking, excellent cross-country skiing, and snowmobiling.

Sports and Recreation

BOATING

The **Clearwater Canoe Trail** is a 3.5-mile (5.6-km) stretch of flatwater that takes paddlers down the Clearwater River from north of the town of Seeley Lake into the lake itself. Magnificent wildflowers, a variety of birds, and other wildlife are often seen along the way. A canoe trip takes 1-2 hours. A roughly 1-mile (1.6-km) hiking trail alongside the river leads paddlers back to the trailhead parking lot. Canoes ($25 for 4 hours, $40 for 8 hours, $55 overnight) and other sporting equipment, including ski boats, pontoon boats, rafts, kayaks, paddleboards, and WaveRunners can be rented from **Rocky Mountain Adventure Gear** (3192 Hwy. 83 S., 406/677 8300, www.rockymtngear.com, 9am-6pm daily).

HIKING AND BIKING

Among the most popular hiking trails in the region is the **Morrell Lake and Falls Trail,** a 5-mile (8-km) round-trip hike on relatively even terrain to a beautiful mountain lake and a series of towering cascades, the largest of which is 90 feet (27 m) high. From Seeley Lake, drive north less than 0.5 mile (0.8 km) to Morrell Creek Road (also known as Cottonwood Lakes Rd. or Forest Rd. 477). Turn right (east), drive 1.1 miles (1.8 km) to the junction of West Morrell Road, and turn left. Drive 5.6 miles (9 km) to another junction and turn right. Drive 0.7 mile (1.1 km) to the trailhead. The trail is well marked and follows the creek to a pond, Morrell Lake, and then the falls.

Mountain biking is permitted on a variety of Forest Service roads and trails, including a 14-mile (22.5 km) round-trip ride at the **Seeley Creek Nordic Ski Trails** (www.seeleylakenordic.org). From Highway 83, turn east onto Morrell Creek Road (also known as Cottonwood Lakes Rd. or Forest Rd. 477) and drive 1.1 miles (1.8 km) to the trailhead on the north side of the road. Bikes can be rented from **Rocky Mountain Adventure Gear** (3192 Hwy. 83 S., 406/677-8300, www.rockymtngear.com, 9am-6pm daily, $20 for

The area around Seeley Lake is like a step back in time.

4 hours, $30 for 8 hours, $40 overnight, $185 weekly). It also offers guide services for any kind of adventure you want to have.

For more information on Forest Service trails, contact the **Seeley Lake Ranger District** (3583 Hwy. 83, 406/677-2233, www. fs.usda.gov).

WINTER RECREATION

Seeley Lake is a cross-country skier's paradise. Several of the local resorts, including the **Double Arrow Lodge** (301 Lodge Way, 2 mi/3.2 km south of Seeley Lake, 406/677-2777 or 800/468-0777, www.doublearrowresort. com), offer groomed ski trails. The cream of the crop in this region is the **Seeley Creek Nordic Ski Trails** (www.seeleylakenordic. org). This trail system has been under development since the 1970s, initially created from old logging camps and hilly logging roads, and has a degree of difficulty that resulted in the slogan, "Get good or eat wood." With 20 miles (32 km) of groomed classic and skate trails that can be combined to form some impressive routes, the area offers something for every ability level, and an annual 50-kilometer race is held the last Saturday in January. From Highway 83, turn east onto Morrell Creek Road (also known as Cottonwood Lakes Rd. or Forest Rd. 477) and drive 1.1 miles (1.8 km) to the trailhead on the north side of the road. Nearby are dogsled and snowmobile trails.

For backcountry skiers who want plenty of adventure with a side of luxury, **Yurtski** (406/721-1779, www.yurtski.com) offers a wide range of services. From extraordinary guided trips for newer skiers to gourmet-catered trips, self-service trips, or just shuttling gear, Carl and his team make use of their awesome backcountry yurts, local knowledge, and mad culinary skills.

Around Seeley Lake are more than 350 miles (565 km) of snowmobile trails. For information on specific trails and snowmobile-specific maps, contact the **Seeley Lake Ranger Station** (3583 Hwy. 83, 406/677-2233, www.fs.usda.gov/lolo) at Lolo National Forest. Snowmobiles, as well as

snowshoe packages, snowbikes, ice fishing gear, and guided tours, are available at **Rocky Mountain Adventure Gear** (3192 Hwy. 83 S., 406/677-8300, www.rockymtngear.com, 9am-6pm daily).

CONDON

Just 27 miles (43 km) up Highway 83 from Seeley Lake is tiny Condon (population 351; elevation 3,785 ft/1,154 m), another gem in the string of lake towns between the Mission and Swan Ranges. Condon is surrounded by the **Mission Mountains Wilderness Area** to the west and the **Bob Marshall Wilderness Complex** to the east, making the region a favorite for outdoor recreation. Holland Lake is a gorgeous 400-acre (161.9-hectare) lake with prime opportunities for fishing and boating.

Sports and Recreation

The stunning **Holland Lake** is the main attraction here and offers plenty of recreational opportunities, including boating, fishing, and swimming. The relatively easy and well-traveled **Holland Falls Trail** leads hikers on a 3-mile (4.8-km) round-trip hike to a waterfall. From the trailhead on Holland Lake Road just beyond the Holland Lake Campground, the trail skirts the north shore of the lake and climbs roughly 600 feet (183 m) before reaching the 40-foot (12.2-m) falls. There are natural seating areas for picnickers and waterfall gazers. The trail is often used by outfitters packing into Upper Holland Lake and the Bob Marshall Wilderness Complex.

SWAN LAKE

An hour's drive north of Seeley Lake and 16 miles (26 km) south of Bigfork is the quaint little village of Swan Lake (population 113; elevation 3,198 ft/975 m), on Highway 83 at the southern end of the lake of the same name. The area is a natural stopping point for migrating birds, making the Swan River National Wildlife Refuge a wonderful place for avid birders. The lake itself offers excellent fishing for northern pike, kokanee salmon, and rainbow trout. A few services are available in town, including lodging and dining options, but most people come to Swan Lake for recreation. There are 50 miles (81 km) of trails for cross-country skiers and many options for hiking.

Sports and Recreation

From Swan Lake, numerous lengthy trails get hikers and horseback riders into the Bob Marshall Wilderness Complex. The **Upper Holland Loop,** from the trailhead on the north shore of Holland Lake, is a steep and rugged trail that climbs nearly 4,000 feet (1,219 m) over nearly 7 miles (11.3 km) or 13.3 miles (21.4 km) round-trip, which can be tackled on a well-planned full-day hike. The trail passes the Sapphire Lakes and Upper Holland Lake before descending again down along Holland Creek. For maps and information, contact the **Swan Lake Ranger District** (200 Ranger Station Rd., off Hwy. 35, Bigfork, 406/837-7500).

The **Swan River National Wildlife Refuge** (Hwy. 83, 1 mi/1.6 km south of Swan Lake, 406/727-7400, www.fws.gov/refuge/swan_river) is nearly 1,800 acres (728.4 hectares) of glacially carved grassy floodplain that provides habitat for more than 170 species of birds, including waterfowl, bald eagles, various types of hawks, owls, and songbirds. The bald eagles generally arrive in February, and visitors can often see eaglets fledging in mid-May. There are also plenty of other animals—moose, elk, beavers, bobcats, and the occasional grizzly bear—wandering through this quiet and undeveloped place. The refuge is closed for nesting season (Mar. 1-July 15), except for the viewing platforms.

Swan Mountain Outfitters (26356 Soup Creek Rd., on Hwy. 83 between mile markers 64 and 65, 406/387-4405, www.swanmountainoutfitters.com) offers everything from two-hour trail rides ($70) in the national forest to daylong rides into Glacier ($255) to six-day pack fishing trips ($2,220/person). It also leads dinner rides, llama treks, and snowmobiling adventures in winter.

FOOD

For a hearty meal, the **Hungry Bear Steakhouse** (6287 Hwy. 83, between mile markers 38 and 39, Condon, 406/754-2240, 8am-9pm daily, $18-23) serves steak, seafood, and pizza with a full-service bar and kids' menu. Breakfast ($4.25-9) and lunch ($7-11) are served as well. The **Swan Valley Cafe** (6798 Hwy. 83, 406/754-3663, 8am-3pm Sat.-Thurs., 8am-8pm Fri. May-Nov., $6-21) is a great family-style restaurant with a six-page menu that is sure to please. For a real culinary and visual treat, dine lakeside on gourmet fare at ★ **Holland Lake Lodge** (1947 Holland Lake Rd., Condon, 406/754-2282, www.hollandlakelodge.com, 8:30am-9:45am, noon-2pm, and 5:45pm-8:45pm daily mid-June-late Oct.). The beautiful inn serves breakfast ($6-12), lunch ($7-15), and dinner ($23-35) with entrées like gruyère egg bake, green chili burger with cheese and lodge salsa, and pecan-crusted pork tenderloin. Reservations are required as hours can change depending on special events and guest occupancy. The **Laughing Horse Lodge** (71284 Hwy. 83, Swan Lake, 406/886-2080, www.laughinghorselodge.com, 5pm-9pm Wed.-Sun., May-Dec., days and hours can vary with private functions, $14-38) is a wonderful place to eat (and you can stay there as well). Chef Kathleen cooks up everything from double-Frenched pork chops to huckleberry peach pie. On the second and fourth Tuesday between late June and September, the lodge hosts a six-course tasting menu spotlighting cuisine and wines from around the globe. Nights are limited to 32 diners and sell out months in advance, so book ahead.

In Seeley Lake, the local favorite is the lakefront **Lindey's Prime Steak House** (Hwy. 83, 406/677-9229, 5pm-10pm daily May-Sept., 5pm-9pm daily Oct.-May, $23-31), where the steaks are of the same caliber as the great view. There is not much on the menu besides steak, but meat lovers will be exceedingly happy with this authentic Montana steak house. Another reliable spot for a meal in Seeley Lake almost any time of day is the **Filling Station Restaurant** (3189 Hwy. 83, 406/677-2080, 11am-2am Mon.-Fri., 8am-2am Sat.-Sun., $7-12.50); the bar offers karaoke on Friday and Saturday nights. The award-winning menu and wine list in the Double Arrow Resort's **Seasons Restaurant** (301 Lodge Way, 2 mi/3.2 km south of Seeley Lake, 406/677-2777, www.doublearrowresort.com/dining, $23-30) feature classic country cuisine—from rattlesnake and rabbit sausage to baby back ribs and bison tri-tip—in a welcoming and warm environment.

ACCOMMODATIONS

For the most part, the accommodations in the Seeley-Swan Valley are lovely and somewhat rustic. The **Double Arrow Resort** (301 Lodge Way, 2 mi/3.2 km south of Seeley Lake, 406/677-2777, www.doublearrowresort.com, cabins $100-800, main lodge rooms $110-165) is a handsome log lodge with history and character in a ranch-like setting. The accommodations are beautiful cabins and lodge rooms, all with private baths. A variety of activities, including fishing, golf, sleigh rides, horseback riding, and winter sports, can be arranged on-site. Another great old-school family resort in the area is **Tamaracks Resort** (3481 Hwy. 83 N., Seeley Lake, 406/677-2433 or 800/477-7216, www.tamaracks.com, $145-450), which has 17 great old-school cabins that can accommodate up to 10 people. RV sites are also available as are boat rentals. **Seeley Lake Motor Lodge** (3206 Hwy. 83 N., 406/677-2335, www.seeleylakemotorlodge.com, $60-70 winter, $110-145 summer) is what good roadside motels used to be: comfortable, clean, and convenient.

By far the fanciest spot in the region is the exclusive **Holland Lake Lodge** (1947 Holland Lake Rd., Condon, 406/754-2282, www.hollandlakelodge.com, cabins $320, lodge rooms $200) where the rates include phenomenal meals. Activity options at this lakefront idyll include hiking, canoeing, horseback riding, swimming, fishing float trips, and float plane excursions. The cabins are modest for the steep price, but the meals, scenery, and solitude more than make up for it. The **Laughing Horse Lodge** (71284 Hwy. 83, Swan Lake, 406/886-2080, www.laughinghorselodge.com, May-Dec., $126-495) is a cozy and fun bed-and-breakfast where pets are welcome and the activity menu is unlimited. Chef Kathleen whips up farm-to-table masterpieces in the kitchen, and the lodge also offers a six-course tasting menu on the second and fourth Tuesday, June-September.

CAMPING

With so much public forest and wilderness in the vicinity, the multitude of camping options in the area attracts large numbers of campers on summer weekends. **Placid Lake State Park** (5001 N. Placid Lake Rd., 406/542-5500, $14-28) has 40 sites, flush toilets, and drinking water; it is 3 miles (4.8 km) south of Seeley Lake on Highway 83, then 3 miles (4.8 km) west on a county road. **Salmon Lake State Park** (2329 Hwy. 83, 5 mi/8 km south of Seeley Lake, 406/677-6804, May-Nov., $10-34) is another of the better options.

The **Holland Lake Campground** (Holland Lake Rd., 406/646-1012, www.recreation.gov, Memorial Day-Labor Day, $18) has 40 sites, flush toilets, and lake access. The **Swan Lake Campground** (Hwy. 83, Swan Lake, 877/444-6777, www.recreation.gov, $18) is a Forest Service campground 0.5 mile (0.8 km) northwest of Swan Lake on Highway 83.

INFORMATION AND SERVICES

The **Seeley Lake Chamber of Commerce** (2920 Hwy. 83, 406/677-2880, www.seeleylakechamber.com) is in a beautiful old barn on Highway 83 at mile marker 12.5, just south of the town. The **Swan Lake Chamber of Commerce** (22778 Hwy. 83, 406/886-2303, www.swanlakemontana.org) is located in the town of Swan Lake.

TRANSPORTATION

The Seeley-Swan Valley is a 91-mile (147-km) corridor along Highway 83 between the Mission Mountains to the west and the Swan Mountains to the east. From Missoula, Highway 200 leads to Highway 83. The distance from Missoula to Seeley Lake is 55 miles (89 km). From the north, U.S. 93 in Kalispell accesses Highway 82, which then turns into Highway 83. From Kalispell to Swan Lake, the distance is 35 miles (56 km). From Swan Lake to Seeley Lake is 57 miles (92 km).

Kalispell and Whitefish

The northern town of Kalispell (population 22,761; elevation 2,956 ft/901 m) exists because of James Hill's Great Northern Railway and survives in spite of it. Freight and mercantile baron Charles Conrad founded the town of Kalispell when he convinced his friend Hill to run the railroad through it in 1891. By 1904, the Great Northern had abandoned its Kalispell route in favor of the more geographically amenable Whitefish line just 15 miles (24 km) to the north. The people of Kalispell were furious, but the town's economy survived due to Conrad's National Bank and the booming timber industry. Today it is still rather industrial compared to Whitefish's resort-like atmosphere—a nuts-and-bolts kind of town that serves as a natural supply and shopping center and has some wonderful museums, parks, and an ideal location between Flathead Lake and Glacier National Park.

Given a great boost when the train was rerouted from Kalispell in 1904, Whitefish (population 6,649; elevation 3,036 ft/925 m) grew up around Whitefish Mountain (long called Big Mountain) and the sport of skiing, and today is Montana's largest year-round resort community. Although Whitefish is clearly a ski town, it is also an art town, a gateway to Glacier, a summer hot spot, and a great place to find gourmet cuisine.

SIGHTS

The Conrad Mansion National Historic Site

Just a block from Woodland Park in Kalispell sits the palatial historic home of Charles Conrad, the founder of the city. The **Conrad Mansion** (330 Woodland Ave., Kalispell, 406/755-2166, www.conradmansion.com, 10am-5pm Wed.-Sun. mid-May-mid-June, 10am-5pm Tues.-Sun. mid-June-mid-Oct., $15 adults, $14 seniors 65 and over, $8 students 12-17, $6 children 11 and under) was completed in 1895 and designed by the renowned Spokane, Washington, architect Kirtland Cutter. The Conrads made sure that the residents of Kalispell felt some connection to the house: On Christmas Day of the year it was finished, the Conrad family invited people from around town who would otherwise have spent the holiday alone to share in their feast. The entire city was invited to a grand New Year's Eve ball a week later. Over the years, Alicia Conrad hosted famous parties, including a Halloween gathering just after a fire had burned through the roof of the mansion. Alicia decorated the hole with Spanish moss, artificial bats, and volcanoes. After her death in 1923, the family continued to occupy the home until the mid-1960s. Conrad himself had only lived in the house for seven years before his death at age 52. In 1974, his youngest daughter donated the residence to the city of Kalispell. The 26-room, nine-bedroom Norman-style mansion has been beautifully restored and is furnished with the family's original furniture. There is also a large collection of family clothing and three generations of children's toys.

Hockaday Museum of Art

The **Hockaday Museum of Art** (302 2nd

Kalispell

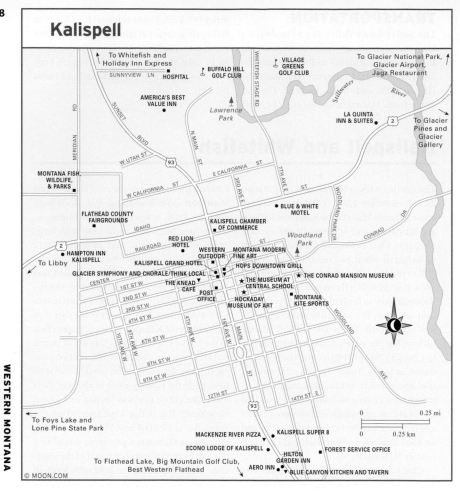

To Whitefish and
Holiday Inn Express

SUNNYVIEW LN   BUFFALO HILL   VILLAGE
HOSPITAL   GOLF CLUB   GREENS
GOLF CLUB

To Glacier National Park,
Glacier Airport,
Jagz Restaurant

AMERICA'S BEST
VALUE INN

Lawrence
Park

Stillwater
River

LA QUINTA
INN & SUITES

To Glacier
Pines and
Glacier
Gallery

MERIDIAN RD

SUNSET

BLVD

W UTAH ST

93

N MAIN ST

W CALIFORNIA   ST

E CALIFORNIA   ST

7TH AVE E.

ST

WHITEFISH STAGE RD

WOODLAND PARK DR

MONTANA FISH,
WILDLIFE,
& PARKS

3RD AVE E.

BLUE & WHITE
MOTEL

FLATHEAD COUNTY
FAIRGROUNDS

IDAHO

KALISPELL CHAMBER
OF COMMERCE

Woodland
Park

CONRAD

DR

2   RED LION
HOTEL
HAMPTON INN   RAILROAD
KALISPELL
To Libby

WESTERN   MONTANA MODERN
OUTDOOR   FINE ART
KALISPELL GRAND HOTEL   HOPS DOWNTOWN GRILL

WOODLAND PARK DR

GLACIER SYMPHONY AND CHORALE/THINK LOCAL

CENTER   THE KNEAD
1ST ST W   CAFE
POST
2ND ST W   OFFICE

THE MUSEUM AT
CENTRAL SCHOOL

HOCKADAY
MUSEUM OF ART

MONTANA
KITE SPORTS

THE CONRAD MANSION MUSEUM

3RD ST W
4TH ST W
6TH ST W
8TH ST W
9TH ST W

9TH AVE W
10TH AVE W

4TH AVE W

1ST AVE W
MAIN

WOODLAND

12TH ST

AVE

14TH ST E.

ST

To Foys Lake and
Lone Pine State Park

93

0   0.25 mi
0   0.25 km

MACKENZIE RIVER PIZZA   KALISPELL SUPER 8

ECONO LODGE OF KALISPELL   FOREST SERVICE OFFICE

To Flathead Lake, Big Mountain Golf Club,
Best Western Flathead

HILTON
GARDEN INN

AERO INN   BLUE CANYON KITCHEN AND TAVERN

© MOON.COM

Ave. E., Kalispell, 406/755-5268, www.
hockadaymuseum.org, 10am-5pm Tues.-Fri.,
10am-4pm Sat., $5 adults, $4 seniors 60 and
over, $2 college students, free for children
K-12) was originally begun by local artists
in the late 1960s, and today it is a well-estab-
lished public museum known for showcasing some of the region's most important art
and artists. Visitors will find works by T. J.
Hileman, John Fery, and Charles M. Russell,
among others. It has the largest collection
of Glacier Park art in the country and also a
large permanent collection dedicated to the
Blackfeet. Public tours of the museum are

offered for free, with admission, on Thursday
and Saturday at 10:30am. Hockaday hosts
the **Arts in the Park** program each July, and
the gift shop has a broad selection of original
works, including jewelry, pottery, and prints
by local artists.

The Museum at Central School

The Central School building was opened in
1894 and for more than 100 years housed
different educational institutions. Slated
for demolition in the early 1990s, the city
of Kalispell instead invested more than $2

Whitefish

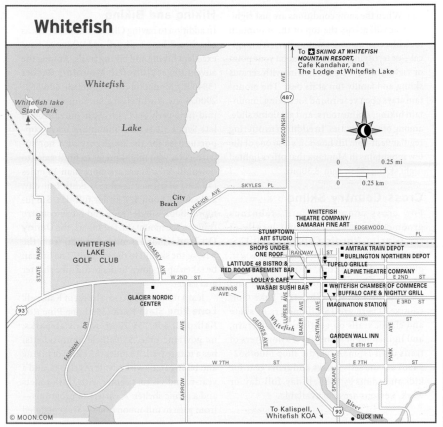

To ✚ **SKIING AT WHITEFISH MOUNTAIN RESORT**, Cafe Kandahar, and The Lodge at Whitefish Lake

Whitefish

Whitefish lake State Park

Lake

SKYLES PL

City Beach

WHITEFISH THEATRE COMPANY/ SAMARAH FINE ART

EDGEWOOD

STUMPTOWN ART STUDIO

PL

WHITEFISH LAKE GOLF CLUB

SHOPS UNDER ONE ROOF

■ AMTRAK TRAIN DEPOT
■ BURLINGTON NORTHERN DEPOT

RAILWAY

LATITUDE 48 BISTRO & RED ROOM BASEMENT BAR

TUPELO GRILLE

ALPINE THEATRE COMPANY

W 2ND ST

E 2ND ST

LOULA'S CAFE

JENNINGS AVE

WASABI SUSHI BAR▼

WHITEFISH CHAMBER OF COMMERCE
BUFFALO CAFE & NIGHTLY GRILL

GLACIER NORDIC CENTER

IMAGINATION STATION

E 3RD ST

E 4TH ST

GARDEN WALL INN

E 6TH ST

W 7TH ST

E 7TH ST

To Kalispell, Whitefish KOA ↘

DUCK INN

To Kalispell, Whitefish River

© MOON.COM

0   0.25 mi
0   0.25 km

WESTERN MONTANA
KALISPELL AND WHITEFISH

million renovating the historic building. Since 1999 it has been used by the Northwest Montana Historical Society, which oversees the **Museum at Central School** (124 2nd Ave. E., Kalispell, 406/756-8381, www. yourmuseum.org, 10am-5pm Mon.-Fri., 10am-2pm Sat. June-Aug., $5 adults, $4 seniors, free for children). The museum is dedicated to preserving the unique history of northwestern Montana and especially the history of Kalispell. Permanent exhibits include a historical examination of the Flathead Valley and the growth of the logging industry in Montana. On Thursdays 5pm-8pm late June-late August, live music, food vendors, arts and crafts, a farmers market, and beer and wine garden converge on the grounds of the museum.

SPORTS AND RECREATION

TOP EXPERIENCE

★ Skiing at Whitefish Mountain Resort

When it comes to skiing in Montana, it doesn't get much better than skiing at the **Whitefish Mountain Resort** (3840 Big Mountain Rd., 406/862-2900, www.skiwhitefish.com, full-day $79 adults 19-64, $68 seniors 65-69 and teens 13-18, $40 juniors 7-12, free for ages 70 and over and 6 and under, half-day $69 adults, $60 seniors and teens, $33 juniors), which offers 94 trails, 11 lifts, 2,353 feet (717 m) of vertical drop, and a 3.3-mile (5.3-km) run. When the snow conditions are just right, the trees all across the top of the mountain look like enormous snow monsters. It's magical—or terrifying, depending upon your point of view. This is a *big* mountain, with serious skiing and family fun at its best. The mountain stays open year-round for hiking, mountain biking, zipline tours, and an alpine slide, among other activities. In addition to offering regular 9am-4pm lift hours, it's also one of the few mountains in Montana that offers lighted night skiing ($23), 4pm-8:30pm.

Cross-Country Skiing

For cross-country skiers, fabulous groomed trails can be found locally at the **Glacier Nordic Center** (1200 U.S. 93 W., Whitefish, 406/862-9498, www.glaciernordicclub.com, $10 adults 18-69, $5 children 8-17, free for 70 and over and 7 and under) on the Whitefish Lake Golf Course. There are 15 kilometers of skate and classic trails on gently rolling terrain, and lighted night skiing on 4 kilometers of trails until 11pm. A Nordic shop (406/862-9498) on-site sells passes and rents gear for kids and adults by the half-day, full-day, or week. Lessons are also available.

Hiking and Biking

In addition to having Glacier National Park as a backyard, both Kalispell and Whitefish have excellent hiking and biking trails. Among the adventures at **Whitefish Mountain Resort** (3840 Big Mountain Rd., Whitefish, 406/862-2900, www.skiwhitefish.com, 8am-6pm daily mid-June-early Sept., Fri.-Sun. only through late Sept.) are serious mountain biking opportunities for the hard-core and not-so-hard-core, who might prefer to limit rides to downhill only. There are more than 30 miles (48 km) of lift-accessed ($31 adult full-day, $22 adult 2-hour, $22 junior full-day, $18 junior 2-hour) single-track and cross-country trails on the mountain. For hikers, the **Danny On Trail** winds 3.8 miles (6.1 km) from the base of the ski hill to the summit. The lift can be taken up or down to make the hike shorter and easier.

Just 4 miles (6.4 km) southwest of Kalispell, **Lone Pine State Park** (300 Lone Pine Rd., Kalispell, 406/755-2706, www.stateparks.mt.gov/lone-pine, $6/vehicle nonresidents) has a nature trail, 7.5 miles (12.1 km) of hiking and biking trails with scenic overlooks, and a year-round visitors center with flush toilets and a picnic shelter. A variety of programs—from yoga to full-moon hikes—are scheduled

Whitefish Mountain Resort

throughout the summer at the visitors center and picnic shelter. Young kids, ages 4-7, will be excited about the **Junior Ranger Club**, where they can learn about the natural world through activities and games.

Golf

Both Kalispell and Whitefish are big golfing destinations as soon as the snow melts. Public courses in Whitefish include the North and South Courses at the **Whitefish Lake Golf Club** (1200 U.S. 93 N., 406/862-5960, 406/862-4000 for tee times, www.golfwhitefish.com, $49-63 for 18 holes, $26-33 for 9 holes, $40 for 18 holes on the South Course after 2pm). Five public courses are in Kalispell, including the **Northern Pines Golf Club** (3230 U.S. 93 N., 406/751-1950, www.northernpinesgolfclub.com, $30-72 for 18 holes, $20-40 for 9 holes), the 36-hole **Buffalo Hill Golf Club** (1176 N. Main St., 888/342-6319, www.golfbuffalohill.com, $35-70 for 18 holes, $21-27 for 9 holes), and the **Village Greens Golf Club** (500 Palmer Dr., 406/752-4666, www.montanagolf.com, $45-55 for 18 holes, $27-32 for 9 holes).

ENTERTAINMENT AND EVENTS

With so much to do year-round in this part of the state, the calendar is always full with seasonal events. In northwestern Montana, summertime means farmers markets, and a good one is the **Kalispell Farmers Market** (777 Grandview Dr., 406/881-4078, www.kalispellfarmersmarket.org, 9am-12:30pm Sat. early May-mid.-Oct.), held on the campus of Flathead Valley Community College. In Whitefish, summer brings the **Downtown Farmers Market** (1 Central Ave., 406/407-5272, www.whitefishfarmersmarket.org, 5pm-7:30pm Tues. late May-late Sept.), which offers local produce and art, handmade crafts, prepared food, and a variety of entertainment, often including live music.

Another market, which focuses on locally made arts and crafts, is the **Artists and Craftsmen of the Flathead Summer Outdoor Show** (920 S. Main St., Kalispell,

406/881-4288, www.artistsandcraftsmen.org), held over a weekend in the first part of July. Among the annual festivals celebrating local art, food, and culture are the **Whitefish Arts Festival** (504 Railway St., Whitefish, 406/862-5875, www.whitefishartsfestival.org), which is usually held the first weekend in July in Depot Park; the **Festival Amadeus** (600 2nd St., Whitefish, 406/407-7000, www.gscmusic.org), a weeklong classical music festival held in late July or August; and the **Huckleberry Days Art Festival** (Depot Park, Whitefish, 406/862-3501, www.whitefishchamber.org), held over three days in mid-August, which celebrates the juicy purple berry with music, entertainment, an art fair, and lots of family fun.

In mid-May, the annual **Feast Whitefish** (O'Shaughnessy Center, 1 Central Ave., Whitefish, across from the train station, 406/862-3501, www.feastwhitefish.com, $110) is the region's premier food event. It includes a weeklong dinner series with exquisite nightly meals by regional chefs, and a one-day distiller's fest (tickets from $30) that focuses on local vodkas, whiskeys, and other spirits by seven regional distilleries.

Perhaps the most anticipated event of the year is the **Northwest Montana Fair & Rodeo** (fairgrounds, 265 N. Meridian Rd., Kalispell, 406/758-5810, www.nwmtfair.com, from $32 adults, $20 children 6-12), usually held in mid-August and kicked off with a parade. The nearly weeklong event includes plenty of local agricultural exhibits, a carnival, three nights of professional rodeo, and a variety of entertainment, all of which attract visitors from across the region. For year-round entertainment, check out the **Glacier Symphony and Chorale** (69 N. Main St., Kalispell, 406/407-7000, www.gscmusic.org), which produces an interesting range of musical events.

In winter, the area celebrates the snow with festivities like the **New Year's Eve Rockin' Rail Jam and Torchlight Parade** (Whitefish Mountain Resort, 406/862-2900, www.skiwhitefish.com) and the **Whitefish Winter**

Carnival (www.whitefishwintercarnival. com), a silly and fun event held annually in early February.

Despite its small size, Whitefish has a remarkably savvy theater crowd with offerings from both the **Alpine Theatre Project** (600 2nd St. E., 406/862-7469, www.atpwhitefish. org), a highly respected repertory theater company, and **Whitefish Theatre Company** (1 Central Ave., 406/862-5371, www.whitefishtheatreco.org), which offers eight community plays annually plus concerts, professional dance, improv performances, workshops, camps, and films.

SHOPPING

Western Outdoor (48 Main St., Kalispell, 406/756-5818 or 800/636-5818, www. westernod.com, 9am-6pm Mon.-Sat., 10:30am-4:30pm Sun. summer, 10am-6pm Mon.-Sat., 10:30am-4:30pm Sun. fall-spring) is one of the most popular shopping attractions. This Western goods store boasts more than 2,500 pairs of boots and close to 1,500 hats in every size, shape, and style imaginable. If you've always wanted real cowboy duds, the salespeople here are very attentive and will do their best to make sure you are outfitted properly.

Think Local (140 Main St., Kalispell, 406/260-4499, 10am-5:30pm Tues.-Sat., extended summer and holiday hours) showcases amazingly diverse works by 51 local artists including photographers, painters, rope and barnwood artists, and copper jewelers, all of them from Montana. A coffee shop in the back makes time spent browsing all the more enjoyable. A perfect winter shop in Kalispell is **Montana Kite Sports** (405 3rd Ave. E., 530/356-2758), which introduces the sports of "power kiting" and "ice boating" to the willing. Hours here can change with the weather, so call ahead. In addition to sales, you can take a lesson! For art lovers, Kalispell's **Montana Modern Fine Art** (127 S. Main St., 406/755-5321, www.montanamodernfineart.

1: downtown Kalispell 2: downtown Whitefish

com, 11am-6pm Tues.-Sat.) is a rare way to see phenomenal artworks and meet artists like Marshall Noice. He works in oils and pastels and captures the western landscape in brilliant color and luscious form.

The streets of downtown Whitefish are filled with bars, restaurants, spas, and art galleries. Several galleries line Central Avenue, including **Stumptown Art Studio** (145 Central Ave., 406/862-5929, www. stumptownartstudio.org, 10am-6pm Mon.-Sat., noon-5pm Sun.), a marvelous gallery for buying, learning about, and even making art. **Samarah Fine Art** (100 Central Ave., 406/862-3339, www.samarahfineart. com,10am-6pm Mon.-Sat.) is a gallery that represents about 30 artists from across the state working in various traditional and contemporary media. Both galleries participate in the popular **Whitefish Gallery Nights** (www.whitefishgallerynights.org) the first Thursday evening of each month May-October. Thirteen galleries are involved, each sponsoring a different artist each night of the event. It's a great way to view art, meet the artists, sample good food, and experience the community.

The **Imagination Station Toys** (221 Central Ave., Whitefish, 406/862-5668, 9:30am-8pm Mon.-Sat., 11am-5pm Sun.) began about 20 years ago when the owners realized that they missed the toys of their youth. Their classic toy selection has grown over the years and is a lot of fun for adults and children alike. They also stock their store with the latest wooden toys from Europe, have a good selection of educational toys, and like to keep a lot of puzzles and board games on hand as well. Like a toy store for grown-ups, **The Shops Under One Roof** (205 Central Ave., Whitefish, 406/862-7253, 10am-5pm Mon.-Sat.) is a labyrinth of wonderful antiques and design shops.

If you have the time, a stop at **Kettle Care Organics** (3575 Hwy. 93, Whitefish, 888/556-2316, www.kettlecare.com, 9am-6pm Mon.-Fri., 10am-3pm Sat.) is well worth the visit. This business is committed to producing fine all-natural body-care products while remaining conscious of its carbon footprint. The ingredients come from its certified organic farm and are created, packaged, and labeled for sale on-site. The store has a small showroom stocked with products; a trip to this store provides visitors an opportunity to see a successful homegrown green business in action.

FOOD

In keeping with the number of strip malls in town, Kalispell has an abundance of chain restaurants, many of them quite good, like **Mackenzie River Pizza** (2230 U.S. 93 S., 406/756-0060, www.mackenzieriverpizza.com, 11am-10pm daily, and 45 Treeline Rd., 406/756-3030, 11am-10pm Sun.-Thurs., 11am-11pm Fri.-Sat., $8-20.50), which serves pies from the traditional to the gourmet and rounds out the menu with a healthy selection of sandwiches, pasta dishes, salads, and appetizers. Adjacent to the Hilton Garden Inn, **Blue Canyon Kitchen & Tavern** (1840 Hwy. 93 S., 406/758-2583, www.bluecanyonrestaurant.com, 4pm-10pm Tues.-Sat., 4pm-9pm Sun.-Mon., $14-36) offers everything from flatbread and salads to bison shepherd's pie and elk meat loaf. It also offers half portions of many of the savory entrées, which is easier on the waistband and the wallet.

Some fantastic local restaurants also are well worth finding. **The Knead Café** (21 5th St. E., 406/752-8436 www.theknead.com, 8am-3pm Tues.-Sat., $8-15) is a great little Mediterranean-inspired breakfast and lunch joint that rightly calls itself a "spirited fusion of food, art, and music." An excellent choice for a gourmet dinner is the family-friendly **Jagz Restaurant** (3796 Hwy. 2 E., 406/755-5303, www.jagzrestaurant.com, 4:30pm-9pm daily, $9-38), which serves a wide assortment of steaks, seafood, and pasta. **Hops Downtown Grill** (121 Main St., 406/755-7687, www.hopsmontana.com, 5pm-9pm Sun.-Thurs., 5pm-9:30pm Sat.-Sun., $10-19) is known for a wide selection of craft beer and gourmet burgers—from wild boar and

buffalo to yak and good ol' American Kobe beef. Chicken, lasagna, ribs, and steak round out the menu.

Whitefish has a surprising number of excellent restaurants. One of the all-around best places to go for a hearty, delicious meal is the budget-friendly **Buffalo Café & Nightly Grill** (514 3rd St. E., 406/862-2833, www.buffalocafewhitefish.com, 7am-2pm and 5pm-9pm Mon.-Sat., 8am-2pm Sun., $12-25). From old-fashioned milk shakes and blueberry granola pancakes to Mexican specialties and baby back ribs, this local favorite has mastered comfort food for more than 30 years. And the service is first-class and speedy.

When breakfast or pie (or any meal whatsoever) is on the docket, one should not overlook the incredible ★ **Loula's Café** (300 2nd St. E., 406/862-5614, www.whitefishrestaurant.com, 7am-3pm Sun.-Mon., 7am-3pm and 5pm-9:30pm Tues.-Sat., $11-22). Breakfast ($5.50-12.50) is everything from Chubby Yuppie Scrambles to Ski Bum Biscuits and Gravy, eggs Benedict, and breakfast burritos. Save room for pie. Lunch ($8.50-13) is a selection of mouthwatering burgers, sandwiches, soups, and salads. And pie. Don't forget the pie. Dinner ($10.50-22) can be a more sophisticated affair with changing menus that pair specials with wine. And pie! If you happen to be in Loula's when the pies come out of the oven and you don't jump to buy at least one, you will regret it for the remainder of your trip. I'm not kidding. Eating a huckleberry cherry pie, straight from the box and still a bit warm, on the shores of Lake McDonald is a memory that will stay with you forever.

Although Montana is not known for its sushi, Whitefish residents could not live without **Wasabi Sushi Bar** (419 E. 2nd St., 406/863-9283, www.wasabimt.com, from 5pm daily May-Oct., from 5pm Mon.-Sat. Nov.-Apr., rolls $5-16), with classic nigiri and sashimi, a contemporary twist on sushi and tempura, and plenty of grill items that include steak, duck, scallops, fish tacos, and more.

While a handful of elegant high-end eateries are in Whitefish, **Tupelo Grille** (17

Central Ave., 406/862-6136, www.tupelogrille. com, 5pm-10pm daily, lounge daily from 4pm, $18-42) is a unique choice with a wonderfully Southern-inspired menu and an exceptional wine list. Just down the block is another gem: **Latitude 48 Bistro and Red Room Basement Bar** (147 Central Ave., 406/863-2323, www.latitude48bistro.com, 5pm-10pm daily, $7-32) is an urban oasis with a phenomenal menu that offers small plates like seared beef tips and lamb sirloin, creative wood-fired pizzas, and substantial main courses in a fusion of traditional and contemporary trends.

For foodies looking for another unforgettable meal, **Café Kandahar** (3824 Big Mountain Rd., 406/862-6247, www.cafekandahar.com, 5:30pm-9:30pm daily mid-Dec.-late Mar. and mid-June-late Sept., market prices) on the ski hill cannot be overtouted. The menus change nightly, but in addition to the à la carte masterpieces, the chef always offers a 5- and 7-course tasting menu and an 11-course degustation menu. Sample dishes include pork belly confit, Hudson Valley foie gras, and elk roulade. But it is the way that Chef Andy Blanton masterfully combines delicate flavors and exquisite ingredients that captivates diners. Make no mistake, this will be a pricey meal—but a phenomenal one.

ACCOMMODATIONS

Kalispell is definitely the best place to find an assortment of more budget-friendly chain hotels and motels, but prices can rise when the town is packed with travelers en route to or from Glacier or Flathead. Next to the airport, the **Aero Inn** (1830 U.S. 93 S., 406/755-3798 or 800/843-6114, www.aeroinn.com, $50-145) has 61 no-frills guest rooms and is reasonably priced. Another good value can be found at the 106-room pet-friendly **Blue & White Motel** (640 E. Idaho St., 406/755-4311 or 800/382-3577, www.blueandwhitemotel. com, $43-95), which, in addition to cool neon signage, has decent rooms, standard amenities, and a 24-hour restaurant next door (making it a favorite with truckers).

Among the larger chain hotels and motels are **America's Best Value** (1550 Hwy. 93 N., 406/756-3222, www.abvkalispell.com, $129-169), **Best Western Plus Flathead Lake Inn and Suites** (4824 Hwy. 93 S., 406/857-2400 or 888/226-1003, www.bestwestern.com, $170-369), **Econo Lodge of Kalispell** (1680 Hwy. 93 S., 406/752-3467 or 800/843-7301, www. choicehotels.com, $120-212), **Hampton Inn Kalispell** (1140 Hwy. 2 W., 406/755-7900 or 800/426-7866, www.hamptoninn3.hilton. com, $179-354), the fairly glamorous for these parts **Hilton Garden Inn** (1840 Hwy. 93 S., 406/756-4500, www.hiltongardeninn3.hilton. com, $179-299), **Holiday Inn Express** (275 Treeline Rd., 406/755-7405, www.ihg.com, $160-270), **Kalispell Super 8** (1341 1st Ave. E., 406/203-1905, www.wyndhamhotels.com, $160-189), and **La Quinta Inn & Suites** (255 Montclair Dr., 406/257-5255 or 800/753-3757, www.lq.com, $166-224).

For a more historic experience, try the pet-friendly **Kalispell Grand Hotel** (100 Main St., 406/755-8100 or 800/858-7422, www. kalispellgrand.com, $75-183) downtown. This stately brick property is the last of eight hotels that once lined downtown. Less historic but reliable and pet-friendly, the **Red Lion Hotel** (20 N. Main St., 406/751-5050 or 800/733-5466, www.redlion.com, $209-329) is conveniently located next to the Kalispell Center Mall in the heart of downtown.

Given its proximity to Whitefish Mountain, Whitefish Lake, and Glacier National Park, it's no surprise that Whitefish has an abundance of accommodations—but true to its resort-town vibe, beds don't come cheap. The largest and most diverse, without a doubt, is the **Whitefish Mountain Resort** (3840 Big Mountain Rd., 406/862-2900, www. skiwhitefish.com, $109-1,500), the resort community around Whitefish Mountain with eight different lodging options, 90 percent of which are condominiums that range from modest and economical guest rooms in the **Hibernation House** to palatial five-bedroom town houses. Rates are generally higher in winter, and particularly around holidays.

Navigating the reservation system can be a feat, so practice patience and be clear about what you want and what your budget is.

Another sizable full-service resort, on the shores of Whitefish Lake and just over 1 mile (1.6 km) from downtown, is the ultra-appealing **Lodge at Whitefish Lake** (1380 Wisconsin Ave., 406/863-4000 or 877/887-4026, www.lodgeatwhitefishlake.com, $130-721). The lodge is pretty spectacular, and the rooms are all luxurious. The attached condos are sizable and great for larger groups, but somewhat less romantic. The immediate lake access is a disincentive to ever leave, and the on-site restaurants will keep you well fed and happy.

Smaller options for lodging in the town of Whitefish include the riverfront 15-room **Duck Inn** (1305 Columbia Ave., 406/862-3825 or 800/344-2377, www.duckinn.com, $199-289) and the charming five-bedroom **Garden Wall Inn** (504 Spokane Ave., 406/862-3440 or 888/530-1700, www.gardenwallinn.com, $155-395).

CAMPING

There are quite a few camping options, both public and private, around Kalispell, but nothing for tent campers in town. Among the largest full-service RV parks and the only one with a heated swimming pool is the shady and private **Glacier Pines** (120 Swan Mountain Dr., Kalispell, 406/752-2760, www.glacierpines.com, from $39 plus $2 pp), with 80 full-service sites, free Wi-Fi, a playground for small kids, horseshoes, and fire pits. A good primitive option for tent campers is the **Ashley Lake Campgrounds** (North Shore Rd., off Ashley Lake Rd., 17 mi/27.4 km west of Kalispell, 406/758-5204, www.fs.usda.gov, Memorial Day-Labor Day, no fees for day use or overnight camping), which offers 11 lakefront sites with no services other than a vault toilet.

By far the most economical accommodations in Whitefish are the campgrounds. There are a number of beautiful national forest campgrounds as well as two private campgrounds, including the **Whitefish KOA** (5121 U.S. 93 S., 2 mi/3.2 km south of Whitefish, 406/862-4242 or 800/562-8734, www.glacierparkkoa.com, mid-May-mid-Sept., $46-89 RV and tent sites, $99-205 cabins), which has every imaginable amenity. **Tally Lake** (913 Tally Lake Rd., 17 mi/27 km west of Whitefish, 406/646-1012, www.recreation.gov, late May-late Sept., from $18) is a gorgeous and popular spot with a nice campground. Closer to town, **Whitefish Lake State Park** (1615 E. Lakeshore Dr., 406/862-3991 or 406/751-4590, www.stateparks.mt.gov, year-round, water and showers available May-Sept., from $10) offers 25 waterfront tent and RV sites that go quickly at this beautiful, convenient spot.

INFORMATION AND SERVICES

The **Kalispell Chamber of Commerce** (406/758-2800, www.kalispellchamber.com, 8am-5pm Mon.-Fri.) and **Flathead Convention and Visitor Bureau** (406/756-9091, www.fcvb.org, 8:30am-4pm Mon.-Fri.) are housed in the historic Great Northern Depot building (15 Depot Park, Kalispell). The **Whitefish Chamber of Commerce** (307 Spokane Ave., Whitefish, 406/862-3501, www.whitefishchamber.org, 9am-5pm Mon.-Fri.) is open year-round.

The **Flathead National Forest Headquarters** (650 Wolf Pack Way, Kalispell, 406/758-5208, www.fs.usda.gov/flathead, 8am-4:30pm Mon.-Fri.) has helpful information for campers and hikers.

Kalispell has the **Flathead County Library** (247 1st Ave. E., 406/758-5820, www.imagineiflibraries.org, 10am-8pm Mon.-Wed., 10am-6pm Thurs.-Fri., 10am-5pm Sat.), and the **main post office** (248 1st Ave. W., 800/275-8777, 9am-4pm Mon.-Fri.) is at the corner of 3rd Street.

The **Kalispell Regional Medical Center** (310 Sunnyview Ln., 406/752-5111, www.krh.org) has a 24-hour emergency room and is just north of downtown Kalispell. There are also several urgent care facilities in town, including

MedNorth Urgent Care (2316 Hwy. 93, 406/755-5661, www.mymednorth.com, 7:30am-7:30pm Mon.-Fri., 9am-3pm Sat.-Sun.) and **Family Health Care** (1287 Burns Way, 406/752-8120, www.mymednorth.com, 8am-6pm Mon.-Fri., 9am-2pm Sat.-Sun.).

TRANSPORTATION
Getting There

Just 14 miles (22.5 km) south of Whitefish, Kalispell is the larger of the two cities and has commercial flights and bus service, while Whitefish has daily train service. Both cities have taxi services.

The **Glacier Park International Airport** (FCA, 4170 U.S. 2 E., Kalispell, www.iflyglacier.com) is served by Delta, Alaska, United, and Allegiant. There are on-site car-rental counters for **Avis, Budget, Hertz,** and **National/Alamo; Dollar,** (406/892-0009, www.dollar.com), **Enterprise** (406/755-4848, www.enterprise.com), and **Thrifty** (406/257-7333, www.thrifty.com) are off-site but near the airport.

Greyhound (2075 Hwy 2 E., Kalispell, 406/755-7447) offers daily bus service in and out of Kalispell.

Amtrak (500 Depot St., Whitefish) runs the *Empire Builder* from Chicago to Seattle with daily stops in Whitefish in each direction.

Kalispell and Whitefish are easily accessible by car: Kalispell is 115 miles (185 km) north of Missoula at the junction of U.S. 2 and U.S. 93; Whitefish is just 14 miles (22.5 km) farther north on U.S. 93.

Getting Around

Eagle Transit (406/758-5728, http://flathead. mt.gov/eagle, 7am-7pm Mon.-Fri., $1) operates the buses in Kalispell. **Glacier Taxi** (406/250-3603, www.glaciertaxi.com, 24/7) covers all of Flathead County from Flathead Lake to Whitefish Mountain, Glacier National Park, Kalispell, and everything in between.

Butte, Helena, and Southwest Montana

From the first major discovery of gold along

Grasshopper Creek in 1862, southwestern Montana attracted prospectors, miners, and those who would build communities around them.

Within a year of that major gold discovery, President Abraham Lincoln signed a bill creating Montana Territory. In many ways, this region gave rise to the state.

Two of the state's best-known mining camps, Helena and Butte, prospered and diversified, becoming a pair of Montana's most interesting and historically significant cities. Others, like Virginia City and Bannack, all but disappeared before rising again as well-maintained tourist attractions. Indeed, history comes to life in southwestern Montana, from the mines in and around Butte to the battlegrounds

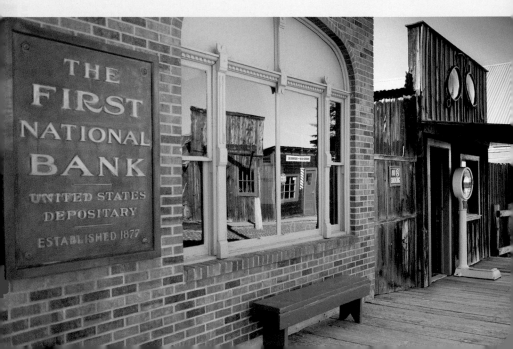

Highlights

Look for ★ to find recommended sights, activities, dining, and lodging.

★ **Old Butte Historical Adventures:** Spend some time with one of the passionate and knowledgeable guides here, where you'll see history both above and below the ground (page 224).

★ **World Museum of Mining:** This museum, built atop the Orphan Girl mine yard, is packed with artifacts from more than a century of hard-rock mining (page 227).

★ **Philipsburg:** This fabulous mining town is experiencing a rebirth, with a couple of fantastic restaurants and a cool hotel (page 239).

★ **Big Hole National Battlefield:** A memorial to the Nez Perce and U.S. Army soldiers who died in battle, this site is both gorgeous and moving. The tipi frames stand where they did the fateful morning of the attack (page 245).

★ **Skiing Maverick Mountain:** A well-kept secret, Maverick has tow ropes, Carhartt, and the most family-friendly ski atmosphere you can imagine (page 249).

★ **Fishing the Big Hole:** Flowing 155 miles (250 km), the Big Hole River is one of the classics in the Montana fishing oeuvre, filled with rainbow, brown, and brook trout as well as rare native grayling (page 249).

★ **Virginia City and Nevada City:** These neighboring mining towns boast more than 100 historic buildings, a 1910 steam locomotive, and plenty of locals willing to re-create the rowdy mining era (page 253).

★ **Lewis and Clark Caverns:** Montana's first state park is a fine example of limestone caves (page 255).

★ **Last Chance Gulch and Reeder's Alley:** One of the few pedestrian malls in Montana is both the historic and modern heart of Helena (page 261).

along the Big Hole River, the ghost towns above Philipsburg, and the cobblestone streets of Montana's capital city of Helena.

But there's much more to this corner of the state than museums and mine shafts. Vast open spaces, like the glorious Big Hole, are dotted with cattle and lined with blue-ribbon trout waters. There are plentiful hot springs, old-school family-oriented ski hills, and some of the region's most scenic drives. And although the region is developing—a hip contemporary art scene in Helena, for example, and a Jack Nicklaus golf course built into the Old Works smelting site in Anaconda—there are stretches that look and feel untouched. The ranchers in the Big Hole Valley still use big wooden beaver-slide contraptions during haying season, and the Beaverhead-Deerlodge National Forest is a vast swath of breathtaking scenery that encompasses 3.5 million acres (1.4 million hectares) and two pristine wilderness areas. Southwest Montana and its best-known cities offer visitors a unique look into Montana's past and an authentic view of Montana's most appealing present.

PLANNING YOUR TIME

This corner of the state is vast and relatively diverse, both geographically and in terms of its offerings. History buffs will be easily sated just about anywhere, from the big cities of Helena and Butte to the tiny ghost towns that dot the landscape. And while southwestern Montana could easily absorb a week or more, it can also be appreciated in three days or less for visitors trying to see more of the state.

Butte is a fascinating destination, not so much for its present-day incarnation, which can be fairly described as a bit rowdy and somewhat bleak, but for its older glory: the remarkable architecture that still stands, the underground city that is just coming to light, and the mines that made Butte the "richest hill on earth" and one of the country's largest cities west of the Mississippi for nearly 50

years. Butte is a marvelous place to spend at least a day, and more if you are interested in mining or history.

For good reason, nature lovers and outdoors enthusiasts will be itching to get out of Butte. The **Big Hole,** southwest of the city, is a natural wonderland of wide-open spaces, supremely good fishing, a ski hill, an important Native American battle site, and a couple of great hot springs. Indeed, this region could be a vacation on its own, and it requires at least a day to cover the terrain.

Farther west, **Philipsburg,** less than 1 mile (1.6 km) from the ghost town of **Granite** and just 10 miles (16.1 km) from **Georgetown Lake** and **Discovery Ski Area,** is an ideal spot to enjoy a sumptuous meal, get a good night's rest, and perhaps even catch a show.

Finally, a host of other places in the region make great add-ons or stand-alone destinations. **Virginia City, Nevada City,** and **Bannack** are meticulously preserved ghost towns. The state's capital, **Helena,** is a bustling city that has successfully transitioned into modernity while still carefully preserving its past. As is true almost anywhere in Montana, the recreational opportunities just outside the city are plentiful, from **Gates of the Mountains,** named by Lewis and Clark, to **Holter, Hauser,** and **Canyon Ferry Lakes,** which offer boating, fishing, and only-in-Montana activities like ice sailing during winter.

HISTORY

Although this area's past was dominated by mining, southwestern Montana's history predates the first precious-metal find. The region long had great appeal to both mountaineers and fur trappers. On their epic journey west, this is where Lewis and Clark were given vital assistance by the Native Americans who frequented the region. Just 14 miles (22.5 km) north of present-day Dillon, Sacagawea recognized Beaverhead Rock as the area where

---

Previous: Virginia City, one of the most well-preserved and lively ghost towns in the state; a general store in Virginia City; The Big Hole.

Butte, Helena, and Southwest Montana

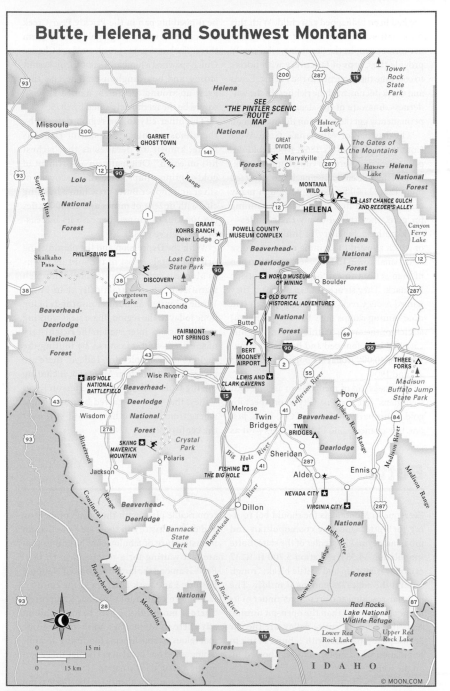

Tower Rock State Park

Helena

SEE "THE PINTLER SCENIC ROUTE" MAP

Holter Lake

Missoula

National

GREAT DIVIDE

The Gates of the Mountains

GARNET GHOST TOWN

Marysville

Hauser Lake

Helena National Forest

Garnet Range

Forest

Lolo

MONTANA WILD

LAST CHANCE GULCH AND REEDER'S ALLEY

Sapphire Mtns

National

HELENA

Canyon Ferry Lake

Forest

GRANT KOHRS RANCH

Deer Lodge

POWELL COUNTY MUSEUM COMPLEX

Beaverhead-

Helena National Forest

Skalkaho Pass

PHILIPSBURG

Lost Creek State Park

Deerlodge

DISCOVERY

WORLD MUSEUM OF MINING

Boulder

Beaverhead-

Georgetown Lake

Anaconda

OLD BUTTE HISTORICAL ADVENTURES

National

Deerlodge

Butte

Forest

National

FAIRMONT HOT SPRINGS

Forest

BERT MOONEY AIRPORT

THREE FORKS

BIG HOLE NATIONAL BATTLEFIELD

Wise River

LEWIS AND CLARK CAVERNS

Madison Buffalo Jump State Park

Beaverhead-

Pony

Deerlodge

Melrose

Twin Bridges

Beaverhead-

Wisdom

National

TWIN BRIDGES

Dearlodge

Forest

SKIING MAVERICK MOUNTAIN

Crystal Park

Sheridan

Jackson

Polaris

FISHING THE BIG HOLE

Alder

Ennis

NEVADA CITY

Dillon

VIRGINIA CITY

National

Bannack State Park

Forest

Beaverhead-

Deerlodge

National

Red Rocks Lake National Wildlife Refuge

Forest

Lower Red Rock Lake

Upper Red Rock Lake

0   15 mi

0   15 km

I D A H O

she had been kidnapped as a child. With this information, the men set out to encounter her former people, the Shoshone, who would provide the Corps of Discovery with horses to continue their journey to the Pacific. Lewis and Clark documented the richness of the wilderness, unaware of the element that would permanently put the region on the map—gold.

The history of Montana's Gold West Country begins in July 1862, when gold deposits were discovered in Grasshopper Creek. A year later, the city of Bannack had attracted more than 3,000 residents. Although many initially arrived to try their luck at panning for gold, they stayed to ply their trades—blacksmithing, butchery, or innkeeping—all of which allowed the mining camp to evolve into a small town. In May 1863, a small group of men set out to explore the area outside Bannack. They struck gold in a stream they named Alder Creek. Alder Gulch quickly had nine mining camps on a 14-mile (22.5-km) stretch of the creek. Within a year, Virginia City had been founded and boasted a population of 10,000 (today its population hovers around 190).

Next, a group of men known as "the four Georgians" left Virginia City to prospect for gold in uncharted territory. "OK, boys, just one last chance," one of the miners said as he dipped his pan in the Prickly Pear Creek and came up with enough gold to keep them there. The word soon spread, and Last Chance Gulch spawned a jumble of saloons, makeshift stores, and boardinghouses. The city that grew up around the gulch, named Helena, would be the territorial capital by 1875.

The other city in the region defined by the almost maniacal pursuit of riches is Butte, known for decades as the "richest hill on earth." Originally an assortment of gold-mining camps, with the discovery of silver and copper Butte grew into a bustling city with dozens of mines and 10,000 miles (16,100 km) of tunnels beneath its increasingly urban streets.

With the Depression and the plummeting price of metals, most of the mining towns in Montana suffered similar fates, although significantly less dramatically than Butte. While a limited amount of mining is being done today in the region, the state is working to draw visitors interested in the rich history of the area—and, of course, by touting the region's natural splendor. Indeed, there are places in southwestern Montana, including the Big Hole Valley and the Jefferson River Valley, that were unscarred by mining and where time seems to have stood still over the centuries.

Butte

Everyone in Montana is (or should be) rooting for Butte. Once the cosmopolitan and urban moneymaking center of the state, Butte (population 34,553; elevation 5,700 ft/1,737 m) today is beat-up and a little bleak; "rough around the edges" is putting it mildly. The most far-reaching and present reminder of its former glory, other than the open-pit mining scars that rend the entire valley, are the car license plates that start with 1, Butte's rank in population when motor vehicles showed up on the scene.

Despite its diminished status, Butte is a remarkable place with the most compelling and diverse history in the state as well as an infrastructure of fabulous old buildings that are just waiting for a renaissance. In fact, Butte is among the largest registered National Historic Landmark Districts in the country, with more than 4,000 historic structures. There is more culture here than just about anywhere in Montana, and there are some marvelous establishments for dining and imbibing—and one hotel in particular that is enjoying a second incarnation.

Unless you are a history fanatic, Butte is not

Butte

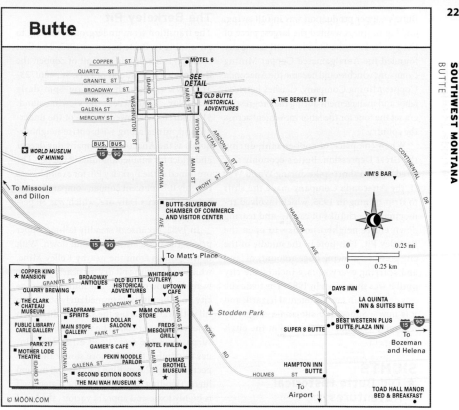

© MOON.COM

a place you'll want to spend an entire week; to see Montana, you need to get out in the fresh air and enjoy the natural beauty. A weekend in Butte gives visitors to the state an incredible opportunity to learn about Montana's past and see firsthand what happens to a place when all of its natural resources are exploited as quickly as possible. Indeed, there is something of *The Lorax* in Butte, and something of *The Giving Tree*. But no copper king or corporation can rob this place of its fascinating past and modern-day spirit. And no one is willing to rule out a renaissance—least of all the citizens of Butte.

HISTORY

Like many of the towns in this part of the state, Butte grew up as a mining camp after a gold strike in 1864. After discovery of both

silver and copper ores, many big companies moved into town to extract, process, and distribute the metals, making Butte the state's first industrialized city. Urban and fiercely proud, Butte residents were known to describe their city as "Butte, America," rather than "Butte, Montana," to distinguish themselves from the rural sensibilities of the rest of the state. By the late 1800s, Butte was one of the world's largest silver and copper producers and among the most populated cities in the United States. Throughout the boom, a diverse range of immigrants flooded into the area looking for opportunities. Irish, Italian, Eastern European, and Chinese newcomers all contributed to the culture and history of the city.

By the early 1900s, with the introduction of electricity and the demands of World War I,

Butte's copper production was in full swing, and big business wanted the largest piece of the pie. In 1899 the Standard Oil Company founded the Amalgamated Copper Mining Company, which would become the Anaconda Copper Mining Company. Clashes between labor and management during the Progressive era set the tone for the labor movement across the country.

When the price of copper sank during the Great Depression, Butte's economy suffered. After a short spike during World War II, the Anaconda Company made the shift to strip-mining in 1955, which involved removing large chunks of earth—and tearing down entire neighborhoods—to open the Berkeley Pit. This hole in the middle of the city grew, swallowing huge amounts of land and scarring every square inch of the city until it was shut down in 1982. The toxic site was declared an environmental hazard, and it is now a Superfund site and a tragic, irreparable reminder of the end of the city's mining era.

SIGHTS
★ Old Butte Historical Adventures

If you only have one day to spend in Butte, plan to attend one of the walking tours put on by **Old Butte Historical Adventures** (117 N. Main St., 406/498-3424, scheduled tours 10am-2pm Mon.-Sat., by reservation only Sun. Apr.-Oct., by reservation only Nov.-Mar., $20 adults; $17.50 seniors, military, and students with ID; $10 children 5-11). It offers a variety of walking tours of Butte's underground city, complete with a speakeasy, a barbershop, and an old city jail. Other tours stay aboveground and visit the gorgeous Finlen Hotel, an old brothel, and the Mai Wah Museum in Chinatown. Ghost tours, labor history tours, and ethnic culture walking tours can also be arranged. What makes these tours so compelling, other than the mind-blowing history, is the passion and knowledge of the guides—you may just fall in love with Butte. Reservations are strongly recommended.

The Berkeley Pit

The transition from underground mining to pit mining in Butte began in 1955. The first open-pit mine dug in pursuit of copper, the **Berkeley Pit** (east end of Park St., 406/723-3177, www.pitwatch.org, 9am-5pm daily Mar.-Nov., $2 to access the viewing stand, $1 children) swallowed several of the underground mines along with entire neighborhoods as the Anaconda Company dug deeper and wider for smaller amounts of copper. The ore mined at the Berkeley Pit, for example, was roughly 0.75 percent copper, compared to the original Marcus Daly ore, which was 30 percent copper.

In 1982, because of steadily falling copper prices, the Berkeley Pit was shut down. With it, the pumps from the nearby Kelley Mine, which had kept the pit dry for nearly 30 years, were shut down as well. The mines under the city and the pit itself immediately started to fill with water bearing the same acidity levels as lemon juice or cola. The water depth today surpasses 5,346 feet (1,629 m) and continues to climb—though more slowly than expected—with 2.6 million gallons (9.8 million liters) flooding in every day. The water itself is highly toxic and appears various shades of brown, blue, green, and red, depending on the concentration of chemicals and subsequent chemical reactions.

In 1994, the EPA established a "critical water level" of 5,410 feet (1,649 m), stipulating that when the water in the pit reaches that level, it could seep into Silver Bow Creek or the alluvial groundwater aquifer and contaminate the region's water supply. The government requires the parties responsible for treating the groundwater to pump and treat the water before it reaches that level, or incur fines of $25,000 per day. Current projections predict the water will reach critical level in 2023.

In November 1995, a flock of snow geese landed in the Berkeley Pit; fog and snow kept them from flying off, and after several days

1: uptown Butte 2: the World Museum of Mining in Butte

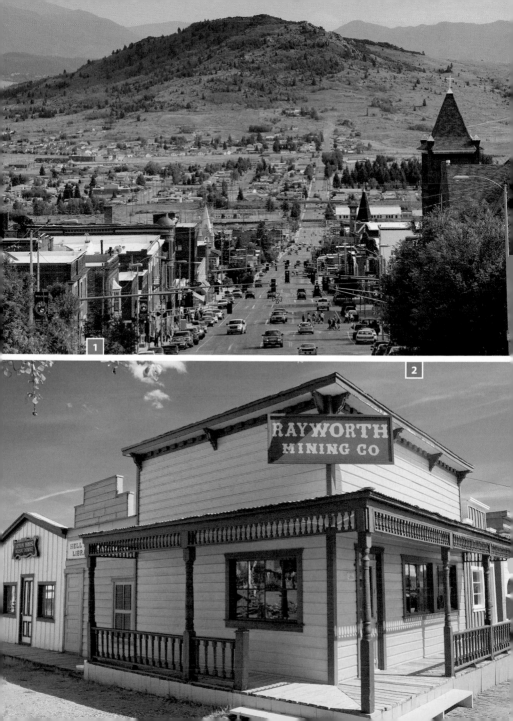

Montana's Superfund Sites

Big Sky Country is most often associated with images of pristine lakes, majestic mountains, and wide-open grasslands. But toxic wastelands? And the worst in the country? It seems far-fetched. However, Montana's mining industry wreaked havoc on the natural environment, scarring the landscape and contaminating both water and soil.

The 1980 Superfund program was created to clean up hazardous waste sites posing a threat to public health and the environment. The area surrounding the Upper Clark Fork River, which encompasses Butte, Anaconda, and Missoula, is the largest Superfund area in the country.

In the late 1800s, Butte's smelters were adjacent to the mines, and the toxic fumes created massive amounts of thick smoke. In mines without smelters, the copper sulfide ore was spread over large piles of logs and ignited in toxic piles that burned for weeks, contaminating air, soil and water. The mining and smelting in Butte decimated not only Butte Hill but was carried downstream and downwind as far as Milltown, 120 miles (193 km) northwest.

Butte was famously without vegetation and its citizens were often sick with burning eyes, bloody noses, gagging, and lung disease. The copper baron William Andrews Clark was quoted as saying, "I must say that the ladies are very fond of this smoky city...because there is just enough arsenic there to give them a beautiful complexion." Eventually an antismoke ordinance was passed, but never enforced because smelter operators threatened to shut down if the laws were applied. No one questioned who had the power in Butte.

When the copper smelter was erected in Anaconda in 1894 by Marcus Daly, Butte's air improved dramatically. But Deer Lodge ranchers and farmers who lived in the valley between Butte and Missoula suffered devastating crop failures and livestock losses. The Anaconda Company built an enormous smokestack in 1918 (at 585 ft/178 m, it surpasses the Washington Monument) to disperse the smoke, but farmers argued it was just spreading the poison over a wider area. The case went all the way to the Supreme Court, and the company won.

By the 1970s it was apparent that the air and water pollution was still hurting livestock and agricultural soil throughout the Deer Lodge Valley. The EPA rated the area the most polluted in the country, worse than Love Canal in New York, and although the cleanup is underway, it will likely last decades and cost hundreds of millions of dollars.

342 birds were found dead in the water. Since then, a program has discouraged migrating birds from landing on the pit water. In November 2016, more snow geese landed in the pit in a single day than often do in an entire year. Crews employed a number of ways to encourage the birds to leave after a short rest—fireworks, bird wailers, drones—but several thousand stayed for a few days and, sadly, perished as a result.

One curious creature that managed to live in and around the pit for years was a dog known by miners as "The Auditor." He greeted workers daily for 17 years but never came close enough for anyone to touch. He was a white (OK, gray) dog with dreadlocks that dragged on the ground. The miners built him a shanty and left food and water; they pointed to The Auditor as proof that there were indeed things able to withstand the toxicity of the Superfund site. The pit's unofficial mascot died in 2003, but not before the community raised enough money to commission a bronze statue of the mangy mutt, which is on display at the pit viewing stand.

Our Lady of the Rockies

High atop the crest of the Continental Divide is **Our Lady of the Rockies** (tours leave from 3100 Harrison Ave., 406/782-1221, www. ourladyoftherockies.net, 10am and 2pm daily weather permitting, gift shop 9am-5pm daily June-Oct., $16 adults, $14 seniors, clergy, and military, $12 children 13-17, $8 children 5-12, $2 children under 5), a 90-foot (27-m) statue of the Virgin Mary meant to watch over this predominantly Catholic town. Between 1979 and 1985, the statue was built and erected entirely by volunteers, many of them miners who had lost their jobs when the Berkeley Pit, Butte's last operating mine, closed down. Bob O'Bill, who worked for the Anaconda Mining Company for years, vowed that if his wife recovered from illness, he would hoist a statue of the Virgin Mary on the East Ridge overlooking the city. When the final piece was set in place by helicopter, Butte came to a screeching halt to watch in proud silence. Indeed, the statue is a reflection of this city's indomitable spirit. The roughly 2.5-hour tours leave from the gift shop on Harrison Avenue and include a trip inside the metal sculpture.

★ World Museum of Mining

Off West Park Road, across from the Montana Tech campus, is the **World Museum of Mining** (155 Mining Museum Rd., 406/723-7211, www.miningmuseum.org, 9am-6pm daily Apr.-Oct., $8.50 adults, $7.50 seniors 65 and over, $5 students 5-17, free for children under 5), which sits on the now-defunct Orphan Girl mine yard. It houses numerous large-scale exhibits, and the mine yard is filled with a variety of equipment covering a century of use, including smelter cars, ore carts, and trucks. When you purchase your entry ticket to the museum, you may also want to buy a ticket for the **underground mine tours** that take place three times a day at 10:30am, 12:30pm, and 3pm. Visitors to the underground mine wear hard hats, cap lamps, and battery belts and descend 65 feet (19.8 m) into the mine. The tours are led by former mine workers who tell their personal stories. They also explain how equipment was used and how the ore was mined and removed from the pit. Combined tickets can be purchased for the museum and the underground tour ($15 adults, $12 seniors 65 and over, $8 students 5-17). Children under five are not permitted on the underground tour.

A highlight of the museum is its **Hell Roarin' Gulch,** a full-scale, authentic reproduction of an 1890s mining town. There are 50 buildings on the site, 15 of which are original historic buildings that have been relocated

to the museum. Visit a bank, general store, school, and Chinese herbalist whose shelves are stocked with original herbs and medicines. The buildings have been painstakingly re-created using as many antiques and original materials as possible. There's also a rock and mineral room in the museum that will delight rock hounds and a remarkable doll and dollhouse collection.

Copper King Mansion

The **Copper King Mansion** (219 W. Granite St., 406/782-7580, www.thecopperkingmansion.com, tours 10am-4pm daily May-Sept., by appointment Oct.-Apr., $10 adults, $5 children) is both a museum and bed-and-breakfast ($105-150). Guided tours show off this 34-room Victorian home built in 1898 for the infamous King of Copper, William Andrews Clark. Considered one of the wealthiest men in the world in his day, Clark could easily afford to import all the material for the house's construction as well as the European artisans needed to do the work. The cost to construct the mansion is estimated at around $500,000, which represents one-half day's wages for Clark at the peak of his career. His personal fortune is thought to have exceeded $50 million by 1900. Each room has a fresco painted on its ceiling by artists personally commissioned by Clark. There is elaborate woodwork throughout the house, including the fireplaces, bookcases, and stairways. Tiffany stained-glass windows and magnificent chandeliers enhance the elegance. It is an exquisite way to truly appreciate the wealth in this city around the turn of the 20th century.

Clark Chateau Museum

W. A. Clark's son, Charles, also commissioned a house in 1898. The **Clark Chateau Museum** (321 W. Broadway, 406/565-5600, www.clarkchateaubutte.wordpress.com, noon-4pm Thurs.-Sun. May-mid-Sept., tours at 1pm and 3pm, by appointment fall-spring, $10 guided tour, $7 general admission, free for children 10 and under, discounts for students, seniors, and military) is a replica of a chateau Charles had admired in France. Today the house is a period museum and Butte's community arts center. Up the gorgeous spiral staircase to the 2nd and 3rd floors is the museum's permanent collection, dedicated to showcasing the diverse cultural and ethnic heritage of the city. Two galleries offer current shows, and the exhibits change over the course of the season. Tours can be arranged off-season by emailing clarkchateau@gmail.com.

Dumas Brothel Museum

Butte also happens to be home to "America's longest-running house of prostitution." The Dumas Brothel was the center of Butte's red-light district back in its mining heyday. Opened in 1890, it only closed its doors in 1982. The brothel reopened as the **Dumas Brothel Museum** (45 E. Mercury St., 406/530-7878, 11:30am-5:30pm Wed.-Sun., $10 admission, children 5 and under free with adult, discounts available for military, seniors, students, and groups), allowing visitors to get a glimpse into the seedier side of the city's history. At its height, the brothel used all 43 rooms and was open 24 hours a day to cater to the miners, who worked around the clock. There were even underground tunnels that led to other downtown buildings, providing secret entry for some of its more distinguished clientele. Since the building was actually constructed to serve as a brothel, it has some unique design elements, including windows lining the hallway. The rooms themselves, known as "cribs," are small enough to hold a bed and not much more. Naturally, the brothel is rife with ghost stories, including the tale of Madame Elenor Knott, who agreed to run away with her married lover in 1955. When he didn't show up for their rendezvous, Elenor took her own life. Her ghost is often reported, and even photographed, in the building. The museum was purchased in 2012 by Travis Eskelsen and Michael Piche, who committed themselves to its preservation and restoration. Tragically, Piche died in 2018.

Eskelsen will continue his work in restoring the museum. Always call before visiting, since the restoration process often requires closures, and museum hours change regularly depending on the number of visitors. This is a labor of love in every way imaginable, like so much of Butte's restoration. Be patient and flexible—it's worth it.

Mai Wah Museum

The **Mai Wah Museum** (17 W. Mercury St., 406/723-3231 or 406/565-1826 off-season, www.maiwah.org, 10am-4pm Tues.-Sat. June-Sept., $5 adults, $3 children under 12) is dedicated to documenting and preserving Butte's Chinese heritage. By 1910, Butte's Chinatown had more than 2,000 Chinese residents, and the 1914 directory listed 62 Chinese businesses that included gambling parlors, noodle shops, herbalists, and grocery stores. The permanent exhibit tells the story of Chinese immigrants to the city who came in search of lucrative jobs in the mining industry 1860-1940. It houses exhibits containing photos, artifacts, and interpretive materials. The museum is in the Wah Chong Tai and Mai Wah buildings, just off China Alley, the heart of Butte's Chinatown. Originally the buildings were a mercantile store and noodle shop that historically served as meeting places and a major point of social interaction for the Chinese immigrant community.

SPORTS AND RECREATION

United States High Altitude Sports Center

A unique facility with an outdoor speed-skating rink and a training facility for Olympic athletes from all over the world, the **United States High Altitude Sports Center** (1 Olympic Way, 406/723-4839, free) hosts various competitions and is open to the public.

Stodden Park

During Butte's mining heyday, the only greenery in town could be found at the beloved Columbia Gardens, which sadly burned down. Today there is plenty of green space in town, and **Stodden Park** (Sampson St. and Utah St., 406/494-3686 or 406/494-6200) tops the list with a swimming pool, tennis courts, horseshoes, a playground, and a nine-hole golf course.

Hiking and Bouldering

Hikers and climbers driving into Butte from the east over Homestake Pass might get tingly as they see the hoodoos scattered across the terrain. A wonderful and quite similar place to explore, without the distraction of highway traffic, is the **Humbug Spires Wilderness Trail,** 26 miles (42 km) south of Butte in the Humbug Spires wilderness area. This is primitive Bureau of Land Management territory that has granite outcroppings, for which the area is named, in addition to primeval Douglas fir forest and a small stream chockfull of little cutthroat trout. The relatively flat 9-mile (14.5-km) round-trip trail can be accessed by taking I-15 to exit 99 for Moose Creek and then heading east on Moose Creek Road for 3.4 miles (5.5 km) to the parking lot and trailhead.

ENTERTAINMENT AND EVENTS
Nightlife

Like a puckish teenager, Butte's reputation has always preceded it. This is a scrappy town where no one likes to back down. Even the most elegant older women love to tell of carrying pearl-handled revolvers every time they traveled into or through Butte. It's a fighting town, which means Butte is a drinking town.

Butte has numerous bars, many of them good ones, with the best being the **M&M Cigar Store** (9 N. Main St., 406/530-6020 or 406/299-3998, 24 hours daily), witness to Butte's glory days from a front-row seat. Opened in 1890, the M&M remained unlocked for more than 100 years. There was once a bowling alley in the basement, a dining and drinking room on the 1st floor, and a gambling lounge upstairs. The cigars were added during Prohibition as a polite show of compliance, but the liquor was never locked up. In a 1970 *Esquire* article, Jack Kerouac wrote a poignant description of a late night spent at the M&M, summing it up: "It was the end of my quest for an ideal bar." The M&M fell on hard times over the years and had to close down for a short period, but it reopened in 2005 with a beautiful restoration and the same spirit it has always had. So far, the doors have not been locked again since.

The **Silver Dollar Saloon** (133 S. Main St., 406/782-7367, 4pm-2am daily) is another legendary Butte watering hole, established on the border between Chinatown and the red-light district. The adjacent building was both a brothel and a boardinghouse for Chinese laborers. One of the hubs of the St. Patrick's Day festivities, the Silver Dollar is known for its live music offerings.

For a more family-friendly place with outstanding beer, try **Quarry Brewing Company** (124 W. Broadway St., 406/723-0245, www.wedig.beer, 3pm-8pm Mon.-Fri., 1pm-8pm Sat., 1pm-6pm Sun.) in the old Grand Hotel. Its five different German-style beers are brewed on-site, and kids will appreciate the play area, free popcorn, and homemade root beer and orange cream soda.

Jim's Bar (2720 Elm St., 406/782-3431, 3pm-2am Sun.-Thurs. 2pm-2am Fri.-Sat.) is kind of a biker bar, with plenty of fun and rowdy events such as biker rodeos and beach volleyball. Closing hours here are dependent on the number of customers.

The Arts

For a selection of contemporary gems, try **Main Stope Gallery** (8 S. Montana St., 406/723-9195, www.mainstopegallery.com, 10am-5pm Tues.-Sat.), which sells pottery, paintings, photography, and other fine art by contemporary Montana artists. Located on the 3rd floor of the Butte public library, the **Carle Gallery** (226 W. Broadway, 406/723-3361, www.buttepubliclibrary.info, 10am-5pm Mon. and Fri.-Sat., 10am-8pm Tues.-Thurs.) pays tribute to Butte artist John Carle, known for his paintings of the city's buildings and people, and hosts monthly shows. The gallery also hosts rotating exhibits from the World Museum of Mining and Mai Wah Museum.

MOTHER LODE THEATRE

Seeing an event at the **Mother Lode Theatre** (316 W. Park St., 406/723-3602, http://buttearts.org) is an event in itself. Built entirely with private funds by the Masons in 1923 as the 1,200-seat Temple Theatre, the glorious building was converted into a movie house during the Depression. As the mines were abandoned, so was the theater. In the 1980s, the only other theater in town was condemned and razed. True to form in Butte, people made it a priority to restore the building. The only more pressing project at the time was a complete overhaul of the city's water system. The Butte Center for the Performing Arts formed as a nonprofit organization to raise the funds necessary and oversee the construction work. The Masons donated the building to the city, and $3 million was raised for the overhaul, completed in 1996. A 106-seat children's theater known as the Orphan Girl Theatre (named for a mine in Butte) was added in 1997 thanks to another big donation.

Today, the Mother Lode provides performance space for the Butte Symphony, Montana Repertory Theatre, Missoula Children's Theatre, traveling Broadway productions, concerts, and numerous other events and organizations.

SILVER BOW DRIVE IN

Since 1977, the **Silver Bow Drive In** (116054 S. Buxton Rd., 406/782-8095, www.silverbowdrivein.com, spring-early-Sept., $6 adults, $4 children 3-11, cash only) has been an absolute classic. There really isn't a better way to see a movie under the Big Sky. Two screens allow for a capacity of nearly 500 cars. Don't bring food with you—a concession stand (that until 1973 was at a drive-in theater in Deer Lodge) serves great popcorn and other goodies including Tombstone pizza and ice cream. The audio can be found on your FM dial, or a few portable radios are available to rent for those without a working car radio or who want to sit outside. This is old-timey goodness.

Festivals and Events

CHINESE NEW YEAR

A reflection of Butte's diverse population and cosmopolitan history, each **Chinese New Year** the community gathers to celebrate with a parade from the courthouse to the **Mai Wah Museum** (17 W. Mercury St., 406/723-3231, www.maiwah.org). For the year of the dragon, the Mai Wah pulls out its 60-foot (18.3-m) paper dragon—a gift from the people of Taiwan—to dance through the streets of uptown Butte. The event is punctuated by 10,000 fireworks, and in 2009 it was voted among the six most interesting parades in the country by *Reader's Digest*. Alongside St. Patrick's Day, this is one of the city's most fascinating and defining events.

ST. PATRICK'S DAY

In a town largely composed of Sullivans, Shannons, Harringtons, O'Neills, Sheas, Driscolls, and O'Briens, is it any wonder that the annual **St. Patrick's Day** celebration is probably the biggest party of the year? Some 30,000 people descend on the city in March to celebrate the strong Irish community with a parade in uptown Butte led by the Ancient Order of Hibernians. Events are held all over the city, including a piper luncheon, concerts, dances, and, of course, no shortage of places to fill up on frosty green beer.

MONTANA FOLK FESTIVAL

The largest free outdoor music festival in the Northwest, the **Montana Folk Festival** (406/497-6464, www.montanafolkfestival.com, free) is held annually early-mid-July and features performances by more than 200 musicians, dancers, and craftspeople. There are six stages including a family stage, a dancing pavilion for participatory dancing, as well as marketplaces and a food court. Music styles run the gamut from Ethiopian funk to Western swing, Latin dance, gospel, blues,

The Irish in Butte

Sometimes referred to as Ireland's fifth province, Butte has long had a significant Irish influence. Of the city's 47,635 residents in 1900, some 12,000—nearly one-quarter of the population—were Irish. For many years, despite its wildly disparate climate and geography, Butte maintained the largest concentration of Irish immigrants in the United States. Copper king Marcus Daly, himself an immigrant from Ireland, was known to preferentially hire Irish workers in his mines and smelters whenever possible. Other well-known Irish figures in Butte included Cornelius "Con" Kelly, a lawyer who ran both the Anaconda Company and later the Montana Power Company; William McDowell, Montana's lieutenant governor and eventually U.S. ambassador to Ireland; and Jeremiah J. Lynch, a local judge who was an important leader of the Irish community in Butte. At times, being Irish was practically a prerequisite for success. Consider a rug merchant named Mohammed Akara, who in the early 1900s changed his last name to Murphy "for business reasons."

The majority of the Irish in Butte came from western Ireland—Cork, Mayo, and Donegal. Of the 1,700 people who emigrated between 1870 and 1915 from County Cork to the United States, 1,138 landed in Butte. A collection of Irish neighborhoods developed around the mines, Corktown and Dublin Gulch among them. Irish pubs sprang up on just about every corner, many of which still stand today. The Irish Times Pub, a modern-day addition, has booths made out of church pews that originally stood in a Dublin church. A stone at the front door, imported from County Clare, allows patrons to touch Irish rock as they enter. Other bars with Irish influence include Maloney's, the Silver Dollar Saloon, and the M&M Cigar Store.

But Irish culture in Butte extends beyond drinking establishments, thankfully. Each summer the community gathers to celebrate their Irish heritage at the An Rí Rá Montana Irish Festival, an outdoor celebration of Celtic music and dance complete with footraces, concerts, and dance performances. Another Butte program, Project Children, brings Irish children and young adults of different faiths to Butte to work on projects like Habitat for Humanity to show them that religious differences need not prevent cooperation and communication.

Undoubtedly the best-known Irish event in Butte is the annual St. Patrick's Day celebration. Some 30,000 people descend on the city, creating bedlam that some see as a fabulous party. The day kicks off with a parade in uptown Butte led by the Ancient Order of Hibernians. There's a piper luncheon, concerts, and dances, and the city's plentiful bars host massive crowds for green beer and Irish festivities. This Montana version of New Year's Eve in Times Square is more than a little rough-and-tumble: One gets a real sense of what life as a Butte miner must have been like around the turn of the 20th century.

and, of course, bluegrass. For history buffs (who will love the setting) and music lovers, this is a fantastic event.

EVEL KNIEVEL DAYS

An only-in-Butte event is the free **Evel Knievel Days** (http://evelknieveldays.org, free) held annually in mid-late July. The perfect platform for daredevils and thrill seekers, the event includes all sorts of crazy stunts that would make its namesake proud. Someone is always likely to lose an eye, whether from freestyle motorcycle jumps, snowmobile and four-wheeler stunts, or BASE jumps, among other activities. In 2016, there was a stunt

dog show, a downhill urban mountain bike race, and plenty of live music. As only seems right at an event honoring Knievel—a Butte native, whose old jail cell can be visited on one of the Old Butte Historical Adventures walking tours—some drama comes even with the organization, and when a couple of major stunts went wrong in 2015, city officials got concerned and now require the biggest, most dangerous stunts to happen outside of Butte's city streets.

AN RÍ RÁ

Held annually the second week of August, **An Rí Rá** (Park St. between N. Main St. and

N. Montana St., www.mtgaelic.org, free) is the less bawdy cousin to St. Patrick's Day. The event focuses less on drinking (there are no alcohol sponsors and no alcohol sold at the festival itself) and more on Irish culture and traditions, with music and dancing, drama, and historical lectures along with lots of events geared to families with children. The event is sponsored by the Montana Gaelic Cultural Society and includes a 1-mile (1.6-km) fun run as well as 5K and 10K races. The festival culminates in an Irish mass held outdoors in the Irish language, often with crowds of more than 1,000 people. The Montana Gaelic Cultural Society sponsors education and entertainment opportunities throughout the year as fundraisers for the festival.

CHRISTMAS STROLL AND ICE SCULPTING FESTIVAL

Held on successive weekends in December, the **Christmas Stroll** and the **Ice Sculpting Festival** celebrate the past, present, and future of uptown Butte. The Christmas Stroll usually takes place the first Friday evening in December and offers a number of activities for the whole family. It is a community-centered event with food vendors, music, dancing, a parade, a visit from Santa, and a tree-lighting ceremony. Many businesses get involved by offering treats and special events to strollers. There are also plenty of places along the parade route to stop in for a toddy.

Resulting in dozens of marvelous ice sculptures placed around town, the annual Ice Sculpting Contest is another family-oriented event that kicks off with a breakfast with Santa and culminates in the judging of the sculptures. Progress on the carving can be monitored throughout the day as you stroll around uptown Butte.

Information on both events is available from **Mainstreet Uptown Butte** (66 W. Park St., Ste. 211, 406/497-6464, www. mainstreetbutte.org).

SHOPPING

Once home to 100,000 people and a number of copper kings, it's no surprise that Butte offers plenty of antiques shopping in the historic uptown. Several antiques stores are located in the area bounded by Main, Montana, Granite, and Galena Streets. **Broadway Antiques** (45 W. Broadway St., 406/723-4270, 10am-5pm Tues.-Sat.) is packed with trinkets and treasures. Not exactly an antiques store, but more of an antique, **Whitehead's Cutlery** (73 E. Park St., 406/723-9188, www. whiteheadscutlery.com, 11am-5pm Mon.-Sat.) was founded in 1890 and is considered to be the oldest continuously operated family-owned small business in the state. Its founder, Joseph Whitehead, made his living by traveling to mining camps in the region selling and sharpening knives. His first grinder in Butte was powered by a St. Bernard that ran on a treadmill to run the wheel. While his own line of products expanded from knives to include straight razors, barber supplies, and hockey and figure skates, Joseph's son Edward collected knives and swords from around the world. The impressive collection is on display and worth a visit. Another Butte treasure is **Second Edition Books** (112 S. Montana St., 406/723-5108, www.secondeditionbooks.com, 9:30am-5:30pm Mon.-Sat.), a second-generation, family-run used bookstore. In addition to a great selection of Butte books, both common and rare, Second Edition Books carries a nice selection of books on Montana, mining, engineering, geology, Yellowstone, and Glacier. There is also a children's section.

If you lack space in your suitcase for antique treasures and have a taste for spirits, stop into **Headframe Spirits** (21 Montana St., 406/299-2886, www.headframespirits. com, 10am-8pm daily), founded in 2010 but steeped in Butte history. You can sip and sample the Neversweat Bourbon Whiskey, Destroying Angel Whiskey, Anselmo Gin, High Ore Vodka, and Orphan Girl Bourbon Cream Liquor. Tours of the distillery are offered Thursday at 5pm, Friday at 4pm, Saturday at 2:30pm and 4:30pm, and Sunday in July only at 2pm. Or you can skip the tour and relax with a cocktail in the tasting room. It's really quite a fitting way to spend an afternoon in Butte.

FOOD

No other Montana town can match the culinary history and culture of Butte. The Butte pasty, inspired by the Cornish dish, is a flaky pastry filled with meat and potatoes for the ultimate miner's lunch; when in Butte, it is the thing to try. The **Gamer's Café** (15 W. Park St., 406/723-5453, 7am-2pm Mon.-Sat., $3-8) is a quaint little spot, founded in 1905, that feels like an old ice-cream parlor. There are no irritating keno machines, despite the name (those are next door in the casino), and the home-cooked food is excellent. Breakfast is served all day, and lunches include homemade soups, burgers, and sandwiches. Still, this is Butte, and you've got to try a pasty: The ones here are made with New York steak from Montana beef and potatoes grown just down the road in Twin Bridges. Don't miss the apple dumpling for dessert, warm with a scoop of ice cream.

For a rare treat and a step back in time, head to ★ **Matt's Place** (2339 Placer St., 406/782-8049, 11:30am-6:30pm Tues.-Sat. first Mon. in Mar.-week before Christmas, $5-10). Open since 1930 and run by only two families in all that time, Matt's is famous for nut burgers (topped with ground peanuts and mayonnaise) and pork chop sandwiches, both of which ought to be washed down with one of its world-class milk shakes; the ice cream is made daily on-site. The place only seats 18 at a counter, so you'll likely make some new friends. Although not exactly healthy, a meal at Matt's is a unique, delicious, and entirely worthwhile experience.

Another fun and historic establishment is the **Pekin Noodle Parlor** (117 Main St., 406/782-2217, 5pm-10:30pm Sun.-Mon. and Wed.-Thurs., 5pm-3am Fri.-Sat., $6-17), Butte's oldest Chinese restaurant, open since 1911. The place is casual and utterly authentic with private booths hidden behind curtains.

Everything is the color of a Creamsicle. Reading the menu is a lesson in history, and an evening in the parlor is time well spent. Hours can vary depending on the number of customers, so call ahead.

The locals love **Fred's Mesquite Grill** (205 S. Arizona St., 406/723-4440, 11am-8pm daily, $8-30), a casual place with ample outdoor seating and the best ribs and kebabs in town. Fred was a salty character with a heart of gold and had a penchant for motorcycles and great food. Though he died in 2007, his legacy is still alive—and delicious.

Long considered the best restaurant in Butte, the ★ **Uptown Café** (47 E. Broadway, 406/723-4735, www.uptowncafe.com, 11am-2pm and 5pm-9pm Mon.-Fri., 5pm-9pm Sat.-Sun., $13-37) is a gourmet restaurant with sophisticated style and plenty of Butte spirit. The creative and mouthwatering dinner menu offers pasta, beef, poultry, and seafood entrées, and daily changing specials are posted online. If you want to believe the renaissance in Butte is imminent, enjoy a meal at the Uptown Café.

A decidedly interesting place for upscale dining, craft cocktails, and excellent wine in Butte is **Park 217** (217 W. Park St., 406/299-3570, www.park217.com, 5pm-close Tues.-Sat., wine bar from 4pm, $15-33), which opened in 2015. Housed in a restored hotel with an exposed granite foundation and wood accents, the below-street-level restaurant has a metropolitan ambience and harkens back to the days when much of Butte's nightlife happened beneath the streets. The menu features excellent steaks and seafood and changes regularly to make the most of fresh, seasonal ingredients. The wine bar features an impressive wine list that spans the globe, plus spirits and craft beers.

ACCOMMODATIONS

Although Butte has quite an assortment of nice chain-type hotels, there are a couple of places that will have significantly more appeal to those caught up in the saga of Butte's past and present. William Andrews

Clark's ★ **Copper King Mansion** (219 W. Granite St., 406/782-7580, www. thecopperkingmansion.com, $105-150) is also a bed-and-breakfast. Guests sleep in the butler's room to the Clarks' master bedroom. Because it is a functioning museum, check-in is at 4pm and guests must check out by 9am to accommodate the tour schedule. Guided tours are free for guests, and a full breakfast is served in the formal dining room.

In the heart of uptown Butte is another fantastic old building striving to achieve its former glory. **Hotel Finlen** (100 E. Broadway, 406/723-5461 or 800/729-5461, www.finlen. com, $80-102) was built in 1924 on the site of the old McDermott Hotel, one of the grandest in the Northwest. Modeled after the Astor Hotel in New York City, the Finlen is a nine-story Second Empire building with a copper-shingled roof. Over the years, Hotel Finlen was visited by Charles Lindberg, Harry Truman, John F. Kennedy, and Richard Nixon. As is true of all of Butte, Hotel Finlen fell into disrepair and neglect as the mining economy dried up. The Taras family purchased the hotel in 1979 and has worked hard to restore the lobby and mezzanine, both of which are more beautiful than ever. The 30 guest rooms are basic, and the 25 guest rooms

in the motor inn are dated; still, there is history here, and with some luck, a future.

For classic charm on the lush grounds of the Butte Country Club, **Toad Hall Manor Bed & Breakfast** (1 Green Ln., 406/494-2625 or 866/443-8623, www.toadhallmanor.com, $130-185) is an excellent choice. From a goblet of sherry or port upon arrival to feather beds, Jacuzzi tubs, and decadent breakfasts, Toad Hall Manor offers classic B&B style.

Butte also has its fair share of reliable chain hotels, but none of them capture the town's amazing history as well as the independent hotels and inns that can be found uptown. Options spread along Harrison Avenue and close to the interstate include the **Best Western Plus Butte Plaza Inn** (2900 Harrison Ave., 406/494-7611 or 800/543-5814, www.bestwestern.com, $100-154), **Days Inn Butte** (2700 Harrison Ave., 406/494-7000 or 800/225-3297, www.daysinn.com, $71-160), **Hampton Inn** (3499 Harrison Ave., 406/494-2250, www.hamptoninn3.hilton.com, $99-172), **La Quinta Inn & Suites** (1 Holiday Park Dr., 406/494-6999, www.laquintabutte.com, $109-139), **Motel 6** (220 N. Wyoming St., 406/723-4391, www.motel6.com, $53-79), and **Super 8** (2929 Harrison Ave., 406/494-6000 or 800/454-3213, www.super8.com, $59-119).

the historic Hotel Finlen

INFORMATION AND SERVICES

The front of the **Butte-Silver Bow Chamber of Commerce and Visitor Information Center** (1000 George St., 406/723-3177 or 800/735-6814, www.buttechamber.org, 8am-6pm Mon.-Sat, 9am-4pm Sun. summer, 10am-5pm Mon. and Fri.-Sat. winter) is stocked with brochures, pamphlets, and tour information; in back, you can usually find a helpful chamber employee to answer questions. A terrific Butte online resource is www.butteamerica.com.

The **Butte-Silver Bow Public Library** (226 W. Broadway, 406/723-3361, www.buttepubliclibrary.info, 10am-5pm Mon. and Fri.-Sat., 10am-8pm Tues.-Thurs.) is at Broadway and Idaho Street. The **main post office** (406/494-2107, 8:30am-5:30pm Mon.-Fri., 9am-1pm Sat.) is at 701 Dewey Boulevard.

The emergency room at **St. James Hospital** (400 S. Clark St., 406/723-2627) is open 24 hours every day. Butte has walk-in medical facilities, including **St. James Rocky Mountain Clinic** (435 S. Crystal St., #300, 406/496-3600, 8am-5pm Mon. Fri.) and **Express Care** (435 S. Crystal St., #200, 406/723-6889, 8am-5:30pm Mon.-Fri.).

For laundry, coffee, and tanning, the **Suds McClean Laundry Tanning and Coffee** (740 W. Park St., 406/221-7039, 8:45am-9pm Mon.-Thurs., 9am-6pm Fri.-Sun.) is the spot.

TRANSPORTATION
Getting There

The **Bert Mooney Airport** (BTM, 101 Airport Rd., 406/494-3771, www.butteairport.com) in Butte is served by Delta and Alpine Air Express, with daily direct flights to and from Salt Lake City, Billings, Bozeman, and Helena. NetJets also serves the airport. The car-rental agencies at the airport are **Avis, Budget, Enterprise,** and **Hertz.**

Bus service from **Greyhound** and **Rimrock Stages** (406/723-3287) is available at 1324 Harrison Avenue. Butte is 64 miles (103 km) south of Helena, 82 miles (132 km) west of Bozeman, and 120 miles (193 km) southeast of Missoula.

Getting Around

The **Butte-Silver Bow Transit System** (406/497-6515, www.buttebus.org, free) offers bus service 6:45am-6:15pm Monday-Friday, with shorter hours on Saturday. You can pick up a bus schedule at the public library or download a copy online. **Mining City Taxi** (406/723-6511) offers service 24 hours every day.

The Pintler Scenic Route

This stretch of the state is wide open, with sweeping valleys, soaring mountains, and some authentic small communities that were involved in different stages of Montana's boom-and-bust economy.

Set in a grassy valley that was known by Native Americans for its abundance of deer, Deer Lodge was both a mining town and a ranching community during its evolution. It has also long been a county seat, giving Deer Lodge an interesting if somewhat random collection of specialized museums.

Historic and charming Philipsburg is another study in Montana's boom, bust, and renewal economy. Today's visitors come for proximity to wild beauty, quaint architecture, and good food.

Named for the Anaconda Copper Mining Company, Anaconda was by all accounts a company town. But it's managed to hang on and is working to redefine itself since the company pulled out in 1980. Structures like the **Anaconda City Hall, Deer Lodge County Courthouse,** and **Washoe Theatre** hark back to the town's glory days, when it vied for the status of state capital. Its

The Pintler Scenic Route

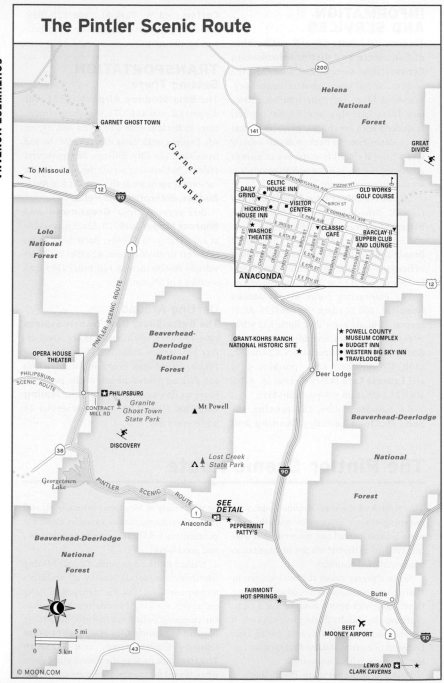

200

Helena

National

Forest

GARNET GHOST TOWN

141

GREAT
DIVIDE

G a r n e t

To Missoula

12   90

R a n g e

E PENNSYLVANIA AVE   PIZZINI WY

CELTIC
HOUSE INN

DAILY
GRIND

OLD WORKS
GOLF COURSE

VISITOR
CENTER

BIRCH ST

E COMMERCIAL AVE

HICKORY
HOUSE INN

E PARK AVE

E 3RD ST

Lolo

National

Forest

1

WASHOE
THEATER

CLASSIC
CAFÉ

BARCLAY II
SUPPER CLUB
AND LOUNGE

MAIN ST   OAK ST   CHERRY ST   HICKORY ST   BIRCH ST   ALDER ST   ASH ST

E 4TH ST

E 5TH ST

E 6TH ST

E 7TH ST

E E 7TH ST

WASHINGTON ST   ADAMS ST   JEFFERSON ST   MADISON ST

ANACONDA

12

Beaverhead-

Deerlodge

GRANT-KOHRS RANCH
NATIONAL HISTORIC SITE

★ POWELL COUNTY
MUSEUM COMPLEX
● BUDGET INN
● WESTERN BIG SKY INN
● TRAVELODGE

OPERA HOUSE
THEATER

National

Forest

Deer Lodge

PINTLER SCENIC ROUTE

PHILIPSBURG
SCENIC ROUTE

PHILIPSBURG

Granite
Ghost Town
State Park

Mt Powell

Beaverhead-Deerlodge

CONTRACT
MILL RD

38

DISCOVERY

National

Forest

*Georgetown
Lake*

Lost Creek
State Park

PINTLER   SCENIC   ROUTE

90

SEE
DETAIL

Beaverhead-Deerlodge

Anaconda

1

PEPPERMINT
PATTY'S

National

Forest

FAIRMONT
HOT SPRINGS

Butte

0   5 mi

0   5 km

43

BERT
MOONEY AIRPORT

2

90

© MOON.COM

LEWIS AND
CLARK CAVERNS

proximity to **Georgetown Lake** and the Jack Nicklaus-designed **Old Works Golf Course** keep Anaconda hopping with visitors in the warmer months, and **Discovery Ski Area** is a marvelous place to spend a winter's day.

DEER LODGE

Nestled between the Flint Creek and Garnet mountain ranges sits the small, and shrinking, town of Deer Lodge (population 2,994; elevation 4,521 ft/1,378 m). Although initially a trading and trapping town like the other towns in the area, Deer Lodge grew when gold was discovered just a few miles outside town. With the gold and quartz mining, businesspeople, among them copper king W. A. Clark, flocked in to set up mills.

Today Deer Lodge is best known for being home to the state penitentiary. But that fact aside, it also proclaims itself the museum capital of Montana, and it does have more museums per capita than any other city in the state. Old West aficionados and collectors will definitely find Deer Lodge worth a stop.

Sights
GRANT KOHRS RANCH
The **Grant Kohrs Ranch** (266 Warren Ln., 406/846-2070, ext. 250, www.nps.gov, 9am-5:30pm daily Memorial Day-Labor Day, 9am-4:30pm daily Labor Day-Memorial Day, free) is a National Historic Site and a wonderful piece of Montana history. Originally, cattle were grazed in these lush grasslands on the open range. Canadian Richard Grant and his sons Johnny and James were able to build up their herd trading with pioneers moving west along the Oregon Trail. They offered travelers a nicely fattened cow for two of their travelworn brutes.

In 1862 Johnny established a base ranch on the grounds, and as fortune would have it, the area soon flooded with hungry beefeating gold prospectors. In 1866, Grant sold the ranch to Conrad Kohrs, who went on to become the King of Cattle, making the ranch the headquarters of a 10-million-acre (4-million-hectare) cattle empire that stretched

over three states. Although it was reduced in size over time, the ranch stayed in the Kohrs family until 1972, when it was bought by the National Park Service to preserve its historical significance.

Today it is a 1,600-acre (647.5-hectare) small-scale working cattle ranch with 80 historic buildings, walking trails, guided tours, and ranger-led talks. You can take a tour of the 23-room main house, built in 1862 and later expanded by Kohrs. Sign up for the tours at the visitors center; tour size is limited to 12 people, and they do fill up quickly in the summer. Ranger talks are also available in the summer and cover topics such as the life of cowboys on the open range, the importance of the chuck wagon to cowboys on the trail, and the role of the blacksmith. **Wagon tours** (1pm, 1:30pm, 2pm, 2:30pm, 3pm, 3:30pm Wed. late June-Aug.) are a fun way to see a good portion of the park with a ranger as your guide.

POWELL COUNTY MUSEUM COMPLEX
The real highlight of a trip to Deer Lodge is the **Old Prison Museum** (1106 Main St., 406/846-3111, www.pcmaf.org, 8am-6pm daily summer, 10am-4pm Wed.-Sun. fall-spring), which is part of the larger **Powell County Museum Complex** (www.pcmaf.org, $15 adults, $8 children 10-15, free for children under 10, guided tours at 11am and 2pm in summer). Tickets are a two-day pass that grants visitors admission to all the museums.

Deer Lodge was home to the first prison in Montana Territory, built in 1871. The impressive redbrick, iron-gated prison you see today was built in the 1890s using inmate labor. Prisoners also made the 1.2 million bricks used to build the cell block and other buildings. Visitors can take self-guided tours through the rows of vacant cell blocks, the maximum-security area, the "galloping gallows," and learn about the rules and daily regimen for both prisoners and guards. There are a few macabre histories of some of the more interesting characters who occupied these

Dude Ranch Vacations

Southwest Montana is a natural destination for ranch vacations, with an age-old ranching history, wide-open spaces, and spectacular mountain scenery. Indeed, the challenge is choosing among the dozens of wonderful and welcoming ranches in the region. One of the best resources available, aside from a good friend who will steer you to a personal favorite, is the **Montana Dude Ranchers' Association** (888/284-4133, www.montanadra.com). In addition to a number of ways to choose a ranch (by location, type of experience, and so on), the website offers some helpful advice in finding the best fit for you.

- **Location:** Imagine yourself on horseback, and then think about the type of landscape you want to explore. Do you want to lope through open meadows or wind up mountain trails? Do you want to be out in the middle of sublime nowhere, or would you like to be just a quick ride from town? Determine where you want to be, and then look for ranches in the immediate vicinity. Consider distance from the nearest airport, too.

- **Type of riding:** What is your main objective, and your comfort level, for your time in the saddle? Would you like to be on a working ranch, helping with daily chores like rounding up cattle? Or are you more interested in working on your riding skills in clinics? There are ranches that can accommodate both. There are also places where you can just ride as the means to take in the incredible scenery. Your choice will come down to working ranches, dude ranches, and ranch resorts.

- **Size and season:** Think about size. Do you want to be among just a handful of guests, or would you like to be among a much larger group of people? And when would you most like to go—summer, spring, or fall?

- **Activities:** Are you exclusively interested in horseback riding, or do you want other options as well—fishing, golf, activities for kids? Sightseeing and day trips away from the ranch?

- **Accommodations:** You'll need to decide whether you want to immerse yourself in ranch life and cowboy style (a working ranch or some dude ranches), whether you just want to casually play cowboy or cowgirl for a week (a dude ranch), or whether you want some serious luxury with a little bit of Western flavor tossed in for good measure (a ranch resort). Accommodations can range from lodge rooms to individual cabins, and amenities vary dramatically, from no cell service or TV to full-on wireless Internet, massages, and luxury accommodations.

cells. Prisoners who were seen as potential escapees, for example, were forced to wear work shoes with concrete soles, each weighing about 20 pounds (9.1 kg), to inhibit their flight. The building itself is actually impressive and somewhat beautiful (but bleak and very cold), resembling a castle with turreted stone towers at each corner. Also housed in this building is the **Montana Law Enforcement Museum,** which pays tribute to officers who have lost their lives in the line of duty. For visitors who love to be scared, the prison offers **ghost tours** (406/846-3111, 9:30pm-2:30am, reservations required, $50 pp).

The **Montana Auto Museum** was recently recognized by *USA Today* as one of the best auto museums in the country. It houses more than 150 cars, many of them beautifully restored, hard-to-find vintage models, including a 1911 Ford Model T.

The other museums are open during summer but closed during winter. **Frontier Montana** covers the history of the Old West and displays a vast and impressive gun collection. **Desert John's Saloon Museum** has a large amount of whiskey memorabilia and brings the saloons of the Old West to life. The **Powell County Museum** covers local history, which includes mining history, of course; exhibits include antique furniture, historical photos, and a weapons collection from both World Wars. **Yesterday's Playthings** is a toy and doll museum with a fun collection of antique dolls, mohair teddy bears, baby carriages, horse-drawn carriages, and tea sets that date back to the mid-1800s. The newest attraction in the museum complex is **Cottonwood City,** a completely reconstructed historic mining town with a school, a mortuary, and a blacksmith's shop where blacksmithing demonstrations take place daily in season.

GARNET GHOST TOWN

About 40 miles (64 km) outside Deer Lodge, off I-90 at the head of First Chance Creek, you can explore the tucked-away mining ghost town of Garnet. Named after the semiprecious stone mined in the area, Garnet is an unspoiled, well-restored, authentic Montana ghost town. Founded in 1895, about 30 buildings are on-site along with a visitors center to welcome guests. It is open all year, but the road is closed to wheeled vehicles January-April, making it a popular cross-country ski trip. In its heyday around 1898, the town had a population of 1,000, with a school, hotels, saloons, and even a Chinese laundry. By 1950 the town was virtually abandoned. In the summer, visitors can take guided tours, walk in and out of the buildings, and rent cabins to stay overnight. If you are interested in ghost sightings, Kelly's Saloon reportedly has spectral sounds of laughter, music, and voices even in the dead of winter.

Food

The **Broken Arrow Steak House** (317 Main St., 406/846-3400, 10:30am-midnight daily, $9-30) serves a variety of steak platters for lunch and dinner. **Yak Yaks** (200 Main St., 406/846-1750, 7am-2pm Mon.-Fri., 8am-2pm Sat., $5-9) offers fresh deli sandwiches with fresh-cut veggies, gyros, tacos, wraps, and a plethora of different lattes, Italian sodas, and milk shakes.

Accommodations

All the accommodations in Deer Lodge fall in the budget-motel category. The most centrally located (across from the Old Prison Museum) is the **Budget Inn** (809 Main St., 406/846-2810, $60-75). Motel rooms in this clean mom-and-pop establishment are equipped with microwaves, fridges, and a high-speed Internet connection. The pet-friendly **Western Big Sky Inn** (210 N. Main St., 406/846-2590 or 866/244-7590, www.westernbigskyinn.com, $69-83) is at the other end of town, nicely located for a trip out to the Grant Kohrs Ranch. It also offers free breakfast muffins, fruit, yogurt, granola bars, and the like. The only chain hotel in town is the **Travelodge** (1150 N. Main St., 406/846-2370 or 800/525-4055, www.travelodge.com, $71-99).

Information

A good source of visitor information is the **Powell County Chamber of Commerce** (529 Main St., 406/846-2094, www.powellcountymontana.com, 8am-4pm Mon.-Fri.). The Old Prison Museum also has a **visitors center** (1106 Main St., 406/846-3111, 9am-6pm daily summer, 10am-4pm Wed.-Sun. fall-spring).

Transportation

Deer Lodge is immediately off I-90. It is 37 miles (60 km) northwest of Butte and 83 miles (134 km) southeast of Missoula.

★ PHILIPSBURG

The little town of Philipsburg (population 920; elevation 5,280 ft/1,609 m) is something of a hidden gem. Off the main drag but right on the Pintler Scenic Route, also known as Highway 1, P-burg, as it is known locally, is an 1890s silver-mining town ideally located just minutes from recreational hot spots like **Georgetown Lake, Discovery Ski Area,** and the **Old Works Golf Course.** Still, P-burg can stand on its own merits. Surrounded by mountains—the Pintler Range to the south, the Sapphire Mountains to the west, and the Flint Range to the east—Philipsburg is populated by a beautiful collection of brightly painted Victorian brick buildings that have been brought back from the dead—the state's oldest operating school, jail, and theater are all here—by an exceedingly proud and active local population, many of whom are transplants from faraway places. There is a wonderfully restored hotel, a couple of great restaurants, a fantastic brewery, a candy store straight out of your childhood dreams, and many other reasons to come to Philipsburg and stay awhile. Like all mining towns in these parts, P-burg has seen its own rise and fall. The ups and down are immortalized in a poignant poem by Richard Hugo titled "Degrees of Gray in Philipsburg." Before you go, look it up.

Sights

The **Opera House Theatre** (140 S. Sansome St., 406/859-0013, www.operahousetheatre. com) was built in 1896, complete with a sod basement, elaborate dressing rooms, and indoor plumbing. Countless performers played the stage here for throngs of culture-hungry miners. In 1919 the elegant boxes were removed to make way for sound equipment, and the theater continued to attract a wide range of entertainers. It is still undergoing an extensive restoration that started in the late 1990s. This is the oldest continually operating theater in the state, with one of the youngest theater companies, the **Opera House Theatre Company** ($20 adults, $10 children 15 and under), performing live theater and vaudeville shows to much fanfare every summer. Inside, look for five original backdrops painted by Charlie Russell contemporary Edgar S. Paxson.

Just northeast of town, off Highway 1 near mile marker 36, is a marked but rough dirt road that leads 4 miles (6.4 km) up the mountain to **Granite Ghost Town State Park** (347 Granite Rd., 406/287-3541, www. stateparks.mt.gov, dawn-dusk May-Sept., $6/vehicle nonresidents), once the site of one of the world's richest silver-mining districts.

Today it's a fascinating and entirely abandoned ghost town.

Granite's first silver strike came in 1865 at the hands of Hector Horton. In the fall of 1872, the Granite mine was established, then relocated in 1875. But when the mine failed to produce anything of substance, a telegram was sent from mine owners on the East Coast that it should be shut down; the telegram was fatefully delayed. As foreman Charles D. McClure prepared to give his workers the bad news, the miners struck silver ore that would produce 1,700 ounces (48,194 g) of silver to the ton, yielding $40 million. Because of the great demand for silver by the U.S. government for coinage, the population of Granite swelled to more than 3,000 almost overnight with miners in pursuit of the $4-per-shift wages. The town grew on the steep mountainside with a two-level main street and many buildings on stilts. Local establishments included the usual abundance of saloons, brothels, and churches, but there was also a sophisticated reading room, bathhouse, and toboggan run that zoomed 2,000 vertical feet (610 m) down the mountain to Philipsburg.

Two mines ran full-bore, making Montana the country's largest silver producer until 1893, when Congress voted to end silver purchases, leading to a rapid mass exodus from Granite. The barely staffed mines eventually merged and produced a modest supply of silver for another decade or so until they flooded in 1915. A 1958 fire demolished what was left of the buildings. Today the town is like a graveyard, filled with brick foundations, rusting equipment, and the faded memories of Montana's biggest silver boom.

By far the most scenic—if somewhat hair-raising—way to get from Philipsburg's Flint Creek Valley to the Bitterroot Valley south of Missoula is by way of **Skalkaho Pass,** a largely graveled 50-mile (81-km) high-mountain road. Highway 38 heads up through the thickly forested Sapphire Mountains 6 miles (9.7 km) south of P-burg and brings adventurous drivers down 3 miles (4.8 km) south of Hamilton. The road is primitive, not for trailers or the faint of heart (particularly driving east, which puts cars along some pretty precipitous cliffs), seasonal, and well worthwhile.

Skalkaho Pass was long used as a trail by Native Americans traveling between the valleys. A more permanent road was built in 1924 to connect the mining areas around Philipsburg with the agricultural resources in the Bitterroot. There are two campgrounds along the road as well as the spectacular **Skalkaho Falls.** The summit is at 7,260 feet (2,213 m), and the region is home to an abundance of wildlife, including moose, elk, deer, black bears, and mountain goats. Though not well traveled due to its altitude and spotty road conditions, the area does offer incredible recreation opportunities, including hiking, mountain biking, cross-country skiing, and snowmobiling on the plentiful trails.

Sports and Recreation

With all the rivers and lakes in this region—Rock Creek, the Clark Fork, Blackfoot, and Bitterroot Rivers, Georgetown Lake, and more—there are plenty of good places to wet a line. You can get geared up in Philipsburg at **Flint Creek Outdoors** (116 W. Broadway, 406/859-9500, www.blackfootriver.com, 9am-6pm daily summer, 10am-5pm Fri.-Sun. fall-spring), a fishing aficionado's version of The Sweet Palace across the street. The owners of Flint Creek also offer guided fishing trips as **Blackfoot River Outfitters** (from $460 for half-day floats, from $550 for all-day walk/wade trips). Once you're geared up, head out to **Rock Creek,** a gorgeous 29-mile (47-km) stream known for its late May-early June salmonfly hatch, 15 miles (24 km) west of town. The creek, which looks and fishes more like a river, is chock-a-block with rainbow, cutthroat, and brown trout. You'll likely be wade fishing here, and although the Rock Creek Road is bumpy and winding, and the fish tend to be a bit smaller than they are closer to the confluence with the Clark Fork River, the access is broad and the anglers are fewer than on other stretches.

Food

Visitors to Philipsburg are advised to arrive in town with an empty belly; the town has a couple of great places to eat. The first stop should always be at ★ **The Sweet Palace** (109 E. Broadway, 406/859-3353, www.sweetpalace. com, 10am-6pm Sun.-Fri. June-Aug., 10am-5pm Sun.-Fri. Sept.-May), itself a Victorian confection. The store is all nostalgia and sugar, and it is certainly among the best candy shops in the state.

The **Doe Brothers Restaurant** (120 E. Broadway, 406/859-6676, 11am-6pm daily, $8-17) is a malt shop in its most classic form, housed in a faithfully restored 1887 drugstore. The counter is lined with sweetheart chairs, and the tables come with boards for chess and checkers. The owners, transplants from North Carolina, have lovingly intertwined some of their own family history with that of Philipsburg. The service is beyond compare, and the food is terrific. The homemade bread is dusted with sugar, the ice cream is all Montana-made, and the entrées—ranging from mouthwatering buffalo burgers and elk stew to Butte-style pasties, crab cakes, and specials like teriyaki salmon—are large and savory. Don't miss the onion rings, which are served hanging on little stands, or the beer-battered fried pickles. And whatever you do, don't forgo dessert.

The **UpNSmokin BBQ House** (127 E. Broadway, 406/240-1616, 11am-8pm daily) serves up mouthwatering small-batch applewood-smoked barbecue—from brisket and prime rib to pulled pork ribs, sausage, and chicken—for true aficionados.

If you need a delicious, easy-on-the-palate craft beer to wash down the succulent barbecue, head over to **Philipsburg Brewing Company** (101 W. Broadway, 406/859-2739, 10am-8pm daily) for a pint or a growler. Opened in 2012 in a stunning Victorian building, the bar even boasts a copper plate, cooled with glycol lines, so that mugs set on the bar never get warm. Not unlike the dance floors on springs that Philipsburg was once known for, this is P-burg technology at its best.

Accommodations

For such a tiny town, P-burg has no shortage of wonderful and unique accommodations, with nary a chain hotel to be found.

The frontrunner in town is ★ **The Broadway Hotel** (103 W. Broadway, 406/859-8000, www.broadwaymontana. com, $85-170), a cozy hotel with individually themed guest rooms in a beautifully restored 1890 building. There are only nine guest rooms and a couple of cabins, so book early. Some of the rooms are pet-friendly, but you'll need to announce Fido well in advance to guarantee his accommodations. Guests enjoy amenities that include a continental breakfast, a coffee bar, ample common areas, wireless Internet, and a local library. TVs and DVD players are in every room. Ski packages for nearby Discovery Ski Area can be arranged and are a great deal.

The newest hotel in town is also the oldest: **The Kaiser House Lodging** (203 E. Broadway, 406/859-2004, www. kaiserhouselodging.com, $94-180). Completed in 1881, the building was a fine restaurant and hotel. The basement was a game room, where high-stakes billiards and cards were played. The place has been beautifully restored, and each of the five rooms has historic charm and modern amenities including telephone, satellite TV, free Wi-Fi, and air-conditioning. The morning breakfasts are a treat.

Nestled creekside along the Skalkaho Pass Road is the ultra-swanky **Ranch at Rock Creek** (79 Carriage House Ln., off Hwy. 38, 877/786-1545, www.theranchatrockcreek. com, $900-1,700 pp/night all-inclusive), which offers an unmatched setting, exquisite service and amenities, and extraordinary accommodations including riverfront cabins, glamorous wall tents, rooms in a converted hayloft, and a five-bedroom riverfront home. Luxury is infused in every detail.

Information

A good source of information on the local area is the **Philipsburg Chamber of Commerce** (109 E. Broadway, 406/859-3388, www. philipsburgmt.com, 9am-5pm Sun.-Fri.).

Transportation

Philipsburg is 78 miles (126 km) southeast of Missoula and 55 miles (89 km) northwest of Butte. From either city, I-90 leads to Highway 1, which can be accessed at Drummond. From Drummond, Philipsburg is 27 miles (43 km) south.

ANACONDA

The much smaller sibling of Butte, Anaconda (population 9,085; elevation 4,756 ft/1,450 m) boomed with the mines and suffered when the company hurriedly pulled out of the region. But this fierce little town has not given up: The population is rising slowly, after a downturn of more than 6 percent between 2000 and 2010. The townspeople are working to restore some of their most glorious buildings, and they've transformed slag heaps and mining refuse into recreational opportunities including the **Old Works Golf Course,** built on the black sand of the slag heap, littered with interesting pieces of old equipment, and one of the finest in the state. Anaconda is working to make the most of their location too, just minutes from **Georgetown Lake** and **Discovery Ski Area.** In winter, the scene in the town's central park, **Kennedy Commons**—ice skaters, the community Christmas tree—looks like a tableau in the *Saturday Evening Post.* Not an obvious destination for anything other than golf, Anaconda is a proud and tight-knit community that is not ready to be ruled out.

Sights

A fantastically pink art deco building, the **Washoe Theatre** (305 Main St., 406/563-6161, movies and frequent live performances daily year-round, check Facebook for schedule) was built in 1936 with massive murals as well as silver, copper, and gold leaf to be a movie palace in the truest sense. It is one of the few art deco theaters standing today and was ranked fifth in the nation for its architectural value by the Smithsonian Institution.

The only Jack Nicklaus signature course in the state, the publicly owned **Old Works** (1205 Pizzini Way, 406/563-5989, www. oldworks.org, $50-135 for 18 holes, discounts for booking online 5 or more days in advance) is a fabulous and challenging course built entirely on a Superfund site. The design makes impressive use of the black slag for all its bunkers along with many relics from the original smelter, including the remains of flues and ovens. The course offers generous fairways and beautifully maintained greens, and the fishable Warm Springs Creek offers water challenges on several holes. If you only play one course in Montana, this is the one.

Georgetown Lake

A vast artificial lake that dates back to the mining era and has been a longtime respite for residents of Butte, Georgetown Lake is a popular but relatively uncrowded recreation area for boating, fishing, camping, and windsurfing. The elevation here tops 6,000 feet (1,829 m)—the local ski area is visible from the lake—so the wind can pick up and the weather can change quickly. In addition to rainbow trout, the lake has a healthy population of kokanee salmon. There are four public boat ramps and a number of campgrounds, and in the winter ice fishing and snowmobiling are among the most popular activities. There are not a huge number of services, but that is part of Georgetown's charm. The lake feels like something out of the 1950s, when people went to their cabins or brought their campers and simply enjoyed the great outdoors.

Boats can be rented, and flies or worms acquired, at the tiny **Moose Marina** (14411 Hwy. 1 W., 406/563-3277, 8am-8pm Mon.-Sat., 8am-6pm Sun. May-Sept.), the only marina on the lake. In addition to docks, a boat launch, and boat rentals that range from canoes to small motorized fishing boats, Moose Marina offers gasoline, fishing licenses, hand-tied flies, and a small assortment of food and sundries.

SKIING AND WINTER RECREATION

Just across from Georgetown Lake is **Discovery Ski Area** (180 Discovery Basin Rd., 406/563-2184, www.skidiscovery.com, $49 adults full-day, $39 adults half-day, $36 seniors 65 and over with ID, $26 children 12 and under, free for children 5 and under), a diverse mountain with varied terrain for all ability levels. There are seven lifts and 67 runs, with a vertical drop of 2,388 feet (728 m). This is a very family-friendly ski hill, with the longest run being 1.5 miles (2.4 km) and an annual average snowfall of 215 inches (546 cm). There is also a terrain park and 3 miles (4.8 km) of groomed cross-country ski trails. On summer weekends, the mountain and lifts are open for mountain bikers (11am-5pm Sat.-Sun.).

For Nordic skiing enthusiasts, **Mt. Haggin Nordic Ski Area** (Mill Creek Rd./Hwy. 274, 11 mi/17.7 km south of Hwy. 1, 406/498-9615, www.milehighnordic.org, donations appreciated) offers more than 17 miles (27 km) of groomed trails in what used to be a series of logging camps. This is not an ideal place for new skiers, but hard-core enthusiasts and racers will be delighted. A number of fantastic loops are available on varied terrain. The trails also provide access to backcountry skiing along the Continental Divide. Naturally, the wildlife-rich area is ideal for hiking when the snow melts. Maintained by volunteers, usually on Saturday morning, the trails are not patrolled. Though Mt. Haggin isn't dog-friendly, Fido is welcome on the groomed trails at **Moulton Reservoir** (Moulton Reservoir Rd., 406/498-9615, www. milehighnordic.org) above Butte. The trails aren't groomed to the same standards as Mt. Haggin, but the skiing is excellent.

Food

Though far from elegant (or even inviting, to be perfectly frank), **Barclay II Supper Club and Lounge** (1300 E. Commercial Ave., 406/563-5541, 5pm-9pm daily summer, closed Mon. off-season, $15-39) is the most popular fine-dining restaurant in town. In the classic tradition of seven-course meals, what this establishment lacks in ambience it more than makes up for with friendly service, hearty food, and good old-fashioned relish trays. Entrées include steak, seafood, chicken, veal, and pasta.

For big burgers, made-from-scratch pizza, sandwiches, salads, and an extremely family-friendly atmosphere (you can eat in a Volkswagen Bug or on a table made from an engine block), **Classic Café** (627 E. Park Ave., 406/563-5558, 11am-9pm Tues.-Thurs., 11am-10pm Fri., 8am-10pm Sat., 8am-9pm Sun., $6-21) is an excellent choice for friendly service and a diverse menu; the food is consistently good.

Another good bet for a satisfying meal in Anaconda is **The Daily Grind Deli & Mesquite Grill** (100 Main St., 406/563-2393, 11am-3pm Mon.-Fri.) which serves everything from homemade soups and rolls to deli sandwiches and baby back ribs.

Almost as much a tradition as the pasty in Butte is the pork chop sandwich in Anaconda. For an excellent version with gravy fries, the place to go is **Peppermint Patty's** (1212 E. Park Ave., 406/563-7428, 11am-8pm daily, $5-10).

Accommodations

Anaconda's glorious hotels are a thing of the past, sadly, and most of the offerings in the area are roadside motels that are decidedly past their prime. One notable exception is the **Hickory House Inn** (218 E. Park St., 406/563-5481, www.hickoryhouseinnanaconda.com, $90-125), a bed-and-breakfast that has been beautifully maintained. The house was originally the rectory of St. Paul's Church and offers five lovely guest rooms. Another historic option is the **Celtic House Inn** (23 Main St., 406/563-2372, $60-80), a brick building that was a bordello at the turn of the 20th century. The hotel has 10 basic guest rooms, some with kitchenettes; because it is located over the Harp Pub, light sleepers should request

one of the quieter guest rooms or, better yet, find another place.

Outside town is a great option for a family-friendly, full-service resort. ★ **Fairmont Hot Springs** (I-90 exit 211 and follow the signs, 800/332-3272, www.fairmontmontana.com, $179-205, suites $225-450) is a sizable property built around the hot springs. Guest rooms are nothing fancy, but it's the water that makes this place special. An enormous, warm (88-94°F/31.1-34.4°C) indoor pool, with one end shallow enough for toddlers to walk around, is complemented by a smaller indoor hot pool (100-104°F/37.8-40°C) and two outdoor pools, one warm, one hot. Fairmont's enclosed three-story, 350-foot (107-m) waterslide ($1/run or $17 all-day adults Mon.-Thurs., $19.75 all day adults Fri.-Sun., $13 all day kids 10 and under Mon.-Thurs., $16 all day kids 10 and under Fri.-Sun., half-session passes available) is a blast, particularly when cold weather causes so much steam that you can't see what's right in front of your face. The pools are open 24 hours daily for hotel guests, for whom entrance is included at no additional charge. Nonguests can swim 8am-8:30pm daily (hours change seasonally, $9.75 adults Mon.-Thurs., $11.75 adults Fri.-Sun., $5.75 seniors 65 and over Mon.-Thurs., $6.75 seniors Fri.-Sun., $6.75 children 10 and under Mon.-Thurs., $8.50 children 10 and under Fri.-Sun.). There are two restaurants and a snack bar in the hotel and a small game room. There is also a golf course, a small spa, tennis courts, an outdoor playground, and a small petting zoo.

At Georgetown Lake, the way to go is **vacation rentals,** where you can provide your own meals. A few websites for perusing vacation rentals in the area are www.georgetownlakevacations.com, www.airbnb.com, and www.vbro.com.

Camping

Two miles (3.2 km) east of Anaconda is a surprisingly lush and beautiful campground at **Lost Creek State Park** (5750 Lost Creek Rd.,

406/287-3541, www.stateparks.mt.gov, May-Nov., $6-34), set amid pink and white granite cliffs that soar 1,200 feet (366 m) above the canyon floor. There is a lovely waterfall, and campers can often spot bighorn sheep and mountain goats on the cliffs. There are 25 sites, vault toilets, fire rings, picnic tables, and drinking water. Campers can also rent a cabin ($54-66), a yurt ($54-72), or a tipi ($30-42).

Numerous campgrounds, both public and private, are at Georgetown Lake. Among the closest to the lake is **Lodgepole Campground** (10.75 mi/17.3 km south of Philipsburg on Hwy. 1, 406/210-8199, www.reserveamerica.com, May-Sept., $15), which has 31 sites, fire pits, picnic tables, and vault toilets. The campground is across the highway from the lake.

Information

Visitor information is available from the **Anaconda Chamber of Commerce and Visitors Center** (306 E. Park Dr., 406/563-2400, www.anacondamt.org, 10am-4pm Mon., 10am-4:30pm Tues.-Fri.). The visitors center offers a wonderful two-hour antique bus tour of the city (1pm Mon.-Sat. summer, $10 adults, $4 children under 12) mid-May through mid-September. A printed guide for walking tours is also available.

Transportation

Anaconda is just a short jog off I-90 on Highway 1, the Pintler Scenic Highway. The town is 108 miles (174 km) southeast of Missoula and 24 miles (39 km) northwest of Butte.

The Big Hole

The Big Hole Valley is high, wide, and handsome, not unlike Montana's larger breadbasket to the east, but the emphasis here is on high. Most of this massive valley is a relatively high mountain plateau, entirely flat terrain at or above 6,000 feet (1,829 m) ringed by mountains that soar more than 10,000 feet (3,048 m) into the sky. It's beautiful in the most sweeping sort of way and relatively untouched by the developments of our modern world; technology runs a distant second to tradition.

The oldest town in the valley, Wisdom (population 98), was settled in 1898. Located on the Big Hole River, Melrose (population 123) is an angler's paradise, as is Wise River (population 297), which is set at the confluence of the Wise River and the Big Hole. Jackson (population 144), known for its hot springs resort and awesome snowmobile terrain, is a winter haven. Polaris (population 73) is considered a populated mining ghost town with a wonderful old-school hot springs resort, Elkhorn Hot Springs, and a classic ski hill, Maverick Mountain.

The Big Hole is a unique corner of the state

with virtually all the attractions Montana is known for: big skies, vast agricultural lands, towering mountains, historically significant sites, world-class fishing, and rugged but charming small towns.

★ BIG HOLE NATIONAL BATTLEFIELD

Among the most moving historic sites in the state, the **Big Hole National Battlefield** (16425 Hwy. 43, 10 mi/16.1 km west of Wisdom, 406/689-3155, www.nps.gov, visitors center 9am-5pm daily summer, 10am-5pm fall-spring, battlefield sunrise to sunset daily, free) is an important stop for visitors interested in the state's Native American history and, more specifically, the flight of the Nez Perce. The site bears the ghosts of the battle on August 9, 1877, between Chief Joseph's band of Nez Perce, often referred to as the nontreaty Nez Perce, who were fleeing the U.S. Army and their own homeland in the Wallowa Valley in Oregon rather than be sent to a reservation, as the U.S. government insisted. Thinking they were safe once they had crossed the border from Idaho into Montana, the Nez Perce set up camp on the picturesque stream to celebrate their freedom and rest after the rugged journey. Thanks to the invention of the telegraph, the Army was able to learn of their movements and catch up to them during the night. The Nez Perce lost nearly 90 people, many of them women and children, in the early morning ambush, and Col. John Gibbon lost 31 of his soldiers. Visitors learn the tragic details as they amble around the well-preserved battlefield.

All visits should start at the visitors center, where rangers are on hand to answer questions in addition to showing an excellent 18-minute video and museum exhibit on the battle, the key players, the events leading up to the Nez Perce War, and the fateful encounter at the Big Hole.

Several excellent self-guided trails (buy the printed guide available in the visitors center or at the trailhead; the details it provides are more than worth the $1-2) lead visitors to various scenes of the battle. On hot summer days or wet spring days when the river bottom is soggy or buggy, one trail leads up into the forest for a firsthand look at the location from which the Army mounted its surprise attack. You can still see small mounds, called rifle pits, where the soldiers scratched the earth by hand or with their rifles to protect themselves from the Nez Perce's return fire. The Nez Perce sniper areas are pointed out, as well as the location where the Nez Perce managed to take control of an Army cannon. When the lower trail along the river bottom is dry, visitors can walk among the tipi frames erected where historians have learned the 89 camps stood. Markers indicate where numerous Nez Perce died.

The battlefield is as serene and beautiful today as it is haunting. The National Park Service has done an extraordinary job of presenting information about the Nez Perce War and this battle in particular. Because so little has changed in this region—from the actual landscape to the overall view—it is easy to imagine the events that gave this spot its bloody legacy.

MELROSE

Once a mining outpost and then a railroad town, today Melrose (population 123; elevation 5,184 ft/1,580 m) is a fishing town midway between Butte and Dillon. Easy access to both the Wise River and the Big Hole River ensure a steady stream of anglers in this otherwise tiny village.

tipi frames at Big Hole National Battlefield

The Sportsman Hotel (540 N. Main St., 406/835-2141, www.sportsmanmt.com, motel rooms $78-95, cabins $115-150, houses $150-300) offers one-stop shopping: In addition to the pet-friendly motel and cabins, there is an RV park with tent sites ($29 full hookups, $15 tent sites), plus you can hire a guide and rent a raft on the premises. Hunters are just 10 minutes from the Beaverhead-Deerlodge National Forest. Owners Tony and Janet Wagner can point you toward some great adventures, including hikes to the otherworldly **Canyon Creek Charcoal Kilns,** a series of beehive-shaped kilns built in the 1870s to produce charcoal for the silver and lead smelters. There are also a few buildings still standing in what was the mining town of **Farlin** on Birch Creek, including some old mining cabins, a school, a butcher shop, and the old smelter.

Another terrific option for anglers just steps away from the Big Hole River is the **Pioneer Mountain Cabins** (47 Trapper Creek Rd., 406/596-1007 or 406/835-2711, www.pioneermountaincabins.com, $90/night or $540/week), which are modern, clean, and very comfortable with air-conditioning, satellite TV, microwave, refrigerator, and coffee machine—all the standard amenities that feel like luxuries when you're out in the middle of nowhere.

WISE RIVER

Although it's too small to be an incorporated town, Wise River is another fishing paradise. The non-town—a collection of modest drinking establishments that are long on character—grew up around the place where the Wise River flows into the Big Hole.

While the area around Wise River offers no end of opportunities for entertainment—fishing, hunting, rockhounding, hiking, snowmobiling—the facilities in Wise River are rather sparse. The notable exception is the **Wise River Club** (65013 Hwy. 43, 406/832-3258, www.wiseriverclub.net, $65 rooms with shared bath, $85 cabins with private bath), which has been a restaurant, bar, hotel, and unofficial community center, all in one since

1896. The menu in the restaurant (8am-9pm Sun.-Thurs., 8am-1am Fri.-Sat., $9.50-34) lists standard Montana fare, including burgers, steaks, and chicken-fried steak; Friday is always prime rib night. The bar is open from noon daily, and there is live music Friday nights 7pm-10pm and Sunday afternoons 2pm-6pm. The countless antlers on the ceiling in the club actually came from a single elk that lived across the street for years. People came from miles around to visit the bull, and each year when he shed his antlers, someone would bring them to hang up in the club.

In the nondrinking hours—meaning during fly-fishing time—the best resource in town is **The Complete Fly Fisher** (66771 Hwy. 43, 406/832-3175 or 435/659-1069), a beautiful facility that caters to discriminating anglers for five-day, six-night all-inclusive guided fishing stays ($4,500). The gourmet meals are exquisite (including streamside lunches where your guide will wow you with linens and a menu), and the accommodations are top-notch. Shorter stays or day trips (from $900/day) can be arranged. The guides are absolute pros, and everything you could possibly need—from fishing licenses to the latest and greatest fly—is available on-site. As a lodge, it can also arrange other activities including horseback riding, hiking, and nature tours.

WISDOM

Another great fishing town in a spectacular setting, Wisdom (population 98; elevation 6,050 ft/1,844 m) is the name that Lewis and Clark initially gave to the Big Hole River. The Beaverhead and Ruby Rivers were named Philosophy and Philanthropy. Together the three formed the Jefferson River, and the names were meant to honor the three "cardinal virtues" possessed by President Thomas Jefferson.

Wisdom has no cell phone coverage, but there is a wonderful restaurant, well worth the drive. **The Crossing Bar & Grill at Fetty's** (327 County Rd., 406/689-3260, 7am-9pm daily May-Nov., 8am-8pm daily Dec.-Apr., $11-40) was established in 1932 as Fetty's and reopened in 2011 by the Havig family, whose own restaurant and art gallery across the street burned down in 2010. The Havigs spruced the place up quite a bit and expanded the menu with more gourmet options, but they still keep true to Fetty's promise of "authentic cowboy cuisine since 1932." Never mind that the building dates to 1960; the black-and-white photos tell a treasured history of the area. The Crossing is as famous for its burgers as for its Rocky Mountain oysters (don't ask, just try them). From the kitchen you can hear the muffled sound of the local police scanner, and the snickerdoodles are homemade and always available to go. What could be better than such old-school goodness? The Havigs also have a cozy one-bedroom cabin they rent out, **The Wisdom Cabin,** for $86 per night or $525 per week.

JACKSON

From the cool little town of Jackson (population 144; elevation 6,407 ft/1,953 m), it's 25 miles (40 km) to Idaho on foot and 45 miles (72 km) by car. More to the point, though, why leave? There is a great hotel, restaurant, and hot springs complex, not to mention spectacular scenery and terrain worth exploring in every direction along with fishing access. This is an outdoors lover's paradise at any time of year.

The best place to launch an adventure—or recover from one—is the ★ **Jackson Hot Springs Lodge** (108 Jardine Ave., 406/834-3151, www.jacksonhotsprings.com, $126-156 fireplace cabins and suites, $30 tent site). The rooms are not fancy, by any stretch, but the outdoor pool fed by natural hot springs is divine, and the gigantic Western bar and dance hall are authentic and welcoming. Live bands often play, and the massive Montana-size dance floor invites fancy footwork.

POLARIS

Essentially a ghost town with a surprising number of people (mostly ranchers) still in residence, Polaris (population 73; elevation 6,352 ft/1,936 m) was an important silver-mining center near Grasshopper Creek as early as 1885. The smelter was destroyed in 1922, and by 1955 the only structure left standing was the **Polar Bar,** a small white cabin on the side of the road that served up frosty beers to weary travelers. It's been closed since the 1990s.

Most people coming through Polaris today are headed for skiing at **Maverick Mountain** or soaking at **Elkhorn Hot Springs,** both worthwhile pursuits.

Elkhorn Hot Springs

After a full day of skiing, nothing is better than submerging in naturally heated mineral waters, and **Elkhorn Hot Springs** (Hwy. 284, 13 mi/20.9 km north of Hwy. 278, 800/722-8978, www.elkhornhotsprings.com, from $80 single-room rustic cabin, from $130 multiroom rustic cabin, $130-150 modern cabin, from $35 single and $60 double B&B-style rooms) is just the place to do so. Set in the forest and very basic (the rustic cabins do not have running water, and heat is provided by a fireplace or wood-burning stove), Elkhorn Hot Springs is a playground for outdoors enthusiasts. The two outdoor pools (8am-9pm Sun.-Thurs., 8am-10pm Fri.-Sat., $7 adults 16 and up, $5 children, free for children 3 and under, admission included with any lodging package) range 92-102°F (33.3-38.9°C), and an indoor wet sauna ranges 104-106°F (40-41.4°C). These are not sparkling clear pools; dark green algae grows on the bottom of them. But the water is natural and right out of the ground. So if you prefer greenery to chemicals, this is the place. A restaurant on the premises serves standard Montana fare for three meals daily in summer (breakfast buffet is $7/adult, $5/kids), and lunch and dinner Friday-Sunday in winter (lunch $7-12, dinner $12-26).

In addition to all the other amenities at this relatively time-worn resort, there is immediate access to more than 200 miles (320 km) of groomed snowmobile trails and 20 miles (32 km) of cross-country ski trails.

SPORTS AND RECREATION

★ Skiing Maverick Mountain

North of the town of Polaris, **Maverick Mountain** (1600 Maverick Mountain Rd., 406/834-3454, www.skimaverick.com, Thurs.-Sun. and holidays Dec.-late Mar., full-day $38 adults, $25 seniors 70 and over, $24 juniors 12 and under, half-day $28 adults, $25 seniors, $18 juniors) boasts 24 trails, 450 skiable acres (182.1 hectares), and just over 2,000 feet (610 m) of vertical drop. There are two lifts, one of which is a rope tow, and a nice breakdown of beginner runs (30 percent), intermediate (40 percent), and expert runs (30 percent). The area receives an average of 200 inches (508 cm) of the white stuff annually.

An antidote to ski areas like Aspen and Sun Valley, the real charm of Maverick is its total lack of pretense: You're likely to ride a chairlift with a rancher in Carhartt coveralls or a Hutterite girl in a dress and braids. Skiing at Maverick is a little bit like skiing somewhere small but fantastic in about 1968, with no lift lines and wide-open skiing. It is as family-friendly as a ski hill gets, and the terrain is excellent.

★ Fishing the Big Hole

If Butte is a city built on mining, the Big Hole is a region defined by fishing and hunting. For generations, the land and rivers here have provided pristine habitat for an abundance of wildlife and terrific access for anglers and hunters.

The 155-mile-long (250-km) **Big Hole River** is spectacularly beautiful and offers a diversity of terrain, from its origin high in the Bitterroot Range through the wide flats of the Big Hole Valley. It is known for early-season salmonfly hatches and then a golden stone hatch in late June-early July. It is also considered the last river where an angler can catch all five species of trout.

The access to the river is pretty good, thanks to designated fishing access sites and informal road access sites. Considered the most scenic of the stretches, the upper river from its origin to Squaw Creek is known for huge brook trout and smaller cutthroat and rainbows. There are native grayling here too, which can be caught but must be released. Brookies, which can exceed 16 inches (41 cm) on this stretch, are primarily fished higher up on the upper river, while rainbows and cutts, usually 12 inches (31 cm) or less, are more plentiful downstream from Wisdom. Don't forget to pack your mosquito repellent, especially in June and July. The skeeters love all this water and are delighted with the fresh blood of anglers. By August, they are usually not as much of a problem.

The stretch of river from Wise River to the Salmon Fly Fishing Access Site is ideally suited to big browns and can be accessed along Highway 43 or from various fishing access sites.

There are numerous outfitters eager to introduce anglers to the trout in the Big Hole River. Among them are **Sunrise Fly Shop** (472 Main St., Melrose, 406/835-3474, www.sunriseflyshop.com, 7am-7pm daily, $555-575 full-day guided float trip for 1-2 anglers) and **Troutfitters** (62311 Hwy. 43, 2 mi/3.2 km west of Wise River, 406/832-3212, www.bigholetroutfitters.com, $515-540 full-day guided float trip for 1-2 anglers, $75 rod fee for trophy ponds), both of which can also provide lodging.

Rockhounding

There is a reason this part of the state is known locally as Gold West Country. There are a number of places still open to rockhounding. One of the best places to look for gems is at **Crystal Park** (Pioneer Mountains Scenic Byway/Rd. 73, 406/683-3900, www.fs.usda.gov, May 15-Sept. 30 depending on road conditions, $6/vehicle day use), at 7,800 feet (2,377 m) high in the Pioneer Mountains, where visitors can dig for quartz crystal and amethyst, among other stones. There are picnic benches and grills on-site as well as toilets.

Hiking

The Big Hole is surrounded by the **Beaverhead-Deerlodge National Forest** (406/683-3900, www.fs.usda.gov), the state's largest national forest, which encompasses several mountain ranges and innumerable phenomenal hiking trails. Three of the longest running through the region are the **Continental Divide National Scenic Trail,** the **Nez Perce National Historic Trail,** and the **Lewis and Clark National Historic Trail.**

A great day hike near Elkhorn Hot Springs is the trail to beautiful **Sawtooth Lake,** filled with colorful lake trout. It's a 4-mile (6.4-km) hike to the lake (and 4 mi/6.4 km back), climbing just over 1,500 vertical feet (457.2 m). The trailhead is off Willman Creek Road (Forest Rd. 7441). Go east on Willman Creek Road through the Taylor subdivision for 1.8 miles (2.9 km) until it forks; keep right for 0.3 mile (0.5 km) to the trailhead, where you'll see the parking lot and vault toilet. The trail crosses the creek twice, which can be treacherous at high water or anytime the logs are wet.

CAMPING

There are countless campsites in the vast **Beaverhead-Deerlodge National Forest** (406/683-3900, www.fs.usda.gov). You can choose RV campgrounds, tent sites, or even cabin rentals by location on the website.

The **Boulder Creek Campground** (406/832-3178, $8 summer, free in winter) near Wise River has 13 sites in a high-elevation and heavily wooded site; another with only 5 sites but set right on the Big Hole River is the **East Banks Recreation Site** (Hwy. 43, 8 mi/12.9 km west of Wise River, 406/533-7600, no fees for day use or camping).

INFORMATION

The website of the **Big Hole Tourism Association** (www.bigholevalley.com) offers information on the towns, businesses, attractions, and accommodations in the region. Information is also available through the **Beaverhead Chamber of Commerce** (10 W. Reeder St., Dillon, 406/683-5511, www.beaverheadchamber.org, 8am-5pm Mon.-Fri.).

TRANSPORTATION

The Big Hole Valley can be accessed most directly from Butte via I-15 south to Highway 43 and Highway 278, and from Dillon via I-15 south to Highway 278.

Dillon and the Southwest Corner

This part of the state is where mining meets agriculture, and where history and adventure are intertwined. There are wide-open spaces, snowcapped peaks, and limestone caves that snake deep underground. It is an area that will enchant history buffs with preserved mining settlements like Virginia City, Nevada City, and Bannack, and transfix lovers of sports and nature with incredible wildlife habitat, phenomenal fishing in rivers and lakes, and plenty of wild space just to get lost in for a while.

Dillon, the economic and service hub of the region, was an important stopping point for the Lewis and Clark expedition. Lewis and Clark met the Shoshone in Dillon, and were able to cache their canoes and some supplies for the return trip. In the latter part of the 19th century, Dillon was an important shipping point between the goldfields of Montana and Utah. Agriculture has also shaped the area. Cattle were first brought to Dillon in 1865, followed by sheep in 1869. The University of Montana Western, which emphasizes agriculture, thrives in Dillon today and adds youthful energy to the town. Dillon's downtown offers the largest number of shops (including the Patagonia Outlet), hotels, and eateries in the region.

DILLON

The area around Dillon (population 4,257; elevation 5,096 ft/1,553 m) was significant on Lewis and Clark's westward journey. One site earned the name Camp Fortunate when Lewis and Clark met the Shoshone and managed to cache supplies for their return voyage.

After gold strikes in Bannack, Helena, and Butte, the area around what is now Dillon became an important shipping route between the booming mining camps and more-developed Utah, often the source of equipment, supplies, and labor. Eventually the railroads came through the region, but not until a deal was struck between Irish rancher Richard Deacon, the railroad owners, and the merchants who made their living following the railroad construction crews. A staunch opponent of the railroad and a shrewd businessman, Deacon raised the price on his land to a whopping $10,500, which the railroad agreed to pay. The town of Dillon, named for Sidney Dillon, president of the Utah and Northern Railway, grew quickly as the construction crews completed the rail line during the winter of 1880-1881. Its longevity was ensured when the county seat was moved to Dillon from nearby Bannack later that year. The town prospered with the construction of a teachers college in 1892, leading some to predict that Dillon would become "the very Athens of the West."

If not quite Athens, today Dillon is a thriving (and growing!) little community and home to the University of Montana Western. The town has preserved its local history—from Native American influences to agriculture and mining—and achieved a reputation as an excellent launching point for outdoor adventures that include hunting, fishing, hiking, biking, and rockhounding. Mostly, though, it is Dillon's proximity to historic mining centers like Bannack, Virginia City, and Nevada City that make it an obvious destination.

More reliable than the first frost, Montanans mark the end of summer with the **annual Labor Day weekend sale** at the **Patagonia Outlet** (16 S. Idaho St., 406/683-2580, www.patagonia.com, 10am-6pm Mon.-Sat., 11am-5pm Sun.). Sales on the already reduced selection of ecofriendly and always cutting-edge outdoor gear jump to 40 percent discounts. Just as Montanans buy their ski passes before the first flake falls, so too do they get their gear when the getting's cheap.

BANNACK STATE PARK

Twenty-five miles (40 km) west of Dillon is **Bannack State Park** (4200 Bannack Rd., 406/834-3413, www.bannack.org, visitors center 10am-7pm daily Memorial Day-Labor Day, 10am-5pm daily Labor Day-Sept. 31, 10am-5pm weekends only Oct.; park 8am-9pm daily Memorial Day-Labor Day, 8am-dusk Labor Day-Oct., 8am-5pm Nov.-Mar., 8am-dusk Daylight Saving Time-Memorial Day, $6/vehicle nonresidents), which comprises the original mining settlement of Bannack. First established in 1862 when John White discovered gold on Grasshopper Creek, the town waxed and waned for years until World War II, when all nonessential mining was prohibited. In 1954, much of the area and its 50-plus buildings were donated to the state for preservation.

The town site is well preserved but not restored or commercialized, which makes it an interesting place to visit. Bannack's history is fascinating, and many of its stories come to life in the buildings and grounds in the state park. Henry Plummer, the sheriff of both Bannack and Virginia City, was famously hanged here by a group of vigilantes in 1864. He is reportedly buried at the site. The gallows and cemetery can be visited, and nearly all the buildings can be entered.

Two types of guided tours are on offer at Bannack when staff are available: **Mill Tours** (about 50 minutes, noon Sat.-Sun. summer, $4 pp) and **Town Tours** (about 60 minutes, 2pm Mon.-Fri., 10:30am and 2pm Sat.-Sun.

summer, free with park admission). The visitors center is open 11am-5pm on weekends only in May and October and 10am-6pm daily late May until the first week in September. Held annually the third weekend in July, **Bannack Days** is a celebration of the way life was when Bannack was in its prime. The weekend kicks off with a breakfast (7am Sat.) at **Hotel Meade.** Throughout the day there are a variety of pioneer demonstrations, including quilting, basket making, blacksmithing, and shooting a black-powder rifle. Lots of old-time delicacies—think kettle corn, fry bread, and fresh lemonade—are available, along with live music and an abundance of theatrics.

There are two campgrounds in Bannack State Park as well: **Vigilante Campground** and **Road Agent Campground** (855/922-6768, $28 summer, discounts available for Montana residents). Restrooms, water, picnic tables, and fire rings are available, and a tipi (mid-May-early Oct., $42 for nonresidents) can be reserved at the Vigilante Campground.

RED ROCK LAKES NATIONAL WILDLIFE REFUGE

Known for its alpine and riparian beauty and its phenomenal habitat for birds and other wildlife, including bears, wolves, and moose, the **Red Rocks Lake National Wildlife Refuge** (27650B S. Valley Rd., Lima, 406/276-3536, www.fws.gov, 7:30am-4pm Mon.-Fri. year-round except federal holidays) is a spectacular area for naturally inspired recreation. Some 232 bird species have been recorded at the refuge, including 53 that are rare or considered accidental. The refuge was founded in 1935 to protect the majestic trumpeter swans, which are still happily in residence. In 1932, there were thought to be fewer than 70 in existence worldwide, half of them in this area. Today there are nearly 46,000 trumpeter swans, including roughly 500 that live in Montana, Wyoming, and Idaho. Up to 2,000 tundra and trumpeter swans gather in the refuge in early fall along with 50,000 ducks and geese. Springtime provides opportunities to see (and hear!) nesting sandhill cranes. Hunting and fishing are permitted at specific places and seasons within the refuge, but regulations change frequently and can be found through **Montana Fish, Wildlife & Parks** (406/444-2535 or 406/444-2950 for out-of-state licensing, www.fwp.mt.gov). One of the few marshland wilderness areas in the country, the area is in its original natural state. Physical facilities are kept to a minimum,

Bannack State Park has been well preserved.

and formal trails are not maintained or designated. This is a place to get away from the crowds and explore at your own pace with minimal impact. To get to the refuge, turn off I-15 at Monida and drive 28 miles (45 km) east on the gravel and dirt road. Primitive camping ($7) is available at the **Upper** and **Lower Red Rocks Lake Campgrounds.**

★ VIRGINIA CITY AND NEVADA CITY

Another 57 miles (92 km) east of Dillon are Virginia City and Nevada City, two thriving ghost towns left over from Montana's glorious gold-mining era. In May 1863, a party of six prospectors left Bannack after a string of bad luck. While they set up camp for the night along Alder Creek, the men discovered what would become one of the richest gold deposits in North America. Nine camps grew up along the creek almost overnight, the largest of which would be named Virginia City.

Within a year, the town had upward of 10,000 residents and became the first territorial capital. It was also the site of the state's first newspaper, the first public school, and the first Masonic Lodge. The town's history is intertwined with the Vigilantes of Montana, the group that would hang Sheriff Henry Plummer, among others, in 1864.

By 1875, much of the mining activity in the region had abated, and Virginia City's population had dwindled to less than 800. Over the years, as new technologies developed, including the mining dredges, the area was mined over and over for traces of what might be left. Still, between 1863 and 1889, some $90 million worth of gold had been extracted from the region. Today, that amount of gold would be worth $40 billion.

In 1961, Virginia City was designated a National Historic Landmark and protected as an important historic site. Since then, many of the buildings have been restored to function as shops, restaurants, and a hotel. The display of artifacts in both Virginia and Nevada City constitutes the largest collection of Old West memorabilia outside the Smithsonian.

The population of 198 people works hard to re-create the atmosphere of Virginia City at its peak. Throughout the summer, nightly cabaret entertainment at **Brewery Follies at Gilbert Brewery** and nightly 19th-century melodrama courtesy of the **Virginia City Players at the Opera House** entertain visitors. There are **train rides** on a 1910 locomotive between the cities, and an abundance of living history exhibits scattered around the sites. Plenty of services—accommodations and restaurants—are available for visitors who plan to stay.

For more than six decades, the illustrious **Virginia City Players** (338 W. Wallace St., Virginia City, 406/843-5312 or 800/829-2969, ext. 2, www.virginiacityplayers.com, 4pm Tues.-Thurs., 7pm Fri.-Sat., 2pm Sat.-Sun., times can vary year to year so check the website or call ahead, $20 adults, $18 college students, seniors, and military, $12 children 17 and under) have been entertaining the crowds at the Virginia City Opera House with turn-of-the-20th-century-style melodrama and variety acts. They generally offer three shows over the course of the summer season and also play silent movies on one of only two operating photoplayers in the world. Reservations are strongly encouraged.

For more outlandish theater and comedy geared strictly to adults, the **Brewery Follies** (200 E. Cover St., Virginia City, 800/829-2969, ext. 3, www.breweryfollies.net, 8pm Tues.-Wed., 4pm and 8pm Thurs.-Mon. Memorial Day weekend-Sept., $20) at the Old H. S. Gilbert Brewery offers the unique setting of a restored 1864 brewery with bawdy entertainment and excellent microbrews.

Visitor services are available at four staffed areas throughout summer: **Virginia City Depot Visitors Information Center, Virginia City Depot Gift Store, Nevada City Open Air Museum,** and the **Alder Gulch Shortline Railroad.** More information is available from the **Montana Heritage Commission** (406/843-5247, www.montanaheritagecommission.mt.gov).

Cell service is not available in Virginia City or Nevada City.

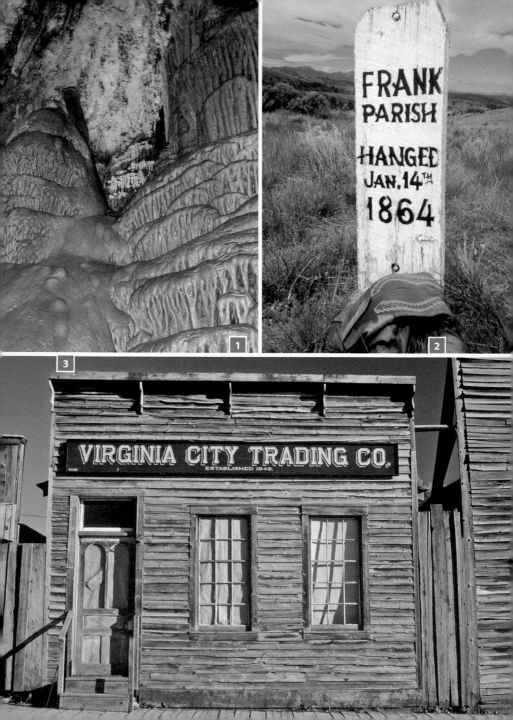

SHERIDAN AND THE RUBY RIVER VALLEY

Nestled between the Ruby and Tobacco Root mountain ranges, the Ruby River Valley is lush, fertile, and known for its fishing and bird hunting. Among the small but scenic hamlets in this valley are **Silver Star, Twin Bridges, Sheridan,** and **Alder.** Between Sheridan and Alder is **Robber's Roost,** a notorious hangout for thieving road agents in the gold rush era. The landmark hideout cabin is marked by a roadside sign and can be toured in a matter of minutes.

JEFFERSON RIVER VALLEY

The Beaverhead, Big Hole, and Ruby Rivers come together at Twin Bridges to form the Jefferson River, which flows 77 miles (124 km) through dry, scrubby, and relatively untouched country before joining the Missouri alongside the Madison and Gallatin Rivers at Three Forks. Along the way are small, nondescript towns like **Whitehall, Cardwell, LaHood,** and the tiny but charming **Willow Creek.** Much of the valley looks the same as it did when Lewis and Clark made their way through it more than 200 years ago.

★ Lewis and Clark Caverns

Among the sights Lewis and Clark missed on their travels through the region is the **Lewis and Clark Caverns** (25 Lewis and Clark Caverns Rd., 17 mi/27 km east of Whitehall off Hwy. 2, 406/287-3541, www.stateparks. mt.gov, $6/vehicle nonresidents), a phenomenal limestone cave several hundred yards above the Jefferson River on which the explorers traveled. The caverns are among the largest in the Northwest and were Montana's first state park. Filled with several rooms and lined with stalactites, stalagmites, columns, and helictites, the temperature in these colorful caverns stays at around 50°F (10°C)

1: Lewis and Clark Caverns **2:** cemetery overlooking Virginia City **3:** storefront in ghost town Virginia City

year-round, making them the perfect spot to escape the rare blisteringly hot days in southwest Montana.

The caves can only be accessed on a **two-hour guided tour** (9am-4:30pm daily May 1-mid-June and mid-Aug.-Sept., 9am-6:30pm daily mid-June-mid-Aug., $12 ages 12 and up, $5 children 6-11) that includes a roughly 2-mile (3.2 km) hike up to and down from the caverns. On hot days, the hike can be grueling, but the cool, dark, moist caverns are the perfect reward. The natural bat nursery inside is daunting to some, but fascinating to others. Wait times can be anywhere from a half hour or less in early and late season, and on weekday mornings and evenings during peak season. During midday peak season, wait times can be well over an hour. **Wild Cave Tours** ($30 ages 12 and up) can be reserved ahead of time.

A **campground** at the caves has 40 sites ($18-34), restrooms with showers, a dump station, three **cabins** ($54-66), two **yurts** ($54-72) and a **tipi** ($30-42) for rent. Within the 3,000-acre (1,214-hectare) park are 10 miles (16.1 km) of hiking trails with trailheads at the campground, a fishing access site, two picnic areas, and a gift shop and restaurant.

SPORTS AND RECREATION

With so many fantastic rivers in the region, it's no surprise that southwest Montana is known as a fishing paradise. Anglers can choose from the Beaverhead, Big Hole, Jefferson, Ruby, and Red Rock Rivers, all within this corner of the state. The Beaverhead, which is easily accessed from Dillon, is among the state's most productive and prolific tailwaters, with dense bug populations and upward of 4,000 fish per mile. The Jefferson River does not give up its savvy fish easily, but streamer fishing and terrestrial fishing are fantastic. The Ruby River offers great wading and superb caddis and mayfly hatches. It's a serene river that offers small stream-like settings. The Red Rock River flows out from Lillian Lake into the Centennial Valley. Its upper portion, known for cutthroat, rainbows, and grayling, is narrow and ideally suited for wading. There is also great brown and rainbow trout fishing beneath the Lima Reservoir.

With so many fish, there are numerous outfitters in the region eager to get anglers on the water. Among them is Justin Hartman of **Tight Line Adventures** (406/925-1684, www.tightlinemontana.com, from $690 full-day for 2 anglers), who can guide you to the huge trout and also offers accommodations. Another excellent resource is **Frontier Anglers** (680 N. Montana St., Dillon, 800/228-5263, www.frontieranglers.com, from $525 full-day float/walk/wade for 1 angler, from $575 for 2 anglers), a full-service fly shop offering everything from boat and gear rentals to equipment and supplies, guide services, fly-fishing lessons, and even vacation home rentals.

FOOD

Paula and Bill Kinoshita, owners of ★ **The Old Hotel** (101 E. 5th Ave., Twin Bridges, 406/684-5959, www.theoldhotel.com, 5pm-9pm Tues.-Fri., 8am-1pm and 5pm-9pm Sat., 9am-2pm Sun. mid-May-mid-Oct., 5pm-9pm Thurs.-Sat., 9am-2pm Sun. mid-Oct.-mid-May, $21-34), are phenomenal chefs who have mastered everything from Le Cordon Bleu classics to Pacific Rim flavors and their own brilliant invention, cowboy sushi—a classic nigiri roll filled with thinly sliced vegetables and their own barbecue beef then dipped in tempura batter and fried, served with red chili aioli. The creative menu changes weekly and is always paired with carefully selected wines from around the world. The restaurant serves anglers, ranchers, and range-roving foodies year-round. Because the tiny size and remote location of The Old Hotel is entirely disproportionate to the incredible fusion of flavors, reservations are strongly recommended.

While the cuisine at The Old Hotel is surely the most surprising and remarkable in the region, this is not plain burger-and-fries country (although the beef in southwestern Montana is notably good). There is fine dining

at **Wells Fargo Steakhouse** (314 W. Wallace St., Virginia City, 406/843-5556, 5pm-10pm Tues.-Sun. mid-May-mid-Sept., $18-35), a stately building with tall, tin ceilings and a grand horseshoe bar. In addition to gourmet cuisine like crispy cumin-crusted chicken, seared duck breast with brown ale glacé, and of course mouthwatering steaks, the Wells Fargo often hosts live music in its ballroom-size dining room.

The ★ **Star Bakery Restaurant** (1576 Hwy. 287, Nevada City, 406/843-5777, www.aldergulchaccommodations.com, 7am-7pm Thurs.-Mon. Memorial Day-Labor Day, $15-30) has been serving delicious and hearty meals since 1863 when it was a hot spot with miners. Today the clientele is more family-oriented, and the menu has plenty to appeal to everyone, including homemade sandwiches, beer-battered shrimp, and sodas from the early-1900s soda fountain. The restaurant is known for its fried pickles, so you might want to indulge. The emporium offers quick sugary goodies like ice cream, fudge, and penny candy, too.

In Dillon, a good bet for a relatively quick bite (depending on the crowd of hungry college students) is **Sparky's Garage** (420 E. Poindexter St., 406/683-2828, 11am-9:30pm Mon.-Thurs. and Sun., 11am-10pm Fri.-Sat., $9-16), a neat little barbecue joint with tender brisket, mouthwatering pulled pork, and delicious sweet-potato fries.

In the Ruby River Valley, all roads lead (or ought to lead) to the **The Shovel & Spoon** (108 S. Main St., Sheridan, 406/842-7999, 11am-7pm Mon.-Fri., $12.50), a great little spot for old-fashioned comfort food—ham, scalloped potatoes, biscuits and gravy, plus excellent sandwiches and baked goods. They also have frozen meals that you can take to-go.

ACCOMMODATIONS

While Dillon is home to what was once a grand railroad hotel, the **Metlen Hotel & Saloon** is much the worse for wear: an interesting place to see and ripe for restoration but not a great place to stay. A better choice is the budget-friendly and pet-friendly **Sundowner Motel** (500 N. Montana St., 406/683-2375, $48-73), which offers 32 basic rooms with continental breakfast and Wi-Fi included. It is the best rate in town, the staff are super-friendly, and the rooms are consistently clean and comfortable. There's a coin laundry across the street and the **taco bus** is just steps away.

Among the chain hotels and motels in Dillon are **Best Western Paradise Inn of Dillon** (650 N. Montana St., 406/683-4214, www.bestwestern.com, $123-289), **Comfort Inn** (450 N. Interchange, 406/683-6831 or 800/442-4667, www.comfortinndillon.com, $99-154), and **Motel 6 of Dillon** (20 Swenson Way, 406/683-5555, www.motel6.com, $82-90).

For a more historical lodging experience, the **Fairweather Inn** (305 W. Wallace St., Virginia City, 406/843-5377 or 800/829-2969, ext. 4, www.aldergulchaccommodations.com, June-mid-Sept., $120-164) is a historic building from 1863 with plenty of charm. There are 14 guest rooms, six of which have en suite baths; the others share facilities. Don't expect to find a bed larger than a double in this property. The ★ **Nevada City Hotel & Cabins** (1578 Hwy. 287, Nevada City, booking 855/377-6823, or 406/843-5377 or 800/829-2969, ext. 4, mid-May-late Sept., $120-175) has a more rustic exterior with slightly more elegant interiors. All the guest rooms have private baths, and two Victorian suites have their own balconies. The cabins are true sod-roofed pioneer cabins that have been updated with comfortable accommodations and modern amenities. Both hotels offer ideal access to all the sights in Virginia City and Nevada City plus some local discounts.

INFORMATION AND SERVICES

The **Beaverhead Chamber of Commerce** (496/683-5511, www.beaverheadchamber.org, 8am-5pm Mon.-Fri.) is at 10 West Reeder Street in Dillon.

The **Virginia City Chamber** (406/843-5555 or 800/829-2969, www.virginiacity.com) does not have a physical address but provides information by phone and on its website. The **Montana Heritage Commission** (300 W. Wallace St., Virginia City, 406/843-5247, www.montanaheritagecommission.mt.gov, summer) is a good source of information because it manages most of the sights in Virginia City and Nevada City.

For information about the towns in the Ruby River Valley, the **Greater Ruby Valley Chamber of Commerce and Agriculture** (www.rubyvalleychamber.com) makes visitor information available at the public library (206 S. Main St.) in Twin Bridges.

TRANSPORTATION

The closest airport to Dillon is the **Bert Mooney Airport** (BTM, 101 Airport Rd., 406/494-3771, www.butteairport.com) in Butte. Car-rental agencies at the airport include **Avis, Budget** and **Hertz. Enterprise** has an agency offsite.

Greyhound bus service is available to Dillon from various cities in Montana. The station is located at 1324 Harrison Avenue (406/723-3287 or 800/454-2487).

Dillon is about 65 miles (105 km) south of Butte and 115 miles (185 km) southwest of Bozeman. Virginia City and Nevada City are both 70 miles (113 km) southeast of Butte or southwest of Bozeman.

Helena

Montana's capital, Helena (population 31,169; elevation 4,090 ft/1,247 m) is an elegant city, the demure little sister to Butte. The city has done a particularly good job of preserving its history by maintaining architecture. The State Capitol Building, for example, is Greek Renaissance style, and the myriad mansions around town are largely Victorian. With its soaring spires and remarkable stained glass, the **St. Helena Cathedral** would look at home in Europe. There are also humble miners' cabins and historic businesses lining the streets in Last Chance Gulch, the site of the city's origins.

But Helena is not living in the past. The city is growing rapidly, and with that growth comes culture. Helena is becoming recognized as the arts capital of the state, with an edgy, contemporary fine arts scene in addition to extensive performing arts. And the tourism office is not shying away from technology: Look for its self-guided walking tour app that tells the juicy stories behind the city's stately buildings and mansions, or go on a geocaching adventure.

But it's not technology that draws people to Montana. Located as it is in a wide-open valley surrounded by mountains, lakes, and rivers, Helena also offers endless opportunities to get out of the city and into the wilderness.

HISTORY

Founded in 1864 with a gold strike on a site that would become the heart of the city, Helena was initially named Crabtown by the four prospectors who made the discovery. Eventually, as the camp filled with miners, the name was changed to St. Helena after a town in Minnesota. It was a gold-mining town, after all, so the saint was eventually dropped.

As was common at the time, these small towns would boom and bust, and commerce and government would move from one gold strike to the next; by 1875 the territory's capital was in Helena, the city that had grown up around Last Chance Gulch. The city of Helena persisted because just as its gold supply dwindled, other valuable materials were discovered, including quartz, silver, and lead. Helena had also established itself as an important center of trade for the region, and when Montana became a state in 1889, Helena had more millionaires per capita than any other city in the country. Although there had been a fierce battle between Helena and Anaconda, pitting copper kings Marcus Daly and William Andrews Clark against each other, Helena was named the capital of Montana Territory, and 13 years later ground was broken on the State Capitol Building.

SIGHTS
Last Chance Tour Train

One of the best ways to get an overview of the city and some historical perspective is by hopping on one of the **Last Chance Tours** (tours depart from Montana Historical Society, 225 N. Roberts, on the corner of E. 6th Ave., 406/442-1023, www.lctours.com, Mon.-Sat. June 1-Sept. 15, $9 ages 13-59, $8 seniors 60 and over, $7 children 4-12, free for children under 4). The wheeled trains and trolley cruise around town with commentary on places like Reeder's Alley, the Old Fire Tower, Last Chance Gulch, and the city's tree-lined Mansion District. Tours depart at 11am and 3pm June 1-14 and September 1-15; 11am, 1pm, and 3pm June 15-30; 11am, 1pm, 3pm, and 5:30pm July-August. Plan to arrive 15 minutes before departure time for any tour.

Montana State Capitol

Visible for miles around with its weathered copper dome, the **Montana State Capitol** (225 N. Roberts St., 406/444-2694 or

1: Montana State Capitol building in Helena 2: St. Helena Cathedral 3: Helena at dusk

Helena

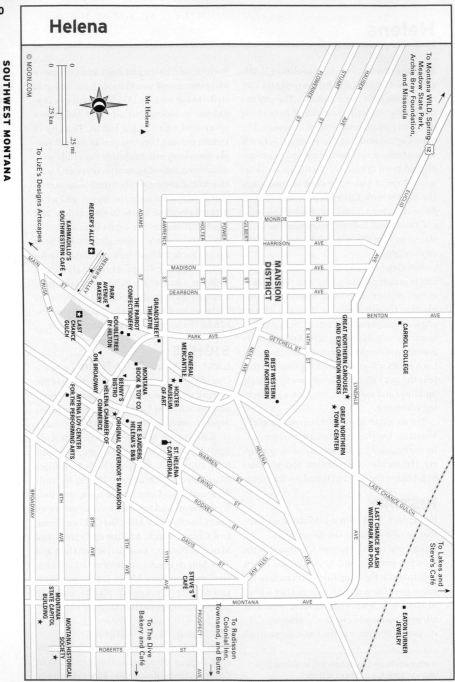

© MOON.COM

To Montana WILD, Spring
Meadow State Park,
Archie Bray Foundation,
and Missoula

Mt. Helena ▲

To LiZe's Designs Artscapes

0   .25 km
0   .25 mi

ADAMS ST

LAWRENCE ST

MADISON ST

DEARBORN

REEDER'S ALLEY

KARMADILLO'S
SOUTHWESTERN CAFÉ

REEDER'S ALLEY

MAIN ST

CRUSE ST

BROADWAY

6TH AVE

8TH AVE

9TH AVE

11TH AVE

MONROE ST

HARRISON AVE

MANSION
DISTRICT

HOLTER

POWER

GILBERT

MADISON AVE

AVE

PARK AVENUE
BAKERY

THE PARROT
CONFECTIONERY

GRANDSTREET
THEATRE

LAST
CHANCE
GULCH

DOUBLETREE
BY HILTON

ON BROADWAY

PARK AVE

GENERAL
MERCANTILE

MONTANA
BOOK & TOY CO.

HOLTER
MUSEUM
OF ART

BENNY'S
BISTRO

HELENA CHAMBER OF
COMMERCE

ORIGINAL GOVERNOR'S MANSION

THE SANDERS,
HELENA'S B&B

ST HELENA
CATHEDRAL

MYRNA LOY CENTER
FOR THE PERFORMING ARTS

GETCHELL ST

E 14TH ST

NEILL AVE

WARREN ST

EWING ST

RODNEY ST

DAVIS ST

15TH AVE

HELENA AVE

STEVE'S
CAFÉ

MONTANA
STATE CAPITOL
BUILDING

MONTANA HISTORICAL
SOCIETY

ROBERTS ST

PROSPECT AVE

To The Dive
Bakery and Café

To Radisson
Colonial Inn,
Townsend, and Butte

MONTANA AVE

BENTON AVE

CARROLL COLLEGE

GREAT NORTHERN CAROUSEL
AND EXPLORATION WORKS

GREAT NORTHERN
TOWN CENTER

BEST WESTERN
GREAT NORTHERN

LYNDALE AVE

LAST CHANCE GULCH

LAST CHANCE SPLASH
WATERPARK AND POOL

To Lakes and
Steve's Café

EATON TURNER
JEWELRY

EUCLID AVE

HAUSER

STUART

FLOWERREE ST

12

406/444-4789, www.visit-the-capitol.mt.gov, 7am-6pm Mon.-Sat., 11am-5pm Sun.) unites Montana's past and present in a very ornate and interesting way. The building itself is something of a Greek Renaissance masterpiece. Started in 1898, the main portion of the building was completed in 1902, and the wings were unveiled 10 years later. The building is filled with dramatic art by some of Montana's most recognizable legends, among them Charles M. Russell and Edgar Paxson.

Self-guided tours are possible 9am-5pm daily. **Guided tours** (free) are offered on the hour 10am-2pm Monday-Saturday in summer, and on the hour 10am-2pm Saturday only mid-September-mid-May. When the legislature is in session, in odd-numbered years, tours are offered 9am-2pm Monday-Saturday January-April. The capitol is always closed on state holidays and on Sunday when the legislature is in session.

Montana Historical Society

With a phenomenal collection spanning 12,000 years of history, the **Montana Historical Society** (225 N. Roberts St., 406/444-2964, www.montanahistoricalsociety.org, 9am-5pm Mon.-Wed. and Fri.-Sat., 9am-8pm Thurs., $5 adults, $1 children, $12 family, free admission the second Sat. of every month) is the best historical resource in the state. There is an impressive art gallery, photo archives, a Native American collection, and decorative arts—more than 50,000 artifacts in all. A wonderful long-term exhibit explores what Montana must have been like at the time of Lewis and Clark. There are also several special exhibits and traveling exhibits. The institution was founded in 1865, making it among the oldest of its kind in the western United States.

Original Governor's Mansion

Built in 1888 by a wealthy businessman, this Queen Anne-style mansion was owned by a number of important Helena residents before it was acquired by the state of Montana in 1913 as the **Original Governor's Mansion**

(304 N. Ewing St., 406/444-4789, www.montanahistoricalsociety.org, guided tours hourly noon-3pm Tues.-Sat. summer, noon-3pm Sat. only mid-Sept.-mid-May, $4 adults, $1 children, $10 family, combination tickets for museum and tour $8 adults, $1.50 children, $19 family). Since 1959, the mansion has been owned, meticulously restored, and maintained by the Montana Historical Society.

★ Last Chance Gulch and Reeder's Alley

Rarely in the West have important gold or other mineral discovery sites gone on to become the center of big modern cities. Helena is an exception. Four prospectors (known as "the four Georgians") discovered gold in a small tributary of Ten Mile Creek. A mining camp quickly grew up around them, and the discovery site became the camp's main drag. Businesses sprouted up around the creek and never left.

Nearly 150 years after that first discovery, **Last Chance Gulch** (between W. 6th Ave. and Pioneer Park) is still at the heart of the city. But rather than a dusty collection of saloons and brothels, the area has been transformed into a marvelous pedestrian mall that includes dozens of great eateries, a few museums and galleries, wonderful shopping, and one of the most popular candy shops in the state. The area is even home to the **Last Chance Splash Waterpark and Pool** (1203 N. Last Chance Gulch, 406/447-1559, www.lastchancesplash.com, 12:15pm-7pm Mon.-Fri., 1pm-5pm Sat.-Sun., lap swim 9:30am-7pm Mon.-Fri., 1pm-5pm Sat.-Sun. mid-June-mid-Aug, $4.50 adults, $3.50 children 4-12 and seniors, free for children under 3), a welcome stop on a hot day, only about 1 mile (1.6 km) from the mall. If your time in Helena is limited, Last Chance Gulch should be your first stop.

Nearby, **Reeder's Alley** (between S. Park Ave. and S. Benton Ave., across from Pioneer Park, www.reedersalley.com) is a unique little corner of downtown that reflects its more humble origins. The area has remained authentic visually, while some of the small miners' shacks, tenements, stables, and other buildings have been transformed into upscale shops and eateries. The buildings have been designated a historic district on the National Register of Historic Places and are maintained by the Montana Heritage Commission (406/843-5247, www.montanaheritagecommission.mt.gov). Both areas are worth spending an afternoon or evening, enjoying a meal and some shopping.

Montana WILD

On the west side of Helena, near Spring Meadow Lake State Park, **Montana WILD** (2668 Broadwater Ave., 406/444-9944, http://fwp.mt.gov/education/montanawild, 8:30am-5pm Mon.-Fri.) is the state's flagship education and conservation center, dedicated to all things wild. The 7,000-square-foot refurbished historic building sits on 5 acres (2 hectares) and includes a wildlife rehabilitation center. Naturally a favorite destination with local schoolchildren, it's a great place to get an overview of the wildlife that lives in every corner of the state.

Great Northern Carousel and Exploration Works

The must-see corner of town for kids includes the **Great Northern Carousel** (989 Carousel Way, 406/457-5353, www.gncarousel.com, 11am-8pm Mon.-Fri., 11am-9pm Sat., 11am-7pm Sun., $1.50), a modern, hand-built, Montana lovers' carousel with 37 animals including a grizzly bear, bobcats, bison, and trout, as well as the hands-on **Exploration Works** (995 Carousel Way, 406/457-1800, www.explorationworks.org, 10am-5pm Mon.-Sat., noon-5pm Sun. June-Aug., check website or call ahead for winter hours, $9 adults, $6.50 seniors and students with ID, $5.50 children 2-18, free for children under 2). The museum is an interactive science center with frequently changing exhibits like space exploration, waterworks, and amazing airways. After you've exhausted your brain in the museum, head next door to the carousel for a leisurely ride and a fantastic ice-cream cone. It's kid paradise.

Marysville

Forty-five minutes northwest of Helena is the once-booming town of Marysville. The story is familiar: Gold was discovered in the 1880s, and a town grew up around it almost overnight until there were 4,000 souls eking a living out of the earth. Over the course of 20 years, the town exploded with dozens of businesses, including competing newspapers, a dozen saloons, three churches, two doctors, and two hotels. But by century's end, mining had all but ceased, and the prosperous town withered quickly as its residents fled elsewhere for opportunities.

Surprisingly, a great restaurant is to be found amid the slowly decaying ghost town. **Marysville House** (153 Main St., 406/443-6677, www.marysvillemontana.com, kitchen 5pm-9pm, bar 4pm-11pm if there are patrons, Wed.-Sun., $9-37) is a rustic but wonderful destination with good food in plentiful quantities. There is quite a selection of seafood and steaks, and the restaurant makes sure to point out that you won't need a salad with this meal. Dessert is roasted marshmallows over the bonfire out back. You won't find an experience like this anywhere else. The **Marysville Guest House** (406/442-5141, $120 or $225 for the weekend) is nearby if you want to spend the night. To reach Marysville, take I-15 north to Highway 279 then west for 23 miles (37 km) and follow the signs for Marysville.

SPORTS AND RECREATION

Gates of the Mountains

Just outside Helena is one of the loveliest canyons in Montana. Named Gates of the Mountains by Lewis and Clark in 1805 because of the 1,200-foot (366-m) limestone cliffs that tower on either side of the Missouri River, it has become a favorite recreation area for Helena residents.

There are many ways to enjoy this scenic area on your own, but for those interested in

The Fire at Mann Gulch

Not far from the Gates of the Mountains is a small but haunting little draw known as Mann Gulch. The tragedy at Mann Gulch happened on August 5, 1949, when a small fire grew with blistering hot winds into an inescapable wall of fire.

Fifteen U.S. Forest Service smokejumpers embarked on a fairly routine call that day. As they departed from their base in Missoula, temperatures in Helena hit 97°F (36.1°C) and the wind picked up. The cargo drop did not go as planned—heavy turbulence forced a higher than usual jump, the crew's radio was broken, and much of their equipment was scattered over a wide area—but within about an hour, by 5pm, the smokejumpers had gathered their gear, rendezvoused with a local recreation and fire prevention guard who had initially called in the fire, and headed down the slope toward the fire, which was burning up from the river. When their path to the Missouri River was blocked by fire around 5:30pm, the crew turned around and headed back uphill. At 5:53pm, with the fire rapidly gaining on them, foreman R. Wagner Dodge advised the firefighters to drop their tools in an attempt to speed their flight. The men were literally running up the mountain, a 76 percent grade in places, trying to escape 20-foot (6.1-m) flames that were traveling an estimated 280-610 feet (85-186 m) per minute. The fire was seconds away when, at 5:55pm, Dodge lit what has come to be known as an escape fire in an open grassy area. Despite his pleas for the men to stay with him in the burned-out area he was creating, the crew continued their mad dash uphill away from the flames. Thirteen of the men were overtaken and burned to death between 5:56 and 5:57pm. Dodge survived by lying in his burned-out area, although he was lifted off the ground three separate times by the wind created by the main fire. The only other survivors, Sallee and Rumsey, escaped by taking the shortest and steepest route through a crack in the rimrock to the summit.

The shocking tragedy—the first deaths in the relatively new field of smokejumping—was not without meaning. Copious research was done at the site to determine more about fire science and, in particular, firefighter safety. The best book on the subject is the posthumously published *Young Men and Fire* (1992) by legendary Montana writer Norman Maclean. Modern safety techniques—including safety zones, individual fire shelters, and survival training—were created in the aftermath of the disaster and are still relied on today. In August 1985, 73 firefighters were trapped while they fought a fire near Salmon, Idaho. Because of the knowledge that came out of the Mann Gulch tragedy, all 73 survived. It's worth noting that despite technology, no amount of experience can eliminate the danger from fighting unpredictable wildfires, something the nation learned again in the summer of 2013 with the tragic loss of 19 hotshots in Yarnell, Arizona.

Hikers and horseback riders can access Mann Gulch from three separate Forest Service trails leading from the north, east, and south end of the gulch. The trails range 7-18 miles (11.3-29 km) in length. For more information on the trails, contact the **U.S. Forest Service in Helena** (2880 Skyway Dr., 406/449-5201).

tours, **Gates of the Mountains Boat Tours** (3131 Gates of the Mountains Rd., 20 mi/32 km north of Helena at I-15 exit 209, 406/458-5241, www.gatesofthemountains.com, 8am-8pm daily) has 120-minute cruises ($16 adults 18-59, $14 seniors 60 and over, $10 children 4-17, free for children under 4, dinner cruise $44) from the marina; schedules change daily, so call or go online for details. Abundant wildlife inhabit the area, including bighorn sheep, mountain goats, and more than 120 bird species. You can bring a picnic lunch and

get off the boat at Meriwether Picnic Area, returning later on another one. It is also possible to hike from here to **Mann Gulch,** where 13 firefighters were killed by a fast-moving wildfire in 1949.

Canyon Ferry, Hauser, and Holter Lakes

All three lakes were created by dams on the Missouri River, and all three have become important recreational areas for people from all over southwest Montana.

South of Helena off U.S. 287, **Canyon Ferry Lake** is the largest of the three and the newest, dating to the 1950s. Canyon Ferry covers 25 square miles (64.8 sq km) and offers 80 miles (129 km) of shoreline along with endless boating and fishing opportunities. The nearby **Canyon Ferry Wildlife Management Area** provides habitat for a diversity of animals including foxes, moose, ospreys, and geese. Plentiful campgrounds and services are located around the lake, but things fill up quickly on hot summer weekends, so book in advance.

A scenic 3,200-acre (1,295-hectare) reservoir 7 miles (11.3 km) north of Helena on I-15, then 4 miles (6.4 km) east on Highway 453 and 3 miles (4.8 km) north on a county road, **Hauser Lake** is home to record-breaking kokanee salmon, rainbow and brown trout, walleye, and perch. Two public campgrounds, **White Sandy Recreation Area** (6563 Hauser Dam Rd., 406/458-4744, 32 sites, $5-15/vehicle) and **Black Sandy State Park** (406/495-3260, www.stateparks.mt.gov, $12-34 May-Nov., $6/vehicle nonresidents) offer terrific access to the reservoir.

Holter Lake (406/533-7600) is the most beautiful of the reservoir lakes, within view of the Gates of the Mountains north of Helena. There are three public campgrounds and recreation areas along the shoreline, designated swimming areas, two boat ramps, and plenty of fish waiting to be caught. From Helena, take I-15 north toward Great Falls to exit 226 at Wolf Creek. Turn right toward Recreation Road, then left onto Recreation Road. After crossing over the bridge, turn right on Beartooth Road and continue 2.3 miles (3.7 km) to Holter Lake Campground.

Skiing

Despite the fact that Helena is rather dry compared to many parts of Montana, it does have a pretty impressive ski hill when the weather cooperates. **Great Divide** (7385 Belmont Dr., Marysville, 406/449-3746, www.skigd.com, $48 adults, $40 students and military, $20 seniors and children grades 1-5, free for preschoolers, $10/hour for anyone) has 140 trails and four terrain parks spread across three peaks and three valleys. There is terrain for everyone from toddlers testing out their ski legs to triple-black-diamond adrenaline junkies. The mountain is 23 miles (37 km) northwest of Helena.

Hiking

Considered by many to be the best urban hiking trail in the state, the over 7-mile (11.3-km) one-way trail along the **Mount Helena Ridge** leads gradually up and along the forested ridge overlooking the Helena Valley. It can be accessed 5 miles (8 km) south of town from the Park City trailhead or in town at the Mount Helena trailhead: Drive south on Park Avenue until you see the sign for Mount Helena City Park. Drive through the Reeders Village subdivision to get to the parking lot. Arrange a shuttle (or turn around partway) if you don't want to hike the full 14.8 miles (23.8 km) round-trip. If you depart from the Mount Helena parking area, there are roughly 20 miles (32 km) of hiking trails in the 620-acre (250.9-hectare) park to explore. For more information, contact the **Helena Ranger District** (2880 Skyway Dr., 406/449-5490, www.fs.usda.gov).

ENTERTAINMENT AND EVENTS
The Arts

In a town that is becoming known for its art, the **Holter Museum of Art** (12 E. Lawrence St., 406/442-6400, www.holtermuseum.org, 10am-5:30pm Tues.-Sat., noon-4pm Sun., free) is a fascinating place to spend some time. The building was constructed in 1914 and expanded in 1999 to add 6,000 square feet (557.4 sq m) of gallery space. The museum's contemporary collection includes art in a variety of media displayed in over 25 exhibitions annually, creating a unique voice in the Northwest art scene. The museum makes art education a priority and has managed to keep admission free.

Another cutting-edge artists workshop

Boulder Hot Springs and Radon Mines

In a town that is somewhat jokingly referred to by locals as "Institutionville" for its plethora of, well, institutions (the Montana Developmental Center, Elkhorn Treatment Center, and Riverside Youth Correctional, to name a few), Boulder is home to some fascinating therapies indeed.

Indisputably, one of the best is the mineral-rich water at **Boulder Hot Springs** (31 Hot Springs Rd., 406/225-4339, www.boulderhotsprings.com, hours vary daily and seasonally, $7 adults, $5 seniors 60 and over, $4 children 3-12), a historical gem about 30 miles (48 km) south of Helena off Highway 69. Backing on the Beaverhead-Deerlodge National Forest, the landmark inn was first built as a bathhouse and saloon in 1863 by a prospector who hoped to lure local miners in for a warm bath and a cold drink or two. The Victorian hotel was built in 1881 and enlarged in 1890. In 1910, under the eye of a Butte millionaire and banker, the hotel was renovated and redecorated in Spanish mission style by a snazzy New York firm. The hotel and hot springs attracted presidents and celebrities, among them Teddy Roosevelt. After countless owners and some neglect, including a temporary closure in the late 1980s, the hotel has been renovated (although not to its former glory, it must be noted) and updated, and it provides guests with simple accommodations, fantastic food, and some of the best soaking waters anywhere.

There are both indoor plunge pools and an outdoor swimming pool, varying in temperature 70-106°F (21.1-41.1°C). The indoor pools are separate for men and women and are bathing-suit-optional, giving it almost a European feel. The water is constantly moving, replenishing itself every four hours, so no chemicals are needed. Steam rooms also are available on both the men's and women's sides. Spa services, including massages, are also among the amenities.

The rooms are simple and "technology-free," and the focus here is truly on healing. Bed-and-breakfast rooms range $99-139 and include a full nutritious breakfast. Guest rooms without breakfast, and often with shared bath, range $65-70 for a single and $85-90 for a double and are more basic than the B&B rooms.

Slightly more controversial than the soothing hot springs waters are the **radon mines** in Boulder, which many people believe are the best alternative treatment for relieving chronic pain and diseases that range from gout and lupus to eczema, asthma, arthritis, and even cancer. There are a number of radon mines in town thanks to an abundance of the natural radioactive gas. One of the oldest is the **Free Enterprise Radon Health Mine** (149 Depot Hill Rd., 406/225-3383, hours vary, by appointment, $8 for 1 hour, $275 for unlimited hours over 10 days), founded in 1924 as a silver and lead mine. Visitors travel in an Otis elevator 85 feet (26 m) below the surface to sit or sleep and breathe in the radon. There is even a special area for pets to be treated. Wireless Internet is available even underground, and motel accommodations are available for those undergoing full treatment.

and gallery is the **Archie Bray Foundation** (2915 Country Club Ave., 406/443-3502, www.archiebray.org, 10am-5pm Mon.-Sat. year-round, 1pm-5pm Sun. June-Aug., free), an international hotbed of ceramic art in what was once a brick factory. Hundreds of well-known artists have come to work and exhibit here. Classes and workshops are available for people of all ages and abilities, and some of the studio spaces are open to visitors. The grounds are open daily, year-round, during daylight hours.

There are two marvelous theaters in town that host both musical and dramatic events. The **Myrna Loy Center for the Performing Arts** (15 N. Ewing St., 406/443-0287, www.myrnaloycenter.com) presents contemporary media and performing arts from its glorious theater in the castle-like old county jail. The **Grandstreet Theatre** (325 N. Park Ave., 406/442-4270, www.grandstreettheatre.com) presents classic plays and musicals in a beautifully restored Unitarian church.

Festivals and Events

For a full listing of daily events in Helena, visit www.helenamt.com or www.helenaevents.com.

Every Wednesday throughout summer, a different block of Helena comes to life for **Alive at 5** (406/447-1535, www. downtownhelena.com, 5pm-9pm June-Aug.), a fun and family-oriented event that combines live music, food, and drink for a fantastic summer evening. Happening the first Friday of every month is **First Friday** (406/447-1535, www.downtownhelena.com, 5pm-9pm), which invites visitors to explore downtown shops, galleries, and restaurants.

Once each summer, in late July, the Helena Symphony joins Carroll College in presenting **Symphony Under the Stars** (406/442-1860, www.helenasymphony.org, date varies, show starts 8:30pm, free) on the hillside at Carroll College. Concerts feature classical, opera, or Broadway-oriented music, and all of them end with a spectacular fireworks display.

In late July-early August, Helena puts on the annual **Last Chance Stampede and Fair** (98 W. Custer Ave., 406/457-8516, www. lewisandclarkcountyfairgrounds.com) at the fairgrounds. In addition to big country-music concerts, the fair holds a rodeo, a carnival, food, and a variety of entertainment.

SHOPPING

Eaton Turner Jewelry (1735 N. Montana Ave., 406/442-1940, www.eatonturnerjewelry. com, 10am-5:30pm Mon.-Fri.) is the oldest jeweler in the state and has been family owned and operated since 1885. History aside, this is a special store and offers a great selection of jewelry, including local stones like Montana and Yogo sapphires.

A wonderful independent bookstore, **Montana Book & Toy Co.** (331 N. Last Chance Gulch, 406/443-0260 or 877/844-0577, www.mtbookco.com, 9:30am-6pm Mon.-Fri., 9:30am-5pm Sat.) offers a diverse collection of books for all readers and children's toys.

The **General Mercantile** (413 N. Last Chance Gulch, 406/442-6078, www. generalmerc.com, 8am-5:30pm Mon.-Fri., 9am-5pm Sat., 11am-4pm Sun.) is like a step back in time. The Merc serves every variety of coffee and tea, including espresso from vintage machines, and there are all sorts of cozy nooks to sip a latte while perusing a book. The store has gifts and cards galore, but it's the atmosphere in the Merc that makes it so welcoming.

Another unique destination in Helena is **LizE Designs Artscapes** (330 Fuller Ave., 406/459-4081, 10am-5:30pm Wed.-Fri., 10am-4pm Sat.), which sells fine and funky art as well as one-of-a-kind gifts, many of which are crafted from found objects. In addition to her own mixed-media work, Liz showcases various guest artists who work in raku pottery, photography, painting, and jewelry, among other media.

For a real taste of Montana, look no farther than **The Parrot Confectionery** (42 N. Last Chance Gulch, 406/442-1470, www. parrotchocolate.com, 9am-6pm Mon.-Sat.), an absolute Montana standard when it comes to candy shops and diners. The shop makes 130 different varieties of candy, and its reputation for hand-dipped chocolates has won customers worldwide. Try a cherry phosphate from the original soda fountain, and sit up at the bar for a bowl of the secret-recipe chili. A local favorite since 1922, The Parrot should not be missed.

FOOD

For a quick bite between sights, and breakfast all day, try **Steve's Café** (1225 E. Custer, 406/444-5010, and 630 N. Montana Ave., 406/449-6666, both locations 6:30am-2:30pm daily, $5-15) for wonderful huckleberry pancakes, breakfast burritos, steak and eggs, burgers, sandwiches, and the like. Another good spot for a quick bite is **The Dive Bakery & Café** (1609 11th Ave., 406/442-2802, www. thedivebakery.com, 6am-4pm Mon.-Fri., $3-9), which is known for its from-scratch pastries, bread, and soup, plus delicious crepes and salads.

For the best artisan bread in town (or maybe anywhere) try **Park Avenue Bakery** (44 S. Park Ave., 406/449-8424, www. parkavenuebakery.net, 7am-6pm Mon.-Fri., 7am-5pm Sat., 8am-2pm Sun., $4-8) where you can fill up on gorgeous European-style breads, pastries, pizza, quiche, calzone, homemade soups, salads, and dessert.

On the top of a hill overlooking Last Chance Gulch and the Helena Valley, ★ **Karmadillo's Southwestern Café** (139 Reeder's Alley, 406/442-2595, 11am-9pm Tues.-Sat.) is a perfect spot to sit outside and enjoy a summer afternoon or evening. The food is sensational, all slow-cooked with salsas and crèmes prepared fresh daily. Lunch ($7-14) options include nachos, homemade chicken tortilla soup, tacos, enchiladas, and even a savory barbecue-beef sandwich. Dinner ($8-16) offers some of the same items as well as tamales, chiles rellenos, and combo plates. As good as its slow-cooked meats are, Karmadillo's also has a number of vegetarian items and a children's menu. Even if the food weren't so good, you would come just for the incredible view and the spacious outdoor seating. Check their Facebook page for the code word of the day to receive free chips and salsa.

For fine dining in Helena, **On Broadway** (106 Broadway, 406/443-1929, www. onbroadwayinhelena.com, 5:30pm-close Mon.-Sat., $18-43) is the elegant favorite, with mouthwatering pasta dishes, steaks, and seafood, and live jazz on Thursday evenings. For great Italian food, **Lucca's** (56 N. Last Chance Gulch, 406/457-8311, www. luccasitalian.com, 5pm-close Wed.-Sun., $22-34) is a gustatory delight.

Another nice spot just off Last Chance Gulch is ★ **Benny's Bistro** (108 E. 6th St., 406/443-0105, www.bennysbistro.com, 11am-3pm Mon.-Tues., 11am-3pm and 5:30pm-9pm Wed.-Sat., lunch $9-14, dinner $21-31). Set in a renovated historic building, Benny's does a phenomenal job of catering to the "locavore" movement by using as many fresh, locally grown ingredients as possible. Its list of Montana suppliers is vast. You can taste the best of the state in dishes like Mediterranean lamb burger with Montana lamb and local greens, pork and beans with candied bacon made with ginger-rubbed Montana pork loin and a Flathead cherry reduction, plus jerk chicken with chicken from the Hutterite colony. This is Montana cuisine at its best.

ACCOMMODATIONS

While Helena is long on hotels (perhaps for all the legislators who come to govern for four months every other year), most fall into the category of nice upscale chain hotels or nice upscale bed-and-breakfasts.

Still, there are plenty of nice rooms all around town. The **Best Western Great Northern** (835 Great Northern Blvd., 800/829-4947, $153-304) is shiny and new, with decor intended to conjure the Great Northern Railway days. It has all the amenities you could want in a city hotel, and small pets (under 25 pounds/11.3 kg) are welcome for $15 per night per animal for up to two animals. The hotel is ideally located in the **Great Northern Town Center** within walking distance of an eight-plex theater, shopping, a children's museum, and a carousel.

Closer to the highway is the **Radisson Colonial Hotel** (2301 Colonial Dr., 406/443-2100, www.radisson.com, $135-244), a large, full-service, very comfortable hotel.

Additional chain hotels and motels that line the major thoroughfares here include the pet-friendly **Baymont Inn & Suites** (750 Fee St., 406/443-1000, www.baymontinns. com, $89-129), the **Comfort Suites** (3180 N. Washington St., 406/495-0505, www. comfortsuiteshelena.com, $99-150), **Days Inn** (2001 Prospect Ave., 406/442-3280, www. wyndhamhotels.com, $76-120), **Holiday Inn Express & Suites** (3170 N. Sanders St., 406/442-7500, www.ihg.com, $134-178), and **Super 8** (2200 11th Ave., 406/443-2450, www. wyndhamhotels.com, $62-80). Situated right downtown in the heart of Last Chance Gulch is the pet-friendly **Doubletree by Hilton Helena Downtown** (22 N. Last Chance Gulch, 406/443-2200, www.doubletree3. hilton.com, $124-213).

For a more historic option near downtown and the state capitol, **The Sanders, Helena's Bed and Breakfast** (328 N. Ewing St., 406/442-3309, www.sandersbb.com, $145-165) offers seven guest rooms in its beautifully appointed 1875 Queen Anne mansion. Many of the furnishings are original to the home, and the owners are gracious and welcoming.

INFORMATION AND SERVICES

A good source of visitor information is the **Helena Chamber of Commerce** (225 Cruse Ave., 406/442-4120 or 800/743-5362, www. helenachamber.com, 8am-5pm Mon.-Fri.). The **Helena Tourism Alliance** (406/449-1270, www.helenamt.com) is located at 105 Reeder's Alley. Hours are determined daily, so call ahead. A terrific website for planning a trip to Helena is www.helenamt.com. The site allows you to plug in your dates of travel and shows you all the available hotels and their average nightly rates.

The **main post office** (406/443-3304, 8am-6pm Mon.-Fri., 9am-noon Sat.) is at 2300 North Harris Street, and the **Lewis and Clark Library** (406/447-1690, www. lewisandclarklibrary.org, 10am-9pm Mon.-Thurs., 10am-6pm Fri., 10am-5pm Sat., 1pm-5pm Sun.) is at 120 South Last Chance Gulch.

St. Peter's Hospital (2475 Broadway, 406/442-2480, www.stpetes.org) has a 24-hour emergency room. The hospital also runs the **St. Peter's Urgent Care Clinic** (2475 Broadway, 406/447-2488, www.stpetes. org, 9am-8pm daily) and **North Clinic** (3330 Ptarmigan Ln., 406/495-7901, www.stpetes. org, 7am-6pm daily).

The **Clean and Coin Laundromat** (1411 11th Ave., 406/442-9395, 6am-8:50pm) has a Ms. Pac-Man machine to entice you while your duds dry.

TRANSPORTATION
Getting There

The **Helena Regional Airport** (HLN, 2850 Skyway Dr., 406/442-2821, www. helenaairport.com) is just 2.5 miles (4 km) from the city center and is served by Delta/SkyWest, Alaska/Horizon, and United. The car-rental agencies at the airport are **Alamo, Avis, Budget, Hertz,** and **National.**

Shuttles to the airport are provided by hotels in town. The courtesy phone to contact them is located in the baggage claim area. There is also a courtesy phone to call **Capitol Taxi** (406/449-5525). **Helena Towncar** (406/437-8585, www.helenatowncar.com) is another option.

Greyhound (1415 N. Montana Ave.) runs several bus routes to and from nearby cities, including Bozeman, Billings, and Butte.

Helena is accessible from I-15, and U.S. 12 and 287. The city is 68 miles (109 km) north of Butte and 115 miles (185 km) southeast of Missoula.

Getting Around

Capital Transit (406/447-8080, www. ridethecapitalt.org, $0.85 single ride, $2.60 all-day pass) operates fixed route bus service (7am-6pm Mon.-Fri.), with nine loops around the city.

Capitol Taxi (406/449-5525) and **Helena Towncar** (406/437-8585, www.helenatowncar. com) provide service throughout the city.

Bozeman and the Gateway to Yellowstone

The gateway to the nation's first national park, south-central Montana is a playground bursting with mountains to climb, rivers to fish, and trails to hike.

This region is home to a number of noteworthy mountain towns, including Bozeman, Big Sky, and Red Lodge. Big Timber, Livingston, and Three Forks offer more of a big plains mentality despite their immediate proximity to some very impressive mountains.

The diversity of the region's geography and climate allows for a compelling range of activities. From Bozeman, you can drive 30 miles (48 km) west and hike the sacred ground at Madison Buffalo Jump State Park; head just 15 miles (24 km) south from there and you can fish along the Madison River. Just a few miles north of Bozeman is Bridger

Highlights

Look for ★ to find recommended sights, activities, dining, and lodging.

★ **Museum of the Rockies:** Renowned for its impressive dinosaur collection, this museum is also home to a planetarium and a living history farm (page 274).

★ **Emerson Center for the Arts and Culture:** A 1900s school rehabbed as an arts hub, the Emerson has more than 30 studios, a fab restaurant, and special events (page 276).

★ **Madison Buffalo Jump State Park:** A hike on this cliff is a lesson in Native American history and an exercise in solitude (page 276).

★ **Floating the Madison River:** This river's warm water is perfect for floaters, weaving through beautiful rolling terrain (page 279).

★ **Chico Hot Springs Resort:** Chico has all the trappings of a resort—hiking, riding, pool, day spa, and sumptuous cuisine—with none of the attitude (page 300).

★ **Beartooth Scenic Highway and Pass:** This highway offers room for spontaneous adventures. Bring your bike, hiking boots, binoculars, and even your skis on this summit-topping stunner (page 305).

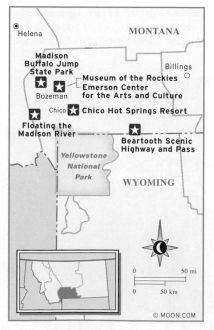

Canyon and the legendary Bridger Bowl, where you can ski deep powder on the ridge. Or head 20 miles (32 km) south of town to find yourself up Hyalite Canyon, an impressive recreation area known for its challenging ice climbs. All of these activities are possible in the same month, March; few regions in the state allow you to choose your season as easily as your activities.

While the main draw is the natural splendor and recreational opportunities, as well as the high probability of sunny weather to enjoy them, there are a multitude of ways to get to know this area: The Sweet Pea Festival of the Arts in Bozeman, the Fourth of July Rodeo in Livingston, and the "Running of the Sheep" in normally sleepy Reed Point show that south-central Montana is a distinctive blend of the Old and New West. As the hub of the region and the home of Montana State University, Bozeman is an increasingly sophisticated mountain town with a welcoming mix of outdoor junkies, old-time cowboys, and blissed-out transplants.

PLANNING YOUR TIME

As is true across Montana and Wyoming in general, this region is vast and can require significant driving to get from one destination to the next. With its fairly central location, ease of air or highway access, and abundance of accommodations, **Bozeman** is a superb launching point for the region. You could easily spend three days here, checking out the arts scene and nightlife and enjoying the spectacular recreational opportunities in every direction. Nearby **Big Sky** is a popular destination for skiing in winter as well as for biking, hiking, and horseback riding in summer. **Three Forks** and **Manhattan** offer an excellent taste of small-town Montana and are worthwhile stops, especially if you can be there for a favorite local event: Manhattan's **Potato Festival** in late August, or **Three Fork's Christmas Stroll**.

Just over the pass from Bozeman is **Livingston,** a small but vibrant community with a lot of character (and plenty of characters). You could happily spend a morning or afternoon browsing the shops and galleries downtown, and Livingston has an inordinate number of excellent restaurants to sample. The town explodes with enthusiasm and visitors over the **Fourth of July,** and if you can secure a parking spot for the parade and a ticket to the rodeo, dealing with the crowds (this is Montana, remember) will be well worth the effort.

Aptly named **Paradise Valley** links Livingston with the northernmost entrance to Yellowstone National Park at Gardiner. The mountains are spectacular and beg to be hiked. **Chico Hot Springs Resort** is the place to stay and boasts some of the best dining in the state and a long list of activities.

The plains seem to unfurl themselves, green and then golden, as you drive from Livingston through **Big Timber.** Anyone interested in Norwegian immigrant history in Montana should not miss the **Crazy Mountain Museum,** and a meal at the historic **Grand Hotel** right downtown is a treat. In **Columbus** the sheer bulk of the Beartooths dominates the horizon. There are wonderful side trips en route: a riverside hike in the **West Boulder Valley,** a burger at **Holly's Road Kill Saloon** in McLeod, and if you time it right (Labor Day Sunday), the **Great Montana Sheep Drive** in Reed Point.

Red Lodge is itself a wonderful destination for skiers, bikers, hikers, and even driving enthusiasts who want to tackle the **Beartooth Highway.** It would be an easy and worthwhile place to spend a couple of days before heading back to civilization in Billings or Bozeman, or into the wilds of Yellowstone through the northeast entrance at Cooke City.

HISTORY

Called the "Valley of the Flowers" by the Native Americans—including Shoshone,

---

Previous: Beartooth Scenic Highway; a guest ranch near Big Sky; Missouri Headwaters State Park in Three Forks.

Bozeman and the Gateway to Yellowstone

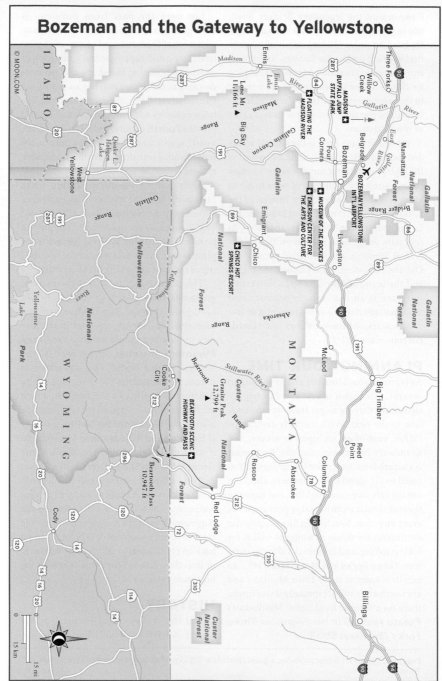

© MOON.COM

IDAHO

Three Forks

Willow Creek

Madison

Ennis

MADISON BUFFALO JUMP STATE PARK

FLOATING THE MADISON RIVER

Ennis Lake

Lone Mt. 11,166 ft

Big Sky

Madison Range

Gallatin Canyon

Four Corners

Belgrade

Bozeman

Manhattan

Gallatin National Forest

Bridger Range

BOZEMAN YELLOWSTONE INTL. AIRPORT

MUSEUM OF THE ROCKIES

EMERSON CENTER FOR THE ARTS AND CULTURE

Gallatin National Forest

Emigrant

Livingston

Chico

CHICO HOT SPRINGS RESORT

Absaroka Range

MONTANA

West Yellowstone

Quake L. Hebgen Lake

Gallatin Range

Yellowstone

Yellowstone River

Yellowstone National Park

Yellowstone Lake

WYOMING

Cooke City

Beartooth

Granite Peak 12,799 ft

Custer Range

Stillwater River

McLeod

Big Timber

BEARTOOTH SCENIC HIGHWAY AND PASS

Beartooth Pass 10,947 ft

Roscoe

Absarokee

Custer National Forest

Columbus

Red Point

Cody

Red Lodge

Billings

Custer National Forest

0   15 km

0   15 mi

Gallatin River

Easy Gallatin River

Gallatin River

Nez Perce, Blackfeet, Flathead, and Sioux—the Gallatin Valley around Bozeman was known as a peaceful place; no wars or skirmishes are known to have occurred in the valley. Trappers may have entered the valley in the late 18th century, most likely in pursuit of prized beaver pelts. Lewis and Clark camped in the valley in 1805 and 1806.

The discovery of gold at Alder Gulch in 1863 prompted John Bozeman of Georgia to establish the Bozeman Trail, a spur of the Oregon Trail. On July 7, 1864, Daniel E. Rouse and William J. Beall proposed the site for the town that would be named for Bozeman. Some of Bozeman's earliest residents include mountain man Jim Bridger and cattle baron Nelson Story, who herded his cattle from Texas to Bozeman.

Founded along the Yellowstone River in 1882 and named for the pioneer director of the Northern Pacific Railway, Johnston Livingston, the city of Livingston grew up around mining, the railroad, and agriculture. Its proximity to Yellowstone National Park, founded in 1872, ensured a constant stream of visitors and established Livingston's ongoing reputation as a tourist-friendly town.

In the 18th century, Red Lodge was inhabited by the Crow, who had steadily been moving westward to outrun their Sioux enemies. It is believed the city's name derives from the red clay used to paint the council tipi. Although it was part of the territory assigned to the Crow Nation by the 1851 Fort Laramie Treaty, the U.S. government reneged on its agreement and opened it to settlers and prospectors when coal was discovered in the region. The discovery of this precious resource, attributed to James "Yankee Jim" George, would change the fabric of this town and put it on the map. The town of Red Lodge was officially established in 1884, and by 1887 the Rocky Fork Coal Company opened the area's first mine. By 1889 the Northern Pacific Railway had extended its line to Red Lodge, allowing it to become a major shipping and trade center.

In its heyday, Red Lodge was a high-spirited frontier town with miners, ranchers, cowboys, and Indians creating a rather rowdy and at times lawless atmosphere. Both Buffalo Bill Cody and Calamity Jane were known to frequent the town. By the early 20th century, as other mines and sources of energy were being developed, Red Lodge's prominence as a mining town began to fade. When the West Side mine closed during the Great Depression, further economic hardship hit and the end of coal mining in the area was marked by a methane explosion in the Smith Mine, which killed 74 miners in 1943.

Life came back to this town when construction began on the Beartooth Highway in 1931, linking Red Lodge to Yellowstone Park. The highway was officially opened in 1936 and has ensured that the town remains a vibrant destination.

Bozeman and the Gallatin Valley

With Montana State University anchoring it and a geographical setting that has always appealed to outdoors enthusiasts and nature lovers, over the last 25 years Bozeman (population 45,250; elevation 4,820 ft/1,469 m) has grown from a cow town to a town of wine bars and art. The historic downtown is the heart of the community and attracts locals for numerous special events. There are a number of excellent restaurants and bars that appeal to everyone from broke and thirsty students to whiskey and wine connoisseurs. A handful of galleries and some very unique shops round out downtown's offerings.

Although the city is expanding exponentially and always on the list of Montana's fastest-growing cities, and Gallatin County (which encompasses the geography of Gallatin Valley) was ranked the fastest-growing county of its size in the United States in

2018, the original draw—nature—is still intact. Bridger Bowl and Big Sky are two excellent alpine skiing destinations nearby. The Gallatin, Madison, and Yellowstone Rivers, three blue-ribbon trout streams, are also nearby, in addition to numerous smaller streams. And there are literally hundreds of hiking and biking trails, enough to satisfy the most hard-core enthusiast.

SIGHTS
★ Museum of the Rockies

Best known for its paleontology exhibit curated by dinosaur guru Jack Horner, **Museum of the Rockies** (600 W. Kagy Blvd., 406/994-2251, www. museumoftherockies.org, 8am-6pm daily Memorial Day-Labor Day, 9am-5pm Mon.-Sat., noon-5pm Sun. Labor Day-Memorial Day, $14.50 adults, $13.50 seniors 65 and over, $10 MSU students with ID, $9.50 children 5-17, free for children 4 and under) is a fantastic resource for the entire state. The museum tackles 500 million years of history, no small feat, with permanent exhibits that reflect Native American culture, 19th- to 20th-century regional history, an outdoor living history farm (open only in summer), a planetarium, and, of course, the dinosaurs.

The Siebel Dinosaur Complex includes hundreds of important fossils and an array of impressive life-size reproductions. The traveling exhibitions vary widely—think polar obsession, the villas of Oplontis near Pompeii, guitars, *National Geographic*'s 50 greatest photos, and even chocolate—but typically offer excellent contrast to the permanent exhibits.

The Martin Children's Discovery Center upstairs offers a great place for preschool and elementary schoolchildren to play in hands-on Yellowstone exhibits. They can camp in a tent, listen for the eruption of Old Faithful (beware—it's loud, surprising, and often scary for little ones), recline in an eagle's nest, cook up a feast in a log cabin, fish for magnetic fish, and dress up as a park ranger or firefighter. For kids with vivid imaginations, this may be the highlight of the museum. In addition, the museum offers several engaging classes for children as young as infants and excellent day camps for elementary age kids.

The gift shop is outstanding and includes a great selection of local jewelry, science-oriented toys, art, books, and even candy.

Some argue that the admission fees are too steep, particularly if you come when there is no traveling exhibit, but on a rainy day in Bozeman, the museum can provide hours of compelling exploration. Additionally, admission provides unlimited access for two consecutive days.

Downtown Bozeman

Historic downtown Bozeman is interesting architecturally and compelling culturally. It is without a doubt the heart and soul of the city, and more often than not it is the gathering point for the most celebrated events, including **Bite of Bozeman, Music on Main, Crazy Days,** various parades, and **Christmas Stroll.** Businesses have faced some stiff competition from big-box stores on the perimeter of town, and there is significant turnover in retail and restaurants, but local residents support downtown in meaningful ways, even starting a petition campaign to fight to keep staple businesses, like the Owenhouse Ace Hardware, on Main Street. A natural-gas explosion rocked downtown in March 2009, killing one woman and destroying several businesses. Residents showed up in droves to support downtown business owners, workers, and residents alike. For a list of businesses and a calendar of weekly, annual, and special events that really showcase Main Street, visit www.downtownbozeman.org.

Gallatin History Museum

Touted as the place "where history and Main Street meet," the **Gallatin History Museum** (317 W. Main St., 406/522-8122, www.gallatinhistorymuseum.org, 11am-5pm Tues.-Sat. Memorial Day-Labor Day, 11am-4pm Tues.-Sat. Labor Day-Memorial Day, $7.50 adults, free for children under 12,

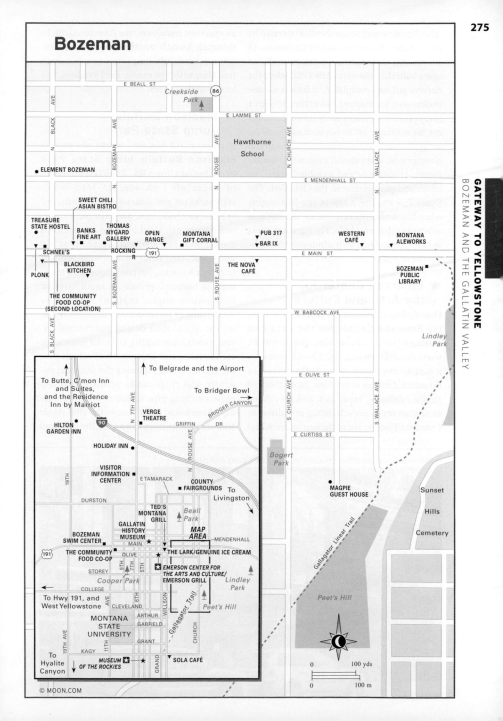

Bozeman

E BEALL ST

Creekside Park

86

E LAMME ST

Hawthorne School

E MENDENHALL ST

ELEMENT BOZEMAN

SWEET CHILI ASIAN BISTRO

TREASURE STATE HOSTEL

BANKS FINE ART

THOMAS NYGARD GALLERY

OPEN RANGE

MONTANA GIFT CORRAL

PUB 317

BAR IX

WESTERN CAFÉ

MONTANA ALEWORKS

SCHNEE'S

ROCKING R

191

E MAIN ST

BLACKBIRD KITCHEN

THE NOVA CAFÉ

BOZEMAN PUBLIC LIBRARY

PLONK

THE COMMUNITY FOOD CO-OP (SECOND LOCATION)

W BABCOCK AVE

Lindley Park

E OLIVE ST

To Belgrade and the Airport

To Butte, C'mon Inn and Suites, and the Residence Inn by Marriot

To Bridger Bowl

VERGE THEATRE

BRIDGER CANYON

HILTON GARDEN INN

90

GRIFFIN DR

E CURTISS ST

HOLIDAY INN

VISITOR INFORMATION CENTER

Bogert Park

E TAMARACK

COUNTY FAIRGROUNDS

MAGPIE GUEST HOUSE

Sunset Hills Cemetery

To Livingston

DURSTON

TED'S MONTANA GRILL

Beall Park

MAP AREA

GALLATIN HISTORY MUSEUM

BOZEMAN SWIM CENTER

MAIN

MENDENHALL

THE COMMUNITY FOOD CO-OP

191

OLIVE

THE LARK/GENUINE ICE CREAM

STOREY

EMERSON CENTER FOR THE ARTS AND CULTURE/ EMERSON GRILL

Cooper Park

Lindley Park

COLLEGE

Gallagator Trail

Peet's Hill

To Hwy 191, and West Yellowstone

CLEVELAND

ARTHUR

MONTANA STATE UNIVERSITY

GARFIELD

GRANT

KAGY

To Hyalite Canyon

MUSEUM OF THE ROCKIES

SOLA CAFÉ

Gallagator Linear Trail

Peet's Hill

0   100 yds

0   100 m

© MOON.COM

school groups, and researchers) is operated by the Gallatin Historical Society in Bozeman's 1911 county jail building. The museum shared space with the prisoners 1979-1982 before the current jail was completed. It boasts a comprehensive permanent collection of items that reflect Bozeman's early history, including an authentic 1870s homesteader's cabin, an agricultural room, substantial historical photographs, and a sheriff's room that houses plenty of artifacts and exhibits related to crime and punishment in the Old West. The Silsby Fire Engine, a top-of-the-line engine when it was manufactured in the late 1800s, is a favorite exhibit for kids. The museum offers weekly lectures, free with admission, throughout the summer.

★ Emerson Center for the Arts and Culture

Operated as an elementary school 1918-1991, the **Emerson Center for the Arts and Culture** (111 S. Grand Ave., 406/587-9797, www.theemerson.org), or The Emerson, as it is more commonly called, is the nucleus of Bozeman's robust arts scene. More than 30 studios, galleries, boutiques, and art-related businesses reside in the building in addition to Crawford Theater, one of the best in town, and

an excellent restaurant, the Emerson Grill. In summer, **Lunch on the Lawn** (11:30am-1:30pm Wed July-Aug., free) is a Bozeman tradition with live music, food vendors, and lots of smiling faces.

★ Madison Buffalo Jump State Park

Farther afield but well worth the visit is **Madison Buffalo Jump State Park** (6990 Buffalo Jump Rd., 7 mi/11.3 km south of Logan off I-90, 406/285-3610, www. stateparks.mt.gov, sunrise-sunset daily, $6/ vehicle nonresidents, $4/walk-in, bicycle, bus passenger). Used by Native Americans some 2,000 years ago (and as recently as 200 years ago), long before horses were brought to North America, buffalo jumps are a testament to human ingenuity. A small, covered interpretive display explains how Native Americans persuaded bison up the hill and off the cliff to their deaths, but the real lesson comes from hiking the trail (watch for rattlesnakes and cacti, both of which love the sun here) and exploring the site independently. Tipi rings can be identified, as can eagle-catching pits. Splinters of bison bone have been found at the base of the cliff. Aside from the compelling history of the area and

Downtown Bozeman offers excellent strolling, shopping, and dining.

the magnificent views from the top, the park's location limits traffic, and you are likely to have the place to yourself.

SPORTS AND RECREATION

Bozeman is a town of relatively young, active people, a fact that the infrastructure in town reflects.

Pools and Parks

The **Bozeman Swim Center** (1211 W. Main St., 406/582-2994, www.bozeman.net, $4 adults, $3 children and seniors) is a 50-meter Olympic-size pool inside the high school open to the public at designated times daily. The water is kept at a cool 84°F (28.9°C), ideal for lap swimming.

During summer, the outdoor pool at **Bogert Park** (303 S. Church Ave., 406/582-0806, $4 adults, $3 children under 14) is packed with families and their children. A couple of waterslides keep the energy (and the crowds) at peak levels. In the park itself, an extensive playground entices children. A band shell is used for Tuesday evening concerts, and the pavilion becomes an ice rink in winter.

Farther down Church Avenue from Bogert is the **Gallagator Trail**, which follows a former railroad line abandoned in the 1930s. Entirely flat, the gravel trail weaves through some lovely residential and forested areas along Bozeman Creek. Just before the Gallagator is **Peet's Hill**, the city's most popular in-town spot for a hike. A quick cruise up the hill leads you to a network of nice trails, a chance to commune with just about anyone and their dog, and ultimately to **Lindley Park**, an excellent destination year-round. In summer, there is picnicking and the fanfare of the Sweet Pea Festival. Two wonderful green areas in the city's historic neighborhoods are **Beall Park** (N. Bozeman Ave. and E. Villard St.), which is popular with kids and has an arts center, a playground, and an ice rink in winter; and **Cooper Park** (S. 8th Ave. and W. Koch St.), a favorite with dogs. The city of Bozeman (www.bozeman.net) has a list of city and county parks online.

Hiking

Many of Montana's cities and towns have constructed an enormous letter on a mountain or hill nearby. Bozeman's B has faded away over time, but the **M** (for Montana State University) is one of the community's favorite, and often most crowded, hiking spots. Accessed from a small parking lot on the west side of Bridger Drive, just past and across the road from the Bozeman Fish Technology Center, the M is hard to miss and well worth the hike. There is a steep route up (20-30 minutes) or a longer, gentler route (45 minutes-1 hour), making mix-and-match loops a possibility. The diehards can follow the trail 21 miles (34 km) to the **Fairy Lake Campground** near the end of Bridger Canyon.

Just across Bridger Canyon Drive from the M is the **Bozeman Fish Technology Center** (4050 Bridger Canyon Rd., 406/587-9265, www.fws.gov), one of the community's best-kept secrets. In addition to classes and kid-centered festivals (the Kid Fishing Derby and the Community Watershed Festival), the site offers a great newer trail called **Drinking Horse Mountain.** Slightly less steep and more shaded than the M trail, and with a summit view that looks north into Bridger Canyon rather than south into the Gallatin Valley, the trail is 1.6 miles (2.6 km) to the top and offers loop options.

Hikers eager to put some serious miles on their legs and get some elevation under their belts can continue 21 miles (34 km) down Bridger Canyon to the turnoff for Fairy Lake. At the end of a bumpy 6-mile (9.7-km) road is the Fairy Lake campground and a couple of great trailheads. The 1.2-mile (1.9-km) loop around beautiful **Fairy Lake** is easy and can be loaded with huckleberries in late July and August. The water is cold but swimmable. Another trailhead at the campground takes hikers up 2,000 feet (610 m) of elevation gain over 2 miles (3.2 km) one-way to **Sacajawea Peak,** the highest point in the Bridger Range at 9,665 feet (2,946 m). The trail winds through a conifer forest and climbs several rocky switchbacks.

At 8,963 feet (2,732 m) is the Bridger Divide with signed turnoffs to Hardscrabble Peak (9,575 ft/2,918 m), North Cottonwood Creek, Corbly Creek, and Sacajawea to the south. Follow the trail to the left and watch for mountain goats. From the summit, there are magnificent views in every direction. The there-and-back hike is only 4 miles (6.4 km), but with so much elevation gain, it can easily take three hours. For hikers who want to keep going (and have the ability to set up shuttle vehicles), between the Bridger Divide junction and Sacajawea Peak is a junction for the 19.9-mile (32-km) **Bridger Mountains National Recreation Trail,** running along the spine of the Bridger Range all the way to the M trailhead.

South of town is another excellent recreation area, **Hyalite Canyon** (south on S. 19th Ave. to Hyalite Canyon Rd.), one of the most popular in the state. There are excellent opportunities for boating on the reservoir, fishing in Hyalite Creek, and hiking on the various trails, including the stunning **Palisades Falls** trail, which is paved for wheelchair access. Other recreational opportunities include mountain biking, ice climbing, and backcountry skiing in winter.

Skiing

One of only two nonprofit ski areas in Montana, **Bridger Bowl** (15795 Bridger Canyon Rd., 406/587-2111, www.bridgerbowl.com, 9am-4pm daily during ski season, full-day $63 adults, $35 seniors, $25 children 7-12, free for children 6 and under and seniors 80 and over) is only 16 miles (26 km) north of Bozeman and offers 2,000 acres (809.4 hectares) of exceptional terrain and first-class facilities for about half of what you would pay at Aspen or Vail. Multiple-day tickets and ski school options are available, and there are 75 marked trails and eight lifts to get you on the mountain, including **Schlasman's,** which summits the ridge, an area long known as an "earn your turns" mecca. Though the area is hugely popular with locals and a seat in the cafeteria can be hard to find at lunchtime, lift lines are rarely longer than 10-15 people. With so much terrain and a local tendency to ski in the trees, Bridger Bowl offers what feels like wide-open space. The mountain offers diverse terrain but is slightly more geared toward advanced skiers, with 42 percent of the trails rated "expert." The longest run is 3 miles (4.8 km), and the average annual snowfall is 350 inches (889 cm). In the

Hyalite Canyon is a popular recreation spot.

summer, trails are open to hikers and mountain bikers. In early October, usually before the snow flies, the ski hill hosts the **Bridger Raptor Fest** (bridgerraptorfest.org), a series of films, walks, talks, and demonstrations that coincides with the largest golden eagle migration in the United States.

Just north of Bridger Bowl is the **Crosscut Mountain Sports Center** (16621 Bridger Canyon Rd., 406/586-9070, www.crosscutmt.org, 9am-4pm daily, $20 adults, $10 children 12-18, free for children under 12), a wonderful place for cross-country novices and racers alike. Crosscut boasts 16 miles (26 km) of impeccably groomed trails suitable for both classic and skate skiers, and it's also hosted numerous competitions, including the U.S. Olympic Qualifying Championship in 2002 and national NCAA events. In summer, Crosscut transforms its trails into excellent hiking, mountain biking, and horseback riding trails. It also has a championship biathlon course and a disc golf course.

In downtown Bozeman, **Lindley Park** (E. Main St. and Buttonwood Ave.) offers extensive groomed cross-country ski trails courtesy of the Bridger Ski Foundation. The best place to park is the northwest parking lot of Bozeman Deaconess Hospital (915 Highland Blvd.). Season passes can be purchased online (www.bridgerskifoundation.org, $50 individual, $100 family), or donations can be made in the boxes at the various trailheads.

The 18-hole golf course at **Bridger Creek** (2710 McIlhattan Rd., 406/586-2333, www.bridgercreek.com) is also groomed for skiers in the winter. Buttons, which are the wear-on-your-jacket equivalent of a ski pass, can be purchased at a variety of locations in town, including **Bangtail Bike & Ski** (137 E. Main St., 406/587-4905, www.bangtailbikes.com), an excellent cycle and Nordic ski shop that also rents cross-country skis. During winter, the **Bridger Ski Foundation** (www.bridgerskifoundation.org) grooms miles of trails that bring out racers and novices alike to make tracks around the city's hospital.

Fishing

Bozeman is a trout lover's paradise, with several blue-ribbon streams nearby. The **Gallatin, Jefferson,** and **Madison Rivers** flow through the valley, forming the headwaters of the Missouri River in aptly named Three Forks (31 mi/50 km west of Bozeman on I-90). Al Gadoury of **6X Outfitters** (406/586-3806, www.6xoutfitters.com, wade or float trips $500 for 1-2 people, $600 for 3-4 people, $40-120 private water rod fee) is widely considered to be among the region's best outfitters, particularly when it comes to spring creeks and private water. As an aside, his shore lunches (think grilled moose burgers) are second to none.

Other local outfitters can offer excellent advice and guide services. **The River's Edge** (2012 N. 7th Ave., 406/586-5373, www.theriversedge.com, 8am-6pm daily) is one of Bozeman's oldest and most venerated. **Montana Troutfitters** (1716 W. Main St., 406/587-4707, www.troutfitters.com, 7am-7pm daily) has been guiding fly-fishing excursions since 1978 and offers excellent online fishing reports. **Yellow Dog Flyfishing Adventures** (406/585-8657 or 888/777-5060, www.yellowdogflyfishing.com) offers first-class trips in the region and mind-blowing fishing adventures around the world.

★ Floating the Madison River

In a college town with an active and outdoorsy population, floating the rivers is a popular pastime. The calm and relatively warm **Madison River** is easily the most popular, followed by the slightly more remote **Jefferson River.** For an idyllic half-day float on the Madison, rent a 3- to 6-person raft (from $85) or inner tubes (from $12) from **Big Boys Toys All Terrain Rentals** (8254 Huffine Ln., 406/587-4747, www.bigboystoysrentals.com). Or rent tubes with coolers (from $10), kayaks (from $35), stand-up paddleboards (from $40), or canoes (from $40). Tubes (from $10), stand-up paddleboards (from $35), and rafts (from $50) are also available from **Pink Cowboy Recreation Rentals** (8191 Huffine Ln.,

406/219-8823, www.pinkcowboy.net), which donates 5 percent of profits to the fight against breast cancer. Delivery can be arranged within 50 miles (81 km) of Bozeman on reservations of $150 or more.

From either place, drive 30 minutes west on Highway 84 (also known as Norris Rd.) to the Warm Springs access. Float time down to Black's Ford is 2-3.5 hours, depending on the time of year and water flow. If you only have one vehicle, make sure to arrange a shuttle through one of the rental shops. Try to schedule your float on a weekday, if possible, or early in the morning on the weekend if you don't want to get caught up in the college booze-cruise flotilla.

Golf

There are three private golf courses in and around Bozeman (Valley View Golf Club, Riverside Country Club, and Black Bull Run Golf Club), and two that are open to the public. The 18-hole **Bridger Creek Golf Course** (2710 McIlhattan Rd., 406/586-2333, www. bridgercreek.com, weekdays $21 for 9 holes and $34 for 18 holes, weekends and holidays $23 for 9 holes and $36 for 18 holes) offers 6,511 yards (5,954 m) of golf from the longest tees for a par of 71. Special family nights are ideal for little ones just picking up the game, and novice nights provide a non-stressful atmosphere for new players. Its camp offerings for kids and its group and private lessons for anyone are highly rated. **Cottonwood Hills Golf Course** (8955 River Rd., 406/587-1118, www.cottonwoodhills.com) offers a 9-hole, 1,181-yard (1,080-m), par-3 course ($10 adults, $8 children 6-12) as well as an 18-hole, 6,751-yard (6,173-m) course with a par of 70 ($24 for 9 holes, $44 for 18 holes).

Fitness and Yoga

The largest gym in the area—which has a pool, racquetball and basketball courts, and a fantastic kid's drop-off playroom—is **The Ridge** (4181 Fallon Ave., 406/586-1737, www.ridgeathletic.com, 5:15am-10pm Mon.-Thurs., 5:15am-9pm Fri., 7am-8pm Sat.-Sun.,

$20 day pass), an impressive facility with every class you can imagine and numerous trainers on the floor at all times. A smaller branch, known as **The Ridge Downtown** (111 E. Mendenhall St., 406/586-0077, www. ridgeathletic.com, 5:30am-9pm Mon.-Thurs., 5:30am-8pm Fri., 8am-7pm Sat., noon-7pm Sun., $15 day pass) is just off Main Street and limited to strength training and cardio equipment plus various yoga and fitness classes. Also downtown is **Main Street Fitness** (7 W. Main St., 406/556-2200, www. mainstreetfitness.net, open 24 hours) where, for $10, visitors can have full access to the gym and its range of classes, including kickboxing, ski conditioning, and yoga.

Find your center at **Your Yoga** (20 E. Main St., 406/599-5005, www.youryoga. com). Choose from a variety of classes—from meditation and vinyasa to kundalini, hatha, and restorative. Sweat-inducing Bikram yoga can be found at **Bend Beyond Yoga** (705 E. Mendenhall St., 406/219-3837, www. bendbeyondyoga.com). Drop-ins are welcome for $20. Discounts are available for seniors, students, and veterans. Mats and towels can be rented for $2 each. Worth noting is the meditation garden behind the studio. **Pure Barre Bozeman** (34 E. Mendenhall St., 406/577-2918, www.purebarre.com) provides an hour-long, full-body workout that uses a ballet bar and small repetitive movements with upbeat music and encouraging instructors. Drop-in classes are $23 or $105 for five classes.

ENTERTAINMENT AND EVENTS
Nightlife

In downtown Bozeman, **Plonk** (29 E. Main St., 406/587-2170, www.plonkwine.com, 11:30am-2am daily) is an elegant wine bar as known for its tapas and desserts—start with the cheese board or ploughman's platter and finish with the chef's chocolate board for dessert—as for its remarkably global selection of more than 600 wines. The atmosphere is a captivating integration of 100-year-old architecture, contemporary original works of art, minimalist urban design, and an eclectic collection of well-played vinyl records. In the summertime, the crowd spills outside to a handful of sidewalk tables. In a mostly family-friendly town, this is one establishment that does not welcome children or babies.

Also downtown, **Bar IX** (311 E. Main St., 406/551-2185, www.bar-ix.com, 2pm-2am Mon.-Fri., 11am-2am Sat.-Sun.) is both industrial and rustic, and it's usually hopping. Its happy hour specials and Bucket Nights are well known locally. Appealing to Bozeman's athletic crowd, **Pub 317** (321 E. Main St., 406/582-8898, www.pub317.com, 11am-2am daily) is one of the few bars that hosts running races. Twice each year, the Irish pub sponsors 10K or half-marathons that end back at the bar. There's usually live Irish music on Sunday, live bluegrass on Tuesday, and trivia nights on Wednesday. An ideal spot for a gourmet Montana meal or just a mean cocktail, **Open Range** (241 E. Main St., 406/404-1940, www.openrangemt.com, dining 5pm-10pm daily, drink service 10pm-close daily) is an upscale favorite.

Popular with the college (and alumni) crowds is the **Rocking R Bar** (211 E. Main St., 406/587-9355, www.rockingrbar.com, 11am-2am daily), a favorite hangout since the 1940s.

Theater

For a relatively small Rocky Mountain town, Bozeman has a decent number of theater offerings. The best is certainly **Broad Comedy** (406/522-7623, www.broadcomedy.com), which produces irreverent and side-splitting satire by a female cast (and geared to mature audiences only). The company has achieved global recognition and plenty of YouTube followers. If you are in town when the company is performing, be there. Broad Comedy was also the founder of (and still runs) the highly respected and always full Camp Equinox, an incredible theatre experience for kids in summer.

Verge Theater (2304 N. 7th Ave., 406/587-0737, www.vergetheater.com) has been around for more than 20 years (until

2013 as Equinox Theatre Company) and produces eclectic and original shows, many of which are hilariously funny. The company produces eight main stage shows each year and six children's matinees. It is also home to the region's only full-time improv comedy troupe.

There are also shows produced by students at **Montana State University** (406/994-3904) and professional theater brought to the **Brick Breeden Fieldhouse** (1 Bobcat Cir., 406/994-7117) through **Broadway in Bozeman** (406/994-2287, www.brickbreeden.com).

One of the state's most beloved troupes, **Montana Shakespeare in the Parks** (www.shakespeareintheparks.org) is based out of Montana State University and travels all over the state bringing fantastic, outdoor (when weather permits), and free Shakespearean theater to parks and even cow pastures around the Northern Rockies in small, underserved communities. The company, which travels around to do school workshops in the off-season, has been bringing the Bard to the people since 1973. Bill Pullman is one of the company's most famous alumni. You can always catch a glimpse of them at Bozeman's Sweet Pea Festival, but going to see them anywhere in Montana or Wyoming is worth doing.

Music

Thanks to the eager audiences provided by the university, Bozeman also has a lively and impressive music scene. **Intermountain Opera Bozeman** (104 E. Main St., Ste. 101, 406/587-2889, www.intermountainopera.org) has been producing two professional shows annually since 1978. The shows feature world-class performers and conductors with a local chorus and orchestra and are staged at the **Willson Auditorium** (404 W. Main St., 406/587-2889) in the spring and fall. The **Bozeman Symphony Orchestra and Symphonic Choir** (406/585-9774, www.bozemansymphony.org) presents a number of performances each season, starting in September, that range from late Renaissance pieces through the 20th century. It also performs annually with the Montana Ballet Company in *The Nutcracker.* **Vootie Productions** (406/586-1922, www.vootie.com) brings outstanding performers to town regularly.

Live from the Divide (627 E. Peach St., www.livefromthedivide.com, show dates vary, tickets from $20) is an independently produced hour-long public radio program celebrating the songwriters of American roots music. Tickets are sold to 50 lucky music lovers who get to sit in on the taping. Check the calendar online for the next show.

Festivals and Events

Held annually the first full weekend in August, **Sweet Pea Festival of the Arts** (406/586-4003, www.sweetpeafestival.org) is Bozeman's answer to Mardi Gras. No one is parading around half-naked—this is Montana, after all—but there is plenty of food (don't miss the tater pigs, a Sweet Pea classic), live music, theater, dance, an arts and crafts fair, both juried and open art shows, and a flower show. The weekend events are held at **Lindley Park** (east end of Main St.). Events leading up to the festival include the **Sweet Pea Ball** (Sat. before Sweet Pea weekend), **Chalk on the Walk** (Tues. before Sweet Pea), **Bite of Bozeman** (Wed. before Sweet Pea), and the **Children's Run and Sweet Pea Parade** (Sat. morning of Sweet Pea). Packed into three days, the nearly 40-year-old festival is organized by more than 1,500 volunteers and draws more than 16,000 visitors annually. Wristbands (from $20 adults, $10 children 7 and older) are required for entry to Lindley Park, and one wristband enables you to access all the events in Lindley Park over the course of the weekend. Children six and under are free.

Founded in 2011, in response to the increasing competition and expense for local artists to get into Sweet Pea, **SLAM Fest** (406/219-7773, info@slamfestivals.org, free), which stands for Support Local Artists and

Music, runs in Bogert Park the same weekend as the other festival. Like a smaller and free version of Sweet Pea, SLAM hosts more than 50 artists and artisans from around the state, plus live music, readings, dance, food, and a beer garden.

Although Bozeman residents joke about the "nine months of winter and three months of houseguests," people take summertime recreation very seriously, and the town of Bozeman (www.downtownbozeman.org) has created numerous ways to celebrate outside as much as possible. Residents and visitors gather on the lawn at the Emerson Center for the Arts and Culture for **Lunch on the Lawn** (11:30am-1:30pm Wed. July-Aug., free), a concert series that attracts 100-200 people and an interesting mix of food vendors. **Music on Main** (6:30pm-8:30pm Thurs. July-Aug., free) is an opportunity for folks to gather downtown on closed-off streets and enjoy live music, food vendors, and early evening activities for kids. On the second Friday of every month June-September, art lovers gather for the **Downtown Bozeman Art Walk** (406/586-4008, 6pm-8pm), an opportunity to stroll through the galleries downtown, sipping wine and tasting hors d'oeuvres along the way. Another summer event, **Crazy Days** (downtown, 406/586-4008), is a price-slashing shopping extravaganza that happens each year the third weekend in July.

Bozeman also boasts two fabulous **farmers markets.** The original is the **Bogert Farmers' Market** (S. Church Ave., www.bogertfarmersmarket.org, 5pm-8pm Tues.), held in Bogert Park. It includes everything from produce, arts, and crafts to gourmet food trucks, entertainment, and activities (like reverse bungee jumping and rock climbing for kids). The park is packed, so plan to stay in immediate contact with little ones. For a more relaxing evening, bring a blanket and park yourself away from the masses. A larger market, the **Gallatin Valley Farmers' Market** (901 N. Black Ave., 406/388-6701, ext. 101, www.gallatinvalleyfarmersmarket.com,

9am-noon Sat. mid-June-early Sept.) runs at the Gallatin County Fairgrounds.

Other annual events worth checking out are the **Big Sky Country State Fair** (406/582-3270, www.406statefair.com, $10 adults, $3 children 6-12, free for children under 6), held at the county fairgrounds (901 N. Black Ave.) the third week in July, which offers carnival rides, entertainment, animals, contests (where else can your kid ride a sheep or wrestle a piglet?), and food; October's **MSU Homecoming** and **Downtown Trick or Treat** (both on Main St.); and February's **Wild Winter Fest** (Gallatin County Fairgrounds, 901 N. Black Ave.). Bozeman's **Christmas Stroll** brings the town out the first Saturday of December to eat, shop, and enjoy the festive season.

SHOPPING

Like most regional hubs in Montana, Bozeman offers an abundance of shopping opportunities for every taste and budget level. Major stores include Target and Costco on North 19th Avenue as well as Walmart and Murdoch's Ranch & Home Supply on North 7th Avenue. **Downtown Bozeman** (www.downtownbozeman.org), however, is by far the best place to go for unique items and pure charm.

The **Country Bookshelf** (28 W. Main St., 406/587-0166, www.countrybookshelf.com, 9am-7pm Mon.-Fri., 9am-6pm Sat., 10am-5pm Sun.) is Bozeman's most beloved bookstore and the state's largest independent bookstore. It is especially geared to local and regional authors, many of whom are willing to show their affection for the place with readings and book signings. On the same block is **Vargo's Jazz City & Books** (6 W. Main St., 406/587-5383, 9:30am-7pm Mon.-Fri., 10am-6pm Sat., 11am-5pm Sun.), an excellent place to get lost. The shop specializes in slightly more obscure books, CDs, and vinyl, both new and used.

For marvelous gifts and cards, there are three excellent boutiques downtown. **Perspectives** (424 E. Main St., 406/522-7125, www.perspectivesmt.com, 10am-5:30pm Mon.-Sat.) offers an adorable selection of baby clothes, shoes, and gifts in addition to distinctive bags, cards, stationery, and jewelry. Touted as a shop "for the everyday celebration," **HeyDay** (7 W. Main St., 406/586-5589, www.heydaybozeman.com, 10am-7pm Mon.-Sat., 10am-5pm Sun.) specializes in timeless home decor and elegant gifts. From gardening to personal grooming, cooking, and entertaining, this stylish little shop is sure to make you smile. For gifts that could only come from Montana, **Montana Gift Corral** (237 E. Main St., 406/585-8625, www.giftcorral.com, 9am-8pm Mon.-Fri., 9am-6pm Sat., 10am-5pm Sun.) is the place to go.

For the hunters and outdoors enthusiasts, downtown Bozeman offers top-of-the-line shopping. Occupying two beautifully restored 1903 storefronts is an outstanding local shoe store and something of a Bozeman institution. Poised to make shoe snobs out of nearly anyone, **Schnee's** (35 E. Main St., 406/587-0981, www.schnees.com, 8am-8pm Mon.-Fri., 9am-6pm Sat., 10am-5pm Sun.) sells everything from locally made bombproof hunting boots to a selection of very hip street shoes and sandals. It also sells clothes and accessories, leather bags, and hunting and fishing gear, and takes its 100 percent satisfaction guarantee very seriously.

Bozeman has a number of notable art galleries. **Thomas Nygard Gallery** (133 E. Main St., 406/586-3636, www.nygardgallery.com, 9am-5pm Mon.-Fri.) specializes in Western, wildlife, and sports art. Just down the street, **A. Banks Gallery** (127 E. Main St., 406/586-1000, www.abanksgallery.com, 10am-5:30pm Mon.-Fri., 10am-4:30pm Sat., noon-4pm Sun.) displays an outstanding collection of American, Western, and sports art. **Visions West Contemporary** (34 W. Main St., 406/522-9946, www.visionswestcontemporary.com, 10am-5:30pm Mon.-Wed., 10am-6pm Thurs.-Sat.) is a dynamic space that focuses on contemporary artists in the West.

Bozeman's most significant shopping

event is **Crazy Days** (downtown Bozeman, 406/586-4008), an annual event held on the third weekend in July. Merchants reduce their inventory prices by up to 75 percent and put much of it out on the street. Early birds are the winners here; it's not uncommon to see several brand-new pairs of last year's skis being carried away by happy new owners.

FOOD

If you have recently traveled through rural Montana, Bozeman seems like a food lover's mecca. With everything from sushi to tapas, the town affords diners much more than the burgers and steaks for which the state is so well known (although there is an outstanding selection of those as well).

The ★ **Community Food Co-op** (908 W. Main St., 406/587-4039, www.bozo.coop, 7:30am-10pm Mon.-Sat., 8am-10pm Sun., deli counter 8am-8pm daily) is a cornerstone of the community, and its **downtown branch** (44 E. Main St., 406/922-2667, 7:30am-8pm Mon.-Sat., 8am-8pm Sun.) is not only convenient but also offers an excellent hot bar, salad bar, and sandwich and smoothie counter. Everything the Co-op does—gourmet and often locally produced groceries, mouthwatering prepared foods, and a primo coffee shop, juice bar, and bakery—is done brilliantly. The homemade soups are excellent, as is the salad bar and just about everything in the sprawling deli case. Exotic hot lunches and dinners are often available at prices that cannot be matched elsewhere.

Just down the block, the super-casual and family-friendly **Naked Noodle** (27 S. Willson Ave., 406/585-4501, 11am-9:30pm Mon.-Tues. and Thurs.-Sat., 11am-9pm Sun., $8.25-14.25) dishes up pasta that is cooked and topped to order as you stand watch. The hearty salads—like Korean beef—are excellent too.

Another spot for fresh, creative cuisine is right across the street from the Museum of the Rockies. **Sola Café** (290 W. Kagy Ave., 406/922-7652, www.solacafe.com, 7am-8pm Mon.-Thurs., 7am-4pm Sat.-Sun., $5-15) is

a good place for salads, panini, soups, sandwiches, daily entrée specials, and an assortment of fresh-baked goodies. Sola is also a full-service coffee bar. Online and text ordering along with a drive-through window make gourmet takeout dinners a great option.

Right downtown and worth noting is **Ted's Montana Grill** (105 W. Main St., 406/587-6000, www.tedsmontanagrill.com, 11am-10pm Sun.-Thurs., 11am-11pm Fri.-Sat., $11-36) in the historic Baxter hotel. It is the flagship restaurant of local part-time resident and unequivocal philanthropist and land steward Ted Turner. Everything is made from scratch, and each meat cut is available in bison or beef. The apple cobbler is extremely good.

For excellent (but pricey!) Asian food, **Sweet Chili Asian Bistro** (101 E. Main St., 406/582-1188, www.sweetchilibistro.com, 11am-9pm Mon.-Thurs., 11am-9:30pm Fri.-Sat., noon-9pm Sun., $15-27) serves up an extensive menu of fresh and flavorful Asian cuisine along with sushi and a full bar. The room is dimly lit with red lights, lending some romantic ambience. This is still Bozeman though, and any restaurant is fairly casual.

★ **Blackbird Kitchen** (140 E. Main St., 406/586-0010, www.blackbirdkitchen.com, 5pm-9pm Mon.-Thurs., 5pm-9:30pm Fri.-Sat., $12-30) is a tiny little spot that is usually standing room only. From the kale Caesar salad to the Willow Spring lamb chop, the wood-fired pizza, and handmade pasta, the country Italian flavors are sensational. The wine list is extensive, and if you leave without sampling the chocolate *budino* (pudding) sprinkled with sea salt and drizzled with olive oil, you've made a mistake.

On the east end of town, **Montana Ale Works** (611 E. Main St., 406/587-7700, www. montanaaleworks.com, 4pm-10pm Sun.-Thurs., 4pm-11pm Fri.-Sat., bar until midnight daily, $10.50-24) combines a hip eatery with an extremely popular smoke-free bar and pool lounge. The menu offers inventive takes on Western staples like burgers and steaks, and the atmosphere, in a beautifully rehabbed 100-year-old railroad warehouse, is energetic and suitable for everyone from toddlers to grandparents; it can be loud at any time of the week, so a separate dining room is a good option for those with noise issues.

As Bozeman has evolved from its ranching and agricultural heritage, many of the classic diners have been lost to trendier eateries, but two have stood the test of time. The **Western Café** (443 E. Main St., 406/587-0436, 6am-2pm daily, $6-12) is an old-timers classic for breakfast and lunch, including its famed chicken-fried steak and cinnamon rolls.

For a more upscale breakfast or lunch option downtown, **The Nova Café** (312 E. Main St., 406/587-3973, www.thenovacafe. com, 7am-2pm daily, $6.50-13.25) is considered the best breakfast place in town. The café uses fresh, healthy ingredients and gets almost everything—from meats and produce to salsa—locally. The service and the food are consistently outstanding. Also downtown are two more excellent breakfast and lunch offerings. The elegant **Little Star Diner** (548 E. Babcock St., 406/624-6463, www. littlestardiner.com, 8am-2pm Tues.-Sun., $6-14) boasts a frequently changing menu with lots of local produce and meats, plus delicious, atypical breakfast fare like crème fraiche donuts with rhubarb sauce, yellow lentil dal, and grilled mushroom toast. With lovely ambience and a bar, it's like dinner for morning people. The always-bustling **Jam** (312 E. Main St., 406/587-3973, www.jamonmain.com, 7am-3:30pm daily, $4-14) often has a long line of diners waiting for a table. It offers a big menu of more traditional fare, including crepes, pancakes, a variety of eggs Benedict, and omelets for breakfast, and sandwiches, burgers, salads, and tacos for lunch. You won't leave hungry. At Jam, lunch is served Monday through Friday only; breakfast is served all day every day.

A few steps off Main Street, tucked into the Emerson Center for the Arts and Culture, the **Emerson Grill** (111 S. Grand Ave., 406/586-5247, 5pm-9pm Mon.-Thurs., 5pm-10pm Sat.-Sun., $15-43) is a perfect spot for a bite. With walls the color of acorn squash and high-backed wooden booths that recall a 100-year-old schoolhouse, this northern Italian restaurant offers a warm, intimate ambience and excellent, uncomplicated food. The flatbread pizzettes—one of the Grill's signature dishes—are especially good (try the pear, white sauce, caramelized onions, and gorgonzola version), and the extensive boutique-style wine list boasts descriptions like "Sophia Loren in a glass."

A great spot for gourmet wood-fired pizza is **Pizza Campania** (1285 N. Rouse Ave., 406/404-1270, 11am-9:30pm Mon.-Fri., 4pm-9:30pm Sat.-Sun., $10-16). Toppings include such delicacies as fennel sausage, fig preserves, goat gorgonzola, and brie. The restaurant also serves great salads and desserts, and opens up to the outside with a glass garage-style door. Patio diners can sit by the fire with a great bottle of wine.

ACCOMMODATIONS

For a long time, Bozeman's accommodations were lacking in charm, for a town with seemingly sophisticated tastes. That changed with the addition of two terrific contemporary hotels in 2015. Still, for those willing to look, there are numerous and diverse offerings, from roadside motels to upscale chains, cozy vacation rentals, and, farther afield, a historical gem.

Newer is better in Bozeman, when it comes to hotels. ★ **The Lark** (122 W. Main St., 866/464-1000, www.larkbozeman.com, $187-349) considers itself a base camp and works hard at getting guests out of its modern, art-filled rooms and into the wilds of Bozeman and its surrounds. A map room helps with planning, and motel employees are called guides. Still, your time inside The Lark will be a pleasure with 38 unique rooms, each filled with work by local artists and craftspeople. Kids will love the bunk room, and everyone will appreciate the heart-of-downtown location, which is within walking distance to everywhere. Look out for the **Genuine Ice Cream** (www. genuineicecream.com) truck just outside the hotel, dishing up handmade ice cream in flavors like fresh mint chip, matcha green tea, honey lavender, and Nutella crunch.

Another newer property in downtown Bozeman with a decidedly Scandinavian feel is ★ **Element Bozeman** (25 E. Mendenhall St., 406/582-4972, www.elementbozeman. com, from $234) a Starwood Hotel. Just a block off Main Street, this high-rise (for Bozeman, anyway) hotel has spacious rooms, a complimentary breakfast bar, evening reception, and fully stocked kitchenettes, as well as a patio grill, an indoor pool, a fitness center, and bikes to borrow.

Offering an ideal location right downtown, and the cheapest rooms anywhere, the **Treasure State Hostel** (27 E. Main St., 406/624-6244, www.treasurestatehostel.com, dorm bed from $28, private room from $38) is a find in Bozeman. Just 20 minutes from Bridger Bowl and an hour from Big Sky, the hostel is popular with skiers in winter.

The **Magpie Guest House** (323 S. Wallace Ave., 406/585-8223, www.magpiegh. com, $160-175) offers charming accommodations for up to four people in an ideal downtown location, sandwiched between the library and Peet's Hill, with all the comforts of home.

At the 19th Street exit on I-90, visitors will find the extremely comfortable all-suites **Residence Inn by Marriott** (6195 E. Valley Center Rd., 406/522-1535, www.marriott.com, from $179) with 115 suites. The hotel offers a hot breakfast each morning and social hours Monday-Thursday. Other reliable chain hotels in the area include **C'Mon Inn Hotel & Suites** (6139 E. Valley Center Rd., 406/587-3555 or 866/782-2717, www.cmoninn.com, from $150), the upscale **Hilton Garden Inn** (2032 Commerce Way, 406/582-9900, http://hiltongardeninn3.hilton.com, $189-316) on the northwest side of town, and the older but well-maintained **Holiday Inn** (5 E. Baxter Ln., 406/587-4561 or 800/315-2621, www. holidayinn.com, from $121). **Travelodge** (1200 E. Main St., 406/586-8534, www. wyndhamhotels.com, from $149) is a hotel at the east end of downtown, not far from the interstate, with clean, spacious rooms.

Bozeman Cottage Vacation Rentals (406/580-3223, www.bozemancottage.com) offers a broad array of properties to meet individual preferences for location, price, size, and style—from a lodge near Bridger Bowl to downtown cottages and riverfront cabins. There are plenty of pet-friendly offerings, and last-minute bargains can be had for those inclined to wing it. **Mountain Home** (406/586-4589 or 800/550-4589, www.mountain-home. com) has an excellent array of vacation rentals in and around Bozeman and across southwestern Montana.

INFORMATION AND SERVICES

A good place for information, travel services, and maps is the **Bozeman Chamber of Commerce** (2000 Commerce Way, southeast corner of N. 19th St. and Baxter Ln., 406/586-5421 or 800/228-4224, www. bozemancvb.com, 8am-5pm Mon.-Fri.). The chamber also staffs a **visitors center** at Bozeman Yellowstone International Airport, which offers the same assortment of information, brochures, and maps as at the chamber. Downtown shoppers can find an abundance of information at the **Downtown Bozeman Visitor Center** (222 E. Main St., 406/586-4008, 9am-5pm Mon.-Fri.).

The **main post office** (2201 Baxter Ln. at 19th St., 8:30am-5pm Mon.-Fri., 9am-1pm Sat.) offers a 24-hour automated postal service that accepts major credit and debit cards. The old post office still operates downtown at 32 East Babcock Street, one block south of Main Street.

The **Bozeman Public Library** (626 E. Main St., 406/582-2400, www. bozemanlibrary.org, 10am-8pm Mon.-Thurs., 10am-6pm Fri., 10am-5pm Sat., 1pm-5pm Sun.) boasts a modern and green architectural design with lots of space to work, a nice coffee shop, and an excellent children's section. The library is one of the few places in town that offers **free Internet access**. Internet access can also be found at either of the Community Food Co-op (908 W. Main St. or 44 E. Main St., 406/587-4039, www.bozo. coop) locations. Both restaurants turn their Wi-Fi off during the busy lunch hour so that diners can get tables.

Bozeman Deaconess Hospital (915 Highland Blvd., 406/585-5000, www. bozemanhealth.org) has a 24-hour emergency room. Another option is Bozeman Urgent Care Center (1006 W. Main St., Ste. E, 406/414-4800, 8am-7pm Mon.-Fri., 9am-5pm Sat.-Sun.).

Coin-operated washers and dryers can be found at Duds-n-Suds (502 S. 23rd Ave., 406/586-3837, 7:30am-9pm Sun.-Thurs., 7:30am-8pm Fri.-Sat.), which also boasts a car wash, a dog wash, and free Wi-Fi; and at The Clothesline (815 W. Main St., 406/586-3070, 7am-10pm daily), which offers drop-off laundry service as well.

TRANSPORTATION
Getting There
Bozeman Yellowstone International Airport (BZN, 406/388-8321, www. bozemanairport.com) is 8 miles (12.9 km) northwest of downtown Bozeman in the nearby town of Belgrade. Delta, Alaska, American, Allegiant, Frontier, Jet Blue, and United all offer daily nonstop service to and from major U.S. cities, including Salt Lake City, Minneapolis, Seattle, Atlanta, Chicago, and Denver. Seasonal nonstop flights serve Houston, Las Vegas, Los Angeles, New York, Phoenix, Portland, and San Francisco.

Greyhound travels to almost 40 towns and cities in Montana from the bus depot (1205 E. Main St., 612/499-3468, 10am-3pm daily).

Off I-90, Bozeman is easily accessible by car. It is 142 miles (229 km) west of Billings, 202 miles (320 km) southeast of Missoula, and 85 miles (137 km) east of Butte. The driving distances are slightly farther from Wyoming: Jackson is 215 miles (345 km) south, Sheridan is 270 miles (435 km) southeast, and Cody is 214 miles (345 km) southeast of Bozeman.

Getting Around
From the airport, the Best Western, Comfort Inn, and Hampton Inn offer shuttle service. A number of car-rental agencies are at the airport too; the car-rental center is located next to the baggage claim. Alamo, Avis, Budget, Enterprise, Dollar, Hertz, Thrifty, and National have on-site counters.

The only ground transportation provider within the terminal, Karst Stage (406/556-3540 or 800/845-2778, www.karststage. com) offers daily bus service in winter to Big Sky, West Yellowstone, and Mammoth Hot Springs. Shuttles are by reservation only in non-winter months.

Greater Valley Taxi (406/388-9999 or 406/587-6303, www.greatervalleytaxi.com) has a courtesy phone next to the baggage claim area. Rides into Bozeman cost $3.50 per mile plus a $6.00 pick up fee. Each additional passenger is $5. It is also a good option for getting around town while you are in Bozeman. Shuttle to Big Sky & Taxi (406/995-4895 or 888/454-5667, www.bigskytaxi.com) provides private van and SUV transportation to, from, and around Big Sky. Uber (www.uber.com) also serves the Bozeman area.

VICINITY OF BOZEMAN
Belgrade
Nine miles (14.5 km) west of Bozeman on I-90, and often unfairly labeled a bedroom community of Bozeman, Belgrade (population 8,254; elevation 4,459 ft/1,359 m) is a great little Montana town with plenty of character. Lewis and Clark Park (Main St.) is the hub of the city and provides a covered picnic area, a wonderful playground, and a wildly popular splash park geared to small children. The Belgrade Bandits are the local baseball team, and with Little League and high school offerings, there is always a ball game to watch.

Belgrade has a couple of good restaurants. Long the town's most popular eatery, The Mint Bar & Cafe (27 E. Main St., 406/924-6017, www.mintcafebar.com, 4:30pm-9:30pm Sun.-Thurs., 4:30pm-10pm Fri.-Sat., $12-37) is a good place for a martini and steak.

Two other standouts, which have eateries in Bozeman as well, are **Mackenzie River Pizza** (409 W. Main St., 406/388-0016, www.mackenzieriverpizza.com, 11am-10pm daily, $7-19), known for their inventive pizzas, sandwiches, pasta, and salad, and **Bar 3 Bar-B-Q** (100 S. Broadway, 406/388-9182, www.bar3bbq.com, 11am-8pm Mon.-Fri., 9am-8pm Sat.-Sun., $11-18) which serves phenomenal barbecue and also brews their own beer on-site.

The **Fall Festival,** normally held the third weekend of September, brings out the crowds for a parade, a street dance, and a host of fun family activities. The **Festival of Lights,** the first Friday of December, is another highlight with a craft show and horse-drawn wagon rides. The **Belgrade Chamber of Commerce** (10 E. Main St., 406/388-1616, www.belgradechamber.org, 9am-5pm Mon.-Fri.) is a good source for local information and a friendly chat.

Manhattan

Twenty minutes west of Bozeman on I-90, Manhattan (population 1,691; elevation 4,245 ft/1,294 m) is a welcoming little community surrounded by potato and dairy farms, wheat fields, and mountains. The town was settled by immigrants from the Netherlands but named by New Yorkers who operated the Montana Malting Company. Most folks in the state associate Manhattan with its most famous eatery, **Sir Scott's Oasis** (204 W. Main St., 406/284-6929, 4:15pm-midnight Mon., 11am-midnight Tues.-Sun., from $21), an old-school supper club with relish trays to start and sundaes for dessert. The hearty steak and potatoes you get in between will satiate even the most discerning meat lovers.

During the summer, the **Manhattan Farmers Market** (406/641-0883, 4pm-7pm Wed.) fills the small downtown with local produce, baked goods, arts and crafts, and live entertainment. The third Saturday in August is the annual **Potato Festival,** which features a Friday night street dance, pancake breakfast, a parade, 5K and 10K races, cooking competitions, an invitational car show, and music throughout the day. In December, the whole town comes together for an old-fashioned **Christmas Stroll** featuring strolling carolers, horse-drawn hayrides, the lighting of the Christmas tree and fireworks. For visitor information, contact the **Manhattan Chamber of Commerce** (406/284-4162, www.manhattanareachamber.com, 11am-1pm, 9:30am-11:30am Fri.).

Three Forks and Willow Creek

Named for the three rivers that form the headwaters of the Missouri River, Three Forks (population 1,944; elevation 4,075 ft/1,242 m) was put on the map by Lewis and Clark in 1805. The town is rich in fur trapping and trading history and equally distinguished today by a tightly knit community and a mild climate that locals refer to as the "banana belt."

The **Three Forks Rodeo** is held annually the third weekend in July at the fairgrounds and includes a parade, two nights of rodeo, plenty of food, and entertainment. The town's **Christmas Stroll** is what every small town should aspire to: the crowning of a Christmas King and Queen, fireworks, horse-drawn wagon rides, a community cookie exchange, and s'mores around the bonfire.

A couple of great outings just beyond town include **Madison Buffalo Jump State Park** (6990 Buffalo Jump Rd., 7 mi/11.3 km south of Logan, 406/285-3610, www.stateparks.mt.gov, sunrise-sunset daily, $6/vehicle nonresidents) and **Missouri Headwaters State Park** (1585 Trident Rd., Three Forks, 406/285-3610, www.stateparks.mt.gov, dawn-dusk daily, $6/vehicle nonresidents), which offers hiking, biking, interpretive trails, camping, and river access for boating and fishing.

For a historical treat in Three Forks, the ★ **Sacajawea Hotel** (5 N. Main St., 406/285-6515, www.sacajaweahotel.com, $150-254) is one-of-a-kind. Lovingly restored in 2010 by the Folkvord family, local farmers who own the enormously successful Wheat Montana Bakeries, the Sac is a historic gem. There are 29 charming and comfortable rooms, some of which are pet-friendly, ranging from full beds to kings. The amenities are pretty plush and the food is sensational. Visit the Sac for a meal or just a cocktail, at **Pompey's Grill** (4:30pm-9pm Mon.-Thurs., 4:30pm-10pm Fri.-Sat., 4pm-9pm Sun., $18-46).

Six miles (9.7 km) south of Three Forks, the small community of Willow Creek (population 210; elevation 4,153 ft/1,266 m) has plenty of charm. The creek that runs through town was originally named Philosopher's River by William Clark, but the town wisely renamed it and the town for the willows that grow along the banks. The town's half-dozen artists organize the **Willow Creek Art Walks** the third Friday of each month June-August. A local gallery not to be missed is **Aunt Dofe's Hall of Recent Memory** (102 Main St., 406/285-6996, www.auntdofe.com, hours vary), which supports the work of contemporary local artists. Across the street, the **Willow Creek Café and Saloon** (21 N. Main St., 406/285-3698, noon-10pm Mon., 4am-10pm Tues.-Fri., 11am-10pm Sat.-Sun., $9.50-29) draws diners from far and wide for its quaint ambience and savory cuisine, including the best ribs in the valley, maybe the whole state. You can't go wrong with the daily specials—everything is made from scratch. And if you can time your dinner on a night when **Montana Rose** is playing, you're in for a real treat.

Ennis

In the heart of the Madison Valley, and in the thick of some of the state's best fly-fishing, is Ennis (population 890; elevation 4,941 ft/1,506 m), 45 miles (72 km) southwest of Bozeman on U.S. 287. The town hosts a wonderful **Fourth of July Rodeo and Parade** (for reserved-seat tickets, call 406/599-4705 after Memorial Day) each year at the fairgrounds. There is also an excellent weekly **Madison Farm to Fork Farmers Market** (First Interstate Bank, 118 W. Williams St., www.madisonfarmtofork.com, 5pm-7pm Fri. July-Sept.) and the much-touted **Ennis on the Madison Fly Fishing Festival** (406/682-3148, www.madisonriverfoundation.org), held annually over Labor Day weekend. A benefit for the Madison River Foundation, the three-day event offers plenty of art, food, music, fly-fishing instruction, and camaraderie.

The **fishing** is indeed the thing in these parts, and a number of good outfitters can lead you to gulpers on the Madison River and in Ennis Lake, Hebgen Lake, Quake Lake,

The historic Sacajawea Hotel recalls another era.

Cliff Lake, and Wade Lake. A good place to start is **The Tackle Shop** (127 Main St., 800/808-2832, www.thetackleshop.com, 7am-7pm daily), which touts itself as the oldest fly shop in Montana.

There is excellent **hiking** in every direction—the Tobacco Root Mountains and the Madison Range ring the town—and you'll find trail maps and helpful advice west of town at the local **USDA Forest Service Ranger Station** (5 Forest Service Rd., 406/682-4253).

For dining, Ennis offers a number of good choices including **Alley Bistro** (59 Hwy. 287, 406/682-5695, 4pm-9pm daily, $8-25), which dishes up everything from fish tacos to pot roast and veggie pizza. A great spot for diner-style breakfast or lunch right on the main drag is **Yesterday's Soda Fountain** (124 Main St., 406/682-4246, 6am-4pm daily Sept.-May, 6am-3pm daily June-Aug., $5-10), which is part restaurant, part pharmacy, part antiques store.

After filling your belly, the creek-side cabins south of town at **El Western** (4787 U.S. 287, 406/682-4217, www.elwestern.com, $129-489) are an excellent place to hang your hat for the night. It has everything from single rooms to lodges with four bedrooms.

For more information about Ennis, contact the **Ennis Chamber of Commerce** (201 E. Main St., 406/682-4388, www.ennischamber.com, 8am-4:30pm Mon.-Fri. fall-spring, 9am-6pm Mon.-Sat. summer hours).

Big Sky

In the shadow of Lone Peak, tucked in the winding and rugged beauty of Gallatin Canyon, the resort town of Big Sky (population 2,308; elevation 7,218 ft/2,200 m) actually has three resorts: Big Sky, Moonlight Basin, and the entirely private Yellowstone Club. Although there are not any sights per se, the town and resorts are clearly geographically blessed with mountains for skiing, hiking, climbing, and biking; rivers for fishing and floating; and trails aplenty for horses, hiking, cross-country skiing, and mountain biking. Visitors can take solace in the fact that mountains make up for museums, and the area can be used as a launching point for Yellowstone National Park (51 mi/82 km south) or Bozeman (50 mi/81 km north).

Although Big Sky has more activities than any visitor could dream of pursuing in a single trip—golf, horseback riding, fishing, skating, skiing, kayaking, wildlife-watching—it has a slight identity crisis in that there is no real center of town, which the community has been working hard to remedy with the 2009 completion of its own K-12 school (so that kids don't have to be bussed 50 winding mi/81 km to Bozeman) and the 2013 opening of the impressive 282-seat Warren Miller Performing Arts Center. Though the community is growing stronger by the year, Big Sky still feels a bit like a collection of enclaves, resorts, and villages dotting the mountainside. The uniting factor in this area is a zeal for outdoor adventuring.

SPORTS AND RECREATION
Skiing
One thing that distinguishes Big Sky from other ski destinations in the Rockies is the plentiful elbow room—there are fewer skiers per skiable acre than in most places. **Big Sky Resort** (snow phone 406/995-5900, reservations 800/548-4486, snowsports school 406/995-5743, www.bigskyresort.com, $139 adults; $119 children 11-17, college students with ID, and seniors 70 and over; $88 children 6-10; free for children 5 and under) calls itself a ski resort without limits. It has 5,800 skiable acres (2,347 hectares) and 4,350 vertical feet (1,326 m), and the area averages over 400 inches (1,016 cm) of the

fluffy stuff annually. The ski season generally lasts from Thanksgiving to mid-April. With virtually nonexistent lift lines (except during holidays), this is an ideal place for ambitious skiers and families.

The resort's **Lone Peak Tram** takes daring skiers 16 feet (4.9 m) shy of the mountain's summit and offers 300 degrees of skiing from the top of Lone Peak. Manicured terrain parks with many groomed features are available for snowboarders. Even with some of the steepest terrain in the country, Big Sky offers plenty of groomers for beginning and intermediate skiers and snowboarders.

In addition to the Mountain Sports School, which offers a wide range of ski and snowboard lessons and programs in winter, Big Sky Resort has the **Basecamp** (406/995-5769), an activity center offering two zipline courses, a high ropes course, a bungee trampoline, a climbing wall, and snowshoeing.

Down the mountain is **Lone Mountain Ranch** (750 Lone Mountain Rd., 406/995-4644 or 800/514-4644, www.lonemountainranch. com, $20 adults, $15 children 13-17 and seniors, free for children 12 and under and adults 70 and over), a cross-country skier's paradise with 85 kilometers of beautifully groomed and forested trails on 5,000 skiable acres (2,023 hectares) with 2,200 vertical feet (671 m). Snowshoeing is another option, as are guided naturalist tours, lessons, and clinics. Rental equipment (skis and snowshoes) and lessons are available, and with such magnificent terrain, this is one of the biggest bargains around. The trails are sublime, and wildlife-viewing can be excellent. For winter solitude and exploration, this is a marvelous place to be.

Fishing and Floating

The **Gallatin River** runs through the canyon beneath Big Sky and offers up a plethora of recreational opportunities. Since U.S. 191 runs parallel to the river for 40 miles (64 km), fishing access is easy. The road is not meant for casual driving—no stopping and looking here—but there are several pullouts that can double as parking lots. Float fishing is prohibited, but the wade fishing is enticing, if somewhat tricky given the number of rapids created as the water tumbles down the canyon over beautiful car-size boulders.

Rainbows, browns, and cutthroats can all be found in these chilly waters, and the fish have to be lean and mean to battle the currents. They tend to be slightly less selective than downriver in Bozeman, where the decline slows and the water flattens out. There

BIG SKY GATEWAY TO YELLOWSTONE

The Gallatin River runs between Big Sky and Bozeman and is known for great rafting.

are caddis hatches practically all summer, and a killer salmonfly hatch in mid-June to early July. Late in the season, whopping terrestrials are the way to go. **Wild Trout Outfitters** (U.S. 191, 0.5 mi/0.8 km south of the turnoff to Big Sky, 406/995-2975 or 800/423-4742, www. wildtroutoutftters.com, half-day Gallatin River wade trip $240 for 1 angler, $280 for 2 anglers, all-day Gallatin River wade trip $350 for 1 angler, $400 for 2 anglers) can offer professionally guided trips—wading or floating—including into Yellowstone National Park. **East Slope Outdoors** (44 Town Center Ave., 406/995-4369 or 888/359-3974, www. eastslopeoutdoors.com, 8am-8pm daily, half-day Gallatin River wade trip $250 for 1 angler, $290 for 2 anglers, all-day Gallatin River wade trip $350 for 1 angler, $400 for 2 anglers) offers equipment, rental gear, and guided fly-fishing trips.

If the tranquility of fishing appeals less than the mayhem of white water, rafting on the Gallatin River is a good option. **Montana Whitewater** (63960 Gallatin Rd., 800/799-4465, www.montanawhitewater.com, half-day $61 adults, $50 children 6-12, full-day $98 adults, $78 children 6-12) offers a range of trips to suit any adrenaline level, including half-day scenic floats, full-day white-water trips, and paddle-and-saddle overnighters. Plus, from the Gallatin Canyon base camp—which is like a small outdoors-loving city—you can mix and match adventures including rafting, ziplining, fly-fishing, and horseback riding. Its on-site café, **Blazin' Paddles Café,** is a convenient food truck. **Geyser Whitewater** (46651 Gallatin Rd., next to Buck's T-4 on U.S. 191, 406/995-4989, www. raftmontana.com, half-day $68 adults, $58 children 12 and under, full-day $109 adults, $89 children 12 and under, minimum age restrictions vary with water conditions) is another superb local outfitter that specializes in Gallatin River trips. It also offers kayak trips, horseback riding, bike rentals, rock climbing, and ziplining adventures.

Hiking and Mountain Biking

In the summer, the mountain at Big Sky unfolds into a network of mountain bike and hiking trails. The **Big Sky Scenic Lift** (406/995-5769, $26 adults, $18 children 13-17 and seniors, free for children 12 and under) gives riders and hikers a lift up (and down, if they choose) and a chance to tackle some thrilling terrain for every skill level. Bikes and helmets are available for rent at **Big Sky Sports** (Mountain Mall, 50 Big Sky Resort Rd., 406/995-5840, www.bigskyresort.com).

The hiking opportunities are endless around Big Sky, with three mountain ranges, the Gallatin National Forest, the Lee Metcalf Wilderness Area, and Yellowstone National Park all nearby. Some local favorites include **Ousel Falls,** an easy up-and-down 1.8-mile (2.9-km) stroll to a beautiful waterfall. (Find the parking lot and trailhead on Ousel Falls Rd., 2 mi/3.2 km beyond the intersection of Ousel Falls Rd. and Spur Rd.) Picnic benches along the way make the path a good one for small children. For more ambitious hikers, **Beehive Basin** offers some excellent options. (Find the parking lot and trailhead by following the Beehive Basin turnoff—1.3 mi/2.1 km beyond Big Sky Mountain Village and 30 yards (27.4 m) before the entrance gate to Moonlight Basin—for 2.8 mi/4.5 km.) The trail is sky high at 9,200 feet (2,804 m) and offers unrivaled 360-degree views. As with all of Montana, the weather can change quickly—snow can fall in July—and hikers need to be fully prepared for whatever Mother Nature sends their way. Farther north in the Gallatin Canyon is **Lava Lake,** a somewhat steep hike that leads you to a crystalline icy-cold mountain lake. (From Big Sky, the trailhead is 13.5 mi/21.7 km north on U.S. 191, just north of the Gallatin River Bridge, but since left turns cannot be made from there, you will need to turn around at the first turnout and approach the gravel turnoff from the north.) The 6-mile (9.7-km) there-and-back trail is almost entirely shaded and an excellent choice on a sweltering day.

Golf

For those who choose to hoof it around the links instead of a mountain trail, the 18-hole Arnold Palmer-designed **Big Sky Golf Course** (Meadow Village, 406/995-5780, www.bigskyresort.com, $79-159, $49 twilight play after 3pm) is open to nonguests and is well worth playing. There is abundant wildlife often sharing the par-72 course. A driving range, bar and grill, and full pro shop are available.

ENTERTAINMENT AND EVENTS

Although it is set up as a winter resort, Big Sky does an excellent job of capitalizing on the relatively short summer with events that draw crowds from near and far. There are few better venues in the state for live music: Concerts are held in a glorious meadow surrounded by rocky peaks at the free **Music in the Mountains** series (changing venues, 406/995-2742, www.bigskyarts.org, June-Sept.). Past headliners in Big Sky have included Willie Nelson, Bonnie Raitt, and the Doobie Brothers. Other annual musical events sponsored by the Arts Council of Big Sky include **Strings under the Big Sky** (chamber music) and the **Bozeman Symphony Orchestra Pops** concert.

The weekly **Big Sky Farmers Market** (Firepit Park, Big Sky Town Center, 406/480-6579, www.bigskytowncenter.com, 5pm-8pm Wed. June-Sept.) features lots of local vendors in addition to prepared food, a great kids' area, musical entertainment, and personal enrichment that includes yoga and massage.

FOOD

Something about the high mountain air produces serious appetites, and Big Sky has a substantial selection of eateries for every taste. From the top of the mountain to the bottom, you're never more than a quick jog from your next mouthwatering meal.

The Corral (42895 Gallatin Rd., 5 mi/8 km south of Big Sky, 406/995-4249, www.corralbar.com, 8am-10pm daily, bar until 2am

daily, $17-38) offers up an excellent take on the classic Montana menu. From buffalo T-bones to Delmonico steaks, prime rib, and good ol' hamburgers, The Corral's food is consistently good, with plenty of chicken, seafood, and pasta options available. You can't go wrong with the smoked trout appetizer.

For great barbecue with a view, the **Gallatin Riverhouse Grill** (45130 Gallatin Rd., 406/995-7427, www.gallatinriverhousegrill.com, 3pm-close daily, $8-26) is known for its excellent smoked barbecue. From their fried pickles, okra, and sweet corn nuggets to beef brisket, baby back ribs, and pulled pork, owners Kyle and Greg don't let anyone leave hungry. As if the sound of the rushing Gallatin weren't enough, this wonderful riverfront venue hosts plenty of live music.

For an elegant meal, **Olive B's Big Sky Bistro** (151 Center Ln., 406/995-3355, www.olivebsbigsky.com, 11am-9pm Mon.-Fri., 4pm-9pm Sat., $25-37) is a great choice. Owned by a couple from the East Coast, the restaurant offers an abundance of good seafood including lobster mac 'n' cheese, ahi, and shrimp and grits. But the spot also serves up the best of the West: Rocky Mountain elk with huckleberry demi-glace, pheasant, and beef tenderloin.

Blue Moon Bakery (3090 Big Pine Dr., 406/995-2305, www.bigskybluemoonbakery.com, 7am-10pm daily, $5-10) is a good bet for everything from breakfast sandwiches and baked goods to salads and gourmet pizza pies. Another good spot for breakfast or lunch is **Bugaboo Café** (47995 Gallatin Rd., Ste. 101, 406/995-3350, 7:30am-2:30pm Wed.-Mon., $8-12), an unassuming little place featuring comfort food with an inventive twist. The menu changes seasonally to take advantage of local products and includes such favorites as blue crab omelets and chicken potpie. The Bugaboo is probably the best value in Big Sky.

★ **Buck's T-4** (46625 Gallatin Rd., 1 mi/1.6 km south of Big Sky, 800/822-4484, www.buckst4.com, 5:30pm-9:30pm daily summer, 6pm-9pm daily winter, $14-40) is fairly unassuming but serves up some of the best cuisine in the region. Known statewide and beyond for wild game—think duck, pheasant, bison, and red deer—Buck's menu reflects Montana culinary traditions with more contemporary, lighter fare. It even packages up duck bacon for diners to take home. Buck's has an extensive and impressive wine list, and its drinks make the most of the local harvest; try a wild huckleberry martini or bacon bourbon old-fashioned. Buck's keeps limited hours in the fall and spring, between ski season and summer.

For a truly unique meal during the ski season, try the sleigh-ride dinner at ★ **Lone Mountain Ranch** (750 Lone Mountain Rd., 406/995-4644 or 800/514-4644, www.lonemountainranch.com, $145-185 pp), which whisks diners up a snowy trail to a candlelit cabin in the woods for a steak and potato dinner. Or try **dinner in a yurt** (via snowcat instead of horse-pulled sleigh) high atop Lone Mountain (406/995-3880, www.bigskyyurt.com, $114 adults, $99 children), which also includes time for sledding. Both experiences offer hearty meals and unparalleled ambience, and both sell out well in advance—so book ahead.

ACCOMMODATIONS

Big Sky was built as a resort, and it caters to visitors and vacationers. There is a wide range of accommodations, from ski-in/ski-out mountainside lodging to rustic roadside motels, inviting guest ranches, luxe resorts, and condo or cabin rentals, that can address your specific needs—staying put or traveling around, skiing or golfing, walking or driving to dinner.

For the best bang for your buck, try the **Corral Motel** (42895 Gallatin Road, 5 mi/8 km south of Big Sky, 406/995-4249 or 888/995-4249, www.corralbar.com, from $100 single, $20 each additional person), which also has a terrific restaurant and bar open year-round. The guest rooms are basic but clean and comfortable, with honeyed pine paneling that evokes the best of Western hospitality.

During the winter, a shuttle runs from the motel to Big Sky Resort and Meadow Village.

Closer to Big Sky is **Buck's T-4 Lodge** (46625 Gallatin Rd., 1 mi/1.6 km south of Big Sky, 800/822-4484, www.buckst4.com, $169-319), a very comfortable hotel with newly remodeled rooms, a great bar, and one of the best restaurants in the region. The roadside location leaves something to be desired in ambience and views, but it is convenient.

On top of the mountain is the **Summit at Big Sky** (Mountain Village Center, 800/548-4486, www.bigskyresort.com, studio rooms from $293), a deluxe slopeside facility with the convenience of a hotel and the amenities of a condo. It offers both residences and temporary lodging, all in a comfortable and sophisticated atmosphere. There are indoor and outdoor pools, hot tubs, a sauna and fitness facility, and fireplaces in most accommodations. Lodging packages can include lift tickets. **Big Sky Resort** (800/548-4486) can arrange a variety of lodging from slopeside rooms and condos to ski-in/ski-out cabins and homes for rent.

INFORMATION AND SERVICES

The **Big Sky Chamber of Commerce** (55 Lone Mountain Trail, 406/995-3000 or 800/943-4111, www.bigskychamber.com, 8:30am-5:30pm daily summer, 8:30am-5:30pm Mon.-Fri. fall-spring) is an excellent resource for local information.

The **post office** (800/275-8777, 10am-5pm Mon.-Fri., 10am-1pm Sat.) is conveniently located at 55 Meadow Center Drive, Suite 2.

Your best bet for free **Internet access** is at the **Big Sky Community Library** (45465 Gallatin Rd., 406/995-4281). The library sets aside hours for community use (1pm-5pm Sun., 10am-6pm Mon., 4pm-8pm Tues.-Wed.).

The **Mountain Clinic of Big Sky** is in the ski patrol building at Big Sky Resort (100 Beaverhead Trail, 406/995-2797, 9am-5pm Mon.-Fri.). For more serious medical emergencies, **Bozeman Deaconess Hospital** (915 Highland Blvd., 406/585-5000, www.

bozemandeaconess.org) has a 24-hour emergency room about an hour's drive from Big Sky.

To wash your clothes and have a few drinks while you wait, **Sit & Spin Laundry Lounge** (115 Aspen Leaf Dr., 1F, 406/600-8416, 11am-2am Wed.-Sun.) is the place. They have great bloody Marys, fresh-squeezed juices, and house specialty shots that look like Tide pods. They also serve specialty coffees.

TRANSPORTATION

Getting There

Big Sky is about 50 miles (81 km) south of Bozeman off U.S. 191. The closest airport is **Bozeman Yellowstone International Airport** (BZN, 406/388-8321, www.bozemanairport.com) in Belgrade, about 50 miles (81 km) north.

A variety of shuttle services run from the airport. **Karst Stage** (406/556-3540 or 800/845-2778, www.karststage.com) has a counter next to National Rent-a-Car and provides shuttles ($54 one-way with two-fare minimum, $82 round-trip) to Big Sky. **Shuttle to Big Sky & Taxi** (406/995-4895 or 888/454-5667, www.bigskytaxi.com) offers shuttles from the airport ($82 for two people). Another luxury shuttle service is **Big Sky Shuttle** (406/624-3332, www.bigskyshuttle.net).

Getting Around

Once in Big Sky, take advantage of the free bus service, **Skyline** (406/995-6287, www.skylinebus.com). In addition to covering the Big Sky area, buses also run between Bozeman and Big Sky. Hours vary by season.

Shuttle to Big Sky & Taxi (406/995-4895 or 888/454-5667, www.bigskytaxi.com) offers taxi service around Big Sky.

Dollar Rent-a-Car (1 mi/1.6 km from the airport, Belgrade) will deliver a vehicle to any Big Sky location.

Livingston and Paradise Valley

Rough and tumble Livingston (population 7,401; elevation 4,501 ft/1,372 m) has always been a crossroads of cultures. A railroad town, it was long the launching point for expeditions—both professional and leisurely—into Yellowstone National Park. Paradise Valley, the stunning agricultural and recreational corridor linking Livingston to the north entrance of Yellowstone National Park, was the stomping ground of the Crow, a prized region for fur trappers, and the end point of the great cattle drive from Texas. The town was surrounded by mines, which drew a unique crowd, and today it probably has more literary figures and artists per capita than any other community in the state.

At one point in the early 1880s, there were 40 businesses in town, 30 of which were saloons. Such legendary characters as Calamity Jane and Madame Bulldog were residents. Evidence of those wild days is still visible in various establishments—for example, as bullet holes through the ceiling. The town still has a healthy number of bars, but in a nod to foodies, there are now an equal number of excellent restaurants.

Livingston's transformation into a haven for legendary artists, writers, and actors probably started in the 1960s. Iconic film director Sam Peckinpah took up residence in the town's Murray Hotel, and writers Tom McGuane, Doug Peacock, Tim Cahill, and Richard Brautigan all called Livingston home—and some still do. Actors including Peter Fonda, Jeff Bridges, Michael Keaton, and Dennis Quaid have ranches outside town.

Indeed, Livingston has a rich blended culture that is evident in everything from its sophisticated galleries and gourmet restaurants to its bawdy bars, rollicking rodeo, and fly-fishing paradise.

SIGHTS

The town's **Depot Center** (200 W. Park St., 406/222-2300, www.livingstonmuseums. org, 10am-5pm Mon.-Sat., 1pm-5pm Sun. Memorial Day-Labor Day, donation) is a majestic building anchoring the town to its railroad heritage. In addition to being something of a community center where the town gathers for concerts and special events, the depot houses a worthwhile museum featuring history, art, and culture of the region. Electric-train buffs should ask for a tour of the basement, where the region's train fanatics have built a wonderland.

On the other side of the tracks, the **Yellowstone Gateway Museum** (118 W. Chinook St., 406/222-4184, www. yellowstonegatewaymuseum.org, 10am-5pm daily Memorial Day-Sept., 10am-5pm Thurs.-Sat. Oct.-Memorial Day, $5 adults, $4 seniors 55 and over, free for children 18 and under), housed in a historic schoolhouse, holds the county's archives and presents

some excellent local exhibits on railroad history, pioneer life, Native American cultures, and military history.

SPORTS AND RECREATION

Fishing and Floating

If art defines Livingston, fishing feeds it. The **Yellowstone River** curves around the town and always makes its presence known. Paradise Valley lives up to its name in countless ways, fishing among them. **Nelson's, Armstrong's,** and **De Puy's Spring Creeks** are just minutes from town and offer some of the best and most consistent fishing in the state. Winter is an especially good time to fish the spring creeks because the springs flow constantly at a consistent temperature, the crowds are gone, and the rod fees go down significantly. Matson Rogers's **Angler's West Flyfishing** (206 Railroad Ln., off U.S. 89 S., Emigrant, 406/333-4401, www. montanaflyfishers.com), 7am-7pm daily summer, 8am-6pm daily spring and fall) is a great resource, with both a fly shop and complete guiding service for the Yellowstone River and waters around the state. In Livingston, **Dan Bailey's Fly Shop** (209 W. Park St., 406/222-1673, www.dan-bailey.com, 8am-6pm

Livingston is a railroad town, an art mecca, and an angler's paradise.

Mon.-Sat., 8am-noon Sun. summer, 8am-6pm Mon.-Sat. winter) is as venerable a fly shop as ever there was, anywhere. In addition to a living history lesson—the shop was established in 1938—the staff at Dan Bailey's can offer superbly qualified advice along with renowned gear and world-famous flies.

To cover a lot of water in this country, with or without a rod, floating on a raft or drift boat can be a great option. While just about any outfitter can arrange to float and fish, **Flying Pig Adventure Company** (888/792-9193, www.flyingpigrafting.com, half-day trips $43 adults, $33 children 12 and under, full-day trips $90 adults, $69 children) and **Montana Whitewater** (603 Scott St., Gardiner, 800/799-4465, www. montanawhitewater.com, half-day $43 adults, $32 children 12 and under, full-day $82 adults, $62 children) both offer scenic and white-water floats on the Yellowstone River. In addition to its standard menu of day trips, Flying Pig also offers half-day, all-day, and three-day "Paddle and Saddle" trips.

Hiking

With mountains towering in every direction—the Absarokas and the Gallatins south of town, the Bridgers to the west, and the Crazies to the northeast—and a stiff wind usually blowing, heading out for a hike is never a bad idea in Livingston. Six miles (9.7 km) south of town on the east side of River Road in Paradise Valley, **Pine Creek** is a stunning and popular spot with camping (spots fill up early) and hiking options for every ability level. A nice leisurely amble is the 2-mile (3.2-km) out-and-back trail to **Pine Creek Falls.** Hard-core hikers could hike the steep but mostly shaded 10 miles (16.1 km) to **Pine Creek Lake. Suce Creek, Deep Creek,** and **Mill Creek** all have first-rate trails and stunning scenery, but be aware of bears in the region. For gear or just good ideas, talk to Dale at **Timber Trails** (309 W. Park St., 406/222-9550, noon-6pm Tues., 9am-6pm Wed.-Mon.), on the main thoroughfare into downtown Livingston. His wonderful little gem of a store also rents mountain bikes.

ENTERTAINMENT AND EVENTS
The Arts

One of the area's best-kept secrets is **Music Ranch Montana** (4664 Old Yellowstone Trail N., 9 mi/14.5 km south of Livingston, 406/222-2255, www.musicranchmontana. net), a unique music venue for indoor/outdoor

the Yellowstone River

Cranky Yankee Jim's Road

James George, who earned the moniker Yankee Jim as well as a reputation for being more than a little cantankerous, came to Montana Territory as a young prospector in 1863. When gold eluded him, Jim began to hunt professionally, for meat for the Crow Indian Agency. In 1873, Jim took possession of the road from Bottler's Ranch in Paradise Valley, near present-day Emigrant, to Mammoth by squatting in the canyon along the Yellowstone when the road builders stopped construction. Jim set up a toll booth in the narrowest section of the canyon, today called Yankee Jim Canyon, and charged exorbitant fees to all travelers passing through. At the time, it was the only way for travelers to get from Livingston to Gardiner, Montana, and the brand-new Yellowstone National Park. By all accounts, Yankee Jim made a lot of money but few friends in those days.

In 1883, the Northern Pacific Railway appropriated his roadbed, much to Yankee Jim's chagrin. He negotiated the construction of another road through the canyon (parts of which are still visible along the west side of U.S. 89 South) and used his location above the train tracks reportedly to spit on, curse at, and occasionally fire rifle shots at passing trains. His tirades were supposedly fueled by copious amounts of whiskey.

By 1893, with his road in disrepair and his penchant for alcohol steadily on the rise, Yankee Jim agreed to surrender his road for a lump sum of $1,000. Local lore inserts Teddy Roosevelt, a frequent visitor to Yellowstone National Park, as the person who convinced Yankee Jim to give up his road and his antics (or else). In 1924, Yankee Jim died penniless in Fresno, California. There are many who believe that his fortune, amassed by all those years of price-gouging in the canyon that bears his name, is buried in the hills between Emigrant and Gardiner.

concerts in summer. Founded by a well-known entrepreneur and his wife in 1995, Music Ranch has a large barn with both indoor and outdoor seating, including terraces built into the hillside. Talk about an amphitheater with a view! The ticket prices for the concerts, largely country and folk musicians, are reasonable, and a dance floor right next to the stage keeps the energy up for each concert. Family-owned and operated in the best possible way, attending a concert at Music Ranch feels like a festive family reunion.

ART GALLERIES

Livingston is a railroad town, but to its core it is also an artists' town. There are over a dozen galleries and many more artists, both brilliant amateurs and sophisticated professionals.

The **Livingston Art Museum** (106 N. Main St., 406/222-6510, www.livingstonartmuseum.org, 11am-5pm Tues.-Fri., noon-5pm Sat., extended summer hours) is the town's oldest gallery. The well-respected gallery focuses on contemporary art with constantly changing exhibitions, and it even promotes school-age child artists through some inspired installations.

Local character and talented artist Parks Reece captures the beauty of the region with a delightful and often mischievous sense of humor. The **Parks Reece Gallery** (119 S. Main St., Ste. A3, 406/222-5724, www.parksreece.com, 9am-5pm Tues.-Fri., 4pm Sat.) should not be missed.

Festivals and Events

Since 1924, the annual **Livingston Roundup Rodeo** (406/222-3199, www.livingstonroundup.com) has enticed cowboys from across the country with its fat purse on the Fourth of July holiday. As crowds overtake the town's fairgrounds with rabid rodeo fever, regular events include barrel racing, bareback team roping, tie-down roping, saddle bronc, steer wrestling, and bull riding. The three-day event—held July 2-4—kicks off with a hometown parade and ends each evening with fireworks. This is without a doubt when Livingston most shines. General admission and reserved seating rodeo tickets are available online or by calling, but both sell out well before July.

In a town as food-savvy as Livingston, it's no surprise that there are a handful of great events to sample the local offerings. The wonderful community-centered **Livingston Farmers Market** (at the band shell in Sacajawea Park, River Dr., 406/222-0730, 4:30pm-7:30pm Wed. early June-mid-Sept.) offers up the region's fresh local bounty in a friendly and festive environment. Live music is performed until 9pm. Sponsored by the Western Sustainability Exchange (www.northrock.org), the event supports a Young Entrepreneur Leadership Program that teaches kids about the intricacies of business and the value of giving back to the community, and a Senior Farmers Market Nutrition Program provides local low-income seniors with $50 vouchers for locally grown veggies, herbs, fruit, and honey at the market.

If you want a fantastic overview of the art scene, and consequently the entire community, hit the town **art walks,** held the fourth Friday of every month late June-September; there is also a single holiday art walk each year in November-December. The town comes out in force to celebrate the arts.

SHOPPING

Downtown Livingston is a wonderful place to shop, with stores all within walking distance of one another offering a convenient escape from the town's ever-present wind along with an eclectic assortment of wares, from art and clothes to books and equipment. Most shops are closed on Sunday.

Sax & Fryer (109 W. Callender St., 406/222-1421, 9am-5pm Mon.-Fri.) is an anchor for the town and a direct link to its origins. Founded in 1883, the year after Livingston was incorporated, and still run by the Fryer family, the store offers a meaty selection of books from regional and local authors as well as magazines, cards, gifts, and office supplies. An excellent section is devoted to children's books.

B-Hive Artisan Cooperative (113 W.

Park St., 406/222-5996, 10am-5pm Mon.-Sat.) is a hip little boutique that is artist-owned and staffed. The collection blends various media—jewelry, yard art, ceramics, hand-blown glass, handbags, and bronze sculpture—perfect for those who don't necessarily want their gifts detailed with rusty nails or old barbed-wire.

The Obsidian Collection (108 N. Second St., 406/222-2022, www.theobsidiancollection.com, 10am-6pm Mon.-Sat.) offers an appealing selection of gifts, children's items, jewelry, cards, stationery, soaps, and lotions. Customers are loyal, often driving significant distances to see the latest and greatest collections.

FOOD

If the pools bring people to ★ **Chico Hot Springs Resort** (163 Chico Rd., off U.S. 89 S., 23 mi/37 km south of Livingston, 406/333-4933, www.chicohotsprings.com, $28-50), the food is what transforms them into regulars. From the first taste of baked brie en croûte with Montana huckleberry coulis, through the house-smoked rainbow trout and the gorgonzola filet mignon to the legendary flaming orange, Chico has gone a long way in defining Montana cuisine with fresh local ingredients in simple, hearty, and outstanding dishes. The Chico cookbook, available at the resort, should be in every kitchen.

Closer to town but still set in the grandeur of Paradise Valley, the ★ **Pine Creek Lodge & Café** (2496 E. River Rd., 10 mi/16.1 km south of Livingston, 406/222-3628, www.pinecreeklodgemontana.com, 4pm-9pm Mon.-Fri., 10am-9pm Sat.-Sun., $9-24), is a longtime favorite and an off-the-beaten-path gem. The menu changes frequently but boasts such fare as pasta with elk sausage and rainbow trout tacos you won't soon forget. Live music and outdoor barbecues take place in summer, and readings by local authors in winter. The place was nearly burned down in a big 2012 forest fire, but this little enclave continues to be a wonderful part of the community. Call for reservations.

Not gourmet by any stretch of the

imagination, **Mark's In & Out Drive-In** (801 W. Park St., Livingston, 406/222-7744, 11am-10pm daily late spring-early fall, $2-5) just might be the town favorite. There is no seating at this seasonal walk-up or drive-up joint right out of the 1950s, but the burgers, fries, and shakes are so good that you won't mind.

Housed in the venerable Murray Hotel, **2nd Street Bistro** (123 N. 2nd St., 406/222-9463, www.secondstreetbistro.com, 5pm-close Wed.-Sun., $16-38) serves simple but inspired cuisine—both small and large plates—with French flair and Western attitude. The Mediterranean fish stew is a local favorite, as are the upscale pizzas. All of the meat served is raised locally, as is much of the produce. On Friday and Saturday nights, Montana prime rib is served all night.

An excellent regional chain is the **Rib & Chop House** (305 E. Park St., 406/222-9200, www.ribandchophouse.com, 11am-9:30pm Mon.-Thurs., 11am-10pm Fri.-Sat., 4pm-9:30pm Sun., $15-45), which serves excellent steak, seafood, and, obviously, ribs. It's a popular spot (in all of its six Montana and Wyoming locations, plus Pennsylvania and Utah), so reservations are strongly recommended.

Every Western town worth its salt should have a **Stockman** (118 N. Main St., 406/222-8455, 11am-2pm and 5pm-9pm Mon.-Thurs., 11am-2pm and 5pm-10pm Fri.-Sat., $9-29). It is an old-school bar with the essence of a supper club. The steaks, prime rib, and burgers are second to none; this is the real Montana.

ACCOMMODATIONS

It's true that Livingston has quite a collection of funky roadside motels that have seen better days, but there are some treasures around town and down the valley. Right in town, the **Murray Hotel** (201 W. Park St., 406/222-1350, www.murrayhotel.com, from $229, pets welcome for $25) is a Montana standard. It hasn't been glamorously overhauled, but the authenticity works well, and the place is rich with history, including the story of Will Rogers and Walter Hill trying to bring a saddle horse to the 3rd floor in a 1905 hand-cranked elevator. Guest rooms are well appointed, with elegant details.

Nestled between town and Paradise Valley is the **Blue Winged Olive Angler's Rest** (5157 U.S. 89 S., 3 mi/4.8 km south of Livingston, 406/222-8646, Apr.-Oct., $110 s, $150 d, 3-night minimum), a cute vacation rental geared to anglers (you can hang your waders on the deck to dry). The owners also have a fully outfitted year-round vacation rental cabin ($1,250/week), which can sleep up to four, along Mill Creek, not far from the Yellowstone River. Either place offers a quiet, comfortable respite for hard-core anglers.

For travelers who long to stay in one place and experience life as a dude, **Mountain Sky Guest Ranch** (480 National Forest Development Rd. 132, Emigrant, 406/333-4911, www.mountainsky.com, all rates weekly Sun.-Sun., $4,430-5,860 adults, $3,790-4,790 children 7-12, $2,950-3,510 children 6 and under) sets the gold standard for summertime family ranch vacations. Set on 10,000 acres (4,047 hectares) of mountains and forests, Mountain Sky offers impeccable service, gourmet dining, charming log cabins, and fantastic activity possibilities, including golf on a Johnny Miller course, a high-energy kids' program, endless alpine trails for horseback riding and hiking, swimming, and even a spa. With such superlative options for balancing family time and adult relaxation, it's small surprise that 87 percent of the guests return year after year, and that entire summers are often booked more than a year in advance.

★ Chico Hot Springs Resort

Built around a natural hot spring that was discovered in the late 1800s, the **Chico Hot Springs Resort** (163 Chico Rd., 23 miles (37 km) south of Livingston in Pray, 406/333-4933, www.chicohotsprings.com) has become a Montana icon, as much for its sensational food and raucous saloon as for its heavenly year-round outdoor pools. The resort got its start when Bill and Percie Knowles offered weary miners a clean bed, a hot bath, and fresh strawberries with every meal. The resort has stayed true to its humble origins by offering simple, no-frills guest rooms with shared baths in the main lodge starting at $73-110. Modern accommodations are available in Warren's Wing (from $155), the Lower Lodge (from $155), and in elegant cabins ($245) or pet-friendly rustic cabins ($125-135). Cottages, houses, and chalets (from $260-525) can accommodate larger parties.

For travelers in search of more than a memorable meal and a luxurious soak, Chico offers a number of activities, all of which take advantage of its spectacular location just north of Yellowstone National Park in Paradise Valley. From horseback riding and dogsledding to hiking and cross-country skiing, Chico affords every visitor ample opportunity to earn their dinner.

INFORMATION AND SERVICES

The **Livingston Chamber of Commerce** (303 E. Park St., 406/222-0850, www.livingston-chamber.com, 9am-5pm Mon.-Fri., 9am-1pm Sat.-Sun. Memorial Day-Labor Day, closed weekends Labor Day-Memorial Day) is housed in the former crew quarters of the Burlington Northern Railroad. It offers a wide assortment of information about summer and winter activities, including a brochure titled "What to Do in Livingston." Stop by to meet the friendly people and pick up information on restaurants, accommodations, fishing, dude ranches, and more. A computer is available for visitors to check their email or browse the internet.

The **Livingston-Park County Public Library** (228 W. Callender St., 406/222-0862, www.livingstonparkcountylibrary.blogspot.com, noon-8pm Mon.-Tues., 10am-8pm Wed.-Thurs., 10am-6pm Fri., 10am-5pm Sat.) offers cozy spaces to work or browse through your guidebook. It has a terrific collection of fly-fishing material and even offers a genealogy service for visitors in the summer. It also has **free Internet access.** Computers are available for up to an hour at a time.

Internet access can also be found at the chamber of commerce and the internet café **Chadz** (104 N. Main St., 406/222-2247, 6:30am-2:30pm daily).

The **main post office** (406/222-0912, 8:30am-5pm Mon.-Fri., 10:30am-12:30pm Sat.) is at 105 North 2nd Street.

Livingston HealthCare (320 Alpenglow Ln., 406/222-3541) has a 24-hour emergency room. For nonemergency medical

Chico Hot Springs Resort, just north of Yellowstone, is a classic Montana lodge.

care, visit **Urgent Care** (104 Centennial Dr., 406/222-0030, 8am-7pm Mon.-Fri., 8am-4pm Sat.-Sun.).

Wash clothes at **Off the Cuff** (322 E. Park St., 406/222-7428, 24 hours daily). It has coin-operated washers and dryers, laundry drop-off service, dry cleaning, and free Wi-Fi.

TRANSPORTATION
Getting There
Livingston is 116 miles (187 km) from the **Billings Logan International Airport** (BIL, 406/247-8609, www.flybillings.com) and 38 miles (61 km) from **Bozeman Yellowstone International Airport** (BZN, 406/388-8321, www.bozemanairport.com).

From Bozeman, **Greater Valley Taxi** (406/587-6303, www.greatervalleytaxi.com)

has a stand outside the baggage claim area, and rides to Livingston are around $130 for a single passenger. Livingston's lone taxi service, **Amazing Taxi** (406/223-5344, 7am-11pm daily), also offers taxi service within 125 miles (201 km) of Livingston.

From the Billings airport, **Phidippides Shuttle Service** (307/527-6789, www.codyshuttle.com) will transport you to Livingston (call for rates).

Getting Around
Both airports have car-rental companies on-site. At Bozeman's airport, **Alamo, Avis, Budget, Enterprise, Dollar, Hertz, Thrifty,** and **National** have on-site counters. At Billing's airport, **Enterprise, Thrifty, Dollar, Hertz, National, Alamo, Avis,** and **Budget** all have a presence.

Livingston to Red Lodge

This stretch of highway is a smooth ribbon between dramatic mountains ranges—the Absarokas, the Crazies, and the behemoth Beartooths. The views stretch for miles in every direction, and although many of the scarce exits off I-90 lead to nothing more than a jumble of ranch buildings, there are some wonderful old towns that appear every now and then. **Big Timber,** still heavily populated by Norwegian immigrants, is a mining town with a railroad history and a grand old hotel. Tiny **Reed Point** is an agricultural town with big attitude. **Columbus** and **Roscoe,** barely dots on the map, offer, respectively, a well-known watering hole, the New Atlas Bar, and a great restaurant, the Grizzly Bar & Grill.

MCLEOD AND THE BOULDER VALLEY
Just east of Livingston is **Swingley Road** (from Livingston, head southeast from E. Park St. before you get to the easternmost entrance to I-90)—as far as this writer is concerned, it

is the portal to paradise. The road meanders through age-old farmsteads and stunning ranches, with the Boulder River carving the valley deeper into jagged peaks. The trail at **West Boulder,** which starts from the campground, offers a scenic but moderately easy 6-mile (9.7-km) round-trip hike through forest and meadow to **Boulder Meadows,** a tranquil spot with the occasional cow that is perfect for wetting a line or setting up camp. You could continue another 5 miles (8 km) to the junction of **Falls Creek Trail,** or farther into the **Mill Creek drainage** of Paradise Valley, but the meadows are a hard place to leave. Right near the trailhead is **West Boulder Cabin** (406/222-1892 for last-minute booking, www.recreation.gov for advance reservations, $35), maintained by the U.S. Forest Service. The three-bedroom, no-bath cabin is supremely rustic (it does have electricity, a refrigerator, and cook stove, but no cell service), complete with mice-eaten mattresses, but there is no better place to wake up if early morning hiking is your thing.

Reservations are required and can be made up to six months in advance.

If you can manage to drag yourself out of West Boulder, head northeast on Highway 295 to McLeod and the renowned **Holly's Road Kill Saloon** (1557 Main Boulder Rd., 406/932-6174, noon-8pm Thurs.-Mon., $11-30). It serves everything from thick, hand-cut steaks and barbecued chicken dinners to enormous hoagies and juicy Philly cheesesteaks. In addition to the food, it's the people and the atmosphere (and the name!) that make it worth stopping.

From Big Timber, McLeod is 16 miles (26 km) south on Highway 298.

BIG TIMBER

Not only is it perfectly situated for a roadway coffee break between Bozeman and Billings, but Big Timber (population 1,645; elevation 4,091 ft/1,247 m) is also an interesting little town and a worthwhile stop, with some nice galleries, a good shop or two, a great museum, and a beautiful old railroad hotel that anchors the community. An old-school agricultural community with strong mining and railroad ties, it is flat as a pancake but surrounded on either side by dramatic mountains and encircled by the Boulder and Yellowstone Rivers. Oh, and trees—thus the name.

Right off the highway is the **Crazy Mountain Museum** (2 S. Frontage Rd., southeast of I-90 exit 367, 406/932-5126, www.crazymountainmuseum.com, 10am-4:30pm Mon.-Sat., 1pm-4:30pm Sun. Memorial Day-Sept. 30, donations appreciated), a thoughtfully laid-out collection that pays tribute to the town's Norwegian heritage. Several old buildings are on-site, including the Sourdough Schoolhouse and a Norwegian *stabbur*. There's a diorama of Big Timber in 1907, a Chinese archaeological exhibit, a gun collection, and an exhibit on the local sheep industry, among other permanent exhibits, and also plenty of rotating exhibits. The staff of volunteer docents bring the collection to life with wonderful stories and often personal reflections.

In the heart of town is **The Grand Hotel Bed & Breakfast** (139 McLeod St., 406/932-4459, www.thegrand-hotel.com, $73-175), a stately Victorian-style railroad hotel. The guest rooms are traditional and fairly small with period antiques and private or shared bath. Downstairs, the **restaurant** (lunch $9-17, dinner $19-41) and saloon attract visitors from around the state with butter-knife steaks, elk rellenos, Montana morel chicken breast, and an award-winning wine list. The food is sumptuous, and the atmosphere—with rich, dark mahogany and 1890s furnishings—leaves nothing to be desired.

Greycliff Prairie Dog Town State Park (I-90 exit 377, Greycliff, 406/247-2940, www.stateparks.mt.gov, $6/vehicle nonresidents) is just what the name suggests—a remarkable metropolis constructed and inhabited by thousands of black-tailed prairie dogs. These furry little creatures are endearing if you watch them interact for even just a few minutes. A picnic area is available, but remember to keep Fido in the car.

REED POINT

Every Labor Day weekend, the population of Reed Point swells from about 100 to more than 5,000. People come from far and wide to watch a couple of thousand sheep make their way, leaping and running, down Main Street. It's called the **Great Montana Sheep Drive** (406/322-4505, www.stillwatercountychamber.com), and it is an afternoon well spent. The annual event includes a mutton cook-off, a parade and car show, a street dance, a kids' carnival and petting zoo, local crafts sales, and a variety of entertainment. Even though it's this one-day event that puts little Reed Point on the map, it is a nice town to explore if you have time.

COLUMBUS, ABSAROKEE, AND ROSCOE

For anglers and adventurers in search of good water, high mountains, and a friendly bar with decent grub, these three hamlets fit

Running of the Sheep

It's not exactly Pamplona's Running of the Bulls, but Reed Point's Great Montana Sheep Drive (406/322-4505, www.stillwatercountychamber.com), also known as "Running of the Sheep," is a Montana classic. Though history might suggest this was a reaction to conflict between sheepherders and cattle ranchers, a tongue-in-cheek thumbing of the nose perhaps, the truth is that this event was started in 1980 when the town (population, according to one sign posted in town, "about 100: 99 good folks and one real jerk") gathered to auction off an 89-year-old bachelor in hopes of finding him a companion. The sheep were introduced in 1989, Montana's centennial celebration of statehood during which the relatively nearby town of Roundup was planning a cattle drive. One resident (possibly the jerk?) had the idea of a sheep drive that would actually cross in front of the cattle. The cattle confrontation was quashed, but the idea of the sheep drive took hold, and the event has been growing every year since. Roughly 2,000 sheep make their way down Main Street, sandwiched between thousands of spectators and more than 70 food vendors. The annual event also includes a mutton cook-off, a parade, a car show, a street dance, a kids' carnival and petting zoo, local crafts sales, and a variety of entertainment. The event is scheduled annually the Sunday of Labor Day.

the bill brilliantly. With the Stillwater and Yellowstone Rivers nearby, Columbus is a fishing town, and the 100-year-old New Atlas Bar (528 E. Pike Ave., 406/322-4033, 10am-2am daily) is one of the coolest but least-visited bars in the state. There never seem to be more than a couple of old-timers bellied up to the beautiful old bar, and with more than 60 mounts on the walls and a couple of oddities here and there (a stuffed two-headed calf, for example), this place has the feel of a cool but somewhat dingy old museum.

Heading down Highway 78 toward Red Lodge is Absarokee, a quaint little town near the Stillwater River with a handful of B&Bs and a similar number of outfitters. Absaroka River Adventures (113 Grove St., 800/334-7238, www.absarokariver.com) offers scenic floats (half-day $45 adults, $30 children 12 and under, full-day $105 adults, $80 children) on the lower Stillwater and on the more dramatic upper section (half-day $45 adults, $30 children), which is only floatable in early summer. Paintbrush Adventures (86 N. Stillwater Rd., 406/328-4158, www.paintbrushadventures.com) offers guided horseback riding ($40 for 1 hour, $65 for 2 hours, $200 full-day) and hiking ($85 day hike with lunch). It also offers saddle-to-paddle

trips ($110 adults, $70 children), which include a full day of rafting and horseback riding, as well as two- to seven-day pack trips, drop camps, and working ranch vacations. Cabin accommodations are available as well.

The Grizzly Bar & Grill (1 Main St., 406/328-6789, noon-10pm daily, $11-30), along the East Rosebud River in Roscoe, offers a perfect setting for a delicious Montana meal. The cuisine is classic—relish trays and steaks large enough to hang off the edges of your plate—and the ambience is idyllic. Diners can enjoy a great meal on the deck overlooking the tumbling river. Ah, summer in Montana—short but so sweet.

INFORMATION

As you drive west off I-90 exit 367 to Big Timber, you can't miss the Sweet Grass County Chamber of Commerce (1350 Hwy. 10 W., 406/932-5131, www.bigtimber.com, 9am-4pm Mon.-Sat., noon-4pm Sun. Memorial Day-Labor Day). In a small log cabin with stunning views of the Crazy Mountains, you will find a well-informed and friendly staff ready to answer any questions you may have about the area. The center also offers a good selection of maps, brochures, and travel magazines.

Red Lodge and the Beartooth Plateau

At the edge of the massive Beartooth Plateau, Red Lodge (population 2,237; elevation 5,568 ft/1,697 m) is a mountain town with the Great Plains spread out at its feet. There are a couple of great resorts and some world-class skiing just beyond town, but downtown Red Lodge is a worthwhile destination on its own. Cute shops and wonderful restaurants line Broadway, and the spectacle of nature—the rush of Rock Creek and the drama of the Beartooths—is evident from every part of the street. The town's Western hospitality combined with historic zeal for a good time make Red Lodge a wonderful getaway or a fun launching point to the wildness of the Beartooth Plateau and Yellowstone National Park.

SIGHTS
★ Beartooth Scenic Highway and Pass

Considered one of the most beautiful roadways in the country, the **Beartooth Scenic Highway** begins in Red Lodge, climbs and twists its way through 60-million-year-old

mountains, and ends 65 miles (105 km) later in Cooke City at the northeast entrance to Yellowstone National Park. The scenic road has numerous switchbacks and steep grades that, once you're driving on it, clearly demonstrate why it is closed during winter. As you ascend, you come upon magnificent vistas of the Beartooth Plateau, Glacier Lake, and the canyons forged by the Clarks Fork River. After about 30 miles (48 km), you reach the mountain summit at 10,947 feet (3,337 m). Here you will encounter the aptly named **Top of the World** rest area, which provides the only services on the route. Keep an eye out for a herd of mountain goats that frequents the area.

If you plan to drive this byway, keep in mind that it is not about getting from A to B—the drive itself is the destination, and it should be undertaken with plenty of time; it lasts about three hours without stops. You will encounter an array of wildlife, including black bears, bighorn sheep, and mountain goats, as well as a broad display of vibrant wildflowers, depending on the season and moisture levels. Take time to pull over and enjoy the vistas or

lake near Beartooth Pass

explore the hiking trails and accessible lakes. With snow falling almost year-round, skiing is popular in the area June through July. Because of the extreme conditions of the mountains, the highway is only open May to October, weather permitting. Contact the **Montana Department of Transportation** (406/444-6200) or the **Red Lodge Visitors Center** (406/446-1718) for opening and closing dates.

Yellowstone Wildlife Sanctuary

This wildlife refuge is the only one of its kind in Montana. It houses indigenous animals that cannot be released back into the wild due to an injury or unfortunate dependency on humans. The **Yellowstone Wildlife Sanctuary** (615 2nd St. E., 406/446-1133, www.yellowstonewildlifesanctuary.com, 10am-4pm Tues.-Sun. May-Sept., 10am-2pm Tues.-Sun. Oct.-Apr., $30 adults, $15 children 3-12, free seniors, military, and children under 3) cares for some 60 animals that include wolves, black bears, bison, elk, bald eagles, mountain lions, and many more. The center says in its mission that its "primary focus is to educate the public about the protection and conservation of Montana's wildlife and its habitats" by allowing visitors an up close and intimate perspective of some of Montana's most beautiful species. The center's location also affords some spectacular views of the Beartooth Mountains.

SPORTS AND RECREATION
Beartooth Plateau

High atop these massive mountains is the vast and rugged grandeur of the Beartooth Plateau. It's a nature lover's paradise with spectacular scenery, unrivaled vistas, abundant wildlife, and a tangle of trails and lakes to get out and enjoy. The **Beartooth Scenic Highway** makes this remarkable place a Sunday drive destination. But if you have the time, this is a wonderland that begs to be discovered. Take a hike, wet a line—heck, throw

on your skis in midsummer; just get out and enjoy this magnificent place.

The truth of the matter is, you're already pretty much on top of the world here, so you don't need to aspire much when planning a hike. The plateau is crisscrossed with trails, and as long as you are amply prepared, you can't choose a bad one. The **Clay Butte Fire Lookout Tower** is only 1 mile (1.6 km) from the highway and can be accessed by a trail that takes hikers up and above 11,000 feet (3,353 m). The views are incredible, and an interpretive display gives great perspective on the 1988 Yellowstone fires and how they impacted the entire region. **Crazy Creek Cascade** is another nice short hike, and the **Clarks Fork Trailhead,** just 3 miles (4.8 km) from Cooke City, offers an abundance of longer trails. Near the summit, an 8-mile (12.9-km) loop around **Beartooth Lake** offers easy terrain and lovely scenery. For trail maps, stop by the **U.S. Forest Service ranger station** (6811 U.S. 212, Red Lodge, 406/446-2103).

Biking the Beartooth Plateau is not for the faint of heart. Never mind the insane elevation climbs and descents, the vast grizzly habitat, and the possibility of a blizzard on virtually any day of the year; the real danger is the automobiles, which are plentiful, often wide, and driven by people who can't help but ogle the mountain vistas instead of the bike traffic. You can eliminate that danger by getting off the road and onto a network of trails.

In order to fish any of the mountain lakes on the Beartooth Plateau, many of which have been stocked with trout, you'll need a Wyoming fishing license, which can be purchased at the **Top of the World Resort** (2823 Hwy. 212, 307/587-5368, www.topoftheworldresort.com) or in Red Lodge or Cooke City. Rental gear is also available ($10/day spincasting setup, $20/day fly rod and reel setup, $10/hour and $40/day paddleboat or canoe) at the Top of the World Resort.

Skiing

Situated in a glacial valley surrounded by the Beartooth Mountains, Red Lodge offers superb downhill and cross-country skiing. **Red Lodge Mountain** (305 Ski Run Rd., 406/446-2610 or 800/444-8977, www.redlodgemountain.com) is just 6 miles (9.7 km) from downtown Red Lodge and boasts a mountain free of crowds and with reasonable lift ticket prices ($57 adults 19-64, $47 seniors 65-69, $20 seniors 70 and over, $44 juniors 13-18, $24 children 6-12, free for children 5 and under) as well as ski runs for beginners to experts. The mountain offers a higher base elevation (7,433 feet/2,266 m) than any other ski hill in the state, a spine-chilling 2,400-foot (731.5-m) vertical drop, 69 runs, and six chairlifts to keep you up to your elbows in the white stuff all day. The diverse terrain is groomed regularly, and the runs' features are frequently upgraded or even changed. Red Lodge offers a full-service lodge, with ski lessons, ski rentals, child care, a restaurant, two bars, and two cafeterias, all on the hill. The resort also has two cross-country trails that offer about 11 miles (17.7 km) of skiing. On top of the outstanding terrain and the jaw-dropping views, one of the things that makes this hill so special is the small-town friendless of just about everyone here, from the lift ops to the people sharing a chair with you. This feels like what skiing in Montana should be.

Probably the best-known place for cross-country skiing in Red Lodge is the **Red Lodge Nordic Center** (406/446-1771, www.beartoothtrails.org, 8:30am-4:30pm daily in season, $5/day payable at the trailhead) 2 miles (3.2 km) west of downtown off Highway 78. The center is operated by the nonprofit Beartooth Recreational Trails Association (which also maintains several excellent trails for hiking when snow isn't covering the ground) and offers more than 9.3 miles (15 km) of groomed classic and skate trails rated from easy to most difficult. Rentals and lessons can be arranged prior to your arrival via online booking. Other than a porta potty, there are no services at the Nordic Center, so plan ahead.

Hiking and Fishing

There are a number of rivers, creeks, and lakes worth fishing or just ambling along in the vicinity of Red Lodge, and with surroundings as spectacular as these, the catching may not be the point. **Rock Creek** flows through town and is a surprisingly good place to catch rainbows or browns. Public access can be found just north of town. The north-flowing **Stillwater River,** west of town toward Absarokee, is a medium-size tributary of the Yellowstone River with relatively few people fishing it and a healthy number of rainbows and browns.

Wild Bill Lake is stocked regularly and makes a fantastic family outing or introduction to fly-fishing. The area is fully accessible for wheelchairs and can be found 2 miles (3.2 km) south of Red Lodge on U.S. 212, then 5 miles (8 km) west on Forest Road 2071.

While there are numerous gnarly trails on the Beartooth Plateau for hard-core hikers, you'll find plenty of trails just outside town that are a bit more mellow but equally beautiful. The **Nichols Creek Trail** (West Fork Rd. to Forest Rd. 2478), for example, is a 4-mile (6.4-km) round-trip out-and-back hike that follows Nichols Creek through aspen and pine forests with moderate elevation gain (1,100 feet/335.3 m) and a marvelous view of the West Fork Canyon.

Another popular option is the well-traveled **Basin Lakes Trail #61.** The steep, 5.1-mile (8.2-km) there-and-back trail leads to two lakes with a 1,500-foot (457-m) elevation gain. Beautiful waterfalls are along the way and, if you time it right, you can pick wild raspberries as you go. Abundant wildlife is also in the area—moose are commonly seen—so do bring bear spray and keep your eyes open. You will like run into plenty of other hikers and anglers. The upper lake is the better of the two for fishing. To get to the trailhead, drive south on U.S. 212 from Red Lodge to West Fork Drive and head west for 2.8 miles (4.5 km). Stay left and follow the signs another 4.1

miles (6.6 km) to the Basin Lakes trailhead. Note that the West Fork Road is closed from early December-mid-April.

For a professional fishing guide—or just the right gear and good advice—contact **Rocky Fork Outfitters & Guide Service** (108 Obert Rd., 406/445-2598, www.rockyforkoutfittersguide.com, full-day float or wade for 1-2 anglers from $400, half-day from $250) or **Montana Trout Scout** (406/855-3058, www.montanatroutscout.wordpress.com, full-day float or wade for 1-2 anglers from $500, half-day wade from $350).

Golf

To hit the links, head to the 18-hole course at **Red Lodge Resort and Golf Club** (828 Upper Continental Dr., southwest of Red Lodge, 406/446-3344, www.redlodgemountain.com, $39 for 18 holes walking Mon.-Thurs., $50 for 18 holes walking Fri.-Sun., discounts for booking 48 hours in advance, juniors 18 and under, and twilight play after 4pm). On top of the jaw-dropping scenery around this challenging course, your ball will travel farther because of the altitude.

ENTERTAINMENT AND EVENTS

Since 1950, the **Festival of Nations** has been a Red Lodge tradition celebrating the wide diversity of ethnic groups that first came to the town during the late-1800s mining boom. The cultural groups honored include both southern and northern Europeans—German, Irish, Finnish, Italian, Norwegian, Scottish, Greek—and a variety of others. The festival takes place in late July or August over two and a half days, with cultural exhibits, dancing, ethnic food, music, children's activities, and a wide assortment of daytime and nighttime entertainment. People who wear ethnic costumes get admitted free. Contact the **Red Lodge Visitors Center** (406/446-1718) for this year's dates and location.

The **Winter Carnival** (305 Ski Run Rd., 406/446-2610 or 800/444-8977, dates vary each year) takes place at the Red Lodge Mountain Resort and has become a favorite event among locals and visitors alike. Although the carnival selects a different theme each year (in 2016 the theme was "Space Wars" in celebration of the seventh Star Wars film), many tried-and-true events make an annual appearance. The Cardboard Classic race tests the skills of its participants as they guide their original crafts—made only from cardboard, duct tape, and glue—in a competitive downhill race. Other popular activities include a scavenger hunt, a snow sculpture contest, a parade of costumes, a jalapeño-eating contest, and a dazzling fireworks show. You may even be crowned King or Queen of Red Lodge Mountain if you can telemark, alpine race, and snowboard yourself to victory.

The **Home of Champions Rodeo and Parade** (406/446-1718, www.redlodgerodeo.com, July 2-4, $15-30, $30 admits 4 on Family Day July 2) takes place each year at the fairgrounds west of Red Lodge just off Highway 78, and the parades run daily in downtown Red Lodge. Rodeo competition in the area dates back to the 1890s, when cowboys used to get together on Sunday to ride broncos at the local stockyards. Formed in 1930, the Red Lodge Rodeo Association has been hosting this annual celebration ever since. The name, Home of Champions, was coined in 1954 after a local cowboy, Bill Linderman, won his third title as World All Around Champion. A different theme is selected for the event every year, and a parade takes place at noon each day; participation is open and there are categories for all age groups. The rodeo is part of the Professional Rodeo Cowboys Association circuit, so you will see many of the nation's top champions compete in a number of different events, including bareback, bull riding, calf roping, and barrel racing.

Lovers of classical music and fine art are in for a wildly unexpected treat at **Tippet Rise Art Center** (96 S. Grove Creek Rd., Fishtail, www.tippetrise.org, June-Sept.), which brings together nature, art, and music in magnificent ways. Set on an 11,500-acre

(4,654-hectare) working ranch, in the shadow of the Beartooths, Tippet Rise brings world-class musicians to the area for intimate performances throughout summer at a variety of indoor and outdoor venues, all of them small and visually spectacular. Tickets for concerts and films are limited to just 100 seats at most—and are available online only for as little as $10, and free for ages 21 and younger—but sell out months in advance. Tickets to the art center are available for free, online, but also in very limited quantities.

SHOPPING

Shopping in Red Lodge is a leisurely stroll through the historic downtown district. Broadway has still managed to retain the charm and vibrancy of the coal-mining days with a diverse assortment of stores. **Sylvan Peak Mountain Shop** (9 N. Broadway Ave., 406/446-1770, 9am-6pm daily) is a perfect starting point for anyone in need of adventure-related gear. The store carries its own line of clothing as well as more familiar brands such as Marmot, Mountain Hardware, and Osprey. An outlet store on the main floor and a Mountain Shoppe downstairs not only sell equipment but also rent cross-country skis, telemark skis, and snowshoes. From climbing gear to boating gear, fleeces or bear spray, you will find it—plus the best insider's advice anywhere and a true commitment to protecting the great outdoors—at Sylvan Peak.

Right next door, you'll find the irresistible **Montana Candy Emporium** (7 N. Broadway Ave., 406/446-1119, 9am-9pm daily Memorial Day-Labor Day, 9am-7pm Sun.-Thurs., 9am-9pm Fri.-Sat. Labor Day-Memorial Day). The mouthwatering window displays will draw you in to this world of sweets. It is said to be the largest candy store in Montana, which is easy to believe meandering through its selection of more than 800 sugary treats. Located in the former Park Theater, decorated with nostalgic memorabilia, and selling old-fashioned candies, this store will take you back to a simpler time.

Since 1990, **Kibler and Kirch** (101 N. Broadway Ave., 406/446-2226, www.kiblerandkirch.com, 9am-5pm Mon.-Sat.) has been a pillar of the downtown shopping scene in Red Lodge. A home-furnishings store with a nice selection of Western artwork and accessories, the offerings include pottery, glassware, and handcrafted leather. Since many of its products are made in Montana, you may find the perfect gift to take home.

FOOD

The fanciest place in town these days is the dining room at **The Pollard Hotel** (2 N. Broadway Ave., 406/446-0001, www.thepollard.com, 7am-10am and 5pm-9pm daily, $17-36). Though it offers a nightly vegetarian special, most of the fare is classic Montana meat and potatoes. Think porcini-rubbed beef tenderloin, bison brisket, and beef rib eye. **The Pub at the Pollard** (5pm-9pm daily, $7-15) is a much more casual place for a bite. The atmosphere is great, especially when the place hosts live music.

A new farm-to-table restaurant that opened in 2016 to great reviews is **Ox Pasture** (7 Broadway N., 406/446-1212, www.oxpasture.com, 11:30am-10pm Tues.-Sun., $14-32). The small menu changes frequently to make the most of seasonal produce. From Sicilian specialties like arancini, fritto misto, and eggplant parmesan to grilled sea bass and a variety of handmade pastas, this foodie heaven puts together phenomenal flavors.

For a casual, inexpensive, old-fashioned drive-in—or better yet, walk-up—experience, head to the **Red Box Car** (1300 S. Broadway Ave., 406/446-2152, 11am-8pm daily early Apr.-Sept., $3.60-13.50). Based in an actual 1906 boxcar from the Rocky Fork Railway, this stand serves some of the best shakes, malts, chili, and burgers you could imagine. Sit outside and enjoy your meal as you take in views of nearby Rock Creek. The Red Box Car may close at any time due to weather, so call ahead or check its Facebook page before visiting.

Set in a cool old Conoco gas station, **Más Taco** (304 N. Broadway Ave., 406/446-3636,

11am-7pm Tues.-Sat., $3-9) is the place for authentic Mexican cuisine in Red Lodge. It has lots of vegetarian options and makes everything from scratch, including the corn tortillas and sour cream. The wet burritos are legendary, and the restaurant is also known for its five versions of al pastor, pork roasted with pineapple and paper-thin slices of onion. Sit outside in the summer to enjoy the view, or plant yourself at the counter and watch them cook!

Attached to the Regis Grocery and known for outstanding breakfasts and organic, whole foods, ★ Café Regis (501 Word Ave. S., 406/446-1941, www.caferegis.com, 7am-2pm Wed.-Sun., $5-12) is an excellent spot for a hearty, healthy, and very reasonably priced meal. The service is quick and friendly, and every delicious item on the menu—from omelets and breakfast burritos to soup, sandwiches, salads, and mouthwatering daily blue plate specials—is available to go. Grab a ready-to-go picnic lunch or find all the gourmet fixings for whatever adventure you have planned. The Regis Grocery has a huge selection of organic, gluten-free, and other specialty products.

Thirty-five miles (56 km) northeast of town is the tiny hamlet of Fromberg (drive east of Red Lodge on Hwy. 308 to Belfry, then north on Hwy. 72 past Bridger) and the **Little Cowboy Bar & Museum** (105 W. River St., 406/668-9502, noon-2am daily), a rare find. This special place combines a wonderful collection of rodeo and local memorabilia with a good old-fashioned Montana bar. After a fire in December 2013 destroyed much of the memorabilia, the bar was rebuilt and made use of what it could save by hanging it on the walls. Can you imagine a better way to learn about Montana history than with an ice-cold bottle of beer in hand?

ACCOMMODATIONS

In historic downtown Red Lodge, ★ **The Pollard Hotel** (2 N. Broadway Ave., 406/446-0001, www.thepollard.com, $160-300) should not be overlooked. The hotel was the first brick building constructed in Red Lodge and dates to 1893. It has played host to some of the West's most famous legends, including Calamity Jane, Buffalo Bill Cody, and famed orator William Jennings Bryan. Each of the 39 guest rooms and suites are individually decorated, more traditional than modern, and can come with mountain views, jetted tubs, and balconies. All stays include a full breakfast in The Pollard's excellent dining room.

Rock Creek Resort (6380 U.S. 212 S., 800/667-1119, www.rockcreekresort.com, $97-409) is about 5 miles (8 km) south of Red Lodge in a gorgeous canyon at the base of the Beartooth Mountains. The resort has 87 rooms sprawled over a 30-acre (12.1-hectare) site and offers many outdoor activities. The facility has a heated indoor pool, tennis courts, a soccer field, a fully stocked fish pond, and numerous trails for hiking and biking (along with bikes for rent). Accommodations range from hotel rooms and condos to cabins and larger homes. Most have impressive views of the mountains.

If you want to stay close to downtown Red Lodge without breaking the bank, try the pet-friendly ★ **Yodeler Motel** (601 S. Broadway Ave., 406/446-1435, www.yodelermotel.com, $105-155). This historic, Swiss-themed chalet, owned by delightful former guides Mac and Tulsa Dean, is only three blocks from downtown. Remodeled guest rooms offer nice amenities that include cable TV, free Wi-Fi, jetted tubs, steam showers, and even a wax room to work on your skis. The rooms on the lower level are more budget-friendly and do not have balconies like the upper level, but every room is clean, comfortable, and well maintained.

CAMPING

Thirteen campgrounds along U.S. 212 offer 226 sites between Red Lodge and Cooke City. Because of the elevation and volume of snow, many do not open until late June or July. **Beartooth Lake Campground** (21 sites, $15, July-mid-Sept.) and **Island Lake**

Campground (21 sites, $15, July-mid-Sept.) are two excellent choices very near the summit. Campsites along the Beartooth Highway are managed by the **Custer National Forest** (406/446-2103, www.fs.usda.gov/custergallatin) and range in price free-$20 per night, depending on the site.

INFORMATION AND SERVICES

The **Red Lodge Chamber of Commerce** (701 N. Broadway Ave., 406/446-1718 or 888/281-0625, www.redlodgechamber.org, 9am-5pm Mon.-Fri., 10am-4pm Sat.-Sun. summer, winter hours vary) is at the intersection of U.S. 212 and Highway 78. It has a 24-hour brochure room that offers a variety of local information. Inside the center you will find knowledgeable staff and plenty of state publications, visitors guides, and maps.

Access the Internet at **Red Lodge Carnegie Library** (3 8th St. W., 406/446-1905, 10am-6pm Tues.-Fri., noon-6pm Sat.). The library has several Internet-connected computers available to the public. You can also stop by the **Coffee Factory Roasters** (22 S. Broadway Ave., 406/446-3200, www.coffeefactoryroasters.com, 6:30am-6pm daily), where the Wi-Fi is free.

The **Beartooth Billings Clinic** (2525 N. Broadway Ave., 406/446-2345, 7:30am-6pm walk-in care) offers 24-hour emergency care.

U.S. 212 climbs another 5,000 feet (1,524 m) past Red Lodge. If you want to know the road conditions for the Beartooth Highway, you can stop by the chamber of commerce or check with the state of Montana **Traveler Road Information** (800/226-7623, TTY 800/335-7592, www.mdt.mt.gov).

TRANSPORTATION

The two major airports closest to Red Lodge are **Billings Logan International Airport** (BIL, 406/247-8609 or 406/657-8495, www.flybillings.com) and **Bozeman Yellowstone International Airport** (BZN, 406/388-8321, www.bozemanairport.com). One of the best options for getting to Red Lodge is by car; both airports have a selection of car-rental companies.

From the Billings airport, **Phidippides Shuttle Service** (307/527-6789, www.codyshuttle.com) transports visitors to Red Lodge.

Driving from Billings, take I-90 West to U.S. 212/310 South. Red Lodge is 60 miles (97 km) southwest of Billings, and the drive time is about an hour. From Bozeman, take I-90 East to Highway 78 south. Bozeman is about 150 miles (242 km) and 2.5 hours north and then west of Red Lodge.

Yellowstone National Park

Yellowstone National Park is at the heart of our country's relationship with wilderness. It's also the largest intact ecosystem in the Lower 48—all of the species that have roamed this plateau are still (or once again) in residence.

Yellowstone was our nation's first national park. Signed into being by President Ulysses S. Grant after a series of important and legendary scouting expeditions through the area, the region's history is lengthy and very much alive, from its prehistoric supervolcanic eruptions, to its occupation by the U.S. Army in the 1880s, to the controversial reintroduction of wolves in the 1990s and the more recent snowmobile usage, bison, and grizzly delisting quagmires. The stories, both far-fetched and true, and characters that have emerged from the park

Highlights

Look for ★ to find recommended sights, activities, dining, and lodging.

★ **Boiling River:** In a stretch of the Gardner River at the park's north entrance, hot water flows over waterfalls and via springs, mixing with the river water to create a perfect soaking temperature (page 326).

★ **Mammoth and the Mammoth Hot Springs Terraces:** The travertine terraces here look like an enormous cream-colored confection. Since the springs shift and change daily, a walk around the colorful terraces is never the same experience twice (page 330).

★ **Grand Canyon of the Yellowstone:** The sheer cliffs and dramatic coloring of this canyon have inspired millions of visitors. In the summer, get a rare bird's-eye view of several osprey nests (page 331).

★ **Watching the Wolves:** The wolves put on a spectacular show—with at least one reported sighting daily since 2001. The sagas of the 11 packs are dramatic, heart-wrenching, and captivating (page 338).

★ **Lamar Valley:** Known as the "Little Serengeti of North America," this scenic, glacially carved valley offers spectacular wildlife-watching year-round (page 340).

★ **Yellowstone Lake:** This beautiful lake was touted by early mountain men as perhaps the only place where you could catch a fish and cook it without ever taking it off the line (page 345).

★ **Old Faithful:** If you can see just one thing in Yellowstone, make it this world-famous geyser that erupts every 45-90 minutes (page 346).

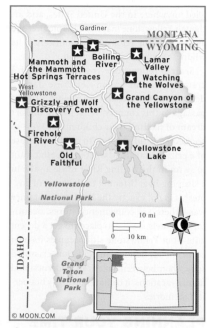

★ **Firehole River:** This river offers a stunning, heated swimming area surrounded by cliffs. The twists and turns of the cascading canyon are worth seeing even if you don't get wet (page 348).

★ **Grizzly and Wolf Discovery Center:** You're guaranteed an up-close look at two of the park's biggest and most fascinating predators at this home to grizzly bears and wolves that can't survive in the wild (page 353).

are as colorful and compelling as the landscape itself.

A vast 2.2 million acres (890,308 hectares), Yellowstone is indeed a wonderland, filled with steaming geysers and boiling mud pots, packed with diverse and healthy populations of wildlife, and crisscrossed by hundreds of miles of hiking and skiing trails. A stretch of the park called the Lamar Valley is known as the "Little Serengeti of North America," and for good reason: At certain times of the year, in a single day visitors can spot grizzly and black bears, moose, wolves, bison, elk, coyotes, bald eagles, and the occasional bighorn sheep or mountain goat. In fact, the opportunities for viewing wildlife in the park are unparalleled anywhere in the United States, and although Yellowstone may not be as picturesque as Glacier or the Tetons, it is magnificent in its wildness and uniquely American.

Seeing Yellowstone from the back of a cramped station wagon—or these days, a decked-out Winnebago—is almost a rite of passage in this country. What parent doesn't dream of hauling their children out West to see Old Faithful erupt or to catch a glimpse of a grizzly bear? And what kid doesn't want to swim in the Boiling River or lie awake in a sleeping bag, listening to the howl of coyotes? It is not exactly the last frontier it once was—there are convenience stores, beautiful old hotels, and even places to get a decent latte—but Yellowstone still occupies its own corner of our national imagination; classified somewhere between American wilderness and family vacations, it conjures up foggy but perfect memories.

PLANNING YOUR TIME

One could quite literally spend a lifetime in Yellowstone without being able to cover every last corner of this magnificent wilderness, but the reality is that most visitors only have a couple of days, at best, to spend exploring the park. Something like 98 percent of visitors never get more than a mile from the road, but it's easier than you might think—and incredibly worthwhile. Three days in the park is ideal, but if you have less time, there are ways to maximize every minute.

One important consideration in planning your time in Yellowstone is to know the season you'll be traveling. Summer offers magnificent scenery, usually good weather, and the inevitable "bear jam," when drivers hit the brakes as soon as someone spots anything resembling a brown furry creature. Summer visitors to Yellowstone need to plan for traffic and often for road construction delays. Fall and spring are fantastic times to see wildlife, but the weather can change in a heartbeat—at Yellowstone's high elevation, blizzards can strike nearly any month of the year. Winter is a magical time in the park, but cars are only permitted on one road in the northeast corner. All other travel is done via snow coach, guided snowmobile tour, or on skis and snowshoes. There is no wrong time to visit the park, but knowing the advantages and disadvantages of the various seasons will help you manage your expectations.

Assuming you'll be in Yellowstone when the roads are open to car traffic, there are five entrances and exits to Yellowstone, making loop trips relatively easy. From Montana, you can enter or exit the park from the northeast at Cooke City, from the north at Gardiner, or from the west at West Yellowstone. From Wyoming, you can enter the park from the east entrance nearest Cody or from the south through Grand Teton National Park. If you're going from one state to the next, there is no more spectacular route than through the heart of Yellowstone.

A cursory glance at a Yellowstone map will reveal the main roads, which form a figure eight in the heart of the park, and the access roads leading to and from the entrances. The majority of the park's big-name highlights—**Old Faithful, West Thumb Geyser**

Previous: Grand Prismatic Spring; the Roosevelt Arch in Gardiner; herd of bison along the Firehole River.

Basin, Fishing Bridge, Grand Canyon of the Yellowstone, Norris and Mammoth Geyser Basins—are accessible from the main loops. Depending on your time and your plan for accommodations, you could easily spend a full day driving each of the two loops. A third day would permit an opportunity for deeper exploration—perhaps a hike—and a leisurely exit from the park.

If time won't permit even one night in the park, it is still well worth driving through, just to get a sense of this tremendously diverse place. Consider choosing one feature and pursuing it. To give yourself the best chance of seeing wolves, traveling between the north and northeast entrances is an excellent route during non-summer months. Geothermal aficionados will have no shortage of choices for seeing the park's impressive features, but to swim in them, try the **Boiling River,** a stretch of the Gardner River near Mammoth, which is swimmable year-round except during spring and early summer runoff. The **Firehole River** also offers excellent summer swimming not far from Old Faithful. Landlubbers might prefer a short hike into a less-famous geyser like **Lone Star,** just a few flat miles from Old Faithful.

The best advice is this: Get off the road, get out of your car, be smart, and come prepared to give yourself the opportunity to see and understand what makes Yellowstone America's first wonderland.

INFORMATION AND SERVICES

The best resource to familiarize yourself with the park and to help plan your trip is the **National Park Service** (307/344-7381, www.nps.gov/yell). On the website, click on the link titled Plan Your Visit. The site also posts information about the different **Ranger Programs** being offered, including educational lectures and hikes.

Park Fees and Passes

Admission to the park is $35 per vehicle for seven days, $30 for motorcycles, and $20 for hikers and bicyclists. In 2018, entrance fees to the park were waived on 4 days, including Martin Luther King Jr. Day, April 21 to celebrate the start of National Park Week, September 22 for National Public Lands Day, and Veterans Day. Check the Yellowstone website before you travel to see if any fee-free days are on the horizon. The park is open year-round, but during the winter, cars can only access the park through the north and northeast entrances.

Visitors Centers

There are 10 visitors centers in and around the park. Since days and hours vary seasonally, it's a good idea to check the website (www.nps.gov/yell) before you go into the park.

The **Albright Visitor Center at Mammoth Hot Springs** (Grand Loop Rd., 307/344-2263, 8am-6pm daily mid-June-Labor Day, 9am-5pm daily Labor Day-mid-June) is open year-round and houses a bookstore, wildlife and history exhibits, and films on the park and its early visitors. Free Wi-Fi is available.

The **Canyon Visitor Education Center** (Canyon Village, 307/344-2550, 8am-6pm daily mid-June-early Oct., 9am-5pm daily mid-Apr.-mid-June and early Oct.-early Nov.) offers the best overview of the park's geology, including phenomenal supervolcano exhibits and a dynamic film. During the season, the bathrooms remain open 24 hours a day.

The **Fishing Bridge Visitor Center** (East Entrance Rd., 307/344-2450, 8am-5pm daily late May-June 1, 8am-7pm daily June 2-Labor Day, 8am-1pm Labor Day-early Oct.) is home to a bookstore, birds and wildlife exhibits, plus information on the lake's geology.

The **Grant Village Visitor Center** (west shore of Yellowstone Lake, 307/344-2650, 8am-5pm daily Memorial Day-June 1, 8am-7pm daily June 2-Labor Day, 9am-5pm daily Labor Day-early Oct.) offers information on fire in Yellowstone.

The **Madison Information Station and Trailside Museum** (307/344-2821, 9am-5pm daily late May-early Oct.) at Madison Junction

Yellowstone National Park

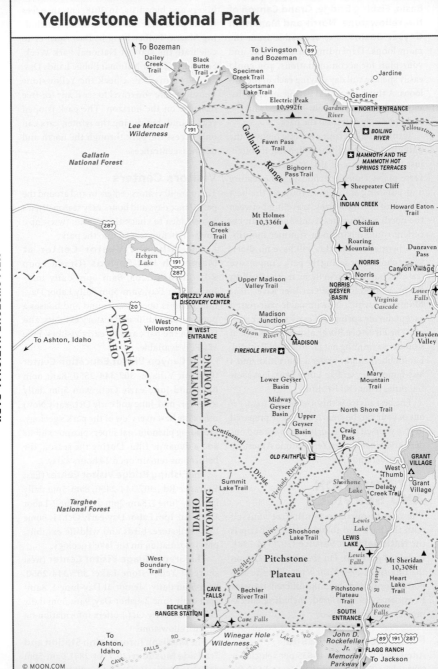

To Bozeman

Dailey Creek Trail

Black Butte Trail

To Livingston and Bozeman

89

Jardine

Specimen Creek Trail

Sportsman Lake Trail

Electric Peak 10,992ft

Gardiner

Gardner River

■ NORTH ENTRANCE

Lee Metcalf Wilderness

191

Gallatin Range

Fawn Pass Trail

✪ BOILING RIVER

Yellowstone

Gallatin National Forest

✪ MAMMOTH AND THE MAMMOTH HOT SPRINGS TERRACES

Bighorn Pass Trail

✚ Sheepeater Cliff

∧ INDIAN CREEK

Howard Eaton Trail

287

Gneiss Creek Trail

Mt Holmes 10,336ft ▲

✚ Obsidian Cliff

Roaring ✚ Mountain

Dunraven Pass

Hebgen Lake

191

287

Upper Madison Valley Trail

∧ NORRIS

Canyon Village

★ Norris

Lower Falls

NORRIS GESYER BASIN

Virginia Cascade

20

MONTANA IDAHO

West Yellowstone

✪ GRIZZLY AND WOLF DISCOVERY CENTER

■ WEST ENTRANCE

Madison River

Madison Junction

∧ MADISON

Hayden Valley

To Ashton, Idaho

MONTANA WYOMING

✪ FIREHOLE RIVER

Lower Geyser Basin

Mary Mountain Trail

Midway Geyser Basin

Continental

Upper Geyser Basin

North Shore Trail

Craig Pass

GRANT VILLAGE

✚ OLD FAITHFUL ✪

Divide

Firehole River

Shoshone Lake

West Thumb

∧ Grant Village

Targhee National Forest

IDAHO WYOMING

Summit Lake Trail

Delacy Creek Trail

Lewis River

Shoshone Lake Trail

Lewis Lake

LEWIS LAKE

West Boundary Trail

Bechler River

Shoshone Lake Trail

Lewis Falls

Mt Sheridan 10,308ft ▲

Heart Lake Trail

Pitchstone Plateau

Pitchstone Plateau Trail

Lewis R

CAVE FALLS

Bechler River Trail

SOUTH ENTRANCE

Moose Falls

BECHLER RANGER STATION

∧ Cave Falls

To Ashton, Idaho

Winegar Hole Wilderness

FALLS RD

CAVE

LAKE RD

GRASSY

John D. Rockefeller Jr. Memorial Parkway

89 191 287

■ FLAGG RANCH

To Jackson

© MOON.COM

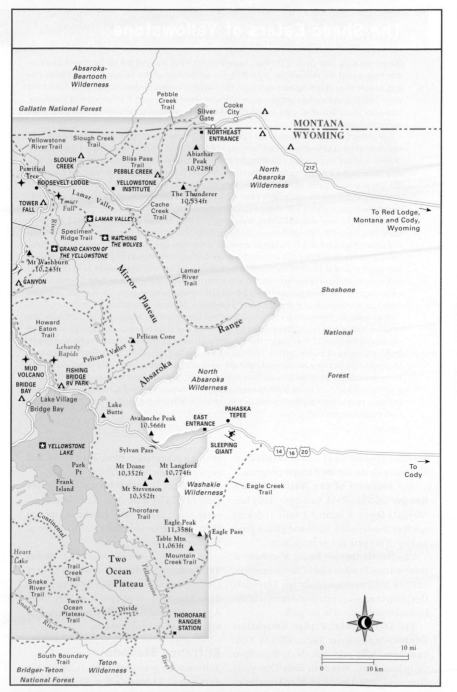

Absaroka-
Beartooth
Wilderness

Gallatin National Forest

Pebble
Creek
Trail

Silver
Gate

Cooke
City

Cooke City

MONTANA
WYOMING

NORTHEAST
ENTRANCE

Yellowstone
River Trail

Slough Creek
Trail

SLOUGH
CREEK

Bliss Pass
Trail

PEBBLE CREEK

Abiathar
Peak
10,928ft

North
Absaroka
Wilderness

212

To Red Lodge,
Montana and Cody,
Wyoming

Petrified
Tree

ROOSEVELT LODGE

YELLOWSTONE
INSTITUTE

The Thunderer
10,554ft

TOWER
FALL

Tower
Fall

Lamar Valley

LAMAR VALLEY

Cache
Creek
Trail

River

Specimen
Ridge Trail

WATCHING
THE WOLVES

Mt Washburn
10,243ft

GRAND CANYON OF
THE YELLOWSTONE

CANYON

Mirror Plateau

Lamar
River
Trail

Shoshone

Howard
Eaton
Trail

Pelican Cone

Range

National

Lehardy
Rapids

Pelican Valley

Absaroka

North
Absaroka
Wilderness

Forest

MUD
VOLCANO

FISHING
BRIDGE
RV PARK

BRIDGE
BAY

Lake Village
Bridge Bay

Lake
Butte

PAHASKA
TEPEE

Avalanche Peak
10,566ft

EAST
ENTRANCE

SLEEPING
GIANT

YELLOWSTONE
LAKE

Sylvan Pass

14 16 20

To
Cody

Park
Pt

Mt Doane
10,352ft

Mt Langford
10,774ft

Washakie
Wilderness

Eagle Creek
Trail

Frank
Island

Mt Stevenson
10,352ft

Thorofare
Trail

Eagle Peak
11,358ft

Eagle Pass

Continental

Table Mtn
11,063ft

Mountain
Creek Trail

Heart
Lake

Two
Ocean
Plateau

Trail
Creek
Trail

Yellowstone

Snake
River
Trail

Two
Ocean
Plateau
Trail

Divide

THOROFARE
RANGER
STATION

Snake
River

South Boundary
Trail

River

Bridger-Teton
National Forest

Teton
Wilderness

0   10 mi

0   10 km

The Sheep Eaters of Yellowstone

During the early 18th century, the horse was introduced to many of the Native American tribes that frequented the Yellowstone area. With the acquisition of this new, strong, and agile animal, people were able to spread out across the plains, traveling farther and longer to follow the bison. Hunting and warfare became more efficient almost overnight. A small group of Shoshone chose not to use horses or guns, however, and instead remained committed to their traditional mountain living.

The Sheep Eaters, also known as the Tukudika, were forest dwellers considered to be the only Native Americans to have inhabited Yellowstone year-round. They lived in *wikiups*—temporary shelters made of aspen poles, pine boughs, and other brush—rather than animal-hide tipis, and they traveled the mountain ridges rather than the river paths as their counterparts on the plains did. Living in small bands of 10-20 people, they relied on their wolf dogs to help them move provisions up and down the mountains. They were named for the animal whose migration they followed: the bighorn sheep. The Sheep Eaters developed highly effective sheep traps, the remains of which can be seen around Dubois, Wyoming, and they utilized the animal for both food and tools. They heated the sheep's horns in the hot springs of Yellowstone to mold them into exquisite and strong bows, powerful enough to drive an arrow through a bison. The reputation of these bows spread to other tribes and were highly sought-after. The European outsiders who made their way into the park during the early and mid-1800s described the Sheep Eaters as destitute and forlorn, not owning or seeming to want the modern trappings of the Plains Indians. Contemporary views suggest that these people revered their environment and ancestors' way of life and were more intent on maintaining their customs than competing and conquering.

Unfortunately, their traditions did not allow the Sheep Eaters to escape the same ultimate fate as other Native Americans. Devastated by smallpox and considered an obstacle to westward expansion, the Sheep Eaters fought the U.S. Army in the last Indian war in the Pacific Northwest. Unfairly accused of murdering five Chinese miners, the last remaining Sheep Eaters, a group of 51 people that included woman and children, were relentlessly pursued in the Idaho wilderness along the Middle Fork of the Salmon River in the fall of 1879. When the Army purportedly captured a woman who had just given birth, the remaining members of the tribe surrendered to save her and were sent to the Wind River Shoshone Reservation in Wyoming and Fort Hall Shoshone Bannock Reservation in Idaho.

provides a bookstore as well as detailed information on the **Junior Ranger** program.

The **Museum of the National Park Ranger** (307/344-7353, 9am-5pm daily late May-late Sept.) is located 1 mile (1.6 km) north of Norris Geyser Basin and gives a good history of the park ranger profession.

The **Norris Geyser Basin Museum & Information Station** (east of Norris Junction, 307/344-2812, 9am-6pm daily late May-early Oct.) offers visitors an excellent overview of the hydrothermal features in the park.

The **Old Faithful Visitor Education Center** (Upper Geyser Basin, 307/344-2751, 9am-6pm daily mid-Apr.-May, 8am-8pm daily June-Sept., 9am-5pm daily Oct.-early Nov. and mid-Dec.-mid-Mar.) includes

exhibits, information, films, a bookstore, and geyser eruption predictions.

The **West Thumb Information Center** (307/344-2876, 9am-5pm daily late May-early Oct.) offers information about the West Thumb Geyser Basin on the shore of Yellowstone Lake.

In West Yellowstone, the **West Yellowstone Visitor Information Center** (30 Yellowstone Ave., 307/344-2876, 8am-8pm daily May-Sept., 8am-8pm Mon.-Fri. Oct.-Apr.) hosts a National Park Service desk, plus information and publications.

Entrance Stations

Yellowstone National Park is open 365 days a year, 24 hours a day. There are five entrance stations, three in Montana and two in Wyoming.

- The **North Entrance,** at Gardiner, Montana, is the only one open year-round to wheeled vehicles.

- The **Northeast Entrance** is near the small communities of Cooke City and Silver Gate, Montana, and generally open late May to mid-October, depending upon weather and road conditions.

- The **West Entrance,** in West Yellowstone, Montana, is open to wheeled vehicles generally from the third Friday in April until the first Sunday in November.

- The **South Entrance,** 49 miles (79 km) north of Jackson, Wyoming, at the border between Grand Teton National Park and Yellowstone, is open to wheeled vehicles typically the second Friday in May through the first Sunday in November, and to snow coaches and snowmobiles mid-December to mid-March.

- The **East Entrance,** 53 miles (85 km) west of Cody, Wyoming, is generally open to wheeled vehicles from the first Friday in May to the first Sunday in November.

All entrances can be closed at any time due to weather and unscheduled changes. Visit www.nps.gov/yell before your trip for up-to-date road information, or call 307/344-2117 for recorded road and weather information.

Services

Yellowstone National Park Lodges (307/344-7311, www.yellowstonenationalparklodges.com) is the official concessionaire of Yellowstone, and all reservations for lodging, dining, and special activities in the park can be made through them.

If you encounter an **emergency** when traveling through the park, dial 911, but be aware that cell coverage is spotty. Emergency medical services are attended to by rangers. There are three **urgent care facilities** inside Yellowstone. The clinic at **Mammoth**

(307/344-7965, 8:30am-5pm Mon.-Fri. June-late Sept., 8:30am-5pm Mon.-Thurs, 8:30am-1pm Fri. late Sept.-May) is open year-round, and the clinics at **Lake** (307/242-7241, 8:30am-8:30pm daily mid-May-mid-Sept., 10am-6:30pm daily mid-Sept.-late Sept.) and **Old Faithful** (307/344-7325, 7am-7pm daily mid-May-mid-Sept., 8:30am-5pm daily mid-Sept.-early Oct.) are open in prime visiting season.

TRANSPORTATION
Getting There
BY AIR
Yellowstone is about 90 miles (145 km) from the airports in Bozeman and Billings, 49 miles (79 km) from the airport in Jackson Hole, and 52 miles (84 km) from the airport in Cody. The **Yellowstone Airport** (WYS, 607 Airport Rd., West Yellowstone, www.yellowstoneairport.org, 406/646-7631) is served by Delta with regular service to Salt Lake City, and is only open late May-late September.

BY CAR
The North Entrance at Gardiner, which is the only entrance open year-round to cars, is 83 miles (134 km) south of Bozeman and 170 miles (275 km) southwest of Billings. The Northeast Entrance at Cooke City is 124 miles (200 km), including the spectacular Beartooth Highway, from Billings. The West Entrance at West Yellowstone is 90 miles (145 km) south of Bozeman. The East Entrance is 53 miles (85 km) west of Cody. The South Entrance is 49 miles (79 km) north of Jackson.

BY BUS
Shuttle service with **Karst Stage** (800/845-2778, www.karststage.com) is available from Bozeman to West Yellowstone year-round and to Gardiner during the winter and summer seasons.

Getting Around
PRIVATE VEHICLES
Your best bet to see the park on your own terms is to go by car. The nearest car-rental

agencies are **Budget, Avis,** and **Big Sky Car Rentals** (800/231-5991), available in West Yellowstone. Cars can also be rented from airports in Billings, Bozeman, Cody, and Jackson Hole.

When planning your drive through Yellowstone, it is best to fill up your tank outside the park. Once inside, the gas prices you'll encounter tend to be extremely high, and options are quite limited. Gas stations are located within the park at Canyon, Fishing Bridge, Grant Village, Mammoth, Upper and Lower Old Faithful, and Tower Junction. They are generally open late spring-early fall.

One of the things that makes Yellowstone so wild and enchanting is its utter unpredictability—something that relates to wildlife, weather, and, unfortunately, road conditions. A 20-year $300-million plan is currently afoot to address the structural deficiencies of Yellowstone's roads. Keep a close watch on road closures and delays that can happen at any time of year because of construction, bad weather, or even fire. For a 24-hour road report, check **Road Construction Delays and Closures** (307/344-2117, www.nps.gov/yell). Information on state roads is available from the **Montana Department of Transportation** (800/226-7623, www.mdt511.com) and **Wyoming Department of Transportation** (888/996-7623, www.wyoroad.info). **National Weather Service** (www.crh.noaa.gov) reports are available for Yellowstone and Grand Teton National Parks.

TOURS

Xanterra/Yellowstone National Park Lodges (307/344-7311 or 866/439-7375, www.yellowstonenationalparklodges.com) offers a variety of different bus tours of the park during the summer, including historic Yellow Bus tours that range 1-12 hours. The **Grand Loop Tour** ($118-124.50 adults, $59-62.50 kids 3-11) departs daily from Gardiner, Mammoth, and the Old Faithful Inn and covers the entire park in one day. Other options include early morning or evening wildlife tours, lake sunset tours, geyser gazers, Lamar Valley wildlife expeditions, photo safaris, boat tours, fishing trips, and custom guided tours.

Depending upon your particular interests, there are a range of companies outside the park that offer specialized tours of Yellowstone. The only one inside the park, and an outstanding option, is the **Yellowstone Forever Institute** (406/848-2400, www.yellowstone.org). Courses are broken into summer and winter semesters, and single-day course fees begin around $139. Multiday tours are also available. The courses are engaging and are taught by experts in their fields. Using Yellowstone as their classroom, the instructors concentrate on "individual aspects of the ecosystem." During the summer, you can take the "Introduction to Wolf Management and Ecology" course led by a wolf biologist or "Mammal Signs: Interpreting Tracks, Scat, and Hair" with an animal tracker. There's also a three-week naturalist guide certificate program offered. Classes can focus on flora with courses such as "The Art of Wildflower Identification"; other options include "Yellowstone's Geoecosystem" and "Wilderness First Aid." The institute can provide unique (and inexpensive) lodging in its two field campuses, in Gardiner and the Lamar Valley. Or it can include standard hotel lodging at park hotels.

A newer offering for Yellowstone Forever is **Yellowstone Day Adventures** (May 30-Aug., $79 adults, $49 children) in which guests are picked up at dawn, whisked to the Lamar Valley with a wildlife expert for the chance to see elk, pronghorn, bison, and maybe bears and wolves, and returned by day's end to Gardiner. Tours are offered Wednesdays and Fridays during peak summer season and include breakfast, hot beverages, expert instruction, all transportation, use of scopes, binoculars and digiscoping equipment. If you take the time to browse through the course catalog, you will likely find something geared to your interests. Any of the Yellowstone Forever Institute tours are one of the best ways to get an in-depth insider's view of Yellowstone.

Other tour operators that offer a range of excursions in the park include **Yellowstone Tour & Travel** (800/221-1151, www. yellowstone-travel.com), a full-service travel agency in West Yellowstone that can book everything from accommodations and tours to complete packages, and **Yellowstone Alpen Guides** (555 Yellowstone Ave., 406/646-9591 or 800/858-3502, www.yellowstoneguides. com, from $95 adults, $90 seniors, $85 children under 16), also in West Yellowstone, which offers a fantastic array of naturalist-guided tours year-round.

PLANTS AND ANIMALS

Yellowstone is a living, breathing, evolving ecosystem that is home to a diversity of high-alpine, subalpine, and forest plants (more than 1,000 native species of flowering plants) and an extraordinary number of animals (including 67 mammal species). It is fascinating to understand how the flora and fauna relate—and react—to one another throughout the park.

Plants

What makes the plantlife in Yellowstone so interesting is neither the abundance nor the variety but rather the relationship between the plants and their environment and the way they are determined and shaped by forces of geology, climate, fire, insect infestation, drought, flood, and not least of all, wildlife. In various places throughout the park, for example, visitors will notice small fenced areas where grazing animals like elk, deer, and bison do not have access. The flora is decidedly different when it is protected from herbivores. The massive burns of 1988 and, more recently in 2016, have given rise to a plant lover's paradise where hot pink fireweed is among the first to recolonize the blackened areas. The geothermal areas have their own rare and unique plant communities. And the reintroduction of wolves caused the movements of elk to be more sporadic as they tried to avoid being eaten, which led to an increase in the number of willows and a resulting increase in various

animals, including beavers, that thrive on willows. These chains of events linking plants, animals, and the natural forces that control the park are endless and fascinating.

Animals

For many, the fauna in Yellowstone is the main event. With large mammals such as elk, bison, bighorn sheep, pronghorn, bears, wolves, and mountain lions, Yellowstone is among the best areas in the country to see wildlife in its natural habitat. For those willing to get up early and be patient enough to wait, sometimes for hours, Yellowstone is like the Discovery Channel brought to life.

There are a few species of reptiles and amphibians known to inhabit the park—10 in all—thanks to Yellowstone's cool, dry climate, and some 330 species of birds have been documented since the park's 1872 founding, ranging from tiny calliope hummingbirds to majestic trumpeter swans.

But it's the big animals that draw more than four million people to the park annually. The omnipresent bison are the largest animal in the park, with males (bulls) weighing upward of 1,800 pounds (817 kg) and females (cows) averaging about 1,000 pounds (454 kg). Yellowstone is the only place in the Lower 48 where wild bison have existed since prehistoric times. The herd dropped to near-extinction levels at the turn of the 20th century with only 50 animals within the park boundaries. The importation of 21 bison from private herds and the subsequent 50 years of repopulation efforts led to a marked increase in numbers. By 2006 some 3,500 of these wild, woolly behemoths once again roamed the high prairies of Yellowstone, but significant population fluctuations occur, primarily because of fears surrounding the disease brucellosis. In a given year, the bison population in Yellowstone ranges 2,300-5,000 animals, with the population in August 2016 hovering above the high end at 5,500.

The most recent official count in 2016 placed the number of grizzly bears in the

The Ecology of Fire

In 1988, wildfires blazed through Yellowstone National Park. To quell the flames, the largest firefighting effort in U.S. history was organized, involving 25,000 people and $120 million, but it was the first snowfall of the season that would eventually rein in the fire. The fires began in July and burned until November. More than 793,000 acres (320,916 hectares), roughly one-third of the park, were affected, 67 structures were destroyed, and 345 elk and 63 other large mammals died as a direct result of the fire. The entire nation watched in horror as the first national park burned. The park's fire management plan consequently came under intense scrutiny. The question on everyone's lips was, "How could this have happened?"

During the first half of the 20th century, it was widely believed that nothing good came of wildfire. In the 1940s and 1950s, all fires in Yellowstone were immediately suppressed. During the 1960s, however, the tide shifted as studies showed that fire was a natural condition helping to cleaned out understory and residual dead plant matter, creating less competition between tree species for important nutrients and natural elements. It was determined that wildfires had always been a part of the ecosystem and were necessary to preserve healthy and continuous life cycles of plants and trees.

By the 1970s, the park allowed wildfires caused by lightning to burn under controlled conditions. Until 1988, 235 fires had burned; only 10 of which were larger than 100 acres (40.5 hectares). In June 1988, the driest year in the park's history, early summer storms produced lightning that ignited 20 fires. Eleven self-extinguished, and the rest were monitored; by mid-July only 8,500 acres (3,440 hectares) had burned. Within a week, park managers agreed to extinguish all fires due to extremely dry conditions. Strong winds made that impossible and, within a week, 99,000 acres (40,064 hectares) had burned. By September, in order for emergency workers to battle the blaze, the park had to close to visitors for the first time in its history.

By spring, the earth was green and vibrant amid the fire-blackened swaths. With the exception of moose, which lost a significant portion of their forested habitat, the animal populations appeared as if nothing had ever happened. Elk were even reported munching on the burned bark. Yellowstone, it seemed, was different—better and healthier.

park at 150, with another 690 living within the Greater Yellowstone Ecosystem, and likely three to four times as many black bears. Gray wolves were reintroduced to the park (after being entirely killed off in the area) in 1995, and in 2016 there were 108 wolves in 11 packs living primarily within the park boundaries, and as many as 528 living in the Greater Yellowstone Ecosystem. Wolverines and lynx live within the park but are rarely seen. Coyotes are plentiful and often visible from cars, and somewhere between 25-35 mountain lions inhabit the northern range. Elk populations soar in the summer months to 10,000-20,000 animals in six or seven herds, compared to the roughly 5,000 elk that winter in the park, while moose, hard hit by the fires of 1988, number fewer than 200. In the northern Yellowstone ecosystem, there are 329 bighorn sheep, with 163 counted inside the

park. There are also 208 nonnative mountain goats in and around Yellowstone.

Finding the animals means knowing their habitats, being willing to wait during the edges of daylight, and oftentimes just plain getting lucky. A number of excellent wildlife-spotting guides are available through **Yellowstone Forever** (www.yellowstone. org), but the most obvious place to start is by asking any of the rangers at the park's various visitors centers. They can tell you about recent predatory kills, bear and wolf activity, elk and bison migrations, and the most up-to-date sightings of any number of animals.

As is true with nearly every feature of the park, the importance of safety in the face of wildlife cannot be overstated. Just check out YouTube for any number of videos highlighting ill-advised visitor interactions with wildlife. Be certain to stay at least 25 yards (22.9

m) away from bison and elk and at least 100 yards (91.4 m) away from bears, wolves, and other predators. If the animals change their behavior because of your presence, if they stop eating to look at you, for example, you are too close and are creating a significant and perhaps even life-threatening hazard for both the animal and yourself. Always remember that you are the visitor here and they are the residents; show proper respect.

GEOTHERMAL FEATURES

If the animals are what bring people to Yellowstone, the geothermal features are what transfix them and lure them back year after year.

The world's largest concentration of thermal features—more than 10,000 in all—Yellowstone bursts to life with geysers, hot springs, fumaroles (steam vents), and mud pots. There are six grand geysers, of which **Old Faithful** is the most famous, and more than 300 lesser geysers. Throughout the park are a number of basins where visitors can see all four types of thermal features, including **Norris Geyser Basin.**

The thermal features in Yellowstone are an indication of the region's volcanic past, present, and future, and as such they are in constant states of change. Small but daily earthquakes cause shifts in activity and temperature. The travertine **Mammoth Terraces** are literally growing and changing on a daily basis to the point that the boardwalks have had to be altered to protect visitors from different flows of searing hot water.

As miraculous as these water features are to see—with dramatic color displays and water dances that put Las Vegas's Bellagio fountains to shame—and to smell (think rotten eggs), what you can't see is perhaps even more compelling: thermophiles, heat-loving microorganisms that inhabit the geothermal features throughout the park. A source of ongoing scientific study, these thermophiles are modern examples of the earth's first life-forms and responsible for the discovery of DNA fingerprinting.

As spellbinding as they are, particularly in winter when the warm steam beckons, it is critically important to stay on boardwalks in geothermal areas and never touch the water. In addition to being boiling hot, many features are highly acidic or alkaline and could cause extreme chemical burns. The ground around the features is often thin and unstable, occasionally allowing animals to break through and be cooked. Twenty-one people have died in Yellowstone's thermal features, including one man who strayed off the boardwalk in 2016 to get a closer look and broke through the thin crust; the water was so hot that by the time help arrived, there were no remains to collect.

HISTORY
Tracing Human History

Evidence from archaeological sites, trails, and even oral histories suggests that humans inhabited the region of Yellowstone as far back as 11,000 years ago. And although the land is rich with history, not much has changed since the park was created in 1872, the invaluable blessing of having been protected as the nation's first national park. The unique geothermal features, pristine lakes and waterfalls, abundant wildlife, and the different ecosystems have endured through the years.

Yellowstone was traversed by various Native American tribes, including the Crow, Blackfeet, Nez Perce, and Shoshone, whose oral history teaches that they originated in this area. Although these nomads passed through the area, only a branch of the Shoshone, known as the "Sheep Eaters," made Yellowstone their home. The first Europeans to have visited the area were most likely fur traders and trappers who seem to have missed the unusual geothermal activity. Lewis and Clark's expedition bypassed the region completely. On their return voyage in 1806, however, John Colter separated from the group and ventured alone into the region. He is considered the first non-Native American to

Yellowstone's Supervolcano: Waiting for the Big One?

It's always interesting to watch visitors' expressions when you tell them that in Yellowstone National Park they are standing atop one of the world's largest active supervolcanoes … and that it is overdue for an apocalyptic eruption. While these facts are true, the reality is much less threatening. Indeed there have been three phenomenal eruptions over the course of the last two million years, and the patterns do indicate that the volcano is overdue to erupt. But scientists agree that the chances of a massive eruption in the next 1,000 or even 10,000 years are very slight. For the time being, anyway, the supervolcano that gives rise to Yellowstone's extraordinary geothermal features is all bark and no bite—thankfully.

A SUPER HISTORY

The first supervolcanic eruption 2.1 million years ago was 6,000 times more powerful than the 1980 eruption of Mount St. Helens, spouting rock and ash in every direction from Texas to Canada, Missouri to California. The eruption emptied the magma chamber located just underneath the park and caused a massive sinking of the earth, known as a caldera, within the confines of what is now the park. Small lava flows filled in the perimeter of the Huckleberry Ridge Caldera over the course of hundreds of thousands of years.

The second major eruption occurred 1.3 million years ago and created the Henry's Fork Caldera. The most recent massive eruption took place roughly 640,000 years ago and created the Yellowstone Caldera, which is 30 by 45 miles (48 by 72 km) in size. The perimeter of the Yellowstone Caldera is still visible in places throughout the park. Hike up Mount Washburn on Dunraven Pass between Canyon and Tower, look south, and you will see the vast caldera formed by the most recent eruption. The caldera rim is also visible at Gibbon Falls, Lewis Falls, and Lake Butte. As you drive between Mammoth and Gardiner, look at Mount Everts to the east and you will see layers of ash from the various eruptions.

TODAY'S EARTHQUAKES ARE HINTS

But volcanic activity is not a thing of the past in Yellowstone. The magma, which some scientists think is just 5 miles (8 km) beneath the surface of the park in places as opposed to the typical 40, has created two enormous bulges, known as resurgent domes, near Sour Creek and Mallard Lake. The Sour Creek Dome is growing at an impressive rate of 1.5 inches per year, causing Yellowstone Lake to tip southward, leaving docks on the north side completely out of the water and flooding the forested shore of the south side. In addition, there are roughly 2,000 earthquakes every year centered in Yellowstone, most of which cannot be felt. In 2014, however, a 4.8-magnitude quake occurred 4 miles (6.4 km) from Norris Geyser Basin. The earthquakes shift geothermal activity in the park and keep the natural plumbing system that feeds the geyser basins flowing. They also suggest volcanic activity. In early 2010, a series of more than 3,200 small earthquakes (the largest registered 3.8 on the Richter scale) rocked the park, with 16 quakes registering a magnitude greater than 3.0. A 1985 swarm recorded more than 3,000 earthquakes over three months, with the largest registering at 4.9 on the Richter scale.

DON'T WORRY!

Still, the scientists at the Yellowstone Volcano Observatory have no reason to suspect that an eruption, or even a lava flow, is imminent. For more than three decades, scientists have been monitoring the region for precursors to volcanic eruptions—earthquake swarms, rapid ground deformation, gas releases, and lava flows—and although there is activity, none of it suggests anything immediately foreboding. Current real-time monitoring data, including earthquake activity and deformation, are available online at http://volcanoes.usgs.gov. The bottom line is that the volcano is real and active, but certainly not a threat in the immediate future, and not a reason to stay away from this awe-inspiring place.

have seen the thermal features in the park. When Colter returned home three years later, his stories were considered suspicious. His tales of "bubbling ground," "mountains made of glass," and rivers where you could catch a fish and cook it without ever removing it from the water seemed preposterous to Easterners. Colter's descriptions of fire and brimstone quickly earned the place the nickname of "Colter's Hell." However, as more fur traders moved into the region, the stories of boiling mud, steaming land, and hot pools of water continued. Jim Bridger explored the area in 1856 and is considered by some the "first geographer" of the region. He too shared wild descriptions that were met with similar skepticism.

Expeditions into Yellowstone

The first organized expeditions into the Yellowstone area were made in 1869 and 1870. It was the 1871 government-sponsored expedition into the region led by Ferdinand Vandeveer Hayden, however, that produced a detailed account of the area. The Hayden Geological Survey was accompanied by William Henry Jackson photographs and artwork by Henry W. Elliott and Thomas Moran. Photographs and spectacular paintings and drawings were splashed across magazines and newspapers around the East so that people could see the wonders of the region for the first time. It was this report, coupled with the earnest pleas of the men who had seen the area, that prodded Congress to grant the region national park status in 1872. That year, the park had 300 visitors.

Nathaniel Langford was the park's first superintendent, but without proper funding and staff he had difficulty protecting the land. Poachers and vandals exploited the park's natural resources, creating a state of general lawlessness. By 1886 the U.S. Army had entered the park to help regain control of the region. They built park structures, strengthened and enforced regulations, encouraged visitors, and made sure the land and wildlife were protected. Transportation infrastructure improvements also helped attract more visitors to the park. The Northern Pacific Railway extended to the town of Cinnabar, north of modern-day Gardiner, near the northern entrance of the park, and in 1915 automobiles were allowed into Yellowstone, making it more accessible to the masses. Following World War II, car travel exploded, and more than one million visitors came to the park in 1948.

Shaping Park Policy

The Army's leadership was not a long-term solution to managing the new national park, and in 1916 the National Park Service was created. (The birthday of the Park Service is still celebrated every year on August 25 with a smattering of hilariously decorated Christmas trees around the park.) Since then, the park's boundaries have been redrawn to encompass 2.2 million acres (890,308 hectares, roughly equivalent in size to the state of Connecticut), and wildlife management has been continuously refined as new science emerges. One fundamental change came as a result of the 1963 Leopold Report, which suggested that "natural regulation" was superior to the long-held unnatural management in which park managers controlled animal populations and altered the course of naturally occurring events like fire. Ecological Process Management, as it has come to be called, is still the core philosophy behind park management today.

Both the grizzly bear and the gray wolf (reintroduced to the park in 1995) have seen enormous improvements to their endangered status due to Yellowstone's wildlife policies. In 1988 the park experienced the largest wildfires in its history, affecting more than a third of its land, and once again sparking furious debates about management of public resources and the value of natural ecosystems. In the spring of 2016, the U.S. Fish and Wildlife Service proposed removing grizzlies from the endangered species list in the Greater

Yellowstone Ecosystem, a controversial decision that will likely be tied up in courts for years to come.

Modern-day Yellowstone is every bit as spellbinding as it was for John Colter and Jim Bridger and the scores of Native Americans who had traveled through the park long before them. But it is increasingly complex. Issues like bioprospecting, bison management in the face of the disease brucellosis, and the delisting criteria of endangered species loom large. Despite the fact that, thankfully, the physical features of Yellowstone—its mountainscapes, geothermal features, and wildlife populations—remain largely untouched, an area of this size with more than four million visitors annually (nearly three times the populations of Montana and Wyoming combined!) cannot be immune to human influence. The challenge as we move forward is to determine a way to let Yellowstone age and evolve in its own way, on its own time, while giving people around the world access to this unique and spectacular place. It is we, the visitors, who have an opportunity to be changed forever by time spent in Yellowstone, and not the other way around.

Gardiner

Named rather inauspiciously for a cannibalistic mountain man who allegedly got rid of his wives year after year by, ahem, eating them, Gardiner (population 875; elevation 5,314 ft/1,619 m) is actually a cute little town with plenty of places to stay, eat, and stock up and has ideal proximity to the park. The only year-round entrance to Yellowstone for automobiles, this scrubby little tourist town has a charm and an identity all its own. The Yellowstone River cuts a canyon beside the main drag, which allows for plenty of river-runner hangouts. Few other places in the world have elk congregating in the churchyard or on the front lawns of most of the motels in town. And where else do high school football players have to dodge bison dung as they're running for a touchdown? The town's architecture is a combination of glorious wood and stone "parkitecture" buildings alongside old-school Western-style buildings complete with false fronts. The towering **Roosevelt Arch,** built in 1903 and dedicated by Yellowstone champion Teddy Roosevelt himself, welcomes visitors to the park with its inspiring slogan, "For the Benefit and Enjoyment of the People." Yes, Gardiner is built around its proximity to the park, but the town has maintained its integrity by preserving its history and making the most of its surroundings.

SIGHTS
★ Boiling River

Halfway between Gardiner and Mammoth Hot Springs, straddling the Montana-Wyoming border and the 45th parallel, the halfway point between the equator and the North Pole, is the Boiling River, one of only two swimmable thermal features in Yellowstone. From the clearly marked parking area, visitors amble upstream along a 0.5-mile (0.8-km) rocky path running parallel to the Gardner River. Where the trail ends and the steam envelops almost everything, a gushing hot spring called the Boiling River flows into the otherwise icy Gardner River. The hot and cold waters mix to a perfect temperature that can be enjoyed year-round. The area is open during daylight hours only, and all swimmers must wear a bathing suit. The Boiling River is closed each year during spring and early summer runoff, when temperature fluctuations and rushing water put swimmers at risk. Alcohol is not permitted.

Kids and adults alike marvel at the floating Day-Glo green algae. The water should not be ingested. Bison and elk frequent the area, and despite the regular crowds of people (note that 20 people constitute a crowd in this part of the West), this is one of the most unique and unforgettable ways to enjoy a few hours in Yellowstone.

SPORTS AND RECREATION

Fishing and Boating

The Yellowstone is the longest free-flowing river in the Lower 48, and as such it offers excellent boating and fishing opportunities. With the river plunging through town on its way to Yankee Jim Canyon, Gardiner is home to several outfitters that can whet your appetite for adventure, trout, or both. The **Flying Pig Adventure Company** (511 Scott St., 888/792-9193, www.flyingpigrafting. com, May-Sept., 2-hour raft trip $43 adults, $33 children 12 and under) is a full-service outfitter offering guided white-water rafting, horseback rides, wildlife safaris, and cowboy cookouts. **Yellowstone Raft Company** (111 2nd St., 406/848-7777 or 800/858-7781, www.yellowstoneraft.com, May-Sept., half-day raft trip $43 adults, $33 children 6-12) was established in 1978 and has an excellent reputation for experienced guides and top-of-the-line equipment. For adrenaline junkies, Yellowstone Raft Company offers sit-on-top kayak instruction and adventures.

For anglers eager to wet a line in or out of the park in search of native cutthroats or brown trout, **Park's Fly Shop** (202 2nd St. S., 406/848-7314, www.parksflyshop.com, 8am-6pm daily summer, 9am-5pm Mon.-Sat., 10am-4pm Sun. fall-spring) is the best place to start. This is an old-school shop with a 1920s cash register—nothing fancy here. It offers half-day trips for two people starting around $425, and full-day trips for two from $525. Anglers can pick up their licenses and any supplies in the retail shop, which stays open year-round. And since Park's has been serving the area since 1953, its guides are keenly aware of the spots where the fish greatly outnumber the anglers.

Hiking

Yellowstone is a hiker's paradise, and unless you have a pet that needs to stretch its legs, hiking just outside the park is like spending the day in the Disney World parking lot. Not that there isn't stunning country in every direction, but there is something particularly alluring about hiking within the boundaries of the park.

That said, some 4.7 miles (7.6 km) south of the terraces at Mammoth Hot Springs, on the left-hand side after the Golden Gate Bridge, is the **Glen Creek Trailhead** and a small dirt parking lot. A range of wonderful hikes start from this point. Across the street on the west side of the road, a trail leads through **The Hoodoos,** massive travertine boulders that look otherworldly in this setting, and down the mountain 3.8 miles (6.1 km) back to Mammoth. If you cannot arrange either a drop-off at the trailhead or a shuttle, the return trip, another 3.8 miles (6.1 km), climbs constantly for nearly 1,000 vertical feet (305 m). Another more ambitious hike is the 9.2-mile (14.8-km) round-trip to **Osprey Falls.** The first 4 miles (6.4 km) are easy and flat, following an abandoned roadbed popular with mountain bikers. A blink-and-you'll-miss-it spur trail off the south side of the road leads hikers down into Sheepeater Canyon and the remaining 0.6 mile (1 km) to the mesmerizing 150-foot (45.7-m) falls. Relax, have a snack, and save your energy for the 800-vertical-foot (244-m) climb back up to the road. **Bunsen Peak** offers hikers an interesting walk through an entirely burned forest and all of its colorful rebirth, as well as a stunning view from the 8,500-foot (2,591-m) summit. The climb is steep: 1,300 vertical feet (396 m) over 2.1 miles (3.4 km). Try to ignore the hum of the radio tower near the summit, easily accomplished when the summit view fills your senses.

ENTERTAINMENT AND EVENTS

The biggest event of the year in this gateway community is the **Annual NRA Gardiner Rodeo** (406/848-7971, $10 adults), usually held in June over Father's Day weekend. The rodeo is held in the Jim Duffy arena at the northern end of town off U.S. 89 and includes the usual competitions such as bull riding and bareback bronc riding. Women and juniors compete in barrel racing and breakaway roping. The first night of the rodeo is followed by a dance at the Gardiner Community Center, and the following day the chamber of commerce hosts a parade downtown. This is a great small-town rodeo.

But Gardiner is far from a one-event town. In late February, the **Jardine Ski Run** (406/848-7971) is a 5-mile (8-km) groomed track race where outlandish costumes are appreciated as much, if not more than, speed. Another worthwhile pursuit for the active is the **Park to Paradise Triathlon** (406/848-7971) in early May, which includes a 17.5-mile (28.2-km) bike, 4-mile (6.4-km) run, and 7-mile (11.3-km) river paddle. The much less demanding and very family-friendly **Annual Brewfest** (406/848-7971, $20) happens in mid-August and raises money for the local chamber with live entertainment, food, crafts, microbrews, and fun kids' activities like soda-tasting, face-painting, horseshoes, and kites. For more information on these events, contact the **Gardiner Chamber of Commerce** (406/848-7971, www.gardinerchamber.com).

FOOD

Known since 1960 for its "Hateful Hamburgers" and the huge personality of its owner, Helen, this fabulous burger joint was sold to the Wild West Rafting Company and is now known as ★ **Wild West Corral** (Hwy. 89 S., across from the Super 8 Motel, 406/848-7627, 11am-10pm daily May-Oct., burgers $7-17). Even without Helen, this is still the kind of place you might easily drive 100 miles (161 km) to for the burgers, shakes, and old-school ambience. The limited seating is mostly outside, and there is often a line of people waiting to order. But none of that will matter when you take your first bite of a bison bacon cheeseburger or a perfectly grilled elk burger. Wild West Corral even managed to improve on Helen's by expanding the menu and cleaning the place up a bit. This is still a little slice of hamburger paradise—if you like that sort of thing.

Just over the river toward the park, the

K-Bar Pizza (202 Main St., 406/848-9995, www.kbarmontana.com, 4pm-9pm Mon.-Thurs., 4pm-10pm Fri., 11am-11pm Sat.-Sun., large pizzas $18-24) is a classic bar that's been dishing up surprisingly good homemade pizza since 1953. **The Raven Grill** (118 Park St., 406/848-9171, 5pm-10pm daily mid-Apr.-mid-Oct., $10-28) boasts a small but excellent menu long on comfort food and made from scratch. It also serves cocktails, including a mean Montana Huckleberry Moscow Mule. For a good, hearty breakfast, excellent pastries, fresh Mexican food, and burgers, the **Yellowstone Grill** (404 Scott St., 406/848-9433, 7am-2pm Tues.-Sat., 7am-noon Sun., $7-12) is sure to please. Remember though, this is small-town Montana. Sometimes the place closes when short-staffed. Or when the owners' youngest son has a Legion baseball game. Be glad for that; the important stuff still matters here. You can always have a late lunch.

ACCOMMODATIONS

Gardiner is built to accommodate the overflow from the park, but in reality, many of the little motels have more charm and much better value, particularly in non-summer months, than those inside the park. For the most part, it's hard to go wrong in Gardiner. There are plenty of small cabins and larger vacation rentals in the area. The folk Victorian ★ **Gardiner Guest House** (112 Main St. E., 406/848-9414, $95-165 summer, $75-115 winter) welcomes both children and pets and offers three modest but comfortable guest rooms and a cabin. Owners Richard and Nance Parks are longtime residents and an extensive source of information on the area. His fly shop and guiding company, **Park's Fly Shop** (202 2nd St. S., 406/848-7314, www.parksflyshop.com), is one of the oldest businesses in town. **Yellowstone Park Riverfront Cabins** (505 S. Yellowstone, 406/570-4500, www.cabinsontheyellowstone.com, $350/night) offers comfortable cabins in a quiet location above the river. Another option for small, basic, and reasonably priced cottages right in town is **Hillcrest Cottages**

(400 Scott St., 406/848-7353 or 800/970-7353, www.hillcrestcottages.com, early May-mid-Oct., $95-187). The cottages come in various sizes that can sleep 1-5 people. The **Flying Pig Adventure Company** (511 Scott St. W., 866/264-8448, www.flyingpigrafting.com) offers a host of higher-end vacation rentals ranging from cozy canvas wall tents on a nearby ranch ($200) and cabins ($175-300) to an enormous private lodge ($599) that can sleep up to 15. Minimum nights apply.

For more standard hotels, there is a decent selection ranging from the riverfront **Absaroka Lodge** (310 Scott St., 406/848-7414, www.yellowstonemotel.com, $85-190), where each room has its own balcony, and the **Comfort Inn** (107 Hellroaring St., 406/848-7536 or 800/424-6423, www.comfortinn.com, $162-325) to the barebones but clean and pet-friendly **Super 8** (702 Scott St. W., 406/848-7401, www.wyndhamhotels.com, $71-221).

CAMPING

The difference between camping outside the park and inside Yellowstone is simply that you need to focus on reservations and availability instead of permits and regulations. There are six campgrounds in Gardiner—four national forest campgrounds and two private ones.

The private **Yellowstone RV Park & Campground** (121 U.S. 89 S., 406/848-7496, May-Oct., 46 sites including pull-through and tent sites, tent sites $30-40, RV sites $48-72) is ideally situated on the Yellowstone River just 1.3 miles (2.1 km) north of the park entrance. The other private campground is **Rocky Mountain RV Park & Cabins** (14 Jardine Rd., 406/848-7251, www.

rockymountainrvpark.com, May-Sept., standard RV sites $46-59, deluxe RV sites $52-67, cabins $75-195), just four blocks from the park entrance.

Those in search of a more rustic experience might enjoy checking out a national forest campground. The pack-in, pack-out **Bear Creek Campground** (Forest Rd. 493, 10.5 mi/16.9 km northeast of Gardiner, 406/848-7375, 4 sites with no services, mid-June-late Oct. depending on weather, free) and the **Timber Camp Campground** (Forest Rd. 493, 9.5 mi/15.3 km northeast of Gardiner, 406/848-7375, no services, mid-June-late Oct. depending on weather, free) are both small, isolated, and pleasantly rustic. The other Forest Service campgrounds in Gardiner are Eagle Creek Campground and Canyon Campground, both of which charge $7 per night (plus $3 per additional vehicle) and are about 15 minutes outside of town.

INFORMATION AND SERVICES

For information on Gardiner and the area around it, the **Gardiner Chamber of Commerce** (216 Park St., 406/848-7971, www.gardinerchamber.com, 9am-5pm Mon. and Wed.-Thurs., 9am-noon Tues. and Fri., extended summer hours) is an excellent and welcoming resource. Just a couple of doorways down, the headquarters of the **Yellowstone Forever** (308 Park St., 406/848-2400, www.yellowstone.org, 8am-8pm daily) offers information about the park, as well as its own phenomenal educational tours. A great gift shop also is on-site, and the nicest bathrooms you have likely seen in a while.

The Northern Loop

With striking panoramas, wonderful thermals, plentiful wildlife, and year-round vehicle access between the north and northeast entrances, this is one of the most underappreciated parts of the park. The accommodations and dining are not as fancy as elsewhere, but the crowds are more manageable, and the experience is just as good or better. Phenomenal highlights include Mammoth Hot Springs, the Lamar Valley, Tower Falls, Dunraven Pass, the Grand Canyon of the Yellowstone, and Norris Geyser Basin.

SIGHTS
★ Mammoth and the Mammoth Hot Springs Terraces

Just 5 miles (8 km) into the park and up the road from Gardiner, Mammoth is the primary northern hub of Yellowstone National Park. It is also an interesting little community in its own right, with a small medical center, the most beautiful post office in the West, and a magnificent stone church. The town of Mammoth, once known as Fort Yellowstone, was essentially built by the U.S. Army during its 1886-1918 occupation. Thinking they were on a temporary assignment, the soldiers erected canvas wall tents and lived in them through five harsh winters. In 1890, Congress set aside $50,000 for the construction of a permanent post, a stately collection of stone colonial revival-style buildings, most of which are still in use today.

The 2015 renovated **Albright Visitor Center** (307/344-2263, 8am-6pm daily mid-June-Labor Day, 9am-5pm daily Labor Day-mid-June) is a must-see. There are films, history and wildlife exhibits, and a small but excellent selection of books and videos in the shop run by **Yellowstone Forever** (406/848-2400, www.yellowstone.org). While at the center, don't miss seeing some of the artwork produced during the 1871 Hayden Geological Survey of the park, including quality reproductions of painter Thomas Moran's famous watercolor sketches and original photographs by William Henry Jackson. Rangers on staff can usually give you up-to-date animal sightings and activity reports. The flush toilets downstairs are the last for a while.

The primary ecological attraction in Mammoth (other than the elk often seen lounging around and nibbling on the green grass) can be found on the **Mammoth Hot Springs Terraces.** Since the days of the earliest stagecoach trails into the park, they have been a visual and olfactory marvel for visitors. The Hayden Expedition named the area White Mountain Hot Spring for the cream-colored, steplike travertine terraces.

Beneath the ground, the Norris-Mammoth fault carries superheated water rich in dissolved calcium and bicarbonate. As the water emerges through cracks in the surface, carbon dioxide is released as a gas, and the carbonate combines with calcium to form travertine. The mountain is continuously growing as travertine is deposited and then shifted as the cracks are sealed and the mineral-laden water emerges somewhere else. For frequent visitors to the park, vast changes are noticeable from one visit to the next. In addition to changes in shape and water flow, the colors at Mammoth can vary dramatically from one day to the next. Not only does travertine morph from bright white when it is new to cream and then gray as it is exposed to the elements, the cyanobacteria create fabulous color shifts too—from turquoise to green and yellow to red and brown, depending on water temperatures, available sunlight, and pH levels.

Liberty Cap, at the base of the terraces, is an excellent example of a dormant spring, where all but the core cone has been eroded away. **Minerva Terrace** and **Canary Spring** are two other springs worth seeing. Their temperatures average around 160°F, and when they are flowing, they often put on marvelous color displays.

Tower Falls

Eighteen scenic miles (29 km) down the road from Mammoth Hot Springs—past **Undine Falls** and **Blacktail Plateau,** where you can see deer, elk, and bison along with some impressive lookouts—is **Tower Junction** and the breathtaking Tower Falls. The waterfall itself cascades 132 feet (40.2 m) from volcanic basalt. A popular spot with visitors and just steps from the parking lot, this is not the ideal place for solitude, but it is lovely to see.

Dunraven Pass

Between Tower and the dramatic Grand Canyon of the Yellowstone is one of the most nerve-racking and perhaps most beautiful drives in the park. Climbing up the flanks of **Mount Washburn,** Dunraven Pass is the highest road elevation in the park. The spectacular summit of the road tops out at 8,859 feet (2,700 m) and offers impressive views of Yellowstone's caldera rim. Eagle eyes can also spot the nearby Grand Canyon of the Yellowstone. Hikers will have no shortage of trailheads to start from. The whitebark pines that grow along the road are a critical and dwindling food source for grizzly bears, so keep your eyes open. Because of its extreme altitude and relative exposure, Dunraven Pass is one of the last roads to open in the spring and one of the first to close when bad weather hits. For current road information, call 307/344-2117.

★ Grand Canyon of the Yellowstone

Yellowstone's most recent volcanic explosion, some 600,000 years ago, created a massive caldera and subsequent lava flows, one of which was called the Canyon Rhyolite flow, in the area that is now known as the Grand Canyon of the Yellowstone. This particular lava flow was impacted by a thermal basin, which altered the rhyolite and created the beautiful palette of colors in the rock through constant heating and cooling. Over time, lakes, rivers, and glaciers formed in the region, and the relatively soft rhyolite was easily carved away. Roughly 10,000 years ago, the last of the area's glaciers melted, causing a rush of water to carve the canyon into the form it has today. The 20-mile-long (32-km) canyon is still growing thanks to the forces of erosion, including water, wind, and earthquakes. A

Canary Spring at Mammoth Hot Springs Terraces

number of terrific lookouts are on both the North and South Rims of the canyon.

Before setting out for the canyon itself, visitors are advised to visit the **Canyon Visitor Education Center** (307/344-2550, 8am-6pm daily mid-June-early Oct., 9am-5pm daily mid-Apr.-mid-June and early Oct.-early Nov.), which has an outstanding and vast exhibit on Yellowstone's supervolcano, geothermal activity, and other natural history. In fact, this should be a mandatory stop for every visitor who might otherwise have no appreciation for the region's fascinating geology.

On the **North Rim,** don't miss **Inspiration Point,** a natural viewing platform that gives a bird's-eye view both up and down the river. Nathaniel Langford, who would go on to be the park's first superintendent, stood in the same spot with the Washburn Expedition in 1870. He wrote:

> Standing there or rather lying there for greater safety, I thought how utterly impossible it would be to describe to another the sensations inspired by such a presence. As I took in the scene, I realized my own littleness, my helplessness, my dread exposure to destruction, my inability to cope with or even comprehend the mighty architecture of nature.

Look down, if you dare, among the nooks and crannies of rock to try to spot nesting ospreys.

Another phenomenal viewing platform can be found at **Lookout Point,** where visitors can gaze from afar at the thundering Lower Falls of the Yellowstone. Visitors who want to get closer to the spray of the falls and don't mind a long hike down, and back up again, can head toward the base of the falls at **Red Rock Point.** It's a 0.5-mile (0.8-km) trip one-way that drops more than 500 vertical feet (152.4 m). There is another platform at the top of the 308-foot (94-m) falls aptly named the **Brink of the Lower Falls.** This lookout also involves a 0.5-mile (0.8-km) hike and a 600-foot (183-m) elevation loss. The **Upper Falls** are just over one-third the size of the lower falls, at 109 feet (33.2 m), but they are worth a gander and can be easily accessed at

the **Brink of the Upper Falls.** Mountain man Jim Bridger purportedly regaled friends with tales of the Upper Falls as early as 1846 and urged them to see it for themselves.

From the **South Rim,** visitors can see the Upper Falls from the **Upper Falls Viewpoint.** A trail that dates back to 1898, **Uncle Tom's Trail** still takes hardy hikers to the base of the **Lower Falls.** The trail down loses 500 vertical feet (152.4 m) through a series of 300 stairs and paved inclines, but what goes down must come up again. From **Artist Point,** one of the largest and most inspiring lookouts, visitors get a glorious view of the distant Lower Falls and the river as it snakes down the pinkish canyon. It was long thought that Artist Point was where painter Thomas Moran made sketches for his 7 by 12-foot (2.1 by 3.7-m) masterpiece *Grand Canyon of the Yellowstone.* More likely, say historians, he painted from a spot on the North Rim now called **Moran Point.**

Norris Geyser Basin

Both the hottest and the most unpredictable geyser basin in the park, Norris Geyser Basin is a fascinating collection of bubbling and colorful geothermal features. A 2.3-mile (3.7-km) web of boardwalks and trails leads visitors through this remarkable basin. From the **Norris Geyser Basin Museum** (307/344-2812, 9am-6pm daily mid-Apr.-Sept., 9am-5pm daily Oct.-early Nov., free), which carefully unravels the geothermal mysteries of the region, there are two loop trails guiding visitors safely through the basin. The 1930s log and stone building that houses the museum has been designated a National Historic Landmark. There is also an information desk and a Yellowstone Association bookstore inside the building.

Porcelain Basin is a stark, barren setting with a palette of pink, red, orange, and yellow mineral oxides. Some of the features of note include **Africa Geyser,** which had been

---

1: Norris Geyser Basin 2: Lower Falls 3: view from Inspiration Point

a hot spring in the shape of its namesake continent and started erupting in 1971. When it is active, **Whirligig Geyser,** named in 1904 by the Hague Party, erupts in a swirling pattern for a few minutes at irregular periods with a roar and hiss. The hottest steam vent in the hottest geothermal basin in the park is **Black Growler,** which has measured 280°F. The second-largest geyser in Norris, **Ledge Geyser** erupts irregularly to heights up to 125 feet (38.1 m).

In Norris's **Back Basin** you'll find the world's tallest geyser, **Steamboat Geyser,** which can erupt more than 300 feet (91.4 m) in the air. Minor eruptions of 10-40 feet (3-12.2 m) in height are more common. The eruptions can last 3-40 minutes and be separated by days or decades (in the past, Steamboat has gone more than 50 years without an eruption, but in 1964, it erupted 29 times). A major eruption in September 2014 happened at 11pm and was witnessed by a park ranger. Prior to that, the last major eruption occurred in 2013, and before that in 2005. In 2018, Steamboat entered an active phase with eruptions starting in March (after 3.5 years of silence), followed by two in April, four in May, three in June, and one in July. Just down the boardwalk, **Cistern Spring** is linked to Steamboat Geyser and drains in advance of a major eruption. The color is a beautiful blue, enhanced by as much as 0.5 inch of gray sinter deposited annually. By comparison, Old Faithful only deposits 0.5-1 inch of sinter every century. **Echinus Geyser** is the world's largest acid geyser and is almost as acidic as vinegar. Eruptions since 2007 have been rare and unpredictable, typically lasting about 4 minutes, but large ones have been known to reach heights of 80-125 feet (24.4-38.1 m).

SPORTS AND RECREATION

Yellowstone is indeed a hiker's paradise, with ubiquitous brown signs pointing to trailheads. Look for them anytime your legs need a stretch. In the northern loop, there are some fantastic trails in an otherwise nondescript stretch between Norris and Canyon. Drive east of Norris Junction 3.5 miles (5.6 km) or 8.5 miles (13.7 km) west of Canyon Junction to the **Ice Lake Trailhead** on the north side of the road. It is a fairly popular 4.5-mile (7.2-km) loop with minimal elevation gain. In fact, the entire trail to Ice Lake is wheelchair accessible and leads to the only wheelchair-accessible backcountry campsite in the park. Avid hikers will want to continue on to **Little Gibbon Falls,** a 25-foot (7.6-m) waterfall that is not even on the USGS topographic map. Another way to see this hidden gem is to find the Little Gibbon Falls Trailhead 0.4 mile (0.6 km) east of the Ice Lake Trailhead. There is a small pullout on the south side of the road. The trail starts about 100 feet (30.5 m) east of the pullout on the north side of the road. From here, Little Gibbon Falls is a 1.2-mile (1.9-km) out-and-back hike.

A lengthier hike in the vicinity of Tower Junction is along the **Hellroaring Trail,** a beautiful but strenuous hike through wide open sagebrush and along fishable water. The trailhead is 3.5 miles (5.6 km) west of Tower Junction and starts with a steep descent to a suspension bridge over the Yellowstone River. Day hikers can enjoy a 6.2-mile (10-km) there-and-back stretch through scenic sagebrush plateau to the confluence of Hellroaring Creek and the Yellowstone River. This is Yellowstone, so best to come prepared: Bring bear spray and a fly rod!

FOOD

By far the most unique meal available in the park is the ★ **Old West Dinner Cookout** (307/344-7311, www.yellowstonenationalparklodges. com) which departs daily early June-mid-Sept. from the Roosevelt Lodge and is served in Yellowstone's wilderness. The hearty steak-and-potatoes dinner with all the cowboy trimmings can be attended on horseback (1-hour rides from $87 ages 12 and over, $72 children 8-11, 2-hour rides from $94 ages 12 and over, $86 children 8-11) or via covered wagon (from $63 ages 12 and over, $50 children 3-11, free for children under 3).

Be Safe and Smart in the Backcountry

Hiking and camping in the Yellowstone backcountry is undoubtedly the best way to understand and appreciate this magnificently wild place. But with this opportunity comes the responsibility to keep yourself safe, protect the animals from human-caused altercations, and preserve this pristine environment.

When hiking, prevent erosion and trail degradation by hiking single file and always staying on the trail. Don't take shortcuts or cut corners on switchbacks. If you do have to leave the trail, disperse your group so that you don't inadvertently trample the vegetation and create a new, unwanted trail.

Chances are good that you will encounter some kind of wildlife in the backcountry, so you need to be prepared to react. Never approach an animal: Remember to always stay at least 25 yards (22.9 m) away from all wildlife, and at least 100 yards (91.4 m) away from predators, including bears. Make noise as you hike along to give animals the opportunity to depart before an encounter. Do not hike at the edges of day—dawn or dusk—or at night, as these are the most active times for bears and other predators. Always be aware of your surroundings. Look for overturned rocks and logs, dug-out areas, and, of course, carcasses, all of which suggest bear activity.

If you do encounter a bear, know what to do. If there is some distance between you and the bear, give the bear an opportunity to leave, or take the opportunity to redirect your own party. If you run into a bear at close range, be as nonthreatening as possible. Talk calmly and back away. Never turn your back, and never run. Make sure you have your bear spray accessible. If the bear charges, stand your ground. Bears will often bluff charge to determine whether you will run and are thus prey. If the bear does attack, keep your pack on, fall to the ground on your belly, protect your head and neck with your arms, and play dead. When the bear leaves, get up and retreat. In the very uncommon circumstance that a bear provokes an attack or enters a tent, fight the bear with every resource you have.

Go to great lengths to avoid attracting bears by hanging all food, cooking utensils, and scented items (toothpaste, deodorant, other toiletries, and trash) in a bear bag in a tree or atop a bear pole. Designate a separate cooking and eating area away from the sleeping tents. Dispose of your trash and personal waste properly.

You need to plan your trip carefully and secure all permits and backcountry campsites through any one of nine backcountry permit offices: Bechler Ranger Station, Canyon Visitor Center, Grant Village Visitor Center, Bridge Bay Ranger Station, Mammoth Visitor Center, Old Faithful Ranger Station, South Entrance Ranger Station, Tower Ranger Station, and the West Yellowstone Visitor Information Center (307/344-2160, www.nps.gov/yell, permits available 8am-4:30pm daily June-Aug., $25 annual backcountry pass, $3 pp over 9 years old per night). Some of Yellowstone's roughly 300 backcountry campsites can be reserved in advance either in person, by fax, or through the mail. Backcountry use permits are required for all overnight stays and can only be attained in person no more than 48 hours before your trip. A park booklet titled *Beyond Road's End* is available online and will help familiarize you with the backcountry regulations and restrictions.

Breakfast, lunch, and dinner are served daily throughout the season in the **Roosevelt Lodge Dining Room, Canyon Lodge Dining Room, Cafeteria, and Deli,** and the **Mammoth Hotel Dining Room and Terrace Grill** (866/439-7375, www.yellowstonenationalparklodges.com). Each restaurant has its own flair—Roosevelt Lodge tends to be heartier, with options like barbecue beef, bison chili, and Wyoming cheesesteak, while Mammoth is known for elaborate buffets and inventive small plates like goat cheese sliders, mini trout tacos, and Thai curry mussels. Canyon offers a wok station and slow food fast, with ready-made entrées like barbecued ribs, country-fried steak and rotisserie chicken. Breakfasts include entrées ranging from pancakes and eggs to biscuits and gravy ($6-12). Lunches range $9-16, and dinners are generally $12-36. Generally, breakfast is served 6:30am-10am, lunch 11:30am-2:30pm, and dinner 5:30pm-10pm. Hours vary seasonally by restaurant and are subject to change. Call ahead for reservations or to check on hours; menus are available on the website.

ACCOMMODATIONS

There are three accommodations in the northern loop. The largest is the **Mammoth Hot Springs Hotel and Cabins** (late Apr.-early Oct. and mid-Dec.-early Mar., $109-213 rustic 1- to 2-bedroom cabin without bath, $183 frontier cabin, $177 standard room, $305 hot tub cabin, $587 suite), which has 79 guest rooms and another 116 cabins, four with hot tubs. Mammoth is undergoing a renovation; its cabins are expected to be completed in summer 2019. After the renovation, all 79 rooms will have a private bathroom. Set amid historic Fort Yellowstone, Mammoth provides convenient access to restaurants, gift shops, a gas station, and the visitors center, so guests may forget they're somewhat out in the wild. Despite human and car traffic in Mammoth, wolves have been known to sneak onto the green watered lawns at night to take down an unsuspecting well-grazed elk. You can imagine the surprise when early risers spotted the carcass on their way to get a breakfast burrito.

Named for Yellowstone champion Theodore Roosevelt, the ★ **Roosevelt Lodge Cabins** (early-June-early Sept.) offer a timeless rustic setting reminiscent of a great old dude ranch in a quiet corner of the park. The Roughrider Cabins (from $102) usually offer double beds and a wood-burning stove. What they lack in amenities they make up for with charming authenticity. Toilets and communal showers are available nearby. The Frontier Cabins (from $170) are slightly larger and include a private bathroom with a shower, toilet, and sink.

Set adjacent to the spectacular Grand Canyon of the Yellowstone, **Canyon Lodge & Cabins** (early June-late Sept.) is the largest single lodging property in the park. The facilities were built in the 1950s and 1960s, added onto and renovated significantly in 2016 to bring the total to 590 rooms and cabins. In the lodges, there are standard rooms ($210), premium rooms ($340), superior rooms ($360), superior lodge rooms with patios ($370), and 2-bedroom suites ($700). The modest Western Cabins ($204) are basic motel-style units with private full bathrooms.

Reservations for all hotels inside the park should be made through **Yellowstone National Park Lodges** (307/344-7311, www.yellowstonenationalparklodges.com). Nature is the draw here: There are no televisions, radios, or air-conditioning. Internet access can be purchased in the public areas of some hotels in the park.

CAMPING

The only campground in the park's northern loop that can be reserved in advance, operated by Xanterra, the park's concessionaire, is the 270-site **Canyon** (307/344-7901 for same-day reservations, 307/344-7311 for advance reservations, late May-early Sept., $30 nightly rate includes two showers/night), which has 15 public restrooms with flush toilets, faucets with cold running water, and pay showers. The other six sites—at Mammoth, Tower Falls, Slough Creek, Pebble Creek, Indian Creek, and Norris—are available on a first-come, first-served basis and cost $15-20. These sites fill up quickly; your best bet is to arrive before 11am. Mammoth is the only campground open all year; all the campgrounds have some RV sites. A great feature on the Yellowstone website shows current availability and also what time any given site closed the day before (www.nps.gov/yell).

In addition to the campgrounds, more than 300 backcountry campsites are scattered throughout the park. Overnight permits, which are available at all ranger stations and visitors centers, are only issued in person up to 48 hours in advance; they are required for all the sites. Backcountry campsites can be reserved January 1-October 31 by paying a $25 reservation fee. All requests to

Camping in Yellowstone

As accommodations cannot meet the demand of Yellowstone's four million visitors each year, camping is an excellent option, particularly for those spontaneous souls who want to see the park without planning months in advance. More than 2,000 campsites spread over 12 campgrounds are located in the park. The five largest—Bridge Bay, Canyon, Fishing Bridge RV Park, Grant Village, and Madison—are run by Xanterra; all inquiries and reservations should be made by calling Xanterra (same-day reservations 307/344-7901, advance reservations 307/344-7311); these campgrounds have additional sales and utility tax fees. The other sites are assigned on a first-come, first-served basis. Try to arrive early to secure your spot; sites often fill up by 11am, especially in the busy summer months. Yellowstone also has more than 300 backcountry campsites, which require permits.

Campground	Number of Sites	Dates (Approx.)	Fees	RV Sites
Bridge Bay	432	late May-mid Sept.	$25.25	call for availability and reservations
Canyon	273	late May-mid-Sept.	$30	call for availability and reservations
Fishing Bridge RV Park	340	early May-early Sept.	$47.75	call for availability and reservations
Grant Village	430	mid-June-mid-Sept.	$30	call for availability and reservations
Indian Creek	70	mid-June-mid-Sept.	$15	10 for 35-foot (10.7 m); 35 for 30-foot (9.1 m), walk through to assess site
Lewis Lake	85	mid-June-early Nov.	$15	25-foot (7.6-m) limit
Madison	278	late Apr.-mid-Oct.	$25.25	call for availability and reservations
Mammoth	85	year-round	$20	most pull-through, 30-foot (9.1-m) limit
Norris	111	late May-late Sept.	$20	2 for 50-foot (15.2 m), 5 for 30-foot (9.1 m)
Pebble Creek	27	mid-June-late Sept.	$15	some long pull-throughs
Slough Creek	16	mid-June-early Oct.	$15	14 for 30-foot (9.1 m), walk through to assess site
Tower Falls	31	late May-late Sept.	$15	all 30-foot (9.1 m) or less; hairpin turn

reserve sites must be made in person, faxed, or mailed in. Pertinent forms and information for backcountry camping in Yellowstone are available online at the National Park Service Backcountry Trip Planner (www.nps.gov/yell).

The Northeast Corner

With arguably the best wildlife-viewing in the park, especially in winter, this region is known as the "Little Serengeti of North America." The wide-open spaces of the Lamar Valley and much of the northeast corner of the park also offer some pretty dramatic mountain vistas. There is excellent fishing and hiking in the region, and just outside the park's northeast entrance is Cooke City, a cool little community with tremendous appeal to backcountry skiers, snowmobilers, and other outdoors enthusiasts.

TOP EXPERIENCE

★ WATCHING THE WOLVES

When visitors list the animals they most want to see in Yellowstone, wolves rank second, right behind grizzly bears. Since their return to Yellowstone in 1995, wolves have surprised park-goers and wildlife experts alike by being much more visible than anyone anticipated. In fact, since their reintroduction, wolves have been spotted in Yellowstone by at least one person nearly every day. Much of that is thanks to wolf researchers, including the indefatigable Rick McIntyre, who is out in the field an average of 11 hours per day seven days per week, and the ever-passionate wolf watchers (who tend to follow Rick), armed with massive scopes and camera lenses that look strong enough to spot wildlife on other planets.

The bad news is that there are roughly 108 wolves in 11 packs, plus a few lone wolves, roaming throughout Yellowstone, an area that is approximately the size of Connecticut. It's always a good idea to bear those figures in mind when you have only a couple of hours and a keen desire to spot one of these majestic canines.

But there's good news too. If seeing the wolves is a high priority for you, here are five ways to improve your odds:

- **Visit in winter.** Wolves are most active and most visible (nearest to the roads and against a white backdrop) in the winter when they have significant advantages over their prey, including elk and bison. Spring and fall can offer viewing opportunities as well, but summer visitors are at a disadvantage because the wolves are often way up in the high country, far from roads. Whenever you go, don't forget your binoculars or a scope if you have one.

- **Do your homework or hire a guide.** Stop at the visitors center in Mammoth in winter (or any of the visitors centers at other times of year) and inquire about recent activity. Rangers can often tell you where packs have been spotted, if kills have recently occurred, and so forth. You could also consider hiring a guide that specializes in wolf-watching. **Yellowstone Wolf Tracker** (406/223-0173, www.wolftracker.com, $630/day for 1 person, $660/ 2 people, $700/4 people) offers 6- to 8-hour tours led by wildlife biologists. The **Yellowstone Forever Institute** (406/848-2400, www.yellowstone.org) offers a variety of courses that focus on wolves.

- **Visit the Lamar Valley.** The only road open to car traffic year-round, the stretch of asphalt that winds through the Lamar Valley takes visitors through the heart of some of the park's best winter wolf terrain.

Cinderella: The Real-Life Fairy Tale of Wolf 42

In 1926 the last known wolf in Yellowstone was killed, bringing to a conclusion a decades-long campaign to rid the region of an animal widely considered a worthless pest. The murderous eviction was a tragic end to a noble creature. It took nearly 70 years for wolves to be seen not only for their intrinsic worth but their value in making the Yellowstone ecosystem whole again. This was their home, after all, and they had been unnaturally removed. Thirty-one Canadian gray wolves—*Canis lupus*—were reintroduced to the park in 1995-1996 with loud cheers and simultaneous objections.

Among the wolves brought into the park from Canada was a female who would come to be known as wolf number 42. Her sister, wolf 40, was the alpha female of the Druid Peak pack and known to rule the pack with an iron paw. She was suspected of running off her mother, number 39, and her sister, number 41. Number 42, the pack's beta female, managed to stay in the group, likely as a result of her unmatched speed and excellent hunting ability, but she could not get into her sister's good graces. The two fought constantly for four years. Both bred with wolf 21, the pack's alpha male, and wolf 40 reportedly killed her sister's first litter of pups in 1999. Wolf watchers nicknamed 42 "Cinderella" and flocked to the Lamar Valley to watch the drama unfold. Much of Cinderella's life was captured on film by Bob Landis for two *National Geographic* specials.

In a story that plays out like a fairy tale, wolf 42 got her nieces to den with her in 2000 when she had another litter of pups with 21, and after researchers saw wolf 40 approaching the den just before the pups were weaned, ostensibly to kill this second litter of pups, 42 and her nieces attacked. Wolf 40 was found dying of her wounds, and 42 not only rose to alpha status overnight, paired for life with wolf 21, but also moved into 40's den and adopted her dead sister's seven pups as her own. That year 42 and 21 raised 20 pups.

Over the course of her life—eight years, which is more than double wolf lifespan averages—she birthed 32 pups and held her alpha-female status over the Druid Pack, which climbed to 37 members in 2000, becoming one of the largest wolf packs ever recorded. She was known for her faithful and patient parenting, even coaching younger wolves in the middle of an elk hunt. When she was killed by another pack in February 2004, wolf watchers noted wolf 21, her constant companion, atop a ridgeline howling for two days straight. The wolf watchers mourned along with him.

After receiving a mortality signal from 42's radio collar, chief park wolf biologist Doug Smith hiked up the 9,000-foot (2,743-m) Specimen Ridge on a blustery winter day. There he found Cinderella dead. She was the last remaining member of the 31 wolves imported from Canada, but her legacy and story will be forever entwined with the Yellowstone wilderness and the saga of *Canis lupus* finally coming home.

There are numerous pullouts along the road for viewing, but be sure to park safely out of traffic without blocking other visitors. In the summer, along the stretch of road near the confluence of the Lamar River and Soda Butte Creek, the road is often closed to stopping thanks to a wolf-denning site not far from the pavement. Your chances to see a wolf—even pups—is good.

- **Wake up early.** Like most wildlife, wolves are most active at the edges of day. Putting yourself in the heart of the Lamar Valley before sunrise greatly improves your odds of seeing the wolves. The same is true at sunset. In this game, patience pays.

- **Watch for the wolf watchers.** They often have significant advantages, including radio telemeters that allow them to track collared wolves. These people know much about the wolves and can regale you with dramatic sagas of individual animals and entire packs. Don't be shy about pulling over when you see them; they are often willing to let you peer through their scopes. But do be safe and courteous; turn off your engine and remain quiet.

★ LAMAR VALLEY

One of my favorite corners of the park, the **Lamar Valley** is stunningly beautiful with wide valleys carved by rivers and glaciers as well as views to the high rugged peaks around Cooke City. Generally uncrowded (save for the ever-growing number of bespectacled and bescoped wolf watchers), some of the best hiking, fishing, and camping can be had at Slough Creek. And the wolf-watching, particularly in the winter, is unrivaled anywhere else in the world. There are also grizzlies, black bears, mountain lions, coyotes, red foxes, elk, bison, bighorn sheep, and pronghorn in the area. In early summer, on occasion, there can be as many as 2,000 bison dotting the wide green expanse; it's a miraculous sight.

Lamar Buffalo Ranch

The **Lamar Buffalo Ranch Field Campus** of the **Yellowstone Forever Institute** (406/848-2400, www.yellowstoneassociation. org) is located away from the large crowds (of two-legged creatures, anyway) in the idyllic Lamar Valley. The institute offers field seminars at this private and unique campus year-round. If you bring your own sleeping bag and pillow, you can stay at the ranch in one of its log cabins ($41.20 pp shared cabin in summer, $85 for 1-2 people private cabin in winter, sleeping bag and pillow rental $20). Propane heaters, a communal bathhouse with individual showers, and a fully equipped kitchen are housed in the common building. It's quite comfortable but not fancy. The best part is waking up each morning in the Lamar Valley, an opportunity very few people have. You can also stay in a nearby campsite or hotel while taking a course at the ranch. Field seminars also take place at hotels throughout the park. The institute holds rooms in various lodges until 30 days before the course.

COOKE CITY

Named for a miner and populated by hardcore modern-day prospectors in search of snow, **Cooke City** (population 22; elevation 7,600 ft/2,316 m) is a jumble of old buildings and some fairly salty characters, all with true Western flavor. At the end of a one-way road for most of the year (except during the height of summer when the Beartooth Highway leads visitors up and over the towering peaks), Cooke City has a remarkable sense of community, unlimited recreational opportunities, plenty of accommodations,

bison on the move in Lamar Valley

The Brucellosis Problem

Yellowstone is the only place in the continental United States where bison have existed since prehistoric times. Current policy mandates that the animals stay within the park's unfenced boundaries, and how best to enforce this is a matter of constant debate.

The park's management of the bison has changed throughout the years, just as bison numbers have fluctuated. Prior to 1967, park authorities would trap and reduce the herd to keep it manageable. After 1967, however, the guiding philosophy changed, and the bison were managed by nature alone. By 1996 the number of bison in the park had grown to 3,500. The size of the herd, coupled with winters that brought significant snowfall, led many of the bison to migrate out of the park in order to find better grazing and calving grounds. The problem of brucellosis played out on the national stage.

Brucellosis is a bacterial infection present in the bison and elk in the Greater Yellowstone area. The disease can cause spontaneous abortions, infertility, and lowered milk production in the infected animal, but the Yellowstone elk and bison populations seem relatively unscathed by the disease, despite the number of animals infected. The same tolerance of the disease is not common among cattle, however. The overwhelming fear is that bison exiting Yellowstone could infect neighboring cattle; this would be gravely detrimental to Montana, Wyoming, and Idaho beef production. Brucellosis cannot be treated in cattle and can be passed on to humans in the form of undulant fever. The government created a fairly simple inoculation program to eradicate the disease in cattle as early as 1934, but brucellosis has never been eliminated from wildlife.

Starting in the 1980s, when more than 50 percent of the park's bison tested positive for the disease, the park's approach was to control the borders with hazing to limit the number of bison that left the park. When hazing was unsuccessful, the bison were shot. The winter of 1996-1997 brought record cold and snow, and bison left the park in large numbers to forage for food; 1,079 bison were shot and another 1,300 starved to death inside the park's boundaries. This incident magnified the problem of maintaining a healthy herd while preventing the spread of brucellosis.

The National Park Service, the U.S. Department of Agriculture, and Montana, Wyoming, and Idaho are working together to see how brucellosis can be eliminated and free-roaming bison protected. A vaccination program has been implemented, with a 65 percent success rate, and the use of quarantine has proven fairly successful. Local bison rancher and wildlife advocate Ted Turner has agreed to accept some of the quarantined bison on his property. A small and highly regulated hunting season on bison is carried out each winter just outside the park boundaries.

But while there are no easy or obvious solutions, there are questions: What about elk, which also carry the disease and have been identified as the source of brucellosis outbreaks among horses in Wyoming and cattle in Idaho? No efforts to limit their natural migration in and out of the park have ever been attempted. Why are bull bison—who can carry the disease but cannot spread it through milk or birthing fluids as females do—quarantined and killed? For now, it seems, we watch, wait, and hope for a healthy, wild, and free-roaming bison population.

and some excellent places to fill your belly. Nearby **Silver Gate** is equally scenic and even quieter, the Connecticut to Cooke's New York City. Pilot, Index, and Beartooth Peaks are three of the impressive summits that loom over these twin settlements, beckoning adventurers.

Sports and Recreation

The northeastern corner of the park and the area just outside it are a natural playground for fishing, hiking, cross-country skiing, and snowmobiling.

HIKING AND FISHING

One short but worthwhile hike can be found 1.8 miles (2.9 km) west of the Pebble Creek Campground at **Trout Lake.** The hike itself is short and steep, just 1.2 miles (1.9 km) round-trip, and leaves from the Trout Lake Trailhead on the north side of the road. Anglers can bring a rod after July 15 when it opens to catch-and-release fishing for native cutthroats. In late spring-early summer, trout can be seen spawning in the inches-deep inlet, a fairly miraculous sight. There is an excellent trail around the 12-acre (4.9-hectare) lake and shallow inlet and a decent chance of spotting playful otters, but hikers should take great care not to disturb the fish, especially during spawning. Bear awareness and a can of bear spray are necessary, as the bruins like fish too.

Another great place to combine fishing, hiking, and wildlife-watching—perhaps the perfect Yellowstone trifecta—is along the trail at **Slough Creek.** East of Tower Junction 5.8 miles (9.3 km) or west of the northeast entrance is an unpaved road on the north side of the road leading to Slough Creek Campground. The trailhead is 1.5 miles (2.4 km) down the road on the right side, just before the campground. The trail itself is a double-rutted wagon trail that leads to Silver Tip Ranch, a legendary private ranch just outside the park. The trail is maintained for 11 miles 17.7 km) one-way and only gains 400 feet (122 m) in elevation. All along the trail there is world-class fishing in slow-moving Slough Creek, home to a healthy population of native cutthroat trout. You may meet elk, bison, wolves, and even grizzlies along the trail, so be prepared and be safe.

MOTORIZED RECREATION

With an average of 500 inches of snowfall each year, mountainous terrain with elevation that ranges 7,000-10,000 feet (2,134-3,048 m), and a nearly interminable winter, Cooke City is a winter mecca with 60 miles (97 km) of groomed snowmobile trails and endless acres of ungroomed terrain for skiing and snowmobiling. Some favorite trails are **Daisy Pass, Lulu Pass,** and **Round Creek Trail.**

A number of places in town rent snowmobiles and all the necessary gear. Most important, you'll need to talk with experts about local conditions, trail closures, and avalanche dangers. **Cooke City Motorsports** (203 Eaton St., 406/838-2231, www. cookecitymotorsports.com, snowmobiles

from $205/day) and **Cooke City Exxon** (204 Main St., 406/838-2244, www.cookecityexxon. com, snowmobiles from $220/day) are obvious choices in town. When the snow melts, you can rent ATVs from **Bearclaw Sales and Service** (309 E. Main St., 406/838-2244, www.bearclawsalesandservice.com, single ATVs from $35/hour, $100/half-day, $160/ full-day, and side-by-side ATVs from $75/ hour, $200/half-day, $275/full-day) as another way to get out and cover a lot of ground.

Entertainment and Events

Among the biggest events of the year in Cooke City is the annual **Sweet Corn Festival,** a gathering for backcountry skiers and snowboarders usually held in April on the weekend after the nearby ski hills have closed for the season. The weather is often sublime—think blue skies, cold nights, and warm afternoons—and the snow is like, well, sweet corn. Accommodations are not easy to come by this weekend (even floor space is pretty much spoken for), so plan ahead or bring a tent. Plenty of snowmobilers are on hand to act as taxis, enabling telemark skiers not to have to earn their turns for once. With some of the best backcountry skiing in the West when the conditions are right, this is a welcome event.

The **Annual Hog Roast** happens in mid-March and attracts a throng of hungry snowmobilers, backcountry skiers, and more recently, a healthy number of cross-country skiers to Cooke City. The event includes an auction, dinner, and live music.

The popular **Firemen's Picnic** is held annually on July 4, just east of town, with a good old-fashioned parade on Main Street, food, kids' games, and fireworks after dark. Another great small-town event, the **Mount Republic Chapel Bazaar** is held annually on a Friday and half-day Saturday in mid-July.

For some culture on the periphery of Yellowstone's wilderness, check out **Shakespeare in the Parks** in Silvergate Park in July or August.

For more information on any of these events, call or visit Donna—who is as knowledgeable as she is friendly—at the chamber-run **visitors center** (206 W. Main St., 406/838-2495, www.cookecitychamber.org, year-round, hours change seasonally), on the west end of town on the north side of the street; the center also has flush toilets.

Food

There are a million ways to work up an appetite in and around Cooke City. Be assured you won't go hungry (or thirsty, for that matter). ★ **Beartooth Café** (14 U.S. 212, 406/838-2475, www.beartoothcafe.com, 11am-9:30pm daily late May-late Sept., $13-27) offers excellent mountain fare—think steak and trout—with just a hint of Asian flair. The front-porch outdoor dining is a treat. Another great spot for a quick bite anytime (except April, May, October and November when it's closed) is the **Bearclaw Bakery** (309 E. Main, 406/838-2040, 5am-10:30am daily, rolls and coffee served from 5am, hot breakfasts from 6am), which makes from-scratch baked goods, full hearty breakfasts, and light lunch. The bakery also offers a full coffee bar.

The **Prospector Restaurant** (210 U.S. 212, 406/838-2251, www.cookecity.com, 7am-10pm daily, $13-35), inside the Soda Butte Lodge, is open year-round and particularly known for steak and prime rib—not a stretch in these parts. Finally, for those wanting to pick up some supplies, the ★ **Cooke City Store** (101 Main St., 406/838-2234, www.cookecitystore.com, 8am-8pm daily mid-May-Sept., hours may vary slightly based on customers and local activity) is as much a local museum and community center as it is a place to pick up some bread and a bottle of sunscreen. There's also a fly shop inside, **Trout Rider Fly Shop,** where you can get fishing licenses for Montana, Wyoming, or Yellowstone National Park as well as picking up some flies and other supplies. It's a wonderful place and worth a visit; plus the nearest grocery store is 90 minutes away.

Accommodations

For a town with a population that is only barely in the double digits, Cooke City has an impressive number of places to hang your hat. Lodging runs the gamut from cabins and vacation rentals to roadside motels, chain hotels, and small resorts, although not all of them are open year-round. Most of the photo galleries on the accommodations' websites are images of moose and bears or snowmobiles buried in powder rather than pictures of beds and baths. Clearly, Cooke City has morphed from a mining town into a tourist destination.

Big Moose Resort (715 U.S. 212, 406/838-2393, www.bigmooseresort.com, $95-150) is 3 miles (4.8 km) east of town and a great place to set up a base camp if you want to explore the region's trails and rivers. Open year-round, the lodge has a collection of seven old and new cabins, all of which are quite comfortable and can accommodate up to four people. There are no phones in the cabins (and no cell service in the area), but free Wi-Fi is provided, and you can schedule a Swedish massage on-site.

The **Cooke City Super 8** (303 E. Main St., 406/838-2070, $125-174) is owned by Bearclaw Bob who also owns the Bearclaw Bakery and Bearclaw Sales and Service. The rooms are basic and clean, and the service is exceptionally friendly.

In the heart of bustling Cooke City is the **Soda Butte Lodge** (210 E. Main St., 406/838-2251, www.cookecity.com, $110-180), a full-service hotel with 32 guest rooms, a saloon, and a restaurant. The guest rooms are basic, but you didn't come to Cooke City to hang out in your hotel room.

In nearby Silver Gate, ★ **Silver Gate Lodging** (109 U.S. 212, 406/838-2371, www.pineedgecabins.com, $120-300) offers 29 great cabins, plus motel rooms and a big lodge that can accommodate any size group and welcomes pets. The setting is both quiet and communal, with barbecue grills, horseshoe pits, and a playground. And because this is Yellowstone, you can also rent scopes, which will come in plenty handy.

Camping

Three Forest Service campgrounds are in the vicinity of Cooke City. **Soda Butte** (406/848-7375, www.fs.usda.gov, July-Sept. depending on weather, $9/vehicle) is 1 mile (1.6 km) east of Cooke City on U.S. 212. It has 27 sites, restrooms, and drinking water, and fishing is available nearby. Please note that due to bear activity, this is a hard-sided campground only, and advance reservations are not accepted. Also strictly a hard-sided campground, **Colter Campground** (406/848-7375, www.fs.usda.gov, July 15-Sept. 7 depending on weather, $8/vehicle) is just 2 miles (3.2 km) east of Cooke City and gives campers access to 18 sites, restrooms, drinking water, and nearby fishing and hiking trails. Reservations are not accepted, so arrive early and have a backup plan in place.

Fox Creek Campground (307/527-6921, www.fs.usda.gov, July 15-Sept. 7 depending on weather, $20-60) is a 33-site campground 6.7 miles (10.8 km) east of Cooke City on the Beartooth Highway with awesome views of Pilot and Index Peaks. Water is available here but cell service is not. The campground is closed due to construction on the highway until the summer of 2020.

The Southern Loop

Some of the park's biggest highlights are found in the southern loop, along with a significant number of visitors and plentiful wildlife. There are a lot of trees, many of them burned, and not as much dimension to the land as elsewhere, but the southern loop is what many people picture when they think of Yellowstone. From the sweeping Hayden Valley and the otherworldliness of West Thumb Geyser Basin to the sheer size of Yellowstone Lake and the well-deserved hubbub around Old Faithful, this section of the park has an abundance of dynamic features—some world-famous, others hidden gems—for every visitor.

SIGHTS
Hayden Valley

South of Canyon is the expansive and beautiful Hayden Valley, a sweep of grassland carved

The vast Hayden Valley is a lush paradise in summer.

by massive glaciers named for the famed leader of the 1871 Hayden Expedition and occupied by copious amounts of wildlife that includes grizzly bears, wolves, and in summer, thundering herds of bison. The Yellowstone River weaves quietly through the valley, and because the soil supports grasses and wildflowers instead of trees, this is one of the most scenic drives in the park, especially during the bison rut and migration in late summer. Besides driving, hiking is an excellent way to explore the valley, either on your own (pay very close attention for signs of bear activity) or with a ranger on weekly **guided hikes** (4-5 hours, early July-late Aug., free). The hikes are limited to 15 people, and reservations must be made in advance at the **Canyon Visitor Education Center** (307/344-2550, 8am-6pm daily mid-June-early Oct., 9am-5pm daily mid-Apr.-mid-June and early Oct.-early Nov.) in Canyon Village.

Fishing Bridge

What was once the epicenter of Yellowstone fishing is today a relic of the past and a touchstone for the ongoing struggle between nature and human meddling. Fishing Bridge was built in 1937 and for years considered the best place to throw a line for native cutthroat trout. Humans were not the only ones fishing in the area, and human-grizzly encounters led to 16 grizzly bear deaths. To protect the bears and the fish, fishing in the vicinity was banned in 1973. Today, because of the sharp decline of cutthroat as a direct result of the introduction of nonnative lake trout, grizzlies are not seen as often fishing in the river.

There are some services—an RV park, a gas station, and a general store—and a 1931 log and stone structure that serves as the **Fishing Bridge Visitor Center** (307/242-2450, 8am-5pm daily late May-June 1, 8am-7pm daily June 2-Labor Day, 8am-1pm Labor Day-early Oct.). On the National Register of Historic Places, the visitors center has a collection of stuffed bird specimens worth seeing and an exhibit on the lake's geology, including a relief map of the lake bottom.

★ Yellowstone Lake

Covering 136 square miles (352 sq km), Yellowstone Lake is North America's largest freshwater lake above 7,000 feet (2,134 m). In addition to being spectacularly scenic—both when it is placid and when the waves form whitecaps—the lake is a fascinating study in underwater geothermal activity. Beneath the water—or ice, much of the year—the lake bottom is littered with faults, hot springs, craters, and the miraculous life-forms that can thrive in such conditions. There is also a rather large bulge, some 2,000 feet (610 m) long, that rises 100 feet (30.5 m) above the rest of the lake bottom. The uplift is related to the ever-present geothermal activity beneath Yellowstone. Whether the bulge is gaseous or potentially volcanic in nature is the subject of ongoing research.

Aside from its geological significance, Yellowstone Lake also offers plenty of recreational opportunities, primarily in the form of boating and fishing. The water is bitter cold, though, typically 40-50°F, and not suitable for swimming. Outboards ($57/hour) can be rented mid-June-early September at **Bridge Bay Marina** (307/344-7311 or 866/439-7375), just south of Lake Village or 21 miles (34 km) north of West Thumb. There is great fishing for native cutthroat trout as well. It's worth mentioning that early visitors to the park loved to tell stories about catching fish at the edge of the lake and then dipping their catch in the hot springs at West Thumb Geyser Basin to cook them without taking the fish off the line—a practice that would be seriously frowned upon today.

The rambling pale-yellow **Lake Yellowstone Hotel** was built in 1891 and is an elegant reminder of Yellowstone's bygone era. The lobby and deck, which overlook the lake, are worth seeing, even if you are not staying here. Grab an iced tea and soak in the views; this is a stunning spot. If you can, stay for a meal and enjoy the live piano music. The crowds will fade as you gaze on the scenery.

West Thumb Geyser Basin

On the western edge of Yellowstone Lake is the eerie West Thumb Geyser Basin, a collection of hot springs, geysers, mud pots, and fumaroles that dump a collective 3,100 gallons (11,735 liters) of hot water into the lake daily. An excellent boardwalk system guides visitors through the area, but there have been injury-causing bison and bear encounters on the boardwalk, so keep your eyes open.

Abyss Pool is a sensational spring, some 53 feet (16.2 m) deep, that transforms in color from turquoise to emerald green to brown and back, depending on a variety of factors. Similarly beautiful, **Black Pool** is no longer black because the particular thermophiles that caused the dark coloration were killed in 1991 when the water temperature rose. **Big Cone** and **Fishing Cone,** surrounded by lake water, are the features that led to the stories of fishing and cooking the catch in a single cast. Called "Mud Puffs" by the 1871 Hayden Expedition, **Thumb Paint Pots** are like miniature reddish mud volcanoes (depending on rainfall, after which they can get soupier) and are an excellent example of mud pots. Throughout the last several years, the mud pots have been particularly active, forming new mud cones and even throwing mud into the air. **Surging Spring** is fun to watch as the dome of water forms and overflows, unleashing a torrent of water on the lake.

Grant Village

On the West Thumb of Yellowstone Lake, Grant Village is a fairly controversial development dating to the 1970s and built in the heart of grizzly bear habitat and among several cutthroat spawning streams. The architecture is ugly, and the location is better suited to wildlife than visitors. In addition to the **Grant Village Visitor Center** (307/344-2650, 8am-5pm daily Memorial Day-June 1, 8am-7pm daily June 2-Labor Day, 9am-5pm daily Labor Day-early Oct.), which houses an exhibit dedicated to fire in the Yellowstone ecosystem, accommodations, a campground, and food services are available.

★ Old Faithful

Though often crowded, the **Old Faithful** complex brings together so many of the phenomena—both natural and human-made—that make Yellowstone so special: the landmark geyser and the incredible assortment of geothermal features surrounding it, the wildlife, the grand old park architecture of the Old Faithful Inn, and even the mass of people from around the world who come to witness the famous geyser.

An obvious stop at the Old Faithful complex is the **Old Faithful Visitor Education Center** (307/344-2751, 9am-6pm daily mid-Apr.-May, 8am-8pm daily June-Sept., 9am-5pm daily Oct.-early Nov. and mid-Dec.-mid-Mar.), which showcases Yellowstone's hydrothermal features. The $27 million facility hosts 2.6 million visitors annually. Efficient travelers (who are fighting an uphill battle here most of the time) can call ahead for a recorded message about daily geyser eruption predictions (307/344-2751).

Known as the **Upper Geyser Basin,** the area surrounding Old Faithful is the largest concentration of geysers anywhere in the world. By far the most famous is Old Faithful because of its combination of height (although it is not the tallest) and regularity (although it is not the most frequent or most regular). Intervals between eruptions are generally between 60-110 minutes and can be predicted according to duration of previous eruptions. Eruptions can last anywhere from 90 seconds to five minutes. It spouts 3,700-8,400 gallons (14,006-31,797 liters) of hot water at heights of 106-184 feet (32.3-56.1 m). Signs inside the nearby hotel lobbies and the visitors center, and a Twitter feed (@GeyserNPS), keep visitors apprised of the next expected eruptions, of which there are an average of 17 in any 24-hour period. Keep in mind that Old Faithful doesn't stop being predictable just because people go to bed or the weather turns cold—some of the most magical eruption viewings can happen

---

1: Black Pool in West Thumb Geyser Basin 2: crowd at Old Faithful

without crowds. Choose a full-moon night, any time of year, and be willing to get up in the middle of the night. The vision of Old Faithful erupting in winter with snow and ice, frost, and steam in every direction is unforgettable.

If you take the time to come to Yellowstone to see Old Faithful, take the time—an hour or more is ideal—to walk through the other marvelous features of the Upper Geyser Basin. **Giantess Geyser** can erupt up to 200 feet (61 m) high in several bursts. The irregular eruptions happen 2-6 times each year and can occur twice hourly, continuing 4-48 hours, and changing the behavior of many of the other geysers in the region. **Doublet Pool,** a colorful hot spring with numerous ledges, is lovely and convoluted. You can actually hear Doublet vibrating and collapsing beneath the surface. Looking something like a fire hose shooting 130-190 feet (39.6-57.9 m) in the air, **Beehive Geyser** typically erupts twice daily, each eruption lasting 4-5 minutes. **Grand Geyser** is the world's tallest predictable geyser, erupting every 7-15 hours, lasting 9-12 minutes, and reaching heights up to 200 feet (61 m). Visible from the road into the Old Faithful complex if you look back over your shoulder, **Castle Geyser** is thought to be the park's oldest. It generally erupts every 10-12 hours, reaches 90 feet (27.4 m) in height, and lasts roughly 20 minutes. A 30- to 40-minute noisy steam phase follows the eruptions.

★ Firehole River

Since swimming in Yellowstone Lake is not an option unless you are a trained member of the polar bear club, a dip in the heated (but far from hot!) waters of the Firehole River is one of the nicest ways to spend an afternoon. The designated and somewhat popular swimming area is surrounded by high cliffs and some fast-moving rapids both upstream and downstream, so the area is not recommended for new or young swimmers. The water temperature averages 80°F (26.7°C), but this avid swimmer would argue that the temperatures feel more like the 70s (about 23.9°C). Though quite limited, parking is accessible

from Firehole Canyon Drive, which leaves the main road south of Madison Junction, less than 1,000 feet (305 m) after crossing the river. There is a toilet available but no lifeguards, so you will be swimming entirely at your own risk.

Midway and Lower Geyser Basins

Between Old Faithful and Madison Junction, along the pastoral Firehole River, are the Midway and Lower Geyser Basins, technically considered part of the same basin. In 1889, Rudyard Kipling dubbed Midway Geyser Basin "hell's half-acre" for its massive hot springs and geysers. Among the most significant features at Midway is **Grand Prismatic Spring,** a colorful and photogenic spring that was immortalized by painter Thomas Moran on the Hayden Expedition. It releases some 560 gallons (2,120 liters) of water into the Firehole River every minute. At 250 by 380 feet (76.2 by 115.8 m), Grand Prismatic is the third-largest hot spring in the world and the largest in Yellowstone. Now dormant, **Excelsior Geyser Crater** was once the largest geyser in the world, soaring up to 300 feet (91.4 m) high. Major eruptions in the 1880s led to a dormancy that lasted more than a century. In 1985, Excelsior erupted continuously for two days but never topped 80 feet (24.4 m). Today, acting as a spring, it discharges more than 4,000 gallons (15,142 liters) of heated water every minute.

Compared to the much smaller Midway Geyser Basin, the Lower Geyser Basin is enormous, spanning 12 square miles (31.1 sq km) and including several clusters of thermal features. Among them are the notable **Fountain Geyser,** a placid blue pool that erupts on average every 4.5-7 hours for 25-50 minutes and sprays up to 50 feet (15.2 m) high, the temperamental **White Dome Geyser,** the almostconstant **Clepsydra,** and the **Pocket Basin Mud Pots,** which are the largest collection of mud pots in the park. **Great Fountain Geyser** in the Firehole Lake area is the only predictable geyser in the Lower Geyser Basin and erupts every 10 hours and 45 minutes, give or take two hours, for up to an hour, reaching heights of 70-200 feet (21.3-61 m).

SPORTS AND RECREATION

Fishing and Boating

Some 80,000 anglers are lured to Yellowstone each year by the promise of elusive trout, and they are seldom disappointed by the offerings at Yellowstone Lake. In addition to the prized native cutthroat, the lake is home to a population of nonnative lake trout that is devastating the cutthroat trout population and endangering all the animals that eat the cutthroat trout. Introduced in 1890 into Lewis and Shoshone Lakes by the U.S. Fish Commission, the lake trout were first documented in Yellowstone Lake in the mid-1990s; scientists believe they were illegally introduced from a nearby lake in the 1980s. The average lake trout live and spawn in deep waters, feeding on as many as 40 cutthroat each year. By comparison, cutthroat trout spawn in the shallow tributaries of the lake, making them an important food source for a variety of creatures that include eagles and bears. Since the lake trout have no enemies in the deep waters of Yellowstone Lake, they are creating a serious food shortage by devouring the cutthroat. As a result, the eagles are having to eat other birds instead of fish, and Yellowstone is facing the complete elimination of some nesting bird species. All lake trout caught in Yellowstone Lake must be killed. Pick up your **fishing permit** at one of the visitors centers along with a copy of the Yellowstone fishing regulations.

There are a number of ways to see Yellowstone Lake by boat. Scenic or fishing boat tours as well as outboard motor ($57/hour) rentals are available from **Bridge Bay Marina,** south of Lake Village or 21 miles (34 km) northeast of West Thumb. Hour-long cruises ($18 adults, $10.50 children 3-11, free for children under 3) depart regularly from the marina mid-June-mid-September. Reservations can be made through **Xanterra** (307/344-7311 or 866/439-7375, www.yellowstonenationalparklodges.com).

Hiking

The southern loop of the park offers plentiful hiking opportunities, most of which can be combined with other interests. The **Hayden Valley** has great trails for wildlife lovers, but precautions against bear encounters must be taken. The **Alum Creek Trail,** 4.4 miles (7.1 km) south of Canyon at the north end of the

Grand Prismatic Spring

Hayden Valley, is a good hike. Wide open and relatively flat, the trail offers a 10-mile (16.1-km) out-and-back trip through prime bison and grizzly habitat. There are also some thermal features along Alum Creek.

Among the geysers in the Upper Geyser Basin is **Lone Star Geyser,** named for its lonely location 5 miles (8 km) from Old Faithful. An old once-paved road leads to the geyser and makes a nice level hike or bike trip. The entire out-and-back trip is 4.6 miles (7.4 km). There is parking at the trailhead on the south side of the road, 3.5 miles (5.6 km) east of the Old Faithful interchange. Lucky viewers will get to see a 30- to 50-foot (9.1- to 15.2-m) eruption, which happens every 2-3 hours and tends to last 10-15 minutes.

FOOD

As the southern loop is generally the most heavily traveled section of the park, there are plenty of dining opportunities. In the park restaurants, breakfast and lunch are on a first-come, first-served basis, but reservations are strongly recommended for dinner, particularly if 5pm or 9pm are not your ideal dining hours. In almost all the venues, you will find some good vegetarian options and many items made with sustainable or organic ingredients; these are identified on each menu. If you are planning a day activity away from the center of things, the restaurants or cafeterias offer box lunches for travelers to take with them. Place your order the night before, and it will be ready in the morning. The Yellowstone General Stores at Grant Village, Lake Village, and Old Faithful also have fast-food service, groceries, and snacks.

The **Grant Village Dining Room** (866/439-7375, 6:30am-10am, 11:30am-2:30pm, and 5pm-10pm daily late May-Sept., $17-32) offers a pleasant view of the lake, good service, and a nice variety of American cuisine. In addition to the à la carte menu for breakfast, a buffet is available ($13.95 adults, $7.25 children). Lunch and dinner include dishes such as prime rib sliders, smoked bison bratwurst, or spinach ravioli. Reservations are required for dinner.

The **Lake House** at Grant Village (6:30am-10:30am and 5pm-9:30pm daily high season, shortened hours early/late seasons) sits right on the lake, with great views and a casual ambience. Breakfast ($13.95 adults, $7.25 children) is buffet only, and the dinner menu ($10-25) consists of regional fare like huckleberry chicken, wild game meat loaf, prime rib, and lemon pepper trout.

The ★ **Lake Yellowstone Hotel Dining Room** (307/344-7311 or 866/439-7375, 6:30am-10am, 11:30am-2:30pm, and 5pm-10pm daily mid-May-early Oct., reservations required for dinner, $16-45, breakfast buffet $15.75 adults, $7.25 children) is the most elegant dining room in the park, with a gorgeous view of the lake. The restaurant is committed to creating dishes with fresh, local, organic, and sustainable ingredients. Lunch ($11-15) is a good way to sample some of the gourmet fare without putting too large a dent in your pocketbook. Try the delicious organic lentil soup or blackened wild Alaska salmon wrap. Dinner at the hotel is sure to be a memorable experience with options like Montana elk chops, bison tenderloin and lamb sliders.

Directly inside the hotel is the **Lake Hotel Deli** (6:30am-9pm daily mid-May-early Sept., shortened hours early/late seasons, $8-11), which serves a nice selection of soups, salads, and sandwiches. The **Lake Lodge Cafeteria** (6:30am-10pm daily early June-late Sept., shortened hours early/late seasons, $7-17) is a casual place for a quick bite. It serves basic breakfast standards, plenty of kids' favorites, and comfort food dishes ranging from spinach pie and fried chicken to apple-glazed pork loin.

Five eateries are located in the Old Faithful complex, but by far the most desirable is the **Old Faithful Inn Dining Room** (307/344-7311, 6:30am-10am, 11:30am-2:30pm, and 4:30pm-10pm daily early June-early Sept., shortened hours in May, Sept., early Oct., $17-30), which offers a buffet for each of the main meals daily (breakfast $13.95 adults and

$7.25 children, lunch $16.25 adults and $7.95 children, dinner $30.50 adults and $11.50 children) as well as an à la carte menu. You can dine in the historic inn while enjoying its distinct rustic architecture and Western-style ambience. Lunch is a "Western buffet" with items such as farm-raised pan-fried trout, pulled pork and wild game sausage. If you don't opt for the dinner buffet (featuring prime rib and trout), you could try pork osso buco, penne with local lamb ragout, wild Alaska sockeye salmon, and New York strip steak. Reservations are required for dinner.

The **Bear Paw Deli** (6am-9pm daily late May-early Sept., shortened hours early/late seasons, $4-9), also inside the inn, is perfect for on-the-go meals. It offers a continental breakfast including bagel sandwiches, and sandwich and salad deli fare for lunch, as well as serving up several flavors of ice cream. In addition to these two eateries at the inn, there is a cafeteria and bakeshop in the lodge and a dining room and grill in the Old Faithful Snow Lodge.

ACCOMMODATIONS

★ **Lake Yellowstone Hotel** (mid-May-early Oct., rooms $515-590, suites $820-980) is both grand and picturesque, perched on the shores of Yellowstone Lake. Originally built in 1891 and completely renovated in 2014 to celebrate its colonial revival influences, the hotel houses the nicest rooms in the park. As is true everywhere in the park, though, the appeal comes from the location and the views. If you are staying in the hotel, request a room with a view of the lake. There is an adjacent building, **The Sandpiper Lodge** ($320), that also offers recently renovated rooms. Individual cabins, called Lake Cottages, are behind the hotel but part of the Lake Lodge operation. These duplexes were remodeled in 2004 and are simple and modest.

The **Lake Lodge Cabins** (mid-June-late Sept., $158 Pioneer cabins, $209 Lake cottages, $246 Western cabins) are clean and simple and many underwent renovation in 2016. Located just off the lake, the cabins are

clustered around the main lodge, which is an inviting common area for guests to gather. It has a large porch that beckons guests to take a seat in one of the rocking chairs and soak in the view, as well as two fireplaces, a gift shop, and a cozy lounge. The Western cabins are a bit more spacious, with two beds and a shower-tub in each bathroom. The Pioneer cabins are older and more spartan, with shower-only bathrooms and 1-2 double beds. (They'll be available in 2020 once renovations are complete.) The Lake cottages underwent renovations in 2018. The setting is tranquil and quiet, and early risers may spot a herd of bison wandering through the property.

The ★ **Old Faithful Inn** (early May-early Oct., $320 standard room, $350-370 premium rooms, $390 superior room near geyser, $260-400 Old House rooms with bath, $160-320 Old House rooms with shared bath, $800 suites, $690 junior suites) is the most popular lodging inside the park, and for good reason. The original part of the lodge, known as the Old House, was built in 1904 by acclaimed architect Robert Reamer. Situated close to the Old Faithful geyser, the lodge epitomizes rustic beauty, originality, and strength. It has a large front lobby that houses a massive stone fireplace. The larger rooms are in the wings of the inn, built in the 1910s and 1920s, while the more modest rooms are in the Old House. The inn has a wide assortment of guest rooms and rates, ranging from two-room suites with sitting rooms and fridges to simple rooms without individual baths. Since this is the most sought-after lodging in the park, make reservations well in advance.

Close to the inn are the **Old Faithful Lodge Cabins** (mid-May-late Sept., $96-159), offering much simpler and rustic lodging. If you are looking for budget-friendly accommodations that put you in the center of park activity, these are a good option. The cabins are small motel-style units that vary in condition. Many of them were renovated in 2016. The lower-priced cabins do not come with baths, but there are communal showers nearby. The cabins are scattered around a main log cabin-style lodge. Built in the 1920s, the main lodge has a large cafeteria, bakery, and fully stocked gift shop, making it popular with park visitors throughout the day.

The **Old Faithful Snow Lodge and Cabins** (late Apr.-mid Oct. and mid-Dec.-late Feb., in summer $301-323 premium lodge rooms, $202 Western cabin, $129 Frontier cabin; and in winter $336-358 premium lodge rooms, $219 Western cabin, $167 Frontier cabin) are among the newest accommodations in the park. The original lodge was torn down and a new structure was built in 1999. Its architecture is intended to complement, though not duplicate, the Old Faithful Inn, and the lodge won a Cody Award for Western Design. It offers comfortable, modern rooms decorated with Western flair. It also has a few motel-style cabins, built in 1989. The Western cabins are a good value for the money; they're large rooms with two queen beds and a full bath. This is one of only two lodges (the other is Mammoth Hot Springs Hotel) open during the winter season in Yellowstone.

Grant Village is about 20 miles (32 km) southeast of Old Faithful on the West Thumb of Yellowstone Lake. Although the accommodations do not have the same rustic feel or character of the other lodges, they do offer a comfortable and modern place to stay away from the crowds. The complex is made up of six small condo-like buildings. Each building

has 50 nicely furnished hotel rooms ($270) that come with either two double beds or one queen and full baths. The rooms and exteriors were renovated in 2016.

Reservations for all hotels inside the park should be made through **Xanterra/Yellowstone National Park Lodges** (307/344-7311 or 866/439-7375, www.yellowstonenationalparklodges.com). Note that there are no televisions, radios, or air-conditioning.

CAMPING

Five of the 12 campsites in the park are in this southern region: **Bridge Bay** (between West Thumb and Lake, late May-early Sept., flush toilets, $25.25); **Fishing Bridge RV Park** (at Fishing Bridge north of Lake Village, early May-late Sept., flush toilets and pay showers, $47.75), the only campground offering water and sewer, for hard-sided vehicles only; **Grant Village** (at Grant Village south of West Thumb, late June-mid-Sept., flush toilets, $30); **Lewis Lake** (at Lewis Lake south of Grant Village, early-June-early Nov., vault toilets, $15); and **Madison** (at Madison Junction between the west entrance and Old Faithful, late Apr.-mid-Oct., flush toilets, $25.25). Advance reservations (307/344-7311 or 866/439-7375) or same-day reservations (307/344-7901) can be made at Bridge Bay, Fishing Bridge RV Park, Grant Village, and Madison.

West Yellowstone

West Yellowstone (population 1,353; elevation 6,667 ft/2,032 m) has something of a split personality—hard-core athletes training for the Olympics next to hard-core snowmobilers aiming for high-marking honors; get-too-close tourists alongside bison activists who try to put themselves in the line of fire. The winters are huge, with snow that buries everything but this town's spirit. The region shines with sensational recreational opportunities,

from guided snow coach and cross-country skiing excursions to snowmobiling and dogsledding. The winters look interminable with piles of snow still scattered around town well into May and sometimes June, but with so much sun and so much to do, residents never complain about the cold.

The summers tend to be crowded as most people going to Old Faithful come through "West," as the town is known locally. With crystal clear alpine lakes and rivers in every direction, there is no shortage of summer recreation—fishing opportunities are phenomenal, and there are plenty of places to cycle. As the hub of the region and the busiest entrance to Yellowstone National Park, there is plenty of good grub plus lots of comfortable beds in and around town.

SIGHTS
★ Grizzly and Wolf Discovery Center

If you have your heart set on seeing a grizzly or a wolf in Yellowstone, here's my advice: Get it out of the way before you even go into the park, like a first kiss on a first date before you order dinner. The **Grizzly and Wolf Discovery Center** (201 S. Canyon St., 406/646-7001 or 800/257-2570, www.grizzlydiscoveryctr.org, 8:30am-8:30pm daily mid-May-early Sept., 8:30am-7pm daily early Sept.-late Sept. and late Apr.-mid-May, 8:30am-6pm daily late Sept.-late Oct., 8:30am-4pm daily Nov.-late Apr., $13 ages 13 and over, $12.25 seniors 62 and over, $8 children 5-12, free for children under 5, admission valid for two consecutive days) is a nonprofit organization that acts something like an orphanage, giving homes to problem, injured, or abandoned animals that have nowhere else to go. Although there is something melancholy about watching these incredible beasts confined to any sort of enclosure, particularly on the perimeter of a chunk of wilderness as massive as Yellowstone, there is also something remarkable about seeing them close enough to count their whiskers. Watching a wolf pack interact from a comfy bench behind floor-to-ceiling windows in the warming hut is a worthwhile way to spend an afternoon. The naturalists on staff are excellent at engaging with visitors of all ages and have plenty to teach everyone. One fantastic opportunity for curious children ages 5-12 is the **Keeper Kids** program, which is offered twice daily during the summer season. For roughly 45 minutes, the kids learn about grizzly eating habits and behavior. They get

to then go into the grizzly enclosure, while the bears are locked away obviously, and hide buckets of food for the bears. When the kids exit and the bears come racing out to search for their treats—overturning massive logs and boulders in the process—the kids (and their parents!) are mesmerized. The **Keeper Crew**, for kids 13-17, helps the keepers prepare the bears' enrichment for the Keeper Kids program. Enroll with a naturalist as space is limited. The center has gone to great lengths to share the personal story of each animal and why it cannot survive in the wild. They also give the bears all sorts of games and tasks—aiding in the design of bear-proof garbage cans is one example. Since these bears do not hibernate, this is a stop absolutely worth making any time of the year. Ultimately, this is a really nice place to learn a lot about bears, wolves, and raptors before heading into the park to look for them in the wild.

Yellowstone Giant Screen Theatre

Montana's first giant screen, the **Yellowstone Giant Screen Theatre** (101 S. Canyon St., 406/646-4100 or 888/854-5862, www.yellowstonegiantscreen.com, premium seating $13.75 adults, $13.25 seniors, $11 children 4-12; regular seating $9.75 adults, $9.25 seniors, $7 children) boasts a six-story-high screen with stereo surround sound that makes any subject larger than life. Nature-oriented movies rotate in and out, as do popular movies like the newest *Star Wars* and *Jurassic Park* flicks that benefit from the massive screen, but *Yellowstone* is frequently on the playlist and offers an extraordinary introduction to the park's history, wildlife, geothermal activity, and mountainous beauty with giant screen grandeur. The biggest bargain in town is the $0.50 soft serve ice cream available daily at the theater.

SPORTS AND RECREATION
Fishing

The fishing around West tends to be as plentiful as it is phenomenal. In addition to the

West Yellowstone

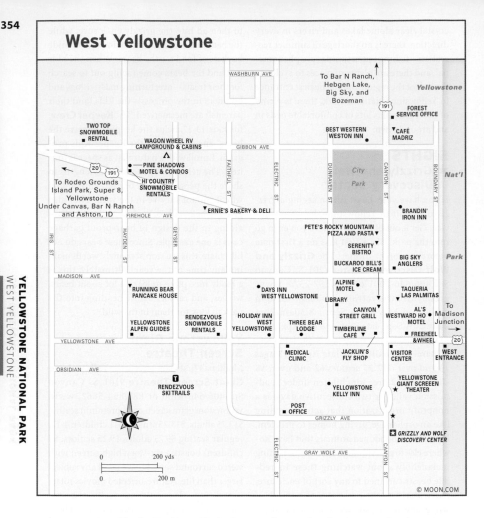

WASHBURN AVE

To Bar N Ranch, Hebgen Lake, Big Sky, and Bozeman

Yellowstone

191

FOREST SERVICE OFFICE

TWO TOP SNOWMOBILE RENTAL

WAGON WHEEL RV CAMPGROUND & CABINS

GIBBON AVE

BEST WESTERN WESTON INN

CAFÉ MADRIZ

20 191

PINE SHADOWS MOTEL & CONDOS

HI COUNTRY SNOWMOBILE RENTALS

To Rodeo Grounds Island Park, Super 8, Yellowstone Under Canvas, Bar N Ranch and Ashton, ID

FAITHFUL ST

ELECTRIC ST

DUNHAVEN ST

City Park

CANYON ST

BOUNDARY ST

Nat'l

FIREHOLE AVE

ERNIE'S BAKERY & DELI

BRANDIN' IRON INN

IRIS ST

HAYDEN ST

GEYSER ST

MADISON AVE

PETE'S ROCKY MOUNTAIN PIZZA AND PASTA

SERENITY BISTRO

BUCKAROO BILL'S ICE CREAM

BIG SKY ANGLERS

Park

RUNNING BEAR PANCAKE HOUSE

DAYS INN WEST YELLOWSTONE

ALPINE MOTEL

LIBRARY

TAQUERIA LAS PALMITAS

To Madison Junction

YELLOWSTONE ALPEN GUIDES

RENDEZVOUS SNOWMOBILE RENTALS

HOLIDAY INN WEST YELLOWSTONE

THREE BEAR LODGE

CANYON STREET GRILL

TIMBERLINE CAFÉ

AL'S WESTWARD HO MOTEL

FREEHEEL &WHEEL

20

YELLOWSTONE AVE

OBSIDIAN AVE

MEDICAL CLINIC

JACKLIN'S FLY SHOP

VISITOR CENTER

WEST ENTRANCE

RENDEZVOUS SKI TRAILS

YELLOWSTONE KELLY INN

YELLOWSTONE GIANT SCREEEN THEATER

POST OFFICE

GRIZZLY AVE

GRIZZLY AND WOLF DISCOVERY CENTER

ELECTRIC ST

GRAY WOLF AVE

CANYON ST

0   200 yds

0   200 m

© MOON.COM

big-name rivers like the **Madison, Firehole, Yellowstone,** and the nearby **Henry's Fork** across the border in Idaho, there are all sorts of small streams and beautiful lakes of all sizes. **Hebgen Lake** and **Quake Lake** are two favorites for year-round fishing.

You won't have any difficulty finding guides and gear in the town of West Yellowstone. Among the best is **Big Sky Anglers** (formerly Bud Lilly's Trout Shop, 39 Madison Ave., 406/646-7801, www. bigskyanglers.com, 7am-10pm daily during the season), which has been outfitting and

guiding anglers for 60 years. Another pretty famous name among anglers is Bob Jacklin of **Jacklin's Fly Shop** (105 Yellowstone Ave., 406/646-7336, www.jacklinsflyshop.com, 7am-10pm summer, $550 full-day guided float for 2 people; $450 half-day guided walk/wade for 2 people). Both outfitters are licensed to guide in and out of Yellowstone National Park, and both carry an excellent assortment of top-of-the-line gear. Jacklin's Fly Shop also hosts free fly-casting lessons every Sunday evening in summer 7pm-8pm. Anglers do not need state fishing licenses in Yellowstone, but a

Spring Biking Through the Park

For a few magical weeks between the end of the snowmobile season and the onset of the summer car traffic, Yellowstone's roads are open exclusively to nonmotorized users. This means that bicyclists, walkers, runners, inline skaters, and roller skiers can cruise through the park in near silence with eyes focused on bison traffic as opposed to wide Winnebagos. Depending on the seasonal snow, the road between the west entrance and Mammoth Hot Springs typically opens the last Friday in March and stays open to nonmotorized users until the third Thursday in April. Opening can be delayed in heavy snow years due to the need for plowing.

Sometime in May there is normally a brief period of bicycle-only traffic permitted from the east entrance to the east end of Sylvan Pass, and from the south entrance to West Thumb Junction. The roads between Madison Junction and Old Faithful, and Norris Junction to Canyon, remain closed to all traffic during this spring season for human safety and bear management.

There is something truly spellbinding about being on the open road in the park, the wind whistling through your helmet. The relative silence allows some unrivaled wildlife-viewing and necessitates great care. As nerve-racking as it can be to get engulfed by a herd of bison while driving in your car, coming across them on your bike is an entirely different scenario. Still, if you are cautious and respectful, being on your bike can allow you to feel somewhat less like an intruder and more like a resident. You can fall into sync with the flow of the rivers, the movement of the breeze, and the calls of the animals. It is an unforgettable way to experience the park.

With that said: Respect, restraint, and absolute caution are of vital importance to your safety and the well-being of the animals. Keep a good distance from all wildlife—25 yards (22.9 m) from ungulates and 100 yards (91.4 m) from predators. Remember that bison can run at speeds topping 30 mph (48.3 kph), and they can jump a 6-foot (1.8-m) fence. Harbor no illusions about your immunity from an attack. The fact that you have approached silently allows for more of a startle factor for the animals and increases the likelihood of a conflict. Wear a helmet, and dress in layers: Yellowstone in spring can go from blue skies to blizzard conditions in a staggeringly short period of time. Be prepared for anything, and understand that there are no services in the park at this time. Enjoy this unique opportunity to savor the park up close. For specific information about road conditions, call 307/344-2109 from 8am-4:30pm on weekdays.

Yellowstone fishing permit—available at any of the visitors centers in the park—is required.

Mountain Biking and Cross-Country Skiing

Sandwiched between Yellowstone and the Gallatin National Forest on a high plateau, West Yellowstone offers excellent terrain for mountain biking. Because of its high altitude and location at the top of a reasonably flat plateau, West Yellowstone is also known for its cross-country ski trails. The town's excellent **Rendezvous Ski Trails** (look for the archway at the south end of Geyser St., www.skirunbikemt.com) offer roughly 22 miles (35 km) of gently rolling terrain, groomed for both skate and classic skiers, which easily converts to a single-track for mountain bikers and trail runners when the snow melts.

Athletes from around the world come to train in West thanks in large part to this trail system. And it should be noted that the proximity to Yellowstone opens up a whole new world of opportunity for both mountain bikers and skiers.

The best bike and ski shop in town—which also has surprisingly stylish clothes, great gear, a Pilates studio, and killer coffee—is the **Freeheel & Wheel** (33 Yellowstone Ave., 406/646-7744, www.freeheelandwheel.com, 9am-7pm Mon.-Sat., 9am-6pm Sun.). It rents, sells, and services bikes and skis and can offer any advice you could possibly need on the region's best rides and trails. Front suspension kid and adult mountain bikes ($10/hour, $35/day) and road bikes ($10/hour, $40/day) can be rented and come with a helmet and water bottle.

Other Winter Recreation

Although snowmobiling inside the park has shifted with the four-stroke engine and guide requirements along with daily entry limits, West Yellowstone is still considered the snowmobile capital of the world for its proximity to the 200 miles (320 km) of groomed trails in the park as well as hundreds of miles of groomed terrain in the national forests surrounding West.

There are numerous places in town to rent a snowmobile, and since the park mandates that all snowmobilers within park boundaries use a guide, several outfits also offer guiding services both in and out of the park. **Two Top Snowmobile Rental** (645 Gibbon Ave., 800/646-7802, www.twotopsnowmobile.com) has rentals for self-guided tours outside the park from $129 per day and guided tours into the park from $219. It also has licensed guides, Yellowstone-mandated four-stroke engines, and other rental equipment. Another full-service rental outfit in West is **Rendezvous Snowmobile Rentals** (415 Yellowstone Ave., 406/646-9564 or 800/426-7669, www.yeloowstonevacations.com), renting snowmobiles at $129-225 per day for travel outside the park or $225 for a single/double snowmobile on a guided trip to Old Faithful. For

deep-powder backcountry touring options outside the park, **Hi Country Snowmobile Rentals** (229 Hayden St., 406/646-7541 or 800/624-5291, www.hicountrysnowmobile.com) is an excellent bet, with snowmobile rentals from its entirely new fleet each year, guided trail rides, and guided backcountry tours. Rates vary throughout the year, so call for information.

For those who want to explore the backcountry outside Yellowstone National Park in a slightly quieter way, dogsledding might be the perfect choice. **Yellowstone Dog Sled Adventures** (406/223-5134, www.yellowstonedogsledadventures.com) offers half-day "Learn to Mush" tours ($235 adults, $150 children 5-12) where guests get to drive their own sled, which are appropriate for ages 5 and up. Other offerings allow guests to cuddle up in a sled while an experienced musher does the driving.

Another amazing way to see the park is on a guided snow coach tour. There are numerous providers, but **Yellowstone Alpen Guides** (555 Yellowstone Ave., 406/646-9591 or 800/858-3502, www.yellowstoneguides.com, from $145 adults, $135 seniors, $110 children under 16, prices do not include national park passes) offers classic 10-passenger

Touring Yellowstone in winter by snow coach is a magical way to see the park.

Bombardiers, a fantastic array of tours, and some of the best naturalist guides anywhere. Snow coach tours can be combined with some cross-country skiing in the park. Alpen Guides can also package lodging and meals.

ENTERTAINMENT AND EVENTS

There is plenty for visitors to do year-round in West Yellowstone. Before you arrive, you may want to visit the chamber of commerce **events calendar** (www.westyellowstonechamber. com) to scope out the current happenings. The **West Yellowstone Visitor Information Center** (30 Yellowstone Ave., 406/646-7701) also has information on programs like ranger-led educational Yellowstone National Park afternoon and evening programs and snow-shoe walks through the park in winter, free Music in the Park evenings, and weekly West Yellowstone rodeo shows in summer.

The **World Snowmobile Expo** (www. snowmobileexpo.com) is the largest snow-mobile exposition in the West. All the major manufacturers descend on West Yellowstone in early spring (usually early to mid-March) to unveil their latest and greatest. The show is combined with racing and evening events.

The **Yellowstone Rendezvous Race** (www.rendezvousskitrails.com or www. skirunbikemt.com), a one-day cross-country ski competition, is the largest event of the year. It usually takes place in early March, and 600-900 skiers come to participate. Six races are held concurrently, based on age and ability, over distances of 2-50 kilometers (1.2-31 miles). The **Kids 'N' Snow Youth Ski Festival** (www.kidsnsnow.org) is a newer event held the day after the Rendezvous Race. To encourage families to stay after the race, there are a series of ski events (including a relay race, an obstacle course, and even musical chairs) for children 13 and younger. The **Equinox Ski Challenge** (www. equinoxsnowchallenge.com) is the final ski event, held biennially (in odd years) on one of the last weekends in March. Skiers can participate as individuals or in relay teams

of up to eight people and compete to see how many laps they can complete in the time allotted. There is a 24-minute Kids Race and 3-hour, 6-hour, 12-hour, and 24-hour races for adults. A potluck and bonfire are held on Saturday night to mark the midpoint of the 24-hour race. All proceeds are donated to local charities.

The **Annual Mountain Bike Biathlon** (406/599-4464, www.skirunbike.com) takes place in June or July. There are two divisions, and first-timers are welcome to participate. The Match Class is for participants with experience and their own rifles; the Sport Class is for novices. The race covers 7.5 kilometers (4.7 miles) with two bouts of shooting. If you'd like to get some practice in before the event, you can sign up for the **Biathlon Shooting Camp** (406/599-4465) in August.

The **Wild West Yellowstone Rodeo** (175 Oldroyd Rd., 406/560-6913, www. yellowstonerodeo.com, $15 adults, $8 children) is another summertime event that runs June-August. Shows begin at 8pm and are held Tues.-Sat. June-Aug.; tickets are available online or at the gate.

FOOD

A great spot for a full breakfast, hot lunch, or terrific sack lunches is the long-standing **Ernie's Bakery & Deli** (409 Firehole Ave., 406/646-9467, www.erniesbakery.com, 7am-3pm daily summer, 7am-2pm daily winter, $8-18). **Running Bear Pancake House** (538 Madison Ave., 406/646-7703, www. runningbearph.com, 6:30am-2pm daily, $8-14) offers family-style dining for breakfast and lunch.

For the best soup, salad, and potato bar in town, try the **Timberline Café** (135 Yellowstone Ave., 406/646-9349, www. my.montana.net/timberlinecafe/, 6:30am-4pm and 5pm-10pm daily mid-May-early Oct., breakfast and lunch $6-14, dinner $11-31), an old-school establishment that has been feeding Yellowstone visitors and locals during the summer season since the early 1900s. Don't miss the homemade pie.

A real surprise in this tourist town is the wonderful ★ **Café Madriz** (311 N. Canyon St., 406/646-9245, late May-mid-Sept., 5pm-9pm Mon.-Sat., $11-30), which serves authentic Spanish dishes, from paella and tortilla española to hot and cold tapas, and makes the most of fresh, local ingredients. The salads are killer.

Another West Yellowstone institution is **Buckaroo Bill's Ice Cream & BBQ** (24 N. Canyon St., 406/646-7901, 10:30am-10pm Mon.-Sat. May-Oct., $7.75-29), which has excellent bison burgers, steaks, and sandwiches in addition to mouthwatering Montana-made ice cream. The joint is popular, though, and it's not always easy to get a seat; the outside patio is a lively place for a meal.

Canyon Street Grill (22 N. Canyon St., 406/646-7548, 8am-8pm daily May-Oct., reduced hours in off season, $5-12) is a 1950s-style diner with delicious burgers, fries, and milk shakes. **Pete's Rocky Mountain Pizza and Pasta** (112 Canyon St., 406/646-7820, www.petesrockymountainpizza.com, 11am-10pm summer, seasonal hours vary, delivery available after 5pm, large pizzas $20-27) serves up good pizza and hearty pasta dishes like elk sausage spaghetti and Italian buffalo ravioli. They do have gluten-free pizza offerings too.

If you like Mexican street food, the best place within a day's drive from Yellowstone is, without a doubt, ★ **Taqueria Las Palmitas** (21 N. Canyon St., 406/640-0172, 10am-10pm daily early Apr.-mid-Oct., $5-10), known locally as "The Taco Bus." We're talking soft tacos, beans, and more, piled onto paper plates and served in an old-school bus. It couldn't be less fancy or more satisfying.

For a more gourmet experience, **Serenity Bistro** (38 N. Canyon St., 406/646-7660, www.sydneysbistro.com, 11am-3pm and 5pm-close daily May-Oct., $8-30) is undoubtedly the place. It serves excellent, fresh meals utilizing local ingredients whenever possible. Entrées include the bistro burger, Panang chicken seafood pasta, trout escalope, buffalo tortellini, elk tenderloin, and twice-cooked quail.

Pasta lovers won't want to miss the butternut squash. The bistro also offers gourmet salads and sandwiches for lunch and boasts the most extensive wine list in town.

Six miles (9.7 km) outside of town is **Bar N Ranch** (970 Buttermilk Creek Rd., 406/646-9445, www.bar-n-ranch.com, 7am-10am and 5pm-10pm daily mid-May-mid-Oct., $15-45), a wonderful place for a meal. With beautiful views all around, you can indulge in terrific Western gourmet cuisine including game burgers, bison stir-fry, steaks, and pasta. One favorite is the campfire tacos with pulled pork, jalapeño slaw, and barbecue aioli. Gourmet picnic lunches are available too.

ACCOMMODATIONS

In the summer months there are more than 2,000 hotel rooms to be found in West and about 1,300 when the snow covers the ground. Guest ranches, bed-and-breakfasts, and cabin rentals are also available. **Yellowstone Tour & Travel** (800/221-1151, www.yellowstone-travel.com) is a full-service travel agency in West Yellowstone that can book everything from accommodations and tours to complete packages. The **West Yellowstone Chamber of Commerce** (406/646-7701, www.destinationyellowstone.com) also has an excellent website that shows all lodging availability.

Just seven blocks from the west entrance to Yellowstone National Park, the pet-friendly **Pine Shadows Motel & Condos** (229 Hayden St., 406/646-7541 or 800/624-5291, www.pineshadowsmotel.com, $79-250) is open year-round and has a selection of motel rooms and newly built, spacious condos, all of which are clean and comfortable. As is true in much of the town, free Wi-Fi is available. Also open year-round, the **Three Bear Lodge** (217 Yellowstone Ave., 406/646-7353 or 800/646-7353, www.threebearlodge.com, $79-264) offers 44 guest rooms in its recently remodeled pet-friendly motel unit and 26 in the lodge, where no two rooms are alike. All guest rooms have a refrigerator, a microwave, an LCD TV, handmade furniture, and fluffy duvets.

The **Alpine Motel** (120 Madison Ave., 406/646-7544, www. alpinemotelwestyellowstone.com, $79-189) is a budget-friendly choice with a variety of units, some including kitchens, just two blocks from the park entrance. The service by owners Brian and Patty is noticeably good. Another good independent property, which is only open mid-May-mid-October, is **Al's Westward Ho Motel** (16 Boundary St., 888/646-7331, www.alswestwardhomotel. net, $129-179), which is just across the street from the park entrance and the Yellowstone Giant Screen Theatre. A couple of blocks farther from the entrance, but a long-standing and reliable choice in town is the 79-room, pet-friendly **Brandin' Iron Inn** (201 Canyon, 406/646-9411 or 800/217-4613, www. brandiniron.com, $69-299).

There are a number of larger, chain hotels in town, including three Best Western options, the nicest of which is probably the **Best Western Weston Inn** (103 Gibbon Ave., 406/646-7373, www.bestwestern.com, $223-369). Other options include **Holiday Inn West Yellowstone** (315 Yellowstone Ave., 406/646-7365 or 800/315-2621, www. ihg.com, $141-468), **Days Inn West Yellowstone** (301 Madison, 406/646-7656, www.daysinn.com, $113-332), **Yellowstone Kelly Inn** (104 S. Canyon, 406/646-4544, www.yellowstonekellyinn.com, $90-350), and, 7.5 miles (12.1 km) from town, **West Yellowstone Super 8** (1545 Targhee Pass, 406/646-9584, www.wyndhamhotels.com, $187-269).

CAMPING

With nearly two dozen private and public campgrounds in the vicinity of West, campers have plenty of choices, although most are geared to RV campers. The nearest U.S. Forest Service campground is **Baker's Hole Campground** (U.S. 191, 3 mi/4.8 km northwest of West Yellowstone, 406/823-6961, www.hebgenbasincampgrounds.com, May 15-Sept. 30 depending on weather, $16 for 1 vehicle, $7 for each additional vehicle, plus $6 for electrical sites), with 73 sites (33 with electricity) set on a scenic oxbow of the Madison River. Basic services such as water and trash pickup are provided, there is firewood for sale ($6), and the fishing is excellent.

Right in town, just six blocks from the park's west entrance, is **Wagon Wheel RV Campground & Cabins** (408 Gibbon Ave., 406/646-7872, www.yellowstonervcabin.com, camping May 15-Sept. 30, cabins May 1-Oct. 31, $46-85 full-hookup pull-through sites), offering a forested and quiet setting for RV camping only. The nine cabins ($189-399), reminiscent of the 1930s and '40s architecture found throughout the park, are small but charming. Note that they get booked up quickly and require three- and five-night stays. At peak season here, there isn't much elbow room. Free Wi-Fi is available in some public areas.

For a truly unique experience outside of town, ★ **Yellowstone Under Canvas** (890 Buttermilk Creek Rd., 406/219-0441, www. mtundercanvas.com, Memorial Day-Labor Day) offers "glamping" (glamour-camping) options ($219-634) ranging from modest tipis and safari tents to luxury safari suite tents with king-size beds, private baths with freestanding tubs, and woodstoves. A variety of options are available, from shared bathrooms (the hot water showers are provided by a generator that runs from 6am to 11pm and is not quiet) to private but separate baths, influencing the price. But all of these tents and tipis are set in a mountain-ringed meadow with a creek running through. And the bedding is nothing short of luxurious. The guests here are largely international, and it can be a treat to listen to campfire or next-tent pillow talk in several different languages. The only downside is that snoring is universally annoying, and with all but the most expensive tents situated so close together, light sleepers are bound to hear plenty of snorers. Still, this is comfortable camping without the work.

INFORMATION AND SERVICES

The **West Yellowstone Chamber of Commerce** (406/646-7701, www. destinationyellowstone.com), **Montana State Visitors Center**, and **Yellowstone Park Visitors Center** (307/344-2876) are all housed under the same roof at 30 Yellowstone Avenue. You can get all the information you need about the city and the state, and you can even buy your park permits. The visitors center also has a lot of information about the regular and special events held in town.

The **West Yellowstone Public Library** (23 N. Dunraven St., 406/646-9017, 10am-6pm Tues.-Fri., 10am-2pm Sat. mid-May-Sept.; 10am-5pm Tues.-Fri., 10am-1pm Sat. winter) is between Yellowstone and Madison Avenues.

It offers free Wi-Fi and has three computers with Internet access.

The town's only **post office** (209 Grizzly Ave., 406/646-7704, 8:30am-5pm Mon.-Fri.) is at the corner of Electric Street and Grizzly Avenue.

Swan Cleaners (520 Madison Ave., 406/646-7892, 8am-8pm daily) is just east of the Running Bear Pancake House. It has coin-operated machines and wash-and-fold laundry services (9am-3pm Mon.-Fri.).

For nonemergency medical care, you can walk into the **Community Health Partners-West Yellowstone Clinic** (11 Electric St., 406/646-9441, www.chphealthmt.org, 9am-6pm Mon. and Thurs., 8am-5pm Tues.-Wed. and Fri. in high season, winter hours start Oct. 30). There is 24-hour paramedic emergency service available in town by calling 911.

Grand Teton National Park

Just south of Yellowstone, Grand Teton National Park is even more dazzling in alpine splendor than its more prominent neighbor. The Tetons soar skyward, 3 in a sea of 12 peaks topping 12,000 feet (3,658 m).

The mountains are young—still growing, in fact—and utterly spectacular, perhaps the most dramatic anywhere in the Lower 48. The park itself contains approximately 310,000 acres (125,453 hectares, roughly 15 percent the size of Yellowstone), 100 miles (161 km) of paved road, and much to the delight of hikers, some 200 miles (320 km) of trails.

Like Yellowstone, Grand Teton is home to healthy populations of wildlife—this is among the best places in the West to see a moose—but the rugged terrain and limited number of roads afford the animals

Highlights

Look for ★ to find recommended sights, activities, dining, and lodging.

★ **Cruise to Elk Island:** Lure yourself out of bed and into this wonderland with an early morning cruise (page 371).

★ **Oxbow Bend:** This hairpin curve of slow-moving backwater from the Snake River is perfect for novice boaters, wildlife watchers, and photographers (page 373).

★ **Signal Mountain:** Follow this exciting drive with expansive views of the entire valley (page 373).

★ **Jenny Lake:** Resting like a mirror at the base of the Tetons, this alpine lake is a gem for hikers, boaters, and picnickers (page 379).

★ **Hidden Falls and Inspiration Point:** The glorious views along this popular hike are worth every step (page 379).

★ **Craig Thomas Discovery and Visitor Center:** This architectural gem—complete with video rivers running beneath your feet and walls of windows that showcase the Tetons—offers a stunning introduction to the park (page 384).

★ **Laurance S. Rockefeller Preserve:** The longtime summer home of the Rockefeller family, this lovely preserve exemplifies the family's commitment to stewardship (page 384).

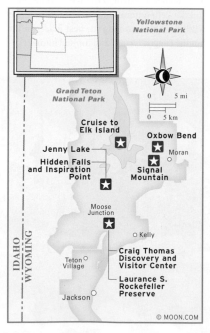

better places to hide. Still, you always need to be prepared for bear encounters in the park. Beyond the fascinating natural and geological history of the region, Grand Teton offers some interesting human-built attractions—including the historic and elegant Jenny Lake Lodge, the Chapel of the Transfiguration, and the Laurance S. Rockefeller Preserve—that are well worth seeing. At the end of the day, though, Grand Teton is a place for nature lovers and outdoors enthusiasts. The vistas are unparalleled, as are the recreational opportunities.

PLANNING YOUR TIME

Grand Teton National Park is smaller, and in some ways more manageable, than its northerly neighbor. There are only 100 miles (161 km) of paved road, all of which can be driven easily in less than a day's time. With fewer accommodations than Yellowstone, Grand Teton lends itself to easy day trips from various locations in Wyoming, such as **Jackson Hole** or **Dubois,** 65 miles (105 km) from the east entrance. **Cody** is about a three-hour drive from the park, via Yellowstone, so overnighting there is an option when rooms can not be found any closer. A destination in its own right, Grand Teton is a paradise for outdoors enthusiasts. Hikers, bikers, boaters, and in winter, cross-country skiers will have no problem coming up with marvelous weeklong itineraries. Still, for those on a time budget, you can get an excellent sampling of the park in two days, but even if you are just driving through, there are a few places that should not be missed.

While summer is by far the busiest time in the park, spring and fall can be magnificent with wildflowers, golden aspens, and more active wildlife. **Hiking** and **climbing** in the Tetons is best done in summer and early fall, after the winter snow has melted and before it starts flying again. Still, snow squalls and bad weather can surprise hikers at any time of year, so come prepared. Park rangers offer educational programs throughout the year that are an excellent way to make the most of the time you have. In the fall, for example, drivers can join ranger-led **wildlife caravans** from the Craig Thomas Discovery and Visitor Center that guide visitors to the best places to see wildlife that day. **Ranger-led hikes and eco-talks** are geared to the seasons and offer visitors an insiders' look at the park.

The National Park Service offers an excellent **trip-planning tool online** (www.nps. gov), or you can order a booklet by mail by calling 307/739-3600.

INFORMATION AND SERVICES

Visit the website of the **National Park Service** (www.nps.gov) to help plan your trip to Grand Teton. In the section titled Plan Your Visit, you'll find answers to most of your pressing questions. When you enter the park, you will receive a copy of the park newspaper, *Grand Teton Guide*, which has a lot of useful information about park facilities, hours of operation, and programs and specific activities offered daily or weekly. If you need additional information before you go, you can call the **visitors information line** (307/739-3300, ext. 1). For campground information, call the **Grand Teton Lodge Company** (307/543-3100 or 307/543-2811) and for **backcountry** information, contact the permits office (307/739-3309) or book backcountry sites online (www.recreation.gov) in advance.

Park Fees and Passes

Single-entry entrance fees are $35 per vehicle, $20 per person for hikers or bicyclists, and $30 per motorcycle for seven days in both Grand Teton National Park and Yellowstone National Park.

With more than 200 miles (320 km) of maintained trails in the park, backpacking and backcountry camping provide a

---

Previous: Grand Teton National Park; canoes at Jenny Lake; Hidden Falls.

Grand Teton National Park

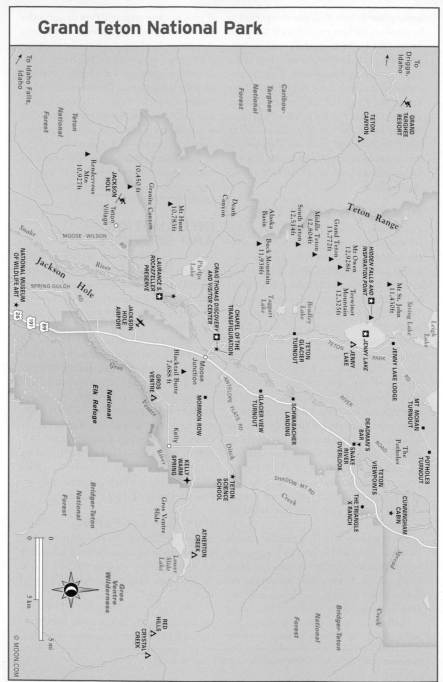

To Driggs, Idaho

GRAND TARGHEE RESORT

TETON CANYON

Caribou-Targhee National Forest

To Idaho Falls, Idaho

Teton National Forest

Rendezvous Mtn 10,927ft

JACKSON HOLE

Teton Village

10,450 ft

Granite Canyon

Death Canyon

Mt Hunt 10,783ft

Alaska Basin

South Teton 12,514ft

Middle Teton 12,804ft

Grand Teton 13,772ft

Mt Owen 12,928ft

Teton Range

Buck Mountain 11,938ft

HIDDEN FALLS AND INSPIRATION POINT

Mt St. John 11,430ft

Teewinot Mountain 12,325ft

Snake

River

MOOSE - WILSON RD

Jackson Hole

SPRING GULCH RD

NATIONAL MUSEUM OF WILDLIFE ART

26 191 89

LAURANCE S. ROCKEFELLER PRESERVE

Phelps Lake

CRAIG THOMAS DISCOVERY AND VISITOR CENTER

CHAPEL OF THE TRANSFIGURATION

Taggart Lake

Bradley Lake

TETON GLACIER TURNOUT

String Lake

Leigh Lake

JENNY LAKE

JENNY LAKE LODGE

TETON PARK RD

JACKSON HOLE AIRPORT

Blacktail Butte 7,688 ft

Moose Junction

Gros Ventre

GROS VENTRE

National Elk Refuge

MORMON ROW

Kelly

KELLY WARM SPRING

ANTELOPE FLATS RD

Ditch

GLACIER VIEW TURNOUT

SCHWABACHER LANDING

GLACIER VIEW TURNOUT

SNAKE RIVER

RIVER

MT MORAN TURNOUT

The Potholes

POTHOLES TURNOUT

DEADMAN'S BAR

SNAKE RIVER OVERLOOK

TETON VIEWPOINTS

CUNNINGHAM CABIN

ROAD

Gros Ventre River

Gros Ventre Slide

TETON SCIENCE SCHOOL

SHADOW MT RD

Creek

THE TRIANGLE X RANCH

ATHERTON CREEK

Bridger-Teton National Forest

Lower Slide Lake

0

0

5 Km

5 mi

Gros Ventre Wilderness

RED HILLS

CRYSTAL CREEK

Bridger-Teton National Forest

Spread

Creek

© MOON.COM

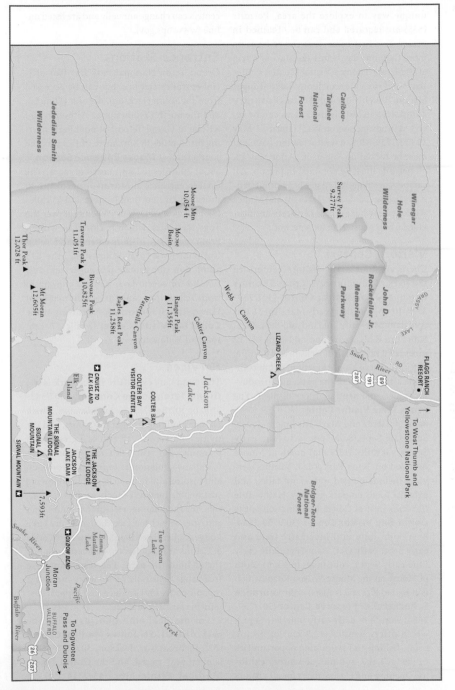

GRAND TETON NATIONAL PARK

unique way to explore the area. Permits ($35) are required and can be obtained in person on a first-come, first-served basis no more than one day before the start of a trip at the Craig Thomas Visitor Center, Colter Bay Visitor Center, or Jenny Lake Ranger Station. Roughly one-third of **backcountry campsites** in heavily used areas can be reserved in advance online ($45) January 1-May 15 (307/739-3309, www.recreation.gov) and must be picked up in person. After May 15, all permits must be obtained in person. All campers are required to use bear-proof canisters below 10,000 feet (3,048 m) and at sites without bear boxes. Free canisters are provided when registering for a permit.

Visitors Centers

There are four main visitors centers in the park. The impressive **Craig Thomas Discovery and Visitor Center** (307/739-3399, 10am-4pm daily early Mar.-Apr., 8am-5pm daily May-early June and mid-Sept.-Oct., 8am-7pm daily early June-mid-Sept.) is 12 miles (19.3 km) north of Jackson and 0.5 mile (0.8 km) west of Moose Junction. Exhibits include a relief map of the park, an introductory video, and natural history displays. The **Jenny Lake Visitor Center** (307/739-3392, 8am-5pm daily mid-May-early June and early Sept.-late Sept., 8am-7pm early June-early Sept.) is 8 miles (12.9 km) north of Moose Junction on Teton Park Road. Visitors' services include guided walks and talks, and exhibits focus on park geology. Half a mile (0.8 km) west of Colter Bay Junction is the **Colter Bay Visitor Center** (307/739-3594, 8am-5pm daily mid-May-early June and early Sept.-early Oct., 8am-7pm daily early June-early Sept.). Four miles (6.4 km) south of Moose on the Moose-Wilson Road (which is closed to RVs and trailers) is the **Laurance S. Rockefeller Preserve Center** (307/739-3654, 9am-5pm daily early June-late Sept.), which offers 8 miles (12.9 km) of hiking trails, fishing and swimming opportunities in Phelps Lake, and unique sensory exhibits. Opening and closing dates for all visitors centers can change annually and are listed online (www.nps.gov).

Entrance Stations

Grand Teton National Park has two official entrance stations, but can be accessed from the south (Jackson), the east (Dubois), and the north (Yellowstone). Although you will be in Grand Teton National Park starting just 5 miles (8 km) north of Jackson, the southernmost **Moose Entrance Station** is about 20 miles (32 km) north of town. The eastern entrance at **Moran Junction** is 30 miles (48 km) north of Jackson and 55 miles (89 km) west of Dubois, Wyoming, over the Togwotee Pass, which is closed in winter. From the north, visitors enter Grand Teton National Park from Yellowstone; the $35 admission (for private passenger vehicles) is valid for seven days. Visitors coming in from Yellowstone can stop for information at **Flagg Ranch Information Station** or the **Colter Bay Visitor Center** 18 miles (29 km) south of Yellowstone.

Services

The main concessionaire in the park is the **Grand Teton Lodge Company** (307/543-3100 or 307/543-2811, www.gtlc.com), which operates lodging, restaurants, tours, and activities. Its website can also be a great aid in planning your visit. The Grand Teton Lodge Company's mission is to preserve, protect, and inspire, and to do so in part by following sustainable business practices. It is responsible for the lodging, restaurants, tours, and activities at Jackson Lake Lodge, Jenny Lake Lodge, Colter Bay Village, Headwaters Lodge & Cabins at Flagg Ranch, and campgrounds throughout the park. The restaurants use free-range, naturally raised meat and dairy, organic coffee and produce, and support sustainable farming practices.

For **medical emergencies** within the park, dial 911. **St. John's Medical Center** (625 E. Broadway, Jackson, 307/733-3636) is open year-round, and the **Grand Teton Medical Clinic** (307/543-2514 during

Bear #399 and the Grizzlies of Grand Teton

In July 1975, grizzly bears were listed as "threatened" under the Endangered Species Act. At that time, and for several years afterward, not a single grizzly was known to wander the wilds of Grand Teton National Park. Estimates put the number of grizzlies in Yellowstone around 136 at the time, but in Grand Teton, there wasn't even one.

The animal's listing and, thankfully, passionate involvement by good people have changed that. In early 2016, the number of grizzlies in the Greater Yellowstone Ecosystem—which includes Yellowstone and Grand Teton National Parks and their surrounds—hovered somewhere around the 700 mark. And at the end of 2015, Grand Teton National Park was home to some 60 of these totemic animals.

Because it's true that we protect what we love, and love what we know, perhaps no bear has done as much for grizzly protection as #399. First captured and collared in 2001 when she was five years old, #399 has become the most famous grizzly in the world. She has had more than 15 cubs and grandcubs and been watched along roadsides by thousands upon thousands of park visitors over the years. "Along with her cubs, she made you want to protect her," said acclaimed photographer Tom Mangelsen, who, with writer Todd Wilkinson, put out a marvelous book on #399, *Grizzlies of Pilgrim Creek* (www.mangelsen.com).

Because she is so visible, Bear #399 has shown us the challenges bears face to simply survive. According to Wilkinson, nearly 75 percent of her descendants have died as a result of human encounters—struck by cars, killed illegally by big-game hunters, euthanized for preying on cattle or for coming too close to human development. She has lost other cubs to starvation or encounters with dominant males. But it's the day-to-day glimpses of #399, often with her cubs, that endear her to people the world over and give people a vision of something worth fighting for.

Even with postcard bears like #399 and citizen advocates, the fight to protect bears is far from won. After the success of their recovery over the last 40 years, in the early part of 2016, the U.S. Fish and Wildlife Service proposed that grizzly bears be removed from the federal List of Endangered and Threatened Wildlife, which strips away various protective measures and eventually opens grizzlies up for hunting. In 2017, 56 grizzlies died from poachers, conflicts with hunters and ranchers, and car collisions. Even so, with all the threats, in the fall of 2018, plans for the sport hunt will endanger as many as 22 grizzlies, 12 of them females, which can be shot on public or private land outside the national parks. As the status of grizzly bears is questioned, their value in our wild world should not be.

While scientists call the grizzly an "umbrella" or "indicator" species—meaning that when the grizzlies thrive, so too do the other plants and animals that inhabit their world—naturalist and writer Doug Peacock, who has dedicated his life to making the world a safer place for grizzlies, goes further in asserting the importance of their survival. "Really, we are as much endangered as the grizzly bears. The fate of humans and grizzlies is a single, collective one," he said.

Twenty-two years old in 2018, when she emerged from hibernation with year-old twin cubs, Bear #399 will not be around much longer. But let us hope—and fight—to make sure grizzly bears still are.

GRAND TETON NATIONAL PARK

business hours or 307/733-8002 after hours, 9am-5pm daily mid-May-mid-Oct.) is located in the Jackson Lake Lodge.

TRANSPORTATION

Getting There

BY AIR

The only airport within a national park, **Jackson Hole Airport** (JAC, 1250 E. Airport Rd., Jackson, 307/733-7682, www.jacksonholeairport.com) is served by American, Delta, United, and Frontier. The schedules change seasonally but include regular flights from Salt Lake City, Denver, Seattle, Chicago, Minneapolis, Dallas, Houston, Phoenix, San Francisco, and Los Angeles.

The airport has on-site car rentals from **Alamo, National, Hertz,** and **Enterprise.**

Avis/Budget, Dollar, and Thrifty are available off-site.

Somewhat amazingly for this part of the country, Jackson has 32 taxi companies serving the area, including **Broncs Taxi** (307/413-9863, www.jackson-hole-taxi.com), **Snake River Taxi** (307/413-9009, www.snakerivertaxi.com), and **Teton Mountain Taxi** (307/699-7969, www.jacksonholecab.com). Transportation to Jackson from the airport runs roughly $40 for 1-2 people. A taxi to Teton Village averages $70. A complete list of taxi services can be found under the transportation heading on the airport website.

BY CAR

Grand Teton National Park is 20 miles (32 km) from Jackson, 195 miles (315 km) from Bozeman through Yellowstone, 290 miles (465 km) from Salt Lake City, and 550 miles (890 km) from Denver. Grand Teton National Park is immediately south of Yellowstone and about 100 miles (161 km) southwest of Cody when the park roads are open and 323 miles (360 km) in the winter when park roads are closed. If you are driving from Yellowstone, take U.S. 89 South, which will lead you directly into the park. If you are coming from Idaho Falls, from I-15 take U.S. 26 East to ID 31 East, continuing to Highway 33 East. This will take you through the scenic Teton Pass, where it becomes WY 22. Continue until you reach U.S. 89, taking it north into the park. An alternate route, flatter but slightly longer, is to take U.S. 26 until it hits U.S. 89 and head north.

BY BUS

Alltrans/Jackson Hole Express (307-733-3135 or 800/443-6133, www.jacksonholealltrans.com) offers shuttles between Jackson Hole, eastern Idaho, and Salt Lake City. The nearest **Greyhound** stop is in Idaho Falls.

Getting Around

PRIVATE VEHICLES

If you are driving through the park, don't forget to keep an eye on your fuel gauge. The only gas station open year-round is at **Dornan's** (10 Moose Rd., gas pumps available 24 hours if paying with a credit card) in Moose. Other gas stations open May-October are at Signal Mountain, Jackson Lodge, and Colter Bay.

For up-to-date road information and closures in the park, call 307/739-3682, or 307/344-2117 for Yellowstone road reports. For Wyoming road information, contact the **Wyoming Department of Transportation** (888/996-7623, www.wyoroad.info).

TOURS

The **Grand Teton Lodge Company** (307/543-3100 or 307/543-2811, www.gtlc.com) offers any number of tours throughout the park, including four-hour tours departing from Jackson Lake Lodge during summer.

A great educational opportunity is provided by the **Teton Science Schools** (307/733-1313, www.tetonscience.org), based in Jackson. The organization is committed to creating a deeper appreciation and understanding of the wilderness and natural ecosystems found in the Greater Yellowstone area. Its experts provide classes and programs to engage every type of learner from small children to adults. The courses focus on everything from ecology and geology to unique plant and animal life. Even if you only plan to be in the park for a day or two, visit the website to see what is being offered. Regular programs can include hikes, campfires, canoe tours, and wildlife-viewing. The school also offers renowned **Wildlife Expeditions** (877/404-6626). These can be half-day, full-day, or multiple-day guided tours with professional wildlife biologists who provide you with an up close and unique opportunity to experience the natural wonders of the park.

Another tour company that focuses on getting visitors up close and personal with the park's wildlife in comfy 4x4 vehicles is **EcoTour Adventures** (307/690-9533, www.jhecotouradventures.com). Guided half-day tours, often at sunrise or sunset, run roughly four hours and start at $130 for adults and $95 for children 10 and under. Full-day trips last approximately eight hours and can take visitors into Grand Teton and Yellowstone. These tours include lunch at one of the park lodges and start at $225 for adults and $190 for children 10 and under.

PLANTS AND ANIMALS

Despite the fact that every square inch of Grand Teton National Park is at or above 6,400 feet (1,951 m) in elevation, there is a remarkable diversity of both plant and animal life in the three main growing zones and four distinct habitat regions. Throughout the short summer, the valleys are awash in colorful wildflowers. And although animals aren't quite as visible as they are in the vast open spaces or burned-out forests of Yellowstone, wildlife watchers will have terrific opportunities in the park.

All three of Grand Teton's growing zones—alpine, subalpine, and valley—fall between 6,400 feet (1,951 m) and 13,770 feet (4,197 m) in elevation, meaning harsh climates and a short growing season. Still, upward of 1,000 species of vascular plants grow in the park. Porous soil allows for an abundance of colorful wildflowers. And even in the high reaches of the mountains, delicate jewels like alpine forget-me-nots grow close to the ground in mats.

Because of the short growing season, the vast majority of trees in the park are conifers—as in Yellowstone, lodgepole pine is the most common tree—but aspens and cottonwoods have chlorophyll in the bark, allowing them to photosynthesize before putting out leaves. As a result, Grand Teton National Park is illuminated in the fall by changing leaves. Sagebrush is everywhere, lending an almost minty smell to the crisp air.

Along with Yellowstone, Grand Teton National Park is a critical part of the more than 11-million-acre (4.5-million-hectare) Greater Yellowstone Ecosystem, considered one of the last nearly intact temperate ecosystems on earth. As such, it provides critical home habitat and migratory routes for a number of species.

The park's four main habitat types are alpine, sagebrush, forest, and aquatic. The alpine habitat, above 10,000 feet (3,048 m), is home to some of the park's hardiest creatures: yellow-bellied marmots, pikas, and bighorn sheep. In the ubiquitous sagebrush areas, with more than 100 species of grasses and wildflowers, wildlife watchers can look for pronghorn, coyotes, bison, badgers, elk, and Uinta ground squirrels. While not as easy to explore, the park's forested regions are home to elk, mule deer, red squirrels, black bears, and snowshoe hares. And finally, in and around the plentiful lakes, rivers, and ponds of Grand Teton National Park are populations of moose, river otters, beavers, muskrat, coyotes, bison, and mule deer.

HISTORY

The history of this region dates back 11,000 years, when it was a seasonal hunting ground for such tribes as the Shoshone, Gros Ventre, Flathead, and Blackfeet. John Colter was likely the first European to explore the region; he is thought to have traveled through the area in 1808, guided by wildlife and Native American trails. By the 1820s the area was widely known for its abundance of beavers, and mountain men arrived with traps in hand. Trapper David E. Jackson spent the winter of 1829 along the shores of Jackson Lake; the valley, the lake, and the nearby town of Jackson bear his name. Many of the park's features were named by the Hayden Geological Survey in 1871.

The region was sparsely settled and farmed due to the climate and the soil, but it was used for cattle ranching in the late 1800s. The area was also well known among hunters and eventually became the setting for a handful of dude ranches.

In 1897, President Grover Cleveland established the Teton Forest Reserve, and the Teton National Forest was created in 1908. The park itself—96,000 acres (38,850 hectares) in its first incarnation—was set aside by Congress in 1929 and included primarily the mountains and alpine lakes. There were some attempts through the 1930s to add to the park, none of which were successful. John D. Rockefeller Jr., however, was quietly purchasing land in the Teton Valley through his Snake River Land Company. Between 1926 and 1946, Rockefeller bought 35,000 acres (14,164 hectares) adjacent to the park, and in 1949 he deeded all but 2,000 acres (809.4 hectares) to the federal government, which had established the 210,000-acre (84,984 hectares) Jackson Hole National Monument under President Franklin Roosevelt in 1943. In 1950, Congress agreed to merge the monument and the Rockefeller-donated land with the park, bringing it to its current boundaries.

Flagg Ranch and Colter Bay

Just south of the Yellowstone border, Flagg Ranch was at one time a U.S. Cavalry outpost. Converted to a guest ranch in 1910 and now known as Headwaters Lodge & Cabins at Flagg Ranch, it is ideally situated for visitors looking to explore both Yellowstone and Grand Teton National Parks from one location. In addition to full resort lodging and services—Flagg Ranch offers activities and services—a gas station, a grocery store, a deli and coffee shop—for those just passing through.

One of the busiest spots in the park, with a marina, lodging, a campground, a visitors center, and a museum on the shores of Jackson Lake, Colter Bay is a practical, if not exactly quiescent, place to stay, and it is a worthwhile region to explore.

SIGHTS
Colter Bay Indian Arts Museum
The unassuming **Colter Bay Indian Arts Museum** (307/739-3594, 8am-7pm daily early June-Labor Day, 8am-5pm daily Labor Day-early Oct., free) is tacked onto the visitors center almost as an afterthought. But the relatively unknown gem includes important Native American artifacts that belonged to tribes across the country. The David T. Vernon collection—which includes more than 1,000 objects ranging from dolls, shields, pipes, and weapons to photography—was donated by the Rockefeller family with the provision that it be displayed permanently in Grand Teton National Park. In 2012, almost the entire collection was sent to a conservation facility but is slowly coming back to the park, at both the Colter Bay and Craig Thomas Visitor Centers. As of 2016, more than 80 objects had been returned to the park, and digital images of many of the artifacts are available online through the **Google Cultural Institute** (www.google.com/culturalinstitute). It is a remarkable collection that could just as easily be on display at the Smithsonian were it not for the wishes of an extremely generous family. Meanwhile, Native American artisans practice their crafts in the museum intermittently through the summer, and a number of prominent lecturers and daily educational events are scheduled on-site.

SPORTS AND RECREATION
Boating and Fishing
On the shores of **Jackson Lake,** by far the largest body of water in the park, Colter Bay and the **Colter Bay Village Marina** (307/543-2811, ext. 1097, or 307/543-2811, www.gtlc.com) are excellent launching points for a variety of boating expeditions. From the marina, you can arrange cruises, canoe or kayak excursions, motorboat rentals, and guided fishing trips.

Guided fly-fishing tours can be arranged through the marina as well. Guided Jackson Lake **fishing** (307/543-2811) can be arranged from Colter Bay Marina starting at $110 per hour for 1-2 adults with a two-hour minimum and $22 per hour per additional person; day trips start at $475 for 1-2 people for four hours, or $575 for 1-2 people for eight hours.

★ Cruise to Elk Island

Since nothing builds an appetite like time spent on an alpine lake, there are wonderful breakfast cruises and dinner cruises (307/543-2811, www.gtlc.com) departing from the marina that whisk guests across the lake to Elk Island, in the shadow of Mount Moran. Each cruise takes approximately three hours. The **breakfast cruise** ($49 adults, $24 children 3-11), offered daily except Thursday (which can change from year to year), serves hearty fare with eggs and trout, pancakes, pastries, fresh fruit, and the all-important cowboy coffee. Typically, it departs at 7:15am from June to August and at 8am late August to early September. The **lunch cruise** ($47 adults, $24 children 3-11) includes a sack lunch and plenty of time to explore the island. It departs Monday, Wednesday, Friday, and Saturday at 12:15pm. The **dinner cruise** (5:15pm Fri.-Wed. June-Sept. 5, $70 adults, $40 children 6-11) includes such delectable mountain fare as steak and trout, baked beans, corn on the cob, a salad bar, roasted potatoes, and mouth-watering fruit cobbler. Scenic **lake cruises** (10:15am, 1:15pm, and 3:15pm daily, $34

adults, $14 children 3-11), which last about 90 minutes and are geared to different aspects of the park (with one cruise designed especially for kids). An extra tour departs at 6:15pm on Thursdays.

Hiking and Biking

There is a lot of marvelous terrain in every corner of the park for hiking and biking, and the northern section near Colter Bay is no exception. The hike to **Hermitage Point** is one of the most significant hikes (and long, at nearly 9 mi/14.5 km round-trip). The elevation gain is minimal (980 vertical ft/299 m), and the trail, which starts immediately across from the boat launch at the southern end of the parking lot, meanders through forest, meadow, and alongside ponds and streams. The easy **Lakeshore Trail** is only 2 miles (3.2 km) long round-trip and circumnavigates Colter Bay with stunning views in every direction.

North of Colter Bay, near the Flagg Ranch, is **Grassy Lake Road,** a 52-mile (84-km) dirt road—great for mountain biking—that follows an ancient Indian thoroughfare all the way to Ashton, Idaho. Along the way are hiking trails, streams, ponds, and splendid scenery.

Jackson Lake

FOOD

The main lodge at Headwaters Lodge & Cabins at Flagg Ranch is the center of all activity at the ranch. It has a gas station, a general store, and **Sheffields Restaurant & Bar** (800/443-2311, www.gtlc.com, 6:30am-10am, 11:30am-2pm, and 5:30pm-9:30pm daily June-late Sept., $20-31), which serves a solid range of local cuisine—including bison and elk meat loaf and Wyoming prime rib—in a family-friendly setting.

The **Café Court Pizzeria** (11am-10pm daily late May-early Sept., $8-24) in Colter Bay Village serves up specialty salads, toasted subs, and pizza, both by the slice and whole pies. Also at Colter Bay is the **Ranch House Restaurant** (6:30am-10:30am, 11:30am-1:30pm, and 5:30pm-10pm late May-late Sept.). The restaurant offers family-style meals with an emphasis on barbecue. The breakfast buffet ($10-16 adults, $7-9 children) can include eggs, French toast, hot specials, and organic oatmeal, or if you want to order à la carte ($7-15), you can easily fill up on the New York steak and eggs, pan-fried oatmeal, or the breakfast burrito. Lunch ($11-17) consists of a good selection of salads, burgers, and sandwiches, while dinner ($18-25) offers hearty steaks, chops, and seafood dishes. The bar is open 11:30am-10:30pm daily and has a small food menu as well.

ACCOMMODATIONS AND CAMPING

The **Headwaters Lodge & Cabins at Flagg Ranch** (307/543-2861 or 307/543-3100, www.gtlc.com, June-Sept.) is touted as the oldest continuously operating resort in upper Jackson Hole. It is ideally situated to take advantage of both Yellowstone and Grand Teton National Parks. The accommodations options include deluxe or premium log cabins ($301-320); camper cabins (from $77), which are a four-walled structure with a permanent roof and cots; and RV sites (from $74). Log cabins have two queen or one king bed, coffeemakers, private baths, and patios furnished with rocking chairs. The camper cabins (built in 2012), RV sites, and campsites all include access to 24-hour hot shower and laundry facilities. Note there is no cell service or Wi-Fi in the area.

Colter Bay Village (307/543-3100, www.gtlc.com, late May-early Oct.) on the northern shore of Jackson Lake offers some of the park's most affordable lodging. The village has rustic cabins ($179-265), an RV site, and a tent village. The original homestead cabins, purchased by the Rockefellers and moved to the area, have been refurbished but still offer a glimpse into the past. Each cabin displays a description of its own history. While most of the one-room cabins sleep 2, one can sleep up to 6 people, and the two-room cabin can sleep up to 10 with rollaways. Prices vary depending on the number of occupants in the room and the arrangement of double, twin, and rollaway beds. Pull-through RV sites are available for $72. The tent cabins ($74) consist of two log walls, two canvas walls and a canvas roof, a single lightbulb, and a wood-burning potbellied stove. Each log wall has two pull-down bunks with thin mattresses; additional cots can be rented. Guests are encouraged to bring their own bedding, but a limited number of sleeping bags can be rented from the cabin office. Each tent cabin has a picnic and grilling area, and showers are located in the launderette with a fee for use. The **Colter Bay Campground** (800/628-9988, late May-late Sept., $31/vehicle, $12 pp for hikers or bicyclists) has 330 sites. All tent cabins, campsites, and RV sites are discounted up to 50 percent with the presentation of a Golden Access Pass. Electric RV sites are $53/night.

Located 30 miles (48 km) north of Moose between Flagg Ranch and Colter Bay Village, the **Lizard Creek Campground** (307/543-2831, mid-June-early Sept., $30) has 60 individual sites with no hookups and rarely fills.

Jackson Lake Lodge and Signal Mountain

Its breathtaking setting, coupled with excellent amenities and access to hiking and sightseeing in the park's northeastern corner, make Jackson Lake Lodge a vacation destination all its own. Though the lodge is not adjacent to Jackson Lake in the way that the Colter Bay Village is, the views over the lake to the Tetons are magnificent. Nearby, the rustic Signal Mountain Lodge is situated immediately on the water, offering unlimited opportunities for enjoying Jackson Lake and its proximity to hiking and adventuring.

SIGHTS

TOP EXPERIENCE

★ Oxbow Bend

Just southeast of Jackson Lake Lodge on the main road is Oxbow Bend, a picturesque river area created when the Snake River carved a more southerly route. One of the most photographed areas in the park, the slow-moving water perfectly reflects towering Mount Moran. The serenity of the area attracts an abundance of wildlife, including moose, beaver, and otters along with a vast number of birds. White pelicans can occasionally be spotted passing through, as can sandhill cranes, majestic trumpeter swans, nesting great blue herons, and bald eagles. Avid boaters like to paddle the area in their canoes and kayaks. Don't forget your binoculars and your camera.

★ Signal Mountain

One mile (1.6 km) south of Signal Mountain Lodge is the turnoff to Signal Mountain Road and one of the greatest viewpoints in Grand Teton National Park. The winding 5-mile (8-km) road is completely **unsuitable for RVs**

and trailers. Along the way, there are ample spots for wildlife-viewing—look for moose in the pond on the right as you start up the road, and the pond lilies blooming in June. Two small parking lots are near the summit. The first offers the best view of the Tetons: Sunsets are sensational. From the second, a short walk takes you down to an overlook with a view of Oxbow Bend. Visitors in August might even have a chance to pick some succulent huckleberries as they ripen in the late-summer sun.

The story of Signal Mountain's name is a rather tragic one. Around the turn of the 20th century, a local rancher named Roy Hamilton got lost when he was out hunting. Rescuers agreed to light a fire on the mountain as soon as anyone found Hamilton. After nine days, a fire was lit atop the mountain, signaling the end of rescue efforts. Tragically, Hamilton's body was found in the Snake River, and some speculated his business partner had suggested he cross the river in a particularly dangerous spot.

SPORTS AND RECREATION
Fishing

Anglers will be pleased with the varied offerings in this stretch of the park. From the lunkers in Jackson Lake, which can be fished on shore or by boat, to the healthy but discerning trout in the Snake River, guided trips can be arranged through **Grand Teton Lodge Company** (307/543-2811 and ask for the marina, www.gtlc.com), from $110 per hour for 1-2 adults with a two-hour minimum and $22/ hour per additional person; day trips start at $575 per day for 1-2 anglers. From **Signal Mountain Lodge** (307/543-2831, www. signalmountainlodge.com), anglers can go out with experienced guides (late May-mid-Sept.)

in pursuit of Jackson Lake's cutthroat, brown, and lake trout for $115 per hour for 1-2 people with a two-hour minimum and $35/hour per additional person; half-day trips are $312 for 1-2 people and $109 per additional person. Half-day and multiple-day fishing trips on Jackson Lake can also be arranged through **Grand Teton Fly Fishing** (307/690-0910 or 307/690-4347, www.grandtetonflyfishing. com, all-day floats from $595, half-day floats from $525 for two people). A Wyoming fishing license is required for all fishing in the park and can be purchased at **Snake River Angler at Dornan's** (12170 Dornan Rd., 307/733-3699, www.snakeriverangler.com), **Signal Mountain Marina** (307/543-2831, www. signalmountainlodge.com), and **Colter Bay Marina** (307/543-3100, www.gtlc.com). Pick up a fishing brochure from any of the visitors centers to learn about all park regulations.

Boating

With so much beautiful water in the park, boating is a fantastic way to explore. Rafting on the **Snake River,** canoeing or kayaking on any number of lakes, or cruising across **Jackson Lake**—there are options for adrenaline junkies and die-hard landlubbers alike.

Scenic 10-mile (16.1-km) floats down the Snake can be arranged through **Signal Mountain Lodge** (307/543-2831, www. signalmountainlodge.com, $77 adults, $50 children 6-11), **Grand Teton Lodge Company** (307/543-3100 or 307/543-2811, www.gtlc.com), or **Solitude Float Trips** (307/733-2871, www.grand-teton-scenic-floats.com, $80 adults, $60 children 5-15, $900 for a private boat for up to 12 guests). Most floats on the Snake River inside the park last about two hours. Both GTLC and Solitude offer a wonderful sunrise float, perfect for spotting wildlife. GTLC also offers four-hour luncheon floats Mon.-Sat. May-Labor Day ($78 adults, $55 children 6-11) and dinner floats (4:30pm Tues.-Thurs. and Sat.

May-early Sept., $95 adults, $65 children 6-11) with fun riverside cookouts.

Human-powered boats like kayaks and canoes are permitted on Emma Matilda Lake and Two Ocean Lake, east of Jackson Lake Lodge. Jackson Lake is open to motorboats, human-powered boats, sailboats, waterskiing, and windsurfers. Permits are required for motorized boats ($40) and nonmotorized crafts ($10), including SUPs, and can be purchased at the visitors centers in Moose, Jenny Lake (cash only), or Colter Bay. A variety of boats can be rented through **Signal Mountain Lodge** (307/543-2831, www.signalmountainlodge. com), including deck cruisers ($139/hour, $699/day for up to 10 people), pontoon boats ($105/hour, $509/day for up to 10 people), runabouts ($69/hour, $339/day for up to 5 people), fishing boats ($42/hour, $185/day for up to 5 people), canoes ($25/hour, $99/day for up to 3 people), and sea kayaks ($20/hour, $79/day single, or $25/hour, $99/day for 2 people). The **Grand Teton Lodge Company** (307/543-3100 or 307/543-2811, www.gtlc.com) can also arrange various boat rentals throughout the park.

Hiking and Biking

Sandwiched between Jackson, Emma Matilda, and Two Ocean Lakes, the area around Jackson Lake Lodge offers some wonderful hiking. The **Christian Pond Loop** is a relatively flat and easy 4.3-mile (6.9-km) round-trip hike through prime waterfowl habitat. The trailhead is east of the parking lot adjacent to the Jackson Lake Lodge corrals. Nearby, **Two Ocean Lake** offers a moderate 6.4-mile (10.3-km) round-trip hike around the lake though forest and meadow. **Emma Matilda Lake** offers an even longer 9.1-mile (14.7-km) hike, with fabulous Teton views from the north shore ridge.

A nice area for visitors who travel with their bicycles is in the vicinity of **Two Ocean Road,** southeast of Jackson Lake Lodge and northeast of Signal Mountain Lodge. The road itself is just 3 miles (4.8 km) long, but the scenery is sublime for a short, sweet ride.

Finding a Guide

Setting off into the wilds of Grand Teton National Park can be slightly intimidating, making guided tours a good option. The Park Service maintains a list of licensed, permitted, and park-approved guides.

For any type of technical **rock climbing,** a guide is as necessary as a helmet and rope. **Exum Mountain Guides** (307/733-2297, www.exumguides.com) has been offering instruction and guided mountain climbing since 1931, making it the oldest guide service in North America and certainly one of the most prestigious. Exum offers numerous programs, from easy day climbing for families with kids to guided expeditions up the 13,770-foot (4,197-m) Grand Teton. Detailed information, including climbing routes and trail conditions, can be found at www.tetonclimbing.blogspot.com.

The Hole Hiking Experience (307/690-4453, www.holehike.com) offers a range of **guided hikes** and **snowshoe or ski tours** in and around the park for all interests and ability levels, from sunrise or sunset discovery tours to all-day wildlife-watching hikes. Kids will love the family day hikes with fun survival-like activities that include eating "lemon drop" ants and using butterfly nets. Winter cross-country ski and snowshoe tours are guided by naturalists and show off the best winter has to offer.

There are several options for guided **horseback riding** trips, May-September, from a number of lodges in the park, including Colter Bay Village, Flagg Ranch, and Jackson Lake Lodge. The **Grand Teton Lodge Company** (307/543-3100 or 307/543-2811, www.gtlc.com) can arrange everything from a one-hour ($45-90 1-3 hours) horseback ride to breakfast wagon rides ($45) and dinner rides ($79-84 adults, $59-64 children 8-13) to pony rides ($5). All riders in the park must be at least eight years old and under 225 pounds (102 kg).

With so many varied bodies of water, there are a number of **fishing** outfitters that can guide any type of trip you can dream up. A good place to start is the **Grand Teton Lodge Company** (307/543-3100 or 307/543-2811, www.gtlc.com), which can arrange trips from any of the accommodations inside the park. Fishing trips on the Snake River or Jackson Lake can also be arranged through the lakefront **Signal Mountain Lodge** (307/543-2831, www.signalmountainlodge.com) or **Grand Teton Fly Fishing** (307/690-0910, www.grandtetonflyfishing.com).

Rafting is popular in Grand Teton National Park, and there are 11 licensed outfitters to guide visitors down the Snake River. As with all activities, **Grand Teton Lodge Company** (307/543-3100 or 307/543-2811, www.gtlc.com) can make arrangements for the park's most popular 10-mile (16.1-km) scenic float. Other outfitters include **Barker-Ewing** (307/733-1800 or 800/448-4202, www.barker-ewing.com) and **Solitude Float Trips** (307/733-2871, www.grand-teton-scenic-floats.com).

Throughout the year, Park Service rangers offer excellent **naturalist-guided tours.** Late December-March, depending on conditions, daily guided **snowshoe hikes** depart from the **Craig Thomas Discovery and Visitor Center** (307/739-3399, reservations required, $5 donation suggested). During the summer months, the range of offerings is vast—from 30-minute map chats and campfire programs to three-hour hikes, evening astronomy programs, and tipi demos. For more information on ranger programs, pick up the park newspaper at any of the entrance stations, call 307/739-3300, or check out the visitors centers in Moose, Jenny Lake, Colter Bay, and the Laurance S. Rockefeller Preserve.

River Road is 15 miles (24 km) of gravel running along the west side of the Snake River between Signal Mountain and Cottonwood Creek. Do remember that this is bear country and every precaution—including bear spray—should be taken.

Horseback Riding

The **Grand Teton Lodge Company** (307/543-3100 or 307/543-2811, www.gtlc.com) can arrange one-hour ($45) or two-hour ($75) horseback tours that depart from Jackson Lake Lodge and can include trips to Emma Matilda Lake and an overlook of Oxbow Bend. All riders must be at least eight years old and under 225 pounds (102 kg).

FOOD

There are a lot of options for dining at the **Jackson Lake Lodge** (307/543-3100, www. gtlc.com). The **Mural Room** (307/543-3463, 7am-9:30am, 11am-2:30pm, and 5:30pm-9pm daily mid-May-early Oct., $22-46) has unmatched ambience with its windowed wall looking out onto the lake, Mount Moran, and the Teton Range along with the colorful murals by famed artist Carl Routers depicting life out West. The food is upscale and innovative—also known as Rocky Mountain cuisine—and when coupled with the view, it makes this one of the most pleasurable dining experiences in the park. Breakfast includes classic eggs Benedict and huckleberry French toast. Lunch is a mix of sandwiches and salads as well as regional cuisine including Idaho rainbow trout and beef Bourguignon. Dinner is a hearty affair with delectable main entrée items including grilled elk loin, Idaho ruby red trout, and wild mushroom saffron risotto. A delightful end to the meal is the flourless dark chocolate cake or the huckleberry pound cake.

Kids menus are available. Dinner reservations are recommended.

Also in the lodge is the much more casual and less pricey **Pioneer Grill** (6am-10pm daily mid-May-early Oct., $10-26), a true-to-style 1950s diner; supposedly it has the largest soda fountain counter still in use. A fun place for a meal, the counter snakes 200 feet (61 m) through the room and encourages guests to interact with other diners. The Pioneer Grill offers American cuisine with a slight gourmet twist (try the poutine) and has a takeout service if you decide you'd rather watch the sunset while munching on your burger. Its famous desserts keep customers returning, and you should not leave without ordering a huckleberry shake.

The **Blue Heron Lounge** (307/543-2811, 11am-midnight daily mid-May-early Oct., food served until sunset, $11-26) is another casual dining experience in Jackson Lake Lodge. It has a bar menu with a good selection of appetizers and creative sandwiches and even offers sustainable draft beer from local breweries. Enjoy your meal on the deck with a huckleberry mojito and a beautiful view of the mountains.

If you are at the pool or with your kids at the playground, you may want to fill up on the terrific Mexican food at the outdoor **Poolside Cantina** (food service 11am-4pm, beverage

Floating on the Snake River offers quite a backdrop.

service 11am-8pm daily early June-late Aug. depending on weather, $6-12), which also serves salads, plus burgers and hot dogs for the kids.

There are three options for dining at the **Signal Mountain Lodge** (307/543-2831, www.signalmountainlodge.com) as well. **The Trapper Grill** (7am-10pm daily early May-early Oct., $11-18) has a large menu for all three meals of the day. It mostly sticks to American fare with some Tex-Mex thrown in. The nachos are a favorite. The breakfast menu is vast, with an egg menu, an omelet menu, and griddle options. The lunch and dinner menu is filled with specialty sandwiches, salads, and burgers, but the restaurant prides itself on its homemade desserts. You may want to share an entrée so that you'll have room for the Wyoming Whiskey chocolate pecan pie. **The Peaks Restaurant** (5:30pm-10pm daily early May-early Oct., $18-41) serves delicious dinners and is committed to offering an environmentally sustainable menu. Dine on Snake River Farms Kurabota pork shank, bison meatball, or grilled Colorado white bass. **Leek's Pizzeria** (11am-10pm daily late May-early Sept., $10-25) is at the marina on Jackson Lake. It serves specialty pizzas and calzones, sandwiches, salads, and microbrews in a fantastic outdoor setting. For a drink, snack, and a glimpse of television, you may want to stop at **Deadman's Bar** (noon-midnight daily), which serves the largest plate of fully loaded nachos you've ever seen. They pair perfectly with a blackberry margarita and a Wyoming sunset.

ACCOMMODATIONS

The **Jackson Lake Lodge** (307/543-3100, www.gtlc.com, mid-May-early Oct., $330-449 cottages, $330-439 lodge rooms) is one of the largest resorts in the park and commands an unparalleled view of Jackson Lake and the Teton Range from the lobby's panoramic 60-foot-high (18.3-m) windows. There are 385 guest rooms in the main lodge and surrounding cottages, and the grounds also house a playground and swimming pool. The cottages are in clusters and come in a range of styles. The classic cottage guest room has one king bed and sleeps a maximum of three. The cottage guest room with a view of the Tetons can sleep up to five people and has a minifridge and a patio or balcony. The mountain-view suite has a spectacular view of Willow Flats, where moose often meander, and the majestic range; it comes with a king bed and a comfortable sitting area. The lodge guest rooms are on the third floor and also come in three price ranges. Unlike the cottages, these guest rooms do not accommodate rollaways.

The **Signal Mountain Lodge** (307/543-2831, www.signalmountainlodge.com, early May-mid-Oct.) is an independently owned resort on the banks of Jackson Lake with a gorgeous view of the Tetons. It has a variety of options for lodging, ranging from rustic log cabins (1-room cabin $217-242, 2-room $247-277) and motel-style rooms ($261-367) to one- or two-room bungalows ($261-407) on the beach. The two-room lakefront retreats ($367-407) are ideal for families; they overlook the lake with fantastic views of the mountains and have kitchenettes. Many of the rooms in the lodge were remodeled in 2015, and all of them are carpeted and comfortably furnished. There is one three-bedroom cabin aptly named Home Away from Home ($492); if you are lucky enough to get it, you'll have a bedroom, dining area, living room with a gas fireplace, kitchen, and small laundry room all to yourself; the only drawback is that there is no view.

CAMPING

The **Signal Mountain Campground** (800/672-6012, early mid-May-mid-Oct., $32/vehicle standard site, $54 electric site) is nestled among spruce and fir trees with views of the mountains, lakes, and hillside. It is also wildly popular and often fills up between 8am-10am on a first-come, first-served basis. There are 86 smallish sites, each with a picnic table and fire ring, and RVs up to 30 feet (9.1 m) in length are permitted. Restrooms with cold running water are available but no showers.

Jenny Lake and Vicinity

Carved some 12,000 years ago by the same glaciers that dug out Cascade Canyon, Jenny Lake is perhaps the most picturesque and popular spot in the park. The hiking—to places like Inspiration Point and the even more beautiful Leigh Lake—is sublime, and the water activities—scenic cruising, canoeing, kayaking, swimming, and fishing—are plentiful. The park's fanciest and most expensive lodging and dining can be found at the historic Jenny Lake Lodge.

In much the same way that Old Faithful embodies the Yellowstone experience for many visitors, so too does Jenny Lake conjure up all that is wonderful about Grand Teton. A scenic drive from North Jenny Lake to South Jenny Lake skirts the water and affords breathtaking views of the Grand Teton, Teewinot, and Mount Owen. Those who are more interested in solitude would be well advised to get off the main drag here, away from the crowds and into the wilderness.

SIGHTS
★ Jenny Lake

In 1872 an English-born mountain man, known widely as "Beaver Dick" Leigh for his enormous front teeth and his penchant for the animal, guided Ferdinand Hayden around the Tetons. Hayden named the alpine lake for Dick's wife, Jenny, a member of the Shoshone tribe. In the fall of 1876, pregnant Jenny took care of an ailing Native American woman, not knowing the woman had smallpox. Jenny and all four of her children became ill. Her baby was born just before Christmas and, along with Jenny and the other four children, died within a week. Beaver Dick buried his family in Jackson Hole.

Despite its tragic namesake, Jenny Lake is indeed one of the most beautiful and visited spots in the park. From cruising across the lake to hiking along its shores, there are an endless number of ways to enjoy this idyllic spot.

Set between two parking areas, and with easy walking access to the lake, trails and campground, the Jenny Lake Visitor Center is 8 miles (12.9 km) north of Moose at South Jenny Lake.

★ Hidden Falls and Inspiration Point

One of the area's most popular hikes is to the spectacular **Hidden Falls.** From Jenny Lake's south shore, the hike follows a moderate 2.5-mile (4-km) trail (one way) with 550 feet (168 m) of elevation gain to the cascade. Visitors who want to put fewer miles on their feet can take the **Jenny Lake Shuttle** (307/734-9227, www.jennylakeboating.com, 10am-4pm mid-May-early June, 7am-7pm early June-early Sept., round-trip $15 adults 12-61, $12 seniors, $8 children 2-11 years, one-way $9 adults, $6 children), which runs every 10-15 minutes throughout the day, to shorten the hike to 1 mile (1.6 km) with 150 feet (45.7 m) of elevation gain. The hike to **Inspiration Point,** a breathtaking overlook 5.8 miles (9.3 km) round-trip with 700 feet (213.4 m) of elevation gain from the trailhead, or 2.2 miles (3.5 km) round-trip with 420 feet (128 m) of elevation gain from the boat shuttle, earns its name. In summer 2018, a horizontal crack in a rock buttress was measured at 100 feet (30.5 m) long. The route remains accessible (after a brief closure); the park service continues to monitor the crack. Hikers can also get to Cascade Canyon via the horse trail along Jenny Lake.

Leigh Lake

Named for mountain man "Beaver Dick" Leigh, Leigh Lake is much quieter and perhaps even more beautiful than the more southerly Jenny Lake. The lake offers unrivaled views of Mount Moran, Mount Woodring, and

Rockchuck Peak, and it is dotted with sandy beaches ideal for picnics. The 5.4-mile (8.7-km) round-trip (out-and-back) trail is flat and weaves in and out of the forest with a constant water view. The Leigh Lake Trailhead is at the northwest corner of the String Lake Picnic Area. The trail can be hiked as early as May or June, depending on snowmelt, and is typically passable well into September. Although popular, Leigh Lake does not attract the crowds that Jenny Lake does.

SPORTS AND RECREATION
Fishing

Fishing is permitted in Jenny, String, Leigh, Bradley, and Taggart Lakes. A Wyoming fishing license is required and can be purchased at **Snake River Angler at Dornan's** (12170 Dornan Rd., 307/733-3699, www.snakeriverangler.com), **Signal Mountain Marina** (307/543-2831, www.signalmountainlodge.com), and **Colter Bay Marina** (307/543-3100, www.gtlc.com). Pick up a fishing brochure from any of the visitors centers to learn about all park regulations.

Boating

Scenic one-hour **cruises** (noon and 2pm daily mid-May-early June and early Sept.-late Sept.; 11am, 2pm, and 5pm daily early June-early Sept., $19 adults, $17 seniors 62 and over, $11 children 2-11), **shuttles** to Cascade Canyon hiking trails (round-trip $15 adults, $8 children, depart every 10-15 minutes), and canoe or kayak **rentals** ($20/hour, $75/day) can be arranged through **Jenny Lake Boating** (307/734-9227, www.jennylakeboating.com).

Hiking and Biking

Jenny Lake is at the heart of the park's largest concentration of popular hiking trails. In addition to the **Hidden Falls, Inspiration Point,** and **Leigh Lake** trailheads, there are a number of excellent trails in the region. The mostly level **Jenny Lake Loop Trail** circumnavigates the lake with a 6.6-mile (10.6-km) round-trip hike. The **Lupine Meadows Trailhead** offers hikers a number of ways to get up into the Teton Range.

The multiuse pathway from South Jenny Lake to Taggart Lake Trailhead offers bikers (and all nonmotorized travelers) 16 miles (26 km) round-trip of smooth, level pavement. Bike racks are available at Taggart Lake Trailhead and in Moose. Bicycles can be rented from **Dornan's** (12170 Dornan Rd. in Moose, 307/733-2415, www.dornans.

the view from Inspiration Point

com, 9am-6am daily). In addition to a range of adult bikes ($16-25/hour, $38-55/half-day, $44-65/day or 24 hours), Dornan's rents kids' bikes, Trail-a-Bikes, bike racks, and Burley carriers for toddlers.

FOOD

The **Jenny Lake Lodge Dining Room** (307/543-3352, www.gtlc.com, 7:30am-10am, 11:30am-1:30pm, and 6pm-9pm daily June-early Oct.) offers a fine-dining experience in an original log cabin. Reservations are required for all three meals and should be booked well in advance. Men are required to wear dinner jackets. The food is incredibly creative and incorporates local flavors. Crab cake Benedict and a prime rib cowboy skillet appear on the breakfast menu ($12-18), and lunch ($15-20) consists mostly of upscale sandwiches and salads. The main event at the restaurant is the prix fixe five-course dinner ($94, not including gratuity or alcohol). There are options for each course that rotate every night. Depending on the day, you may be dining on Lockhart beef tartare, Heluka pork tenderloin, Alaskan Pacific halibut, or duck leg confit—no matter what's on the menu, it is sure to be a memorable meal (and an expensive one!).

ACCOMMODATIONS

A former dude ranch for sophisticated Easterners, **Jenny Lake Lodge** (307/543-3100, www.gtlc.com, mid-May-early Oct., cabins $530-1,000/night for 2 people) is the finest lodging in the park and the only four-diamond eco-resort. The cabins have authentic log walls, renovated baths, and touches such as handmade bed quilts that add to the charm of each room. Situated among the three lakes, the lodge is comfortably secluded but offers beautiful vistas in all directions. The rooms are pricey, but guests get a lot for their dime. A gourmet breakfast, five-course dinner, horseback riding,

and access to bicycles are all included in the rates. Each week, different activities are available and include options such as live raptor displays on the front patio, stargazing, interpretive programs, live musicians, and garden games like bocce ball and croquet. If you are looking for a romantic getaway, consider booking one of the suites, which come with wood-burning stoves.

A much more affordable, and truly rustic, option is the **Grand Teton Climbers Ranch** (307/733-7271, www.americanalpineclub.org, June-Sept. 10, $17.28 AAC members, $27 nonmembers), owned by the American Alpine Club and located just 3 miles (4.8 km) south of Jenny Lake. The ranch has small log cabins that serve as dormitories for 4-8 people. Guests must bring their own sleeping bags and pads, towels, cooking equipment, and food. Cooking and dishwashing facilities, toilets, and showers with hot water are available. No camping is allowed. There is also a general store on the grounds where you can stock up on groceries as well as hiking and camping supplies. The ranch often offers a work week in early June which allows volunteers to remain at the ranch for free.

CAMPING

The **Jenny Lake Campground** (307/543-3100 or 307/543-2811, early May-Sept., $29/vehicle, $12 hikers and bicyclists) is the smallest in the park and is available on a first-come, first-served basis only; it is usually full by 8am. It has 49 sites that can each accommodate one vehicle, two tents, and up to six campers. Ten additional sites are set aside for hikers or bicyclists. There are no large group sites, nor are trailers, campers, or generators allowed in the area. Because of its size and popularity, the maximum stay is seven days (at the other campgrounds it is 14 days). Flush toilets are available but no shower facilities. Payment is by cash or check only; credit cards are not accepted.

Moran to Moose

The stretch of road between Moran Junction and the southernmost entrance to the park at Moose is scenic and full of interesting sights, both natural and artificial. From the historic crossing at **Menors Ferry** to the architecturally inspired **Craig Thomas Discovery and Visitor Center** and the wildlife-rich **Antelope Flats,** this part of the park is heavily traveled for a good reason: There is so much to see.

SIGHTS

Cunningham Cabin

A relic of hardscrabble ranching days before the turn of the 20th century—and the site of the murder of two alleged horse thieves— **Cunningham Cabin** is 6 miles (9.7 km) south of Moran Junction. The cabin reflects the common building materials and style of 1890, the year it was built. Known as a "dogtrot," it consists of two small structures connected by a breezeway and topped with a dirt roof.

Pierce Cunningham built a modest home for his family on Flat Creek in 1888. A neighbor introduced Cunningham to two strangers, George Spenser and Mike Burnett, asking if they could buy hay for their horses. Cunningham sold them 15 tons of hay and arranged for them to winter in his cabin near Spread Creek. The rumor among the locals was that the men were in fact horse thieves.

In April 1893, Spenser and Burnett were the target of a posse of vigilantes from Montana. Sixteen men on horseback rode up to the little cabin on Spread Creek under cover of darkness and waited in silence for dawn. Spenser and Burnett's dog barked in the early morning hours, perhaps warning the men of the ambush that awaited them. Spenser dressed, armed himself, and walked out the front door. When the posse called for him to hold his hands up, Spenser fired his revolver in the direction of the speaker and was immediately shot. He propped himself up on one elbow and continued to fire until he collapsed. Burnett came out next, armed with a revolver and a rifle. The men shot at him, but Burnett managed to shoot the hat off one of the posse members and "crease his scalp" with the bullet. Burnett was shot and killed moments later. The two men were buried in unmarked graves a few hundred yards southeast of the cabin on the south side of a draw. Some of their bones were eventually excavated by badgers.

Mormon Row and Antelope Flats

Interesting both for its wildlife and human history, the area around **Mormon Row** is instantly recognizable from some of the region's most popular postcards, featuring a weathered barn leaning into the jagged mountains behind it. Listed on the National Register of Historic Places, Mormon Row is a collection of six fairly dilapidated homesteads that can be explored on a **self-guided tour** (brochures are available near the pink house). The area was settled around the turn of the 20th century by a handful of Mormon families who built homes, a church, a school, and a swimming hole. The settlement was abandoned and left to the elements when the Rockefellers bought up much of the land and transferred it to the National Park Service. In the 1990s the historical and cultural value of the site was recognized; the area was added to the National Register of Historic Places in 1997, and steps were taken to preserve the structures.

The **Antelope Flats** area—excellent for walking or biking on a flat, unpaved road—offers prime habitat for pronghorn, bison, moose, coyotes, ground squirrels, northern harriers, kestrels, and sage grouse. In the

1: old barn at Mormon Row **2:** view from Antelope Flats winter, the first mile (1.6 km) of Antelope Flats Road is plowed to a small parking area, giving visitors easy snowshoe or cross-country ski access to Moulton Ranch, one of the homesteads on Mormon Row. On the NPS website, visitors can access **audio tours** (www.nps.gov/grte/learn/photosmultimedia/audio-descriptions.htm) of Mormon Row and other historical spots and places of interest.

★ Craig Thomas Discovery and Visitor Center

Twelve miles (19.3 km) north of Jackson in Moose, the **Craig Thomas Discovery and Visitor Center** (307/739-3399, 10am-4pm daily early Mar.-Apr., 8am-5pm daily May-early June and mid-Sept.-Oct., 8am-7pm daily early June-mid-Sept.) is, among other things, an architectural masterpiece, mimicking the nearby natural masterpiece of the Teton Range. The $21.6 million structure has more than 22,000 square feet (2,044 sq m) and is being used as a model for other national parks—in that more than half the funds used to build the center were donated by private individuals. The state-of-the-art facility, including video rivers that flow beneath your feet, places emphasis on the connection between humans and the natural world. Fantastic interpretive displays include a large relief model of the park that uses technology to show glacier movement and animal migration; there is also a photographic tribute to mountaineering in the region. Many of the excellent ranger-led hikes and tours depart from the Craig Thomas Discovery and Visitor Center.

Menors Ferry Historic District

In 1894, William D. Menor came to Jackson Hole and built a homestead along the Snake River. He built a ferryboat on cables to carry settlers and hopeful miners across the river, which was otherwise impassable during spring runoff. Entire wagon teams crossed on the ferry, paying $0.50 per trip, while a horse and rider paid $0.25. In 1918, Menor sold the ferry operation to Maud Noble, who doubled the fares ($1 for automobiles with local plates,

$2 for out-of-staters) in the hope of attracting more tourists to the region. When a bridge was built in 1927, the ferry became obsolete, and in 1929 Noble sold her land to the Snake River Land Company, the same year the park was created. She had already donated a portion of her land for the construction of the Chapel of the Transfiguration.

Today, a replica of the ferryboat and cables has been built on-site, and visitors can meander down the 0.5-mile (0.8-km) self-guided **Menors Ferry Trail** past Menor's cabin, which doubled as a country store. On the NPS website, there are **audio tours** (www.nps.gov/grte/learn/photosmultimedia/audio-descriptions.htm) of Menors Ferry, Mormon Row, and the Murie Ranch, along with other historical spots and places of interest.

Chapel of the Transfiguration

Built in 1925 to serve the ranchers and dudes in the Teton Valley, the **Chapel of the Transfiguration** (307/733-2603, services 8am and 10am Sun. Memorial Day-Sept.) is a humble log cabin structure with the most spectacular mountain view framed in the window behind the altar. An Episcopal church, operated by St. John's in Jackson, it was built on land donated by Maud Noble and is a favorite spot for summer weddings. A candle-lit Christmas night service and sunrise Easter service are particularly wonderful ways to experience this historic place of worship.

★ Laurance S. Rockefeller Preserve

Four miles (6.4 km) south of Moose on the Moose-Wilson Road, the former JY Ranch and longtime summer home of the Rockefeller family, known as the **Laurance S. Rockefeller Preserve** (307/739-3654, 9am-5pm daily late May-late Sept., center closed late Sept.-late May, trails open year-round) offers 8 miles (12.9 km) of trails through forest, wetlands, and meadows on reclaimed property along Phelps Lake and Lake Creek. The preserve is 1,106 acres (447.6 hectares) and was donated to the Park

Service in 2007 by the Rockefeller family with the mission of giving people access to the natural world that Laurance Rockefeller found so inspiring and sustaining.

The Laurance S. Rockefeller Preserve Center is the first platinum-level LEED-certified building constructed in a national park and was constructed to give visitors a sensory experience of the natural elements found on the preserve. A poem by beloved writer Terry Tempest Williams features prominently, and visitors can learn about the preserve and Rockefeller's beliefs about land stewardship in a comfortable and environmentally sustainable building. Several ranger programs, including sunrise hikes and children's programs, are available from the center daily throughout summer. The preserve is accessible by car from May to October.

Murie Ranch

The onetime STS Ranch and former residence of wilderness champions Olaus and Mardy Murie, the **Murie Ranch** (1 Murie Ranch Rd., Moose, 307/732-7752, www.tetonscience.org/murie-center/home, 9am-5pm Mon.-Fri. mid-Mar.-mid-Oct.) is dedicated to connecting people and wilderness. It is where the Wilderness Act was authored in the 1950s and early 1960s. The ranch itself is a National Historic Landmark and the site of ongoing conservation seminars and educational workshops. On-site accommodations are available to participants, and the entire facility can be rented for conservation education programs. An excellent library and bookstore is on-site, and rangers host naturalist programs throughout the summer. Free tours of the Murie home are given from 2:30pm-3:30pm daily in summer.

SPORTS AND RECREATION

Like most of Grand Teton National Park, there is an abundance of excellent hiking terrain to be discovered between Moran and Moose, and many easy strolls can combine with historic sites like the Cunningham Cabin, Menors Ferry, and Mormon Row.

For more substantial hikes, try the **Taggart Lake Trailhead,** 3 miles (4.8 km) northwest of Moose. The trail is 3.2 miles (5.2 km) round-trip with 410 feet (125 m) of elevation gain. If that isn't enough, continue on to **Bradley Lake** (4 mi/6.4 km round-trip with a 650-ft/198-m elevation gain) or Beaver Creek. Three miles (4.8 km) south of Moose is the **Death Canyon Trailhead,** not nearly as

The Chapel of the Transfiguration was built in 1925.

ominous as the name would imply. The road is not suitable for trailers or RVs and very rough for vehicles in general. However, the hike to **Phelps Lake** is perfect for families, only 1.8 miles (2.9 km) round-trip with 420 feet (128 m) of elevation gain. Black bears, moose, and marmots frequent the area, so have your bear spray at the ready.

There are plenty of biking opportunities on the paved and unpaved roads in the region, including **Antelope Flats Road** all the way to Kelly, the **Shadow Mountain Road,** and the **Moose-Wilson Road** linking Moose and the Laurance S. Rockefeller Preserve. The **multiuse pathway** from Moose or the Taggart Lake Trailhead to South Jenny Lake is popular for good reason.

FOOD

You'll find most of your food options in this area at Dornan's ranch. ★ **Dornan's Moose Chuck Wagon** (307/733-2415, ext. 203, 7am-11am, noon-3pm, and 5pm-9pm daily, mid-June-Labor Day, weather dependent) serves up hearty "cowboy cuisine" during the summer. Dornan's uses beef from its own butcher shop and Dutch ovens heated over wood fires. Breakfast ($7-10) offers great sourdough pancakes, and dinner ($25-29 adults, $13-15 children 5-11) is an all-you-can-eat affair with prices based on your choice of barbecued beef or chicken, pork ribs, or trout. Lunch ($8-16) is served as well. The restaurant is used for private events on weekend evenings. And Monday night is the hootenanny starting at 6pm, an evening of acoustic delight. There's often live music Tues.-Sat. between 5:30pm and 8:30pm. It's a good idea to call ahead for evening reservations and check that it's not privately booked for the evening.

Dornan's Pizza and Pasta Company (307/733-2415, ext. 204, 11:30am-9pm daily, $9-17) offers a large variety of salads, hot sandwiches, gourmet pizzas, rich pasta dishes, and calzones. If you are looking to pick up something to eat on your hike, stop at **Dornan's Moose Trading Post & Deli** (307/733-2415, ext. 201, 8am-8pm daily) for

everything from freeze-dried meals and cold drinks to gourmet groceries and any camping equipment you might need. The deli is open May-September; it's a good option for a quick meal or a sweet treat. If you have the time, don't miss a visit to **Dornan's Wine Shoppe** (307/733-2415, ext. 202, 10am-9pm daily in summer, reduced hours off-season). It is a find for wine connoisseurs and novices alike, with an award-winning selection of around 1,600 varieties of wines and 150 types of cheese. *Food & Wine* magazine named it one of the 50 most amazing wine experiences in the country, and *Wine Spectator* has bestowed its Wine Award on the shop for 28 consecutive years and counting.

ACCOMMODATIONS

★ **The Triangle X Ranch** (2 Triangle X Ranch Rd., 307/733-2183, www.trianglex. com, late May-mid-Oct., and Dec. 26-mid-Mar., $1,958-2,713 pp/week summer when paid with credit card, discounts for paying in cash, $150 pp/night winter) has been in operation since 1926. Twenty-six miles (42 km) north of Jackson and 32 miles (52 km) south of Yellowstone, it is the only authorized guest ranch concessionaire in the entire National Park System and sits right inside Grand Teton National Park. Not surprisingly, the setting is gorgeous, and you can see the entire mountain range from this secluded getaway.

The lodge, which is the center of activity and meals, is the original main house used by two generations of the Turner family. The 20 log cabins are also originals that once housed families in different parts of Jackson Hole. The cabins come with 1-3 bedrooms; all have modern amenities and are decorated with cozy Western charm.

The ranch is also the only concession in the park that is open during winter. During the peak season (early-June-late Aug.), the minimum stay is one week (Sun.-Sun.). During the spring and fall seasons, the ranch requires a minimum four-night stay but offers reduced rates, and during the winter season, visitors can book per night. All meals, served family-style in the main lodge, are included in the price, as are the endless horseback rides, cookouts, square dancing, and special programs for children. Winter activities include cross-country skiing, snowshoeing, and snowmobiling. Regardless of the season, there are always great opportunities for wildlife-viewing.

Dornan's Spur Ranch Cabins (12170 Dornan Rd., Moose, 307/733-2522, www.dornans.com, year-round) sits idyllically on the Snake River in the middle of a wildflower meadow, and gives alpine views in all directions. This is a small, family-owned business that provides quality service with personal touches, and the location affords easy access to fly-fishing and floating adventures. There are eight one-bedroom cabins ($235-275 summer, $150-170 fall-spring) and four two-bedroom duplexes ($375 summer, $175-225 fall-spring) on the premises. The cabins were built in the early 1990s and are bright, airy, and furnished with lodgepole pine furniture. They each have queen beds, kitchens, living-dining areas, and covered porches with a barbecue grill nearby. Also on these 10 acres (4 hectares) of property are a grocery and camping store, two restaurants, and an award-winning wine shop. Visitors can rent mountain bikes, canoes, and kayaks during the summer and cross-country skis and snowshoes in the winter to make the most of the surrounding area.

CAMPING

Gros Ventre (307/543-2811 or 307/543-3100, www.gtlc.com, early May-early Oct., tent and dry RV sites $29, electric sites $53) is the closest park campground to Jackson and among the largest campgrounds in the park, situated at the southeast end, 11.5 miles (18.5 km) southeast of Moose. Booked on a first-come, first-served basis, the 318 individual sites and five large group sites usually fill between noon and 5pm mid-June-mid-Aug., and rarely fill outside that time frame. All campsites and RV sites are discounted up to 50 percent with the presentation of a Golden Access Pass. Each individual site has a fire pit and picnic table and can accommodate two tents, two vehicles, and up to six people. The campground isn't far from the river, and there are sites to be had in the cottonwoods and open sage. Nearby bathrooms include flush toilets, but no shower facilities are available. A grocery store and service station are within 2 miles (3.2 km) of the campground.

Jackson Hole, Cody, and the Wind Rivers

Northwest Wyoming swings dramatically from stunning vistas and a sublime outdoor culture to the arts scene and high style of Jackson and Cody.

Some of the state's most exquisite lodgings and legendary ranches can be found in this corner of Wyoming. The area is jam-packed with obvious destinations such as world-class museums—Cody's Buffalo Bill Center of the West and Jackson's National Museum of Wildlife Art are among the best—as well as landmarks like Sinks Canyon near Lander, Hot Springs State Park near Thermopolis, the Wind River Range, and a string of scenic drives. The region provides a marvelous launching point into both Grand Teton and Yellowstone National Parks. Naturally, opportunities to explore the great outdoors here are

Highlights

Look for ★ to find recommended sights, activities, dining, and lodging.

★ **Jackson Town Square:** Surrounded by archways constructed entirely out of elk antlers, this is the heart of the community for shoppers, art lovers, and diners (page 394).

★ **National Museum of Wildlife Art:** This collection is dedicated to all things wild, spanning George Catlin's bison to incredible works by Georgia O'Keeffe, Charlie Russell, and marvelous contemporary artists (page 394).

★ **National Elk Refuge:** Most magical in winter under a blanket of snow, this refuge is home to more than 11,000 elk. Tour the area by horse-drawn sleigh (page 396).

★ **Rafting on the Snake River:** The Snake winds through the valley, giving floaters unparalleled access to the area's most stunning views (page 399).

★ **Sinks Canyon State Park:** This natural wonder occurs where the Middle Fork of the Popo Agie River "sinks" into a cave and then emerges again in a great spring (page 417).

★ **Hot Springs State Park:** This park has fabulous limestone terraces as well as public baths in therapeutic waters (page 423).

★ **Wyoming Dinosaur Center and Dig Sites:** Here, you can learn about dinosaurs, see their remains up close, and even dig for a day. There's a chance you'll find a fossil (page 425).

★ **Buffalo Bill Center of the West:** Here, five remarkable museums capture the art, natural

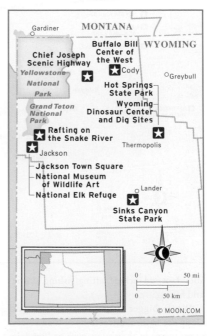

history, Native American cultures, and legends of the Old West. If you can visit only one museum in the West, this should be it (page 428).

★ **Chief Joseph Scenic Highway:** This scenic drive has high mountain plateaus speckled with wildflowers, cascading rivers, and narrow canyons teeming with wildlife (page 432).

Jackson Hole, Cody, and the Wind Rivers

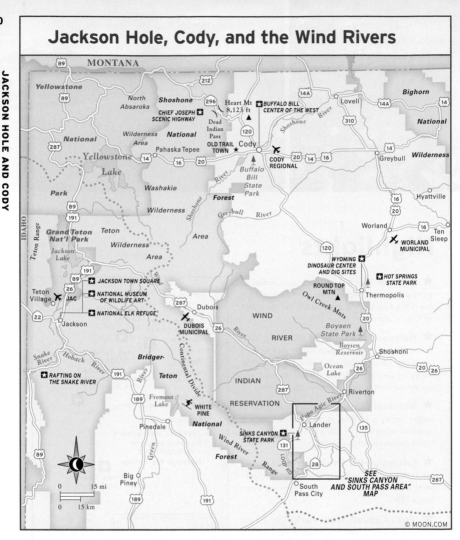

MONTANA

Yellowstone

North Absaroka
Wilderness Area

Shoshone

CHIEF JOSEPH SCENIC HIGHWAY

Heart Mt 8,123 ft

BUFFALO BILL CENTER OF THE WEST

Lovell

Bighorn

National

Wilderness

Yellowstone National Park

Pahaska Tepee

Dead Indian Pass

OLD TRAIL TOWN ★

Cody

Shoshone River

Greybull

Hyattville

Washakie Wilderness Area

Buffalo Bill State Park

CODY REGIONAL

Jackson Lake

Greybull River

Worland

Ten Sleep

Grand Teton Nat'l Park

Teton Wilderness Area

WYOMING DINOSAUR CENTER AND DIG SITES

ROUND TOP MTN

WORLAND MUNICIPAL

HOT SPRINGS STATE PARK

Teton Village

JAC

JACKSON TOWN SQUARE

NATIONAL MUSEUM OF WILDLIFE ART

NATIONAL ELK REFUGE

Dubois

DUBOIS MUNICIPAL

WIND

RIVER

Owl Creek Mtns

Boysen State Park

Thermopolis

Boysen Reservoir

Shoshoni

Jackson

Ocean Lake

Bridger-

Teton

INDIAN

Riverton

RAFTING ON THE SNAKE RIVER

Fremont Lake

WHITE PINE

RESERVATION

Pinedale

National

SINKS CANYON STATE PARK

Lander

Wind River

Forest

Big Piney

0   15 mi

0   15 km

South Pass City

SEE "SINKS CANYON AND SOUTH PASS AREA" MAP

© MOON.COM

abundant and include rafting, fishing, skiing, and hiking.

While bigger towns like Jackson and Cody are natural attractions in themselves, other towns in the region, such as Pinedale, Thermopolis, and tiny Ten Sleep, offer an authentic Wyoming experience with great museums, hot springs, historical monuments, and hole-in-the-wall cafés. Though towns like Lander and Powell lack the glitz and pomp of Jackson and Cody, they possess so much of what defines the state—rugged beauty, open space, rich history, and unrivaled wilderness access. In Wyoming, the journey from one town to the next is often the destination

Previous: performers at Eastern Shoshone Indian Days on the Wind River Reservation; Chief Jospeh Scenic Highway; the Wyoming Dinosaur Center.

itself, and by far the best way to appreciate this sparsely populated state.

PLANNING YOUR TIME

Jackson Hole and Cody are obvious destinations, with easy (but pricey) air access; each could easily occupy visitors for 2-3 full days, and both are excellent launching pads for day trips into Yellowstone and Grand Teton National Parks. Both have their own distinctive cultures that include art and entertainment, the great outdoors, and elegant accommodations and eateries. The dude ranches outside both Jackson and Cody offer tremendous opportunities to experience the state's vast open spaces in close proximity to the hustle and bustle of town. For many people, this is the ideal way to spend a week enjoying the best of Wyoming's offerings.

The charm of Jackson is that it is pretty much anything you want it to be. Boutique shopping? Check. Gallery strolls? Check. Kitschy bars with saddle-topped stools? Check. Gourmet dining? Hard-core outdoor pursuits? Quiet afternoons in the museum? Check. Check. Check. Jackson is a great destination because it is geared to visitors who want to be entertained, pampered, challenged, and wined and dined. A few hours in

the **National Museum of Wildlife Art** is time well spent. And you will want to allow an afternoon to stroll around town, browsing the shops and galleries—but don't let Jackson's shopping sirens lure you away from the majestic wilderness in every direction. In winter, try skiing at Jackson's original ski hill, **Snow King,** right in town, or at **Jackson Hole Mountain Resort** in nearby Teton Village. In summer you'll find trails to hike and dirt roads to bike, and two of the world's most incredible national parks are just up the road. Make sure to book a raft trip on the Snake River, and consider a wagon or sleigh ride on the sprawling **National Elk Refuge.**

Decidedly less glitzy than Jackson and more for the working cowboy than the urban variety (except during Rendezvous Royale), Cody is a rugged Western town with a rich history and just enough refinement to appeal to sophisticated travelers. The **Buffalo Bill Center of the West** is far and away the heart of Cody and should not be missed. A quick tour at a breakneck pace could probably be accomplished in two hours, but history buffs and Western art lovers could spend several days in the museum and not see the same exhibit twice. Cody's **nightly rodeos** in summer are a treat for the entire family, and a trip

Wind River

to Buffalo Bill's town would not be complete without a visit to the beautiful old hotel he built and named for his daughter, the **Irma Hotel**. The restaurant and saloon are open to nonguests, and if you go in the evening, watch the old **Cody Gunfighters** hash it out right outside the hotel Monday-Saturday at 6pm.

While disparate in philosophy, perhaps, the energy boomtown of Pinedale and the outdoor mecca of Lander both offer excellent access to the spectacular Wind River Mountains. The region is absolutely worth exploring as a destination for outdoor and nature lovers and as a beautiful setting for travelers en route from one place to the next.

HISTORY

While Wyoming had long been home to the Sioux, Crow, Cheyenne, Arapaho, Shoshone, Gros Ventre, Bannock, and Ute, a party of Frenchmen, traveling and trapping in the northwestern corner of the state as early as 1743, are thought to be the first Europeans in the area. Perhaps the most influential visitor in encouraging other trappers and mountain men to visit the region was John Colter, a member of the Lewis and Clark expedition who plied his skills as a trapper in the vicinity of what is now Jackson Hole in 1807-1808. His exploits and subsequent stories opened the area to an influx of mountain men, trappers, and traders, and by 1825 folks like Jedediah Smith, David Jackson, and Bill Sublette had made names for themselves as fearless explorers and shrewd businesspeople.

By 1840, the demand for beaver pelts had bottomed out, leaving little incentive for mountain men in the region. The population temporarily swelled with pioneers headed west on the Oregon Trail. Conflicts with Native Americans were inevitable as settlers encroached on traditional hunting grounds and, more importantly, nearly wiped out the bison altogether. There were great battles that always ended tragically, most often for the Native Americans, and a series of treaties that reduced the size of their lands until there was virtually none left. Today Wyoming is home to two recognized tribes—the Shoshone and Arapaho—once enemies and now neighbors sharing the Wind River Reservation.

By the 1880s, cattle ranching had taken hold, and sheep ranchers moved in just over a decade later. Both Jackson and Cody were settled much later, closer to the turn of the 20th century, because of the harsh snowy winters in Jackson and the desertlike conditions around Cody. What irrigation did for Cody by increasing the population, the creation of Grand Teton National Park did for Jackson in 1929 by attracting tourists and jump-starting dude ranching in the area.

Wyoming's biggest boom, however, came in the form of energy—oil, gas, and coal, the production of which still dominates the state's economy despite plummeting prices and subsequent layoffs. Oil was discovered outside Cody in 1904. The largest coal deposits in the country are being mined in the Powder River Basin, and much of the western portion of the state produces natural gas.

Wyoming's motto—"Equal Rights"—attests to the fact that Wyoming was the first territory to grant voting rights to women, in 1869, more than 20 years before its statehood was established. It was also the first state to elect a woman as governor, Nellie Tayloe Ross, who served 1923-1925. A darker time in Wyoming's history includes the creation of the Heart Mountain Relocation Camp, between Powell and Cody, where more than 10,000 Japanese Americans were held during World War II.

Chief Washakie and the Shoshone

Born around the turn of the 19th century to a Flathead (Salish) father and a Shoshone (Lemhi) mother, Washakie lived through the most tumultuous century for Native Americans. When his father was killed during a Blackfeet raid, the young boy and his mother left to live with the Lemhi people in Idaho. During his adolescence, Washakie joined a nomadic band of Bannocks, and eventually settled with the Shoshone in southwest Wyoming's Green River Basin. During the early 1820s Washakie befriended Jim Bridger, who would become a celebrated explorer and mountain man. Together they hunted, trapped, and traded. Their friendship was so great that one of Washakie's daughters became Bridger's third wife. Although trading and trapping ingratiated him with the settlers and explorers, Washakie also earned the respect of his fellow Indians as a skilled warrior.

Chief Washakie of the Shoshone

By the mid-1800s, Washakie was already an influential leader, having forged an alliance between the Shoshone and the Europeans. The skills Washakie acquired through his friendship with Bridger and other traders and trappers served him well as a leader. He was able to negotiate for the best interests of his people, getting them much-needed supplies. When younger warriors questioned his leadership after his alliances with settlers, Washakie left camp, only to return a week later with seven Sioux scalps, challenging anyone who questioned him to match the feat.

Washakie was also considered forward-thinking. When their land was threatened in the early 1850s by the influx of settlers, he suggested to leaders, including Brigham Young, that land be set aside for the Shoshone. By the end of the decade, he was negotiating directly with the U.S. government. In 1863 the Treaty of Fort Bridger designated land for the tribe.

On the reservation, Washakie continued to lead, maintaining a balance between the new reservation life and their traditions. Living in a log cabin rather than a tipi, Washakie sent his children to the agency schools and even farmed a small piece of land. But he also made sure his children joined him on buffalo hunts. He defended Native American practices and led his fellow Shoshone warriors in the U.S. Army battles against the Sioux and Cheyenne. In 1900, Chief Washakie was buried with full military honors. A warrior and peacemaker, a diplomat and an advocate for change, Chief Washakie is considered the last of the great Shoshone leaders. Wyoming has paid tribute by naming various public places in his honor.

Jackson Hole

Visitors love Jackson (population 10,529; elevation 5,672 ft/1,729 m) because it encompasses the best of the West in a charming town with a spectacular setting. Western indeed, Jackson boasts a classic boardwalk around town, saloons with swinging doors and saddles for bar stools, and architecture built on elk antlers. At the same time, Jackson is clearly mountain chic, with a number of high-end boutiques and art galleries, a phenomenal performing arts center, gourmet dining, and ritzy accommodations.

The valley itself, known as Jackson Hole because it is entirely surrounded by mountains, is 48 miles (77 km) long and up to 8 miles (12.9 km) wide in places. With the

Tetons as the most significant landmark, Jackson Hole gives rise to the headwaters of the Snake River, fed abundantly by numerous mountain streams. Because of its remarkable setting, Jackson Hole is a natural playground with offerings for just about anyone. In winter, outdoors enthusiasts can ski downhill at two well-known ski areas, Snow King and Jackson Hole Mountain Resort, or go the cross-country route just about anywhere, including nearby Grand Teton National Park. For those less interested in working up a sweat, a sleigh ride in the National Elk Refuge is a memorable experience. When the snow melts, there is no end to the amount of adventurous options this valley offers, with fly-fishing and wildlife-watching among the less exhausting. From hiking and mountain biking to rafting and rock climbing, Jacksonians do it all.

SIGHTS
★ Town Square

Almost European in its layout with a central square, Jackson's **Town Square** is uniquely distinguished by four dramatic archways constructed in 1932 entirely from naturally shed and sun-bleached elk antlers. It is the focal point of town and a good meeting spot, with shady trees and the occasional musician. In the summer, late May-early September, Town Square is the site of the free **Jackson Hole Shootout,** a spirited reenactment of frontier justice, which plays for crowds Monday-Saturday 6-6:30pm. In winter, the arches are illuminated by strings of lights, creating a magical setting.

Within easy walking distance of the square are more than 70 eateries—from mouthwatering pizza joints with ski-bum prices to the very tony—and a number of fine art galleries and shops that sell everything from high-end furs to T-shirts and knickknacks. There are also plentiful espresso and ice-cream shops for those in need of instant energy.

Jackson Hole Historical Society and Museum

Just down Cache Street from Town Square, the **Jackson Hole Historical Society and Museum** (225 N. Cache St., 307/733-2414, www.jacksonholehistory.org, 10am-5pm Tues.-Sat., $6 adults, $4 seniors over 60 and students, free for children 6 and under) is actually two museums within easy walking distance of one another. One is dedicated to the history of homesteading and dude ranches in the area, and the other to Indians of the Greater Yellowstone (the latter is open only in summer). The collections include historical photos of the region, Indian artifacts, fur trade-era tools, and firearms. Admission is good for both museums. The society also operates the hands-on Mercill Archaeology Center, which is open on a program basis only. In summer, the historical society offers free Jackson **walking tours** (10:30am Tues.-Fri., Memorial Day-last full week in Sept.). Tours depart from the center of Town Square. For a historical perspective on the town and valley, this is the best place to begin.

★ National Museum of Wildlife Art

Just 3 miles (4.8 km) north of Town Square overlooking the National Elk Refuge, the **National Museum of Wildlife Art** (2820 Rungius Rd., 307/733-5771, www.wildlifeart.org, 9am-5pm daily May-Oct., 9am-5pm Tues.-Sat., 11am-5pm Sun. winter, $14 adults, $12 seniors 60 and over, $6 for one child 5-18, $2 each additional child, free for children under 5) is an absolute find. In existence in various forms since 1984, the museum's 14 galleries represent the lifetime study and collection of wildlife art by Bill and Joffa Kerr. More than 5,000 objects reside in the permanent collection, primarily paintings and sculptures by artists that range from early Native American artists to masters both past and present, including Pablo Picasso, Carl Rungius, John James Audubon, Robert Bateman, and Kent Ullberg. A 0.8-mile (1.3-km) sculpture trail, which is free and open to the public, was added in 2013. The trail combines marvelous art with the stunning landscape around Jackson, and often plays

Downtown Jackson

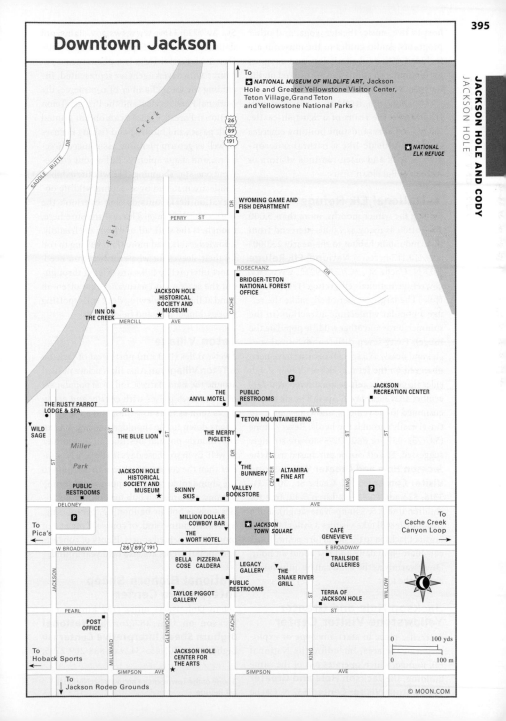

To
★ NATIONAL MUSEUM OF WILDLIFE ART, Jackson Hole and Greater Yellowstone Visitor Center, Teton Village, Grand Teton and Yellowstone National Parks

★ NATIONAL ELK REFUGE

WYOMING GAME AND FISH DEPARTMENT

PERRY ST

ROSECRANZ

BRIDGER-TETON NATIONAL FOREST OFFICE

JACKSON HOLE HISTORICAL SOCIETY AND MUSEUM ★

INN ON THE CREEK

MERCILL AVE

THE ANVIL MOTEL

PUBLIC RESTROOMS

JACKSON RECREATION CENTER

THE RUSTY PARROT LODGE & SPA

GILL AVE

TETON MOUNTAINEERING

WILD SAGE

THE BLUE LION

THE MERRY PIGLETS

THE BUNNERY

ALTAMIRA FINE ART

Miller Park

JACKSON HOLE HISTORICAL SOCIETY AND MUSEUM ★

PUBLIC RESTROOMS

SKINNY SKIS

VALLEY BOOKSTORE

DELONEY

MILLION DOLLAR COWBOY BAR

★ JACKSON TOWN SQUARE

CAFÉ GENEVIEVE

To Pica's

THE WORT HOTEL

To Cache Creek Canyon Loop

W BROADWAY

26 89 191

E BROADWAY

BELLA PIZZERIA COSE CALDERA

LEGACY GALLERY

THE SNAKE RIVER GRILL

TRAILSIDE GALLERIES

PUBLIC RESTROOMS

TAYLOE PIGGOT GALLERY

TERRA OF JACKSON HOLE

PEARL ST

POST OFFICE

To Hoback Sports

JACKSON HOLE CENTER FOR THE ARTS ★

SIMPSON AVE

SIMPSON AVE

To Jackson Rodeo Grounds

0   100 yds
0   100 m

© MOON.COM

host to live music, theater, yoga, and other programs. Audio guides to the museum are included with paid admission, and coupons for discounts on admission are offered on the museum's website.

The museum itself is a work of art: Inspired by the ruins of a Scottish castle, the red Arizona sandstone building emerges from the hillside like a natural outcropping of rock and often reminds visitors of Ancestral Puebloan ruins.

★ National Elk Refuge

During the winter months, more than 5,000 elk—often as many as 7,000—descend from their mountain habitat to the nearly 25,000-acre (10,117-hectare) **National Elk Refuge** (532 N. Cache St., 307/733-9212, www.fws.gov/refuge/national_elk_refuge/) in Jackson Hole. The large number of elk make the refuge a popular wintertime attraction (in the summer, birds and other wildlife populate the range). Forty-seven different mammal species and nearly 175 species of birds have been observed on the refuge. Horse-drawn sleigh rides through the refuge are offered mid-December-first Saturday in April. The elk are accustomed to the vehicles, allowing visitors to travel easily through the herds. Reservations (307/733-0277 or 800/772-5386) are strongly suggested. Tickets can be purchased from the **Jackson Hole and Greater Yellowstone Visitor Center** (532 N. Cache St., 307/733-3316, $23 adults, $15 children 5-12, free for children under 5, $400/private sleigh), and a free shuttle will take visitors 3 miles (4.8 km) north of Jackson to the departure point. Tours run 10am-4pm daily and last about an hour. Dress warmly as the wind can be quite biting during the tour.

Jackson Hole and Greater Yellowstone Visitor Center

A terrific place to start any type of exploration of the area, including the National Elk Refuge, which operates out of the same building, the **Jackson Hole and Greater Yellowstone Visitor Center** (532 N. Cache

St., 307/733-3316, www.fws.gov, 8am-7pm daily Memorial Day-Sept. 30, 9am-5pm daily Oct. 1-Memorial Day) is a phenomenal resource with seven agencies represented, including the local chamber of commerce, the National Park Service, and the Bridger-Teton National Forest. Visitors can obtain annual park passes and hunting and fishing licenses as well as get trip planning assistance, directions, and maps aplenty. Talk about convenient one-stop shopping. The wildlife exhibits inside are matched by sweeping wildlife observation decks outside that overlook the National Elk Refuge. The real treasure here, though, is the staff, all of whom are friendly, knowledgeable, and more than willing to roll up their sleeves for whatever help you need. Short interpretive talks are offered throughout the season, and naturalists are often on hand at the upper viewing deck with spotting scopes, binoculars, and field guides.

Teton Village

Twelve miles (19.3 km) northwest of Jackson is **Teton Village,** an Alps-like enclave nestled around the state's largest and most popular ski hill. The area pulses with energy and activity as soon as the snow flies, and although it quiets down in the shoulder seasons, it is an enormously popular destination in summer as well. Even so, these days it's quite a bit quieter than the center of Jackson. In addition to the abundant lodging, shopping, and dining options, the area is a hub for outdoor activities such as hot-air ballooning, paragliding, horseback riding, and, of course, a myriad of mountain-oriented sports. Plenty of concerts and special events are also held year-round.

National Bighorn Sheep Interpretive Center

Set in Dubois, 85 miles (137 km) east of Jackson on U.S. 287/26, the **National Bighorn Sheep Interpretive Center** (10 Bighorn Ln., 307/455-3429 or 888/209-2795,

1: one of the Town Square archways 2: National Elk Refuge

The Elk Conundrum

Established in 1912, the National Elk Refuge was the first Wyoming state-run feeding ground for elk. In the 1930s and 1940s, more feeding grounds were created to help the animals survive the harsh winters, and in part to keep them from entering areas reserved for cattle grazing. The thriving herd in Jackson ultimately was used to replenish other herds of elk and aid the reintroduction of elk throughout the country. However, as a result of the large number of elk concentrated in these feeding grounds, the animals are much more susceptible to contagious diseases including brucellosis and, more recently, chronic wasting disease. Wyoming lost its federal brucellosis-free status in 2004 when cattle acquired the disease after coming into contact with elk from the refuge.

In 2005 the U.S. Department of Agriculture's Animal Plant Health Inspection Service reported that there was a 50-80 percent rate of brucellosis infection among elk on feedlots, and though that number has dropped to 30 percent in more recent reports, it is still substantially higher than the 1-3 percent infection rate in wild free-ranging elk. Before the National Elk Refuge was created, the elk from southern Yellowstone would migrate and spread past the area of the refuge into southwestern Wyoming. As the winter came to a close, they moved back to their summer habitat. Today it's believed that the 11,000 elk in the Jackson herd alone migrate to and from the refuge at the risk of spreading both brucellosis and chronic wasting disease. As of 2018, the National Elk Refuge is one of 22 feeding grounds for elk in the western part of the state. A study published in 2016 showed that four of the five strains of brucellosis are found on Wyoming feeding grounds, a discovery that pinned the blame for the spread of brucellosis outside Yellowstone on the elk, as opposed to the bison that have long been treated as the culprits.

The question now is, what can be done? The argument has been made that the elk should return to their historic migration routes and original winter ranges rather than being concentrated in the feedlots. Today, however, many of those routes and ranges have been developed for housing, ranches, or other businesses. Furthermore, the idea of elk and cattle competing for food on the open range is worrisome to many Wyoming ranchers. So, although the scientific consensus is that it would be best for the elk to return to their natural migration patterns, the challenge is finding places in the wild that can sustain them throughout the year.

www.bighorn.org, 9am-6pm daily late May-early Sept., 10am-4pm Mon.-Sat. early Sept.-mid-Dec. and Apr.-late May, 10am-4pm Tues.-Sat. late Dec.-late Mar., $6 adults, $3 children 8-17, free for children under 8) is dedicated to educating the public about these majestic creatures and their habitats. Visitors are welcomed by a stunning bronze of a ram and led inside to several hands-on exhibits that will delight little ones and fascinate animal lovers. There are 16 mounts of wild sheep from around the world and a great little gift shop with everything from T-shirts to children's toys and wares by local artists. November-March, the center offers tours to the winter range of the **Whiskey Mountain Habitat Area,** providing an excellent opportunity to see the bighorn sheep in their natural, windswept environment. Reservations for the 3- to 5-hour tours should be made at least

48 hours in advance by calling the center. The cost is $100 per person for 2 or more.

SPORTS AND RECREATION
Fishing

Surrounded by abundant rivers and streams, including the Snake River and its myriad mountain tributaries, plus Grand Teton and Yellowstone National Parks, Jackson has become something of a fly-fishing mecca.

The best-known trout stream in the region is the Snake River, which winds more than 60 miles (97 km) on lazy flats and then blasts through the Snake River Canyon, which offers more white-knuckle rafting than graceful casting. The Upper Snake, much of which is in Grand Teton National Park, is characterized by braided channels with cutbanks and logjams, and the water holds native cutthroats.

Drift boating is popular as a way to maximize the water covered (and scenery enjoyed), but there are ample opportunities to get out and wade-fish. The section of the river that goes through the canyon is almost exclusively fished by boat (self-bailers come in handy in the Class II-III rapids), and despite the action of the waves, the fish are more plentiful in the canyon, though not always easy to catch.

Jackson has no shortage of fly-fishing guides or fly shops. Among the best is a small outfit, **Teton Fly Fishing** (544 Clark St., 307/413-1215, www.tetonflyfishing.com), run by Nate Bennett, who loves teaching his clients about the art of fishing as much as he loves hooking a fish. He books only one trip daily so that the pace can be less breakneck and far more enjoyable. Bennett gets his clients on a variety of types of water and, like a good fish whisperer, somehow gets the fish to bite. An artist by training, Bennett ties all his own flies and loves to share. His trips ($495 half-day, $535 full-day for up to 2 anglers) on the Snake, Salt, and Green Rivers include all equipment, flies, transportation, streamside lunch, and full access to his unlimited knowledge and expertise.

Another great resource for fishing would be the friendly folks at **JD High Country**

Outfitters (50 E. Broadway, 307/733-3270, www.jdhcoutfitters.com, 9am-8pm daily summer, reduced hours in winter). The staff are experts on waters all over the region, and in addition to guiding services on the Snake River ($475/half-day, $575/full-day), the shop has a great selection of flies, equipment, and clothing. They even teach casting lessons for novices.

TOP EXPERIENCE

★ Rafting on the Snake River

One of the greatest attractions for summertime visitors to Jackson is rafting the Snake River. There are close to two dozen rafting companies to choose from in the area, and most are open mid-May-September. Below are a few options for those who are interested in experiencing the river, whether it be a tranquil day float through Grand Teton National Park or white-water adventure a little farther south in the canyon. Most adult fares average $80-90 for an 8-mile (12.9-km) trip. Increasingly popular are combination trips, which include a scenic float or white-water raft trip with other activities ranging from wildlife tours to horseback rides to gourmet Dutch-oven meals.

Barker-Ewing (307/733-1000 or

rafting the Snake River

800/448-4202, www.barker-ewing.com, $82-88 adults, $65-88 children) is a family-operated business that has been running small trips for more than 50 years.

Dave Hansen Whitewater (800/732-6295, www.davehansenwhitewater.com, $82-88 adults, $65-88 children) has been in the business since the late 1960s. Dave actually named two of the largest waves on the river, the Lunch Box and the Big Kahuna.

Another option with a variety of trips down the Snake River is **Mad River Boat Trips** (800/458-7328, www.mad-river.com, $79-99 adults, $59-94 children).

For experienced floaters who want to tackle the Snake unguided, **Rent-a-Raft** (U.S. 89, Hoback Jct., 13 mi/20.9 km south of Jackson, 307/733-2728, www.rentaraft.net) offers 11-foot (3.4 m, $65), 12.5-foot (3.8 m, $90), 13-foot (4 m, $105), and 14-foot rafts (4.3 m, $125) as well as sit-on-top kayaks, one- and two-person ducks ($40) and shuttle service from its headquarters.

TOP EXPERIENCE

Skiing and Mountain Sports

Jackson's reputation among the West's premier ski towns is not hard to explain. There are three developed downhill ski resorts, the closet one being right in town.

Snow King Mountain (400 E. Snow King Ave., 307/201-5464, www.snowkingmountain.com, full-day $55 adults, $35 high schoolers 15-18 and seniors 65 and over, free for children 5 and under, half-day $45 adults, $30 high schoolers and seniors 65 and over; night skiing 4pm-7pm $30 adults, $25 high schoolers and seniors, discounts available for multi-day passes) soars skyward just six blocks from Town Square, so Jackson is a ski town in the most literal sense. The mountain was developed for skiing in 1939, making it the first in the Jackson area and one of the first in the country. The area boasts 1,571 feet (479 m) of vertical drop over 400 acres (161.9 hectares) with two double chairlifts, one triple lift, a surface tow, and the ever-popular **Snow**

Tubing Park ($20 adults 15 and over, $15 children, $5 each additional hour). The area is open for day and night skiing. Discounts are available for lodging guests. Nonskiers can pay to ride the lift ($20 adults, $15 children 12 and under and seniors 65 and over) just to enjoy the breathtaking views of town and the valley from the summit. In the summer, the trails and lifts are open for hiking, mountain biking, and paragliding, plus a cowboy rollercoaster, an alpine slide, and a ropes course.

In nearby Teton Village, the ski area at **Jackson Hole Mountain Resort** (307/733-2292 or 888/DEEP-SNOW, www.jacksonhole.com, $104-149 adults, free for children 5 and under, prices rise as the season progresses, especially around the holidays, discounts available by purchasing online) is in fact two mountains, Apres Vous and Rendezvous, which together offer skiers 2,500 skiable acres (1,012 hectares), a vertical drop of 4,139 feet (1,262 m), and open access to more than 3,000 acres (1,214 hectares) of backcountry terrain. There are 129 trails, of which a whopping 50 percent are geared to experts, 40 percent for intermediate skiers, and 10 percent for beginners. The ski hill averages 459 inches (1,166 cm) of snow annually. In 2018, they topped 500 inches (1,270 cm)! In Jackson, this is the mountain to ski and be seen.

The **aerial tram** (307/733-2292, 9am-5pm daily late May-mid-June, 9am-6pm daily mid-June-early Sept., single ride $35 adults when purchased online, $29 seniors 65 and older, $22 children 6-17, $89 family with up to four children, free for children under 6), known as Big Red or the Red Heli, takes hikers, bikers, paragliders, backcountry skiers, and lookie-loos up to the summit of Rendezvous Peak (4,139 ft/1,262 m in 9 minutes). At the top, **Corbet's Cabin** (307/739-2688, 9am-4:30pm daily in season), a fabulous little waffle hut, makes you wish you had hiked the whole way.

Although you need to go through Idaho to get there, **Grand Targhee Resort** (3300 Ski Hill Rd., 307/353-2300, www.grandtarghee.com, full-day $85-90 adults, $60-65 seniors 65 and over, $39-44 juniors 6-12, free for children under 6) in Alta, Wyoming, is a destination in itself. The skiing in winter is out of this world, with huge dumps of powder and expansive terrain. The resort also offers Nordic skiing, tubing, guided snowcat tours, sleigh-ride dinners, snowmobile tours, and ice climbing. In summer, the mountain stays awake for hiking, mountain biking, horseback riding, and a couple of renowned musical events, including **Targhee Fest** and the **Grand Targhee Bluegrass Festival.**

For avid Nordic skiers, the blanket of snow transforms many favorite local hiking trails into first-rate ski trails. From hitting the groomers at local golf courses, including **Teton Pines** (3450 N. Clubhouse Dr., 307/733-1733 or 800/238-2223, www.tetonpines.com, $15 adults, $10 seniors, $5 children 6-12, rentals available for $25 cross-country ski package, $35 skate ski package, $15 kids skate or classic, $30 backcountry touring package) to hoofing into the backcountry in Grand Teton National Park, there is terrain for everyone. The **Jackson Hole Nordic Center** (3395 Village Dr., 307/739-2629, www.jhnordic.com) at Teton Village offers 11 miles (17.7 km) of groomed trails for classic and skate skiers. Rentals are available on-site. In town, alpine, cross-country, skate, or snowshoeing gear can be purchased or rented from **Skinny Skis** (65 W. Deloney Ave., 307/733-6094 or 888/733-7205, www.skinnyskis.com, general touring package $20/full day, skate skiing package $25/full day) or **Teton Mountaineering** (170 N. Cache St., 307/733-3595, www.tetonmtn.com).

Hiking and Mountain Biking

Although plenty of hikers choose to hit the trails in Grand Teton and Yellowstone National Parks, with so many mountains in every direction around Jackson, there is no shortage of amazing hikes outside the parks. Many of the trails outside the parks are open to mountain bikers as well.

One trail with immediate proximity to town that skirts the Gros Ventre Wilderness Area is the **Cache Creek Canyon Loop,** which is part of the Greater Snow King Trail Network. It is a popular trail for hikers, mountain bikers, and in winter, cross-country skiers. To get to the trailhead, drive east on Broadway to Redmond Street, across from the hospital; turn right and go 0.4 mile (0.6 km) to Cache Creek Road. Turn left and continue just over 1 mile (1.6 km) to the parking lot at road's end. Hikers can amble along both sides of the creek on this 4-mile (6.4 km) loop, gaining only 350 vertical feet (106.7 m). Connecting trails lead to Game Creek and Granite Falls, or back to Snow King in Jackson.

Ten miles (16.1 km) west of town near Teton Pass is **Phillips Pass,** an incredible and somewhat strenuous day hike at the edge of the Tetons and the Jedediah Smith Wilderness Area. The trail is open to hikers and mountain bikers. To get to the trailhead, head west to Teton Pass on Highway 22. Two miles (3.2 km) east of the summit is Phillips Canyon Road (Forest Rd. 30972). There is no parking at the trailhead, which is 0.5 mile (0.8 km) down this road, so park safely across the highway in a small pullout or on Phillips Canyon Road close to the highway. The 8-mile (12.9 km) out-and-back trail starts at 8,000 feet (2,438 m) in elevation and is spectacularly beautiful, particularly in late summer, as it winds through flower-drenched meadows and forest to the alpine country above the tree line. As always in this part of the country, be prepared for significant weather changes and encounters with wild animals.

For excellent guided hiking in the Tetons and around the valley, contact **The Hole Hiking Experience** (307/690-4453 or 866/733-4453, www.holehike.com, half-day from $240 for up to 2 hikers, $92 pp for 3 or more, full-day $450 for up to 2 hikers, $182 pp for 3 or more), which offers a wide variety of trips from half-day naturalist-guided trips geared to families to strenuous all-day hikes and even yoga-hiking combinations. For guided mountain bike trips for the whole family (including kids on Trail-a-Bikes and in trailers) or more extreme riders, contact **Teton Mountain Bike Tours** (545 N. Cache

St., 307/733-0712, www.tetonmtbike.com) for half-day (from $75 pp), full-day (from $115-165 pp plus $10 box lunch), multiple-day, and specialty trip offerings. It also rent bikes.

Hoback Sports (520 W. Broadway Ave., 307/733-5335, www.hobacksports.com, 9am-7pm daily) has all kinds of rental bikes for adults and kids, from road bikes ($59-79 for 3 hours, $69-89 full day) and hybrids ($39 for hours, $49 full day) to full-suspension mountain bikes ($69-79 for 3 hours, $79-89 full day), and can point bikers in the direction of any kind of ride they seek.

Horseback Riding

Another popular way to experience the great outdoors in Jackson is on horseback. Several options, including hourly rentals, half-day trail rides, or overnight pack trips, are available from the many local outfitters in and around town. For half-day trail rides, expect to pay around $120-150 per person.

Located 35 miles (56 km) south of Jackson, **Jackson Hole Outfitters** (307/699-3541, www.jacksonholetrailrides.com, early June-early Sept.) starts its trail rides in the secluded Greys River camp and follows trails through the Bridger-Teton National Forest. It offers half-day rides ($120), full-day rides ($175), five-and-a-half-hour extreme rides ($210), and overnight stays ($95) in comfortable canvas tents and real beds.

Spring Creek Ranch (1600 N. East Butte Rd., 307/733-8833 or 800/443-6139, www.springcreekranch.com, mid-May-mid-Oct.) offers one-hour rides ($49), two-hour rides ($69), and half-day rides ($159) along the East Gros Ventre Butte. It also offers wagon rides to a chuck wagon dinner ($75 adults, $45 children 12 and under) Sun., Tues., and Thurs. nights at 6pm. Age restrictions vary for the different rides.

Mill Iron Ranch (307/773-6390 or 888/808-6390, www.millironranch.net) 10.5 miles (16.9 km) south of Jackson on U.S. 89/191 offers two-hour ($80), four-hour ($140), or full-day trips ($220-280) that can

be combined with breakfast, lunch, fishing, or a steak dinner for an additional charge.

Golf

Golf is becoming increasingly popular in Jackson Hole (maybe because the ball seems to fly so much farther at altitude), and there are a couple of world-class public courses. The **Jackson Hole Golf & Tennis Club** (5000 Spring Gulch Rd., 307/733-3111, www.jhgtc.com, $70-190 with twilight discounts after 2pm) offers an award-winning 18-hole course designed by Bob Baldock and renovated twice by Robert Trent Jones II, most recently in 2004. Local conservation hero Laurance Rockefeller once owned the course, which says a lot about its natural beauty. The 18-hole course at **Teton Pines Country Club** (3450 Clubhouse Dr., 307/733-1005 or 800/238-2223, www.tetonpines.com, $130-175 for 18 holes, $85 for 9 holes) in Teton Village was designed by Arnold Palmer and has been highly ranked by *Condé Nast Traveler, Audubon International,* and *Golf Digest,* among others.

ENTERTAINMENT AND EVENTS
The Arts

Among the most impressive facilities in the state is the **Jackson Hole Center for the Arts** (265 S. Cache St., 307/734-8956 or 307/733-4900, www.jhcenterforthearts.org), a truly inspired art campus in the heart of downtown that offers educational programs and facilities along with professional theater, dance, and music as well as a remarkable space for major community events. Check out the schedule online—there is always something happening. Of particular note at the Center for the Arts is the **Off Square Theatre Company** (240 S. Glenwood St., 307/733-3021, www.offsquare.org), which produces excellent and wildly diverse shows ranging from family-favorite American musicals (*Beauty and The Beast*) and dramatic masterpieces (*Macbeth*) to side-splitting improv by Laff Staff. Regardless of the offerings, a night at the theater in Jackson is a night well spent.

ART GALLERIES

The art scene in Jackson is both rarefied and approachable, and an increasingly important part of both the community and the local economy. There are more than 30 galleries in town. Among the favorites are **Trailside Galleries** (130 E. Broadway, 307/733-3186, www.trailsidegalleries.com, 10am-5:30pm Mon.-Sat., noon-5pm Sun. June-Oct., 10am-5:30pm Mon.-Sat. Nov.-May) and **Legacy Gallery** (75 N. Cache St., 307/733-2353, www.legacygallery.com, 10am-5pm Mon.-Sat.), both with classic examples of Western art in its traditional and contemporary forms. **Altamira Fine Art** (172 Center St., 307/739-4700, www.altamiraart.com, 10am-5pm daily or by appointment) has a more loftlike urban feel and represents groundbreaking contemporary artists, including Rocky Hawkins, Duke Beardsley, Ed Mell, Mary Roberson, and John Nieto. The **Tayloe Piggot Gallery** (62 S. Glenwood St., 307/733-0555, www.jhmusegallery.com, 10am-6pm Mon.-Wed., 10am-8pm Thurs.-Sat., 11am-5pm Sun.) is cutting-edge cool with both emerging and mid-career artists in a variety of media. For more information on all the galleries in Jackson, visit the **Jackson Hole Gallery Association** (www.jacksonholegalleryassociation.com).

Festivals and Events

Weekly events in Jackson during the summer season (Memorial Day-Labor Day) include the **Jackson Rodeo** (447 Snow King Ave., 307/733-7927, www.jhrodeo.com, 8pm Wed. and Sat. June, 8pm Wed., Fri., and Sat. July-Labor Day, $20-35), a fun family event with bull riding, team roping, barrel racing, bareback broncs, and plenty of other action. Food and refreshments are sold at the chuck wagon.

For one of Jackson's favorite regular events, check out the **Town Square Shootout** (6pm Mon.-Sat.) on the Town Square. It's free and a lot of fun for visitors.

An annual event built around the well-known Boy Scout Elk Antler Auction, where the boys sell the shed antlers they collect from the National Elk Refuge, **Elk Fest** (307/733-5935 or 300/733-3316, www.elkfest.org) takes place the weekend before Memorial Day and includes plenty of food, community concerts, children's activities, and many opportunities to learn about elk.

Happening each year over Memorial Day weekend all around town is Jackson's long-running **Old West Days** (307/733-3316, www.jacksonholechamber.com), which features a horse-drawn parade, old-town entertainment, a rodeo, a mountain man rendezvous, and a host of other events that celebrate Jackson's rough-and-tumble origins.

Happening in late July-early August, the nearly weeklong **Teton County Fair** (Teton County Fairgrounds at 305 West Snow King Ave., 307/733-5289, www.tetoncountyfair.com) includes family-friendly events like pig wrestling ($5-15), a rodeo ($15-25), a demolition derby ($15-30), concerts, a carnival, and plenty of agricultural and animal exhibits.

The equivalent of Cody's Rendezvous Royale, Jackson's **Fall Arts Festival** (307/733-3316, www.jacksonholechamber.com) is a 10-day event in mid-September that unites the community and attracts a crowd of art lovers with a phenomenal range of art-related events, including the prestigious **Jackson Hole Art Auction** (www.jacksonholeartauction.com) and **Western Design Conference** (www.westerndesignconference.com), gallery walks, open-air art fairs, historic ranch tours, and culinary coups.

The **Grand Teton Music Festival** (McCollister Dr., Teton Village, 307/733-1128, www.gtmf.org, $15-85, free for students) takes place annually during July-August. It is held in the all-wooden Walk Festival Hall, which recently underwent a $4.85 million renovation to improve the intimate setting and provide top-notch acoustics. Known as one of the top classical music festivals in the country, it showcases an impressive list of musicians and singers. Running annually since 1962, past performers include Sarah Chang, Itzhak Perlman, the New York Philharmonic, and the Mormon Tabernacle Choir. In addition to the summer festival, the organization hosts concerts during the winter. Family concerts are free, as are students, and open rehearsals (Friday mornings at 10 am) can be attended for as little as $15.

One of the most renowned bluegrass festivals in the country takes place on the western slopes of the Grand Tetons in Targhee during mid-August. The **Grand Targhee Bluegrass Festival** (3300 Ski Hill Rd., 307/353-2300, www.grandtarghee.com, 3-day pass from $239, day passes also available starting at $85, camping $40-110) draws a large number of the best bluegrass musicians in the country, including Brother Mule, Danny Barnes, and Sarah Jarosz, along with a large number of fans. Held at the Grand Targhee Resort (800/827-4433), tent and RV camping is allowed in the national forest during the festival weekend. In addition to performances all day long, there is also plenty of food, arts, and crafts available.

Also taking place at Grand Targhee Resort, in mid-July, the decade-old **Targhee Fest** (www.grandtarghee.com, 3-day pass from $239, day passes also available from $85, camping $40-110) is a lively three-day music festival with an eclectic mix of artists such as Los Lobos and John Hiatt. Camping is also allowed in the national forest during this event.

The **Jackson Hole Film Festival** (307/200-3286, www.jhfestival.org) is a biennial event dedicated to nature conservation, held in late September-early October. The six-day festival attracts leaders in science, conservation, and media as numerous films are screened and related social events and activities are organized throughout the week. The festival is held at the Jackson Lake Lodge, except for the final event, which screens selected finalists at the Center for the Arts in downtown Jackson. The festival is slated to run in 2019, 2021 and 2023.

Winter Fest (307/733-3316, www.jacksonholechamber.com) gives residents and visitors alike one more reason to celebrate the snow. Happening over two weeks in February, the celebration includes events like snow sculpting, skiing, ice-skating, and wine-tasting.

Another winter event everyone looks forward to is the **Pedigree Stage Stop Dog Race** (307/734-1163, www.wyomingstagestop. org). It takes place from the last weekend in January through the first week of February. Begun in 1996, it is the largest U.S. dogsled race outside Alaska. The race begins in Jackson and runs 500 miles (805 km) to Park City, Utah. It is unusual in that the participants stop for the night in towns along the way, including Lander, Pinedale, Big Piney-Marbleton, Alpine, Kemmerer, Lyman, Evanston, and Uinta County. Each town along the route celebrates with different festivities as they greet and cheer on the racers.

SHOPPING

For those with time and money, shopping can practically be an athletic pursuit in Jackson, particularly in the streets and alleyways around **Town Square.** In the early 1990s, Jackson was populated with a number of outlet stores, but today most of those have been pushed out by more sophisticated boutiques. There are lots of fascinating little shops to pop into, from gorgeous high-end art galleries to the few remaining tacky but fun T-shirt and tchotchke shops.

For an independent bookstore, **Valley Bookstore** (125 N. Cache St., 307/733-4533, www.valleybookstore.com, 9am-9pm daily June-Aug., 9am-7pm Mon.-Sat., 10am-6pm Sun. Sept.-May) is pretty great and has been providing local readers with fabulous books and stellar recommendations for nearly 50 years. The owners grew up in Jackson and have a superb local and regional section.

For top-of-the-line women's and children's clothes in a spacious, almost Zen-like setting, visit **Terra of Jackson Hole** (105 E. Broadway, 307/734-0067, www.terrajh.com, 11am-6pm Mon.-Sat., noon-5pm Sun.), which would not be out of place in Manhattan or San Francisco. Another glorious place filled with beautiful things is **Bella Cose** (48 E. Broadway, 307/733-2640, www.bellacose.com,

10am-6pm Mon.-Sat., noon-5pm Sun.), which offers elegant home decor as well as kitchen and dining items; it clearly caters to the second-home crowd. For a chance to actually play with some cool toys, visit the **Jackson Hole Toy Store** (165 Center St., 307/734-2663, www.jacksonholetoystore.com, 10am-8pm daily in high season, 10am-6pm daily in off-season). There's a wireless Wild West shooting gallery ($5) and the owner can tell you anything about any of the creative toys they stock from all over the world.

One of the most exquisite design studios anywhere, **WRJ Design** (30 S. King St., 307/200-4881, www.wrjdesign.com, 10am-6pm Mon.-Fri., weekends by appointment) has a Jackson showroom filled with furnishings, unique objects, fine art, and curated lines from around the world. Owned by renowned designers Klaus Baer and Rush Jenkins, WRJ's style is elegant, earthy, and contemporary.

FOOD

For every opportunity this region provides to exert energy by skiing, hiking, biking, or other pursuits, Jackson offers many more ways to replenish your supply. The number of outstanding restaurants in this town puts just about every other town in Wyoming—and many Western states—to shame.

As a rule, every day in Jackson should start with a trip to **The Bunnery** (130 N. Cache Dr., 307/733-5474, www.bunnery.com, 7am-3pm daily, $10-17). The food is entirely made from scratch and utterly scrumptious. The baked goods—including its trademark OSM (oats, sunflower, millet) bread and homemade granola—are beyond compare, and the enormous and diverse menu offers plenty of healthy options as well as a few decadent ones. The "Get Your Buns in Here" bumper stickers are also good for a laugh. Be prepared to wait, however; The Bunnery is beloved by visitors and locals alike.

Just as the best days in Jackson should start at The Bunnery, so too should they finish at the **Million Dollar Cowboy Bar** (25 N. Cache Dr., 307/733-2207, www.milliondollarcowboybar.com, 11am-2am daily summer, noon-2am daily winter, Fri.-Sat. 9pm-1:30am off-season, bar food $9-17), right on Town Square. The bar has been a centerpiece of Jackson since 1937 when the first liquor license was issued in the state. The saddle bar stools should absolutely be sat upon and visitors are encouraged to check out the impressive collection of Western memorabilia

The Million Dollar Cowboy Bar in Jackson is a classic.

adorning the bar. There is live music is regularly, and patrons who don't want to go too far can enjoy a hearty meal next door in the **Million Dollar Cowboy Steakhouse** (307/733-4790, www.jhcowboysteakhouse. com, 5:30-10pm daily, $24-29), featuring specialties like beer and bone marrow fondue, short rib nachos, grilled halibut, and any kind of steak you can imagine. Reservations are recommended. During the "Hidden Hour" from 8pm-9pm daily, take half off the Den Menu ($13-17), well cocktails, and wines by the glass.

Inspired by New York's EATALY, but every bit Jackson Hole, **Bin 22** (200 W. Broadway, 307/739-9463, www.bin22jackson.com, wine bar 11am-10pm Mon.-Sat., 3pm-10pm Sun., retail shop 10am-10pm daily, $9-16) is a great spot for a light bite or to pick up a bottle of wine to go. It has all sorts of salamis and cheeses, plus appetizers and tapas-style plates.

Newer on the Jackson scene, and often with a line out front, **Persephone Bakery** (145 E. Broadway, 307/200-6708, www. persephonebakery.com, 7am-3pm daily, pastry case and beverages 7am-6pm Mon.-Sat. and 7am-5pm Sun. summer, call ahead for winter hours, $9-14) is an artisanal bakery and café, known for French-style rustic, elegant breads and pastries, and excellent salads and sandwiches for lunch. It also offers afternoon high tea service (reservations required) and a nice wine list and cocktail menu. How's that for a Jackson Hole bakery?

One of the most interesting places for craft cocktails, excellent wine, and a gourmet meal is **The Rose** (50 W. Broadway, 307/733-1500, www.therosejh.com, 8pm-1:30am Sun.-Wed., 5:30pm-1:30am Thurs.-Sat., $11-30) founded by the same team who created the insanely hip Death & Co. in New York City. Everything here is artisanal and local, from the food and cocktails to the dinner plates and art. Adjacent to the bar and restaurant is the **Pink Garter Theatre,** an excellent venue for a diverse range of live music and special events.

Set in a 1910 log cabin, one of the oldest residential structures in town, **Café**

Genevieve (135 E. Broadway, 307/732-1910, www.genevievejh.com, 8am-9pm daily, $24-38) serves inspired home cooking with dishes like red curry baby back ribs, smoked turkey leg and steak frites. It serves a killer breakfast until 3pm with specialties like grits and eggs, sweet and spicy candied bacon (known as pig candy), corned beef hash and fried chicken and waffles. Fido will appreciate the pet-friendly deck. There's also a daily happy hour (3pm-5:30pm).

A fresh and delicious arrival on Jackson's culinary scene is **Pica's Mexican Taqueria** (1160 Alpine Ln., 307/734-4457, www. picastaqueria.com, 11am-10pm daily summer, 11am-10pm Mon.-Sat. winter, $9-16), which offers the freshest take on tacos, burritos, great salads, and authentic Mexican dishes. Their margaritas are outstanding. Another terrific Mexican restaurant right in town is **The Merry Piglets** (160 N. Cache St., 307/733-2966, www.merrypiglets.com, 11:30am-9pm daily, $10-26), which serves classic taco, burrito, chimichanga, and enchilada plates with fresh salsas, sauces, and tortilla chips, all made in-house daily. The fish is wild, the meat is pasture-raised, and no partially hydrogenated oils are used. The portions are big, and the flavors are very satisfying.

Known for its rack of lamb, but accomplished at everything on the menu, **The Blue Lion** (160 N. Millward St., 307/733-3912, www.bluelionrestaurant.com, 5:30pm-9pm daily, $23-44) has been a staple of the Jackson food scene for more than two decades, with menu items ranging from elk and buffalo tenderloin and Idaho trout to rack of lamb and hazelnut-crusted chicken. There's also a children's menu. Reservations are recommended.

For burger lovers, the best spot in town is **MacPhail's Burgers** (399 W. Broadway, 307/733-8744, www.macphailsburgers.com, 4pm-9pm Tues.-Sat., $14-32), a classic burger joint, but not cheap! They use premium Angus beef from local ranches and ground fresh daily. They also serve bison burgers, cheesesteaks, chicken sandwiches, and steak meals, plus salads and smaller meals. As is true at any good burger joint, the milk shakes are great. But so too are the locals brews.

Every ski town worth its salt needs a good hometown pizza joint. **Pizzeria Caldera** (20 W. Broadway, 307/201-1472, www. pizzeriacaldera.com, 11am-9:30pm daily, $10-17) serves up thin-crust Napoletana-style pizza baked over stone-hearth fires. Options range from classic Italian margherita to pure Jackson Hole, like the Bisonte, with bison sausage and fresh sage. There is also a great beer and wine list, plus yummy salads, pastas, and tapas.

Although it is every inch a Four Seasons, this is still Wyoming, and there is a casualness that puts visitors at ease here. The hotel has some exquisite restaurants, **Westbank Grill** (serving breakfast, lunch, and dinner) among them, but a great little spot is the **Ascent Lounge** (7680 Granite Loop Rd., Teton Village, 307/732-5000, www.fourseasons. com/jacksonhole, 3pm-11pm daily, $13-29), which feels like an oversize living room and serves casual but still elegant light fare with pan-Asian flair, including Thai chicken lettuce cups, tuna poke bowl, and salmon-hamachi avocado roll. It's smaller than the resort's other restaurants, with seating for 38. As it's quite popular with the locals, the overflow spills out onto the gorgeous mountainside patio that is heated in winter.

Also in Teton Village, a longtime favorite is the **Mangy Moose Restaurant and Saloon** (3295 Village Dr., 307/733-4913, www.mangymoose.com, 8am-9pm daily, saloon 11:30am-late daily summer and ski season, $17-40). The menu is packed with upscale pub fare including a bison burger with truffle fries, prime rib, baby back ribs, and grilled rainbow trout.

Right on the Town Square is one of Jackson's most celebrated eating establishments, the **Snake River Grill** (84 E. Broadway, 307/733-0557, www.snakerivergrill.com, 5:30pm-9:30pm daily summer, from 6pm daily winter, $21-66). A visual feast in addition to being a gastronomical delight, the Snake River Grill has largely defined Jackson

Hole cuisine with offerings like crispy pork shank, cast-iron roasted elk chop, and Wagyu boneless beef ribeye. The menu is diverse, constantly changing, and completely mouthwatering. It's worth noting that although children are welcome in the restaurant, no high chairs or children's menus are available.

Another elegant option for an unforgettable meal is at the Rusty Parrot's **Wild Sage** (175 N. Jackson St., 307/733-2000, www.rustyparrot. com, 5:30pm-9:30pm daily, $29-41). With only eight tables, the service is as notable as the food. From dry-aged duck to bison short ribs, Wild Sage has made quite a name for itself in the Intermountain West culinary scene. Reservations are strongly recommended.

ACCOMMODATIONS

While there are plenty of places to hang your hat in Jackson, during the prime seasons those places will not come cheap. In summer, there really is no such thing as a good deal. Just off Town Square, the **Anvil Motel** (215 N. Cache St., 800/234-4507, www.anvilmotel.com, $94-375), might be as close as you can get. The rooms are mountain-rustic with thoughtful details, custom furnishings, and some have air-conditioning.

Almost as close to Town Square but quite a bit higher on the luxury scale is **The Wort Hotel** (50 N. Glenwood St., 800/322-2727, www.worthotel.com, $158-799), built in 1941 and a landmark in town, complete with the legendary Silver Dollar Bar & Grill, which has more than 2,000 inlaid silver dollars as time capsule-type decorations. The rooms are plush, and the location is great. Just down the street, the **Rusty Parrot Lodge & Spa** (175 N. Jackson St., 307/733-2000 or 888/739-1749, www.rustyparrot.com, $230-515) is like a little oasis at the edge of town. From the onsite spa to the world-class dining at Wild Sage Restaurant, every little detail is well considered. The 31 rooms and suites are luxurious; some even have fireplaces and jetted tubs.

Just four blocks from Town Square, **Rustic Inn Creekside Resort & Spa** (475 N. Cache, 800/323-9279 or 307/733-2357, www.

rusticinnatjh.com, double queen rooms $149-809) is an oasis of calm. The creekside cabins are farther from the road and quieter, but the whole property is lovely on 12 acres (4.9 hectares) of beautiful landscaping. The log cabins are cozy and elegantly appointed. The spa is excellent, as are on-site dining options.

Although independent hotels and inns tend to reflect more of Jackson's charm, there are plenty of nice chain hotels, some of which can offer good deals, particularly in the off-season. Among them are **Hampton Inn** (350 S. Hwy. 89, 307/733-0033, www.hamptoninn3.hilton.com, $149-458); **Jackson Hole Super 8** (750 S. Hwy. 89, 307/733-6833, www.jacksonholesuper8.com, $79-284), which is steps away from the free bus service in town; and **Motel 6** (600 S. Hwy. 89, 307/733-1620, www.motel6.com, $82-209).

A comfortable bed-and-breakfast with easy access to both town and country is **Inn on the Creek** (295 N. Millward, 307/739-1565, www.innonthecreek.com, $149-359), which offers balconies, fireplaces, king beds, and private Jacuzzis in some of its rooms. Another very peaceful place to stay with a babbling creek to help lull you to sleep is the **Wildflower Lodge at Jackson Hole** (3725 Shooting Star Ln., Wilson, 307/733-4710, www.jhwildflowerlodge.com, 2 nights from $598), which boasts cozy handcrafted log beds, fluffy comforters, and delicious food. There's even a kids' bunk room with eight beds for families traveling together. There are minimum stays for the various accommodations.

For unparalleled luxury in the heart of this mountain village, Jackson has plenty of options. **Amangani** (1535 NE Butte Rd., 307/734-7333, www.amanresorts.com, from $800-2,450) is perched on the edge of a butte with stunning views from every window of meadows and mountains. In addition to deluxe suites and first-class service, Amangani rents spectacular homes. In Teton Village at the base of the ski hill, the five-star **Four Seasons Resort** (7680 Granite Loop Rd., 307/732-5000, www.fourseasons.com, from $315-3,500) offers ski-in/ski-out access with exquisite amenities including exquisite dining, a spa, and flawless service.

Away from the hustle and bustle of town, perched on a ridge overlooking the entire valley is the **Spring Creek Ranch** (1800 Spirit Dance Rd., 307/733-8833 or 800/443-6139, www.springcreekranch.com, from $200 spring and fall, $320 early summer, $400 summer, $200 winter), which boasts a variety of accommodations, including hotel rooms, cabins, condos, and exclusive mountain villas. The property is entirely self-contained with two restaurants on-site, a spa, and a slew of activities. The views from here beat just about everything else in the region, and the quiet gives Spring Creek Ranch tremendous appeal.

At Teton Village, **Hotel Terra** (3335 W. Village Dr., 307/201-6065 or 800/318-8707, www.hotelterrajacksonhole.com, $188-1,200) is a hip choice, at once luxurious and sustainable. The ecofriendly rooms have clean lines, retro-funky appointments, and lots of gadgets for techies, including iPod docking stations, flat-screen high-definition TVs, and Bose surround sound. The 132 guest rooms and suites range in size and style from urban studios and Terra guest rooms to one- to three-bedroom suites. There are two restaurants on-site, a lively bar, a rooftop swimming pool and hot tub, a day spa, and a fitness center.

GUEST RANCHES

For many visitors, the best way to enjoy Jackson Hole is to while away the days at a scenery-soaked dude ranch somewhere in the valley. After all, it was the dude ranches that jump-started Jackson's economy in the 1920s and 1930s. A multitude of wonderful choices are available, ranging from the historic and rustic, like the **Flat Creek Ranch** (15 bumpy mi/24 km from Jackson in isolated splendor, 307/733-0603 or 866/522-3344, www.flatcreekranch.com, 3-night stays in summer from $3,150 for 2 people, all-inclusive, 3-night stays in spring or fall $2,400 for 2 people, all inclusive, 7-night stays in summer $7,350 for 2 people, all inclusive), to the extravagant, like **Lost Creek Ranch & Spa** (17820 Old Ranch

Rd., Moose, 30 minutes north of Jackson, 307/733-3435, www.lostcreek.com, cabins from $5,500/week per cabin for 1-2 people), to the family-oriented, like the **Heart Six Guest Ranch** (Moran, 35 mi/56 km north of Jackson, 307/543-2477, www.heartsix.com, 1- to 3-bedroom cabins $199-299 nightly). There are options for every preference: proximity to town, emphasis on riding, this century or last, weekend or weeklong stays, and more.

For a comprehensive listing of the dude ranches in the vicinity of Jackson Hole, contact the **Dude Ranchers' Association** (866/399-2339 or 307/587-2339, www. duderanch.org).

CAMPING

Camping is by far the most economical way to stay in and around Jackson, and there are 14 campgrounds within a 15-mile (24-km) radius of downtown. Among the closest to town is the **Curtis Canyon Campground** (Flat Creek Rd., 8 mi/12.9 km northeast of Jackson, 307/739-5400, www.fs.usda.gov/ btnf, mid-May-early Sept., $15), which offers phenomenal views of the Tetons, immediate access to the National Elk Refuge, and terrific mountain hiking trails.

For more information on specific public campgrounds, contact the **Bridger-Teton National Forest** (340 N. Cache Dr., Jackson, 307/739-5500, www.fs.usda.gov).

For RV parks in Jackson, try the large and conveniently located **Virginian Lodge** (750 W. Broadway, 307/733-2792 or 800/262-4999, May 1-Oct. 15, www.virginianlodge.com), which has both motel rooms ($159-259 summer, $64-175 winter) and 103 RV sites (full hookups $110) in addition to all the amenities you could want, including laundry, a pool, a hot tub, a salon, a restaurant, and a saloon.

INFORMATION AND SERVICES

The most comprehensive spot to get information on the area is the **Jackson Hole and Greater Yellowstone Visitor Center** (532 N. Cache St., 307/733-3316, www.fws.

gov, 8am-7pm daily Memorial Day-Sept. 30, 9am-5pm daily Oct. 1-Memorial Day), which houses representatives from the Jackson Hole Chamber of Commerce (307/733-3316), the National Park Service, the Bridger-Teton National Forest, and four other agencies all under the same sod roof.

TRANSPORTATION
Getting There

The only airport within a national park, **Jackson Hole Airport** (JAC, 1250 E. Airport Rd., Jackson, 307/733-7682, www. jacksonholeairport.com) is served by American, Delta, United, and Frontier. The schedules change seasonally but include regular flights from Salt Lake City, Denver, Seattle, Chicago, Minneapolis, Dallas, Houston, Phoenix, San Francisco, and Los Angeles.

The major routes into Jackson Hole—including U.S. 89/191/287 from Yellowstone and Grand Teton National Parks, U.S. 26/287 from the east, Highway 22 from the west over Teton Pass, and U.S. 189/191/89 from the south—can all experience weather closures in the winter, particularly over Teton Pass. There is no car traffic in the southern portion of Yellowstone during the winter. For Wyoming **road reports,** call 800/WYO-ROAD (800/996-7623, www.wyoroad.info).

Jackson is roughly 240 miles (385 km) south of Bozeman, 177 miles (280 km) southwest of Cody through Yellowstone National Park, and 275 miles (445 km) northeast of Salt Lake City. Keep in mind that while distances through the national parks may be shorter in actual mileage, the time is often extended by lower speed limits, traffic congestion, and animal jams. In addition, most of the park roads are closed in winter, and car travel is not possible between Bozeman and Jackson or between Cody and Jackson. Driving distances around the parks increase significantly.

Getting Around

The airport has on-site car rentals from **Alamo, National, Hertz,** and **Enterprise.**

Avis/Budget, Dollar, and Thrifty are available off-site.

In town, **Alltrans** (307/733-3135 or 800/443-6133, www.jacksonholealltrans. com) provides airport shuttles and a variety of tours. Shuttles can also be arranged through **Jackson Hole Shuttle** (307/200-1400, www. jhshuttle.com).

Somewhat amazingly for this part of the country, Jackson has 32 taxi companies serving the area, including **Broncs Taxi** (307/413-9863, www.jackson-hole-taxi.com), **Snake River Taxi** (307/413-9009, www. snakerivertaxi.com), and **Teton Mountain Taxi** (307/699-7969, www.jacksonholecab. com). Transportation to Jackson from the airport runs roughly $40 for 1-2 people. A taxi to Teton Village averages $70. A complete list of taxi services can be found under the transportation heading on the airport website.

Pinedale

Like so many small communities that dot the West, Pinedale (population 1,895; elevation 7,201 ft/2,195 m) started as a ranch that doubled as a post office. Organized in 1904 and incorporated in 1912, the small community has an interesting mix of people and, thanks to the state's energy boom and extraction of natural gas nearby, some unavoidable growing pains.

Nestled between the western flank of the staggeringly beautiful Wind River Mountains and the 11-mile-long (17.7-km) Fremont Lake, Pinedale is a natural playground for hiking, climbing, sailing, and fishing. The other great pastime in these parts is history, and the town has done an excellent job of preserving it with the Museum of the Mountain Man and annual events like the Green River Rendezvous in July. Not necessarily a well-known destination, Pinedale, which is the county seat for Sublette County, is a natural stopping point between Jackson (78 mi/126 km north) and Rock Springs (100 mi/161 km south), with great access to some of Wyoming's most extraordinary mountains and lakes.

SIGHTS
Museum of the Mountain Man
The **Museum of the Mountain Man** (700 E. Hennick St., 307/367-4101 or 877/686-6266, www.museumofthemountainman. com, 9am-5pm daily May-Oct., $10 ages 13 and over, $8 seniors, free for children 12 and under) is dedicated to preserving the history of the fur trapping and trading era. Its exhibits are full of interesting artifacts and interpretive materials related to the Western fur trade and the life of Native Americans in the region during this period. Visitors can view Jim Bridger's rifle, learn about beaver trapping and the processing of fur, and see a full-size buffalo hide tipi (there are not many of these remaining in the United States) that has been extensively and authentically furnished. The museum also houses exhibits related to local history, including the settling of Sublette County and the development of Pinedale over the last 100 years.

Granite Hot Springs
En route from Jackson to Pinedale, some 12 miles (19.3 km) south of Hoback Junction on U.S. 189/191, is the turnoff for **Granite Hot Springs** (307/690-6323, 10am-8pm daily summer, 10am-6pm daily winter, $8 adults, $5 children). The 10-mile-long (16.1-km) scenic drive is on a gravel road that ends at the parking lot for the hot springs. Camping is allowed along the road but not within the last 1.5 miles (2.4 km) before the springs. In the winter the road is groomed to allow access on skis, snowshoes, snowmobiles, or dogsleds. The pool is situated below the Gros Ventre mountain range and was built by the Civilian Conservation Corps in 1933. The water is usually about 93°F (33.9°C) in the summer

and 112°F (44.4°C) in winter. There is a nice deck for lounging, and changing rooms are available. There is also a nearby 51-site campground (mid-May-late Sept., $15), run by the same people who manage the hot springs.

If you are visiting during the winter, a popular way to access the hot springs is by dogsled. **Jackson Hole Iditarod Sled Dog Tours** (307/733-7388 or 800/554-7388, www.jhsleddog.com), run by eight-time veteran of the Iditarod Frank Teasley, offers full-day trips to the hot springs and include a hearty lunch and a steak or trout dinner (prepared on-site while you are enjoying a dip in the springs). Other options include snowmobiling, cross-country skiing and fat-tire biking.

SPORTS AND RECREATION

Fremont Lake

The second-largest natural lake in the state, **Fremont Lake** (3.2 mi/5.2 km north of Pinedale, www.pinedale.com) was formed glacially and is more than 600 feet (183 m) deep in places. The lake was named for John C. Fremont, who mapped the area in 1842 in advance of the Oregon Trail. The lake is a natural recreation site with opportunities for boating, sailing, waterskiing, fishing, and camping. Though there are no designated hiking trails around the lake, most of the shoreline is undeveloped and can be walked on. The 54 RV and tent campsites at **Fremont Lake Campground** ($12-24), operated by the U.S. Forest Service at the lower end of the lake, are generally open late-May-early September and can be reserved through www.recreation.gov (877/444-6777). Also at the lower end of the lake, the **Sandy Beach** picnic area is for day use only.

For an incredibly scenic drive or bike ride, **Skyline Drive** is a 16-mile (26-km) paved road along the lake's eastern shore that leads to a campground and hiking trails at the edge of the Bridger Wilderness.

The only commercial facility at Fremont Lake is the idyllic **Lakeside Lodge Resort & Marina** (99 Forest Service Rd.

111, 307/367-2221 or 877/755-5253, www.lakesidelodge.com, year-round), which offers 12 beautiful cabins ($59-179), a full-service restaurant (307/367-3555, lunch and dinner daily summer, dinner daily winter), and fishing boat rentals ($60 half-day, $95 full-day), pontoon boats ($200 half-day, $375 full-day), and ski boats ($60/hour, $250 half-day, $425 full-day), plus stand-up paddleboards, kayaks, and canoes.

Fishing and Boating

There are literally hundreds of lakes in the vicinity of Pinedale that contain several species of trout and a few Montana grayling, as well as an assortment of freestone waterways that include the world-class Green, Hoback, and New Fork Rivers. Wild trout abound in smaller streams too, including Faler Creek, Fish Creek, and North Cottonwood Creek in the Wyoming Range, some of which are private-lease streams.

The best place to start any fishing expedition is at **Two Rivers Emporium** (211 W. Pine St., 307/367-4131, www.2rivers.net, 8am-7pm daily in high season, reduced hours off-season), which can outfit you from rod to leader to fly and offers a range of guided trips (float fishing from $399/half-day, $499/full day for 1-2 people), including wading on private waters, backcountry and llama treks. Trips can include lodging and gourmet meals.

With so many lakes in the region, canoeing is a wonderful and quiet way to navigate the myriad waterways. Lake-use canoe and kayak rentals ($35/day) and stand-up paddleboards ($45/day) are available in town from the **Great Outdoor Shop** (332 W. Pine St., 307/367-2440, www.greatoutdoorshop.com, 8am-9pm Mon.-Sat., 8am-8pm Sun.). It also offers an amazing range of services, including guided fishing trips and gear rental, shuttles to the best trailheads and the airport in Jackson, backpacking, and gear rentals for rock or ice climbing.

Motorized and nonmotorized boats are available for rent on Fremont Lake at **Lakeside Lodge Resort & Marina** (99 FS

Rd. 111, 877/755-5253, www.lakesidelodge. com, $15-60/hour with 2-hour minimum).

Hiking and Rock Climbing

The Wind River and Wyoming Ranges, which include the Jim Bridger and Gros Ventre Wilderness Areas, offer some of the best hiking and climbing in the state. Hundreds of miles of trails crisscross the area and give hikers and backpackers access to hundreds of thousands of acres of gorgeous alpine and subalpine terrain. Many of the trailheads are at 9,000 feet (2,743 m) and higher, so be prepared for significant and immediate changes in the weather. Prime hiking season this high is short—mid-July-mid-September—and it can snow any day of the year. Average daytime summer temperatures peak in the 70s and 80s Fahrenheit, with nighttime lows dropping into the 30s Fahrenheit. Afternoons often bring rainstorms with lightning, so be prepared to get lower in a hurry. Always be aware that this is black bear and grizzly bear country, so plan ahead to bring pepper spray.

Among the favorites in the area is the easily accessible **Elkhart Park Trail,** the only one accessed by a paved road, just 15 miles (24 km) northeast of Pinedale. The heavily hiked trail departs from the **Trails End Campground** at 9,100 feet (2,774 m) in elevation. Great day hikes will lead you into the Wind River Mountains and places like **Photographer's Point** and **Miller Lake.** A staffed Forest Service visitors center at the Elkhart Park trailhead can provide information about trails and trail conditions.

Another excellent series of trails is in the **Green River Lakes,** 52 miles (84 km) north of Pinedale (31 paved mi/50 km and 21 mi/34 km of good gravel). The **Hiline Trail,** among others, starts at a 39-site campground at 8,000 feet (2,438 m) in elevation and runs almost the length of the Winds, 80 miles (129 km) south over jaw-droppingly beautiful terrain. There are several fishable lakes in the area and an abundance of ways to enjoy a day hike.

For more information on specific trails, conditions, and maps, contact the **Bridger-Teton National Forest office** (29 E. Fremont Lake Rd., Pinedale, 307/367-4326, www.fs.usda.gov).

Mountain Biking

The 2,700-mile (4,345-km) **Great Divide Mountain Bike Route** from Banff, Alberta, to the U.S.-Mexican border, along the spine of the Rockies, passes directly through Pinedale. There is plenty of good rugged terrain to be explored by mountain bike. Due to the weather, however, most trails are only good for biking 3-5 months of the year. **Sweeny Creek** and **Grouse Mountain Trails** have some good short rides, or for the more adventurous (and fit), try the ride up **Half Mountain.** From the top you can bike almost the entire length of the ridge and take in some spectacular views. Other favorite local spots for mountain biking include **Kelly Park, Fortification Mountain,** and **The Old Skyline Drive.**

During the summer, **White Pine Ski Resort** (74 White Pine Rd., 10 mi/16.1 km northeast of Pinedale, 307/367-6606) is open to mountain bikers who aren't afraid of a good climb or fast downhill ride. Special biking trails for all levels of experience have been groomed for the ride downhill. For a more tranquil and scenic ride, opt for one of the flatter cross-country trails. There are also plenty of trails in the vicinity, including some which lead to Kelly Park.

For more trail ideas in the Pinedale area, visit www.singletracks.com.

Skiing

The state's oldest ski area, **White Pine Ski Resort** (74 White Pine Rd., 10 mi/16.1 km northeast of Pinedale, 307/367-6606, www. whitepineski.com, all-day $48 adults, $35 youth and seniors, $6 children 5 and under) is tucked in the Bridger-Teton National Forest above Fremont Lake. Though relatively small

---

1: hiking in the Green River Lakes area
2: performers at Eastern Shoshone Indian Days
3: kayak on Green River Lakes

JACKSON HOLE AND CODY
PINEDALE

when compared to others in the Jackson area, the resort is a wonderful family-oriented ski hill with lodging, two restaurants, rentals, and free cross-country skiing in winter.

In summer, the mountain is open for mountain biking, hiking, horseback riding, and, because of its proximity to the lake, fishing.

Horseback Riding

The Bridger-Teton National Forest is a wonderful experience on horseback. The **White Pine Ski Resort** (74 White Pine Rd., 10 mi/16.1 km northeast of Pinedale, 307/367-6606, www.whitepineski.com) offers multi- and single-night pack trips. One amazing option is the overnight pack trip to Sweeney Lake (from $450 pp), during which anglers can fish for prized golden trout. An excellent outfitter with a stellar reputation for everything from horseback riding and snowmobiling trips to hunting and fishing is **Green River & Bridger-Teton Outfitters** (138-2 Forty Rod Rd., 307/733-1044, www.grbto.com). Among the offerings are two-hour rides (from $85 pp) through meadows and thick timber, half-day-plus (from $185 pp) rides through mountain meadows and along a stream to a historic log cabin for lunch, and all-day rides (from $250 pp) through alpine terrain. Those who want to book an exclusive trip (without other guests) have that option for increased rates (2-hour rides from $150 pp with 4-person minimum, half-day from $295 pp with 4-person minimum, and full day from $495 pp with 4-person minimum.)

Golf

At the west end of town, **Rendezvous Meadows Golf Course** (Club House Rd., 307/367-4252, www.golfpinedale.com, $20 for 9 holes, $27 for 18 holes, carts $10 for 9 holes and $15 for 18 holes) is a nice nine-hole public course.

ENTERTAINMENT AND EVENTS

The **Green River Rendezvous** (307/367-2242, www.meetmeonthegreen.com) is a huge community event that takes place the second full weekend of July. The city prides itself on the fact that 6 of the 15 Rocky Mountain Rendezvous were held here in the Green River Valley at Horse Creek. The first rendezvous was held in 1825 and continued each summer until 1840. For about three weeks trappers, traders, and Native Americans would come together to trade and resupply their outfits, exchange stories, catch up with old friends, get incredibly drunk, and participate in all sorts of boisterous behavior.

Today the Green River Rendezvous is more family-friendly while still bringing the era of the mountain man to life. There are plenty of games, crafts, living history demonstrations, guest speakers, a mountain man encampment, programs for children, and a rodeo. The pageant, which is usually held on Sunday, should not be missed. It is an entertaining reenactment of an 1830s rendezvous. The participants, in original costumes, are lively characters who barter, trade, and duel.

A newer addition to the summer lineup is the **Wind River Mountain Festival** (www.windriverfest.com), held in late July. In addition to concerts, you'll find music, yoga, hiking, camping, gear demos and workshops, a craft beer fest, and other adventures. The events are held in Pinedale at the American Legion Park. On the Sunday of the festival, adventurers can compete in the three-person-team Surly Pika Adventure Race—a biking, hiking, boating extravaganza to various checkpoints—in either the 6-hour or 12-hour divisions.

FOOD

For authentic Mexican and big, juicy burgers, **Los Cabos** (120 W. Pine St., 307/367-6781, 11am-9pm Sun.-Thurs., 11am-10:30pm Fri.-Sat., $10-15) is the spot. Tuesday nights are burger specials that bring a lot of locals out.

For a fun evening with excellent beer, try the **Wind River Brewing Company** (402 W. Pine St., 307/367-2337, www.windriverbrewingco.com, 11am-11pm Sun.-Thurs., 11am-midnight Fri.-Sat., $10-26) for great salads, appetizers, sandwiches, burgers, and steaks. Its award-winning handcrafted ales are the icing on the cake.

A good place for a filling meal for the whole family is **Old Stones Smokehouse & Country Pizza** (4 Country Club Ln., 307/367-6760, www.windriverpizza.com, 11am-9pm Mon.-Sat., 11am-8pm Sun., $13-27), which serves barbecue and gourmet stone-hearth pizza, plus calzones, pasta, salads, and all variety of bar-type appetizers. There's also a salad, soup, and pizza buffet ($5 children 3-8, $9-10 adults).

A unique dinner option that reflects the people and culture of Pinedale is the family-run ★ **Pitchfork Fondue** (9888 U.S. 191, 307/367-3607, www.pitchforkfondue.com, 5pm-8:30pm Thurs.-Sat., late May into Sept., $30 adult steak or chicken, $16 buffet only), an ingenious Western outdoor cookout at the fairgrounds south of town. Tender steaks are seared in large cast-iron cauldrons of oil (yes, on pitchforks) and served with fondue sauces, hot homemade potato chips, fruit salad, green salad, beverages, and homemade brownies. There are options for vegetarians too. The picnic tables can accommodate 240 people, but call ahead for reservations and current pricing.

ACCOMMODATIONS

Because of a population boom driven by the energy industry, there are quite a few accommodations in and around Pinedale, particularly given the size of the town. **The Log Cabin Motel** (49 E. Magnolia St., 307/367-4579, www.thelogcabinmotel.com, $59-179) is as charming as it is conveniently located. Built in 1929, the motel lives up to its name by remaining true to Pinedale's architectural style. The cabins vary in size, but most are quite spacious with partial or full kitchens, covered porches, satellite TV, and Wi-Fi. A comfortable and more modern option is the pet-friendly **Sundance Motel** (148 E. Pine St., 307/367-4789, $79-145), which offers singles, doubles, triples, and even a bunk room. The doubles and triples have kitchenettes.

The **Chambers House Bed & Breakfast** (111 W. Magnolia St., 307/367-2168, www.chambershouse.com, $89-189) is a charming inn, the oldest in the state, and run by a historian. There are seven cozy rooms and great breakfasts. Pets are welcome for a fee.

Three-and-a-half miles (5.6 km) out of town, a great lakeside resort is the **Lakeside Lodge Resort & Marina** (99 Forest Service Rd. 111, 307/367-2221 or 877/755-5253, www.lakesidelodge.com, year-round), which offers 12 beautiful cabins ($59-179), and a full-service restaurant (307/367-3555, lunch and dinner daily summer, dinner daily winter), all with immediate waterfront access and splendid views.

CAMPING

Sublette County is 80 percent public land, making camping in the region a viable option. The closest (and happily, the most scenic) RV and tent campsites can be found at **Fremont Lake Campground** (5 mi/8 km northeast of Pinedale, www.recreation.gov, late May-early Sept., $12-24) and the **Half Moon Lake Campground** (10 mi/16.1 km northeast of Pinedale, late May-early Sept., 877/444-6777, www.recreation.gov, $7). There is no potable water at Half Moon Lake, and 11 of its spots can be reserved.

For more information on U.S. Forest Service campgrounds and backcountry camping, contact the **Bridger-Teton National Forest office** (29 E. Fremont Lake Rd., Pinedale, 307/367-4326, www.fs.usda.gov).

INFORMATION AND SERVICES

The **Sublette County Visitor Center** (19 E. Pine St., 307/367-2242 or 888/285-7282, www.sublettechamber.com, 9am-6pm daily summer, 9am-5pm Mon.-Fri. winter) can provide information about the local area and the region for everything from hiking trails to fishing guides and up-to-date event calendars.

Two comprehensive websites for activities and businesses in the area are www.pinedaleonline.com and www.visitpinedale.org.

The **Sublette County Library** (155 S. Tyler Ave., 307/367-4114, www.sublettecountylibrary.org, 10am-8pm Mon.-Fri., 10am-5pm Sat.) offers plenty of interesting events in addition to its sizable collection. Free Wi-Fi is provided, and public computers with free internet access are available for 30 minutes at a time.

Though the nearest hospital is 78 miles (126 km) north in Jackson, Pinedale is served by the **Pinedale Medical Clinic** (625 E. Hennick St., 307/367-4133, 8am-5pm Mon.-Fri.).

TRANSPORTATION
Getting There
The nearest commercial airports are in Jackson (78 mi/126 km), Rock Springs (100 mi/161 km), Idaho Falls, Idaho (190 mi/305 km), and Salt Lake City (250 mi/405 km). Private jets can be accommodated at **Pinedale Wenz Field** (307/367-4136 or 307/367-6425).

Rental cars are available in Jackson and Rock Springs. The closest Greyhound bus service is also in Rock Springs.

Getting Around
For shuttle service in Pinedale, the **Great Outdoor Transportation Company** (322 W. Pine St., www.gotcoshuttle.com, 307/367-1764) offers taxi service, gear drops, and fishing shuttles, and shuttles from the airports in Jackson and Rock Springs.

Lander

Tucked in the foothills of the Wind River Mountains on the banks of the Popo Agie (po-PO-zhuh) River and adjacent to the Wind River Indian Reservation, Lander (population 7,665; elevation 5,357 ft/1,633 m) is an outdoors lover's town and a vibrant, growing community. The area was first visited by fur trappers as early as 1811, and oil was discovered in 1824 but not developed until the mid-1880s. The area was the home ground of Chief Washakie and his Shoshone. In 1869 a small military post was established here to protect the Shoshone from enemies that included the Sioux and Arapaho. The valley, once known by Native Americans as Pushroot for its fertile soil, was farmed early on to great success thanks to the soil, relatively mild winters, and little wind.

Not a large town by any stretch, Lander is a welcoming place with friendly people, a decidedly outdoor-oriented culture, and immediate access to some of the most stunningly rugged wilderness in the country.

SIGHTS
Wind River Reservation
The **Wind River Reservation** sits on 2.2 million acres (890,308 hectares) and is home to more than 8,600 Northern Arapaho (www.northernarapahoe.com) and 3,900 Eastern Shoshone (www.easternshoshone.org) tribal members. It surrounds the city of Riverton, with the towns of Lander, Shoshoni, and Thermopolis close to its borders. There is not a lot of intermingling between the native and nonnative communities, or between the Arapaho and Shoshone themselves, for that matter; the arrangement to leave both tribes on the same reservation was decided by the U.S. government without their consent. The western part of the reservation, including the towns of Fort Washakie, Burris, and Crowheart, is occupied by the Shoshone, and the eastern part, including the towns of Ethete and Arapaho, are occupied by the Arapaho. Although the reservation struggles with problems of poverty and unemployment, it is also home to an incredibly rich history, important traditions, and pristine wilderness.

A drive through the reservation affords visitors magnificent views of Wyoming's undeveloped natural beauty and the majestic Wind River Mountains. The reservation is easily accessible by car, and its roads are open to visitors. If you'd like to hike, fish, camp, or boat, however, access is restricted to certain parts of the reservation, and a recreation fee or fishing permit is required. Hunting by nonnatives is not allowed. The chambers of commerce in Lander, Riverton, and Dubois can provide more information about fees and permits. Fort Washakie is also the location of the **Shoshone Tribal Cultural Center** (90 Ethete Rd., 307/332-3515, 9am-4pm Mon.-Fri.) and the gravesites of the two most prominent Shoshone, Chief Washakie (it was his hometown) and Lewis and Clark's fearless guide Sacagawea. Be sure to call ahead since the cultural center is located in the school library and closes when school is not in session.

The biggest draw to the reservation is the powwows held throughout the summer season. These large cultural celebrations usually take place over a three-day weekend and include dancing, singing, parades, and traditional games. Competitors come from across the country, and both tribes host their own powwows. The largest Shoshone powwow is the **Eastern Shoshone Indian Days Powwow and Rodeo** (307/332-9106 or 307/349-7089), an all-Indian rodeo usually held the fourth weekend in June. The event hosts more than 700 dancers and 15 professional drumming groups. The largest Arapaho powwow is the **Ethete Celebration** (307/223-6430 or 307/438-3706) in late July. For additional information about the powwows and weekly events, contact the **Wind River Heritage Center** (307/856-0706, www.windriverheritagecenter. com) or the **Wind River Visitor's Council** (307/332-5546, www.windriver.org).

★ Sinks Canyon State Park

A place that is as beautiful as it is fascinating, **Sinks Canyon State Park** (3079 Sinks Canyon Rd., 6 mi/9.7 km south of Lander, 307/332-6333 or 307/332-3077, www.

sinkscanyonstatepark.org, sunrise-10pm daily, visitors center 9am-6pm daily Memorial Day-Labor Day, free) is filled with recreational opportunities and one of the state's geological wonders. Here in the canyon is where the Middle Fork of the Popo Agie River plunges into a cave, only to emerge 0.5 mile (0.8 km) away in an area known as the Rise. What makes it so interesting is that geologists have determined that it takes more than two hours for the water to make the journey. In addition, there is plenty of water emerging at the Rise that did not enter at the Sinks. Adding yet another layer of mystery is that the water is a couple of degrees warmer when it emerges than when it disappeared.

Aside from its geological and scenic attributes, Sinks Canyon is a fantastic place for hiking, rock climbing, fishing (but not in the trout-laden waters at the Rise, where vending machines dole out food for these lunkers), and wildlife-watching. Keep your eyes peeled for transplanted bighorn sheep, moose, and any number of bird species.

Loop Road

Among the most scenic drives in the region, and perhaps the state, is a roughly 70-mile (113-km) seasonal route known locally as the **Loop Road.** From Lander, follow the signs to Sinks Canyon State Park via Highway 131. Just beyond Bruce's Camp parking area, the 32-mile (52-km) Loop Road climbs past Frye Lake, Fiddler's Lake, and Louis Lake to a junction that leads south to South Pass City Historic Site or north to Atlantic City and Highway 28, which brings travelers 35 miles (56 km) back to Lander. Along the way, the Wind River Range unfolds in all its majesty, and hikers will have no shortage of trailheads to amble down. Because of its extreme altitude, the road is often not open until July due to snow, and it closes as early as September again because of snow.

South Pass City Historic Site

One of the region's few gold mines, **South Pass City Historic Site** (125 S. Pass Main St.,

Peaceful Coexistence:
The Shoshone and the Arapaho

The Treaty of Fort Bridger, signed in 1863, designated 44 million acres (17.8 million hectares) as "Shoshone Country." This large parcel of land not only included territory in Wyoming but also crossed into Colorado, Utah, and Idaho. However, there was no formal demarcation, and settlers and migrants continued to settle the land in the south, up into the Green River Valley, forcing the Shoshone into Arapaho territory in order to hunt. Furthermore, gold was discovered near South Pass, and coal near Rock Springs, and both mining towns and farms were popping up along the Wind River drainage.

In 1868, another treaty was signed, establishing the much smaller 2.2-million-acre (890,308-hectare) Wind River Reservation. For a variety of reasons, land continued to be ceded to the government, including the Popo Agie Valley and the present-day towns of Shoshoni and Thermopolis. Shoshone Chief Washakie bartered determinedly to improve life on the reservation for his people. He asked for specific physical improvements, goods, and protection from their Indian enemies. (Fort Brown, renamed Fort Washakie in 1878, resulted from this bargaining.) Today the reservation stretches 70 miles (113 km) west-east and 55 miles (89 km) north-south and is home to about 3,900 Eastern Shoshone and 8,600 Northern Arapaho.

Understanding why two tribes, historically great enemies, would share the same reservation requires a history lesson and some imagination. By 1877, most Native Americans had been relocated to reservations, yet the Northern Arapaho remained landless. With winter rapidly approaching, the U.S. government turned to Chief Washakie, requesting that the Shoshone share their reservation with the Arapaho just for the winter. Washakie conceded, but made it clear that by spring the visitors must be relocated. Spring came and went with Washakie repeatedly demanding that the Arapaho be removed from the reservation. His pleas fell on deaf ears, and the former archenemies were forced to make the best of the situation.

They each established their own governments and mostly occupied separate parts of the reservation. The Arapaho settled the eastern part of the land, with the towns of Ethete and Arapaho as their hubs; the Shoshone developed the western portion, which includes the towns of Fort Washakie, Burris, and Crowheart. Although there have been few major conflicts, the two cultures tend to keep to their own with little interest in intermixing.

Today the reservation has some incredibly beautiful vistas of the Wind River Valley and its craggy mountains. Standing in the middle of its pristine wilderness, it's not evident that oil and gas fields are the primary source of revenue for the reservation. Although plagued by unemployment and poverty, the two tribes possess great cultural pride, explicitly expressed each May-September through a series of powwows and other cultural celebrations.

For more information on the Wind River Reservation, or to plan a visit, contact the **Wind River Heritage Center** (1075 S. Federal Blvd., Riverton, 307/856-0706, www.windriverheritagecenter. com, 10am-4pm Mon.-Sat.).

35 mi/56 km south of Lander, 2 mi/3.2 km off Hwy. 28, 307/332-3684, www.southpasscity. com, early May-Sept., $4 nonresidents, $2 residents) is a beautifully restored site with 20 original log, frame, and stone structures including the jail, a livery, a stable, a school, saloons, and homes. The city was founded in 1867 and, in addition to its mining legacy, is well remembered for its pivotal role in women's suffrage. A territorial representative from South Pass City, William Bright, introduced the bill that made Wyoming the first territory to grant women the right to vote in 1869; South Pass City's justice of the peace, Esther Hobart Morris, was the first woman to hold political office in the United States.

The South Pass Hotel has been refurbished to give visitors a sense of 1880s Wyoming. The Smith-Sherlock General Store is open for shopping, and the Miner's Exchange Saloon

Sinks Canyon and South Pass Area

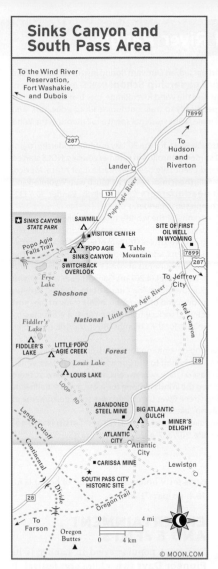

To the Wind River Reservation, Fort Washakie, and Dubois

7899

287

To Hudson and Riverton

Lander

131

SINKS CANYON STATE PARK

SAWMILL

VISITOR CENTER

SITE OF FIRST OIL WELL IN WYOMING

Popo Agie Falls Trail

POPO AGIE SINKS CANYON

Table Mountain

7899

287

SWITCHBACK OVERLOOK

Frye Lake

To Jeffrey City

Shoshone

Red Canyon

Fiddler's Lake

National

Little Popo Agie River

FIDDLER'S LAKE

LITTLE POPO AGIE CREEK

Forest

28

Louis Lake

LOUIS LAKE

LOOP RD

Lander Cutoff

ABANDONED STEEL MINE

BIG ATLANTIC GULCH

MINER'S DELIGHT

Continental

ATLANTIC CITY

Atlantic City

CARISSA MINE

Lewiston

SOUTH PASS CITY HISTORIC SITE

28

Divide

Oregon Trail

To Farson

Oregon Buttes

0   4 mi

0   4 km

© MOON.COM

offers visitors a chance to shoot pool on an 1840s billiards table.

Every year in mid-July, **Gold Rush Days** celebrates the town's heritage with a vintage baseball tournament, food, entertainment, and interpretive programs. The town's **Carissa Mine** was purchased by the state, overhauled significantly for safety, and can

now be toured. There's also a nice 1.6-mile (2.6-km) trail, the **Flood & Hindle Mining Trail,** which winds along the creek through willows and pine forest. Guided walks are offered at 11am every Saturday in July and August. Reservations are strongly suggested and can be made online.

SPORTS AND RECREATION

Hiking and Rock Climbing

Known as the roof of Wyoming and the spine of the Rockies, the Wind River Range offers phenomenal hiking and climbing from Lander. Among the trails accessible from the Loop Road between Sinks Canyon State Park and South Pass City are the easy 7-mile (11.3-km) **Christina Lake Trail,** the easy-to-moderate 6.5-mile (10.5-km) **Louis Lake Trail,** and the difficult 17-mile (27-km) multiuse **Shoshone Lake Trail.**

For hiking that is somewhat closer to Lander, with scenery no less dramatic, **Sinks Canyon State Park** (www.sinkscanyonstatepark.org) offers 6 miles (9.7 km) of easy-to-moderate trails in a figure-eight layout.

For expert guidance and equipment related to rock climbing, the best resource in town is **Wild Iris Mountain Sports** (166 Main St., 307/332-4541, www.wildirisclimbing.com, 9am-7pm Mon.-Fri., 9am-6:30pm Sat., 10am-5pm Sun.), named for one of the region's best-known climbing areas. Another renowned spot for climbers is Sinks Canyon State Park.

For more information on trails and conditions, contact the Shoshone National Forest's **Washakie Ranger Office** (333 Hwy. 789 S., 307/332-5460, www.fs.usda.gov, 8am-4:30pm Mon.-Fri.).

Fishing

With the Wind River Range as an impressive backdrop to Lander, the fishing in this part of the state varies from crystalline alpine lakes to small but productive rivers, including the **Wind River, Bull Lake Creek,**

NOLS and the Wind River Range

In 1965, one year after the Wilderness Act had passed, an Outward Bound instructor named Paul Petzoldt founded the **National Outdoor Leadership School** (NOLS) in Sinks Canyon. Having spent much of his youth in the Tetons and the Wind River Range, much of which was not even mapped, Petzoldt created a school specifically to train outdoor leaders, educators, and conservationists. That year, a small group of male NOLS students spent a full month in the Wind River Range.

Within a year, female students were admitted to NOLS for the 30-day outdoor leadership training in the Winds, and in 1970, more than 750 students enrolled in summer courses. NOLS started branching out in the 1970s with programs (and eventually bases) in Alaska, East Africa, Mexico, Idaho, and Washington's Northern Cascades. Still, the school never lost touch with Wyoming and the Winds, and in 2002 an impressive **world headquarters** (284 Lincoln St., Lander, 307/332-5300 or 800/710-6657, www.nols.edu) was completed in Lander.

So what are these mountains that gave rise to one of the world's most esteemed wilderness education programs?

The Wind River Range cuts through Wyoming with 100 miles (161 km) of jagged peaks, crystal-line lakes, boulder-strewn meadows, two national forests, and three pristine wilderness areas. The range has 48 summits topping 12,000 feet (3,658 m), 8 summits above 13,500 feet (4,115 m), and seven of the largest glaciers in the Lower 48. At 13,804 feet (4,207 m), Gannett Peak is the crown of this magnificent range and the highest peak in the state. The Cirque of the Towers, 10 miles (16.1 km) into the Bridger Wilderness at the southern end of the range, offers some of the most scenic hiking in the Lower 48, and plenty of technical rock climbing. The Winds are bisected by the Continental Divide to form three major drainages for the Columbia River, the Colorado River, and the Missouri River.

The area has long been a favorite backpacking destination for the adventurous, and access is possible from both the east and west sides. In addition to the Continental Divide Trail, which traverses the range from South Pass to Union Pass on its way between Canada and Mexico, there are hundreds of miles of hiking trails crisscrossing the Winds. Among the more popular trailheads are Big Sandy, Boulder Creek, Elkhart Park, and Green River Lakes. For more solitude, try some of the low-use trailheads like Burnt Lake, Half Moon Lake, and Meadow Lake.

For information on trails and backcountry regulations, contact the **Bridger-Teton National Forest office** (29 E. Fremont Lake Rd., Pinedale, 307/367-4326, www.fs.usda.gov).

the **Sweetwater River,** and various forks of the **Popo Agie River.** Unlike most of the state, the fishing around Lander is exclusively wade fishing.

Daily guided fishing trips can be arranged through **Sweetwater Fishing Expeditions** (2939 Sinks Canyon Rd., 307/332-3986, www.sweetwaterfishing.com), which offer a variety of adventures that include day trips ($460-495 for 1-2 anglers), 5- to 10-day expeditions ($1,955-2,755 pp), and horseback ($1,000-1,500 pp) trips. Shorter trips can be arranged.

Golf

The **Lander Golf Club** (1 Golf Course Dr., 307/332-4653, $21 for 9 holes, $27 for 18, $10 carts for 9 holes, $18 carts for 18 holes) is an 18-hole, par-71 course.

ENTERTAINMENT AND EVENTS

The most popular event in Lander is its **Pioneer Days** (www.lotra.org) festival. It takes place around the Fourth of July and includes a parade, Indian dancing, a buffalo barbecue, fireworks, and a nightly rodeo ($10 adults, $5 children 6-12). The rodeo celebrates 125 years in 2019, making it the oldest paid rodeo in the world.

A much younger but also entertaining event is the **Lander Brew Fest** (307/332-3892 or 800/433-0662, www.landerbrewfest.com), which takes place in mid-June. More than 28 breweries from the Rocky Mountain region participate, allowing visitors to sample more than 80 different types of beer while enjoying family-friendly music, food, and games.

The **International Climber's Festival** (307/349-1561, www.climbersfestival.org,) is held each July and attracts outdoors enthusiasts from around the world. The festival features lectures, activities, social events, and a trade show. Visit the website to check which events require tickets.

Lander is also a stop on the **Pedigree Stage Stop Dog Race** (307/734-1163, www.wyomingstagestop.org), which takes place late January-early February.

Stop by the **Lander Area Chamber of Commerce** (160 N. 1st St., 307/332-3892 or 800/433-0662, http://landerchamber.org, 8am-5pm Mon.-Fri., 10am-4pm Sat.-Sun. summer, 8am-5pm Mon.-Fri. fall-spring) to get more information or to buy tickets for any of the events in town.

FOOD

With so many ways to burn energy, it's surprising that there aren't more eateries to refuel. Still, you won't starve in Lander. **The Breadboard** (1350 W. Main St., 307/332-6090, 11am-7pm Mon.-Fri., 11am-4pm Sat.-Sun., $4-12) has been serving up soup and subs for more than 30 years. Don't miss the green chili! A hub of the community in more ways than one, The Breadboard donates proceeds from refills ($0.25) to local charities.

Foodies in Lander need look no farther than four wonderful establishments, owned by the same folks and sharing one historic block downtown. ★ **Cowfish** (148 Main St., 307/332-8227, www.cowfishlander.com; 8am-2pm and 5pm-9pm daily, $17-31) offers an assortment of fresh seafood, salads, steaks, pasta, and homemade desserts impressive enough to make you forget you are in Wyoming; it's impossible to leave hungry. Right next door, the **Gannett Grill/Lander Bar** (126 Main St., 307/332-8228, www.landerbar.com, 11am-9pm daily, $7-29) is a local favorite with hand-tossed pizzas, juicy burgers made from local beef, gorgeous salads from the on-site organic garden, and locally brewed beer. The outdoor dining option is insanely popular when the weather is good. **Scream Shack** (11am-10pm daily summer) at the Gannett Grill operates in the summer, serving delicious ice cream and thick shakes. The choke cherry shake is delicious. For drinks, **Coalter Loft** (5pm-10pm Thurs.-Fri.) is an elegant bar with a second-story deck overlooking Main Street; its trivia night (7pm-10pm Thurs.) is good fun.

ACCOMMODATIONS

Since it's a great launching point into the Winds, Lander's number of accommodations is growing. Chain hotels include the shiny new and extremely comfortable **Holiday Inn Express & Suites** (1002 11th St., 307/332-4005 or 800/465-4329, www.ihg.com, $122-183), plus the **Inn at Lander** (260 Grand View Dr., 307/332-2847 or 866/452-6337, www.book.bestwestern.com, $72-140), which has 101 guest rooms as well as an on-site restaurant, guest laundry, and a year-round hot tub. The **Rodeway Inn Pronghorn Lodge** (150 E. Main St., 307/332-3940 or 800/424-6423, www.choicehotels.com, $88-108) is another good bet in town.

For a more historical and completely unique option, the **Miner's Delight Inn Bed & Breakfast** (290 Atlantic City Rd., Atlantic City, 307/332-0248, www.minersdelightinn.com, 2-night minimum in summer, $100-130) offers both rooms and cabins, which share a bathroom in the inn. The inn was still for sale as of 2018, so keep an eye on the website.

Five miles (8 km) outside of town, at the foot of the Winds, are the ★ **Outlaw Cabins** (2411 Squaw Creek Rd., 307/332-9655 or 877/732-9655, www.outlawcabins.com, $125, year-round), two cozy, handcrafted log cabins set on the Wunder Ranch. Each cabin is private and comes with a kitchenette and loft area. A stream runs through the property, and there is plenty of wildlife to be watched. The hosts are warm and friendly and will gladly tell you stories of the four outlaws who were supposedly buried on the property.

CAMPING

As evidence of the community's commitment to the outdoor experience, free overnight camping is permitted for up to three nights in Lander's **City Park** (405 Fremont St.). RVs are invited to park in the parking lot.

The best public camping is found in **Sinks Canyon State Park** (3079 Sinks Canyon Rd., 6 mi/9.7 km south of Lander, 307/332-6333 or 307/332-3077, www.sinkscanyonstatepark. org, $11 nonresidents, $6 residents), which has two primitive state park campgrounds: **Sawmill** and **Popo Agie.** Four camping yurts ($40/night plus the camping fee), with a bunk bed, futon, dining table and two chairs, electric lighting and grill, can be reserved year-round at www.wyo-park.com. There is also one campground on the national forest, **Sinks Campground** ($15). Several national forest campgrounds are located along the Loop Road, including sites at **Louis Lake** ($15), **Fiddlers Lake** ($15), and **Worthen Meadow** ($15). No advanced reservations are available. **Showers** are available in town at the community swimming pool (450 S. 9th St.) and the NOLS campus (284 Lincoln St.).

Sleeping Bear RV Park and Campground (715 E. Main St., 307/332-5159 or 888/757-2327, www.sleepingbearrvpark. com) offers 4 tent sites ($24), 40 full RV hookup sites ($43-46), 6 water and electric hookup sites ($37.50), cabins with shared bath ($48), and cabins with private bath ($58). Amenities include Wi-Fi, picnic tables, and fire rings, plus access to clean bathrooms with showers.

INFORMATION AND SERVICES

The **Lander Area Chamber of Commerce** (160 N. 1st St., 307/332-3892 or 800/433-0662, http://landerchamber.org, 8am-5pm Mon.-Fri., 10am-4pm Sat.-Sun. summer, 8am-5pm Mon.-Fri. fall-spring) acts as a visitors center.

For information and maps related to back-country hiking and camping, contact the Shoshone National Forest's **Washakie Ranger Office** (333 Hwy. 789 S., 307/332-5460, www. fs.usda.gov, 8am-4:30pm Mon.-Fri.).

The **Fremont County Library** (307/332-5194, 10am-7pm Mon.-Thurs., 10am-4pm Fri.-Sat.) is located at 200 Amoretti Street.

The largest medical facility in the area is the **Lander Regional Hospital** (1320 Bishop Randall Dr., 307/332-4420, www. sagewesthealthcare.com), which has a 24-hour emergency department. The **Lander Medical Clinic Urgent Care** (307/332-2941, www.landermedicalclinic.com, 7am-5pm Mon.-Fri., 9am-1pm Sat.) is at 745 Buena Vista Drive.

TRANSPORTATION
Getting There

The closest commercial airport to Lander is 26 miles (42 km) away, the **Riverton Regional Airport** (RIW, 4830 Airport Rd., Riverton, 307/856-7063, www.flyriverton.com). **Denver Air Connection** (866/373-8513, www. denverairconnection.com, 30-seat jets) operates daily flights to and from Denver and regular flights to Sheridan. Private air travel is available at **Hunt Field Airport-Lander** (KLND, 307/332-2870).

Shuttles to and from nearby airports can be arranged through **Share-a-Ride Wyoming** (307/696-6116, www.sharearidewyoming. com) in Riverton ($38 for first passenger one-way), Jackson ($350 for first passenger one-way), and Casper ($170 first passenger one-way). Reductions apply for more than one passenger, and additional fees apply for late night arrivals.

By road, Lander is 163 miles (265 km) south of Cody, 160 miles (260 km) southeast of Jackson, 157 miles (250 km) southeast of Yellowstone National Park, 136 miles (219 km) east of Pinedale, and 79 miles (127 km) southwest of Thermopolis.

Getting Around

The **Wind River Transportation Authority** (307/856-7118, www.wrtabuslines.com) offers fixed-route bus service around town.

Thermopolis

At the south end of the Bighorn Basin, Thermopolis (population 2,937; elevation 4,504 ft/1,373 m) is a notably sunny town with 235 sunny days on average each year; it also has natural hot water forming the world's largest mineral hot spring.

The town was originally called Old Town Thermopolis, one of two Wyoming settlements built around mineral hot springs; the other is Saratoga. Around the turn of the 20th century, when an analysis of the water suggested potential health benefits, the town's name was shortened to Thermopolis in a calculated marketing move. Local mineral deposits—including coal, copper, and oil—plus the arrival of the railroad bolstered the Thermopolis economy, but for the most part tourism was and continues to be the major economic force. Teddy Roosevelt and Butch Cassidy and his gang were among the most famous frequent visitors to Thermopolis.

A surprising number of fantastic attractions can be found in this small, friendly town surrounded by the Owl Creek Mountains. At **Hot Springs State Park,** mineral terraces create a stunning background for herds of grazing bison. The **Wyoming Dinosaur Center** is among the best paleontology sites in the state. And the **Legend Rock Petroglyph Site** (which can only be opened in the off-season with a key from the Hot Springs State Park headquarters or the Thermopolis-Hot Springs Chamber of Commerce!) has some of the most compelling examples of prehistoric rock art in the state. From fishing and rafting on the Bighorn to horseback riding in the Owl Creek Mountains, there are a variety of ways to enjoy the natural beauty surrounding town. This is small-town Wyoming in its truest and best form.

SIGHTS
★ Hot Springs State Park
Hot Springs State Park (538 N. Park St.,

307/864-2176, http://wyoparks.state.wy.us, 6am-10pm daily) is a natural phenomenon featuring terrain with brilliant hues, unique rock formations, and, of course, hot springs. The mineral deposits and various life-forms paint the park different shades of red, orange, green, brown, and yellow. In summer the park explodes with vibrant flower gardens. Because the two national parks in the state's northwest corner draw the large crowds, if you make it to this park, you're guaranteed a more leisurely, chaos-free visit.

Originally part of the Wind River Reservation, the hot springs were believed by the Shoshone to be a gift from the Great Spirit. The U.S. government bought Big Springs and the surrounding territory from the Arapaho and Shoshone in 1896. Chief Washakie, who signed the agreement, had one stipulation: The waters should be freely available to all so that anyone could receive the great health and healing benefits. As a result, Wyoming's first state park was created along with the State Bath House, which is free and open to the public to this day. Although one might argue that the 20 minutes that come free with entry to the pool is not exactly what Chief Washakie had in mind, it's still a great place that reflects his deep respect for these medicinal waters.

Big Spring, considered the largest hot spring in the world, is the main attraction in the park. The water's temperature is 128°F (53.3°C), and more than 8,000 gallons (30,283 liters) per day trickle and gush freely over large mineral-painted terraces into the Bighorn River. Boardwalks allow visitors to walk along the terraces, springs, and cooling pools; they lead to a long suspension bridge that crosses the Bighorn and provides great views of the area.

The **State Bath House** (538 N. Park St., 307/864-3765, 8am-5:30pm Mon.-Sat., noon-5:30pm Sun.) has the only free thermal pools in the park, for 20 minutes, every two hours if you like. Those who stay more than 20 minutes will pay a fee. There is an indoor and outdoor soaking pool, although the outdoor pool is closed in the winter, along with smaller private tubs in the locker rooms. The water from the hot springs is piped to these mineral pools and is kept at 104°F (40°C). Open year-round, the pools are small but clean and well maintained. Lockers, towels, and even swimsuits (if you dare) can be rented for a nominal charge. If you are looking for more elaborate swimming facilities (including slides, steam rooms, and hot tubs), there are several commercial facilities inside the park, including **Hellie's Tepee Spa** (144 Tepee St., 307/864-9250, www.tepeepools.com, 9am-9pm daily, $12.50 ages 5-62, $10 seniors 63 and over, $6 children 4 and under) and **Star Plunge** (115 Big Springs Dr., 307/864-3771, www.starplunge. com, 11am-5pm Mon.-Fri., 11am-6pm Sat.-Sun. Memorial Day-Labor Day, 9am-9pm daily winter, $12.50 ages 5-64, $10 seniors 65 and over, $6 children 4 and under), the latter having indoor and outdoor pools and slides. Part of being in this community is feeling like you have stepped back into the 1980s. You'll rock out to Journey and Whitesnake while you soak, but if you go with it, you will love this place. Most of the pools do not take credit cards, so come prepared with cash or a checkbook, and bring coins for the lockers too.

Hot Springs County Museum and Cultural Center

This small town has done an impressive job of collecting and displaying artifacts from its lively past. **Hot Springs County Museum and Cultural Center** (700 Broadway, 307/864-5183, www.hschistory.org, 9am-5pm Mon.-Sat. May-Sept., 9am-4pm Tues.-Sat. Oct.-Apr., $5 adults, $3 seniors 60 and over and children 16 and under, free kids 5 and under) consists of the two-story main museum building and five additional structures in the vicinity. The museum building was, in various incarnations, a Ford garage, a Coke bottling plant, and a technical college before opening as the county museum in 1980.

One of the museum's more interesting exhibits is dedicated to the outlaws of Wyoming. Thermopolis was frequented by outlaws such as Butch Cassidy and the Sundance Kid. The museum has the cherrywood bar from the Hole in the Wall Saloon and the stained-glass windows from Hack Hollywood's Saloon, two of their favorite watering holes in town. There are also exhibits highlighting the town's varied sources of

Hot Springs State Park

revenue, including coal mining, oil drilling, and petroleum extraction. The 1st floor of the main museum re-creates businesses from an early 1900s Main Street, including a dentist's office, a post office, a general store, and a jail. They have been designed mostly using artifacts from the time period and even from the original stores. The cultural center has rotating exhibits by local artists.

★ Wyoming Dinosaur Center and Dig Sites

Located at the Warm Springs Ranch, where dinosaur fossils from the Jurassic period have been unearthed, the **Wyoming Dinosaur Center** (110 Carter Ranch Rd., 307/864-2997 or 800/455-3466, www.wyodino.org, 8am-6pm daily mid-May-mid-Sept., 10am-5pm daily mid-Sept.-mid-May) is a 16,000-square-foot (1,486-sq-m) complex that houses more than 200 displays. In addition to 20-some full-size dinosaur skeletons and casts from the local site and from around the world, there is also a preparation lab on-site. Visitors can watch technicians cleaning recently discovered fossils. One of the special features of the museum is its proximity to the **Warm Springs Dig Site.** Excavations still take place here each summer.

During the summer, visitors can take a tour of the site, or participate in the **Dig for a Day Program** (307/864-2997 for reservations, $150 adults, $100 children with paying adult), which allows you to work at the actual dig site, learning about the process and the science involved. Advanced registration is required, and digs happen daily late spring-early fall. Specific days throughout the summer also are set aside for the **Kids' Dig Program,** which caters to budding archaeologists.

Admission to the museum is $10 adults and $8 children 4-12 and seniors 60 and over. The dig site tour is $12 adults and $10.50 children 4-12 and seniors 60 and over. The best option is to purchase the combination package, which includes entrance to the museum and the tour, for $18.50 adults and $14.50 children and seniors. Families of four can pay a flat rate of $60, which includes both the museum and the tour.

Legend Rock Petroglyph Site

Although it may seem like a small adventure just to find the prehistoric drawings at **Legend Rock Petroglyph Site,** 21 miles (34 km) outside Thermopolis, the sheer number and variety make it a worthwhile visit. The easiest way to visit the petroglyphs is first to stop at the **Hot Springs State Park office** (at the corner of Park St. and Hwy. 789, 307/864-2176, http://wyoparks.state.wy.us), where you can pick up a map to the site (the unmarked route can be difficult to locate) and a gate key in non-summer months. Once at the parking lot for Legend Rock, you can choose to hike the 0.5 mile (0.8 km) to the petroglyphs or drive down the hill (in non-summer months when there is no host at the site, you will need the key to unlock the gate). A host is on-site 8am-6pm daily in summer. Etched along the sandstone cliffs are numerous animal and human figures that have been linked to different time periods throughout history, some dating back 2,000 years. There are more than 92 prehistoric petroglyph panels and upward of 300 petroglyph figures. Unfortunately, not all visitors to the site have treated the paintings respectfully, and it's important not to touch or try to remove the petroglyphs.

SPORTS AND RECREATION

Hiking

Although there is no national forest in immediate proximity to Thermopolis, the locals like to hike around their landmark **Round Top Mountain.** In Hot Springs State Park, there are 6.2 miles (10 km) of accessible walking and hiking trails, the most popular being **Spirit Trail,** which meanders through the park.

Boating and Fishing

Both white-water and scenic river trips are offered on the Wind and Bighorn Rivers and can be arranged exclusively through the Indian-owned **Wind River Canyon**

Whitewater and Fly Fishing (210 Hwy. 20 S., Ste. 5, 307/864-9343 or 888/246-9343, www.windrivercanyon.com). Roughly two-hour white-water trips on the dramatic upper or lower canyon sections start at $59 per person, and all-day trips covering the whole canyon are $109 per person. Scenic two-hour trips are $39 per person. Trips run Memorial Day-Labor Day. As the only outfitters on the Wind River, the company also offers a variety of guided fishing trips. All-day float-fishing trips on the upper or lower canyon are $795 for 1-2 people with lunch included. Full-day trips on the Bighorn are $525 and half-days are $400.

Golf

There is a nine-hole public course at **Legion Town and Country Club** (141 Airport Rd., 307/864-5294, $17 for 9 holes and carts $8 pp, $26 for 18 holes and carts $14 pp).

ENTERTAINMENT AND EVENTS

The **Gift of the Waters Pageant** is held during the first weekend in August and re-creates the selling of the hot springs by the Shoshone and Arapaho to the U.S. government, based on a play written in 1925. The pageant suggests it was a fair transaction between equal partners, which wasn't exactly the case. However, Native Americans from the Wind River Reservation do participate in the event, which is followed by a powwow. The event is a one-hour performance on both Friday and Saturday nights, starting at 6pm. Contact the **Thermopolis-Hot Springs Chamber of Commerce** (220 Park St., 307/864-3192 or 877/864-3192, www.thermopolis.com) for more information.

The **Thermopolis Cowboy Rendezvous** (www.thermopoliscowboyrendezvous.com) is a PRCA rodeo held the weekend after Father's Day and includes a pancake breakfast, street dance, parade, and more, in addition to riding events. This is real rodeo with events including bull riding, bareback riding, saddle bronc, steer wrestling, and team roping.

FOOD

Widely considered the best restaurant in town, **One Eyed Buffalo Brewing Company** (528 Broadway St., 307/864-3555, www. oneeyedbuffalobrewing.com, 4pm-9:30pm Mon., 11am-9:30pm Tues.-Sat., 11am-8pm Sun., $9-24) offers everything from loaded nachos and salads to burgers, steaks, pasta, prime rib and pork Jäger-schnitzel.

For a speedy and delicious meal almost any time of day, **Thermopolis Café** (109 S. 6th St., 307/864-3686, 6am-2pm Tues.-Wed., 6am-2pm and 5pm-8pm Thurs.-Sat., $6-14) is a great bet. It offers breakfast all day, superfast service, a salad bar, and hearty and delicious items ranging from sandwiches to burgers.

Serving bistro-style sandwiches, panini, and mouthwatering burgers along with homemade kettle chips, soups, and salads, the **Front Porch Deli and Grill** (536 Arapahoe St., 307/864-3494, www.fpdeli.com, 11am-8pm Tues.-Sat., $8-24) serves delicious meals made to order, plus offers a great kids' menu. Their daily homemade soups are worth writing home about.

Another place for a satisfying meal is the **Black Bear Café** (111 N. 5th St., 307/864-3221, 6:30am-3pm Mon.-Thurs., 6:30am-3pm and 5pm-8pm Fri., 7am-3pm and 5pm-8pm Sat., 7am-3pm Sun., $4-12). It serves up the biggest cinnamon rolls you can imagine, plus a delicious buffalo breakfast plate, homemade chili, and milk shakes you'll dream about.

No matter where you fill your belly in Thermopolis, always save room for an ice-cold treat from **Dairyland** (510 Park St., 307/864-2757, 11am-10pm Mon.-Sat., 1pm-10pm Sun. Apr.-Sept.), which serves delicious frozen yogurt and ice cream the old-fashioned way. It offers burgers and fries too, but it is the ice cream that brings people back.

ACCOMMODATIONS

With its history of attracting visitors to its medicinal waters, Thermopolis has quite a large, if not necessarily diverse, number of accommodations.

The snazziest hotel by far is the ★ **Best**

Western Plaza Hotel (116 E. Park St., 307/864-2939, www.bestwesternwyoming. com, $103-249), a historic hotel in Hot Springs State Park. It's the only hotel in town where pets are not permitted, but it is by far the nicest hotel.

Right across the street in this beautiful parklike setting is the pet-friendly **Days Inn Thermopolis** (115 E. Park St., 307/864-3131, www.thermopolisdaysinn.com, $97-145). Hunters will flip for the vast number and types of taxidermied mounts throughout the property and the hunting photos that line the walls. Vegetarians, however, may want to reconsider a meal at the hotel's **Safari Club Restaurant & Lounge.** The hotel is slightly run-down (perhaps just the pet-friendly rooms), but the location is ideal.

Some of the more budget-friendly options in town include the recently remodeled **Paintbrush Inn** (605 S. 6th St., 307/864-3155 or 877/621-7811, www.paintbrushinn.com, $49-86), which features basic air-conditioned ground-floor rooms with Wi-Fi and kitchenettes, and the very comfortable and homey **Elk Antler Inn** (501 Hwy. 20, 307/864-2325, www.elkantlerinn.com, $70-125), with two- and three-bed suites and two-bedroom suites. There is also a nice **Quality Inn** (166 S. Hwy. 20 S., 307/864-5515, www.choicehotels.com, $87-189) in town.

CAMPING

While there is no camping permitted in the most desirable of spots—Hot Springs State Park—there are a few RV parks in Thermopolis that allow tent camping as well. The **Fountain of Youth RV Park** (250 U.S. 20 N., 307/864-3265) is open year-round and offers RV sites ($40-45), tent sites ($30 for up to 2 campers), a cabin and a guest house ($140 for up to 4 people, bring your own bedding), and a bunkhouse (from $45 for 2 people). There is also a large hot springs pool on-site, laundry facilities, and free Wi-Fi.

The **Eagle RV Park** (204 U.S. 20 S., 307/864-5262 or 888/865-5707, www. eaglervpark.com) features a shady

campground with RV sites (from $39-43), tent sites (from $20.50), and air-conditioned camping cabins (from $44-78 for 2 people). Amenities include free Wi-Fi, a game room and playground, and laundry facilities.

The nearest public campgrounds to Thermopolis are 17 miles (27 km) south of town in **Boysen State Park** (15 Ash St., Shoshoni, 307/876-2796, http://wyoparks. state.wy.us, $17 for nonresidents) in the Wind River Canyon. Though barren by every definition, the reservoir is beautiful and offers great swimming and colorful rockhounding.

INFORMATION AND SERVICES

The **Thermopolis-Hot Springs Chamber of Commerce** (220 Park St., 307/864-3192 or 877/864-3192, www.thermopolis.com, 8am-5pm Mon.-Fri. summer, 9am-5pm Mon.-Fri. winter) is the very best place to get interesting and accurate information on the area. You will walk away with 100 ideas of cool things to do.

The **Hot Springs County Library** (307/864-3104, 9am-6pm Mon.-Fri., 10am-2pm Sat., closed holidays) is at 344 Arapahoe Street. They have an active Facebook page and regularly post fun activities.

There is a 24-hour emergency room at **Hot Springs County Memorial Hospital** (150 E. Arapahoe St., 307/864-3121, www. hscmh.org).

TRANSPORTATION

The closest commercial airport to Thermopolis is in Riverton (65 mi/105 km). **Denver Air Connection** (866/373-8513, www. denverairconnection.com, 30-seat jets) offers daily service between Riverton and Denver and regular service to Sheridan, Wyoming.

No bus service is available to or from Thermopolis.

By road, Thermopolis is 82 miles (132 km) southeast of Cody, 150 miles (242 km) southeast of the east entrance to Yellowstone National Park, and 190 miles (305 km) south of Billings.

Cody

It seems somehow fitting that this Western town was the brainchild of one of the West's most colorful and dynamic entertainers. Indeed, Cody (population 9,836; elevation 5,088 ft/1,551 m), named for Buffalo Bill Cody, is a small town that packs a lot of punch. Set as it is in the arid Bighorn Basin, you might expect Cody to be all dust and tumbleweeds. But that couldn't be further from reality, although there are plenty of both when the Wyoming wind kicks up. Cody is high style with shiny boots and fringe on almost everything. Cody is Molesworth furniture, a little gaudy sometimes, but an absolute classic. Cody is a nightly rodeo and old-time gunslingers. In many ways, Cody is the Old West, the *cinematic* West, that visitors want to see and experience.

An obvious destination in and of itself, Cody is home to what is arguably the best Western art and history museum in the world. The Buffalo Bill Center of the West is beyond compare. Visitors could spend a week in the complex's five separate museums and never see the same exhibit twice. The compact downtown is scenic and historic, with world-class art galleries, fun tourist shops, and great eateries. There are plenty of Western entertainment options as well across the valley.

Just outside town, the landscape shifts into the lush South Fork and then into the high country the closer one gets to Yellowstone National Park. There are a hundred reasons to go to Cody, including its proximity to Yellowstone.

SIGHTS
★ Buffalo Bill Center of the West

The West's version of the Smithsonian, the **Buffalo Bill Center of the West** (720 Sheridan Ave., 307/587-4771, www.centerofthewest.org, 10am-5pm Thurs.-Sun.

Dec.-Feb., 10am-5pm daily Mar.-Apr., 8am-6pm daily May-Sept. 15, 8am-5pm daily Sept.16-Oct., 10am-5pm daily Nov., $19.50 adults, $18.50 seniors 65 and over, $18 students over 18 with ID, $13 children 6-17, free for children under 6, small discounts available by purchasing tickets online) is a collection of five extraordinary museums plus a research library. The **Buffalo Bill Museum** celebrates the private and public life of town father W. F. "Buffalo Bill" Cody. The **Whitney Gallery of Western Art** reflects the diverse history of art of the American West from the early 19th century to today with original paintings, sculpture, and prints by some of the best-known deceased masters and contemporary geniuses. The **Plains Indian Museum** examines the culture and history of the Arapaho, Crow, Cheyenne, Blackfeet, Sioux, Shoshone, and others through an impressive collection of Native American art and artifacts. The **Cody Firearms Museum** is home to the world's largest assemblage of American arms along with some European arms dating back to the 1500s. The museum is undergoing an extensive renovation as of August 2018. The **Draper Museum of Natural History** offers exhibits that interpret the Greater Yellowstone Ecosystem from human and natural science perspectives. Finally, the **Harold McCracken Research Library** is an extraordinary resource for studies of the American West.

This complex is indeed the grande dame of Western history and art. In addition to its own unrivaled permanent collections, the museums feature a constantly shifting assortment of compelling traveling exhibits and special events. Check the website for events before you arrive. If you only see one museum on your journey out West, this one is it.

The BBCW also has two restaurants, the Eatery and the Coffee Bar, for quick bites and caffeine fixes.

Cody and Vicinity

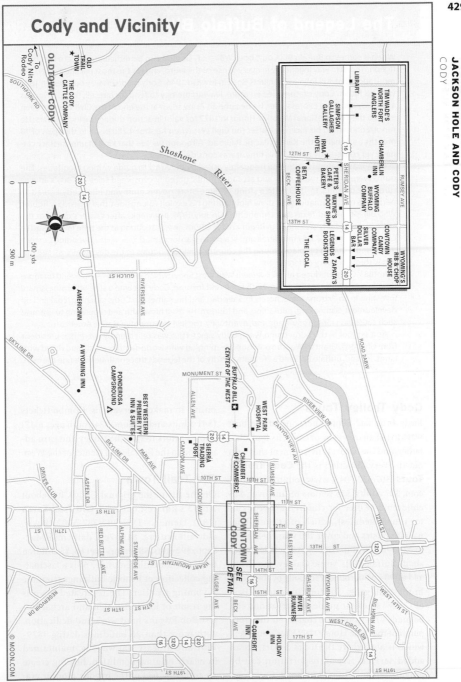

DOWNTOWN CODY *(detail inset)*

- LIBRARY
- TIM WADE'S NORTH FORT ANGLERS
- SIMPSON GALLAGHER GALLERY
- CHAMBERLIN INN
- IRMA HOTEL
- WYOMING BUFFALO COMPANY
- PETER'S CAFÉ & BAKERY
- WAYNE'S BOOT SHOP
- BETA COFFEEHOUSE
- COWTOWN CANDY COMPANY
- SILVER DOLLAR BAR
- COWTOWN HOUSE
- WYOMING'S RIB & CHOP HOUSE
- LEGENDS ZAPATA'S BOOKSTORE
- THE LOCAL
- SHERIDAN AVE
- RUMSEY AVE
- BECK AVE
- 12TH ST
- 13TH ST

Main map labels:

- OLD TRAIL TOWN
- THE CODY CATTLE COMPANY
- To Cody Nite Rodeo
- SOUTHFORK RD
- OLDTOWN CODY
- Shoshone River
- AMERICINN
- A WYOMING INN
- PONDEROSA CAMPGROUND
- BEST WESTERN PREMIER IVY INN & SUITES
- SIERRA TRADING POST
- BUFFALO BILL CENTER OF THE WEST
- WEST PARK HOSPITAL
- CHAMBER OF COMMERCE
- RIVER RUNNERS
- COMFORT INN
- HOLIDAY INN
- MONUMENT ST
- ALLEN AVE
- CANYON VIEW AVE
- RIVER VIEW DR
- ROAD 2ABW
- GULCH ST
- RIVERSIDE AVE
- SKYLINE DR
- DRIVERS CLUB
- ASPEN DR
- PARK AVE
- CANYON AVE
- CODY AVE
- SHERIDAN AVE
- BLEISTEIN AVE
- SALSBURY AVE
- WYOMING AVE
- RED BUTTE AVE
- ALPINE AVE
- STAMPEDE AVE
- HEART MOUNTAIN ST
- ALGER AVE
- BECK AVE
- RESERVOIR DR
- WEST 14TH ST
- BIG HORN AVE
- WEST CIRCLE DR
- 10TH ST
- 11TH ST
- 12TH ST
- 13TH ST
- 14TH ST
- 15TH ST
- 16TH ST
- 17TH ST
- 19TH ST
- **SEE DETAIL**

- 0   500 yds
- 0   500 m

- © MOON.COM

The Legend of Buffalo Bill

When it comes to Buffalo Bill Cody, born William F. Cody, it can be difficult to discern fact from fiction. The man was legendary in every sense of the word, and for the most part he earned the reputation that still follows his name. Born in Iowa in 1846, Cody made his way out west in 1857 with his father. Cody's father died en route, leaving the boy to fend for himself, finding work as a cowboy and Pony Express rider. He became an Army scout at the end of the Civil War and even earned the Congressional Medal of Honor in 1872 for valor in action during the Indian Wars. He reportedly earned his nickname after the Civil War when he shot 4,280 bison in the span of 18 months on behalf of the Kansas Pacific Railroad. Although we see that kind of unnecessary carnage very differently today, in his time, it was considered a feat.

Cody was a natural hunter and frequently asked by the Army to guide visiting dignitaries. The hunts were greatly publicized, and an eager public greedily consumed tales of Cody's adventuresome pursuits. In 1873, with a string of dime-store novels glorifying him, Cody agreed to perform a melodramatic stage show highlighting his exploits alongside other legendary figures Wild Bill Hickok and Texas Jack Omohundro. In July 1876, just weeks after Custer's defeat at the Little Bighorn, Cody and the Fifth Regiment for whom he was scouting at the time met a band of Cheyenne warriors. Cody murdered and scalped a warrior named Yellow Hair, avenging Custer's death and securing his place among the country's military heroes of the day. Again, we see this today through a very different lens.

In 1883, Cody produced his well-known Wild West Show, which would travel the world for more than three decades, earning him both fame and fortune. Cody became a shrewd businessman, investing in an Arizona mine, hotels in Sheridan and his namesake Cody, ranching, coal and oil development, filmmaking, publishing, and tourism. He used his wealth and reputation to espouse such causes as women's suffrage and, eventually, the just treatment of Native Americans.

As a symbol of the burgeoning West, Cody's expertise was relied on by every U.S. president from Ulysses S. Grant to Woodrow Wilson. He mingled with world-famous artists and dined with kings. Indeed, Buffalo Bill lived a life quite worthy of the legends that continue to define the man.

Cody Trolley Tours

Early June-late September, one of the best ways to get an overview of Cody, its founding father, and the natural environment that rolls out in every direction is the **Cody Trolley Tours** (307/527-7043, www.codytrolleytours. com, $27 adults, $25 seniors 65 and over, $15 children 6-17, free for children under 6, call for tour schedules), which offer hour-long narrated tours and cover 100 years of history in 22 miles (35 km). Highlights include stories about Buffalo Bill, Annie Oakley, the Crow, and a 1904 bank robbery in Cody by the Hole-in-the-Wall gang. The tour includes a "Best of Cody" souvenir guide. Reservations can be made and tickets purchased on the front porch of the Irma Hotel (1192 Sheridan Ave.), which is also where the tours depart. As an added service, free transportation can be provided to and from your hotel. Call or go online to make reservations. Combo tickets ($41 adults and seniors, $24 youth ages 6-17) allow visitors to ride the trolley and gain admission to the Buffalo Bill Center of the West.

Old Trail Town

On the site of the original Cody City (about 2 mi/3.2 km west of Cody), **Old Trail Town** (1831 Demaris Dr., 307/587-5302, www. oldtrailtown.org, 8am-7pm daily mid-May-Sept., $9 adults, $8 seniors over 65, $5 children 6-12, free for children under 6) is a fascinating collection of historic buildings from the Wyoming frontier. The re-created town is the result of local historian and archaeologist Bob Edgar's hard work and dedication, with more than 26 buildings dating 1879-1901 and at least 100 wagons, maintained in nearly original condition, helping create an authentic feel of the bygone pioneer era.

Among the highlights is the old Rivers Saloon, its walls still marked by bullet holes (it was a favorite meeting place of Butch Cassidy and the Sundance Kid) and a cabin from Hole-in-the-Wall country. A graveyard in the Old Trail Town complex has the reinterred bodies of many infamous characters of the Old West, including that of John "Liver Eating" Johnston (frequently spelled Johnson). The reburial of his body in Old Trail Town was attended by more than 2,000 people including the actor Robert Redford, who played the famous mountain man in the 1972 movie *Jeremiah Johnson*.

Irma Hotel

Naming it after his beloved youngest daughter and calling it "just the sweetest hotel that ever was," Buffalo Bill built the stately **Irma Hotel** (1192 Sheridan Ave., 307/587-4221 or 800/745-4762, www.irmahotel.com, $80-225) in 1902 with the idea that tourists from around the world could stay here en route to Yellowstone National Park. The hotel was designed by a well-known church architect from Nebraska, and some exterior walls are made of local river rock. The cherrywood bar, one of the most photographed features in town, was built in 1902 as well. Additions were added in 1929 and 1976-1977. Still the heart of downtown, the Irma is starting to show her age a little bit. The rooms are basic but still charming, and it's fun to stay in Buffalo Bill's original suite or imagine the royalty that stayed in many of the other rooms. You don't need to spend a night, though, to get a real sense of the history. Visitors can enjoy a drink at the bar or a full meal at **The Irma restaurant,** which serves breakfast, lunch, and dinner and is known for prime rib and delicious steaks. The atmosphere alone is worth the price of the meal.

Heart Mountain

Heart Mountain lies halfway between Cody and Powell and takes its name from the twin summits atop the mountain range that resemble a heart. Driving east on U.S. 14A, the mountains become clearly visible. The range is a puzzle for many geologists and has inspired heated debate. It seems to be part of rock formations found in Yellowstone National Park, 60 miles (97 km) away, but how they ended up in their present location is unclear. Furthermore, it is an "upside down" mountain, with strata of limestone appearing at the top with younger strata below.

Heart Mountain was the site of a Japanese American internment camp during World War II. Between 1942 and 1945, more than 14,000 people of Japanese descent (at least two-thirds of whom were American citizens) were relocated to this isolated terrain. Confined by barbed-wire fences and armed prison guards, they did their best to create a sense of community and normalcy under difficult living conditions. Of the 120,000 people detained in the 10 internment camps across the country, not one was ever found guilty of espionage or conspiring with the enemy. The camps were a result of heightened wartime hysteria, the fearmongering of politicians, and acute racism.

Opened in 2011, the **Heart Mountain Interpretive Center** (1539 Road 19, Powell, 307/754-8000, www.heartmountain.org, 10am-5pm daily May 15-Oct. 1, 10am-5pm Wed.-Sat. Oct. 2-May 14, $9 adults, $7 seniors/students, free for children under 12) is dedicated to preserving the memory of this dark period in American history and telling the stories of those it affected.

Today, in addition to the interpretive center and a short, paved walking trail, there are three buildings in various stages of decay and different plaques noting the memories of the victims, including one honoring the more than 600 internees who left the camp to fight in the U.S. Army during the war.

Also in this region is the **Heart Mountain Ranch** (307/754-8446, www.nature.org), a 13,000-acre (5,261-hectare) plot of land managed by The Nature Conservancy. It has a large number of rare plants, numerous species of birds, and large mammals such as elk and mule deer. In late spring 2018, the trail was closed for a while due to bear activity. A

Heart Mountain Relocation Center

Situated between the towns of Cody and Powell, in the midst of some overgrown barley fields, stand a few dilapidated buildings. Utterly abandoned, they are remnants of a dark period in U.S. history.

With the bombing of Pearl Harbor in December 1941, war hysteria and anti-Japanese fervor peaked in the United States. There had been anti-Asian sentiment along the West Coast for decades, primarily directed at hardworking Chinese laborers. When the government stopped Chinese immigration, Japanese immigrants quickly became the targets of racism. The attack on Pearl Harbor somehow cemented the racism. President Roosevelt signed Executive Order 9066 in February 1942, authorizing the roundup and removal of all people of Japanese ancestry, regardless of their U.S. citizenship status.

By the early spring, Japanese immigrants and Japanese Americans were given 10 days to gather their families, packing only what they could carry, and report to makeshift assembly centers where they would be deported to camps. Heart Mountain was one such camp.

The camp covered more than 4,600 acres (1,862 hectares) and housed 468 barracks. These poorly assembled, tar-papered buildings provided little relief from Wyoming's searing summers and frigid winters. Also constructed on the site were mess halls, communal bathrooms, laundry rooms, a hospital, a sewage plant, two places of worship, and even a high school. The camp at Heart Mountain became Wyoming's third-largest city.

More than 14,000 internees entered the camp from 1942-1945. Despite dire conditions and human rights violations, life at Heart Mountain proved to be a testament to the human spirit. The internees demonstrated a deep resilience and determination to create and maintain a community within its ragged confines. There were general stores, two movie theaters, barbershops, high school athletic teams, a weekly newspaper, and a democratically elected camp government. They also made the most of their barren surroundings, extending the irrigation system, planting 27 different types of fruits and vegetables, and raising profitable hog and poultry farms. During the three years the camp was open, 552 births and 185 deaths were registered.

Internees were allowed to leave beginning January 1945. Each internee was granted $25 and a bus ticket to his or her destination, though many internees no longer had any other place to call home. The last internees left the camp on November 10, 1945. In 1990, all survivors of Heart Mountain were issued a check for $20,000 and a signed apology from President George H. W. Bush.

7-mile (11.3-km) easy-to-moderate hiking trail takes hikers to the mountain's summit. Dogs are not permitted. An **interpretive cabin** (8am-5pm Thurs.-Sun. May-Sept.) offers information about the geology, cultural significance, and ecology of Heart Mountain and the surrounding land.

TOP EXPERIENCE

★ Chief Joseph Scenic Highway

Linking Cody with the northeast entrance to Yellowstone National Park is the seasonally open 47-mile (76-km) **Chief Joseph Scenic Highway.** It is a winding and at times hair-raising drive that cuts through mountainous country, providing views of spectacular waterfalls and mountain vistas of the Absarokas, Cathedral Cliffs, and the mouth of Sunlight Basin and occasionally a glimpse of wildlife. Interpretive signs along the way tell the story of the Nez Perce's 1877 flight from the U.S. Army under the leadership of Chief Joseph, for whom the highway is named. For adventurers, the highway gives unparalleled access to some incredible hiking trails.

From Cody, drive north 17 miles (27 km) on Highway 120, turning left (west) onto Highway 296, known as the Chief Joseph Scenic Highway. The road climbs over Dead Indian Summit, above 8,000 feet (2,438 m), and then drops into the magnificent Clarks Fork Valley. The road ends at Crandall,

Wyoming, the only place on the highway to buy provisions or find lodging. Ten miles (16.1 km) west of Crandall on the Beartooth All American Road (known locally as the Beartooth Highway) is Cooke City and the northeast entrance to Yellowstone National Park. Plan on spending at least two hours to drive the full 74 miles (119 km) or so from Cody to Cooke City.

Buffalo Bill Scenic Byway

The shorter of two routes to Yellowstone, this one to the east entrance, the 52-mile (84-km) **Buffalo Bill Scenic Byway** winds through the rugged North Fork Canyon along the Shoshone River. President Theodore Roosevelt was among its admirers, calling the road the most beautiful 50 miles (81 km) in the United States.

From Cody, head west on U.S. 20/14/16. The road ends at the east entrance to Yellowstone.

SPORTS AND RECREATION
Hiking

Even though Cody itself is in something of a desertlike bowl, there is abundant hiking in the beautiful forests and mountains to the north, south, and west of town.

There are several districts of the Shoshone National Forest within relatively close proximity to town. Trails worth pursuing include the **Bald Ridge Trail** (County Rd. 7RP, off Hwy. 120, 18 mi/29 km north of Cody). The 5-mile (8-km) trail climbs nearly 4,000 vertical feet (1,219 m) through Bureau of Land Management territory to the summit of Bald Ridge. The views, naturally, are breathtaking. The area is closed December-April to protect critical winter habitat for elk and mule deer. And remember, this is grizzly bear territory, so you should take all necessary precautions.

For more information on trails and conditions, contact the **Shoshone National Forest** (808 Meadow Lane Ave., 307/527-6241, www.fs.usda.gov) or the **Bureau of Land Management** (1002 Blackburn Ave., 307/578-5900, www.blm.gov).

For less vigorous hiking, visit the **Cody Country Chamber of Commerce** (836 Sheridan Ave., 307/587-2777 or 800/393-2639, www.codychamber.org, 8am-7pm daily summer, 8am-5pm Mon.-Fri. fall-spring) and pick up the "Cody Pathways" brochure and map of nonmotorized trails in the region.

Fishing and Rafting

The Shoshone River runs right through

view from Chief Joseph Scenic Highway

the heart of Cody, offering both white-water rafting opportunities and plenty of excellent fishing. Among the rafting companies in town that offer everything from two-hour white-water floats and half-day scenic tours to weeklong trips are **River Runners** (1491 Sheridan Ave., 800/535-7238, www.riverrunnersofwyoming.com, $36 adults, $32 children 12 and under for 2 hours, $78 adults, $68 children half-day), **Wyoming River Trips** (233 Yellowstone Ave., 307/587-6661 or 800/586-6661, www.wyomingrivertrips.com, $36 adults, $34 children 12 and under for 2 hours, $65-80 half-day), and **Red Canyon River Trips** (1119 12th St., 307/587-6988 or 800/293-0148, www.codywyomingadventures.com, $34 adults, $32 children for 2 hours, discounts for families, $70-75 half-day, $119 adult full-day white water, $99 adult full-day scenic float).

There is an abundance of prime fishing waters within an easy drive from Cody, including the Shoshone River, the Clarks Fork of the Yellowstone River, and hundreds of lakes. For fishing gear or advice on local hatches and water conditions, head to **Tim Wade's North Fork Anglers** (1107 Sheridan Ave., 307/527-7274, www.northforkanglers.com, 8am-8pm daily in summer, 9am-6pm Mon.-Sat. fall-spring). In addition to all the gear, the shop offers guided wading trips or float trips. Hours here can change according to the weather, so call first.

Mountain Biking

If you are looking to do some exploring on bikes, **Absaroka Bikes** (2201 17th St., 307/527-5566, 10am-6pm Mon.-Thurs., 10am-4pm Fri.-Sat., Memorial Day-Labor Day, 10am-5pm Tues.-Thurs., 10am-4pm Fri., 10am-2pm Sat. Labor Day-Memorial Day) offers bike rentals, guided bike tours, and maps of bike trails around the area.

Horseback Riding

Head out 1 mile (1.6 km) past the rodeo grounds on the left to **Cedar Mountain Trail Rides** (12 Spirit Mountain Rd., 307/527-4966,

$35 for 1 hour, $50 for 2 hours), where you will be attended by knowledgeable and friendly guides who are especially good with beginners. The trails wind up Cedar Mountain and provide great views of the town below. If you are interested in a full-day ride, guides take the horses and riders by trailer 35 minutes north to Elk's Fork; lunch is provided.

Golf

Golfers can hit the links at the 18-hole semi-private **Olive Glenn Golf & Country Club** (802 Meadow Lane Ave., 307/587-5551, www.oliveglengolfclub.com, $68 for 18 holes with cart, rental clubs available with two sleeves of balls for $20) or at the **Powell Golf Club** (600 WYO Hwy. 114, 7 mi/11.3 km east of Powell, 307/754-7259, www.powellgolfclub.com, $35-59 for 18 holes).

There is also a great miniature course for the whole family at **Cody Miniature Golf** (Cody's City Park, 307/587-3685, $5 adults 16 and over, $4 youth).

ENTERTAINMENT AND EVENTS
Nightlife

Although drinking while driving was only outlawed in Wyoming in 2002, drive-through liquor stores are still a surprise to many visitors. People often take their parties to go. For traditionalists who like to have a drink in a more stationary location, Cody offers plenty of great bars. Among them, in the historic Irma Hotel is the **Silver Saddle Saloon** (1192 Sheridan Ave., 307/587-4221 or 800/745-4762, 11am-2am daily) and, down the street, the **Silver Dollar Bar** (1313 Sheridan Ave., 307/527-7666, kitchen 11am-9pm daily, 11am-2am Mon.-Sat., 11am-midnight Sun., if there are customers), which often has live country music and serves good bar food.

For family-oriented nightlife, try **Dan Miller's Cowboy Music Revue** (720 Sheridan Ave., 307/578-7909, www.cowboymusicrevue.com, 4pm-5:15pm Mon.-Sat. May, 6:30pm-7:45pm Mon.-Sat. June-Sept., $17 pp for music only, $41 pp includes buffet dinner at 5:30pm prior to 6:30pm show, $59.50 combo ticket includes buffet dinner, musical revue, and admission to the Buffalo Bill Center of the West), which features a night of music, comedy, and poetry. The event takes place in the Dining Pavilion of the Buffalo Bill Center of the West.

Festivals and Events

Making this Western town one of the best places in the state to see rodeo, the **Cody Nite Rodeo** (421 W. Yellowstone Ave., 307/587-5155, www.codystampederodeo.com, June-Aug., $20 adults, $10 kids 7-12, free for kids 6 and under) is held nightly in summer at the rodeo grounds except July 1-5 during the Cody Stampede. Running every summer since 1938, the rodeo is two hours filled with daring cowboys and cowgirls looking to make a name for themselves on the circuit. Kids are invited to join in on the calf scramble. Gates open at 7pm, and the action begins at 8pm.

The town's rodeo fever hits its high over the Fourth of July during the annual **Cody Stampede Rodeo** (519 Yellowstone Ave., 307/587-5155, www.codystampederodeo.com, grandstand seats $20-25 adults, $10 children 12 and under). The Stampede has been running for 100 years, as of 2019, and was inspired by Buffalo Bill's own Wild West Show. This is one of the biggies for pro rodeo cowboys and cowgirls, with the bull-ride purse alone bringing the winner $50,000. For world-class rodeo action, it's hard to beat.

One of the few towns to stage nightly gun-fights in summer (Jackson is another), Cody enchants visitors with Old West characters that stage a hilarious, silly, and at times gripping street performance and gunfight known as the **Cody Gunfighters** (6pm Mon.-Sat. June-Sept.). The shows are free and performed adjacent to the Irma Hotel (1192 Sheridan Ave.).

By far the biggest arts-related event of the year in Cody is the **Rendezvous Royale** (307/587-5002 or 888/598-8119, www.rendezvousroyale.com), which happens in mid-September and ushers in the last hurrah of Cody's almost manic summer season. The week is packed with events that include **Cody High Style,** which celebrates Western design in its myriad forms, and the **Buffalo Bill Art Show and Sale,** which boasts its own impressive line of events, with a quick draw in the park and studio tours. The town is full of style icons, design gurus, and blissed-out art collectors, and the energy pulses nearly around the clock. Several galleries and shops host concurrent events. Some of the best shows by contemporary Western masters open at **Simpson Gallagher Gallery** (1161 Sheridan Ave., 307/587-4022, www.simpsongallaghergallery.com).

SHOPPING

Cody is a great town for shopping, particularly if fine art or Western fashion is your thing. A stroll up and down **Sheridan Avenue** can be very productive, and expensive.

Start at **Wayne's Boot Shop** (1250 Sheridan Ave., 307/587-5234, www.waynesbootshop.com, 9am-8pm Mon.-Sat.) for the right pair of kicks. Wayne's has been selling the best-quality cowboy, hiking, and hunting boots since 1955. Now owned by Wayne's son, the store also sells casual and comfort shoes, as well as hats.

For outdoor gear and casual wear at great prices, visit **Sierra Trading Post** (1402 8th St., 307/578-5802, www.sierratradingpost.com, 9am-8pm Mon.-Sat., 10am-6pm Sun.), which sells everything from clothing and footwear to outdoor gear, luggage, and home goods at deep discounts. Quilters will delight in an afternoon at **Friends and Co. Quilt Shop** (402 E. Warren, 307/527-7217, www.friendsandco.net, 10am-5pm Mon.-Fri., 10am-4pm Sat.), which offers classes, private lessons, and more fabric than you can imagine. Book lovers will want more time at **Legends Bookstore** (1350 Sheridan Ave., 307/586-2320, www.legendsbooks.com, 9:30am-9pm Mon.-Sat. and 10am-8pm Sun. in summer, 10am-8pm Mon.-Sat. and noon-7pm Sun. in winter), an outstanding independent bookstore with plenty of events featuring local and regional authors, plus gifts, cards, and great toys.

Cody has an impressive number of fine art galleries, and you should wander Sheridan Avenue to see many of them. But be sure not to miss **Simpson Gallagher Gallery** (1161 Sheridan Ave., 307/587-4022, www.simpsongallaghergallery.com, 10am-5:30pm Mon.-Sat.), which carries the work of contemporary Western masters including Clyde Aspevig, Carol Guzman, T. D. Kelsey, T. Allen Lawson, William Matthews, Julie Oriet, and Kathy Wipfler. The gallery has marvelous rotating shows and features both painting and sculpture.

If shopping wears you out, fuel up on made-in-Wyoming smoked elk and bison jerky or summer sausage, barbecue sauces, jams, spices, and other local specialties at **Wyoming Buffalo Company** (1270 Sheridan Ave., 307/587-8708, www.wyobuffalo.com, 10am-6pm Mon.-Sat.). Or appease your sweet tooth at **Cowtown Candy Company** (1323 Sheridan Ave., 307/587-8212, www.cowtowncandy.com, 10am-9pm Mon.-Sat. in summer, shortened hours fall-spring), which specializes in turtles, fresh cream and butter truffles, and homemade fudge.

FOOD

Although much of the state can be classified as meat and potatoes only, Cody leans toward slightly more variety. For a great cup of coffee and a light breakfast of homemade pastries and bagels (admittedly the homemade cinnamon rolls may not count as light), stop into the **Beta Coffeehouse** (1450 Sheridan Ave., 307/587-7707, 6:30am-4pm Mon.-Fri., 8am-4pm Sat., 9am-2pm Sun. $2-7). A favorite community gathering spot, the Beta often hosts live music and open-mic nights. In the winter, the homemade soups are beyond compare. **Peter's Café & Bakery** (1219 Sheridan Ave., 307/527-5040, 7am-7pm Mon.-Sat., $4-12) is another great place for a quick bite, whether breakfast, burgers, espresso, or ice cream. Daily soups, specials, and desserts should not be missed. You can find them on

Facebook. Another solid breakfast choice in Cody is **Our Place** (148 Yellowstone Ave., 307/527-4420, 6am-2pm daily, $4-12, cash only) which dishes up veggie egg white omelets, hash browns, pancakes, and all the classics. They have great lunch specials too. Try the chili. But bring cash because they don't take credit cards.

For Mexican food, nothing beats **Zapata's** (1362 Sheridan Ave., 307/527-7181, www.zapatascody.com, 11am-9pm Mon.-Sat., noon-8pm Sun., $7-17), which serves outstanding New Mexico-style Mexican food including fish tacos, snow crab enchiladas, and homemade salsas and sauces you can buy and take home.

Open only in summer, **The Cody Cattle Company** (1910 Demaris St., 307/272-5770, www.thecodycattlecompany.com, doors open at 5:15pm daily June-mid-Sept., dinner and show $30 adults, $15 children 3-12) serves up a bountiful all-you-can-eat chuck wagon dinner—including brisket, steak, potato, beans, and more—and a live country music show starting nightly at 6:30pm. You can pair your dinner and a show with tickets to the nightly rodeo, which is within walking distance, for the cowboy trifecta.

Among the best places for steak, ribs, and chops in town is **Wyoming's Rib & Chop House** (1367 Sheridan Ave., 307/527-7731, 11am-9pm Sun.-Thurs., 11am-10pm Fri.-Sat., $14-36), an excellent (and expanding) regional chain. From its buffalo rib eye to the cedar plank salmon, the food is always great. They serve brunch on Saturday and Sunday from 11am-2pm. Reservations are strongly suggested.

Cody's best-kept culinary secret is likely ★ **The Local** (1134 13th Ave., 307/586-4262, 8:30am-2pm and 5pm-9pm Tues.-Sat., $14-38), an American bistro with inventive creations relying on ingredients sourced from local producers. This is farm-to-table cuisine in its best Wyoming iteration. The salads are phenomenal, as are the elk gyro flatbread, the Ishawooa Mesa beef burgers, and the yam chips.

An absolute must for at least one meal (if you are not staying at the hotel) is **The Irma** (1192 Sheridan Ave., 307/587-4221, www.irmahotel.com, 7am-9pm daily year-round, $11-33). The prime rib dinner buffet (5pm-8:30pm daily May-June 15, 5pm-9pm daily mid-June-Aug., 5:30pm-8pm Fri.-Sat. Sept.-Apr., $26 adults, $10 children 7-10, free for children 6 and under) is famous, but it's really the history and ambience of the place that make it a must. The Irma also serves a breakfast buffet (7am-11am daily June-Sept., 7am-11am Sat.-Sun. Oct.-May, $11 adults, $5 children 7-10, free for children under 6) and lunch buffet (11:30am-2pm Mon.-Sat. summer, $11 adults, $6 children 7-10, free for children 6 and under, 11:30am-2pm Sun. year-round $15 adults, $7 children 7-10, free for children 6 and under).

It doesn't get more local or more traditional than **Cassie's Supper Club** (214 Yellowstone Ave., 307/527-5500, www.cassies.com, 11am-10pm daily, Sunday brunch 11am-2pm, $7-36), named for its original proprietor, Cody's most beloved madam. When the city asked her to close her brothel in the early 1930s, Cassie complied, sort of: She opened her supper club at the west end of town, where it stands today. The atmosphere is dark, the mood light, the food hearty, and the history rich. It is Cody's hot spot for two-stepping and has three bars to help lubricate dancers. It should be stated that Cassie's brothel business died with her in 1952.

ACCOMMODATIONS

Geared as it is toward the flocks of visitors headed to Yellowstone, Cody has an abundance of accommodations, many of them newer. Among the best deals in town is the basic but appealing and independently owned **A Wyoming Inn** (720 Yellowstone Ave., 307/587-4208, www.hotelcody.com, May-Oct., $110-125). Among the chain hotels in town are **AmericInn** (508 Yellowstone Ave., 307/587-7716, www.wyndhamhotels.com, $119-249), **Comfort Inn** (1601 Sheridan Ave., 307/587-5556,

www.comfortinn.com, $93-219), **Holiday Inn** (1701 Sheridan Ave., 800/315-2621, www.ihg.com, $102-237), and the very upscale **Best Western Premier Ivy Inn & Suites** (1800 8th St., 307/587-2572, www.bestwesternwyoming.com, $110-285).

For significantly more charm, the ★ **Chamberlin Inn** (1032 12th St., 307/587-0202 or 888/587-0202, www.chamberlininn.com, $145-650) is a stately complex built in 1904 and beautifully restored in 2007. There are 21 individual rooms, including several suites, a cottage and a house, all of which are unique. Ernest Hemingway spent the night in one of them in 1932—his signature is still in the guest register.

Buffalo Bill's beloved **Irma Hotel** (1192 Sheridan Ave., 307/587-4221 or 800/745-4762, www.irmahotel.com, $80-225) is another classic in Cody. Showing a few more signs of wear than the Chamberlin, but with its own marvelous history and central location, Irma is an important landmark and central to this community.

Just outside Yellowstone's east entrance, **Pahaska Tepee** (183 North Fork Hwy., 307/527-7701 or 800/628-7791, www.pahaska.com, $99-1,250) is another of Buffalo Bill's historic lodges. The complex is vast, with the old 1904 lodge, newer housekeeping cabins, and deluxe modern condos and a seven-bedroom family reunion lodge, but so are the recreational opportunities. From horseback riding to cross-country skiing, Pahaska Tepee is like a giant playground with immediate proximity to Yellowstone.

GUEST RANCHES

Since Cody is cowboy country, after all, it's fitting that there are a number of guest ranches in the area. Most are geared heavily toward horseback riding and provide lodging in individual and often charmingly rustic cabins. Other activities such as fishing and hiking are regularly available. Things like cell phone coverage, satellite TV, and Wi-Fi are simply not on the menu. These ranches provide true opportunities to get away from life as you know it in some of the most spectacular country on the planet.

Forty miles (64 km) west of Cody, the **Absaroka Mountain Lodge** (1231 North Fork Hwy., 307/587-3963, www.absarokamtlodge.com, $135-250 cabins) dates back to 1917 and is one of the largest and best-known. Unlike many guest ranches in the area, the Absaroka Mountain Lodge is not all-inclusive; guests select and pay for activities, including fishing and horseback riding, and eat meals in a restaurant.

Founded by the grandson of Buffalo Bill, the **Bill Cody Ranch Resort** (2604 North Fork Hwy., 26 mi/42 km west of Cody, 307/587-2097 or 800/615-2934, www.billcodyranch.com, $120-225 cabins) is exactly halfway between Cody and Yellowstone in the magnificent North Fork Valley. Meals and activities are paid for separately for standard cabins. Packages are also available and include breakfast, dinner, a four-hour horseback ride with lunch, and overnight accommodations ($185 pp for 2 people).

The **7D Ranch** (774 Sunlight Rd., 307/587-9885, www.7dranch.com, from $2,310/week for 1 adult in a cabin) is a small, remote ranch in the Sunlight Basin, 50 miles (81 km) northwest of Cody, offering cozy, rustic accommodations, horseback riding and fishing, pack trips, and hunting trips.

For more guest ranches in the Cody area, contact the **Wyoming Dude Ranchers' Association** (1122 12th St., Cody, 307/587-2339, www.wyomingdra.com).

CAMPING

Buffalo Bill State Park (47 Lakeside Rd., 307/587-9227, http://wyoparks.state.wy.us, May-Sept., $17 nonresidents), 11 miles (17.7 km) west of Cody, offers the closest public campgrounds. Situated below the Absaroka Mountains, the park has two campgrounds: North Shore Bay Campground has 37 sites, and North Fork Campground has 62 sites.

A good, fully equipped private facility in town is the **Ponderosa Campground** (1815 8th St., 307/587-9203, www.codyponderosa.

com, mid-Apr.-mid-Oct., $30 tents, $37-50 RVs, $38 tipis, $65 cabins for 2 people). There is a cowboy cappuccino bar, a convenience store, a playground, clean restrooms and showers, and many other amenities in this large complex.

INFORMATION AND SERVICES

The **Cody Country Chamber of Commerce** (836 Sheridan Ave., 307/587-2777 or 800/393-2639, www.codychamber.org, 8am-7pm daily summer, 8am-5pm Mon.-Fri. fall-spring) acts as a visitors center and a ticket outlet for events around town, and avid walkers can pick up a map of trails. Excellent planning tools are also available online at www.yellowstonecountry.org.

For information on recreational trails and public camping in the region, contact the **Shoshone National Forest** (808 Meadow Lane Ave., 307/527-6241, www.fs.usda.gov) or the **Bureau of Land Management** (1002 Blackburn Ave., 307/578-5900, www.blm.gov).

The main **post office** (307/527-7161, 8am-4:30pm Mon.-Fri., 9am-noon Sat.) may be found at 1301 Stampede Avenue.

The airy and bright **Park County Library** (307/527-1880, www.parkcountylibrary.org, 9am-8pm Mon.-Thurs., 9am-5:30pm Fri., 9am-5pm Sat., 1pm-4pm Sun.) is at 1500 Heart Mountain Street.

Cody's **West Park Hospital** (707 Sheridan Ave., 307/527-7501 or 800/654-9447, www.codyregionalhealth.org) has a 24-hour emergency room. The hospital also runs an **Urgent Care Clinic** (424 Yellowstone Ave., 307/578-2903, 8am-6:30pm Mon.-Fri., 9am-5:30pm Sat., 9am-3:30pm Sun.) for illnesses and injuries that do not require hospital care.

Visitors can do laundry at **Cody's Laundromat** (1728 Beck Ave., 307/587-8500, www.codylaundromat.weebly.com, 24 hours daily).

TRANSPORTATION
Getting There

The Cody area is served commercially by the

Yellowstone Regional Airport (COD, 2101 Roger Sedam Dr., 307/587-5096, www.flyyra.com), just a two-minute drive from downtown, which has daily flights on **Delta** and **United**. The airport is 52 miles (84 km) from the east entrance to Yellowstone National Park. Air and shuttle services are also available from Billings (107 mi/172 km). Long-term and short-term outdoor vehicle parking at the airport is free.

By road, Cody is 177 miles (280 km) northeast of Jackson, 163 miles (265 km) north of Lander, 84 miles (135 km) northwest of Thermopolis, and 52 miles (84 km) east of Yellowstone National Park.

Getting Around

Car-rental companies operating at the Yellowstone Regional Airport include **Avis, Budget, Dollar, Hertz,** and **Thrifty.**

For travel between Cody and Billings, local taxi service in town, and tours to Yellowstone, contact **Phidippides Shuttle Service** (307/527-6789 or 866/527-6789, www.codyshuttle.com).

For regular taxi service, contact **Cody Cab** (307/272-8364) or **Town Taxi** (307/250-8090). Tours of Yellowstone and Grand Teton National Parks can also be arranged.

Sheridan and Northeast Wyoming

Northeast Wyoming encompasses rocky peaks,

meadows full of wildflowers, river-carved canyons, and wide-open spaces, as well as classic Western town Sheridan and the Powder River Basin towns of Gillette and Buffalo.

Long a prime buffalo hunting territory for Native Americans, the area has seen great conflict between Indians and encroaching settlers. Today that relationship is dynamic and evident throughout much of the region, even at Devils Tower, where climbers are making strides toward working in cooperation with the Native Americans who consider the feature sacred.

The economy here is based almost entirely on natural resources: coal and coal-bed methane, livestock production, and tourism in these vast

Highlights

Look for ★ to find recommended sights, activities, dining, and lodging.

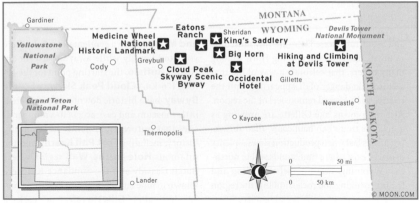

MONTANA
WYOMING
NORTH DAKOTA

Gardiner
Yellowstone National Park
Grand Teton National Park
Cody
Greybull
Thermopolis
Lander
Kaycee
Newcastle
Gillette
Sheridan

★ Medicine Wheel National Historic Landmark
★ Eatons Ranch
★ King's Saddlery
★ Big Horn
★ Cloud Peak Skyway Scenic Byway
★ Occidental Hotel
★ Hiking and Climbing at Devils Tower
Devils Tower National Monument

0   50 mi
0   50 km

© MOON.COM

★ **King's Saddlery:** Part museum, part Western tack store, this is the hub of Sheridan (page 445).

★ **Medicine Wheel National Historic Landmark:** High in the Big Horns on a narrow ridge is this mysterious, Stonehenge-esque feature thought to be 500-800 years old (page 447).

★ **Eatons Ranch:** The oldest dude ranch in the world is certainly one of the most traditional (page 453).

★ **Big Horn:** This tiny little town is full of character, with a gem of an art museum, plenty of polo, and wonderful Western celebrations (page 455).

★ **Occidental Hotel:** Catch a glimpse of what the good life looked like in the Old West (page 457).

★ **Cloud Peak Skyway Scenic Byway:** This stunning road climbs over and cuts through the Big Horn Mountains, passing by beautiful spots and providing access to historic sites (page 459).

★ **Hiking and Climbing at Devils Tower:** Rising more than 1,200 feet (366 m) above the Belle Fourche River, the nation's first national monument is a magnet for hikers and climbers (page 471).

Sheridan and Northeast Wyoming

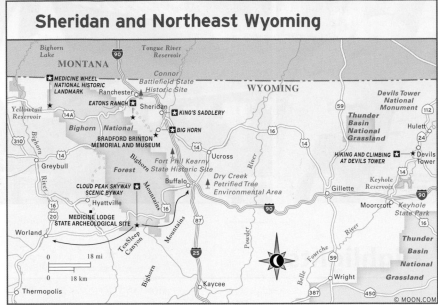

© MOON.COM

and beautiful places. There are tiny museums in towns like Sheridan and Big Horn, among many others, that celebrate a way of life that seems in no danger of disappearing, with the relative vastness and remote feel of the region. Although towns like Gillette are growing as quickly as trains can haul coal—then shrinking just as fast when production slows—plenty of places exist where time stands still in northeast Wyoming. From horseback riding and fishing to hiking and rock climbing, the region has no shortage of recreational opportunities.

PLANNING YOUR TIME

Travelers heading east or west on I-90 will have easy access to much of the region. **Sheridan** is a wonderful town to visit and a terrific hub for many of Wyoming's **dude ranches.** Although most ranches are busiest in summer, a few open in May, and some stay open into fall for hunters. Just down the road from Sheridan, the tiny town of **Big Horn** is home to the **Bradford Brinton Memorial**

and Museum, on a gentleman's ranch where you could easily while away an afternoon. Nearby **Buffalo,** the starting point for the 47-mile (76-km) **Cloud Peak Skyway Scenic Byway,** has a historic downtown with a great little museum and easy access to a number of sites that feature prominently in Wyoming history, including **Fort Phil Kearny** and the infamous **Hole-in-the-Wall** region where Butch Cassidy and the Sundance Kid were known to hide out. Though not exactly a touristy destination, **Gillette** offers nice parks, a terrific public pool and waterslide. Summer, late spring, and early fall are the best times to hit this corner of the state because of the blue skies and easy opportunities to be outdoors. They're still here in the winter, of course, but one gets the feeling that everyone is hunkered down, waiting for spring.

Though **Devils Tower** is not exactly on the way to anywhere, it is for many the highlight of a trip to Wyoming as an obvious recreation spot for climbers, hikers, and campers. The

Previous: Devils Tower; climber scaling Devils Tower; horses at Eatons Ranch.

trip can be made fairly easily in a day from just about anywhere in northeast Wyoming. It's wise to plan your visit to Devils Tower sometime other than June, when the voluntary ban on hiking and climbing is in place, or the first and second weeks in August, when bikers headed to or from the huge Sturgis Motorcycle Rally in South Dakota's Black Hills can descend on the tower in crowds of hundreds and even thousands.

HISTORY

Stretching from the eastern flank of the Big Horn Mountains east to the Black Hills and bordered on the south by the North Platte River, the Powder River Basin was prime hunting territory for a number of different Native American groups. In order to bypass inevitable conflict, most miners traveling through the region to Montana's goldfields steered south of the Powder River Basin on the Oregon Trail. In 1864, however, as mining towns were booming overnight in Montana, John Jacobs and John Bozeman built the first trail through the area. The Bozeman Trail became known as the "Bloody Bozeman."

The area was essentially a war zone as early as 1854, during the first of three Sioux wars. Only after the 1876-1877 Great Sioux War, which included Crazy Horse's surrender, and the Ghost Dance War, which ended with the Massacre at Wounded Knee in 1890, did the Sioux commit to living on the reservation. During those decades numerous battles flared between significant leaders on both sides, including Sioux chief Red Cloud, Dull Knife, and Col. H. B. Carrington. The 1876 "Dull Knife Fight" robbed the Cheyenne of all their winter supplies, including winter food storage. Part military tactic, part revenge for the recent death of Custer and his men at the Battle of the Little Bighorn in June of that year, the U.S. Army destroyed everything the Cheyenne had gathered for winter, and the surviving Indians, women and children included, fled on foot in temperatures that fell below -30°F (-34.4°C). The Cheyenne surrendered a few weeks later.

The reservation spread into the Black Hills, much of which was thought to be gold-rich and so was seized by the government from the Sioux in 1876. Although the Indian Peace Commission had originally offered $6 million, and the Sioux, understanding the value the settlers saw in the soil, had asked for $70 million, in the end the government reclaimed the land without paying the tribe a penny. The case was still being argued in 1980 when the U.S. Supreme Court ruled that the government owed the Sioux $106 million for the land they had stolen.

With the Indian Wars winding down, a new type of conflict arose between the moneyed cattle ranchers and the hardscrabble homesteaders across the Powder River Basin. Texas cattle had come into the region between 1875 and 1884. They were grazed on the open range until homesteaders started fencing off pastureland and watering holes. The cattle herds continued to increase while the open rangeland decreased. With drought followed by freezing temperatures, more than 500,000 cattle died over the winter of 1886-1887, later referred to as the "Great Die-up." Ranchers became even more resolved to make their outfits profitable.

While the ranchers were trying to rid themselves of pesky rustlers and homesteaders, a hired group called the Regulators pursued a "dead list" of ambitious and outspoken homesteaders and people believed to be rustlers. Known as the Johnson County War, there were major conflicts between ranchers and townspeople who supported the outspoken homesteaders.

The last Indian battle in Wyoming took place on October 31, 1903, southwest of Newcastle, when Sioux returning to their reservation from Montana ran into lawmen from Newcastle. At stake was the issue of whether or not the Sioux were violating game laws by hunting off the reservation. Three lawmen were killed, and the Sioux eventually surrendered, were put on trial, and were ultimately acquitted.

Throughout the 20th century, the story of

this corner of Wyoming centered on cattle and sheep production and, more recently (and far more lucratively), coal and coal-bed methane production. With wide-open ranch country and Devils Tower as the country's first national monument, it's not a stretch to see why tourism, too, continues to play an important role in the region.

Sheridan and Vicinity

Although Sheridan (population 17,954; elevation 3,753 ft/1,144 m) continuously touts itself as the midpoint between Yellowstone National Park and the Black Hills, it sells itself short. It's true that it is conveniently located, but this authentic Western town has much more to offer than proximity to other places.

Rich with history, Sheridan is the town where Martha Jane Canary transformed herself into Calamity Jane. The iconic Sheridan Inn was opened in 1893; Buffalo Bill operated it for two years; using the inn as a place to audition acts for his Wild West Show.

One of the most charming towns in the state, Sheridan has the feel of the Old West, although that is slowly beginning to change as traditional Main Street businesses are gradually replaced by high-end art galleries and gourmet eateries. Still, Wyoming's best-known saddlery is here and in no danger of leaving, as are some classic watering holes like the Mint Bar, along with numerous historic sites.

The tiny (and unincorporated) town of Big Horn (population 490; elevation 4,081 ft/1,244 m) is on the eastern slopes of the Big Horn Mountains, with Little Goose Creek running through. The town was settled in the late 1880s by such well-known sheep and cattle ranchers as the Moncreiffe brothers, the Wallop family, the Gallatin family, and Bradford Brinton, whose home is a gem of a museum and one of the best reasons to visit Big Horn. The other reason to visit is to check out a polo match, a favorite pastime of the town.

Downtown Sheridan

SIGHTS
Trail End State Historic Site
The **Trail End State Historic Site** (400 Clarendon Ave., 307/674-4589, www.trailend. co, 1pm-4pm daily Apr.-May, 9am-6pm daily June-Aug., 1pm-4pm daily Sept.-mid-Dec., 10am-5pm Memorial Day and Labor Day weekends, $4 nonresidents, $2 residents, children 17 and under free if accompanied by

an adult) is situated high on a bluff overlooking town. The 4-acre (1.6-hectare) grounds are impeccably manicured and have retained much of their original landscaping, designed nearly a century ago. The museum is the former home of John B. Kendrick, one of Wyoming's most famous sons. Kendrick was orphaned early in life and got his start at age 15 as a ranch hand. Originally from Texas, he followed cattle into Wyoming and, taken with its beauty, decided to stay. He went on to become a successful rancher and businessman, accumulating more than 200,000 acres (80,937 hectares) of land. Kendrick would become Wyoming's first governor and later a U.S. senator. Kendrick referred to the house, begun in 1908 and completed in 1913, as the "end-of-the-trail mansion," and it's where he would spend the last 20 years of his life when he wasn't in Washington DC.

The house is built in the Flemish revival style, with rich mahogany walls, exposed-beam ceilings, and 18 beautifully decorated rooms. What is unique to this historic house is that almost everything on display (furniture, rugs, magazines, books, and photographs) is the original property of the Kendrick family. Self-guided tours are available; for groups larger than eight, reservations for guided tours can be made two weeks in advance.

Sheridan Inn

When the **Sheridan Inn** (856 Broadway, 307/655-7861, www.sheridaninn.com) opened in 1893, it was considered the finest hotel between Chicago and San Francisco. Designed after a Scottish inn and with a bar imported from England, the inn was the only hotel in Sheridan to have electric lights (200 of them, to be exact). The porch runs the full 130-foot (40-m) length of the hotel, and there are 62 dormer windows.

Buffalo Bill Cody helped inaugurate the hotel—chilled champagne was served—and went on to become a co-owner. He would hold auditions for his Wild West Show on the hotel's veranda, and the Sheridan Inn quickly became the social center for Sheridan's affluent residents.

The hotel has hosted famous guests, including presidents Theodore Roosevelt, Howard Taft, and Herbert Hoover. Its longest resident, however, is said to still reside in the hotel: Catherine B. Arnold worked and lived at the inn for 64 years, from her arrival in 1901 until she left, only when the hotel closed, in 1965. She had worked as a desk clerk, seamstress, housekeeper, and hostess, and her dying request was to be buried in the hotel. When she died three years later, her ashes were placed in the wall of the 3rd-floor room she often occupied. According to local lore, the presence of "Miss Kate" is still felt. From the sound of footsteps and lights turning on and off to doors being opened and shut, the rumor is that she still likes to manage the inn.

The hotel reopened in 1967 and continued to operate for another 20 years before closing its doors again. In 1991 a restaurant opened in the inn and tours of the building were available, but it no longer functioned as a hotel. In the fall of 2012, the property was completely shuttered until Bob and Dana Townsend of Oklahoma purchased it, continued the restoration, and reopened the hotel in 2015. Today the hotel is, once again, at the center of the Sheridan community.

★ King's Saddlery

In a town full of Western stores, **King's Saddlery** (184 N. Main St., 307/672-2702 or 800/443-8919, www.kingssaddlery.com, 8am-5pm Mon.-Sat.) is indeed aptly named. A legendary tack store established by the King family in the late 1940s, its founder Don King is a local hero and was a renowned saddle maker. Many of his saddles are on display in the store's **Don King Museum** (8am-5pm Mon.-Sat., donation requested) as well as at the National Cowboy Hall of Fame and the PRCA Rodeo Hall of Fame. For six years, Don handcrafted the PRCA World Championship saddles.

In addition to the store's dizzying selection of rope, hats, and Western tack, the museum

houses hundreds of saddles, wagons, coaches, Native American artifacts, cowboy memorabilia from around the world, and original art. Don't leave without a King Ropes baseball cap, which promotes the saddlery's most famous product; it will connect you with other cowboy aficionados the world over.

Ucross Foundation

Twenty-seven miles (43 km) east of Sheridan, nestled in the midst of a 20,000-acre (8.094-hectare) working cattle ranch (half of the land is protected by The Nature Conservancy), is the artists' haven known as **Ucross** (30 Big Red Ln., 307/737-2291, www.ucrossfoundation.org). About 80 artists from around the globe are invited to take up residence at the foundation each year, since 1981, for a few weeks at a time. The foundation's mission is simply to provide a workplace where writers, composers, painters, and other artists can live and work uninterrupted for an extended period of time. There are usually eight to nine residents on the grounds at the same time. Pulitzer Prize-winning author Annie Proulx has been a significant supporter of Ucross, and Elizabeth Gilbert wrote part of her novel *Eat, Pray, Love* while in residence.

Big Red was the main house of the original ranch and now serves as an important part of the complex. It is decorated with antique furniture and houses a gallery (8:30am-4pm Mon.-Fri., 10am-4pm Sat. July-Labor Day) that hosts four annual exhibitions, which are open to the public. The gallery is closed between exhibitions, so call ahead or check online before you go.

Bighorn Scenic Byway

One stretch of stunning road between Yellowstone to the west and Mount Rushmore and the Black Hills to the east is the **Bighorn Scenic Byway,** a 45-mile (72-km) stretch of road that starts at Shell, Wyoming, in the dramatic Shell Canyon. Winding up through the Bighorn National Forest past Shell Falls, the byway slips through narrow canyons past red chimney rocks and towering cliffs. The highest point on the drive is Granite Pass, just above the Antelope Butte Ski Area. North of the pass, the byway intersects with U.S. 14A, known as the Medicine Wheel Passage for its access to Medicine Wheel National Historic Landmark. In addition to a diversity of landscapes—rangeland, forest, subalpine, and alpine—there is an abundance of wildlife in the region; travelers can watch for elk, moose, and deer. The access to public campgrounds and hiking trails is better on this byway than just about anywhere in the Bighorn National Forest. The byway's eastern end (although U.S. 14 continues on) is just west of Ranchester.

★ Medicine Wheel National Historic Landmark

High atop a bluff in the Big Horn Mountains, some 70 miles (113 km) or about a 90-minute drive west of Sheridan on U.S. 14A, **Medicine Wheel National Historic Landmark** is an 82-foot-wide (25-m) stone circle with 28 interior spokes connecting the exterior with an interior circular mound. Made of limestone slabs and boulders, the Medicine Wheel is a mysterious landmark that has spiritual but unexplained significance to many Native American groups. First seen by Eastern explorers in the late 1800s, thoughts on its origins are vast and varied: some link it back to the worship of the Aztecs; others attribute it to early French or Russian explorers. The most common viewpoint, however, is that it was built by one of the tribes in the region: Crow, Arapaho, Shoshone, Sheep Eater, or Cheyenne. The star alignments suggest the medicine wheel could have been constructed as early as the 13th century, and the solstice alignments are accurate even today. The only carbon dating from the site, done on a piece of wood, suggests a minimum age of 1760. There are tipi rings around the site and worn travois trails to the site, suggesting heavy usage.

1: the western store King's Saddlery **2:** Medicine Wheel National Historical Landmark

Stone markers in the shape of arrows point to a number of nearby medicine wheels, including those in Meeteetse and Steamboat Mountain in southwest Wyoming near Rock Springs.

Although the site was designated a National Historic Landmark in 1970, little was done to protect the artifacts from the elements, livestock, and, rather unfortunately, disrespectful visitors. Today the **U.S. Forest Service** (2013 Eastside 2nd St., Sheridan, 307/674-2600, www.fs.usda.gov) is responsible for protecting and preserving the area, and Native American guides have been hired to interpret the site for visitors. Driving to the site itself is restricted, so plan to park at the ranger station and walk about 1.5 miles (2.4 km) on a gravel road.

SPORTS AND RECREATION

Hiking

With the Big Horn Mountains looming so close to town, there is plenty of country to get lost in within an easy drive from Sheridan. To plan a good hike or backpacking trip, visit the **U.S. Forest Service** (2013 Eastside 2nd St., Sheridan, 307/674-2600, www.fs.usda.gov/bighorn) for maps and advice. Right downtown, **The Sport Shop** (208 N. Main St., 307/672-5356, 9am-5:30pm Mon.-Fri., 9am-5pm Sat.) can outfit hikers and backpackers or just offer friendly advice.

For adventurous types keen to head out, there are hundreds of trails in the **Bighorn National Forest,** many of which can be accessed from the Bighorn Scenic Byway on U.S. 14. One such trail is the **Tongue River,** an 18.2-mile (29.3-km) out-and-back hike that leaves from a trailhead roughly 9 miles (14.5 km) west of Ranchester on County Road 92 in the Tongue River Canyon. Though the trail climbs more than 3,000 vertical feet (914 m) over 9 miles (14.5 km), hikers looking for a shorter route will be delighted with the 2-mile (3.2-km) round-trip hike along the gushing river and up a set of switchbacks to a rather large limestone cave that can be explored if you have the right equipment (headlamps are essential). Be on the lookout, however, for livestock, poison ivy, and rattlesnakes; even with them, this is a beautiful spot.

An interactive map of the trails and campgrounds in the area is available online (www.sheridanwyoming.org).

Fishing

There is no shortage of fantastic fishing spots around Sheridan. Anglers have long flocked to the region to wet a line on the **Tongue River, Little Goose Creek,** and **Big Goose Creek** as well as any of the dozens of pristine alpine lakes in the region, including **Sibley Lake** and **Lake DeSmet.**

For up-to-date information and all the gear you could possibly need, stop into **Fly Shop of the Bighorns** (334 N. Main St., 307/672-5866, www.sheridanflyfishing.com, 7am-7pm Mon.-Sat., 7am-3pm Sun., shortened hours off-season). It offers guided walks and wades as well as float trips to blue-ribbon trout waters on both public and private lands as **Rock Creek Anglers.** Half-day wade fishing trips start at $275 for one angler, $415 for two, and $675 for three. All-day wade fishing trips are $425 for one angler, $525 for two, and $775 for three. All-day float trips are $500 for one angler and $550 for two. Private water leases can add fees of $100 per rod to the cost.

Horseback Riding

While Sheridan is surrounded by some of the best guest ranches in the country that focus on riding, there aren't many options for visitors to town who are looking for a riding opportunity without the full-on ranch experience. About 20 minutes from Sheridan is **Rangeland Enterprises** (394 Beaver Creek Rd., 307/672-6717, www.rangelandhuntingadventures.com, $40/hour, minimum age 6, reservations required). Day trips, overnight adventures, and hunting expeditions are also offered. Outside of Buffalo on U.S. 16 West, **South Fork Mountain Lodge & Outfitters** (307/267-2609, www.lodgesofthebighorns.com/south-fork-mountain-outfitters-wyoming.php) offers a range of activities and amenities,

The Mustangs of the Pryor Mountains

One of the most unforgettable experiences you can have in the West is to witness the wild mustangs of the Pryor Mountains that straddle Montana and Wyoming. The majority of these horses share the hereditary line of those brought by Spanish explorers to the Americas more than five centuries ago. The mustangs are small horses with narrow but deep chests and strong, short backs. They are often distinguished by a solid stripe running down their backs or the unique "zebra" stripes across their legs.

Although initially wary of the animals that the conquistadores rode, Native Americans quickly learned to prize them. Through the years they were traded and often stolen in raids. Horses used by the Indians or settlers were known to stray, and by the mid-1800s enough free stallions and mares had mated that there were more than two million wild horses living west of the Mississippi. At the same time, however, homesteaders were staking out their land and settling in the area. The mustangs' land was needed for houses, farms, and cattle grazing. Seen as an impediment to progress, the wild horses quickly began to disappear, hunted for sport or captured alive, where they were sent to slaughter and used by pet food companies. By the 1950s, only a handful of herds were left.

In response to the work of grassroots organizations and public outcry, the U.S. government sanctioned the **Wild Horse Range** in 1968. Some 31,000 acres (12,545 hectares) were set aside to protect these majestic animals in the Pryor Mountains. Three years later, the Wild Free Roaming Horse and Burro Act stipulated that these horses were "an integral part of the natural system of the public land" and were to be protected from future harassment.

Today around 155 mustangs live on a now 38,000-acre (15,378-hectare) range, which is maintained by the Bureau of Land Management (BLM). The mustangs live in small social units known as harems, which consist of a dominant stallion, a head mare, other mares, and colts. There are currently estimated to be about 30 harems, which produce 20-30 foals each year. In order to balance the well-being of the horses with the well-being of the public land, the BLM has overseen a wild horse adoption program since 1973.

The best place to launch a visit to the Pryor Range is the **Pryor Mountain Wild Mustang Center** (U.S. 14A, Lovell, Wyoming, 307/548-9453, www.pryormustangs.org, 9am-5pm Mon.-Sat. summer, 10am-3pm Mon.-Fri. winter), where staff can tell you about current sightings and locations.

If you drive north along Highway 37 from U.S. 14A east of Lovell into the Bighorn Canyon Recreation Area, you may get lucky and see some mustangs. Sightings are more frequent on East Pryor Mountain, but travel is much more difficult and requires four-wheel drive. There are outfitters willing to take you into the backcountry for a better chance of seeing these wild and beautiful creatures. It is critical that your presence does not impact or change their behavior in any way. The standard distance to keep from the mustangs is 100 feet (30.5 m).

included horseback riding options ($125/pp two-hour ride, $300/pp four-hour ride, including lunch), June-September.

Golf

One semiprivate and one public golf course are in the vicinity of Sheridan. The **Hidden Bridge Golf Club** (550 Mydland Rd., 307/752-6625, www.hiddenbridgegolf.com, $30 for 9 holes including cart, $45 for 18 holes including cart) is close to downtown. The municipal **Kendrick Golf Course** (65 Golf Course Rd., 307/674-8148, $30 for 9 holes with cart, $46 for 18 holes with cart) offers 18 holes with discounts for families and twilight play.

ENTERTAINMENT AND EVENTS
Nightlife

Whether you are cruising in a beat-up pickup truck or on foot, you don't have to leave Main Street for a taste of Sheridan's nightlife. The most famous of all the watering holes, and for good reason, is the **Mint Bar** (151 N. Main St., 307/674-9696, www.mintbarwyo.com, 10am-2am Mon.-Sat.), which boasts hundreds of artifacts and mounts, furniture made in the tradition of Thomas Molesworth, hundreds of local cattle brands on the wall, and ambience that cannot be beat. Don't leave without a pair of satin underpants that touts the Mint as a place "where good friends meet."

The craft brew scene is gaining steam in Sheridan with two excellent brewpubs. **Blacktooth Brewing Company** (312 Broadway, 307/675-2337, www.blacktoothbrewingcompany.com, noon-10pm Mon.-Thurs., noon-11pm Fri.-Sat., noon-7pm Sun.) pours brown ales, amber ales, wheat beers, IPAs, and a variety of seasonal offerings in a very cool space. Just down the street, **Luminous Brewhouse** (504 Broadway, 307/655-5658, www.luminousbrewhouse.com, 2pm-10pm Mon.-Thurs., noon-midnight Fri.-Sat., 1pm-5pm Sun.) brews a variety of beers including red ale, coffee ale, IPA, session ale, a roasted pueblo chile ale, and a handful of seasonal brews. They also offer live local music every Wednesday from 5pm-7pm, bluegrass jams on Tuesday nights at 7pm, and an open-mic night Thursdays at 7:30pm. There is root

beer made on premises for the kids and non-beer drinkers can order cold press coffee, kombucha, and soft drinks.

The Arts

Sheridan is home to two theaters, the **Carriage House Theater** (419 Delphi Ave., 307/672-9886) and the **WYO Theater** (42 N. Main St., 307/672-9084), the oldest vaudeville theater in the state.

Festivals and Events

Sheridan is a strong community of locals and regular yearly visitors that supports a multitude of weekly events, including the Thursday **Sheridan Farmers Market** (307/672-8881, www.downtownsheridan.org, 5pm-7pm Thurs. mid-June-mid-Sept.) at Grinnell Plaza Park (W. Algers St. and N. Brooks St.) and Tuesday evening **Concerts in the Park** (www.sheridanwyoming.org) at Kendrick Park. The third Thursday of each month is the **Third Thursday Street Festival** (www.downtownsheridan.org), with music and food vendors in the heart of downtown. For much bigger-name entertainment over a weekend in mid-June, **Big Horn Country USA** (www.bighorncountry.us) is a popular camping and music festival.

The Mint Bar is "where good friends meet."

Since 1930, the **Sheridan WYO Rodeo** (www.sheridanwyorodeo.com) has been one of the most celebrated events in the state, and its renowned posters hang as graphic art all across the West. The mid-July event entails four nights of PRCA rodeo, multiple concerts, a traditional Indian Relay with a $50,000 payout, a parade, and a footrace. The **First People's Pow Wow and Dance** (www. sheridanwyoming.org) is a celebration with traditional dancers and drum teams held over the course of several days during the Sheridan WYO Rodeo on the lawn at the Sheridan Inn.

Held annually the first week of August, the **Sheridan County Fair** (1650 W. 5th St., Sheridan, 307/672-2079, www.sherfair.com, free) offers games, contests, and events to entertain the whole family, including a pancake breakfast, horse and livestock shows, community exhibits, inflatable games and slides, and the usual 4-H and FFA events.

Later in the summer, typically in early to mid-August, the **Sheridan County Rodeo** (www.sherfair.com) is held at the local fairgrounds. Less flashy than the Sheridan WYO Rodeo, this old-school small-town rodeo showcases the abundant local talent the region is known for. Events are open to adults and kids in more than two dozen events, including roping, racing, pole bending, goat tying, and steer wrestling.

The **Suds n' Spurs Brew Fest** (307/672-2485, www.sheridanwyoming.org) is an end-of-summer event with live music, food vendors, and, of course, plenty of beer. Held in Whitney Commons Park (200 W. Alger St.) in late August, a $30 ticket buys unlimited samples from more than 20 breweries. Transportation is available from the Sheridan Trolley.

SHOPPING

After a requisite stop at **King's Saddlery** (184 N. Main St., 307/672-2702 or 800/443-8919, www.kingssaddlery.com, 8am-5pm Mon.-Sat.), shoppers can stroll up and down historic **Main Street** with its abundance of art galleries, boutiques, and classic Western stores.

For appropriate cowboy and cowgirl duds, stop into the **Custom Cowboy Shop** (1286 Sheridan Ave., 800/487-2692, www. customcowboyshop.com, 9am-6pm Mon.-Sat. Oct.-May, 9am-8pm Mon.-Sat., 10am-7pm Sun. June-Sept.), which was founded by cattle rancher and saddle maker Don Butler in 1976 as a way to make ends meet. Today this store, as well as another location in Cody, carries everything from saddles and tack to hats, buckles, scarves, clothing, jewelry, and housewares.

A couple of great Main Street shops worth visiting are **Little Willow Traders** (166 N. Main St., 307/672-0200, www. littlewillowtraders.com, 10am-5:30pm Mon.-Sat.), which sells rustic home furnishings, gifts, clothing, and more, and **Over the Moon Boutique** (176 N. Main St., 307/673-4821, www.shopoverthemoon.com, 10am-5:30pm Mon.-Thurs., 10am-5:30pm Fri.-Sat.), which sells women's clothing, jewelry, bath and body products, handmade jewelry, baby clothing, and gifts.

The Sugar Boot (198 N. Main St., 307/675-1825, 10am-7pm Mon.-Sat.) is an old-timey candy shop with hand-dipped ice cream and retro toys, too.

For sporting goods, try **The Sport Shop** (208 N. Main St., 307/672-5356, 9am-5:30pm Mon.-Fri., 9am-5pm Sat.).

FOOD

Unlike much of rural Wyoming, Sheridan is quite cosmopolitan when it comes to dining options. There is plenty of variety—think Chinese, Korean, and Mexican—plus some sophisticated gourmet eateries. Even so, it's never hard to find a juicy burger or steak in this cattle country.

A high-end restaurant in the Sheridan community since 2013 is **Frackelton's** (55 N. Main St., 307/675-6055, www.frackeltons. com, 10am-2pm and 4pm-10pm Mon.-Sat., 10am-2pm Sun., $12-34) with the comfort-gourmet cuisine. The restaurant serves American bistro cuisine featuring familiar, mouthwatering burgers, salads, pastas, and juicy steaks. Among the local favorites are penne pasta with gorgonzola sauce, pan-roasted beef tenderloin, and the Original Bar & Grill Burger.

A tried-and-true favorite in town (and across Montana and Wyoming) is **Wyoming's Rib & Chop House** (847 N. Main St., 307/673-4700, www.ribandchophouse.com, 11am-9pm Sun.-Thurs., 11am-10pm Fri.-Sat., $14-45), which is known for its steaks, seafood, and baby back ribs.

For classic Western fare all day long, look no further than the **Cowboy Cafe** (138 N. Main St., 307/672-2391, www.cowboycafewyo.com, 7am-9pm daily, $9-18). Some of their specialties include soft tacos, corned beef hash, burgers, the Reuben sandwich and the Cowboy Cuban sandwich.

A good local place for a quick breakfast or lunch with Mexican flair is **Oliva's Kitchen** (437 N. Main St., 307/673-0986, 6am-9pm Mon.-Sat., $7-23). Locals line up for enchiladas and Oliva's famous *alambre,* grilled beef topped with chopped bacon, peppers, onions, cheese, salsa, and avocado.

For another gourmet, and rather unexpected treat for weekday lunches, try the **Wyoming Culinary Institute** (1841 S. Sheridan Ave., 307/764-3388, www.sheridan.edu, 11:30am-2pm Mon.-Fri., $8-14) at Sheridan College. Specialties include risotto croquettes, starburst grapefruit salad, shrimp sliders, and lobster thermidor penne. There's even a kids' menu.

ACCOMMODATIONS

Sheridan has a broad assortment of roadside hotels and motels. One of the most interesting is the ★ **Mill Inn** (2161 Coffeen Ave., 307/672-6401 or 888/357-6455, www.sheridanmillinn.com, $85-125), cleverly built in an 1890s flour mill and listed on the National Register of Historic Places. The modern rooms are standard and comfortable. For historic charm though, nothing beats the **Sheridan Inn** (856 Broadway, 307/674-2178, www.sheridaninn.com, $179-349). Built in

1893 and reopened as a hotel in 2015, the hotel has long been a hub of the community. Buffalo Bill even auditioned performers for his Wild West Show on the rambling front porch. The 22 rooms and suites are named for important people in Buffalo Bill's storied life.

Among the best budget-friendly options in town is the **Super Saver Inn** (1789 N. Main St., 307/672-0471, www.supersaverinn.com, $65-77), near the VA Medical Center; it is clean and very basic, offering microwaves, coffeemakers, refrigerators, free Wi-Fi, and a coin laundry on-site. The 37 guest rooms are pet-friendly (for $8 additional), and the inn's rates are the lowest in town.

At the other end of the spectrum, the **Comfort Inn** (1950 E. 5th St., 307/675-1101, www.choicehotels.com, $129-164) is geared to business travelers and has spacious over-size rooms with nice amenities, including a complimentary continental breakfast buffet, a fitness room, free Wi-Fi, a pool, and a self-service business center. Every room offers either a view of the Big Horn Mountains or the prairie. Located on a hilltop east of I-90, the Comfort Inn is quiet with easy access to town.

Among the other chain hotels in town are **Baymont by Wyndham** (911 Sibley Cir., 307/673-9500, www.wyndhamhotels.com, $114-134), **Days Inn** (1104 E. Brundage Ln., 307/672-2888, www.wyndhamhotels.com, $82-125), **Best Western Sheridan Center** (612 N. Main St., 307/674-7421, www.bestwestern.com, $119-140), and **Holiday Inn** (1809 Sugarland Dr., 307/672-8931 or 800/315-2621, www.ing.com, $123-169).

For a unique experience just 15 miles (24 km) south of Sheridan (take Hwy. 335 to County Rd. 77 to Canyon Ranch Rd.), the 3,000-acre (1,214-hectare) **Canyon Ranch** (59 Canyon Ranch Rd., Big Horn, 307/751-6785 or 307/751-3580, www.canyonranchbighorn.com) has been run by the Wallop family for more than a century and offers ranch-type accommodations and vacation rentals as well as activities like fly-fishing, polo, and wildflower viewing. From the Foreman's House ($1,500/week) and the Hay Meadow House

($2,350/week), upgraded with all the modern amenities—flat-screen TVs, Wi-Fi, modern kitchens, and laundry rooms—to the Canyon Ranch Lodge ($2,400/week), this is ranch living at its most beautiful.

GUEST RANCHES

One beloved dude ranch in the area, operating for more than a century, is the **HF Bar** (1301 Rock Creek Rd., 307/684-2487, www.hfbar. com, $350/day ages 13 and over, $250/day children 5-12, all-inclusive, 7-day minimum June-Sept.), located about 35 miles (56 km) from Sheridan or 20 miles (32 km) northwest of Buffalo. The cabins are at once rustic and comfortable, and activities include horseback riding, fishing, hiking, and sporting clays, among others.

Another option is the **Wyoming High Country Lodge** (Forest Rd. 13, 307/529-0914, www.wyhighcountry.com, $90-100 Nov.-May, $90-125 June-Oct.), which is about 30 miles (48 km) outside of Lovell in the Bighorn National Forest. This year-round ranch offers rustic rooms or cute cabins and any number of activities (except horseback riding!) including fishing, hiking, mountain biking, ATV trips, hunting, snow-kiting, cross-country skiing, and snowmobiling.

For a comprehensive list of dude ranches across the region, contact the **Dude Ranchers' Association** (866/399-2339 or 307/587-2339, www.duderanch.org), which represents more than 100 of the West's most respected ranches. Another excellent resource for finding the ideal dude ranch vacation is **Gene Kilgore's Ranchweb** (www. ranchweb.com).

★ Eatons Ranch

A half-hour's drive from Sheridan, nestled along Wolf Creek in the Big Horn Mountains, is **Eatons Ranch** (270 Eaton Ranch Rd., 307/655-9552, www.eatonsranch.com, $260-325/day pp early June-mid-Aug., $240-285/day pp early June and mid-Aug.-Sept., all-inclusive), the oldest dude ranch in the world and the cream of the crop. The cabins are old and

charming, and the wonder of Eatons is that it rarely changes through the decades. The founding family is still running the ranch, which can accommodate up to 125 guests, and many of the dudes' families have been coming for generations as well. The riding is excellent, and Eatons is among the only ranches where riders can take to the mountains or prairies without a wrangler (although one is always available). The setting is magnificent and diverse—with mountains, canyons, and prairies to ride—and the traditions here are time-tested. In the winter, bed-and-breakfast packages are available for single night or longer stays.

CAMPING

There are numerous public campgrounds in the Bighorn National Forest, many of which are easily accessed from the Bighorn Scenic Byway. For information about specific sites and, in some cases, to make reservations, contact the **U.S. Forest Service** (2013 Eastside 2nd St., Sheridan, 307/674-2600, www.fs.usda. gov/bighorn). Reservations can be booked at some sites through www.recreation.gov.

A handful of RV parks are scattered around town. The **Sheridan KOA** (63 Decker Rd., 307/674-8766 or 800/652-7621, www.koa.com, $45-80) offers tent and RV sites, one- to two-room cabins, bike rentals, fishing, miniature golf, a swimming pool, and free Wi-Fi.

INFORMATION AND SERVICES

The office of **Sheridan Travel and Tourism** (1517 E. 5th St., 307/673-7120, www. sheridanwyoming.org, 8am-5pm daily summer, 8am-5pm Mon.-Fri. fall-spring) is conveniently located at the **State of Wyoming Information Center** (just east of I-90 at exit 23) and can offer very helpful advice in person or over the phone.

For information on hiking, camping, and other recreation in the Bighorn National Forest, contact the **U.S. Forest Service** (2013 Eastside 2nd St., Sheridan, 307/674-2600, www.fs.usda.gov/bighorn). Information on

The Nation's First Dude Ranch

In 1868, a trio of brothers left Pittsburgh in pursuit of more adventure than their father's dry goods store promised. Howard Eaton settled in the Badlands of North Dakota; his brothers Alden and Willis joined him a few years later, and together the three established a small ranch near what would become the town of Medora, North Dakota. On the Custer Trail Ranch, the brothers made their living by supplying wild game to railroad workers and hay to the nearby U.S. Army fort, all while establishing their own herds of horses and cattle.

Stories of their adventures trickled east, and before long the much-loved brothers hosted an endless string of friends. In 1882, realizing the financial strain he and others were placing on the hospitable Eatons, Bert Rumsey insisted on paying for the privilege of staying on the ranch. In so doing, Rumsey became the world's first "dude," a term coined by Howard Eaton. Modest as it was—guests slept several to a bed or on the floor, paying $25 per month for the right to do chores—the dude ranching industry was born.

The brutal winter of 1886-1887 changed dude ranching from a practicality to a necessity: The Eatons lost all but 150 of their 1,500 cattle to the cold and snow. The paying guests kept the Eatons afloat.

In 1904, the Eaton brothers bought 7,000 acres (2,833 hectares) of land on the northeastern slope of the Big Horn Mountains. They announced to their friends that they'd be taking a year off to build structures on the ranch: cabins, barns, and a dining hall. Some 70 dudes showed up anyway and for about $100 apiece built many of the cabins that stand today. Although Howard and Willis remained lifelong bachelors, Alden married and set into motion the family that would run the ranch for more than a century. His great-great-grandson, Jeff Way, is the ranch general manager today, and like those before him, he and his own family welcome guests every summer.

Not much has changed since 1903. Days start early with the thunder of horses being brought down from night pasture. The clanging of an old locomotive wheel signals the start of hearty meals served family-style in the old dining hall. There are still Saturday-night cookouts and West-

fishing and hunting is available through the **Wyoming Game and Fish Department** (700 Valley View Dr., 307/672-7418, http://wgfd.wyo.gov).

The **main post office** (307/672-0714, 7:30am-5:30pm Mon.-Fri., 8am-noon Sat.) in Sheridan is at 101 East Loucks Street.

The **Sheridan County Fulmer Public Library** (335 W. Alger St., 307/674-8585, www.sheridanwyolibrary.org, 9am-9pm Mon.-Thurs., 9am-5pm Fri.-Sat.) has both Internet-connected computers and free Wi-Fi available.

Sheridan Memorial Hospital (1401 W. 5th St., 307/672-1000, www.sheridanhospital.org) has a 24-hour emergency room. There are also two urgent care facilities in town: **Cedars Health Sheridan Clinic** (813 Highland Ave., 307/673-5501, 8am-8pm Mon.-Fri., 8am-5pm Sat.) and **Sugarland Walk-in Clinic** (1005 Sugarland Dr., 307/675-7777, 8:30am-5:30pm Mon.-Fri.).

Do laundry at **Wash Yer Wooleys Laundry** (2220 Coffeen Ave., Unit D, 307/752-0389, 24 hours daily).

TRANSPORTATION

Getting There

The tiny **Sheridan County Airport** (SHR, 908 W. Brundage Ln., 307/674-4222) offers daily flights to and from Denver on **Denver Air Connection** (866/373-8513, www.flysheridan.com). The nearest larger airports are about 135 miles (217 km) away (2 hours by car) in Billings (BIL) and Casper (CPR).

Bus service in the region is provided by **Jefferson Bus Lines** (307/674-6188 or 800/451-5333, www.jeffersonlines.com). The non-ticketing bus stop in Sheridan is at Good 2 Go Food Store (1229 Brundage Ln.,

Horses are wrangled each morning and released each evening at Eatons Ranch in Wolf.

ern dances, picnics, softball games, rodeos, and more riding than the horsiest Easterner could ever dream of.

The dude season at **Eatons Ranch** (307/655-9285, www.eatonsranch.com) runs late May-September, and the ranch can accommodate 125 guests in 47 cabins and three suites in the main ranch house. Depending on the dates and cabin selected, adult nightly rates for a six-night stay range $240-325, children 6-17 are $215-240 per night, and children under 6 are not charged. Rates include transportation to and from Sheridan, accommodations, all meals, and riding.

307/672-6802). The nearest ticketing stop is in Buffalo, Wyoming.

By car, Sheridan is 103 miles (166 km) northwest of Gillette, 147 miles (237 km) east of Cody, 199 miles (320 km) east of Yellowstone National Park, and 324 miles (525 km) northeast of Jackson.

Getting Around

Rental cars are available from **Avis, Budget,** or **Enterprise.** Local taxi service is available by calling **WYO Rides Sheridan Taxi** (307/675-8294).

★ BIG HORN

On the eastern flank of the Big Horns, the tiny town of **Big Horn** (population 490; elevation 4,081 ft/1,244 m) packs a lot of punch. The town was initially settled by upper-class ranchers and European aristocrats; among them was the Moncreiffe family, who raised prize sheep in the region. Although the town never officially incorporated, at one time the population purportedly passed 1,000 but rapidly dwindled in 1893 when the railroad came to Sheridan, 9 miles (14.5 km) northeast. Still, with its heritage of gentleman ranchers and a significant population boom since 2000, Big Horn has an assortment of fascinating sites and a unique culture that make a stop in town worthwhile.

Sights

For starters, **The Brinton Museum** (239 Brinton Rd., 307/672-3173, www.thebrintonmuseum.org, 9:30am-5pm Wed.-Sun., $10 adults, $8 seniors 62 and over and students 13 and over with ID, free for children under 13) is an exquisite museum housed on the grounds of a genteel 1920s and

The Bozeman Trail

Although the Bozeman Trail was not given a name until John Jacobs and John Bozeman plowed through the region to give optimistic miners and settlers access to the quickest route through the Powder River Basin, the trail was an ancient migratory route long used by animals and Paleo-Indians. Today this modern transportation corridor is rich with evidence from the past: pictographs, petroglyphs, and ledger art. There are oral histories of trappers and traders in the area that date back to the mid-1700s; written records from Lewis and Clark, who zigzagged across the trail; and evidence that mountain men, missionaries, and the U.S. military all used the trail that, until the first gold rush in southwest Montana in 1862, probably resembled a well-used, age-old game trail.

Enter Jacobs and Bozeman in 1863. Leading a wagon train toward the goldfields in Montana, the men were just 140 miles (225 km) beyond Deer Creek when they met a large party of Northern Cheyenne and Sioux warriors. Although the bulk of the wagon train turned back toward the Oregon Trail crossing southern and central Wyoming, Bozeman and a few of the men continued on horseback through the region. The following year, Bozeman again led a wagon train through the region, this time with help from Allen Hurlbut and mountain man Jim Bridger. Although non-native traffic through the area was illegal under the Fort Laramie Treaty of 1851, military support for the Bozeman Trail was evident in various campaigns throughout the region. The treaties signed at Fort Sully in 1865 gave the military unchecked authority to build roads and forts along the Bozeman Trail, and in 1866 alone, more than 2,000 people traveled on it to Montana, with Fort Reno and Fort Phil Kearny established to protect civilians. On December 21, with tensions high between Native Americans and the military, an entire command of 81 men, under Capt. William J. Fetterman, was demolished by Sioux warriors.

In 1868, after several more battles, the Bozeman Trail and the forts along it were abandoned as indefensible by the U.S. Army. Still, the trail saw traffic from expeditions sent to scout the Yellowstone area and the Black Hills. When the Cheyenne were ultimately defeated by General Crook in November 1876 and forced to live on a reservation, the Bozeman Trail once again opened the region to significant settler traffic. Gradually, it became the preferred route for telegraph lines, stagecoaches, and eventually, an interstate highway.

'30s working ranch. Bradford Brinton was a wealthy businessman from Chicago when he bought the ranch in 1923. He turned it into an elaborate estate to showcase his ever-growing collection of art, which he left to his sister when he died. She meticulously maintained the home and collection and left both to the Northern Trust Company of Chicago. Tours through the 20-room Brinton home are available. And inside the 24,000-square-foot (2,230-sq-m), eco-conscious rammed-earth museum is one of the most important collections of Native American and Western art in the Rocky Mountains. It showcases the largest collection of works by Hans Kleiber in the world, in addition to a surprising number of works by Charlie Russell and Frederic Remington. In addition to four galleries on three floors, the museum has a gift store and farm-to-table bistro, which utilizes fresh produce grown on-site and, in good weather, opens onto a lovely patio with views to the mountains.

Another surprising museum in this tiny little town is the **Bozeman Trail Museum** (335 Johnson St., 307/674-6363 or 307/674-8050, 11am-4pm Sat.-Sun. Memorial Day-Labor Day, free). Built in what was a log blacksmith shop to serve travelers along the trail, the museum includes Native American artifacts, photos, pioneer clothing, books, tools, and other artifacts.

Sports and Recreation

Big Horn is also the **polo** hotbed of Wyoming, with practice games on Wednesday and Friday at 1pm and 3pm, and tournament games on Sunday at 2pm in June and at 1pm and 3pm in July and August, at the noteworthy **Big Horn Equestrian Center** (932 Bird Farm Rd.,

307/673-0454, www.thebhec.org). Admission to the announced matches is free, and concessions are available. Every year on Labor Day Sunday-Monday, the center closes out the season with **Don King Days,** a classic Western celebration with polo, championship steer roping, bronco riding, and wild-cow milking. The center is also one of the local favorite places to spend the **Fourth of July,** with a phenomenal fireworks display.

Buffalo and Vicinity

A neat little Western town with a lot of history and a surprising Basque influence, Buffalo (population 4,590; elevation 4,645 ft/1,416 m) was settled in 1879. Historically it is among Wyoming's biggest sheep towns, which was true as recently as the 1980s, until a late-spring storm after shearing in 1984 caused major losses and reminded locals of the Great Die-up of 1886-1887. Political and environmental conditions never allowed ranchers to recover. Instead, Buffalo makes the most of its beautiful location in the foothills of the Big Horn Mountains, its easy access to scenic drives and outdoor adventures, and its historic buildings and museums.

SIGHTS
Jim Gatchell Memorial Museum
The origins of the **Jim Gatchell Memorial Museum** (100 Fort St., 307/684-9331, www.jimgatchell.com, 9am-5pm Mon.-Sat., noon-5pm Sun. May 26-Sept. 2, 8am-4pm Mon.-Fri. Sept. 4-May 25, $7 adults, $5 seniors, $5 children 12-18, $3 children 6-11, free for children under 6) can be traced back to the opening of the Buffalo Pharmacy in 1900, the first of its kind in town. People from all walks of life—cattle barons, outlaws, and homesteaders—frequented Jim Gatchell's drugstore, and many would give him small mementos, which he kept. Over time, they began entrusting him with pieces of Johnson County history. He also befriended the local Indians, and they too would bestow on him different cultural and personal artifacts.

After Gatchell passed away in 1954, his family donated his collection to Johnson County with the condition it would be shared with the public. The museum was established three years later. Its focus is on Johnson County's frontier-era history, and more than 15,000 pieces are on display. There is a large array of Native American artifacts and many pieces that can be traced back to the U.S. Cavalry, plus a variety of wagons, historical photos, a model of Fort Phil Kearny, artifacts from the fateful Fetterman Fight, and many interpretive materials related to the Bozeman Trail.

★ Occidental Hotel
Entering the **Occidental Hotel** (10 N. Main St., 307/684-0451, www.occidentalwyoming.com, $110-285), many visitors feel as if they've stepped back in time. The hotel has been painstakingly restored to its original 1880s splendor, which includes many of its original furnishings such as light fixtures, the back bar, tin ceilings, a piano, and stained glass. Even the bullet holes throughout the bar are mementos of rowdier days. The place is said to be part museum, part hotel, part bar and restaurant. Visitors can follow a brochure for a self-guided tour or take a free 15-minute guided tour. Hotel guests have a variety of individual suites to choose from, each uniquely decorated with different antiques and features to match the original era. On Thursday nights, the saloon hosts a jam session featuring high-caliber bluegrass, Western, and folk musicians.

Dry Creek Petrified Tree Environmental Area
To find the unusual Dry Creek Petrified Forest, drive east from Buffalo 7 miles (11.3 km) on

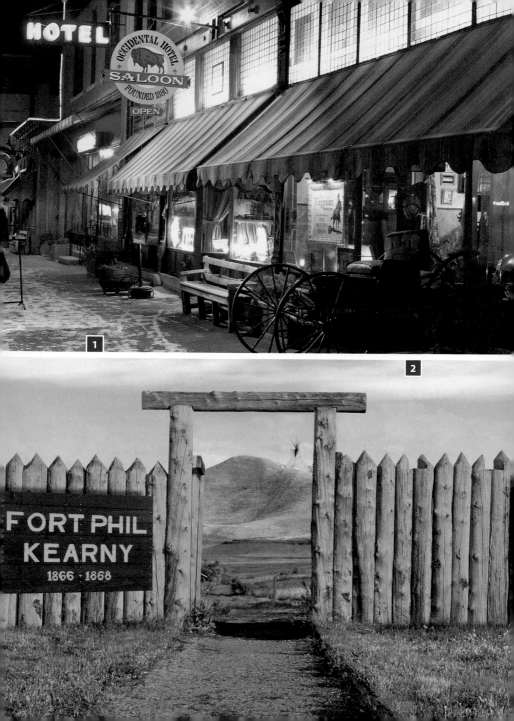

I-90, take the Red Hills Road exit (exit 65), and drive north on Tipperary Road for 5 miles (8 km) to the Petrified Tree Area access road. In the midst of this sagebrush country, you can follow a 0.8-mile (1.3-km) loop that winds through the remnants of petrified trees that date back 60 million years to when the area was swampland covered by metasequoia trees. Some of the stumps are larger than 4 feet (1.2 m) in diameter, and the numerous rings can be identified. The loop that takes visitors through the area is also an eight-station ecological trail with information about the process of petrifaction and the unique history of the land.

Fort Phil Kearny State Historic Site

Between Sheridan and Buffalo off I-90, the **Fort Phil Kearny State Historic Site** (528 Wagon Box Rd., Banner, 307/684-7629, www. fortphilkearny.com, grounds dawn-dusk daily, $4 nonresidents, $2 residents, free for children under 18) commemorates the fort that stood on the site 1866-1868.

The fort was commissioned at the height of the Indian Wars when the Sioux stood by their vow to fight for their traditional hunting grounds against anyone who dared cross into the Powder River Basin. Although Col. H. B. Carrington attempted to get permission for the fort's construction from Sioux chief Red Cloud, it was never given. The soldiers lived with nearly constant attacks by the Sioux. In the first six months, some 154 people were killed by Indians, and 700 horses, mules, and cattle were stolen.

At 17 acres (6.9 hectares), the fort was a complete settlement, with a stockade, variety of living quarters, social club, guardhouse, hospital, even a laundress row. But the structures alone were little help in keeping the soldiers safe. The battles that took place in close proximity to the fort include the Fetterman Fight and the Wagon Box Fight. By 1868 the railroad had made the Bozeman Trail

---

1: the Occidental Hotel **2:** Fort Phil Kearny State Historic Site

obsolete, and the military abandoned the fort as indefensible. It was burned to the ground, likely by the Cheyenne, in 1868.

At the site of the fort today are an **interpretive center and museum** (8am-6pm daily May-Sept., noon-4pm Wed.-Sun. Oct.-Dec. 21) that provide information for self-guided tours of the grounds and outlying sites. A cabin built by the Civilian Conservation Corps was crafted to resemble officers' quarters. Several of the battlefields are accessible within 5 miles (8 km) of the fort.

TOP EXPERIENCE

★ Cloud Peak Skyway Scenic Byway

Traveling from Buffalo on U.S. 16 over the southern portion of the Big Horn Mountains toward Ten Sleep and Worland, the 45-mile (72-km) paved Cloud Peak Skyway Scenic Byway offers breathtaking scenery of the Cloud Peak Wilderness and the only view of Cloud Peak itself, the highest mountain in the Big Horns. This remarkable stretch of road is the southernmost route across the Big Horns. The summit is at 9,666 feet (2,946 m), and the road also winds through the spectacular Tensleep Canyon. Multiple turnouts are along the way for travelers to stretch their legs and enjoy the view; the road also passes **Fort McKinney** and runs just 20 miles (32 km) south of **Medicine Lodge State Archeological Site**, known for its ancient petroglyphs, pictographs, and idyllic campgrounds. There is also ample access to hiking trails in the Bighorn National Forest.

SPORTS AND RECREATION

Hiking

In addition to the wealth of trails in the nearby **Bighorn National Forest** (www. fs.usda.gov), Buffalo has an excellent 12-mile (19.3-km) trail system in town. Known as the **Clear Creek Trail System,** the well-marked trails can be accessed around town at various spots, including the historic shopping district

The Fetterman Fight of 1866

During the 1860s onslaught of eager gold seekers looking for a quick route to riches in Montana, John Bozeman led many travelers along the trail that would eventually bear his name, taking them from southeast Wyoming across the Powder River Basin into Montana. The Sioux who inhabited the region had fought and removed the Crow and were determined to prevent settlers from moving in as well. Travelers were warned not to venture past the Northern Platte River, and the military felt that in order to protect the Bozeman Trail, new forts would need to be established.

In June 1866 the military met with the Sioux chief Red Cloud, to attain permission to build forts in the area. Though he refused, and despite a warning by the Sioux, the commander of the area, Col. H. B. Carrington, gave orders to build a fort at the fork of Big Piney and Little Piney Creeks. The fort was named after Civil War general Phil Kearny. Both the Cheyenne and Jim Bridger had warned Carrington that it was a death wish to build the fort in the middle of the Sioux's hunting ground. But the warnings went unheeded.

True to their word, the Sioux made numerous attacks on the fort. Within the first five months, there were many civilian and military losses as well as the theft of horses, mules, and cattle. The fort's construction required timber and logs to be shipped in from the nearby Big Horn Mountains, and the trains were easy targets for the Sioux.

In mid-December 1866, Capt. William J. Fetterman and his 18th Cavalry were stationed at the fort. Fetterman did not think highly of the Sioux's fighting skills and was convinced that if given the opportunity, his 80 men "could ride through the whole Sioux nation." In response, Jim Bridger reminded Fetterman and his men that although they had fought in the South during the Civil War, "they don't know anything about fighting Indians."

On December 21, 1866, the Sioux attacked a lumber train heading toward the fort. Fetterman and his men responded to the cries for help, intending to ward off the attackers. The 18th Cavalry pursued the attackers, chasing the Indians who dared to taunt them, and rode right into a well-designed ambush about 5 miles (8 km) from the fort. The 81 men were dead within 30 minutes. No one would see such an obliteration of U.S. troops until Custer's last stand at the Battle of the Little Bighorn 10 years later.

For this brief period, the Sioux had successfully defended their territory. The Bozeman Trail was no longer used, and by 1868 Fort Kearny was abandoned.

Today the site of the fight, which is 2 miles (3.2 km) from the fort along Old Highway 87, is marked by a stone monument. The site of **Fort Phil Kearny** (528 Wagon Box Rd., Banner, 307/684-7629, www.fortphilkearny.com, grounds dawn-dusk daily, $4 nonresidents, $2 residents, free for children under 18) has been designated a National Historic Landmark. Although the original fort was burned to the ground, most likely by Indians, it was partially reconstructed in 2000. There is also a small **museum** (8am-6pm daily May-Sept., noon-4pm Wed.-Sun. Oct.-Dec. 21).

on Main Street, the motel circle near the intersection of I-25 and U.S. 16, the city park, and the Mosier Gulch picnic area. Mountain bikes are welcome on the trail, and maps are available through the **Buffalo Chamber of Commerce** (307/684-5544 or 800/227-5122, www.buffalowyo.com).

Swimming

Buffalo has a wonderful free public outdoor swimming pool, the largest in the state, attracting locals and visitors alike on warm summer days. The enormous pool at **Washington** **Memorial Park** (S. Burritt Ave. and W. Angus St., free) is surrounded by trees, walking trails, and prime picnic spots. There is also a water park for kids and a snack shack. The pool is open midmorning-sunset June-August.

Fishing

For fishing gear and current conditions on such varied water as **Clear Creek, Rock Creek,** the **Powder River,** and a variety of mountain and prairie lakes, stop in at **The Sports Lure** (66 S. Main St., 307/684-7682, www.sportslure.com, 8am-6pm Mon.-Sat., 10am-4pm Sun.).

Buffalo offers an excellent way to pair two of the state's favorite pastimes. For guided fishing trips on horseback to any of 200 mountain lakes and streams in the Big Horns, contact **South Fork Mountain Lodge & Outfitters** (U.S. 16 W., 16 mi/26 km west of Buffalo, 307/267-2609, www.lodgesofthebighorns.com, $500 full-day). Its guides know how to find the rainbows, brookies, native cutthroats, browns, and golden trout.

To leave the horse behind and just focus on the fish, **Rock Creek Anglers** (1301 Rock Creek Rd., Saddlestring, 888/945-3876, www.rockcreekanglers.com, half-day wading trip for 1 angler $250, all-day wading trip for 1 angler $400, all-day drift boat trip for 1 angler $475) can get you onto any number of rivers, plus private waters, for a chance at hauling in some trout. It can also arrange accommodations.

Horseback Riding

Outside of Buffalo on U.S. 16 West, the **South Fork Mountain Lodge & Outfitters** (307/267-2609, www.lodgesofthebighorns.com) offers the full range of activities and amenities, including two-hour rides ($125), four-hour rides with lunch ($300), and full-day wilderness rides

including lunch ($500), June-September. It also offers pack trips, drop camps, fishing and hunting trips, plus overnight accommodations in streamside log cabins.

Golf

Golfers can hit the links at the 18-hole **Buffalo Golf Course** (500 W. Hart St., 307/684-5266, www.buffalowygolf.com, $40 for 18 holes, $15 cart/rider). In 2009, this course was voted the best municipal golf club in Wyoming by *Golf Digest.*

ENTERTAINMENT AND EVENTS

The biggest event in Buffalo is the week-long annual **Johnson County Fair and Rodeo** (307/684-7357, www.johnsoncountyfairgrounds.com), held at the Johnson County Fairgrounds during the end of July and first week of August; it culminates with a three-day rodeo. There are also two rodeos weekly in the region: The **Cowgirl Rodeo** (www.johnsoncountyfairgrounds.com), featuring women, girls, and boys under 16, is held each Tuesday night at the Johnson County Fairgrounds June-August, and the **Kaycee Lion's Club Rodeo** (7pm-10pm, $5 admission) is held every Friday night at

The Cloud Peak Skyway Scenic Byway travels over some of the highest points of the Big Horn Mountains.

Harold Jarrard Park in nearby Kaycee; call the **Buffalo Chamber of Commerce** (307/684-5544) or **Kaycee Chamber of Commerce** (307/738-2444), respectively, for more information. Also in the area, the tiny town of Ten Sleep has been hosting regular rodeos since 1908, when audience members circled their covered wagons to form a makeshift arena. The Ten Sleep **Beauty and the Beast Rodeo** (307/366-2311, www.wtschamber.org) is held over Memorial Day, and the **Fourth of July Rodeo** (307/366-2311, www.wtschamber.org) happens over two days.

Since 2012, **Longmire Days** (307/684-5544, www.buffalowyo.com) has become the biggest event of Buffalo's summer season. A celebration of all things Longmire—the books by local author Craig Johnson and popular TV adaptation on Netflix—this event includes a 5K race, autograph sessions with the author and actors, an arts and crafts show, food vendors, and plenty of other entertainment. It's like an Old West version of Comic-Con, if such a thing is possible.

FOOD

Known for its hearty breakfasts and great burgers, **Main Street Diner** (41 N. Main St., 307/684-5627, 7am-1pm Tues.-Fri., 7am-noon Sat., 8am-noon Sun., $6-12) has a full menu and a homey small-town feel.

Up in Smoke (94 S. Main St., 307/217-2290, www.upinsmokebuffalowy.com, 11am-10pm Thurs.-Sat., serving until 10pm, $8-30) offers a unique approach to barbecue. It incorporates organic produce, dairy, and chicken whenever possible; all dishes are made from scratch; and takeout containers, made from cornstarch, are biodegradable. In other words, if there is such a thing as healthy and green barbecue, this is it. Sit outside on warm summer evenings and savor the delicious food with a regional microbrew or a premium Scotch. And there's live music on Friday and Saturday nights. Up in Smoke accepts cash and local checks only.

For family dining and three square meals a day, this Western states chain restaurant,

Bozeman Trail Steakhouse (675 E. Hart St., 307/684-5555 or 888/351-6732, www.thebozemantrailsteakhouse.com, 11am-9pm daily, $10-30), is a safe bet for everyone. Little ones will love the kids' menu, and adults will appreciate the variety from steaks and game to Mexican specialties, huge salads, and good old-fashioned favorites like chicken-fried steak.

By far the most upscale dining experience in town is **The Virginian** (10 N. Main St., 307/684-0451, www.occidentalwyoming.com, from 5pm Tues.-Sat., $22-55), named for Owen Wister's iconic novel and housed in the historic Occidental Hotel. The ambience is 1890s chic, and the food is globally gourmet, with offerings including bison rib eye, elk tenderloin, and filet mignon Occidental. The beer and wine list is impressive too. For an unforgettable meal in a one-of-a-kind setting, this is a marvelous place for dinner. Also in the Occidental, a wonderful spot for breakfast, lunch, dinner, or an ice-cream treat anytime is the **Busy Bee Café** (7am-8pm daily summer, 7am-4pm off-season, hours may be shorter depending on patronage, $7-12), which serves hearty Western fare including biscuits and gravy, bison burgers, and world-class root beer floats.

ACCOMMODATIONS

For such a small town, Buffalo has a surprising number of chain hotels and motels, which indicates its popularity with travelers. A great mom-and-pop option with the best rates in town is the **Big Horn Motel** (209 N. Main St., 307/684-7822, www.bighorn-motel.com, $75-132). Rooms are clean and comfortable. There's a little art gallery on-site, and the personal touches—including baked goods made with eggs from the owners' chickens—make this a wonderful place to stay. Among the chain hotels are the pet-friendly **Days Inn** (333 E. Hart St., 307/684-2219, www.wyndhamhotels.com, $77-99) and the **Holiday Inn Express Hotel & Suites** (106 U.S. 16 E., 307/684-9900, www.ihg.com, $127-185).

The ★ **Occidental Hotel** (10 N. Main St., 307/684-0451, www.occidentalwyoming.com, $110-285) is an upscale historic gem that is worth every penny. From its historical ties to such figures as Owen Wister and Teddy Roosevelt, among others, to its fantastic restaurant, this is a uniquely Wyoming getaway.

GUEST RANCHES

For an authentic cowboy and cowgirl experience at a working ranch, try the **TA Guest Ranch** (28623 Old Hwy. 87, 307/684-5833, www.taranch.com), south of Buffalo off I-25 on Crazy Woman Creek. Established as a working ranch in 1883, this 8,000-acre (3,237-hectare) working cattle ranch offers beautifully restored Victorian accommodations, gourmet meals, riding twice daily, fly-fishing, and a variety of other dude ranch activities. The ranch focuses on local history and takes guests to tipi rings and Bozeman Trail sites on the property as well as important battlefields nearby. Since guests get to work, ride, and even share meals with the ranch crew, there is a real sense of camaraderie. The TA Ranch is one of the few in the area that does not require a weeklong stay, so visitors can enjoy the ranch's activities and amenities for as little as one night. All-inclusive rates start at $350 per day for adults (25 percent discounts are available for stays of longer than four days); bed-and-breakfast rates that don't include riding or meals range $175-275 based on double occupancy.

Another wonderful family-oriented ranch in the area is the **HF Bar Ranch** (1301 Rock Creek Rd., Saddlestring, 307/684-2487, www.hfbar.com, from $350/day ages 13 and up, $250/day children 5-12, all-inclusive), which offers wonderful riding and an assortment of fun activities for kids. The HF Bar is the second-oldest dude ranch in the country after Eatons Ranch in Wolf.

CAMPING

Thirty-two inexpensive public campgrounds ($13-20) can be found nearby in the **Bighorn National Forest** (877/444-6777, www.recreation.gov), about 15 miles (24 km) west of Buffalo on U.S. 16. Right in town is the **Indian Campground & RV Park** (660

E. Hart St., 307/684-9601 or 866/808-9601, www.indiancampground.com, mid-Apr.-mid-Oct., $31 tents, $42-45 RVs, $53 camping cabins) offers shaded sites and a stream running through. There's a large swimming pool, a 24-hour coin laundry, clean hot showers, Wi-Fi, and, dear to any reader's heart, a Trade-a-Book exchange program.

INFORMATION AND SERVICES

The **Buffalo Chamber of Commerce** (307/684-5544 or 800/227-5122, www.buffalowyo.com, 8am-6pm Mon.-Fri., 10am-4pm Sat.-Sun. Memorial Day-Labor Day, 8am-5pm Mon-Fri. Labor Day-Memorial Day) is at 55 North Main Street. The **Summer Info Center** (187 U.S. 16 E., 307/425-1025, 9am-6pm daily June-Oct.) is a great place for local information.

For information on hiking, camping, and other recreation in the Bighorn National Forest, contact the **U.S. Forest Service** (2013 Eastside 2nd St., Sheridan, 307/674-2600, www.fs.usda.gov/bighorn).

The **Johnson County Library** (307/684-5546, www.jclwyo.org, 10am-8pm Mon.-Thurs., 10am-5pm Fri.-Sat. year-round, 1pm-4pm Sun. Sept.-May) is at 171 North Adams Avenue.

The **Johnson County Healthcare Center** (497 W. Lott St., 307/684-5521, www.jchealthcare.com) has a 24-hour emergency room.

TRANSPORTATION

Although Buffalo does have a small airport, the nearest commercial and charter air service is available in Sheridan (33 mi/53 km north) and Gillette (72 mi/116 km east).

Bus service throughout the region is provided by **Jefferson Bus Lines** (307/674-6188 or 800/451-5333, www.jeffersonlines.com).

By car, Buffalo is 123 miles (198 km) northeast of Thermopolis, 182 miles (290 km) east of Cody, 234 miles (380 km) east of Yellowstone National Park, and 341 miles (545 km) northeast of Jackson.

Gillette

Founded as a livestock center and transformed into a minerals hub with one of the largest and most easily accessible coal seams in the world, Gillette (population 32,398; elevation 4,550 ft/1,387 m) was organized in 1869 and named for a railroad engineer, Edward Gillette. After a significant oil boom in the late 1960s, coal extraction in the area was boosted by the 1970 Clean Air Act, which mandated cleaner-burning low-sulfur coal. But like so many other communities in the West, only more so, Gillette has experienced intense booms and busts related to energy production.

This is a working town with all sorts of growing pains related to coal, oil, and gas extraction. While it certainly has the infrastructure for people traveling through, Gillette is not typically on the top of the vacation radar. Still, it does make an excellent launching point to some of northeast Wyoming's wide-open spaces, and with its enormous tax base, it has managed to develop some phenomenal recreational facilities, many of which are free. The Avenue of Arts on 4J Road, for example, is a walking path lined with ever-changing sculptures. Visitors learn quickly that community means everything here—and Gillette residents are quick to point out that people came for the job, stayed for the money, then never left because of the community.

SIGHTS

Campbell County Rockpile Museum

The exhibits at the **Rockpile Museum** (900 W. 2nd St., 307/682-5723, www. rockpilemuseum.pastperfectonline.com, 9am-5pm Mon.-Sat., free) are focused on the local history of Campbell County. The museum has accrued a wide array of artifacts and displays them creatively. Visitors can see the inside of a general store, the tools and trade of an early medical clinic, and a large rifle collection. An actual homestead cabin and tiny one-room schoolhouse have been moved to the grounds, and there is an impressive collection of wagons, carriages, and even an old horse-drawn hearse. Hands-on activities for children are available, including a fun dress-up area with old-time garb. Since this is the heart of coal country, watch the short film about coal excavation and distribution; the large-scale explosions are sure to catch any viewers' attention.

CCSD Science Center

The **Campbell County School District's Science Center** (525 W. Lakeway Rd., 307/686-3821, www.sites.google.com/ ccsd1schools.net/adventurarium, 9:30am-3:30pm Tues.-Thurs., 9:30am-noon Fri. summer, 9:30am-3:30pm Mon.-Fri. fall-spring, closed late May-mid-June, free) is open to the public. Housed in the Lakeway Learning Center, the science center occupies almost 10,000 square feet (929 sq m) and offers young visitors numerous opportunities to discover, inquire, experiment, and learn. There are live animal displays (children can visit with an African pygmy hedgehog, an African bullfrog, ferrets, exotic birds, and even a python) and more than 60 interactive exhibits.

Wright Centennial Museum

Thirty-five miles (56 km) south of Gillette in the small town of Wright, the **Wright Centennial Museum** (104 Ranch Ct., 307/464-1222, www. wrightcentennialmuseum.org, 10am-5pm Mon.-Fri., 10am-2pm Sat. mid-May-early Oct., free) houses a small collection of artifacts from the surrounding area. The museum's collection has been largely amassed from the donations of residents. On display are vintage clothes, kitchen and bathroom furnishings from old homesteads, tools, saddles, and even a prostitute's "dresser box" with her personal items (including a gun). The town was established by the Atlantic Richfield mining company, and so there are many exhibits and interpretive materials dedicated to the mining industry.

SPORTS AND RECREATION

Swimming

With a soaring tax base in the 2000s, it's no surprise Gillette built up a wealth of terrific public facilities, including the outdoor **Gillette City Pool** (909 S. Gillette Ave., 307/682-1962, www.gillettewy.gov, 10am-8pm Mon.-Fri., 10am-4:30pm Sat., 1pm-4:30pm Sun., June-early Sept. weather-dependent, free). Admission is free to the massive outdoor pool and all of its facilities, which includes a deep-diving well, zero-depth entry for toddlers, waterslides, a bathhouse, a concession area, a sand playground, climbing structures, and a sunbathing area. The **Campbell County Recreation Center** (250 W. Shoshone Ave., 307/682-8527, www.ccgov.net, 5am-10pm Mon.-Thurs., 5am-9pm Fri., 8am-5pm Sat., 1pm-5pm Sun., $6 adults, $4 junior and senior high school students, $3.50 children, $13 family) is a phenomenal facility that has a climbing wall, a kids' zone, an aerobics room, a gymnasium, a lap pool, a leisure pool, and a sports complex. Call for swim session hours, which include open swim and lap swim.

Kids will be deliriously happy at the **Caribbean Cove Indoor Water Park** (2577 S. Douglas Hwy., 307/682-1717, 4pm-10pm Mon.-Fri., 8am-11pm Sat.-Sun., free for hotel guests, $8.40 pp nonguests), an 11,000-square-foot (1,022-sq-m) indoor water park with a lazy river, waterslides galore, a kiddie pool, and an activity pool. The water park is inside the Fairfield Inn & Suites.

Golf

Golfers do not lack options in Gillette. The nine-hole **Gillette Golf Club** (1800 Country Club Rd., 307/682-4774, $20 for 9 holes, $30 for 18 holes) and the 18-hole **Bell Nob Golf Club** (4600 Overdale Dr., 307/686-7069, $53 for 18 holes with cart, $37 for 9 holes with cart), which underwent a vast remodel in 2013 with added putting greens and a clubhouse, are both open to the public. The Bell Nob course also has a par 3 9-hole course ($8 adults, $2 children, $1 children with an adult).

ENTERTAINMENT AND EVENTS

Most of Gillette's large-scale events take place in the massive facility known as **Cam-Plex** (1635 Reata Dr., 307/682-0552, www.cam-plex.com), which hosts concerts, theater productions, conventions, expos, sporting events, public ice-skating, and good ol' Wyoming rodeos. Visit the website to see what events are scheduled when you're in town.

Rodeos are held almost every weekend during the summer at Cam-Plex. The **PRCA Rodeo**, which takes place in late July or early August, is quite popular, and the **National High School Rodeo Finals** in July are also a huge draw. Almost 6,000 people descend on Gillette for this annual weekend event.

Head out to the **Gillette Thunder Speedway** (13002 Hwy. 51, 307/257-9589, www.gillettespeedway.com) for stock-car races almost every Saturday night during the summer; check the website for the current schedule.

In the winter, the **Powder River Symphony Orchestra** (307/257-5105, www.prsymphony.org) performs concerts at Cam-Plex, including family-friendly events.

FOOD

A great but tiny spot for breakfast, lunch, and sensational homemade pies, among other specialties, is **Lula Belle's Café** (101 N. Gillette Ave., 307/682-9798, 5am-3pm Mon.-Sat., 6am-2pm Sun., $5-12). Another popular spot for lunch and dinner is **Humphrey's Bar & Grill** (408 W. Juniper Ln., 307/682-0100, www.humphard.net, 11am-10pm Mon.-Thurs., 11am-11pm Fri.-Sat., 10am-9pm Sun., $9-23), which has an enormous menu and more than 50 beers on tap. After a significant expansion, **The Prime Rib Restaurant**

Gillette

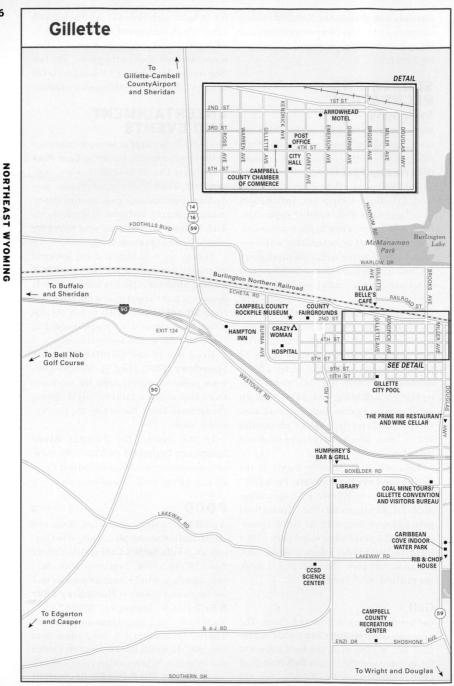

DETAIL

To
Gillette-Cambell
CountyAirport
and Sheridan

1ST ST
2ND ST
ARROWHEAD
MOTEL
3RD ST
KENDRICK AVE
ROSS AVE
WARREN AVE
GILLETTE AVE
EMERSON AVE
OSBORNE AVE
BROOKS AVE
MILLER AVE
DOUGLAS HWY
POST
OFFICE
4TH ST
CITY
HALL
CAREY AVE
5TH ST
CAMPBELL
COUNTY CHAMBER
OF COMMERCE

14
16
59

FOOTHILLS BLVD

HANNUM RD

McManamen
Park

Burlington
Lake

WARLOW DR

Burlington Northern Railroad

To Buffalo
and Sheridan

ECHETA RD

GILLETTE AVE
BROOKS AVE

LULA
BELLE'S
CAFÉ

RAILROAD ST

90

EXIT 124

CAMPBELL COUNTY
ROCKPILE MUSEUM

COUNTY
FAIRGROUNDS
2ND ST

KENDRICK AVE
GILLETTE AVE
MILLER AVE

HAMPTON
INN

BURMA AVE

CRAZY
WOMAN

4TH ST

HOSPITAL

6TH ST

SEE DETAIL

To Bell Nob
Golf Course

50

9TH ST
10TH ST

GILLETTE
CITY POOL

WESTOVER RD

S 4 J RD

DOUGLAS HWY

THE PRIME RIB RESTAURANT
AND WINE CELLAR

HUMPHREY'S
BAR & GRILL

BOXELDER RD

LIBRARY

COAL MINE TOURS/
GILLETTE CONVENTION
AND VISITORS BUREAU

LAKEWAY RD

CARIBBEAN
COVE INDOOR
WATER PARK

LAKEWAY RD

RIB & CHOP
HOUSE

To Edgerton
and Casper

CCSD
SCIENCE
CENTER

CAMPBELL
COUNTY
RECREATION
CENTER

59

ENZI DR

SHOSHONE AVE

S 4-J RD

SOUTHERN DR

To Wright and Douglas

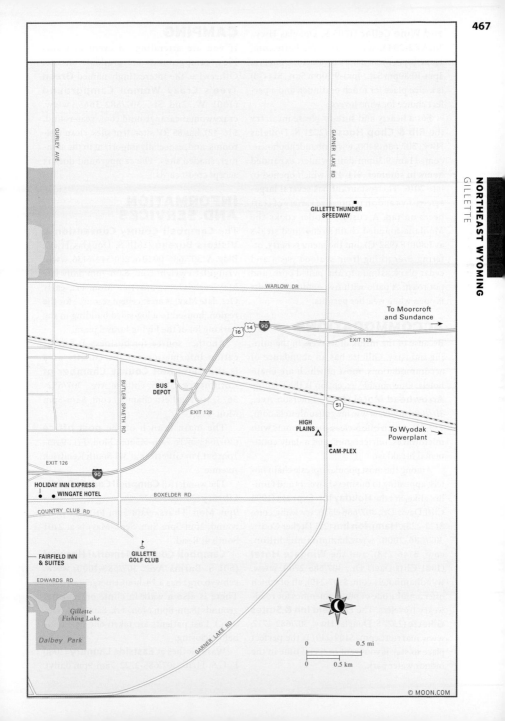

GURLEY AVE

GARNER LAKE RD

GILLETTE THUNDER
SPEEDWAY

WARLOW DR

To Moorcroft
and Sundance

16 14 90

EXIT 129

BUTLER SPAETH RD

BUS
DEPOT

EXIT 128

51

To Wyodak
Powerplant

HIGH
PLAINS

CAM-PLEX

EXIT 126

90

HOLIDAY INN EXPRESS
WINGATE HOTEL

BOXELDER RD

COUNTRY CLUB RD

FAIRFIELD INN
& SUITES

GILLETTE
GOLF CLUB

EDWARDS RD

Gillette
Fishing Lake

Dalbey Park

GARNER LAKE RD

0   0.5 mi

0   0.5 km

© MOON.COM

and **Wine Cellar** (1205 S. Douglas Hwy., 307/682-2944, www.primeribgillette.com, 11am-10pm Mon.-Thurs., 11am-10:30pm Fri., 4pm-10:30pm Sat., 4pm-9:30pm Sun., $14-50) is a nice place for lunch or dinner, and a perfect choice for wine lovers.

For a hearty and sure-to-please meal, try the **Rib & Chop House** (2721 S. Douglas Hwy., 307/686-9400, www.ribandchophouse.com, 11am-9:30pm daily winter, expanded hours in summer, $14-45), which opened in late 2016. The restaurant has several large-screen TVs and an impressive variety of craft beers on tap. A custom broiler cooks the Montana-founded chain's renowned steaks at 1,800°F (982°C), but the menu is hefty, offering everything from seafood pasta and cedar plank salmon to ahi, pulled pork, and pot roast. A patio with five outdoor fire pits is open when weather permits.

ACCOMMODATIONS

Because of the influx of workers in the mining industry, Gillette has an abundance of accommodations, most of which are chain hotels. One notable exception is the friendly **Arrowhead Motel** (202 S. Emerson Ave., 307/686-0909, www.magnusonhotels.com, $39-71), which offers clean, basic rooms with microwaves, refrigerators, and a daily continental breakfast.

Among the most popular upscale chain hotels, appealing to business travelers and families alike, are the **Holiday Inn Express** (1908 Cliff Davis Dr., 307/686-9576, www.ihg.com, $122-228), **Hampton Inn** (211 Decker Court, 307/686-2000, www.hamptoninn3.hilton.com, $146-258), and the **Wingate Hotel** (1801 Cliff Davis Dr., 307/685-2700, www.wyndhamhotels.com, $107-249), all of which offer a multitude of plush amenities for road-weary travelers. The **Fairfield Inn & Suites Gillette** (2577 S. Douglas Hwy., 307/682-1717, www.marriott.com, $109-219) is the perfect place to stay if you want to spend time in the indoor water park.

CAMPING

If you are attending an event at Cam-Plex, campgrounds are available on-site. Otherwise, the interestingly named **Green Tree's Crazy Woman Campground** (1001 W. 2nd St., 307/682-3665, www.crazywomancampground.com, year-round, $16-42), has 85 RV sites, tent sites, clean restrooms, and, especially important in the summer, shaded sites. The campground doesn't accept credit cards.

INFORMATION AND SERVICES

The **Campbell County Convention & Visitors Bureau** (1810 S. Douglas Hwy., Bldg. A, 307/686-0040 or 800/544-6136, www.visitgillettewright.com, 8am-7pm daily late May-early Oct., 9am-4pm Mon.-Fri. early Oct.-late May) is an excellent resource for the region, housed in a log-sided building in the parking lot of the Flying J travel plaza.

Another source for business and relocation information for the Gillette area is the **Campbell County Chamber of Commerce** (314 S. Gillette Ave., 307/682-3673, www.gillettechamber.com, 8am-5pm Mon.-Fri.).

The main branch of the **post office** (307/682-3727, 7am-5:30pm Mon.-Fri., 9am-1pm Sat.) in Gillette is at 311 South Kendrick Avenue.

The wonderful **Campbell County Public Library** (307/682-3223, www.ccgov.net, 9am-9pm Mon.-Thurs., 9am-5pm Fri.-Sat. year-round, 1pm-5pm Sun. Sept.-May) is at 2101 South 4J Road.

Campbell County Memorial Hospital (501 S. Burma Ave., 307/688-1000, www.cchwyo.org) has a 24-hour emergency room. There is also a walk-in clinic on hospital grounds (8am-8pm Mon.-Fri., 8am-6pm Sat.-Sun.). Last patients are taken one-half hour before closing.

Wash clothes at **Eastside Laundry** (1080 E. U.S. 14/16, 307/685-2722, 7am-9pm daily).

Another laundry with free Wi-Fi is **Surf'n Suds** (203 S. Richards Ave., 307/686-9266, 7am-9pm daily).

TRANSPORTATION
Getting There
The **Gillette-Campbell County Airport** (GCC, 2000 Airport Rd., 307/686-1042, www.ccgov.net) offers daily flights to and from Denver and Salt Lake City. Carriers include **United** and **Delta**.

Bus service in the region is provided by **Powder River Transportation** (307/682-0960), **Trailways** (www.trailways.com), and **Greyhound** (800/451-5333, www.greyhound.com).

By car, Gillette is 70 miles (113 km) east of Buffalo, 136 miles (219 km) north of Casper, 250 miles (405 km) east of Cody, 301 miles (485 km) east of Yellowstone National Park, and 411 miles (660 km) northeast of Jackson.

Getting Around
Car rentals are available in town from **Enterprise** (603 E. 2nd St., 307/686-5655, www.enterprise.com), **Avis** (2000 Airport Rd., 307/682-8588, www.avis.com), and **Rent-A-Wreck** (513 E. 2nd St., 307/363-4388, www.rentawreck.com).

Taxis are available through **City Cab** (307/685-1000), but note that only cash is accepted.

Devils Tower National Monument

Rising 1,267 feet (386 m) above the Belle Fourche River, Devils Tower is an iconic rocky sentinel that was formed some 50-60 million years ago and has fascinated people for generations. The tower was instantly recognizable in the 1977 film *Close Encounters of the Third Kind,* where it bridged human and alien life-forms. Composed of phonolite porphyry, which is a volcanic rock created by magma and similar to granite without the quartz, the massive columnar feature looks like an otherworldly cat-scratching post. Scientists refer to it as a laccolith, or igneous intrusion, meaning that magma welled up into a pocket of sedimentary rock, where it cooled and hardened. Over millions of years, the sedimentary rock was eroded away by natural forces, leaving the phenomenal tower.

The country's first national monument, Devils Tower is both a sacred site to many Native Americans and a climbing mecca for rock hounds from around the globe. The two groups have managed a hard-won, if somewhat delicate, respect for each other through a voluntary climbing closure in June every year, the month traditionally known for the greatest number of Native American ceremonies.

Climbers are strongly encouraged to refrain from climbing or hiking around the tower during the closure.

Still, Devils Tower is a recreational hot spot with several climbing routes for beginners and experts alike, plus some 8 miles (12.9 km) of hiking trails that circle the tower and wind through the nearby forests and meadows. Although it's not exactly conveniently located, 33 miles (53 km) north of I-90, Devils Tower is the type of destination—like Mount Rushmore—that visitors are happy to go out of their way to see. Especially for those with an interest in hiking or climbing, it's easy to make a day of Devils Tower.

HISTORY
According to the National Park Service, more than 20 Native American tribes have historically attached cultural and spiritual significance to Devils Tower. Many of the tribes have sacred stories related to the tower, which often determined their name for the feature. The Arapaho, for example, called the tower Bear's Tipi. Similarly, the Cheyenne referred to it as Bear's Lodge, Bear's House, and Bear Peak. The Crow are known to refer to it as

Bear's Lair, and the Lakota, who often had winter camps at the tower, called it a variety of names that include Bear Lodge, Grizzly Bear's Lodge, Ghost Mountain, and funnily enough, Penis Mountain. The Kiowa called the feature Tree Rock or Aloft on a Rock, and their origin story for the rock is among the best known. The story goes that the tribe was camped along the river, and seven sisters and their brother were playing when the brother turned into a bear, forcing the sisters to flee in search of safety. They climbed onto a rock and prayed for divine intervention. The rock began to grow skyward as the bear clawed at it to get to the sisters. Eventually, the girls were so high that they became the stars in the Big Dipper, and the tower still bears the scars of the bear's ferocious claws.

Many tribes conducted their most sacred events—including sun dances, sweat lodges, vision quests, and funerals—in the shadow of the tower, and they still do. In 2014 and 2015, formal requests were made by both the Lakota and Oglala Sioux tribes to officially change the name of the monument from Devils Tower to Bear Lodge. Politicians in Wyoming have repeatedly rejected the request. As of March 2018, a resolution to make the name "Devils Tower" permanent was put before the House of Representatives by Wyoming congresswoman Liz Cheney, Dick Cheney's daughter. A final vote had not yet occurred at the time of publication.

First studied in 1875 by scientists H. Newton and Walter P. Jenney, who were commissioned to complete a geological survey of the area, the land surrounding the tower was wisely pulled from homestead acreage in 1892, and the government created Devils Tower Reserve the following year. President Theodore Roosevelt dedicated Devils Tower as the country's first national monument in 1906.

Although it is constantly overrun by people, the area around and on top of the tower is ecologically significant. A colony of threatened black-tailed prairie dogs, who today occupy only 2 percent of their former habitat, make their home in the soft soils around the tower. Prairie falcons are known to nest in the cracks of the tower, requiring temporary closures to protect their young. Even on the grassy top of the tower, which is about the size of a football field, many wildlife species have been recorded, including chipmunks, mice, pack rats, and snakes.

Playing into the "because it's there" mentality, adventurers have long looked at ways to climb the soaring monolith. The first

Devils Tower was the first national monument in the United States.

recorded ascent involved an oak peg ladder on July 4, 1893, by local ranchers Bill Rogers and W. A. Ripley, much to the delight of local revelers. Rogers's wife, Linnie, was the first woman to climb it (using the ladder) two years later on July 4, 1895. Both spectacles included crazy patriotic costumes, some 2,000 spectators, and live music. Although the ladder was no longer used after 1927, portions of it are still visible on the southwest side of the tower.

Technical rock climbers made the first ascent in 1937 in just four hours and 46 minutes, opening the tower to scores of climbers and dozens of firsts, including George Hopkins, who parachuted onto the summit in 1941 without an exit plan. Hopkins was stranded on the summit for six days before he was rescued. Since then, numerous routes have been established up the rock, and the fastest free climb of Devils Tower was in the 1980s by Todd Skinner, who made the climb without ropes or protection in an astonishing 18 minutes. Today's average climb for two people requires 4-6 hours up and 2 hours for the rappel down.

SPORTS AND RECREATION

★ Hiking and Climbing

Nonclimbers interested in hiking will delight in the 1.5-mile (2.4-km) **Joyner Ridge Trail,** which offers beautiful views of the tower, particularly at sunset. There are an additional 7 miles (11.3 km) of trails that meander through the nearby forest and meadows. Trail maps are available at the visitors center (307/467-5283, www.nps.gov/deto). The 2.8-mile (4.5-km) **Red Beds** trail winds through meadows and ponderosa pines, with a significant elevation gain, to Joyner Ridge Trail. Plan on two hours for the Red Beds hike.

Each year the tower is climbed by some 5,000 people who come to slip their fingers and toes into the hundreds of parallel cracks that divide the hexagonal columns of Devils Tower. Although the entire tower offers more than 200 routes with technical difficulties ranging 5.7-5.13, the **Durrance Route,** first

pioneered in 1938, is the most common. A few bolted face climbs were established in the 1980s and 1990s, but new bolts and fixed pitons are prohibited. Only a handful of fatalities have occurred over the years, most of which happened on the descent.

All climbers must register at the **climber registration office** next to the visitors center; registration is free.

Climbing is strongly discouraged during the **June voluntary climbing closure,** advocated by the National Park Service out of respect for the many Native American cultures that recognize the tower as a sacred place.

CLIMBING GUIDES

For inexperienced climbers, hiring a licensed guide is the best way to approach the monolith. About seven companies are licensed to guide climbers on Devils Tower, a list that can change from year to year. Among them is **Above All Climbing School & Guides** (307/467-5267 or 888/314-5267, www.devilstowerclimbing.com, $500 for 1 climber to summit, discounts for additional climbers). The school offers excellent instruction and guiding through play days, instruction days, and summit days. Combination specials that include lodging are available. Other guiding companies licensed to work in the monument include **Above Ouray Ice and Tower Rock Climbing Guides** (307/756-3516 or 888/345-9061, www.towerguides.com, $300 for 1 climber, $210 pp for 4 climbers, no credit cards) which requires a paid training day ($210 for 1 climber) before summiting; and **Sylvan Rocks Climbing School and Guide Service** (605/484-7585, www.sylvanrocks.com), which requires two-day courses ($791 for 1 climber, $525 pp for 3 climbers) to attempt the summit.

ENTERTAINMENT AND EVENTS

A tradition since the early 1880s, when settlers would descend on the area for a few days at a time to camp, picnic, and enjoy one another's company, the **Old Settler's Picnic** was formalized as an annual event in 1932 on Father's Day weekend. The tradition continues today, after a 40-year lapse starting in the 1960s, with a large gathering of locals and visitors who come to enjoy food, Western music, cowboy poetry, kids' activities, and nondenominational church.

The annual **Cultural Program Series** changes from year to year but consistently offers fascinating lectures, entertainment, and living history displays over the course of the summer season (May 31-Aug. 31). For information on current happenings, contact the visitors center at the base of the tower (307/467-5283) or look online at the *Park News* newsletter (www.nps.gov/deto).

The National Park Service hosts a fantastic spectrum of ranger-guided programs throughout the summer season. Offerings include a 1.3-mile (2.1-km) guided **Tower Walk,** a variety of 20-minute **Interpretive Talks,** hour-long **Evening Programs,** and fantastic 90-minute **Full Moon Walks** that leave from the Joyner Ridge Trail parking lot. For information on any of the regularly scheduled events, contact the visitors center at the base of the tower (307/467-5283, www.nps.gov/deto).

FOOD

No food is sold inside the monument, so you will have to bring your own supplies or eat before you arrive at Devils Tower. Restaurants and grocery-convenience stores are in Moorcroft (33 mi/53 km), Sundance (28 mi/45 km), and Hulett (9 mi/14.5 km).

ACCOMMODATIONS

Other than the Belle Fourche Campground, there are no accommodations inside the monument. The **Devils Tower Lodge Bed & Breakfast** (just north of the monument, 307/467-5267 or 888/314-5267, www. devilstowerlodge.com, $150-250) is owned by climbing guide Frank Sanders and offers comfortable rooms with unparalleled access to the tower.

CAMPING

The only campground in the monument proper is the 50-site **Belle Fourche Campground** (307/467-5283, ext. 635, $20), open in the summer season for tent campers and RVs on a first-come, first-served basis. Running water is available, but no RV hookups.

Just outside the monument, the **Devils Tower KOA** (60 Hwy. 110, 307/467-5395 or 800/562-5785, www.devilstowerkoa.com) has RV hookups ($53-65), cabins ($77-172), and tent sites ($32-42), plus an on-site heated swimming pool, snack bar, nightly hayrides, and free Wi-Fi. With the tower looming in the background, the nightly outdoor showing of *Close Encounters of the Third Kind,* filmed largely at the campground, is an unforgettable experience.

INFORMATION AND SERVICES

Vehicular **entrance fees** for seven days are $20. Motorcyclists can enter for seven days for $15, pedestrians and bicyclists for $10.

The National Park Service operates a great **visitors center** (307/467-5283, www.nps.gov/ deto, 8am-7pm daily Memorial Day-Labor Day, 9am-5pm daily Labor Day-Sept., 9am-4pm daily Oct.-Memorial Day) in the parking lot beneath the tower. Housed in a classic 1938 Park Service log cabin constructed by the Civilian Conservation Corps, the visitors center is staffed and has a number of interesting geological, natural, and cultural history exhibits.

While the number of visitors to the monument continues to grow, it is generally not overcrowded. That changes in August; be prepared to wait in long entrance lines in the weeks surrounding the Sturgis Motorcycle Rally in nearby Sturgis, South Dakota, each summer. If you don't like crowds, this is not the time to go to Devils Tower. To check on dates for the rally, visit www.sturgismotorcyclerally.com.

The nearest health care facilities are the **Hulett Medical Clinic** (122 Main St., Hulett, 307/467-5281), 7 miles (11.3 km) north of Devils Tower, and the **Moorcroft Clinic**

(101 W. Crook St., Moorcroft, 307/756-3414), 33 miles (53 km) south of Devils Tower. The nearest hospital to treat trauma is **Campbell County Memorial Hospital** (501 S. Burma Ave., Gillette, 307/688-1000, www.cchwyo. org), 61 miles (98 km) away in Gillette.

The speed limit in the monument is 25 mph (40 kph). Each year, dozens of wild animals are hit and killed by cars. Reduced speed can positively impact the number of fatalities.

Do not feed the wildlife. Prairie dogs are especially sensitive and can die from eating any human food.

TRANSPORTATION

By car, **Devils Tower National Monument** is 33 miles (53 km) northeast of the I-90 exit at Moorcroft and 27 miles (43 km) northwest of Sundance. The monument is 61 miles (98 km) northeast of Gillette, 131 miles (211 km) northeast of Buffalo, 309 miles (500 km) east of Cody, and 363 miles (590 km) east of Yellowstone National Park.

The nearest commercial airports are located in Gillette (61 mi/98 km southwest) and Rapid City, South Dakota (120 mi/193 km east).

Southern Wyoming

An enormous expanse of diverse terrain that

includes everything from vast prairie and rugged mountain peaks to red desert and windblown dunes, southern Wyoming in many ways defines the state.

It has celebrated events, an important intellectual culture, and a wealth of historic sites. This region is also at the heart and soul of Wyoming's agricultural tradition, both past and present. But interestingly, the lower half of the state is less traveled *to* and more often traveled *through*.

With I-80 in the far south and a series of smaller roads bisecting the landscape east-west and north-south, it seems this section of Wyoming is thick with travelers on their way someplace else, which has been

Highlights

Look for ★ to find recommended sights, activities, dining, and lodging.

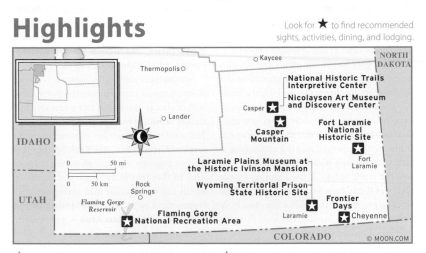

© MOON.COM

★ **Nicolaysen Art Museum and Discovery Center:** With an impressive collection of more than 6,000 works by contemporary artists, The Nic is a phenomenal tribute to the current art scene in the West (page 480).

★ **National Historic Trails Interpretive Center:** Among the best museums in the state, this place gives visitors a sense of pioneer life on many of the historic trails that crisscross the state (page 481).

★ **Casper Mountain:** The skiing, hiking, camping, and fascinating local folklore give this area its own magical identity (page 482).

★ **Laramie Plains Museum at the Historic Ivinson Mansion:** This museum is a labor of love for the people who operate it and a gift to visitors (page 491).

★ **Wyoming Territorial Prison State Historic Site:** Part agriculture exhibit, part broom factory, and part Old West town, this is also the best old prison in the West (page 492).

★ **Fort Laramie National Historic Site:** This was a fur trading fort, a military outpost, and an important witness to the dramatic conflicts and sweeping change of the 19th century in the American West (page 504).

★ **Frontier Days:** The big daddy of Wyoming rodeos draws thousands of eager spectators to its big-name country music concerts, carnival, parades, and world-class professional rodeo (page 507).

★ **Flaming Gorge National Recreation Area:** Fed by the Green River, this natural playground composed of cliffs and Technicolor desert rock formations surrounds a 91-mile-long (147-km) reservoir (page 516).

true for more than a century. Most of the West's great travel routes—the Oregon Trail, the Overland Trail, the Bozeman Trail, and eventually the Northern Pacific Railway—cut through this dramatically shifting landscape, exposing travelers, if only briefly, to the diversity of terrain.

In the southeast corner around Cheyenne—the state's capital, known for its festive, even rowdy, rodeo, called Frontier Days—the landscape shifts, greens, and begins to look more like Colorado. Just north and west of Cheyenne, Laramie presents an interesting blend of university counterculture and age-old Western tradition in a literary-meets-cowboy dance. Beyond town, three impressive mountain ranges offer prime climbing opportunities, then give way to the plains and prairies where sheep and cattle rather than trees dot the horizon. Farther north on I-25, the frontier town of Casper is experiencing a renaissance as a fishing and outdoor-loving town.

Heading west on I-80, the landscape is loaded with minerals, and the entire area is rich with mining history, dinosaur fossils, and the stark beauty of the Flaming Gorge National Recreation Area. There are wildlife refuges, endless spots to wet a line, and little ranching communities and outposts that give southern Wyoming its flavor.

PLANNING YOUR TIME

Cheyenne, Casper, and Laramie are all sizable cities for Wyoming and could occupy visitors for at least a full day each. In Cheyenne, a number of museums are worth seeing, including the **Wyoming State Museum** and the **Frontier Days Old West Museum,** among others. In this part of the state, summer is the most popular time to travel thanks to sunny, warm days and easy road conditions. Bear in mind, however, that Cheyenne's population explodes during **Frontier Days,** the second half of July, and accommodations can be tough to find.

In Laramie, there are more museums including the outstanding **Wyoming Territorial Prison,** plenty of opportunities to get out and experience some of Wyoming's most beautiful landscapes, and a fascinating university culture that brings with it abundant entertainment and a lively downtown with some darn good eateries. Laramie can be a bit windy and bleak, even frigid, in winter, but the university culture keeps things lively with concerts, lectures, sporting events, and other happenings. In Casper, the state's second-largest city after Cheyenne, there is a growing interest in the region's fishing on the **North Platte River** and plenty of year-round recreational opportunities in the nearby **Laramie Mountains, Medicine Bow National Forest,** and **Casper Mountain.**

Southwest Wyoming, by contrast, is a series of small towns experiencing the boom-and-bust of energy extraction and a vast swath of starkly beautiful land primed for recreation. There are indeed a number of museums in the areas of Green River and Rock Springs, but the vast majority of people who come to spend time in this region do so for the outdoors, which can be pleasant mid-spring-late fall. Summer can be hot, but the **Flaming Gorge National Recreation Area** is a gateway to the dramatic Green River country and offers plenty of places and ways to cool down.

HISTORY

Southern Wyoming is a land of corridors, home to the Oregon, Mormon, California, Cherokee, and Overland Trails. The Pony Express crossed through here, as did the nation's first transcontinental railroad and the first transcontinental automobile route. It makes sense that early Wyoming was defined not by settlers so much as by travelers.

What initially attracted Native Americans to this region also attracted traders, trappers, and immigrants. The North Platte and Sweetwater Rivers created natural

---

Previous: buttes in Sweetwater County; hikers in Medicine Bow National Forest; Ivinson Mansion.

Southern Wyoming

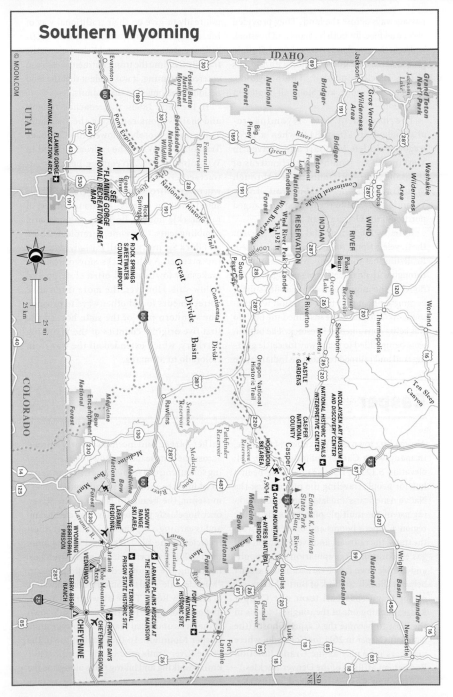

IDAHO

UTAH

COLORADO

Evanston

Jackson

Grand Teton Nat'l Park

Jackson Lake

Gros Verdes

Wilderness Area

Teton

Bridger-

National

Forest

Fossil Butte National Monument

Seedskadee National Wildlife Refuge

Big Piney

Fontenelle Reservoir

Green River

Pony Express

Green

River

Bridger-

Teton

National

Forest

Fremont Lake

Pinedale

Continental Divide

Wind River Range

Gannett Peak 13,192 ft

South Pass City

Lander

Washakie

Wilderness

Area

Dubois

WIND

RIVER

INDIAN

RESERVATION

Pilot Butte

Ocean Lake

Boysen Reservoir

Worland

Thermopolis

Ten Sleep Canyon

Rock Springs

SEE "FLAMING GORGE NATIONAL RECREATION AREA" MAP

FLAMING GORGE NATIONAL RECREATION AREA

ROCK SPRINGS SWEETWATER COUNTY AIRPORT

Great

Divide

Basin

Continental Divide

Oregon National Historic Trail

Riverton

Shoshoni

Moneta

CASTLE GARDENS

CASPER NATRONA COUNTY

NATIONAL HISTORIC TRAILS INTERPRETIVE CENTER

NICOLAYSEN ART MUSEUM AND DISCOVERY CENTER

Casper

Rawlins

Seminoe Reservoir

Pathfinder Reservoir

Alcova Reservoir

HOGADON SKI AREA

CASPER MOUNTAIN 7,904 ft

AYRES NATURAL BRIDGE

Edness K. Wilkins State Park

N. Platte River

Encampment

Medicine Bow National Forest

Medicine Bow Mtns

Medicine Bow River

Medicine Bow National Forest

Douglas

Glenrock

Thunder Basin National Grassland

Wright

Newcastle

Lusk

SNOWY RANGE SKI AREA

LARAMIE REGIONAL

Laramie

Wheatland Reservoir

Pole Mountain Area

VEDAUWOO

WYOMING TERRITORIAL PRISON

TERRY BISON RANCH

CHEYENNE

CHEYENNE REGIONAL

LARAMIE PLAINS MUSEUM AT THE HISTORIC IVINSON MANSION

WYOMING TERRITORIAL PRISON STATE HISTORIC SITE

FORT LARAMIE NATIONAL HISTORIC SITE

Fort Laramie

Glendo Reservoir

FRONTIER DAYS

0   25 mi

0   25 km

passageways across the land. They provided water and food for both humans and livestock and kept the grasslands well irrigated. Buffalo grazed across the grassy plains with Indians always in close pursuit. The Shoshone, Arapaho, Cheyenne, and Sioux all hunted in the region.

The movement into Wyoming really picked up after 1843, when a large wagon train left Missouri and arrived in Washington six months later. Hundreds of thousands of immigrants passed through Wyoming over the Oregon Trail. Today Wyoming is home to the longest unchanged portion of the Oregon Trail.

Initially, the Indians did little to prevent the travelers from crossing the land they used. Realizing that the wagons were just moving through with no intention of staying, they did not view the migrants as a threat. But soon it became evident that the migration was taking a toll. The grass that sustained the buffalo was being consumed by livestock. The buffalo were being killed to make way for cattle grazing land and railroad tracks. The Indians were not ready to give up their traditional way of life; confrontations ensued, and by the 1860s military stations were established along the trail. By the time the transcontinental railroad entered Wyoming, it was evident that the land no longer belonged to the Indians.

In the early 1860s, stagecoaches, freight, and mail wagons ran along the Overland Trail, which loosely followed the Cherokee Trail of 1848. When the railroad arrived in Wyoming in 1867, Wyoming began to attract settlers. Tent cities sprang up overnight wherever railroad crews laid tracks. These small "hell on wheels" towns consisted of ramshackle houses, brothels, saloons, and gambling tents. Cheyenne, Laramie, Carbon, and Rock Springs were all initially settled in this manner. As the tracks moved west, the makeshift towns would often close up and follow suit. However, the more innovative entrepreneurs found other ways to prosper. The southern part of the state housed the first five original counties of the Wyoming Territory, which extended all the way from Colorado to Montana.

Casper

A sprawling town near the center of the state, in many ways Casper (population 59,324; elevation 5,123 ft/1,561 m) has long been a hub for people traveling the region, first the Native Americans and later the settlers making use of the multiple pioneer trails in the region. Casper's booms and busts came with the trails, the railroad, and eventually oil and gas exploration. Its reputation as a rough-and-tumble town is well earned, and one can't help but chuckle to think of Butte, Montana's minor league baseball team, the Copper Kings, ditching one of the roughest towns in the West to become the Casper Ghosts (the team left Casper in 2011 for Colorado, where members now play as the Grand Junction Rockies, an affiliate of the Denver Rockies.)

Although Casper is indeed industrial, rather large, and perhaps overly spread across the landscape, the town is experiencing something of a renaissance in recent years. In addition to a world-class contemporary art museum, the beautiful North Platte River, once hopelessly polluted, has been cleaned up and is earning a reputation as one of the best fisheries in the West. The river boasts more than 4,000 fish per mile on most stretches, including the renowned 5.5-mile (8.9-km) "Miracle Mile" and the blue-ribbon tailwaters of the "Grey Reef." There is a wealth of incredible outdoor opportunities just outside town at the city's unofficial year-round playground, Casper Mountain. In the heart of town, the Platte River Trails offer nearly 10 miles (16.1 km) of walking and biking trails alongside the river, an ideal spot to stretch your legs or take

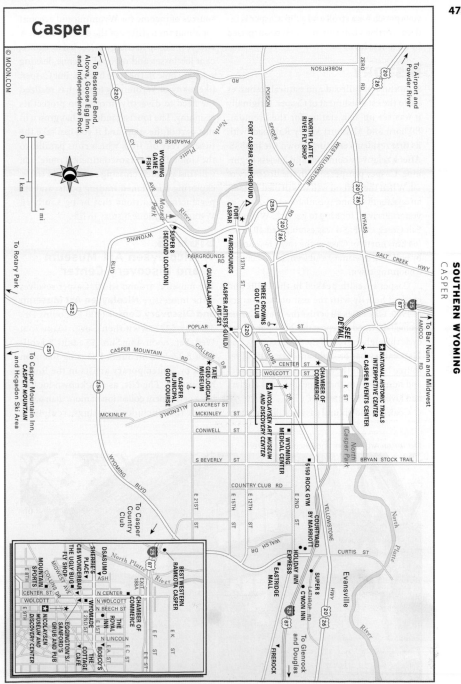

Casper

© MOON.COM

To Bessemer Bend,
Alcova, Goose Egg Inn,
and Independence Rock

To Airport and
Powder River

To Rotary Park

To Bar Nunn and Midwest

To Casper Mountain Inn,
CASPER MOUNTAIN
and Hogadon Ski Area

To Glenrock
and Douglas

To Casper
Country
Club

ROBERTSON RD

ZERO RD

POISON RD

SPIDER RD

PARADISE DR

WESTYELLOWSTONE RD

SALT CREEK HWY

AMOCO RD

BYPASS

20
26
258
20/26
20/26
87
25
220

CY AVE

MORMON AVE

WYOMING BLVD

North Platte River

Morad Park

NORTH PLATTE
RIVER FLY SHOP ▪

FORT CASPAR CAMPGROUND ▲

WYOMING
GAME &
FISH ▪

FORT
CASPAR ▪

SUPER 8
(SECOND LOCATION) ▲

FAIRGROUNDS ▪
FAIRGROUNDS RD

GUADALAJARA ▪

CASPER ARTISTS GUILD/
ART 321 ▪

THREE CROWNS
GOLF CLUB

13TH ST

COLLINS DR

CENTER ST

WOLCOTT ST

CHAMBER OF
COMMERCE ■

★ NATIONAL HISTORIC TRAILS
INTERPRETIVE CENTER

■ CASPER EVENTS CENTER

E ST
K ST

NICOLAYSEN ART MUSEUM
AND DISCOVERY CENTER ★

POPLAR ST

TATE
GEOLOGICAL
MUSEUM ▪

CASPER
MUNICIPAL
GOLF COURSE

CASPER MOUNTAIN RD

COLLEGE DR

ALLENDALE DR

OAKCREST ST

MCKINLEY

MCKINLEY ST

CONWELL ST

S BEVERLY ST

COUNTRY CLUB RD

WYOMING
MEDICAL
CENTER ▪

5150 ROCK GYM ▪

BRYAN STOCK TRAIL

North Casper Park

North Platte River

E 21ST ST

E 15TH ST

E 12TH ST

E 2ND ST

WALSH DR

COURTYARD
BY MARRIOTT ■

HOLIDAY INN
EXPRESS ■

EASTRIDGE
MALL ■

SUPER 8 ■

C'MON INN ■

LATHROP RD

YELLOWSTONE HWY

CURTIS ST

Evansville

FIREROCK

20/26
25
87

To Casper Mountain Inn

0   1 km
0   1 mi

220
220
251
258
252

SEE DETAIL

BEST WESTERN
RAMKOTA CASPER ■

EXIT
188A

CHAMBER OF
COMMERCE ■

North Platte River

25
87

COLLINS DR

MIDWEST AVE

CENTER ST

WOLCOTT ST

NICOLAYSEN ART
MUSEUM AND
DISCOVERY CENTER ★

DSASUMO ▼
SHERRIE'S
PLACE ▼

C85 WONDERBAR ▼
THE UGLY BUG
FLY SHOP ▪

MOUNTAIN
SPORTS ▪

EGGINGTON'S/
SANFORD'S
GRUB AND PUB ▼

ASH

N CENTER

N WOLCOTT ST

N BEECH ST

N LINCOLN ST

WYOMADE ▼

THE
ROYAL
INN ■

THE
COTTAGE
CAFE ▼

BOSCO'S ▼

E 6TH
E 7TH
E 8TH
E 9TH

E 1ST ST
E 2ND ST

E F ST
E G ST
E K ST

E C ST
E D ST
E E ST

your pooch for a stroll and a dip. Casper is indeed worth a visit; you may well be surprised by all that is here.

HISTORY

A mixture of railroad and natural resources led to the establishment of Casper. Originally it was set up as a station for the Fremont, Elkhorn and Missouri Valley Railroad, with its first residents creating a town site in 1888. After a relatively common and lawless beginning, Casper prospered with the discovery of oil. When the first oil well was drilled in 1887, an onslaught of land speculators and other investors arrived, looking to get rich. When the Salt Creek Oil Field was established 40 miles (64 km) north of Casper, the town responded by building a refinery and went on to become a booming town.

Casper's wealth peaked in the 1920s and crashed heavily with the rest of the country in 1929. Like cities all across the West, Casper seemed destined to repeat this boom-and-bust cycle through the rest of the 20th century. The 21st century has brought another natural resource boom in the form of rehabbed rivers and hungry trout that appeal to avid anglers and lovers of the outdoors.

Coal, oil, and natural gas are still important sources of income for Wyoming and account for about three-fifths of the state's budget. A two-year slump in energy prices led to significant job losses and reduced revenue, leaving a gaping hole in the state budget. But Casper, like many of Wyoming's towns, has realized the need to diversify in order to protect its economy. The tourism industry has grown in this part of the state, and if you can take the time to veer off I-80, which runs parallel to the Union Pacific transcontinental route, you will find yourself crossing century-old trails, exploring abandoned trading posts, and experiencing traditions that bring southern Wyoming's unique history to life.

SIGHTS
★ Nicolaysen Art Museum and Discovery Center

The museum around which Casper revolves is the impressive **Nicolaysen Art Museum and Discovery Center** (400 E. Collins Dr., 307/235-5247, www.thenic.org, 10am-5pm Wed.-Sat., noon-4pm Sun., $5 adults, $3 children 3-17, free on Sun.). Focusing solely on work by contemporary artists in the Rocky Mountains, The Nic, as it is known locally, has a permanent collection of more than 6,000 works that includes paintings, sculpture,

Nicolaysen Art Museum and Discovery Center

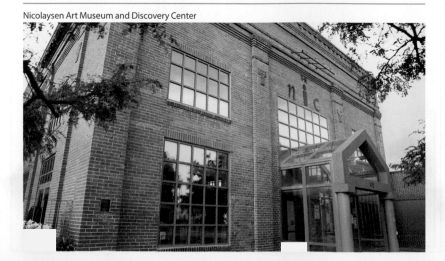

textiles, drawings, photos, and prints; it features the region's most important traveling exhibitions related to their mission. The Discovery Center offers hands-on art activities for visitors of all ages along with a lineup of classes and special programs. The museum is very invested in the Casper community and often serves as host to some favorite local events. In summer the **Casper Downtown Farmers Market** (5pm-7:30pm Tues. mid-July-mid-Sept.) is held on the museum grounds. There's also a wonderful festival, **Nic Fest,** held over a weekend in early June that offers artist booths, live music and activities for kids. The museum's annual art auction and ball is held in early September.

Tate Geological Museum

A great little free museum associated with Casper College since 1980 is the **Tate Geological Museum** (125 College Dr., 307/268-2447, www.caspercollege.edu/tate, 9am-5pm Mon.-Fri., 10am-4pm Sat., free), which houses nearly 3,000 fossil and mineral specimens. The museum is also home to "Dee," an 11,600-year-old Columbian mammoth (the oldest and largest mounted specimen in the world) who was likely 65 or 70 years old when he died. The collection includes dinosaur bones and fossilized footprints found in Wyoming. A fossil prep lab allows visitors to watch and ask questions of working paleontologists, and an interactive "Dino Den" will delight kids.

Fort Caspar

Positioned at a critical river crossing for the Oregon, Mormon, Pioneer, California, and Pony Express Trails, **Fort Caspar** (4001 Ft. Caspar Rd., 307/235-8462, www.fortcasparwyoming.com, museum 8am-5pm and fort buildings 8:30am-4:30pm daily May-Sept., museum 8am-5pm Tues.-Sat. Oct.-Apr., $3 adults, $2 children 13-18 May-Sept., $2 adults, $1.50 seniors and teens, Oct.-Apr., always free for children under 13) was built in 1862 to protect travelers through the area and was occupied by the military until 1867. When the Army decommissioned the site and took as many of the materials as they could with them to build Fort Fetterman in 1867, Native Americans burned what remained to the ground. In 1936, a Works Progress Administration crew rebuilt several of the buildings on the original site. The fort and museum are operated by the city of Casper.

Exhibits at the fort include reconstructions of the Mormon Ferry, Guinard Bridge, and Richard Bridge that predated the fort, as well as fort history, pioneer trail history, and other agricultural, oil, and gas exhibits related to the region. The museum also hosts interesting traveling exhibitions.

★ National Historic Trails Interpretive Center

Among the state's most renowned museums, the **National Historic Trails Interpretive Center** (1501 N. Poplar St., 307/261-7700, www.blm.gov, 8am-5pm Tues.-Sun. late May-early Sept., 9am-4:30pm Tues.-Sat. early Sept.-late May, free) tells the gritty story of Manifest Destiny and westward expansion on the historic pioneer trails through interactive exhibits and multimedia presentations. The museum's exhibits are both indoors and out, and they succeed in giving visitors a real sense of what day-to-day life was like for the early pioneers. The museum's seven distinct galleries are dedicated to four of the trails that cut through the region, as well as Native Americans, mountain men, explorers, and the trails today. There's even a virtual river crossing experience. Wyoming's BLM manages more than 340 miles (545 km) or 60 percent of the Oregon, California, Mormon, Pioneer, and Pony Express Trails in the state, and this museum celebrates both the heritage of those trails and the remarkable ability to still see and experience them in much the same way. For information on all of Wyoming's trails, their rich history, and ways to experience them, visit www.wyoshpo.state.wy.us/trailsdemo.

Ayres Natural Bridge

Some 50 miles (81 km) southeast of Casper and 10 miles (16.1 km) west of Douglas is one of Wyoming's earliest tourist attractions, **Ayres Natural Bridge** (208 Natural Bridge Rd., 307/358-3532, 8am-8pm daily Apr.-Oct., free), a natural arch where LaPrele Creek worked its way through a 100-foot-long (30.5-m), 50-foot-high (15.2-m) solid rock wall over the centuries. It is set in a lovely 22-acre (8.9-hectare) park. The Native Americans of the region thought of the natural bridge as a sinister place because of a tale about a young brave being struck by lightning in the canyon. The legend developed until it was widely believed among the Indians that an evil spirit lived beneath the bridge. Travelers on the Mormon Trail, which crossed the creek 2 miles (3.2 km) north of the site, discovered the bridge and the legend, and often visited the area to escape the Native Americans.

There are 12 beautiful campsites (free) within the park boundaries; pets are not allowed in the park.

★ Casper Mountain

When Casper residents are eager to flee the city, particularly in the heat of summer, they head to **Casper Mountain,** an alpine oasis just minutes from town. In addition to the popular **Hogadon Ski Area,** several campgrounds and parks, and miles of beautiful, forested hiking and biking trails, Casper Mountain is also rich with history and culture.

An early settler from Missouri, Elizabeth "Neal" Forsling, fled a horrible marriage with her two young daughters to homestead on the top of Casper Mountain in the 1920s. An artist and writer, Forsling was strong, independent, and loved the mountain with all of her being. She fell in love with and married a local rancher, Jim, who joined her in her happy life on the mountaintop, but when he froze to death at the age of 38 while skiing home from town with supplies, Neal dedicated herself even more to the land on which she lived. She painted and wrote stories about the spirits, trolls, fairies, and other beings that lived on Casper Mountain. She hosted a summer solstice party in 1930 that would become the Mid-Summer's Eve Celebration that continues today. Single-handedly, Neal Forsling created a mythical culture on the mountain that persists today.

Forsling donated her land and cabin to Natrona County in 1973. She died a few years later, and the county turned her home into a

cabin at Casper Mountain

wonderful museum named for the book of stories she created about the mountain: The **Crimson Dawn Museum** (1620 Crimson Dawn Rd., 307/235-1303, museum 10am-7pm Sat.-Sun. June-Sept., park 8am-8pm daily June-Sept.) is at the center of the Mid-Summer's Eve Celebration. Keep an eye on their Facebook page for news and events.

SPORTS AND RECREATION

Hiking and Biking

In addition to the abundance of hiking and biking trails just outside the city in places like Casper Mountain, there are a number of green trails within city limits. The **Platte River Trails** (www.platterivertrails.com) wind nearly 10 miles (16.1 km) along the river's edge and can be accessed in a number of parks, including **Morad Park** and **Casper Whitewater Park,** as well as at the Holiday Inn on the River. **Rotary Park,** just south of town at the base of Casper Mountain, is home to the beloved Garden Creek Falls and 4.5-mile (7.2-km) **Bridle Trail,** which climbs 1,200 feet (366 m) and offers views of the falls and the city below.

Just 6 miles (9.7 km) east of town on Highway 252, **Edness K. Wilkins State Park** (S. Poplar St., 307/577-5150, http://wyoparks.state.wy.us, $6 nonresidents) is a serene spot with giant cottonwoods, swimmable river access, ideal picnic spots, fishing, boat access, and a playground. There are also 2.8 miles (4.5 km) of paved trails for walkers, and birders will delight in the more than 40 species that can be counted in a single day in the park.

Casper Mountain is the best place for serious hiking and biking. Among the many popular trails in the area is the unique **Lee McCune Braille Trail** for both sighted and visually impaired hikers.

Avid bikers without wheels can rent great mountain bikes from **Mountain Sports** (543 S. Center St., 307/266-1136, www.caspermtnsports.com, 9am-6pm Mon.-Sat., 11am-4pm Sun.).

Skiing

Casper's easy access to the mountains makes this town an ideal winter getaway. Just 15 minutes from town is **Hogadon Ski Area** (2500 W. Hogadon Rd., Casper Mountain, 307/235-8499, www.hogadon.net, 9am-4pm Wed.-Sun., full-day $42 adults, $37 youth; half-day $34 adults and youth; $32 seniors 65-69 and active military, free for seniors 70 and over), a small, family-friendly mountain that offers 20 percent beginner terrain and 40 percent each intermediate and advanced. There are 27 trails and two lifts, and a snowboard terrain park for more adventurous riders. Group and private lessons are available, as are rentals. In summer, the mountain is open to mountain bikers and hikers.

For Nordic skiers, the **Casper Mountain Trails Center** (9301 S. Circle Dr. on Casper Mountain, 307/237-5014 or 307/259-0958, www.natrona.net/238/trails-center, sunrise-10pm daily, day pass $10) offers 26 miles (42 km) of groomed trails for both classical and skate skiers, in addition to a 0.7-mile (1.2-km) lighted loop. There are an additional 30 miles (48 km) of backcountry and snowshoe trails in the area as well. A map of Casper Mountain Nordic trails is available at www.natrona.net.

For equipment rentals for just about any sport in any season, head to **Mountain Sports** (543 S. Center St., 307/266-1136, www.caspermtnsports.com, 9am-6pm Mon.-Sat., 11am-4pm Sun.).

Rock Climbing

As Casper's status among outdoor junkies continues to climb, rock climbing is another of the region's well-known offerings. **Fremont Canyon** (www.fremontcanyon.com) has world-class granite climbing for people of all ability levels (5.6-5.13d in difficulty), with cliffs ranging 40 to over 400 feet (12.2 to over 122 m). The area is known for its steep crack climbs but does offer some sport climbing and bouldering problems. To get to the canyon, which overlooks Alcova Reservoir, head south from Casper on Highway 220 to the town of Alcova; the canyon is 10 miles (16.1

km) farther south, accessed by the Fremont Canyon Bridge.

To practice or get information on other area climbs, visit Casper's in-town climbing gym, **5150 Rock Gym** (408 N. Beverly St., 307/337-2166, www.5150rockgym.com, 2pm-9pm Mon.-Sat., $10 day use, $2 harness rental, $3 shoe rental).

Fishing

Fishing in the cold waters of the **North Platte River** is something of a comeback story. Around the turn of the 20th century, the North Platte was known as one of the great trout fisheries of the West; as an example, a celebration in Saratoga in 1907, known as the Railroad Days Celebration and Fish Fry, required more than 3,000 fish to be caught in two days to feed visitors. The river was thick with trout, and anglers flocked to the area to catch them. As industrialization spread across the country, feedlots and oil refineries increasingly dotted the landscape and polluted the North Platte until it was nearly uninhabitable. Only since 1997 have sweeping measures been taken to restore the river, an effort that has, by all accounts, been enormously successful. In fact, *American Angler* magazine voted the Grey Reef section of the North Platte River

the number one big fishery in the world in 2005. The area is widely considered the best rainbow trout tailwater in the Lower 48. The largest trout caught in the North Platte, in the fabled Grey Reef section, was a 22-pound (10-kg) brown trout. Average rainbows in this river weigh upward of 5 pounds (2.3 kg) and measure 16 to 18 inches (41-46 cm), and trophies range 25 to 30 inches (64-76 cm).

Today, in part because of its shallow depth and slow current, the river can be fished for hundreds of miles, and anglers can expect to see the noses of rainbows, browns, Snake River cutthroats, walleye, and the occasional cutbow, a rainbow-cutthroat hybrid.

Casper offers an abundance of fly shops and guides. A good place to start for a license and regulations is **Wyoming Game and Fish** (3030 Energy Ln., Ste. 100, 307/473-3400, http://wgfd.wyo.gov, 8am-5pm Mon.-Fri.). For gear or guided trips, contact the **Ugly Bug Fly Shop** (240 S. Center St., 307/234-6905, www.crazyrainbow.net, 9am-5:30pm Mon.-Fri., 8am-4pm Sat.), which has full-day ($475-500/boat) and half-day ($375/boat) guided fly-fishing trips. A full-day guided float trip on the Miracle Mile is $500 per boat. Discounts are available in the off-season (Nov.-Mar.), when the weather can be lousy but the fishing

The North Platte River runs from Colorado through Wyoming and into Nebraska.

great. The **North Platte River Fly Shop** (7400 Hwy. 220, 307/237-5997 or 307/277-6282, www.wyomingflyfishing.com, 9am-4pm Mon.-Fri., 9am-2pm Sat.) offers all-day guided trips in boats ($450-525 for 2 anglers) or wade fishing ($450 for 2 anglers). Single anglers and off-season trips are discounted.

Golf

Casper has 90 holes for avid golfers, including a world-class course designed by Robert Trent Jones Jr. built on an old remediated oil refinery: The **Three Crowns Golf Club** (1601 King Blvd., 307/472-7696, www.threecrownsgolfclub.com, $70 for 18 holes, $40 for 9 holes Mon.-Thurs., $75 for 18 holes, $50 for 9 holes Fri.-Sun., $46 for 18 holes after 3pm every day, prices include carts) is a par-72 course that opened in 2005 and has a resort-like feel.

Another course worth playing is the **Casper Municipal Golf Course** (2120 Allendale Blvd., 307/223-6620, www.casperwy.gov, $32 for 18 holes, $20 for 9 holes Mon.-Fri., $34 for 18 holes, $22 for 9 holes Sat.-Sun.), which has 27 holes on three distinct nines. Opened in 1929, the course is consistently ranked among the best municipal courses in the state.

ENTERTAINMENT AND EVENTS

Theater

Performing in an intimate theater-in-the-round, Casper's **Stage III Community Theatre** (900 N. Center St., 307/234-0946, www.stageiiitheatre.org) is an entirely volunteer organization that produces six productions annually between September and June. The company has been entertaining Casper since 1980, with evening and matinee offerings ranging from classic dramas to mysteries and comedies.

Founded in 2014, **Casper Theater Company** (735 Cy Ave., 307/267-7243, www.caspertheatercompany.net) is a semiprofessional theater company offering four productions each season, including original works.

Rodeos

Rodeo is serious business in this part of the state—or anywhere in Wyoming, for that matter. One of the biggest is the **College National Finals Rodeo** (509/529-4402, www.cnfr.com), held annually at the Casper Events Center (800/442-2256) in mid-June. More than 400 cowboys and cowgirls from 100 universities and colleges compete for champion status in saddle bronc riding, bareback riding, bull riding, tie-down roping, steer wrestling, team roping, barrel racing, breakaway roping, and goat tying.

Another big rodeo in Casper is the **PRCA Rodeo** held annually in conjunction with the **Central Wyoming Fair** (1700 Fairgrounds Rd., 307/235-5775 or 888/225-2600, www.centralwyomingfair.com) in mid-July. The fair has been in operation since 1904 and comes with all the hoopla and community spirit you'd expect.

Mid-Summer's Eve Celebration

Held each year on June 21, the summer solstice, the **Mid-Summer's Eve Celebration** (Crimson Dawn Park, 1620 Crimson Dawn Rd., 307/235-9311) is a unique event that showcases the history and spirit of Casper. The stories around this event, started in 1930 by Casper Mountain resident, artist, and author Neal Forsling, are considered by some to be Wyoming's only folklore. The event starts with a storytelling walk through the forest, amid a network of rock shrines, and culminates with a bonfire that everyone is invited to throw red dirt into, in hopes of seeing their fondest wish granted. It is a charming celebration of the witches, spirits, and trolls said to inhabit the mountain.

Beartrap Summer Festival

Undoubtedly one of the best outdoor music festivals in the region, the **Beartrap Summer Festival** (307/266-5252, www.beartrapsummerfestival.com) brings Casper Mountain to life with bluegrass music the first weekend in August. The event hosts big-name bands and musicians for two days midmorning-dusk. Rounding out the festival are musical workshops, an arts and crafts marketplace, an open-air food court, and supervised children's activities. Pets are welcome on a leash. Discounted tickets can be purchased in advance by phone.

SHOPPING

A central shopping locale for much of the region, Casper has every sort of shopping imaginable, from big malls and shopping centers to box stores and downtown boutiques. The largest facility in the region by far is the **Eastridge Mall** (601 SE Wyoming Blvd., 307/265-9392, www.shopeastridge.com), anchored by Target, Best Buy, Macy's, Bed Bath and Beyond, Sears, Dick's Sporting Goods, and J. C. Penney.

There are some smaller stores too that should not be missed. **WYOMade** (116 E. 2nd St., 307/337-1186, www.wyomade.com, 10am-5pm Tues.-Fri., 10am-4pm Sat.) sells apparel, gifts, jewelry, candles and art, all made in Wyoming. A terrific place to find work by local artists is the **Casper Artists Guild/Art 321** (321 W. Midwest Ave., 307/265-2655, www.casperartguild.com, 10am-4pm Tues.-Sat.), which hosts regular shows in a variety of media as well as active workshops for artists (including regular Sunday afternoon painting sessions). The gift shop is an excellent place to pick up one-of-a-kind works by local artists.

For a sweet tooth or an espresso with a side of chocolate, the best spot in Casper is **Donells Candies** (201 E. 2nd St., 307/234-6283, www.donellschocolates.com, 9am-6pm Mon.-Fri., 9am-5pm Sat.), which has been churning out delectable handmade chocolates, savory nuts, and all flavors of popcorn since 1956. The store is still owned and operated by the founding family, and with brisk Internet sales it has found admirers the world over. The Donells expanded the downtown store and added an espresso bar where candy lovers can also order hand-dipped ice cream.

FOOD

Casper is a breakfast lover's town: You'll find a number of great places to start the day right. **Eggington's** (229 E. 2nd St., 307/265-8700, www.eggingtons.com, 6am-2pm Mon.-Sat., 7am-2pm Sun., $6-15) serves breakfast and lunch to a bustling crowd. It offers everything from omelets and pastries to burgers and salads. A somewhat hidden but marvelous spot for lunch is ★ **The Cottage Café** (116 S. Lincoln St., 307/234-1157, www.cottagecafe.com, 11am-1:30pm Mon.-Fri., $11-13), which is tucked into a residential neighborhood and serves delicious homemade soups, panini, pastas, and more. Another weekday-only place that offers up great, classic breakfasts and lunches is **Sherrie's Place** (310 W. Yellowstone Hwy., 307/235-3513, 6:30am-2pm Mon.-Fri., $5-10). From cinnamon rolls and stuffed French toast to fried chicken and good old-fashioned malts, this place is the real deal.

For good Mexican food, which southern Wyoming seems to have no shortage of, try **Guadalajara** (3350 CY Ave., 307/234-4699, www.guadalajaramexicanwyoming.com, 11am-9pm Sun.-Thurs., 11am-10pm Fri.-Sat., $9-17). **Bosco's** (847 E. A St., 307/265-9658, 11am-1:30pm and 5pm-9:30pm Tues.-Sat., $12-30) serves wonderful Italian meals (including gluten-free options) in an intimate setting. Another favorite in town is the Wyoming/Dakotas chain **Sanford's Grub & Pub** (61 SE Wyoming Blvd., 307/315-6040, www.thegrubandpub.com, 11am-10pm daily, $9-26), which has an outrageously big menu featuring Cajun twists on American food, and plenty of beer; its $1 pints are well known among beer lovers. Kids will delight in the fact that every square inch of wall is covered with memorabilia and garage sale finds. For a high-end steak, chops, and seafood place, try the **FireRock Steakhouse** (6100 E. 2nd St., 307/234-2333, 11am-10pm Mon.-Thurs., 11am-11pm Fri.-Sat., 11am-9pm Sun., $10-43), serving aged steaks cooked over a wood-fired grill, rack of lamb, pork chops, and all sorts of toppings and sides including shrimp and lobster. They also offer a nice selection of burgers, sandwiches, salads, and pasta. FireRock Steakhouse also has a full-service bar.

Part Asian bistro and part sushi bar, **Dsasumo** (320 W. First St., 307/237-7874, www.dsasumo.com, 11am-2:30pm and 4:30pm-9pm Mon.-Fri., 11am-9pm Sat., noon-2:30pm and 3:30-9pm Sun., $14-22) is a great find in Casper. Most of the food is Thai, but there are plenty of fusion choices and a great sushi menu. Don't miss the specialty cocktails.

Starting in 1942, cowboys would ride up to the bar known as **C85 Wonderbar** (256 S. Center St., 307/333-6890, www.c85group.com, 11am-midnight Mon.-Sat., $13-38) for a beer for themselves and their mount. Then they would ride through the bar and out the back alley. Joe Lowndes, a member of the famed "Wild Bunch," was a regular. Today you don't see horses and riders in the bar, but the place is still a popular watering hole for locals and was beautifully remodeled recently. And the restaurant serves creative starters, cast-iron steaks, sandwiches, salads, pizza, Mexican food, and anything you could want to wet your whistle. They specialize in smoked cocktails. The informal slogan is, "It's more fun to eat in a bar than drink in a restaurant." How true.

ACCOMMODATIONS

Casper has no shortage of places to stay, and many chain hotel options are available. The **Best Western Ramkota Casper** (800 N. Poplar St., 307/266-6000 or 800/528-1234, www.casper.ramkota.com, $101-159) is a large facility that caters both to business travelers (in-room desks, free Wi-Fi, and a business center) and to families with the Castaway Bay Indoor Water Playground, geared to young children. The pet-friendly hotel also offers complimentary breakfast. Among the other chain hotels in Casper are **C'Mon Inn** (301 E. Lathrop Rd., 307/472-6300 or 866/782-2690, www.cmoninn.com/casper, $110-160) with king Jacuzzi suites, the newer 100-room **Courtyard by Marriott** (4260 Hospitality Ln., 307/473-2600, www.marriott.com/cprcy, $96-139), **Holiday Inn**

Express (4250 Legion Ln., exit 185 on I-25, 307/237-4200, www.hiexpress.com, $143-183), and two pet-friendly **Super 8** motels (www.wyndhamhotels.com, 739 Luker Lane, Evansville, 307/462-0775, from $53 or 3838 CY Ave., 307/266-3480, $71-101).

A more budget-friendly option downtown is **The Royal Inn** (440 E. A St., 307/234-3502, www.caspermotel.com, $40-50), which offers basic rooms with microwaves and refrigerators, free Wi-Fi, and on-site laundry machines. The inn also provides gas grills and a briquette for guests who want to cook out.

For an unforgettable wilderness B&B experience just out of town, ★ **Sunburst Lodge** (2700 Micro Rd., 307/235-9086, www.sunburst-lodge.com, $135-165) is on Casper Mountain next to Hogadon Ski Area and just 20 minutes from town. There is much exploring to be done year-round just outside the lodge along with cozy accommodations and sumptuous meals inside.

CAMPING

The closest public camping in the vicinity of Casper is 10 miles (16.1 km) south of town on **Casper Mountain,** a breezy, forested all-season playground for locals. There are four campgrounds on the mountain; **Beartrap Meadow** (Casper Mountain Rd., 307/235-9311, $10) is the only one with water and also the nicest of the four. Various campsites maintained by the **Bureau of Land Management** (307/261-7500, www.wy.blm.gov, $7) include the **Rim** and **Lodgepole Campgrounds** in the Muddy Mountain Environmental Education Area, which can be accessed from gravel roads off Casper Mountain Road. Both have vault toilets, and the campgrounds are connected by a 2-mile (3.2-km) interpretive nature trail.

For a scenic lakeside locale 28 miles (45 km) west of Casper on County Road 407, off Highway 220, **Alcova Reservoir** has numerous **campgrounds** (County Rd. 407/ Kortes Rd., 307/235-9311, www.natrona.net, $35 full hookups, $10 unserviced), including **Westside Campground, Black Beach,** and **Cottonwood.** Unserviced sites are first-come, first-served, and sites with hookups are by reservation only.

A few private campgrounds and RV parks are also available right in town. Set along a bend in the North Platte River, the **Fort Caspar Campground** (4205 Fort Caspar Rd., 307/234-3260 or 888/243-7709, www.ftcasparcamp.com, tent site $25, RV $44 full hookups) offers basic tent and RV sites on gravel, a lodge, ponds, and several walking trails; it also provides free Wi-Fi.

INFORMATION AND SERVICES

The **Natrona County Travel and Tourism Council** (139 W. 2nd St., Ste. 1B, 307/234-5362 or 800/852-1889, www.visitcasper.com, 8am-5pm Mon.-Fri.) has a wealth of information for visitors. The **Casper Area Chamber of Commerce** (500 N. Center St., 307/234-5311 or 866/234-5311, www.casperwyoming.org, 8am-5pm Mon.-Fri.) is an excellent resource for local businesses and relocation information.

Post offices are located at 411 North Forest Drive (307/237-8556, 8:30am-5pm Mon.-Fri., 9am-noon Sat.) and at 150 East B Street (9am-5:30pm Mon.-Fri., 9am-noon Sat.).

The **Natrona County Public Library** (307/577-7323, www.natronacountylibrary.org, 9am-6pm Mon.-Thurs., 9am-5pm Fri.-Sat.) is at 307 East 2nd Street.

Wyoming Medical Center (1233 E. 2nd St., 307/577-7201 or 800/822-7201, www.wyomingmedicalcenter.org) is the largest health care facility in the state and offers everything from 24-hour emergency medicine to highly specialized care.

Laundry facilities are available at **Hilltop Laundromat** (2513 E. 3rd St., 307/234-7331, 9am-9pm daily) and **CY Laundromat** (2300 CY Ave., 307/265-2151, 7:30am-8pm daily).

TRANSPORTATION

Getting There

The **Casper/Natrona County International Airport** (CPR, 8500 Airport Pkwy., 307/472-6688, www.iflycasper.com) is on U.S. 20/26 approximately 9 miles (14.5 km) west of downtown. Two carriers, **United** and **Delta,** provide daily flights to and from Denver and Salt Lake City.

Car-rental agencies at the airport include **Enterprise, National,** and **Hertz. Avis and Budget** have offices off-site.

Regular bus service to and from Casper is available on **Greyhound** (601 N. Center St., 307/265-2353) and **Black Hills Stage Lines** (601 N. Center St., 307/265-2353, www.blackhillsstagelines.com).

By car, Casper is 145 miles (233 km) east of Lander, 148 miles (238 km) north of Laramie, 178 miles (290 km) northwest of Cheyenne, 240 miles (385 km) northeast of Green River, 242 miles (385 km) south of Gillette, 284 miles (460 km) east of Jackson, and 267 miles (425 km) southeast of Yellowstone National Park.

Getting Around

The easiest public transportation in Casper is **The Bus** (307/265-1313, www.catcbus.com, 6:30am-6:30pm Mon.-Fri., $1 general, $0.75 students, $0.50 reduced for elderly and disabled, free for children 5 and under), a fixed-route transit system. The Casper Area Transportation Coalition also offers **Dial-a-Ride,** which must be reserved before 3pm at least one day in advance; it's better to reserve two days early. The cost is $5, or $2 for seniors and people with special needs, $1 for children 12 and under accompanied by an adult.

Local taxi service is provided by **Casper Cabs** (307/577-7777, www.caspercabs.com) and **Eagle Cab** (307/797-3818, www.eaglecab.net).

Laramie

Nestled in a high basin between the Laramie and Medicine Bow Mountains, Laramie (population 32,382; elevation 7,173 ft/2,186 m) is a charming combination of Old West frontier town and sophisticated university town, all with immediate proximity to the natural rocky playground that envelops the city.

Even with a relatively lawless history, Laramie continues to be among the most progressive cities in the state, although it hasn't lost any of its cowboy swagger. The 150 year-old downtown buildings are beautiful and authentic examples of the finest frontier architecture. From old-school quilt shops to herb stores, cowgirl yarn shops to outdoor stores, downtown Laramie is a charming mix of the Old and New West. For proof, look no further than Ivinson and First Streets, where cowboy and motorcycle bars share customers with a vegetarian café and a global cuisine bistro. The town is full of important historic sites and an arresting spectrum of museums. The university gives Laramie just enough academic culture to keep the town young and vibrant with concerts, lectures, sports, and coffeehouses, and the surrounding wilderness is well used without becoming overcrowded.

HISTORY

Like so many cities in the region, Laramie can trace its roots back to a fort: Fort John Buford, built in 1866 to protect travelers on the pioneer trails, most notably the Overland Trail. In 1867, railroad workers plotting the course through the Laramie Valley rumbled into town, bringing with them numerous businesses to support their way of life. When the first passengers disembarked from the Union Pacific train in Laramie City in 1868, there were 23 saloons ready for them to wet their whistles.

Fort John Buford, by then known as Fort Sanders, was abandoned in 1882, but other significant structures had been built in Laramie. The Wyoming Territorial Prison was first built in 1872 as a response to the lawlessness of the area. And in 1887, Wyoming University, now known as the University of Wyoming, opened its doors to both men and women. It's worth pointing

Downtown Laramie

Laramie

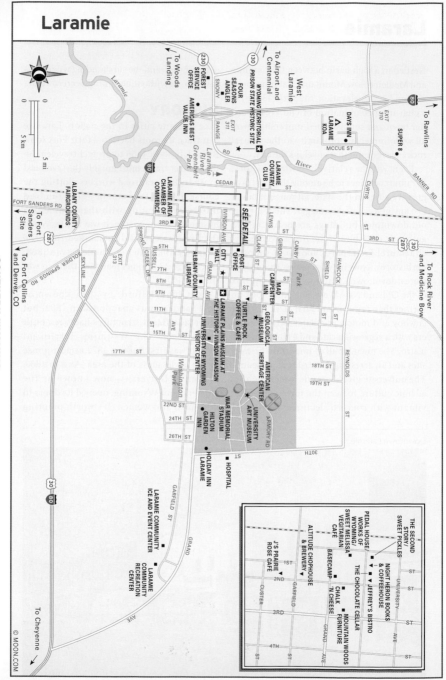

To Woods Landing

To Airport and Centennial

West Laramie

To Rawlins

230 FOREST SERVICE OFFICE

130

WYOMING TERRITORIAL/ PRISON STATE HISTORIC SITE

FOUR SEASONS ANGLER

SNOWY

AMERICAS BEST VALUE INN

RANGE

EXIT 311

80

EXIT 310

DAYS INN

LARAMIE KOA

SUPER 8

MCCUE ST

To Fort Sanders Site

287

FORT SANDERS RD

ALBANY COUNTY FAIRGROUNDS

LARAMIE AREA CHAMBER OF COMMERCE

SOLDIER SPRINGS RD

SKYLINE RD

EXIT 313

SPRING CREEK DR

RUSSELL AVE

GRAND AVE

5TH

7TH

8TH

9TH

11TH

15TH

17TH

3RD

PARK

CEDAR

Laramie River Greenbelt Park

80

Laramie River

LARAMIE COUNTRY CLUB

VINSON AVE

SEE DETAIL

CLARK ST

LEWIS ST

GIBBON

CANBY ST

HANCOCK

SHIELD

ST

ST

3RD ST

30 287

To Rock River and Medicine Bow

BANNER RD

CURTIS

River

Park

REYNOLDS ST

ALBANY COUNTY LIBRARY

CITY HALL

POST OFFICE

MAD CARPENTER INN

GEOLOGICAL MUSEUM

18TH ST

19TH ST

TURTLE ROCK COFFEE & CAFÉ

LARAMIE PLAINS MUSEUM AT THE HISTORIC IVINSON MANSION

UNIVERSITY OF WYOMING VISITOR CENTER

Washington Park

WAR MEMORIAL STADIUM

AMERICAN HERITAGE CENTER

UNIVERSITY ART MUSEUM

ARMORY RD

30TH

22ND ST

24TH ST

26TH ST

HILTON GARDEN INN

HOLIDAY INN LARAMIE

HOSPITAL

ST

To Fort Collins and Denver, CO

GARFIELD ST

GRAND AVE

LARAMIE COMMUNITY ICE AND EVENT CENTER

LARAMIE COMMUNITY RECREATION CENTER

30 80

To Cheyenne

© MOON.COM

0
0

5 km

5 mi

J'S PRAIRIE ROSE CAFÉ

ALTITUDE CHOPHOUSE & BREWERY

PEDAL HOUSE

WORKS OF WYOMING/ SWEET MELISSA VEGETARIAN CAFÉ

THE SECOND STORY/ SWEET PICKLES

THE CHOCOLATE CELLAR

NIGHT HERON BOOKS & COFFEEHOUSE

JEFFREY'S BISTRO

BASECAMP

CHALK 'N CHEESE

MOUNTAIN WOODS FURNITURE

1ST

2ND

3RD

4TH

CUSTER

GARFIELD

GRAND AVE

UNIVERSITY

ST

ST

ST

ST

AVE

out that women in Laramie were the first in the United States to sit on a jury and to vote, both in 1870.

SIGHTS

American Heritage Center

Established in 1945, the **American Heritage Center** (2111 Willett Dr., 307/766-4114, www.ahc.uwyo.edu, 8am-7pm Mon., 8am-5pm Tues.-Fri., 10am-5pm Sat. 2nd-floor loggia only, free) houses one of the most extensive nongovernmental historical collections in the country. In addition to the manuscripts collections, a rare book center has more than 55,000 items that date back to medieval times. Topics range from the American West, an obvious and natural specialty, to British and American literature, natural history, conservation, women authors, and book arts, among countless others. The center is open to the public and is utilized constantly by scholars from all over the world. The center also hosts an array of fascinating events from lectures and symposia to rare and important exhibits. The website offers viewers a meaningful look into the digital collection, audiovisual collection, and virtual exhibits.

University of Wyoming Art Museum

Housed in the same architecturally interesting complex as the American Heritage Center, the **University of Wyoming Art Museum** (2111 Willett Dr., 307/766-6622, www.uwyo.edu/artmuseum, 10am-5pm Mon.-Sat. May-Aug. and Dec.-Jan., 10am-7pm Mon. and 10am-5pm Tues.-Sat. Feb.-Apr. and Sept.-Nov., free) brings art from around the world to Wyoming. Its permanent collection houses more than 7,000 objects, including European and American paintings, prints, and drawings; 19th-century Japanese prints; 18th-19th-century Persian and Indian miniature paintings; 20th-century photography; and African and Native American artifacts. The museum also hosts important exhibitions focused on everything from regional art to international museum collections.

University of Wyoming Geological Museum

In a university with several compelling museums covering everything from anthropology to insects, another great one is the **University of Wyoming Geological Museum** (West Campus, near N. 9th St. and E. Lewis St., 307/766-3386, www.uwyo.edu/geomuseum, 10am-4pm Mon.-Sat., free). The museum houses some of the best fossils in the country and dedicates plenty of space to Wyoming's earliest inhabitants: the dinosaurs. In addition to the usual suspects—from the allosaurus to the *T. rex*—the museum lays claim to one of only six apatosaurus skeletons on display worldwide. This one is 145-160 million years old and was discovered in Albany County in 1901. There are also skeletons of *Diatryma gigantea,* a prehistoric carnivorous flying dinosaur more than 7 feet (2.1 m) tall, found in 1876. One of the most unique exhibits is the fossilized remains of a dinosaur that died giving birth. The bones of the baby are clearly visible. Dozens of displays tell the stories of the more than 50 species of dinosaur whose remains have been found in Wyoming soil. And when displays are missing here, they are often on loan to the Museum of Natural History in New York City. These are serious bones in a very unassuming package.

★ Laramie Plains Museum at the Historic Ivinson Mansion

Entrepreneur and banker Edward Ivinson was a local hero in Laramie, not only for his ethical business practices and his community-minded role in the construction of the prison and the university, but also for the home that he built in 1892, the same year he lost the Wyoming gubernatorial race. Indeed, the **Ivinson Mansion** (603 E. Ivinson Ave., 307/742-4448, www.laramiemuseum.org, tours 9am-5pm Tues.-Sat. and 1pm-4pm Sun. in summer, 1pm-4pm Tues.-Sat. fall-spring, hours can change for private events, $10 adults, $7 seniors, $5 students and military, $25 families, free for children under 6) is among Laramie's most impressive buildings. The house was designed by architect W. E. Ware and built for $40,000 with then-unheard-of amenities that included central heating, electricity, and running water. Jane Ivinson, Edward's wife, decorated the home with elegant appointments from around the world. After his beloved wife died, Ivinson donated their regal residence to the Episcopal Missionary District of Wyoming with the understanding that it be used as a school-home for teenage ranch girls who otherwise might not be educated. The school operated until 1958, at which point the house sat vacant at the mercy of vandals for more than a decade.

In 1972 the Episcopal Church sold the mansion to the Laramie Plains Museum Association. Under the museum's care, the home has been beautifully restored and is open to the public as the Laramie Plains Museum. The home is filled with artifacts from all over the state, including the largest collection of Wyoming Territorial Prison furnishings, gorgeous wood pieces made by Swedish prisoner Jan Hjorth, a regional gun collection spanning more than a century, period furnishings, and more. Seeing the artifacts in such a stunning home setting makes this museum absolutely worth seeing. The only way to see the house is on a docent-led tour.

★ Wyoming Territorial Prison State Historic Site

Built in 1872 to deal with the ruffians in lawless Laramie, the **Wyoming Territorial Prison** (975 Snowy Range Rd., 307/745-3733, http://wyoparks.state.wy.us, 8am-7pm daily May-Sept., 8am-5pm Mon.-Sat. Apr., 8am-5pm daily Oct., $5 adults, $2.50 children 11-17, free for children under 11) was restored in 1989 and made into a 190-acre (76.9-hectare) state historic site. The prison was in use 1872-1903, during which time more than 1,000 men and 12 women were imprisoned there. Among the most famous residents was Butch Cassidy. When Wyoming achieved statehood in 1890, work was already underway on a new state prison in Rawlins. When the Wyoming Frontier Prison opened in 1901, the transition began, and prisoners in the territorial prison were slowly replaced by animals from the University of Wyoming's experimental stock farm, which were housed in the prison for more than 70 years.

Rounding out the historic site are an entirely re-created frontier town; a number of buildings in various stages of restoration,

the Wyoming Territorial Prison State Historic Site

including the broom factory where many of the prisoners worked on a variety of different jobs, authentic pioneer cabins, a schoolhouse, and agricultural buildings where kids can stick their arms into a simulated (and gooey!) cow's belly.

Still, the prison is the main attraction, and visitors should plan to spend at least 90 minutes touring the facility. A brochure in the gift shop provides a self-guided tour through furnished cells, the prisoner dining room, guards' quarters, women's quarters, the warden's office, and a number of other rooms and exhibit galleries. The warden's house on the grounds can also be toured.

Several things make this experience both unique and unforgettable. For starters, willing visitors are assigned the identity of a former prisoner upon entering and can find out about their prisoner throughout the facility, something that keeps kids fully involved. The prisoner ID card can be stamped at the end of the visit for a fun take-home souvenir. The museum itself is spotlessly clean and easy to explore. There are also numerous volunteers throughout the property, dressed as late 19th-century prisoners, who answer questions and tell fascinating stories. This is just a wonderful place to spend an afternoon.

SPORTS AND RECREATION
Rock Climbing

A mecca for rock climbers and nature lovers alike, **Vedauwoo** (off I-80 exit 329, about 20 mi/32 km east of Laramie, 307/745-2300, www.vedauwoo.org) is an otherworldly jumble of enormous boulders that offer some of the best wide-crack climbing in the West. More than 500 sport climbs were documented in the first guidebook for the area, written in 1994 and no longer available. Today there are more than 900 climbs, many of which are detailed on the Vedauwoo website, and the number continues to grow. For nonclimbers, the area is ideal for hiking, trail running, and even wildlife-viewing. Among the animals sighted here are pronghorn, deer, moose, and even black bears and cougars. A U.S. Forest Service campground is available at the site. The elevation here is surprisingly high, at 8,200 feet (2,499 m) above sea level.

Hiking and Biking

Although it is primarily known for its climbing opportunities, Vedauwoo offers excellent hiking for those who like to stay in contact with the ground. The **Turtle Rock Loop** is a 2.8-mile (4.5-km) trail that climbs only 314 feet (96 m) through forest and alongside the famed red rocks. The trail got its name from its proximity to the base of Turtle Rock, an outcrop of Sherman granite that is as old as the Rocky Mountains. Along the route, the Snowy Mountains are visible to the east. To get to the trailhead from Laramie, drive east on I-80 for 12 miles (19.3 km) to Vedauwoo Road. Turn left and cross under the interstate. Stay on Vedauwoo Road for 1.2 miles (1.9 km) to the campground entry gate. Turn left into the campground and continue 0.5 mile (0.8 km) to a small gravel parking lot on the left.

In addition to meandering hikes in town along the Laramie River Greenbelt and at nearby Vedauwoo, the **Pole Mountain Area** (Forest Rd. 705, off I-80 exit 323, 13 mi/20.9 km east of Laramie) in the Sherman Mountains offers terrific trails for hiking and biking. The **Headquarters National Recreation Trail Loop** can be a 4-mile (6.4-km) or 8-mile (12.9-km) round-trip loop, depending on your time and energy level. The trail winds through a number of environments, from sage and grassy meadows to pine forests, and there is plenty of opportunity for bouldering among the pink granite rocks that are reminiscent of Vedauwoo. A brochure, "Pole Mountain Summer-Use Trails," is available at the **Laramie Ranger District** (2468 W. Jackson St., 307/745-2300, 8am-4:30pm Mon.-Fri.).

You'll have to bring your own bike to Laramie, unless you are a student or faculty member of the University of Wyoming, in which case you can rent from the ingenious Bike Library through the **Outdoor Program**

(307/766-2402), but if you need service, repairs, or just some good advice, head into the **Pedal House** (207 S. 1st St., 307/742-5533, www.pedalhouse.com).

Fishing

While Laramie isn't quite the hotbed of fishing that can be found in other parts of the state, its location makes access to varied waters relatively easy. For lake fishing, options include **Laramie Plains Lakes** (15 mi/24 km west of town off Hwy. 230) and **Lake Hattie** (20 mi/32 km southwest of Laramie off Hwy. 230). Nearby rivers filled with trout include the **Big Laramie River** and the **Upper North Platte River.** For fishing gear or guided trips, contact **Four Seasons Angler** (334 S. Fillmore St., 307/721-4047, www.fourseasonsanglers. com). Half-day wade trips for two anglers start at $400; full-day trips for two start at $500 including lunch.

Golf

Golfers can hit the links in Laramie at the nine-hole **Fox Run** (489 Hwy. 230, 307/745-4161, www.foxrunlaramie.com, $35 for 18 holes, $25 for 9 holes) or the **Jacoby Park Golf Course** (3501 Willett Dr., 307/745-3111, www.jacobygc.com, $40 for 18 holes, $32 for 9 holes) on the University of Wyoming campus.

Skiing

Thirty-two miles (52 km) west of town in the Medicine Bow National Forest, **Snowy Range Ski Area** (3254 Hwy. 130, Centennial, 307/745-5750, www.snowyrangeski.com, full-day $49 adults, $42 teens 13-17 and military, $30 children 5-12, free for kids under 5 and seniors 70 and over) has four ski lifts covering 27 trails on 250 acres (101.2 hectares): 7 beginner trails, 12 intermediate trails, 8 expert trails and 2 terrain parks. The area receives an average of 245 inches (622 cm) annually, with a base elevation of 8,798 feet (2,682 m) and summit of 9,663 feet (2,945 m).

While Laramie is not known as a cross-country ski destination, there are miles upon miles of groomed trails just 15 minutes from town. **Tie City** and **Happy Jack Trailheads,** which give skiers access to some 30 miles (48 km) of trails, are found off I-80, exit 323, then north on Happy Jack Road for 1 mile (1.6 km). A $5 parking fee is required. More information and maps for these trails and others can be found online at www. visitlaramie.org and medicinebownordic. org. A terrific store for all kinds of gear, daily or weekly rentals, and first-rate advice for Nordic skiers is the **Basecamp** (222 S. 2nd St., 307/721-2851, www.laramiesbasecamp. com, 9am-6pm Mon.-Thurs., 8am-7pm Fri.-Sat., 8am-4pm Sun.).

Spectator Sports

When it comes to recreation, one cannot forget that Laramie is a college town and somewhat fanatical about its football. Attending a **Wyoming Cowboys** game at War Memorial Stadium (E. Grand Ave. and N. 22nd St.) is a true Wyoming experience. It's likely the only place in Wyoming you'll ever feel crowded. For schedule and tickets, contact the **Athletic Ticket Office** (877/996-3261, www.wyomingathletics.com).

Perhaps small beans compared to the Cowboys, collegiate baseball is played at **Cowboy Field** (2623 Willet Dr., just east of War Memorial Stadium, www.laramiecolts. com). The Laramie Colts are part of the Rocky Mountain Baseball League, play upward of 40 games per season, and still live with local families willing to take them in and feed them home-cooked meals between games.

Recreation Centers

When the wind blows in Laramie, and it will, the **Laramie Community Recreation Center** (920 Boulder Dr., 307/721-5269, www. cityoflaramie.org, 5am-9pm Mon.-Fri., 8am-8pm Sat., noon-8pm Sun., nonmember fitness class $8 adults, daily visit $6.50 adult, $6.25 seniors 60 and over, $5.50 children 13-18, $3.75 children 3-12, free for kids under 3) offers an indoor leisure pool, an eight-lane lap pool, an outdoor pool with waterslides and a lazy river, a full-court gymnasium, weights, an indoor playground, and an abundance of classes and activities. Check the website for pool and gym hours.

Accessed from a trailhead at West Garfield Street and South Spruce Street, the **Laramie River Greenbelt Park** offers 5.8 miles (9.3 km) of paved walking, running, biking, and inline skating paths.

When winter comes to town, the **Laramie Community Ice and Event Center** (3510 Garfield St., 307/721-2161, www.cityoflaramie. org, 5am-9pm Mon.-Fri., 8am-8pm Sat., noon-8pm Sun., weekly schedules posted online, $5 nonresident adults, $2.50 children 3-5, drop-in figure skating $8 nonresidents, drop-in hockey $8 nonresident adults 18 and up) offers ice-skating, broomball, curling, and skate rentals. When there is no ice, mid-March-September, usually, roller-skating is available.

ENTERTAINMENT AND EVENTS

With such a young, vibrant population, Laramie has loads of events going on year-round. From scholarly lectures on campus to concerts and meditation gatherings, offerings are plentiful and diverse. A great way to get warmed up to the history of the region is with the living history tour **Legends of Laramie** (www.visitlaramie.org), available on your smartphone or tablet. Organized by the Albany County Tourism Board, the tour includes 15 stops around Laramie highlighting everything from railroad romances and shootouts to the ghost town of Sherman 18 miles (29 km) south of town.

On Wednesday nights throughout summer, the **Laramie Municipal Band,** made up primarily of students and teachers from the university, puts on free concerts in Washington Park (Sheridan St. between S. 18th St. and S. 21st St.) starting at 7:30pm. On Friday afternoon and evening July-September, the town comes downtown for the weekly and festive **farmers market** (307/742-3774, www. laramiemainstreet.org, 3pm-7pm). For cultural events held throughout the year at the university, including the **University of**

Wyoming Symphony Orchestra, theater and dance performances, and major concerts, contact the **Fine Arts Box Office** (307/766-6666, www.uwyo.edu/finearts).

For more than 70 years, **Laramie Jubilee Days** (www.laramiejubileedays.com) has been the annual hometown celebration that draws revelers from across the region. Often scheduled in the week leading up to the anniversary of Wyoming's statehood on July 10, the event offers Fourth of July celebrations, including the biggest fireworks display in the state. Other Jubilee Days events include street dances, a classic parade, bull riding, and three nights of professional rodeo.

The **Albany County Fair** is held annually late July-early August at the fairgrounds (3520 U.S. 287, 307/742-3224, www. albanycountyfair.org) and has all the family-friendly fun visitors expect from a Western fair, including a carnival, entertainment, and 4-H activities.

SHOPPING

While the shopping options are quite varied around town, from marvelous bookstores to hippie outposts and classic Western saddleries, the experience of shopping in Laramie's historic and charming downtown cannot be beat. **The Second Story** (105 E. Ivinson Ave., 307/745-4423, 10am-6pm Mon.-Sat., Sun. during Christmas season only), for example, is a gem of an independent bookstore housed in a public hall built in 1889. Since then, it has been a hotel, a bordello, a saloon, a senior center, and now a bookstore. The children's book selection is particularly good. As a bonus, with every book purchase comes a free espresso drink, made to order. Watch their Facebook page for special events. Right next door, **Night Heron Books & Coffeehouse** (107 E. Ivinson Ave., 307/742-9028, www. nightheronbooks.com, 7am-7pm daily) offers a great selection of rare and used books. Plus, the coffee shop serves up a rotating menu of quiche, soups, sandwiches, and baked goods.

For a delectable treat, stop by **The Chocolate Cellar** (113 Ivinson Ave.,

307/742-9278, 10am-5:30pm Mon.-Sat.), which has been creating handcrafted goodies since 1982. Plus they have an extensive collection of gifts, including chocolate and candy tins. **Mountain Woods Furniture** (1512 Hwy. 230, 866/689-6637, www.mountainwoodsfurniture.com, 10am-6pm Mon.-Sat.) sells rustic log furniture handcrafted by artisans from across North America. **Chalk n' Cheese** (209 2nd St., 307/742-1800, www.chalkncheesewy.com, 10am-6pm Tues.-Sat.) is a great cheese and gourmet food shop that sells kitchenware and antiques, as well as offers fun cooking classes. Stop by on Thursday and Friday evenings to taste from their elaborate charcuterie platters. **Works of Wyoming** (300 S. 2nd St., 307/460-3304, www.worksofwyoming.org, 10am-6pm Mon.-Sat.) has an excellent selection of fine art, crafts, and gifts made by Wyoming artists and artisans. **Sweet Pickles** (117 E. Ivinson St., 307/745-4114, 10am-6pm Mon.-Sat., noon-4pm Sun.) is a wonderful spot for kids, with both toys and clothes. And if the shopping wears you out, there's wonderful homemade ice cream at **Big Dipper Ice Cream** (111 E. Ivinson St., 307/460-3358, 11am-9pm Mon.-Sat., noon-9pm Sun.) a few doors down.

FOOD

Like all college towns worth their salt, Laramie has an abundance of good, relatively cheap places to enjoy a meal. For breakfast or lunch, a local favorite is **J's Prairie Rose Café** (410 S. 2nd St., 307/745-8140, 7am-3pm Mon.-Sat., 7am-noon Sun., $5-11). The Prairie Rose, as it is known, has the best green chili in town, plus phenomenal breakfast burritos, Philly cheesesteaks, and, like all good diners, homemade pie. Its off-menu specials include everything from Italian dishes to eggs Benedict. Breakfast is served all day.

For a smattering of reasonably priced global cuisine, try ★ **Jeffrey's Bistro** (123 E. Ivinson Ave., 307/742-7046, www.jeffreysbistro.com, 11am-9pm Mon.-Sat., $10-17), which offers hearty salads, creative daily specials like ancho-cherry barbecue chicken or

hot-and-spicy Thai shrimp, and delicious entrées such as potpie, enchiladas, Thai burritos, and jambalaya, many of which can be made vegetarian. For serious vegetarians, **Sweet Melissa Vegetarian Café** (213 S. 1st St., 307/742-9607, 11am-9pm Mon.-Thurs., 11am-10pm Fri.-Sat., $9-15) is like green heaven in the middle of cow country. Tons of salads, pastas, and sandwiches are on the menu, as expected, but there is also plenty of gluten-free options as well as good old-fashioned comfort food like smothered sweet potato and black bean burritos, seitan fajitas, caprese linguini, and Thai peanut stir-fry with tofu. There's a kid's menu and the desserts include specialties like fried banana bread, peanut butter pie, and vegan chocolate cake. Check Facebook for daily specials and events. The fact that Sweet Melissa adjoins a popular watering hole, **Front Street Tavern** (11am-close Mon.-Sat.), is just icing on the cake.

Serving upscale brewpub cuisine that ranges from the traditional (hickory burgers, seafood pasta, bacon-wrapped tenderloin, and cedar-plank salmon) to the unusual (Vietnamese barbecue, orange-braised pork loin, and Thai salmon burgers), **Altitude Chophouse & Brewery** (320 S. 2nd St., 307/721-4031, www.altitudechophouse.com, 11am-10pm Mon.-Sat., $9-29) perfectly pairs sensational beer with delicious and creative cuisine. There's a kid's menu, plenty of options for vegetarians and even a vegan menu.

Set in the lovely, tree-lined university area, **Turtle Rock Coffee & Café** (270 N. 9th St., 307/745-3741, www.turtlerockcoffee.com, 7am-9pm Mon.-Thurs., 7am-8pm Fri.-Sat., 8am-6pm Sun.) serves up yummy sandwiches, pastries, ice cream, and, of course, the requisite college coffee. The outdoor seating is delightful, and the Geological Museum at the University of Wyoming is just steps away.

ACCOMMODATIONS

Laramie has more than 2,000 guest rooms in town, of which several hundred are just a few years old. Accommodation options include hotels, motels, bed-and-breakfasts, and guest ranches.

For the best value in town, the **Americas Best Value Inn** (523 S. Adams St., 307/721-8860, www.redlion.com, from $64) offers clean, no-frills guest rooms with air-conditioning and free Wi-Fi. Another good budget option is the **Laramie Valley Inn** (1104 S. 3rd St., 307/721-8860, www.laramievalleyinn. com, $79-109) owned by University of Wyoming alumni. Most of the rooms have been renovated; those that haven't are less expensive. Pets are welcome in a few rooms.

At the other end of the spectrum, the ★ **Hilton Garden Inn** (2229 Grand Ave., 307/745-5500, www.uwconferencecenter.com, $99-236) offers all the frills you are going to find in Laramie. From Egyptian cotton sheets and ergonomic chairs to flat-screen TVs and cushy bathrobes, this hotel sets the standard for luxury.

Standard chain hotels in town include the newer **Holiday Inn Laramie** (204 S. 30th St., 307/721-9000, www.ihg.com, $159-270), the pet-friendly **Days Inn** (1368 McCue St., 800/329-7466, www.wyndhamhotels.com, $79-169), and **Super 8** (1987 Banner Rd., 307/745-8901, www.super8.com, $59-132).

A few unique lodging options are the fabulously quirky **Mad Carpenter Inn** (353 N. 8th St., 307/742-0870, www.madcarpenterinn. net, $95-145), a B&B near the university where the creative and delightful innkeepers have a passion for carpentry, cooking (a gourmet continental breakfast is included), and poetry. In addition to three rooms, there is a three-bedroom house available. For those who want more of the rustic, backwoods-type experience, **Brooklyn Lodge** (3540 Hwy. 130, Centennial, 307/742-6916, www. brooklynlodge.com, from $199) is the ticket. Designated a National Historic Site and set in the Medicine Bow National Forest right near the ski area, the two king-bedded rooms at this bed-and-breakfast are cozy, rustic, and abundantly comfortable. Although pets are not allowed, horses can stay for $25 per night.

CAMPING

There are plenty of fantastic opportunities for camping or renting a cabin in the **Medicine Bow-Routt National Forest,** which surrounds Laramie to the east (Pole Mountain) and west (Snowy Range). The closest public campgrounds to town are the nicely forested **Yellow Pine Campground** (Forest Rd. 719, 13.2 mi/21.2 km west of Laramie, $10) and otherworldly **Vedauwoo Campground**

camping in Vedauwoo

(Vedauwoo Rd., 17.3 mi/27.8 km east of Laramie, $10). Both campgrounds have potable water.

Equidistant between Laramie and Cheyenne is **Curt Gowdy State Park** (1319 Happy Jack Rd., 307/632-7946 or 877/996-7275, http://wyoparks.state.wy.us, $4 residents, $6 nonresidents, camping $10 residents, $17 nonresidents, includes day use), 24 miles (39 km) east of Laramie at the edge of the Laramie Mountains. Historically, the area served as prime hunting and camping grounds for numerous Native American tribes. There are 35 RV sites that can be reserved, 15 with water hookups, none with electricity. The remaining sites are first-come, first-served. Set on three lovely reservoirs, the park offers trout and kokanee salmon fishing as well as hiking and biking trails and prime picnicking spots. Dogs are not permitted off-leash or in the water.

For information on sites in the Laramie Ranger District or other nearby areas, contact the **U.S. Forest Service** (2468 W. Jackson St., 307/745-2300, 8am-5pm Mon.-Fri.).

Just north of I-80, the **Laramie KOA** (1271 W. Baker St., 307/742-6553, www.koa.com) has tent sites ($31), RV sites ($47-50), and cabins ($60-65) in addition to free Wi-Fi, various organized activities, and a playground.

INFORMATION AND SERVICES

The **Albany County Tourism Board** (210 E. Custer St., 307/745-4195, www.visitlaramie. org, 8am-5pm Mon.-Fri., 9am-1pm Sat. June-Sept., 8am-5pm Mon.-Fri. Oct.-May) operates a convention and visitors bureau and is happy to send a visitor guide in advance of your trip. The **Laramie Area Chamber of Commerce** (800 S. 3rd St., 307/745-7339 or 866/876-1012, www.laramie.org, 8am-4:30pm Mon.-Fri.) can provide useful information on local businesses and relocation.

For information on recreation in the nearby **Medicine Bow-Routt National Forest** and the **Thunder Basin National Grassland,** both of which are managed by the U.S. Forest Service, visit the **headquarters**

(2468 W. Jackson St., 307/745-2371, 8am-5pm Mon.-Fri.).

The **Albany County Public Library** (310 S. 8th St., 307/721-2580, www. albanycountylibrary.org, 1pm-6pm Mon. and Fri., 10am-7pm Tues.-Thurs., 1pm-5pm Sat.) has nine Internet terminals available for free.

The main **post office** may be found at 152 North 5th Street (307/721-8837, 8am-5:15pm Mon.-Fri., 9am-1pm Sat.).

Ivinson Memorial Hospital (255 N. 30th St., 307/742-2141, www.ivinsonhospital.org) offers 24-hour emergency care plus specialized medicine. **Grand Avenue Urgent Care** (3236 E. Grand Ave., 307/760-8602, www. grandaveurgentcare.com) is open 9am-8pm Mon.-Fri., 9am-6pm Sat., and 9am-4pm Sun.

This is a college town, with no shortage of laundries, including **Spic and Span Laundromat** (272 N. 4th St., 307/745-3939, 7:30am-10pm daily, last load in by 8:30pm), which offers plasma TVs, Wi-Fi, and double- and triple-load machines.

TRANSPORTATION
Getting There

The **Laramie Regional Airport** (LAR, 555 General Brees Rd., 307/742-4164, www. laramieairport.com) offers daily 40-minute flights to and from Denver on **United.**

The only car-rental agency at the airport is **Hertz. Enterprise** (517 S. 3rd St.) has a location in town.

Greyhound serves Laramie from the Diamond Shamrock Gas Station at 1952 Banner Road.

By car, Laramie is 49 miles (79 km) west of Cheyenne, 130 miles (209 km) north of Denver, 148 miles (238 km) southeast of Casper, 207 miles (340 km) east of Rock Springs, 380 miles (610 km) southeast of Yellowstone National Park, and 383 miles (620 km) southeast of Jackson.

Getting Around

Laramie's taxi service is provided by **Snowy Range Taxi** (307/343-2323, www. snowyrangetaxi.com, 6pm-6am Tues.-Sat.).

Cheyenne

Just a few miles from the Colorado border is Cheyenne (population 64,019; elevation 6,062 ft/1,848 m), the state capital and an important historical and modern crossroads. The town was named by the Sioux, who used the word to define another tribe, which we know as the Cheyenne, that they considered alien. A settlement sprang up on July 4, 1867, in advance of the Union Pacific Railroad's arrival; the town's population thrived and culture flourished. Influential people and performers traveling across the West by train often stopped in Cheyenne, making it a rather progressive town. Today I-80 and I-25 cross in Cheyenne, bringing visitors from every direction into its historic folds.

The city's defining event, Frontier Days, was founded in 1897 and today brings nearly 250,000 people (and 6,000 animals!) to town for 10 days in late July. Cheyenne is still a rodeo town, with one of the only visitor bureaus that lists horse-boarding stables along with hotels and motels. After all, if you're coming to Cheyenne, why not bring your horse?

High and windswept, Cheyenne is not a classic Wyoming beauty in the same way as Jackson or Sheridan, but it has a compelling setting with more urban culture than in most of the state, some wonderful museums, and a smattering of ways to enjoy the great outdoors.

HISTORY

The first makeshift railroad town to be settled in Wyoming was Cheyenne in July 1867. Initially a boisterous, mayhem-filled tent city, it soon began to blossom. By November, when the railroad arrived, it had 4,000 residents and was dubbed the "magic city" for its large population boom. Because Cheyenne was an "end-of-tracks town" for longer than any other Wyoming town, it was marked by rapid growth and lawlessness. Fort D. A. Russell was

established nearby, and the military presence helped to settle things down.

In 1869, Cheyenne was named the territorial capital, a title challenged unsuccessfully by Laramie and Evanston. The cornerstone for the Wyoming Capitol was laid in May 1887. After the arrival of both sheep and cattle in the 1870s, Cheyenne became an important shipping center, exporting cattle and supplies to the East and importing the latest fashions and desirables. Thanks to the cattle barons, by the 1880s Cheyenne was considered one of the wealthiest cities per capita in the world.

SIGHTS

As a wonderful prelude to this historic city, jump on the **Cheyenne Street Railway Trolley** (121 W. 15th St., 307/778-3133 or 800/426-5009, www.cheyennetrolley.com, 90-minute tours 10am, 11:30am, 1pm, 2:30pm, and 4pm Mon.-Fri., 2-hour tours 10am, noon, and 2pm Sat., noon and 2pm Sun., May-Sept., $12 adults, $6 children 2-12), departing from the beautiful old rail depot (121 W. 15th St.). The ride gives visitors a narrated overview of the city, stopping by many of the best sights, including the Nelson Museum, Wyoming State Museum, the state capitol, Cheyenne Botanic Gardens, Old West Museum, and Historic Governors' Mansion. Visitors are welcome to hop off and hop on the next trolley, 90 minutes later on weekdays or two hours later on weekends.

Wyoming State Capitol

The cornerstone of the **Wyoming State Capitol** (200 W. 24th St. and Capitol Ave., 307/777-7220, 8am-5pm Mon.-Fri.) was laid on May 18, 1887, when Wyoming was still a territory. Modeled after the capitol in Washington DC, this National Historic Landmark went through various phases of construction, the last being the addition of the senate and house chambers, completed

Cheyenne

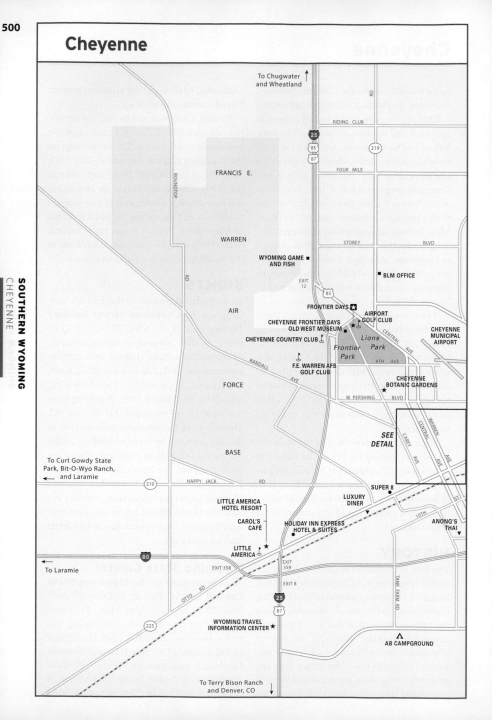

To Chugwater and Wheatland

RIDING CLUB

25
85
87

219

FOUR MILE

FRANCIS E.

ROUNDTOP

WARREN

STOREY

BLVD

WYOMING GAME AND FISH

BLM OFFICE

EXIT 12

85

AIR

FRONTIER DAYS

AIRPORT GOLF CLUB

CHEYENNE FRONTIER DAYS OLD WEST MUSEUM

CENTRAL AVE

CHEYENNE MUNICIPAL AIRPORT

CHEYENNE COUNTRY CLUB

Lions Park

Frontier Park

8TH AVE

RANDALL AVE

F.E. WARREN AFB GOLF CLUB

CHEYENNE BOTANIC GARDENS

FORCE

W PERSHING BLVD

BASE

SEE DETAIL

CAREY AVE

WARREN AVE

CENTRAL AVE

To Curt Gowdy State Park, Bit-O-Wyo Ranch, and Laramie

210

HAPPY JACK RD

SUPER 8

LUXURY DINER

LITTLE AMERICA HOTEL RESORT

I-25

10TH

CAROL'S CAFÉ

HOLIDAY INN EXPRESS HOTEL & SUITES

ANONG'S THAI

80

LITTLE AMERICA

To Laramie

EXIT 358

EXIT 359

EXIT 8

OTTO RD

TANK FARM RD

225

25
87

WYOMING TRAVEL INFORMATION CENTER

AB CAMPGROUND

To Terry Bison Ranch and Denver, CO

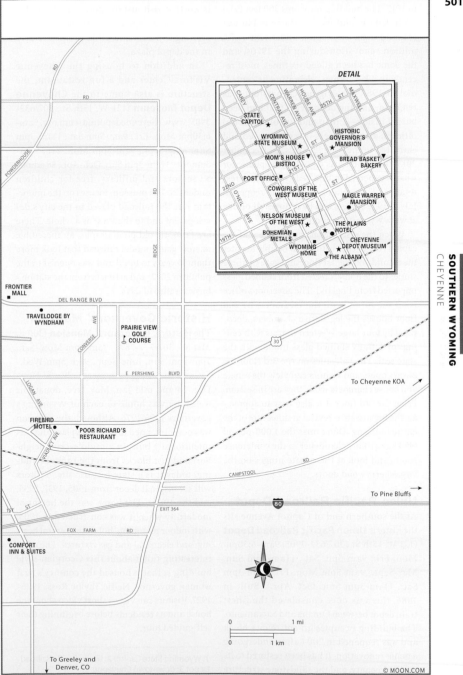

DETAIL

STATE
CAPITOL ★

WYOMING
STATE MUSEUM ★

HISTORIC
GOVERNOR'S
★ MANSION

MOM'S HOUSE ▼
BISTRO

BREAD BASKET ▼
BAKERY

POST OFFICE ■

COWGIRLS OF THE
WEST MUSEUM

NAGLE WARREN
● MANSION

NELSON MUSEUM
OF THE WEST ★

THE PLAINS
★ HOTEL

BOHEMIAN
METALS ■

CHEYENNE
★ DEPOT MUSEUM

WYOMING
HOME ▼

THE ALBANY ▼

CAREY
CENTRAL AVE
WARREN AVE
HOUSE AVE
25TH ST
MAXWELL
21ST
O'NEIL AVE
22ND
RIDGE
CAPITOL AVE

FRONTIER
MALL ■

DEL RANGE BLVD

TRAVELODGE BY ●
WYNDHAM

CONVERSE AVE

PRAIRIE VIEW
GOLF
COURSE

30

E PERSHING BLVD

To Cheyenne KOA →

LOGAN AVE

FIREBIRD
MOTEL ●

VIADUCT AVE

▼ POOR RICHARD'S
RESTAURANT

CAMPSTOOL RD

To Pine Bluffs →

1ST ST

EXIT 364

80

FOX FARM RD

COMFORT ●
INN & SUITES

0   1 mi

0   1 km

To Greeley and
↓ Denver, CO

© MOON.COM

in 1917. The building measures 300 feet (91.4 m) in length, and its gold dome is 146 feet (44.5 m) high. The capitol underwent a $7.6 million renovation during the 1970s, and the dome has been gilded six times, most recently in 1988. When celebrating its centennial in 1987, the original cornerstone was removed, and the documents that had been buried inside—a map and list of territorial officers, among others—were removed and entrusted to the state archives. In December 2015, the capitol was closed to the public for what is expected to be a nearly four-year restoration. The capitol is expected to reopen in July 2019. Progress can be monitored online at www.wyomingcapitolsquare.com.

When the restoration is complete and the capitol reopened, visitors will be able to enter the rotunda on the 1st floor and gaze up three stories to the dome, created from stained glass imported from England. The governor's office is off the rotunda on the 1st floor. The 2nd floor houses the legislative chambers, decorated by four large Western murals with ceilings of Tiffany stained glass inlaid with the state seal. The balconies on the 3rd floor are always open, and visitors can view the senate and house chambers while they are in session. From the 3rd floor it is also easy to appreciate the Renaissance-revival architecture of the entire building. Don't miss the 1,000-pound (454 kg) Tiffany chandelier in the conference room, and look at the ornate hinges on the large cherrywood doors.

Union Pacific Railroad Depot

At the southern end of Capitol Avenue sits the historic **Union Pacific Railroad Depot** (121 W. 15th St., 307/632-3905, 9am-6:30pm Mon.-Fri., 9am-5pm Sat., 11am-3pm Sun. May-Sept., 9am-5pm Mon.-Fri., 9am-3pm Sat., 11am-3pm Sun. Oct.-Apr.). Built in 1886, this was once considered the finest train depot between Omaha and Sacramento. The building occupies an entire city block and was reopened in 2004 after undergoing a major renovation. It has been restored to its original beauty, and the sandstone structure is worth a visit just to appreciate the architecture and design. During the summer, free evening concerts and other events are held in the depot plaza.

In addition to housing the Cheyenne Visitors Center and a fun restaurant, the structure is also home to the **Cheyenne Depot Museum** (121 W. 15th St., 307/632-3905, www.cheyennedepotmuseum.org, 9am-6:30pm Mon.-Fri., 9am-5pm Sat., 11am-3pm Sun. May-Sept., 9am-5pm Mon.-Fri., 9am-3pm Sat., 11am-3pm Sun. Oct.-Apr., $8 adults, $7 seniors and military, free for children under 12). The museum focuses on the important role the railroad played in the city's development and to the West as a whole. There are fantastic old photographs, an incredible narrow gauge model railroad that took more than 30 years to build and was opened to the public in 2012, and artifacts from the station's busiest railroad days.

Historic Governors' Mansion

The **Historic Governors' Mansion** (300 E. 21st St., 307/777-7878, 9am-5pm Mon.-Sat., 1pm-5pm Sun. June-Sept., 9am-5pm Wed.-Sat. and Tues. by appointment only mid-Nov.-Dec. 24 and mid-Jan.-May, free, donations welcome) was home to each of Wyoming's governors 1905-1976. Although the mansion was never intended to be a showplace and was intentionally built in a middle-class neighborhood just blocks from the capitol building, today it is a state historic site. Visitors will see original decor from 1905, 1937, 1955, and the 1960s. The home was the height of modernity when it was constructed in 1905, with indoor plumbing, hot water, central heating, and electrical and gas fixtures. The most interesting tidbit about this Georgian-style building is that it housed the country's first woman governor, Nellie Tayloe Ross, 1925-1927. Visitors can view a short video about the house and its residents before beginning their self-guided tour.

1: Wyoming State Capitol **2:** Union Pacific Railroad Depot **3:** downtown Cheyenne

Wyoming State Museum

The **Wyoming State Museum** (2301 Central Ave., 307/777-7022, http://wyomuseum.state.wy.us, 9am-4:30pm Mon.-Sat., free) is dedicated to documenting the state's history from its earliest inhabitants to the present day. In addition to the permanent collection, 3-4 traveling exhibits are showcased at a time. Always on display are exhibits dedicated to prehistoric Wyoming and its dinosaurs, the wildlife of Wyoming, the state's mining history (including an explanation of how coal is created in nature), and a social history of the state. Other exhibits include beautiful Native American beadwork and pottery, a vast firearms collection, and a copy of the act granting women the right to vote in the Wyoming Territory. A hands-on history room for children is well equipped with vintage clothing, a child-size tipi, a chuck wagon, and dinosaur and other interactive displays. As you tour the museum, you can dial up an audio tour at 307/316-0077. The museum also holds a free Thursday Night Lecture Series.

Cheyenne Frontier Days Old West Museum

Frontier Days is such an important part of Cheyenne's local history that a museum was created to tell the story of this Western celebration. The **Old West Museum** (4610 Carey Ave., 307/778-7290, www.oldwestmuseum.org, 9am-5pm daily year round, 8am-6pm daily during Frontier Days, $10 adults, $9 seniors and military, free for children under 12) is filled with memorabilia from the rodeo and focuses on frontier life in Wyoming. It has more than 150 horse-drawn carriages and wagons dating back over a century, along with large Western art exhibits and some 60,000 artifacts. There is also a fun children's history room with clever interactive displays. The museum has extended hours during the Frontier Days festival and is conveniently located in Frontier Park adjacent to the rodeo. A terrific store is also on-site for gift shopping.

Nelson Museum of the West

If you are interested in viewing more cowboy and Native American memorabilia, head over to the **Nelson Museum of the West** (1714 Carey Ave., 307/635-7670, www.nelsonmuseum.com, 9am-4:30pm Mon.-Sat. June-Aug., 9am-4:30pm Mon.-Fri. May and Sept.-Oct., $5 adults, $4 seniors or $2 for seniors on Sat., free for children under 13). There are more than 20 exhibits created from the eclectic personal collection of Robert C. Nelson, including the art of the Plains Indians, firearms of the West, and furnishings from the homes of cattle barons. Look for the stuffed big-game animals scattered throughout the three floors. Audio tours are available on your phone at 307/316-0069.

Cheyenne Botanic Gardens

Should the days get hot and dusty in Cheyenne, find a stunning oasis at the **Cheyenne Botanic Gardens** (710 S. Lions Park Dr., 307/637-6458, www.botanic.org, grounds open dawn-dusk daily, conservatory 10am-6pm Wed.-Sat., free). The plant diversity is stunning, and there is a unique children's village (10am-5pm Tues.-Sun., free) with drop-in activities, a pond and labyrinth, a solar conservatory, community gardens, and more.

★ Fort Laramie National Historic Site

An indelible part of Wyoming's history, **Fort Laramie** (307/837-2221, www.nps.gov, 9am-7pm daily Memorial Day-Labor Day, 8am-4:30pm daily Labor Day-Memorial Day, free) sits at the confluence of the Laramie and North Platte Rivers. It was a major trading center, a military garrison, and the site where the infamous Treaty of 1868 between the U.S. government and the Plains Indians was signed. People from all walks of life, including Native Americans, trappers, missionaries, and homesteaders, passed through the fort during its almost 50 years of existence.

Today there are 22 original structures on

the 830 acres (335.9 hectares) of this National Historic Site. The first stop at the fort should be the **visitors center** in the old commissary building. There is an 18-minute video that describes the fort's rich history along with exhibits with artifacts from frontier times, including weapons, uniforms, and historical photos. A free brochure is available to help visitors with a self-guided tour, or experience the audio tour ($3), which includes voices and sounds from the past.

While at the fort, visit the **cavalry barracks,** which give a clear sense of the cramped living quarters of the soldiers, and **Old Bedlam,** initially the fort headquarters and later used as officers' quarters. The officers were known to host wild parties in the building, hence its name. Also on the grounds is an old stone **guardhouse** where prisoners were kept, a model of the original **Fort John** building erected in 1841, and the old fort **bakery.**

To get to the fort from Cheyenne, head north on I-80 for 80 miles (129 km) to exit 92 for Guernsey and Torrington. Drive east for 27.9 miles (44.9 km), turn right onto Highway 160, and follow the signs. The drive is just over 113 miles (182 km) and should take about an hour and 45 minutes.

SPORTS AND RECREATION

For a city known for its rodeo, Cheyenne has a vast array of recreational opportunities beyond the chutes.

Hiking and Biking

For being in the middle of a high desert, Cheyenne has a remarkable number of green parks to explore and enjoy on two feet or two wheels. The **Greater Cheyenne Greenway** links several of the parks with 10 miles (16.1 km) of paved trails open to hikers and bikers. Sections of trail wind through Crow Creek, Dry Creek, Sun Valley, Lions Park, and Allison Draw, among other parts of town. The trails also serve as a wildlife corridor, so keep your eyes peeled.

Halfway between Cheyenne and Laramie on the Happy Jack Road, **Curt Gowdy State Park** (1319 Happy Jack Rd., 307/632-7946, http://wyoparks.state.wy.us, $4 residents, $6 nonresidents, camping $10 residents, $17 nonresidents, includes day use) contains more than 35 miles (56 km) of trails connecting three reservoirs as well as four open free-ride areas. The trails were given an Epic designation by the International Mountain Biking Association, and all are open to both

Fort Laramie National Historic Site

The Grand Old Post

Originally built as a fur trading post in 1834, **Fort Laramie** was established as a military fort in 1849 when the U.S. government purchased the old Fort John. As was true of most of the forts across the region, its mission was to ensure the safety of pioneers traveling west on the established trails, the closest of which was the Oregon Trail. The second military fort constructed for this purpose, Fort Laramie was unique in that it was always an open fort, meaning there was no wall or fence enclosing the structures.

In 1854, three years after the Treaty of 1851, which was meant to bring peace between the Native Americans and the United States, 29 soldiers from Fort Laramie, an officer, and an interpreter were killed in the Grattan Fight. The event fueled a new ferocity in the war that raged throughout the 1860s and 1870s between Native Americans and the U.S. military. As the battles grew larger, Fort Laramie was often a staging ground and command post.

By the late 1880s, when the Indian Wars were mostly a thing of the past, Fort Laramie became more of a village than a fort. Trees were planted on the otherwise barren landscape. Boardwalks were built in front of the officers' quarters. In March 1890, when the Union Pacific Railroad was routed south of the fort, with no enemy to fight and no trails to protect, the military decommissioned the fort and sold many of its buildings at auction.

For decades, Fort Laramie existed as a small village, attracting a few curious history buffs, but not much else. Three homesteaders secured and used some of the existing buildings for businesses or agricultural purposes, preventing them from the fate of many of the buildings, which were to be stripped and sold for lumber and other materials. By the numbers, nine original buildings survived by being useful while more than 50 were demolished, moved, or stripped. In 1938, after much wrangling among federal and state officials and private landowners, including a battle over turning the fort into a golf resort, the 214 acres (86.6 hectares) that had once been Fort Laramie were made a national monument. In 1960, the monument was increased to 571 acres (231.1 hectares) and named a National Historic Site by Congress. A great deal of restoration took place at the fort 1950-1970.

Today, visitors can amble around the grounds and peek into several of the restored buildings. Admission is free. A very worthwhile audio tour, including readings from journals of people who lived at the fort, is available for $3 at the **visitors center** (9am-7pm daily Memorial Day-Labor Day, 8am-4:30pm daily Labor Day-Memorial Day). The fort offers a Living History Military Weekend (visit www.nps.gov for dates and details), which brings the fort to life with reenactments and various educational events. The weekend is also the time for the annual Moonlight Tour. Other events throughout the year include Haunted Prison Tours in October and Horse Barn Dinner Theater evenings in summer.

hikers and bikers. Among the longer trails are **Canyon's Trail** (5.4 mi/8.7 km), **Stone Temple Circuit** (3.8 mi/6.1 km), **Lariat** (2.9 mi/4.7 km), and **Shoreline** (2.6 mi/4.2 km). The area is also open to horses. A map is available online or at the park. Pets are not permitted in the water at Gowdy, and the area is usually packed on warm weekends with campers and recreationists.

Golf

Cheyenne has a number of golf courses, including the 18-hole **Airport Golf Club** (4801 Central Ave., 307/638-3700, $25 for 18 holes, $18 for 9 holes, twilight and off-season discounts), **Cheyenne Country Club** (800 Stinner Rd., 307/637-2204, www.cheyennecountryclub.com, $70 for 18 holes as an unaccompanied guest), 18-hole **F. E. Warren AFB Golf Club** (6110 Golf Course Dr., 307/773-3556, www.funatwarren.com, $25 civilian guests for 18 holes, $24 civilian seniors, $18 civilian guests for 9 holes or twilight play, advance reservations required) at the air force base, 9-hole municipal **Prairie View Golf Course** (3601 Windmill

Rd., 307/637-6420, $12), and 9-hole **Little America Golf Course** (2800 W. Lincolnway, 307/775-8500, $28-30 for 18 holes).

ENTERTAINMENT AND EVENTS
★ Frontier Days

The biggest event in Cheyenne—the biggest in Wyoming—is **Frontier Days** (www.cfdrodeo.com), an affair that has been defining Wyoming's capital city since 1897. The largest outdoor rodeo in the country today, the celebration's origins are rather humble. Union Pacific passenger agent F. W. Angier and the editor of the local Cheyenne newspaper claimed to have dreamed up the idea based on Greeley, Colorado's "Potato Day."

The first Frontier Days was held on September 23, 1897, and drew a substantial crowd for events that ranged from a bucking horse contest to a mock stagecoach robbery and mock hanging. The troops from Fort Russell lit cannons, and the crowd quickly followed suit by firing their own guns, sending horses and other livestock into a panic. No one was killed, and the event only reinforced Wyoming's reputation for rowdiness.

By far the most popular event at early Frontier Days was the bucking bronc contest, which allowed ranchers to pit their cowboys against each other to determine who had the best ones. Although riders could use a saddle, they had to wait until the horse came to a complete standstill before finishing their ride. They weren't allowed to hold on to any part of the saddle, but they could fan the horse with their hats, whip it, or use their spurs.

More than 120 years later, Frontier Days carries on with much the same spirit. It is now a 10-day event spanning two weekends. In recent years more than 250,000 people have shown up to attend events that include parades, major rock and country music concerts, free pancake breakfasts, tours of an Indian village, a Western art show, a carnival, dances, and nine days of PRCA rodeo. This event has clearly earned its nickname, "the daddy of 'em all."

The event is held annually the last two weekends in July at the rodeo grounds (4610 Carey Ave.) and around town. For more information, contact the **Frontier Days office** (307/778-7222 or 800/227-6336, 9am-5pm Mon.-Fri.).

Other Events

At the end of May and beginning of June is the **Hispanic Festival** (www.cheyennehispanicfestival.com), celebrating Hispanic culture with educational exhibits, games, mariachis, food and craft vendors, and live performances. It's free and fun for the whole family.

Happening over a weekend each year in mid-June, Cheyenne gathers on the beautiful Depot Plaza to celebrate beer at the **Wyoming Brewer's Festival** (www.wyobrewfest.com). The event includes a delicious Taster's Party, which pairs beer with food from Cheyenne's varied culinary scene. There is also live music both nights and plenty of festivities. The proceeds from this event benefit the Cheyenne Depot.

For 13 days in early August, the **Laramie County Fair** (3967 Archer Pkwy., 307/633-4670, www.laramiecountyfair.com), which calls itself the oldest and largest county fair in the state, offers up family entertainment with everything from a demolition derby and dock diving for dogs to horse events and 4-H. After all the flash and sparkle of Frontier Days, the Laramie County Fair is bunny shows over bronc riding, a refreshingly traditional small-town event.

In mid-August, the **Cheyenne Arts Festival** (www.cheyenneartsfestival.com, 307/222-4091) is a three-day event with artist booths, live music, food, and art workshops.

For information on regularly scheduled events such as Tuesday-night **Movies in the Park** or **symphony orchestra concerts** in the amphitheater at Lions Park, check out the Visit Cheyenne website at www.cheyenne.org.

Throughout summer, May-September, free **horse-drawn carriage rides** are offered from 15th Street and Capitol Avenue,

11am-5pm daily. Rides are dependent on weather and other downtown activities. For daily updates, call 307/778-3133.

SHOPPING

Because of its size, Cheyenne has plenty of the major superstores, but there are also some smaller and wonderful boutiques to check out. **Bohemian Metals** (314 W. 17th St., 307/778-8782, www.bohemianmetals.com, 10am-6pm Mon.-Fri., 10am-5pm Sat.) specializes in handmade jewelry, including vintage Native American pieces, gemstones and minerals, and fossils.

A wonderful place for browsing and shopping is the **Cowgirls of the West Museum & Emporium** (205 W. 17th St., 307/638-4994, www.cowgirlsofthewestmuseum.com, 11am-4pm Tues.-Fri., 11am-3pm Sat. May-Aug., extended hours during Frontier Days, free), a nonprofit museum dedicated to informing visitors about the contribution that women made to the settlement of the Old West and the contributions being made by women today. The gift shop features Wyoming-made collectibles, jewelry, Western art, antiques, and wonderful kids' items. Set in a beautiful, historic building, **Wyoming Home** (216 W. Lincolnway, 307/638-2222, www.wyominghome.com, 9am-6pm Mon.-Fri., 9am-5pm Sat., noon-5pm Sun. summer, 10am-6pm Mon.-Fri., 10am-5pm Sat. fall-spring) has an enormous selection of Wyoming-made gifts and housewares.

The largest shopping mall in the region is **Frontier Mall** (1400 Dell Range Blvd., 307/638-2290, www.frontiermall.com, 10am-9pm Mon.-Sat., 11am-6pm Sun.), which has more than 80 stores.

FOOD

As Wyoming's largest city by far, Cheyenne has quite a few restaurants and no shortage of chain establishments to choose from, and there are some wonderful gems worth seeking out.

One of the best local spots for breakfast or lunch is **Luxury Diner** (1401 W. Lincolnway, 307/638-8971, 6am-2pm Mon.-Thurs., 6am-3pm Fri.-Sun., $6-15), a tiny railroad-themed place announced by a "Wyoming Motel" sign nearly as large as the restaurant. It's crowded but completely delightful, and the food explains the wait; try the corned beef hash and eggs or Santa Fe breakfast burrito. The **Bread Basket Bakery** (1819 Maxwell Ave., 307/432-2525, www.breadbasketbakery.com, 6am-6pm Tues.-Fri., 6am-4pm Sat., $4-8.50) offers wonderfully fresh pastries, breads, cakes, and other goodies along with a selection of sandwiches and soups. Another great spot for a quick bite, cup of joe, or delicious frappe is **Carol's Café** (2800 W. Lincolnway, 307/775-8400, www.cheyenne.littleamerica.com, 6am-9pm daily) in the Little America Hotel & Resort. You might have seen billboards across the state touting their $0.75 cones.

Just across from the historic depot on the corner of 15th and Capitol, **The Albany** (1506 Capitol Ave., 307/638-3507, www.albanycheyenne.com, 11am-2pm and 5pm-9pm Mon.-Sat., $10-25) has been serving locals since 1942. Owned by the same family all those years, The Albany looks more charming from the outside than it does the inside, but the food is good and hearty, from burgers, salads, sandwiches, and Mexican fare to steaks, chops, and seafood. The chicken-fried steak and Jack Daniel's bread pudding earn regular raves. There are extensive offerings for vegetarians and gluten-free sandwiches.

Despite the fact that **Anong's Thai** (620 Central Ave., 307/638-8597, www.anong-thai.com, 11am-3pm and 5pm-9pm Mon.-Sat., 11am-3pm and 5pm-8pm Sun., $10-18) looks like a strip club from the outside, with only two tinted windows and lots of attention-grabbing signage, the dishes here are authentically delicious, and the service is excellent. Anong's Thai has two other locations as well, one in Laramie and the other in Rawlins. Thai food lovers won't be disappointed by the big menu and wonderful cuisine at any of the three.

Perhaps Cheyenne's most well-known restaurant, **Poor Richard's Restaurant**

(2233 E. Lincolnway, 307/635-5114, www. poorrichardscheyenne.com, 11am-2:30pm and 5pm-close Mon.-Sat., $12-27) has been dishing up classic fare since 1977. The menus are extensive with steaks, seafood, and pasta. Garlic, cream, and butter are appreciated here.

For a rustic Western dinner theater experience, try the **Bit-O-Wyo Ranch Horse Barn Dinner Show** (470 Happy Jack Rd., 307/638-6924, 6pm Sat. July-Aug., and Wed. during Frontier Days, $50 pp, free for children under 7, reservations required), which includes a classic chuck wagon dinner of steak, baked beans, and applesauce, followed by a two-hour performance of cowboy music and comedy. The entire season is often sold out by July so be sure to book ahead.

ACCOMMODATIONS

Built in 1888 when Cheyenne was among the richest cities of its size in the world, the ★ **Nagle Warren Mansion** (222 E. 17th St., 307/637-3333 or 800/811-2610, www.naglewarrenmansion.com, $192-265) is an exquisite bed-and-breakfast boasting 12 rooms in the mansion and the adjacent carriage house. While the ambience and furnishings are a wonderful reflection of the elegant Victorian era in which the mansion was built, the amenities—including central air-conditioning, private baths, telephone, TV, and wireless Internet in each room—are decidedly 21st century. Each room is uniquely appointed and named for an important figure in the mansion's fascinating history. A sumptuous breakfast is served each morning; lunches and dinners can be arranged as well. The mansion's Murder Mystery Dinners are great fun and wildly popular, as are a variety of getaway weekends and special events.

Undoubtedly one of the coolest signs at any motel just about anywhere is the one at the **Firebird Motel** (1905 E. Lincolnway, 307/632-5505, $50-100). The dated rooms are as basic as can be, and the motel has been hit hard by the economic downturn, but the sign is worth seeing. A good and more reliable budget-friendly choice in town is the

Travelodge by Wyndham (1625 Stillwater Ave., 307/274-3666, $76-104).

An important part of the Cheyenne community since 1911, **The Historic Plains Hotel** (1600 Central Ave., 307/638-3311 or 866/275-2467, www.theplainshotel.com, $93-194) is a handsome establishment with 130 lovely rooms and suites. The hotel is decorated with art by Wyoming artists and offers a full restaurant, bar, coffee shop, and an on-site fitness center and spa. A multimillion-dollar renovation in 2003 restored the hotel to its glory, and The Historic Plains is an excellent value for your money in Cheyenne.

Cheyenne also has a number of comfortable, convenient chain hotels. Both the **Red Lion Cheyenne** (204 W. Fox Farm Rd., 307/638-4466, www.redlion.com, $84-149) and **Holiday Inn Express Hotel & Suites** (1741 Fleischli Pkwy., 307/433-0751 or 800/315-2621, www.ihg.com, $118-184) are good choices. **Comfort Inn & Suites** (201 W. Fox Farm Rd., 307/514-6051, www.choicehotels.com, $121-221) and **Super 8** (1900 W. Lincolnway, 307/635-8741, www.wyndhamhotels.com, $81-212) are a bit more budget-friendly.

The website for the **Cheyenne Convention and Visitors Bureau** (800/228-6063, www.cheyenne.org) has a handy tool where travelers can input their travel dates to see all available accommodations in the city. The tool is particularly useful the closer one gets to Frontier Days, as accommodations fill up entirely.

CAMPING

Thanks to the massive numbers of people that roll into town for Frontier Days, Cheyenne has abundant RV and tent campgrounds, not all of which are necessarily great. Among those that are really special is ★ **Curt Gowdy State Park** (1319 Happy Jack Rd., 307/632-7946 or 877/996-7275, http://wyoparks.state.wy.us, $4 residents, $6 nonresidents, camping $10 residents, $17 nonresidents, includes day use), 24 miles (39 km) west of Cheyenne, at the edge of the Laramie Mountains. There are 35 sites that can be reserved, 15 RV sites with water hookups, none with electricity, and the remaining sites are first-come, first-served. In addition to camping and picnicking spots, the park—set on three lovely reservoirs—offers trout and kokanee salmon fishing as well as hiking and biking trails.

Another worthwhile camping spot, particularly for families with children, is the **Terry Bison Ranch Campground** (51 E. I-25 Service Rd. E., 307/634-4171, www.terrybisonranch.com), just 7 miles (11.3 km) south of Cheyenne. There is an abundance of activities available, including horseback riding, fishing, train tours to see the ranch's population of bison, ostriches, and camels, and even bison hunts in winter. With a restaurant on-site, the place is fully self-contained. Accommodations options include cabins ($81-115, or $125-250 during Frontier Days), RV sites ($30-60, or $34-95 during Frontier Days), and tent sites ($23-28). You can board your horse here too. Indoor stalls are $25/night and outdoor stalls are 18/night. Wood chips are $10/bag and after-hours check-in (7pm summer, 5pm fall-spring) is $25 or $100 if you and your steed arrive after midnight.

Other options right in Cheyenne are the nicely shaded **A.B. Campground** (1503 W. College Dr., 307/634-7035, www.campcheyenne.com, Apr.-Oct., $23 tent and RV sites, $30-46), which offers nightly barbecues, and **Cheyenne KOA** (8800 Archer Frontage Rd., 307/638-8840 or 800/562-1507, www.koakampgrounds.com, $39 tent and $54-58 RV sites, $84 cabins w/o bathrooms), which has an outdoor swimming pool in summer.

INFORMATION AND SERVICES

Cheyenne's well-organized convention and visitors bureau has a downtown **visitors center** (121 W. 15th St., Ste. 202, 307/778-3133 or 800/426-5009, www.cheyenne.org, 8am-7pm Mon.-Fri., 9am-5pm Sat., 11am-3pm Sun. summer, 8am-5pm Mon.-Fri., 9am-5pm Sat., 1pm-3pm Sun. fall-spring).

The **Southeast Wyoming Welcome Center** (5611 High Plains Rd., 307/777-7777 or 800/225-5996, 8am-5pm daily June-Sept., 8am-5pm Mon.-Fri., 9am-3pm Sat.-Sun. Oct.-May) is headquartered at the rest area at exit 4 on I-25 and offers abundant parking, a dump station, fresh water, clean bathrooms, picnic tables, and more information than you could possibly take in.

The main downtown **post office** (307/772-7080, 7:30am-noon Mon., 7:30am-5:30pm Tues.-Fri.) is at 2120 Capitol Avenue.

The **Laramie County Library** (307/634-3561, www.lclsonline.org, 10am-9pm Mon.-Thurs., 10am-6pm Fri.-Sat., 1pm-5pm Sun.) is at 2200 Pioneer Avenue.

The **Cheyenne Regional Medical Center** (214 E. 23rd St., 307/634-2273, www.cheyenneregional.org) is a major medical facility with 24-hour emergency care. Another option is **College Drive Urgent Care** (4136 Laramie St., 307/637-2800, www.collegedriveurgentcare.com, 8am-8pm Mon.-Fri., 9am-4pm Sat.-Sun.).

Wash clothes at **Easy Way Laundry** (900 W. Lincolnway, 307/638-2177, 7am-10pm daily).

TRANSPORTATION
Getting There

Although Cheyenne does have an airport, **Cheyenne Regional Airport** (CYS, 200 E. 8th Ave., 307/634-7071, www.cheyenneairport.com), commercial service ended in March 2018 when Great Lakes Airlines shut down operations. The city been given a grant and is building a new terminal to try to secure regular airline service. Keep an eye on the website for updates. For shuttle service to Denver, contact **Green Ride** (307/459-4433 or 888/472-6656, greenrideco.com).

Car rentals are available from **Avis, National,** and **Hertz.**

By car, Cheyenne is 49 miles (79 km) east of Laramie, 100 miles (161 km) north of Denver, 256 miles (410 km) east of Rock Springs, 291 miles (465 km) southwest of Rapid City, 393 miles (635 km) southeast of Cody, 429 miles (690 km) southeast of

Yellowstone National Park, and 456 miles (735 km) southeast of Billings.

Daily bus service in and out of Cheyenne is provided from the Rodeway Inn by **Greyhound** (5401 Walker Rd., 307/635-1327, www.greyhound.com) and **Express Arrow** (5401 Walker Rd., 877/779-2999, www.expressarrow.com).

Getting Around

Local public transportation is available in Cheyenne from **Cheyenne Transit** (307/637-6253, www.cheyennecity.org). There are also a handful of taxi companies, including **Cowboy Shuttle** (307/638-2468) and **TI Shuttle** (307/778-4066, www.tishuttle.com).

Sweetwater County

Sweetwater County in the southwest corner of Wyoming is a mix of the desert Southwest—think kaleidoscopic rock formations, mesas, and canyons—and the rugged Western appeal of rodeo, wild mustangs, and vast open spaces. Though not a tourist destination in the way that northwest Wyoming is—the region is shifting with the boom-and-bust of the energy sector—this part of the state offers constant and abundant recreational opportunities. This is not so much cowboy country as mining country, mountain biking country, and river rafting country.

A high-alpine desert, Rock Springs (population 23,755; elevation 6,271 ft/1,911 m) parallels Gillette in some ways—it is in the thick of an energy boom-and-bust cycle—but it is located next to some pretty phenomenal country, including the unrivaled and scenic **Flaming Gorge National Recreation Area.** The city itself has a few good museums and an interesting international flavor that dates back to coal mining and railroad development around the turn of the 20th century.

Green River (population 12,305; elevation 6,109 ft/1,862 m) is an old railroad town that got its start as a station along the Overland and Pony Express routes. It has a rather industrial history spanning the railroads and mines in the region, but it is best known for its namesake river, which runs right through town. The Green River forms the headwaters of the Colorado River basin and was for years a prime shipping route for timber. Major John Wesley Powell launched two of his biggest expeditions from here, including his first into the unexplored Grand Canyon in 1869. Surrounded by magnificent multicolored buttes and outcroppings, the town is still very much centered around the river and a popular launching spot for raft and kayak expeditions.

SIGHTS
Museums

There are a number of museums in this region worth a visit. The **Sweetwater County Historical Museum** (3 E. Flaming Gorge Way, Green River, 307/872-6435, www.sweetwatermuseum.org, 10am-6pm Mon.-Sat. mid-May-mid-Oct., 9am-5pm Tues.-Sat. mid-Oct.-mid-May, free) will surprise visitors with its vast and thorough displays. The museum has done a good job of documenting the history of the region and exhibits many artifacts from the daily life of ranchers, miners, and the numerous immigrants who came here. Visitors can see everything from a dinosaur's fossilized footprint to a rifle from Butch Cassidy's gang to an RCA Victor Victrola phonograph and a wedding dress from 1903. There is also an engaging video and display about the horrific Chinese Massacre in Rock Springs.

In Rock Springs, the **Rock Springs Historical Museum** (201 B St., 307/362-3138, www.rswy.net, 10am-5pm Mon.-Sat., free) is situated in the stately city hall, built from sandstone in 1894 for a total cost of $28,200. The museum documents the city's diverse immigrant population, its coal-mining history, and the illegal activity and outlaws it also attracted. The **Western Wyoming Community College Natural History Museum and Weidner Wildlife Museum** (2500 College Dr., 307/382-1600, 7am-9:30pm daily May-Aug., 9am-10pm daily Sept.-Apr., free) houses a small collection of fossils, minerals, and Native American artifacts from the area. A large number of big-game heads from around the world are also on display. The **Community Fine Arts Center** (400 C St., 307/362-6212, www.cfacf4art.com, 10am-6pm Mon.-Thurs., noon-5pm Fri.-Sat., free) is an unexpected gem with works by Norman Rockwell, Conrad Schwiering, and Grandma Moses, among other prominent American artists.

Pilot Butte Wild Horse Scenic Tour

There are 1,100-1,600 wild horses roaming the stark landscape of the 392,000-acre (158,637-hectare) **White Mountain Herd Management Area** around Rock Springs and Green River. Although they can often be spotted from I-80, a scenic road affords better opportunities for wild horse sightings. County Road 53 can be accessed either from Rock Springs or Green River; it is a 24-mile (39-km) gravel road that takes about 90 minutes to drive as it winds across the White Mountains with spectacular vistas. The most likely view of the horses comes between Rock Springs and 14-Mile Hill and all the way across the top of White Mountain. Early morning and late afternoon are the best times to view wildlife. The road is only open May-October. For more information about the scenic drive, contact the Bureau of Land Management's **Rock Springs Field Office** (280 Hwy. 191 N., 307/352-0256, www.blm.gov).

Rich Nobles of **Green River Wild Horse Tour & Eco Safari** (307/875-2923 or 307/875-5711, www.greenriverwildhorsetours.com) works hard to get his customers views of the wild mustangs. For half-day tours ($75 pp), he takes passengers off the normal route in his imported all-terrain vehicle to view the wildlife up close. The trip usually covers about 70 miles (113 km) and can last up to six hours.

White Mountain Petroglyphs

Some 26 miles (42 km) north of Rock Springs on County Road 4-17 is one of the state's premier rock art sites, the **White Mountain Petroglyphs.** On a 300-foot (91.4-m) cliff, hundreds of images—portraying everything

Rock Springs is a cute town in Sweetwater County.

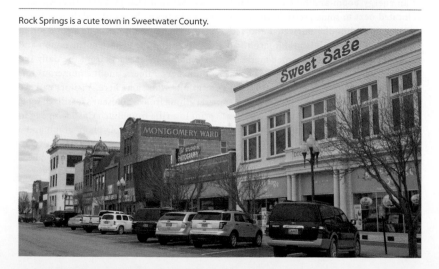

The Chinese Massacre

MINING AT ROCK SPRINGS AND CARBON

Mining was essential to the success of the Union Pacific Railroad: Closed mines threatened coal supplies and trains required a steady supply of fuel to meet their schedules. In 1875, when miners in Rock Springs and Carbon organized to demand better wages, their strike shut down Union Pacific's two largest mines. It was no surprise the railroad looked for a quick yet cheap solution. Until this point, all the miners in Rock Springs had been white, but two weeks after the strike started, Union Pacific brought in 150 Chinese men to work the mines. By month's end, some 50 white miners had returned to work, strike organizers had been fired, and the two races were expected to work side by side. Although there was underlying resentment and racism—Chinese miners worked for less, plus this was the era when the Chinese Exclusion Act of 1882, restricting immigration and barring those already in the country from obtaining U.S. citizenship, was passed—tensions did not come to a head until a decade later.

RISING TENSION

By 1885 the number of Chinese miners outnumbered whites as much as 2:1. Since they were paid by the ton, mine assignments were important. On September 2, some white miners were upset that Chinese miners had been assigned to prime areas. They met the Chinese men outside the mine and prevented them from entering. The altercation quickly turned violent, with one Chinese miner dying from his injuries. The mob mentality quickly picked up momentum. Many Chinese victims were scalped, mutilated, dismembered, and even burned alive. In an effort to escape the violence, many Chinese miners fled into the surrounding desert.

VIOLENCE AND RACISM

The white miners entered Chinatown, attacking its occupants and setting fire to the buildings. The entire neighborhood burned to the ground: 79 homes were destroyed, 28 Chinese were killed, and 15 were injured. The violence shocked the nation, but it also ignited anti-Chinese violence in other small towns in the West. Reaction in Wyoming was mixed. The local newspaper supported the attacks; other papers criticized the massacre while empathizing with the plight of the white miners. The territorial governor, Francis E. Warren, requested federal help to restore peace.

When the mines reopened, 45 men were fired for their role in the violence. Sixteen men were arrested and held in Green River. Although a grand jury was called, no indictments were handed out, and the men were released a month later to a heroes' welcome.

REPARATION ATTEMPTS

The only form of justice came as a response by the U.S. government to appease the Chinese government. With much finagling, President Grover Cleveland persuaded Congress to issue financial compensation to China for $149,000. During the 1920s and 1930s, the Union Pacific Coal Company paid retirement packages and purchased tickets for retired miners to return to China. Only one of the miners chose to live his final days in Rock Springs.

For more information on the Chinese Massacre or other episodes in Wyoming's storied history, visit www.wyohistory.org, an outstanding resource.

from bison and elk hunts to geometric shapes and even tiny footprints—tell the stories of the Plains and Great Basin Indians who lived and traveled through the region as many as 1,000 years ago. Depictions of horses and swords suggest the natives' first contact with Europeans. The site is remote and primitive with no facilities. Pack plenty of water and food. Four-wheel drive is recommended, and you will be on foot for the last quarter mile to the site. For more information, contact the Bureau of Land Management's **Rock Springs Field Office** (280 Hwy. 191 N., 307/352-0256, www.blm.gov).

Seedskadee National Wildlife Refuge

The **Seedskadee National Wildlife Refuge** (www.fws.gov) sits along 36 miles (58 km) of the Green River and encompasses over 26,000 acres (10,522 hectares) of land. The Shoshone first called the Green River "Sisk-a-dee-agie," or "River of the Prairie Chicken." Fur traders changed the name to Seedskadee. The refuge consists of marshes, wetlands, and uplands, and more than 200 different bird species have been sighted in the area. The riparian areas have become an important nesting ground for a variety of migratory birds, including Canada geese, great blue herons, and swans. In springtime, the prairie is filled with the strange pops and whistles of the greater sage-grouse males, pining for mates. The refuge is a popular spot for fishing, wildlife-viewing, and short float trips. It is 37 miles (60 km) north of Green River on Highway 372. The refuge headquarters is just 2 miles (3.2 km) north of the junction of Highways 372 and 28.

Killpecker Sand Dunes

Thirty-seven miles (60 km) from Rock Springs is one of Wyoming's most unique natural wonders, complete with a herd of rare desert elk not found anywhere else in the United States. The 109,000-acre (44,111-hectare) **Killpecker Sand Dunes** are the largest active dunes in the United States. The massive hills of white sand stretch more than 55 miles (89 km) and offer a fun playground for hikers. There are two wilderness study areas in the dunes—Buffalo Hump and Sand Dunes—but elsewhere on the shifting sands, off-road vehicle enthusiasts can explore this natural playground. However, go prepared with water, food, a compass, and a map—people can easily get disoriented in the desert setting. If approaching the dunes from Rock Springs, you will pass the area office of the **Bureau of Land Management** (280 U.S. 191 N., Rock Springs, 307/352-0256); it's worth stopping in to get more information and a map of the area. Don't forget to ask about the wild horses and

how you can have the best chance of seeing them in their desert habitat. Sightings often occur in the Leucite Hills area.

Also at the dunes, rock climbing enthusiasts will enjoy a visit to the volcanic plug known as **Boar's Tusk.** This towering rock formation measures 400 feet (122 m) in height; Devils Tower is the only other geological feature like this in the state.

Fossil Butte National Monument

Known as "America's Aquarium in Stone," **Fossil Butte National Monument** (864 Chicken Creek Rd., Kemmerer, 80 mi/129 km west of Green River, 307/877-4455, www.nps.gov, free) sits in the middle of what was once a subtropical habitat. During the Eocene epoch, 50 million years ago, this was a large lake area, home to alligators, turtles, fish, and even palm trees. Over the eons, animal and plant remains sank to the bottom of the lake bed, where they were covered with sediment and fossilized. When the lake dried up and the bed was eventually pushed to the surface, some of the best-preserved fossils in the world were revealed.

The **visitors center** (9am-6pm daily May-Sept., 9am-4:30pm daily early Sept.-Nov. and Mar.-late May, 9am-4:30pm Mon.-Sat. Dec.-Feb.) displays more than 80 fossils, including two types of bats, numerous species of fish, and even a 13-foot (4-m) crocodile. There is also an area where visitors can handle the fossils and make rubbings of them. During summer, experts conduct fossil preparation demonstrations and take questions from the public. Two short trails take visitors through the unique history of the park and allow for some wildlife-viewing. From late June-August, plan to visit 11am-3pm Friday-Saturday to assist paleontologists as they collect fossils at the research quarry. Plan to spend about 90 minutes at the quarry and note that there are no bathrooms and no

1: Killpecker Sand Dunes 2: Fossil Butte National Monument

shade. Bring your own water, sunscreen, and bug repellent.

★ Flaming Gorge National Recreation Area

The **Flaming Gorge National Recreation Area** is full of beautiful rock formations, spectacular land, and rich natural colors. The area was aptly named by a group led by John Wesley Powell, who started their famous journey down the Green River from where the town of Green River now stands. The explorers floated through the rocky canyons and were stunned by the striking red hues, particularly in Utah.

The area consists of more than 200,000 acres (80,937 hectares) and crosses southwestern Wyoming into northeastern Utah. The landscape in Wyoming is primarily high desert, and the more impressive and dramatic sights are found over the border in Utah. Three roads—Highway 530, U.S. 191, and UT 44—connect to form a loop around the national recreation area. The visitors center is on the Utah side at Red Canyon.

Activity in Wyoming is largely based around the 91-mile-long (147-km) **Flaming Gorge Reservoir,** with more than 300 miles (485 km) of shoreline. Constructed in 1964, the reservoir is a popular destination for waterskiing, fishing, camping, and boating. Its trout-filled waters make it an attractive year-round fishing spot; licenses can be bought in Wyoming or Utah. There are also campgrounds nearby (43 campgrounds with 700 individual sites and more than 30 group sites in the entire recreation area), and many boat launches around the reservoir.

If approaching the reservoir from Highway 530 south of Green River, the road follows the west side of the lake just a few miles from the shore. Various dirt-road turnoffs lead to the water, and many end at isolated beaches where you can camp for free. There are also commercial services, including **Lucerne Valley Marina** (5570 E. Lucerne Valley Rd., off Hwy. 530, 435/784-3483, 8am-6pm daily in season, www.flaminggorge.com) and

Buckboard Marina (Hwy. 530, 25 mi/40 km south of Green River, 307/875-6927, www.buckboardmarina.com), that take visitors to the recreation area's campsites and docks. If you continue south, heading to Utah, the road passes **Haystack Buttes,** rocky moundlike formations that resemble haystacks, and **Devil's Playground,** a barren badlands of rough terrain.

The loop can also be started at U.S. 191, heading south from Rock Springs. This approach is more mountainous and therefore more scenic, but it is also farther from the reservoir. Early on, a paved road turnoff will take you to **Firehole Canyon.** Here you can see the rocky spires known as **North and South Chimney Rocks** and other interesting geological features. U.S. 191 continues south, climbing 8,000 vertical feet (2,438 m), and has good views of the rolling hills and

Flaming Gorge National Recreation Area

valleys to the east and west. From here the reservoir is about 15 miles (24 km) from the road. However, when crossing Spring Creek, the water becomes visible, and there is a turn-off leading 4 miles (6.4 km) to the shore.

Both routes cross the Wyoming-Utah border and lead to UT 44, which takes visitors through the dramatic canyons. One other approach to the loop is from Highway 414, heading southeast from the town of Mountain View. This road traverses badlands, fields filled with sage and juniper, and large open pastures and leads to Henry's Fork, the site of the first mountain man rendezvous in the country.

SPORTS AND RECREATION

Recreation Centers

Thanks to the energy boom around the turn of the 21st century and subsequent growth of the tax base, Rock Springs built plentiful facilities, so recreational opportunities abound. The **Rock Springs Family Recreation Center** (3900 Sweetwater Dr., 307/352-1440, www.rswy.net, 5am-7pm Mon.-Thurs., 5am-5pm Fri., noon-6pm Sat.-Sun., $7 adults, $4 students 7-18, free for children under 7) offers an indoor swimming pool with a fun splash area for little ones and slides for bigger ones; a full-size ice arena; a full gym with basketball, volleyball, racquetball, and handball courts; an indoor putting course; and various classes and fitness programs.

Golf

Golfers can tee off at the 27-hole championship **White Mountain Golf Course** (1501 Clubhouse Dr., 307/352-1415, www.rswy.net, sunrise-sunset daily late Mar.-early Nov.), considered among the best public golf courses in the state. Nonresidents pay $51 for 18 holes with cart or $29 for 9 holes with cart. There is also an 18-hole course in Green River, the **Rolling Green Country Club** (29 Country Club Rd., 307/875-6200, greens fees vary).

Hiking and Mountain Biking

Although this is wide-open desert, there are some interesting places to hit the trail. For starters, the **Green Belt** and **Scotts Bottom Nature Area,** running through Green River, offer lovely trails to stretch your legs and enjoy the views. The trails are easily accessed from **Expedition Island,** the launching point for Powell's famous river trips through the Grand Canyon.

For more of an adventure, Sweetwater

Flaming Gorge National Recreation Area offers high-desert beauty.

County has more still-visible pioneer trails running through it than anywhere else in the country, and hikers and mountain bikers can follow the double ruts at a variety of points in the big open countryside. Trails in the region include the Oregon and California Trails, the Mormon Trail, and the Pony Express Trail. All adventurers need to be well prepared for the vast undeveloped stretches of land and should bring maps, adequate clothing, and plenty of water.

The mountain biking in the area is sublime, with hundreds of miles of trails ranging from the scenic to the gnarly. Green River is known for some of its hairier trails, including the extremely technical 4-mile (6.4-km) **Lunatic Fringe** (with lots of ladder bridges and areas of exposure) and the slightly less insane 5-mile (8-km) **Macbones Trail,** both of which can be scouted on www.singletracks.com.

Among the most popular trails is the 20-mile (32-km) **Cherokee Trail/Currant Creek Ranch Loop,** which starts and ends at the Currant Creek Ranch off County Road 33. It is part of a wider 250-mile (405-km) network of trails on Little Mountain, south of Rock Springs.

For excellent advice or service, visit **The Bike and Trike** (612 Broadway, Rock Springs, 307/382-9677, www.bikeandtrike.com, 9am-5pm Mon.-Fri., 9am-3pm Sat.). They also have a great coffee shop (7am-4pm Mon.-Fri., 9am-2pm Sat.).

Without a doubt, the **Flaming Gorge National Recreation Area** offers the densest concentration of recreational opportunities, including miles upon miles of trails for hikers and mountain bikers. The scenic 5-mile (8-km) **Canyon Rim Trail** is accessible from the Red Canyon Visitors Center and is open to both hikers and mountain bikers. The **Dowd Mountain-Hideout Canyon Trail** is significantly steeper and also open to both hikers and mountain bikers. A trail map for these and other trails in the gorge is available for free at the **U.S. Forest Service** offices in

Green River (132 Buck Board Rd., 307/875-4641) and Manila, Utah (intersection of Hwys. 43 and 44, 435/784-3445). For a list of other hiking trails, visit www.flaminggorgecountry.com. For **mountain bike rentals** in the Flaming Gorge, visit the **Red Canyon Lodge** (2450 W. Red Canyon Lodge, Dutch John, Utah, 435/889-3759, www.redcanyonlodge.com, $12/hour, $20 half-day, $36 full-day), 4 miles (6.4 km) west of the junction of Highway 44 and U.S. 191.

Fishing

There are a couple of ways to fish this part of the state, but for anglers looking to hook the big one—the really big one—**Flaming Gorge Reservoir** is the place to go. The lake trout in the reservoir can grow to weigh more than 50 pounds (22.7 kg), and 20-pounders (9 kg) are common. Lake trout generally like deeper waters and are more easily fished from boats. The rainbows in the reservoir, on the other hand, can be fished from shore. Other fish in the reservoir include smallmouth bass, kokanee, and burbot. The reservoir drops into Utah, and fishing licenses are required in both Wyoming and Utah; special-use stamps are available for fishing in both states.

The fishing on the **Green River** around its namesake town produces cutthroat, lake trout, and the occasional whitefish. For current conditions, information, and licenses, visit the **Wyoming Game and Fish Department** (351 Astle Ave., Green River, 307/875-3223, http://wgfd.wyo.gov).

For equipment and guided fishing trips on the Green River, contact **Trout Creek Flies** (1155 Little Hole Rd., Dutch John, Utah, 435/885-3355 or 435/885-3338, www.troutcreekflies.net, 7am-7pm daily) at the corner of U.S. 191 and Little Hole Road. In addition to being a full-service fly shop, Trout Creek Flies offers half-day ($400) and full-day ($500) float trips that are discounted in winter, plus lodging, shuttling, overnight camping trip options, and pretty much anything an avid angler might need.

Rafting and Boating

For the high desert, Sweetwater County has an awful lot of ways to enjoy the water. Kayakers get their thrills at the **Green River Whitewater Park and Tubing Channel** (www.cityofgreenriver.org) near Expedition Island in Green River. In addition to the splash park, there is a 1,200-foot-long (366-m) tubing channel for beginning boaters and swimmers with a series of 4.5-foot (1.4-m) drops and three pools. In the main river, a white-water park with eight gates is geared to advanced boaters. The park and channel can close due to river conditions so check the website or call the Parks and Recreation Department (307/872-6148 or 307/872-6151) before you go.

Most of the boating action in the area, however, happens at Flaming Gorge, and boats can be rented at three locations: **Buckboard Marina** (Hwy. 530, 25 mi/40 km south of Green River, 307/875-6927, www.buckboardmarina.com), **Cedar Springs Marina** (2685 Cedar Springs Boat Ramp, off U.S. 191, 2 mi/3.2 km from the dam, 435/889-3795, www.cedarspringsmarina.com), and **Lucerne Valley Marina** (5570 E. Lucerne Valley Rd., off Hwy. 530, 435/784-3483, www.flaminggorge.com). All three marinas also offer lodging options.

ENTERTAINMENT AND EVENTS

Known as **Wyoming's Big Show**, the **Sweetwater County Fair,** held annually at the **Sweetwater Events Center** (3320 Yellowstone Rd., Rock Springs, 307/352-6789, www.sweetwaterevents.com, $15 adults, $9 children 6-12, free for children under 6, discounts for advance purchase), is a 10-day event that includes rodeo action, 4-H livestock competitions, entertainment, and a carnival. Comparable in size to the Wyoming State Fair, the event attracts some 80,000 attendees annually. The Sweetwater Events Center is also home to a variety of rodeo events and stock-car, motocross, and BMX racing.

Rock Springs has a healthy representation of the performing arts, including the **Sweetwater County Concert Association** (307/350-5697 or 307/382-5035), which produces four to five musical performances annually as well as fundraisers that pair music with festive dining. Check their Facebook page for events. The city also programs a solid lineup of musical performances with **Rock Springs Concerts in the Park** (Friday nights at 7pm in Bunning Park, Evans St. between Elk St. and Noble Dr., 307/352-1500, www.rswy.net) June-August, as well as **Movies in the Park** (Bunning Park). Also in Bunning Park in mid-August is the **Annual Sweetwater Blues 'n Brews Festival** (307/352-1434, www.downtownrs.com, $5 pp), which combines a daylong lineup of blues music with local hoppy libations.

As a nod to the town's 56 different ethnicities, the Rock Springs Chamber of Commerce hosts a free **International Day** (307/362-3771, www.rsinternationalday.com, free) in Bunning Park early-mid-July. The daylong family-oriented event includes international food and beer plus entertainment and activities.

In the middle of July, the **National High School Finals Rodeo** (307/352-6789, www.nhsra.com) is held at the Sweetwater Events Complex in Rock Springs. The event is known as the "world's largest rodeo" and features 1,500 from the U.S., Canada, and Australia competing for national titles, prizes, and scholarship awards.

In Green River, the biggest event of the year is **Flaming Gorge Days** (800/354-6743, www.fgdays.com), held annually the last weekend of June. The event includes a country concert and a rock concert along with basketball and volleyball tournaments, a parade, a festival in the park, and children's entertainment. Concert tickets are available in advance at discounted rates from the chambers of commerce in Rock Springs (1897 Dewar Dr., 307/362-3771, www.rockspringschamber.com, 8am-5pm Mon.-Fri.) and Green River (1155

Flaming Gorge Way, 307/875-5711, www. grchamber.com, 8:30am-5:30pm Mon.-Fri.) or at full price at the gate.

Another big event in Green River is the **Annual River Festival** (307/875-5711, www. grchamber.com) held in late August. This two-day event includes a Cajun shrimp boil, kids' games, a horseshoe tournament, a car and bike show, dog and bike events, a number of races including a marathon and half marathon, and plenty of food.

SHOPPING

With the major slump in both coal and oil prices, the economy in the region is hurting, and many of the local galleries and gift shops are shuttering. Little gems remain, however. **Tynsky's Rocks & Jewelry** (706 Dewar Dr., Rock Springs, 307/389-7246, noon-3pm daily or by appointment) has a nice selection of locally quarried rock, fossils, jewelry, and tumbling supplies. **Busy Bee Bath Essentials** (535 N. Front St., Rock Springs, 307/851-9862, www.busybeebathessentials.com, 11am-6pm Tues.-Fri., noon-4pm Sat.) is known for its handmade body care and beauty products, but it also features handmade crafts by local artists including jewelry, home decor, blankets, and unfinished wood.

FOOD

For a relatively remote Wyoming town, Rock Springs has an impressive number of international eateries, the origins of which date back to the town's population diversity. **Bonsai** (1996 Dewar Dr., 307/362-1888, 11am-9pm daily, $8-16) feeds the community's appetite for Asian cuisine. In addition to Chinese and Thai specialties, the restaurant serves decent sushi.

For southwest Wyoming's favorite hamburgers, fries, and shakes, hit **Grub's Drive In** (415 Paulson St., Rock Springs, 307/362-6634, www.grubsdrivein.com, 6am-8pm Mon.-Fri., $4-10). It's not healthy, and you may have to wait in a good-size line, but the shamrock burgers are juicy, the fries come with a side of brown gravy, and the milk shakes are something to write home about.

Another local favorite in Rock Springs is **Cowboy Donuts** (1573 Dewar Dr. #4, 307/362-3400, www.cowboydonuts.com, 5am-2pm Mon.-Sat.), which serves 55 different varieties baked daily, from hand-chopped apple fritters to blueberry cake and glazed doughnut holes. It also offers an excellent selection of *kolaches*—slightly sweet butter bread stuffed with meats and cheeses.

Among the hippest dining options in

one of the many options from Cowboy Donuts in Rock Springs

town is ★ **Bitter Creek Brewing** (604 Broadway, Rock Springs, 307/362-4782, www. bittercreekbrewing.com, 11am-9pm Mon.-Sat., $9-32), which offers a large and varied menu—think chicken wings, Thai nachos, pizza, and mouthwatering baby back ribs—in a casual, fun, and family-friendly environment. It also has a nice selection of seasonal microbrews on tap.

In Green River, hungry diners head to **Penny's Diner** (1170 W. Flaming Gorge Way, Green River, 307/875-3500, ext. 550, 24 hours daily, $8-10), adjacent to the Oak Tree Inn, a classic 1950s-style diner open 24 hours a day that serves up everything from omelets and sandwiches to burgers and pie. Another local favorite is the family-friendly **Hitching Post Restaurant and Saloon** (580 E. Flaming Gorge Way, Green River, 307/875-2246, restaurant 6am-10pm daily, saloon 6am-2am Mon.-Sat. and 10am-midnight Sun., $8-23), which has an enormous menu with burgers, pasta, steaks, sandwiches, baskets, and a salad bar with more than 40 items to choose from.

ACCOMMODATIONS

Rock Springs has a number of chain hotels, but among the best is the pet-friendly **Best Western Outlaw Inn** (1630 Elk St., 307/362-6623, www.bestwestern.com, $121-188), which has a variety of room configurations, standard amenities, a pool, an on-site restaurant, and complimentary breakfast. Another option in Rock Springs is the **Days Inn** (1545 Elk St., 307/362-5646, www.wyndhamhotels. com, $66-91).

The **Western Inn** (890 W. Flaming Gorge Way, Green River, 307/875-2840, $55-90) offers clean, basic accommodations with friendly staff, Wi-Fi, refrigerators, microwaves, and a nice continental breakfast included. Chains in Green River include the **Hampton Inn & Suites Green River** (1055 Wild Horse Canyon Rd., 307/875-5300, www.hamptoninn3.hilton.com, $99-163) and **Super 8** (280 W. Flaming Gorge

Way, 307/875-9330, www.wyndhamhotels. com, $56-87).

The most appealing place to stay in the region is actually over the border near Dutch John, Utah. The ★ **Red Canyon Lodge** (2450 W. Red Canyon Lodge, Dutch John, Utah, 435/889-3759, www.redcanyonlodge. com, cabins $129-159) has attractive and cozy cabins with front porches perfect for enjoying the tranquil scenery. The resort offers excellent dining with stunning views and daily wild-game specials, plus a host of activities that range from horseback riding and mountain biking to boat trips and fishing tours.

CAMPING

The **Rock Springs/Green River KOA** (86 Foothill Blvd., Rock Springs, 307/362-3063, www.koa.com) is open year-round and offers tent sites ($38) with electricity, RV sites ($42-60), and cabins without bathrooms ($66). The campground also has Wi-Fi, a swimming pool, a playground, and a variety of games. Pets are permitted.

There is phenomenal public camping in the Flaming Gorge National Recreation Area. Among the favorites is the ★ **Red Canyon Campground** (early May-late Sept., $15), which offers front-row seats for the area's spellbinding sunsets. There are lodgepole and ponderosa pines for shade, abundant wildflowers in summer, and nearby Greens Lake for recreation. The red Canyon Rim Trail starts nearby and is excellent for hikers and mountain bikers. To reserve one of the more than 700 campsites throughout Flaming Gorge, visit www.recreation.gov or call 877/444-6777. To read more about individual campsites in the recreation area, go to www.flaminggorgecountry.com.

INFORMATION AND SERVICES

The **Rock Springs Chamber of Commerce** (1897 Dewar Dr., Rock Springs, 307/362-3771, www.rockspringswyoming. net, 8am-5pm Mon.-Fri.) doubles as a visitors center. The **Green River Chamber of Commerce** (1155 W. Flaming Gorge Way, Green River, 307/875-5711, www.grchamber.com, 8:30am-5:30pm Mon.-Fri.) also operates as a visitors center.

There are **post offices** in Rock Springs (2829 Commercial Way, 307/362-9792, 9am-5pm Mon.-Fri., 9am-noon Sat.) and in Green River (350 Uinta Dr., 307/875-4920, 8:30am-5:30pm Mon.-Fri., 9:30am-1pm Sat.).

Medical care is available 24-7 at **Memorial Hospital of Sweetwater County** (1200 College Dr., Rock Springs, 307/362-3711, www.sweetwatermemorial.com). Walk-in care is offered at **Red Desert Insta Care** (2761 Commercial Way, Rock Springs, 307/382-3064, www.reddesertinstacare.com, 7am-7pm Mon.-Fri., 8am-5pm Sat.) and **Big Horn Urgent Care** (1453 Dewar Dr., Rock Springs, 307/382-2466, 8am-8pm Sun. only).

In Rock Springs, wash clothes at the **Sweetwater Laundry** (2528 Foothill Blvd., Rock Springs, 307/382-6290, 7am-9pm daily, last wash at 7:30pm). In Green River, big, clean machines (and a nice kids' play area) are available at **Wash and Play Laundromat** (1315 Bridger Dr., Green River, 307/364-0479, 24 hours daily).

TRANSPORTATION

Getting There

The **Rock Springs-Sweetwater County Airport** (RKS, 382 Hwy. 370, 307/352-6880, www.flyrks.com) has daily nonstop flights to Denver on **United**.

Rental cars are available at the Rock Springs-Sweetwater County Airport from **Avis** and **Budget**.

Green River is 14 miles (22.5 km) west of Rock Springs, 113 miles (182 km) south of Pinedale, 209 miles (340 km) southwest of Thermopolis, 240 miles (385 km) southwest of Casper, and 247 miles (395 km) south of Yellowstone National Park.

Daily bus service is provided by **Greyhound** (1695 Sunset Dr., Ste. 118, Rock Springs, 307/362-2931).

Getting Around

Public transportation across Sweetwater County is available through **STAR Transit** (307/382-7827, www.ridestartransit.com).

For taxi service in and around Sweetwater County, contact **All City Taxi** (307/382-1100, www.allcitytaxiwy.com, 5am-2am daily, or by appointment) which has been serving the region for 25 years.

Background

The Landscape

Not only do Montana and Wyoming share borders, they also share many of the same characteristics when it comes to the geographic and cultural lay of the land. While both are well known for their spectacular mountains, rivers, and valleys, the eastern part of both states is remote, rural, and based on agriculture. Both states have Native American reservations and the stories that go with them—many of the West's fiercest battles took place here—and they share many of the same industries: agriculture, mining, oil and gas, tourism, and forestry. Although Montana and Wyoming have many similarities, it's

their subtle differences that make them stand out on their own.

GEOGRAPHY

Montana is the fourth-largest state in area, with just over 147,000 square miles (380,278 sq km) of land, but ranks near the bottom in population—44th, to be exact, with an estimated 1,050,493 people as of July 2017. To the north is Canada, with Montana sharing borders with Saskatchewan, Alberta, and British Columbia, while Wyoming is to the south. The western and southwestern part of the state is bordered by Idaho, and North and South Dakota flank its eastern edge. Montana is bisected by the Continental Divide, which runs diagonally from the northwest to the south-central part of the state. The big peaks and expansive valleys dominating the landscape of western Montana, from Yellowstone to Glacier National Parks, inspired the state's name, which comes from the Spanish word for mountains. Central Montana acts as a transition to the flatter part of the state, with the Yellowstone and Missouri Rivers flowing out of the mountains and into the wide-open spaces that make up remote eastern Montana and the northern plains. Eye-catching badlands, buttes, terraces, and old grain silos dominate the horizon here, a stark contrast to the coniferous forests found farther west. Granite Peak in the Beartooth Mountains is the highest point in the state at 12,799 feet (3,901 m).

Wyoming is the least populous state in the union with only 579,315 people as of 2017, but is 10th in land area—just over 97,000 square miles (251,229 sq km). One of only three states (Colorado and Utah are the others) that have borders along straight latitudinal and longitudinal lines, Wyoming is bordered on the north by Montana and on the south by Utah and Colorado. Nebraska and South Dakota border Wyoming on the east, while Idaho makes up most of the western border with a little slice of Utah. Like Montana, the western part of Wyoming is made up of mountainous terrain covered by coniferous forests, and similarly the Continental Divide continues its diagonal run through the state. Eastern Wyoming consists of the High Plains, an expanse of high-elevation prairie that is home to large cattle ranches and oil and gas wells. Wyoming is the third-highest state in the nation (behind Alaska and Colorado), with an elevation range of 3,125-13,804 feet (953-4,207 m). Gannet Peak in the Wind River Range is the highest point in the state at 13,804 feet (4,207 m).

GEOLOGY

Montana and Wyoming (as well as parts of Idaho) converge around the Greater Yellowstone Ecosystem, widely regarded as the largest biologically intact temperate ecosystem in North America. Centered around Yellowstone National Park, this 31,000-square-mile (80,290-sq-km) area, or nearly 20 million acres (8 million hectares), consists of a diverse landscape with geothermal activity and native wildlife; it is considered by scientists as a natural laboratory for landscape ecology, geology, and wildlife preservation.

Visiting the Greater Yellowstone area provides the opportunity to see a natural environment much like it was hundreds and even thousands of years ago. Yellowstone National Park itself is on a high plateau, the remnants of a volcano that last exploded more than 640,000 years ago, leaving a giant caldera. Yellowstone is one of the most geothermic places on earth, containing a majority of the world's types of geothermal features, including geysers, hot springs, mud pots, and fumaroles.

If you are worried that Yellowstone could erupt during your vacation, you're not alone. Scientists are constantly measuring the amount of pressure in the magma chamber,

---

Previous: Traditional tipis remind visitors of the region's long history.

1: geyser eruption in Yellowstone **2:** Glacier's Hidden Lake Trail **3:** clear day in Grand Teton National Park

which actually raises the floor of the caldera plateau—nearly 7 inches (18 cm) between 1976 and 1984, and almost 10 inches (25 cm) from 2004 to 2009. Since 2010, the rate of growth has significantly slowed down. But as if the caldera could breathe, the growth is up and down. The dome rises and falls, then rises again. Theoretically, the volcano could erupt, but most scientists seem to think there is little evidence that a cataclysmic explosion will occur anytime soon. Due to its volcanic nature, the Yellowstone area experiences upward of 1,000-3,000 measurable earthquakes each year, but you are unlikely to feel one.

Outside Yellowstone Park, the rest of the ecosystem is mountainous and filled with large tracts of roadless land, jagged peaks, broad valleys, and flowing rivers—exactly why many people live here and even more choose to visit. Wildlife abounds, offering a rare glimpse into the lives of everything from the pine marten to the grizzly bear. Of course, people live here too, and the interaction between humans and nature is important not only historically but in contemporary matters as well.

In addition to mountains, both states have large tracts of prairies that contain mostly dry grasses and shrubs. The iconic big sagebrush plant can be found at nearly every elevation—more sage grows in Wyoming than anywhere else—and many land areas seem almost desertlike, right down to the tumbleweeds that roll along in the breeze. Wyoming actually includes two areas that are classified as desert: the Red Desert near Rock Springs and a large part of the Bighorn Basin.

CLIMATE

Montana and Wyoming have similar weather patterns, influenced predominantly by each state's diverse topography. Generally, summers are hot and dry, often punctuated by brief but intense afternoon thunderstorms. Winters are cold and see a healthy amount of snow, particularly in the western portions of the states. Daytime highs in a Montana and Wyoming summer are in the 80s and 90s, with triple digits occasionally setting in. During the winter, it can get downright cold in either state—the coldest recorded temperature in the lower 48 states was -70°F (-56.7°C) at Rogers Pass, northwest of Helena, Montana, on January 20, 1954. For both states, July and August are the warmest months, while January and February are the coldest. Snow can fall at any time of the year, but most occurs November-March. May and June are often the rainiest months of the year. Humidity is generally on the low side, making the hot summer days a little more bearable. It's important to realize that when engaging in outdoor activities during the summer, you should always plan for bad weather—it can happen almost instantly at any time in Montana or Wyoming, even during the hottest part of the summer.

Temperatures decrease with higher altitude, so it's not uncommon in the mountains for the weather to be drastically different from lower elevations. Storms can move in on a moment's notice and can often be fierce—driving hail in the summer and blizzard conditions in the winter. Rain in the valleys can often mean snow in the mountains, especially in the spring when a storm can dump several feet of heavy snow in a relatively short amount of time.

Chinook winds can blow in both states. These unusually warm, dry winter winds blow down the east slopes of the Rockies and across the plains. They occur when moist Pacific air rises over the mountains, loses its moisture in the form of precipitation, and then warms rapidly on the leeward side. Chinooks can quickly melt snow and raise the temperature, as evidenced in January 1972, when the temperature in Loma, Montana, went from -56°F (-48.9°C) to 49°F (9.4°C) in 24 hours.

In general, both states are known for being on the windy side. Great Falls, Montana, and Casper and Cheyenne, Wyoming, all rank among the windiest cities in the country. Winter winds can turn an average cold day into a bone-chilling one, while summer gusts often keep outdoor event planners working overtime.

Plants and Animals

PLANTS

Both Montana and Wyoming encompass a variety of habitats, ranging from grasslands and desert shrublands to forests, mountain meadows, and alpine tundra. Though both states are fairly arid, Wyoming has some 2,200 plant species and Montana has 2,063 species in 176 plant families.

Trees

In Wyoming, forests account for roughly one-fifth of the state's land. In the lower-elevation mountains in the eastern part of the state, ponderosa pine is the primary species. Farther west, **Douglas fir** is prominent in the lower elevations. Higher up, where the climate is cooler and wetter, **lodgepole pine, Engelmann spruce, subalpine fir,** and **aspen** are among the most common species. Timberline in the northern part of Wyoming is at about 8,900 feet (2,713 m), and at about 11,500 feet (3,505 m) in the southern part of the state. Engelmann spruce, subalpine fir, whitebark pine—an important and dwindling food source for grizzly bears—and **limber pine** grow at high elevations as shrubs, rather than trees.

In Montana, forests cover roughly 22.3 million (9 million hectares) of the state's 93.3 million acres (37.8 million hectares). Conifers—or cone-producing trees—grow most abundantly in drier areas. Montana's most prevalent conifers include similar species to Wyoming's: ponderosa pine, Douglas fir, lodgepole pine—which combined make up some 66 percent of Montana's forests—subalpine fir, and **western larch,** which actually lose their needles every fall like deciduous trees and can live to be more than 500 years old. In both states, an infestation of mountain pine beetles has caused massive pine die-offs, increasing the threat of catastrophic forest fires. The tallest tree in Montana is a 203-foot (61.9-m) Engelmann spruce in Sanders County, and the runner-up is a 194-foot (59.1-m) ponderosa pine—incidentally, the ponderosa pine is the state's official tree—in Mineral County.

Flowers

What they lack in fall foliage colors, thanks to an abundance of evergreens, Montana and Wyoming more than make up for with spring and summer displays of wildflowers. Wyoming has more than 150 varieties including purple **New England asters, bluebells, California poppies, camas, black-eyed Susans, fireweed, wild blue flax,** and **sticky geraniums.** Montana has many of the same species, as well as **fireweed, goldenrod, Indian paintbrush,** and **yellow monkeyflower.** The **bitterroot** is Montana's state flower, while Indian paintbrush is the state flower of Wyoming.

Vegetation

Wyoming's alpine tundra, found above timberline, is home to a variety of grasses and other herbaceous plants that can tolerate freezing temperatures at any time of year. **Big sagebrush,** the most dominant of Wyoming's species of sagebrush, covers much of the western two-thirds of the state. Other plants with a wide range in Wyoming include **western wheatgrass, blue grama, needleleaf sedge, scarlet globemallow, fringed sagewort, phlox, milkvetch, rabbitbrush,** and **prickly pear cactus.** In the driest parts of the state, shrubs like **juniper, mountain mahogany, saltbush, winterfat,** and **spiny hopsage** occur alongside various species of sagebrush. The most abundant vegetation in this part of the state is found along rivers and streams and can include **cottonwood trees** and **willows.**

In Montana, much of the eastern, central, and northern parts of the state consist of vast swaths of plains grassland, on which grow various species of grasses including blue grama, **bluebunch wheatgrass, needle-and-thread,** and little bluestem. In Montana's shrubby grasslands, where the temperatures can be extreme and soils are generally fragile, dominant species include blue grama, **fringed sagewort, rubber rabbitbrush, broom snakeweed,** and **Rocky Mountain juniper.**

ANIMALS

Both Montana and Wyoming are known for their abundant wildlife, and it's only fitting that residents and visitors want to see them in their natural habitat. Both herbivores and predators roam the land, and with the right information a savvy traveler can seek out views of these animals. Keep in mind that it is not acceptable to approach wildlife for any reason—keep a safe distance away and never feed any animal.

Bison

Two herds fluctuating from 2,300 to 5,500 bison roam within the borders of Yellowstone National Park, a far cry from the millions that once lived throughout central North America from Canada to Mexico. These massive creatures graze on grasses, and males can weigh up to 2,000 pounds (907 kg), while females can weigh as much as 1,000 pounds (454 kg). Bison can commonly be seen almost any time of the year in Yellowstone, often causing traffic jams as they stand on the road. The National Bison Range wildlife refuge in Moiese, Montana, also supports a herd of 300-400 animals and has a visitors center and interpretive displays.

Elk

Elk are found throughout the mountainous region, and between 10,000 and 20,000 roam free in Yellowstone National Park in 6-7 different herds. These regal creatures are fairly common and can be found at higher elevations in the summer and lower elevations in the winter. The Northern Yellowstone elk herd numbered 7,579 animals during the winter of 2018, up 42 percent since 2017's count of 5,349; the herd spends its winters just north of the park. The National Elk Refuge in Jackson, Wyoming, is home to 5,000-7,000 wintering elk, as well as an educational visitors center and winter sleigh rides that travel among the herd.

Deer, Antelope, and Sheep

White-tailed deer and the large-eared **mule deer,** as well as **pronghorn antelope,** can be found throughout the region and are as often seen on the sides of highways as they are in the wild. **Bighorn sheep** are impressive, stocky animals. The rams (males) are known for their massive curled horns, which give the rugged creatures their distinctive look. Herds of bighorn sheep can be found in and around Yellowstone—near the north entrance of the park and around Big Sky, Montana, in particular—and Wyoming's Whiskey Basin Habitat Area near Dubois.

Mountain Goats

Mountain goats inhabit many of the high peaks of Montana and Wyoming and can often be seen clinging to impossibly steep sides of rocky cliffs. Considered nonnative species, mountain goats were introduced to Montana in the 1940s and 1950s, and to Yellowstone in the 1990s.

Moose

Some of the largest animals you'll encounter are **moose,** which typically inhabit river bottoms, wetlands, and willowed areas and graze on grasses, brush, and leaves. Moose can surprise you on the trail, as they are typically quiet and private creatures. Their docile nature can quickly turn deadly if they charge; give them plenty of room, especially if you encounter a female with young.

1: bison 2: beargrass near Logan Pass 3: grizzly bear 4: bighorn sheep

The Wyoming Jackalope

As much a design staple as statewide lore, the famed jackalope is to Wyoming what bigfoot is to the Pacific Northwest. Does it exist? Could it possibly? Stop into nearly any roadside tavern and you are bound to see a mount of the creature. Ask around and the locals will gladly play along.

Popularized by Douglas Herrick in 1939, the jackalope is supposed to be an extinct antlered rabbit species, a cross between a pygmy deer and some sort of killer rabbit. Among the beliefs surrounding these legendary creatures are that jackalopes can travel at speeds of 90 mph and can mimic human sounds when chased.

Sighted in Colorado, New Mexico, and Nebraska in addition to Wyoming, jackalopes have cousins in Germany (called the *wolperdinger*) and in Sweden (the *skvader*). Drawings of antlered rabbit-like creatures date back to the 16th century in scholarly European works, so it is not just the stuff of goofy Wyoming calendars.

Those who sit on the fence between believing and not believing cite a disease called papillomatosis, which indeed lead parasite-caused growths on the top of a rabbit's head to harden, perhaps resembling antlers.

For those who prefer lore to science, the story of Herrick, a taxidermist from Douglas, seems a believable origin. Herrick and his brother Ralph returned from a hunt one day and slid their catch onto the floor. A hare landed next to a set of antelope antlers, and a pop-culture idea was born. The brothers mounted the antlered bunny, and the rest is history.

Jackalopes became so popular in the 1940s that Douglas was known far and wide as the "Jackalope Capital of the World." The city has stayed true to the legend with public art and signage all over town, as well as an annual Jackalope Day in June. Each year the local chamber issues thousands of jackalope hunting licenses, which specify that hunters cannot have an IQ higher than 72 and can only hunt between midnight and 2am on June 31. In the works now? There's been talk for years of a giant 80-foot (24.4-m) fiberglass jackalope sculpture to tower over I-25. This is a story so entwined with Wyoming culture that it will never fade away.

Horses

The region is also home to a large herd of **wild horses,** located in the Pryor Mountains south of Billings along the Montana-Wyoming border. One of just 10 herds left in the country, many of the Pryor Mountain horses have primitive striping on their backs, withers, and legs; they are thought to be descendants of colonial Spanish horses. In 1968, interested individuals and groups convinced the government to set aside 31,000 acres (12,545 hectares) in the Pryor Mountains as a public range for the wild horses, which had been living there for more than a century. The Pryor Mountain Wild Mustang Center in Lovell, Wyoming, houses a museum where visitors can learn about the history, behavior, and life of the animals. The center can also direct visitors on where and how to catch a glimpse of these beautiful creatures running free in the wild.

Bears

Montana and Wyoming are perhaps best known for the predators that visitors most want to glimpse. **Black bears** can be found in forested areas and often see much more human interaction than their larger counterpart, the **grizzly bear.** Grizzlies once roamed the entire Northern Hemisphere, and when Lewis and Clark traversed the area, there were likely more than 50,000 grizzlies across the West. Although there are still healthy populations in western Canada and Alaska, grizzly numbers in the Greater Yellowstone Ecosystem dropped to as few as 136 animals in 1975. Since the U.S. Fish and Wildlife Service listed them as a threatened species, the population has recovered to include an estimated 690 bears in the region. The Northern Continental Divide Ecosystem in western and northwestern Montana is believed to be home to the largest number of grizzlies—approximately 1,000 as of 2017. The grizzlies along the Rocky Mountain Front have, in the last several years, started coming out of their alpine habitat to regain their status as residents of the plains, something not seen since Lewis and Clark traveled the region at the turn of the 19th century. Indeed, grizzlies today have been reported east of Great Falls, more than 100 miles (161 km) from the nearest mountain range. But despite their successes, grizzlies in the region face enormous hurdles including habitat destruction and climate change, both of which put them in danger of human conflict. According to the USGS, in 2016 there were at least 43 human-caused deaths for grizzlies in the Greater Yellowstone Ecosystem with reasons ranging from roadkill and self-defense, to management for livestock depredations and those mistaken by hunters for black bears. Add that to the fact that grizzlies are the second-slowest reproducing land mammal in North America, and the hurdles for their survival look insurmountable. Even so, in 2017 the U.S. Fish and Wildlife Service delisted the Yellowstone grizzly population, and while the bears will be protected inside park boundaries, a hunting season is slated for fall 2018 where both males and females can be shot outside the park in Wyoming. More than 7,000 hunting permit applications were received, which is but a trickle compared to the 850,000 public comments submitted on the 2016 delisting proposal, 99 percent of which opposed delisting. It's time for humans to protect the grizzlies, and what is wild, or lose them forever.

Wolves and Coyotes

The reintroduction of the gray wolf is one of the greatest—and most controversial—wildlife success stories of the 20th century. Numbers went from zero—gray wolves were last seen in Montana and Wyoming in the 1930s—to more than 1,915 in some 300 packs living throughout Montana, Wyoming, Idaho, Washington, and Oregon by the end of 2016. Yellowstone National Park is the best place to catch a glimpse of the elusive wolf. The Lamar and Hayden Valleys are especially good places to view one of the 104 or so wolves that roam through Yellowstone in 11 different packs.

You'll often see coyotes walking along the roadsides in Yellowstone or strolling in an open meadow stalking their prey. These doglike predators have a longer and more pointed nose than wolves, a much fluffier tail, and are noticeably smaller and more delicate in appearance. Their numbers in Yellowstone decreased substantially with the reintroduction of the wolf, thanks to food competition and conflicts between the two species.

Mountain Lions

Mountain lions, also known as cougars, are present in the region. Though their numbers dwindled to almost zero with the predator removal campaigns in the early 1900s, they managed to hang on thanks to their shy nature. These elusive cats are becoming slightly more common, and human confrontations have risen over the years. The largest cat in North America, with a length of up to 7.5 feet (2.3 m) from nose to tail, male cougars can weight 145-170 pounds (66-77 kg), and females generally weigh 85-120 pounds (39-54 kg). If you see one in the wild, chances are it will be crossing the road on a late-night hunting excursion.

Pikas and Marmots

The high country is home to the smallish pika and the larger, fuzzier yellow-bellied marmot. Both can be spotted running along rocky outcrops and scree fields at higher elevations. Listen for their high-pitched chirp.

Birds

Both states have numerous species of birds, including raptors. Attentive visitors can expect to see **bald** and **golden eagles, ospreys, hawks, falcons, owls, woodpeckers, grouse, herons, pelicans,** and more. Smaller species include **jays, mountain bluebirds, warblers, western tanagers,** and **magpies.** The Red Rock Lakes National

Wildlife Refuge in southwestern Montana is home to one of the largest habitats of the majestic **trumpeter swan.** For information on the excellent birding opportunities, visit www.audubon.org.

Snakes

The only venomous snake in Montana is the **prairie rattlesnake,** found in the eastern part of the region, typically in open arid country. In addition to the prairie rattlesnake, Wyoming also has an endangered population of its cousin, the **midget faded rattlesnake,** which lives only around the Flaming Gorge area. Prairie rattlesnakes tend to den on south-facing slopes with rock outcrops and consume rodents as their main meal.

Environmental Issues

As in many Western states, the environment is a controversial topic in Montana and Wyoming. While both states are on the conservative side politically, many of the people who have moved here in the past two decades have a decidedly more liberal view, particularly when it comes to land, air, and water issues.

MINING

The effects of irresponsible hard-rock mining operations can be found throughout Montana, marked by a scarred landscape and contaminated water. The 1-mile-wide (1.6-km) Berkeley Pit, a former open-pit copper mine in Butte, is one of the country's largest Superfund sites. Since it closed in 1982, contaminated water has been filling the pit, which could eventually contaminate the entire Clark Fork River basin. In 1998, voters in Montana approved a law that phased out the process of cyanide leaching in open-pit mines, although mining companies are trying to get the decision reversed. Twelve of the 17 Superfund sites in Montana are related to mining operations.

In the early 2000s, Wyoming's mining and gas industries experienced a major boom. In 2004, Wyoming ranked 16th in the country in total nonfuel mineral production value and first in the production of coal, which is mined primarily in the Powder River Basin. Together, this was a $7.8 billion piece of the state's economic pie. The state has nearly 200 mines and is the country's largest producer of soda ash and bentonite clays. Wyoming also has the world's largest deposit of trona, from which soda ash is refined. In spring 2016, however, the bust could not be ignored. When low natural gas prices damaged coal's dominance in the electricity sector, the country's largest coal mine, south of Gillette, laid off 15 percent of its workers, as did another major mine nearby. More than 1,000 mining jobs were lost and several mining companies in the area filed for bankruptcy amid the plummeting market. In all of 2017, only five full-time mining jobs were added in Wyoming. Even the companies that survived were still reducing production as of 2018. The Black Thunder Mine cut production by 15 million tons, and Cloud Peak's Cordero Rojo mine went from producing 9 million tons in the fourth quarter of 2012 to 3.9 million tons in the fourth quarter of 2017.

One of the most tragic reminders of the mining industry's legacy is the situation of the northwest Montana town of Libby, where a former vermiculite mine was found to have poisoned the town's residents with a rare form of asbestos that was present in the mining dust. Health workers estimate that more than 400 people died from asbestos-related cancers, and some 3,000 residents have been sickened from exposure. There was local and national outrage when the news was made public in 2000 that the W. R. Grace Company, which owned the mine, knew all along that the asbestos was sickening workers and their families and yet said nothing. The company has since filed for bankruptcy, blaming the large number of personal-injury lawsuits, and a 20-year emergency cleanup of the town is being managed by the Environmental Protection Agency with a price tag that reached $575 million in 2017. When the EPA wraps up its work in 2019, the state of Montana will be taking over the job of cleanup and handling future asbestos discoveries. Two documentary films have been made and several books written about the case and the tragic events surrounding the town.

AIR POLLUTION

Air quality in Montana and Wyoming is another concern, in particular emissions from coal-fired power plants and, in places, ongoing tire burning. Proponents of banning snowmobiles in Yellowstone National Park succeeded in lowering the number of machines allowed to enter, as well as requiring all snowmobiles to be the cleaner four-stroke variety. This has divided towns where the winter economy has traditionally relied on the snowmobile tourism industry. Global warming has also affected Glacier National Park, as the number of glaciers larger than 25 acres (10.1 hectares) has decreased from 150 in 1850 to 25 in 2010—and some prediction models, based on a 2003 USGS study and 1992 temperature predictions, suggest that the park's glaciers could disappear altogether by 2030. A significant problem for air quality in both states during most summers is smoke from massive forest fires. The Department of Environmental Quality (DEQ) for both states (www.deq.mt.gov, deq.wyoming.gov) monitors air quality.

WATER QUALITY

Major environmental issues in Wyoming also include water quality, especially associated with coal-bed methane, a form of natural gas. Wyoming is the country's third-largest coal-bed methane producer, much of it coming from the Powder River Basin in the northeast part of the state. Wyoming is also the seventh-largest oil-producing state, with five large refineries and the fourth-largest volume of oil reserves. Like Montana, Wyoming faces issues with hard-rock mining and coal-fired power plants. And as is true around the country, and the world, the process of fracking—extracting natural gas from shale rock layers using hydraulic fracturing—is stirring up significant controversy in these resource-rich states. Montana is not immune to significant water quality concerns either, with mining, oil extraction, and agricultural use of pesticides, among other dangers. Various reports on impaired waters are available through each state's DEQ (www.deq.mt.gov, deq.wyoming.gov).

FOREST MANAGEMENT

Perhaps nothing divides Westerners more than how to use and manage the forests. Whether the topic is the creatures that live in them, logging operations, forest fires, recreation, or potential wilderness, residents are passionate about their beliefs. Both sides of any issue typically have ardent followers, making legislation a painstaking process. Whether it's clear-cutting issues or motorized-vehicle access, forestry can be touchy subjects at the lunch counter. Check any newspaper in either state and you're bound to see articles and letters to the editor about these topics.

WOLF REINTRODUCTION

Another contentious issue in both states is the government-sponsored reintroduction of the wolf, which started in 1995 when 66 Canadian wolves were transplanted to Yellowstone National Park and central Idaho. The population has rebounded and, in some people's minds, become a threat to humans and livestock. At last count, there were close to 1,915 wolves across five states and about 104 in Yellowstone National Park. Area ranchers say wolves prey on livestock and elk herds; environmentalists say the animals have a right to thrive on land that was once theirs. Wolves were relieved of their endangered-species status in Montana and Idaho by 2011,

Leave No Trace

Leave No Trace is an educational program that teaches outdoors enthusiasts how to protect the places they love from human-caused recreational impact. However, the Leave No Trace ethic extends far beyond backcountry and wilderness areas. As more and more people are recreating in "front country" settings, knowledge of how to apply Leave No Trace principles becomes increasingly important.

Planning ahead is the easiest way to protect outdoor places and to enjoy a safe visit. Use a map, bring a small first-aid kit, remember to bring additional clothing to keep you warm and dry, and wear suitable shoes or boots on the trails. When hiking, stay on designated trails, especially if they pass through private property. Shortcutting around corners causes erosion and damages trailside plants, especially if it's wet or muddy. Dispose of trash and biodegradable materials, such as orange peels, apple cores, and food scraps, in a bear-proof trash container. Remember, animals that become dependent on human food often have to be relocated or destroyed. Two easy slogans to remember are "Pack it in, pack it out," and "Leave it as you find it." By leaving the natural world as you find it, you will be protecting the habitat of plants and animals as well as the outdoor experience of millions of visitors.

In the backcountry, you must carry all trash out with you. Use a biodegradable soap when washing dishes, and avoid using soap within 200 feet (61 m) of a stream or spring. Allow others a sense of discovery by leaving rocks, plants, archaeological artifacts, and other objects of interest as you find them. Minimize campfire impacts by instead using portable camp stoves or fire pans. Use designated fire grates if available, and always make sure the fire is completely out before you leave camp. If you make a fire ring with rocks, disperse the rocks before you leave camp, and try hard to "leave no trace" of your being there.

Finally, always respect wildlife and be considerate of other visitors to help protect the quality of their experience. The last thing you want to do is ruin somebody else's trip of a lifetime. Keep noise to a minimum and let nature's sounds prevail; everyone will be happier for it.

and Wyoming by 2012, but Wyoming wolves were re-listed in 2014 as a nonessential experimental population since the state could not abide by post-delisting rules. They were delisted again in 2017, and in the first hunt since 2013, 44 Wyoming wolves were killed.

History

MONTANA

When examining the history of Montana, it's important to note the role geology played in creating the mountains, rivers, lakes, and valleys that are so treasured by residents and visitors alike. The Rocky Mountains were created about 100 million years ago, when giant masses of molten rock deep inside the earth began to push to the surface. The ensuing tectonic pressure stretched the land in every direction, allowing large blocks of rock to thrust upward and create the massive jumble of mountains we see today.

These new mountains were eventually buried under ice and water during several ice ages—the last one starting roughly 20,000 years ago—that carved out many of the details of today's landscape. The remnants of these glaciers can still be seen throughout the high country of Montana and Wyoming, particularly in Glacier National Park, Grand Teton National Park, and the Wind River Mountains.

Prehistoric Residents

Dinosaurs played an important role in the region's early history. Some of the most recent and important fossil discoveries have been made here, including the largest known skull of a *Tyrannosaurus rex*. At Bozeman's Museum of the Rockies, an excellent exhibit highlights Montana's prominent role in dinosaur discovery.

The region's geologic history has made Montana a perfect laboratory for finding fossils from the Cretaceous and Jurassic periods. As the dinosaurs were dying off, the formation of the mountains caused sediment to slough off the rising peaks to form a layer over their remains. Receding glaciers then scoured the land and removed many of the layers, leaving behind fossils that can be found at or near the surface. And since much of the region remains undeveloped, most fossils have been undisturbed by humans.

The first humans most likely appeared 10,000-30,000 years ago, when Asiatic people came to North America across the Bering Strait land bridge. These people traveled south from Alaska to the Great North Trail, which ran along the eastern slopes of the Rockies. Some wandered all the way to South America. Those who stayed in the north hunted big game, including the extinct mammoth, and used tools made of chipped stone. They lived on the plains and foothills until a climatic change around 5000 BC turned the plains into a desert, and the people and animals all but disappeared.

As the climate slowly became more moderate, people returned from the south and northwest, bringing with them new techniques and cultural ideals. Bison roamed the land, providing a much-needed food source. These last prehistoric migrants are thought to be the direct ancestors of today's Native Americans. Evidence of their culture can be found in the tipi rings, pictographs (rock paintings), and petroglyphs (rock carvings) that still adorn the landscape. Buffalo jumps (also called pishkuns) were used during this period; entire herds were stampeded off rocky cliffs and then slaughtered for their meat and hides. Two of the most remarkable buffalo jumps can be seen at First Peoples Buffalo Jump State Park near Great Falls and Madison Buffalo Jump State Park outside Three Forks.

Native Americans

Although the Flathead Indians lived west of the Continental Divide, the Indians that we associate with Montana today did not arrive until the early 1600s, moving westward after European settlement forced them from their traditional homelands. These new migrants—Plains Indians, as we refer to them today—mostly came from the Great Lakes and Mississippi Basin region, where their sedentary life was uprooted by westward expansionism. Many Native Americans abandoned their agricultural lifestyle and developed a culture of hunting as they were forced west onto the plains, where the bison was plentiful and the newly developed tipi provided a means to move around and follow the herds.

The Shoshone were among the first Plains Indians to enter Montana, displacing the resident Salish farther north. They brought with them the first horses and were fierce warriors. The Crow followed shortly after, moving throughout the valleys around the Yellowstone River. The Blackfeet brought the rifle with them when they settled in Montana during the early 1700s, and together with their allies, the Gros Ventre and Assiniboine, they quickly came to dominate the northern plains. Other groups that came to settle in Montana were the Sioux, Northern Cheyenne, Cree, and Chippewa, causing tensions with so many squeezed into a limited area as settlers moved farther west.

Lewis and Clark

It is hard to envision what a monumental change would come when President Thomas Jefferson purchased the Louisiana Territory from France in 1803. This large part of the western United States was viewed as an important acquisition, and Jefferson hoped to explore this new territory to find a safe trade route from the Missouri River to the headwaters of the Columbia River and the Pacific. In other words, the West would soon be open for business.

Jefferson charged his personal secretary, Meriwether Lewis, and William Clark with the task of putting together a Corps of Discovery to explore the West. On May 14, 1804, the two set out from St. Louis with 45 men. Traveling up the Missouri River, the party spent the following winter in a Mandan village in North Dakota. Here they recruited French trader Toussaint Charbonneau, who spoke several native languages and had traveled extensively along the Missouri. One of Charbonneau's wives was the young Shoshone named Sacagawea, who accompanied the party as an interpreter and guide.

The Corps entered Montana in April 1805 and followed the Missouri to its headwaters, near the present-day town of Three Forks. Lewis encountered the expedition's first Native American shortly thereafter, a Shoshone who led them to Sacagawea's brother and the tribe from which she had been kidnapped as a girl. The Shoshone led the party down the Bitterroot Valley and over the mountains through Lolo Pass near the Montana-Idaho border. The party then followed the Clearwater, Snake, and Columbia Rivers to the Pacific Ocean, where they built a fort and spent a long cold winter on the coast.

In the spring, the Corps backtracked across Oregon, over Lolo Pass, and into Montana in June 1806. The expedition then split into two parties, with Lewis taking the northeast route toward Great Falls and Clark taking the more southern route to explore the Yellowstone River. The two parties met at the confluence of the Yellowstone and Missouri Rivers in August, and they were back in St. Louis by the end of September.

The Fur Trade and the Gold Rush

Although Lewis and Clark's famous expedition failed to find a manageable passage to the Pacific, it opened the door to fur trading, which would come to dominate the first half of the 19th century in the region. Trading posts sprang up along the Missouri and Yellowstone Rivers, and fashionable beaver pelts were soon finding their way to the East and Europe. By 1840, however, the mountain man era was over as beavers were trapped nearly to extinction and demand waned.

Catholic missionaries established posts near Stevensville and St. Ignatius and attempted to teach the Native Americans a different way of life. Some of these missions were successful, others were not, but their presence alone signaled that the traditional Native American way of life would soon be changed forever as settlers expanded farther into their territory.

If the beaver trade and missionary work marked the initial changes to the Native American way of life, the 1860 discovery of gold in Gold Creek near Deer Lodge signified the end of Native American autonomy. Gold was soon found near Bannack, the first territorial capital, and Virginia City, the second capital, and settlers began flocking to Montana to seek their fortunes. In 1860 there were fewer than 100 settlers in the state, but by 1870 that number had jumped to more than 20,000. Soon Montana became a postcard of the Wild West, where miners, settlers, Indians, and thieves interacted to create a dangerous, hostile atmosphere built on greed. The Bozeman Trail, established in the 1860s as an alternative to the more southern Oregon Trail, became known as the "Bloody Bozeman" for its perilous route through Indian country and several famous battles along its path.

By the 1870s, the gold rush was in full swing and the U.S. government was waging a full-on war against the Indians, forcing them onto reservations and land that was not traditionally theirs. Many famous battles were fought in Montana, including George Custer's infamous "last stand" at the 1876 Battle of the Little Bighorn, where the 7th Cavalry fought several thousand Lakota and Cheyenne warriors and suffered heavy losses.

In 1877, the Nez Perce fled Oregon hoping to settle in Canada. Under the leadership of Chief Joseph, the tribe traveled across Idaho and into Montana, where they engaged with U.S. soldiers near the Big Hole River, a battle that left nearly 90 Indians dead. The Nez Perce continued to flee, passing through Yellowstone National Park and north toward Canada, only to be captured near Chinook just 40 miles (64 km) from the Canadian border. Even though they were originally from the Pacific Northwest, the Nez Perce were sent to reservations in Oklahoma.

As gold and other minerals were being plundered, the railroad came to Montana when the Union Pacific built a line from Utah to Butte in 1881. The Northern Pacific linked Chicago with Portland by 1883, opening up Montana's fortunes to the rest of the world. The Great Northern linked Minneapolis to Seattle in 1893, while the Milwaukee Road route across the center part of the state was completed in 1909.

Mining, Agriculture, and the Montana Economy

Fueled by investors from all over the country, the large deposits of gold, copper, and other minerals quickly created vast wealth in Montana. Butte became known as the "richest hill on earth," and its three copper kings— Marcus Daly, William Clark, and Augustus Heinze—were among the richest men in the world. The competition between them to control Butte's copper mines is worth a book on its own—several have been written—and sounds like something out of a Hollywood movie. Each tried to buy courts, newspapers, politicians, banks, law enforcement, and anything and anyone that could help them or damage their opponents. In 1899, Daly teamed up with Standard Oil to create a behemoth mining company, which soon bought out Heinze's and Clark's interests and became the Anaconda Copper Mining Company. Named after the smelter town to the northwest, the company would dominate Butte for most of the 20th century.

Copper production in Butte peaked in 1917

and then started to decline, leaving the city in shambles as Anaconda began to shift jobs to places with cheaper labor like Asia and South America. The riches of Butte, once the envy of the West, were leaving town just as fast as the mine workers. Anaconda stopped mining the massive Berkeley Pit in 1982, and it has since become one of the largest contaminated waste sites in the country.

As the mining industry gained and then lost ground, cattle and sheep ranches continued to take advantage of Montana's abundant grasslands. By the late 1880s, there were nearly 700,000 head of cattle in the state. The passage of the Enlarged Homestead Act in 1909 brought thousands of homesteaders into the state looking for inexpensive land. Wheat farming was popular until an extended drought and a drop in market prices after World War I ruined many farmers, who were forced to abandon their farms.

Montana's post-World War I depression extended through the 1920s into the Great Depression of the 1930s. President Franklin D. Roosevelt's New Deal then brought relief to the state in the form of various projects and agencies: the building of Fort Peck Dam, the Civilian Conservation Corps (CCC), the Works Projects Administration (WPA), and the Agricultural Adjustment Administration (AAA). These "alphabet agencies" mark the first real dependence of the state on federal spending in the 20th century, a reliance that would only build.

Since World War II, Montana can be characterized by a slow shift from an economy that relied on the extraction of natural resources to one that is service-based. Such traditional industries as copper, petroleum, coal, and timber have suffered wild market fluctuations and unstable employment patterns. Agriculture has remained Montana's primary industry throughout the era. Tourism supplanted mining as the state's second-largest industry in the early 1970s. This era also saw an important shift in the state's transportation system from railroads to cars, trucks, and highways.

Montana's history contributes to its current way of life. Gone are the days of the Wild West, but each year thousands of visitors flock to see a real ghost town or an Indian battlefield. Large ranching operations hark back to the days of the cowboy, and the same rivers Lewis and Clark navigated now provide a thrilling ride to white-water boaters.

WYOMING

Like Montana, Wyoming is a young state with a long history. Both states share many of the same historical traits—cowboys and Indians, cattle barons and miners, railroads and ranching. As the least populous state in the union, some parts of Wyoming have remained unchanged since the first settlers came into the area, allowing those who live and visit here today a glimpse into the state's rich and varied past.

Geology and Early Life-Forms

Much like Montana, Wyoming's geologic history includes the creation of the Rocky Mountains and the impact of glaciers on the landscape. Of course, Yellowstone National Park is the state's biggest geologic claim to fame, created when a series of three massive volcanic explosions—2.1 million, 1.3 million, and 640,000 years ago—spewed gases and hot ash across North America. Some experts suggest the most recent blast alone was more than 10,000 times larger than the well-known 1980 eruption of Mount St. Helens in Washington. Geothermal forces are still at work underneath Yellowstone's surface, giving the park its trademark geysers, hot springs, fumaroles, and mud pots, making it the earth's most active geothermal area.

Wyoming is also a hotbed for dinosaur fossils. A fossil of a giant allosaurus—among the first meat-eating dinosaurs—was found in 1991, providing valuable insight into this carnivore that roamed the earth during the Jurassic period 130-190 million years ago. The excellent Wyoming Dinosaur Museum (www.wyodino.org) in Thermopolis features more than 200 displays and more than 30 mounted skeletons of various dinosaurs. Fossils of fish, insects, birds, plants, and reptiles are on display at the Fossil Butte National Monument, a 50-million-year-old lake bed near Kemmerer that holds the largest deposit of freshwater fish fossils in the Western Hemisphere.

By most accounts, humans have inhabited what is now Wyoming for at least 13,000 years. Stone fossils have been found that indicate the presence of early human cultures, including the Plano, a tribe of hunter-gatherers that inhabited the Great Plains 9000-6000 BC. There is also evidence of the Clovis culture, people that lived in the area nearly 13,000 years ago. Their distinctive bone and ivory "Clovis points" have been found in both Wyoming and Montana.

An interesting, but still somewhat mysterious discovery in Wyoming was the Bighorn Medicine Wheel in the north-central part of the state. This giant stone ring is thought to have been sacred to indigenous people and believed to have been used for astronomical, teaching, and healing purposes. Constructed between 900 and 700 years ago, the Bighorn wheel is 80 feet (24.4 m) in diameter and is one of the best-preserved stone rings in the world.

Native Americans and Mountain Men

As in Montana, Plains Indians didn't move into the area until the early 1600s, when Native Americans around the Great Lakes and Canadian plains were forced west. The arrival of horses and rifles created nomadic hunters who followed the massive herds of buffalo, and the culture began to change as villages grew larger and tribes had more interaction. Indian society grew more turbulent by the 19th century, and it was soon greeted by early American explorers who sought control of the state's vast geographic and natural resources.

Although French explorers crossed into northern Wyoming in the mid-1700s, two of the most famous names in Wyoming's early history are John Colter and Jim Bridger. Colter, a member of the Lewis and Clark expedition, was most likely the first person of European descent to enter the region in 1807, and he gave birth to the term *mountain man*. He explored what would become Yellowstone National Park and was one of the first nonnatives to see the Grand Tetons, spending a winter alone in the wilderness as he recorded his discoveries. Colter's most legendary story is when he escaped from a group of Blackfeet, running naked and evading capture for 12 days.

Another mountain man, Jim Bridger, had a profound effect on Wyoming's early frontier days in the 19th century. Bridger established the Rocky Mountain Fur Company in 1830 and spent the next 30 years in the West as a fur trader and guide, establishing a trading post on the banks of Wyoming's Green River. Bridger married Indian women—the last being the daughter of Shoshone chief Washakie—and discovered new trading routes, including shortcuts on the Oregon and Bozeman Trails. He later served as a U.S. Army guide and scout in their campaign against the Sioux and Cheyenne, who were attacking parties along the Bozeman Trail.

Blazing Trails Across the State

The famous Oregon Trail passed through central and southern Wyoming on its way from Missouri to the Northwest. Today, Wyoming contains the longest and least-changed stretch of trail—487 miles (790 km)—that can be recreated by traveling on various state and federal highways. The Oregon Trail was one of the main trading routes for those migrating west and used by an estimated 400,000 people. Large wagon trains left Missouri as early as 1841 and usage peaked in 1850, but the trail practically disappeared when the first transcontinental railroad was completed in 1869.

With the arrival of the railroad, population gradually began to increase, and the Wyoming Territory was created in 1869. Yellowstone was made the first national park in 1872, and visitors slowly started trickling in from the East. Coal was discovered near Rock Springs in 1885, but no large deposits of

minerals like gold or silver were ever discovered. Wyoming's lack of a gold rush limited its population growth, but in 1890 the territory was officially recognized as the 44th state.

Wyoming played a large role in the women's suffrage movement, being the first to grant women the right to vote in 1869. Wyoming also had the first female justice of the peace, the first female court bailiff, and the first female governor in the country.

Livestock and Energy

The devastation of the West's bison herds and the subsequent placement of Native Americans on reservations led to the development of what would become Wyoming's hallmark industry in the late 19th century: cattle. Millions of cattle were driven into Wyoming in the 1870s and 1880s, and cattle barons soon dominated the natural and political landscape, basically buying off any and all forms of government. Sheep soon followed, taking advantage of vast tracts of grasslands, and by 1902 there were more than six million sheep roaming throughout Wyoming. Conflicts between sheepherders and cattlemen often escalated into violence, but these died down as the government enacted policies and divided up the land.

Wyoming's first oil well was drilled in 1884, and by the time of the first oil boom in 1908, the state was pumping out nearly 18,000 barrels per year. Production continued to climb, peaking in 1970, when more than 150 million barrels were pumped. It has mostly declined since then, leveling off at around 51-55 million barrels per year. But in 2014, another boom bounced production up to 69 million barrels of crude oil annually. And in 2017, production topped 75 million barrels. The boom-and-bust oil cycle of the 1970s and 1980s had a profound effect in Wyoming as so-called oil-patch towns like Green River, Rock Springs, and Casper grew rapidly on the promise of high-paying oil jobs, then fell flat as the industry bubble collapsed in the early 1980s. The bust left many of these cities struggling to survive.

After its peak in the 1970s, the oil industry in Wyoming was surpassed by coal, of which the state is still the nation's leading producer. In 2012, the state provided 40 percent of the country's coal. Much of the coal is located in the Powder River Basin and used for coal-fired power plants. The state produced more than 438 million tons of coal in 2011—a decrease from 2010—but still has billions, maybe even trillions, of tons in reserves. But the bust is obvious. Massive mine layoffs in 2016, plus bankruptcy filings for two of the largest coal producers, are in line with the 32 percent decrease in production from 2014 to 2015. After more than 1,000 layoffs in 2016, and significant population reductions in Wyoming's biggest mining towns, only five full-time mining jobs were added in Wyoming in 2017. Things don't look good for the mining industry in Wyoming at present.

The natural gas boom of the first decade of the 21st century seems to be over as well, with production falling seven years in a row starting in 2009. Production decreases in Wyoming can be attributed to several things: plummeting prices for natural gas, increased stores nationwide, aging wells, and perhaps most of all, an inability to compete with the cheaper production costs back East via fracking.

Even wind power, on the rise nationally as a clean and cheap source of energy, hit a wall in Wyoming in 2015. Despite the state's natural windiness, no new capacity was been added since 2010 because of the expense of building transmission lines. The production is easy, but how to get it moved out of state? Other issues besides transmission have stalled further development of wind energy production. The U.S. Fish and Wildlife Service offered to not prosecute wind producers for eagle deaths that come as a result of the turbines. The permits they wanted to dole out would have been good for 30 years, but a federal judge in California said the repercussions of that had not been carefully analyzed and limited the permits to five years. There are also tax credits that have expired and other things that make profit from wind production less certain. Even with the hurdles, researchers from the Wind Energy Research Center at the University of Wyoming expect as much as 5,000 megawatts of new wind power could take form over the next five to seven years, an amount three times the power potential of the state's current fleet of wind projects. Currently underway is an estimated $8 billion project near Rawlins and the Transwest Express transmission lines that will carry the power to the Southwest. The first half of the wind farm and a lower capacity version of the transmission line are expected to be functional by 2021. Several others are in the works as well.

Just as people migrated west and settled in Wyoming hundreds of years ago, people today come to visit Yellowstone National Park, travel the Oregon Trail, or climb one of the majestic peaks of the Teton Mountains. Tourism is now the state's second-largest industry, worth more than $3.5 billion annually. Wyoming saw 8.7 million visitors in 2017, nearly doubling the national average visitation growth rate. Visitation in Wyoming has gone up 48 percent in the last decade. Towns like Jackson Hole and Cody reap the benefits of being adjacent to Yellowstone, while the park itself attracts more than four million visitors annually.

Like Montana, Wyoming's balance among energy development, agriculture, and tourism is the face of the New West, where people move for a better quality of life while still trying to preserve the cultural heritage. Just like the settlers who established trading posts hundreds of years ago, these new immigrants are chasing a dream of living in an unspoiled part of the world and doing anything necessary to pay the bills. As you explore Wyoming, you'll notice that history is never far behind, and that the future holds unlimited possibilities.

Government

MONTANA

Montana became a territory in 1864 and was named the 41st state in 1889. Originally, the state's constitution reflected the mining and timber interests that seemed to run daily life in the early years, but in 1972 Montanans held a second Constitutional Convention, where the earlier, dated document was replaced with a more populist set of laws that placed more responsibility on the individual voter and made significant strides in protecting Montana's environment.

Montana granted women the right to vote in 1914, and two years later elected the first woman representative to the U.S. Congress. Jeannette Rankin, a lifelong pacifist and the only member of Congress to vote against entering World War II, is still the only woman Montana has elected to Congress. She served one term, worked as a lobbyist in Washington DC for 20 years, and then was elected again to Congress in 1940. Her antiwar stance fell out of favor, and she served one more term before retiring.

The Montana State Legislature is a bicameral body that meets in Helena each odd-numbered year for no longer than 90 days. It consists of a 100-member House and a 50-seat Senate. Montana is often characterized as a swing state, and the legislature has been split along party lines consistently throughout its history, especially since the new state constitution was enacted in 1972. Both parties have enjoyed similar successes over the years, and the legislature often changes hands. Montana's term-limits law survived in 2004 when 70 percent of voters shot down a measure that would have repealed term limits in the state legislature. Originally passed in 1992, the law limits representatives to four two-year terms and senators to two four-year terms. However, the term limit is for consecutive, not lifetime, terms.

Montana's postwar politics have seen some remarkable national politicians, including Mike Mansfield, Lee Metcalf, and Pat Williams. Democrat Mansfield was the longest-serving majority leader of the U.S. Senate (1961-1977) and the U.S. ambassador to Japan for more than a decade. Lee Metcalf, another Democrat, was instrumental in creating three new wilderness areas in Montana. The Lee Metcalf Wilderness Area was named for his efforts in 1983, after his death. Williams was yet another Democrat who had a hand in expanding wilderness designation and served in the U.S. House 1979-1997.

Present-day Montana politicians are also gaining notoriety on the national scene. Former governor Brian Schweitzer is a Democrat who appeals to members of both parties. In fact, his running mate in 2004 was Republican John Bohlinger. Schweitzer is known for his down-to-earth persona and in 2008 gave a speech at the Democratic National Convention that was widely acclaimed. Senator Max Baucus, a Democrat, served in the U.S. Senate 1978-2014 and, as chair of the Senate Committee on Finance, played a pivotal role in the debate over health care reform. Baucus was the U.S. ambassador to China under President Obama until 2017. Montana's current governor, Steve Bullock, is also a Democrat. Montana has two senators, one Republican and one Democrat, and a single representative in Congress, who is a Republican. Since the state has recently crossed the one million mark in population, a second congressional representative should be on the horizon.

By some accounts, Montana is becoming a "purple" state on the national scene—once primarily red but slowly turning blue. Maybe. Montanans have voted for the Republican presidential candidate in every election since 1968, except when they chose Democrat Bill Clinton over Republican George H. W. Bush in 1992. In 2008, Montana voters gave John

Changing Politics

The political history of Montana and Wyoming is as colorful as the Wild West and has changed over the years to reflect the shifting population, economy, and culture that exist here.

Wyoming's political history is a study in contrasts. It was the first state to grant women the right to vote—in 1869, nearly 50 years before Montana did!—and the first state to elect a woman as governor. Yet the state remains largely conservative and has only voted for one Democratic president since 1960 (Lyndon B. Johnson in 1964). Even though more than half of Wyoming's residents consider themselves Republicans, and Republicans have held a majority in the state senate continuously since 1936 and in the state house since 1964, Democrats have owned the governor's seat for all but 14 years since 1975. Democratic governor Dave Freudenthal, in office 2002-2011, had one of the highest approval ratings in the country. Still, as recently as 2017, a Gallup poll ranked Wyoming the most conservative state in the country.

As in many states in the West, Democratic strongholds tend to exist in slightly more urban areas or areas that have a large number of transplants and a younger population. In Wyoming, Teton County is the only reliably Democratic county, which is no surprise as it includes Jackson Hole. The town's population has boomed over the years, boosted by younger transplants from more liberal parts of the country who come for the skiing, fly-fishing, and outdoor lifestyle the town offers.

Montana is a little harder to figure out. At first glance, it may come across as a decidedly Republican state, but its history shows that both parties have had successes. Montana lagged behind Wyoming in the women's suffrage movement, but Montanan Jeannette Rankin became the first woman elected to the U.S. Congress in 1916 as a Republican.

Sometimes characterized as a swing state, Montana has had long-term shifts in party control throughout its history. Five of its first six governors were Democrats, and between 1952 and 1984 it elected only Democratic senators. Republicans held the governorship 1953-1969 and again 1989-2005, with current Democratic governor Steve Bullock elected in 2012. In the 2000 election, Republican Judy Martz became the first woman governor of Montana.

The swing-state nature of Montana continues today. Montana overwhelmingly supported George W. Bush in 2000 and 2004, and Mitt Romney in 2012, and Donald Trump in 2016. As of 2018 Montana's U.S. senators were Republican and Democrat. A big change came in 2006 when Democrat John Tester defeated longtime senator Conrad Burns, one of the crucial races that allowed the party to regain control of the U.S. Senate. Montana's lone U.S. representative, Greg Gianforte, is a Republican. Montanans last supported a Democratic president in 1992 (Bill Clinton), although in 2008 the margin was just 2 percent in favor of Republican John McCain.

As university towns like Bozeman and Missoula gain population and the state's economy shifts toward tourism and the high-tech industry, Montana may become a purple state. The lines between political parties are becoming blurred but seem to be shifting slowly toward blue. But then again, as history has proved, it may only last so long.

McCain a narrow margin—just over 2 percent—over Barack Obama. The 2012 election results from Montana swayed much more heavily on the side of Mitt Romney over President Obama. In 2016, Donald Trump won by a landslide in Montana, 56.5 percent to Secretary Clinton's 36 percent.

An easy characterization of the shift in politics follows the state's population trends. The eastern part of the state—more rural, less industrialized—is more Republican but is losing population. The western part of Montana, from Bozeman west toward Butte and Missoula, is seeing rapid population expansion and more liberal influences taking root. Many observers argue that the younger, more intellectual western part of the state will soon "take over" Montana politics. Only time will tell.

WYOMING

Wyoming Territory was formed in 1869, but the road to statehood did not begin until 1888. After a few statehood bills failed to pass, the

House finally approved the bill on March 27, 1890, making Wyoming the 44th state after President Benjamin Harrison signed the bill into law soon after. Its capital is Cheyenne.

During the territorial era, the Wyoming Legislature played a pivotal role in the U.S. suffrage movement. In 1869, just 4 years after the Civil War and 35 years before women's suffrage became a highly visible political issue in the United States, Wyoming granted all women age 21 and older the right to vote; the territorial government was the first in the world to secure this right for women. Democrat Nellie Tayloe Ross became the first female governor in the country when she won a special election in 1924 after then-governor William Ross died in office. She later became the first woman to serve as director of the U.S. Mint, appointed in 1933 by President Franklin D. Roosevelt, a position she held until her retirement in 1953.

Like Montana, Wyoming remains one of the few states that has a true part-time citizen legislature, meaning its members don't enjoy the same accommodations provided to full-time legislators in larger states. As of 2017, for example, legislators were paid just $150 per day, when convening, and a proposal to raise payment to $175 per day was rejected. There are 60 state representatives elected for two-year terms along with 30 state senators that serve four-year terms. There are no term limits. The state legislature meets in odd-numbered years beginning the second Tuesday in January. The general session is limited to 40 legislative days. The offices of governor, secretary of state, auditor, treasurer, and superintendent of public instruction are all elected every four years.

The Wyoming Legislature passed a bill limiting the office of governor to two consecutive terms after Democrat Edgar Herschler served three terms in the mid-1980s. In 1992 voters approved term limits in a ballot initiative, but neither action constituted an amendment to the Wyoming constitution. In 2004 two state legislators challenged the term-limit law in the courts, and the Wyoming Supreme Court subsequently invalidated the limits in a unanimous decision, ruling that a constitutional amendment would be required to establish such a law. Popular Democrat Dave Freudenthal, who served two terms as governor after being elected in 2002 and 2006, did not use the same challenge to seek a third term.

Freudenthal's election and popularity—his approval rating was a staggering 82 percent in the months before the 2010 election—defy Wyoming's Republican nature. In fact, the governorship in general has seen its fair share of Democrats, but Republicans have dominated both houses of the legislature almost since statehood. Wyoming has only voted for one Democratic president in the last half century (Lyndon B. Johnson in 1964), and Republicans have held a majority in the state senate continuously since 1936 and in the state house since 1964. Despite its tendency to elect Democrats as governor—though current governor Matt Mead is a Republican—Wyoming is considered a red state at the national level and was named the country's most conservative state in a 2017 Gallup poll.

Dick Cheney is Wyoming's best-known political figure. Born in Casper, Cheney was the White House chief of staff during the Nixon and Ford administrations and was then elected to the U.S. House of Representatives in 1978. He served five terms and was then selected to be the secretary of defense during the first Bush presidency and later served as the vice president 2001-2009 under George W. Bush. In 2016, his daughter, Republican Liz Cheney, ran for Wyoming's lone seat in the U.S. House of Representatives and won. Despite the fact that Donald Trump earned only 7 percent of the Republican primary vote, behind Ted Cruz at 66.3 percent and Marco Rubio at 19.5 percent, he beat Hillary Clinton handily with 70.1 percent of the vote to her 22.5 percent.

The Wind River Indian Reservation is home to the Eastern Shoshone Tribal Government, a sovereign government that operates under its own constitution. The Business Council of the Eastern Shoshone Tribe consists of a chair, vice chair, and four additional council members who are elected by the tribe. The tribal council chair is the administrative head of the tribe and serves a two-year term with the vice chairman and the other members of the council. Both the Eastern Shoshone and Northern Arapaho are represented.

INDIAN RESERVATIONS

The Native American population plays an important role in both Montana and Wyoming government and politics. Tribal law prevails within reservation boundaries, and Indian reservations are federally recognized as independent political units with their own structure and legislation. As sovereign nations, tribes can have their own school systems, constitutions, police and court systems, and legislative councils. They can also regulate transport and trade within reservation boundaries. The state can't tax land or transactions that occur on reservations.

What does this mean to the visitor? Essentially, some state laws may not apply on reservations. Goods and services—mainly gasoline and tobacco—can be much cheaper on the reservations since there are no state taxes enforced. Not all land may be open to the public, and there may be additional fees for recreation, including hunting and fishing. It's best to inquire at a local store or gas station if you are traveling on reservation land in Montana or Wyoming.

Economy

MONTANA

Montana was founded on rural traditions and industries: farming, ranching, mining, and forestry. To a large extent, these industries are still dominant. Agriculture is one of the state's leading industries, with large-scale farming and ranching operations responsible for more than $4.58 billion in income in 2017 on 27,100 farms and ranches. In 2017, the number one export from Montana was cigarettes, up more than 18 percent from 2016. Other top cash crops include wheat, hay, barley, lentils, sugar beets, corn, oats, cherries, and seed potatoes. Beef cattle dominate the ranching sector, although hogs, sheep, dairy cattle, llamas, and horses are also raised. It should be noted that there are about three cows for every person in Montana.

Cities like Butte and Helena benefited from the mining boom of the late 19th and early 20th centuries. Butte was once one of the richest cities in the country, spurred by the large amount of copper in the area. Today, mining and resource extraction are a dwindling part of Montana's economy, even though its coal reserves are the largest in the nation, and the mountain ranges of central, southern, and western Montana hold large ore deposits of copper, gold, lead, silver, and zinc. The Stillwater Mine in Columbus is the only palladium and platinum producer in the country. Montana is the 7th-largest producer of coal in the nation and 13th in crude oil production. As of 2017, mining made up 6.1 percent of Montana's GDP.

Tourism is Montana's second-ranked and fastest-growing industry. An estimated 12.2 million visitors in 2017 generated $3.29 billion in income for the state. The nonresident travel industry in Montana accounts for roughly 53,000 jobs and makes up 7.3 percent of the state's GDP.

The timber industry has played a large and important part in Montana's economic growth but has fallen on hard times. Montana lumber production in 2009 was the lowest since the end of World War II. The number of solid-wood sawmills has decreased from 30 to 8 over the last three decades. Lumber prices roared back in 2017, 22 percent higher than the previous year's prices because of a strong housing market and the reconstruction of hurricane-damaged properties in the South.

Other industries that contribute significantly to Montana's economic output are construction, the retail trade, real estate, health care, education, and government. Montana also has a growing high-tech sector, particularly in Bozeman, Missoula, and Kalispell. The universities in Missoula and Bozeman are two of the state's largest employers, as are Costco, First Interstate Bank, Northwestern Energy, and Town Pump. Many of the top 20 employers are in the health care field—including hospitals and clinics in Billings, Great Falls, Kalispell, Missoula, Bozeman, and Helena. There were more than 91,200 government—local, state, and federal—employees in June 2018.

A remarkably strong economy in 2015 did not carry into 2016, in part due to continued deterioration in energy and natural resources. Inflation-corrected wages for the first half of 2016 grew only 1.6 percent, as opposed to 5.5 percent in the second half of 2015. In the same period, the U.S. GDP was barely growing at 1 percent. The biggest losses were in the mining industry which saw wages decline by 19.3 percent the first half of 2016. Broad patterns that began in 2014 suggest growth in the more populous western counties in the state, driven by a sizable, and widening, list of industries.

WYOMING

The economy in Wyoming is similar to Montana's in that natural resource extraction, agriculture, and tourism play major roles. Oil production and coal and natural gas extraction fell dramatically in the middle part of the decade, making Wyoming's economy one of only four states in the country to shrink in the first half of 2015. In 2017, Wyoming current-dollar GDP was $40.3 billion, compared to $36.3 billion in 2007, ranking the state 49th and 46th respectively in the U.S. Growth of the real GDP in 2017 hit 2 percent, compared to 2.1 percent change nationally for 2016-2017. In 2017, Wyoming's largest industry was still

mining, quarrying, and oil and gas extraction, which accounted for 23.3 percent of the state's GDP and had 12.7 percent real growth. Government and government enterprises were the second-largest industry, accounting for 15.5 percent of the GDP, and showed a 2.2 percent real decline.

Tourism is still one of the largest contributors of tax revenue to the state. Since 2005, tax revenues generated by tourism and hospitality in Wyoming have grown by 86 percent. In 2017, 8.7 million people visited the state, up 2.4 percent from 2016. Travel spending topped out at $3.6 billion in 2017, up 8.5 percent over the previous year. Yellowstone and Grand Teton National Parks play a big role in tourism for the state, adding more than four million visitors annually.

Since most of Wyoming can be classified as rural, it's no surprise that agriculture plays a vital role in the state's economy—more than $1 billion in cash receipts annually every year since 2010. There are more than 11,600 farms and ranches operating in Wyoming, occupying 30.4 million acres (12.3 million hectares). Wyoming ranks 11th nationally in total land in farms and ranches, and 1st in the United States for the average size of farms and ranches. The number of ranches and farms peaked at more than 18,000 in the 1930s, then slowly declined, but the industry has leveled off in the past few decades and is now starting to grow again.

Hay is the leading crop in Wyoming in terms of value, with 2.48 million tons produced in 2017, followed by sugar beets, barley, corn, wheat, and dry beans. Dryland winter wheat is grown primarily in the eastern part of the state. Other more specialized commodities in the state include oats, hogs, bison, and sunflowers.

The cattle industry produces the largest agricultural commodity—mainly beef cattle—and dates back to the mid-1880s, when settlers first came to the West. After the Civil War, cattle ranching flourished, and Cheyenne became a world trade center for the beef industry.

Wind Power: Wyoming's Next Boom?

Having prospered from the boom and then endured the bust of energy production cycles count-less times over the last century or more, Wyoming is at the forefront of a new boom, this one based on what has for eons been at the center of the state's frequently harsh climate: wind. Wind power technology as we now know it started in the early 1980s. As the seventh-windiest state, ac-cording to the American Wind Energy Association, Wyoming ranks 15th in installed wind capacity, and the numbers are growing slowly but steadily. In 2017, wind energy provided 9.4 percent of all in-state electricity production, or enough to power 408,700 homes. In addition to constant wind, the vast tracts of public land and low population density make Wyoming an ideal wind energy producer. Benefits of wind power to Wyoming include jobs and electricity produced without greenhouse gases. The DOE Wind Vision Scenario projects that wind energy from Wyoming could power the equivalent of 3.4 million average American homes by 2030.

However, the challenge is trying to sell that wind energy to major urban areas that need it, such as Las Vegas and locations in California and Arizona. The distances are vast, and as of 2018, there is still a significant lack of transmission capacity. A consortium of companies, some of them affiliates of the privately held Anschutz Corp., which is building the biggest wind farm in the country in Carbon County, are proposing the building of three major transmission lines—Transwest Express, Zephyr, and Gateway West—to send the energy to the Southwest and California.

Spend a few days in Wyoming, particularly in the southern half of the state, and you will agree it has some of the most consistent wind in the country. The state has the highest per capita wind-power capacity in the country, followed by Minnesota in 2nd place and Montana in 18th place. In 2018, there were over 1,000 wind turbines installed in Wyoming, according to the American Wind Energy Association, and hundreds more were under construction. Estimates put the eventual tally as high as 10,000 towers across the state, which will clearly change the landscape of Wyoming.

Somewhat controversially, Wyoming is the first state to put a tax on wind energy production. Proposed by Governor Dave Freudenthal, the $1 per megawatt hour tax went into effect in 2012 after a sales tax exemption for renewable energy projects expired in 2011. In its first year alone, the tax generated roughly $2.6 million for the state. As of 2017, more than $18 million in revenue had been collected. Experts expect this number to grow significantly as the state's ability to sell and transport the energy expands. The crux of the controversy is that some feel this makes Wyoming unfriendly to wind power producers, but the governor and his supporters argued that the produc-ers are going to make a lot of money but that Wyomingites will bear the environmental—primarily visual—and socioeconomic burden. They point to the benefits gained statewide by tax revenues from oil, gas, coal, and coal-bed methane.

As the wind power boom takes off, there is something of a land rush in southeastern Wyoming, where the greatest number of wind farms exist, transforming the local agricultural and ranching culture. In an effort to prevent bad deals with a strength-in-numbers approach, ranchers and farmers have joined together to form associations to bargain collectively. One of a dozen or so such cooperatives, the Bordeaux Wind Energy Association asserts that everyone is going to be impacted, whether the turbines are on their property or not, so everyone should benefit. Just as the massive wind turbines are undoubtedly altering the landscape of Wyoming, so too are the proactive ranchers and farmers working together to transform the business of agriculture. Indeed, income from wind farms can often be the deciding factor in whether a family can hold on to their ranch or not. As a result, some argue that wind farms are in fact strengthening Wyoming's agricultural tradition by keeping farmers and ranchers on their land.

Wyoming's high plains and mountain meadows are recognized for their role in pro-ducing high-quality sheep. According to the National Agricultural Statistics Service, in 2017 Wyoming ranked fourth in the country in stock sheep and the lamb crop, and third in wool production. Wyoming's wool is among the most desirable in the world.

The University of Wyoming is the largest government employer in the state with 5,225 jobs. The largest private employers are Rio Tinto Energy America with 1,795 employees, the Powder River Coal Co. with 1,459 employees, and the Cheyenne Regional Medical Center with 1,324 employees. In 2017, Wyoming's per capita personal income was $56,724, 113 percent above the national average. A vast departure from Montana, whose per capita income ranked 35th in the country in 2017, Wyoming ranked 8th in the United States in the same year. In May 2018, Wyoming's unemployment rate was 3.7 percent, compared to the national average of 3.9 percent.

Local Culture

Since Montana and Wyoming are two of the newest states in the union (41st and 44th, respectively), it's no surprise that their people and culture are largely tied to the settling of the West and the Native Americans who inhabited the area. It wasn't until the 1860s that settlers started building permanent communities—both were some of the last states to see an influx of outsiders—as the gold rush, the railroad, and the Homestead Act lured those seeking a different and potentially lucrative way of life. Many areas were settled by immigrants and still retain their European heritage.

Both are largely considered conservative states, and both have a population that is around 90 percent Caucasian—89 percent for Montana and 93 percent for Wyoming. More than 10 percent of Wyoming's population is listed as Hispanic or Latino in origin, while less than 4 percent is listed as Hispanic in Montana. In Montana, more than 6 percent of the population is Native American.

NATIVE AMERICANS

Although farming, ranching, and natural resource extraction certainly contributed to the growing cultural landscape, it's the rich Native American history that gives these states a proud and colorful representation of the past that transcends today's modern American culture. Before trappers and settlers came west, Indian people roamed freely across the land, following the huge bison herds that once covered the plains. Each tribe has unique customs and traditions. While Native Americans have worked to adapt to the changing world around them, they have also tried to keep the culture and traditions of their past alive. Their culture is celebrated through dance, songs, games, language, and religious ceremonies. This rich heritage contributes to the distinct flavors of Montana and Wyoming.

There are several museums in each state that pay tribute to the American Indian, and many reservation towns host annual powwows, rodeos, and celebrations. Today, 6.6 percent of Montana's population and 2.7 percent of Wyoming's are classified as Native American.

There are 11 different tribes represented in Montana, the majority living on seven different reservations. There is only one reservation in Wyoming, which is home to two different tribes. The following is a list of the Native American groups and the reservations that they inhabit today.

Blackfeet

The 1.5-million-acre (607,028-hectare) Blackfeet Reservation is in northwestern Montana along the eastern slopes of the Rocky Mountains, bordered on the north by Canada and on the west by Glacier National Park. More than 16,500 members make up the tribe, with about 10,405 living on or near the reservation. The Blackfeet are thought to have acquired their name from the characteristic black color of their moccasins, painted or darkened with ashes, and once inhabited land near the Great Lakes before they migrated west. During this migration, the various tribes of

Climbing the Alphabet

One of the things you'll notice fairly quickly when driving around Montana is the seemingly end-less number of large white letters on the hillsides or mountains. These hillside letters—sometimes called "geoglyphs" or "mountain monograms"—are a source of pride for many Montana localities, and in most cases highlight the first letter of the adjacent town, school, or university. Over the years the letters have become not just visible landmarks but cultural ones as well.

Montana has the largest number of hillside letters in the country, almost 90 that represent everything from Anaconda to Whitehall. The most popular hillside letter is the M in Missoula, which sits about halfway up Mount Sentinel overlooking the University of Montana campus. It's a moderate 1.5-mile (2.4-km) hike up a well-used trail and provides a panoramic view of the Clark Fork and Bitterroot Rivers and the surrounding mountains. On Saturdays in the fall, the M is often packed with students watching the football game—it offers a great aerial view of the 25,000-seat stadium.

The largest letter is the M in Bozeman, which represents Montana State University and is a popular hike for residents and visitors. The 200-foot (61-m) letter sits on a steep hillside on the south end of the Bridger Mountains, accessed by a trail that is also the start of the 21-mile (34-km) Bridger Mountains National Recreational Trail.

The M in Butte is actually electric, and the C near Cut Bank is one of the smallest letters in the state. The town of Anaconda actually has two letters: a C for Central High School and an A for the town's name. Even the tiny towns of Bainville and Froid—population 153 and 195, respectively—in northeastern Montana have letters. The town of Brockton has three letters—BHS—that represent the local high school. And Livingston, set amid the twists and turns of the Yellowstone, has a fish on its hillside to designate itself as the "trout capital of the world."

Montana isn't the only state with a plethora of hillside letters. It's a common sight throughout the West, with only a few erected east of the Mississippi River and nearly all of them built in a community-wide effort. Most are made of painted rocks or concrete, some are just painted on existing rock faces, and others are cut out of the vegetation. Wyoming has 22 letters at last count.

The first letter to appear in the West was the C that overlooks the University of California, Berkeley, built in 1905. Missoula's M was built in 1908, originally of rocks, then again with wood in 1912. A blizzard destroyed that one in 1915, and it was replaced by a whitewashed granite letter that lasted until 1968, when the current concrete M was erected. Each fall the letter is lit up at the homecoming football game to welcome former students back to campus.

An interesting read on this subject is Evelyn Corning's *Hillside Letters A to Z: A Guide to Hometown Landmarks*, which explains the history of 60 letters in 14 Western states.

the Blackfeet joined together to form the Blackfeet Confederacy, made up of the Piegans, the Bloods, and the Northern Blackfeet. Soon they became one of the largest and most feared Indian tribes and were great hunters of the buffalo that roamed the northern plains. The Blackfeet were notoriously leery of the settlers moving into their territory.

A worthy detour on the reservation is the Museum of the Plains Indian in Browning, where a permanent exhibit displays artifacts of the Northern Plains Indians and two spe-cial galleries feature rotating presentations.

Crow

The Crow Indian Reservation is the fifth-larg-est reservation in the United States, home to nearly 7,900 residents on its 2.2 million acres (890,308 hectares) south of Billings. The tribe originally lived in the Great Lakes region, but was one of the first to enter Montana in the early 1600s. The tribe was called Apsáalooke, which means "children of the large-beaked bird," and are also called Absarokee. Today, nearly 85 percent of the tribe speaks Crow as their first language.

The Sacred Sun Dance

Very little is known about the Native American sun dance, a highly revered and often secretive traditional ceremony performed by various tribes in North America. In Montana, the Arapaho, Sioux, Assiniboine, Crow, and Blackfeet are among the nations that hold this practice sacred. The sun dance represents a spiritual rebirth and regeneration of the land. Participants acquire spiritual powers, often experiencing visions, and invoke blessings for the whole community. In 1875, Lakota chief Sitting Bull formed an alliance with the Cheyenne during a sun dance in which he had a vision of U.S. soldiers falling from the sky. Many saw his vision as foretelling the defeat of the U.S. Army at the Battle of the Little Bighorn in June 1876.

Although each tribe's sun dance has its own characteristics, there are some common elements. Sun dances involve construction of a lodge, dancing, singing, strict fasting among the dancers and subsequent feasting, the erection of a sacred pole, often body painting, and the sacrificial piercing of the chest or back. The sponsor of the dance, along with other leaders, works for months planning the event and performing certain critical rites beforehand. The sun dances themselves are known to last 3-8 days.

Before the introduction of reservation life, the sun dance ceremony provided an opportunity for the various hunting bands within a tribe to come together. Today, it serves a similar purpose in Native American communities. Often members travel from different regions of the country, and regardless of social status or religious affiliation, the sun dance provides an occasion for tribe members to reaffirm their cultural identity. Many would argue that important rituals such as the sun dance contribute to the longevity and preservation of Native American culture.

With the introduction of reservations and the determination of the U.S. government to assimilate Native Americans, many practices, including the sun dance, were banned in 1885. Some tribes did not continue with their rituals and ceremonies, and others did so in secret. When the Commission of Indian Affairs lifted the ban on ceremonies in 1934, certain tribes immediately returned to performing this sacred ceremony in public. The Shoshone in Wyoming had not lost the practice, for example, and they reintroduced it to the Crow. The 50th anniversary performance of the Crow sun dance was held in Pryor, Montana, in 1991. Among the Assiniboine and Sioux, the sun dance is done annually on the Fort Peck Indian Reservation.

Flathead

The Flathead Indian Reservation is home to the Confederated Salish and Kootenai Tribes, a combination of the Salish, Pend d'Oreille, and Kootenai. There are 7,443 registered members, with about 63 percent living on or near the reservation. The 1.3-million-acre (526,091-hectare) piece of land is in Montana between Missoula and Kalispell, north of I-90 among the majestic peaks of the Mission Mountains and along the shores of beautiful Flathead Lake, the largest natural freshwater lake west of the Mississippi.

These Salish-speaking people moved east from Columbia River valleys and adopted a way of life based on hunting bison while maintaining the religious and social traditions of the Northwest coast. They were generally friendly to settlers as they entered Montana.

Assiniboine

The Fort Belknap Reservation in north-central Montana is home to two tribes: the Assiniboine, or Nakoda, and the Gros Ventre. There are about 7,000 people in these two tribes spread over the 652,000-acre (263,855-hectare) reservation.

The Assiniboine originated in the Lake of the Woods and the Lake Winnipeg area of Canada and became allied with the Cree. A division between the two tribes happened in 1744, and some bands moved west into the valleys of the Assiniboine and Saskatchewan Rivers in Canada, while others moved south into the Missouri River valley. The tribes inhabited an area from Minnesota to Montana. The Assiniboine were typically large-game hunters, dependent on bison for a considerable part of their diet and living in tipis made from the animal's hide.

The 2-million-acre (809,371-hectare) Fort Peck Reservation is in northeastern Montana, 40 miles (64 km) west of the North Dakota border and 50 miles (81 km) south of the Canadian border, with the Missouri River defining its southern perimeter. About 6,800 Assiniboine and Sioux live on the reservation, with another 3,900 living off the reservation. Though separate, both tribes have similar languages that descended from the same language family.

Gros Ventre

The Gros Ventre are closely affiliated with the Algonquin-speaking Arapaho and Cheyenne. All three were among the last to migrate together into Montana, but they soon split up and went their separate ways. The Gros Ventre became allies of the Blackfeet, dominating the northern plains until settlers moved in and moved the tribe to Fort Belknap in 1878. About 4,000 people from two tribes live on the Fort Belknap Reservation.

Sioux

Nearly 6,800 Assiniboine and Sioux live on the 2-million-acre (809,371-hectare) Fort Peck Reservation in northeastern Montana, with another 3,900 living off the reservation. Though separate, both tribes have similar languages that descended from the same language family.

The Sioux is one of the largest and most famous Indian nations in North America, and its people are divided into three linguistic groups: the Dakota, the Lakota, and the Nakota. All were originally from Canada and didn't arrive in Montana until the beginning of the 19th century, where many settled around the Fort Peck area. Viewed by many as noble yet fearsome, the Sioux were excellent hunters and skilled warriors. The reservation was created in 1888, and today is home to a large industrial park and Fort Peck Community College. The Assiniboine and Sioux Cultural Center and Museum in Poplar

features fascinating displays of their history, arts, and crafts.

Northern Cheyenne

This 445,000-acre (180,085-hectare) reservation is located in southeastern Montana. The tribe comes from Algonquin linguistic ancestry and moved west from the Minnesota area under pressure from other tribes. Today there are more than 11,000 members of the Northern Cheyenne, with about 5,000 living on the reservation. An interesting stop if you're in the area is the St. Labre Indian School and Museum, established in 1884 by the Franciscan order. The building's visitors center, museum, and Ten Bear Gallery are important showplaces of Cheyenne heritage and art.

Chippewa-Cree

The 130,000-acre (52,609-hectare) Rocky Boy's Reservation near the Canadian border in north-central Montana provides a home for about 2,500 members of the Chippewa-Cree tribe. It's Montana's smallest reservation, and in 1916 it was the last to be established in the state. Historically, the Chippewa lived in bands on both sides of what now divides their homelands, the Canadian border and the Great Lakes region. The Cree territory extended from eastern Canada into what are now the provinces of Saskatchewan and Alberta. The tribes began their migrations west in the 1700s, and by the early 1890s they had united in Montana to find a permanent home. The term *Rocky Boy* comes from a misinterpretation of the Chippewa leader's name, Chief Stone Man.

Shoshone

Wyoming's Wind River Reservation, the seventh-largest in the country at more than 2.2 million acres (890,308 hectares), is home to more than 3,900 Eastern Shoshone and 8,600 Northern Arapaho. The Shoshone have been in Wyoming since the 16th century and were some of the first Indians to have horses. The eastern part of the tribe was pushed back west of the Laramie Mountains when their enemies—the Sioux, Crow, and Arapaho—invaded their territory.

Fort Washakie is home to the Shoshone Tribal Cultural Center and the cemeteries where both Shoshone chief Washakie and Lewis and Clark's Shoshone guide, Sacagawea, are buried. Originally called Fort Brown, the name was changed in 1878 to honor the chief who negotiated the treaty establishing the reservation. Ironically, the Shoshone ended up on the same reservation as their former enemies, the Arapaho, after the U.S. government temporarily placed them together—which soon became a permanent situation, betraying Chief Washakie's wishes to end the arrangement.

Arapaho

The Arapaho ended up on Wyoming's Wind River Reservation along with their former enemies, the Shoshone, after the U.S. government placed them together, supposedly temporarily. Today, Wind River is home to more than 3,900 Eastern Shoshone and 8,600 Northern Arapaho.

Like many tribes, the Arapaho were forced out of Minnesota after the arrival of settlers and migrated to the Great Plains in the late 18th century. After many years of trying to fight back against the settlers, the tribe was decimated by the late 1800s and ultimately forced onto a reservation with the Shoshone. The Heritage Center at St. Stephens and the Arapaho Cultural Museum in Ethete both provide insight into the tribe and its traditions.

THE ARTS

Montana and Wyoming are not just filled with cowboys and ungulates; in fact they boast vibrant and varied art scenes with an interesting and colorful history. Towns like Great Falls, Cody, and Jackson are meccas for Western art, while Missoula and Livingston have a decidedly literary bent. From books and music to landscape painting

and sculpture, both states have a remarkable range of fine art to discover.

Literature

Montana has an especially long list of literary heroes, both past and present. Andrew Garcia's *Tough Trip Through Paradise* may be the state's first famous export, a gripping firsthand account of the Nez Perce flight in the 1870s. The writing program at the University of Montana in Missoula—established in 1919 by H. G. Merriam—can largely be credited with putting Montana on the map; students and faculty have included A. B. Guthrie Jr., William Kittredge, Annick Smith, Kevin Canty, Judy Blunt, Rick DeMarinis, James Welch, Deirdre McNamer, and poet Richard Hugo. Contemporary authors that grew up in or call Montana home include Rick Bass (*For A Little While and Why I Came West*), Tom McGuane (*Ninety-Two in the Shade*), Richard Ford (*Independence Day*), Susan Henderson (The Flicker of Old Dreams), Walter Kirn (*Up in the Air*), Joanna Klink (Excerpts From a Secret Prophecy), Maile Meloy (Both Ways is the Only Way I Want It), Prageeta Sharma (Undergloom), Karen Volkman (Spar), and many more. There are thriving writing communities in Bozeman, Livingston, and Missoula, the last hosting the annual Montana Festival of the Book every October.

While Wyoming does not have quite the literary lore that Montana has, it has its share of standouts. Platte Valley resident C. J. Box is one of the top-selling mystery writers in the country, and Annie Proulx won a Pulitzer Prize for her novel *The Shipping News*. Other writers who call Wyoming home include James Galvin (The Meadow), Mark Spragg (*Where Rivers Change Direction*), Kathleen O'Neal Gear (*People of the Longhouse*), and Alexandra Fuller (Don't Let's Go to the Dogs Tonight). In addition, Ernest Hemingway spent a lot of time in Wyoming, where he worked on several novels, including *Death in the Afternoon* and the *Green Hills of Africa*.

Matthew Shepard and *The Laramie Project*

Born in Casper, Wyoming, in 1976, Matthew Shepard was a political science major and the student representative for the Wyoming Environmental Council during his first year at the University of Wyoming in Laramie. Long a champion for equality and an admired peer counselor in high school, Shepard was the kind of kid who wanted to change the world. Tragically, it was his brutal 1998 murder that effected the change Shepard worked to inspire during his short life.

On October 7, Shepard, who was gay, was abducted from a bar in Laramie by Aaron McKinney and Russell Henderson. The two men drove Shepard to a remote area east of town where they robbed and viciously beat their victim with the butt of a handgun. Likely unconscious from countless blows to the face and head, Shepard was tied to a fence and left to die. He was found 18 hours later by a bicyclist who at first mistook Shepard for a scarecrow. Matthew Shepard died on October 12 from his injuries without ever having regained consciousness. Both murderers confessed their crimes using a gay-panic defense strategy and are serving consecutive life sentences in unidentified prisons.

What was a horrific tragedy for Shepard's tight-knit family was seen around the world as a hate crime, inflicted upon the 21-year-old because he was gay. Shepard's parents, Dennis and Judy, created the Matthew Shepard Foundation (www.matthewshepard.org) to honor the memory of their son and to "replace hate with understanding, compassion and acceptance" through educational, outreach, and advocacy programs. Judy Shepard has turned her personal tragedy into a crusade for justice as she travels the world over, speaking on behalf of and advocating for lesbian, gay, bisexual, and transgender youth. To date, Judy has brought Matthew's message of acceptance to more than 300,000 people worldwide. In 2009, the Matthew Shepard and James Byrd Jr. Hate Crimes Prevention Act was passed into federal law, an expansion of the 1969 federal hate-crime law to include crimes motivated by a victim's actual or perceived gender, sexual orientation, gender identity, or disability. It was the first federal law to extend legal protection to transgendered people.

Another response to Shepard's murder was *The Laramie Project,* brought to fruition by Tectonic Theater Project. The small theater company traveled to Laramie and interviewed residents about the events surrounding Shepard's death. What they learned was transformed into a play, *The Laramie Project,* and eventually a movie of the same name that ran on HBO and was seen by more than 30 million people nationwide.

Ten years after the murder, Moisés Kaufman and other members of the theater company traveled back to Laramie to see if and how the community had been transformed by the passage of time. In October 2009, *The Laramie Project Epilogue* premiered across the country in major theaters, as well as at high schools and colleges. Another documentary project, *Matt Shepard is a Friend of Mine,* won an Emmy in 2016.

On the 20th anniversary of his murder, in 2018, Shepard's remains were interred at Washington National Cathedral. Activists say that the site is a symbol of the LGBT movement.

Fine Art

Not surprisingly, both Montana and Wyoming are hotbeds for Western art lovers. Two of the West's premier art events—Jackson's Fall Arts Festival and Cody's Rendezvous Royale— take place each September in Wyoming. Much of the Cody event centers around the Buffalo Bill Center of the West, which houses the impressive Whitney Gallery of Western Art. Collections here include works from the early 19th century to contemporary times that commemorate the events, people, and landscape of the Rocky Mountain region.

One of the best-known Western artists is Charles M. Russell (1864-1926), who left Missouri for Montana in 1880 at age 16. He soon became a working artist whose colorful and detailed scenes captured the landscape, spirit, and culture of the West during the late 1880s-early 1900s. Russell was also a sculptor and writer, and the excellent C. M. Russell Museum in Great Falls houses five galleries of paintings, sculptures, drawings, and illustrations that Russell created from childhood through the end of his life. Every March, around the artist's birthday, the city of Great Falls comes alive with art auctions, exhibitions, and events.

Two particularly art-themed towns are Bozeman, Montana, and Jackson, Wyoming. Both feature quaint streets lined with galleries and shops, offering everything from locally made stationery to the finest in Western photography, sculpture, and painting. The bustling college town of Bozeman is regionally known for its annual Sweet Pea Festival of the Arts and SLAM in August, and it also boasts a well-regarded symphony as well as jazz and opera performances. The Emerson Center for the Arts and Culture houses studios, galleries, classrooms, and restaurants along with a 700-seat theater in a refurbished two-story elementary school.

Jackson's 10-day Fall Arts Festival is home to one of the region's largest auctions, and the Grand Teton Music Festival hosts some of the world's finest classical musicians each summer in nearby Teton Village. Jackson is also home to the National Museum of Wildlife Art, which boasts more than 5,000 works in its permanent collection, and to the Jackson Hole Center for the Arts, a vibrant community center that offers everything from nationally touring musical and dance acts to educational workshops.

Although both states are well known for historical, landscape, and wildlife art, Montana in particular has its fair share of contemporary art galleries and museums. The Holter Museum in Helena, the Paris Gibson Square Museum in Great Falls, and the Yellowstone Art Museum in Billings have some of Montana's best contemporary works on display. The Archie Bray Foundation in Helena is nationally recognized for modern pottery creations from its resident artists, and the town of Livingston boasts "14 galleries and three stop lights" and is famous for its Friday-night, wine-filled art walks.

Performing Arts

Montana is home to numerous small-town theaters as well as the large theaters associated with the universities in Bozeman and Missoula. The Missoula Children's Theatre is nationally recognized, and year-round theaters can be found in many cities, including Billings, Missoula, Bozeman, and Whitefish. Theaters in West Yellowstone, Fort Peck, and Bigfork offer excellent summer programs, and the raucous Brewery Follies in historic Virginia City plays to sold-out crowds May-September.

In Wyoming, Jackson's Off Square Theatre Company is a vibrant year-round company founded in 1998, and Casper's Stage III offers six productions each year September-June. In downtown Sheridan, the historic WYO Theater—which opened in 1929 as the Lotus—was saved from demolition and refurbished, opening again in 1989 as a nonprofit organization. Today it offers an array of musical concerts and theater productions that belie its small-town setting. The University of Wyoming is home to one of the most outstanding undergraduate theater programs in the country along with the University of Wyoming Fine Arts Studio, where some of the region's finest facilities are located. Indirectly, Wyoming is probably best known in the theater world as the setting for *The Laramie Project,* an award-winning play depicting the reaction to the 1998 murder of gay University of Wyoming student Matthew Shepard in Laramie. The play was produced by the New York-based Tectonic Theater Project and was also made into an HBO film of the same name.

Montana Shakespeare in the Parks, a troupe based at the university in Bozeman, takes their show on the road each summer to rural communities in Montana and northern Wyoming. The performances are free and well regarded for their high quality, drawing actors for the cast from Chicago, Seattle, and Montana. Their plays are often summer highlights in small towns that may not see much cultural infusion the rest of the year.

For opera lovers, it doesn't get much better than Intermountain Opera Bozeman, a beloved local company that stages two remarkable productions in the spring and fall. Built under the guidance of renowned baritone Pablo Elvira, the company brings world-class talent from the Met, among others, to small-town Montana for performances in the fall and spring.

Music

While towns in Montana and Wyoming certainly don't have the hip music scenes larger cities may offer, there are plenty of tunes around to keep your toes tapping, especially in the summer. Many communities have free music nights, and local bars and taverns are usually good for a fun country band and the occasional touring act. In Montana, Billings and Missoula have the most offerings, including arena shows, nightclubs, and theaters. In Wyoming, Casper and Cheyenne are home to big arenas, while Cheyenne's Frontier Days rodeo offers nightly performances by favorite country music stars each July.

It seems nearly every small town across both states has a bluegrass festival during the summer, and Wyoming's Grand Targhee Bluegrass Festival is one of the nation's best. Other popular music festivals include Bozeman's Sweet Pea Festival, the Magic City Blues Festival, and Rockin' the Rivers, while Wyoming's Grand Teton Music Festival hosts classical concerts and workshops June-August. Newest on the scene, and stunning if you can get one of very few tickets, are the classical concerts at Tippet Rise Art Center in Fishtail, Montana.

Essentials

Transportation

GETTING THERE

Flying into Montana or Wyoming is easier than you think, and it's by far the best way to get here. Flights into the larger airports are becoming increasingly frequent as the region gains ground as an incredible destination for visitors. Although getting here by train or bus is possible, it's not as convenient, and stops can be far from the main travel areas—best left to hardy travelers or those on a tight budget. If you live in the West, driving to Montana or Wyoming is a great way to get here—major highways will carry you into the state, and

well-traveled back roads will lead you to your final destination.

By Air

In Wyoming, commercial flights are available to and from Casper, Cody, Gillette, Jackson, Laramie, Riverton, Rock Springs, and Sheridan. Jackson has the best service, with jet flights from Atlanta, Denver, Salt Lake City, Dallas, Houston, Chicago, Minneapolis, Phoenix, New York City, Newark, Washington DC, San Francisco, and Los Angeles. Some flights only operate during peak times in the winter and summer, and many people choose to fly into Salt Lake City (275 mi/445 km) or Idaho Falls (90 mi/145 km) and pick up a rental car for the scenic drive to Jackson. Major carriers with service to Wyoming include American, United, Frontier, and Delta.

In Montana, the cities of Billings, Bozeman, Kalispell, Helena, Butte, and Missoula are served by major carriers Delta, United, Alaska/Horizon, and Frontier, although some flights may be seasonal. Low-cost Allegiant Air offers direct flights to Phoenix or Las Vegas from Billings, Bozeman, Great Falls, Missoula, and Kalispell. Cape Air (www.capeair.com) has some flights from Billings on 19- or 32-seat turboprops to the smaller towns of Havre, Glasgow, Wolf Point, Sidney, and Glendive. West Yellowstone's airport is open late May-September and operates daily flights on Delta to and from Salt Lake City.

If budget is your top priority, be sure to look into flights into nearby airports. For travelers going to Bozeman, for example, sometimes flights in and out of Billings (140 mi/225 km) or Butte (85 mi/137 km) can be less expensive or more available during high-traffic seasons. That's not always the case; sometimes smaller airports can be even pricier with more limited schedules, but it's worth looking into. Keep in mind that drivers will often encounter wildlife on the roads, particularly late at night. And weather conditions can be sketchy, especially during winter. In other words, make sure the money saved on the flight is worth your time on the road.

By Car

In Montana, U.S. 191 and U.S. 93 are popular north-south routes that connect Montana with Idaho and Canada. The only major highway running north to south is I-15, which links Great Falls, Helena, and Butte to Canada and Salt Lake City. The I-94/I-90 corridor is the most direct route across the state.

In Wyoming, I-80 runs across the state from Nebraska to Nevada, while I-25 heads north from Colorado up to its intersection with I-90 in Buffalo, then on to Billings, Montana. U.S. 89 is a popular and scenic route to Jackson from Salt Lake City and heads up through Grand Teton and Yellowstone National Parks into Montana.

By Train

For two states that were quite literally built by the railroads, train service today is spotty at best. The *Empire Builder* from **Amtrak** (800/872-7245, www.amtrak.com), which travels in both directions daily through Montana between Chicago, Seattle, and Portland, is the only train service in the two states. Most of the stops are in the far northern part of Montana, which can be acceptable if you are going to Glacier National Park, but otherwise the train stops are long distances from the major population centers. There is no passenger train service in Wyoming on Amtrak, but buses pick up in Cheyenne, Evanston, Laramie, Rawlins, and Rock Springs and can transport travelers to train stations in Utah and Colorado. In Montana, there is bus service from Livingston to train stops in the northern part of the state.

By Bus

In Montana, **Greyhound** (800/231-2222, www.greyhound.com) buses travel

Montana License Plates

You wouldn't know it just by driving around, but Montana's license plates have provided an interesting look at the state's population trends since the first plate was produced in 1914. In the 1930s, the state added a number to the left side of the plate that corresponded to county population—the number 1 was for the county with the highest population, and 56 was for the lowest. If you correlate these with the city that is the county seat, you get a snapshot of the state's population history—and you can tell where people are from just by looking at their plates. In lieu of road trip bingo, a fun game is to see how many plates you can identify while driving around.

When the list for the license plate was created, Silver Bow County was the largest in the state, as Butte—with a population of just under 40,000 people—was a thriving city, booming with the economic flush of mining. Great Falls was number 2, Billings was 3, and Missoula 4. Libby—in northwest Lincoln County—came in last at number 56. In 1930 the total population of the state was just 537,606; the population of Billings was a mere 16,280, and the state capital, Helena, had just under 12,000 residents.

Over the past 80-plus years, the state motor vehicle department has left the number and corresponding counties the same. That is, a car with a number 1 is still from Butte-Silver Bow County, and a truck with a number 56 is from the Libby area. However, the population snapshot paints a dramatically different picture these days. While Butte has lost nearly 7,000 people since 1930, other cities have seen significant increases, leaving Butte now the sixth-largest city in Montana. Billings is the largest city, with more than 110,000 residents, and Missoula has moved up to number 2 with more than 72,000 people.

If the state did change the numbers for the license plate, Butte-Silver Bow would now be 8, and the top five counties would be Yellowstone (Billings), Missoula, Gallatin (Bozeman), Flathead (Kalispell), and Cascade (Great Falls). Lincoln County, now with more than 19,000 residents, jumped up more dramatically than any other. It's moved from last place (56) to 10th largest since 1930. The least populated county in Montana is Petroleum County in eastern Montana, with 523 people spread across more than 1,600 square miles (4,144 sq km). It is the third least populated county in the continental United States. Generally, western Montana is growing in population and eastern Montana is shrinking, except for areas impacted by the oil boom in North Dakota. Also, transplants tend to settle in larger, more urban centers where service-related jobs are typically abundant.

Why aren't the numbers on the plates being changed? Montana drivers have a certain amount of pride regarding their heritage, and the numbers hark back to a different era. Newcomers may not pay much attention to it, but old-timers and natives certainly do. The numbers are part of the state's cultural history—something nobody wants to change anytime soon.

mostly along I-90 and I-94 and north-south on I-15, but service is also available on **Jefferson Lines** (800/451-5333, www.jeffersonlines.com) from Billings, Bozeman, Butte, Glendive, Livingston, Miles City, and Missoula. These routes can also be booked through Greyhound. Greyhound stations are in Arlee, Billings, Bozeman, Butte, Evaro, Glendive, Kalispell, Lakeside, Miles City, Missoula, Pablo, Polson, Ravalli, St. Ignatius, and Whitefish.

Greyhound has service to all major cities and many smaller Wyoming towns, including Buffalo, Casper, Cheyenne, Evanston, Gillette, Jackson, Laramie, Rawlins, Rock Springs, Sheridan, and Wheatland. Bus service is also available on **Jefferson Lines** (800/451-5333, www.jeffersonlines.com) from Buffalo, Gillette (stop is unstaffed), and Sheridan.

Alltrans/Jackson Hole Express (307/733-3135 or 800/443-6133, www.jacksonholealltrans.com) provides daily shuttle service between Salt Lake City, Idaho Falls, Pocatello, and the resort town of Jackson, as well as transfers to and from the Jackson Hole Airport.

The **Wind River Transportation Authority** (307/856-7118, www.wrtabuslines.

com) offers fixed-route and airport shuttles in summer between Riverton, Ethete, Hudson, and Lander.

GETTING AROUND

By far the best way to get around these large states once you're here is by car. Rental cars are available at the major airports, and you'll see more of each state while driving around. Consider an all-wheel-drive vehicle even if you travel only during the summer, as many of the region's most scenic roads are gravel. In addition to better traction, these vehicles typically offer higher clearance.

By Car

Driving around Wyoming and Montana is the most efficient way to experience the scenic grandeur of these two states.

In Montana, the I-94/I-90 corridor follows the Yellowstone and Clark Fork Rivers and is the most direct route across the state. U.S. 191 and 93 are popular north-south routes; the only major highway running north to south is I-15. Some of the state's more famous back roads include U.S. 2, which parallels the Canadian border on Montana's Hi-Line along the old Great Northern rail line, and Highway 200 and U.S. 12, which cut east and west across the central part of the state.

In Wyoming, I-80 runs across the state, while I-25 is primarily a north-south highway, which intersects with I-90 in Buffalo, then goes on to Billings, Montana. U.S. 89 is a popular and scenic north-south route that passes through Jackson, and then up through Grand Teton and Yellowstone National Parks into Montana.

CAR RENTAL

If you plan on renting a car, it's a good idea to reserve one well in advance. Unless you will be driving entirely on paved roads, which is doubtful, a high-clearance or all-wheel-drive vehicle is a good idea. Many Forest Service campgrounds are located along gravel roads, and anytime you venture off the beaten path, you're bound to encounter some type of gravel

or dirt road. In the winter, all-wheel drive is a must. And be aware that rock chips on the windshield are common occurrences at any time of year. Make sure your insurance will cover it, or consider paying for added insurance from the car-rental agency.

Car-rental agencies widely serving Wyoming and Montana include **Alamo** (800/227-7368, www.alamo.com), **Avis** (800/352-7900, www.avis.com), **Budget** (800/527-0700, www.budget.com), **Enterprise** (800/261-7331, www.enterprise.com), **Dollar** (800/800-5252, www.dollar.com), **Hertz** (800/654-3131, www.hertz.com), **Thrifty** (800/847-4389, www.thrifty.com), and **National** (888/868-6204, www.nationalcar.com).

HIGHWAY SAFETY

A few considerations apply when you are planning a road trip to Montana or Wyoming. In general, interstates and major highways are in good condition across the region, although short summers mean road construction can be expected at any time of the day—or night, in some cases. State highways are often narrow and winding, not compatible with drowsy or inattentive drivers. Wildlife is a concern on any road, particularly at twilight and dark, and fallen rocks can be a problem in mountainous areas. For Wyoming road conditions, the **Wyoming Department of Transportation** (888/996-7623, www.wyoroad.info) has a wealth of information. Montana information can be found through the **Montana Department of Transportation** (800/226-7623, www.mdt.mt.gov/travinfo).

Distances between settlements can be great in Montana and Wyoming, especially in the eastern parts of the states. As a rule of thumb, planning ahead is critical. Don't wait until your gas light is on to fill up your tank, and make sure your spare is inflated. Carrying emergency gear is recommended. Rest areas—even on major highways and interstates—can be hundreds of miles apart. Most major towns and cities have reliable mechanics and car

Laws of the Wild West

Both Montana and Wyoming were born of the Wild West, and in many cases there still exists a hands-off, "we don't need no government" mentality. While this may work in some areas, some outdated laws and rules are being updated or eliminated. First of all, there s a speed limit in Montana. While the limit used to be listed as "reasonable and prudent," it was changed in 1999 after the Montana Supreme Court deemed the law too vague. Currently, the speed limit for automobiles is 80 mph on interstates in both states, 70 mph on most two-lane highways, and 65 mph on most interstates within urban areas. In places, nighttime speed limits are lower than daytime.

Believe it or not, it used to be legal to operate a vehicle in Montana and Wyoming with an open container of alcohol, whether you were driving or just along for the ride. In states where distances are often measured in "six-packs," this was a big deal. After much public debate, the Montana law was finally changed in 2005, making it illegal for drivers and passengers to have any amount of open alcohol. Montana had the highest rate of alcohol-related fatalities per vehicle-mile traveled in the nation in 2002-2003, as reported by the National Highway Traffic Safety Administration, and the rates are still high. However, if you're taking a cab, bus, or limo, or riding in the back of a traveling motor home, you can still drink legally. Bottoms up!

Wyoming passed a weak open-container law in 2002, which became known as the "Here, hold my beer while I talk to this officer" law, but passed a stricter version, similar to Montana's, in 2007. It is taken much more seriously these days.

Speaking of alcohol, Wyoming is one of the few states where you can still buy a bottle from a drive-through liquor store—just don't open it in the car. And they no longer serve "to go" cocktails.

In case you're wondering, it's also illegal in Montana to have a sheep in the cab of your truck without a proper "chaperone," and certain animals caught running at large can be castrated if not claimed within five days—at the owner's expense. Montana is still open-range country, so if you hit a black cow standing in the middle of the highway in the middle of the night, it's your responsibility to reimburse the rancher. And in Wyoming, make sure you close the gate if you cross a river or onto private land; otherwise it could cost you $750.

dealerships, but don't expect to find parts for your old Porsche roadster in very many places.

In general, the speed limit in both states is 80 mph on interstates and 70 mph on most two-lane highways, although it can vary quite a bit depending on location and time of day. Many two-lane roads have numerous turn-outs, where slower-moving vehicles can pull over and let cars pass. Montana and Wyoming drivers are used to driving faster on these roads, so if you're getting tailgated by a local, just pull over and let them go by. Increasingly, passing lanes are being incorporated into many state highways, particularly on roads over mountain passes. Be aware that Montana has a "move over law" which requires drivers to slow down and change lanes for stopped emergency or maintenance vehicles. Courtesy would suggest you do the same for any vehicle stopped alongside the road.

WINTER TRAVEL

Winter driving in Montana and Wyoming takes special care, focus, and—at times—lots of caffeine. Roads can be rendered impassable in a matter of minutes by snow and wind, and mountain passes are especially susceptible to fast-changing conditions. Because of the area covered, it may take a while before snowplows clear the roads. And be extremely cautious when driving behind or toward a snowplow, as visibility can be diminished to nothing. Be aware that because of wildlife, salt is rarely used on roads in Montana and Wyoming. Instead, the roads are graveled to provide better traction in icy conditions. Loose gravel often translates into cracked or chipped windshields, so drive with caution, and never get too close to a graveling truck.

Snow tires are a must in many places, and carrying emergency supplies is strongly recommended. A good emergency kit includes a shovel, a first-aid kit, jumper cables, a flashlight, signal flares, extra clothing, some food, water, a tow strap, and a sleeping bag. Don't rely on your cell phone to save you—although service is improving, there are many dead zones across both states.

Both states' transportation websites (www.wyoroad.info, www.mdt.mt.gov/travinfo) have links to current and projected weather patterns, and toll-free information numbers are updated regularly. It's a good idea to carry these numbers in your car. Occasionally weather information can be found on the AM band of your car radio—you'll notice signs along roads indicating when this is possible.

TRAVEL MAPS

Free road maps can be found at visitors centers and rest areas in both states, while an excellent supplement is the **Delorme Gazetteer series** (www.delorme.com), available at bookstores and in many gas stations. These oversize companions are a must for those venturing off the beaten path, as they include topographic data, Forest Service roads and trails, camping and hiking information, fishing areas, scenic drives, and more. Sporting goods stores offer more specialized maps, from national forests and wilderness areas to Bureau of Land Management lands and mile-by-mile river guides. The free road maps you get when you enter the national parks are sufficient to use during your stay.

By Bike

Montana and Wyoming have many options for those cycling through. Numerous back roads and accessible campgrounds make for some fun trips, but be prepared for long-distance rides and not much company. Both the Wyoming and Montana transportation websites (www.wyoroad.info, www.mdt.mt.gov/travinfo) offer excellent information for cyclists. You can order a **Montana Bicycle Touring Packet** online, as well as download maps and road grade information from each site. In Wyoming, information can also be found on www.cyclingwyoming.org.

Recreation

Montana and Wyoming offer some of the best recreational opportunities in the West, from mountain biking and fishing to boating and horseback riding. Vast areas of untouched land make for scenic beauty that can take a lifetime to explore, luring visitors back time and again to experience the outdoors.

In the summer, rivers come alive with white-water boaters, and smaller streams entice fly fishers seeking solitude. Wilderness areas and national forests offer miles of hiking trails, while national parks host visitors from around the world. Surprisingly, excellent golf courses are to be found here and can be relatively uncrowded, even in busy seasons. Look for unusual forms of the sport like the Cow Pasture Open in Wisdom, Montana, where golfers compete in a two-person scramble in for silver belt buckles or cellophane-wrapped cow pies. Lakes buzz with the sound of motorboats, campgrounds are full, and everyone seems to be outside doing something. Summers in the West are short, so people take advantage of them.

It's no surprise, then, that winters are particularly long, but those that live in and visit Montana and Wyoming take advantage of it by enjoying some of the finest and least-crowded ski slopes in the country. Great snow and majestic mountain trails make snowmobiling extremely popular, and Nordic ski centers and trails can be found in most mountain areas. Ice fishing, dogsledding, and backcountry skiing and snowboarding are other activities that keep folks busy when the snow flies.

NATIONAL PARKS

With three of the country's most popular national parks located in Montana and Wyoming, this is where many visitors begin and end their journey. **Glacier National Park** (www.nps.gov/glac) falls entirely within Montana, and its Canadian counterpart, **Waterton Lakes National Park** (www.pc.gc.ca) is directly across the border and shares some of the same trails. Although most of **Yellowstone National Park** (www.nps.gov/yell) is in Wyoming, three of the park's entrances are found in Montana. Just below Yellowstone in Wyoming is **Grand Teton National Park** (www.nps.gov/grte). Each park offers a different type of beauty, from Glacier's receding namesakes and high-alpine scenery to the majestic peaks of the Tetons and Yellowstone's striking geothermal features and abundant wildlife. Visitors will find a variety of accommodations in the parks, including rustic cabins, grand lodges, and tent and RV campgrounds. Popular activities include hiking, boating, fishing, and wildlife-viewing. Informational visitors centers and museums are sited in each park and offer excellent resources for history buffs.

The entrance fee in the summer for each park is $35 for automobiles, which is valid for seven days. An annual America the Beautiful national parks and federal recreation lands annual pass, which permits entrance to more than 2,000 federal recreation sites, costs $80. Campground and other lodging fees are extra. Annual passes for any of the three parks are available for $70.

Each state also has numerous national monuments, historic sites, trails, and recreation areas that fall within the national park system. Consult the National Park Service website (www.nps.gov) for more information on these areas.

STATE PARKS

Montana has **55 state parks** (www.stateparks.mt.gov) that focus on both history and recreation. This diverse selection includes historic ghost towns, Native American cultural sites, and lakeside and riverside retreats. Twenty of the parks have more than 500 camping sites, which are typically open mid-May-mid-September. Camping fees for nonresidents in peak season (third Friday in May-third Friday in Sept.) range from $12 per night for a hike-in or bike-in site to $34 per night for a site with electricity. For residents of Montana, camp fees range $6-24 during peak season. Many parks now offer yurts, tipis,

Discovery Ski Area in Philipsburg, Montana

and cabins ($42-72/night for nonresidents). Camping rates are reduced for both residents and nonresidents during the off-season. Cars with Montana license plates are allowed free admission to all state parks, while nonresidents are charged $6 per vehicle per park.

Wyoming manages **12 state parks** (www.wyoparks.state.wy.us) plus historic sites and landmarks, ranging from battlefields and museums to parks with hot mineral soaking springs. Daily use fees are $4 per adult for historic sites (kids under 18 are free) and $6 per vehicle (nonresident) for state parks. Overnight camping permits start at $17 for nonresidents and include the daily use fee. Camping cabins and yurts start at $40 per night (plus a $50 deposit, $6 daily use fee and $11 camping fee). Sites can be reserved online no more than 90 days in advance for dates May 15-September 15.

NATIONAL FORESTS

Much of the public land in Montana and Wyoming's mountainous areas is administered by the U.S. Forest Service (www.fs.fed.us), including 19.39 million acres (7.8 million hectares) in 10 national forests in Montana and 9.7 million acres (3.9 million hectares) in 8 national forests in Wyoming. The Forest Service is a branch of the United States Department of Agriculture (USDA) and manages much of the nation's forest and rangelands. All national forests contain developed hiking and biking trails, and in the winter the roads and trails can often be used for cross-country skiing. Forest Service ranger stations are good places to obtain information on camping and recreation, while most sporting goods stores sell excellent maps that pertain to specific areas. **Beartooth Publishing** (www.beartoothpublishing.com) offers a popular series of waterproof maps that highlight national forest roads, trails, campgrounds, picnic areas, and fishing access sites for specific regions in Montana and Wyoming. For reference, Montana is located in Region 1 (Northern Region) and Wyoming is located Region 2 (Rocky Mountain Region) and Region 4 (Intermountain Region). You'll notice signs along the highways that indicate when you enter and leave a particular national forest.

Forest Service campgrounds are widespread in Montana and Wyoming and offer some of the finest camping available. Fees range free-$17, depending on the type of site and the amenities offered. Free sites are often very remote and offer limited services. The Forest Service also rents some rustic cabins and lookouts starting at $20 per night. These can be a great way to enjoy the outdoors, as most are in prime locations. These cabins, as well as most campgrounds, can be reserved in advance (with additional fees) at www.recreation.gov.

WILDERNESS AREAS

As of 2018, there are 15 federally designated wilderness areas in Wyoming and 16 in Montana. These are roadless and closed to mechanized use, including mountain bikes. Wilderness areas generally offer solitude and amazing scenery, although some areas may be more heavily used than remote non-wilderness areas. Some wilderness areas may fall under Native American jurisdiction, so make sure you have the necessary permits before hiking, hunting, or fishing in these locations.

BLM PUBLIC LAND

The rest of the public land falls under purview of the Bureau of Land Management (BLM), which offers everything from camping and boating to caving and backcountry scenic byways. The BLM manages multiple resources and uses, including energy and minerals; timber; forage; recreation; wild horse and burro herds; fish and wildlife habitat; wilderness areas; and archaeological, paleontological, and historical sites. There are just over 8 million acres (3.2 million hectares) of BLM land in Montana and more than 18 million acres (7.3 million hectares) in Wyoming. You can find out more about the BLM offerings at www.blm.gov.

Forest Service Cabins and Lookouts

Imagine waking up in your own rustic cabin, nestled in the woods next to a rambling stream. You stoke the fire, mix up a pot of cowboy coffee, and enjoy a sunny breakfast on the porch with a 10,000-foot (3,048-m) peak looming overhead. There is no one else around. Now imagine that you have to pay less than $100 per night for this. Too good to be true? Well, thanks to the U.S. Forest Service cabin rental system, it isn't.

Literally hundreds of these cabins exist in Montana and Wyoming, most situated in locations that people would pay millions of dollars to own a piece of. Many are old ranger stations, very few are still used by the Forest Service, and all have their own unique charms. Cabins come in all different shapes and sizes, from extremely remote backcountry sites and mountaintop fire lookouts to larger cabins with electricity and motor vehicle access. Either way, they offer an unparalleled way to enjoy the outdoors.

Each national forest has a number of cabins for rent. You can find a list for Wyoming cabins and lookouts (www.fs.fed.us/r2/recreation/rentals). In Montana, you need to search the Forest Service website (www.fs.fed.us) by national forest or city. All cabins must be reserved online (www.recreation.gov), where you can enter when you want to stay and a list of available cabins will come up, or over the phone (877/444-6777 or 518/885-3639 outside the U.S.). Cabins range from $20 for small, one-room units to upward of $200 for larger rentals that sleep up to 10 people. There are additional booking fees, both online ($9) and over the phone ($10).

Cabins typically have bunk beds (bring your own bedding), wood stoves, wood, and pots and pans. Some have more, some have less. Toilet facilities are usually outside, and potable water is not always available. When you make your reservation, you'll get a list of what to bring as well as detailed directions.

Some of the more interesting rentals are historic fire lookouts, perched high atop a mountain with commanding views of the surrounding peaks. Sitting inside these lookouts, you can imagine backcountry rangers gazing out over the land trying to spot forest fires. These lookouts are especially beautiful at night, when you're out among the stars feeling like you're on top of the world. It's a must-do experience for those who want to get off the beaten path—and one you'll remember for a lifetime.

HUNTING

Montana and Wyoming are popular destinations for those hunting elk, deer, black bears, bighorn sheep, pronghorn, pheasants, and mountain lions. In 2009 both states also implemented a wolf season, and as of 2018, the hunt continues in both states. Starting in 2018, Wyoming is set to allow the sport hunting of grizzly bears outside Yellowstone and Grand Teton National Parks. More than 7,000 people applied for the first hunting permits, including renowned primatologist Jane Goodall and other conservationists who are willing to fight to protect the last grizzlies rather than see them shot as trophies. Montana also has a bison hunt, for which the time, location, and quotas are determined each year.

For more information on hunting in Montana, contact the **Montana Department of Fish, Wildlife & Parks** (406/444-2535, www.fwp.mt.gov). In Wyoming, contact the **Wyoming Game and Fish Department** (307/777-4600, http://wgfd.wyo.gov). If you would like to enlist a hunting guide, check the websites for recommendations on established outfitters or contact the **Montana Guides and Outfitters Association** (406/449-3578, www.montanaoutfitters.org) or the **Wyoming Outfitters and Guides Association** (307/265-2376, www.wyoga.org).

FISHING

Montana and Wyoming are known throughout the world as premier fishing destinations, mainly due to the popularity of fly fishing on beautiful rivers that flow throughout the region. Legendary trout streams like the Snake,

Great Divide Mountain Bike Route

Created in 1998, the Great Divide Mountain Bike Route is the longest off-pavement bicycle route in the world, running 3,000 miles (4,828 km) from Jasper, Canada, down to Antelope Wells, New Mexico. Developed by the Adventure Cycling Association, the trail is roughly 90 percent unpaved and crosses the Continental Divide as many as 30 times. The elevation gains and losses are equivalent to 220,000 vertical feet (27,056 m), which compares to riding up Mount Everest nearly 10 times.

One stretch of the trail in southern Wyoming from South Pass City near Lander to Rawlins cuts through an area known as the Great Basin, since the water in this area does not drain into the Atlantic or Pacific but rather stays in the playa lakes here or evaporates in the heat. In fact, the Continental Divide splits and is on both sides of the Great Basin. It's the only portion of the route where the terrain is consistently level. But that doesn't make it easy. Riders will need to carry plenty of water on the 131-mile (211-km) stretch and will likely have to deal with significant wind. Temperatures in this high desert can plummet quickly, and rainstorms can make the double-track nearly impassable. Possible wildlife encounters in this stretch of the trail can include prairie dogs, pronghorn, coyotes, and even wild horses.

The Great Basin is a starkly picturesque place that will appeal to those who love wide-open spaces. For maps and detailed route information, start online at www.adventurecycling.org.

Yellowstone, Madison, Big Horn, North Platte, Big Hole, and Gallatin lure anglers looking for lunkers, especially June-September. These rivers can be crowded during the summer, but luckily there are literally hundreds of other rivers and smaller streams on which to wet a line. And for die-hard anglers, plenty of secret spots are around—think spring creeks and alpine lakes—for excellent year-round fishing.

Lake fishing is also popular, with famed walleye fishing in Montana's Canyon Ferry and Fort Peck Reservoirs. In Wyoming, the Flaming Gorge and Buffalo Bill Reservoirs offer lake trout, kokanee salmon, and smallmouth bass. In addition, hundreds of backcountry lakes offer solitude and great fishing in a wilderness setting, and ice fishing is becoming increasingly popular during the winter.

In Wyoming, nonresident fishing permits cost $14 for one day or $56 for five days. Resident fishing licenses cost $27 per year or $6 per day. With the exception of a one-day license, you'll also need to purchase a Wyoming Conservation Stamp for $12.50, which is good for one calendar year. Youth under 14 do not need a license if fishing with an adult who has a valid fishing license. Annual Montana fishing licenses cost $111 for nonresidents

or $50 for two consecutive days, including a $10 Conservation License. Residents pay $31 for the season. Nonresidents under 12 do not need a license if accompanied by an adult who has a valid license. Check the websites for each state (www.fwp.mt.gov, http://wgfd.wyo.gov) for specific stamps you may need when fishing in certain waters. Fishing outfitters and stores sell licenses, as do many gas stations and sporting goods stores.

It's important to remember that you need a separate license to fish in Yellowstone National Park. Anglers 16 years of age and older are required to purchase an $18 three-day, $25 seven-day, or $40 season permit. Children 15 and under may fish without a permit if fishing with an adult who has a valid park permit. Permits are available at park ranger stations, stores, and many businesses in the Greater Yellowstone area.

Outfitters and guide services are abundant in Montana and Wyoming. Although it's not necessary, using one of these outfitters is a good idea if you're new to angling or want to hone your fly-fishing skills. Guides also know the hot spots on the rivers, can tell you what is hatching on any given day, and may have access to private sites along various streams.

Two excellent private websites for general fishing information and a good overview of the region are **Big Sky Fishing** (www. bigskyfishing.com) and **Wyoming Fishing Network** (www.wyomingfishing.net).

For detailed fishing information, contact the **Montana Department of Fish, Wildlife & Parks** (406/444-2535, www.fwp. mt.gov) or the **Wyoming Game and Fish Department** (307/777-4600, http://wgfd. wyo.gov).

TOUR OPERATORS

Wyoming and Montana cover a large geographic area, so it can be difficult to choose what to see in the time you have. There are many tour operators with well-researched itineraries that can cater to your specific needs and wishes. Many of these tours cater to families or a particular interest: biking, cultural and history tours, wildlife, and more. **Austin Adventures** (800/575-1540, www.austinadventures.com), for whom this writer used to guide, offers numerous multiple-sport trips (think biking, hiking, horseback riding, and rafting on one trip) in the region, including Yellowstone and Grand Teton National Parks and Glacier National Park. The Montana-based **Adventure Cycling Association** (800/755-2453, www. adventurecycling.org) offers self-contained and supported bicycle tours in Montana and in Yellowstone and Grand Teton National Parks. **Backroads** (800/462-2848, www. backroads.com) offers multiple-sport tours throughout Greater Yellowstone and in Glacier National Park. **Big Wild Adventures** (406/848-7000, www.bigwildadventures. com) offers backpacking and canoeing trips in Montana, Wyoming, and Yellowstone and Grand Teton National Parks. **Yellow Dog Fly Fishing Adventures** (406/585-8667 or 888/777-5060, www.yellowdogflyfishing.com) offers custom trips around the area. In addition, there are operators in nearly every town that offer specific adventures, such as whitewater rafting, horseback riding, fly-fishing, hiking, biking, and more.

SPECTATOR SPORTS
Rodeo

Most communities in Montana and Wyoming have rodeos at least once during the summer, and some of the larger towns like Jackson, Cody, and West Yellowstone have nightly or weekly rodeos that showcase the sport's nonstop action. Some of the best rodeos are the smaller ones, often called "ranch rodeos," that

fly-fishing in Grand Teton National Park

feature real cowboys and cowgirls from area ranches competing against each other in real-life ranch activities. Many rodeos offer events for kids, such as greased-pig contests or wild-sheep riding. Generally speaking, rodeos are great family-oriented events. **Frontier Days** (307/778-7222 or 800/227-6336, www.cfdrodeo.com) in Cheyenne is the country's largest outdoor rodeo, with attendance of nearly 250,000 people each summer for the 10-day festival. The **Cody Stampede Rodeo** (307/587-5155, www.codystampederodeo.com) in Cody has had bucking broncs since 1919, and the family-friendly **Cody Nite Rodeo** (307/587-5155, www.codystampederodeo.com) runs nightly June-August. Jackson Hole offers rodeos (307/733-7927, www.jhrodeo.com) twice weekly, on Wednesday and Saturday nights, Memorial Day-Labor Day, plus some Friday nights in July and August. The small town of Buffalo offers two weekly rodeos, including an all-women rodeo, the **Cowgirl Rodeo,** on Tuesday nights. West Yellowstone also hosts a rodeo (406/560-6913, www.yellowstonerodeo.com) during each weekend in the summer June-August, and the **Professional Bull Riders** tour (719/242-2800, www.pbr.com) stops in Montana at Big Sky, Livingston, and Eureka, and in Wyoming at Cheyenne.

Minor League Baseball

A popular spectator sport in Montana and Wyoming is professional minor league baseball. The **Pioneer League** (www.pioneerleague.com) has teams in Missoula (Arizona Diamondbacks), Helena (Milwaukee Brewers), Great Falls (Chicago White Sox), and Billings (Cincinnati Reds). This rookie league plays about 70 games June-September, and most players are recent draft picks. Although Casper used to have a Pioneer League team known as the Casper Ghosts, the ball club was replaced by the Casper Cutthroats who are part of the Mountain Collegiate Baseball League, as are the Cheyenne Grizzlies. In both leagues, games often draw good crowds and are enjoyed by baseball aficionados who live in these states that have no major league sports teams.

College Football

Both the **Montana State University Bobcats** (www.msubobcats.com) and the **University of Montana Grizzlies** (www.montanagrizzlies.com) compete in the Football Championship Subdivision (formerly Division 1-AA) of college football. Both teams have won national championships, and there has been a fierce rivalry between them since the first game was played in 1897. The Grizzlies have been one of the top teams in the country for the past two decades, and games often draw crowds of more than 20,000 rowdy fans.

With only one university in the state, it's no great surprise that the NCAA Division I **University of Wyoming Cowboys** (www.wyomingathletics.com) draw rabid fans to its home games in Laramie. The annual "border war" match between Colorado State and Wyoming has been going on since 1899 and is considered the oldest interstate rivalry west of the Mississippi River. Since 1968, the winner of that game takes home the Bronze Boot, one of the best-known and most highly sought-after traveling trophies in college football.

Travel Tips

CANADIAN CROSSINGS AND CUSTOMS

Of the many roads that cross into Canada from Montana, only three border crossings are open 24 hours, year-round. U.S. 93 (Roosville) and I-15 (Sweetgrass) are the busiest, while the remote crossing near Raymond on Highway 16 sees much less traffic. U.S. citizens are now required to carry passports when crossing into Canada; Canadians entering the United States must have a passport, a NEXUS card, an Enhanced Driver's License (EDL), or Enhanced Identification Card (EIC). Citizens of other countries must show their passports and appropriate visas and may be asked to prove that they have sufficient funds for their length of stay. U.S. citizens returning to the United States by air must present a U.S. passport.

When heading north into Canada, travelers age 21 and older can import, duty free, a maximum of 40 ounces (1.2 liters) of liquor or 24 12-ounce (0.4 liter) cans of beer or ale into the country as personal luggage. Up to 50 cigars and 200 cigarettes may be allowed entry duty free for those age 18 or over. U.S. visitors spending more than 48 hours in Canada may bring $400 worth of duty-free goods back with them, or $200 if staying less than 48 hours. If you're carrying more than $10,000, you'll need to declare the amount. Handguns can't be taken into Canada, although hunting rifles are allowed. Bear spray and hunting knives are also prohibited.

TOURIST INFORMATION

Both states have excellent information available for those interested in traveling to the region. Most chambers of commerce and visitors centers (listed for each town in this book) are good sources when driving around, but the online sites are where you should start your research. For Wyoming, visit **Wyoming Tourism** (307/777-7777, www.travelwyoming.

com) for the latest information. You can check out the various towns, attractions, and events, as well as order a **free vacation guide.**

For Montana, the **Montana Office of Tourism** (800/847-4868, www.visitmt.com) is the state's official tourism organization for vacation information and to order the annual free **Montana Guidebook.** Montana has divided the state into six different tourism regions, and specific booklets are available for each one.

COMMUNICATIONS AND MEDIA
Cell Phones

Although Montana and Wyoming may be remote, cell phone coverage is overall very good and getting better each year. That being said, rural and mountainous areas may have spotty coverage. Indeed, check the storefronts in some of the smaller towns in the region (I'm looking at you, Augusta), and you'll see that cell-phone service is just being brought to the area. Verizon is the main carrier, although AT&T is increasingly available.

Internet Access

Many coffee shops and public libraries have computers available for Internet use, and most larger towns have business centers with computers and fax machines.

High-speed Internet connections are generally available, but the service is often slower and more problematic compared to larger metropolitan areas. Wireless Internet is frequently offered at coffee shops, libraries, hotels, and other public places.

Media

USA Today is the one national newspaper that can be found throughout the region, and the **Wall Street Journal** is also popular. If you want a national newspaper like the **New York Times** or the **Washington Post,**

many towns still have smaller newspaper and magazine stores, but you may get a copy that is a few days old at best. Large grocery stores typically have regional dailies. In Montana, the larger dailies are the *Missoulian,* the *Great Falls Tribune,* the *Montana Standard, Helena Independent Record,* and the *Billings Gazette,* although every small town seems to have at least a weekly newspaper, which can be a great source of information on local events and attractions. Other Montana publications to look out for include the *Lively Times* (www.livelytimes. com), a monthly statewide guide to entertainment, and *Montana Magazine,* a good roundup of life in Montana. The *Montana Quarterly* and *Big Sky Journal* are excellent literary reads and feature well-written articles about the Treasure State and the Greater Yellowstone area.

In Wyoming, the larger daily newspapers include the *Casper Star-Tribune* (the only statewide newspaper), the *Wyoming Tribune Eagle* in Cheyenne, and the *Laramie Boomerang.* Other popular papers include the weekly *Jackson Hole News & Guide* and Worland's *Northern Wyoming Daily News.* Other Wyoming publications to watch for include the *Wyoming Magazine* (www.wyomingmagazine.com), which focuses on travel and adventure in the state, and *Wyoming Lifestyle Magazine* (www. wyolifestyle.com).

One of best sources of local and national news is **National Public Radio,** which can be heard in even the smallest of towns in both states. **Montana Public Radio** covers western Montana (www.mtpr.org), while **Yellowstone Public Radio** (www.ypr.org) covers the rest of the state as well as northern Wyoming. **Wyoming Public Radio** (www. wyomingpublicradio.net) also covers much of the state.

FOOD

One thing is certain: This is meat-and-potatoes country, which can be great for those craving a good steak, as you can find one in almost every town. Locally raised beef can be found on the menus of many restaurants, and bison is becoming increasingly popular as well. If you haven't had it, it's highly recommended, and beef lovers will generally enjoy bison. A good bison burger or tenderloin is hard to beat, but if you are asked how you like it cooked, never ask for anything more than medium. Wild-game dishes, mostly elk and venison, are also found at finer establishments, with pheasant and other regional game occasionally on the menu. If you enjoy trying new fare, this can be an exciting option.

With all the meat on the menu, you would think that vegetarians would be out of luck when dining out, but surprisingly, options abound, especially at higher-end restaurants. The "eat local" campaigns are in full swing out West, and many of the best restaurants get as much of their food as possible from local and regional growers. Despite the region being seriously landlocked, seafood is no longer necessarily a bad idea. Fresh seafood is flown in from Hawaii or Seattle daily in many places, and it is generally pretty good. Yes, there are even fresh sushi bars in Montana and Wyoming, and some are darn tasty. Innovative cuisine can be found in every major town, but certainly Jackson, Bozeman, Bigfork, Whitefish, Missoula, and Billings stand out.

Does either state have a well-known meal? Well, not really. Montana is famous for its huckleberries and Flathead cherries, so a good pie or milk shake is a must. Pasties in Butte are considered indispensable regional cuisine, and Rocky Mountain oysters (calf testicles) are usually breaded and fried—not exactly gourmet, and not exactly popular or necessarily worth trying. Delicious Indian tacos load the ingredients onto fry bread, and good Mexican and Chinese restaurants can be found throughout the region. Other regional specialties in both states include wild game, chicken-fried steak, chili, and trout.

You'll also see the standard fast-food establishments, especially near the interstates, but avoid these and try a local restaurant instead.

You'll find the best food at the most random of places—and it will certainly be a more culinary and cultural experience. And remember, folks out here are friendly—if you stop and ask someone about the best place in town, they will happily point you in the right direction and will probably know the owner.

If you are traveling the back roads and small towns and get tired of ordinary bar-type food (burgers, burgers, and more burgers), consider a quest to find the best chicken-fried steak or the best piece of pie. Sometimes a personal challenge can relieve the boredom of limited options. Plus, who doesn't want an excuse to eat homemade pie for breakfast, lunch, and dinner?

ACCOMMODATIONS

Since Montana and Wyoming are both big destinations for visitors, it's no surprise that a wide variety of lodging options are available, from standard hotels and motels to luxury resorts and guest ranches. Generally speaking, all lodging is more expensive in the summer, and rooms fill rapidly—advance reservations are a must, especially around special events like Cheyenne's Frontier Days or Bozeman's Sweet Pea Festival. Rooms, cabins, and even campgrounds in the national parks fill up several months—if not longer—in advance. Shoulder seasons (spring and fall) offer reduced rates and thin crowds, while rooms at the ski resort lodges fill fast in the winter but may be wide open during the summer.

Most larger towns have numerous choices for chain motels, which are typically clustered around the interstate exits. Gateway towns to Yellowstone and Grand Teton National Parks also have chain hotels, as well as a number of mom-and-pop motels sprinkled around town. Travelers used to standard hotels will be happy with these choices, but those who seek a more unique experience will want to try some of the smaller boutique hotels located in towns in both states. It just depends on whether you would rather stay in the usual Super 8 or sleep in a room that once accommodated Ernest Hemingway or Annie Oakley.

An excellent resource is **Historic Hotels of the Rockies** (www.historic-hotels.com).

There are a number of bed-and-breakfasts in Montana and Wyoming, most of which are in the higher-traffic tourist areas. Many are located on the banks of a river or nestled in the pine trees and often make great escapes from the busier hotel atmosphere. A fairly comprehensive listing can be found at **BnBFinder** (www.bnbfinder.com). Very few hostels exist in Montana and Wyoming, but **Hostels.com** (www.hostels.com) has a list of what might be available.

Guest ranches range from traditional horse-and-cowboy dude ranches to luxury "glamping" (a portmanteau of *glamorous* and *camping*) resorts that offer spa services and high-end cuisine. Two excellent resources for those seeking a real Western working vacation are the **Montana Dude Ranchers' Association** (888/284-4133, www.montanadra.com) and the **Wyoming Dude Ranchers' Association** (www.wyomingdra.com). Many of these are focused around horseback riding, fly-fishing, and family activities and often booked in weeklong blocks. In the winter, many of these ranches offer cross-country skiing, snowshoeing, or dogsledding.

Higher-end guest ranches are becoming very popular in Montana and Wyoming, offering guests a chance to experience a more rustic atmosphere with upscale amenities. These are typically set in remote locations with beautiful surroundings and private, in some cases gated from public access. Typically these are the priciest accommodations, ranging from several hundred to $1,000 and more per night.

Cabins and other vacation rentals are becoming increasingly popular, as many travelers are looking for that Western cabin experience. These can range from rustic—just beds, no plumbing—to luxurious—down comforters, a rock fireplace—and are perhaps the best way to stay. Sites like **Airbnb** (www.airbnb.com) and **VRBO** (www.vrbo.com) offer private homes and cabins for rent, while many resorts provide nightly cabin rentals. For Forest Service cabins—which can be quite primitive, but set in phenomenal locations—travelers can check availability and make reservations at www.recreation.gov.

Plenty of RV and tent camping sites in Montana and Wyoming are available for those on the road. From national forest campgrounds to large private RV resorts, there is something for everyone. RV campers will find private campgrounds in most towns, and most national forest campgrounds have room for all but the longest RVs. It's generally legal to camp on national forest land, unless you see a sign indicating that overnight camping isn't allowed. For something closer to back-country experience without hoofing it, drive on a Forest Service road until you find a nice campsite, pull over, and set up camp. Not only is it often scenic, it's also free.

ACCESS FOR TRAVELERS WITH DISABILITIES

For the most part, Montana and Wyoming comply with state and federal guidelines for handicapped access. Most hotels offer accessible rooms, and the national parks and even some state parks feature accessible trails. However, it's important to remember that many parts of both states are rural, and some features may be outdated, less accessible, or nonexistent.

WOMEN TRAVELING ALONE

Overall, Montana and Wyoming can be exciting for a woman traveling alone. For the most part, the West is full of independent and strong women, and you won't seem out of place in most areas. Outgoing and talkative women—as well as men—will feel right at home. Folks are pretty friendly and accommodating around these parts, and in general they like to meet people from other places. Of course, there is always the occasional weirdo, so if a place or a person makes you uncomfortable, the best thing to do is just leave. Use the same precautions and common sense that you would at home. And it's worth noting that bear spray can be just as effective on a creepy dude as it is on a curious grizzly.

LGBTIQ TRAVELERS

It's safe to say that many people in Montana and Wyoming are socially conservative, and same-sex public displays of affection are not very common. You shouldn't necessarily anticipate discrimination or hostility if you are LGBTIQ, but you'll want to be aware of your surroundings. You might not think much of expressing yourself at a back-road Montana or Wyoming bar, but you never know what the patrons in the corner are thinking. Sadly, this is where Matthew Shepard was brutally murdered in 1998 for no other reason than because he was gay. Montana and Wyoming still have a long way to go in terms of recognizing and celebrating alternative lifestyles. In general, "don't ask, don't tell" is the safest policy to assume when traveling here.

That being said, there are thriving—although often underground—gay communities in many Montana and Wyoming towns, particularly college towns like Missoula, Bozeman, and Laramie. Two excellent resources for LGBTIQ travelers are the **Western Montana LGBT Community Center** (406/543-2224, www.gaymontana. org) and the **University of Wyoming's Rainbow Resource Center** (307/766-3478, www.uwyo.edu/RRC).

Health and Safety

While medical services and health care in many of the larger Montana and Wyoming towns are excellent—and in some cases on par with bigger cities—it's important to remember that when traveling around, you'll mostly likely be far away from emergency medical services. Rural and mountainous highways are especially troublesome, as cell phone coverage can be spotty. Most small towns have a local clinic, and services are available in the national parks. Refer to specific areas of the text for emergency numbers, and remember that calling 911 doesn't always work in many rural areas.

In general, **weather, altitude,** and **insect bites** pose the greatest risk traveling here. The summer sun can get extremely hot, and it is easy to get dehydrated, so make sure to drink plenty of water during the day. Hiking—and just walking, for some people—can be a strenuous activity as the altitude increases. It's best to carry plenty of food and water, and take your time getting to your destination. Always let someone know where you are going and when you plan to be back. The earliest and most obvious sign of altitude-related health problems is a headache, and the best remedy is drinking water and moving to a lower elevation if possible.

The common insect nuisances are mosquitoes and ticks. Montana and Wyoming mosquitoes rarely carry any diseases, but they can be annoying at certain times during the summer. While West Nile virus is becoming an increasing threat to livestock across the West, human infection is less common. Still, it's a good idea to carry bug repellent with DEET, especially when hiking or camping near water. Ticks can pose a small threat of Rocky Mountain fever or Lyme disease, and they seem to have become more pervasive in the last 10 years or so. It's a good idea to check every part of your skin after a day of hiking or fishing outdoors—places where you might encounter underbrush, dense trees, and grassy meadows. If you find a tick with its head stuck in your skin, pull gently with tweezers or your fingers until the tick works its way out. Don't forget to check your pets too.

A common backcountry ill is **giardia,** sometimes called "beaver fever," a microscopic parasite that lives in mountain streams and can wreak havoc in your intestinal tract. Avoid drinking unfiltered or untreated water directly from streams, rivers, springs, or lakes. Carry a water filter or water-purifying tablets (iodine or similar products), and you'll have nothing to worry about.

If you're camping or staying in a cabin, **hantavirus** can be a concern. Hantavirus is a potentially fatal disease caused by contact with rodent droppings, particularly those of deer mice. Symptoms include fever, muscle aches, coughing, and difficulty breathing. Campers should avoid sleeping on bare ground, and avoid cabins if you see signs of rodents. For more information, visit the Centers for Disease Control and Prevention (www.cdc.gov).

Winter poses different types of health concerns, namely **hypothermia** and **frostbite.** If you or someone in your party shows any signs of hypothermia—uncontrollable shivering, slurred speech, loss of coordination—get them out of the wind and inside immediately. If you're camping, a dry sleeping bag is your best bet. It's a good idea to dress in layers, avoid cotton clothing, always bring a hat, and—most important—make good decisions *before* you put yourself in a situation where you could be stranded in the wind and cold. If you're outside in the winter, a sign of frostbite is the whitening and hardening of the skin. The best way to warm the affected area is with other skin, but avoid warming it too quickly because thawing can be quite painful.

WEATHER

The old saying is a tad cliché but nonetheless often true: If you don't like the weather in Montana or Wyoming, just wait five minutes. What this means to the traveler is that weather in this part of the West can change dramatically in an unbelievably short amount of time. In the summer, extreme heat can dehydrate the human body rapidly, and in the winter, extreme cold can render your body useless in a matter of minutes. Sudden changes in the weather can happen at any time of the year in mountainous areas. It can snow, sleet, hail, and rain at a moment's notice. If you're heading into the backcountry or getting ready for a three-day river float, check the forecast, but don't rely on it; plan for the worst with extra gear and plenty of food and water.

In general, Montana and Wyoming have a semiarid climate. There is enough moisture at certain times of the year, but summers are typically dry and warm, with July-August being the hottest months. Mountainous areas see heavy snowfall during the winter (to the delight of skiers), while the eastern part of both states can seem downright desertlike much of the year.

WILDLIFE

Although many people visit Montana and Wyoming for the abundant wildlife, with so much human interaction, safety is a real concern. A general rule of thumb is *never* to approach wildlife, no matter what the situation. It's just a bad idea, and each year people are hurt or killed because they ignore this basic rule. Not only are they putting themselves in harm's way, but they are often precipitating imminent doom for the animal as well. The old adage, "A fed bear is a dead bear," can be applied universally to wildlife. The problem of humans getting too close to animals, particularly in Yellowstone National Park, gets plenty of coverage these days on YouTube and the evening news. Do not become a cautionary lesson for other travelers; keep your distance from wildlife. Period.

SAFETY IN BEAR COUNTRY

Grizzly bears and black bears live in many parts of Montana and Wyoming, and although encounters are rare, it is necessary to learn what to do in case it happens to you. It is also important to know how to avoid the situation in the first place. No method is absolutely foolproof, but with caution and

Bear boxes make picnicking safer for people and bears alike.

attentiveness you can avoid most of the common mistakes that lead to bear encounters.

When out in the backcountry, it's the unexpected bear encounter you really want to avoid. The best way to do this is to let them know you are present. Make noise in areas of dense cover and blind spots on hiking or biking trails. Immediately move away from any animal carcass you come across, as there may be a bear nearby protecting it. Avoid hiking or biking in the early morning or at dusk, and travel in larger groups; the more of you there are hiking together, the more likely a bear will sense you and move away. Making noise is a great way to let bears know you are near, and in most cases they will be long gone before you have the chance to get a glimpse of them. Be aware that dogs can provoke bears and bring them right to you. And, of course, never leave food out.

If you're camping in an area frequented by bears, look for bear signs (waste, overturned rocks, decimated fallen timber, claw marks and hair on trees) around the campsite. Since bears are attracted to all kinds of odors—food, toothpaste, soap, deodorant—your cooking, eating, and food storage area should be at least 50 yards (45.7 m) from your tent. It's tempting to bring tasty items like sausage, ham, tuna, and bacon with you, but these smell good to bears too. Freeze-dried foods are your best bet. Store foods in airtight bags, and be sure to hang all food at least 12-15 feet (3.7-4.6 m) off the ground and away from tree trunks. Some designated campsites have bear storage containers or food storage poles.

Carrying **pepper spray** (sold in most sporting goods stores, but it's worth noting that the Grizzly and Wolf Discovery Center in West Yellowstone is the only place you can buy bear spray at cost) is a must in bear country, and it has been proven useful in fending off bear attacks. These sprays only work at close range (10-30 feet/3-9.1 m) and can quickly dissipate in the wind or sometimes blow back in your face. Carry the spray in a holster or on a belt across your chest for easy access. It's important to note that these spray canisters are not allowed on commercial airplanes, they expire after a certain date, and they should not be left in a very hot place like a closed car. Also, test your container every now and then in light or no wind to make sure it works.

If you happen to encounter a bear, and it notices you, try not to panic or make any sudden moves. Do not run—bears can run more than 40 mph in short bursts—or try to climb a tree. Make yourself visible by moving out into the open so the bear can identify you. Avoid direct eye contact with the bear, but talking in a low voice may convince the animal that you are human. If the bear is sniffing the air or standing on its hind legs, it's most likely trying to identify you. If it's woofing and posturing, this could be a challenge. Stand your ground if the bear charges; most charges are bluffs, where the bear will stop short and wander away.

If a grizzly does charge and knocks you to the ground, curl up in the fetal position with your hands wrapped behind your neck and your elbows tucked over your face. Keeping your backpack on may offer some protection. Remain as still as possible, as bears will often only sniff or nip you and leave. This is considered playing "active dead." If the bear rolls you over, as it will likely try to do, roll yourself back over on your stomach and keep your neck as protected as possible. Remain on the ground until you know the bear has vacated the area.

In general, black bears are more common and seem to have more interaction with people. In many places they can be a nuisance—getting into garbage, breaking into homes—but don't think that they are not dangerous. Black bears will generally try to avoid you and are easily scared away, but if you encounter an attacking or aggressive bear, this usually means it views you as food. In this case, most experts recommend fighting back with whatever means possible: large rocks or sticks, yelling, and shouting.

It's a rare event when a bear attacks sleeping campers in tents at night, as tragically happened at the Soda Butte campground near

Cooke City in July 2010, but if you find yourself in that situation, defend yourself as aggressively as you can. In these circumstances, bears are viewing you as prey and may give up if you fight back. Never play dead in this case, and to thwart off an attack, always keep pepper spray and a flashlight handy.

Before you go into the backcountry, brush up on your **bear identification.** You can't tell what kind of bear you see by its color alone. Grizzlies are often larger and have a trademark hump at the top of their neck. Grizzlies also have more of a dish-shaped face profile, compared to a straighter profile of black bears.

OTHER WILDLIFE

Although bears get the majority of the press, there are other animals that you need to be aware of when traveling around Montana and Wyoming. **Moose** are huge animals that are prone to sudden charges when surprised, especially females traveling with young. If you travel through Yellowstone National Park, you'll encounter numerous **bison,** large animals with sharp horns. Although it may be tempting to walk up to them, avoid doing so. While they are not vicious, bison can charge if provoked and have maimed and even killed visitors in the past. Statistically, bison injure more people in Yellowstone than any other animal. Be aware that these lumbering beasts can sprint the length of a football field in six seconds and can leap a 6-foot (1.8-m) fence. Likewise, elk in the park can seem downright

docile, but it's important to remember not to approach them.

Mountain lions generally keep a low profile, but as humans encroach on their habitat, encounters are becoming more frequent in the West. Most attacks have been on unattended children, and they rarely target adults. If you happen to find yourself in a situation with a mountain lion, be aggressive and fight back if necessary, or throw rocks and sticks to try to make it go away.

Rattlesnakes can be found in the central and eastern parts of Montana and Wyoming, especially in the drier prairies. Rattlesnake bites are rarely fatal (less than 4 percent when antivenin is used in time), and the snakes generally avoid humans. Be careful where you step when hiking around these areas, and pay attention if children are with you. If you surprise or step on a rattlesnake—chances are you'll hear its trademark rattle before you do—it may coil and strike. Any bite from a rattlesnake should be regarded as a life-threatening medical emergency that requires immediate hospital treatment by trained professionals.

With all of the incredible wildlife-viewing opportunities around Montana and Wyoming, it can be easy for some people to get complacent when taking pictures or hiking around. Treat all wildlife with respect and care, and never feed or approach any type of wild animal. If you are lucky enough to see many of these critters, observe them in their natural habitat and then carry on. The last thing you want is to become a statistic.

Resources

Suggested Reading

MONTANA

Information and Travel

Davis, Seabring. *Food Lovers' Guide to Montana.* Guilford, CT: Globe Pequot Press, 2010. Beautifully written and broken down into the state's six regions, this smart little book guides foodies to the state's best restaurants, farmers markets and stands, specialty stores, local producers, and food-related events.

Fifer, Barbara, and Vicky Soderberg. *Along the Trail with Lewis and Clark,* second edition. Helena, MT: Farcountry Press and *Montana Magazine,* 2001. Full of colorful maps, this is the most in-depth guide to the Lewis and Clark Trail.

Graham, Keith, and Neil Chaput de Saintonge. *Chasing Time.* Helena, MT: Riverbend Publishing, 2017. This wonderful and engaging photo book tells the story of Montana through its 68 active one-room schoolhouses.

McCoy, Michael. *Montana Off the Beaten Path,* eighth edition. Guilford, CT: Globe Pequot Press, 2010. This book guides travelers to the unexpected, and at times outlandish, places in Montana.

Merrill-Maker, Andrea. *Montana Almanac,* second edition. Guilford, CT: Globe Pequot Press, 2005. Written by a former legislative researcher, this tome compiles thousands of interesting facts about Big Sky Country.

Montanans Inc. *Montana: A Profile in Pictures.* New York: Fleming Publishing, 1941. What I love about this tiny little picture book is that so little has changed in more than 70 years. Swap out newer cars, modern fashions, and perhaps some racier skis, and nearly every one of these photographs could have been taken in the last decade.

Rowland, Russell. *Fifty-Six Counties.* Bozeman, MT: Bangtail Press, 2016. This artful travelogue, told by a fourth-generation Montanan and novelist, visits the strangest and most beautiful corners of the state.

Snyder, S. A. Scenic Driving Montana, second edition. Guilford, CT: Globe Pequot Press, 2005. This book covers 24 jaw-droppingly beautiful drives around the state.

Spencer, Janet. *Montana Trivia.* Helena, MT: Riverbend Publishing, 2005. A quirky and fascinating compendium of factoids about Montana, this book covers geography, history, entertainment, sports, arts, science, and nature.

Therriault, Ednor. *Montana Curiosities: Quirky Characters, Roadside Oddities & Other Offbeat Stuff.* Curiosities Series. Guilford, CT: Globe Pequot Press, 2010. A perfect book to carry along in the car, or in the backpack, this offbeat book highlights so many of the quirky, wonderful, and don't-blink-or-you'll-miss-it places and faces of the state.

Vasapoli, Salvatore. *Montana: Portrait of a State*. Portland, OR: Graphic Arts Books, 2008. If you need nudging on why to choose Montana or want a way to reflect on your trip the rest of the year, this coffee-table picture book of Montana nature porn, and more, is just the ticket.

History and Culture

Ambrose, Stephen E. *Undaunted Courage*. New York: Simon & Schuster, 1996. This has long been considered the definitive account of Lewis and Clark's extraordinary expedition.

Cheney, Roberta Carkeek. *Names on the Face of Montana*. Missoula, MT: Mountain Press Publishing, 1983. In its eighth printing, this is a classic for anyone who wants to know the stories behind names like Freezeout Lake, Ekalaka, Deadman's Basin, and more than 1,000 others.

Colton, Larry. *Counting Coup: A True Story of Basketball and Honor on the Little Bighorn*. New York and Boston: Grand Central Publishing, 2000. This powerful work of nonfiction tells the story of Sharon LaForge, a 17-year-old Native American basketball player fighting to grow up on the reservation.

Egan Jr., Ken. *Montana 1889*. Helena, MT: Riverbend Publishing, 2017. Historian Ken Egan Jr. brings characters to life in this exquisitely crafted history of the year Montana became a state.

Fritz, Harry, Mary Murphy, and Robert Swartout. *Montana Legacy: Essays on History, People and Place*. Helena, MT: Montana Historical Society Press, 2002. This wonderful collection of essays reflects the state's surprising diversity.

Horner, John R. (Jack), and James Gorman. *Digging Dinosaurs*. New York: Harper

Collins, 1990. A popular science book for good reason, it redefined the way we think of dinosaurs as parents.

Howard, Joseph Kinsey. *Montana: High, Wide and Handsome*. Lincoln, NE: University of Nebraska Press, 1943. Before "Big Sky," this compelling text was the source of one of Montana's earliest taglines.

Hungry Wolf, Adolf, and Beverly Hungry Wolf, compilers. *Indian Tribes of the Northern Rockies*. Skookumchuck, Canada: Good Medicine Books, 1993. With historic photos and copies of treaties, this volume offers a well-rounded cultural and historical overview of numerous tribes.

MacDonald, Douglas H. *Montana Before History*. Missoula, MT: Mountain Press Publishing, 2012. An excellent look at archaeological sites across the state, this book dives into the oldest known evidence of humans in Montana and how they lived.

MacGregor, Carol Lynn, editor. *The Journals of Patrick Gass*. Missoula, MT: Mountain Press Publishing, 1997. A well-edited and annotated version of the journals of Patrick Gass, a member of the Lewis and Clark expedition, this work focuses on the day-to-day activities of the Corps of Discovery.

Malone, Michael P., editor. *Montana Century: 100 Years in Pictures and Words*. Helena, MT: Falcon Publishing, 1999. This gorgeous coffee-table book looks at the faces, places, and events that shaped Montana in the 20th century.

Malone, Michael P., Richard B. Roeder, and William L. Lang. *Montana: A History of Two Centuries*. Seattle and London: University of Washington Press, 1991. First written in 1976, this authoritative history of Montana deals with prehistory, Native American studies, ethnic history, women's studies, oral history, and contemporary political history.

Montana Place Names from Alzada to Zortman. Helena, MT: Montana Historical Society Press, 2009. Written over the course of two years by five staff members from the Montana Historical Society Research Center, this book is backed by extensive research and access to the best historians in the state.

Munn, Debra D. *Montana Ghost Stories*. Helena, MT: Riverbend Publishing, 2007. A fun read for ghost lovers, this short volume spins tales of 11 favorite Montana ghosts.

Spritzer, Don. *Roadside History of Montana*. Missoula, MT: Mountain Press Publishing, 1999. Organized insightfully by natural travel routes, this book is filled with nice overviews of towns and regions as well as interesting little anecdotes.

Literature

Bass, Rick. *For a Little While*. New York: Little, Brown and Company, 2016. Though he is most often celebrated for lyrical nonfiction driven by his passion for Montana's Yaak Valley and all things wild, Bass's fiction is second to none. This collection reflects 30 years of his most brilliant short stories, many of them set in Montana.

Bass, Rick. *Winter: Notes from Montana*. Boston: Houghton Mifflin, 1991. Written by one of the state's most well-known contemporary writers, this lovely book celebrates the quietude of Montana's longest season.

Blew, Mary Clearman. *All But the Waltz*. Norman, OK: University of Oklahoma Press, 2001. Clearman Blew is a strong voice for central Montana in this hauntingly beautiful collection of essays spanning five generations of her family in the state.

Blunt, Judy. *Breaking Clean*. New York: Vintage Books, 2002. This unflinching memoir tells the story of Blunt's ranch upbringing and the life she ultimately had to flee.

Doig, Ivan. *This House of Sky: Landscapes of a Western Mind*. New York: Harcourt, 1978. A moving memoir that launched his long career, this work by Ivan Doig captures small-town Montana as it once was.

Fromm, Pete. *Indian Creek Chronicles: A Winter in the Bitterroot*. New York: Picador, 2003. Hired to tend salmon eggs during winter in Montana 40 miles (64 km) from the nearest road, this memoir is the author's exquisite introduction to the icy solitude of a Montana winter.

Grady, James, and Keir Graff. *Montana Noir*. New York: Akashic Books, 2017. This dark short story anthology gives readers a fascinating look into the seedier sides of Big Sky Country from some of its most talented writers.

Guthrie, A. B., Jr. *The Big Sky*. Boston: Houghton Mifflin, 1947. This timeless novel about three frontiersmen gave the state its well-known moniker.

Harrison, Jim. *Legends of the Fall*. New York: Bantam Doubleday Dell Publishing Group, 1978. Perhaps the most well-known of Harrison's works—thanks to the Hollywood adaptation starring Brad Pitt—this novella is a masterpiece, 100 years in 100 pages.

Henderson, Susan. *The Flicker of Old Dreams*. New York: Harper Perennial, 2013. Set against the dying town of Petroleum in eastern Montana, this beautiful novel tells the story of resilience and redemption.

Hugo, Richard. *Making Certain It Goes On*. New York: W. W. Norton, 1984. A collection of Hugo's poems, this is an absolute classic.

Kittredge, William, and Annick Smith. *The Last Best Place: A Montana Anthology*. Helena, MT: Montana Historical Society Press, 1988. This is the ultimate reader's guid to Montana literature, with nearly 1,200 pages of literary selections spanning Native American stories and myths to contemporary fiction and poetry with everything in between.

Maclean, Norman. *A River Runs Through It*. Chicago: University of Chicago Press, 1976. The book that launched a thousand drift boats.

Maclean, Norman. *Young Men and Fire*. Chicago and London: University of Chicago Press, 1992. The posthumously published work by the author of *A River Runs Through It*, this nonfiction work about the fire that claimed 12 airborne firefighters is considered a modern tragedy and a magnificent piece of literature.

McGuane, Thomas. *Crow Fair*. New York: Alfred A. Knopf, 2015. Tom McGuane is a poet, a philosopher, a wild man, a master. His latest collection of short stories, set in the state he loves, should not be missed.

McMurtry, Larry. *Lonesome Dove*. New York: Pocket Books, 1985. Another can't-miss classic about the legendary Texas cattle drives.

Meloy, Maile. *Both Ways Is the Only Way I Want It*. New York: Riverhead Books, 2009. A fresh voice in short fiction, Meloy has a sly and bittersweet understanding of Montana and is a marvelous storyteller.

Stegner, Wallace. *Collected Stories of Wallace Stegner*. New York: Random House, 1990. A wonderful collection of Stegner's masterful fiction.

Stegner, Wallace. *Where the Bluebird Sings to the Lemonade Springs*. New York: Penguin Books, 1992. A classic and luminous Western writer, Wallace Stegner writes about the land and the human condition in these 16 brilliant essays.

Watson, Larry. *Montana 1948*. Minneapolis, MN: Milkweed Editions, 2007. This is a novel about love and courage, of power abused, and the terrible choice between family loyalty and justice.

Welch, James. *Riding the Earthboy 40*. New York: Penguin Books, 1971. The only book of poetry by one of the West's most remarkable poets, this collection is magnificent and timeless. Sherman Alexie called it the most important book of poetry in all of Native American literature.

Welch, James. *Winter in the Blood*. New York: Penguin Books, 1974. Welch's first novel, about a young Native American man living on the Fort Belknap Indian Reservation, is a heartbreaking and beautiful classic.

Zupan, Kim. *The Ploughmen*. New York: Henry Holt & Company, 2014. Zupan's searing novel about an aging killer and a troubled young deputy in Montana has earned him comparisons to Cormac McCarthy.

Recreation

Arthur, Jean. *Winter Trails Montana: The Best Cross-Country Ski & Snowshoe Trails*. Guilford, CT: Globe Pequot Press, 2000. This book offers great suggestions and 42 trails for everyone from newbie skiers and families to pros.

Fischer, Kit. *Paddling Montana*. Guilford, CT: Globe Pequot Press, 2015. Detailed paddling info for more than 30 river trips.

Grossenbacher, Brian, and Jenny Grossenbacher. *Fly Fishing Montana: A No Nonsense Guide to Top Waters*. Tucson: No Nonsense Fly Fishing Guidebooks, 2007. This great guide by an ambitious husband-and-wife guide team covers the entire state.

Lomax, Becky. *Moon Montana, Wyoming & Idaho Camping*. Berkeley, CA: Avalon

Travel, 2014. Hands down, the best and most comprehensive guide for camping in the region.

Schneider, Bill, and Russ Schneider. *Hiking Montana*. Guilford, CT: Globe Pequot Press, 2014. The 35th anniversary edition, this hiking guide offers excellent advice, clear directions, and descriptive details, plus great maps for hiking trails across the state.

Straub, Patrick (Paddy). *Montana on the Fly: An Angler's Guide*. Woodstock, VT: Countryman Press, 2008. A comprehensive guide to Montana waters and outfitters.

Magazines

A longtime literary publication for Montana and the Northern Rockies, including Wyoming and Idaho, *Big Sky Journal* (subscriptions 800/731-1227, www.bigskyjournal.com) is published five times annually and includes special issues devoted to fly-fishing and the arts. Regular features by well-known writers focus on ranching and rodeo, hunting, fishing, art, and architecture.

Published six times annually, *Montana Magazine* (subscriptions 888/666-8624, www.montanamagazine.com) approaches life in Montana with broad strokes.

Montana Outdoors (subscriptions 800/678-6668, www.fwp.mt.gov/mtoutdoors) is an excellent publication produced by Montana Fish, Wildlife & Parks, focusing on the state's natural resources, including fishing and hunting. The magazine has won countless awards and is a fantastic resource for natural historians. You can read the current issue online.

Montana Quarterly (subscriptions 406/333-2154, www.themontanaquarterly.com) is a beautiful magazine that tackles the issues of the state—politics, science, arts, and culture—head on. Their editorial policy is simple: "Montana, warts and all."

For history buffs, there is no better publication than *Montana: The Magazine of Western History* (subscriptions 800/243-9900, www.

mhs.mt.gov/pub), produced quarterly by the Montana Historical Society.

A remarkable literary magazine that captures the beauty and grit of the state, *Whitefish Review* (www.whitefishreview.org) comes out twice annually and includes important interviews with Montana figures and work by the best and brightest across the country.

Maps

Montana Atlas & Gazetteer. Yarmouth, ME: Delorme Publishing, 2013. The most indispensable map book you'll find, these topographic maps cover roads and trails all over the state.

GRAND TETON, YELLOWSTONE, AND GLACIER

History

Black, George. *Empire of Shadows: The Epic Story of Yellowstone*. New York: St. Martin's Press, 2012. Black offers a fascinating look at the gripping and unexpected history of our first national park.

Clayton, John. *Wonderlandscape: Yellowstone National Park and the Evolution of an American Cultural Icon*. New York: Pegasus Books, 2017. Using iconic figures—including painters, naturalists, and entrepreneurs—as the storytelling mechanisms, John Clayton paints a fascinating cultural picture of the park.

Guthrie, C. W. *Glacier National Park, The First 100 Years*. Helena, MT: Farcountry Press, 2008. A marvelous volume compiled to celebrate the park's centennial in 2010, this book features exquisite photos and artwork in addition to compelling history.

Haines, Aubrey. *The Yellowstone Story: A History of Our First National Park*. Yellowstone National Park, WY, and Niwot, CO: The Yellowstone Association for Natural Science, History, and Education and The University Press of Colorado, 1996. This comprehensive volume tackles the park's early years, from primitive exploration to early development.

Righter, Robert W. *Crucible for Conservation: The Struggle for Grand Teton National Park.* Moose, WY: Grand Teton Natural History Association, 1982. This gripping history makes one grateful that things worked out the way they did.

Righter, Robert W. *Wind Energy in America: A History.* Norman, OK: University of Oklahoma Press, 2003. Righter gives readers an excellent, in-depth look at the saga of wind energy across the West.

Saunders, Richard L., editor. *A Yellowstone Reader: The National Park in Folklore, Popular Fiction, and Verse.* Salt Lake City: University of Utah Press, 2003. This volume offers a core sample of historical literature that spans the late 19th century through the 1980s.

Whittlesey, Lee H. *Death in Yellowstone: Accidents and Foolhardiness in the First National Park.* Lanham, MD: Roberts Rinehart Publishers, 1995. Who doesn't love reading about a little gore and some good old-fashioned stupidity when traveling through Yellowstone?

Natural History

Blakeslee, Nate. *American Wolf: A True Story of Survival and Obsession in the West.* New York: Crown Publishing, 2017. There's nothing like a good wolf story, and Blakeslee portrays Yellowstone alpha female O-Six against the backdrop of conservation politics.

Johnsgard, Paul A., and Thomas D. Mangelsen. *Yellowstone Wildife: Ecology and Natural History of the Greater Yellowstone Ecosystem.* Boulder, CO: University Press

of Colorado, 2013. With stunning images by Mangelsen and detailed natural histories of the animals that call the park home, this is an outstanding book for wildlife lovers.

Mangelsen, Thomas, and Todd Wilkinson. *Grizzlies of Pilgrim Creek.* New York: Rizzoli, 2015. The project of famed photographer Tom Mangelsen and environmental writer Todd Wilkinson, this gorgeous, oversized book tells the story of grizzly bear #399, one of the most beloved and oft-seen bruins in Grand Teton National Park.

Murie, Margaret, and Olaus Johan Murie. *Wapiti Wilderness.* Boulder, CO: University Press of Colorado, 1985. A magnificent read by two of the region's now deceased but beloved conservationists, the chapters alternate between his work studying elk and her descriptions of their fascinating life together.

Olsen, Jack. *Night of the Grizzlies.* Moose, WY: Homestead Publishing, 1996. Perhaps better read *after* your camping trip in Glacier, this is the account of a 1967 night in which two campers were killed in Glacier in two different locations by two different bears.

Peacock, Doug. *Grizzly Years: In Search of American Wilderness.* New York: Holt Paperbacks, 1996. A classic by one of Montana's favorite authors who was the model for George Hayduke in Ed Abbey's novels, this narrative tells of one man's 20-year quest to understand and appreciate this magnificent creature.

Phillips, Michael K., and Douglas W. Smith. *The Wolves of Yellowstone.* Stillwater, MN: Voyageur Press, 1996. Told with fabulous color photos and intimate details by the two men who oversaw the project, this book tells the story of the wolves' reintroduction to Yellowstone in 1995.

Riis, Joe, with contributions from Arthur Middleton, Emilene Ostlind, Gretel Ehrlich, and Thomas Lovejoy. *Yellowstone Migrations.* Seattle: Mountaineers Books, 2017. This marvelous photographic exploration of the last great migrations of elk, pronghorn, antelope, and mule deer features rich, meaty essays by some wonderful writers.

Schreier, Carl. *A Field Guide to Yellowstone's Geysers, Hot Springs and Fumaroles.* Moose, WY: Homestead Publishing, 1999. This slightly larger-than-your-pocket book is the authoritative guide to Yellowstone's best-known thermal features, with information about the origin of their names, regular and irregular activity, statistics, and anecdotal histories.

Schullery, Paul. *Searching for Yellowstone: Ecology and Wonder in the Last Wilderness.* Helena, MT: Montana Historical Society Press, 2004. A fascinating and compelling environmental history of the world's first national park.

Schullery, Paul. *Yellowstone Bear Tales.* Boulder, CO: Roberts Rinehart Publishers, 1991. Read this for hair-raising accounts of bear encounters by one of the park's most respected natural historians.

Wilkinson, Todd. *Yellowstone Wildlife: A Watcher's Guide.* Minocqua, WI: NorthWord Press, 1992. This is an excellent guide for where to see wildlife, with fascinating must-know information about each creature.

Recreation

Henry, Jeff. *Yellowstone Winter Guide.* Boulder, CO: Roberts Rinehart Publishers, 1998. This full-color guide is a must for travelers seeing Yellowstone in its quietest and arguably most magical season.

Lilly, Bud, and Paul Schullery. *Bud Lilly's Guide to Fly Fishing the New West.* Portland, OR: Frank Amato Publications, 2000. Written by the father of Western trout fishing and one of the West's most respected natural historians, this book weaves Lilly's personal history as an angler, guide, and conservationist with the history of fly-fishing in the region along with sage advice.

Lomax, Becky. *Moon Glacier National Park.* Berkeley, CA: Avalon Travel, 2017. Lomax wrote the definitive resource for visitors to this phenomenal park.

Lomax, Becky. *Moon Yellowstone & Grand Teton.* Berkeley, CA: Avalon Travel, 2018. This is the ultimate guide to what to see and how to see it in these two national parks.

Marschall, Mark C. *Yellowstone Trails: A Hiking Guide.* Yellowstone National Park, WY: Yellowstone National Park Association, 2008. Another great hiking guide, this one includes descriptions of more than 100 trails ranging from day hikes to backpack trips.

Nystrom, Andrew Dean, Morgan Konn, and Tim Cahill. *Top Trails Yellowstone & Grand Tetons: Must-do Hikes for Everyone.* Berkeley, CA: Wilderness Press, 2009. This book covers 45 wonderful hikes from 0.5-mile (0.8-km) jaunts to 30-mile (48-km) treks.

Schneider, Bill. *Hiking Yellowstone National Park,* third edition. Guilford, CT: Globe Pequot Press, 2012. This excellent hiking guide offers short, moderate, and long hikes throughout Yellowstone.

Watters, Ron. *Winter Tales and Trails: Skiing, Snowshoeing and Snowboarding in Idaho, the Grand Tetons and Yellowstone National Park.* Pocatello, ID: Great Rift Press, 1997. Intertwining guide advice with great stories, you'll wish Ron was along for the trip.

WYOMING

Information and Travel

Fritz, William J. *Roadside Geology of the Yellowstone Country*. Missoula, MT: Mountain Press Publishing, 1985. Even though it was published more than 30 years ago, we're talking about rocks; a couple of decades doesn't make much difference, and this is a fantastic resource for anyone interested in the region's geology.

Kilgore, Gene. *Ranch Vacations: The Leading Guide to Dude, Guest, Resort, Fly Fishing, Working Cattle Ranches and Pack Trips*. Sonoma, CA: Ranchweb, 2016. The best resource for finding a ranch vacation perfectly suited to you and your family.

Pflughoft, Fred. *Wyoming Wild and Beautiful II*. Helena, MT: Farcountry Press, 2003. As in his first book in the series, photographer Fred Pflughoft captures the beauty of the Cowboy State.

Roberts, Stephen L., David L. Roberts, and Phil Roberts. *Wyoming Almanac*. Laramie, WY: Skyline West Press, 2001. Every factoid you could ever want to know about Wyoming.

Trevathan, Mary Ann. *More Than Meets the Eye: Wyoming Along I-80*. Glendo, WY: High Plains Press, 1993. As a marvelous and unique approach to traveling, this book focuses on the people who live and work along the highway and is imbued with the sense that people give places life.

History

Ehrlich, Gretel. *Heart Mountain*. New York: Penguin, 1989. This historical novel by one of Wyoming's best-loved writers is set in the Heart Mountain Relocation Camp.

Haines, Aubrey L. *Historic Sites Along the Oregon Trail*. St. Louis: Patrice Press, 1994. This volume gives readers a look at the historic sites along the trail written by a well-respected historian.

Harris, Burton. *John Colter: His Years in the Rockies*. Lincoln, NE: University of Nebraska Press, 1993. This book, first published in 1952, provides the best look at early explorer and legendary figure John Colter, considered the first nonnative to lay eyes on Yellowstone.

Larson, T. A. *History of Wyoming*, second edition. Lincoln, NE: University of Nebraska Press, 1990. This massive volume covers it all and is considered the best single-volume history of the state in print.

McPhee, John. *Rising from the Plains*. New York: Farrar, Straus and Giroux, 1987. McPhee masterfully parallels Wyoming's geology with frontier history.

Moulton, Candy. *Roadside History of Wyoming*. Missoula, MT: Mountain Press Publishing, 2003. An excellent guide, this book is organized by driving routes across the state.

Munn, Debra D. *Wyoming Ghost Stories*. Helena, MT: Riverbend Publishing, 2008. A fun read for ghost lovers, this short volume rounds up ghost stories from across the state.

Murray, Robert A. *The Bozeman Trail: Highway of History*. Boulder, CO: Pruett Publishing, 1988. Murray gives readers a short but meaty volume on the bloodiest settler route of them all.

Philipps, David. *Wild Horse Country: The History, Myth, and Future of the Mustang*. New York: W.W. Norton, 2017. A reporter for the *New York Times*, Philipps explores how the wild animals captured the imagination of a nation and became central to American identity amid controversy.

Russell, Don. *The Lives and Legends of Buffalo Bill*. Norman, OK: University of Oklahoma Press, 1979. When it comes to biographies of the legendary figure, this is the bible.

Shepherd, Rose, and Susan Marsh. *Saving Wyoming's Hoback: The Grassroots Movement that Stopped Natural Gas*. Salt Lake City: University of Utah Press, 2017. An important book that won the Wallace Stegner Prize in Environmental Humanities tells the story of the 2012 efforts to prevent industrialization of the Hoback and Noble basins in northwestern Wyoming.

Taylor, Tory. *On the Trail of the Mountain Shoshone Sheep Eaters; A High Altitude Archaeological and Anthropological Odyssey*. Scotts Valley, CA: CreateSpace Independent Publishing Platform, 2017. Taylor masterfully combines his own explorations in the high mountain backcountry and his narrative with the history of the Mountain Shoshone who lived in Wyoming's Wind Rivers and Montana's Absarokas before the arrival of Europeans.

Trenholm, Virginia Cole. *The Arapahoes, Our People*. Norman, OK: University of Oklahoma Press, 1986. First published in 1970, this compelling history of the Arapaho tribe follows their ways of life from prehistoric Minnesota and Canada through the 20th century in Montana, Wyoming, and Oklahoma.

Urbanek, Mae Bobb. *Wyoming Place Names*. Missoula, MT: Mountain Press Publishing, 1988. This is the best guide for those who want to know the stories behind names like Bessemer Bend and Tensleep Canyon.

Literature

Ehrlich, Gretel. *A Match to the Heart: One Woman's Story of Being Struck by Lightning*. New York: Penguin, 1995. Another masterpiece from Ehrlich, this one is a memoir about her near death and subsequent reawakening.

Ehrlich, Gretel. *The Solace of Open Spaces*. New York: Viking Penguin, 1985. Arriving in Wyoming to work on a PBS film in 1976, Gretel Ehrlich could barely extricate herself from the independent and hard-won life she created for herself there. This collection of essays is one of the best ever written about Wyoming's landscape, people, and culture.

Forbes, Jamie Lisa. *Unbroken*. Greybull, WY: Pronghorn Press, 2011. An award-winning novelist, Forbes writes about the harshness of Wyoming ranch life.

Fuller, Alexandra. *Quiet Until the Thaw*. New York: Penguin Books, 2017. Though Fuller is better known for her memoirs set in Africa, her Wyoming stories are just as powerfully written. Her first novel tells the story of two Lakota cousins who choose different paths in a complex tale spanning generations and geography.

Galvin, James. *The Meadow*. New York: Henry Holt & Company, 1992. Part novel, part natural history, this poetic book tells the 100-year history of a meadow in the arid mountains that bridge Wyoming and Colorado.

Harrison, Jim. *The English Major*. New York: Grove Press, 2008. Perhaps known more for his poetry and dramatic fiction—like *Legends of the Fall*—Harrison's comedic novel about a 60-year-old, sad sack of a man traveling cross-country is a delight.

Proulx, E. Annie. *Close Range: Wyoming Stories*. New York: Scribner, 2000. Pulitzer Prize-winning Proulx is among the state's best-known writers, and for good reason. The tales are dark and the landscape unforgiving, but the characters in this collection are sublime. "Brokeback Mountain" is just one of the stories in this collection.

Schaefer, Jack. *Shane.* New York: Random House, 1949. It just doesn't get more Wyoming than this cowboy classic.

Shay, Michael. *Deep West: A Literary Tour of Wyoming.* Greybull, WY: Pronghorn Press, 2003. This anthology brings together 19 writers with roots in the state, including Annie Proulx and Robert Roripaugh.

Spragg, Mark: *Where Rivers Change Direction.* New York: Riverhead Books, 2000. A profoundly compelling memoir by one of Wyoming's most beloved contemporary authors, this book tells the story of Spragg's coming-of-age on a Wyoming dude ranch.

Twain, Mark. *Roughing It.* Mineola, NY: Dover, 2013. Published originally in 1872, this nearly 900-page work is an account of Twain's six years in the wild, woolly West.

Wister, Owen. *The Virginian.* Mineola, NY: Dover, 2006. This classic 1902 novel put Wyoming on the map.

Recreation

Birkby, Jeff. *Touring Montana and Wyoming Hot Springs,* second edition. Guilford, CT: Globe Pequot Press, 2013. A comprehensive guide to public and private springs across the region.

Downing, Paul. *Fly Fishing the Southern Rockies: Small Streams and Wild Places.* Fountain Hills, AZ: Majestic Press, 2016. This comprehensive guide by a longtime editor for *Fly Fish America* offers advice on where to fish and what to use, and includes waters in Wyoming, Colorado, and New Mexico.

Hunger, Bill. *Hiking Wyoming.* Guilford, CT: Globe Pequot Press, 2008. This guide carefully outlines 110 of Wyoming's best hiking trails.

Keffer, Ken. *Hiking Wyoming's Bighorn Mountains: A Guide to the Area's Greatest Hiking Adventures.* Guilford, CT: Falcon Guides, 2017. This book lives up to its name with great coverage of dozens of trails, both for day hikers and backpackers.

Lewis, Dan. *Paddle and Portage: The Floater's Guide to Wyoming Rivers.* Douglas, WY: Wyoming Naturalist, 1991. Intended more for less experienced boaters, this book gives an overview of various waters around the state.

Logue, Terrence, and Maria Katherman, Peggy Knittel, Beecher Ed Strube, and Dana Van Burgh Jr.. *A Field Guide to the Casper Mountain Area,* second edition. Casper, WY: Endeavor Books, 2017. A wonderful handbook covering everything from geology, plants, and animals to local history. There are maps, mileage markers, and color photos.

Lomax, Becky. *Moon Montana, Wyoming & Idaho Camping.* Berkeley, CA: Avalon Travel, 2014. The best guide for camping in the region.

Magazines

A longtime literary publication covering Montana, Wyoming, and Idaho, **Big Sky Journal** (subscriptions 800/731-1227, www.bigskyjournal.com) is published five times annually and includes special issues devoted to fly-fishing and the arts. Regular features by well-known writers focus on ranching and rodeo, hunting, fishing, art, and architecture. **The Open Range** (www.openrangemagazine.com) touts itself as a gritty new publication devoted to the realities of living and working in the West, with stories about everything from night calving and blacksmithing to working in the oilfields. **Wyoming Magazine** (www.wyomingmagazine.com) focuses on adventure and travel opportunities across the state, with stories about communities, entertainment, and outdoor pursuits.

Wyoming Wildlife (subscriptions 800/710-8345, http://wgfd.wyo.gov) is an award-winning publication of the Wyoming Game and Fish Department.

Maps

Wyoming Atlas & Gazetteer. Yarmouth, ME: Delorme Publishing, 2013. The most indispensable map book you'll find, these topographic maps cover roads and trails all over the state.

Internet Resources

MONTANA

Montana Office of Tourism
www.visitmt.com
Searchable by region and town, places to go, things to do, and a variety of other user-friendly options, the website is superbly organized and easy to navigate.

Montana Kids
www.montanakids.com
The kids' version of the Montana Tourism site is loaded with fun facts, games, and information on the state.

Montana Travel and Tourism Information
www.travelmt.com
Searchable by region, this website provides hotel, restaurant, shopping, recreation, and business information for each city and town in the state.

Winter Montana
www.wintermt.com
Another product of the state of Montana, this site is invaluable for visitors during Montana's longest season.

National Park Service
www.nps.gov
The NPS website is helpful for making plans to visit any of the national parks.

Montana Fish, Wildlife & Parks
www.fwp.mt.gov
This official state site is useful for finding state

parks, fishing and hunting information, and other recreational opportunities.

U.S. Forest Service
www.fs.fed.us/r1
The Forest Service's website is helpful for pursuing recreational opportunities—including multiuse trails, campgrounds, and cabin rentals—throughout Montana.

Recreation.gov
www.recreation.gov
This government-run site allows visitors to make reservations at public campgrounds.

Montana Outfitters & Guides Association
www.montanaoutfitters.org
An ideal source for visitors looking for professionally guided hunting and fishing trips or other types of outdoors experiences.

Museums Association of Montana
www.montanamuseums.org
A great database of museums across the state.

Montana Bed-and-Breakfast Association
www.mtbba.com
A useful resource for visitors looking for a B&B experience.

Traveler Updates
www.mdt.mt.gov/travinfo
The best resource for up-to-date road information comes courtesy of the Montana Department of Transportation.

WYOMING

State of Wyoming
www.wyoming.gov
Wyoming's official website offers a wealth of information about the state and its government.

Wyoming Travel and Tourism
www.travelwyoming.com
The state's comprehensive offering for visitors, this is a great place to find information on towns, accommodations, travel ideas and itineraries, shopping, and dining.

Wyoming State Parks, Historic Sites, and Trails
www.wyoparks.state.wy.us
Useful information on parks, recreation, and historic preservation.

Wyoming Travel Information
www.wyoroad.info
Up-to-date road information provided by the Wyoming Department of Transportation.

National Park Service
www.nps.gov
The NPS website is helpful for making plans to visit any of the national parks.

Recreation.gov
www.recreation.gov
This government-run site allows visitors to make reservations at public campgrounds.

Wyoming Game and Fish Department
http://wgfd.wyo.gov
The website offers much of what visitors need to know about fishing and hunting in the state.

U.S. Forest Service
www.fs.fed.us
The Forest Service website is helpful for pursuing recreational opportunities—including multiuse trails, campgrounds, and cabin rentals—throughout the eight national forests, recreation areas, and grasslands in Wyoming.

Wyoming Outfitters and Guides Association
www.wyoga.org
A fantastic resource for planning guided outdoor adventures.

Wyoming Dude Ranchers Association
www.wyomingdra.com
An excellent place to look for dude ranch vacations.

Index

M

List of Maps

Photo Credits

Title page photo: brizardh | dreamstime.com;
page 2 © kan1234 | dreamstime.com; page 3 © motbd/donnie sexton; page 12 © (top left) carter g. walker; (top right) motbd/donnie sexton; (bottom) motbd; page 13 © (top) motbd/tim kemple; (bottom left) lorpic99 | dreamstime.com; (bottom right) wyoming office of tourism; page 14 © (top) haveseen | dreamstime.com; page 15 © (top) motbd; (bottom left) wyoming office of tourism/peter adams; (bottom right) motbd/donnie sexton; page 16 © henry turner | dreamstime.com; page 19 © (top) motbd/noah couser; (bottom) valentin armianu | dreamstime.com; page 20 © (top) carter g. walker; (bottom) motbd/christina & eric mcevoy; page 21 © wyoming office of tourism/andy austin; page 22 © (top) wyoming office of tourism; (middle) wyoming office of tourism/jason lindsey; (bottom) coltonstiffler | dreamstime.com; page 23 © alexey kamenskiy | dreamstime.com; page 24 © (bottom) william michael norton | dreamstime.com; page 26 © (bottom) bennymarty | dreamstime.com; page 28 © (bottom) dianebentleyraymond | istock; page 29 © (top) samspicerphotography/123rf; page 31 © brina bunt | dreamstime.com; paul lemke | dreamstime.com; page 32 © wyoming office of tourism/eric lindberg; glenn nagel | dreamstime.com; page 33 © (bottom) keeganconnell | dreamstime.com; page 34 © (bottom) motbd/donnie sexton; page 36 © (top) tracey taylor | dreamstime.com; page 39 © (top) jesse kraft | dreamstime.com; page 41 © (bottom) bradley dailey | dreamstime.com; page 43 © indian memorial dedicated on june 25, 2003; page 49 © motbd/chuck haney; page 52 © (top left) motbd; (top right) motbd; (bottom) jacob boomsma | dreamstime.com; page 61 © motbd; page 65 © (top) motbd; (bottom) motbd; page 75 © (top left) carter g. walker; (top right) motbd/donnie sexton; (bottom) zrfphoto | dreamstime.com; page 84 © (top) carter g. walker; (bottom) pictureguy66 | dreamstime.com; page 88 © carter g. walker; page 90 © motbd/donnie sexton; page 93 © motbd; page 100 © (top) motbd/jacob moon; (bottom) motbd; page 113 © (top) mtnmichelle | istockphoto.com; (bottom) carter g. walker; page 122 © motbd; page 129 © nps/tim rains; page 135 © motbd/noah couser; page 141 © nps/jacob w. frank; page 144 © (top) nps; (bottom) carter g. walker; page 148 © carter g. walker; page 152 © (top) nps/jacob w. frank; (bottom) nps/jacob w. frank; page 155 © nps/tim rains; page 159 © motbd/donnie sexton; page 161 © nps/jacob w. frank; page 163 © skiing at montana snowbowl; page 172 © dspataro | dreamstime.com; page 173 © motbd/mike schirf; page 185 © (top) carter g. walker; (bottom) motbd/donnie sexton; page 194 © steve boice | dreamstime.com; page 195 © victoria ditkovsky | dreamstime.com; page 198 © (top) motbd/bob webster; (left middle)motbd/donnie sexton; (right middle)adeliepenguin | dreamstime.com; (bottom) carter g. walker; page 203 © motbd/donnie sexton; page 210 © ronniechua | dreamstime.com; page 212 © (top) motbd/donnie sexton; (bottom) motbd; page 218 © motbd/donnie sexton; page 225 © (top) motbd/donnie sexton; (bottom) radkol | dreamstime.com; page 234 © jesse kraft | dreamstime.com; page 246 © motbd/donnie sexton; page 252 © mtsue | dreamstime.com; page 254 © (top left) carter g. walker; (top right) carter g. walker; (bottom) joe sohm | dreamstime.com; page 259 © (top left) glenn nagel | dreamstime.com; (top right) motbd/donnie sexton; (bottom) motbd/bob webster; page 269 © bobby j norris | dreamstime.com; page 276 © motbd/donnie sexton; page 278 © flashon studio | dreamstime.com; page 289 © motbd/donnie sexton; page 291 © motbd; page 296 © miroslav liska | dreamstime.com; page 297 © philip bird | dreamstime.com; page 305 © robert crum | dreamstime.com; page 312 © wyoming office of tourism/martin ruegner; page 331 © nps/jacob w. frank; page 333 © (top left) nps/neal herbert; (top right) nps/jacob w. frank; (bottom) nps/neal herbert; page 340 © nps/jacob w. frank; page 344 © nps/jacob w. frank; page 347 © (top) nps/jacob w. frank; (bottom) wyoming office of tourism; page 349 © nps/jim peaco; page 356 © motbd/hunter day; page 361 © f11photo | dreamstime.com; page 371 © wyoming office of tourism; page 374 © (top) randy harris | dreamstime.com; (bottom) steven hardin | dreamstime.com; page 377 © wyoming office of tourism; page 380 © kwiktor | dreamstime.com; page 382 © (top) wyoming office of tourism; (bottom) wyoming office of tourism; page 385 © jackstraw22 | dreamstime.com; page 388 © wyoming office of tourism; page 391 © carter g. walker; page 393 © wyoming office of tourism; page 397 © (top) wyoming office of tourism; (bottom) acoyster | dreamstime.com; page 399 © michael turner | dreamstime.com; page 405 © wyoming office of tourism; page 413 © (top left) wyoming office of tourism/andy austin; (top right) wyoming office of tourism; (bottom) stevehymon | dreamstime.com; page 424 © wyoming office of tourism; page 433 © jimsphotos | dreamstime.com; page 440 © richard collens | dreamstime.com; page 446 © (top) wyoming office of tourism/jason lindsey; (bottom) wyoming office of tourism; page 450 © sandra foyt | dreamstime.com; page 458 © (top) wyoming office of tourism; (bottom) onesmallsquare | dreamstime.com; page 461 © wyoming office of tourism; page 470 © wyoming office of tourism/jason lindsey; page 474 © wyoming office of tourism; page 480 © wyoming office of tourism/jason lindsey; page 482 © wyoming office of tourism/jason lindsey; page 484 © wyoming office of tourism/jason lindsey; page 489 © rolf52 | dreamstime.com; page 492 © wyoming office of tourism; page 497 © wyoming office of tourism; page 503 © (top left) wyoming office of tourism; (top right) wyoming office of tourism; (bottom) wyoming office of tourism; page 505 © wyoming office of tourism; page 512 © wyoming office of tourism; page 515 © (top) wyoming office of tourism/andy austin; (bottom) wyoming office of tourism; page 517 © wyoming office of tourism/andy austin; page 521 © wyoming office of tourism; page 523 © motbd/bob webster; page 525 © (top left) nps/jacob w. frank; (top right) motbd/noah couser; (bottom) kenny tong | dreamstime.com; page 529 © (top) nps/jacob w. frank; (left middle)motbd/donnie sexton; (right middle)motbd/donnie sexton; (bottom) motbd/donnie sexton; page 555 © nps/neal herbert; page 561 © motbd/tim kemple; page 565 © jchutch | dreamstime.com; page 572 © carter g. walker.

Acknowledgments

There is a bottle-top proverb affixed to my desk that reads, "If you want to go quickly, go alone. If you want to go far, go together." During my now years-long journey to create and update this book, I have never wanted for company. There are many people to whom I owe an enormous debt of gratitude.

First and foremost, thanks to the indefatigable Aparna Sundaram, my co-everything for as long as I can remember. Without her—and her patient and amazing family—this book would have been a mountain of notes and a bowl of salty tears at the edge of my cluttered desk. There simply aren't words enough to praise her diligent efforts and unfailing support. The Adams family—Shannon, Dean, Jake, and Bell—are a constant source of love and inspiration: They tell the best stories, play the best music, take the best pictures, and remind my girls and me daily of the beauty in this world. I am grateful to Melanie Viets for making me laugh, for having cameos in my dreams, for letting me imagine us in a cabin somewhere, someday, writing. Then walking. Always laughing. Alex White is just, well, why would I do *anything* without Alex White? She makes everything better. Our early-morning salons make me whole. I'm grateful too to Cam Paterson, for his help with these chapters, and then some.

Thanks also to my conscientious and patient editor—Leah Gordon—and the whole team at Avalon Travel for taking the leap and working so hard on this book. Mike Morgenfeld is a map genius and Kit Anderson does magic with photography (and Luddite writers).

I am grateful to the talented Donnie Sexton for the use of her gorgeous images, and to Kristin Gates from MOTBD for making so many beautiful Montana images available. And thanks to Charles Lammers from Wyoming Office of Tourism, who contributed so many wonderful photos in the book.

Last but certainly not least, I am grateful to my family, the one I came from and the one I made. You all have encouraged and supported and loved me well. I'm grateful too that you had the mettle and wisdom to let me go! Sissel, and Siri: You are what I love most about this place, and this life. Sharing the adventure with you is my greatest blessing.

Travel with Moon in the Rockies, the Southwest, and Texas

ARIZONA & THE GRAND CANYON — TIM HULL

AUSTIN SAN ANTONIO & THE HILL COUNTRY — JOSTIN MARLER

COLORADO — TERRI COOK

DENVER, BOULDER & COLORADO SPRINGS — MINDY SINK

IDAHO — JAMES P. KELLY

MONTANA & WYOMING — CARTER G. WALKER

NEVADA — SCOTT SMITH

NEW MEXICO — ZORA O'NEILL

PHOENIX, SCOTTSDALE & SEDONA

SANTA FE, TAOS & ALBUQUERQUE — STEVEN HORAK

TEXAS — ANDY RHODES

UTAH with Zion, Bryce Canyon, Arches, Capitol Reef & Canyonlands National Parks — W. C. McRAE & JUDY JEWELL

Or go big and go abroad

ANGKOR WAT

FIJI

GALÁPAGOS ISLANDS TRIP OF A LIFETIME

MACHU PICCHU TRIP OF A LIFETIME

ROME, FLORENCE & VENICE

#TravelWithMoon

FIND YOUR ADVENTURE

MOON

USA
NATIONAL
PARKS

THE COMPLETE GUIDE TO ALL

59 PARKS

BECKY LOMAX

Join our travel community!
Share your adventures using **#travelwithmoon**

MOON.COM
@MOONGUIDES

ARCHES & CANYONLANDS
NATIONAL PARKS

ACADIA
NATIONAL PARK

BANFF
NATIONAL PARK

DEATH VALLEY
NATIONAL PARK

GLACIER
NATIONAL PARK

GRAND
CANYON

GREAT SMOKY
MOUNTAINS
NATIONAL PARK

MOUNT RUSHMORE
& THE BLACK HILLS

ROCKY MOUNTAIN
NATIONAL PARK

YELLOWSTONE
& GRAND TETON

YOSEMITE
SEQUOIA &
KINGS CANYON

ZION &
BRYCE

In these books:

- Full coverage of gateway cities and towns
- Itineraries from one day to multiple weeks
- Advice on where to stay (or camp) in and around the parks

MOON MONTANA & WYOMING

Avalon Travel
Hachette Book Group
1700 Fourth Street
Berkeley, CA 94710, USA
www.moon.com

Editor: Leah Gordon
Series Manager: Kathryn Ettinger
Copy Editor: Ashley Benning
Graphics and Production Coordinator: Krista Anderson
Cover Design: Faceout Studios, Charles Brock
Interior Design: Domini Dragoone
Moon Logo: Tim McGrath
Map Editor: Mike Morgenfeld
Cartographers: Brian Shotwell; Karin Dahl
Indexer: Rachel Kuhn

ISBN-13: 9781640491915

Printing History
1st Edition — 2011
4th Edition — May 2019
5 4 3 2 1

Front cover photo: Grinnell Glacier Trail, Glacier National Park © Haizhan Zheng | Getty Images
Back cover photo: Grand Prismatic Spring, Yellowstone National Park © Yun Gao | Dreamstime.com

Printed in China by RR Donnelley